Text Copyright © 2021 by Steve's F
All Rights Reserve

M000032656

Steve's Football Bible offers the best and most informative Trends and Angles information for the sophisticated football handicapper in the nation. We don't offer opinions on who is going to win games. We provide the historical facts and you can use that to form your opinion and handicap games accordingly. We offer Pro and College football handicappers the best and most in-depth books on team trends and angles, pointspread analysis, plus each teams schedule for the upcoming season. You have everything at your fingertips with the **Pro Football Bible** or the **College Football Bible.** The **Pro Football Bible** includes the complete history of the NFL playoffs, Monday Night Football, Sunday Night Football, Thursday games and Saturday games. The **College Football Bible** includes each team's all-time records in the Polls when they were ranked and versus ranked teams. You won't find this type of information anywhere.

We also have numerous published books on College Football History and well as books on Baseball History. All of these are available on our website at: www.stevesfootballbible.com. They are also available at www.barnesandnoble.com as well as www.amazon.com.

2021 College Football Trends and Angles Bible

Copyright © *(Registered) 2021 by Steve's Football Bible, LLC (All Rights Reserved)*

The 2021 College Football Trends and Angles Bible is published by Steve's Football Bible, LLC and may not be re-produced by any means without permission of the Publisher

All information in this publication is for news matter only and is not intended to be used to violate any Local, State or Federal Laws.

Copyright © 2021 by Steve's Football Bible, LLC

Books available from Steve's Football Bible LLC

Print Version $29.99

Print Version $29.99

Print Version $29.99

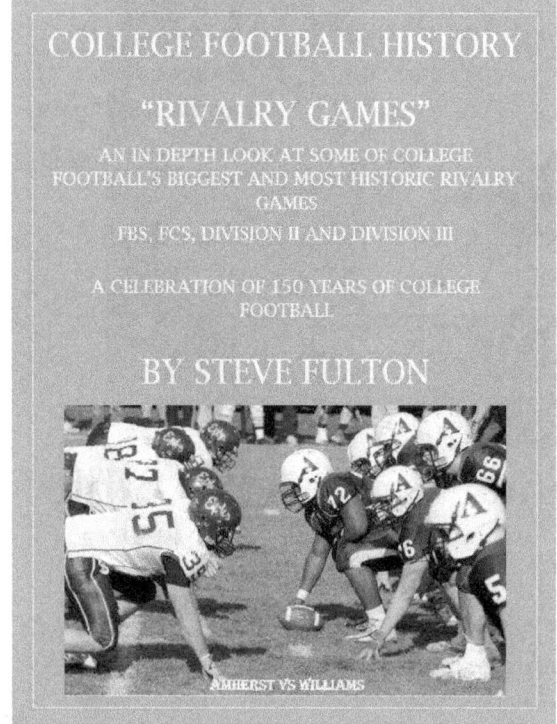

Print Version $24.99

These books available at numerous online retailers

Copyright © 2021 by Steve's Football Bible, LLC

Books available from Steve's Football Bible LLC
Print Version $34.99   Print Version $34.99

Print Version $29.99   Print Version $34.99

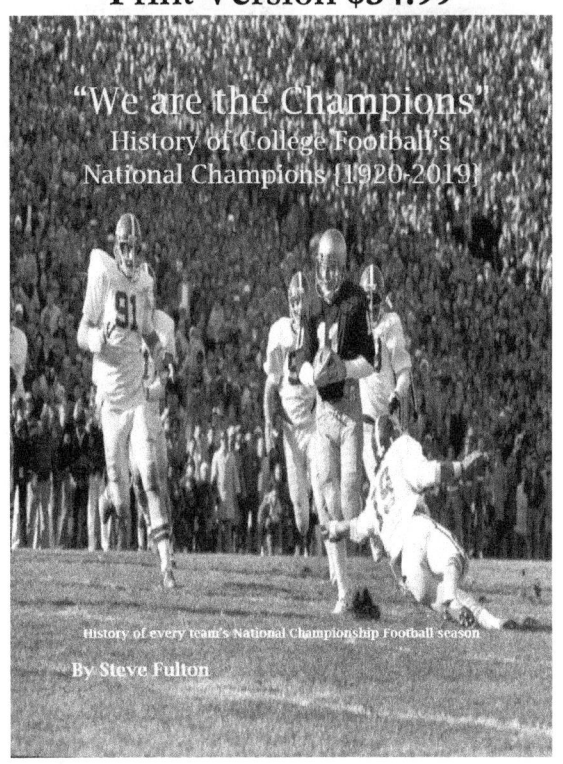

These books available at numerous online retailers

Copyright © 2021 by Steve's Football Bible, LLC

Steve's Football Bible also offers the Pro Football Bible, the Pro football handicapper's best friend for the 2021 football season.

Steve's Football Bible also offers the 2021 FCS College Football Bible for the FCS College Football fans.

To order Go to: www.stevesfootballbible.com

2021 Pro Football Bible $24.95

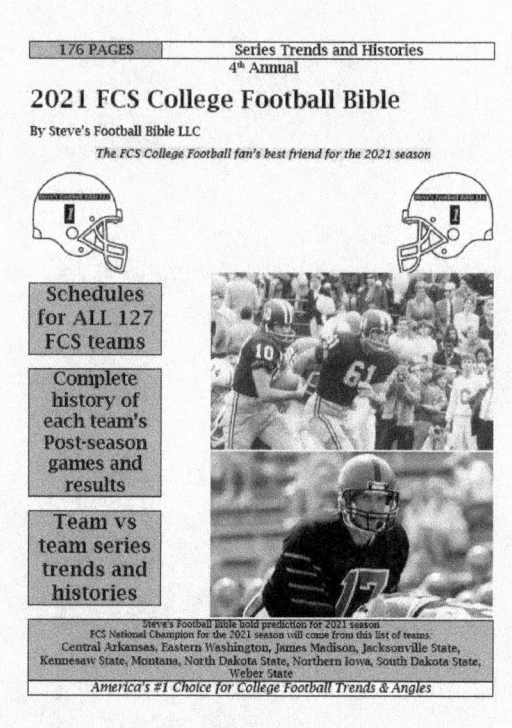

2021 FCS College Football Bible $19.95

www.stevesfootballbible.com

Copyright © 2021 by Steve's Football Bible, LLC

TABLE OF CONTENTS

Key Word definitions

S/U - Straight Up

O/U – Over/Under

ATS – Against The Spread

s/1983 – Since 1983 {or year listed}

Copyright © 2021 by Steve's Football Bible, LLC

AIR FORCE FALCONS   MOUNTAIN WEST Mountain

2020-Air Force		Opponent	AFA	Opp	S/U	Line	ATS	Total	O/U	
10/3/2020	vs	NAVY	40	7	W	6.0	W	47.5	U	
10/24/2020	@	San Jose State	6	17	L	-7.5	L	64.5	U	
10/31/2020	vs	BOISE STATE	30	49	L	12.5	L	48.5	O	
11/21/2020	vs	NEW MEXICO	28	0	W	-8.0	W	55.5	U	
12/3/2020	@	Utah State	35	7	W	-13.5	W	52.5	U	
12/19/2020	@	Army	7	10	L	-2.0	L	37.5	U	
Coach: Troy Calhoun		Season Record >>	146	90	3-3	ATS>>	3-3	O/U>>	1-5	
2019-Air Force		Opponent	AFA	Opp	S/U	Line	ATS	Total	O/U	
8/31/2019	vs	COLGATE	48	7	W	-24.0	W	NT	---	
9/14/2019	@	Colorado	30	23	W	3.0	W	58.0	U	{OT}
9/21/2019	@	Boise State	19	30	L	7.0	L	55.5	U	
9/28/2019	vs	SAN JOSE STATE	41	24	W	-19.0	L	58.0	O	
10/5/2019	@	Navy	25	34	L	-3.0	L	46.5	O	
10/12/2019	vs	FRESNO STATE	43	24	W	-2.5	W	49.5	O	
10/19/2019	@	Hawaii	56	26	W	-3.5	W	65.5	O	"Kuter Trophy"
10/26/2019	vs	UTAH STATE	31	7	W	-3.5	W	60.0	U	
11/2/2019	vs	ARMY	17	13	W	-16.5	L	44.5	U	
11/9/2019	@	New Mexico	38	21	W	-10.5	W	62.0	U	
11/23/2019	@	Colorado State	44	22	W	-24.0	L	56.5	O	"Ram-Falcon Trophy"
11/30/2019	vs	WYOMING	20	6	W	-13.0	W	41.5	U	
12/27/2019	vs	**Washington State**	31	21	W	-2.5	W	71.5	U	Cheez-it Bowl
Coach: Troy Calhoun		Season Record >>	443	258	11-2	ATS>>	8-5	O/U>>	5-7	
2018-Air Force		Opponent	AFA	Opp	S/U	Line	ATS	Total	O/U	
9/1/2018	vs	SUNY-STONY BROOK	38	0	W	-14.5	W	NT	---	
9/8/2018	@	Florida Atlantic	27	33	L	7.5	W	61.5	U	
9/22/2018	@	Utah State	32	42	L	9.5	L	59.5	O	
9/29/2018	vs	NEVADA	25	28	L	-3.5	L	63.0	U	
10/6/2018	vs	NAVY	35	7	W	3.0	W	47.0	U	
10/13/2018	@	San Diego State	17	21	L	11.0	W	42.5	U	
10/19/2018	@	Unlv	41	35	W	-9.5	L	54.0	O	
10/27/2018	vs	BOISE STATE	38	48	L	9.5	L	57.5	O	
11/3/2018	@	Army	14	17	L	4.5	W	41.5	U	
11/10/2018	vs	NEW MEXICO	42	24	W	-13.0	W	55.5	O	
11/17/2018	@	Wyoming	27	35	L	2.5	L	43.0	O	
11/24/2018	vs	COLORADO STATE	27	19	W	-14.5	L	64.0	U	"Ram-Falcon Trophy"
Coach: Troy Calhoun		Season Record >>	363	309	5-7	ATS>>	6-6	O/U>>	5-6	
2017-Air Force		Opponent	AFA	Opp	S/U	Line	ATS	Total	O/U	
9/2/2017	vs	VIRGINIA MILITARY	62	0	W	-34.5	W	55.0	O	
9/16/2017	@	Michigan	13	29	L	23.0	W	52.5	U	
9/23/2017	vs	SAN DIEGO STATE	24	28	L	-1.0	L	48.5	O	
9/30/2017	@	New Mexico	38	56	L	-3.0	L	50.5	O	
10/7/2017	@	Navy	45	48	L	4.5	W	52.0	O	
10/14/2017	vs	UNLV	34	30	W	-9.0	L	64.0	T	
10/20/2017	@	Nevada	45	42	W	-6.0	L	64.0	O	
10/28/2017	@	Colorado State	45	28	W	9.5	W	68.5	O	"Ram-Falcon Trophy"
11/4/2017	vs	ARMY	0	21	L	-6.5	L	53.5	U	
11/11/2017	vs	WYOMING	14	28	L	-2.5	L	50.5	U	
11/18/2017	@	Boise State	19	44	L	17.5	L	60.0	O	
11/25/2017	vs	UTAH STATE	38	35	W	-2.0	W	57.0	O	
Coach: Troy Calhoun		Season Record >>	377	389	5-7	ATS>>	5-7	O/U>>	8-3-1	

Copyright © 2021 by Steve's Football Bible, LLC

AIR FORCE FALCONS   MOUNTAIN WEST Mountain

STADIUM: Falcon Stadium {46,692}		Location: Colorado Springs, CO							COACH: Troy Calhoun
DATE		**Opponent**	**AFA**	**Opp**	**S/U**	**Line**	**ATS**	**Total**	**O/U**	**Trends & Angles**
9/4/2021	vs	*LAFAYETTE*								1st meeting
9/11/2021	@	*Navy*								1-8 S/U @ Navy since 2003
9/18/2021	vs	UTAH STATE								3-0 S/U & ATS @ home vs Utah State since 2015
9/25/2021	vs	*FLORIDA ATLANTIC*								vs Florida Atlantic - FAU leads series 1-0
10/9/2021	vs	WYOMING								Game 1-6 O/U @ home vs Wyoming since 2007
10/9/2021	@	New Mexico								1-3 S/U & ATS @ New Mexico since 2013
10/16/2021	@	Boise State								0-4 S/U @ ATS vs Boise State since 2017
10/23/2021	vs	SAN DIEGO STATE								0-4 ATS @ home vs San Diego State since 2009
11/6/2021	vs	*Army {@ Arlington, TX}*								Game 0-7 O/U since 2014
11/13/2021	@	Colorado State								Game 8-0 O/U @ Colorado State since 2005
11/20/2021	@	Nevada								vs Nevada - Air Force leads series 3-2
11/27/2021	vs	UNLV								6-1 S/U @ home vs UNLV since 2003
12/4/2021	vs									MWC Championship
	vs									BOWL GAME

Pointspread Analysis
Non-Conference

	LAFAYETTE
0-12 S/U vs Non-Conf. as 15.5-20 point Dog since 1988	
0-10 S/U vs Non-Conf. as 10.5-15 point Dog since 1991	
2-9 O/U vs Non-Conf. as 7.5-10 point Dog since 1984	
3-10 O/U vs Non-Conf. as 3 point or less favorite since 1995	
13-1 S/U vs Non-Conf. as 7.5-10 point favorite since 1989	
2-6 ATS vs Non-Conf. as 10.5-15 point favorite since 2000	
31-0 S/U vs Non-Conf. as 15.5 point or more favorite since 1988	
1-10 ATS @ Navy since 1999	
0-3 S/U & ATS @ Navy as 3 point or less Dog since 2005	
Game 4-16 O/U vs Navy since 2001	
vs Navy - Air Force leads series 31-22	
vs Army - Air Force leads series 37-18-1	
3-0 S/U & ATS vs Army as 3 point or less Dog since 1990	
0-4 S/U & ATS vs Navy as 3 point or less favorite since 1993	
4-1 S/U @ Army as 3.5-7 point favorite since 1992	
5-0 S/U & ATS vs Army as 7.5-10 point favorite since 1989	
5-1 S/U vs Navy as 7.5-10 point favorite since 1985	
8-1 S/U vs Army as 10.5-15 point favorite since 1985	
6-0 S/U vs Army as 15.5-20 point favorite since 2002	
4-0 S/U vs Navy as 20.5-25 point favorite since 1994	

Dog

7-2 ATS as home Dog since 2014	
1-7 S/U on road as 20.5 point or more Dog since 1990	
7-1 ATS on road as 20.5 or more Dog since 1990	
0-11 S/U on road as 15.5-20 point Dog since 1988	
2-8 S/U on road as 10.5-15 point Dog since 2000	
5-1 ATS @ home as 7.5-10 point Dog since 2007	
9-3 ATS on road as 7.5-10 point Dog since 1994	
2-12 S/U on road as 3.5-7 point Dog since 2003	

Bowl Games

3-0 S/U & ATS in Independence Bowl	
16-0 S/U in 1st home game of season since 2005	LAFAYETTE
14-3 ATS in 1st road game of season since 2004	Navy
2-11 ATS in final road game of season since 2008	Nevada
11-1 S/U in final home game of season since 2009	UNLV

Favorite

10-0 S/U as 32 point or more favorite since 1988
3-7 ATS as 32 point or more favorite since 1988
4-0 O/U as 32 point or more favorite since 2010
6-0 S/U as 25.5-30 point favorite since 1985
0-3 O/U as 25.5-30 point favorite since 2003
33-0 S/U @ home as 20.5 point or more favorite since 1983
18-3 S/U @ home as 15.5-20 point favorite since 1984

Pointspread Analysis
Conference

vs Boise State - Boise State leads series 6-3
vs Colorado State - Air Force leads series 37-21-1
3-0 ATS vs Colorado State as 7.5-10 point Dog since 2001
3-0 S/U vs CSU as 7.5-10 point favorite since 1988
Game 4-1 O/U vs Nevada since 2012
Game 4-0-1 O/U @ home vs UNLV since 2007
Game 9-1-1 O/U vs UNLV since 2006
Game 4-0-1 O/U @ home vs UNLV since 2007
vs UNLV - Air Force leads series 16-6
5-0 S/U vs UNLV as 3.5-7 point favorite since 2002
5-1 O/U vs UNLV as 3.5-7 point favorite since 2000
3-0 S/U vs UNLV as 15.5-20 point favorite since 1998
3-0 S/U vs UNLV as 20.5-25 point favorite since 1997
Game 6-2 O/U @ New Mexico since 2005
vs New Mexico - Air Force leads series 23-13
Game 6-2 O/U vs New Mexico since 2013
4-0 S/U vs New Mexico as 15.5-20 point favorite since 1985
vs San Diego State - Air Force leads series 20-17
0-8 S/U vs San Diego State since 2010
2-7 ATS vs San Diego State since 2009
1-6 S/U vs San Diego State as 3.5-7 point Dog since 1990
0-4 ATS vs San Diego State as 3 point or less favorite since 1991
0-3 S/U vs SDSU as 3.5-7 point favorite since 2003
0-4 ATS vs SDSU as 3.5-7 point favorite since 1997
vs Utah State - Air Force leads series 6-3
0-3 S/U &ATS vs Utah State as 7.5-10 point Dog since 2013
3-0 O/U &ATS vs Utah State as 7.5-10 point Dog since 2013
vs Wyoming - Air Force leads series 28-26-3
2-8 ATS @ home vs Wyoming since 1999
1-10 ATS vs Wyoming since 2009
4-0 S/U vs Wyoming as 3.5-7 point favorite since 1985
1-5 ATS vs Wyoming as 10.5-15 point favorite since 1986

Favorite

7-1 S/U on road as 15.5-20 point favorite since 1985
10-0 S/U @ home as 10.5-15 point favorite since 2005
2-5 ATS on road as 10.5-15 point favorite since 2012
9-3 O/U as 10.5-15 point favorite since 2012
15-3 S/U @ home as 7.5-10 point favorite since 1989
0-4 ATS @ home as 7.5-10 point favorite since 2010
25-5 S/U on road as 3.5-7 point favorite since 1985
3-9 S/U on road as 3 point or less favorite since 1988
2-6 O/U on road as 3 point or less favorite since 1995

Copyright © 2021 by Steve's Football Bible, LLC

AKRON ZIPS

MAC East

2020-Akron		Opponent	Akr	Opp	S/U	Line	ATS	Total	O/U	
11/4/2020	vs	WESTERN MICHIGAN	13	58	L	20.0	L	**52.0**	O	
11/10/2020	@	Ohio	10	24	L	27.0	W	58.0	U	
11/17/2020	@	Kent State	35	69	L	26.0	L	**60.5**	O	"Wagon Wheel"
11/28/2020	vs	MIAMI-OHIO	7	38	L	14.0	L	55.0	U	
12/5/2020	vs	BOWLING GREEN	31	3	W	-2.5	W	54.5	U	
12/12/2020	@	Buffalo	7	56	L	33.5	L	58.5	O	
Coach: Tom Arth		Season Record >>	103	248	1-5	ATS>>	2-4	O/U>>	3-3	
2019-Akron		Opponent	Akr	Opp	S/U	Line	ATS	Total	O/U	
8/31/2019	@	Illinois	3	42	L	18.0	L	60.0	U	
9/7/2019	vs	ALABAMA-BIRMINGHAM	20	31	L	8.0	L	**46.5**	O	
9/14/2019	@	Central Michigan	24	45	L	2.5	L	**45.0**	O	
9/21/2019	vs	TROY	7	35	L	18.5	L	57.0	U	
9/28/2019	@	Massachusetts	29	37	L	-9.5	L	**60.5**	O	
10/12/2019	vs	KENT STATE	3	26	L	14.5	L	57.5	U	"Wagon Wheel"
10/19/2019	vs	BUFFALO	0	21	L	17.5	L	48.0	U	
10/26/2019	@	Northern Illinois	0	49	L	22.5	L	**41.5**	O	
11/2/2019	@	Bowling Green	6	35	L	3.5	L	48.0	U	
11/12/2019	vs	EASTERN MICHIGAN	14	42	L	17.0	L	**44.5**	O	
11/20/2019	@	Miami-Ohio	17	20	L	28.5	W	45.0	U	
11/26/2019	vs	OHIO	3	52	L	27.5	L	**52.5**	O	
Coach: Tom Arth		Season Record >>	126	435	0-12	ATS>>	1-11	O/U>>	6-6	
2018-Akron		Opponent	Akr	Opp	S/U	Line	ATS	Total	O/U	
9/8/2018	vs	MORGAN STATE	41	7	W	-42.5	L	**NT**	---	
9/15/2018	@	Northwestern	39	34	W	21.0	W	**46.5**	O	
9/22/2018	@	Iowa State	13	26	L	18.5	W	47.0	U	
10/6/2018	vs	MIAMI-OHIO	17	41	L	-5.0	L	**47.5**	O	
10/13/2018	@	Buffalo	6	24	L	11.0	L	54.5	U	
10/20/2018	@	Kent State	24	23	W	-4.5	L	49.5	U	"Wagon Wheel"
10/27/2018	vs	CENTRAL MICHIGAN	17	10	W	-4.0	W	43.5	U	
11/1/2018	vs	NORTHERN ILLINOIS	26	36	L	6.0	L	**37.0**	O	
11/10/2018	@	Eastern Michigan	7	27	L	11.0	L	41.5	U	
11/17/2018	vs	BOWLING GREEN	6	21	L	-6.0	L	47.5	U	
11/23/2018	@	Ohio	28	49	L	23.5	W	**56.5**	O	
12/1/2018	@	South Carolina	3	28	L	28.5	W	56.5	U	
Coach: Terry Bowden		Season Record >>	227	326	4-8	ATS>>	5-7	O/U>>	4-7	
2017-Akron		Opponent	Akr	Opp	S/U	Line	ATS	Total	O/U	
9/2/2017	@	Penn State	0	52	L	30.0	L	62.5	U	
9/9/2017	vs	ARKANSAS-PINE BLUFF	52	3	W	-49.0	T	**NT**	---	
9/16/2017	vs	IOWA STATE	14	41	L	10.0	W	63.0	U	
9/23/2017	@	Troy	17	22	L	17.0	W	55.5	U	
9/30/2017	@	Bowling Green	34	23	W	-3.0	W	58.0	U	
10/7/2017	vs	BALL STATE	31	3	W	-4.5	W	51.5	U	
10/14/2017	@	Western Michigan	14	13	W	12.5	W	54.5	U	
10/21/2017	@	Toledo	21	48	L	14.5	L	**58.5**	O	
10/28/2017	vs	BUFFALO	21	20	W	2.5	W	66.5	U	
11/7/2017	@	Miami-Ohio	14	24	L	11.5	W	50.5	U	
11/14/2017	vs	OHIO	37	34	W	14.5	W	**51.0**	O	
11/21/2017	vs	KENT STATE	24	14	W	-14.5	L	46.0	U	"Wagon Wheel"
12/2/2017	vs	**Toledo**	28	45	L	21.0	W	**61.0**	**O**	MAC Championship
12/19/2017	vs	**Florida Atlantic**	3	50	L	23.0	L	65.5	U	Boca Raton Bowl
Coach: Terry Bowden		Season Record >>	310	392	7-7	ATS>>	8-5-1	O/U>>	3-10	

Copyright © 2021 by Steve's Football Bible, LLC

AKRON ZIPS

MAC East

STADIUM: InfoCision Stadium {30,000}			Location: Akron, OH						COACH: Tom Arth	
DATE		Opponent	Akr	Opp	S/U	Line	ATS	Total	O/U	Trends & Angles
9/4/2021	@	Auburn								Auburn leads series 1-0
9/11/2021	vs	TEMPLE								0-5 S/U & ATS vs Temple since 2007
9/18/2021	vs	BRYANT								1st meeting
9/25/2021	@	Ohio State								Ohio State leads series 7-1
10/2/2021	vs	OHIO								1-12 S/U vs Ohio since 2008
10/9/2021	@	Bowling Green								2-10 ATS vs Bowling Green since 2006
10/16/2021	@	Miami-Ohio								2-11 S/U @ Miami-Ohio since 1994
10/23/2021	vs	BUFFALO								7-2 S/U @ home vs Buffalo since 2000
11/2/2021	vs	BALL STATE								vs Ball State - Series tied 10-10-1
11/9/2021	@	Western Michigan								2-8 S/U @ Western Michigan since 1987
11/20/2021	vs	KENT STATE								12-3 S/U @ home vs Kent State since 1989
11/27/2021	@	Toledo								0-6 S/U @ Toledo since 1947
12/3/2021	vs									MAC Championship
	vs									BOWL GAME

Pointspread Analysis Non-Conference		Pointspread Analysis Conference
2-11 S/U vs Non-Conf. as 20.5-25 point Dog since 1989		vs Bowling Green - BGU leads series 18-9
1-13 S/U vs Non-Conf. as 15.5-20 point Dog since 1989		2-14 S/U vs Bowling Green as Dog since 1992
0-8 S/U vs Non-Conf. as 10.5-15 point Dog since 1987		2-9 S/U vs Bowling Green since 2007
8-3 ATS vs Non-Conf. as 7.5-10 point Dog since 1990		0-3 S/U & ATS @ B. Green as 10.5-15 point Dog since 2009
4-0 O/U vs Non-Conf. as 3.5-7 point Dog since 2008		0-4 S/U & ATS vs B. Green as 3.5-7 point Dog since 2001
1-5 ATS vs Non-Conf. as 3.5-7 point favorite since 1994		3-0 S/U vs B. Green as 7.5-10 point favorite since 1989
Dog		vs Buffalo - Akron leads series 11-9
0-34 S/U as 25.5 point or more Dog since 1990		0-5 ATS vs Kent State since 2016
2-15 S/U on road as 20.5-25 point Dog since 1989		Game 0-5 O/U @ home vs Kent State since 2011
2-34 S/U as 15.5-20 point Dog since 1990		vs Kent State - Akron leads series 35-26-1
6-2 ATS on road as 15.5-20 point Dog since 2012		3-0 S/U & ATS @ home vs Kent as 3 point or less favorite since 1995
3-12-1 O/U as 15.5-20 point Dog since 2010		3-0 S/U vs Kent State as 7.5-10 point favorite since 1998
2-23 S/U on road as 10.5-15 point Dog since 1990		Game 3-10 O/U vs Miami-Ohio since 2006
1-11 S/U @ home as 7.5-10 point Dog since 1997		2-17 S/U vs Miami-Ohio as Dog since 1994
8-1 ATS on road as 7.5-10 point Dog since 2001		vs Miami-Ohio - Miami-Ohio leads series 21-8-1
1-8 S/U @ home as 3.5-7 point Dog since 2008		0-3 S/U vs Miami-Ohio as 15.5-20 point Dog since 1997
Favorite		0-5 S/U vs Miami-Ohio as 10.5-15 point Dog since 1994
6-0 S/U as 25.5 point or more favorite since 2000		0-6 S/U vs Miami-Ohio as 7.5-10 point Dog since 1999
9-2 S/U as 15.5-20 point favorite since 1999		vs Ohio - Ohio leads series 23-12-1
2-9 ATS as 15.5-20 point favorite since 1999		0-4 S/U & ATS vs Ohio as 3.5-7 point Dog since 2002
0-7 O/U as 10.5-15 point favorite since 2012		0-4 O/U vs Ohio as 3.5-7 point Dog since 2002
21-4 S/U as 7.5-10 point favorite since 1989		2-10 S/U vs Toledo since 1994
2-8 S/U & ATS on road as 3 point or less favorite since 1990		vs Western Michigan - WMU leads series 15-4
		0-3 S/U vs Western Michigan as favorite since 1990

1-19 S/U in 1st road game of season since 2000	Auburn
1-12 S/U prior to playing Ohio since 2007	Ohio State
0-10 O/U prior to playing Ohio since 2010	Ohio State
8-3-2 ATS prior to playing Miami-Ohio since 2006	Bowling Green
1-7 O/U after playing Buffalo since 2009	BALL STATE
2-13 S/U in final road game of season since 2005	Toledo

Copyright © 2021 by Steve's Football Bible, LLC

ALABAMA CRIMSON TIDE   SEC West

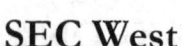

2020-Alabama		Opponent	Bama	Opp	S/U	Line	ATS	Total	O/U	
9/26/2020	vs	MISSOURI	38	19	W	-29.0	L	55.5	O	
10/3/2020	vs	TEXAS A&M	52	24	W	-18.0	W	54.0	O	
10/10/2020	@	Mississippi	63	48	W	-24.0	L	74.0	O	
10/17/2020	vs	GEORGIA	41	24	W	-5.5	W	56.5	O	
10/24/2020	@	Tennessee	48	17	W	-22.0	W	66.5	U	Third Saturday in October Rivalry
10/31/2020	vs	MISSISSIPPI STATE	41	0	W	-29.0	W	63.5	U	
11/21/2020	vs	KENTUCKY	63	3	W	-31.0	W	57.5	O	
11/28/2020	vs	AUBURN	42	13	W	-24.5	W	65.0	U	"Iron Bowl"
12/5/2020	@	Lsu	55	17	W	-28.5	W	63.5	O	
12/12/2020	@	Arkansas	52	3	W	-29.0	W	69.0	U	
12/19/2020	vs	Florida	52	46	W	-16.5	L	74.0	O	SEC Championship
1/1/2021	vs	Notre Dame	31	14	W	-18.0	L	65.5	U	Rose Bowl {CFP Semifinal}
1/11/2021	vs	Ohio State	52	24	W	-9.5	W	75.5	O	CFB Championship Game
Coach: Nick Saban		Season Record >>	630	252	13-0	ATS>>	9-4	O/U>>	8-5	National Champions
2019-Alabama		Opponent	Bama	Opp	S/U	Line	ATS	Total	O/U	
8/31/2019	vs	Duke	42	3	W	-33.5	W	56.5	U	Mercedes Benz Stadium
9/7/2019	vs	NEW MEXICO STATE	62	10	W	-55.0	L	64.0	O	
9/14/2019	@	South Carolina	47	23	W	-26.0	L	59.5	O	
9/21/2019	vs	SOUTHERN MISSISSIPPI	49	7	W	-38.0	W	63.0	U	
9/28/2019	vs	MISSISSIPPI	59	31	W	-37.5	L	62.5	O	
10/12/2019	@	Texas A&M	47	28	W	-17.0	W	61.0	O	
10/19/2019	vs	TENNESSEE	35	13	W	-34.5	L	62.5	U	Third Saturday in October Rivalry
10/26/2019	vs	ARKANSAS	48	7	W	-31.5	W	56.0	U	
11/9/2019	vs	LSU	41	46	L	-4.5	L	65.0	O	
11/16/2019	@	Mississippi State	38	7	W	-19.0	W	61.5	U	
11/23/2019	vs	WESTERN CAROLINA	66	3	W	-57.5	W	NT	---	
11/30/2019	@	Auburn	45	48	L	-3.5	L	51.0	O	"Iron Bowl"
1/2/2020	vs	Michigan	35	16	W	-8.0	W	60.0	U	Citrus Bowl
Coach: Nick Saban		Season Record >>	614	242	11-2	ATS>>	7-6	O/U>>	6-6	
2018-Alabama		Opponent	Bama	Opp	S/U	Line	ATS	Total	O/U	
9/1/2018	vs	Louisville	51	14	W	-23.5	W	60.0	O	Camping World Stadium
9/8/2018	vs	ARKANSAS STATE	57	7	W	-36.5	W	63.0	O	
9/15/2018	@	Mississippi	62	7	W	-22.5	W	71.0	U	
9/22/2018	vs	TEXAS A&M	45	23	W	-23.5	L	58.5	O	
9/29/2018	vs	LOUISIANA-LAFAYETTE	56	14	W	-49.0	L	69.0	O	
10/6/2018	@	Arkansas	65	31	W	-35.0	L	58.0	O	
10/13/2018	vs	MISSOURI	39	10	W	-28.0	W	72.5	U	
10/20/2018	@	Tennessee	58	21	W	-28.5	W	57.5	O	Third Saturday in October Rivalry
11/3/2018	@	Lsu	29	0	W	-13.5	W	51.5	U	
11/10/2018	vs	MISSISSIPPI STATE	24	0	W	-21.5	W	51.0	U	
11/17/2018	vs	THE CITADEL	50	17	W	-51.0	L	NT	---	
11/24/2018	vs	AUBURN	52	21	W	-27.0	W	52.5	O	Iron Bowl
12/1/2018	vs	Georgia	35	28	W	-11.0	L	63.0	T	SEC Championship
12/29/2018	vs	Oklahoma	45	34	W	-15.0	L	80.5	U	Orange Bowl (National Semi-Final)
1/7/2019	vs	Clemson	16	44	L	-5.5	L	57.5	O	CFB Championship Game
Coach: Nick Saban		Season Record >>	684	271	14-1	ATS>>	8-7	O/U>>	8-5-1	SEC Champions
2017-Alabama		Opponent	Bama	Opp	S/U	Line	ATS	Total	O/U	
9/2/2017	vs	Florida State	24	7	W	-7.5	W	51.5	U	Mercedes-Benz Stadium
9/9/2017	vs	FRESNO STATE	41	10	W	-42.5	L	54.5	U	
9/16/2017	vs	COLORADO STATE	41	23	W	-31.0	L	55.5	O	
9/23/2017	@	Vanderbilt	59	0	W	-19.5	W	42.0	O	
9/30/2017	vs	MISSISSIPPI	66	3	W	-29.0	W	55.0	O	
10/7/2017	@	Texas A&M	27	19	W	-25.5	W	56.0	U	
10/14/2017	vs	ARKANSAS	41	9	W	-37.0	L	54.5	U	
10/21/2017	vs	TENNESSEE	45	7	W	-37.0	W	50.5	O	Third Saturday in October Rivalry
11/4/2017	vs	LSU	24	10	W	-20.5	L	46.5	U	
11/11/2017	@	Mississippi State	31	24	W	-14.0	L	49.5	O	
11/18/2017	vs	MERCER	56	0	W	-49.0	W	NT	---	
11/25/2017	@	Auburn	14	26	L	-4.5	L	47.5	U	Iron Bowl
1/1/2018	vs	Clemson	24	6	W	-3.5	W	46.5	U	Sugar Bowl (National Semifinal)
1/8/2018	vs	Georgia	26	23	W	-3.0	T	45.0	O	CFB Championship Game
Coach: Nick Saban		Season Record >>	519	167	13-1	ATS>>	7-6-1	O/U>>	6-7	National Champions

Copyright © 2021 by Steve's Football Bible, LLC

ALABAMA CRIMSON TIDE   SEC West

STADIUM: Bryant-Denny Stadium {101,821}		Location: Tuscaloosa, AL						COACH: Nick Saban	
DATE	Opponent	Bama	Opp	S/U	Line	ATS	Total	O/U	Trends & Angles
9/4/2021	vs	Miami {@ Atlanta}							vs Miami - Alabama leads series 14-3
9/11/2021	vs	MERCER							vs Mercer - Alabama leads series 3-0
9/18/2021	@	Florida							10-2 S/U @ Florida since 1916
9/25/2021	vs	SOUTHERN MISS							vs Southern Miss - Alabama leads series 37-5-2
10/2/2021	vs	MISSISSIPPI							37-2-1 S/U @ home vs Mississippi since 1900
10/9/2021	@	Texas A&M							5-0 S/U @ Texas A&M since 1988
10/16/2021	@	Mississippi State							8-1 S/U @ Mississippi State since 2003
10/23/2021	vs	TENNESSEE							8-0 S/U @ home vs Tennessee since 2005
11/6/2021	vs	LSU							9-1 S/U vs LSU since 2012
11/13/2021	vs	NEW MEXICO STATE							vs New Mexico State - Alabama leads series 1-0
11/20/2021	vs	ARKANSAS							8-0 S/U @ home vs Arkansas since 2005
11/27/2021	@	Auburn							2-6 ATS @ Auburn since 2005
12/4/2021	vs								SEC Championship
	vs								BOWL GAME

Pointspread Analysis Non-Conference		Pointspread Analysis Conference
0-4 S/U & ATS vs Non-Conf. as 3 point or less favorite since 2000		14-0 S/U vs Arkansas since 2007
8-2 S/U vs Non-Conf. as 3.5-7 point favorite since 2001		vs Arkansas - Alabama leads series 23-7
10-2 S/U vs Non-Conf. as 7.5-10 point favorite since 1998		6-1 S/U vs Arkansas as 7.5-10 point favorite since 1980
8-0 S/U vs Non-Conf. as 10.5-15 point favorite since 2005		4-0 S/U vs Arkansas as 15.5-20 point favorite since 2005
1-8 ATS vs Non-Conf. as 15.5-20 point favorite since 1992		5-0 S/U vs Arkansas as 25.5 point or more favorite since 2013
13-1 S/U vs Non-Conf. as 20.5-25 point favorite since 1984		6-1 S/U vs Arkansas as 7.5-10 point favorite since 1980
41-0 S/U vs Non-Conf. as 25.5 point or more favorite since 1986		vs Auburn - Alabama leads series 47-37-1
7-16-1 ATS vs Non-Conf. as 30.5 point or more favorite since 2011		1-3 O/U vs Auburn as 3.5-7 point favorite since 1999
7-0 S/U vs Southern Miss as 10.5-15 point favorite since 1983		Game 5-0 O/U vs Florida since 2011
Dog		9-2-1 ATS vs Florida since 1998
1-11 S/U as 11 point or more Dog since 1996		7-0 S/U vs Florida since 2009
8-1-1 ATS as 11 point or more Dog since 1997		3-0 S/U vs Florida as 3.5-7 point Dog since 1999
0-4 S/U as 7.5-10 point Dog since 2003		4-0 ATS vs Florida as 3.5-7 point Dog since 1994
Favorite		Game 2-7-2 O/U vs LSU since 2011
1-6 ATS @ home as 3.5-7 point favorite since 2002		vs LSU - Alabama leads series 54-26-5
12-1 S/U on road as 7.5-10 point favorite since 1985		3-0 S/U vs LSU as 7.5-10 point favorite since 1991
10-1 S/U @ home as 7.5-10 point favorite since 1998		3-0 S/U & ATS vs LSU as 10.5-15 point favorite since 1990
12-1 S/U on road as 10.5-15 point favorite since 1997		vs Mississippi - Alabama leads series 56-10-2
13-1 S/U @ home as 10.5-15 point favorite since 2007		6-0 S/U vs Mississippi as 10.5-15 point favorite since 1996
25-1 S/U as 15.5-20 point favorite since 2002		0-6 O/U vs Mississippi as 10.5-15 point favorite since 1996
14-0 S/U on road as 15.5-20 point favorite since 1988		vs Mississippi State - Alabama leads series 85-17-3
12-0 S/U @ home as 15.5-20 point favorite since 2002		13-0 S/U vs Mississippi State since 2008
1-5 O/U @ home as 15.5-20 point favorite since 2002		Game 2-11-1 O/U vs Mississippi State since 2007
26-2 S/U @ home as 20.5-25 point favorite since 1986		Game 1-11 O/U @ Mississippi State since 1996
1-6-1 O/U @ home as 20.5-25 point favorite since 2007		11-2 S/U vs Miss. State as 10.5-15 point favorite since 1985
7-0 S/U on road as 20.5-25 point favorite since 1984		6-0 S/U vs Miss. State as 15.5-20 point favorite since 1983
73-0 S/U as 25.5 point or more favorite since 1986		7-0 S/U vs Miss. State as 20.5-25 point favorite since 1987
7-2 ATS on road as 25.5 point or more favorite since 1992		vs Tennessee - Alabama leads series 57-37-8
Bowl Games		14-0 S/U vs Tennessee since 2007
7-2 O/U in Bowl Games as 7.5-10 favorite since 1991		4-0 S/U vs Tennessee as 10.5-15 point favorite since 1986
6-0 S/U in Bowl Game as 10.5-15 point favorite since 1975		3-0 S/U vs Tennessee as 15.5-20 point favorite since 2010
9-2 ATS in Bowl Games as 3.5-7 point favorite since 1981		4-0 S/U vs Tennessee as 25.5 point or more favorite since 2011
19-0 S/U in 1st game of season since 2002	Miami	4-0 ATS vs Tennessee as 25.5 point or more favorite since 2011
19-0 S/U in 1st home game of season since 2002	MERCER	vs Texas A&M - Alabama leads series 11-2
13-1 S/U in 1st road game of season since 2007	Florida	8-0 S/U vs Texas A&M since 2013
17-1 S/U prior to playing Mississippi since 2003	S. MISS	
16-1 S/U prior to playing Arkansas since 2004	NMSU	
10-3 ATS prior to playing Arkansas since 2008	NMSU	
16-1 S/U after playing Mississippi since 2004	Texas A&M	2-14 S/U vs #2 ranked teams all time {0-5 on road}
17-0 S/U prior to playing Tennessee since 2004	M State	54-1 S/U @ home when ranked since 2013
13-0 S/U prior to playing LSU since 2007	TENNESSEE	80-8 S/U when ranked #1 since 2009
13-0 S/U after playing Mississippi State since 2008	TENNESSEE	12-0 S/U on road when ranked #2 since 1992
13-0 S/U prior to playing Auburn since 2008	ARKANSAS	35-0 S/U when ranked #2 vs unranked teams since 1986

Copyright © 2021 by Steve's Football Bible, LLC

ALABAMA-BIRMINGHAM BLAZERS   CONFERENCE USA West

2020-Alabama-Birmingham		Opponent	UAB	Opp	S/U	Line	ATS	Total	O/U	
9/3/2020	vs	CENTRAL ARKANSAS	45	35	W	-20.0	L	49.5	O	
9/10/2020	@	Miami	14	31	L	14.5		54.5	U	
9/26/2020	@	South Alabama	42	10	W	-7.0	W	47.5	O	
10/3/2020	vs	TEXAS-SAN ANTONIO	21	13	W	-21.5	L	55.0	U	
10/17/2020	vs	WESTERN KENTUCKY	37	14	W	-13.5	W	44.5	O	
10/23/2020	vs	LOUISIANA	20	24	L	2.5	L	50.5	U	
10/31/2020	@	Louisiana Tech	34	37	L	-13.0	L	47.0	O	{2 OT}
12/12/2020	@	Rice	21	16	W	-7.0	L	42.0	U	
12/18/2020	@	Marshall	22	13	W	4.0	W	44.0	U	C-USA CHAMPIONSHIP GAME — C-USA CHAMPIONS
Coach: Bill Clark		Season Record >>	256	193	6-3	ATS>>	3-6	O/U>>	4-5	
2019-Alabama-Birmingham		Opponent	UAB	Opp	S/U	Line	ATS	Total	O/U	
8/29/2019	vs	ALABAMA STATE	24	19	W	-39.0	L	NT	---	
9/7/2019	@	Akron	31	20	W	-8.0	W	46.5	O	
9/21/2019	vs	SOUTH ALABAMA	35	3	W	-12.0	W	48.0	U	
9/28/2019	@	Western Kentucky	13	20	L	-3.5	L	47.0	U	
10/5/2019	vs	RICE	35	20	W	-10.0	W	43.5	O	
10/12/2019	@	Texas-San Antonio	33	14	W	-12.5	W	47.0	T	
10/19/2019	vs	OLD DOMINION	38	14	W	-17.0	W	41.5	O	
11/2/2019	@	Tennessee	7	30	L	13.5	L	49.0	U	
11/9/2019	@	Southern Mississippi	2	37	L	7.5	L	50.0	U	
11/16/2019	vs	TEXAS-EL PASO	37	10	W	-14.5	W	42.0	O	
11/23/2019	vs	LOUISIANA TECH	20	14	W	-6.5	L	44.0	U	
11/30/2019	@	North Texas	26	21	W	-3.0	W	49.5	U	
12/7/2019	@	Florida Atlantic	6	49	L	8.0	L	49.0	O	C-USA Championship Game
12/21/2019	vs	Appalachian State	17	31	L	17.0	W	47.5	O	New Orleans Bowl
Coach: Bill Clark		Season Record >>	324	302	9-5	ATS>>	8-6	O/U>>	6-6-1	
2018-Alabama-Birmingham		Opponent	UAB	Opp	S/U	Line	ATS	Total	O/U	
8/30/2018	vs	SAVANNAH STATE	52	0	W	-38.5	W	NT	---	
9/8/2018	@	Coastal Carolina	24	47	L	-8.5	L	54.5	O	
9/15/2018	vs	TULANE	31	24	W	3.5	W	57.0	U	
9/29/2018	vs	CHARLOTTE	28	7	W	-15.5	W	52.0	U	
10/6/2018	@	Louisiana Tech	28	7	W	6.5	W	55.5	U	
10/13/2018	@	Rice	42	0	W	-16.5	W	52.0	U	
10/20/2018	vs	NORTH TEXAS	29	21	W	-1.5	W	53.5	O	
10/27/2018	@	Texas-El Paso	19	0	W	-15.0	W	49.5	U	
11/3/2018	vs	TEXAS-SAN ANTONIO	52	3	W	-21.5	W	42.0	O	
11/10/2018	vs	SOUTHERN MISSISSIPPI	26	23	W	-13.5	L	45.0	O	{OT}
11/17/2018	@	Texas A&M	20	41	L	17.0	L	46.5	O	
11/24/2018	@	Middle Tennessee	3	27	L	-3.0	L	52.0	U	
12/1/2018	@	Middle Tennessee	27	25	W	1.0	W	44.0	O	C-USA Championship Game
12/18/2018	vs	Northern Illinois	37	13	W	-1.0	W	41.0	O	Boca Raton Bowl
Coach: Bill Clark		Season Record >>	418	238	11-3	ATS>>	10-4	O/U>>	6-7	C-USA Champions
2017-Alabama-Birmingham		Opponent	UAB	Opp	S/U	Line	ATS	Total	O/U	
9/2/2017	vs	ALABAMA A&M	38	7	W	-28.0	W	60.5	U	
9/9/2017	@	Ball State	31	51	L	13.5	L	54.0	O	
9/16/2017	vs	COASTAL CAROLINA	30	23	W	1.5	W	53.5	U	
9/23/2017	@	North Texas	43	46	L	9.5	L	59.5	O	
10/7/2017	vs	LOUISIANA TECH	23	22	W	9.5	W	64.5	U	
10/14/2017	vs	MIDDLE TENNESSEE	25	23	W	4.0	W	55.0	U	
10/21/2017	@	Charlotte	24	25	L	-9.5	L	51.5	U	{OT}
10/28/2017	@	Southern Miss	30	12	W	11.5	W	50.5	U	
11/4/2017	vs	RICE	52	21	W	-8.5	W	50.5	O	
11/11/2017	@	Texas-San Antonio	24	19	W	7.0	W	50.0	U	
11/18/2017	@	Florida	7	36	L	10.5	L	48.0	U	
11/25/2017	vs	TEXAS-EL PASO	28	7	W	-21.0	T	47.0	U	
12/23/2017	vs	Ohio	6	41	L	6.5	L	54.5	U	Bahamas Bowl
Coach: Bill Clark		Season Record >>	361	333	8-5	ATS>>	8-4-1	O/U>>	3-10	

Copyright © 2021 by Steve's Football Bible, LLC

ALABAMA-BIRMINGHAM BLAZERS   CONFERENCE USA West

STADIUM: Legion Field {71,594}			Location: Birmingham, AL					COACH: Bill Clark	
DATE		Opponent	UAB	Opp	S/U	Line	ATS	Total	O/U	Trends & Angles
9/1/2021	vs	*JACKSONVILLE STATE*								vs Jacksonville State - UAB leads series 3-2
9/11/2021	@	*Georgia*								vs Georgia - Georgia leads series 2-0
9/18/2021	@	North Texas								4-0 ATS vs North Texas since 2014
9/25/2021	@	*Tulane*								vs Tulane - Series tied 5-5
10/2/2021	vs	*LIBERTY*								1st meeting
10/9/2021	vs	**FLORIDA ATLANTIC**								vs Florida Atlantic - FAU leads series 5-2
10/16/2021	@	Southern Mississippi								4-1 S/U & ATS @ Southern Miss since 2010
10/23/2021	vs	**RICE**								5-0 ATS @ home vs Rice since 2005
11/6/2021	vs	**LOUISIANA TECH**								vs Louisiana Tech - La Tech leads series 6-3
11/13/2021	@	Marshall								1-5 S/U @ Marshall since 2005
11/20/2021	@	Texas-San Antonio								4-0 S/U vs Texas-San Antonio since 2017
11/27/2021	vs	**TEXAS-EL PASO**								5-0 S/U vs UTEP since 2009 {4-0-1 ATS}
12/4/2021										C-USA Championship
	vs									BOWL GAME

Pointspread Analysis Dog		Pointspread Analysis Conference
6-0 ATS on road as 3.5-7 point Dog since 2012		Game 7-0 O/U vs Florida Atlantic since 2008
0-6 O/U as 3.5-7 point Dog since 2017		vs Marshall - Marshall leads series 8-3
5-1 O/U on road as 7.5-10 point Dog since 2010		vs North Texas - UAB leads series 4-1
2-21 S/U as 10.5-15 point Dog since 2003		4-0 S/U vs Rice since 2017
2-10 ATS as 10.5-15 point Dog since 2008		vs Rice - UAB leades series 5-4
0-12 S/U on road as 15.5-20 point Dog since 1997		Game 6-2 O/U vs Rice since 2005
0-29 S/U on road as 20.5 point or more Dog since 1997		7-2 S/U vs Southern Miss since 2009
Favorite		vs Southern Miss - Southern Miss leads series 11-7
20-4 S/U as 15.5 point or more favorite since 1998		vs Texas-San antonio - UAB leads series 4-1
10-2 O/U @ home as 10.5-15 point favorite since 2003		vs Texas-El Paso - UAB leads series 6-1
10-2 S/U @ home as 3.5-7 point favorite since 2001		vs Western Kentucky - Series tied 4-4
6-1 O/U @ home as 3.5-7 point favorite since 2006	JACK. STATE	6-0 S/U in 1st home game of season since 2013
0-9 O/U on road as 3 point or less favorite since 2001	Georgia	1-14 S/U in 1st road game of season since 2004

Print Version $24.99   Print Version $29.99   Print Version $29.99

These books available at numerous online retailers

Copyright © 2021 by Steve's Football Bible, LLC

APPALACHIAN STATE MOUNTAINEERS   SUN BELT East

2020-Appalachian State		Opponent	APP	Opp	S/U	Line	ATS	Total	O/U	
9/12/2020	vs	*CHARLOTTE*	35	20	W	-17.0	L	59.0	U	
9/19/2020	@	*Marshall*	7	17	L	-6.0	L	59.5	U	
9/26/2020	vs	*CAMPBELL*	52	21	W	-32.0	L	53.0	O	
10/22/2020	vs	ARKANSAS STATE	45	17	W	-13.5	W	69.0	U	
10/31/2020	@	Louisiana-Monroe	31	13	W	-29.0	L	56.0	U	
11/7/2020	@	Texas State	38	17	W	-21.5	L	59.0	U	
11/14/2020	vs	GEORGIA STATE	17	13	W	-18.0	L	63.0	U	
11/21/2020	@	Coastal Carolina	23	34	L	3.0	L	48.0	O	
11/28/2020	vs	TROY	47	10	W	-14.0	W	50.5	O	
12/4/2020	vs	LOUISIANA	21	24	L	-3.0	L	51.0	U	
12/12/2020	@	Georgia Southern	34	26	W	-9.5	L	45.0	O	*"Deeper Than Hate Rivalry"*
12/21/2020	vs	**North Texas**	56	28	W	-22.5	W	68.0	O	Myrtle Beach Bowl
Coach: Shawn Clark		Season Record >>	406	240	9-3	ATS>>	3-9	O/U>>	5-7	

2019-Appalachian State		Opponent	APP	Opp	S/U	Line	ATS	Total	O/U	
8/31/2019	vs	*EAST TENNESSEE STATE*	42	7	W	-32.5	W	NT	---	
9/7/2019	vs	*CHARLOTTE*	56	41	W	-23.0	L	54.5	O	
9/21/2019	@	*North Carolina*	34	31	W	2.0	W	58.0	O	
9/28/2019	vs	COASTAL CAROLINA	56	37	W	-14.5	W	58.0	O	
10/9/2019	@	Louisiana-Lafayette	17	7	W	3.0	W	69.0	U	
10/19/2019	vs	LOUISIANA-MONROE	52	7	W	-15.5	W	65.5	U	
10/26/2019	@	South Alabama	30	3	W	-26.5	W	51.0	U	
10/31/2019	vs	GEORGIA SOUTHERN	21	24	L	-13.5	L	41.5	O	*"Deeper Than Hate Rivalry"*
11/9/2019	@	*South Carolina*	20	15	W	6.5	W	51.0	U	
11/16/2019	@	Georgia State	56	27	W	-15.0	W	61.5	O	
11/23/2019	vs	TEXAS STATE	35	13	W	-28.0	L	50.0	U	
11/30/2019	@	Troy	48	13	W	-11.0	W	64.0	U	
12/7/2019	vs	**LOUISIANA-LAFAYETTE**	45	38	W	-5.0	W	57.0	O	SUN BELT CHAMPIONSHIP
12/21/2019	vs	**Alabama-Birmingham**	31	17	W	-17.0	L	47.5	O	New Orleans Bowl
		Season Record >>	543	280	13-1	ATS>>	10-4	O/U>>	7-6	**SUN BELT CHAMPIONS**

2018-Appalachian State		Opponent	APP	Opp	S/U	Line	ATS	Total	O/U	
9/1/2018	@	*Penn State*	38	45	L	24.0	W	54.0	O	{OT}
9/8/2018	@	*Charlotte*	45	9	W	-14.0	W	48.5	O	
9/22/2018	vs	*GARDNER-WEBB*	72	7	W	-49.0	W	NT	---	
9/29/2018	vs	SOUTH ALABAMA	52	7	W	-25.0	W	56.5	O	
10/9/2018	@	Arkansas State	35	9	W	-10.5	W	58.5	U	
10/20/2018	vs	LOUISIANA-LAFAYETTE	27	17	W	-25.5	L	67.0	U	
10/25/2018	@	Georgia Southern	14	34	L	-11.0	L	47.5	O	*"Deeper Than Hate Rivalry"*
11/3/2018	@	Coastal Carolina	23	7	W	-13.5	W	52.0	U	
11/10/2018	@	Texas State	38	7	W	-19.0	W	45.5	U	
11/17/2018	vs	GEORGIA STATE	45	17	W	-27.5	W	54.0	O	
11/24/2018	vs	TROY	21	10	W	-11.5	L	45.5	U	
12/1/2018	vs	**LOUISIANA-LAFAYETTE**	30	19	W	-17.0	L	55.0	U	SUN BELT CHAMPIONSHIP
12/15/2018	vs	**Middle Tennessee**	45	13	W	-6.5	W	49.0	O	New Orleans Bowl
Coach: Scott Satterfield		Season Record >>	1028	481	11-2	ATS>>	9-4	O/U>>	6-6	SUN BELT CHAMPIONS

2017-Appalachian State		Opponent	APP	Opp	S/U	Line	ATS	Total	O/U	
9/2/2017	@	*Georgia*	10	31	L	12.0	L	46.0	U	
9/9/2017	vs	*SAVANNAH STATE*	54	7	W	-51.0	L	NT	---	
9/16/2017	@	Texas State	20	13	W	-21.5	L	49.5	U	
9/23/2017	vs	*WAKE FOREST*	19	20	L	5.0	W	48.5	U	
10/7/2017	vs	NEW MEXICO STATE	45	31	W	-12.5	W	55.5	O	
10/14/2017	@	Idaho	23	20	W	-11.5	L	50.0	U	
10/21/2017	vs	COASTAL CAROLINA	37	29	W	-19.0	L	51.5	O	
10/28/2017	@	*Massachusetts*	27	30	L	-4.0	L	57.0	T	{2 OT}
11/4/2017	@	Louisiana-Monroe	45	52	L	-8.0	L	62.0	O	
11/9/2017	vs	GEORGIA SOUTHERN	27	6	W	-18.0	W	51.5	U	*"Deeper Than Hate Rivalry"*
11/25/2017	@	Georgia State	31	10	W	-6.0	W	51.0	U	
12/2/2017	vs	LOUISIANA-LAFAYETTE	63	14	W	-14.0	W	56.5	O	
12/23/2017	vs	**Toledo**	34	0	W	6.0	W	61.0	U	Dollar General Bowl
Coach: Scott Satterfield		Season Record >>	435	263	9-4	ATS>>	6-7	O/U>>	4-7-1	

Copyright © 2021 by Steve's Football Bible, LLC

APPALACHIAN STATE MOUNTAINEERS   SUN BELT East

STADIUM: Kidd-Brewer Stadium {30,000} | Location: Boone, NC | **COACH:** Shawn Clark

DATE		Opponent	App	Opp	S/U	Line	ATS	Total	O/U	Trends & Angles
9/2/2021	vs	East Carolina {@ Charlotte}								1-5 S/U vs East Carolina since 1962
9/11/2021	@	Miami								vs Miami - Miami leads series 1-0
9/18/2021	vs	ELON								18-0 S/U vs Elon since 1965
9/25/2021	vs	MARSHALL								8-3 S/U @ home vs Marshall since 1977
10/2/2021	@	Georgia State								vs Ga State - App State leads series 7-0 {5-2 ATS}
10/12/2021	@	Louisiana								3-0 S/U @ Louisiana since 2014 {3-0 ATS}
10/20/2021	vs	COASTAL CAROLINA								vs Coast Carolina – App. State leads series 3-1
10/30/2021	vs	LOUISIANA-MONROE								3-0 S/U @ home vs UL-Monroe since 2014
11/6/2021	@	Arkansas State								vs Arkansas State - App State leads series 3-1
11/13/2021	vs	SOUTH ALABAMA								vs South Alabama - App State leads series 2-1
11/20/2021	@	Troy								vs Troy - Appalachian leads series 6-3
11/27/2021	vs	GEORGIA SOUTHERN								5-1 S/U @ home vs Ga. Southern since 2009
12/4/2021	vs									Sun Belt Championship
	vs									BOWL GAME

Pointspread Analysis Dog		Pointspread Analysis Conference
1-6 S/U as 10.5 point or more Dog since 2014		vs Georgia Southern - Appalachian State leads series 19-14-1
Favorite		vs Louisiana - Appalachian State leads series 8-1
4-11 ATS as 21-30 point favorite since 2015		Game 2-7 O/U vs Louisiana since 2014
36-0 S/U as 15.5 point or more favorite since 2014		vs Louisiana-Monroe – App. State leads series 5-1 {2-4 ATS}
16-3 S/U as 10.5-15 point favorite since 2014		Game 0-5 O/U vs Texas State since 2016
8-2 S/U as 3.5-7 point favorite since 2014		
7-2 ATS as 3.5-7 point favorite since 2015		**Non-Conference**
		vs East Carolina - App State leads series 18-8
1-9 S/U in 1st road game of season since 2011	Miami	vs Elon - App State leads series 32-9-1
10-0 S/U in final road game of season since 2011	Troy	vs Marshall - App State leads series 14-7
22-1 S/U in final home game of season since 1998	G. SOUTHERN	
7-3 S/U when ranked all time		

Print Version $34.99   **Print Version $39.99**   **Print Version $39.99**

COLLEGE FOOTBALL HISTORY
"GLORIOUS GAMES OF THE PAST"
A historical look at some of college football's greatest and most memorable games.
A celebration of 150 years of college football
By Steve Fulton

COLLEGE FOOTBALL HISTORY
BOWL GAMES OF THE 20ᵗʰ CENTURY (1902-1999)
THE MOST COMPLETE AND IN-DEPTH HISTORICAL ACCOUNTS OF ALL THE MAJOR BOWL GAMES OF THE 20ᵗʰ CENTURY
A CELEBRATION OF 150 YEARS OF COLLEGE FOOTBALL
BY STEVE FULTON

COLLEGE FOOTBALL HISTORY
BOWL GAMES OF THE 21ˢᵗ CENTURY (2000-2019)
THE MOST COMPLETE AND IN-DEPTH HISTORICAL ACCOUNTS OF ALL THE MAJOR BOWL GAMES OF THE 21ˢᵗ CENTURY
A CELEBRATION OF 150 YEARS OF COLLEGE FOOTBALL
BY STEVE FULTON

These books available at numerous online retailers

Copyright © 2021 by Steve's Football Bible, LLC

ARIZONA WILDCATS   PACIFIC-12 South

2020-Arizona		Opponent	AZ	Opp	S/U	Line	ATS	Total	O/U	
11/14/2020	vs	USC	30	34	L	14.5	W	67.0	U	
11/21/2020	@	Washington	27	44	L	12.5	L	53.5	O	
11/28/2020	@	Ucla	10	27	L	7.5	L	70.5	U	
12/5/2020	vs	COLORADO	13	24	L	9.5	L	55.5	U	
12/11/2020	vs	ARIZONA STATE	7	70	L	8.0	L	58.0	O	Territorial Cup
Coach: Kevin Sumlin		Season Record >>	87	199	0-5	ATS>>	1-4	O/U>>	2-3	
2019-Arizona		Opponent	AZ	Opp	S/U	Line	ATS	Total	O/U	
8/24/2019	@	Hawaii	38	45	L	-10.5	L	70.5	O	
9/7/2019	vs	NORTHERN ARIZONA	65	41	W	-28.0	L	NT	---	
9/14/2019	vs	TEXAS TECH	28	14	W	2.0	W	74.0	U	
9/28/2019	vs	UCLA	20	17	W	-3.0	T	68.0	U	
10/5/2019	@	Colorado	35	30	W	2.5	W	63.5	O	
10/12/2019	vs	WASHINGTON	27	51	L	6.0	L	62.0	O	
10/19/2019	@	Usc	14	41	L	10.0	L	69.0	U	
10/26/2019	@	Stanford	31	41	L	3.0	L	54.0	O	
11/2/2019	vs	OREGON STATE	38	56	L	-5.0	L	71.5	O	
11/16/2019	@	Oregon	6	34	L	27.0	L	68.5	U	
11/23/2019	vs	UTAH	7	35	L	23.5	L	56.5	U	
11/29/2019	@	Arizona State	14	24	L	12.5	W	60.5	U	Territorial Cup
Coach: Kevin Sumlin		Season Record >>	323	429	4-8	ATS>>	3-8-1	O/U>>	5-6	
2018-Arizona		Opponent	AZ	Opp	S/U	Line	ATS	Total	O/U	
9/1/2018	vs	BYU	23	28	L	-11.0	L	59.0	U	
9/8/2018	@	Houston	18	45	L	3.0	L	70.0	U	
9/15/2018	vs	SOUTHERN UTAH	62	31	W	-24.5	W	NT	---	
9/22/2018	@	Oregon State	35	14	W	-4.0	W	73.5	U	
9/29/2018	vs	USC	20	24	L	3.0	L	61.5	U	
10/6/2018	vs	CALIFORNIA	24	17	W	1.0	W	57.0	U	
10/12/2018	@	Utah	10	42	L	13.5	L	52.5	U	
10/20/2018	@	Ucla	30	31	L	10.0	W	57.0	O	
10/27/2018	vs	OREGON	44	15	W	7.5	W	66.0	U	
11/2/2018	vs	COLORADO	42	34	W	-3.0	W	56.5	O	
11/17/2018	@	Washington State	28	69	L	10.5	L	63.5	O	
11/24/2018	vs	ARIZONA STATE	40	41	L	1.5	W	65.5	O	Territorial Cup
Coach: Kevin Sumlin		Season Record >>	376	391	5-7	ATS>>	7-5	O/U>>	4-7	
2017-Arizona		Opponent	AZ	Opp	S/U	Line	ATS	Total	O/U	
9/2/2017	vs	NORTHERN ARIZONA	62	24	W	-27.5	W	70.0	O	
9/9/2017	vs	HOUSTON	16	19	L	2.0	L	65.0	U	
9/15/2017	@	Texas-El Paso	63	16	W	-26.0	W	57.5	O	
9/22/2017	vs	UTAH	24	30	L	5.0	L	61.5	U	
10/7/2017	@	Colorado	45	42	W	7.0	W	58.5	O	
10/14/2017	vs	UCLA	47	30	W	-3.0	W	77.0	T	
10/21/2017	@	California	45	44	W	-4.5	L	65.0	O	{2 OT}
10/28/2017	vs	WASHINGTON STATE	58	37	W	PK	W	63.0	O	
11/4/2017	@	Usc	35	49	L	6.5	L	76.5	O	
11/11/2017	vs	OREGON STATE	49	28	W	-21.0	T	69.5	O	
11/18/2017	@	Oregon	28	48	L	3.0	L	77.5	U	
11/25/2017	@	Arizona State	30	42	L	-2.0	L	75.0	U	Territorial Cup
12/27/2017	vs	**Purdue**	35	38	L	-2.5	L	64.0	O	Foster Farms Bowl
Coach: Rich Rodriguez		Season Record >>	537	447	7-6	ATS>>	5-7-1	O/U>>	8-4-1	

Copyright © 2021 by Steve's Football Bible, LLC

ARIZONA WILDCATS   PACIFIC-12 South

STADIUM: Arizona Stadium {55,675}				Location: Tucson, AZ					COACH: Jedd Fisch
DATE		Opponent	AZ	Opp	S/U	Line	ATS	Total	O/U	Trends & Angles
9/2/2021	vs	Byu {@ Las Vegas}								Game 0-5 O/U vs BYU since 2006
9/11/2021	vs	SAN DIEGO STATE								6-1 S/U @ home vs San Diego State since 1934
9/18/2021	vs	NORTHERN ARIZONA								14-0 S/U vs Northern Arizona since 1933
9/25/2021	@	Oregon								2-11 S/U @ Oregon since 1989
10/9/2021	vs	UCLA								vs Ucla - UCLA leads series 26-17-2
10/16/2021	@	Colorado								4-0 S/U & ATS @ Colorado since 2013
10/22/2021	vs	WASHINGTON								Game 5-1 O/U @ home vs Washington since 2008
10/30/2021	@	Usc								1-8 S/U @ USC since 2004
11/6/2021	vs	CALIFORNIA								5-0 S/U @ home vs California since 2006
11/13/2021	vs	UTAH								0-4 S/U & ATS vs Utah since 2016
11/19/2021	@	Washington State								Game 5-0 O/U vs Washington State since 2014
11/27/2021	@	Arizona State								0-4 S/U @ Arizona State since 2013
12/3/2021	vs									PAC-12 Championship
	vs									BOWL GAME

Pointspread Analysis		Pointspread Analysis
Non-Conference		**Conference**
0-10 S/U vs Non-Conf. as 10.5 point or more Dog since 1988		vs Arizona State - Arizona leads series 49-44-1
6-1 ATS vs Non-Conf. as 7.5-10 point Dog since 1979		0-3 S/U & ATS vs Arizona State as 3.5-7 point favorite since 1992
0-8 S/U vs Non-Conf. as 3.5-7 point Dog since 1995		3-0 S/U vs Arizona State as 10.5-15 point favorite since 1994
0-8 O/U vs Non-Conf. as 3 point or less Dog since 1990		1-5 ATS vs California since 2009
8-1 S/U vs Non-Conf. as 7.5-10 point favorite since 1996		vs California - Arizona leads series 18-14-2
9-3 S/U vs Non-Conf. as 10.5-15 point favorite since 1994		5-0 S/U vs California as 3.5-7 point favorite since 1984
2-10 ATS vs Non-Conf. as 10.5-15 point favorite since 1994		0-4 ATS vs California as 7.5-10 point favorite since 1987
37-0 S/U vs Non-Conf. as 15.5 point or more favorite since 1985		0-5 ATS vs California as 10.5-15 point favorite since 1983
vs BYU - Arizona leads series 12-11-1		7-2 S/U vs Colorado since 2012
vs Northern Arizona - Arizona leads series 15-1		vs Colorado - Colorado leads series 15-8
4-0 S/U vs San Diego State since 1997		6-2 ATS vs Colorado since 2013
vs San Diego State - Arizona leads series 10-5		Game 8-2 O/U vs Colorado since 2011
Bowl Games		Game 5-0 O/U @ Colorado since 2011
1-6 O/U in Bowl Games since 2009		Game 0-7 O/U vs Oregon since 2012
4-0-1 O/U in Bowl Games since 2012		vs Oregon - Oregon leads series since 28-17
Dog		0-4 S/U vs Oregon as 3.5-7 point Dog since 1989
0-3 S/U as 30 point or more Dog since 1991		3-0 S/U & ATS vs Oregon as 7.5-10 point favorite since 1984
3-0 O/U as 30 point or more Dog since 1991		8-2 S/U vs UCLA as favorite since 1994
0-7 O/U as 20.5-29 point Dog since 2003		0-5 S/U vs UCLA as 10.5-15 point Dog since 1987
1-12 S/U as 20.5-29 point Dog since 1988		0-5 S/U @ UCLA as 7.5-10 point Dog since 1995
2-11 S/U on road as 15.5-20 point Dog since 1990		0-4 S/U & ATS vs UCLA as 3.5-7 point Dog since 1993
2-16 S/U on road as 10.5-15 point Dog since 1997		5-0-1 O/U vs UCLA as 3 point or less Dog since 1983
0-6 O/U @ home as 10.5-15 point Dog since 2005		5-23 S/U vs USC as Dog since 1984
3-18 S/U on road as 7.5-10 point Dog since 1984		2-17 S/U vs USC since 2001
8-27 S/U as 3.5-7 point Dog since 1996		vs USC - USC leads series 36-8
4-11 O/U on road as 3 point or less Dog since 1999		Game 1-8 O/U @ home vs USC since 2003
Favorite		0-4 S/U vs USC as 10.5-15 point Dog since 2008
8-2-2 O/U as 3 point or less favorite since 2010		0-4 S/U vs USC as 3 point or less Dog since 1984
11-0 S/U as 7.5-10 point favorite since 2010		0-5 S/U vs USC as 20.5 point or more favorite since 2003
2-18 ATS @ home as 10.5-15 point favorite since 1985		vs Utah - Utah leads series 24-19-2
11-1 S/U @ home as 15.5-20 point favorite since 1986		3-0 ATS vs Washington as 3 point or less Dog since 1987
6-0 S/U on road as 15.5-20 point favorite since 1985		vs Washington State - Arizona leads series 27-17
16-0 S/U @ home as 20.5-25 point favorite since 1985		0-3 S/U vs Washington State as 10.5-15 point Dog since 1997
23-0 S/U as 25.5 or more favorite since 1989		3-0 S/U & ATS vs Wazzu as 3 point or less favorite since 1988
18-1 S/U in 1st home game of season since 2001	SDSU	0-4 ATS vs Washington State as 10.5-15 point favorite since 1993
11-2 O/U prior to playing UCLA since 2007	Oregon	
1-10 S/U after playing Oregon since 2006	UCLA	

Copyright © 2021 by Steve's Football Bible, LLC

ARIZONA STATE SUN DEVILS   PACIFIC-12 South

2020-Arizona State		Opponent	ASU	Opp	S/U	Line	ATS	Total	O/U	
11/7/2020	@	Usc	27	28	L	11.5	W	57.5	U	
12/5/2020	vs	UCLA	18	25	L	-2.5	L	57.5	U	
12/11/2020	@	Arizona	70	7	W	8.0	W	58.0	O	Territorial Cup
12/19/2020	@	Oregon State	46	33	W	-7.5	W	54.5	O	
Coach: Herm Edwards		Season Record >>	161	93	2-2	ATS>>	3-1	O/U>>	2-2	
2019-Arizona State		Opponent	ASU	Opp	S/U	Line	ATS	Total	O/U	
8/29/2019	vs	KENT STATE	30	7	W	-24.5	L	61.0	U	
9/6/2019	vs	SACRAMENTO STATE	19	7	W	-34.5	L	NT	---	
9/14/2019	@	Michigan State	10	7	W	15.5	W	42.0	U	
9/21/2019	vs	COLORADO	31	34	L	-8.0	L	49.0	O	
9/27/2019	@	California	24	17	W	4.5	W	43.0	U	
10/12/2019	vs	WASHINGTON STATE	38	34	W	1.5	W	60.5	O	
10/19/2019	@	Utah	3	21	L	14.5	L	46.0	U	
10/26/2019	@	Ucla	32	42	L	-3.0	L	56.0	O	
11/9/2019	vs	USC	26	31	L	4.5	L	54.0	O	
11/16/2019	@	Oregon State	34	35	L	-1.5	L	56.5	O	
11/23/2019	vs	OREGON	31	28	W	13.5	W	55.0	O	
11/29/2019	vs	ARIZONA	24	14	W	-12.5	L	60.5	U	Territorial Cup
12/31/2019	vs	Florida State	20	14	W	-3.0	W	51.5	U	Sun Bowl
Coach: Herm Edwards		Season Record >>	322	291	8-5	ATS>>	5-8	O/U>>	6-6	
2018-Arizona State		Opponent	ASU	Opp	S/U	Line	ATS	Total	O/U	
9/1/2018	vs	TEXAS-SAN ANTONIO	49	7	W	-17.5	W	52.0	O	
9/8/2018	vs	MICHIGAN STATE	16	13	W	4.5	W	54.0	U	
9/15/2018	@	San Diego State	21	28	L	-5.0	L	47.5	O	
9/22/2018	@	Washington	20	27	L	18.5	W	53.0	U	
9/29/2018	vs	OREGON STATE	52	24	W	-22.0	W	64.5	O	
10/6/2018	@	Colorado	21	28	L	2.5	L	64.5	U	
10/18/2018	vs	STANFORD	13	20	L	2.5	L	57.5	U	
10/27/2018	@	Usc	38	35	W	3.0	W	52.0	O	
11/3/2018	vs	UTAH	38	20	W	7.5	W	54.0	O	
11/10/2018	vs	UCLA	31	28	W	-11.5	L	64.5	U	
11/17/2018	@	Oregon	29	31	L	3.5	W	66.0	U	
11/24/2018	@	Arizona	41	40	W	-1.5	L	65.5	O	Territorial Cup
12/15/2018	vs	Fresno State	20	31	L	6.0	L	53.5	U	Las Vegas Bowl
Coach: Herm Edwards		Season Record >>	389	332	7-6	ATS>>	7-6	O/U>>	6-7	
2017-Arizona State		Opponent	ASU	Opp	S/U	Line	ATS	Total	O/U	
8/31/2017	vs	NEW MEXICO STATE	37	31	W	-25.5	L	68.5	U	
9/9/2017	vs	SAN DIEGO STATE	20	30	L	-3.0	L	53.0	U	
9/16/2017	@	Texas Tech	45	52	L	7.0	T	74.0	O	
9/23/2017	vs	OREGON	37	35	W	15.0	W	75.0	U	
9/30/2017	@	Stanford	24	34	L	16.5	W	60.0	U	
10/14/2017	vs	WASHINGTON	13	7	W	17.5	W	59.0	U	
10/21/2017	@	Utah	30	10	W	10.5	W	54.0	U	
10/28/2017	vs	USC	17	48	L	5.5	L	58.5	O	
11/4/2017	vs	COLORADO	41	30	W	-6.5	W	59.0	O	
11/11/2017	@	Ucla	37	44	L	3.0	L	65.5	O	
11/18/2017	@	Oregon State	40	24	W	-7.0	W	59.0	O	
11/25/2017	vs	ARIZONA	42	30	W	-2.0	W	75.0	U	Territorial Cup
12/29/2017	vs	NC State	31	52	L	4.5	L	62.0	O	Sun Bowl
Coach: Todd Graham		Season Record >>	414	427	7-6	ATS>>	7-5-1	O/U>>	6-7	

Copyright © 2021 by Steve's Football Bible, LLC

ARIZONA STATE SUN DEVILS   PACIFIC-12 South

STADIUM: Sun Devil Stadium {53,599}				Location: Tempe, AZ				COACH: Herman Edwards		
DATE		Opponent	ASU	Opp	S/U	Line	ATS	Total	O/U	Trends & Angles
9/4/2021	vs	*SOUTHERN UTAH*								1st meeting
9/11/2021	vs	*UNLV*								vs UNLV - Unlv leads series 1-0
9/18/2021	@	*Byu*								vs BYU - Arizona State leads series 20-7
9/25/2021	vs	COLORADO								5-1 S/U & ATS @ home vs Colorado since 2007
10/2/2021	@	Ucla								Game 5-0 O/U @ UCLA since 2011
10/8/2021	vs	STANFORD								1-6 S/U vs Stanford since 2009
10/16/2021	@	Utah								5-2 S/U @ Utah since 1975
10/30/2021	vs	WASHINGTON STATE								7-1 S/U @ home vs Wash. State since 2004
11/6/2021	vs	USC								0-3 S/U & ATS @ home vs USC since 2015
11/13/2021	@	Washington								8-0-1 ATS @ Washington since 1995
11/20/2021	@	Oregon State								2-6 S/U @ Oregon State since 2006
11/27/2021	vs	ARIZONA								vs Arizona - Arizona leads series 49-44-1
12/3/2021	vs									PAC-12 Championship
	vs									BOWL GAME

Pointspread Analysis Non-Conference		Pointspread Analysis Conference
0-6 S/U vs Non-Conf. as 10.5-15 point Dog since 1990		3-0 S/U & ATS vs Arizona as 3.5-7 point Dog since 1992
0-5 O/U vs Non-Conf. as 7.5-10 point Dog since 1994		vs Colorado - Arizona State leads series 8-3
1-5 S/U vs Non-Conf. as 3.5-7 point Dog since 2008		7-3 ATS vs Colorado since 2006
7-1 S/U vs Non-Conf. as 3.5-7 point favorite since 2001		8-1 S/U vs Colorado as favorite since 2006
0-5 ATS vs Non-Conf. as 7.5-10 point favorite since 1994		5-0 S/U vs Colorado as 15.5 point or more favorite since 2011
7-0 S/U vs Non-Conf. as 15.5-20 point favorite since 1987		vs Oregon State - Arizona State leads series 30-14-1
18-0 S/U vs Non-Conf. as 25.5 point or more favorite since 1985		19-4-1 S/U vs Oregon State as favorite since 1983
Bowl Games		Game 9-0-1 O/U @ Oregon State since 2003
0-4 S/U in Holiday Bowl		0-3 S/U vs Oregon State as 3.5-7 point Dog since 2003
5-1 S/U in Fiesta Bowl		6-0 S/U vs Oregon State as 10.5-15 point favorite since 1990
6-3 O/U in Bowl Games since 2007		5-0 S/U vs Oregon State as 20.5 point or more favorite since 1983
Dog		Game 1-6 O/U vs Stanford since 2009
0-6 S/U on road as 20.5 point or more Dog since 1988		vs Stanford - Arizona State leads series 17-15
1-7 S/U as 20.5 point or more Dog since 1988		4-0 S/U vs Stanford as 15.5 point or more favorite since 1983
2-12 S/U as 15.5-20 point Dog since 1988		vs UCLA - UCLA leads series 23-13-1
0-11 S/U on road as 15.5-20 point Dog since 1988		Game 8-3 O/U vs UCLA since 2010
7-2 ATS on road as 10.5-15 point Dog since 2009		0-4 S/U vs UCLA as 3.5-7 point Dog since 2000
2-7 S/U @ home as 10.5-15 point Dog since 1990		5-1 O/U vs UCLA as 3.5-7 point Dog since 1987
5-0 ATS @ home as 10.5-15 point Dog since 2005		1-5 ATS vs UCLA as 3.5-7 point favorite since 1983
1-7 S/U & ATS on road as 7.5-10 point Dog since 2003		vs Utah - Arizona State leads series 21-9
3-9 S/U as 7.5-10 point Dog since 2006		8-1 S/U vs Utah as favorite since 1985
3-17 S/U @ home as 3.5-7 point Dog since 1984		3-0 S/U vs Utah as 10.5-15 point favorite since 1985
2-14 S/U on road as 3.5-7 point Dog since 2001		vs USC - USC leads series 24-13
11-5 O/U on road as 3.5-7 point Dog since 2001		4-21 S/U vs USC as Dog since 1985
5-12 S/U as 3 point or less Dog since 2007		Game 4-1 O/U @ home vs USC since 2011
Favorite		0-4 S/U vs USC as 15.5 point or more Dog since 1988
10-2 S/U on road as 3.5-7 point favorite since 1998		1-7 S/U vs USC as 10.5-15 point Dog since 1990
2-10 ATS as 7.5-10 point favorite since 2001		1-6 S/U vs USC as 3.5-7 point Dog since 1998
27-1 S/U @ home as 10.5-15 point favorite since 1985		Game 0-5 O/U vs Washington since 2014
12-5 ATS @ home as 10.5-15 point favorite since 1996		12-0-1 ATS vs Washington since 2002
12-0 S/U @ home as 15.5-20 point favorite since 1987		vs Washington - Arizona State leads series 20-16
6-0 S/U on road as 20.5-25 point favorite since 1991		3-0 ATS vs Washington as 10.5-15 point Dog since 1989
12-2 S/U @ home as 20.5-25 point favorite since 1985		0-4 S/U @ Washington as 15.5 point or more Dog since 1991
11-0 S/U as 25.5-30 point favorite since 1983		vs Wazzu - ASU leads series 28-14-2
24-0 S/U as 25.5 point or more favorite since 1983		3-0 S/U & ATS vs Wazzu as 3 point or less favorite since 1985
14-0 S/U as 30.5 point or more favorite since 1996		4-0 S/U vs Wazzu as 20.5 point or more favorite since 2008

S. UTAH	21-1 S/U in 1st home game of season since 1999
Oregon State	2-10 S/U prior to playing Arizona since 2009
ARIZONA	11-3 ATS after playing Oregon State since 2004
ARIZONA	10-2 S/U after playing Oregon State since 2006

Copyright © 2021 by Steve's Football Bible, LLC

ARKANSAS RAZORBACKS   SEC WEST

2020-Arkansas		Opponent	ARK	Opp	S/U	Line	ATS	Total	O/U	
9/26/2020	vs	GEORGIA	10	37	L	27.5	W	53.0	U	
10/3/2020	@	Mississippi State	21	14	W	17.0	W	68.5	U	
10/10/2020	@	Auburn	28	30	L	13.5	W	46.0	O	
10/17/2020	vs	MISSISSIPPI	33	20	W	1.5	W	75.0	U	
10/31/2020	@	Texas A&M	31	42	L	14.5	W	54.5	O	"Southwest Classic"
11/7/2020	vs	TENNESSEE	24	13	W	2.5	W	54.5	U	
11/14/2020	@	Florida	35	63	L	17.0	L	62.0	O	
11/21/2020	vs	LSU	24	27	L	1.5	L	65.0	U	"The Golden Boot"
12/5/2020	@	Missouri	48	50	L	2.0	T	55.5	O	"Battle Line Trophy"
12/12/2020	vs	ALABAMA	3	52	L	29.0	L	69.0	U	
Coach: Sam Pittman		Season Record >>	257	348	3-7	ATS>>	6-3-1	O/U>>	4-6	
2019-Arkansas		Opponent	ARK	Opp	S/U	Line	ATS	Total	O/U	
8/31/2019	vs	PORTLAND STATE	20	13	W	-30.0	L	NT	---	
9/7/2019	@	Mississippi	17	31	L	5.5	L	50.5	U	
9/14/2019	vs	COLORADO STATE	55	34	W	-9.5	W	64.0	O	
9/21/2019	vs	SAN JOSE STATE	24	31	L	-20.5	L	61.0	U	
9/28/2019	vs	Texas A&M	27	31	L	23.0	W	60.0	U	"Southwest Classic"
10/12/2019	@	Kentucky	20	24	L	3.0	L	52.0	U	
10/19/2019	vs	AUBURN	10	51	L	20.0	L	55.0	O	
10/26/2019	@	Alabama	7	48	L	31.5	L	56.0	U	
11/2/2019	vs	MISSISSIPPI STATE	24	54	L	7.0	L	59.0	O	
11/9/2019	vs	WESTERN KENTUCKY	19	45	L	PK	L	51.5	O	
11/23/2019	@	Lsu	20	56	L	40.0	W	68.5	O	"The Golden Boot"
11/30/2019	vs	MISSOURI	14	24	L	14.5	W	52.5	U	"Battle Line Trophy"
Coach: Chad Morris		Season Record >>	257	442	2-10	ATS>>	4-8	O/U>>	5-6	
2018-Arkansas		Opponent	ARK	Opp	S/U	Line	ATS	Total	O/U	
9/1/2018	vs	EASTERN ILLINOIS	55	20	W	-35.0	T	NT	---	
9/8/2018	@	Colorado State	27	34	L	-14.0	L	70.5	U	
9/15/2018	vs	NORTH TEXAS	17	44	L	-5.5	L	63.0	U	
9/22/2018	@	Auburn	3	34	L	29.5	L	57.5	U	
9/29/2018	vs	Texas A&M	17	24	L	20.0	W	54.0	U	"Southwest Classic"
10/6/2018	vs	ALABAMA	31	65	L	35.0	W	58.0	O	
10/13/2018	vs	MISSISSIPPI	33	37	L	6.5	W	66.5	O	War Memorial Stadium
10/20/2018	vs	TULSA	23	0	W	-7.5	W	53.0	U	
10/27/2018	vs	VANDERBILT	31	45	L	PK	L	53.0	O	
11/10/2018	vs	LSU	17	24	L	13.0	W	49.5	U	"The Golden Boot"
11/17/2018	@	Mississippi State	6	52	L	22.5	L	48.0	O	
11/24/2018	@	Missouri	0	38	L	24.0	L	59.0	U	"Battle Line Trophy"
Coach: Chad Morris		Season Record >>	260	417	2-10	ATS>>	5-6-1	O/U>>	4-7	
2017-Arkansas		Opponent	ARK	Opp	S/U	Line	ATS	Total	O/U	
8/31/2017	vs	FLORIDA A&M	49	7	W	-46.5	L	60.5	U	War Memorial Stadium
9/9/2017	vs	TCU	7	28	L	2.5	L	57.0	U	
9/23/2017	vs	Texas A&M	43	50	L	2.0	L	56.5	O	"Southwest Classic"
9/30/2017	vs	NEW MEXICO STATE	42	24	W	-18.5	L	61.0	O	
10/7/2017	@	South Carolinia	22	48	L	-2.5	L	45.0	O	
10/14/2017	@	Alabama	9	41	L	37.0	W	54.5	U	
10/21/2017	vs	AUBURN	20	52	L	17.0	L	51.0	O	
10/28/2017	@	Mississippi	38	37	W	2.0	W	63.0	O	
11/4/2017	vs	COASTAL CAROLINA	39	38	W	-24.0	L	59.0	O	
11/11/2017	@	Lsu	10	33	L	18.0	L	53.5	U	"The Golden Boot"
11/18/2017	vs	MISSISSIPPI STATE	21	28	L	13.5	W	57.0	U	
11/25/2017	vs	MISSOURI	45	48	L	10.0	W	68.0	O	"Battle Line Trophy"
Coach: Brett Bielema		Season Record >>	345	434	4-8	ATS>>	4-8	O/U>>	7-5	

Copyright © 2021 by Steve's Football Bible, LLC

ARKANSAS RAZORBACKS   SEC WEST

STADIUM: Razorback Stadium {72,000} / War Memorial Stadium {54,120} | **Location:** Fayetteville, AR | **COACH:** Sam Pittman

DATE		Opponent	Ark	Opp	S/U	Line	ATS	Total	O/U	Trends & Angles
9/4/2021	vs	*RICE*								6-1 S/U @ home vs Rice since 1982
9/11/2021	vs	*TEXAS*								1-5 S/U @ home vs Texas since 1983
9/18/2021	vs	*GEORGIA SOUTHERN*								1st meeting
9/25/2021	vs	Texas A&M {Arlington, TX}								0-9 S/U vs Texas A&M since 2012
10/2/2021	@	Georgia								1-8 S/U vs Georgia since 2000
10/9/2021	@	Mississippi								7-1 ATS vs Mississippi since 2013
10/16/2021	vs	AUBURN								0-5 S/U vs Auburn since 2016 {1-4 ATS}
10/23/2021	vs	*ARKANSAS-PINE BLUFF*								1st meeting
11/6/2021	vs	MISSISSIPPI STATE								2-7 S/U vs Mississippi State since 2012
11/13/2021	@	Lsu								2-11 S/U @ LSU since 1995
11/20/2021	@	Alabama								vs Alabama - Alabama leads series 24-7
11/27/2021	vs	MISSOURI								1-7 S/U vs Missouri since 2008
12/4/2021	vs									SEC Championship
	vs									BOWL GAME

Pointspread Analysis
Non-Conference

0-6 S/U vs Non-Conf. as 15.5 point or more Dog since 1987

6-0 ATS vs Non-Conf. as 10.5-15 point Dog since 1991

15-1 S/U vs Non-conf. as 10.5-15 point favorite since 1983

7-0 S/U vs Non-conf. as 15.5-20 point favorite since 1985

12-2 S/U vs Non-Conf. as 20.5-25 point favorite since 1987

31-1 S/U vs Non-Conf. as 25.5 point or more favorite since 1985

16-2 S/U vs Rice since 1974

0-3 S/U & ATS vs Texas as 7.5-10 point favorite since 1983

4-0 S/U vs Rice as 20.5-25 point favorite since 1985

Dog

0-14 S/U as 25.5 point or more Dog since 1996

0-6 S/U as 20.5-25 point Dog since 1995

0-3 S/U @ War Memorial as 15.5-25 point Dog since 1991

1-10 S/U as 15.5-20 point Dog since 2009

0-8 S/U @ home as 15.5-25 point Dog since 1990

1-16 S/U as 10.5-15 point Dog since 2008

0-9 S/U @ home as 10.5-15 point Dog since 2001

1-8 S/U @ home as 7.5-10 point Dog since 2004

1-9 S/U on road as 7.5-10 point Dog since 1997

7-0 O/U @ War Memorial as 3.5-7 point Dog since 1987

7-1 O/U on road as 3 point or less Dog since 2005

1-4 S/U & ATS @ War Memorial as 3 point or less Dog since 1992

Favorite

0-5 O/U @ War Memorial as 3.5-7 point favorite since 1999

6-1 S/U @ War Memorial as 3.5-7 point favorite since 1998

16-1 S/U on road as 3.5-7 point favorite since 1983

5-1 S/U @ War Memorial as 7.5-10 point favorite since 1984

7-0 ATS @ home as 10.5-15 point favorite since 2009

9-2 O/U @ home as 10.5-15 point favorite since 2005

32-2 S/U @ War Memorial as 10.5 point or more favorite since 1994

7-1 S/U on road as 10.5-15 point favorite since 1985

13-0 S/U as 15.5-20 point favorite since 1985

67-3 S/U as 15.5 point or more favorite since 1983

14-0 S/U on road as 10.5 point or more favorite since 1983

19-3 S/U as 20.5-25 point favorite since 1985

13-1 S/U as 25.5-30 point favorite since 1983

24-0 S/U as 30.5 point or more favorite since 1985

Pointspread Analysis
Conference

0-14 S/U vs Alabama as 7.5 point or more Dog since 1996

3-0 O/U vs Alabama as 3 point or less Dog since 1998

vs Auburn - Auburn leads series 18-11-1

Game 6-1 O/U vs Auburn since 2014

1-6 S/U vs Auburn as 15.5 point or more Dog since 1996

0-3 S/U vs Auburn as 7.5-10 point Dog since 2000

0-3 S/U vs Georgia as 3.5-7 point Dog since 1987

vs LSU - LSU leads series 42-22-2

0-5 S/U vs LSU as 15.5 point or more Dog since 1997

0-4 S/U vs LSU as 7.5-10 point Dog since 1996

3-0 ATS vs LSU as 3.5-7 point Dog since 2008

3-0 S/U vs LSU as 3.5-7 point favorite since 1998

10-3 S/U @ home vs Ole Miss since 1994

vs Mississippi - Arkansas leads series 36-27-1

6-1 S/U & ATS vs Ole Miss as 3.5-7 point favorite since 1985

7-0 S/U vs Mississippi as 7.5-10 point favorite since 1986

4-0 ATS vs Mississippi as 7.5-10 point favorite since 1998

vs Mississippi State - Arkansas leads series 17-12-1

0-3 S/U vs Mississippi State as 10.5-15 point Dog since 1992

3-0 ATS vs Mississippi State as 10.5-15 point Dog since 1992

7-0 S/U vs Mississippi State as 10.5-15 point favorite since 1995

1-7 S/U vs Missouri since 2008

vs Missouri - Missouri leads series 9-3

Game 2-7 O/U vs Missouri since 2003

3-0 S/U & ATS vs South Carolina as 3.5-7 point favorite since 2007

vs Texas A&M - Arkansas leads series 41-33-3

0-4 S/U vs Texas A&M as 15.5 point or more Dog since 1990

4-0 ATS vs Texas A&M as 15.5 point or more Dog since 1990

0-3 S/U & ATS vs Texas A&M as 3.5-7 point Dog since 1987

3-0 O/U vs Texas A&M as 3 point or less Dog since 1989

Bowl Games

1-5 S/U in Sugar Bowl

0-4 S/U & ATS vs Big Ten in Bowl Games since 1999

1-10 O/U in Bowl Games since 2002

	RICE	13-1 S/U in 1st home game of season since 2007

Copyright © 2021 by Steve's Football Bible, LLC

ARKANSAS STATE RED WOLVES   SUN BELT West

2020-Arkansas State		Opponent	ASU	Opp	S/U	Line	ATS	Total	O/U	
9/5/2020	@	*Memphis*	24	37	L	18.5	W	72.5	U	"Paint Bucket Bowl"
9/12/2020	@	*Kansas State*	35	31	W	10.5	W	54.0	O	
10/3/2020	@	Coastal Carolina	23	52	L	-3.5	L	64.5	O	
10/10/2020	vs	*CENTRAL ARKANSAS*	50	27	W	-15.5	W	55.5	O	
10/15/2020	vs	GEORGIA STATE	59	52	W	-3.5	W	73.0	O	
10/24/2020	@	Appalachian State	17	45	L	13.5	L	69.0	U	
10/31/2020	vs	TROY	10	38	L	-3.5	L	70.0	U	
11/7/2020	@	Louisiana	20	27	L	14.5	W	68.5	U	
11/21/2020	@	Texas State	45	47	L	-4.5	L	69.0	O	
11/28/2020	vs	SOUTH ALABAMA	31	38	L	-7.0	L	63.5	O	
12/4/2020	vs	LOUISIANA-MONROE	48	15	W	-20.0	W	71.0	U	"Trail of Tears Classic"
Coach: Blake Anderson		Season Record >>	362	409	4-7	ATS>>	6-5	O/U>>	6-5	
2019-Arkansas State		Opponent	ASU	Opp	S/U	Line	ATS	Total	O/U	
8/31/2019	vs	*SMU*	30	37	L	-2.5	L	56.0	O	
9/7/2019	@	*Unlv*	43	17	W	PK	W	64.0	U	
9/14/2019	@	*Georgia*	0	55	L	32.5	L	58.0	U	
9/21/2019	vs	*SOUTHERN ILLINOIS*	41	28	W	-21.5	L	NT	---	
9/28/2019	@	Troy	50	43	W	7.0	W	59.5	O	
10/5/2019	@	Georgia State	38	52	L	-6.0	L	69.0	O	
10/17/2019	vs	LOUISIANA-LAFAYETTE	20	37	L	-6.0	L	68.5	U	
10/26/2019	vs	TEXAS STATE	38	14	W	-11.0	W	60.5	U	
11/2/2019	@	Louisiana-Monroe	48	41	W	1.0	W	69.5	O	"Trail of Tears Classic"
11/16/2019	vs	COASTAL CAROLINA	28	27	W	-13.5	L	60.0	U	
11/23/2019	vs	GEORGIA SOUTHERN	38	33	W	PK	W	52.5	O	
11/30/2019	@	South Alabama	30	34	L	-10.0	L	53.0	O	
12/21/2019	vs	**Florida International**	34	26	W	1.0	W	58.5	U	Camelia Bowl
Coach: Blake Anderson		Season Record >>	438	444	8-5	ATS>>	6-7	O/U>>	6-6	
2018-Arkansas State		Opponent	ASU	Opp	S/U	Line	ATS	Total	O/U	
9/1/2018	vs	*SOUTHEAST MISSOURI*	48	21	W	-31.0	L	NT	---	
9/8/2018	@	*Alabama*	7	57	L	36.5	L	63.0	O	-
9/15/2018	@	*Tulsa*	29	20	W	1.5	W	71.5	U	
9/22/2018	vs	*UNLV*	27	20	W	-8.0	L	66.5	U	
9/29/2018	@	Georgia Southern	21	28	L	-3.0	L	53.5	U	
10/9/2018	vs	APPALACHIAN STATE	9	35	L	10.5	L	58.5	U	
10/18/2018	vs	GEORGIA STATE	51	35	W	-13.0	W	56.5	O	
10/27/2018	@	Louisiana-Lafayette	43	47	L	-3.0	L	70.0	O	
11/3/2018	vs	SOUTH ALABAMA	38	14	W	-14.0	W	61.5	U	
11/10/2018	@	Coastal Carolina	44	16	W	-7.0	W	62.0	U	
11/17/2018	vs	LOUISIANA-MONROE	31	17	W	-8.0	W	68.0	U	"Trail of Tears Classic"
11/24/2018	@	Texas State	33	7	W	-13.0	W	48.5	U	
12/29/2018	vs	**Nevada**	13	16	L	PK	L	57.0	U	Arizona Bowl
Coach: Blake Anderson		Season Record >>	394	333	8-5	ATS>>	6-7	O/U>>	3-9	
2017-Arkansas State		Opponent	ASU	Opp	S/U	Line	ATS	Total	O/U	
9/2/2017	@	*Nebraska*	36	43	L	14.5	W	51.0	O	
9/16/2017	vs	*ARKANSAS-PINE BLUFF*	48	3	W	-52.0	L	NT	---	
9/23/2017	@	*Smu*	21	44	L	2.5	L	72.0	U	
10/4/2017	@	Georgia Southern	43	25	W	-7.5	W	54.5	O	
10/14/2017	vs	COASTAL CAROLINA	51	17	W	-16.0	W	63.0	O	
10/19/2017	vs	LOUISIANA-LAFAYETTE	47	3	W	-12.0	W	65.5	U	
10/28/2017	@	New Mexico State	37	21	W	-3.5	W	71.5	U	
11/11/2017	@	South Alabama	19	24	L	-12.5	L	54.5	U	
11/18/2017	vs	TEXAS STATE	30	12	W	-26.5	L	57.5	U	
11/25/2017	@	Louisiana-Monroe	67	50	W	-8.5	W	69.0	O	"Trail of Tears Classic"
12/2/2017	vs	TROY	25	32	L	1.0	L	60.0	U	
12/16/2017	vs	**Middle Tennessee**	30	35	L	-3.5	L	60.5	O	Camelia Bowl
Coach: Blake Anderson		Season Record >>	848	642	7-5	ATS>>	6-6	O/U>>	5-6	

Copyright © 2021 by Steve's Football Bible, LLC

ARKANSAS STATE RED WOLVES SUN BELT West

STADIUM: Liberty Bank Stadium {30,406}		Location: Jonesboro, AR								COACH: Butch Jones
DATE		Opponent	State	Opp	S/U	Line	ATS	Total	O/U	Trends & Angles
9/4/2021	vs	*CENTRAL ARKANSAS*								vs Central Arkansas - Ark State leads series 4-1
9/11/2021	vs	*MEMPHIS*								3-0 S/U @ home vs Memphis since 2007
9/18/2021	@	*Washington*								1st meeting
9/25/2021	@	*Tulsa*								vs Tulsa - Arkansas State leads series 3-2
10/2/2021	@	Georgia Southern								vs Georgia Southern - Ark State leads series 3-2
10/7/2021	vs	COASTAL CAROLINA								vs Coastal Carolina - Ark State leads series 3-1
10/21/2021	vs	LOUISIANA								2-13 S/U vs Louisiana as Dog since 1990
10/30/2021	@	South Alabama								vs South Alabama - Ark State leads series 6-3
11/6/2021	vs	APPALACHIAN STATE								vs Appalachian State - Appalachian series 3-1
11/13/2021	@	Louisiana-Monroe								11-0 S/U & ATS vs UL-Monroe since 2010
11/20/2021	@	Georgia State								vs Georgia State - Ark State leads series 7-1
11/27/2021	vs	TEXAS STATE								3-0 S/U @ home vs Texas State since 2013
12/4/2021	vs									Sun Belt Championship
	vs									BOWL GAME

Pointspread Analysis Non-Conference		Pointspread Analysis Conference
vs Memphis - HOME team 6-0 S/U since 2007		4-0 S/U vs Georgia State as 10.5 point or more favorite since 2013
0-8 S/U vs Memphis as 15.5 point or more Dog since 1991		Game 1-5 O/U @ home vs Louisiana since 2009
Dog		vs Louisiana - Louisiana leads series 27-21-1
0-59 S/U as 20.5 point or more Dog since 1992		5-1 S/U vs Louisiana as 7.5 point or more favorite since 1999
1-14 S/U on road as 15.5-20 point Dog since 1990		3-0 S/U & ATS vs UL-Monroe as 3.5-7 point Dog since 1998
3-18 S/U on road as 10.5-15 point Dog since 1993		3-0 S/U vs UL-Monroe as 3.5-7 point favorite since 2006
0-5 S/U @ home as 7.5-10 point Dog since 1995		8-0 S/U vs UL-Monroe as 7.5 point or more favorite since 2003
1-7-1 O/U @ home as 3.5-7 point Dog since 2002		6-0 S/U vs North Texas as 7.5 point or more favorite since 2000
Favorite		vs Texas State - Arkansas State leads series 5-2
2-5 S/U & ATS on road as 3 point or less Dog since 2007		Game 1-4 O/U vs Texas State since 2016
4-11 O/U as 3 point or less favorite since 2007		6-0 S/U vs Texas State as 7.5 point or more favorite since 2013
0-4 S/U & ATS as 3 point or less favorite since 2014		vs Troy - Arkansas State leads series 11-7
12-4 S/U @ home as 3.5-7 point favorite since 2004		
14-1 S/U as 7.5-10 point favorite since 2000		
10-1 S/U on road as 10.5 point or more favorite since 1999		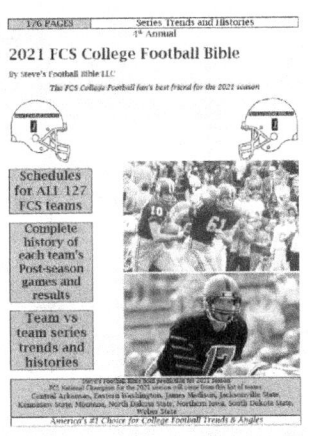
24-1 S/U @ home as 15.5 point or more favorite since 2007		
8-0 O/U as 20.5-25 point favorite since 2012		
2-28 S/U in 1st road game of season since 1991	Washington	
9-2 S/U after playing UL-Monroe since 2009	Georgia State	
9-2 ATS after playing UL-Monroe since 2009	Georgia State	1-23 S/U vs ranked teams since 1994

176 PAGES   Series Trends and Histories
4th Annual
2021 FCS College Football Bible
By Steve's Football Bible LLC
The FCS College Football fan's best friend for the 2021 season

Schedules for ALL 127 FCS teams

Complete history of each team's Post-season games and results

Team vs team series trends and histories

FCS Football Bible bold predictions for the 2021 Season
2021 National Champions for the 2021 season will come from this list of teams:
Central Arkansas, Eastern Washington, James Madison, Jacksonville State,
Kennesaw State Missouri, North Dakota State, Northern Iowa, South Dakota State,
Weber State
America's #1 Choice for College Football Trends & Angles

2021 FCS College Football Bible $19.95

Copyright © 2021 by Steve's Football Bible, LLC

ARMY BLACK KNIGHTS   INDEPENDENT

2020-Army		Opponent	Army	Opp	S/U	Line	ATS	Total	O/U	
9/5/2020	vs	MIDDLE TENNESSEE	42	0	W	-3.5	W	54.0	U	
9/12/2020	vs	LOUISIANA-MONROE	37	7	W	-22.5	W	53.5	U	
9/26/2020	@	Cincinnati	10	24	L	12.0	L	44.5	U	
10/3/2020	vs	ABILENE CHRISTIAN	55	23	W	-31.0	W	49.0	O	
10/10/2020	vs	THE CITADEL	14	9	W	-30.0	L	45.5	U	
10/17/2020	@	Texas-San Antonio	28	16	W	-7.5	W	49.0	U	
10/24/2020	vs	MERCER	49	3	W	-30.0	W	47.5	O	
11/14/2020	@	Tulane	12	38	L	3.0	L	46.5	O	
11/21/2020	vs	GEORGIA SOUTHERN	28	27	W	-3.5	L	38.5	O	
12/12/2020	vs	NAVY	15	0	W	-7.0	W	35.5	U	"Thompson Cup"
12/19/2020	vs	AIR FORCE	10	7	W	2.0	W	37.5	U	
12/26/2020	vs	**West Virginia**	21	24	L	9.0	W	41.0	O	Liberty Bowl
Coach: Jeff Monken		Season Record >>	321	178	9-3	ATS>>	8-4	O/U>>	5-7	
2019-Army		Opponent	Army	Opp	S/U	Line	ATS	Total	O/U	
8/30/2019	vs	RICE	14	7	W	-23.0	L	47.5	U	
9/7/2019	@	Michigan	21	24	L	22.0	W	47.5	U	{2 OT}
9/14/2019	@	Texas-San Antonio	31	13	W	-14.5	W	49.0	U	
9/21/2019	vs	MORGAN STATE	52	21	W	-44.0	L	NT	---	
10/5/2019	vs	TULANE	33	42	L	2.5	L	42.5	O	
10/12/2019	@	Western Kentucky	8	17	L	-5.0	L	43.5	U	
10/19/2019	@	Georgia State	21	28	L	-4.0	L	54.0	U	
10/26/2019	vs	SAN JOSE STATE	29	34	L	-9.5	L	54.0	O	
11/2/2019	@	Air Force	13	17	L	16.5	W	44.5	U	
11/9/2019	vs	MASSACHUSETTS	63	7	W	-34.5	W	61.0	O	
11/16/2019	vs	VIRGINIA MILITARY	47	6	W	NL	---	NT	---	
11/30/2019	@	Hawaii	31	52	L	2.0	L	55.0	O	
12/14/2019	vs	Navy	7	31	L	11.5	L	41.5	U	"Thompson Cup"
Coach: Jeff Monken		Season Record >>	370	299	5-8	ATS>>	4-8	O/U>>	4-7	
2018-Army		Opponent	Army	Opp	S/U	Line	ATS	Total	O/U	
8/31/2018	@	Duke	14	34	L	13.5	L	45.5	O	
9/8/2018	vs	LIBERTY	38	14	W	-7.5	W	59.5	U	
9/15/2018	vs	HAWAII	28	21	W	-7.0	T	62.0	U	
9/22/2018	@	Oklahoma	21	28	L	28.5	W	60.5	U	{OT}
9/29/2018	@	Buffalo	42	13	W	7.0	W	54.5	O	
10/13/2018	@	San Jose State	52	3	W	-17.0	W	57.5	U	
10/20/2018	vs	MIAMI-OHIO	31	30	W	-6.5	L	47.0	O	{2 OT}
10/27/2018	@	Eastern Michigan	37	22	W	-1.5	W	47.5	O	
11/3/2018	vs	AIR FORCE	17	14	W	-4.5	L	41.5	U	
11/10/2018	vs	LAFAYETTE	31	13	W	-46.0	L	NT	---	
11/17/2018	vs	COLGATE	28	14	W	-10.5	W	NT	---	
12/8/2018	vs	Navy	17	10	W	-9.0	L	38.5	U	"Thompson Cup"
12/22/2018	vs	**Houston**	70	14	W	-6.5	W	56.0	O	Armed Forces Bowl
Coach: Jeff Monken		Season Record >>	426	230	11-2	ATS>>	7-5-1	O/U>>	5-6	
2017-Army		Opponent	Army	Opp	S/U	Line	ATS	Total	O/U	
9/1/2017	vs	FORDHAM	64	6	W	-18.5	W	66.0	O	
9/9/2017	vs	BUFFALO	21	17	W	-15.0	L	53.0	U	
9/16/2017	@	Ohio State	7	38	L	31.5	W	54.5	U	
9/23/2017	@	Tulane	17	21	L	3.0	L	45.5	U	
9/30/2017	vs	TEXAS-EL PASO	35	21	W	-22.5	L	47.5	O	
10/7/2017	@	Rice	49	12	W	-13.0	W	47.0	O	
10/14/2017	vs	EASTERN MICHIGAN	28	27	W	-4.0	L	50.5	O	
10/21/2017	vs	TEMPLE	31	28	W	-7.0	L	47.0	O	
11/4/2017	@	Air Force	21	0	W	6.5	W	53.5	U	
11/11/2017	vs	DUKE	21	16	W	3.5	W	50.5	O	
11/18/2017	@	North Texas	49	52	L	2.0	L	59.5	O	
12/9/2017	vs	Navy	14	13	W	2.5	W	44.0	U	"Thompson Cup"
12/22/2017	vs	**San Diego State**	42	35	W	6.5	W	46.0	O	Armed Forces Bowl
Coach: Jeff Monken		Season Record >>	399	286	10-3	ATS>>	7-6	O/U>>	7-6	

Copyright © 2021 by Steve's Football Bible, LLC

ARMY BLACK KNIGHTS INDEPENDENT

STADIUM: Blake Field @ Michie Stadium {38,000}		Location: West Point, NY							COACH: Jeff Monken
DATE		**Opponent**	**Army**	**Opp**	**S/U**	**Line**	**ATS**	**Total**	**O/U**	**Trends & Angles**
9/4/2021	@	Georgia State								vs Georgia State - GA State leads series 1-0
9/11/2021	vs	WESTERN KENTUCKY								vs Western Kentucky - WKU leads series 3-0
9/18/2021	vs	CONNECTICUT								vs Connecticut - UCONN leads series 5-2
9/25/2021	vs	MIAMI-OHIO								vs Miami-Ohio - Series tied 3-3
10/2/2021	@	Ball State								vs Ball State - Series tied 3-3
10/16/2021	@	Wisconsin								1st meeting
10/23/2021	vs	WAKE FOREST								1-9 S/U vs Wake Forest since 1990
11/6/2021	vs	Air Force {Arlington, TX}								vs Air Force - Air Force leads series 37-17-1
11/13/2021	vs	BUCKNELL								vs Bucknell - Army leads series 6-0
11/20/2021	vs	MASSACHUSETTS								vs Umass - Army leads series 3-0
11/27/2021	@	Liberty								vs Liberty - Army leads series 1-0
12/11/2021	vs	Navy {@ East Rutherford}								Game 0-15 O/U vs Navy since 2006
	vs									BOWL GAME

Pointspread Analysis Dog		Pointspread Analysis Non-Conference
0-39 S/U as 20.5 point or more Dog since 1983		0-7 S/U vs Air Force as 15.5-20 point Dog since 1999
10-3-3 ATS on road as 20.5-25 point Dog since 1983		1-7 S/U vs Air Force as 10.5-15 point Dog since 1985
4-33-1 S/U as 15.5-20 point Dog since 1984		0-5 S/U & ATS vs Air Force as 7.5-10 point Dog since 1989
2-10 O/U on road as 15.5-20 point Dog since 2002		0-3 S/U & ATS vs Air Force as 3 point or less favorite since 1990
0-11 S/U @ home as 15.5-20 point Dog since 1994		vs Navy - Navy leads series 61-52-7
1-17 S/U as 10.5-15 point Dog since 2006		1-3 S/U vs Navy at East Rutherford since 1989
3-15 ATS as 10.5-15 point Dog since 2006		1-3 ATS vs Navy at East Rutherford since 1989
2-11 S//U @ home as 10.5-15 point Dog since 1986		Game 1-3 O/U vs Navy at East Rutherford since 1989
4-13-1 O/U as 7.5-10 point Dog since 2002		0-7 S/U vs Navy as 10.5-15 point Dog since 1997
5-23 S/U as 7.5-10 point Dog since 1993		1-5 S/U vs Navy as 3.5-7 point Dog since 1999
2-10 S/U @ home as 7.5-10 point Dog since 1993		3-0 ATS vs Navy as 3.5-7 point Dog since 2011
14-1-1 ATS as 3.5-7 point Dog since 2012		0-3 O/U vs Navy as 3.5-7 point Dog since 2011
4-18 S/U on road as 3.5-7 point Dog since 1984		5-1 S/U vs Navy as 3 point or less favorite since 1984
1-10 S/U @ home as 3 point or less Dog since 2005		5-0 S/U vs Navy as 3.5-7 point favorite since 1987
2-9 ATS @ home as 3 point or less Dog since 2005		0-4 ATS vs Navy as 7.5-10 point favorite since 1988
Favorite		0-4 O/U vs Navy as 7.5-10 point favorite since 1988
9-20 ATS as road favorite since 1986		Game 0-4 O/U vs Wake Forest since 2013
20-2 S/U @ home as 3.5-7 point favorite since 1988		**Bowl Games**
1-7 S/U & ATS on road as 3.5-7 point favorite since 1997		4-1 S/U in Bowl Games since 2010
7-2 S/U as 7.5-10 point favorite since 1999		8-1 ATS in Bowl Games since 1984
5-0 S/U on road as 15.5 point or more favorite since 1985		7-1 O/U in Bowl Games since 1985
16-0 S/U as 20.5 point or more favorite since 1985		
		13-1 S/U @ home when ranked since 1956
		7-0 S/U when ranked vs #15 - #19 ranked teams all time
		0-48 S/U vs ranked teams since 1973
		0-34 S/U on road vs ranked teams since 1963
5-24 S/U prior to playing Navy since 1992	Liberty	0-7 O/U vs ranked teams since 2014

Military Police Insignia

25th Infantry Division – Tropic Lightning

Copyright © 2021 by Steve's Football Bible, LLC

2020-Auburn		Opponent	AUB	Opp	S/U	Line	ATS	Total	O/U	
9/26/2020	vs	KENTUCKY	29	13	W	-6.5	W	48.0	U	
10/3/2020	@	Georgia	6	27	L	7.5	L	44.5	U	"Deep South's Oldest Rivalry"
10/10/2020	vs	ARKANSAS	30	28	W	-13.5	L	46.0	O	
10/17/2020	@	South Carolina	22	30	L	-3.0	L	51.5	O	
10/24/2020	@	Mississippi	35	28	W	-3.5	W	73.5	U	
10/31/2020	vs	LSU	48	11	W	PK	W	63.5	U	
11/21/2020	vs	TENNESSEE	30	17	W	-10.0	W	51.0	U	
11/28/2020	@	Alabama	13	42	L	24.5	L	65.0	U	Iron Bowl
12/5/2020	vs	TEXAS A&M	20	31	L	5.0	L	49.0	O	
12/12/2020	@	Mississippi State	24	10	W	-5.5	W	50.5	U	
1/1/2021	vs	**Northwestern**	19	35	L	3.5	L	45.0	O	Citrus Bowl
Coach: Guz Malzhan		Season Record >>	276	272	6-5	ATS>>	5-6	O/U>>	4-7	
2019-Auburn		Opponent	AUB	Opp	S/U	Line	ATS	Total	O/U	
8/31/2019	vs	Oregon	27	21	W	-3.5	W	55.5	U	AT&T Stadium
9/7/2019	vs	TULANE	24	6	W	-16.0	W	51.0	U	
9/14/2019	vs	KENT STATE	55	16	W	-36.0	W	53.5	O	
9/21/2019	@	Texas A&M	28	20	W	4.0	W	48.0	T	
9/28/2019	vs	MISSISSIPPI STATE	56	23	W	-8.0	W	46.5	O	
10/5/2019	@	Florida	14	23	L	-2.5	L	48.5	U	
10/19/2019	@	Arkansas	51	10	W	-20.0	W	55.0	O	
10/26/2019	@	Lsu	20	23	L	11.5	W	59.5	U	
11/2/2019	vs	MISSISSIPPI	20	14	W	-17.5	L	53.5	U	
11/16/2019	vs	GEORGIA	14	21	L	3.0	L	43.0	U	"Deep South's Oldest Rivalry"
11/23/2019	vs	SAMFORD	52	0	W	-45.5	W	NT	---	
11/30/2019	vs	ALABAMA	48	45	W	3.5	W	51.0	O	Iron Bowl
1/1/2020	vs	**Minnesota**	24	31	L	-7.0	L	53.5	O	Outback Bowl
Coach: Guz Malzhan		Season Record >>	433	253	9-4	ATS>>	9-4	O/U>>	5-6-1	
2018-Auburn		Opponent	AUB	Opp	S/U	Line	ATS	Total	O/U	
9/1/2018	vs	Washington	21	16	W	-1.5	W	50.5	U	Mercedes Benz Stadium
9/8/2018	vs	Alabama State	63	9	W	-62.5	L	NT	---	
9/15/2018	vs	LSU	21	22	L	-10.0	L	45.0	U	
9/22/2018	vs	ARKANSAS	34	3	W	-29.5	W	57.5	U	
9/29/2018	vs	SOUTHERN MISS	24	13	W	-27.0	L	50.0	U	
10/6/2018	@	Mississippi State	9	23	L	-3.0	L	45.0	U	
10/13/2018	vs	TENNESSEE	24	30	L	-14.5	L	47.0	O	
10/20/2018	@	Mississippi	31	16	W	-5.0	W	63.5	U	
11/3/2018	vs	TEXAS A&M	28	24	W	-3.5	W	47.5	O	
11/10/2018	@	Georgia	10	27	L	13.5	L	52.5	U	"Deep South's Oldest Rivalry"
11/17/2018	vs	LIBERTY	53	0	W	-28.5	W	64.5	U	
11/24/2018	@	Alabama	21	52	L	27.0	L	52.5	O	Iron Bowl
12/28/2018	vs	**Purdue**	63	14	W	-3.5	W	58.0	O	Music City Bowl
Coach: Guz Malzhan		Season Record >>	402	249	8-5	ATS>>	6-7	O/U>>	4-8	
2017-Auburn		Opponent	AUB	Opp	S/U	Line	ATS	Total	O/U	
9/2/2017	vs	GEORGIA SOUTHERN	41	7	W	-34.5	L	59.0	U	
9/9/2017	@	Clemson	6	14	L	6.0	L	55.0	U	
9/16/2017	vs	MERCER	24	10	W	-40.0	L	NT	---	
9/23/2017	@	Missouri	51	14	W	-18.0	W	60.5	O	
9/30/2017	vs	MISSISSIPPI STATE	49	10	W	-7.0	W	51.0	O	
10/7/2017	vs	MISSISSIPPI	44	23	W	-21.0	T	55.5	O	
10/14/2017	@	Lsu	23	27	L	-6.5	L	46.5	O	
10/21/2017	@	Arkansas	52	20	W	-17.0	W	51.0	O	
11/4/2017	@	Texas A&M	42	27	W	-15.0	T	52.0	O	
11/11/2017	vs	GEORGIA	40	17	W	2.5	W	48.0	O	"Deep South's Oldest Rivalry"
11/18/2017	vs	LOUISIANA-MONROE	42	14	W	-33.0	L	68.0	U	
11/25/2017	vs	ALABAMA	26	14	W	4.5	W	47.5	U	Iron Bowl
12/2/2017	vs	**Georgia**	7	28	L	2.0	L	48.0	U	SEC Championship
1/1/2018	vs	**Central Florida**	27	34	L	-10.5	L	66.0	U	Chick-Fil-A Peach Bowl
Coach: Guz Malzhan		Season Record >>	474	259	10-4	ATS>>	5-7-2	O/U>>	7-6	

    Copyright © 2021 by Steve's Football Bible, LLC

AUBURN TIGERS   SEC WEST

STADIUM: Jordan-Hare Stadium {87,451}				Location: Auburn, AL				COACH: Brian Harsin		
DATE		Opponent	Aub	Opp	S/U	Line	ATS	Total	O/U	Trends & Angles
9/4/2021	vs	AKRON								vs Akron - Auburn leads series 1-0
9/11/2021	vs	ALABAMA STATE								vs Alabama State - Auburn leads series 1-0
9/18/2021	@	Penn State								vs Penn State - Series tied 1-1
9/25/2021	vs	GEORGIA STATE								1st meeting
10/2/2021	@	Lsu								0-10 S/U @ LSU since 2001
10/9/2021	vs	GEORGIA								3-13 S/U vs Georgia since 2006 {4-12 ATS}
10/16/2021	@	Arkansas								vs Arkansas - Arkansas leads series 16-13-1
10/30/2021	vs	MISSISSIPPI								17-3 S/U @ home vs Ole Miss since 1953
11/6/2021	@	Texas A&M								4-0 S/U @ Texas A&M since 2013 {3-0-1 ATS}
11/13/2021	vs	MISSISSIPPI STATE								5-1 S/U @ home vs M State since 2009
11/20/2021	@	South Carolina								8-1 S/U vs South Carolina since 1996
11/27/2021	vs	ALABAMA								vs Alabama - Alabama leads series 47-37-1
12/4/2021	vs									SEC Championship
	vs									BOWL GAME

Pointspread Analysis Non-Conference		Pointspread Analysis Conference
0-5 S/U vs Non-Conf. as 7.5-10 point Dog since 1989		0-5 S/U vs Alabama as 20.5 point or more Dog since 2011
1-6 S/U & ATS vs Non-Conf. as 3 point or less Dog since 1996		4-0 S/U vs Alabama as 3.5-7 point favorite since 1987
6-0 S/U & ATS vs Non-Conf. as 3 point or less favorite since 2003		3-0 S/U vs Arkansas as 7.5-10 point favorite since 2000
10-1 S/U vs Non-Conf. as 7.5-10 point favorite since 1983		4-1 S/U vs Arkansas as 15.5-20 point favorite since 1996
0-6 ATS vs Non-Conf. as 7.5-10 point favorite since 1990		Game 1-7 O/U vs Georgia since 2014
15-2 S/U vs Non-Conf. as 10.5-15 point favorite since 1992		vs Georgia - Georgia leads series 61-54-8
57-0 S/U vs Non-Conf. as 15.5 point or or more favorite since 1984		1-6 S/U & ATS vs Georgia as 3 point or less Dog since 2002
Bowl Games		3-0 S/U & ATS vs Georgia as 3 point or less favorite since 1983
4-0 S/U vs PAC-12 teams in Bowl Games		3-0 S/U & ATS vs Georgia as 3.5-7 point favorite since 1984
6-12 O/U in Bowl Games since 2001		Game 4-1 O/U @ LSU since 2011
5-0 S/U & ATS in Bowl Games as 3 point or less favorite since 2003		vs LSU - LSU leads series 31-23-1
0-6 S/U vs ranked teams in Bowl Games since 2014		0-4 S/U @ LSU as 3.5-7 point Dog since 2001
Dog		3-0 S/U vs LSU as 3 point or less favorite since 1992
0-6 S/U on road as 20.5 point or more Dog since 1996		vs Mississippi - Auburn leads series 33-10
0-3 S/U @ home as 15.5-20 point Dog since 1999		8-2-1 ATS vs Mississippi since 2009
1-7 O/U on road as 10.5-15 point Dog since 1992		3-0 S/U & ATS vs Ole Miss as 3 point or less Dog since 1998
0-6 S/U @ home as 7.5-10 point Dog since 1991		6-0 S/U & ATS vs Ole Miss as 3.5-7 point favorite since 2001
5-0-1 ATS @ home as 7.5-10 point Dog since 1992		5-0 S/U vs Mississippi as 10.5-15 point favorite since 1985
0-15 S/U as 7.5-10 point Dog since 2000		5-0 S/U vs Mississippi as 15.5-20 point favorite since 1995
5-1 S/U & ATS @ home as 3.5-7 point Dog since 2002		3-0 S/U vs Mississippi as 20.5-25 point favorite since 1997
4-12 S/U on road as 3.5-7 point Dog since 2003		26-5 S/U vs Mississippi State as favorite since 1983
2-11 O/U as 3 point or less Dog since 2009		vs Mississippi State - Auburn leads series 62-29-3
Favorite		Game 2-7 O/U vs Mississippi State since 2012
13-6 S/U as 3 point or less favorite since 2002		5-0 S/U vs Mississippi State as 3.5-7 point favorite since 1993
1-5 O/U as 3 point or less favorite since 2015		6-1 S/U vs Mississippi State as 10.5-15 point favorite since 1984
10-1 S/U @ home as 3.5-7 point favorite since 2007		4-1 S/U vs Mississippi State as 15.5-20 point favorite since 1983
32-6-1 S/U as 7.5-10 point favorite since 1983		1-4 ATS vs Mississippi State as 15.5-20 point favorite since 1983
15-3-1 S/U @ home as 7.5-10 point favorite since 1983		3-0 S/U & ATS vs Mississippi State as 20.5-25 point favorite since 1987
12-0 S/U on road as 10.5-15 point favorite since 1983		Game 6-1 O/U vs South Carolina since 2005
24-4-1 S/U @ home as 10.5-15 point favorite since 1992		vs Texas A&M - ROAD team 8-1 S/U since 2012 {7-1-1 ATS}
12-0 S/U on road as 10.5-15 point favorite since 1983		vs Texas A&M - Texas A&M leads series 6-5
23-5-1 S/U @ home as 10.5-15 point favorite since 1992		
22-0 S/U on road as 10.5 point or more favorite since 1983		
22-2 S/U @ home as 15.5-20 point favorite since 1983		

93-3 S/U @ home as 15.5 point or more favorite since 1983	AKRON	13-1 S/U in 1st home game of season since 2006
7-2 ATS @ home as 25.5-30 point favorite since 1986	G. STATE	15-2 S/U prior to playing LSU since 2003
2-7 ATS as 30.5-40 point favorite since 2014	G. STATE	1-6-1 ATS prior to playing LSU since 2012
	Lsu	10-1 S/U prior to playing Georgia since 2009
43-4 S/U @ home when ranked since 2009	Arkansas	7-0 O/U prior to playing Mississippi since 2013
17-4 S/U @ home when ranked vs ranked teams since 2004	Arkansas	2-10-1 O/U after playing Georgia since 2006
19-0 S/U when ranked vs Mississippi all time	OLE MISS	7-1-1 ATS prior to Texas A&M since 2012

Copyright © 2021 by Steve's Football Bible, LLC

BALL STATE CARDINALS   MAC WEST

2020-Ball State		Opponent	Ball	Opp	S/U	Line	ATS	Total	O/U	
11/4/2020	@	Miami-Ohio	31	38	L	-1.0	L	56.5	O	
11/11/2020	vs	EASTERN MICHIGAN	38	31	W	-8.0	L	61.5	O	
11/18/2020	vs	NOTHERN ILLINOIS	31	25	W	-14.5	L	58.5	U	"Bronze Stalk Trophy"
11/28/2020	@	Toledo	27	24	W	9.5	W	67.0	U	
12/5/2020	@	Central Michigan	45	20	W	-2.5	W	62.5	O	
12/12/2020	vs	WESTERN MICHIGAN	30	27	W	2.0	W	66.0	U	
12/18/2020	@	Buffalo	38	28	W	12.5	W	70.0	U	MAC CHAMPIONSHIP
12/31/2020	vs	San Jose State	34	13	W	7.5	W	66.0	U	Arizona Bowl
Coach: Mike Neu		Season Record >>	274	206	7-1	ATS>>	5-3	O/U>>	3-5	MAC CHAMPIONS
2019-Ball State		Opponent	Ball	Opp	S/U	Line	ATS	Total	O/U	
8/31/2019	vs	Indiana	24	34	L	18.0	W	60.5	U	Lucas Oil Stadium
9/7/2019	vs	FORDHAM	57	29	W	-29.5	L	NT	---	
9/14/2019	vs	FLORIDA ATLANTIC	31	41	L	2.5	L	64.5	O	
9/21/2019	@	NC State	23	34	L	19.5	W	58.5	U	
10/5/2019	@	Northern Illinois	27	20	W	4.0	W	54.5	U	"Bronze Stalk Trophy"
10/12/2019	@	Eastern Michigan	29	23	W	2.0	W	57.0	U	
10/19/2019	vs	TOLEDO	52	14	W	-3.0	W	58.0	O	
10/26/2019	vs	OHIO	21	34	L	-2.0	L	59.5	U	
11/5/2019	@	Western Michigan	31	35	L	6.0	W	65.0	O	
11/16/2019	vs	CENTRAL MICHIGAN	44	45	L	-1.0	L	60.0	O	
11/23/2019	@	Kent State	38	41	L	-3.5	L	67.5	O	
11/29/2019	vs	MIAMI-OHIO	41	27	W	-3.0	W	55.5	O	
Coach: Mike Neu		Season Record >>	418	377	5-7	ATS>>	7-5	O/U>>	6-5	
2018-Ball State		Opponent	Ball	Opp	S/U	Line	ATS	Total	O/U	
8/30/2018	vs	CENTRAL CONNECTICUT	42	6	W	-18.5	W	NT	---	
9/8/2018	@	Notre Dame	16	24	L	34.0	W	60.5	U	
9/15/2018	@	Indiana	10	38	L	15.0	L	60.0	U	
9/22/2018	vs	WESTERN KENTUCKY	20	28	L	-3.0	L	54.0	U	
9/29/2018	vs	KENT STATE	52	24	W	-7.0	W	61.5	O	
10/6/2018	vs	NORTHERN ILLINOIS	16	24	L	3.0	L	53.0	U	"Bronze Stalk Trophy"
10/13/2018	@	Central Michigan	24	23	W	2.5	W	54.5	U	
10/20/2018	vs	EASTERN MICHIGAN	20	42	L	3.0	L	44.0	O	
10/25/2018	@	Ohio	14	52	L	10.0	L	65.5	O	
10/31/2018	@	Toledo	13	45	L	20.0	L	63.5	U	
11/13/2018	vs	WESTERN MCIHIGAN	42	41	W	9.5	W	57.5	O	{OT}
11/20/2018	@	Miami-Ohio	21	42	L	14.5	L	55.0	O	
Coach: Mike Neu		Season Record >>	290	389	4-8	ATS>>	5-7	O/U>>	5-6	
2017-Ball State		Opponent	Ball	Opp	S/U	Line	ATS	Total	O/U	
9/2/2017	@	Illinois	21	24	L	5.5	W	55.5	U	
9/9/2017	vs	ALABAMA-BIRMINGHAM	51	31	W	-13.5	W	54.0	O	
9/16/2017	vs	TENNESSEE TECH	28	13	W	-22.0	L	NT	---	
9/23/2017	@	Western Kentucky	21	33	L	11.0	L	50.0	O	
9/30/2017	@	Western Michigan	3	55	L	12.5	L	54.0	O	
10/7/2017	@	Akron	3	31	L	4.5	L	51.5	U	
10/21/2017	vs	CENTRAL MICHIGAN	9	56	L	3.0	L	48.0	O	
10/26/2017	vs	TOLEDO	17	58	L	26.5	L	54.5	O	
11/2/2017	@	Eastern Michigan	14	56	L	24.5	L	47.5	O	
11/9/2017	@	Northern Illinois	17	63	L	29.0	L	51.0	O	"Bronze Stalk Trophy"
11/16/2017	vs	BUFFALO	24	40	L	17.5	W	53.5	O	
11/21/2017	vs	MIAMI-OHIO	7	28	L	17.5	L	53.5	U	
Coach: Mike Neu		Season Record >>	215	488	2-10	ATS>>	3-9	O/U>>	8-3	

Copyright © 2021 by Steve's Football Bible, LLC

BALL STATE CARDINALS   MAC WEST

STADIUM: Scheumann Stadium {22,500}				Location: Muncie, IN					COACH: Mike Neu	
DATE		Opponent	Ball	Opp	S/U	Line	ATS	Total	O/U	Trends & Angles
9/2/2021	vs	WESTERN ILLINOIS								vs Western Illinois - WIU leads series 3-1
9/11/2021	@	Penn State								1st Meeting
9/18/2021	@	Wyoming								1st Meeting
9/25/2021	vs	TOLEDO								vs Toledo - Toledo leads series 24-21-1
10/2/2021	vs	ARMY								vs Army - Series tied 3-3
10/9/2021	@	Western Michigan								0-3 S/U @ Western Michigan since 2015
10/16/2021	@	Eastern Michigan								7-1 S/U @ E Michigan since 2005 {6-2 ATS}
10/23/2021	vs	MIAMI-OHIO								2-6 S/U @ home vs Miami-Ohio since 1996
11/2/2021	@	Akron								
11/10/2021	@	Northern Illinois								1-5 S/U @ Northern Illinois since 2009
11/17/2021	vs	CENTRAL MICHIGAN								0-3 S/U @ home vs C. Michigan since 2015
11/23/2021	vs	BUFFALO								4-1 S/U @ home vs Buffalo since 1969
12/3/2021	vs									MAC Championship
	vs									BOWL GAME

Pointspread Analysis Non-Conference		Pointspread Analysis Conference
0-57-1 S/U vs Non-Conference as 10.5 point or more Dog since 1989		4-0 S/U vs Akron as 7.5 point or more favorite since 1994
Bowl Games		vs Buffalo - Ball State leads series 10-2
0-8-1 S/U in Bowl Games		11-2-1 S/U vs Central Michigan as favorite since 1989
1-6 ATS in Bowl Games since 1989		8-3 ATS vs Central Michigan since 2010
Dog		vs Central Michigan - Ball State leads series 27-25-1
0-15 S/U as 30.5 point or more Dog since 1993		0-3 S/U vs Central Michigan as 3.5-7 point Dog since 2004
2-11 S/U as 25.5-30 point Dog since 1989		4-1 S/U & ATS vs C. Michigan as 3 point or less favorite since 1996
1-10 S/U as 20.5-25 point Dog since 1996		4-0 S/U vs C. Michigan as 3.5-7 point favorite since 1995
0-7 S/U @ home as 15.5-20 point Dog since 1998		0-4 ATS vs C. Michigan as 10 point or more favorite since 1997
1-33 S/U as 15.5-20 point Dog since 1991		vs Eastern Michigan - Ball State leads series 35-24-2
10-2 ATS on road as 15.5-20 point Dog since 2009		7-1 S/U vs E. Michigan as 3.5-7 point favorite since 1990
1-11 O/U on road as 15.5-20 point Dog since 2009		vs Miami-Ohio - Miami-Ohio leads series 20-13-1
4-22 S/U on road as 10.5-15 point Dog since 1994		1-6 S/U vs Miami-Ohio as 7.5 point or more Dog since 1997
6-32 S/U as 10.5-15 point Dog since 1989		4-0 S/U vs Miami-Ohio as 8 point or more favorite since 1989
1-7 S/U @ home as 10.5-15 point Dog since 1998		2-17 S/U vs Northern Illinois as Dog since 1997
8-22 S/U as 7.5-10 point Dog since 1990		1-8 ATS vs Northern Illinois since 2012
1-7 O/U as 3.5-7 point Dog since 2014		Game 4-1 O/U @ Northern Illinois since 2011
1-7 S/U @ home as 3.5-7 point Dog since 2005		2-10 S/U vs Northern Illinois since 2009
2-11 S/U & ATS @ home as 3 point or less Dog since 1999		1-11 S/U vs Northern Illinois as 7.5 point or more Dog since 1999
Favorite		0-4 S/U vs Northern Illinois as 3 point or less Dog since 2002
8-3 S/U on road as 3 point or less favorite since 1993		5-0 S/U vs N. Illinois as 9 point or more favorite since 1997
11-1 S/U on road as 3.5-7 point favorite since 1990		2-5 S/U vs Toledo since 2014
10-1 S/U on road as 7.5-10 point favorite since 1989		0-8 S/U vs Toledo as 10.5 point or more Dog since 2004
8-0 S/U on road as 10.5-15 point favorite since 1989		2-5 S/U W. Michigan since 2014
3-0 S/U on road as 15.5-20 point favorite since 2008		vs Western Michigan - Western Michigan leads series 26-21
0-3 O/U on road as 15.5-20 point favorite since 2008		0-3 S/U & ATS vs W. Michigan as 3 point or less Dog since 1997
11-0 S/U as 20.5 point or more favorite since 1993		3-0 S/U vs W. Michigan as 7.5 point or more favorite since 1996
1-7 ATS as 20.5 point or more favorite since 2008		

W. ILLINOIS	11-0 S/U in 1st home game of season since 2010
Penn State	1-11 S/U in 1st road game of season since 2009
ARMY	3-10 O/U prior to playing Western Michigan since 2008
W. Michigan	2-10 S/U prior to playing Eastern Michigan since 2009
W. Michigan	3-9 ATS prior to playing Eastern Michigan since 2009
MIAMI-OHIO	12-3 ATS after playing Eastern Michigan since 2006
N. Illinois	3-10 O/U prior to playing Central Michigan since 2008

Copyright © 2021 by Steve's Football Bible, LLC

BAYLOR BEARS

BIG TWELVE

2020-Baylor		Opponent	BAY	Opp	S/U	Line	ATS	Total	O/U	
9/26/2020	vs	KANSAS	47	14	W	-17.5	W	62.0	U	
10/3/2020	@	West Virginia	21	27	L	-1.0	L	54.0	U	{OT}
10/24/2020	@	Texas	16	27	L	10.5	L	61.0	U	
10/31/2020	vs	TCU	23	33	L	2.5	L	47.5	O	
11/7/2020	@	Iowa State	31	38	L	14.0	W	46.5	O	
11/14/2020	@	Texas Tech	23	24	L	1.0	T	54.0	U	
11/28/2020	vs	KANSAS STATE	32	31	W	-5.5	L	44.5	O	
12/5/2020	@	Oklahoma	14	27	L	23.5	W	60.5	U	
12/12/2020	vs	OKLAHOMA STATE	3	42	L	6.0	L	49.5	U	
Coach: Dave Aranda		Season Record >>	210	263	2-7	ATS>>	3-5-1	O/U>>	3-6	
2019-Baylor		Opponent	BAY	Opp	S/U	Line	ATS	Total	O/U	
8/31/2019	vs	STEPHEN F. AUSTIN	56	17	W	-43.0	L	NT	---	
9/7/2019	vs	TEXAS-SAN ANTONIO	63	14	W	-25.0	W	58.0	O	
9/21/2019	@	Rice	21	13	W	-27.0	L	57.5	U	
9/28/2019	vs	IOWA STATE	23	21	W	2.5	W	55.5	U	
10/5/2019	@	Kansas State	31	12	W	PK	W	48.0	U	
10/12/2019	vs	TEXAS TECH	33	30	W	-10.5	L	60.0	O	{2 OT}
10/19/2019	@	Oklahoma State	45	27	W	5.5	W	68.5	O	
10/31/2019	vs	WEST VIRGINIA	17	14	W	-17.5	L	56.5	U	
11/9/2019	@	Tcu	29	23	W	-2.0	W	48.5	O	{3 OT}
11/16/2019	vs	OKLAHOMA	31	34	L	10.5	W	68.5	U	
11/23/2019	vs	TEXAS	24	10	W	-4.0	W	57.5	U	
11/30/2019	@	Kansas	61	6	W	-14.0	W	53.5	U	
12/7/2019	vs	Oklahoma	23	30	L	9.0	W	66.0	U	Big 12 Championship
1/1/2020	vs	Georgia	14	26	L	3.5	L	44.0	U	Sugar Bowl
Coach: Matt Rhule		Season Record >>	471	277	11-3	ATS>>	9-5	O/U>>	5-8	
2018-Baylor		Opponent	BAY	Opp	S/U	Line	ATS	Total	O/U	
9/1/2018	vs	ABILENE CHRISTIAN	55	27	W	-40.5	L	NT	---	
9/8/2018	@	Texas-San Antonio	37	20	W	-17.0	T	55.0	O	
9/15/2018	vs	DUKE	27	40	L	-2.5	L	49.0	O	
9/22/2018	vs	KANSAS	27	6	W	-7.5	W	55.0	U	
9/29/2018	@	Oklahoma	33	66	L	21.0	L	68.0	O	
10/6/2018	vs	KANSAS STATE	37	34	W	-3.5	L	52.5	O	
10/13/2018	@	Texas	17	23	L	13.0	W	58.5	U	
10/25/2018	@	West Virginia	14	58	L	15.0	L	67.0	O	
11/3/2018	vs	OKLAHOMA STATE	35	31	W	6.5	W	68.5	U	
11/10/2018	@	Iowa State	14	28	L	17.0	W	51.0	U	
11/17/2018	vs	TCU	9	16	L	-1.0	L	50.0	U	
11/24/2018	vs	Texas Tech	35	24	W	6.5	W	63.5	U	AT&T Stadium
12/27/2018	vs	Vanderbilt	45	38	W	4.5	W	56.5	O	Texas Bowl
Coach: Matt Rhule		Season Record >>	385	411	7-6	ATS>>	6-6-1	O/U>>	6-6	
2017-Baylor		Opponent	BAY	Opp	S/U	Line	ATS	Total	O/U	
9/2/2017	vs	LIBERTY	45	48	L	-34.5	L	58.0	O	
9/9/2017	vs	TEXAS-SAN ANTONIO	10	17	L	-11.0	L	57.0	U	
9/16/2017	@	Duke	20	34	L	10.5	L	60.5	U	
9/23/2017	vs	OKLAHOMA	41	49	L	28.0	W	60.5	O	
9/30/2017	@	Kansas State	20	33	L	14.5	W	56.0	U	
10/14/2017	@	Oklahoma State	16	59	L	26.0	L	67.5	O	
10/21/2017	vs	WEST VIRGINIA	36	38	L	10.5	W	67.0	O	
10/28/2017	vs	TEXAS	7	38	L	10.0	L	53.5	U	
11/4/2017	@	Kansas	38	9	W	-7.0	W	59.0	U	
11/11/2017	vs	Texas Tech	24	38	L	9.0	L	68.0	U	AT&T Stadium
11/18/2017	vs	IOWA STATE	13	23	L	8.0	L	49.0	U	
11/24/2017	@	Tcu	22	45	L	24.5	W	52.0	O	
Coach: Matt Rhule		Season Record >>	292	431	1-11	ATS>>	5-7	O/U>>	5-7	

Copyright © 2021 by Steve's Football Bible, LLC

BAYLOR BEARS　　　　BIG TWELVE

STADIUM: McLane Stadium {45,140}				Location: Waco, TX					COACH: Dave Aranda
DATE	Opponent	Bay	Opp	S/U	Line	ATS	Total	O/U	Trends & Angles
9/4/2021 @	*Texas State*								vs Texas State - Baylor leads series 7-0
9/11/2021 vs	*TEXAS SOUTHERN*								1st meeting
9/18/2021 @	Kansas								5-0 S/U @ Kansas since 2011
9/25/2021 vs	IOWA STATE								5-1 S/U @ home vs Iowa State since 2008
10/2/2021 @	Oklahoma State								2-12 S/U @ Oklahoma State since 1972
10/9/2021 vs	WEST VIRGINIA								HOME team 8-1 S/U since 2012
10/16/2021 vs	*BYU*								vs BYU - Series tied 1-1
10/30/2021 vs	TEXAS								3-8 S/U @ home vs Texas since 1999
11/6/2021 @	Tcu								3-11 ATS vs TCU since 1995
11/13/2021 vs	OKLAHOMA								0-7 S/U vs Oklahoma since 2015
11/20/2021 @	Kansas State								Game 0-4 O/U @ Kansas State since 2013
11/27/2021 vs	TEXAS TECH								1-6 S/U @ home vs Texas Tech since 1997
12/4/2021 vs									BIG XII Championship
vs									BOWL GAME

Pointspread Analysis Non-Conference		Pointspread Analysis Conference
0-17 S/U vs Non-Conf. as 7.5 point or more Dog since 1989		vs Iowa State - Baylor leads series 10-9
6-0 S/U & ATS vs Non-Conf. as 3 point or less Dog since 1995		3-7 S/U vs Iowa State as Dog since 2000
4-0 S/U vs Non-Conf. as 7.5-10 point favorite since 1995		8-1 S/U vs Iowa State as favorite since 1988
13-1 S/U vs Non-Conf. as 15.5-30 point favorite since 1986		1-6 S/U vs Iowa State as 7.5 point or more Dog since 2000
12-1 S/U vs Non-Conf. as 30.5 point or more favorite since 2010		16-0 S/U vs Kansas as favorite since 1988
Bowl Games		9-0 ATS vs Kansas since 2012
3-0 S/U & ATS in Bowl games as 3 point or less Dog since 1985		11-0 S/U vs Kansas since 2010
0-4 S/U vs Big Ten in Bowl Games		vs Kansas - Baylor leads series 16-4
0-3 S/U in Cotton Bowl		Game 1-5 O/U vs Kansas since 20215
Dog		0-3 S/U vs Kansas as 14 point or more Dog since 1999
0-21 S/U as 30.5 point or more Dog since 1996		6-0 S/U vs Kansas as 3.5-10 point favorite since 1998
6-0 ATS as 30.5 point or more Dog since 2003		9-0 S/U vs Kansas as 15.5 point or more favorite since 1989
0-18 S/U as 25.5-30 point Dog since 1997		vs Kansas State - Series tied 9-9
10-2-1 O/U as 25.5-30 point Dog since 2002		1-5 S/U vs Kansas State as 10.5 point or more Dog since 1998
1-18 S/U as 20.5-25 point Dog since 1997		vs Oklahoma - Oklahoma leads series 28-3
0-43 S/U on road as 15.5 point or more Dog since 1984		2-21 S/U vs Oklahoma as Dog since 1984
2-25 S/U as 15.5-20 point Dog since 1984		Game 5-2 O/U @ home vs Oklahoma since 2009
2-8 ATS on road as 15.5-20 point Dog since 2000		0-19 S/U vs Oklahoma as 7.5 point or more Dog since 1984
3-43-1 S/U as 10.5-15 point Dog since 1983		vs Oklahoma State - Oklahoma State leads series 21-18
12-4 ATS as 10.5-15 point Dog since 2008		3-16 S/U vs Oklahoma State as Dog since 1997
1-14 S/U @ home as 10.5-15 point Dog since 1990		Game 5-1 O/U @ Oklahoma State since 2010
0-11 S/U @ home as 7.5-10 point Dog since 1997		0-14 S/U vs Oklahoma State as 7.5 point or more Dog since 1997
2-9 ATS @ home as 7.5-10 point Dog since 1997		vs Tcu - TCU leads series 57-50-7
3-9 ATS as 7.5-10 point Dog since 2005		0-3 S/U vs TCU as 21 point or more Dog since 2007
2-19 S/U as 7.5-10 point Dog since 1997		3-0 S/U vs TCU as 7.5-10 point favorite since 1983
Favorite		4-1 S/U vs TCU as 10.5-15 point favorite since 1986
12-4 O/U as 3 point or less favorite since 2005		Game 0-8 O/U vs Texas since 2013
12-2 S/U @ home as 3.5-7 point favorite since 2000		vs Texas - Texas leads series 78-27-5
5-0 S/U @ home as 7.5-10 point favorite since 2001		1-16 S/U vs Texas as 7.5 point or more Dog since 1998
26-0 S/U on road as 10.5 point or more favorite since 1984		2-18 S/U vs Texas Tech as Dog since 1988
12-3 S/U as 10.5-15 point favorite since 1994		Game 8-3 O/U vs Texas Tech since 2010
24-2 S/U as 15.5-20 point favorite since 1984		0-7 ATS @ home vs Texas Tech since 1997
9-2 S/U @ home as 20.5-25 point favorite since 1983		vs Texas Tech - Baylor leads series 39-38-1
7-0 S/U @ home as 25.5-30 point favorite since 1994		0-13 S/U vs Texas Tech as 7.5 point or more Dog since 1998
7-1 O/U as 25.5-30 point favorite since 2013		vs West Virginia - West Virginia leads series 6-3
14-1 S/U @ home as 30.5 point or more favorite since 2010		0-4 S/U vs West Virginia as 10.5 point or more Dog since 2012
	OK State	6-2 O/U prior to playing West Virginia since 2012
	Kansas State	8-2 S/U prior to playing Texas Tech since 2010

Copyright © 2021 by Steve's Football Bible, LLC

BOISE STATE BRONCOS   MOUNTAIN WEST West

2020-Boise State		Opponent	Boise	Opp	S/U	Line	ATS	Total	O/U	
10/24/2020	vs	UTAH STATE	42	13	W	-17.0	W	51.0	O	
10/31/2020	@	Air Force	49	30	W	-12.5	W	48.5	O	
11/6/2020	vs	BYU	17	51	L	6.0	L	63.0	O	
11/14/2020	vs	COLORADO STATE	52	21	W	-14.0	W	62.5	O	
11/21/2020	@	Hawaii	40	32	W	-13.0	L	55.5	O	
12/12/2020	@	Wyoming	17	9	W	-9.5	L	47.0	U	
12/19/2020	vs	San Jose State	20	34	L	-6.5	L	59.5	U	MWC CHAMPIONSHIP
Coach: Brian Harsin		Season Record >>	237	190	5-2	ATS>>	3-4	O/U>>	5-2	
2019-Boise State		Opponent	Boise	Opp	S/U	Line	ATS	Total	O/U	
8/31/2019	vs	Florida State	36	31	W	6.5	W	54.5	O	
9/6/2019	vs	MARSHALL	14	7	W	-14.0	L	57.0	U	
9/14/2019	vs	PORTLAND STATE	45	10	W	-33.5	W	NT	---	
9/21/2019	vs	AIR FORCE	30	19	W	-7.0	W	55.5	U	
10/5/2019	@	Unlv	38	13	W	-24.5	W	57.5	U	
10/12/2019	vs	HAWAII	59	37	W	-12.5	W	60.0	O	
10/19/2019	@	Byu	25	28	L	-7.0	L	44.5	O	
11/2/2019	@	San Jose State	52	42	W	-16.5	L	61.0	O	
11/9/2019	vs	WYOMING	20	17	W	-16.5	L	48.0	U	
11/16/2019	vs	NEW MEXICO	42	9	W	-26.0	W	57.5	U	
11/23/2019	@	Utah State	56	21	W	-4.0	W	54.5	O	
11/30/2019	@	Colorado State	31	24	W	-13.0	L	57.0	U	
12/7/2019	vs	HAWAII	31	10	W	-14.0	W	65.0	U	MWC CHAMPIONSHIP GAME
12/21/2019	vs	Washington	7	38	L	4.0	L	48.0	U	Las Vegas Bowl
Coach: Brian Harsin		Season Record >>	486	306	12-2	ATS>>	8-6	O/U>>	5-8	MWC CHAMPIONS
2018-Boise State		Opponent	Boise	Opp	S/U	Line	ATS	Total	O/U	
9/1/2018	@	Troy	56	20	W	-9.0	W	48.0	O	
9/8/2018	vs	CONNECTICUT	62	7	W	-34.0	W	64.0	O	
9/15/2018	@	Oklahoma State	21	44	L	-2.0	L	66.5	U	
9/29/2018	@	Wyoming	34	14	W	-10.0	W	46.0	O	
10/6/2018	vs	SAN DIEGO STATE	13	19	L	-14.0	L	51.0	U	
10/13/2018	@	Nevada	31	27	W	-14.0	L	58.0	T	
10/19/2018	vs	COLORADO STATE	56	28	W	-23.0	W	61.5	O	
10/27/2018	@	Air Force	48	38	W	-9.5	W	57.5	O	
11/3/2018	vs	BYU	21	16	W	-12.0	L	54.0	U	
11/9/2018	vs	FRESNO STATE	24	17	W	2.5	W	55.0	U	"Milk Can"
11/17/2018	@	New Mexico	45	14	W	-22.0	W	61.5	U	
11/24/2018	vs	UTAH STATE	33	24	W	-2.0	W	64.0	U	
12/1/2018	vs	FRESNO STATE	16	19	L	PK	L	51.0	U	MWC CHAMPIONSHIP GAME
12/26/2018	vs	Boston College	-	-	-	-	-	-	-	First Responder Bowl
Coach: Brian Harsin		Season Record >>	460	287	10-3	ATS>>	8-5	O/U>>	5-7-1	
2017-Boise State		Opponent	Boise	Opp	S/U	Line	ATS	Total	O/U	
9/2/2017	vs	TROY	24	13	W	-10.5	W	59.0	U	
9/9/2017	@	Washington State	44	47	L	7.5	W	57.5	O	{3 OT}
9/14/2017	vs	NEW MEXICO	28	14	W	-16.5	L	56.0	U	
9/22/2017	vs	VIRGINIA	23	42	L	-13.5	L	50.5	O	
10/6/2017	@	Byu	24	7	W	-7.0	W	47.0	U	
10/14/2017	@	San Diego State	31	14	W	4.5	W	47.0	U	
10/21/2017	vs	WYOMING	24	14	W	-14.5	L	44.5	U	
10/28/2017	@	Utah State	41	14	W	-13.0	W	51.5	O	
11/4/2017	vs	NEVADA	41	14	W	-20.0	W	61.0	U	
11/11/2017	@	Colorado State	59	52	W	-6.5	W	59.0	O	{OT}
11/18/2017	vs	AIR FORCE	44	19	W	-17.5	W	60.0	O	
11/25/2017	@	Fresno State	17	28	L	-6.5	L	50.0	U	"Milk Can"
12/2/2017	vs	FRESNO STATE	17	14	W	-9.5	L	51.0	U	MWC CHAMPIONSHIP GAME
12/16/2017	vs	Oregon	38	28	W	7.0	W	62.5	O	Las Vegas Bowl
Coach: Brian Harsin		Season Record >>	455	320	11-3	ATS>>	9-5	O/U>>	6-8	MWC CHAMPIONS

Copyright © 2021 by Steve's Football Bible, LLC

BOISE STATE BRONCOS   MOUNTAIN WEST West

STADIUM: Bronco Stadium {36,387}					Location: Boise, ID				COACH: Andy Avalos	
DATE		Opponent	BSU	Opp	S/U	Line	ATS	Total	O/U	Trends & Angles
9/4/2021	@	Central Florida								1st meeting
9/11/2021	vs	TEXAS-EL PASO								vs Texas-El Paso - Boise State leads series 5-0
9/18/2021	vs	OKLAHOMA STATE								vs Ok State - Oklahoma State leads series 1-0
9/25/2021	@	Utah State								7-1 S/U @ UT State since 1999 {8-1 ATS since 1997}
10/2/2021	vs	NEVADA								9-0 S/U @ home vs Nevada since 1999
10/9/2021	@	Byu								vs BYU - Boise State leads series 7-4
10/16/2021	vs	AIR FORCE								vs Air Force - Boise State leads series 6-3
10/30/2021	@	Colorado State								5-0 S/U @ Colorado State since 2011 {4-1 ATS}
11/6/2021	@	Fresno State								Game 0-5 O/U vs Fresno State since 2014
11/13/2021	vs	WYOMING								7-0 S/U @ home vs Wyoming since 2003
11/20/2021	vs	NEW MEXICO								1-4 ATS @ home vs New Mexico since 2011
11/27/2021	@	San Diego State								vs San Diego State - Series tied 3-3
12/4/2021	vs									MWC Championship
	vs									BOWL GAME

Pointspread Analysis Non-Conference		Pointspread Analysis Conference
15-2 S/U vs Non-Conf. as 3.5-10 point favorite since 1999		3-0 S/U vs Air Force as 17.5 point or more favorite since 2011
30-1 S/U vs Non-Conf. as 15.5 point or more favorite since 2001		vs Colorado State - Boise State leads series 10-0
7-2 S/U vs BYU as 2 point or more favorite since 2003		5-0 S/U @ Colorado State since 2011
Bowl Games		4-1 ATS @ Colorado State since 2011
4-1 S/U in Las Vegas Bowl		10-0 S/U vs Colorado State as 6.5 point or more favorite since 2011
3-0 S/U in Fiesta Bowl		1-5 ATS vs Fresno State since 2014
Dog		13-1 S/U vs Fresno State as favorite since 2002
0-5 S/U as 20.5 point or more Dog since 1996		vs Fresno State - Boise State leads series 15-7
4-0 ATS as 15.5-20 point Dog since 1998		13-1 S/U vs Fresno State as 3 point or more favorite since 2002
0-4 S/U @ home as 10.5-15 point Dog since 1996		0-4 ATS vs Fresno State as 6.5 point or more favorite since 2014
0-6 S/U on road as 7.5-10 point Dog since 1998		7-1 ATS vs Hawaii since 2009
2-7 O/U on road as 3.5-7 point Dog since 2001		13-1 S/U vs Hawaii as favorite since 1999
5-0 ATS @ home as 3 point or less Dog since 1998		vs Hawaii - Boise State leads series 14-3
Favorite		16-1 S/U vs Nevada since 1999
10-3 S/U & ATS on road as 3.5-7 point favorite since 2002		vs Nevada - Boise State leads series 30-13
11-0 S/U @ home as 7.5-10 point favorite since 1999		15-1 S/U vs Nevada as 2.5 point or more favorite since 2001
27-3 S/U as 7.5-10 point favorite since 1998		vs New Mexico - Boise State leads series 10-1
16-3 S/U @ home as 10.5-15 point favorite since 2000		9-1 S/U vs New Mexico as 1.5 point or more favorite since 2000
4-10 ATS @ home as 10.5-15 point favorite since 2009		1-5 ATS vs San Diego State since 2011
26-2 S/U as 15.5-20 point favorite since 2000		0-5 ATS vs San Diego State as 6 point or more favorite since 2011
13-0 S/U on road as 15.5-20 point favorite since 2002		Game 5-0 O/U @ Utah State since 2009
10-1 O/U on road as 15.5-20 point favorite since 2005		Game 12-3 O/U vs Utah State since 2002
63-0 S/U as 20.5-30 point favorite since 2000		vs Utah State - Boise State leads series 20-5
3-8 ATS @ home as 30.5 point or more favorite since 2010		16-1 S/U vs Utah State as favorite since 1998
8-0 S/U on road as 30.5 point or more favorite since 2002		17-1 S/U vs Utah State since 1998
33-1 S/U as 30.5 point or more favorite since 2002		vs Wyoming - Boise State leads series 14-1
		1-6 ATS @ home vs Wyoming since 2003
		Game 0-7 O/U @ home vs Wyoming since 2003

19-0 S/U in 1st home game of season since 2002	UTEP	
20-2 S/U in 2nd home game of season since 1999	OK STATE	54-4 S/U @ home when ranked all time
3-11 O/U in 2nd home game of season since 2006	OK STATE	5-0 S/U when ranked vs Colorado State all time
14-1 S/U prior to playing Utah State since 1999	OK STATE	
14-2 S/U prior to playing Nevada since 2001	Utah State	
15-0 S/U after playing Utah State since 1999	NEVADA	
10-1 S/U after playing Nevada since 2003	Byu	
15-0 S/U prior to playing Fresno State since 2001	Colorado State	
21-1 S/U in final home game of season since 1999	NEW MEXICO	
11-3 S/U after playing Wyoming since 2002	NEW MEXICO	
10-4 O/U after playing Wyoming since 2002	NEW MEXICO	

Copyright © 2021 by Steve's Football Bible, LLC

BOSTON COLLEGE EAGLES ACC ATLANTIC

2020-Boston College		Opponent	BC	Opp	S/U	Line	ATS	Total	O/U	
9/19/2020	@	Duke	26	6	W	5.5	W	51.5	U	
9/26/2020	vs	*TEXAS STATE*	24	21	W	-20.5	L	56.5	U	
10/3/2020	vs	NORTH CAROLINA	22	26	L	14.5	W	52.5	U	
10/10/2020	vs	PITTSBURGH	31	30	W	6.0	W	42.0	O	
10/17/2020	@	Virginia Tech	14	40	L	13.5	L	61.5	U	
10/24/2020	vs	GEORGIA TECH	48	27	W	-3.5	W	57.5	O	
10/31/2020	@	Clemson	28	34	L	26.0	W	56.0	O	*"O'Rourke-McFadden Trophy"*
11/7/2020	@	Syracuse	16	13	W	-15.0	L	53.5	U	
11/14/2020	vs	NOTRE DAME	31	45	L	13.0	L	52.0	O	*"Holy War" (Frank Leahy Memorial Bowl)*
11/28/2020	vs	LOUISVILLE	34	27	W	-1.0	W	57.0	O	
12/5/2020	@	Virginia	32	43	L	6.5	L	53.0	O	
Coach: Jeff Hafley		Season Record >>	306	312	6-5	ATS>>	6-5	O/U>>	6-5	

2019-Boston College		Opponent	BC	Opp	S/U	Line	ATS	Total	O/U	
8/31/2019	vs	VIRGINIA TECH	35	28	W	4.0	W	58.0	O	
9/7/2019	vs	*RICHMOND*	45	13	W	-33.5	L	NT	---	
9/13/2019	vs	*KANSAS*	24	48	L	-19.5	L	51.0	O	
9/21/2019	@	*Rutgers*	30	16	W	-7.5	W	57.5	U	
9/28/2019	vs	WAKE FOREST	24	27	L	5.0	W	69.5	U	
10/12/2019	@	Louisville	39	41	L	3.5	W	61.0	O	
10/19/2019	vs	NC STATE	45	24	W	4.0	W	54.5	O	
10/26/2019	@	Clemson	7	59	L	35.0	L	59.0	O	*"O'Rourke-McFadden Trophy"*
11/2/2019	@	Syracuse	58	27	W	3.0	W	59.0	O	
11/9/2019	vs	FLORIDA STATE	31	38	L	-1.0	L	64.0	O	
11/23/2019	@	*Notre Dame*	7	40	L	21.0	L	65.5	U	*"Holy War" (Frank Leahy Memorial Bowl)*
11/30/2019	@	Pittsburgh	26	19	W	8.5	W	51.5	U	
1/2/2020	vs	**Cincinnati**	6	38	L	7.0	L	56.0	U	**Birmingham Bowl**
Coach: Steve Addazio		Season Record >>	377	418	6-7	ATS>>	7-6	O/U>>	7-5	

2018-Boston College		Opponent	BC	Opp	S/U	Line	ATS	Total	O/U	
9/1/2018	vs	*MASSACHUSETTS*	55	21	W	-20.5	W	62.5	O	*"Battle of The Bay State"*
9/8/2018	vs	*HOLY CROSS*	62	14	W	-44.0	W	NT	---	
9/13/2018	@	Wake Forest	41	34	W	-6.5	W	57.5	O	
9/22/2018	@	*Purdue*	13	30	L	-6.5	L	62.5	U	
9/29/2018	vs	*TEMPLE*	45	35	W	-11.5	L	54.0	O	
10/6/2018	@	NC State	23	28	L	6.5	W	60.5	U	
10/20/2018	vs	LOUISVILLE	38	20	W	-12.0	W	56.5	O	
10/26/2018	vs	MIAMI	27	14	W	4.0	W	49.0	U	
11/3/2018	@	Virginia Tech	31	21	W	-2.0	W	57.0	U	
11/10/2018	vs	CLEMSON	7	27	L	17.5	L	51.0	U	*"O'Rourke-McFadden Trophy"*
11/17/2018	@	Florida State	21	22	L	-3.0	L	48.0	U	
11/24/2018	vs	SYRACUSE	21	42	L	-6.0	L	60.5	O	
Coach: Steve Addazio		Season Record >>	384	308	7-5	ATS>>	7-5	O/U>>	5-6	

2017-Boston College		Opponent	BC	Opp	S/U	Line	ATS	Total	O/U	
9/1/2017	@	*Northern Illinois*	23	20	W	-3.5	L	46.0	U	
9/9/2017	vs	WAKE FOREST	10	34	L	PK	L	45.5	U	
9/16/2017	vs	*NOTRE DAME*	20	49	L	14.0	L	53.0	O	*"Holy War" (Frank Leahy Memorial Bowl)*
9/23/2017	@	Clemson	7	34	L	32.5	W	53.0	U	*"O'Rourke-McFadden Trophy"*
9/30/2017	vs	*CENTRAL MICHIGAN*	28	8	W	-10.0	W	52.0	U	
10/7/2017	vs	VIRGINIA TECH	10	23	L	15.5	W	46.5	U	
10/14/2017	@	Louisville	45	42	W	19.0	W	60.0	O	
10/21/2017	@	Virginia	41	10	W	6.5	W	47.5	O	
10/27/2017	vs	FLORIDA STATE	35	3	W	5.5	W	46.5	U	
11/11/2017	vs	NC STATE	14	17	L	3.0	T	52.5	L	
11/18/2017	vs	*CONNECTICUT*	39	16	W	-21.0	W	51.0	O	**Fenway Park**
11/25/2017	@	Syracuse	42	14	W	-4.0	W	56.5	U	
12/27/2017	vs	**Iowa**	20	27	L	2.0	L	46.0	O	**Pinstripe Bowl**
Coach: Steve Addazio		Season Record >>	334	297	7-6	ATS>>	8-4-1	O/U>>	5-8	

Copyright © 2021 by Steve's Football Bible, LLC

BOSTON COLLEGE EAGLES   ACC ATLANTIC

STADIUM: Alumni Stadium {44,500}			Location: Chestnut Hill, MA						COACH: Jeff Hafley
DATE		Opponent	BC	Opp	S/U	Line	ATS	Total	O/U	Trends & Angles
9/4/2021	vs	*COLGATE*								1st meeting
9/11/2021	vs	*MASSACHUSETTS*								12-0 S/U @ home vs Massachusetts since 1967
9/18/2021	@	*Temple*								6-0 S/U vs Temple since 2000
9/25/2021	vs	*MISSOURI*								1st meeting
10/2/2021	@	Clemson								0-6 S/U @ Clemson since 2009
10/16/2021	vs	NC STATE								6-1-1 ATS @ home vs NC State since 2005
10/23/2021	@	Louisville								5-1 ATS @ Louisville since 1990
10/30/2021	@	Syracuse								3-0 S/U @ Syracuse since 2017
11/5/2021	vs	VIRGINIA TECH								7-2 ATS vs Virginia Tech since 2011
11/13/2021	@	Georgia Tech								vs Georgia Tech - G Tech leads series 7-3
11/20/2021	vs	FLORIDA STATE								1-9 S/U vs Florida State since 2010
11/27/2021	vs	WAKE FOREST								0-3 S/U @ home vs Wake Forest since 2015
12/4/2021	vs									ACC Championship
	vs									BOWL GAME

Pointspread Analysis Non-Conference		Pointspread Analysis Conference
0-8 S/U vs Non-Conf. as 10.5-15 point Dog since 1985		vs Clemson - Clemson leads series 18-8-2
42-2 S/U vs Non-Conf. as 15.5 point or more favorite since 1983		0-10 S/U vs Clemson since 2011
10-0 S/U vs Umass since 1979		0-8 S/U vs Clemson as 17.5 point or more Dog since 2011
vs Umass - Boston College leads series 21-5		vs Florida State - Florida State leads series 13-5
vs Temple - Boston College leads series 29-7-2		0-6 S/U vs Florida State as 14.5 point or more Dog since 2010
Bowl Games		4-1 S/U & ATS vs Florida State as 4.0-9.0 point Dog since 2006
1-7 S/U in Bowl Games since 2008		vs Louisville - Louisville leads series 7-6
2-8 ATS in Bowl Games since 2006		Game 8-1 O/U vs Louisville since 1994
4-1 O/U in Bowl Games since 2013		Game 1-5 O/U vs NC State since 2014
2-6 S/U vs ranked teams in Bowl games all time		vs NC State - Boston College leads series 10-7
Dog		3-0 S/U vs NC State as 7.5 point or more favorite since 2007
0-10 S/U as 25.5 point or more Dog since 1990		4-13 S/U vs Syracuse as Dog since 1983
1-14 S/U as 20.5-25 point Dog since 1991		vs Syracuse - Syracuse leads series 32-21
0-4 S/U @ home as 20.5-25 point Dog since 1991		1-4 S/U vs Syracuse as 12 point or more Dog since 1987
9-0 ATS on road as 15.5-20 point Dog since 1993		1-9 S/U & ATS vs Syracuse as 3.5-10 point Dog since 1983
0-7 S/U @ home as 15.5-20 point Dog since 1991		1-5 S/U & ATS vs Syracuse as 6 point or less favorite since 2003
15-3 ATS as 15.5-20 point Dog since 1987		7-2 ATS vs Virginia Tech since 2011
2-9 O/U as 10.5-15 point Dog since 2011		vs Virginia Tech - Virginia Tech leads series 18-10
0-11 S/U @ home as 10.5-15 point Dog since 1986		1-9 S/U vs Virginia Tech as 13.5 point or more Dog since 1997
4-26 S/U as 10.5-15 point Dog since 1985		2-5 S/U vs Virginia Tech as 4.0-10 point Dog since 1998
1-7 S/U @ home as 7.5-10 point Dog since 1985		vs Wake Forest - Boston College leads series 14-11-2
1-9 S/U as 7.5-10 point Dog since 2009		Game 1-9 O/U vs Wake Forest since 2010
4-11 O/U on road as 3.5-7 point Dog since 2007		5-1 S/U & ATS vs Wake F. as 6.5 point or less favorite since 2007
9-2 S/U & ATS on road as 3 point or less Dog since 1995		**Favorite**
		8-2 S/U @ home as 3 point or less favorite since 2000
12-3 S/U in 2nd home game of season since 2006	UMASS	4-12 ATS as 3.5-7 point favorite since 2009
1-9 O/U in 1st road game of season since 2011	Temple	18-3 S/U as 7.5-10 point favorite since 1995
1-11 S/U in 2nd road game of season since 2009	Clemson	7-1 S/U on road as 7.5-10 point favorite since 1995
1-7 O/U after playing Clemson since since 2013	NC STATE	12-0 S/U as 10.5-15 point favorite since 2005
1-9 O/U prior to playing Virginia Tech since 2010	Syracuse	20-2 S/U as 15.5-20 point favorite since 1984
2-10 O/U in final road game of season since 2009	Georgia Tech	13-0 S/U on road as 15.5 point or more favorite since 1984
2-10 O/U prior to playing Wake Forest since 2005	FLORIDA STATE	36-0 S/U as 20.5 point or more favorite since 1983

Copyright © 2021 by Steve's Football Bible, LLC

BOWLING GREEN FALCONS   MAC East

2020-Bowling Green		Opponent	BGU	Opp	S/U	Line	ATS	Total	O/U	
11/4/2020	@	Toledo	3	38	L	24.0	L	63.0	U	*"Battle of I-75 Trophy"*
11/10/2020	vs	KENT STATE	24	62	L	20.5	L	55.0	O	*"Anniversary Award"*
11/17/2020	vs	BUFFALO	17	42	L	31.5	W	57.5	O	
11/28/2020	@	Ohio	10	52	L	22.5	L	55.0	O	
12/5/2020	@	Akron	3	31	L	2.5	L	54.5	U	
Coach: Scott Loeffler		Season Record >>	57	225	0-5	ATS>>	1-4	O/U>>	3-2	
2019-Bowling Green		Opponent	BGU	Opp	S/U	Line	ATS	Total	O/U	
8/29/2019	vs	*MORGAN STATE*	46	3	W	-23.5	W	NT	---	
9/7/2019	@	*Kansas State*	0	52	L	24.5	L	57.5	U	
9/14/2019	vs	*LOUISIANA TECH*	7	35	L	12.5	L	58.5	U	
9/21/2019	@	Kent State	20	62	L	11.5	L	62.0	O	*"Anniversary Award"*
10/5/2019	@	*Notre Dame*	0	52	L	46.0	L	64.5	U	
10/12/2019	vs	TOLEDO	20	7	W	27.0	W	65.0	U	*"Battle of I-75 Strophy"*
10/19/2019	vs	CENTRAL MICHIGAN	20	38	L	10.5	L	54.5	O	
10/26/2019	@	Western Michigan	10	49	L	26.5	L	65.5	U	
11/2/2019	vs	AKRON	35	6	W	-3.5	W	48.0	U	
11/13/2019	@	Miami-Ohio	3	44	L	17.0	L	47.5	U	
11/19/2019	vs	OHIO	24	66	L	21.0	L	55.5	O	
11/29/2019	@	Buffalo	7	49	L	28.0	L	53.5	O	
Coach: Mike Jinks		Season Record >>	192	463	3-9	ATS>>	3-9	O/U>>	4-7	
2018-Bowling Green		Opponent	BGU	Opp	S/U	Line	ATS	Total	O/U	
9/1/2018	@	*Oregon*	24	58	L	34.0	T	70.0	O	
9/8/2018	vs	*MARYLAND*	14	45	L	13.5	L	66.0	U	
9/15/2018	vs	*EASTERN KENTUCKY*	42	35	W	-14.0	L	NT	---	
9/22/2018	vs	MIAMI-OHIO	23	38	L	6.5	L	54.5	O	
9/29/2018	@	*Georgia Tech*	17	63	L	28.5	L	65.0	O	
10/6/2018	@	Toledo	36	52	L	23.0	W	71.0	O	*"Battle of I-75 Trophy"*
10/13/2018	vs	WESTERN MICHIGAN	35	42	L	14.5	W	69.5	O	
10/20/2018	@	Ohio	14	49	L	16.5	L	66.5	U	
10/30/2018	vs	KENT STATE	28	35	L	PK	L	68.0	U	*"Anniversary Award"*
11/10/2018	@	Central Michigan	24	13	W	7.0	W	49.5	U	
11/17/2018	@	Akron	21	6	W	6.0	W	47.5	U	
11/23/2018	vs	BUFFALO	14	44	L	16.0	L	62.5	U	
Coach: Mike Jinks		Season Record >>	292	480	3-9	ATS>>	4-7-1	O/U>>	5-6	
2017-Bowling Green		Opponent	BGU	Opp	S/U	Line	ATS	Total	O/U	
9/2/2017	@	*Michigan State*	10	35	L	17.0	L	56.0	U	
9/9/2017	vs	*SOUTH DAKOTA*	27	35	L	-3.5	L	NT	---	
9/16/2017	@	*Northwestern*	7	49	L	21.0	L	56.0	T	
9/23/2017	@	*Middle Tennessee*	13	24	L	7.0	L	53.5	U	
9/30/2017	vs	AKRON	23	34	L	3.0	L	58.0	U	
10/7/2017	@	Miami-Ohio	37	29	W	16.5	W	50.5	O	
10/14/2017	vs	OHIO	30	48	L	9.5	L	62.0	O	
10/21/2017	vs	NORTHERN ILLINOIS	17	48	L	14.0	L	56.5	O	
10/31/2017	@	Kent State	44	16	W	-1.5	W	48.0	O	*"Anniversary Award"*
11/7/2017	@	Buffalo	28	38	L	7.0	L	60.5	O	
11/15/2017	vs	TOLEDO	37	66	L	17.0	L	65.5	O	*"Battle of I-75 Trophy"*
11/21/2017	@	Eastern Michigan	31	34	L	14.0	W	60.0	O	
Coach: Mike Jinks		Season Record >>	304	456	2-10	ATS>>	3-9	O/U>>	7-3-1	

Copyright © 2021 by Steve's Football Bible, LLC

BOWLING GREEN FALCONS   MAC East

STADIUM: Doyt-Perry Stadium {24,000}									Location: Bowling Green, OH		COACH: Scott Leoffler	
DATE		Opponent	BG	Opp	S/U	Line	ATS	Total	O/U	Trends & Angles		
9/4/2021	@	*Tennessee*								vs Tennessee - Tennessee leads series 1-0		
9/11/2021	vs	*SOUTH ALABAMA*								vs South Alabama - B. Green leads series 1-0		
9/18/2021	vs	*MURRAY STATE*								vs Murray State - B. Green leads series 1-0		
9/25/2021	@	*Minnesota*								vs Minnesota - Minnesota leads series 2-1		
10/2/2021	@	Kent State								8-2 S/U @ Kent State since 2000		
10/9/2021	vs	AKRON										
10/16/2021	@	Northern Illinois								0-4 S/U @ Northern Illinois since 2002		
10/23/2021	vs	EASTERN MICHIGAN								Game 0-5 O/U @ home vs EMU since 2004		
10/30/2021	@	Buffalo								0-4 S/U vs Buffalo since 2017		
11/10/2021	vs	TOLEDO								1-10 S/U vs Toledo since 2010		
11/16/2021	@	Miami-Ohio								4-1 S/U & ATS @ Miami-Ohio since 2009		
11/26/2021	vs	OHIO								0-5 S/U vs Ohio since 2016		
12/3/2021	vs									MAC Championship		
	vs									BOWL GAME		

Pointspread Analysis Non-Conference		Pointspread Analysis Conference
0-32 S/U vs Non-Conf. as 15.5 point or more Dog since 1989		9-1 S/U vs Akron as 8 point or less favorite since 1992
9-3 ATS vs Non-Conf. as 10.5-15 point Dog since 1994		5-1 S/U vs Akron as 11 point or more favorite since 1994
9-1 S/U vs Non-Conf. as 10.5 point or more favorite since 1994		1-6 ATS vs Buffalo since 2014
Dog		vs Buffalo - Bowling Green leads series 11-7
2-9 ATS as 25.5-30 point Dog since 1997		6-2 S/U @ Buffalo since 2005
1-36 S/U as 20.5 point or more Dog since 1989		4-0 S/U vs Buffalo as 8.5 point or less favorite since 2012
1-17 S/U as 15.5-20 point Dog since 1989		0-4 O/U vs Buffalo as 8.5 point or less favorite since 2012
0-7 S/U as 10.5-15 point Dog since 2017		4-0 S/U vs Buffalo as 11.5 point or more favorite since 2001
2-7 S/U @ home as 7.5-10 point Dog since 1990		0-3 ATS vs Buffalo as 11.5 point or more favorite since 2005
1-10 S/U on road as 7.5-10 point Dog since 1997		11-1 S/U vs Eastern Michigan as favorite since 1991
3-10 S/U as 3.5-7 point Dog since 2011		3-0 S/U & ATS vs E. Michigan as 7 point or less favorite since 1991
0-6 S/U @ home as 3.5-7 point Dog since 2010		7-1 S/U vs E. Michigan as 10.5 point or more favorite since 1994
0-5 O/U @ home as 3 point or less Dog since 2010		vs Kent State - Bowling Green leads series 58-23-6
Favorite		Game 5-1 O/U @ Kent State since 2009
9-1 S/U on road as 3 point or less favorite since 2008		6-0 O/U vs Kent State as 7 point or less favorite since 2008
3-8 ATS as 3.5-7 point favorite since 2013		13-1 S/U vs Kent State as 11 point or more favorite since 1991
8-2 S/U on road as 3.5-7 point favorite since 2007		vs Miami-Ohio - Miami-Ohio leads series 45-24-5
13-0 S/U on road as 7.5-15 point favorite since 1991		Game 3-1 O/U @ Miami-Ohio since 2011
10-3 ATS on road as 7.5-15 point favorite since 1991		1-5 O/U vs Miami-Ohio as 9.5 point or less favorite since 2001
22-2 S/U as 10.5-15 point favorite since 1991		1-6 S/U vs Northern Illinois as Dog since 2004
1-7 ATS @ home as 15.5-20 point favorite since 1994		Game 0-4 O/U @ Northern Illinois since 2002
10-1 S/U @ home as 15.5-20 point favorite since 1991		0-3 S/U vs Northern Illinois as 7.5 point or more Dog since 2008
16-3 S/U as 20.5-25 point favorite since 1993		Game 1-4 O/U @ Ohio since 2012
15-0 S/U as 25.5 point or more favorite since 1994		Game 3-7 O/U vs Ohio since 2011
Bowl Games		vs Ohio - Bowling Green leads series 40-30-2
1-5 S/U & ATS in Bowl Games since 2008		0-7 S/U vs Ohio as 9.5 point or more Dog since 2000
5-0 O/U in Bowl Game since 2009		8-0 S/U vs Ohio as 13 point or more favorite since 1992
		6-0-1 ATS vs Ohio as 13 point or more favorite since 1993
		vs Toledo - Toledo leads series 41-40-4
3-10 O/U after playing Kent State since 2008	AKRON	Game 1-6 O/U @ home vs Toledo since 2007
6-2 S/U after playing Akron since 2012	N. Illinois	1-10 S/U vs Toledo as 8.5 point or more Dog since 1990
2-11 O/U after playing Akron since 2001	N. Illinois	0-5 O/U vs Toledo as 8 point or less favorite since 2007

Copyright © 2021 by Steve's Football Bible, LLC

BRIGHAM YOUNG COUGARS   INDEPENDENT

2020-Brigham Young		Opponent	BYU	Opp	S/U	Line	ATS	Total	O/U	
9/7/2020	@	Navy	55	3	W	-1.0	W	48.5	O	
9/26/2020	vs	TROY	48	7	W	-14.0	W	56.5	U	
10/2/2020	vs	LOUISIANA TECH	45	14	W	-24.0	W	61.5	U	
10/10/2020	vs	TEXAS-SAN ANTONIO	27	20	W	-34.0	L	63.0	U	
10/16/2020	@	Houston	43	26	W	-5.0	W	62.5	O	
10/24/2020	vs	TEXAS STATE	52	14	W	-30.0	W	61.5	O	
10/31/2020	vs	WESTERN KENTUCKY	41	10	W	-30.5	W	52.0	U	
11/7/2020	@	Boise State	51	17	W	-6.0	W	63.0	O	
11/21/2020	vs	NORTH ALABAMA	66	14	W	-50.0	W	62.5	O	
12/5/2020	@	Coastal Carolina	17	22	L	-10.0	L	62.0	U	
12/12/2020	vs	SAN DIEGO STATE	28	14	W	-16.5	L	47.5	U	
12/22/2020	vs	**Central Florida**	49	23	W	-5.0	W	80.0	U	**Boca Raton Bowl**
Coach: Kalani Sitake		Season Record >>	522	184	11-1	ATS>>	9-3	O/U>>	5-7	
2019-Brigham Young		Opponent	BYU	Opp	S/U	Line	ATS	Total	O/U	
8/29/2019	vs	UTAH	12	30	L	5.5	L	49.0	U	*"Holy War" (Beehive Boot)*
9/7/2019	@	Tennessee	29	26	W	3.5	W	52.5	O	{2 OT}
9/14/2019	vs	USC	30	27	W	4.5	W	57.5	U	{OT}
9/21/2019	vs	WASHINGTON	19	45	L	6.5	L	51.0	U	
9/28/2019	@	Toledo	21	28	L	-1.5	L	62.5	U	
10/12/2019	@	South Florida	23	27	L	-4.5	L	49.5	O	
10/19/2019	vs	BOISE STATE	28	25	W	7.0	W	44.5	O	
11/2/2019	@	Utah State	42	14	W	3.0	W	52.0	O	*"The Old Wagon Wheel"*
11/9/2019	vs	LIBERTY	31	24	W	-17.0	L	62.0	U	
11/16/2019	vs	IDAHO STATE	42	10	W	NL	---	NT	---	
11/23/2019	@	Massachusetts	56	24	W	-42.0	L	69.0	O	
11/30/2019	@	San Diego State	3	13	L	-4.0	L	38.5	U	
12/24/2019	@	**Hawaii**	34	38	L	-2.5	L	64.5	O	**HAWAI'I BOWL**
Coach: Kalani Sitake		Season Record >>	370	331	7-6	ATS>>	4-8	O/U>>	7-5	
2018-Brigham Young		Opponent	BYU	Opp	S/U	Line	ATS	Total	O/U	
9/1/2018	@	Arizona	28	23	W	11.0	W	59.0	U	
9/8/2018	vs	CALIFORNIA	18	21	L	-2.0	L	47.5	U	
9/15/2018	@	Wisconsin	24	21	W	23.5	W	51.5	U	
9/22/2018	vs	MCNEESE STATE	30	3	W	-24.5	W	NT	---	
9/29/2018	@	Washington	7	35	L	19.0	L	47.5	U	
10/5/2018	vs	UTAH STATE	20	45	L	1.0	L	55.0	O	*"The Old Wagon Wheel"*
10/13/2018	vs	HAWAII	49	23	W	-10.5	W	57.5	O	
10/27/2018	vs	NORTHERN ILLINOIS	6	7	L	-6.5	L	43.0	U	
11/3/2018	@	Boise State	16	21	L	12.0	W	54.0	U	
11/10/2018	@	Massachusetts	35	16	W	-14.0	W	57.5	U	
11/17/2018	vs	NEW MEXICO STATE	45	10	W	-25.5	W	59.0	U	
11/24/2018	@	Utah	27	35	L	10.5	W	44.5	O	*"Holy War" (Beehive Boot)*
12/21/2018	vs	**Western Michigan**	49	18	W	-10.0	W	52.0	O	**Famous Idaho Potato Bowl**
Coach: Kalani Sitake		Season Record >>	354	278	7-6	ATS>>	9-4	O/U>>	4-8	
2017-Brigham Young		Opponent	BYU	Opp	S/U	Line	ATS	Total	O/U	
8/26/2017	vs	PORTLAND STATE	20	6	W	-36.5	L	60.0	U	
9/2/2017	vs	Lsu	0	27	L	14.0	L	47.5	U	**Mercedes Benz Superdome**
9/9/2017	vs	UTAH	13	19	L	5.0	L	46.0	U	*"Holy War" (Beehive Boot)*
9/16/2017	vs	WISCONSIN	6	40	L	14.0	L	41.5	O	
9/29/2017	@	Utah State	24	40	L	1.0	L	49.5	O	*"The Old Wagon Wheel"*
10/6/2017	vs	BOISE STATE	7	24	L	7.0	L	47.0	U	
10/14/2017	@	Mississippi State	10	35	L	23.5	L	50.5	U	
10/21/2017	@	East Carolina	17	33	L	-5.5	L	55.0	U	
10/28/2017	vs	SAN JOSE STATE	41	20	W	-8.5	W	51.0	O	
11/4/2017	@	Fresno State	13	20	L	10.0	W	48.0	U	
11/10/2017	@	Unlv	31	21	W	PK	W	49.0	O	
11/18/2017	vs	MASSACHUSETTS	10	16	L	-3.0	L	51.5	U	
11/25/2017	@	Hawaii	30	20	W	-3.0	W	47.0	O	
Coach: Kalani Sitake		Season Record >>	222	321	4-9	ATS>>	4-9	O/U>>	5-8	

Copyright © 2021 by Steve's Football Bible, LLC

BRIGHAM YOUNG COUGARS   INDEPENDENT

STADIUM: Lavell Edwards Stadium {63,470}										Location: Provo, UT	COACH: Kalani Sitake

DATE		Opponent	BYU	Opp	S/U	Line	ATS	Total	O/U	Trends & Angles
9/2/2021	vs	Arizona {Las Vegas, NV}								vs Arizona - Arizona leads series 12-11-1
9/11/2021	vs	UTAH								0-9 S/U vs Utah since 2010
9/18/2021	vs	ARIZONA STATE								vs Arizona State - ASU leads series 20-7
9/24/2021	vs	SOUTH FLORIDA								vs South Florida - USF leads series 1-0
10/1/2021	@	Utah State								7-2 S/U @ Utah State since 1996
10/9/2021	vs	BOISE STATE								vs Boise State = Boise State leads series 7-4
10/16/2021	@	Baylor								vs Baylor - Series tied 1-1
10/23/2021	@	Washington State								vs Washington State - BYU leads series 3-1
10/30/2021	vs	VIRGINIA								vs Virginia - UVA leads series 3-2
11/13/2021	vs	IDAHO STATE								vs Idaho State - BYU leads series 6-0
11/20/2021	@	Georgia Southern								1st meeting
11/27/2021	@	Usc								vs USC - USC leads series 2-1
	vs									BOWL GAME

Pointspread Analysis

Dog

	Non-Conference
1-6 S/U on road as 21 point or more Dog since 1988	1-7 S/U vs Boise State as 6 point or more Dog since 2003
0-6 S/U as 15.5-20 point Dog since 1992	3-0 ATS vs Boise State as 7.5 point or more Dog since 2004
3-15 S/U as 10.5-15 point Dog since 1976	0-3 O/U vs Boise State as 7.5 point or more Dog since 2004
1-10 S/U on road as 7.5-10 point Dog since 2000	vs San Diego State - BYU leads series 29-8-1
0-5-1 O/U on road as 7.5-10 point Dog since 2005	7-1 S/U vs San Diego State since 2006
2-8 O/U @ home as 3.5-7 point Dog since 2004	3-0 S/U & ATS vs San Diego State as 3 point or less favorite since 1995
9-2 O/U on road as 3 point or less Dog since 1998	0-4 O/U vs San Diego State as 3 point or less favorite since 1986

Favorite

	5-0 S/U San Diego State as 6 point or more favorite since 1999
6-17 O/U as 3 point or less favorite since 2002	Game 2-9 O/U @ home vs Utah since 1997
5-12 ATS as 3.5-7 point favorite since 2011	0-5 ATS @ home vs Utah since 2010
3-9 O/U as 3.5-7 point favorite since 2013	vs Utah - Utah leads series 59-31-4
11-1 S/U as 7.5-10 point favorite since 2009	0-5 S/U vs Utah as 8 point or more Dog since 2002
6-1 S/U on road as 7.5-10 point favorite since 2001	0-3 S/U vs Utah as 4 point or more favorite since 2011
51-4 S/U as 10.5-15 point favorite since 1986	1-9 ATS vs Utah as 3.5 point or more favorite since 1997
20-0 S/U as 15.5-20 point favorite since 1997	22-3 S/U vs Utah State as favorite since 1985
18-0 S/U @ home as 15.5-20 point favorite since 1990	vs Utah State - BYU leads series 49-37-3
28-1 S/U as 20.5-25 point favorite since 1984	21-3 S/U vs Utah State as 4.5 point or more favorite since 1986
5-0 S/U on road as 20.5-25 point favorite since 1984	15-1 S/U @ home vs Utah State as 6.5 point or more favorite since 1986
25-0 S/U as 25.5-30 point favorite since 1985	
7-0 S/U on road as 25.5-30 point favorite since 1985	
17-0 S/U @ home as 30.5 or more favorite since 1988	
21-0 S/U as 30.5 point or more favorite since 1988	

Bowl Games

	Arizona	10-2 S/U prior to playing Utah since 2005
	Baylor	2-9 O/U in 2nd road game of season since 2010
0-3 S/U in Bowl Games as 10.5-15 point Dog since 1976	Utah State	1-8 ATS prior to playing Boise State since 2004
1-6 O/U in Bowl Games as 3 point or less favorite since 1985	Baylor	2-6 O/U after playing Boise State since 2012
1-5-1 S/U vs Big Ten in Bowl Games	IDAHO STATE	14-1 S/U in final home game of season since 2006
2-9-1 S/U vs ranked teams in Bowl games since 1985	Usc	8-3 ATS in final road game of season since 2010

Copyright © 2021 by Steve's Football Bible, LLC

BUFFALO BULLS

MAC East

2020-Buffalo		Opponent	BUFF	Opp	S/U	Line	ATS	Total	O/U	
11/4/2020	@	Northern Illinois	49	30	W	-14.5	W	53.0	O	
11/10/2020	vs	MIAMI-OHIO	42	10	W	-7.0	W	56.0	U	
11/17/2020	@	Bowling Green	42	17	W	-31.5	L	57.5	O	
11/28/2020	vs	KENT STATE	70	41	W	-7.5	W	70.0	O	
12/12/2020	vs	AKRON	56	7	W	-33.5	W	58.5	O	
12/18/2020	vs	BALL STATE	28	38	L	-12.5	L	70.0	U	MAC CHAMPIONSHIP
12/25/2020	vs	Marshall	17	10	W	-5.0	W	53.5	U	Camelia Bowl
Coach: Lance Leipold		Season Record >>	304	153	6-1	ATS>>	5-2	O/U>>	4-3	
2019-Buffalo		Opponent	BUFF	Opp	S/U	Line	ATS	Total	O/U	
8/31/2019	vs	ROBERT MORRIS	38	10	W	-41.5	L	NT	---	
9/7/2019	@	Penn State	13	45	L	31.5	L	55.0	O	
9/14/2019	@	Liberty	17	35	L	-6.0	L	55.0	O	
9/21/2019	vs	TEMPLE	38	22	W	14.0	W	51.0	O	
9/28/2019	@	Miami-Ohio	20	34	L	-2.5	L	48.5	O	
10/5/2019	vs	OHIO	20	21	L	3.0	W	51.5	U	{OT}
10/19/2019	@	Akron	21	0	W	-17.5	W	48.0	U	
10/26/2019	vs	CENTRAL MICHIGAN	43	20	W	-2.0	W	45.5	O	
11/2/2019	@	Eastern Michigan	43	14	W	-1.5	W	49.5	O	
11/14/2019	@	Kent State	27	30	L	-6.0	L	54.5	O	
11/20/2019	vs	TOLEDO	49	30	W	-10.0	W	54.0	O	
11/29/2019	vs	BOWLING GREEN	49	7	W	-28.0	W	53.5	O	
12/20/2019	vs	Charlotte	31	9	W	-7.0	W	51.5	U	Bahamas Bowl
Coach: Lance Leipold		Season Record >>	409	277	8-5	ATS>>	8-5	O/U>>	8-4	
2018-Buffalo		Opponent	BUFF	Opp	S/U	Line	ATS	Total	O/U	
9/1/2018	vs	DELAWARE STATE	48	10	W	-45.0	L	NT	---	
9/8/2018	@	Temple	36	29	W	4.0	W	52.0	O	
9/15/2018	vs	EASTERN MICHIGAN	35	28	W	-3.0	W	54.0	O	
9/22/2018	@	Rutgers	42	13	W	-6.0	W	52.0	O	
9/29/2018	vs	ARMY	13	42	L	-7.0	L	54.5	O	
10/6/2018	@	Central Michigan	34	24	W	-6.5	W	52.5	O	
10/13/2018	vs	AKRON	24	6	W	-11.0	W	54.5	U	
10/20/2018	@	Toledo	31	17	W	3.0	W	62.5	U	
10/30/2018	vs	MIAMI-OHIO	51	42	W	-7.0	W	53.0	O	
11/6/2018	vs	KENT STATE	48	14	W	-17.0	W	48.0	O	
11/14/2018	@	Ohio	17	52	L	2.5	L	65.0	O	
11/23/2018	@	Bowling Green	44	14	W	-16.0	W	62.5	U	
11/30/2018	vs	Northern Illinois	29	30	L	-3.0	L	51.5	O	MAC CHAMPIONSHIP
12/22/2018	vs	Troy	32	42	L	-2.5	L	51.5	O	Dollar General Bowl
Coach: Lance Leipold		Season Record >>	484	363	10-4	ATS>>	9-5	O/U>>	10-3	
2017-Buffalo		Opponent	BUFF	Opp	S/U	Line	ATS	Total	O/U	
8/31/2017	@	Minnesota	7	17	L	22.0	W	51.5	U	
9/9/2017	@	Army	17	21	L	15.0	W	53.0	U	
9/16/2017	vs	COLGATE	33	10	W	-21.0	W	NT	---	
9/23/2017	vs	FLORIDA ATLANTIC	34	31	W	-2.0	W	58.0	O	
9/30/2017	@	Kent State	27	13	W	-7.5	W	40.5	U	
10/7/2017	vs	WESTERN MICHIGAN	68	71	L	7.5	W	50.5	O	{7 OT}
10/14/2017	vs	NORTHERN ILLINOIS	13	14	L	7.0	W	49.5	U	
10/21/2017	@	Miami-Ohio	17	24	L	2.5	L	46.5	U	
10/28/2017	@	Akron	20	21	L	-2.5	L	49.0	U	
11/7/2017	vs	BOWLING GREEN	38	28	W	-7.0	W	60.5	O	
11/16/2017	@	Ball State	40	24	W	-17.5	L	53.5	O	
11/24/2017	vs	OHIO	31	24	W	7.0	W	55.0	T	
Coach: Lance Leipold		Season Record >>	345	298	6-6	ATS>>	9-3	O/U>>	4-6-1	

Copyright © 2021 by Steve's Football Bible, LLC

BUFFALO BULLS   MAC East

STADIUM: UB Stadium {25,013}					Location: Buffalo, NY				COACH: Maurice Linguist	
DATE		Opponent	Buf	Opp	S/U	Line	ATS	Total	O/U	Trends & Angles
9/4/2021	vs	*WAGNER*								vs Wagner - Wagner leads series 1-0
9/11/2021	@	*Nebraska*								1st meeting
9/18/2021	vs	*COASTAL CAROLINA*								1st meeting
9/25/2021	@	*Old Dominion*								1st meeting
10/2/2021	vs	WESTERN MICHIGAN								vs W. Michigan - WMU leads series 7-2
10/9/2021	@	Kent State								6-1-1 ATS @ Kent State since 2003
10/16/2021	vs	OHIO								5-0 ATS @ home vs Ohio since 2011
10/23/2021	@	Akron								6-1 S/U vs Akron as favorite since 2009
10/30/2021	vs	BOWLING GREEN								
11/9/2021	@	Miami-Ohio								Game 8-1 O/U @ Miami-Ohio since 2003
11/17/2021	vs	NORTHERN ILLINOIS								0-5 S/U @ home vs N. Illinois since 1999
11/23/2021	@	Ball State								
12/3/2020	vs									MAC Championship
	vs									BOWL GAME

Pointspread Analysis Non-Conference		Pointspread Analysis Conference
0-24 S/U vs Non-conf. as 20.5 point or more Dog since 1999		1-5 S/U @ Akron as 3.5 point or more Dog since 2000
2-16 S/U vs Non-Conf. as 10.5-20 point favorite since 2000		4-0 O/U @ Akron as 3.5 point or more Dog since 2004
Dog		4-1 S/U vs Akron as 11.5 point or less favorite since 2007
0-25 S/U as 30.5 point or more Dog since 1999		1-6 S/U vs Ball State as 4 point or more Dog since 2000
0-11 S/U as 25-30 point Dog since 2000		1-7 S/U vs Bowling Green as 3.5 point or more Dog since 2001
0-10 S/U on road as 20.5-25 point Dog since 1999		6-1 ATS vs Bowling Green as 3.5 point or more Dog since 2005
2-10 O/U as 20.5-25 point Dog since 2003		0-4 O/U vs Bowling Green as 3.5 point or more Dog since 2012
0-10 S/U on road as 15.5-20 point Dog since 2001		4-0 S/U vs Bowling Green as 3.5 point or more favorite since 2017
0-16 S/U on road as 10.5-15 point Dog since 1999		vs Kent State - Buffalo leads series 14-12
1-11 S/U @ home as 7.5-10 point Dog since 2004		6-1 S/U @ Kent State since 2005
2-8 O/U as 7.5-10 point Dog since 2009		vs Miami-Ohio - Miami-Ohio leads series 15-8
1-12 S/U on road as 3.5-7 point Dog since 2009		8-1 S/U vs Miami-Ohio as favorite since 2008
Favorite		0-13 S/U vs Miami-Ohio as Dog since 1999
14-5 S/U as 3.5-7 point favorite since 2006		0-13 S/U vs Miami-Ohio as 2.5 point or more Dog since 1999
4-0 S/U & ATS as 7.5-10 point favorite since 2011		4-0 O/U @ Miami-Ohio as 5 point or more Dog since 2003
6-1 S/U @ home as 10.5-15 point favorite since 2008		8-1 S/U vs Miami-Ohio as 24.5 point or less favorite since 2008
16-1 S/U as 15.5 point or more favorite since 2010		1-12 S/U vs Northern Illinois since 1970
		0-10 S/U vs N. Illinois as 7 point or more Dog since 1999

10-1 S/U in 1st home game of season since 2010	WAGNER	4-1 S/U @ home vs Ohio since 2011
3-15 S/U in 1st road game of season since 2003	Nebraska	vs Ohio - HOME team 9-1 S/U since 2010
4-15 S/U in 2nd road game of season since 2002	Old Dominion	vs Ohio - Ohio leads series 16-10
9-1 S/U prior to playing Kent State since 2008	W. MICHIGAN	5-1 S/U @ home vs Ohio as 4 point or more Dog since 2001
3-7 O/U prior to playing Akron since 2009	OHIO	4-1 ATS vs Western Michigan since 2009
2-8 S/U prior to playing Akron since 2009	OHIO	0-6 S/U vs W. Michigan as 5.5 point or more Dog since 1999
9-0 O/U after playing Bowling Green since 2009	Miami-Ohio	
2-10 S/U after playing Bowling Green since 2005	Miami-Ohio	
2-8 O/U after playing Miami-Ohio since 2011	N. ILLINOIS	

Copyright © 2021 by Steve's Football Bible, LLC

CALIFORNIA GOLDEN BEARS   PACIFIC-12 North

2020-California		Opponent	CAL	Opp	S/U	Line	ATS	Total	O/U	
11/15/2020	@	Ucla	10	34	L	-3.0	L	58.0	U	
11/21/2020	@	Oregon State	27	31	L	-1.0	L	46.5	O	
11/28/2020	vs	STANFORD	23	24	L	2.0	W	51.0	U	"Big Game" (Stanford Axe)
12/5/2020	vs	OREGON	21	17	W	8.0	W	59.0	U	
Coach: Justin Wilcox		Season Record >>	81	106	1-3	ATS>>	2-2	O/U>>	1-3	
2019-California		Opponent	CAL	Opp	S/U	Line	ATS	Total	O/U	
8/31/2019	vs	CALIFORNIA-DAVIS	27	13	W	-14.5	L	NT	---	
9/7/2019	@	Washington	20	19	W	13.5	W	43.0	U	
9/14/2019	vs	NORTH TEXAS	23	17	W	-14.5	L	50.5	U	
9/21/2019	@	Mississippi	28	20	W	3.0	W	41.5	O	
9/28/2019	vs	ARIZONA STATE	17	24	L	-4.5	L	43.0	U	
10/5/2019	@	Oregon	7	17	L	21.5	W	46.5	U	
10/19/2019	vs	OREGON STATE	17	21	L	-11.0	L	51.0	U	
10/26/2019	@	Utah	0	35	L	21.0	L	36.5	U	
11/9/2019	vs	WASHINGTON STATE	33	20	W	8.5	W	52.0	O	
11/16/2019	vs	USC	17	41	L	4.0	L	48.5	O	
11/23/2019	@	Stanford	24	20	W	-1.0	W	41.5	O	"Big Game" (Stanford Axe)
11/30/2019	@	Ucla	28	18	W	1.0	W	51.0	U	
12/30/2019	vs	Illinois	35	20	W	-6.0	W	48.0	O	Redbox Bowl
Coach: Justin Wilcox		Season Record >>	276	285	8-5	ATS>>	7-6	O/U>>	5-7	
2018-California		Opponent	CAL	Opp	S/U	Line	ATS	Total	O/U	
9/1/2018	vs	NORTH CAROLINA	24	17	W	-7.0	T	58.0	U	
9/8/2018	@	Byu	21	18	W	2.0	W	47.5	U	
9/15/2018	vs	IDAHO STATE	45	23	W	-37.0	L	NT	---	
9/29/2018	vs	OREGON	24	42	L	2.0	L	57.5	O	
10/6/2018	@	Arizona	17	24	L	-1.0	L	57.0	U	
10/13/2018	vs	UCLA	7	37	L	-6.5	L	53.5	U	
10/20/2018	@	Oregon State	49	7	W	-8.5	W	58.5	U	
10/27/2018	vs	WASHINGTON	12	10	W	11.5	W	45.5	U	
11/3/2018	@	Washington State	13	19	L	7.0	W	51.0	U	
11/10/2018	@	Usc	15	14	W	4.0	W	45.5	U	
11/24/2018	vs	COLORADO	33	21	W	-10.5	W	44.5	O	
12/1/2018	vs	STANFORD	13	23	L	3.0	L	46.0	U	"Big Game" (Stanford Axe)
12/26/2018	vs	Tcu	7	10	L	2.5	L	38.0	U	Cheez-it Bowl
Coach: Justin Wilcox		Season Record >>	280	265	7-6	ATS>>	6-6-1	O/U>>	2-10	
2017-California		Opponent	CAL	Opp	S/U	Line	ATS	Total	O/U	
9/2/2017	@	North Carolina	35	30	W	13.0	W	57.0	O	
9/9/2017	vs	WEBER STATE	33	20	W	-25.0	L	NT	---	
9/16/2017	vs	MISSISSIPPI	27	16	W	7.0	W	68.5	U	
9/23/2017	vs	USC	20	30	L	17.0	W	63.0	U	
9/30/2017	@	Oregon	24	45	L	16.5	L	67.0	O	
10/7/2017	@	Washington	7	38	L	28.5	L	55.0	U	
10/13/2017	vs	WASHINGTON STATE	37	3	W	16.5	W	55.0	U	
10/21/2017	vs	ARIZONA	44	45	L	4.5	W	65.0	O	{OT}
10/28/2017	@	Colorado	28	44	L	3.5	L	54.0	O	
11/4/2017	vs	OREGON STATE	37	23	W	-7.0	W	54.5	O	
11/18/2017	@	Stanford	14	17	L	14.0	W	56.0	U	"Big Game" (Stanford Axe)
11/24/2017	@	Ucla	27	30	L	7.0	W	66.0	U	
Coach: Justin Wilcox		Season Record >>	333	341	5-7	ATS>>	8-4	O/U>>	5-6	

Copyright © 2021 by Steve's Football Bible, LLC

CALIFORNIA GOLDEN BEARS   PACIFIC-12 North

STADIUM: Memorial Stadium {62,467}		Location: Berkeley, CA						COACH: Justin Wilcox	
DATE	Opponent	Cal	Opp	S/U	Line	ATS	Total	O/U	Trends & Angles
9/4/2021	vs	NEVADA							17-1-1 S/U @ home vs Nevada since 1904
9/11/2021	@	Tcu							vs TCU - TCU leads series 1-0
9/18/2021	vs	SACRAMENTO STATE							vs Sacramento State - CAL leads series 2-0
9/25/2021	@	Washington							2-5 S/U @ Washington since 2007
10/2/2021	vs	WASHINGTON STATE							7-1 S/U @ home vs Washi. State since 2005
10/13/2021	vs	OREGON STATE							vs Oregon State - California leads series 38-35
10/15/2021	@	Oregon							1-12 S/U @ Oregon since 1989
10/23/2021	vs	COLORADO							4-0 S/U @ home vs Colorado since 1968
11/6/2021	@	Arizona							vs Arizona - Arizona leads series 18-14-2
11/13/2021	vs	USC							0-8 S/U @ home vs USC since 2005
11/20/2021	@	Stanford							1-10 S/U vs Stanford since 2010
11/27/2021	@	Ucla							2-8 S/U @ UCLA since 2001
12/3/2021	vs								PAC-12 Championship
	vs								BOWL GAME

Pointspread Analysis — Non-Conference

0-7 S/U vs Non-Conf. as 15.5 point or more Dog since 1987	
0-5 S/U & ATS vs Non-Conf. as 3 point or less favorite since 2001	
12-1 S/U vs Non-conf. as 3.5-7 point favorite since 1997	
9-1 O/U vs Non-conf. as 3.5-7 point favorite since 2005	
27-0 S/U vs Non-Conf. as 15.5 point or more favorite since 1988	
vs Nevada - California leads series 22-3-1	
15-3 S/U in 1st home game of season since 2002	NEVADA
9-2 O/U in 1st home game of season since 2006	NEVADA
15-4 O/U in 1st road game of season since 2001	Tcu
16-0 S/U in 2nd home game of season since 2004	SACRAMENTO
2-11 S/U in 2nd road game of season since 2008	Washington
0-8 S/U prior to playing Oregon since 2012	OREGON STATE
0-7 S/U after playing Washington State since 2012	OREGON STATE
2-10 S/U after playing Oregon since 2007	COLORADO
2-10 S/U prior to playing UCLA since 2007	Stanford
2-7-1 O/U prior to playing UCLA since 2009	Stanford
1-6 S/U & ATS after playing USC since 2012	Stanford
2-7-1 O/U prior to playing UCLA since 2009	Stanford
1-7 S/U in final road game of season since 2012	Ucla

Dog

0-5 ATS as 30.5 point or more Dog since 1999
0-26 S/U as 20.5 point or more Dog since 1986
1-10 S/U @ home as 15.5-20 point Dog since 1989
0-10 S/U on road as 15.5-20 point Dog since 1997
14-1 ATS on road as 10.5-15 point Dog since 1997
2-10 S/U @ home as 10.5-15 point Dog since 1991
9-1 ATS @ home as 7.5-10 point Dog since 1987
2-11 S/U on road as 7.5-10 point Dog since 1989
4-0 S/U on road as 3 point or less Dog since 2000
4-0 ATS on road as 3 point or less Dog since 2005

Favorite

2-8 S/U on road as 3 point or less favorite since 2003
2-8 ATS on road as 3 point or less favorite since 2003
4-0 S/U & ATS @ home as 3 point or less favorite since 2008
9-0 S/U & ATS @ home as 7.5-10 point favorite since 2006
14-0 S/U as 7.5-10 point favorite since 2005
13-1 ATS as 7.5-10 point favorite since 2005
17-4 S/U @ home as 10.5-15 point favorite since 1987
16-2 S/U as 15.5-20 point favorite since 1983
30-0 S/U as 20.5 point or more favorite since 1988
11-0 O/U as 20.5 point or more favorite since 2006

Pointspread Analysis — Conference

8-0 ATS vs Arizona as 10.5 point or more Dog since 1983
0-4 S/U @ Arizona as 8.5 point or less Dog since 1984
0-5 S/U vs Arizona as 10 point or less Dog since 1998
vs Colorado - California leads series 6-4
Game 6-0 O/U vs Colorado since 2010
3-0 S/U @ home vs Colorado as 10 point or more favorite since 2010
2-10 S/U vs Oregon since 2009
vs Oregon - California leades series 41-40-2
0-9 S/U vs Oregon as 13 point or more Dog since 2000
3-0 S/U vs Oregon as 9.5 point or more favorite since 1991
1-8 S/U vs Oregon State as Dog since 1999
0-3 S/U vs Oregon State as 10.5 point or more Dog since 2001
1-4 S/U vs Oregon State as 6.5 point or less Dog since 2000
1-15 S/U vs USC since 2004
vs Usc - USC leads series 71-31-5
Game 3-13 O/U vs USC since 2004
0-7 S/U vs USC as 14.5 point or more Dog since 2005
2-10 O/U vs USC as 9 point or less Dog since 2007
1-8 S/U vs USC as 7.5 point or less Dog since 2007
3-18-1 S/U vs Stanford as Dog since 1984
vs Stanford - Stanford leads series 60-45-9
0-5 S/U vs Stanford as 10.5 point or more Dog since 2001
0-6 S/U vs Stanford as 10 point or less Dog since 2010
vs Ucla - UCLA leads series 56-34-1
Game 0-8 O/U vs UCLA since 2013
1-10 S/U vs UCLA as 10.5 point or more Dog since 1983
Game 1-10 O/U vs Washington since 2009
2-18 S/U vs Washington as Dog since 1983
vs Washington - Washington leads series 52-41-4
3-14 S/U vs Washington as 11 point or more Dog since 1984
0-5 S/U vs Washington as 10 point or less Dog since 1985
0-5 S/U & ATS vs Washington as 3.5-7 point favorite since 2007
0-4 O/U vs Washington as 3.5-7 point favorite since 2009
5-13 S/U vs Washington State as Dog since 1983
11-3-1 S/U vs Washington State as favorite since 1986
vs Washington State - California leads series 48-28-5
8-0 S/U vs Wazzu as 9 point or more favorite since 2005
1-4 S/U vs Wazzu as 10.5 point or more Dog since 1994

Bowl Games

5-0 S/U in Bowl Games as 3.5-7 point favorite since 2005
9-3 O/U in Bowl Games since 1996

Copyright © 2021 by Steve's Football Bible, LLC

CENTRAL FLORIDA GOLDEN KNIGHTS   AMERICAN

2020-Central Florida		Opponent	UCF	Opp	S/U	Line	ATS	Total	O/U	
9/19/2020	@	Georgia Tech	49	21	W	-8.0	W	63.5	O	
9/24/2020	@	East Carolina	51	28	W	-27.5	L	77.0	O	
10/3/2020	vs	TULSA	26	34	L	-20.0	L	70.0	U	
10/17/2020	@	Memphis	49	50	L	-3.0	L	74.0	O	
10/24/2020	vs	TULANE	51	34	W	-21.5	W	71.0	O	
10/31/2020	@	Houston	44	21	W	-3.0	W	81.0	U	
11/14/2020	vs	TEMPLE	38	13	W	-29.0	L	71.5	U	
11/21/2020	vs	CINCINNATI	33	36	L	4.0	W	65.5	O	
11/27/2020	@	South Florida	58	46	W	-25.0	L	70.5	O	War on I-4 Trophy
12/22/2020	vs	BYU	23	49	L	5.0	L	80.0	U	Boca Raton Bowl
Coach: Josh Heupel		Season Record >>	422	332	6-4	ATS>>	4-6	O/U>>	6-4	
2019-Central Florida		Opponent	UCF	Opp	S/U	Line	ATS	Total	O/U	
8/31/2019	vs	FLORIDA A&M	62	0	W	-44.0	W	NT	---	
9/7/2019	@	Florida Atlantic	48	14	W	-13.5	W	67.5	U	
9/14/2019	vs	STANFORD	45	27	W	-9.5	W	59.0	O	
9/21/2019	@	Pittsburgh	34	35	L	-10.0	L	60.5	O	
9/28/2019	vs	CONNECTICUT	56	21	W	-42.0	L	64.5	O	
10/4/2019	@	Cincinnati	24	27	L	-3.5	L	63.5	U	
10/19/2019	vs	EAST CAROLINA	41	28	W	-34.0	L	64.5	O	
10/26/2019	@	Temple	63	21	W	-10.5	W	61.0	O	
11/2/2019	vs	HOUSTON	44	29	W	-21.0	L	72.5	O	
11/8/2019	@	Tulsa	31	34	L	-16.0	L	68.5	U	
11/23/2019	@	Tulane	34	31	W	-7.0	L	74.0	U	
11/30/2019	vs	SOUTH FLORIDA	34	7	W	-24.0	W	61.5	U	War on I-4 Trophy
12/23/2019	vs	Marshall	48	25	W	-15.5	W	59.5	O	Gasparilla Bowl
Coach: Josh Heupel		Season Record >>	564	299	10-3	ATS>>	6-7	O/U>>	7-5	
2018-Central Florida		Opponent	UCF	Opp	S/U	Line	ATS	Total	O/U	
8/30/2018	@	Connecticut	56	17	W	-24.0	W	69.0	O	
9/8/2018	vs	SOUTH CAROLINA STATE	38	0	W	-52.0	L	NT	---	
9/21/2018	vs	FLORIDA ATLANTIC	56	36	W	-14.0	W	75.0	O	
9/29/2018	vs	PITTSBURGH	45	15	W	-13.0	W	65.5	U	
10/6/2018	vs	SMU	48	20	W	-25.0	W	74.0	U	
10/13/2018	@	Memphis	31	30	W	-5.5	L	80.5	U	
10/20/2018	@	East Carolina	37	10	W	-21.5	W	65.0	U	
11/1/2018	vs	TEMPLE	52	40	W	-10.0	W	60.0	O	
11/10/2018	vs	NAVY	35	24	W	-23.5	L	68.0	U	
11/17/2018	vs	CINCINNATI	38	13	W	-6.5	W	60.5	U	
11/23/2018	@	South Florida	38	10	W	-15.5	W	69.5	U	War on I-4 Trophy
12/1/2018	vs	Memphis	56	41	W	PK	W	65.0	O	AAC Championship
1/1/2019	vs	Lsu	32	40	L	7.0	L	58.5	O	Fiesta Bowl
Coach: Josh Heupel		Season Record >>	562	296	12-1	ATS>>	9-4	O/U>>	5-7	AAC Champions
2017-Central Florida		Opponent	UCF	Opp	S/U	Line	ATS	Total	O/U	
8/31/2017	vs	FLORIDA INTERNATIONAL	61	17	W	-17.0	W	56.0	O	
9/23/2017	@	Maryland	38	10	W	5.0	W	61.5	U	
9/30/2017	vs	MEMPHIS	40	13	W	-5.5	W	68.5	U	
10/7/2017	@	Cincinnati	51	23	W	-15.0	W	52.5	O	
10/14/2017	vs	EAST CAROLINA	63	21	W	-35.0	W	71.0	O	
10/21/2017	@	Navy	31	21	W	-10.0	T	65.0	U	
10/28/2017	vs	AUSTIN PEAY	73	33	W	-43.5	L	NT	---	
11/4/2017	@	Smu	31	24	W	-14.0	L	75.0	U	
11/11/2017	vs	CONNECTICUT	49	24	W	-39.5	L	65.0	O	
11/18/2017	@	Temple	45	19	W	-12.0	W	58.5	O	
11/24/2017	vs	SOUTH FLORIDA	49	42	W	-10.0	L	65.0	O	War on I-4 Trophy
12/2/2017	vs	MEMPHIS	62	55	W	-6.5	W	80.0	O	AAC Championship
1/1/2018	vs	Auburn	34	27	W	10.5	W	66.0	U	Chick-Fil-A Peach Bowl
Coach: Scott Frost		Season Record >>	627	329	13-0	ATS>>	8-4-1	O/U>>	7-5	AAC Champions

Copyright © 2021 by Steve's Football Bible, LLC

CENTRAL FLORIDA GOLDEN KNIGHTS   AMERICAN

STADIUM: Bright House Networks Stadium {44,206}		Location: Orlando, FL				COACH: Gus Malzahn			

DATE		Opponent	UCF	Opp	S/U	Line	ATS	Total	O/U	Trends & Angles
9/4/2021	vs	*BOISE STATE*								1st meeting
9/11/2021	vs	*BETHUNE-COOKMAN*								1st meeting
9/18/2021	@	*Louisville*								vs Louisville - Series tied 1-1
10/2/2021	@	Navy								vs Navy - Central Florida leads series 2-0
10/9/2021	vs	EAST CAROLINA								5-0 S/U vs East Carolina since 2016
10/16/2021	@	Cincinnati								vs Cincinnati - Series tied 3-3
10/22/2021	vs	MEMPHIS								7-0 S/U @ home vs Memphis since 2005
10/30/2021	@	Temple								4-0 S/U vs Temple since 2017
11/6/2021	vs	TULANE								5-0 S/U @ home vs Tulane since 2005 {4-1 ATS}
11/13/2021	@	Smu								vs SMU - UCF leads series 8-1
11/20/2021	vs	*CONNECTICUT*								Game 4-0 O/U @ home vs U Conn since 2013
11/26/2021	vs	SOUTH FLORIDA								4-0 S/U vs South Florida since 2017
12/4/2021	vs									AAC Championship
	vs									BOWL GAME

Pointspread Analysis Non-Conference		Pointspread Analysis Conference
0-13 S/U vs Non-Conf. as 20.5 point or more Dog since 1999		3-1 S/U & ATS vs Cincinnati as 6.5-15 point favorite since 2016
4-18 S/U vs Non-Conf. as 10.5-20 point Dog since 1997		vs East Carolina - East Carolina leads series 10-9
13-0 S/U vs Non-Conf. as 25.5 point or more favorite since 1998		Game 8-2 O/U vs East Carolina since 2010
vs U Conn - Central Florida leads series 5-2		4-0 S/U @ home vs E. Carolina as 8 point or more favorite since 2010
3-0 S/U vs U Conn as 4.5 point or more favorite since 2016		vs Memphis - UCF leads series 13-2
Dog		10-1 S/U vs Memphis as 2.5 point or more favorite since 2006
0-21 S/U as 20.5 point or more Dog since 1997		1-3 ATS @ home vs South Florida since 2013
3-10 ATS as 20.5-25 point Dog since 2001		vs South Florida - Series tied 6-6
0-8 S/U @ home as 15.5 point or more Dog since 1997		0-5 S/U vs South Florida as 7.5 point or more Dog since 2005
2-35 S/U on road as 10.5 point or more Dog since 1997		6-0 S/U vs USF as 10 point or more favorite since 2013
2-8 S/U as 7.5-10 point Dog since 2002		8-0 S/U vs SMU as 9 point or more favorite since 2007
14-4 ATS as 3.5-7 point Dog since 2005		5-2 ATS vs Temple since 2014
2-7 O/U on road as 3 point or less Dog since 2003		Game 6-2 OU vs Temple since 2013
Favorite		vs Temple - UCF leads series 6-2
8-1 S/U @ home as 3.5-7 point favorite since 2007		5-1 S/U vs Temple as 3.5 point or more favorite since 2013
7-2 ATS @ home as 3.5-7 point favorite since 2007		vs Tulane - UCF leads series 8-2
14-3 S/U as 7.5-10 point favorite since 2009		5-0 S/U @ home vs Tulane as 6 point or more favorite since 2005
11-0 S/U on road as 10.5-15 point favorite since 1999		0-3 S/U & ATS vs Tulsa as 3 point or less Dog since 2005
9-1 S/U @ home as 10.5-15 point favorite since 2007		
10-1 S/U @ home as 15.5-20 point favorite since 2001		
16-3 S/U as 15.5-20 point favorite since 1997		
21-2 S/U as 20.5-25 point favorite since 1998		
24-0 S/U as 25.5 point or more favorite since 1998		
11-2 S/U in 1st home game of season since 2008	BOISE STATE	35-4 S/U when ranked all time
9-3 ATS in 1st home game of season since 2005	BOISE STATE	5-1 S/U when ranked vs ranked teams all time
8-3 ATS prior to playing East Carolina since 2009	Navy	11-2 S/U on road when ranked all time
6-0 S/U prior to playing SMU since 2011	TULANE	1-19 S/U on road vs ranked teams all time

Copyright © 2021 by Steve's Football Bible, LLC

CENTRAL MICHIGAN CHIPPEWAS   MAC West

2020-Central Michigan		Opponent	CMU	Opp	S/U	Line	ATS	Total	O/U	
11/4/2020	vs	OHIO	30	27	W	3.0	W	54.5	O	
11/11/2020	@	Northern Illinois	40	10	W	-6.0	W	57.0	U	
11/18/2020	vs	WESTERN MICHIGAN	44	52	L	1.0	L	59.5	O	"Victory Cannon"
11/28/2020	@	Eastern Michigan	31	23	W	-6.0	W	58.0	U	
12/5/2020	vs	BALL STATE	20	45	L	2.5	L	62.5	U	
12/12/2020	@	Toledo	23	24	L	10.0	W	55.0	U	
Coach: Jim McElwain		Season Record >>	188	181	3-3	ATS>>	4-2	O/U>>	3-3	

2019-Central Michigan		Opponent	CMU	Opp	S/U	Line	ATS	Total	O/U	
8/29/2019	vs	SUNY-ALBANY	38	21	W	-14.0	W	NT	---	
9/7/2019	@	Wisconsin	0	61	L	35.0	L	54.0	O	
9/14/2019	@	Miami	45	24	W	-2.5	W	45.0	O	
9/14/2019	vs	AKRON	12	17	L	30.5	W	48.5	U	
9/28/2019	@	Western Michigan	15	31	L	15.0	L	60.0	U	"Victory Cannon"
10/5/2019	vs	EASTERN MICHIGAN	42	16	W	3.5	W	54.0	O	
10/12/2019	vs	NEW MEXICO STATE	42	28	W	-10.5	W	56.5	O	
10/19/2019	@	Bowling Green	38	20	W	-10.5	W	54.5	O	
10/26/2019	@	Buffalo	20	43	L	2.0	L	45.5	O	
11/2/2019	vs	NORTHERN ILLINOIS	48	10	W	1.5	W	49.5	O	
11/16/2019	@	Ball State	45	44	W	1.0	W	60.0	O	
11/29/2019	vs	TOLEDO	49	7	W	-14.5	W	63.5	O	
12/7/2019	vs	Miami-Ohio	21	26	L	-5.5	L	56.5	U	MAC Championship Game
12/21/2019	vs	San Diego State	11	48	L	4.0	L	40.5	O	New Mexico Bowl
Coach: Jim McElwain		Season Record >>	426	396	8-6	ATS>>	9-5	O/U>>	9-4	

2018-Central Michigan		Opponent	CMU	Opp	S/U	Line	ATS	Total	O/U	
9/1/2018	@	Kentucky	20	35	L	17.5	W	49.0	O	
9/8/2018	vs	KANSAS	7	31	L	-3.0	L	48.0	U	
9/15/2018	@	Northern Illinois	16	24	L	14.0	W	48.0	U	
9/22/2018	vs	MAINE	17	5	W	-7.5	W	NT	---	
9/29/2018	@	Michigan State	20	31	L	28.0	W	45.0	O	
10/6/2018	vs	BUFFALO	24	34	L	6.5	L	52.5	O	
10/13/2018	vs	BALL STATE	23	24	L	-2.5	L	54.5	U	
10/20/2018	vs	WESTERN MICHIGAN	10	35	L	6.5	L	54.0	U	"Victory Cannon"
10/27/2018	@	Akron	10	17	L	4.0	L	43.5	U	
11/3/2018	@	Eastern Michigan	7	17	L	14.5	W	46.5	U	
11/10/2018	vs	BOWLING GREEN	13	24	L	-7.0	L	49.5	U	
11/23/2018	@	Toledo	13	51	L	18.5	L	57.5	O	
Coach: John Bonamego		Season Record >>	180	328	1-11	ATS>>	5-7	O/U>>	4-7	

2017-Central Michigan		Opponent	CMU	Opp	S/U	Line	ATS	Total	O/U	
8/31/2017	vs	RHODE ISLAND	30	27	W	-31.5	L	57.0	T	2 OT
9/9/2017	@	Kansas	45	27	W	3.0	W	56.5	O	
9/16/2017	@	Syracuse	17	41	L	8.5	L	66.5	U	
9/23/2017	vs	MIAMI-OHIO	14	31	L	-1.5	L	50.5	U	
9/30/2017	@	Boston College	8	28	L	10.0	L	52.0	U	
10/7/2017	@	Ohio	26	23	W	10.5	W	54.0	U	
10/14/2017	vs	TOLEDO	10	30	L	9.0	L	54.5	U	
10/21/2017	@	Ball State	56	9	W	-3.0	W	48.0	O	
11/1/2017	@	Western Michigan	35	28	W	4.0	W	48.0	O	"Victory Cannon"
11/8/2017	vs	EASTERN MICHIGAN	42	30	W	1.0	W	51.0	O	
11/14/2017	@	Kent State	42	23	W	-17.0	W	44.5	O	
11/24/2017	vs	NORTHERN ILLINOIS	31	24	W	2.5	W	51.5	O	
12/22/2017	vs	Wyoming	14	37	L	2.5	L	47.0	O	Famous Idaho Potato Bowl
Coach: John Bonamego		Season Record >>	370	358	8-5	ATS>>	7-6	O/U>>	7-5-1	

Copyright © 2021 by Steve's Football Bible, LLC

CENTRAL MICHIGAN CHIPPEWAS   MAC West

STADIUM: Kelly-Shorts Stadium {30,255}			Location: Mount Pleasant, MI							COACH: Jim McElwain
DATE		Opponent	CMU	Opp	S/U	Line	ATS	Total	O/U	Trends & Angles
9/4/2021	@	*Missouri*								1st meeting
9/11/2021	vs	*ROBERT MORRIS*								1st meeting
9/18/2021	@	*Lsu*								1st meeting
9/25/2021	vs	*FLA INTERNATIONAL*								1st meeting
10/2/2021	@	Miami-Ohio								0-4 ATS vs Miami-Ohio since 2014
10/9/2021	@	Ohio								9-1-1 S/U @ Ohio since 1981
10/16/2021	vs	TOLEDO								1-10 S/U vs Toledo since 2010 {2-9 ATS}
10/23/2021	vs	NORTHERN ILLINOIS								6-1 S/U & ATS @ home vs N. Illinois since 2007
11/3/2021	@	Western Michigan								1-6 S/U vs Western Michigan since 2014
11/10/2021	vs	KENT STATE								12-2 S/U @ home vs Kent State since 1979
11/17/2021	@	Ball State								
11/26/2021	vs	EASTERN MICHIGAN								4-0 S/U @ home vs E. Michigan since 2013
12/3/2021	vs									MAC Championship
	vs									BOWL GAME

Pointspread Analysis Non-Conference		Pointspread Analysis Conference
0-26 S/U vs Non-Conf. as 20.5 point or more Dog since 1993		1-6 S/U @ Ball State as 20.5 point or less Dog since 1995
2-24 S/U vs Non-Conf. as 7.5-15 point Dog since 1989		5-0 S/U @ Ball State as 15 point or less favorite since 1999
2-10 S/U vs Non-Conf. as 3.5-7 point Dog since 1994		vs Eastern Michigan - CMU leads series 62-30-6
14-0 S/U vs Non-Conf. as 7.5 point or more favorite since 1990		Game 6-1 O/U @ home vs Eastern Michigan since 2007
Dog		Game 5-0 O/U vs Kent State since 2007
0-9 S/U & ATS on road as 30.5 point or more Dog since 1997		4-0 O/U vs Kent State as 17 point or less favorite since 2007
0-8 S/U as 25.5-30 point Dog since 1996		vs Miami-Ohio - Miami leads series 15-13-1
6-0 ATS as 25.5-30 point Dog since 2001		1-5 O/U vs Miami-Ohio as a favorite since 2007
1-16 S/U on road as 20.5-25 point Dog since 1993		1-4 S/U vs Miami-Ohio as 22.5 point or less Dog since 1995
0-7 S/U @ home as 15.5-20 point Dog since 1999		7-0 ATS vs Northern Illinois since 2014
2-8 S/U on road as 15.5-20 point Dog since 1997		6-1 S/U vs Northern Illinois since 2014
0-6 S/U @ home as 10.5-15 point Dog since 1997		vs Northern Illinois - CMU leads series 31-24-1
2-11 S/U as 10.5-15 point Dog since 2010		7-0 ATS vs Northern Illinois as 14 point or less Dog since 2014
3-25 S/U as 7.5-10 point Dog since 1989		9-1 S/U vs Ohio since 2005
1-18 S/U on road as 7.5-10 point Dog since 1989		Game 1-4 O/U vs Ohio since 2013
4-11-1 ATS on road as Dog since 2000		11-0-1 S/U vs Ohio as favorite since 1991
6-2 O/U on road as 3.5-7 point Dog since 2010		5-0 ATS vs Ohio since 2013
1-7 S/U @ home as 3.5-7 point Dog since 2000		1-10 S/U @ home vs Toledo as a Dog since 1995
19-2 O/U as 3 point or less Dog since 2006		3-19 S/U vs Toledo as Dog since 1993
9-0 O/U on road as 3 point or less Dog since 2006		6-0 S/U vs Toledo as favorite since 1992
Favorite		vs Toledo - Toledo leads series 27-19-3
9-0-3 ATS on road as 3 point or less favorite since 1999		Game 0-5 O/U @ home vs Toledo since 2011
12-0 S/U on road as 3 point or less favorite since 1999		vs Western Michigan - WMU leads series 52-39-2
1-7 O/U @ home as 3 point or less favorite since 2007		9-2 S/U vs Western Michigan as favorite since 1990
2-17-1 O/U as 3.5-7 point favorite since 2006		
8-1 S/U @ home as 3.5-7 point favorite since 2005		
7-0 S/U on road as 7.5-10 point favorite since 2001		
11-1 S/U @ home as 7.5-10 point favorite since 1991	Missouri	8-3 ATS in 1st road game of season since 2009
9-0 S/U on road as 10.5-15 point favorite since 1989	ROB MORRIS	12-1 S/U in 1st home game of season since 2007
6-0-1 S/U on road as 15.5-20 point favorite since 1990	ROB MORRIS	1-4-1 O/U in 1st home game of season since 2010
13-1 S/U @ home as 15.5-20 point favorite since 1989	Lsu	0-9 S/U in 2nd road game of season since 2011
8-0 S/U @ home as 30.5 point or more favorite since 1995	W. Michigan	1-8 S/U after playing Northern Illinois since 2010
Bowl Games	E. MICHIGAN	9-0 S/U after playing Ball State since 2011
0-5 S/U in Bowl Games since 2014	E. MICHIGAN	7-1 ATS after playing Ball State since 2012

Copyright © 2021 by Steve's Football Bible, LLC

CHARLOTTE 49ERS   C-USA East

2020-Charlotte		Opponent	Char	Opp	S/U	Line	ATS	Total	O/U	
9/12/2020	@	*Appalachian State*	20	35	L	17.0	W	59.0	U	
10/3/2020	@	Florida Atlantic	17	21	L	4.5	W	63.0	U	
10/10/2020	@	North Texas	49	21	W	-3.0	W	66.5	O	
10/24/2020	vs	TEXAS-EL PASO	38	28	W	-17.5	L	50.5	O	
10/31/2020	@	*Duke*	19	53	L	11.5	L	55.0	O	
12/6/2020	vs	WESTERN KENTUCKY	19	37	L	-3.0	L	47.0	O	
Coach: Will Healy		Season Record >>	162	195	2-4	ATS>>	3-3	O/U>>	4-2	
2019-Charlotte		Opponent	Char	Opp	S/U	Line	ATS	Total	O/U	
8/31/2019	vs	*GARDNER-WEBB*	49	28	W	-31.0	L	NT	---	
9/7/2019	@	*Appalachian State*	41	56	L	23.0	W	54.5	O	
9/14/2019	vs	*MASSACHUSETTS*	52	17	W	-21.0	W	66.5	O	
9/21/2019	@	*Clemson*	10	52	L	41.5	L	61.0	O	
9/28/2019	vs	FLORIDA ATLANTIC	27	45	L	1.0	L	64.5	O	
10/12/2019	@	Florida International	23	48	L	5.0	L	59.5	O	
10/19/2019	@	Western Kentucky	14	30	L	9.5	L	48.5	U	
10/26/2019	vs	NORTH TEXAS	39	38	W	4.0	W	64.0	O	
11/2/2019	vs	MIDDLE TENNESSEE	34	20	W	3.5	W	65.5	U	
11/9/2019	@	Texas-El Paso	28	21	W	-12.0	L	55.5	U	
11/23/2019	vs	MARSHALL	24	13	W	7.0	W	55.5	U	
11/30/2019	@	Old Dominion	38	22	W	-10.0	W	50.5	O	
12/20/2019	vs	**Buffalo**	9	31	L	7.0	L	51.5	U	**Bahamas Bowl**
Coach: Will Healy		Season Record >>	388	421	7-6	ATS>>	6-7	O/U>>	7-5	
2018-Charlotte		Opponent	Char	Opp	S/U	Line	ATS	Total	O/U	
9/1/2018	vs	*FORDHAM*	34	10	W	-16.5	W	NT	---	
9/8/2018	vs	*APPALACHIAN STATE*	9	45	L	14.0	L	48.5	O	
9/13/2018	vs	OLD DOMINION	28	25	W	1.5	W	48.0	O	
9/22/2018	@	*Massachusetts*	31	49	L	6.0	L	55.0	O	
9/29/2018	@	Alabama-Birmingham	7	28	L	15.5	L	52.0	U	
10/13/2018	vs	WESTERN KENTUCKY	40	14	W	9.5	W	49.0	O	
10/20/2018	@	Middle Tennessee	13	21	L	15.0	W	50.0	U	
10/27/2018	vs	SOUTHERN MISSISSIPPI	20	17	W	6.5	W	45.0	U	
11/3/2018	@	*Tennessee*	3	14	L	21.5	W	45.0	U	
11/10/2018	@	Marshall	13	30	L	12.0	L	41.5	O	
11/17/2018	vs	FLORIDA INTERNATIONAL	35	42	L	3.5	L	44.5	O	
11/24/2018	@	Florida Atlantic	27	24	W	17.0	W	55.0	U	
Coach: Brad Lambert		Season Record >>	260	319	5-7	ATS>>	7-5	O/U>>	6-5	
2017-Charlotte		Opponent	Char	Opp	S/U	Line	ATS	Total	O/U	
9/1/2017	@	*Eastern Michigan*	7	24	L	14.0	L	58.0	U	
9/9/2017	@	*Kansas State*	7	55	L	34.0	L	56.0	O	
9/16/2017	vs	*NORTH CAROLINA A&T*	31	35	L	NL	---	NT	---	
9/23/2017	vs	*GEORGIA STATE*	0	28	L	-1.0	L	51.0	U	
9/30/2017	@	Florida International	29	30	L	10.0	W	47.5	O	
10/7/2017	vs	MARSHALL	3	14	L	14.5	W	51.0	U	
10/14/2017	@	Western Kentucky	14	45	L	19.0	L	47.5	O	
10/21/2017	vs	ALABAMA-BIRMINGHAM	25	24	W	9.5	W	51.5	U	{OT}
11/4/2017	@	Old Dominion	0	6	L	9.5	W	50.0	U	
11/11/2017	vs	MIDDLE TENNESSEE	21	35	L	16.0	W	50.0	O	
11/18/2017	@	Southern Miss	21	66	L	17.0	L	47.0	O	
11/25/2017	vs	FLORIDA ATLANTIC	12	31	L	24.0	W	66.0	U	
Coach: Brad Lambert		Season Record >>	170	393	1-11	ATS>>	6-5	O/U>>	5-6	

Copyright © 2021 by Steve's Football Bible, LLC

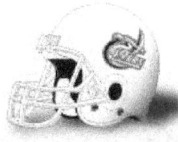

CHARLOTTE 49ERS   C-USA East

STADIUM: Jerry Richardson Stadium {15,314}						Location: Charlotte, NC			COACH: Will Healy	
DATE		Opponent	Char	Opp	S/U	Line	ATS	Total	O/U	Trends & Angles
9/4/2021	vs	DUKE								1st Meeting
9/11/2021	vs	GARDNER-WEBB								vs Gardner-Webb - Charlotte leads series 2-1
9/18/2021	@	Georgia State								vs Georgia State - Series tied 1-1
9/25/2021	vs	MIDDLE TENNESSEE								vs Middle Tennessee - MTSU leads series 4-1
10/2/2021	@	Illinois								1st Meeting
10/9/2021	@	Florida International								vs Florida International - FIU leads series 5-0
10/23/2021	vs	FLORIDA ATLANTIC								vs Florida Atlantic - FAU leads series 4-2
10/30/2021	@	Western Kentucky								vs Western Kentucky - WKU leads series 3-1
11/6/2021	vs	RICE								vs Rice - Rice leads series 2-0
11/13/2021	@	Louisiana Tech								1st Meeting
11/20/2021	vs	MARSHALL								vs Marshall - Marshall leads series 3-2
11/27/2021	@	Old Dominion								vs Old Dominion - Old Dominion leads series 3-2
12/4/2021	vs									C-USA Championship
	vs									BOWL GAME

Pointspread Analysis Non-Conference		Pointspread Analysis Conference
0-13 S/U vs Non-Conf. as 10.0 point or more Dog since 2015		Game 1-5 O/U vs Florida Atlantic since 2015
Dog		Game 3-0 O/U vs Florida International since 2017
0-9 S/U as 20 point or more Dog since 2015		Game 1-4 O/U vs Marshall since 2015
0-5 S/U on road as 3.5-10 point Dog since 2017		3-0 ATS vs Middle Tennessee since 2017
1-3 ATS on road as 3.5-10 point Dog since 2018		4-1 ATS vs Old Dominion since 2015
Favorite		Game 4-1 O/U vs Old Dominion since 2015
6-0 S/U as 10 point or more favorite since 2018		

Steve's Football Bible also offers the Pro Football Bible, the Pro football handicapper's best friend for the 2021 football season.

To order Go to: www.stevesfootballbible.com

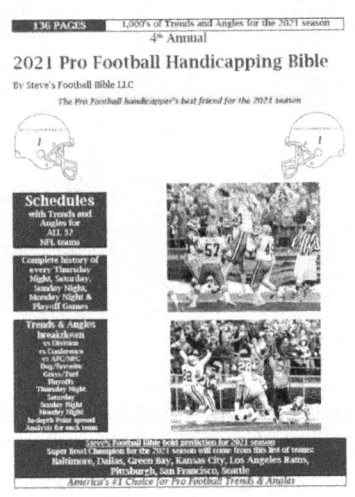

2021 Pro Football Bible $24.95

Copyright © 2021 by Steve's Football Bible, LLC

CINCINNATI BEARCATS   AMERICAN East

2020-Cincinnati		Opponent	Cincy	Opp	S/U	Line	ATS	Total	O/U	
9/19/2020	vs	AUSTIN PEAY	55	20	W	NL	---	NT	---	
9/26/2020	vs	ARMY	24	10	W	-12.0	W	44.5	U	
10/3/2020	vs	SOUTH FLORIDA	28	7	W	-22.5	L	45.5	U	
10/24/2020	@	Smu	42	13	W	-1.0	W	57.5	U	
10/31/2020	vs	MEMPHIS	49	10	W	-6.5	W	56.5	O	
11/7/2020	vs	HOUSTON	38	10	W	-11.5	W	51.5	U	
11/13/2020	vs	EAST CAROLINA	55	17	W	-27.0	W	56.0	O	
11/21/2020	@	Central Florida	36	33	W	-4.0	L	65.5	O	
12/19/2020	vs	**TULSA**	27	24	W	-14.0	L	44.5	O	**AAC CHAMPIONSHIP**
1/1/2021	vs	**Georgia**	21	24	L	8.0	W	43.0	U	**Chick-Fil-A Peach Bowl**
Coach: Luke Fickell		Season Record >>	375	168	9-1	ATS>>	6-3	O/U>>	4-5	**AAC CHAMPIONS**
2019-Cincinnati		Opponent	Cincy	Opp	S/U	Line	ATS	Total	O/U	
8/29/2019	vs	UCLA	24	14	W	-2.5	W	55.5	U	
9/7/2019	@	Ohio State	0	42	L	14.5	L	52.5	U	
9/14/2019	vs	MIAMI-OHIO	35	13	W	-17.5	W	49.5	U	"Victory Bell"
9/28/2019	@	Marshall	52	14	W	-4.0	W	47.5	O	
10/4/2019	vs	CENTRAL FLORIDA	27	24	W	3.5	W	63.5	U	
10/12/2019	@	Houston	38	23	W	-9.5	W	50.0	O	
10/19/2019	vs	TULSA	24	13	W	-15.5	L	47.0	U	
11/2/2019	@	East Carolina	46	43	W	-24.0	L	48.5	O	
11/9/2019	vs	CONNECTICUT	48	3	W	-33.5	W	53.0	U	
11/9/2019	@	South Florida	20	17	W	-13.0	L	46.5	U	
11/23/2019	vs	TEMPLE	15	13	W	-8.5	L	45.5	U	
11/29/2019	@	Memphis	24	34	L	13.5	W	59.5	U	
12/7/2019	@	**Memphis**	24	29	L	8.0	W	58.0	U	**AAC CHAMPIONSHIP GAME**
1/2/2020	vs	**Boston College**	38	6	W	-7.0	W	54.0	U	**Birmingham Bowl**
Coach: Luke Fickell		Season Record >>	415	288	11-3	ATS>>	9-5	O/U>>	3-11	
2018-Cincinnati		Opponent	Cincy	Opp	S/U	Line	ATS	Total	O/U	
9/1/2018	@	Ucla	26	17	W	14.5	W	62.5	U	
9/8/2018	vs	MIAMI-OHIO	21	0	W	1.5	W	45.5	U	"Victory Bell"
9/15/2018	vs	ALABAMA A&M	63	7	W	-44.0	W	NT	---	
9/22/2018	vs	OHIO	34	30	W	-7.0	L	54.5	O	
9/29/2018	@	Connecticut	49	7	W	-16.5	W	62.0	U	
10/6/2018	vs	TULANE	37	21	W	-7.0	W	48.0	O	
10/20/2018	@	Temple	17	24	L	2.5	L	47.0	U	{OT}
10/27/2018	@	Smu	26	20	W	-9.5	L	49.5	U	{OT}
11/3/2018	vs	NAVY	42	0	W	-13.0	W	48.0	U	
11/10/2018	vs	SOUTH FLORIDA	35	23	W	-16.0	L	52.5	O	
11/17/2018	@	Central Florida	13	38	L	6.5	L	60.5	U	
11/23/2018	vs	EAST CAROLINA	56	6	W	-16.5	W	49.5	O	
12/31/2018	vs	**Virginia Tech**	35	31	W	-5.5	L	48.5	O	**Military Bowl**
Coach: Luke Fickell		Season Record >>	454	224	11-2	ATS>>	7-6	O/U>>	5-7	
2017-Cincinnati		Opponent	Cincy	Opp	S/U	Line	ATS	Total	O/U	
8/31/2017	vs	AUSTIN PEAY	26	14	W	-41.5	L	58.0	U	
9/9/2017	@	Michigan	14	36	L	12.0	L	51.0	U	
9/16/2017	@	Miami-Ohio	21	17	W	3.0	W	49.0	U	"Victory Bell"
9/23/2017	@	Navy	32	42	L	7.0	L	52.0	O	
9/30/2017	vs	MARSHALL	21	38	L	-3.0	L	52.5	O	
10/7/2017	vs	CENTRAL FLORIDA	23	51	L	15.0	L	52.5	O	
10/14/2017	@	South Florida	3	33	L	23.5	L	62.5	U	
10/21/2017	vs	SMU	28	31	L	5.5	W	65.5	U	{OT}
11/4/2017	@	Tulane	17	16	W	5.5	W	52.0	U	
11/10/2017	vs	TEMPLE	24	35	L	3.0	L	49.5	O	
11/18/2017	@	East Carolina	20	48	L	-4.5	L	67.0	O	
11/25/2017	vs	CONNECTICUT	22	21	W	-6.5	L	58.5	U	
Coach: Luke Fickell		Season Record >>	251	382	4-8	ATS>>	3-9	O/U>>	5-7	

Copyright © 2021 by Steve's Football Bible, LLC

CINCINNATI BEARCATS   AMERICAN East

STADIUM: Nippert Stadium {40,000}				Location: Cincinnati, OH						COACH: Luke Fickell	
DATE		Opponent	Cin	Opp	S/U	Line	ATS	Total	O/U	Trends & Angles	
9/4/2021	vs	*MIAMI-OHIO*								9-0 S/U @ home vs Miami-Ohio since 2004	
9/11/2021	vs	*MURRAY STATE*								1st meeting	
9/18/2021	@	*Indiana*								0-3 S/U @ Indiana since 1963	
10/2/2021	@	*Notre Dame*								vs Notre Dame - Notre Dame leads series 1-0	
10/8/2021	vs	**TEMPLE**								1-4 S/U vs Temple since 2015	
10/16/2021	vs	**CENTRAL FLORIDA**								vs Central Florida - Series tied 3-3	
10/23/2021	@	**Navy**								vs Navy - Navy leads series 3-1	
10/30/2021	@	**Tulane**								vs Tulane - Tulane leads series 11-6	
11/6/2021	vs	**TULSA**								5-0 S/U @ home vs Tulsa since 1994	
11/12/2021	@	**South Florida**								0-6 ATS vs South Florida since 2015	
11/20/2021	vs	**SMU**								vs Smu - Cincinnati leads series 4-1	
11/27/2021	@	**East Carolina**								8-1 S/U vs East Carolina since 2002	
12/4/2021	vs									AAC Championship	
	vs									BOWL GAME	

Pointspread Analysis Non-Conference		Pointspread Analysis Conference
1-22 S/U vs Non-Conf. as 15.5 point or more Dog since 1984		vs East Carolina - East Carolina leads series 13-11
2-13 S/U vs Non-Conf. as 10.5-15 point Dog since 1985		0-7 S/U vs East Carolina as 7.5 point or more Dog since 1988
6-1 S/U vs Non-Conf. as 3.5-7 point favorite since 2006		3-0 S/U & ATS vs E. Carolina as 4.5 point or less Dog since 1995
34-1 S/U vs Non-Conf. as 10.5 point or more favorite since 1995		4-0 S/U & ATS @ home vs E. Carolina as a favorite since 1993
vs Miami-Ohio - Miami-Ohio leads series 59-58-7		0-4 ATS @ South Florida since 2013
14-0 S/U vs Miami-Ohio since 2006		vs South Florida - Cincinnati leads series 11-7
Game 2-8 O/U vs Miami-Ohio since 2009		4-1 S/U & ATS vs USF as 7 point or less Dog since 2006
0-3 S/U vs Miami-Ohio as 10 point or more Dog since 1991		4-0 S/U @ home vs USF as 10 point or more favorite since 2012
5-1 S/U vs Miami-Ohio as 7 point or less Dog since 1997		3-0 S/U vs SMU as a favorite since 2013
6-0 ATS vs Miami-Ohio as 7 point or less Dog since 1997		Game 0-5 O/U vs SMU since 2013
vs Indiana - Indiana leads series 9-3-1		vs Temple - Temple leads series 13-8-1
0-5 S/U vs Indiana since 1962		Game 4-1 O/U @ home vs Temple since 2003
Dog		0-5 ATS vs Temple since 2015
1-15 S/U as 30.5 point or more Dog since 1984		0-3 S/U vs Temple as 9.5 point or more Dog since 1984
0-7 S/U on road as 25.5-30 point Dog since 1985		5-1 S/U vs Temple as 4.5 point or more favorite since 2002
0-10 S/U on road as 20.5-25 point Dog since 1986		7-1 S/U vs Tulsa since 1993
2-8 ATS as 20.5-25 point Dog since 1987		vs Tulsa - Tulsa leads series 17-16-2
2-54-1 S/U as 15.5 point or more Dog since 1984		5-0 S/U vs Tulsa as 4.5 point or more favorite since 1995
0-9 S/U @ home as 10.5-15 point Dog since 1991		
0-19 S/U as 10.5-15 Dog since 1996		
2-9 ATS as 10.5-15 point Dog since 2004		6-0 S/U when #5 ranked all time
0-6 S/U on road as 7.5-10 point Dog since 2003		20-2 S/U @ home when ranked since 2008
0-6 S/U as 7.5-10 point Dog since 2015		2-31 S/U vs Top 10 ranked teams all time
0-7 O/U as 7.5-10 point Dog since 2015		0-18 S/U on road vs Top 10 ranked teams all time
2-8 S/U as 3.5-7 point Dog since 2012		0-12 S/U vs #10 - #13 ranked teams all time
Favorite		
1-3 S/U & ATS @ home as 3 point or less favorite since 2004		
8-0 S/U as 3.5-7 point favorite since 2017		
14-2 S/U as 7.5-10 point favorite since 2008	MIAMI-OHIO	19-0 S/U in 1st home game of season since 2002
20-0 S/U @ home as 10.5-15 point favorite since 1993	MURRAY STATE	2-5 S/U after playing Miami-Ohio since 2013
2-11 O/U as 10.5-15 point favorite since 2011	ND,Tulane	14-2 ATS in 2nd of B2B road games since 2006
54-0 S/U @ home as 10.5 point or more favorite since 1992	SMU	2-10-1 ATS in final home game of season since 2008
8-0 S/U on road as 15.5 point or more favorite since 2007	East Carolina	7-3 ATS in final road game of season since 2011

Copyright © 2021 by Steve's Football Bible, LLC

CLEMSON TIGERS

ACC Atlantic

2020-Clemson		Opponent	CLEM	Opp	S/U	Line	ATS	Total	O/U	
9/12/2020	@	Wake Forest	37	13	W	-34.0	L	59.0	U	
9/19/2020	vs	THE CITADEL	49	0	W	-50.0	L	55.5	U	
10/3/2020	vs	VIRGINIA	41	23	W	-27.5	L	55.5	O	
10/10/2020	vs	MIAMI	42	17	W	-14.0	W	60.5	U	
10/17/2020	@	Georgia Tech	73	7	W	-27.0	W	63.5	O	
10/24/2020	vs	SYRACUSE	47	21	W	-46.5	L	64.5	O	
10/31/2020	vs	BOSTON COLLEGE	34	28	W	-26.0	L	56.0	O	"O'Rourke-McFadden Trophy"
11/7/2020	@	Notre Dame	40	47	L	-4.5	L	50.5	O	{2 OT}
11/28/2020	vs	PITTSBURGH	52	17	W	-23.5	W	58.5	O	
12/5/2020	@	Virginia Tech	45	10	W	-23.0	W	66.5	U	
12/19/2020	vs	Notre Dame	34	13	W	-11.0	W	58.0	U	ACC CHAMPIONSHIP GAME
1/1/2021	vs	Ohio State	28	49	L	-7.5	L	69.0	O	Sugar Bowl (National Semifinal)
Coach: Dabo Swinney		Season Record >>	522	245	10-2	ATS>>	5-7	O/U>>	7-5	ACC CHAMPIONS
2019-Clemson		Opponent	CLEM	Opp	S/U	Line	ATS	Total	O/U	
8/29/2019	vs	GEORGIA TECH	52	14	W	-36.5	W	61.0	O	
9/7/2019	vs	TEXAS A&M	24	10	W	-16.0	L	62.5	U	
9/14/2019	@	Syracuse	41	6	W	-28.0	W	64.5	U	
9/21/2019	vs	CHARLOTTE	52	10	W	-41.5	W	61.0	O	
9/28/2019	@	North Carolina	21	20	W	-27.5	L	60.0	U	
10/12/2019	vs	FLORIDA STATE	45	14	W	-25.5	W	60.5	U	
10/19/2019	@	Louisville	45	10	W	-25.0	W	62.0	U	
10/26/2019	vs	BOSTON COLLEGE	59	7	W	-35.0	W	59.0	O	"O'Rourke-McFadden Trophy"
11/2/2019	vs	WOFFORD	59	14	W	-48.5	L	NT	---	
11/9/2019	@	NC State	55	10	W	-35.0	W	54.0	O	"Textile Bowl"
11/16/2019	vs	WAKE FOREST	52	3	W	-34.5	W	59.0	U	
11/30/2019	@	South Carolina	38	3	W	-27.0	W	50.5	U	"The Palmetto Bowl"
12/7/2019	vs	Virginia	62	17	W	-30.0	W	57.5	O	ACC CHAMPIONSHIP GAME
12/28/2019	vs	Ohio State	29	23	W	-2.5	W	62.0	U	Fiesta Bowl (National Semi-Final)
1/13/2020	vs	Lsu	25	42	L	4.0	L	66.5	O	CFB Championship Game
Coach: Dabo Swinney		Season Record >>	659	203	14-1	ATS>>	11-4	O/U>>	6-8	ACC CHAMPIONS
2018-Clemson		Opponent	CLEM	Opp	S/U	Line	ATS	Total	O/U	NATIONAL CHAMPIONS
9/1/2018	vs	FURMAN	48	7	W	-49.0	L	NT	---	
9/8/2018	@	Texas A&M	28	26	W	-12.0	L	52.5	O	
9/15/2018	vs	GEORGIA SOUTHERN	38	7	W	-31.5	L	48.5	U	
9/22/2018	@	Georgia Tech	49	21	W	-15.5	W	56.5	O	
9/29/2018	vs	SYRACUSE	27	23	W	-24.5	L	64.5	U	
10/6/2018	@	Wake Forest	63	3	W	-20.5	W	61.0	O	
10/20/2018	vs	NC STATE	41	7	W	-18.5	W	58.0	U	"Textile Bowl"
10/27/2018	@	Florida State	59	10	W	-18.0	W	49.5	O	
11/3/2018	vs	LOUISVILLE	77	16	W	-38.0	W	61.0	O	
11/10/2018	@	Boston College	27	7	W	-17.5	W	51.0	U	"O'Rourke-McFadden Trophy"
11/17/2018	vs	DUKE	35	6	W	-28.5	W	59.5	U	
11/24/2018	vs	SOUTH CAROLINA	56	35	W	-25.5	L	58.5	O	"The Palmetto Bowl"
12/1/2018	vs	Pittsburgh	42	10	W	-27.5	W	53.0	U	ACC CHAMPIONSHIP
12/29/2018	vs	Notre Dame	30	3	W	-10.0	W	58.0	U	Cotton Bowl (National Semi-Final)
1/7/2019	vs	Alabama	44	16	W	5.5	W	57.5	O	CFB Championship Game
Coach: Dabo Swinney		Season Record >>	664	197	15-0	ATS>>	10-5	O/U>>	7-7	ACC CHAMPIONS

Copyright © 2021 by Steve's Football Bible, LLC

CLEMSON TIGERS   ACC Atlantic

STADIUM: Memorial Stadium {81,500}						Location: Clemson, SC			COACH: Dabo Swinney
DATE		Opponent	Clem	Opp	S/U	Line	ATS	Total	O/U	Trends & Angles

DATE		Opponent	Clem	Opp	S/U	Line	ATS	Total	O/U	Trends & Angles
9/4/2021	vs	*Georgia {Charlotte, NC}*								1-6 S/U vs Georgia since 1991 {2-5 ATS}
9/11/2021	vs	SOUTH CAROLINA STATE								vs South Carolina State - Clemson leads series 4-0
9/18/2021	vs	**GEORGIA TECH**								6-0 S/U @ home vs Georgia Tech since 2010
9/25/2021	@	NC State								15-1 S/U vs NC State since 2004
10/2/2021	vs	**BOSTON COLLEGE**								10-0 S/U vs Boston College since 2011
10/15/2021	@	Syracuse								Game 2-7 O/U vs Syracuse since 1996
10/23/2021	@	Pittsburgh								vs Pittsburgh - Series tied 2-2
10/30/2021	vs	**FLORIDA STATE**								8-1 S/U @ home vs Florida State since 2003
11/6/2021	@	Louisville								vs Louisville - Clemson leads series 6-0
11/13/2021	vs	CONNECTICUT								1st meeting
11/20/2021	vs	**WAKE FOREST**								10-0 S/U @ home vs Wake Forest since 2000
11/27/2021	@	*South Carolina*								12-1 S/U @ South Carolina as a favorite since 1983
12/4/2021	vs									ACC Championship
	vs									BOWL GAME

Pointspread Analysis Non-Conference		Pointspread Analysis Conference
1-5 ATS vs Non-Conf. as 7.5-10 point favorite since 2000		11-0 S/U vs Boston College 5 point or more favorite since 2011
1-5 O/U vs Non-Conf. as 7.5-10 point favorite since 2000		6-0 S/U @ home vs B.C. as 5 point or more favorite since 2009
8-1 S/U vs Non-Conf. as 10.5-15 point favorite since 1988		vs Georgia Tech - Georgia Tech leads series 52-32-2
40-0 S/U vs Non-Conf. as 15.5 point or more favorite since 1990		5-0-1 ATS @ home vs Georgia Tech since 2010
0-5 S/U vs South Carolina as Dog since 1987		0-4 S/U vs Georgia Tech as a Dog since 2005
vs South Carolina - Clemson leads series 71-41-4 (6 straight W)		8-2 ATS vs Georgia Tech as a Dog since 1995
0-4 O/U vs South Carolina as Dog since 2001		6-0 S/U vs Georgia Tech since 2015 {5-0-1 ATS}
6-0 S/U vs South Carolina since 2014		5-0 S/U vs Florida State since 2015
Bowl Games		7-2 ATS @ home vs Florida State as a Dog since 1992
0-3 S/U in Gator Bowl since 1996		vs Florida State - Florida State leads series 20-13
0-7 O/U in Peach Bowl since 1993		6-0 S/U vs Florida State as favorite since 2009
0-3-1 O/U in Gator Bowl since 1989		0-5 S/U vs Florida State as a Dog since 2008
4-0 O/U in CFB Championship Game since 2016		4-0 ATS vs Louisville since 2016
8-1 ATS in Bowl Games as 3.5-7 point Dog since 2004		vs NC State - Clemson leads series 59-28-1
1-6 ATS in Bowl Games as 3 point or less favorite since 1993		Game 3-0 O/U @ NC State since 2015
1-5 S/U in Bowl Games as 3 point or less favorite since 1996		15-1 S/U vs NC State as 3.5 point or more favorite since 2000
4-1 S/U & ATS vs Ohio State in Bowl Games		vs Syracuse - Clemson leads series 7-2
3-0 S/U & ATS vs Oklahoma in Bowl Games		Game 1-5 O/U @ home vs Wake Forest since 2009
0-3 O/U vs Oklahoma in Bowl Games		vs Wake Forest - Clemson leads series 68-17-1
0-3 O/U vs Kentucky in Bowl Games		12-0 S/U vs Wake Forest since 2009
10-1 ATS in Bowl Games since 2012	SC STATE	17-0 S/U in 1st home game of season since 2004
9-2 S/U in Bowl Game since 2012	SC STATE	11-3-1 ATS in 1st home game of season since 2004
Dog	G TECH	9-0 S/U prior to playing NC State since 2011
0-5 S/U as 21 point or more Dog since 1993	NC State	10-0 S/U after playing Georgia Tech since 2011
4-0 ATS @ home as 15.5 point or more Dog since 1995	NC State	10-1 S/U prior to playing Boston College since 2010
2-7 S/U as 10.5-15 point Dog since 1993	NC State	9-2 ATS prior to playing Boston College since 2010
0-5 S/U on road as 7.5-10 point Dog since 1994	Syracuse	10-0 S/U in 2nd road game of season since 2011
0-6 S/U as 7.5-10 point Dog since 1998	Syracuse	9-2 S/U after playing Boston College since 2010
10-3 ATS on road as 3.5-7 point Dog since 2001	Pittsburgh	12-0 S/U prior to playing Florida State since 2008
Favorite	Louisville	12-3 ATS after playing Florida State since 2005
8-1 S/U as 3.5-7 point favorite since 2014	Louisville	15-0 S/U after playing Florida State since 2005
9-1 S/U on road as 7.5-10 point favorite since 1996	UCONN	3-9 O/U prior to playing Wake Forest since 2008
21-4 S/U as 7.5-10 point favorite since 1996	WAKE F.	8-0 S/U prior to playing South Carolina since 2012
13-1-1 S/U @ home as 7.5-10 point favorite since 1989		**Favorite**
23-0 S/U as 10.5-15 point favorite since 2010		26-3 S/U as 20.5-25 point favorite since 1987
3-8 O/U on road as 10.5-15 point favorite since 2004		60-0 S/U as 25.5 point or more favorite since 1984
12-0 S/U @ home as 10.5-15 point favorite since 2008		
17-5-1 ATS as 10.5-15 point favorite since 2010		37-1 S/U @ home when ranked since 2014
17-0 S/U as 15.5-20 point favorite since 2006		12-2 S/U when ranked #1 all time
10-0 S/U on road as 15.5-20 point favorite since 1995		22-2 S/U when ranked #2 all time {10-0 @ home}
6-1 O/U on road as 15.5-20 point favorite since 2007		12-1 S/U when ranked vs NC State since 1997 {5-0 @ home}
		27-0 S/U when ranked vs Wake Forest since 1948 {11-0 on road}

Copyright © 2021 by Steve's Football Bible, LLC

COASTAL CAROLINA CHANTICLEERS   SUN BELT East

2020-Coastal Carolina		Opponent	CCU	Opp	S/U	Line	ATS	Total	O/U	
9/12/2020	@	Kansas	35	23	W	40.0	W	56.0	O	
9/19/2020	vs	CAMPBELL	43	21	W	-28.5	L	54.5	O	
10/3/2020	vs	ARKANSAS STATE	52	23	W	3.5	W	64.5	O	
10/17/2020	@	Louisiana	30	27	W	9.0	W	57.0	T	
10/24/2020	vs	GEORGIA SOUTHERN	28	14	W	-1.5	W	48.5	U	
10/31/2020	@	Georgia State	51	0	W	-4.0	W	60.5	U	
11/7/2020	vs	SOUTH ALABAMA	23	6	W	-17.0	T	57.0		
11/21/2020	vs	APPALACHIAN STATE	34	23	W	-3.0	W	48.0	O	
11/28/2020	@	Texas State	49	14	W	-16.5	W	59.0	O	
12/5/2020	vs	BYU	22	17	W	10.0	W	62.0	U	
12/12/2020	@	Troy	42	38	W	-11.5	L	53.0	O	
12/26/2020	vs	Liberty	34	37	L	-6.5	L	60.0	O	FBC Mortgage Cure Bowl
Coach: Joe Moglia		Season Record >>	443	243	11-1	ATS>>	8-3-1	O/U>>	7-4-1	
2019-Coastal Carolina		Opponent	CCU	Opp	S/U	Line	ATS	Total	O/U	
8/31/2019	vs	EASTERN MICHIGAN	23	30	L	4.5	L	54.0	U	
9/7/2019	@	Kansas	12	7	W	7.0	W	54.0	U	
9/14/2019	vs	NORFOLK STATE	46	7	W	-25.5	W	NT	---	
9/21/2019	@	Massachusetts	62	28	W	-17.0	W	62.0	O	
9/28/2019	@	Appalachian State	37	56	L	14.5	L	58.0	O	
10/12/2019	vs	GEORGIA STATE	21	31	L	-3.0	L	63.0	U	
10/19/2019	@	Georgia Southern	27	30	L	7.0	W	43.0	O	{2 OT}
11/2/2019	vs	TROY	36	35	W	PK	W	60.0	O	
11/7/2019	vs	LOUISIANA-LAFAYETTE	7	48	L	14.0	L	58.0	U	
11/16/2019	@	Arkansas State	27	28	L	13.5	W	60.0	U	
11/23/2019	@	Louisiana-Monroe	42	45	L	6.0	W	63.5	O	
11/30/2019	vs	TEXAS STATE	24	21	W	-7.0	L	52.0	U	
Coach: Joe Moglia		Season Record >>	364	366	5-7	ATS>>	7-5	O/U>>	5-6	
2018-Coastal Carolina		Opponent	CCU	Opp	S/U	Line	ATS	Total	O/U	
9/1/2018	@	South Carolina	15	49	L	31.0	L	55.5	O	
9/8/2018	vs	ALABAMA-BRIMINGHAM	47	24	W	8.5	W	54.5	O	
9/15/2018	vs	CAMPBELL	58	21	W	-28.5	W	NT	---	
9/22/2018	@	Louisiana-Lafayette	30	28	W	3.0	W	63.0	U	
9/29/2018	@	Troy	21	45	L	13.5	L	57.0	O	
10/13/2018	vs	LOUISIANA-MONROE	20	45	L	-6.5	L	67.5	U	
10/20/2018	@	Massachusetts	24	13	W	2.0	W	74.0	U	
10/27/2018	@	Georgia State	37	34	W	-2.5	W	60.5	O	
11/3/2018	vs	APPALACHIAN STATE	7	23	L	13.5	L	52.0	U	
11/10/2018	vs	ARKANSAS STATE	16	44	L	7.0	L	62.0	U	
11/17/2018	vs	GEORGIA SOUTHERN	17	41	L	7.5	L	53.0	O	
11/24/2018	@	South Alabama	28	31	L	-1.0	L	58.5	O	
Coach: Joe Moglia		Season Record >>	320	398	5-7	ATS>>	5-7	O/U>>	6-5	
2017-Coastal Carolina		Opponent	CCU	Opp	S/U	Line	ATS	Total	O/U	
9/2/2017	vs	MASSACHUSETTS	38	28	W	2.5	W	56.0	O	
9/16/2017	@	Alabama-Birmingham	23	30	L	-1.5	L	53.5	U	
9/23/2017	vs	WESTERN ILLINOIS	10	52	L	3.0	L	NT	---	
9/30/2017	@	Louisiana-Monroe	43	51	L	7.5	L	54.0	O	
10/7/2017	vs	GEORGIA STATE	21	27	L	PK	L	52.0	U	
10/14/2017	@	Arkansas State	17	51	L	16.0	L	63.0	O	
10/21/2017	@	Appalachian State	29	37	L	19.0	W	51.5	O	
10/28/2017	vs	TEXAS STATE	7	27	L	-9.5	L	54.0	U	
11/4/2017	@	Arkansas	38	39	L	24.0	L	59.0	O	
11/11/2017	vs	TROY	17	42	L	17.0	L	53.0	O	
11/18/2017	@	Idaho	13	7	W	7.0	W	50.5	U	
12/2/2017	vs	GEORGIA SOUTHERN	28	17	W	3.0	W	48.5	U	
Coach: Joe Moglia		Season Record >>	284	408	3-9	ATS>>	4-8	O/U>>	6-5	

Copyright © 2021 by Steve's Football Bible, LLC

COASTAL CAROLINA CHANTICLEERS   SUN BELT East

STADIUM: Brooks Stadium {20,000}					Location: Conway, SC				COACH: Joe Moglia	
DATE		Opponent	CCU	Opp	S/U	Line	ATS	Total	O/U	Trends & Angles
9/4/2021	vs	*THE CITADEL*								vs The Citadel - Series tied 1-1
9/11/2021	vs	*KANSAS*								vs Kansas - Coastal Carolina leads series 2-0
9/18/2021	@	*Buffalo*								1st meeting
9/25/2021	vs	*MASSACHUSETTS*								vs Massachusetts - Coastal Carolina leads series 3-0
10/2/2021	vs	LOUISIANA-MONROE								vs Troy - Series tied 2-2
10/7/2021	@	Arkansas State								vs Georgia State - Series tied 2-2
10/20/2021	@	Appalachian State								vs Louisiana-Monroe - UL-Monroe leads series 3-0
10/28/2021	vs	TROY								vs Texas State - Coastal Carolina leads series 2-1
11/6/2021	@	Georgia Southern								vs Appalachian State - Appalachian leads series 5-1
11/13/2021	vs	GEORGIA STATE								vs Georgia Southern - G. Southern leads series 5-2
11/20/2021	vs	TEXAS STATE								vs Arkansas State - ASU leads series 3-1
11/27/2021	@	South Alabama								vs South Alabama - Series tied 1-1
12/4/2021	vs									ACC Championship
	vs									BOWL GAME

Pointspread Analysis Dog		Pointspread Analysis Favorite
1-10 S/U as 13.5 point or more Dog since 2017		7-0 S/U as 10.5 point or more favorite since 2018
3-8 ATS as 13.5 point or more Dog since 2017		
7-1 O/U on road as 13.5 point or more Dog since 2017		
5-1 S/U & ATS as 3 point or less Dog since 2017	THE CITADEL	9-1 S/U in 1st home game of season since 2011
1-3 O/U as 3 point or less Dog since 2017	TEXAS STATE	10-2 S/U in final home game of season since 2009

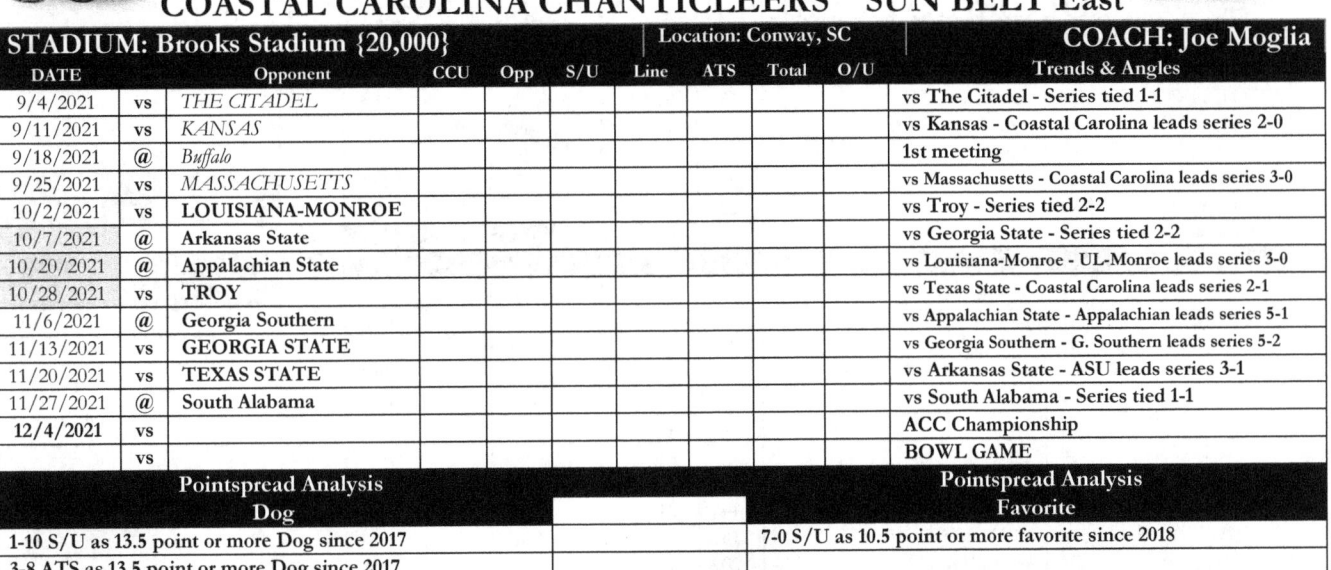

This book takes a Historical look at past College Football games. Game of the Century, Memorable games, Great comebacks, great games of the 20th Century, When number 1 played number 2, when number #1 ranked teams lost to an unranked team. Everything for the College Football fan.

College Football "Glorious Games of the Past" {8.5" x 11"} {293 pages}

{6" x 9"} {473 pages}

$29.95 + $5.00 Shipping & Handling

$34.95

These books available at numerous online retailers

Copyright © 2021 by Steve's Football Bible, LLC

COLORADO GOLDEN BUFFALOES   PACIFIC-12 South

2020-Colorado		Opponent	COL	Opp	S/U	Line	ATS	Total	O/U	
11/7/2020	vs	UCLA	48	42	W	7.0	W	56.0	O	
11/14/2020	@	Stanford	35	32	W	10.0	W	55.5	O	
11/28/2020	vs	*SAN DIEGO STATE*	20	10	W	-6.0	W	51.5	U	
12/5/2020	@	Arizona	24	13	W	-9.5	W	55.5	U	
12/12/2020	vs	UTAH	21	38	L	2.5	L	49.0	O	*"Rumble in the Rockies"*
12/19/2020	vs	**Texas**	**23**	**55**	L	9.0	L	67.0	O	Alamo Bowl
Coach: Karl Dorrell		Season Record >>	171	190	4-2	ATS>>	4-2	O/U>>	4-2	
2019-Colorado		Opponent	COL	Opp	S/U	Line	ATS	Total	O/U	
8/30/2019	vs	*Colorado State*	52	31	W	-13.5	W	55.5	O	*"Rocky Mountain Showdown*
9/7/2019	vs	*NEBRASKA*	34	31	W	4.0	W	64.5	O	{OT}
9/14/2019	vs	*AIR FORCE*	23	30	L	-3.0	L	58.0	U	{OT}
9/21/2019	@	*Arizona State*	34	31	W	8.0	W	49.0	O	
10/5/2019	vs	ARIZONA	30	35	L	-2.5	L	63.5	O	
10/12/2019	@	Oregon	3	45	L	22.5	L	62.0	U	
10/19/2019	@	Washington State	10	41	L	13.0	L	68.5	U	
10/26/2019	vs	USC	31	35	L	10.5	L	64.5	O	
11/2/2019	@	Ucla	14	31	L	6.5	L	64.5	U	
11/9/2019	vs	STANFORD	16	13	W	4.0	W	56.5	U	
11/23/2019	vs	WASHINGTON	20	14	W	14.0	W	53.0	U	
11/29/2019	@	Utah	15	45	L	28.0	L	50.0	O	*"Rumble in the Rockies"*
Coach: Mel Tucker		Season Record >>	282	382	5-7	ATS>>	6-6	O/U>>	6-6	
2018-Colorado		Opponent	COL	Opp	S/U	Line	ATS	Total	O/U	
9/1/2018	vs	*Colorado State*	45	13	W	-7.0	W	66.0	U	*"Rocky Mountain Showdown*
9/8/2018	@	*Nebraska*	33	28	W	3.0	W	63.5	U	
9/15/2018	vs	NEW HAMPSHIRE	45	14	W	-38.0	L	NT	---	
9/28/2018	vs	UCLA	38	16	W	-10.0	W	56.5	U	
10/6/2018	vs	ARIZONA STATE	28	21	W	-2.5	W	64.5	U	
10/13/2018	@	Usc	20	31	L	7.0	L	57.5	U	
10/20/2018	@	Washington	13	27	L	17.0	W	50.5	U	
10/27/2018	vs	OREGON STATE	34	41	L	-24.5	L	60.0	O	{OT}
11/3/2018	@	Arizona	34	42	L	3.0	L	56.5	O	
11/10/2018	vs	WASHINGTON STATE	7	31	L	5.5	L	59.5	U	
11/17/2018	vs	UTAH	7	30	L	7.0	L	45.5	U	*"Rumble in the Rockies"*
11/24/2018	@	California	21	33	L	10.5	L	44.5	O	
Coach: Mike MacIntyre		Season Record >>	325	327	5-7	ATS>>	5-7	O/U>>	3-8	
2017-Colorado		Opponent	COL	Opp	S/U	Line	ATS	Total	O/U	
9/1/2017	vs	*Colorado State*	17	3	W	-3.0	W	68.0	U	*"Rocky Mountain Showdown*
9/9/2017	vs	*TEXAS STATE*	37	3	W	-35.5	L	56.5	U	
9/16/2017	vs	*NORTHERN COLORADO*	41	21	W	-38.5	L	NT	---	
9/23/2017	vs	WASHINGTON	10	37	L	11.0	L	54.5	U	
9/30/2017	@	Ucla	23	27	L	7.5	W	66.0	U	
10/7/2017	vs	ARIZONA	42	45	L	-7.0	L	58.5	O	
10/14/2017	@	Oregon State	36	33	W	-10.0	L	56.0	O	
10/21/2017	@	Washington State	0	28	L	9.0	L	52.0	U	
10/28/2017	vs	CALIFORNIA	44	28	W	-3.5	W	54.0	O	
11/4/2017	@	Arizona State	30	41	L	6.5	L	59.0	O	
11/11/2017	vs	USC	24	38	L	13.5	L	62.5	U	
11/25/2017	@	Utah	13	34	L	9.0	L	57.0	U	*"Rumble in the Rockies"*
Coach: Mike MacIntyre		Season Record >>	317	338	5-7	ATS>>	3-9	O/U>>	4-7	

Copyright © 2021 by Steve's Football Bible, LLC

COLORADO GOLDEN BUFFALOES   PACIFIC-12 South

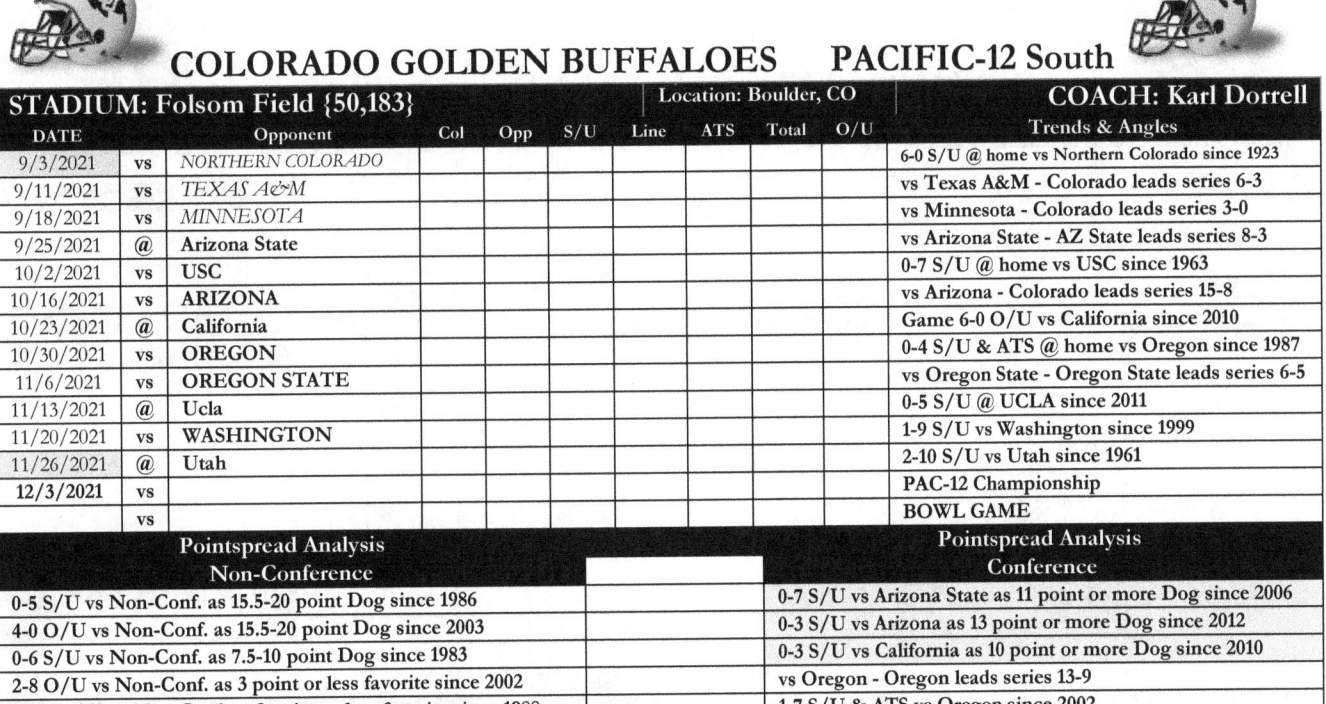

STADIUM: Folsom Field {50,183}					Location: Boulder, CO				COACH: Karl Dorrell	
DATE		Opponent	Col	Opp	S/U	Line	ATS	Total	O/U	Trends & Angles
9/3/2021	vs	NORTHERN COLORADO								6-0 S/U @ home vs Northern Colorado since 1923
9/11/2021	vs	TEXAS A&M								vs Texas A&M - Colorado leads series 6-3
9/18/2021	vs	MINNESOTA								vs Minnesota - Colorado leads series 3-0
9/25/2021	@	Arizona State								vs Arizona State - AZ State leads series 8-3
10/2/2021	vs	USC								0-7 S/U @ home vs USC since 1963
10/16/2021	vs	ARIZONA								vs Arizona - Colorado leads series 15-8
10/23/2021	@	California								Game 6-0 O/U vs California since 2010
10/30/2021	vs	OREGON								0-4 S/U & ATS @ home vs Oregon since 1987
11/6/2021	vs	OREGON STATE								vs Oregon State - Oregon State leads series 6-5
11/13/2021	@	Ucla								0-5 S/U @ UCLA since 2011
11/20/2021	vs	WASHINGTON								1-9 S/U vs Washington since 1999
11/26/2021	@	Utah								2-10 S/U vs Utah since 1961
12/3/2021	vs									PAC-12 Championship
	vs									BOWL GAME

Pointspread Analysis Non-Conference		Pointspread Analysis Conference
0-5 S/U vs Non-Conf. as 15.5-20 point Dog since 1986		0-7 S/U vs Arizona State as 11 point or more Dog since 2006
4-0 O/U vs Non-Conf. as 15.5-20 point Dog since 2003		0-3 S/U vs Arizona as 13 point or more Dog since 2012
0-6 S/U vs Non-Conf. as 7.5-10 point Dog since 1983		0-3 S/U vs California as 10 point or more Dog since 2010
2-8 O/U vs Non-Conf. as 3 point or less favorite since 2002		vs Oregon - Oregon leads series 13-9
2-10-1 ATS vs Non-Conf. as 3 point or less favorite since 1988		1-7 S/U & ATS vs Oregon since 2002
0-5 O/U vs Non-Conf. as 7.5-10 point favorite since 1996		4-1 S/U vs Oregon State as favorite since 1983
10-2 S/U vs Non-Conf. as 10.5-15 point favorite since 1987		Game 1-5 O/U vs Stanford since 2011
2-6 O/U vs Non-Conf. as 10.5-15 point favorite since 2007		0-3 S/U & ATS vs Stanford as 14.5 point or more Dog since 2011
24-1 S/U vs Non-Conf. as 15.5 point or more favorite since 1987		0-3 O/U vs Stanford as 14.5 point or more Dog since 2011
vs Northern Colorado - Colorado leads series 10-2		vs Ucla - UCLA leads series 11-5
0-10 ATS as Non-Conf road favorite since 1988		6-2 ATS vs UCLA since 2013
Bowl Games		Game 1-4 O/U vs UCLA since 2016
6-1 S/U & ATS in Bowl Games as 3.5-7 point favorite since 1993		3-0 S/U vs UCLA as favorite since 2003
0-4 S/U & ATS in Bowl Games as 3 point or less favorite since 1988		0-5 S/U vs UCLA as 7.5 point or more Dog since 2012
Dog		4-0 ATS vs UCLA as 7.5 point or more Dog since 2013
0-6 ATS as 30.5 point or more Dog since 2011		vs Usc - USC leads series 14-0
0-23 S/U as 25.5 point or more Dog since 1983		Game 1-4 O/U vs USC since 2015
2-16 S/U as 20.5-25 point Dog since 1984		0-10 S/U vs USC as 5.5 point or more Dog since 2000
2-26 S/U as 15.5-20 point Dog since 1985		vs Utah - Colorado leads series 33-32-3
5-1 ATS @ home as 15.5-20 point Dog since 1986		0-5 ATS vs Utah since 2016
2-15 S/U @ home as 10.5-15 point Dog since 1983		Game 1-4 O/U @ Utah since 2011
2-15 S/U on road as 10.5-15 point Dog since 2002		0-7 S/U vs Utah as 7 point or more Dog since 2012
3-7 S/U on road as 7.5-10 point Dog since 1997		2-8 ATS vs Washington since 1999
4-0 ATS @ home as 7.5-10 point Dog since 2001		vs Washington - Washington leads series 12-7-1
0-11 S/U on road as 3.5-7 point Dog since 1998		Game 0-4 O/U vs Washington since 2016
1-10 ATS on road as 3.5-7 point Dog since 1998		1-7 S/U vs Washington as 3.5 point or more Dog since 1985
7-18 ATS as 3.5-7 point Dog since 2007		vs Washington State - Wazzu leads series 7-6
4-22 S/U as 3.5-7 point Dog since 2007		Game 0-3 O/U vs Washington State since 2017
4-11 S/U @ home as 3.5-7 point Dog since 2007		**Favorite**
1-7 O/U on road as 3.5-7 point Dog since 2008		3-14-1 O/U as 3 point or less favorite since 2000
1-6 O/U on road as 3 point or less Dog since 2004		10-2 S/U on road as 7.5-10 point favorite since 1985
		6-0 S/U @ home as 7.5-10 point favorite since 2001
11-3 ATS in final home game of season since 2006	WASHINGTON	15-1 S/U as 10.5-15 point favorite since 1999
4-0 O/U prior to playing Oregon State since 2014	OREGON	2-10-1 O/U as 10.5-15 point favorite since 2004
0-6 S/U after playing Oregon State since 2013	Ucla	26-2 S/U as 15.5-20 point favorite since 1987
3-13 S/U in final road game of season since 2005	Utah	24-3 S/U as 20.5-25 point favorite since 1985
		8-0 S/U on road as 20.5-25 point favorite since 1986
4-33 S/U vs ranked teams since 2009		27-0 S/U as 25.5 point or more favorite since 1987
1-31 S/U on road vs ranked teams since 2002		
0-8 S/U vs ranked USC all time		
23-4 S/U @ home when ranked since 1996		

Copyright © 2021 by Steve's Football Bible, LLC

COLORADO STATE RAMS MOUNTAIN WEST West

2020-Colorado State		Opponent	CSU	Opp	S/U	Line	ATS	Total	O/U	
10/31/2020	@	Fresno State	17	38	L	-2.5	L	57.5	U	
11/5/2020	vs	WYOMING	34	24	W	3.5	W	53.0	O	"Bronze Boot"
11/12/2020	@	Boise State	21	52	L	14.0	L	62.5	O	
12/5/2020	@	San Diego State	17	29	L	8.0	L	45.5	O	
Coach: Steve Addazio		Season Record >>	89	143	1-3	ATS>>	1-3	O/U>>	3-1	

2019-Colorado State		Opponent	CSU	Opp	S/U	Line	ATS	Total	O/U	
8/30/2019	vs	Colorado	31	52	L	13.5	L	55.5	O	"Rocky Mountain Showdown"
9/7/2019	vs	WESTERN ILLINOIS	38	13	W	-13.0	W	NT	---	
9/14/2019	@	Arkansas	34	55	L	9.5	L	64.0	O	
9/21/2019	vs	TOLEDO	35	41	L	6.0	T	67.0	O	
9/28/2019	@	Utah State	24	34	L	24.0	W	69.0	U	
10/5/2019	vs	SAN DIEGO STATE	10	24	L	6.5	L	48.0	U	
10/12/2019	@	New Mexico	35	21	W	-5.0	W	66.0	U	
10/26/2019	@	Fresno State	41	31	W	13.5	W	56.5	O	
11/2/2019	vs	UNLV	37	17	W	-7.0	W	64.0	U	
11/16/2019	vs	AIR FORCE	21	38	L	10.5	L	62.0	U	"Ram-Falcon Trophy"
11/23/2019	@	Wyoming	7	17	L	4.0	L	51.0	U	"Bronze Boot"
11/30/2019	vs	BOISE STATE	24	31	L	13.0	W	57.0	U	
Coach: Mike Bobo		Season Record >>	337	374	4-8	ATS>>	6-5-1	O/U>>	4-7	

2018-Colorado State		Opponent	CSU	Opp	S/U	Line	ATS	Total	O/U	
8/25/2018	vs	HAWAII	34	43	L	-17.0	L	58.0	O	
8/31/2018	vs	Colorado	13	45	L	7.0	L	66.0	U	"Rocky Mountain Showdown"
9/8/2018	vs	ARKANSAS	34	27	W	14.0	W	70.5	U	
9/15/2018	@	Florida	10	48	L	21.5	L	59.0	U	
9/22/2018	vs	ILLINOIS STATE	19	35	L	-4.5	L	NT	---	
10/6/2018	@	San Jose State	42	30	W	-3.0	W	59.5	O	
10/13/2018	vs	NEW MEXICO	20	18	W	2.5	W	69.0	U	
10/19/2018	@	Boise State	28	56	L	23.0	L	61.5	O	
10/27/2018	vs	WYOMING	21	34	L	3.0	L	47.5	O	"Bronze Boot"
11/10/2018	@	Nevada	10	49	L	14.0	L	62.0	U	
11/17/2018	vs	UTAH STATE	24	29	L	30.0	W	66.0	U	
11/24/2018	@	Air Force	19	27	L	14.0	W	64.0	U	"Ram-Falcon Trophy"
Coach: Mike Bobo		Season Record >>	274	441	3-9	ATS>>	5-7	O/U>>	4-7	

2017-Colorado State		Opponent	CSU	Opp	S/U	Line	ATS	Total	O/U	
8/26/2017	vs	OREGON STATE	58	27	W	-3.5	W	60.0	O	
9/1/2017	vs	Colorado	3	17	L	3.0	L	68.0	U	"Rocky Mountain Showdown"
9/9/2017	vs	ABILENE CHRISTIAN	38	10	W	-43.0	L	NT	---	
9/16/2017	@	Alabama	23	41	L	31.0	W	55.5	O	
9/30/2017	@	Hawaii	51	21	W	-6.5	W	66.0	O	
10/7/2017	@	Utah State	41	10	W	-9.5	W	65.0	U	
10/14/2017	vs	NEVADA	44	42	W	-24.5	L	65.5	O	
10/20/2017	@	New Mexico	27	24	W	-10.0	L	60.0	U	
10/28/2017	vs	AIR FORCE	28	45	L	-9.5	L	68.5	O	"Ram-Falcon Trophy"
11/4/2017	@	Wyoming	13	16	L	-4.0	L	47.5	U	"Bronze Boot"
11/11/2017	vs	BOISE STATE	52	59	L	6.5	L	59.0	O	{OT}
11/18/2017	vs	SAN JOSE STATE	42	14	W	-32.5	L	67.5	U	
12/16/2017	vs	Marshall	28	31	L	-3.0	L	58.5	O	New Mexico Bowl
Coach: Mike Bobo		Season Record >>	448	357	7-6	ATS>>	4-9	O/U>>	7-5	

Copyright © 2021 by Steve's Football Bible, LLC

COLORADO STATE RAMS MOUNTAIN WEST West

STADIUM: Sonny Lubick Field @ Canvas Stadium {41,000}									Location: Fort Collins, CO	COACH: Steve Addazio
DATE		Opponent	CSU	Opp	S/U	Line	ATS	Total	O/U	Trends & Angles
9/4/2021	vs	*SOUTH DAKOTA STATE*								vs South Dakota State - CSU leads series 2-0
9/11/2021	vs	*VANDERBILT*								1st meeting
9/18/2021	@	*Toledo*								vs Toledo - Toledo leads series 2-1
9/25/2021	@	*Iowa*								1st meeting
10/9/2021	vs	SAN JOSE STATE								1-5 ATS vs San Jose State since 2011
10/16/2021	@	New Mexico								10-0 S/U vs New Mexico since 2010
10/23/2021	@	Utah State								4-0 ATS vs Utah State since 2016
10/30/2021	vs	BOISE STATE								vs Boise State - Boise State leads series 10-0
11/6/2021	@	Wyoming								1-4 S/U & ATS vs Wyoming since 2016
11/13/2021	vs	AIR FORCE								Game 10-3 O/U vs Air Force since 2007
11/20/2021	@	Hawaii								7-1 S/U vs Hawaii since 1995
11/27/2021	vs	NEVADA								8-0 S/U @ home vs Nevada since 1974
12/4/2021	vs									MWC Championship
	vs									BOWL GAME

Pointspread Analysis Non-Conference		Pointspread Analysis Conference
0-14 S/U vs Non-Conf. as 20.5 point or more Dog since 1985		vs Air Force - Air Force leads series 37-21-1
2-9 S/U vs Non-Conf. as 15.5-20 point Dog since 1986		1-7 S/U @ home vs Air Force as 3.5 point or more Dog since 1985
7-2 ATS vs Non-Conf. as 15.5-20 point Dog since 1987		7-2 O/U vs Air Force as 3.5 point or more Dog since 2008
3-12 S/U vs Non-Conf. as 10.5-15 point Dog since 1987		0-6 S/U @ Air Force as 6 point or more Dog since 2006
1-11 S/U vs Non-Conf. as 3.5-7 point Dog since 1993		0-4 ATS vs Air Force as 7.5-11 point favorite since 1997
4-12-1 O/U vs Non-Conf. as 3.5-7 point Dog since 1998		3-0 O/U vs Air Force as 3.5-7 point favorite since 1994
11-1 S/U vs Non-Conf. as 15.5 point or more favorite since 1990		0-10 S/U vs Boise State as 6.5 point or more Dog since 2011
Bowl Games		Game 5-0 O/U vs Hawaii since 2012
0-4 S/U & ATS in Bowl Games since 2014		5-1 ATS vs Hawaii since 1997
0-3 O/U in Liberty Bowl		vs Hawaii - Colorado State leads series 15-10
3-0 O/U in New Mexico Bowl		7-1 S/U vs Hawaii as 30 point or less favorite since 1995
Dog		5-0 O/U vs Hawaii as 20.5 point or less favorite since 2012
0-29 S/U as 20.5 point or more Dog since 1985		vs New Mexico - Colorado State leads series 42-25
0-8 S/U as 15.5-20 point Dog since 1995		9-0 S/U vs New Mexico as favorite since 2010
1-9 S/U @ home as 10.5-15 point Dog since 2006		5-0 S/U @ New Mexico since 2011
3-15 S/U as 7.5-10 point Dog since 1994		7-0 S/U & ATS vs New Mexico as 7 point or less Dog since 1985
2-8 S/U @ home as 7.5-10 point Dog since 1988		5-1 S/U @ New Mexico as 3.5-7 point favorite since 1994
Favorite		10-1 S/U vs Nevada as favorite since 1997
5-1 S/U on road as 3.5-7 point favorite since 2011		vs Nevada - Colorado State leads series 12-4
8-1 S/U on road as 7.5-10 point favorite since 1999		4-0 S/U vs UNLV as 3.5-7 point favorite since 2000
8-1 S/U on road as 10.5-15 point favorite since 1996		Game 5-1 O/U vs San Jose State since 2011
6-0 O/U on road as 10.5-15 point favorite since 1997		vs San Jose State - Colorado State leads series 6-4
2-9 ATS on road as 10.5-15 point favorite since 1986		vs Utah State - Colorado State leads series 39-35-2
20-3 S/U as 15.5-20 point favorite since 1992		5-0 S/U vs Utah State as favorite since 1994
22-0 S/U as 20,5 point or more favorite since 1990		vs Wyoming - Colorado State leads series 59-48-5
6-0 O/U as 20.5-25 point favorite since 2002		0-4 S/U @ home vs Wyoming as 3 point or more Dog since 1988
12-1 S/U in 1st home game of season since 2008	SD STATE	5-1 S/U & ATS vs Wyoming as 3.5 point or less favorite since 1995
8-1 ATS in 1st home game of season since 2012	SD STATE	5-1 S/U vs Wyoming as 9 point or more favorite since 1994
9-2 O/U in 1st home game of season since 2007	SD STATE	0-5 ATS vs Wyoming as 11 point or more favorite since 1994
2-8 ATS after playing New Mexico since 2009	Utah State	
1-9 O/U prior to playing Air Force since 2010	Wyoming	5-0 ATS on road vs ranked teams since 2012
6-2 S/U after playing Boise State since 2012	Wyoming	0-22 S/U vs ranked teams since 2004
7-2 S/U in final home game of season since 2012	NEVADA	0-25 S/U on road vs ranked teams all time

Copyright © 2021 by Steve's Football Bible, LLC

CONNECTICIUT HUSKIES AMERICAN East

2019-Connecticut		Opponent	Uconn	Opp	S/U	Line	ATS	Total	O/U	
8/29/2019	vs	WAGNER	24	21	W	-23.0	L	NT	---	
9/7/2019	vs	ILLINOIS	23	31	L	21.5	W	59.0	U	
9/21/2019	@	Indiana	3	38	L	26.0	L	56.0	U	
9/28/2019	@	Central Florida	21	56	L	42.0	W	64.5	O	
10/5/2019	vs	SOUTH FLORIDA	22	48	L	11.0	L	48.0	O	
10/12/2019	@	Tulane	7	49	L	33.5	L	57.5	U	
10/19/2019	vs	HOUSTON	17	24	L	21.5	W	56.0	U	
10/26/2019	@	Massachusetts	56	35	W	-9.5	W	62.0	O	
11/1/2019	vs	NAVY	10	56	L	26.5	L	54.5	O	
11/9/2019	@	Cincinnati	3	48	L	33.5	L	53.0	U	
11/23/2019	vs	EAST CAROLINA	24	31	L	14.5	W	64.0	U	
11/30/2019	@	Temple	17	49	L	27.0	L	48.0	O	
Coach: Randy Edsall		Season Record >>	227	486	2-10	ATS>>	5-7	O/U>>	5-6	
2018-Connecticut		Opponent	Uconn	Opp	S/U	Line	ATS	Total	O/U	
8/30/2018	vs	CENTRAL FLORIDA	17	56	L	24.0	L	69.0	O	
9/8/2018	@	Boise State	7	62	L	34.0	L	64.0	O	
9/15/2018	vs	RHODE ISLAND	56	49	W	-9.5	L	NT	---	"Ramnapping Trophy"
9/22/2018	@	Syracuse	21	51	L	30.5	W	75.5	U	
9/29/2018	vs	CINCINNATI	7	49	L	16.5	L	62.0	U	
10/6/2018	@	Memphis	14	55	L	36.0	L	76.0	U	
10/20/2018	@	South Florida	30	38	L	33.5	W	67.5	O	
10/27/2018	vs	MASSACHUSETTS	17	22	L	3.5	L	62.5	U	
11/3/2018	@	Tulsa	14	49	L	19.0	L	60.0	O	
11/10/2018	vs	SMU	50	62	L	18.0	W	65.5	O	
11/17/2018	@	East Carolina	21	55	L	17.5	L	71.5	O	
11/24/2018	vs	TEMPLE	7	57	L	31.0	L	69.0	U	
Coach: Randy Edsall		Season Record >>	261	605	1-11	ATS>>	3-9	O/U>>	6-5	
2017-Connecticut		Opponent	Uconn	Opp	S/U	Line	ATS	Total	O/U	
8/31/2017	vs	HOLY CROSS	27	20	W	-21.5	L	59.0	U	
9/16/2017	@	Virginia	16	38	L	11.5	L	51.5	O	
9/24/2017	vs	EAST CAROLINA	38	41	L	-5.0	L	63.5	O	
9/30/2017	@	Smu	28	49	L	16.0	L	74.5	O	
10/6/2017	vs	MEMPHIS	31	70	L	16.0	L	76.0	O	
10/14/2017	@	Temple	28	24	W	10.5	W	57.5	U	
10/21/2017	vs	TULSA	20	14	W	4.0	W	76.5	U	
10/28/2017	vs	MISSOURI	12	52	L	13.0	L	75.5	U	
11/4/2017	vs	SOUTH FLORIDA	20	37	L	23.5	W	63.5	U	
11/11/2017	@	Central Florida	24	59	L	39.5	W	65.0	O	
11/18/2017	@	Boston College	16	39	L	21.0	L	51.0	O	Fenway Park
11/25/2017	@	Cincinnati	21	22	L	6.5	W	58.5	U	
Coach: Randy Edsall		Season Record >>	281	465	3-9	ATS>>	5-7	O/U>>	6-6	
2016-Connecticut		Opponent	Uconn	Opp	S/U	Line	ATS	Total	O/U	
9/1/2016	vs	MAINE	24	21	W	-27.0	L	NT	---	
9/10/2016	@	Navy	24	28	L	3.5	L	44.0	O	
9/17/2016	vs	VIRGINIA	13	10	W	-3.0	T	48.0	U	
9/24/2016	vs	SYRACUSE	24	31	L	-1.5	L	57.5	U	
9/29/2016	@	Houston	14	42	L	27.5	L	48.5	O	
10/8/2016	vs	CINCINNATI	20	9	W	3.0	W	48.5	U	
10/15/2016	@	South Florida	27	42	L	20.0	W	53.5	O	
10/22/2016	vs	CENTRAL FLORIDA	16	24	L	4.5	L	46.5	U	
10/29/2016	@	East Carolina	3	41	L	6.5	L	54.0	U	
11/4/2016	vs	TEMPLE	0	21	L	10.0	L	44.0	U	
11/19/2016	@	Boston College	0	30	L	9.0	L	36.0	U	
11/26/2016	vs	TULANE	13	38	L	1.5	L	36.5	O	
Coach: Bob Diaco		Season Record >>	178	337	3-9	ATS>>	2-9-1	O/U>>	4-7	

Copyright © 2021 by Steve's Football Bible, LLC

CONNECTICIUT HUSKIES   AMERICAN East

STADIUM: Pratt & Whitney Stadium @ Rentschler Field {38,066}			Location: Storrs, CT					COACH: Randy Edsall		
DATE		Opponent	Conn	Opp	S/U	Line	ATS	Total	O/U	Trends & Angles
8/28/2021	@	Fresno State								1st meeting
9/2/2021	vs	HOLY CROSS								vs Holy Cross - Holy Cross leads series 9-7-1
9/11/2021	vs	PURDUE								1st meeting
9/18/2021	@	Army								vs Army - UCONN leads series 5-2
9/25/2021	vs	WYOMING								1st meeting
10/2/2021	@	Vanderbilt								vs Vanderbilt - Vandy leads series 2-1
10/9/2021	@	Massachusetts								3-0 S/U @ Massachusetts since 1997
10/16/2021	vs	YALE								14-2 S/U vs Yale since 1982
10/23/2021	vs	MIDDLE TENNESSEE								vs Middle Tennessee - MTSU leads series 2-0
11/13/2021	@	Clemson								1st meeting
11/20/2021	@	Central Florida								vs Central Florida - UCF leads series 5-2
11/27/2021	vs	HOUSTON								vs Houston – Houston leads series 2-1
	vs									BOWL GAME

Pointspread Analysis Dog		Pointspread Analysis Non-Conference
0-23 S/U as 25.5 point or more Dog since 2000		3-20 S/U vs Non-Conf. as 10.5 point or more Dog since 2000
1-11 S/U as 20.5-25 point Dog since 2000		0-7 S/U vs Non-Conf. as 3 point or less Dog since 2007
0-9 S/U @ home as 15.5 point or more Dog since 2002		25-1 S/U vs Non-conf. as 7.5 point or more favorite since 2000
2-20 S/U as 15.5-20 point Dog since 2000		5-1 S/U vs Army as favorite since 2003
7-0 O/U on road as 15.5-20 point Dog since 2007		0-4 S/U vs Central Florida as Dog since 2016
0-6 S/U @ home as 10.5-15 point Dog since 2000		vs Massachusetts - UMass leads series 37-35-2
2-15 S/U as 10.5-15 point Dog since 2000		vs Yale - Yale leads series 32-17
2-8 ATS on road as 10.5-15 point Dog since 2005	Fresno State	0-7 S/U in 1st road game of season since 2013
0-6 S/U on road as 3.5-7 point Dog since 2012	HOLY CROSS	0-7 ATS in 1st home game of season since 2013
1-8 S/U on road as 3 point or less Dog since 2006	PURDUE	1-5-2 ATS in 2nd home game of season since 2011
2-8 O/U on road as 3 point or less Dog since 2006	Army	0-7 S/U in 2nd road game of season since 2012
Favorite	Army	1-6 ATS in 2nd road game of season since 2012
1-14-1 ATS as favorite since 2013	Clemson	0-6 S/U prior to playing Central Florida since 2013
0-11-1 ATS as home favorite since 2013		
0-11ATS as 3.5-7 point favorite since 2010		
1-9 O/U @ home as 3.5-7 point favorite since 2004		
12-1 O/U as 7.5-15 point favorite since 2003		
10-1 S/U as 10.5-15 point favorite since 2000		
17-1 S/U as 15.5 point or more favorite since 2003		1-22 S/U on road vs ranked teams all time

Print Version $34.99   **Print Version $39.99**   **Print Version $39.99**

These books available at numerous online retailers

Copyright © 2021 by Steve's Football Bible, LLC

DUKE BLUE DEVILS   ACC Coastal

2020-Duke		Opponent	Duke	Opp	S/U	Line	ATS	Total	O/U	
9/12/2020	@	Notre Dame	13	27	L	21.5	W	51.5	U	
9/19/2020	vs	BOSTON COLLEGE	6	26	L	-5.5	L	51.5	U	
9/26/2020	@	Virginia	20	38	L	4.5	L	45.5	O	
10/3/2020	vs	VIRGINIA TECH	31	38	L	10.5	W	54.0	O	
10/10/2020	@	Syracuse	38	24	W	-2.5	W	51.5	O	
10/17/2020	@	NC State	20	31	L	4.5	L	60.0	U	
10/31/2020	vs	CHARLOTTE	53	19	W	-11.5	W	55.0	O	
11/7/2020	vs	NORTH CAROLINA	24	56	L	11.0	L	63.0	O	"Victory Bell"
11/28/2020	@	Georgia Tech	33	56	L	-2.5	L	57.5	O	
12/5/2020	vs	MIAMI	0	48	L	14.0	L	62.5	U	
12/12/2020	@	Florida State	35	56	L	3.0	L	56.5	O	
Coach: David Cutcliffe		Season Record >>	273	419	2-9	ATS>>	4-7	O/U>>	7-4	
2019-Duke		Opponent	Duke	Opp	S/U	Line	ATS	Total	O/U	
8/31/2019	vs	Alabama	3	42	L	33.5	L	56.5	U	Mercedes Benz Stadium
9/7/2019	vs	NORTH CAROLINA A&T	45	13	W	-27.5	W	NT	---	
9/14/2019	@	Middle Tennessee	41	18	W	-6.5	W	51.0	O	
9/27/2019	@	Virginia Tech	45	10	W	2.5	W	51.5	O	
10/5/2019	vs	PITTSBURGH	30	33	L	-3.5	L	47.0	O	
10/12/2019	vs	GEORGIA TECH	41	23	W	-17.5	W	47.5	O	
10/19/2019	@	Virginia	14	48	L	3.0	L	45.0	O	
10/26/2019	@	North Carolina	17	20	L	3.0	T	53.5	U	"Victory Bell"
11/9/2019	vs	NOTRE DAME	7	38	L	7.0	L	49.5	U	
11/16/2019	vs	SYRACUSE	6	49	L	-9.0	L	49.0	O	
11/23/2019	@	Wake Forest	27	39	L	6.0	L	50.0	O	
11/30/2019	vs	MIAMI	27	17	W	9.0	W	44.0	T	
Coach: David Cutcliffe		Season Record >>	303	350	5-7	ATS>>	5-6-1	O/U>>	6-4-1	
2018-Duke		Opponent	Duke	Opp	S/U	Line	ATS	Total	O/U	
9/1/2018	vs	ARMY	34	14	W	-13.5	W	45.5	O	
9/8/2018	@	Northwestern	21	7	W	2.5	W	47.5	U	
9/15/2018	@	Baylor	40	27	W	2.5	W	49.0	O	
9/22/2018	vs	NORTH CAROLINA CENTRAL	55	13	W	-43.0	L	NT	---	
9/29/2018	vs	VIRGINIA TECH	14	31	L	-6.5	L	52.5	U	
10/13/2018	@	Georgia Tech	28	14	W	1.0	W	55.0	U	
10/20/2018	vs	VIRGINIA	14	28	L	-6.5	L	44.5	U	
10/27/2018	@	Pittsburgh	45	54	L	-3.0	L	45.5	O	
11/3/2018	@	Miami	20	12	W	8.5	W	50.5	U	
11/10/2018	vs	NORTH CAROLINA	42	35	W	-7.5	L	58.5	O	"Victory Bell"
11/17/2018	@	Clemson	6	35	L	28.5	L	59.5	U	
11/24/2018	vs	WAKE FOREST	7	59	L	-9.5	L	60.5	O	
12/27/2018	vs	Temple	56	27	W	3.5	W	56.5	O	Independence Bowl
Coach: David Cutcliffe		Season Record >>	382	356	8-5	ATS>>	6-7	O/U>>	6-6	
2017-Duke		Opponent	Duke	Opp	S/U	Line	ATS	Total	O/U	
9/2/2017	vs	NORTH CAROLINA CENTRAL	60	7	W	-35.5	W	49.0	O	
9/9/2017	vs	NORTHWESTERN	41	17	W	2.0	W	54.5	O	
9/16/2017	vs	BAYLOR	34	20	W	-10.5	W	60.5	U	
9/23/2017	@	North Carolina	27	17	W	1.5	W	61.5	U	"Victory Bell"
9/29/2017	vs	MIAMI	6	31	L	5.0	L	55.0	U	
10/7/2017	@	Virginia	21	28	L	PK	L	52.0	U	
10/14/2017	vs	FLORIDA STATE	10	17	L	7.0	T	44.5	U	
10/21/2017	vs	PITTSBURGH	17	24	L	-9.0	L	49.0	U	
10/28/2017	@	Virginia Tech	3	24	L	17.0	L	48.5	U	
11/11/2017	@	Army	16	21	L	-3.5	L	50.5	U	
11/18/2017	vs	GEORGIA TECH	43	20	W	7.0	W	49.0	O	
11/25/2017	@	Wake Forest	31	23	W	10.0	W	58.5	U	
12/26/2017	vs	Northern Illinois	36	14	W	-5.5	W	47.0	O	Quick Lane Bowl
Coach: David Cutcliffe		Season Record >>	345	263	7-6	ATS>>	7-5-1	O/U>>	4-9	

Copyright © 2021 by Steve's Football Bible, LLC

DUKE BLUE DEVILS   ACC Coastal

STADIUM: Wallace Wade Stadium {40,004}							Location: Durham, NC			COACH: David Cutcliffe	
DATE		Opponent	Duke	Opp	S/U	Line	ATS	Total	O/U	Trends & Angles	
9/4/2021	@	*Charlotte*								vs Charlotte - Duke leads series 1-0	
9/11/2021	vs	*NORTH CAROLINA A&T*								vs North Carolina A&T - Duke leads series 1-0	
9/18/2021	vs	*NORTHWESTERN*								1-6 S/U @ home vs Northwestern since 1996	
9/25/2021	vs	*KANSAS*								vs Kansas - Series tied 1-1	
10/2/2021	@	North Carolina								Game 2-7 O/U @ North Carolina since 2003	
10/9/2021	vs	GEORGIA TECH								3-0 S/U & ATS @ home vs Georgia Tech since 2015	
10/16/2021	@	Virginia								0-6 S/U & ATS vs Virginia since 2015	
10/30/2021	@	Wake Forest								4-1 S/U @ Wake Forest since 2012	
11/6/2021	vs	PITTSBURGH								0-6 S/U @ home vs Pittsburgh since 1969	
11/13/2021	@	Virginia Tech								3-17 S/U vs Virginia Tech since 1982	
11/18/2021	vs	LOUISVILLE								vs Louisville - Louisville leads series 2-0	
11/27/2021	vs	MIAMI								2-8 S/U @ home vs Miami since 1983	
12/4/2021	vs									ACC Championship	
	vs									BOWL GAME	

Pointspread Analysis Non-Conference		Pointspread Analysis Conference
2-12 S/U vs Non-Conf. as 15.5 point or more Dog since 1986		vs Georgia Tech - Georgia Tech leads series 52-13-1
10-3 ATS vs Non-Conf. as 10.5-15 point Dog since 1985		6-1 ATS vs Georgia Tech since 2014
1-12-1 S/U vs Non-Conf. as 7.5-10 point Dog since 1984		1-20 S/U vs Georgia Tech as 10.5 point or more Dog since 1984
4-13 S/U vs Non-Conf. as 3.5-7 point Dog since 1984		3-14 S/U vs Miami since 1983
6-0 S/U & ATS vs Non-Conf. as 3 point or less Dog since 1992		vs Miami - Miami leads series 14-4
5-1 S/U vs Non-Conf. as 3 point or less favorite since 1989		0-9 S/U vs Miami as 12.5 point or more Dog since 1983
2-7-1 O/U vs Non-Conf. as 3.5-7 point favorite since 2005		vs North Carolina - UNC leads series 62-40-4
7-1 S/U vs Non-Conf. as 7.5-10 point favorite since 1985		1-12 S/U vs North Carolina as 12 point or more Dog since 1983
10-2 S/U vs Non-Conf. as 10.5-15 point favorite since 1990		0-5 ATS vs N. Carolina as 7.5 point or less favorite since 1990
14-0 S/U vs Non-Conf. as 15.5 point or more favorite since 1987		1-9 S/U vs Pittsburgh since 1969
11-3 ATS vs Non-Conf. as 15.5 point or more favorite since 1987		vs Pittsburgh - Pittsburgh leads series 15-9
vs Northwestern - Series tied 10-10		0-5 S/U & ATS vs Pittsburgh since 2015
3-8 S/U vs Northwestern since 1999		vs Virginia - UVA leads series 39-33
0-4 S/U vs Northwestern as 9 point or less Dog since 1996		1-15 S/U vs Virginia as 10 point or more Dog since 1990
0-3 S/U @ home vs Northwestern as Dog since 1996		3-1 S/U & ATS vs Virginia as 3 point or less Dog since 2010
0-3 S/U & ATS vs Northwestern as 8 point or less favorite since 1999		4-0 O/U vs Virginia as 3 point or less Dog since 2010
3-0 S/U vs Northwestern as 9 point or more favorite since 1988		vs Virginia Tech - VPI leads series 18-10
0-5 ATS vs Northwestern as favorite since 1989		1-11 S/U vs Virginia Tech as 12.5 point or more Dog since 1984
Bowl Games		vs Wake Forest - Duke leads series 58-40-2
8-0 O/U in Bowl Games since 1989		1-13 S/U vs Wake Forest as Dog since 2000
5-0 ATS in Bowl Games since 2013		7-1-1 ATS @ Wake Forest since 2004
Dog		1-10 S/U vs Wake Forest as 6 point or more Dog since 1984
0-35 S/U as 25.5 point or more Dog since 1984		3-0 S/U & ATS vs Wake F. as 13 point or more favorite since 1989
1-27 S/U as 20.5-25 point Dog since 1984		**Favorite**
0-16 S/U @ home as 20.5 point or more Dog since 1987		8-2 O/U as 3 point or less favorite since 2008
2-24 S/U on road as 15.5-20 point Dog since 1983		3-19-1 O/U as 3.5-7 point favorite since 2005
0-12 S/U @ home as 15.5-20 point Dog since 1990		9-1 S/U on road as 7.5 point or more favorite since 1988
2-13 S/U @ home as 10.5-15 point Dog since 2005		15-0 S/U @ home as 15.5 point or more favorite since 1987
3-15 S/U on road as 10.5-15 point Dog since 1998		13-2 ATS @ home as 15.5 point or more favorite since 1987
7-26 S/U as 7.5-10 point Dog since 1996		
2-13 S/U @ home as 7.5-10 point Dog since 1996	Charlotte	1-7 O/U in 1st road game of season since 2013
2-14 S/U @ home as 3.5-7 point Dog since 2004	NC A&T	8-1 S/U & ATS in 1st home game of season since 2012
11-4 S/U as 3 point or less Dog since 2010	KANSAS	6-0 ATS after playing Northwestern since 2008
11-3-1 ATS as 3 point or less Dog since 2010	North Carolina	1-11 S/U prior to playing Georgia Tech since 2009
12-5 O/U as 3 point or less Dog since 2002	North Carolina	3-10 O/U prior to playing Georgia Tech since 2008
	PITTSBURGH	8-3 ATS prior to playing Virginia Tech since 2010

Copyright © 2021 by Steve's Football Bible, LLC

EAST CAROLINA PIRATES   AMERICAN East

2020-East Carolina		Opponent	ECU	Opp	S/U	Line	ATS	Total	O/U	
9/26/2020	vs	CENTRAL FLORIDA	28	51	L	27.5	W	77.0	O	
10/3/2020	@	Georgia State	29	49	L	-1.5	L	70.0	O	
10/10/2020	@	South Florida	44	24	W	5.0	W	58.0	O	
10/17/2020	vs	NAVY	23	27	L	3.0	L	55.5	U	
10/30/2020	@	Tulsa	30	34	L	17.0	W	59.5	O	
11/7/2020	vs	TULANE	21	38	L	3.5	L	63.5	U	
11/13/2020	@	Cincinnati	17	55	L	27.0	L	56.0	O	
11/21/2020	@	Temple	28	3	W	-7.0	W	53.0	U	
11/28/2020	vs	SMU	52	38	W	12.5	W	72.0	O	
Coach: Mike Houston		Season Record >>	272	319	3-6	ATS>>	5-4	O/U>>	6-3	
2019-East Carolina		Opponent	ECU	Opp	S/U	Line	ATS	Total	O/U	
8/31/2019	@	NC State	6	34	L	17.5	L	51.5	U	"Victory Barrel"
9/7/2019	vs	GARDNER-WEBB	48	9	W	-31.0	W	NT	---	
9/14/2019	@	Navy	10	42	L	7.5	L	54.0	U	
9/21/2019	vs	WILLIAM & MARY	19	7	W	-14.0	L	NT	---	
9/28/2019	@	Old Dominion	24	21	W	3.0	W	46.5	U	
10/3/2019	vs	TEMPLE	17	27	L	12.5	W	46.5	U	
10/19/2019	@	Central Florida	28	41	L	34.0	W	64.5	O	
10/26/2019	vs	SOUTH FLORIDA	20	45	L	1.5	L	51.0	O	
11/2/2019	vs	CINCINNATI	43	46	L	24.0	W	48.5	O	
11/9/2019	@	Smu	51	59	L	22.5	W	74.0	O	
11/23/2019	@	Connecticut	31	24	W	-14.5	L	64.0	U	
11/30/2019	vs	TULSA	24	49	L	7.0	L	64.0	O	
Coach: Mike Houston		Season Record >>	321	404	4-8	ATS>>	6-6	O/U>>	5-5	
2018-East Carolina		Opponent	ECU	Opp	S/U	Line	ATS	Total	O/U	
9/2/2018	vs	NORTH CAROLINA A&T	23	28	L	-13.0	L	NT	---	
9/8/2018	vs	NORTH CAROLINA	41	19	W	15.5	W	59.0	O	
9/22/2018	@	South Florida	13	20	L	19.5	W	68.5	U	
9/29/2018	vs	OLD DOMINION	37	35	W	-7.0	L	60.5	O	
10/6/2018	@	Temple	6	49	L	10.5	L	52.0	O	
10/13/2018	vs	HOUSTON	20	42	L	16.0	L	69.5	U	
10/20/2018	vs	CENTRAL FLORIDA	10	37	L	21.5	L	65.0	U	
11/3/2018	vs	MEMPHIS	41	59	L	10.5	L	66.0	O	
11/10/2018	@	Tulane	18	24	L	10.5	L	54.0	U	
11/17/2018	vs	CONNECTICUT	55	21	W	-17.5	W	71.5	O	
11/23/2018	@	Cincinnati	6	56	L	16.5	L	49.5	O	
12/1/2018	@	NC State	3	58	L	26.0	L	60.5	O	"Victory Barrel"
Coach: Scottie Montgomery		Season Record >>	273	448	3-9	ATS>>	3-9	O/U>>	7-4	
2017-East Carolina		Opponent	ECU	Opp	S/U	Line	ATS	Total	O/U	
9/2/2017	vs	JAMES MADISON	14	34	L	1.5	L	68.0	U	
9/9/2017	@	West Virginia	20	56	L	25.5	L	67.5	O	
9/16/2017	vs	VIRGINIA TECH	17	64	L	27.0	L	60.0	O	
9/24/2017	@	Connecticut	41	38	W	5.0	W	63.5	O	
9/30/2017	vs	SOUTH FLORIDA	31	61	L	22.5	L	73.0	O	
10/7/2017	vs	TEMPLE	10	34	L	3.5	L	58.5	U	
10/14/2017	@	Central Florida	21	63	L	35.0	L	71.0	O	
10/21/2017	vs	BYU	33	17	W	5.5	W	55.0	U	
11/4/2017	@	Houston	27	52	L	23.5	L	62.5	O	
11/11/2017	vs	TULANE	24	31	L	6.5	L	64.0	U	{OT}
11/18/2017	vs	CINCINNATI	48	20	W	4.5	W	67.0	O	
11/25/2017	@	Memphis	13	70	L	29.5	L	81.5	O	
Coach: Scottie Montgomery		Season Record >>	299	540	3-9	ATS>>	3-9	O/U>>	8-4	

Copyright © 2021 by Steve's Football Bible, LLC

EAST CAROLINA PIRATES   AMERICAN East

STADIUM: Dowdy-Ficklen Stadium {50,000}		Location: Greenville, NC					COACH: Mike Houston		
DATE		Opponent	ECU	Opp	S/U	Line	ATS	Total	O/U	Trends & Angles

DATE		Opponent	ECU	Opp	S/U	Line	ATS	Total	O/U	Trends & Angles
9/2/2021	vs	*Appalachian State*								vs App. State - App State leads series 18-8
9/11/2021	vs	*SOUTH CAROLINA*								0-4 S/U vs South Carolina since 2011
9/18/2021	@	*Marshall*								vs Marshall - ECU leads series 10-5
9/25/2021	vs	*CHARLESTON SOUTHERN*								1st meeting
10/2/2021	vs	TULANE								8-2 S/U @ home vs Tulane since 1991
10/9/2021	@	Central Florida								vs Central Florida - ECU leads series 10-9
10/23/2021	@	Houston								Game 8-3 O/U vs Houston since 2000
10/30/2021	vs	SOUTH FLORIDA								0-5 S/U @ home vs USF since 2002 {1-4 ATS}
11/4/2021	vs	TEMPLE								1-6 S/U vs Temple since 2014
11/13/2021	@	Memphis								16-3 ATS vs Memphis since 1994
11/20/2021	@	Navy								0-5 S/U & ATS vs Navy since 2012
11/27/2021	vs	CINCINNATI								vs Cincinnati - East Carolina leads series 13-11
12/4/2021	vs									AAC Championship
	vs									BOWL GAME

Pointspread Analysis Non-Conference		Pointspread Analysis Conference
2-36 S/U vs Non-Conf. as 15.5 point or more Dog since 1985		vs Cincinnati - East Carolina leads series 13-11
8-1 O/U vs Non-Conf. as 3.5-7 point favorite since 2000		8-0 S/U vs Cincinnati as 5 point or more favorite since 1988
19-1-1 S/U vs Non-Conf. as 7.5 point or more favorite since 1989		5-0 S/U @ home vs Cincinnati as favorite since 1987
4-0 S/U vs Marshall as favorite since 2008		3-0 S/U @ Central Florida as favorite since 2006
0-10 S/U vs South Carolina as 9 point or more Dog since 1984		0-6 S/U vs UCF as 8 point or more Dog since 2010
vs South Carolina - USC leads series 14-5		vs Houston - Series tied 7-7
Bowl Games		0-3 S/U vs Houston as 11 point or more Dog since 2011
2-7 S/U in Bowl Games since 2001		12-1 S/U & ATS vs Memphis as favorite since 1991
Dog		vs Memphis - East Carolina leads series 15-8
0-9 S/U as 30.5 point or more Dog since 1985		8-2 ATS @ Memphis since 1994
1-13 S/U as 25.5-30 point Dog since 1986		0-7 S/U vs Memphis as 8 point or more Dog since 1992
0-12 S/U on road as 20.5-25 point dog since 1985		Game 5-2 O/U vs Navy since 2010
1-19 S/U as 20.5-25 point Dog since 1985		vs Navy - Navy leads series 7-1
1-17 S/U on road as 15.5-20 point Dog since 1984		vs South Florida - USF leads series 9-2
1-16 S/U as 15.5-20 point Dog since 2003		2-7 ATS vs South Florida since 2004
5-1 ATS @ home as 15.5-20 Dog since 2003		1-7 S/U vs South Florida as Dog since 2003
6-26 S/U on road as 10.5-15 point Dog since 1984		2-5 ATS vs Temple since 2014
2-10 S/U @ home as 10.5-15 point Dog since 1985		Game 2-5 O/U vs Temple since 2014
3-18 S/U on road as 7.5-10 point Dog since 1987		vs Temple - Temple leads series 10-8
3-12 S/U & ATS @ home as 3 point or less dog since 1994		0-3 S/U @ Temple as Dog since 1986
Favorite		0-5 S/U & ATS vs Tulane as Dog since 1997
2-7 S/U @ home as 3 point or less favorite since 2001		11-1 S/U vs Tulane as favorite since 1991 {8-0 @ home}
0-6 ATS on road as 7.5-10 point favorite since 2001		Game 2-10 O/U vs Tulane since 2002
0-7 S/U as 7.5-10 point favorite since 2008		vs Tulane - East Carolina leads series 11-6
7-0 S/U @ home as 7.5-10 point favorite since 1996	Marshall	2-17 S/U in 1st road game of season since 2002
15-3 S/U @ home as 10.5-15 point favorite since 1994	CHARLESTON	11-2 S/U in 2nd home game of season since 2008
9-2 S/U on road as 10.5-15 point favorite since 1988	Central Fla.	13-0 O/U after playing Tulane since 2000
33-2 S/U as 15.5 point or more favorite since 1989	USF	1-7 ATS prior to playing Temple since 1995
	USF	2-9 ATS after playing Houston since 1998
	Navy	2-6 O/U prior to playing Cincinnati since 2002
4-39 S/U on road vs ranked teams all time	Navy	3-8 ATS in final road game of season since 2010
2-25 S/U vs Top 10 ranked teams all time	CINCINNATI	10-1 O/U in final home game of season since 2010

Copyright © 2021 by Steve's Football Bible, LLC

 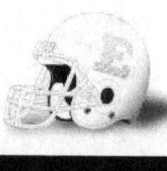

EASTERN MICHIGAN EAGLES   MAC West

2020-Eastern Michigan		Opponent	ECU	Opp	S/U	Line	ATS	Total	O/U	
11/4/2020	@	Kent State	23	27	L	4.5	W	65.5	U	
11/11/2020	@	Ball State	31	38	L	8.0	W	61.5	O	
11/18/2020	vs	TOLEDO	28	45	L	6.5	L	62.5	O	
11/28/2020	vs	CENTRAL MICHIGAN	23	31	L	6.0	L	58.0	U	
12/5/2020	@	Western Michigan	53	42	W	13.0	W	67.5	O	
12/12/2020	vs	NORTHERN ILLINOIS	41	33	W	-6.0	W	55.5	O	
Coach: Chris Creighton		Season Record >>	199	216	2-4	ATS>>	4-2	O/U>>	4-2	
2019-Eastern Michigan		Opponent	ECU	Opp	S/U	Line	ATS	Total	O/U	
8/31/2019	@	Coastal Carolina	30	23	W	-4.5	W	54.0	U	
9/7/2019	@	Kentucky	17	38	L	15.5	L	52.0	O	
9/14/2019	@	Illinois	34	31	W	7.5	W	57.0	O	
9/21/2019	vs	CENTRAL CONNECTICUT	34	29	W	NL	---	NT	---	
10/5/2019	@	Central Michigan	16	42	L	-3.5	L	54.0	O	
10/12/2019	vs	BALL STATE	23	29	L	-2.0	L	57.0	O	
10/19/2019	vs	WESTERN MICHIGAN	34	27	W	9.5	W	61.0	T	
10/26/2019	@	Toledo	34	37	L	2.5	L	53.5	O	{OT}
11/2/2019	vs	BUFFALO	14	43	L	1.5	L	49.5	O	
11/12/2019	@	Akron	42	14	W	-17.0	W	44.5	O	
11/19/2019	@	Northern Illinois	45	17	W	3.5	W	57.5	O	
11/29/2019	vs	KENT STATE	26	34	L	-3.0	L	68.5	U	
12/26/2019	vs	Pittsburgh	30	34	L	12.5	W	51.0	O	Quick Lane Bowl
Coach: Chris Creighton		Season Record >>	379	398	6-7	ATS>>	6-6	O/U>>	9-2-1	
2018-Eastern Michigan		Opponent	ECU	Opp	S/U	Line	ATS	Total	O/U	
8/31/2018	vs	MONMOUTH	51	17	W	-22.5	W	NT	---	
9/8/2018	@	Purdue	20	19	W	15.0	W	50.0	U	
9/15/2018	@	Buffalo	28	35	L	3.0	L	54.0	O	
9/22/2018	@	San Diego State	20	23	L	11.0	W	48.0	U	{OT}
9/29/2018	vs	NORTHERN ILLINOIS	23	26	L	-3.5	L	50.5	U	{3 OT}
10/6/2018	@	Western Michigan	24	27	L	4.5	W	58.5	U	
10/13/2018	vs	TOLEDO	28	26	W	2.0	W	63.0	U	
10/20/2018	@	Ball State	42	20	W	-3.0	W	44.0	O	
10/27/2018	vs	ARMY	22	37	L	1.5	L	47.5	O	
11/3/2018	vs	CENTRAL MICHIGAN	17	7	W	-14.5	L	46.5	U	
11/10/2018	vs	AKRON	27	7	W	-11.0	W	41.5	U	
11/23/2018	@	Kent State	28	20	W	-12.5	L	52.0	U	
12/15/2018	vs	Georgia Southern	21	23	L	3.0	W	45.5	U	Camelia Bowl
Coach: Chris Creighton		Season Record >>	351	287	7-6	ATS>>	8-5	O/U>>	3-9	
2017-Eastern Michigan		Opponent	ECU	Opp	S/U	Line	ATS	Total	O/U	
9/1/2017	vs	CHARLOTTE	24	7	W	-14.0	W	58.0	U	
9/9/2017	@	Rutgers	16	13	W	5.0	W	51.0	U	
9/23/2017	vs	OHIO	20	27	L	-1.5	L	53.5	U	{2 OT}
9/30/2017	@	Kentucky	20	24	L	14.0	W	50.0	U	
10/7/2017	@	Toledo	15	20	L	13.5	W	61.0	U	
10/14/2017	@	Army	27	28	L	4.0	W	50.5	O	
10/21/2017	vs	WESTERN MICHIGAN	17	20	L	2.0	L	51.5	U	{OT}
11/26/2017	@	Northern Illinois	27	30	L	7.5	W	47.0	O	{OT}
11/2/2017	vs	BALL STATE	56	14	W	-24.5	W	47.5	O	
11/8/2017	@	Central Michigan	30	42	L	-1.0	L	51.0	O	
11/15/2017	@	Miami-Ohio	27	24	W	1.5	W	51.0	T	
11/21/2017	vs	BOWLING GREEN	34	31	W	-14.0	L	60.0	O	
Coach: Chris Creighton		Season Record >>	313	280	5-7	ATS>>	8-4	O/U>>	5-6-1	

Copyright © 2021 by Steve's Football Bible, LLC

EASTERN MICHIGAN EAGLES   MAC West

STADIUM: Rynearson Stadium {30,200}			Location: Ypsilanti, MI					COACH: Chris Creighton
DATE		Opponent	EMU	Opp	S/U	Line	ATS	Total	O/U	Trends & Angles

DATE		Opponent	EMU	Opp	S/U	Line	ATS	Total	O/U	Trends & Angles
9/4/2021	vs	*ST. FRANCIS-PA*								1st meeting
9/11/2021	@	*Wisconsin*								vs Wisconsin - Wisconsin leads series 3-0
9/18/2021	@	*Massachusetts*								vs UMASS - UMASS leads series 2-0
9/25/2021	vs	*TEXAS STATE*								1st meeting
10/2/2021	@	Northern Illinois								2-9 S/U @ Northern Illinois since 1999
10/9/2021	vs	MIAMI-OHIO								0-6 S/U @ home vs Miami-Ohio since 1992
10/16/2021	vs	BALL STATE								vs Ball State - Ball State leads series 35-24-2
10/23/2021	@	Bowling Green								
11/2/2021	@	Toledo								0-9 S/U @ Toledo since 2001 {1-8 ATS}
11/9/2021	vs	OHIO								0-4 S/U @ home vs Ohio since 2006
11/16/2021	vs	WESTERN MICHIGAN								2-5 S/U vs Western Michigan since 2014
11/26/2021	@	Central Michigan								vs C. Michigan - CMU leads series 62-30-6
12/3/2021	vs									MAC Championship
	vs									BOWL GAME

Pointspread Analysis — Non-Conference

- 0-50 S/U vs Non-Conf. as 15.5 point or more Dog since 1990
- 1-14 ATS vs Non-Conf. as 20.5-25 point Dog since 1995
- 6-0 O/U vs Non-Conf. as 20.5-25 point Dog since 1995
- 2-8 S/U vs Non-Conf. as 10.5-15 point Dog since 1990
- 1-7 S/U vs Non-Conf. as 7.5-10 point Dog since 1993
- 7-1 S/U vs Non-Conf. as 7.5 point or more favorite since 1995

Dog
- 5-0 O/U as 30.5 point or more Dog since 2013
- 1-72 S/U as 20.5 point or more Dog since 1990
- 0-10 S/U @ home as 20.5 point or more Dog since 2001
- 10-1 O/U on road as 20.5-25 point Dog since 2009
- 2-13-1 ATS as 20.5-25 point Dog since 2009
- 13-3 O/U as 20.5-25 point Dog since 2009
- 0-21 S/U on road as 15.5-20 point Dog since 1991
- 7-0 ATS as 10.5-15 point Dog since 2015
- 2-11 S/U on road as 7.5-10 point Dog since 1998
- 2-12 S/U @ home as 7.5-10 point Dog since 1990
- 3-22-1 S/U @ home as 3.5-7 point Dog since 1990
- 12-2 ATS as road dog last 10 times

Favorite
- 0-6 S/U & ATS @ home as 3 point or less favorite since 2008
- 9-2 S/U as 7.5-10 point favorite since 1989
- 9-0 S/U @ home as 10.5-15 point favorite since 1989
- 20-2 S/U as 15.5 point or more favorite since 1989
- 6-0 S/U @ home as 15.5 point or more favorite since 2000

Pointspread Analysis — Conference

- 1-9 S/U @ home vs Ball State as Dog since 1990
- 0-11 S/U vs Ball State as 2.5-5.5 point Dog since 1989
- 1-10 S/U vs Bowling Green as Dog since 1991
- 0-5 S/U vs C. Michigan as 18.5 point or more Dog since 1992
- 0-6 S/U vs C. Michigan as 7.0-10 point Dog since 1990
- 1-9 S/U vs Miami-Ohio since 1994
- 0-5 S/U @ home vs Miami-Ohio as Dog since 1992
- Game 0-4-1 O/U vs Miami-Ohio since 2005
- 0-4 S/U vs Miami-Ohio as 13.5 point or more Dog since 1991
- 0-7 S/U vs Miami-Ohio as 2.0-11 point Dog since 1990
- 3-17 S/U vs Northern Illinois since 2001 {2W}
- 3-17 S/U vs Northern Illinois as Dog since 1998
- vs Northern Illinois - NIU leads series 33-16-2
- 0-12 S/U vs N. Illinois as 16.5 point or more Dog since 2001
- 1-4 S/U & ATS vs N.Illinois as 7.5 point or less Dog since 1999
- 1-9 S/U vs Ohio as Dog since 1996
- 1-8-1 ATS @ home vs Ohio since 1990
- 5-0 S/U vs Ohio as 4 point or more favorite since 1989
- 0-6 S/U & ATS vs Ohio as 8 point or more Dog since 1997
- 2-19 S/U vs Toledo since 2000
- 1-19 S/U vs Toledo as Dog since 2000
- vs Toledo - Toledo leads series 36-12
- 1-15 S/U @ Toledo as Dog since 1990
- 0-15 S/U vs Toledo as 13 point or more Dog since 1992
- vs Western Michigan - WMU leads series 34-19-2
- 0-10 S/U vs W. Michigan as 15 point or more Dog since 1992
- 0-4 S/U @ home vs W. Michigan as 13 point or more Dog since 2001

4-18 S/U in 1st road game of season since 1999	Wisconsin
6-2 ATS in 2nd road game of season since 2013	Massachusetts
1-12 S/U in 2nd road game of season since 2008	Massachusetts
2-11 ATS in 2nd home game of season since 2008	TEXAS STATE
3-11 S/U prior to playing Ball State since 2007	MIAMI-OHIO
2-11 S/U after playing Ball State since 2008	B. Green
2-9 ATS after playing Ball State since 2010	B. Green
3-10 S/U prior to playing Toledo since 2008	B. Green
2-12 S/U prior to playing Western Michigan	OHIO
9-2 O/U after playing Toledo since 2010	OHIO
9-2-1 ATS after playing Toledo since 2009	OHIO
5-12 ATS in final home game of season since 2004	W. MICHIGAN
2-18 S/U prior to playing Central Michigan since 2000	W. MICHIGAN
4-16 S/U after playing Western Michigan since 2001	C. Michigan
14-2 ATS in final road game of season since 2005	C. Michigan

Copyright © 2021 by Steve's Football Bible, LLC

FLORIDA GATORS  SEC East

2020-Florida		Opponent	FLA	Opp	S/U	Line	ATS	Total	O/U	
9/26/2020	@	Mississippi	51	35	W	-14.0	W	58.5	O	
10/3/2020	vs	SOUTH CAROLINA	38	24	W	-15.0	L	56.5	O	
10/10/2020	@	Texas A&M	38	41	L	-5.5	L	60.0	O	
10/31/2020	vs	MISSOURI	41	17	W	-13.5	W	62.5	U	
11/7/2020	vs	Georgia	44	28	W	2.5	W	51.5	O	"Okefenokee Oar"
11/14/2020	vs	ARKANSAS	63	35	W	-17.0	W	62.0	O	
11/21/2020	@	Vanderbilt	38	17	W	-31.0	L	68.0	U	
11/28/2020	vs	KENTUCKY	34	10	W	-23.5	W	60.5	U	
12/5/2020	@	Tennessee	31	19	W	-18.5	L	63.0	U	
12/12/2020	vs	LSU	34	37	L	-23.0	L	66.0	O	
12/19/2020	vs	Alabama	46	52	L	16.5	W	74.0	O	SEC Championship
12/30/2020	vs	Oklahoma	20	55	L	8.5	L	65.0	O	Cotton Bowl
Coach: Dan Mullen		Season Record >>	478	370	8-4	ATS>>	6-6	O/U>>	8-4	
2019-Florida		Opponent	FLA	Opp	S/U	Line	ATS	Total	O/U	
8/24/2019	vs	Miami	24	20	W	-7.0	L	46.0	U	"Seminole War Canoe Trophy"
9/7/2019	vs	TENNESSEE-MARTIN	45	0	W	-45.0	T	NT	---	
9/14/2019	@	Kentucky	29	21	W	-9.5	L	46.5	O	
9/21/2019	vs	TENNESSEE	34	3	W	-14.0	W	48.5	U	
9/28/2019	vs	TOWSON	38	0	W	-36.5	W	NT	---	
10/5/2019	vs	AUBURN	23	14	W	2.5	W	48.5	U	
10/12/2019	@	Lsu	28	42	L	14.0	T	55.0	O	
10/19/2019	@	South Carolina	38	27	W	-3.5	W	45.0	O	
11/2/2019	vs	Georgia	17	24	L	6.0	L	47.5	U	"Okefenokee Oar"
11/9/2019	vs	VANDERBILT	56	0	W	-27.0	W	49.5	O	
11/16/2019	@	Missouri	23	6	W	-6.5	W	51.0	U	
11/30/2019	vs	FLORIDA STATE	40	17	W	-16.5	W	55.5	O	"Govenor's Cup"
12/30/2019	vs	Virginia	36	28	W	-16.5	L	55.0	O	Orange Bowl
Coach: Dan Mullen		Season Record >>	431	202	11-2	ATS>>	7-4-2	O/U>>	6-5	
2018-Florida		Opponent	FLA	Opp	S/U	Line	ATS	Total	O/U	
9/1/2018	vs	CHARLESTON SOUTHERN	53	6	W	-43.0	W	NT	---	
9/8/2018	vs	KENTUCKY	16	27	L	-13.5	L	52.5	U	
9/15/2018	vs	COLORADO STATE	48	10	W	-21.5	W	59.0	U	
9/22/2018	@	Tennessee	47	21	W	-3.5	W	45.5	O	
9/29/2018	@	Mississippi State	13	6	W	7.0	W	51.0	U	
10/6/2018	vs	LSU	27	19	W	1.5	W	44.5	O	
10/13/2018	@	Vanderbilt	37	27	W	-10.0	T	52.0	O	
10/27/2018	vs	Georgia	17	36	L	7.0	L	52.5	O	"Okefenokee Oar"
11/3/2018	vs	MISSOURI	17	38	L	-5.0	L	58.5	U	
11/10/2018	vs	SOUTH CAROLINA	35	31	W	-6.5	L	54.0	O	
11/17/2018	vs	IDAHO	63	10	W	-41.5	W	NT	---	
11/24/2018	@	Florida State	41	14	W	-4.5	W	52.0	O	"Govenor's Cup"
12/29/2018	vs	Michigan	41	15	W	4.0	W	51.0	O	Chick-Fil-A Peach Bowl
Coach: Dan Mullen		Season Record >>	455	260	10-3	ATS>>	8-4-1	O/U>>	7-4	
2017-Florida		Opponent	FLA	Opp	S/U	Line	ATS	Total	O/U	
9/2/2017	vs	Michigan	17	33	L	4.0	L	46.0	O	AT&T Stadium
9/16/2017	vs	TENNESSEE	26	20	W	-6.5	L	51.0	U	
9/23/2017	@	Kentucky	28	27	W	-3.0	L	44.5	O	
9/30/2017	vs	VANDERBILT	38	24	W	-9.0	W	39.0	O	
10/7/2017	vs	LSU	16	17	L	1.5	W	44.5	U	
10/14/2017	vs	TEXAS A&M	17	19	L	-3.5	L	49.5	U	
10/28/2017	vs	Georgia	7	42	L	13.0	L	43.5	O	"Okefenokee Oar"
11/4/2017	@	Missouri	16	45	L	1.0	L	61.5	U	
11/11/2017	@	South Carolina	20	28	L	4.5	L	40.5	O	
11/18/2017	vs	ALABAMA-BIRMINGHAM	36	7	W	-10.5	W	48.0	L	
11/25/2017	vs	FLORIDA STATE	22	38	L	5.0	L	43.5	O	"Govenor's Cup"
Coach: Jim McElwain		Season Record >>	243	300	4-7	ATS>>	3-8	O/U>>	6-5	

Copyright © 2021 by Steve's Football Bible, LLC

FLORIDA GATORS

SEC East

DATE		Opponent	Fla	Opp	S/U	Line	ATS	Total	O/U	Trends & Angles
STADIUM: Florida Field at Ben Hill Griffin Stadium {88,548}							Location: Gainesville, FL			COACH: Dan Mullen	
9/4/2021	vs	*FLORIDA ATLANTIC*								vs Florida Atlantic - Florida leads series 3-0
9/11/2021	@	*South Florida*								vs South Florida - Florida leads series 1-0
9/18/2021	vs	**ALABAMA**								0-7 S/U vs Alabama as Dog since 1992
9/25/2021	vs	**TENNESSEE**								8-0 S/U @ home vs Tennessee since 2005
10/2/2021	@	Kentucky								16-0 S/U @ Kentucky since 1988
10/9/2021	vs	**VANDERBILT**								22-1-1 S/U @ home vs Vandy since 1951
10/16/2021	@	Lsu								1-4 S/U @ LSU since 2011
10/30/2021	vs	Georgia								vs UGA - Team that wins S/U is 14-0 ATS since 2007
11/6/2021	@	South Carolina								Game 4-0 O/U vs South Carolina since 2017
11/13/2021	vs	*SAMFORD*								vs Samford - Florida leads series 2-0
11/20/2021	@	Missouri								Game 0-4 O/U vs Missouri since 2017
11/27/2021	vs	*FLORIDA STATE*								1-4 S/U & ATS @ home vs Florida State since 2011
12/4/2021	vs									SEC Championship
	vs									BOWL GAME

Pointspread Analysis
Non-Conference

0-7 S/U vs Non.Conf. as 10.5 point or more Dog since 1988

3-10 S/U & ATS vs Non-Conf. as 3.5-7 point Dog since 1984

16-2 S/U vs Non-Conf. as 3.5-7 point favorite since 1983

14-4 ATS vs Non-Conf. as 3.5-7 point favorite since 1983

11-2 S/U vs Non.Conf. as 10.5-15 point favorite since 1984

64-2-1 S/U vs Non-Conf. as 15.5 point or more favorite since 1984

Game 3-0 O/U vs Florida State since 2017

0-9 S/U vs Florida State as 7.5 point or more Dog since 1987

2-7 ATS vs Florida State as 7.5 point or more Dog since 1987

0-5 O/U vs Florida State as 7.5 point or more Dog since 1993

4-0 S/U & ATS vs Florida State as 5.5-7.5 point Dog since 1986

0-6 S/U & ATS vs Florida State as 3 point or less Dog since 1998

12-0 S/U vs Florida State as 3.5-20 point favorite since 1983

11-1 ATS vs Florida State as 3.5-20 point favorite since 1983

vs Florida State - Florida leads series 35-27-2

Bowl Games

4-0 S/U in Orange Bowl

3-0 vs Penn State in Bowl Games

7-2 S/U in Gator Bowl

3-0 S/U in Outback Bowl since 2006

4-1 O/U in Outback Bowl

0-3 S/U in Citrus Bowl since 2000

3-0 O/U in Citrus Bowl since 2000

7-3 S/U & ATS in Bowl Game since 2009

1-5 S/U & ATS in Bowl Games as 3.5-7 point Dog since 1977

4-0 S/U & ATS in Bowl Games as 3 point or less favorite since 2000

7-3 S/U vs ranked teams in Bowl games since 2006

8-2 O/U vs ranked teams in Bowl games since 2006

Dog

0-6 S/U as 15.5 point or more Dog since 1988

2-10 S/U as 10.5-15 point Dog since 1989

1-7 S/U as 7.5-10 point Dog since 2007

1-5 S/U on road as 7.5-10 point Dog since 2007

1-7 S/U & ATS as 3.5-7 point Dog since 2015

7-1 O/U as 3.5-7 point Dog since 2015

4-11 O/U as 3 point or less Dog since 2010

Favorite

10-2 S/U on road as 3.5-7 point favorite since 2006

9-2 ATS on road as 3.5-7 point favorite since 2007

7-0 S/U on road as 7.5-10 point favorite since 2003

26-3 S/U @ home as 10.5-15 point favorite since 1984

17-1 S/U on road as 10.5-15 point favorite since 1984

3-8 ATS @ home as 15.5-20 point favorite since 2001

Pointspread Analysis
Conference

vs Georgia - Georgia leads series 53-44-2

2-5 S/U & ATS vs Georgia as Dog since 2011

12-1 S/U vs Georgia as 9.5 point or more favorite since 1990

33-1 S/U vs Kentucky since 1987

vs Kentucky - Florida leads series 53-18

25-0 S/U vs Kentucky as 14 point or more favorite since 1983

12-0 S/U @ Kentucky as 10 point or more favorite since 1984

vs LSU - Florida leads series 33-31-3

11-2 S/U vs LSU as 10.5 point or more favorite since 1990

vs Missouri - Series tied 5-5

vs South Carolina - Florida leads series 29-9-3

0-3 S/U vs South Carolina as Dog since 2011

23-3 S/U vs South Carolina as favorite since 1992

20-0 S/U vs South Carolina as 7 point or more favorite since 1992

vs Tennessee - Florida leads series 30-20

7-1 ATS vs Tennessee as Dog since 1993

12-0 S/U vs Tennessee as favorite since 2005

15-1 S/U vs Tennessee since 2005

14-0 S/U vs Tennessee as 4.5-16 point favorite since 1984

29-1 S/U vs Vanderbilt since 1989

vs Vanderbilt - Florida leads series 42-10-2

26-0 S/U vs Vanderbilt as 12 point or more favorite since 1983

FLA ATLANTIC	31-0 S/U in 1st home game of season since 1990
ALABAMA	17-1 S/U in 2nd home game of season since 2003
TENNESSEE	13-0 S/U prior to playing Kentucky since 2008
Kentucky	24-3 S/U after playing Tennessee since 1993
VANDERBILT	9-0 S/U prior to playing LSU since 2012 (7-1-1 ATS)
VANDERBILT	2-12 O/U prior to playing LSU since 2007
VANDERBILT	3-9 ATS after playing Kentucky since 2009
SAMFORD	13-4 S/U after playing South Carolina since 2004
Missouri	31-2 S/U prior to playing Florida State since 1987

13-0 S/U @ home when #1 ranked since 1996

21-2 S/U when ranked vs South Carolina all time

24-0 S/U when ranked vs Vanderbilt since 1989

Favorite

38-5-1 S/U as 15.5-20 point favorite since 1983

8-0 S/U on road as 15.5-20 point favorite since 1997

40-6 S/U as 20.5-25 point favorite since 1987

2-11 O/U as 20.5-25 point favorite since 2009

8-0 S/U on road as 25.5 point or more favorite since 1995

74-1 S/U as 25.5 point or more favorite since 1984

Copyright © 2021 by Steve's Football Bible, LLC

2020-Florida Atlantic		Opponent	FAU	Opp	S/U	Line	ATS	Total	O/U	
10/3/2020	vs	CHARLOTTE	21	17	W	-4.5	L	63.0	U	
10/24/2020	@	Marshall	9	20	L	19.5	W	51.0	U	
10/31/2020	vs	TEXAS-SAN ANTONIO	24	3	W	-4.5	W	47.0	U	
11/7/2020	vs	WESTERN KENTUCKY	10	6	W	-6.5	L	37.5	U	
11/13/2020	@	Florida International	38	19	W	-9.5	W	41.5	O	"Shula Bowl" (Don Shula Award)
11/20/2020	vs	MASSACHUSETTS	24	2	W	-34.0	L	50.5	U	
12/5/2020	@	Georgia Southern	3	20	L	2.0	L	41.0	U	
12/10/2020	@	Southern Mississippi	31	45	L	-9.0	L	43.0	O	
12/23/2020	vs	Memphis	10	25	L	9.5	L	52.5	U	Montgomery Bowl
Coach: Willie Taggert		Season Record >>	170	157	5-4	ATS>>	3-6	O/U>>	2-7	
2019-Florida Atlantic		Opponent	FAU	Opp	S/U	Line	ATS	Total	O/U	
8/31/2019	@	Ohio State	21	45	L	27.5	W	65.5	O	
9/7/2019	vs	CENTRAL FLORIDA	14	48	L	13.5	L	67.5	U	
9/14/2019	@	Ball State	41	31	W	-2.5	W	64.5	O	
9/21/2019	vs	WAGNER	42	7	W	-39.0	L	NT	---	
9/28/2019	@	Charlotte	45	27	W	-1.0	W	64.5	U	
10/12/2019	vs	MIDDLE TENNESSEE	28	13	W	-12.5	W	63.5	U	
10/19/2019	vs	MARSHALL	31	36	L	-4.0	L	58.0	O	
10/26/2019	@	Old Dominion	41	3	W	-14.0	W	57.5	U	
11/2/2019	@	Western Kentucky	35	24	W	PK	W	51.0	O	
11/9/2019	vs	FLORIDA INTERNATIONAL	37	7	W	-11.0	W	59.0	U	"Shula Bowl" (Don Shula Award)
11/23/2019	@	Texas-San Antonio	40	26	W	-21.5	L	57.0	O	
11/30/2019	vs	SOUTHERN MISS	34	17	W	-9.0	W	58.5	U	
12/7/2019	vs	ALABAMA-BIRMINGHAM	49	6	W	-8.0	W	49.0	O	C-USA Championship Game
12/21/2019	vs	Smu	52	28	W	7.0	W	63.5	O	Boca Raton Bowl
Coach: Lane Kiffin		Season Record >>	510	318	11-3	ATS>>	10-4	O/U>>	8-5	C-USA Champions
2018-Florida Atlantic		Opponent	FAU	Opp	S/U	Line	ATS	Total	O/U	
9/1/2018	@	Oklahoma	14	63	L	19.0	L	68.0	O	
9/8/2018	vs	AIR FORCE	33	27	W	-7.5	L	61.5	U	
9/15/2018	vs	BETHUNE-COOKMAN	49	28	W	-40.0	L	NT	---	
9/21/2018	@	Central Florida	36	56	L	14.0	L	75.0	O	
9/29/2018	@	Middle Tennessee	24	25	L	-2.5	L	62.0	U	
10/6/2018	vs	OLD DOMINION	52	33	W	-13.0	W	63.5	O	
10/20/2018	@	Marshall	7	31	L	-2.5	L	60.0	U	
10/27/2018	vs	LOUISIANA TECH	13	21	L	-3.5	L	58.5	U	
11/3/2018	@	Florida International	49	14	W	1.5	W	59.5	O	"Shula Bowl" (Don Shula Award)
11/10/2018	vs	WESTERN KENTUCKY	34	15	W	-18.0	L	59.5	U	
11/17/2018	@	North Texas	38	41	L	4.0	W	63.5	O	
11/24/2018	vs	CHARLOTTE	24	27	L	-17.0	L	55.0	U	
Coach: Lane Kiffin		Season Record >>	373	381	5-7	ATS>>	3-9	O/U>>	5-6	
2017-Florida Atlantic		Opponent	FAU	Opp	S/U	Line	ATS	Total	O/U	
8/31/2017	vs	NAVY	19	42	L	8.5	L	65.0	U	
9/9/2017	@	Wisconsin	14	31	L	34.5	L	59.5	U	
9/16/2017	vs	BETHUNE-COOKMAN	45	0	W	-20.0	W	NT	---	
9/23/2017	@	Buffalo	31	34	L	2.0	L	58.0	O	
9/30/2017	vs	MIDDLE TENNESSEE	38	20	W	-2.5	W	60.0	U	
10/7/2017	@	Old Dominion	58	28	W	-5.0	W	57.0	O	
10/21/2017	vs	NORTH TEXAS	69	31	W	-3.5	W	67.0	O	
10/28/2017	@	Western Kentucky	42	28	W	-6.5	W	67.0	O	
11/3/2017	vs	MARSHALL	30	25	W	-6.0	L	63.0	O	
11/11/2017	@	Louisiana Tech	48	23	W	-3.5	W	63.0	O	
11/18/2017	vs	FLORIDA INTERNATIONAL	52	24	W	-14.5	W	66.0	O	"Shula Bowl" (Don Shula Award)
11/25/2017	@	Charlotte	31	12	W	-24.0	L	66.0	U	
12/2/2017	vs	NORTH TEXAS	41	17	W	-10.5	W	71.0	U	C-USA Championship Game
12/19/2017	vs	Akron	50	3	W	-23.0	W	65.5	U	Boca Raton Bowl
Coach: Lane Kiffin		Season Record >>	568	318	11-3	ATS>>	10-4	O/U>>	6-7	C-USA Champions

Copyright © 2021 by Steve's Football Bible, LLC

FLORIDA ATLANTIC OWLS   C-USA East

STADIUM: FAU Stadium {29,419}		Location: Boca Raton, FL							COACH: Willie Taggart

DATE		Opponent	FAU	Opp	S/U	Line	ATS	Total	O/U	Trends & Angles
9/4/2021	@	*Florida*								vs Florida - Florida leads series 3-0
9/11/2021	vs	*GEORGIA SOUTHERN*								vs Georgia Southern - G South leads series 1-0
9/18/2021	vs	*FORDHAM*								1st Meeting
9/25/2021	@	*Air Force*								vs Air Force - FAU leads series 1-0
10/2/2021	vs	FLA. INTERNATIONAL								6-1 S/U @ home vs FIU since 2004
10/9/2021	@	Alabama-Birmingham								vs UAB - Florida Atlantic leads series 5-2
10/23/2021	@	Charlotte								vs Charlotte - FAU leads series 3-1
10/30/2021	vs	TEXAS-EL PASO								vs UTEP - Series tied 1-1
11/6/2021	vs	MARSHALL								vs Marshall - Marshall leads series 7-1
11/13/2021	@	Old Dominion								3-0 S/U @ Old Dominion since 2015
11/20/2021	@	Western Kentucky								5-1 S/U & ATS @ W. Kentucky since 2008
11/27/2021	vs	MIDDLE TENNESSEE								2-10 S/U vs Middle Tennessee since 2008
12/4/2021	vs									Sun Belt Championship
	vs									BOWL GAME

Pointspread Analysis Non-Conference		Pointspread Analysis Conference
0-35 S/U vs Non-Conf. as 15.5 point or more Dog since 2004		vs Florida International - Florida Atlantic leads series 12-5
1-11 ATS vs Non-Conf. as 20.5-25 point Dog since 2006		4-0 S/U & ATS vs FIU as 4.5 point or less Dog since 2009
Bowl Games		7-2 O/U vs FIU as favorite since 2007
4-0 S/U & ATS in Bowl Games		Game 2-6 O/U vs Marshall since 2013
Dog		0-5 S/U vs Marshall as Dog since 2013
0-34 S/U as 20.5 point or more Dog since 2005		vs Middle Tennessee - MTSU leads series 12-4
1-7 O/U as 30.5 point or more Dog since 2011		3-8 ATS vs Middle Tennessee since 2009
1-5 O/U as 25.5-30 point Dog since 2010		0-5 O/U vs Middle Tennessee as favorite since 2007
1-12 ATS as 20.5-25 point Dog since 2006		0-10 S/U vs Middle Tennessee as Dog since 2005
0-11 S/U @ home as 7.5-20 point Dog since 2004		vs Old Dominion - Florida Atlantic leads series 4-2
0-9 S/U as 7.5-10 point Dog since 2005		4-0 S/U vs Old Dominion as favorite since 2015
2-11 S/U on road as 3.5-7 point Dog since 2008		Game 4-1 O/U vs Old Dominion since 2015
12-2 O/U as 3.5-7 point Dog since 2012		3-0 S/U @ Western Kentucky as favorite since 2008
7-0 ATS on road as 3.5-7 point Dog since 2012		vs Western Kentucky - Florida Atlantic leads series 9-3
Favorite		1-6 O/U vs Western Kentucky as favorite since 2008
2-6 ATS on road as 3 point or less favorite since 2008		
10-2 S/U as 3.5-7 point favorite since 2015	Florida	1-15 S/U in 1st road game of season since 2005
19-4 S/U as 7.5-15 point favorite since 2004	Ga SOUTHERN	1-11 ATS in 1st home game of season since 2009
13-1 S/U as 15.5 point or more favorite since 2008	Air Force	3-10 S/U in 2nd road game of season since 2009
7-0 S/U on road as 7.5 point or more favorite since 2007	Air Force	7-3 O/U prior to playing Florida International since 2011
	MIDDLE TENN	3-14 ATS in final home game of season since 2004

Print Version $24.99   Print Version $29.99   Print Version $29.99

These books available at numerous online retailers

Copyright © 2021 by Steve's Football Bible, LLC

FLORIDA INTERNATIONAL   C-USA East

2020-Florida Int.		Opponent	FIU	Opp	S/U	Line	ATS	Total	O/U	
9/26/2020	@	Liberty	34	36	L	7.5	W	60.5	O	
10/10/2020	vs	MIDDLE TENNESSEE	28	38	L	-6.5	L	56.5	O	
10/23/2020	vs	JACKSONVILLE STATE	10	19	L	-9.5	L	55.0	U	
11/14/2020	vs	FLORIDA ATLANTIC	19	38	L	9.5	L	41.5	O	"Shula Bowl" (Don Shula Award)
11/21/2020	@	Western Kentucky	21	38	L	7.0	L	41.5	O	
Coach: Butch Davis		Season Record >>	112	169	0-5	ATS>>	1-4	O/U>>	4-1	
2019-Florida Int.		Opponent	FIU	Opp	S/U	Line	ATS	Total	O/U	
8/29/2019	@	Tulane	14	42	L	3.0	L	58.5	U	
9/7/2019	vs	WESTERN KENTUCKY	14	20	L	-9.0	L	57.0	U	
9/14/2019	vs	NEW HAMPSHIRE	30	17	W	-13.5	L	NT	---	
9/21/2019	@	Louisiana Tech	31	43	L	6.5	L	51.5	O	
10/5/2019	vs	MASSACHUSETTS	44	0	W	-28.0	W	70.0	U	
10/12/2019	vs	CHARLOTTE	48	23	W	-5.0	W	59.5	O	
10/19/2019	vs	TEXAS-EL PASO	32	17	W	-24.5	L	51.0	U	
10/26/2019	@	Middle Tennessee	17	50	L	-1.5	L	57.5	O	
11/2/2019	vs	OLD DOMINION	24	17	W	-17.0	L	47.0	U	
11/9/2019	@	Florida Atlantic	7	37	L	11.0	L	59.0	U	"Shula Bowl" (Don Shula Award)
11/23/2019	@	Miami	30	24	W	21.0	W	51.5	O	
11/30/2019	@	Marshall	27	30	L	10.0	W	49.5	O	
12/21/2019	vs	Arkansas State	26	34	L	-1.0	L	58.5	O	Camelia Bowl
Coach: Butch Davis		Season Record >>	344	354	6-7	ATS>>	4-9	O/U>>	6-6	
2018-Florida Int.		Opponent	FIU	Opp	S/U	Line	ATS	Total	O/U	
9/1/2018	vs	INDIANA	28	38	L	13.0	W	55.0	O	
9/8/2018	@	Old Dominion	28	20	W	-2.5	W	51.5	U	
9/15/2018	vs	MASSACHUSETTS	63	24	W	-3.5	W	66.5	O	
9/22/2018	@	Miami	17	31	L	25.5	W	56.5	U	
9/29/2018	vs	ARKANSAS-PINE BLUFF	55	9	W	-57.5	L	NT	---	
10/13/2018	vs	MIDDLE TENNESSEE	24	21	W	-1.5	W	60.5	U	
10/20/2018	vs	RICE	36	17	W	-23.0	L	53.5	U	
10/27/2018	@	Western Kentucky	38	17	W	-3.0	W	54.0	O	
11/3/2018	vs	FLORIDA ATLANTIC	14	49	L	-1.5	L	59.5	O	"Shula Bowl" (Don Shula Award)
11/10/2018	@	Texas-San Antonio	45	7	W	-10.5	W	47.0	O	
11/17/2018	@	Charlotte	42	35	W	-3.5	W	44.5	O	
11/24/2018	vs	MARSHALL	25	28	L	3.0	T	52.5	O	
12/21/2018	vs	Toledo	35	32	W	7.0	W	57.5	O	Bahamas Bowl
Coach: Butch Davis		Season Record >>	450	328	9-4	ATS>>	9-3-1	O/U>>	8-4	
2017-Florida Int.		Opponent	FIU	Opp	S/U	Line	ATS	Total	O/U	
8/31/2017	@	Central Florida	17	61	L	17.0	L	56.0	O	
9/9/2017	vs	ALCORN STATE	17	10	W	-20.0	L	NT	---	
9/23/2017	@	Rice	13	7	W	PK	W	52.5	U	
9/30/2017	vs	CHARLOTTE	30	29	W	-10.0	L	47.5	O	
10/7/2017	@	Middle Tennessee	17	37	L	8.0	L	53.5	O	
10/14/2017	vs	TULANE	23	10	W	12.0	W	50.5	U	
10/28/2017	@	Marshall	41	30	W	14.0	W	47.0	O	
11/4/2017	vs	TEXAS-SAN ANTONIO	14	7	W	6.5	W	53.0	U	
11/11/2017	vs	OLD DOMINION	30	37	L	-10.5	L	48.0	O	
11/18/2017	@	Florida Atlantic	24	52	L	14.5	L	66.0	O	"Shula Bowl" (Don Shula Award)
11/24/2017	vs	WESTERN KENTUCKY	41	17	W	-3.0	W	57.0	O	
12/2/2017	vs	MASSACHUSETTS	63	45	W	2.5	W	56.5	O	
12/21/2017	vs	Temple	3	28	L	7.0	L	56.5	U	Gasparilla Bowl
Coach: Butch Davis		Season Record >>	333	370	8-5	ATS>>	6-7	O/U>>	5-4	

Copyright © 2021 by Steve's Football Bible, LLC

FLORIDA INTERNATIONAL   C-USA East

STADIUM: FIU Stadium					Location: Miami, FL				COACH: Butch Davis
DATE		Opponent	FIU	Opp	S/U	Line	ATS	Total	O/U	Trends & Angles

DATE		Opponent	FIU	Opp	S/U	Line	ATS	Total	O/U	Trends & Angles
9/2/2021	vs	*LONG ISLAND U.*								1st meeting
9/11/2021	vs	*TEXAS STATE*								1st meeting
9/18/2021	@	*Texas Tech*								vs Texas Tech - Texas Tech leads series 1-0
9/25/2021	@	*Central Michigan*								1st meeting
10/2/2021	@	Florida Atlantic								vs Florida Atlantic - FAU leads series 12-5
10/9/2021	vs	CHARLOTTE								vs Charlotte - FIU leads series 4-0
10/23/2021	vs	WESTERN KENTUCKY								Game 5-1 O/U vs W. Kentucky since 2015
10/30/2021	@	Marshall								vs Marshall - Marshall leads series 6-2
11/6/2021	vs	OLD DOMINION								vs Old Dominion - Series tied 3-3
11/13/2021	@	Middle Tennessee								1-7 S/U @ MTSU since 2006
11/20/2021	vs	NORTH TEXAS								3-0 S/U @ home vs North Texas since 2007
11/27/2021	@	Southern Mississippi								vs Southern Miss - FIU leads series 1-0
12/4/2021	vs									Sun Belt Championship
	vs									BOWL GAME

Pointspread Analysis Non-Conference		Pointspread Analysis Conference
1-20 S/U vs Non-Conf. as 20.5 point or more Dog since 2005		0-5 S/U vs Florida Atlantic as 11 point or more Dog since 2004
2-9 S/U vs Non-Conf. as 3.5-10 point Dog since 2004		vs Middle Tennessee - MTSU leads series 11-5
9-0 S/U vs Non-Conf. as 10.5 point or more favorite since 2011		0-6 S/U @ Middle Tennessee as Dog since 2006
Dog		0-8 S/U vs Middle Tenn. as 8 point or more Dog since 2006
1-25 S/U as 20.5 point or more Dog since 2005		Game 7-1 O/U @ Middle Tennessee since 2005
5-0 O/U as 30.5 point or more Dog since 2009		4-0 S/U & ATS vs North Texas as favorite since 2008
1-8 O/U as 25.5-30 point Dog since 2006		vs North Texas - FIU leads series 5-3
0-5 S/U @ home as 15.5-20 point Dog since 2007		0-4 S/U vs Western Kentucky as Dog since 2012
5-0 O/U as 15.5-20 point Dog since 2014		vs Western Kentucky - WKU leads series 7-6
2-11 S/U on road as 10.5-15 point Dog since 2004		5-2 S/U vs Western Kentucky as favorite since 2008
2-16 S/U on road as 7.5-10 point Dog since 2004		
0-5 S/U @ home as 7.5-10 point Dog since 2004		
2-9 S/U on road as 3.5-7 point Dog since 2007		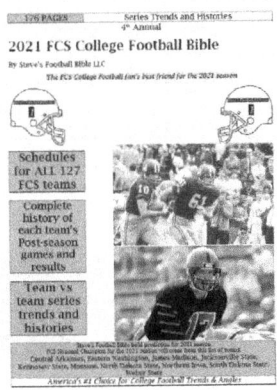
Favorite		
2-5 O/U on road as 3 point or less favorite since 2011		
6-1 S/U @ home as 3 point or less favorite since 2005		
5-1 S/U on road as 3.5-7 point favorite since 2008		
5-2 S/U as 7.5-10 point favorite since 2010		
2-6 O/U as 7.5-10 point favorite since 2006	CHARLOTTE	2-9 S/U prior to playing Western Kentucky since 2008
17-2 S/U as 10.5 point or more favorite since 2011	CHARLOTTE	2-9 ATS prior to playing Western Kentucky since 2005

2021 FCS College Football Bible
By Steve's Football Bible LLC
The FCS College Football Bible's best friend for the 2021 season

Schedules for ALL 127 FCS teams

Complete history of each team's Post-season games and results

Team vs team series trends and histories

2021 FCS College Football Bible $19.95

Copyright © 2021 by Steve's Football Bible, LLC

2020-Florida State		Opponent	FSU	Opp	S/U	Line	ATS	Total	O/U	
9/12/2020	vs	GEORGIA TECH	13	16	L	-13.5	L	50.0	U	
9/26/2020	@	Miami	10	52	L	10.5	L	54.0	O	
10/3/2020	vs	JACKSONVILLE STATE	41	24	W	-26.5	L	53.0	O	
10/10/2020	@	Notre Dame	26	42	L	21.0	W	54.0	O	
10/17/2020	vs	NORTH CAROLINA	31	28	W	13.5	W	65.0	U	
10/24/2020	@	Louisville	16	48	L	5.0	L	62.0	O	
11/7/2020	vs	PITTSBURGH	17	41	L	1.5	L	52.5	O	
11/14/2020	@	NC State	22	38	L	12.0	L	60.5	U	
12/12/2020	vs	DUKE	56	35	W	-3.0	W	56.5	O	
Coach: Mike Norvell		Season Record >>	232	324	3-6	ATS>>	3-6	O/U>>	6-3	
2019-Florida State		Opponent	FSU	Opp	S/U	Line	ATS	Total	O/U	
8/31/2019	vs	Boise State	31	36	L	-6.5	L	54.5	O	TIAA Bank Field
9/7/2019	vs	LOUISIAIANA-MONROE	45	44	W	-23.0	L	65.5	O	{OT}
9/14/2019	@	Virginia	24	31	L	7.0	T	54.5	O	*"Jefferson-Eppes Trophy"*
9/21/2019	vs	LOUISVILLE	35	24	W	-7.0	W	61.0	U	
9/28/2019	vs	NC STATE	31	13	W	-7.0	W	62.0	U	
10/12/2019	@	Clemson	14	45	L	25.5	L	60.5	U	
10/19/2019	@	Wake Forest	20	22	L	-3.0	L	69.0	U	
10/26/2019	vs	SYRACUSE	35	17	W	-12.0	W	59.5	U	
11/2/2019	vs	MIAMI	10	27	L	-3.0	L	50.5	U	
11/9/2019	@	Boston College	38	31	W	1.0	W	64.0	O	
11/16/2019	vs	ALABAMA STATE	49	12	W	-41.0	L	NT	---	
11/30/2019	@	Florida	17	40	L	16.5	L	55.5	O	*"Govenor's Cup"*
12/31/2019	vs	**Arizona State**	**14**	**20**	L	3.0	L	51.5	U	Sun Bowl
Coach: Willie Taggart		Season Record >>	363	362	6-7	ATS>>	4-8-1	O/U>>	5-7	
2018-Florida State		Opponent	FSU	Opp	S/U	Line	ATS	Total	O/U	
9/3/2018	vs	VIRGINIA TECH	3	24	L	-7.5	L	54.0	U	
9/8/2018	vs	SAMFORD	36	26	W	-32.5	L	NT	---	
9/15/2018	@	Syracuse	7	30	L	-3.0	L	69.5	U	
9/22/2018	vs	NORTHERN ILLINOIS	37	19	W	-10.0	W	44.5	O	
9/29/2018	@	Louisville	28	24	W	-5.0	L	46.0	O	
10/6/2018	@	Miami	27	28	L	14.0	W	48.0	O	
10/20/2018	vs	WAKE FOREST	38	17	W	-10.5	W	57.5	U	
10/27/2018	vs	CLEMSON	10	59	L	18.0	L	49.5	O	
11/3/2018	@	NC State	28	47	L	9.0	L	52.0	O	
11/10/2018	@	Notre Dame	13	42	L	17.0	L	51.0	O	
11/17/2018	vs	BOSTON COLLEGE	22	21	W	3.0	W	48.0	U	
11/24/2018	vs	FLORIDA	14	41	L	4.5	L	52.0	O	*"Govenor's Cup"*
Coach: Willie Taggart		Season Record >>	263	378	5-7	ATS>>	4-8	O/U>>	7-4	
2017-Florida State		Opponent	FSU	Opp	S/U	Line	ATS	Total	O/U	
9/2/2017	vs	Alabama	7	24	L	7.5	L	51.5	U	Mercedes-Benz Stadium
9/23/2017	vs	NC STATE	21	27	L	-11.5	L	50.5	U	
9/30/2017	@	Wake Forest	26	19	W	-7.0	T	46.0	U	
10/7/2017	vs	MIAMI	20	24	L	2.5	L	45.0	U	
10/14/2017	@	Duke	17	10	W	-7.0	T	44.5	U	
10/21/2017	vs	LOUISVILLE	28	31	L	-7.0	L	58.5	O	
10/27/2017	@	Boston College	3	35	L	-5.5	L	46.5	U	
11/4/2017	vs	SYRACUSE	27	24	W	-7.5	L	50.5	O	
11/11/2017	@	Clemson	14	31	L	16.0	L	44.5	O	
11/18/2017	vs	DELAWARE STATE	77	6	W	-51.0	W	NT	---	
11/25/2017	@	Florida	38	22	W	-5.0	W	43.5	O	*"Govenor's Cup"*
12/2/2017	vs	LOUISIANA-MONROE	42	10	W	-25.5	W	63.5	U	
12/27/2017	vs	**Southern Mississippi**	**42**	**13**	W	-11.5	W	48.0	O	**Independence Bowl**
Coach: Jimbo Fisher		Season Record >>	362	276	7-6	ATS>>	4-7-2	O/U>>	5-7	

Copyright © 2021 by Steve's Football Bible, LLC

FLORIDA STATE SEMINOLES   ACC Atlantic

STADIUM: Doak Campbell Stadium {79,560}					Location: Tallahassee, FL					COACH: Mike Norvell
DATE		Opponent	FSU	Opp	S/U	Line	ATS	Total	O/U	Trends & Angles
9/5/2021	vs	*NOTRE DAME*								vs Notre Dame - Florida State leads series 6-3
9/11/2021	vs	*JACKSONVILLE STATE*								vs Jacksonville State - FSU leads series 2-1
9/18/2021	@	Wake Forest								7-1 S/U vs Wake Forest since 2012
9/25/2021	vs	LOUISVILLE								10-1 S/U @ home vs Louisville since 1953
10/2/2021	vs	SYRACUSE								6-0 S/U @ home vs Syracuse since 1991
10/9/2021	@	North Carolina								7-1 S/U @ North Carolina since 1985 {6-2 ATS}
10/23/2021	vs	*MASSACHUSETTS*								1st meeting
10/30/2021	@	Clemson								0-7 S/U vs Clemson as Dog since 2009
11/6/2021	vs	NC STATE								6-1 S/U @ home vs NC State since 2007
11/13/2021	vs	MIAMI								1-7 ATS @ home vs Miami as favorite since 1999
11/20/2021	@	Boston College								vs Boston College - Florida State leads series 13-5
11/27/2021	@	*Florida*								0-9 S/U vs Florida as Dog since 1997 {1-8 ATS}
12/4/2021	vs									ACC Championship
	vs									BOWL GAME

Pointspread Analysis
Non-Conference

1-11 S/U vs Non-Conf. as 7.5 point or more Dog since 1980

4-12 S/U vs Non-Conf. as 3.5-7 point Dog since 1981

5-1 S/U & ATS vs Non-Conf. as 3 point or less Dog since 1991

8-0 S/U & ATS vs Non-Conf. as 3 point or less favorite since 1998

0-5 O/U vs Non-Conf. as 3 point or less favorite since 2007

6-2 ATS vs Non-Conf. as 3.5-7 point favorite since 2007

7-0 O/U vs Non-Conf. as 3.5-7 point favorite since 2008

20-6-1 S/U vs Non-Conf. as 3.5-7 point favorite since 1977

9-2 S/U vs Non-Conf. as 7.5-10 point favorite since 1987

20-3 S/U vs Non-Conf. as 10.5-15 point favorite since 1983

2-10 O/U vs Non-Conf. as 10.5-15 point favorite since 1993

57-0 S/U vs Non-Conf. as 15.5 point or more favorite since 1984

vs Florida - Florida leads series 36-26-2

0-12 S/U vs Florida as 3.5-20 point Dog since 1983

1-11 ATS vs Florida as 3.5-20 point Dog since 1983

9-0 S/U vs Florida as 7.5 point or more favorite since 1987 {7-2 ATS}

0-5 O/U vs Florida as 7.5 point or more favorite since 1993

6-0 S/U & ATS vs Florida as 3 point or less favorite since 1998

Dog

0-14 S/U on road as 10.5 point or more Dog since 1986

1-13 S/U as 10.5 point or more Dog since 2007

1-9 S/U as 7.5-10 point Dog since 1980

13-1 O/U as 3.5-7 point Dog since 2006

7-0 O/U on road as 3.5-7 point Dog since 2007

Favorite

7-3 S/U & ATS on road as 3 point or less favorite since 1999

0-6 O/U on road as 3 point or less favorite since 2008

2-10 O/U as 3 point or less favorite since 2008

15-4 S/U as 3.5-7 point favorite since 2013

7-1 S/U @ home as 7.5-10 point favorite since 2007

2-11 O/U @ home as 10.5-15 point favorite since 2005

18-2 S/U on road as 10.5-15 point favorite since 1985

14-1 S/U @ home as 15.5-20 point favorite since 2003

1-7 O/U on road as 15.5-20 point favorite since 2002

9-0 S/U on road as 20.5-25 point favorite since 1986

30-1 S/U on road as 20.5 point or more favorite since 1986

105-0 S/U @ home as 20.5 point or more favorite since 1984

2-7 ATS in 2nd home game of season since 2011

6-1 S/U after playing Clemson since 2012

16-1 S/U after playing Miami since 2003

3-10 O/U in final road game of season since 2007

Pointspread Analysis
Conference

7-0 S/U vs Boston College as 9 point or more favorite since 2010

0-4 S/U & ATS vs B. College as 4.0-6.5 point favorite since 2006

vs Clemson - Florida State leads series 20-13

5-2 O/U vs Clemson as Dog since 2009

5-0 S/U vs Clemson as favorite since 2008

13-1 S/U vs Clemson as 8 point or more favorite since 1996

Game 6-1 O/U vs Louisville since 2014

vs Louisville - Florida State leads series 16-5

4-0 S/U vs Louisville as 24.5 point or more favorite since 1986

2-9 ATS @ home vs Miami since 1999

Game 0-5 O/U @ home vs Miami since 2011

Game 2-8 O/U vs Miami since 2011

vs Miami - Miami leads series 35-29

6-2 ATS vs Miami as Dog since 2005

5-1 S/U vs Miami as favorite since 2011

0-6 O/U vs Miami as favorite since 2011

0-5 S/U vs Miami as 7 point or more Dog since 2001

8-0 S/U vs Miami as 9.5 point or more favorite since 1997

1-6 S/U & ATS vs Miami as 3.5-6 point favorite since 1988

1-5 ATS vs North Carolina as favorite since 2001

9-0 S/U vs N. Carolina as 17.5 point or more favorite since 1992

4-16 ATS vs NC State since 2001

vs NC State - Florida State leads series 27-14

4-14 ATS vs NC State as favorite since 2001

vs Syracuse - Florida State leads series 11-2

11-1 S/U vs Syracuse since 1978

Game 4-1 O/U @ home vs Syracuse since 2005

10-0 S/U vs Syracuse as 5 point or more favorite since 1989

Game 0-6 O/U vs Wake Forest since 2014

vs Wake Forest - Florida State leads series 30-7-1

21-0 S/U vs Wake F. as 10.5 point or more favorite since 1992

NOTRE DAME	27-3 S/U in 1st home game of season since 1990
Wake Forest	1-7-2 ATS in 1st road game of season since 2010
Wake Forest	10-1 S/U prior to playing Louisville since 1986
LOUISVILLE	9-3 S/U after playing Wake Forest since 2008
LOUISVILLE	7-3 S/U prior to playing Syracuse since 1989
North Carolina	4-11-1 ATS in 2nd road game of season since 2004
North Carolina	7-3 S/U after playing Syracuse since 1989
UMASS	7-0 S/U prior to playing Clemson since 2012
UMASS	27-3 S/U in 2nd home game of season since 1990
NC STATE	9-2 S/U prior to playing Miami since 2008
MIAMI	8-1 S/U after playing NC State since 2011 (7-0-1 ATS)
Boston College	13-1 S/U prior to playing Florida since 2006
Florida	8-2 S/U in final road game of season since 2010

Copyright © 2021 by Steve's Football Bible, LLC

FRESNO STATE BULLDOGS   MOUNTAIN WEST West

2020-Fresno State		Opponent	Fres	Opp	S/U	Line	ATS	Total	O/U	
10/24/2020	vs	HAWAII	19	34	L	-3.0	L	64.0	U	"Golden Screwdriver Trophy"
10/31/2020	vs	COLORADO STATE	38	17	W	2.5	W	57.5	U	
11/7/2020	@	Unlv	40	27	W	-11.0	W	57.5	O	
11/14/2020	@	Utah State	35	16	W	-10.5	W	51.5	U	
12/5/2020	@	Nevada	26	37	L	5.5	L	60.0	O	
12/12/2020	vs	New Mexico	39	49	L	-16.5	L	55.5	O	{@ Las Vegas, NV}
Coach: Kalen DeBoer		Season Record >>	197	180	3-3	ATS>>	3-3	O/U>>	3-3	

2019-Fresno State		Opponent	Fres	Opp	S/U	Line	ATS	Total	O/U	
8/31/2019	@	Usc	23	31	L	14.0	W	50.0	O	
9/7/2019	vs	MINNESOTA	35	38	L	3.0	T	46.0	O	{2 OT}
9/21/2019	vs	SACRAMENTO STATE	34	20	W	-24.5	L	NT	---	
9/28/2019	@	New Mexico State	30	17	W	-20.5	L	62.5	U	
10/12/2019	@	Air Force	24	43	L	2.5	L	49.5	O	
10/19/2019	vs	UNLV	56	27	W	-16.0	W	52.0	O	
10/26/2019	vs	COLORADO STATE	31	41	L	-13.5	L	56.5	O	
11/2/2019	@	Hawaii	41	38	W	2.0	W	68.0	O	"Golden Screwdriver Trophy"
11/9/2019	vs	UTAH STATE	35	37	L	-5.5	L	58.0	O	
11/16/2019	@	San Diego State	7	17	L	2.5	L	43.5	U	"Battle for the Oil Can"
11/23/2019	vs	NEVADA	28	35	L	-13.0	L	51.5	O	
11/30/2019	@	San Jose State	16	17	L	2.5	L	59.5	U	"Valley Rivalry"
Coach: Jeff Tedford		Season Record >>	360	361	4-8	ATS>>	4-7-1	O/U>>	8-3	

2018-Fresno State		Opponent	Fres	Opp	S/U	Line	ATS	Total	O/U	
9/1/2018	vs	IDAHO	79	13	W	-24.5	W	NT	---	
9/8/2018	@	Minnesota	14	21	L	PK	L	50.0	U	
9/15/2018	@	Ucla	38	14	W	-2.5	W	51.5	O	
9/29/2018	vs	TOLEDO	49	27	W	-10.0	W	62.0	O	
10/6/2018	@	Nevada	21	3	W	-16.0	W	58.5	U	
10/13/2018	vs	WYOMING	27	3	W	-18.0	W	44.0	U	
10/20/2018	@	New Mexico	38	7	W	-14.0	W	52.5	U	
10/27/2018	vs	HAWAII	50	20	W	-24.0	W	60.0	O	
11/3/2018	@	Unlv	48	3	W	-27.0	W	60.0	U	
11/10/2018	@	Boise State	17	24	L	-2.5	L	55.0	U	"Milk Can"
11/17/2018	vs	SAN DIEGO STATE	23	14	W	-10.0	L	42.0	U	"Battle for the Oil Can"
11/24/2018	vs	SAN JOSE STATE	31	13	W	-32.0	L	52.0	U	"Valley Rivalry"
12/1/2018	@	Boise State	19	16	W	PK	W	51.0	U	MWC CHAMPIONSHIP
12/15/2018	vs	Arizona State	31	20	W	-6.0	W	53.5	U	Las Vegas Bowl
Coach: Jeff Tedford		Season Record >>	485	198	12-2	ATS>>	10-4	O/U>>	3-10	MWC CHAMPIONS

2017-Fresno State		Opponent	Fres	Opp	S/U	Line	ATS	Total	O/U	
9/2/2017	vs	INCARNATE WORD	66	0	W	-36.0	W	56.5	O	
9/9/2017	@	Alabama	10	41	L	42.5	W	54.5	U	
9/16/2017	@	Washington	16	48	L	35.0	W	56.5	O	
9/30/2017	vs	NEVADA	41	21	W	-7.5	W	59.5	O	
10/7/2017	@	San Jose State	27	10	W	-17.0	T	60.0	U	"Valley Rivalry"
10/14/2017	vs	NEW MEXICO	38	0	W	2.0	W	53.0	U	
10/21/2017	@	San Diego State	27	3	W	6.5	W	50.0	U	"Battle for the Oil Can"
10/28/2017	vs	UNLV	16	26	L	-22.5	L	58.0	U	
11/4/2017	vs	BYU	20	13	W	-10.0	L	48.0	U	
11/11/2017	@	Hawaii	31	21	W	-9.5	W	52.5	U	
11/18/2017	@	Wyoming	13	7	W	PK	W	38.5	U	
11/25/2017	vs	BOISE STATE	28	17	W	6.5	W	50.0	U	"Milk Can"
12/2/2017	@	Boise State	14	17	L	9.5	W	51.0	U	MWC CHAMPIONSHIP
12/24/2017	vs	Houston	33	27	W	2.5	W	52.0	O	HAWAI'I BOWL
Coach: Jeff Tedford		Season Record >>	380	251	10-4	ATS>>	11-2-1	O/U>>	4-10	

Copyright © 2021 by Steve's Football Bible, LLC

FRESNO STATE BULLDOGS   MOUNTAIN WEST West

STADIUM: Bulldog Stadium {40,727}					Location: Fresno, CA				COACH: Kalen DeBoer	
DATE		Opponent	Fres	Opp	S/U	Line	ATS	Total	O/U	Trends & Angles	
8/28/2021	vs	CONNECTICUT								1st meeting	
9/4/2021	@	Oregon								0-5 S/U @ Oregon since 1997	
9/11/2021	vs	CAL POLY-SLO								7-0 S/U vs Cal Poly-SLO since 1980	
9/18/2021	@	Ucla								3-0 S/U vs Ucla since 2003	
9/25/2021	vs	UNLV								8-1 S/U @ home vs UNLV since 1985	
10/2/2021	@	Hawaii								6-0 S/U @ Hawaii since 2009	
10/16/2021	@	Wyoming								vs Wyoming - Fresno State leads series 7-5	
10/23/2021	vs	NEVADA								vs Nevada - Fresno State leads series 29-22-1	
10/30/2021	@	San Diego State								4-14 S/U @ San Diego State since 1962	
11/6/2021	vs	BOISE STATE								1-13 S/U vs Boise State as Dog since 2002	
11/13/2021	vs	NEW MEXICO								7-1 S/U @ home vs New Mexico since 1948	
11/27/2021	@	San Jose State								1-3-1 ATS @ San Jose State since 2010	
12/4/2021	vs									MWC Championship	
	vs									BOWL GAME	

Pointspread Analysis Non-Conference		Pointspread Analysis Conference
0-24 S/U vs Non-Conf. as 15.5 point or more Dog since 1987		0-3 S/U & ATS vs Air Force as 3 point or less favorite since 1994
1-10 S/U vs Non-Conf. as 10.5-15 point Dog since 1994		4-0 ATS vs Boise State as Dog since 2014
6-0 O/U vs Non-Conf. as 10.5-15 point Dog since 2002		0-12 S/U vs Boise State as 7 point or more Dog since 2002
7-1 S/U & ATS vs Non-Conf. as 3 point or less favorite since 1985		7-1 ATS @ Hawaii since 2005
1-9 ATS vs Non-Conf. as 3.5-7 point favorite since 2001		5-1 ATS vs Hawaii since 2015
6-1 O/U vs Non-Conf. as 3.5-7 point favorite since 2008		5-1 S/U vs Hawaii as favorite since 2012
10-0 S/U vs Non-Conf. as 7.5-10 point favorite since 1985		5-0 ATS vs Hawaii as Dog since 2007
9-1 S/U vs Non-Conf. as 10.5-15 point favorite since 2005		vs Hawaii - Fresno State leads series 29-23-1
39-1 S/U vs Non-Conf. as 15.5 point or more favorite since 1985		0-5 S/U & ATS vs Hawaii as 9 point or less favorite since 1995
0-4 S/U @ UCLA as 11 point or more Dog since 1987		5-0 S/U & ATS vs Hawaii as 12.5-17.5 point favorite since 1993
0-4 S/U vs UCLA as 10.5 point or more Dog since 1987		vs Unlv - Fresno State leads series 16-7
vs Ucla - UCLA leads series 6-3		0-4 S/U vs Nevada as 7.5 point or more Dog since 2009
0-7 S/U vs Oregon as 2.5 point or more Dog since 1996		4-0 S/U vs Nevada as 19.5 point or more favorite since 2000
Bowl Games		7-1 S/U & ATS vs New Mexico since 1995
2-6 S/U in Bowl Games since 2008		vs New Mexico - Fresno State leads series 13-4
3-0 S/U vs ACC in Bowl Games		6-1 S/U & ATS vs New Mexico as favorite since 1995
0-3 O/U in Las Vegas Bowl		7-1 S/U vs New Mexico as 14 point or more favorite since 1988
Dog		vs San Jose State - Fresno State leads series 42-38-3
0-37 S/U as 15.5 point or more Dog since 1987		Game 0-4 O/U vs San Jose State since 2016
7-1 O/U as 20.5-25 point Dog since 2005		0-5 S/U vs San Jose State as 4 point or more Dog since 1987
0-9 S/U @ home as 10.5 point or more dog since 1994		14-1 S/U @ home vs San Jose State as favorite since 1985
9-0 O/U as 10.5-15 point Dog since 2002		16-0 S/U vs San Jose State as 9.5 point or more favorite since 1985
2-14 S/U on road as 7.5-10 point Dog since 1988		vs San Diego State - San Diego State leads series 30-25-4
3-12 O/U as 3.5-7 point Dog since 2008		Game 0-6 O/U vs San Diego State since 2014
Favorite		0-4 S/U vs San Diego State as 7.5 point or more Dog since 1995
6-2 S/U & ATS as 3 point or less favorite since 2010		5-0 S/U vs San Diego St. as 5.5 point or more favorite since 1993
13-0 S/U @ home as 7.5-10 point favorite since 1986		6-0-1 S/U vs Utah State as 15.5-25.5 point favorite since 1989
8-0 S/U on road as 10.5-15 point favorite since 2005		0-5 ATS vs Utah State as 14.5-20.5 point favorite since 1991
13-2 S/U on road as 15.5-20 point favorite since 1985		3-0 S/U & ATS vs Wyoming as 9 point or less favorite since 1992
23-3 S/U @ home as 15.5-20 point favorite since 1985	UCONN	18-4 S/U in 1st home game of season since 1999
25-3-1 S/U as 20.5-25 point favorite since 1987	CAL POLY-SLO	0-6 ATS prior to playing UCLA since 1987
1-7 O/U as 20.5-25 point favorite since 2009	CAL POLY-SLO	9-3 O/U in 2nd home game of season since 2008
1-5 O/U @ home as 25.5-30 point favorite since 2001	Ucla	8-3 O/U in 2nd road game of season since 2010
22-0 S/U @ home as 25.5 point or more favorite since 1986	NEVADA	2-8 O/U prior to playing San Diego State since 2002
8-1 S/U on road as 25.5-30 point favorite since 1989	San Diego State	8-1-1 ATS prior to playing Boise State since 2005
		2-23 S/U vs ranked teams since 2005
		3-37 S/U on road vs ranked teams all time
		0-6 S/U vs ranked San Diego State all time

Copyright © 2021 by Steve's Football Bible, LLC

GEORGIA BULLDOGS   SEC East

2020-Georgia		Opponent	UGA	Opp	S/U	Line	ATS	Total	O/U	
9/26/2020	@	Arkansas	37	10	W	-27.5	L	53.0	U	
10/3/2020	vs	AUBURN	27	6	W	-7.5	W	44.5	U	"Deep South's Oldest Rivalry"
10/10/2020	vs	TENNESSEE	44	21	W	-12.0	W	63.0	O	
10/17/2020	@	Alabama	24	41	L	5.5	L	56.5	O	
10/31/2020	@	Kentucky	14	3	W	-16.5	L	41.5	U	
11/7/2020	vs	Florida	28	44	L	-2.5	L	54.5	O	"Okefenokee Oar"
11/21/2020	vs	MISSISSIPPI STATE	31	24	W	-26.5	L	44.0	O	
11/28/2020	@	South Carolina	45	16	W	-23.0	W	50.0	O	
12/12/2020	@	Missouri	49	14	W	-14.0	W	54.5	O	
1/1/2021	vs	Cincinnati	24	21	W	-8.0	L	53.0	U	Chick-Fil-A Peach Bowl
Coach: Kirby Smart		Season Record >>	323	200	8-2	ATS>>	4-6	O/U>>	6-4	
2019-Georgia		Opponent	UGA	Opp	S/U	Line	ATS	Total	O/U	
8/31/2019	@	Vanderbilt	30	6	W	-22.5	W	57.0	U	
9/7/2019	vs	MURRAY STATE	63	17	W	-49.0	L	NT	---	
9/14/2019	vs	ARKANSAS STATE	55	0	W	-32.5	W	58.0	U	
9/21/2019	vs	NOTRE DAME	23	17	W	-15.5	L	58.5	U	
10/5/2019	@	Tennessee	43	14	W	-24.0	W	51.0	O	
10/12/2019	vs	SOUTH CAROLINA	17	20	L	-21.0	L	52.5	U	{2 OT}
10/19/2019	vs	KENTUCKY	21	0	W	-24.0	L	45.5	U	
11/2/2019	vs	Florida	24	17	W	-6.0	W	47.5	U	"Okefenokee Oar"
11/9/2019	vs	MISSOURI	27	0	W	-18.5	W	47.5	U	
11/16/2019	@	Auburn	21	14	W	-3.0	W	43.0	U	"Deep South's Oldest Rivalry"
11/23/2019	vs	TEXAS A&M	19	13	W	-12.5	L	43.5	U	
11/30/2019	@	Georgia Tech	52	7	W	-28.5	W	46.0	O	"Clean, old fashioned Hate"
12/7/2019	vs	Lsu	10	37	L	7.0	L	57.0	U	SEC Championship
1/1/2020	vs	Baylor	26	14	W	-3.5	W	44.0	U	Sugar Bowl
Coach: Kirby Smart		Season Record >>	431	176	12-2	ATS>>	8-6	O/U>>	2-11	
2018-Georgia		Opponent	UGA	Opp	S/U	Line	ATS	Total	O/U	
9/1/2018	vs	AUSTIN PEAY	45	0	W	-46.0	L	NT	---	
9/8/2018	@	South Carolina	41	17	W	-8.0	W	59.0	U	
9/15/2018	vs	MIDDLE TENNESSEE	49	7	W	-33.5	W	54.5	O	
9/22/2018	@	Missouri	43	29	W	-14.5	L	68.0	O	
9/29/2018	vs	TENNESSEE	38	12	W	-29.5	L	55.0	U	
10/6/2018	vs	VANDERBILT	41	13	W	-26.0	W	55.5	U	
10/13/2018	@	Lsu	16	36	L	-6.5	L	50.5	O	
10/27/2018	vs	Florida	36	17	W	-7.0	W	52.5	O	"Okefenokee Oar"
11/3/2018	@	Kentucky	34	17	W	-9.0	W	46.0	O	
11/10/2018	vs	AUBURN	27	10	W	-13.5	W	52.5	U	"Deep South's Oldest Rivalry"
11/17/2018	vs	MASSACHUSETTS	66	27	W	-41.5	L	67.0	O	
11/24/2018	vs	GEORGIA TECH	45	21	W	-17.0	W	59.5	O	"Clean, old fashioned Hate"
12/1/2018	vs	Alabama	28	35	L	11.0	W	63.0	T	SEC Championship
1/1/2019	vs	Texas	21	28	L	-13.5	L	60.5	U	Sugar Bowl
Coach: Kirby Smart		Season Record >>	530	269	11-3	ATS>>	8-6	O/U>>	7-5-1	
2017-Georgia		Opponent	UGA	Opp	S/U	Line	ATS	Total	O/U	
9/2/2017	vs	APPALACHIAN STATE	31	10	W	-12.0	W	46.0	U	
9/9/2017	@	Notre Dame	20	19	W	5.0	W	57.0	U	
9/16/2017	vs	SAMFORD	42	14	W	-33.0	L	NT	---	
9/23/2017	vs	MISSISSIPPI STATE	31	3	W	-2.5	W	50.0	U	
9/30/2017	@	Tennessee	41	0	W	-10.0	W	47.0	U	
10/7/2017	@	Vanderbilt	45	14	W	-17.0	W	41.5	O	
10/14/2017	vs	MISSOURI	53	28	W	-28.5	L	58.5	O	
10/28/2017	vs	Florida	42	7	W	-13.0	W	43.5	O	"Okefenokee Oar"
11/4/2017	vs	SOUTH CAROLINA	24	10	W	-23.5	L	45.0	U	
11/11/2017	@	Auburn	17	40	L	-2.5	L	48.0	O	"Deep South's Oldest Rivalry"
11/18/2017	vs	KENTUCKY	42	13	W	-22.5	W	48.5	O	
11/25/2017	@	Georgia Tech	38	7	W	-11.5	W	51.0	U	"Clean, old fashioned Hate"
12/2/2017	vs	Auburn	28	7	W	-2.0	W	48.0	U	SEC Championship
1/1/2018	vs	Oklahoma	54	48	W	-2.5	W	62.5	O	Rose Bowl (National Semifinal)
1/8/2018	vs	Alabama	23	26	L	3.0	T	45.0	O	CFB Championship Game
Coach: Kirby Smart		Season Record >>	531	246	13-2	ATS>>	10-4-1	O/U>>	7-7	SEC Champions

Copyright © 2021 by Steve's Football Bible, LLC

GEORGIA BULLDOGS — SEC East

STADIUM: Sanford Stadium {92,746}					Location: Athens, GA				COACH: Kirby Smart	
DATE		Opponent	UGA	Opp	S/U	Line	ATS	Total	O/U	Trends & Angles
9/4/2021	vs	*Clemson {@ Charlotte}*								5-1 S/U & ATS vs Clemson as Dog since 1984
9/11/2021	vs	*ALABAMA-BIRMINGHAM*								vs UAB - Georgia leads series 2-0
9/18/2021	vs	SOUTH CAROLINA								5-1 S/U vs South Carolina since 2015
9/25/2021	@	Vanderbilt								20-2-1 S/U @ Vanderbilt since 1975
10/2/2021	vs	ARKANSAS								8-1 S/U vs Arkansas since 2000
10/9/2021	@	Auburn								11-1 S/U vs Auburn as favorite since 2007
10/16/2021	vs	KENTUCKY								19-1 S/U @ home vs Kentucky since 1979
10/30/2021	vs	Florida								vs Florida - Georgia leads series 53-44-2
11/6/2021	vs	MISSOURI								7-0 S/U vs Missouri as favorite since 2014
11/13/2021	@	Tennessee								4-1 S/U @ Tennessee since 2011
11/20/2021	vs	*CHARLESTON SOUTHERN*								vs Charleston Southern - UGA leads series 1-0
11/27/2021	@	*Georgia Tech*								15-0 ATS @ Georgia Tech since 1991
12/4/2021	vs									SEC Championship
	vs									BOWL GAME

Pointspread Analysis Non-Conference		Pointspread Analysis Conference
7-2 S/U & ATS vs Non-Conf. as 3 point or less Dog since 1981		8-1 S/U vs Arkansas as 4.5 point or more favorite since 1987
1-7 O/U vs Non-Conf. as 3.5-7 point favorite since 2010		5-0 ATS vs Auburn as 10.5 point or more Dog since 1994
16-2 S/U vs Non-Conf. as 7.5-10 point favorite since 1986		0-9 S/U & ATS vs Auburn as 8 point or less Dog since 1983
11-3 S/U vs Non-Conf. as 10.5-15 point favorite since 1983		1-12 S/U vs Florida as 9.5 point or more Dog since 1990
44-0 S/U vs Non-Conf. as 15.5 point or more favorite since 1985		0-5 O/U vs Florida as 6 point or less Dog since 1984
16-3 S/U vs Georgia Tech since 2001		5-1 O/U vs Florida as 5.5 point or more favorite since 1992
5-1 ATS vs Georgia Tech as Dog since 1991		2-5 O/U vs Florida as 3 point or less favorite since 1988
vs Georgia Tech - Georgia leads series 68-41-5		22-2 S/U vs Kentucky since 1997
10-0 S/U & ATS @ Georgia Tech as favorite since 1993		vs Kentucky - Georgia leads series 60-12-2
9-0 S/U vs Ga Tech as 13.5 point or more favorite since 1983		20-1 S/U vs Kentucky as 10 point or more favorite since 1983
10-0 S/U @ Georgia Tech since 2001		vs Missouri - Georgia leads series 9-1
Bowl Games		0-5 S/U & ATS vs South Carolina as Dog since 1988
9-2 S/U vs Big 10 in Bowl Games since 1989		vs South Carolina - Georgia leads series 51-19-2
4-0 S/U in Citrus Bowl since 1993		7-1 S/U vs S. Carolina as 14 point or more favorite since 1983
5-0 ATS in Citrus Bowl since 1984		vs Tennessee - Georgia leads series 25-23-2
5-0-1 ATS in Bowl Games since 2014		2-10 S/U vs Tennessee as Dog since 1989
3-1 O/U in Peach Bowl since 1995		0-5 S/U vs Tennessee as 3.5-10 point Dog since 1989
4-0 S/U & ATS in Bowl Games as 3 point or less Dog since 1981		vs Vanderbilt - Georgia leads series 58-20-2
3-0 O/U in Bowl Games as 3 point or less Dog since 1998		24-3 S/U vs Vanderbilt since 1995
10-1 S/U in Bowl Games as 7.5-10 point favorite since 1987		8-0 S/U vs Vanderbilt as 7.5-12 point favorite since 1983
0-5 O/U in Bowl Games as 3.5-7 point favorite since 2009		10-0 S/U vs Vanderbilt as 21.5 point or more favorite since 1990
Dog	UAB	23-1 S/U in 1st home game of season since 1997
1-5 S/U & ATS as 3.5-7 point Dog since 2013	UAB	7-2 O/U in 1st home game of season since 2009
0-4 S/U & ATS @ home as 3 point or less Dog since 2000	UAB	9-1 O/U prior to playing South Carolina since 2010
Favorite	S. CAROLINA	8-2 O/U in 2nd home game of season since 2010
18-1 S/U on road as 7.5-10 point favorite since 1989	S. CAROLINA	8-1 S/U prior to playing Vanderbilt since 2010
2-8 O/U on road as 7.5-10 point favorite since 2004	ARKANSAS	11-0 S/U prior to playing Auburn since 2010
26-3 S/U as 7.5-10 point favorite since 2000	ARKANSAS	8-2 S/U after playing Vanderbilt since 2010
16-0 S/U on road as 10.5-15 point favorite since 1983	Auburn	1-8 ATS prior to playing Kentucky since 2012
17-2 S/U @ home as 10.5-15 point favorite since 2008	KENTUCKY	21-3 S/U prior to playing Florida since 1997
6-0 S/U on road as 15.5-20 point favorite since 2005	KENTUCKY	1-9 ATS prior to playing Florida since 2011
24-1 S/U @ home as 15.5-20 point favorite since 1983	KENTUCKY	11-0 S/U after playing Auburn since 2010
21-0 S/U as 15.5-20 point favorite since 1998	Florida	15-2 S/U after playing Kentucky since 2005
63-1 S/U as 20.5 point or more favorite since 1983	Florida	9-1 ATS after playing Kentucky since 2011
	MISSOURI	14-0 S/U after playing Florida since 2007
	CHARLESTON	9-0 S/U prior to playing Georgia Tech since 2011
22-1 S/U @ home when ranked since 2017	Georgia Tech	10-0 S/U in final road game of season since 2011
0-5 S/U vs #1 ranked teams since 1996	Georgia Tech	14-2 ATS in final road game of season since 2005

Copyright © 2021 by Steve's Football Bible, LLC

GEORGIA SOUTHERN EAGLES   SUN BELT East

2020-Georgia Southern		Opponent	GSU	Opp	S/U	Line	ATS	Total	O/U	
9/12/2020	vs	CAMPBELL	27	26	W	-34.0	L	58.5	U	
9/26/2020	@	Louisiana	18	20	L	11.5	W	50.0	U	
10/3/2020	@	Louisiana-Monroe	35	30	W	-18.5	L	49.5	O	
10/17/2020	vs	MASSACHUSETTS	41	0	W	-30.0	W	62.0	U	
10/24/2020	@	Coastal Carolina	14	28	L	1.5	L	48.5	U	
10/29/2020	vs	SOUTH ALABAMA	24	17	W	-3.5	W	51.5	U	
11/7/2020	vs	TROY	20	13	W	2.5	W	52.0	U	
11/14/2020	vs	TEXAS STATE	40	38	W	-13.0	L	50.0	O	
11/21/2020	@	Army	27	28	L	3.5	W	38.5	O	
11/28/2020	@	Georgia State	24	30	L	2.5	L	51.5	O	
12/5/2020	vs	FLORIDA ATLANTIC	20	3	W	-2.0	W	41.0	U	
12/12/2020	vs	APPALACHIAN STATE	26	34	L	9.5	W	45.0	O	"Deeper Than Hate Rivalry"
12/23/2020	vs	Louisiana Tech	38	3	W	-7.5	W	47.5	U	New Orleans Bowl
Coach: Chad Lunsford		Season Record >>	354	270	8-5	ATS>>	8-5	O/U>>	5-8	

2019-Georgia Southern		Opponent	GSU	Opp	S/U	Line	ATS	Total	O/U	
8/31/2019	@	Lsu	3	55	L	27.0	L	52.5	O	
9/7/2019	vs	MAINE	26	18	W	-9.0	L	NT	---	
9/14/2019	@	Minnesota	32	35	L	17.0	W	45.5	O	
9/28/2019	vs	LOUISIANA-LAFAYETTE	24	37	L	3.0	L	55.0	O	
10/3/2019	@	South Alabama	20	17	W	-10.0	L	44.5	U	{2 OT}
10/19/2019	vs	COASTAL CAROLINA	30	27	W	-7.0	L	43.0	O	{2 OT}
10/26/2019	vs	NEW MEXICO STATE	41	7	W	-14.0	W	54.5	U	
10/31/2019	@	Appalachian State	24	21	W	13.5	W	41.5	O	"Deeper Than Hate Rivalry"
11/9/2019	@	Troy	28	49	L	-2.5	L	57.0	O	
11/16/2019	vs	LOUISIANA-MONROE	51	29	W	-6.0	W	58.0	O	
11/23/2019	@	Arkansas State	33	38	L	PK	L	52.5	O	
11/30/2019	vs	GEORGIA STATE	38	10	W	-7.0	W	56.0	U	
12/21/2019	vs	Liberty	16	23	L	-5.0	L	58.5	U	AutoNation Cure Bowl
Coach: Chad Lunsford		Season Record >>	366	366	7-6	ATS>>	5-8	O/U>>	8-4	

2018-Georgia Southern		Opponent	GSU	Opp	S/U	Line	ATS	Total	O/U	
9/1/2018	vs	SOUTH CAROLINA STATE	37	6	W	-27.5	W	NT	---	
9/8/2018	vs	MASSACHUSETTS	34	13	W	-1.5	W	61.0	U	
9/15/2018	@	Clemson	7	38	L	31.5	W	48.5	U	
9/29/2018	vs	ARKANSAS STATE	28	21	W	3.0	W	53.5	U	
10/6/2018	vs	SOUTH ALABAMA	48	13	W	-13.0	W	57.5	O	
10/11/2018	@	Texas State	15	13	W	-17.0	L	51.0	U	
10/20/2018	@	New Mexico State	48	31	W	-10.0	W	52.5	O	
10/25/2018	vs	APPALACHIAN STATE	34	14	W	11.0	W	47.5	O	"Deeper Than Hate Rivalry"
11/3/2018	@	Louisiana-Monroe	25	44	L	-7.0	L	60.5	O	
11/10/2018	vs	TROY	21	35	L	2.5	L	44.5	O	
11/17/2018	@	Coastal Carolina	41	17	W	-7.5	W	53.0	O	
11/24/2018	@	Georgia State	35	14	W	-10.0	W	58.0	U	
12/15/2018	vs	Eastern Michigan	23	21	W	-3.0	L	45.5	U	Camelia Bowl
Coach: Chad Lunsford		Season Record >>	396	280	10-3	ATS>>	9-4	O/U>>	6-6	

2017-Georgia Southern		Opponent	GSU	Opp	S/U	Line	ATS	Total	O/U	
9/2/2017	@	Auburn	7	41	L	34.5	W	59.0	U	
9/9/2017	vs	NEW HAMPSHIRE	12	22	L	-7.5	L	NT	---	
9/23/2017	@	Indiana	17	52	L	22.0	L	50.0	O	
10/4/2017	vs	ARKANSAS STATE	25	43	L	7.5	L	54.5	O	
10/14/2017	vs	NEW MEXICO STATE	27	35	L	5.0	L	58.0	O	
10/21/2017	@	Massachusetts	20	55	L	7.0	L	53.0	O	
10/28/2017	@	Troy	16	38	L	22.5	W	49.0	O	
11/4/2017	vs	GEORGIA STATE	17	21	L	5.0	W	49.0	U	
11/9/2017	@	Appalachian State	6	27	L	18.0	L	51.5	U	"Deeper Than Hate Rivalry"
11/18/2017	vs	SOUTH ALABAMA	52	0	W	6.0	W	43.5	O	
11/25/2017	@	Louisiana-Lafayette	34	24	W	4.5	W	56.0	O	
12/2/2017	@	Coastal Carolina	17	28	L	-3.0	L	48.5	U	
Coach: Tyson Summers		Season Record >>	250	386	2-10	ATS>>	5-7	O/U>>	7-4	

Copyright © 2021 by Steve's Football Bible, LLC

GEORGIA SOUTHERN EAGLES   SUN BELT East

STADIUM: Paulson Stadium {25,000}					Location: Statesboro, GA			COACH: Chad Lunsford	
DATE		Opponent	GSU	Opp	S/U	Line	ATS	Total	O/U
								Trends & Angles	
9/4/2021	vs	GARDNER-WEBB						vs Gardner-Webb - G South leads series 2-1	
9/11/2021	@	Florida Atlantic						vs Florida Atlantic - G South leads series 1-0	
9/18/2021	@	Arkansas						1st meeting	
9/25/2021	vs	LOUISIANA						vs Louisiana - Louisiana leads series 3-1	
10/2/2021	vs	ARKANSAS STATE						vs Arkansas State - ASU leads series 3-2	
10/9/2021	@	Troy						vs Troy - Troy leads series 13-7	
10/14/2021	@	South Alabama						6-1 ATS vs South Alabama since 2014	
10/30/2021	vs	GEORIGA STATE						vs Georgia State - G State leads series 4-3	
11/6/2021	vs	COASTAL CAROLINA						vs Coast Carolina - Ga Southern leads series 5-2	
11/13/2021	@	Texas State						vs Texas State - Ga Southern leads series 4-1	
11/20/2021	vs	BYU						1st meeting	
11/27/2021	@	Appalachian State						vs App. State – App. State leads series 19-14-1	
12/4/2021	vs							Sun Belt Championship	
	vs							BOWL GAME	

Pointspread Analysis Non-Conference				Pointspread Analysis Conference	
0-11 S/U vs Non-Conf. as 15.5 or more Dog since 2014				vs UL-Monroe - Georgia Southern leads series 7-3	
Bowl Games				vs South Alabama - Georgia Southern leads series 7-0	
4-1 S/U in Bowl Games				Game 1-3 O/U vs Texas State since 2014	
Dog				Game 3-1 O/U vs Troy since 2017	
2-13 S/U as 10.5 point or more Dog since 2014					
10-3 O/U as 9.5 point or less Dog since 2017		GARDNER-WEBB		13-1 S/U in 1st home game of season since 2007	
1-7 S/U on road as 9.5 point or less Dog since 2014		Fla Atlantic		1-6 O/U in 1st road game of season since 2014	
Favorite		Fla Atlantic		2-11 S/U in 1st road game of season since 2008	
7-0 S/U @ home as 7.5 point or less favorite since 2018		LOUISIANA		12-1 S/U in 2nd home game of season since 2008	
28-1 S/U as 10 point or more favorite since 2014		BYU		9-3 S/U in final home game of season since 2009	
2-7 O/U on road as 10 point or more favorite since 2014		App State		2-8 S/U in final road game of season since 2011	

Baseball Fans – We have books on Baseball as well

Print Version $39.99

Print Version $39.99

These books available at numerous online retailers

Copyright © 2021 by Steve's Football Bible, LLC

GEORGIA STATE PANTHERS   SUN BELT East

2020 - Georgia State		Opponent	State	Opp	S/U	Line	ATS	Total	O/U	
9/19/2020	vs	LOUISIANA	31	34	L	16.5	W	57.0	O	{OT}
10/3/2020	vs	EAST CAROLINA	49	29	W	1.5	W	70.0	O	
10/15/2020	@	Arkansas State	52	59	L	3.5	L	73.0	O	
10/24/2020	@	Troy	36	34	W	2.5	W	68.5	O	
10/31/2020	vs	COASTAL CAROLINA	0	51	L	4.0	L	60.5	U	
11/7/2020	vs	LOUISIANA-MONROE	52	34	W	-18.5	L	60.0	O	
11/14/2020	@	Appalachian State	13	17	L	18.0	W	63.0	U	
11/21/2020	@	South Alabama	31	14	W	-3.5	W	58.5	U	"Clash of the Claws"
11/28/2020	vs	GEORGIA SOUTHERN	30	24	W	-2.5	W	51.5	O	
12/26/2020	vs	**Western Kentucky**	39	21	W	-3.0	W	49.0	O	**Lending Tree Bowl**
Coach: Shawn Elliott		Season Record >>	333	317	6-4	ATS>>	7-3	O/U>>	7-3	

2019 - Georgia State		Opponent	State	Opp	S/U	Line	ATS	Total	O/U	
8/31/2019	@	Tennessee	38	30	W	24.5	W	58.0	O	
9/7/2019	vs	FURMAN	48	42	W	-6.0	T	NT	---	
9/14/2019	@	Western Michigan	10	57	L	9.0	L	69.5	U	
9/21/2019	@	Texas State	34	37	L	3.0	T	62.5	O	{3 OT}
10/5/2019	vs	ARKANSAS STATE	52	38	W	6.0	W	69.0	O	
10/12/2019	@	Coastal Carolina	31	21	W	3.0	W	63.0	U	
10/19/2019	vs	ARMY	28	21	W	4.0	W	54.0	U	
10/26/2019	vs	TROY	52	33	W	-1.0	W	67.0	O	
11/9/2019	@	Louisiana-Monroe	31	45	L	-2.5	L	76.0	T	
11/16/2019	vs	APPALCHIAN STATE	27	56	L	15.0	L	61.5	O	
11/23/2019	vs	SOUTH ALABAMA	28	15	W	-9.5	W	56.0	U	"Clash of the Claws"
11/30/2019	@	Georgia Southern	10	38	L	7.0	L	56.0	U	
12/31/2019	vs	**Wyoming**	17	38	L	7.0	L	49.0	O	**Arizona Bowl**
Coach: Shawn Elliott		Season Record >>	406	471	7-6	ATS>>	6-5-2	O/U>>	6-5-1	

2018 - Georgia State		Opponent	State	Opp	S/U	Line	ATS	Total	O/U	
8/30/2018	vs	KENNESAW STATE	24	20	W	-2.0	W	NT	---	
9/8/2018	@	NC State	7	41	L	24.5	L	56.0	U	
9/14/2018	@	Memphis	22	59	L	28.5	L	59.0	O	
9/22/2018	vs	WESTERN MICHIGAN	15	34	L	9.0	L	61.0	U	
9/29/2018	vs	LOUISIANA-MONROE	46	14	W	5.5	W	65.5	U	-
10/4/2018	@	Troy	20	37	L	17.0	T	55.5	O	
10/18/2018	@	Arkansas State	35	51	L	13.0	L	56.5	O	
10/27/2018	vs	COASTAL CAROLINA	34	37	L	2.5	L	60.5	O	
11/3/2018	vs	TEXAS STATE	31	40	L	-7.0	L	52.5	O	
11/10/2018	@	Louisiana-Lafayette	22	36	L	13.0	L	70.0	U	
11/17/2018	@	Appalachian State	17	45	L	27.5	L	54.0	O	
11/24/2018	vs	GEORGIA SOUTHERN	14	35	L	10.0	L	58.0	U	
Coach: Shawn Elliott		Season Record >>	287	449	2-10	ATS>>	2-9-1	O/U>>	6-5	

2017 - Georgia State		Opponent	State	Opp	S/U	Line	ATS	Total	O/U	
8/31/2017	vs	TENNESSEE STATE	10	17	L	-14.0	L	56.0	U	
9/16/2017	@	Penn State	0	56	L	38.0	L	54.5	O	
9/23/2017	@	Charlotte	28	0	W	1.0	W	51.0	U	
10/7/2017	@	Coastal Carolina	27	21	W	PK	W	52.0	U	
10/14/2017	@	Louisiana-Monroe	47	37	W	3.5	W	57.0	O	
10/21/2017	vs	TROY	10	34	L	7.0	L	50.5	U	
10/26/2017	vs	SOUTH ALABAMA	21	13	W	-1.0	W	51.0	U	"Clash of the Claws"
11/4/2017	@	Georgia Southern	21	17	W	-5.0	L	49.0	U	
11/11/2017	@	Texas State	33	30	W	-5.5	L	51.0	O	
11/25/2017	vs	APPALACHIAN STATE	10	31	L	6.0	L	51.0	U	
12/2/2017	vs	IDAHO	10	24	L	-7.0	L	45.0	U	
12/16/2017	vs	**Western Kentucky**	27	17	W	5.0	W	54.5	U	**AutoNation Cure Bowl**
Coach: Shawn Elliott		Season Record >>	244	297	7-5	ATS>>	5-7	O/U>>	3-9	

Copyright © 2021 by Steve's Football Bible, LLC

GEORGIA STATE PANTHERS   SUN BELT East

STADIUM: Georgia State Stadium {24,333}								Location: Atlanta, GA		COACH: Shawn Elliott		
DATE		Opponent	State	Opp	S/U	Line	ATS	Total	O/U	Trends & Angles		
9/4/2021	vs	ARMY								vs Army - Georgia State leads series 1-0		
9/11/2021	@	North Carolina								1st meeting		
9/18/2021	vs	CHARLOTTE								vs Charlotte - Series tied 1-1		
9/25/2021	@	Auburn								1st meeting		
10/2/2021	vs	APPALACHIAN STATE								vs App State - App State leads series 7-0		
10/9/2021	@	Louisiana-Monroe								vs Louisiana-Monroe - Series tied 3-3		
10/23/2021	vs	TEXAS STATE								Game 3-0 O/U @ home vs Texas State since 2014		
10/30/2021	@	Georgia Southern								vs Georgia Southern - G State leads series 4-3		
11/4/2021	@	Louisiana								vs Louisiana - Louisiana leads series 5-0		
11/13/2021	@	Coastal Carolina								vs Coastal Carolina – Ga. State leads series 3-1		
11/20/2021	vs	ARKANSAS STATE								vs Arkansas State – Ark. State leads series 6-1		
11/27/2021	vs	TROY								vs Troy - Troy leads series 5-3		
12/4/2021	vs									Sun Belt Championship		
	vs									BOWL GAME		

Pointspread Analysis Non-Conference		Pointspread Analysis Conference	
0-14 S/U vs Non-Conf. as 20.5 point or more Dog since 2010		vs Texas State - Texas State leads series 4-3	
Dog		Game 4-0 O/U vs Texas State since 2016	
1-17 S/U as 20.5 point or more Dog since 2010			
1-22 S/U as 10.5-20 point Dog since 2013			
0-5 S/U & ATS as 7.5-10 point Dog since 2013			
0-15 S/U as home Dog of 5 pts or more since 2013	Alabama	2-8 S/U in 1st road game of season since 2011	
Favorite	CHARLOTTE	3-8 S/U in 2nd home game of season since 2010	
6-1 S/U & ATS as 3 point or less favorite since 2015	Auburn	2-9 S/U in 2nd road game of season since 2010	
3-0 S/U on road as 3.5-7 point favorite since 2017	ARKANSAS STATE	5-1 ATS prior to playing Troy since 2015	

This book is a definitive account of College Football Trophy games across all divisions in FBS, FCS, Division 2 and Division 3. Full of historical information and game recaps of some of the memorable and notable games for each trophy game/rivalry. This book is for College Football fans of all ages, being both entertaining and educational, it is a must read if you love college football.

College Football History "Trophy Games"

{8.5" x 11"} {430 pages}

Price $29.99 + $5.00 Shipping & Handling

$34.99

These books available at numerous online retailers

Copyright © 2021 by Steve's Football Bible, LLC

2020-Georgia Tech		Opponent	Tech	Opp	S/U	Line	ATS	Total	O/U	
9/12/2020	@	Florida State	16	13	W	13.5	W	50.0	U	
9/19/2020	vs	CENTRAL FLORIDA	21	49	L	8.0	L	63.5	O	
9/26/2020	@	Syracuse	20	37	L	-7.0	L	51.5	O	
10/9/2020	vs	LOUISVILLE	46	27	W	4.5	W	63.0	O	
10/17/2020	vs	CLEMSON	7	73	L	27.0	L	63.5	O	
10/24/2020	@	Boston College	27	48	L	3.5	L	57.5	O	
10/31/2020	vs	NOTRE DAME	13	31	L	20.5	W	58.0	U	
11/28/2020	vs	DUKE	56	33	W	2.5	W	57.5	O	
12/5/2020	@	NC State	13	23	L	7.0	L	61.0	U	
12/10/2020	vs	PITTSBURGH	20	34	L	7.0	L	56.0	U	
Coach: Geoff Collins		Season Record >>	239	368	3-7	ATS>>	4-6	O/U>>	6-4	
2019-Georgia Tech		Opponent	Tech	Opp	S/U	Line	ATS	Total	O/U	
8/29/2019	@	Clemson	14	52	L	36.5	L	61.0	O	
9/7/2019	vs	SOUTH FLORIDA	14	10	W	-4.5	L	58.5	U	
9/14/2019	vs	THE CITADEL	24	27	L	-26.5	L	NT	---	{OT}
9/28/2019	@	Temple	3	24	L	9.5	L	48.0	U	
10/5/2019	vs	NORTH CAROLINA	22	38	L	10.0	L	47.0	O	
10/12/2019	@	Duke	23	41	L	17.5	L	47.5	O	
10/19/2019	@	Miami	28	21	W	18.0	W	46.0	O	{OT}
11/2/2019	vs	PITTSBURGH	10	20	L	9.0	L	44.0	U	
11/9/2019	@	Virginia	28	33	L	16.0	W	45.5	O	
11/16/2019	vs	VIRGINIA TECH	0	45	L	6.0	L	51.5	U	"Battle of the Techs"
11/23/2019	vs	NC STATE	28	26	W	2.5	W	46.5	O	
11/30/2019	vs	GEORGIA	7	52	L	28.5	L	46.0	O	"Clean, old fashioned Hate"
Coach: Geoff Collins		Season Record >>	201	389	3-9	ATS>>	3-9	O/U>>	7-4	
2018-Georgia Tech		Opponent	Tech	Opp	S/U	Line	ATS	Total	O/U	
9/1/2018	vs	ALCORN STATE	41	0	W	-42.0	L	NT	---	
9/8/2018	@	South Florida	38	49	L	-3.0	L	60.0	O	
9/15/2018	@	Pittsburgh	19	24	L	-3.5	L	54.5	U	
9/22/2018	vs	CLEMSON	21	49	L	15.5	L	56.5	O	
9/29/2018	vs	BOWLING GREEN	63	17	W	-28.5	W	65.0	O	
10/5/2018	@	Louisville	66	31	W	-5.5	W	56.0	O	
10/13/2018	vs	DUKE	14	28	L	-1.0	L	55.0	U	
10/25/2018	@	Virginia Tech	49	28	W	3.0	W	58.5	O	"Battle of the Techs"
11/3/2018	@	North Carolina	38	28	W	-3.5	W	65.0	O	
11/10/2018	vs	MIAMI	27	21	W	-1.0	W	50.5	U	
11/17/2018	vs	VIRGINIA	30	27	W	-6.5	L	52.0	O	{OT}
11/24/2018	@	Georgia	21	45	L	17.0	L	59.5	O	"Clean, old fashioned Hate"
12/26/2018	vs	Minnesota	10	34	L	-5.0	L	57.0	U	Quick Lane Bowl
Coach: Paul Johnson		Season Record >>	437	381	7-6	ATS>>	5-8	O/U>>	8-4	
2017-Georgia Tech		Opponent	Tech	Opp	S/U	Line	ATS	Total	O/U	
9/4/2017	vs	Tennessee	41	42	L	4.0	W	54.0	O	2 OT
9/9/2017	vs	JACKSONVILLE STATE	37	10	W	-16.0	W	NT	---	
9/23/2017	vs	PITTSBURGH	35	17	W	-7.5	W	54.0	U	
9/30/2017	vs	NORTH CAROLINA	33	7	W	-10.0	W	58.0	U	
10/14/2017	@	Miami	24	25	L	6.5	W	53.0	U	
10/21/2017	vs	WAKE FOREST	38	24	W	-3.5	W	49.0	O	
10/28/2017	@	Clemson	10	24	L	14.0	T	51.0	U	
11/4/2017	@	Virginia	36	40	L	-7.5	L	50.5	O	
11/11/2017	vs	VIRGINIA TECH	28	22	W	3.0	W	47.5	O	"Battle of the Techs"
11/18/2017	@	Duke	20	43	L	-7.0	L	49.0	O	
11/25/2017	vs	GEORGIA	7	38	L	11.5	L	51.0	U	"Clean, old fashioned Hate"
Coach: Paul Johnson		Season Record >>	309	292	5-6	ATS>>	7-3-1	O/U>>	5-5	

Copyright © 2021 by Steve's Football Bible, LLC

GEORGIA TECH YELLOWJACKETS ACC Coastal

STADIUM: Bobby Dodd Stadium @ Historic Grant Field {55,000}					Location: Atlanta, GA			COACH: Geoff Collins		
DATE		Opponent	Tech	Opp	S/U	Line	ATS	Total	O/U	Trends & Angles
9/4/2021	vs	*NORTHERN ILLINOIS*								1st meeting
9/11/2021	vs	*KENNESAW STATE*								1st meeting
9/18/2021	@	Clemson								0-7 S/U @ Clemson as Dog since 2006
9/25/2021	vs	NORTH CAROLINA								9-2 S/U @ home vs UNC since 1999
10/2/2021	vs	PITTSBURGH								Game 0-4 O/U vs Pittsburgh since 2017
10/9/2021	@	Duke								vs Duke - Georgia Tech leads series 52-13-1
10/23/2021	@	Virginia								2-12 S/U @ Virginia since 1992
10/30/2021	vs	VIRGINIA TECH								1-4 S/U @ home vs VPI since 2011 {1-4 ATS}
11/6/2021	@	Miami								1-5 S/U @ Miami since 2009
11/13/2021	vs	BOSTON COLLEGE								vs Boston College - G Tech leads series 7-3
11/20/2021	@	*Notre Dame*								1-8 S/U @ Notre Dame since 1968
11/27/2021	vs	*GEORGIA*								vs Georgia - Georgia leads series 68-41-5
12/5/2020	vs									ACC Championship
	vs									BOWL GAME

Pointspread Analysis Non-Conference		Pointspread Analysis Conference
0-7 S/U vs Non-Conf. as 15.5 point or more Dog since 1983		vs Clemson - Georgia Tech leads series 51-33-2
3-13 S/U vs Non-Conf. as 10.5-15 point Dog since 1983		9-3 S/U vs Clemson as 6.5 point or less Dog since 1984
1-7 O/U vs Non-Conf. as 3 point or less Dog since 1993		10-2 ATS vs Clemson as 6.5 point or less Dog since 1984
0-4 S/U vs Non-Conf. as 3 point or less Dog since 2010		1-12 S/U vs Clemson as 7.0-15.5 Dog since 1983
7-1 S/U vs Non-Conf. as 10.5-15 point favorite since 1993		0-5 ATS vs Duke as favorite since 2014
20-2 S/U vs Non-conf. as 15.5 point or more favorite since 1998		23-1 S/U vs Duke as 8 point or more favorite since 1984
0-9 S/U vs Georgia as 13.5 point or more Dog since 1983		1-6 S/U vs Miami as Dog since 2009
5-1 ATS vs Notre Dame since 1997		3-8 S/U vs Miami since 2009
Game 1-8 O/U vs Notre Dame since 1979		vs Miami - Georgia Tech leads series 13-12
Bowl Games		vs North Carolina - Georgia Tech leads series 30-22-3
4-0 S/U in Sugar Bowl		13-2 S/U vs North Carolina as favorite since 1991
2-7 S/U vs SEC in Bowl Games since 1960		0-6 S/U vs North Carolina as 8 point or more Dog since 1983
0-4 S/U in Chick-Fil-A Peach Bowl		8-0-1 S/U vs UNC as 10 point or more favorite since 1989
2-7 O/U in Bowl Games since 2008		vs Pittsburgh - Pittsburgh leads series 10-5
6-1 O/U in Bowl Games as 3 point or less favorite since 1991		vs Virginia - Georgia Tech leads series 21-20-1
Dog		2-8-1 ATS @ Virginia since 1999
0-11 S/U as 20.5 point or more Dog since 1993		0-6 S/U @ Virginia as Dog since 1992
2-13 S/U as 15.5-20 point Dog since 1983		1-8 S/U vs Virginia as 3.5-7 point Dog since 1988
0-6 S/U @ home as 10.5-15 point Dog since 1992		6-0 S/U vs Virginia as 9.5-12 point favorite since 2000
0-5 O/U @ home as 10.5-15 point Dog since 1998		vs Virginia Tech - Virginia Tech leads series 10-7
1-8 S/U @ home as 7.5-10 point Dog since 1985		4-1 S/U vs Virginia Tech as Dog since 2014
1-7 O/U @ home as 3.5-7 point Dog since 2009		0-4 ATS vs Virginia Tech as favorite since 1990

Favorite		
5-0 S/U @ home as 3.5-7 point favorite since 2016	N. ILLINOIS	24-2 S/U in 1st home game of season since 1995
5-0 S/U & ATS @ home as 7.5-10 point favorite since 2010	KENNESAW	8-3 S/U in 2nd home game of season since 2011 (7-2 ATS)
14-2 S/U @ home as 10.5-15 point favorite since 2005	UNC	6-1 O/U prior to playing Pittsburgh since 2013
7-2 O/U on road as 10.5-15 point favorite since 2001	Duke	3-9 O/U prior to playing Virginia since 2007
20-3 S/U as 10.5-15 point favorite since 2005	Duke	10-2 S/U prior to playing Virginia since 2008
19-0 S/U as 15.5-20 point favorite since 1990	Virginia	3-9 S/U after playing Duke since 2009
8-0 S/U on road as 15.5-25 point favorite since 1984	VA TECH	2-5 O/U prior to playing Miami since 2013
15-1 S/U as 25.5 point or more favorite since 1991	Notre Dame	13-2 S/U prior to playing Georgia since 2005
2-14 S/U on road vs ranked teams since 2009		1-7 O/U when ranked vs Georgia since 2000
1-8 S/U on road vs #1 ranked teams all time		
1-8-1 S/U vs #2 ranked teams all time		
1-10 S/U vs #3 ranked teams all time {0-5 at home}		
1-10 S/U vs #4 ranked teams all time		

Copyright © 2021 by Steve's Football Bible, LLC

HAWAII RAINBOW WARRIORS   MOUNTAIN WEST West

2020-Hawaii		Opponent	HAW	Opp	S/U	Line	ATS	Total	O/U	
10/24/2020	@	Fresno State	34	19	W	3.0	W	64.0	U	"Golden Screwdriver Trophy"
10/30/2020	@	Wyoming	7	31	L	-3.0	L	59.5	U	"Paniolo Trophy"
11/7/2020	vs	NEW MEXICO	39	33	W	-13.0	L	66.5	O	
11/14/2020	@	San Diego State	10	34	L	9.5	L	51.0	U	
11/21/2020	vs	BOISE STATE	32	40	L	13.0	W	55.5	O	
11/28/2020	vs	NEVADA	24	21	W	7.0	W	63.0	U	
12/5/2020	vs	SAN JOSE STATE	24	35	L	2.5	L	59.5	U	
12/12/2020	vs	UNLV	38	21	W	-18.5	L	60.0	U	
12/24/2020	vs	Houston	28	14	W	7.0	W	61.0	U	New Mexico Bowl
Coach: Todd Graham		Season Record >>	236	248	5-4	ATS>>	4-5	O/U>>	2-7	

2019-Hawaii		Opponent	HAW	Opp	S/U	Line	ATS	Total	O/U	
8/24/2019	vs	ARIZONA	45	38	W	10.5	W	70.5	O	
9/7/2019	vs	OREGON STATE	31	28	W	-7.0	L	77.0	U	
9/14/2019	@	Washington	20	52	L	21.5	L	59.0	O	
9/21/2019	vs	CENTRAL ARKANSAS	35	16	W	-14.5	W	NT	---	
9/28/2019	@	Nevada	54	3	W	1.5	W	63.0	U	
10/12/2019	@	Boise State	37	59	L	12.5	L	60.0	O	
10/19/2019	vs	AIR FORCE	26	56	L	3.5	L	65.5	O	"Kuter Trophy"
10/26/2019	@	New Mexico	45	31	W	-10.0	W	71.5	O	
11/2/2019	vs	FRESNO STATE	38	41	L	-2.0	L	68.0	O	"Golden Screwdriver Trophy"
11/9/2019	vs	SAN JOSE STATE	42	40	W	-7.5	L	78.5	O	
11/16/2019	@	Unlv	21	7	W	-7.0	W	72.5	U	
11/23/2019	vs	SAN DIEGO STATE	14	11	W	1.5	W	46.5	U	
11/30/2019	vs	ARMY	52	31	W	-2.0	W	55.0	O	
12/7/2019	@	Bosie State	10	31	L	14.0	L	65.0	U	MWC CHAMPIONSHIP GAME
12/24/2019	vs	BYU	38	34	W	2.5	W	64.5	O	HAWAI'I BOWL
Coach: Nick Rolovich		Season Record >>	508	478	10-5	ATS>>	8-7	O/U>>	9-5	

2018-Hawaii		Opponent	HAW	Opp	S/U	Line	ATS	Total	O/U	
8/25/2018	@	Colorado State	43	34	W	17.0	W	58.0	O	
9/1/2018	vs	NAVY	59	41	W	13.0	W	61.5	O	
9/8/2018	vs	RICE	43	29	W	-17.0	L	68.5	O	
9/15/2018	@	Army	21	28	L	7.0	T	62.0	U	
9/22/2018	vs	DUQUESNE	42	21	W	-37.5	L	NT	---	
9/29/2018	@	San Jose State	44	41	W	-9.5	L	62.0	O	{5 OT}
10/6/2018	vs	WYOMING	17	13	W	3.0	W	53.0	U	"Paniolo Trophy"
10/13/2018	@	Byu	23	49	L	10.5	L	57.5	O	
10/20/2018	vs	NEVADA	22	40	L	-2.0	L	67.5	U	
10/27/2018	@	Fresno State	20	50	L	24.0	L	60.0	O	"Golden Screwdriver Trophy"
11/3/2018	vs	UTAH STATE	17	56	L	18.0	L	72.0	O	
11/17/2018	vs	UNLV	35	28	W	-7.0	T	72.5	U	
11/24/2018	@	San Diego State	31	30	W	18.5	W	54.0	O	{OT}
12/22/2018	vs	Louisiana Tech	14	31	L	-1.0	L	61.5	U	HAWAI'I BOWL
Coach: Nick Rolovich		Season Record >>	431	491	8-6	ATS>>	4-8-2	O/U>>	8-5	

2017-Hawaii		Opponent	HAW	Opp	S/U	Line	ATS	Total	O/U	
8/26/2017	@	Massachusetts	38	35	W	3.0	W	59.5	O	
9/2/2017	vs	WESTERN CAROLINA	41	18	W	-23.5	W	NL	---	
9/9/2017	@	Ucla	23	56	L	24.0	L	62.5	O	
9/23/2017	@	Wyoming	21	28	L	4.5	L	55.0	U	"Paniolo Trophy"
9/30/2017	vs	COLORADO STATE	21	51	L	6.5	L	66.0	O	
10/7/2017	@	Nevada	21	35	L	-3.5	L	62.5	U	
10/14/2017	vs	SAN JOSE STATE	37	26	W	-17.0	L	58.5	O	
10/28/2017	vs	SAN DIEGO STATE	7	28	L	8.0	L	54.5	U	
11/4/2017	@	Unlv	23	31	L	7.0	L	58.5	U	
11/11/2017	vs	FRESNO STATE	21	31	L	9.5	L	52.5	U	"Golden Screwdriver Trophy"
11/18/2017	@	Utah State	0	38	L	10.0	L	56.0	U	
11/25/2017	vs	BYU	20	30	L	3.0	L	47.0	O	
Coach: Nick Rolovich		Season Record >>	273	407	3-9	ATS>>	2-10	O/U>>	5-6	

Copyright © 2021 by Steve's Football Bible, LLC

HAWAII RAINBOW WARRIORS   MOUNTAIN WEST West

STADIUM: Ching Complex {20,000}						Location: Honolulu, HI			COACH: Todd Graham	
DATE		Opponent	Haw	Opp	S/U	Line	ATS	Total	O/U	Trends & Angles
8/28/2021	@	*Ucla*								vs UCLA - UCLA leads series 3-0
9/4/2021	vs	*PORTLAND STATE*								vs Portland State - Hawaii leads series 4-1
9/11/2021	@	*Oregon State*								1-4 S/U vs Oregon State since 2006
9/18/2021	vs	SAN JOSE STATE								0-5 ATS @ home vs San Jose State since 2013
9/25/2021	@	*New Mexico State*								vs New Mexico State - Hawaii leads series 8-0
10/2/2021	vs	FRESNO STATE								vs Fresno State - Fresno leads series 29-23-1
10/16/2021	@	Nevada								2-8 S/U @ Nevada since 2001
10/23/2021	vs	*NEW MEXICO STATE*								7-0 S/U vs NMSU as favorite since 2005
10/30/2021	@	Utah State								0-5 S/U & ATS vs Utah State since 2011
11/6/2021	vs	SAN DIEGO STATE								2-11 ATS @ home vs San Diego State since 1985
11/13/2021	@	Unlv								1-5 S/U @ UNLV since 2009
11/20/2021	vs	COLORADO STATE								1-7 S/U vs Colorado State as Dog since 1995
11/27/2021	@	Wyoming								0-5 S/U @ Wyoming as Dog since 1993
12/4/2021	vs									MWC Championship
	vs									BOWL GAME

Pointspread Analysis Non-Conference		Pointspread Analysis Conference
0-27 S/U vs Non-Conf. as 15.5 point or more Dog since 1991		7-26-1 ATS @ home vs Conference since 2013
6-0 O/U vs Non-Conf. as 3 point or less Dog since 2003		5-0 O/U vs Colorado State as Dog since 2012
9-0 S/U vs Non-Conf. as 3.5-7 point favorite since 2002		1-5 S/U vs Fresno State as Dog since 2012
8-1 S/U vs Non-Conf. as 15.5-20 point favorite since 1990		1-9 S/U vs Fresno State as 12.5 point or more Dog since 1993
1-7-1 ATS vs Non-Conf. as 15.5-20 point favorite since 1990		5-0 S/U & ATS vs Fresno State as 9 point or less Dog since 1995
20-1 S/U vs Non-Conf. as 20.5 point or more favorite since 1989		5-0 S/U vs Fresno State as 4 point or less favorite since 1986
Game 1-6 O/U vs Oregon State since 1989		vs Nevada - Nevada leads series 14-11
0-3 S/U vs Oregon State as 9.5 point or more Dog since 2008		1-5 S/U @ Nevada as Dog since 2005
Dog		Game 0-8 O/U vs Nevada since 2013
0-12 S/U as 30.5 point or more Dog since 1996		1-5 S/U vs Nevada as 7 point or more Dog since 2009
0-12 S/U as 25.5 point or more Dog since 1996		4-0 S/U vs Nevada as 10.5 point or more favorite since 2000
0-14 S/U @ home as 20.5 point or more Dog Since 1991		0-6 S/U @ UNLV as Dog since 1997
4-15 S/U as 15.5-20 point Dog since 1985		1-5-1 ATS vs UNLV since 2014
9-1 O/U as 15.5-20 point Dog since 2011		vs Unlv - Hawaii leads series 18-12
3-17 S/U as 10.5-15 point Dog since 2000		2-7 S/U vs New Mexico since 1993
4-16 S/U @ home as 10.5-15 point Dog since 1985		2-8 ATS vs New Mexico since 1991
1-8 S/U on road as 7.5-10 point Dog since 2009 {2-7 ATS}		vs San Jose State - Hawaii leads series 22-20-1
2-8 O/U on road as 7.5-10 point Dog since 1992		Game 4-1 O/U @ home vs San Jose State since 2013
2-14 S/U @ home as 7.5-10 point Dog since 1987		0-4 S/U & ATS vs San Jose State as 4.0-8.5 point Dog since 1998
3-15 S/U as 3.5-7 point Dog since 2012		10-0 S/U vs San Jose St. as 9.5 point or more favorite since 2001
Favorite		4-20-1 ATS vs San Diego State since 1985
1-18-1 ATS as a favorite since 2015		1-8 ATS vs San Diego State as favorite since 1985
2-7 O/U @ home as 3 point or less favorite since 2007		4-16 S/U vs San Diego since 1990
0-6 O/U on road as 3.5-7 point favorite since 2010		vs San Diego State - SDSU leads series 22-11-2
10-2 S/U @ home as 3.5-7 point favorite since 2002		2-14 S/U vs San Diego State as Dog since 1986
23-2 S/U as 10.5-15 point favorite since 1985		vs Utah State - Utah State leads series 10-6
14-1 S/U @ home as 15.5-20 point favorite since 1989		0-4 S/U & ATS vs Utah State as Dog since 2013
0-7 ATS @ home as 15.5-20 point favorite since 2006		vs Wyoming - Wyoming leads series 14-10
36-1 S/U as 20.5 point or more favorite since 1987		2-7 S/U vs Wyoming since 1993
4-0 S/U on road as 20.5 point or more favorite since 2006		0-6 S/U vs Wyoming as 6.5 point or more Dog since 1987
9-1 ATS in 1st home game of season since 2006	PORTLAND STATE	
1-12 S/U in 2nd road game of season since 2008	Oregon State	
2-8-1 ATS in 2nd road game of season since 2010	Oregon State	5-0 S/U on road when ranked since 2007
10-2 O/U in 2nd home game of season since 2009	SAN JOSE STATE	8-0 S/U @ home when ranked since 2007
3-9 S/U prior to playing Fresno State since 2008	New Mexico State	1-20 S/U on road vs ranked teams all time
1-7 ATS prior to playing Fresno State since 2012	New Mexico State	
1-9 S/U prior to playing Nevada since 2011	FRESNO STATE	
1-9 ATS after playing Fresno State since 2011	Nevada	
5-12 S/U prior to playing San Diego State since 1993	Utah State	
0-9 S/U after playing San Diego State since 1997	Unlv	
0-6 S/U prior to playing Colorado State since 1996	Unlv	
10-3 O/U in final home game of season since 2008	COLORADO STATE	3-8 S/U prior to playing Wyoming since 1992

Copyright © 2021 by Steve's Football Bible, LLC

HOUSTON COUGARS   AMERICAN West

2020-Houston		Opponent	HOU	Opp	S/U	Line	ATS	Total	O/U	
10/8/2020	vs	TULANE	49	31	W	-7.0	W	58.0	O	
10/16/2020	vs	BYU	26	43	L	5.0	L	62.5	O	
10/24/2020	@	Navy	37	21	W	-15.5	W	57.0	O	
10/31/2020	vs	CENTRAL FLORIDA	21	44	L	3.0	L	81.0	U	
11/7/2020	@	Cincinnati	10	38	L	11.5	L	51.5	U	
11/14/2020	vs	SOUTH FLORIDA	56	21	W	-15.0	W	58.5	O	
12/12/2020	@	Memphis	27	30	L	-4.5	L	63.0	U	
12/24/2020	vs	Hawaii	14	28	L	-7.0	L	61.0	U	New Mexico Bowl
Coach: Dana Holgerson		Season Record >>	240	256	3-5	ATS>>	3-5	O/U>>	4-4	
2019-Houston		Opponent	HOU	Opp	S/U	Line	ATS	Total	O/U	
8/31/2019	@	Oklahoma	31	49	L	22.0	W	79.5	O	
9/7/2019	vs	PRAIRIE VIEW A&M	37	17	W	-37.5	L	NT	---	
9/13/2019	vs	Washington State	24	31	L	8.5	W	74.0	U	NRG Stadium
9/19/2019	@	Tulane	31	38	L	4.5	L	57.5	O	
9/28/2019	@	North Texas	46	25	W	8.0	W	59.0	O	
10/12/2019	vs	CINCINNATI	23	38	L	9.5	L	50.0	O	
10/19/2019	@	Connecticut	24	17	W	-21.5	L	56.0	U	
10/24/2019	vs	SMU	31	34	L	12.0	W	65.0	T	
11/2/2019	@	Central Florida	29	44	L	21.0	W	72.5	O	
11/16/2019	vs	MEMPHIS	27	45	L	9.5	L	71.5	O	
11/23/2019	@	Tulsa	24	14	W	6.5	W	57.0	U	"Battle for the Best City"
11/30/2019	vs	NAVY	41	56	L	9.5	L	56.5	O	
Coach: Dana Holgerson		Season Record >>	368	408	4-8	ATS>>	6-6	O/U>>	7-3-1	
2018-Houston		Opponent	HOU	Opp	S/U	Line	ATS	Total	O/U	
9/1/2018	@	Rice	45	27	W	-26.0	L	56.0	O	"Bayou Bucket Classic"
9/8/2018	vs	ARIZONA	45	18	W	-3.0	W	70.0	U	
9/15/2018	@	Texas Tech	49	63	L	PK	L	69.0	O	
9/22/2018	vs	TEXAS SOUTHERN	70	14	W	-55.0	W	NT	---	
10/4/2018	vs	TULSA	41	26	W	-17.5	L	70.0	U	"Battle for the Best City"
10/13/2018	@	East Carolina	42	20	W	-16.0	W	69.5	U	
10/20/2018	@	Navy	49	36	W	-11.0	W	58.5	O	
10/27/2018	vs	SOUTH FLORIDA	57	36	W	-9.5	W	77.5	O	
11/3/2018	@	Smu	31	45	L	-13.5	L	70.5	O	
11/10/2018	vs	TEMPLE	49	59	L	-3.5	L	69.5	O	
11/15/2018	vs	TULANE	48	17	W	-7.5	W	68.0	U	
11/23/2018	@	Memphis	31	52	L	9.5	L	74.5	O	
12/22/2018	vs	Army	14	70	L	6.5	L	56.0	O	Armed Forces Bowl
Coach: Major Applewhite		Season Record >>	571	483	8-5	ATS>>	6-7	O/U>>	8-4	
2017-Houston		Opponent	HOU	Opp	S/U	Line	ATS	Total	O/U	
9/9/2017	@	Arizona	19	16	W	-2.0	W	65.0	U	
9/16/2017	vs	RICE	38	3	W	-22.5	W	54.0	U	"Bayou Bucket Classic"
9/23/2017	vs	TEXAS TECH	24	27	L	-7.0	L	68.0	U	
9/30/2017	@	Temple	20	13	W	-10.5	L	44.0	U	
10/7/2017	vs	SMU	35	22	W	-10.0	W	60.0	U	
10/14/2017	@	Tulsa	17	45	L	-14.0	L	63.5	U	"Battle for the Best City"
10/19/2017	vs	MEMPHIS	38	42	L	PK	L	62.0	O	
10/28/2017	@	South Floirda	28	24	W	10.0	W	52.5	U	
11/4/2017	vs	EAST CAROLINA	52	27	W	-23.5	W	62.5	O	
11/18/2017	@	Tulane	17	20	L	-9.5	L	47.0	U	
11/24/2017	vs	NAVY	24	14	W	-6.5	W	55.0	U	
12/24/2017	vs	Fresno State	27	33	L	-2.5	L	52.0	O	HAWAI'I BOWL
Coach: Major Applewhite		Season Record >>	339	286	7-5	ATS>>	6-6	O/U>>	3-9	

Copyright © 2021 by Steve's Football Bible, LLC

HOUSTON COUGARS AMERICAN West

STADIUM: TDECU Stadium {40,000}					Location: Houston, TX		COACH: Dana Holgerson			
DATE		Opponent	Hou	Opp	S/U	Line	ATS	Total	O/U	Trends & Angles
9/4/2021	vs	*Texas Tech*								1-8 S/U vs Texas Tech since 1991
9/11/2021	@	*Rice*								0-4 ATS @ Rice since 2006
9/18/2021	vs	*GRAMBLING STATE*								vs Grambling State - Houston leads series 2-0
9/25/2021	vs	**NAVY**								vs Navy - Houston leads series 5-2
10/1/2021	@	Tulsa								Game 1-6 O/U @ Tulsa since 2005
10/7/2021	@	Tulane								6-2 S/U & ATS @ Tulane since 2003
10/23/2021	vs	**EAST CAROLINA**								12-2 S/U prior to playing SMU since 2005
10/30/2021	vs	**SMU**								10-2-1 S/U @ home vs SMU since 1989
11/6/2021	@	South Florida								5-0 S/U vs South Florida since 2013
11/13/2021	@	Temple								3-0 S/U @ Temple as favorite since 1987
11/19/2021	vs	**MEMPHIS**								0-6 ATS vs Memphis since 2015
11/27/2021	@	*Connecticut*								vs U Conn - Houston leads series 2-1
12/4/2021	vs									AAC Championship
	vs									BOWL GAME

Pointspread Analysis Non-Conference		Pointspread Analysis Bowl Games
0-14 S/U vs Non-Conf. as 20.5 point or more Dog since 1993		4-1 O/U in Armed Forces Bowl since 2005
2-14 S/U vs Non-Conf. as 15.5-20 point Dog since 1986		1-6 S/U in Bowl Games as 3.5-7 point Dog since 1979
8-0 O/U vs Non-Conf. as 3.5-7 point Dog since 2003		**Conference**
1-7 O/U vs Non-Conf. as 3.5-7 point favorite since 2008		3-0 S/U vs UCF as 9.5 point or more favorite since 2006
13-2 S/U vs Non-Conf. as 10.5 point or more favorite since 1983		vs Cincinnati - Houston leads series 15-12
vs Texas Tech - Houston leads series 18-13-1		vs Memphis - Houston leads series 15-14
Game 4-0 O/U @ Rice since 2006		3-0 S/U @ home vs Memphis as favorite since 2009
vs Rice - Houston leads series 31-11		0-5 S/U vs Memphis since 2016
5-0 S/U vs Rice since 2011		Game 5-1 O/U vs Navy since 2015
13-0 S/U vs Rice as 10.5 point or more favorite since 1983		vs Smu - Houston leads series 21-13-1
4-0 S/U vs Texas Tech as 7.5 point or more favorite since 1983		Game 1-5-1 O/U @ home vs SMU since 2007
0-4 S/U vs Texas Tech as Dog since 1992		vs South Florida - Houston leads series 5-2
Dog		Game 0-3 O/U @ South Florida since 2001
0-18 S/U as 20.5 point or more Dog since 1986		6-0 S/U @ home vs SMU as 16.5 point or more favorite since 1989
4-27 S/U as 15.5-20 point Dog since 1983		vs Tulane - Houston leads series 18-7
2-16 S/U on road as 15.5-20 point Dog since 1985		Game 2-5 O/U @ Tulane since 2005
2-17 S/U on road as 10.5-15 point Dog since 1986		10-1 S/U vs Tulane as 12.5 point or more favorite since 1999
5-1 ATS on road as 10.5-15 point Dog since 2005		3-10 ATS vs Tulsa as favorite since 1985
0-6 S/U @ home as 10.5-15 point Dog since 1983		vs Tulsa - Houston leads series 24-19
8-3 ATS on road as 7.5-10 point Dog since 1995		1-5 S/U & ATS vs Tulsa as 2.5-4.5 point favorite since 1985
3-10 S/U on road as 3.5-7 point Dog since 1999		
5-1 S/U & ATS on road as 3 point or less Dog since 1999	GRAMBLING	14-2 S/U in 1st home game of season since 2005
12-3 O/U as 3.5-7 point Dog since 2005	GRAMBLING	7-1 S/U & ATS after playing Rice since 2007
Favorite	E. CAROLINA	11-3 S/U after playing Tulane since 2006
	E. CAROLINA	10-4 ATS after playing Tulane since 2007
1-7 S/U on road as 3.5-7 point favorite since 2008	Tulane	7-1 S/U prior to playing East Carolina since 2003
0-9 ATS on road as 3.5-7 point favorite since 2007	MEMPHIS	14-2 S/U in final home game of season since 2005
1-13 O/U as 7.5-10 point favorite since 2013	MEMPHIS	8-2 ATS in final home game of season since 2011
13-1 S/U @ home as 7.5-10 point favorite since 1999	Connecticut	2-12 S/U in final road game of season since 2007
15-5 S/U as 10.5-15 point favorite since 2006		
24-4 S/U as 15.5-20 point favorite since 1984		
18-0 S/U @ home as 20.5-25 point favorite since 1989		3-32 S/U on road vs ranked teams since 1985
9-0 S/U as 25.5-30 point favorite since 1988		1-5 S/U vs ranked SMU all time
17-1 S/U @ home as 25.5 point or more favorite since 1988		29-1 S/U @ home when ranked since 1988
6-0 S/U on road as 25.5 point or more favorite since 1988		10-0 S/U when ranked vs Rice all time

Copyright © 2021 by Steve's Football Bible, LLC

ILLINOIS FIGHTING ILLINI   BIG TEN West

2020-Illinois		Opponent	ILL	Opp	S/U	Line	ATS	Total	O/U	
10/23/2020	@	Wisconsin	7	45	L	20.5	L	51.5	O	
10/31/2020	vs	PURDUE	24	31	L	10.0	W	54.5	O	"Purdue Cannon"
11/7/2020	vs	MINNESOTA	14	41	L	7.5	L	64.5	U	
11/14/2020	@	Rutgers	23	20	W	5.5	W	51.5	U	
11/21/2020	@	Nebraska	41	23	W	16.5	W	62.0	O	
12/5/2020	vs	IOWA	21	35	L	13.5	L	53.0	O	
12/12/2020	@	Northwestern	10	28	L	13.0	L	41.0	U	"Land of Lincoln Trophy"
12/19/2020	@	Penn State	21	56	L	16.0	L	53.5	O	
Coach: Lovie Smith		Season Record >>	161	279	2-6	ATS>>	3-5	O/U>>	5-3	
2019-Illinois		Opponent	ILL	Opp	S/U	Line	ATS	Total	O/U	
8/31/2019	vs	AKRON	42	3	W	-18.0	W	60.0	U	
9/7/2019	@	Connecticut	31	23	W	-21.5	L	59.0	U	
9/14/2019	vs	EASTERN MICHIGAN	31	34	L	-7.5	L	57.0	O	
9/21/2019	vs	NEBRASKA	38	42	L	13.0	W	63.0	O	
10/5/2019	@	Minnesota	17	40	L	14.5	L	57.0	T	
10/12/2019	vs	MICHIGAN	25	42	L	24.5	W	48.5	O	
10/19/2019	vs	WISCONSIN	24	23	W	31.0	W	52.0	U	
10/26/2019	@	Purdue	24	6	W	9.5	W	53.5	U	"Purdue Cannon"
11/2/2019	vs	RUTGERS	38	10	W	-18.5	W	48.5	U	
11/9/2019	@	Michigan State	37	34	W	15.5	W	47.5	O	
11/23/2019	@	Iowa	10	19	L	15.5	W	48.5	U	
11/30/2019	vs	NORTHWESTERN	10	29	L	-6.0	L	39.0	T	"Land of Lincoln Trophy"
12/30/2019	vs	California	20	35	L	6.0	L	48.0	O	Redbox Bowl
Coach: Lovie Smith		Season Record >>	347	340	6-7	ATS>>	8-5	O/U>>	5-6-2	
2018-Illinois		Opponent	ILL	Opp	S/U	Line	ATS	Total	O/U	
9/1/2018	vs	KENT STATE	31	24	W	-18.0	L	57.0	U	
9/8/2018	vs	WESTERN ILLINOIS	34	14	W	-7.0	W	NT	---	
9/15/2018	vs	SOUTH FLORIDA	19	25	L	14.0	W	58.5	U	Soldier Field
9/21/2018	vs	PENN STATE	24	63	L	27.0	L	60.0	O	
10/6/2018	@	Rutgers	38	17	W	-4.5	W	50.5	O	
10/13/2018	vs	PURDUE	7	46	L	10.0	L	64.0	U	"Purdue Cannon"
10/20/2018	@	Wisconsin	20	49	L	24.0	L	53.0	O	
10/27/2018	@	Maryland	33	63	L	16.5	L	53.5	O	
11/3/2018	vs	MINNESOTA	55	31	W	10.0	W	62.0	O	
11/10/2018	@	Nebraska	35	54	L	17.5	L	71.0	O	
11/17/2018	vs	IOWA	0	63	L	15.0	L	59.5	O	
11/24/2018	@	Northwestern	16	24	L	14.5	W	57.5	U	"Land of Lincoln Trophy"
Coach: Lovie Smith		Season Record >>	312	473	4-8	ATS>>	5-7	O/U>>	7-4	
2017-Illinois		Opponent	ILL	Opp	S/U	Line	ATS	Total	O/U	
9/2/2017	vs	BALL STATE	24	21	W	-5.5	L	55.5	U	
9/9/2017	vs	WESTERN KENTUCKY	20	7	W	5.0	W	51.0	U	
9/15/2017	@	South Florida	23	47	L	16.5	L	55.0	O	
9/30/2017	vs	NEBRASKA	6	28	L	6.0	L	46.5	U	
10/7/2017	@	Iowa	16	45	L	16.0	L	41.5	O	
10/14/2017	vs	RUTGERS	24	35	L	1.5	L	47.0	O	
10/21/2017	@	Minnesota	17	24	L	13.5	W	48.0	U	
10/28/2017	vs	WISCONSIN	10	24	L	27.0	W	51.5	U	
11/4/2017	@	Purdue	10	29	L	14.0	L	49.5	U	"Purdue Cannon"
11/11/2017	vs	INDIANA	14	24	L	10.5	W	50.0	U	
11/18/2017	@	Ohio State	14	52	L	41.0	W	41.0	O	"Illibuck Trophy"
11/25/2017	vs	NORTHWESTERN	7	42	L	15.5	L	46.0	O	"Land of Lincoln Trophy"
Coach: Lovie Smith		Season Record >>	185	378	2-10	ATS>>	5-7	O/U>>	5-7	

Copyright © 2021 by Steve's Football Bible, LLC

ILLINOIS FIGHTING ILLINI   BIG TEN West

STADIUM: Memorial Stadium {60,670}							Location: Champaign, IL			COACH: Bret Bielema
DATE		Opponent	ILL	Opp	S/U	Line	ATS	Total	O/U	Trends & Angles
8/28/2021	vs	Nebraska {Dublin, IRE}								2-8 S/U vs Nebraska since 1985
9/4/2021	vs	TEXAS-SAN ANTONIO								1st meeting
9/11/2021	@	Virginia								vs Virginia - Illinois leads series 2-0
9/18/2021	vs	MARYLAND								vs Maryland - Maryland leads series 1-0
9/25/2021	@	Purdue								Game 1-6 O/U @ Purdue since 2005
10/2/2021	vs	CHARLOTTE								1st meeting
10/9/2021	vs	WISCONSIN								2-14 S/U vs Wisconsin since 2003
10/23/2021	@	Penn State								1-10 S/U @ Penn State since 1993
10/30/2021	vs	RUTGERS								vs Rutgers - Illinois leads series 5-2
11/6/2021	@	Minnesota								0-4 S/U @ Minnesota since 2011
11/20/2021	@	Iowa								0-6 S/U @ Iowa since 2003
11/27/2021	vs	NORTHWESTERN								0-6 S/U vs Northwestern since 2015
12/4/2021	vs									Big Ten Championship
	vs									BOWL GAME

Pointspread Analysis Non-Conference

0-5 S/U vs Non-Conf. as 15.5 point or more Dog since 1986
1-17 S/U vs Non-Conf. as 3.5-7 point Dog since 1982
2-7 ATS vs Non-Conf. as 3.5-7 point favorite since 2003
31-1 S/U vs Non-Conf. as 10.5 point or more favorite since 1991

Bowl Games
0-3 S/U vs SEC in Bowl Games

Dog
1-20 S/U @ home as 15.5 point or more Dog since 1999
1-10 S/U on road as 25.5 point or more Dog since 1997
1-19 S/U as 20.5-25 point Dog since 1986
3-24-1 S/U as 15.5-20 point Dog since 1986
3-9 ATS as 15.5-20 point Dog since 2012
10-1 O/U on road as 15.5-20 point Dog since 2009
1-18 S/U @ home as 10.5-15 point Dog since 1987
0-11 S/U on road as 10.5-15 point Dog since 2008
0-21 S/U as 10.5-15 point Dog since 2008
5-13-1 O/U as 10.5-15 point Dog since 2009
2-12 S/U @ home vs Big Ten as 7.5-10 point Dog since 2000
14-6 O/U as 7.5-10 point Dog since 2004
3-9 S/U on road as 7.5-10 point Dog since 1993
2-9 O/U @ home as 3.5-7 point Dog since 2009
8-30 S/U as 3.5-7 point Dog since 1996
3-13 S/U on road as 3.5-7 point Dog since 1996
3-10 S/U @ home vs Big Ten as 3 point or less Dog s/1988 {3-10 ATS}
5-17-1 S/U vs Big Ten as 3 point or less Dog since 1986

Favorite
0-6 O/U on road as 3 point or less favorite since 2003
2-8 ATS @ home as 3.5-7 point favorite since 2003
2-6 O/U as 3.5-7 point favorite since 2001
5-16-1 ATS as 7.5-10 point favorite since 1985
26-1 S/U as 10.5-15 point favorite since 1985
18-2 S/U as 15.5-20 point favorite since 1985
14-0 S/U as 25.5 point or more favorite since 1983
2-8 S/U prior to playing Purdue since 2011
0-9 S/U prior to playing Penn State since 2009
1-13 O/U prior to playing Penn State since 2002
0-10 S/U prior to playing Minnesota since 2010
4-15 S/U prior to playing Iowa since 1995
1-12 S/U in final home game of season since 2008

Pointspread Analysis Conference

Team	
	vs Nebraska - Nebraska leads series 13-4-1
	vs Purdue - Series tied 45-45-6
	1-8 S/U vs Purdue as Dog since 2003
	1-6 O/U vs Purdue as Dog since 2005
	vs Purdue - ROAD team 8-1 S/U since 2012
	0-10 S/U vs Purdue as 6 point or more Dog since 1997
	3-0 S/U & ATS vs Purdue as 3.5 point or less Dog since 1993
	5-0 S/U vs Purdue as 6.5-8.5 point favorite since 1984
	vs Penn State - Penn State leads series 20-5
	0-12 S/U vs Penn State as 9.5 point or more Dog since 1993
	Game 0-3 O/U @ home vs Wisconsin since 2015
	1-10 S/U @ home vs Wisconsin as Dog since 1993
	1-13 S/U vs Wisconsin as Dog since 2003
	vs Wisconsin - Wisconsin leads series 42-37-7
	9-0 S/U vs Wisconsin as 2.5 point or more favorite since 1983
	1-15 S/U vs Wisconsin as 7 point or more Dog since 1996
	5-14 S/U vs Minnesota since 1996
	3-11 S/U vs Minnesota as Dog since 1996
	vs Minnesota - Minnesota leads series 40-29-3
	0-5 S/U vs Minnesota as 4.5 point or less Dog since 1996
	vs Iowa - Illinois leads series 38-35-2
	0-14 S/U vs Iowa as Dog since 1996
	1-12 S/U vs Iowa since 2003
	3-0 S/U vs Iowa as 6.5 point or more favorite since 1994
	vs Northwestern - Illinois leads series 55-53-5
UTSA	2-13 S/U vs Northwestern as Dog since 1996
UTSA	Game 7-3-1 O/U vs Northwestern since 2010
Virginia	0-5 S/U vs Northwestern as 14.5 point or more Dog since 2005
MARYLAND	0-4 S/U & ATS vs Northwestern as 5 point or less favorite since 1995
Purdue	11-2 S/U vs Northwestern as 10.5 point or more favorite since 1984
CHARLOTTE	0-9 S/U after playing Nebraska since 1986
CHARLOTTE	22-1 S/U in 1st home game of season since 1998
WISCONSIN	2-7 S/U in 1st road game of season since 2012
RUTGERS	8-3 S/U in 2nd home game of season since 2010
Minnesota	2-10 S/U in 2nd road game of season since 2009
Iowa	2-9 S/U after playing Purdue since 2010
	3-9 ATS prior to playing Penn State since 2005
	11-2 O/U after playing Penn State since 2001
	3-14 S/U after playing Wisconsin since 2002
	2-12 O/U after playing Wisconsin since 2005
NORTHWESTERN	2-11 S/U in final road game of season since 2008
	2-10-1 O/U after playing Iowa since 2003

Copyright © 2021 by Steve's Football Bible, LLC

 **INDIANA HOOSIERS** **BIG TEN East**

2020-Indiana		Opponent	IND	Opp	S/U	Line	ATS	Total	O/U	
10/24/2020	vs	PENN STATE	36	35	W	6.5	W	61.5	O	{OT}
10/31/2020	@	Rutgers	37	21	W	-11.5	W	54.0	O	
11/7/2020	vs	MICHIGAN	38	21	W	4.5	W	54.5	O	
11/14/2020	@	Michigan State	24	0	W	-7.5	W	52.5	U	"Old Brass Spittoon"
11/21/2020	@	Ohio State	35	42	L	20.5	W	67.0	O	
11/28/2020	vs	MARYLAND	27	11	W	-12.0	W	64.5	U	
12/5/2020	@	Wisconsin	14	6	W	13.0	W	44.5	U	
1/2/2021	vs	Mississippi	20	26	L	-7.5	L	67.5	U	Outback Bowl
Coach: Tom Allen		Season Record >>	231	162	6-2	ATS>>	7-1	O/U>>	4-4	
2019-Indiana		Opponent	IND	Opp	S/U	Line	ATS	Total	O/U	
8/31/2019	vs	Ball State	34	24	W	-18.0	L	60.5	U	Lucas Oil Field
9/7/2019	vs	EASTERN ILLINOIS	52	0	W	-35.5	W	NT	---	
9/14/2019	vs	OHIO STATE	10	51	L	17.5	L	60.5	O	
9/21/2019	vs	CONNECTICUT	38	3	W	-26.0	W	56.0	U	
9/28/2019	@	Michigan State	31	40	L	14.0	W	43.0	O	"Old Brass Spittoon"
10/12/2019	vs	RUTGERS	35	0	W	-27.5	W	49.5	U	
10/19/2019	@	Maryland	34	28	W	-6.5	L	59.0	O	
10/26/2019	@	Nebraska	38	31	W	2.5	W	54.5	O	
11/2/2019	vs	NORTHWESTERN	34	3	W	-8.5	W	44.0	U	
11/16/2019	@	Penn State	27	34	L	14.5	W	55.0	O	
11/23/2019	vs	MICHIGAN	14	39	L	10.0	L	54.0	U	
11/30/2019	@	Purdue	44	41	W	-7.0	L	56.5	O	"The Old Oaken Bucket"
1/2/2020	vs	Tennessee	22	23	L	3.5	W	56.0	U	Gator Bowl
Coach: Tom Allen		Season Record >>	413	317	8-5	ATS>>	8-5	O/U>>	6-6	
2018-Indiana		Opponent	IND	Opp	S/U	Line	ATS	Total	O/U	
9/1/2018	@	Florida International	38	28	W	-13.0	L	55.0	O	
9/8/2018	vs	VIRGINIA	20	16	W	-5.0	L	50.0	U	
9/15/2018	vs	BALL STATE	38	10	W	-15.0	W	60.0	U	
9/22/2018	vs	MICHIGAN STATE	21	35	L	6.5	L	51.0	O	"Old Brass Spittoon"
9/29/2018	@	Rutgers	24	17	W	-16.5	L	49.0	U	
10/6/2018	@	Ohio State	26	49	L	28.0	W	64.5	O	
10/13/2018	vs	IOWA	16	42	L	3.5	L	52.5	O	
10/20/2018	vs	PENN STATE	28	33	L	14.0	W	57.0	O	
10/26/2018	@	Minnesota	31	38	L	-2.5	L	54.0	O	
11/10/2018	vs	MARYLAND	34	32	W	-1.0	W	55.0	O	
11/17/2018	@	Michigan	20	31	L	28.0	W	53.5	U	
11/24/2018	vs	PURDUE	21	28	L	3.5	L	65.0	U	"The Old Oaken Bucket"
Coach: Tom Allen		Season Record >>	317	359	5-7	ATS>>	5-7	O/U>>	7-5	
2017-Indiana		Opponent	IND	Opp	S/U	Line	ATS	Total	O/U	
8/31/2017	vs	OHIO STATE	21	49	L	20.5	L	55.0	O	
9/9/2017	@	Virginia	34	17	W	-4.0	W	55.0	U	
9/23/2017	vs	GEORGIA SOUTHERN	52	17	W	-22.0	W	50.0	O	
9/30/2017	@	Penn State	14	45	L	18.5	L	60.5	U	
10/7/2017	vs	CHARLESTON SOUTHERN	27	0	W	-28.5	L	NT	---	
10/14/2017	vs	MICHIGAN	20	27	L	7.0	T	44.0	O	{OT}
10/21/2017	@	Michigan State	9	17	L	6.5	L	47.0	U	"Old Brass Spittoon"
10/28/2017	@	Maryland	39	42	L	-6.5	L	53.0	O	
11/4/2017	vs	WISCONSIN	17	45	L	10.5	L	49.0	O	
11/11/2017	@	Illinois	24	14	W	-10.5	L	50.0	U	
11/18/2017	vs	RUTGERS	41	0	W	-10.5	W	46.5	U	
11/25/2017	@	Purdue	24	31	L	1.0	L	51.0	O	"The Old Oaken Bucket"
Coach: Tom Allen		Season Record >>	322	304	5-7	ATS>>	3-8-1	O/U>>	6-5	

Copyright © 2021 by Steve's Football Bible, LLC

INDIANA HOOSIERS   BIG TEN East

| STADIUM: Memorial Stadium {52,626} | | Location: Bloomington, IN | | | | | | COACH: Tom Allen | |

DATE		Opponent	IND	Opp	S/U	Line	ATS	Total	O/U	Trends & Angles
9/4/2021	@	Iowa								3-17 S/U vs Iowa as Dog since 1983
9/11/2021	vs	IDAHO								1st meeting
9/18/2021	vs	CINCINNATI								3-0 S/U & ATS vs Cincinnati as favorite since 1994
9/25/2021	@	Western Kentucky								vs Western Kentucky - Indiana leads series 3-0
10/2/2021	@	Penn State								0-11 S/U @ Penn State since 1993
10/16/2021	vs	MICHIGAN STATE								2-8 S/U @ home vs MSU since 1995 {3-7 ATS}
10/23/2021	vs	OHIO STATE								0-12 S/U @ home vs Ohio State since 1992
10/30/2021	@	Maryland								vs Maryland - Indiana leads series 7-2
11/6/2021	@	Michigan								2-39 S/U vs Michigan since 1968
11/13/2021	vs	RUTGERS								5-0 S/U vs Rutgers since 2016
11/20/2021	vs	MINNESOTA								8-2 S/U @ home vs Minnesota since 1988
11/27/2021	@	Purdue								Game 6-0 O/U @ Purdue since 2008
12/4/2021	vs									Big Ten Championship
	vs									BOWL GAME

Pointspread Analysis — Non-Conference

2-14 S/U vs Non-Conf. as 3.5-7 point Dog since 1983

32-2 S/U vs Non-conf. as 10.5 point or more favorite since 1986

vs Cincinnati - Indiana leads series 9-3-1

Bowl Games

4-8 S/U in Bowl Games

Dog

3-0 ATS @ home as 25.5 point or more Dog since 1994

0-48 S/U as 20.5 point or more Dog since 1983

1-19 S/U on road as 15.5-20 point Dog since 1984

2-12 S/U @ home as 15.5-20 point Dog since 1992

1-16 S/U @ home as 10.5-15 point Dog since 1986

9-1 O/U @ home as 10.5-15 point Dog since 2005

3-20 S/U on road as 10.5-15 point Dog since 1989

8-1 O/U as 7.5-10 point Dog since 2008

2-12 S/U on road as 7.5-10 point Dog since 1987

0-12 S/U @ home as 7.5-10 point Dog since 2000

0-7 ATS as 7.5-10 point Dog since 2011

0-5 S/U & ATS on road as 3.5-7 point Dog since 2012

5-25 S/U @ home as 3.5-7 point Dog since 1983

3-12 S/U on road as 3 point or less Dog since 1984

Favorite

19-4-1 S/U @ home as 3.5-7 point favorite since 1986

7-1 S/U on road as 7.5-10 point favorite since 1986

25-3 S/U as 10.5-15 point favorite since 1991

20-2 S/U @ home as 10.5-15 point favorite since 1986

33-1 S/U as 15.5 point or more favorite since 1987

16-2 S/U in 1st home game of season since 2002

8-0 O/U after playing Iowa since 2008

0-8 S/U after playing Iowa since 2008

2-9 ATS in 2nd road game of season since 2010

4-11 S/U prior to playing Penn State since 2004

10-1 O/U prior to playing Michigan State since 2008

5-12 S/U prior to playing Michigan State since 2002

10-2 O/U after playing Penn State since 2008

3-12 ATS after playing Penn State since 2004

2-16 S/U after playing Michigan State since 2001

14-1 ATS prior to playing Michigan since 2000

4-10 S/U after playing Michigan since 2003

6-1 ATS prior to playing Purdue since 2013

4-19 S/U in final road game of season since 1997

IDAHO	
IDAHO	
IDAHO	
W. Kentucky	
W. Kentucky	
Penn State	
Penn State	
MICHIGAN ST.	
MICHIGAN ST.	
Ohio State	
Maryland	
RUTGERS	
MINNESOTA	
Purdue	

Pointspread Analysis — Conference

1-7 S/U vs Iowa since 2008

6-1 S/U vs Iowa as favorite since 1988

Game 12-3 O/U vs Iowa since 2000

vs Iowa - Iowa leads series 45-28-4

9-1 O/U vs Iowa as Dog since 2005

0-6 S/U & ATS vs Iowa as 6.5 point or less Dog since 1987

1-9 S/U vs Iowa as 13.5 point or more Dog since 1983

Game 5-1 O/U vs Maryland since 2015

vs Michigan - Michigan leads series 59-10

0-24 S/U vs Michigan as 9 point or more Dog since 1983

vs Rutgers - Indiana leads series 5-2

vs Penn State - Penn State leads series 22-2

1-19 S/U vs Penn State as 4.5 point or more Dog since 1993

0-26 S/U vs Ohio State since 1991

vs Ohio State - Ohio State leads series 77-12-5

8-2 ATS vs Ohio State since 2011

0-23 S/U vs Ohio State as 16 point or more Dog since 1983

0-8 S/U vs Ohio State as 14 point or less Dog since 1985

4-19 S/U vs Michigan State since 1994

vs Michigan State - Michigan State leads series 49-16-2

Game 10-3 O/U vs Michigan State since 2006

Game 5-1 O/U @ home vs Michigan State since 2006

1-16 S/U vs Michigan State as 8 point or more Dog since 1984

0-3 S/U & ATS vs Michigan St. as 3 point or less favorite since 1988

9-3 S/U vs Minnesota as favorite since 1983

3-9 S/U vs Minnesota as Dog since 1984

vs Minnesota - Minnesota leads series 39-26-3

0-4 ATS vs Purdue since 2016

9-0 S/U vs Purdue as favorite since 1990

Game 9-3 O/U vs Purdue since 2008

vs Purdue - Purdue leads series 74-42-6

0-12 S/U vs Purdue as 6.5 point or more Dog since 1984

3-14 S/U after playing Penn State since 2002

2-19 S/U prior to playing Purdue since 1999

3-8 S/U & ATS after playing Minnesota since 1997

Copyright © 2021 by Steve's Football Bible, LLC

2020-Iowa		Opponent	Iowa	Opp	S/U	Line	ATS	Total	O/U	
10/24/2020	@	Purdue	20	24	L	-3.0	L	52.5	U	
10/31/2020	vs	NORTHWESTERN	20	21	L	1.0	T	43.0	U	
11/7/2020	vs	MICHIGAN STATE	49	7	W	-5.5	W	45.5	O	
11/14/2020	@	Minnesota	35	7	W	-3.0	W	58.0	U	"Floyd of Rosedale"
11/21/2020	@	Penn State	41	21	W	-1.0	W	45.5	U	
11/27/2020	vs	NEBRASKA	26	20	W	-12.5	L	53.0	U	"Heroes Trophy"
12/5/2020	@	Illinois	35	21	W	-13.5	W	53.0	O	
12/12/2020	vs	WISCONSIN	28	7	W	1.0	W	39.5	U	"Heartland Trophy"
Coach: Kirk Ferentz		Season Record >>	254	128	6-2	ATS>>	5-2-1	O/U>>	3-5	
2019-Iowa		Opponent	Iowa	Opp	S/U	Line	ATS	Total	O/U	
8/31/2019	vs	MIAMI-OHIO	38	14	W	-24.5	L	47.0	O	
9/7/2019	vs	RUTGERS	30	0	W	-18.0	W	48.0	U	
9/14/2019	@	Iowa State	18	17	W	-1.0	T	42.0	U	"Cy-Hawk Trophy"
9/28/2019	vs	MIDDLE TENNESSEE	48	3	W	-23.5	W	51.0	T	
10/5/2019	@	Michigan	3	10	L	4.0	L	49.0	U	
10/12/2019	vs	PENN STATE	12	17	L	3.5	L	43.5	U	
10/19/2019	vs	PURDUE	26	20	W	-17.5	L	48.0	U	
10/26/2019	@	Northwestern	20	0	W	-8.5	W	36.5	U	
11/9/2019	@	Wisconsin	22	24	L	7.5	W	37.5	O	"Heartland Trophy"
11/16/2019	vs	MINNESOTA	23	19	W	-3.0	W	45.0	U	"Floyd of Rosedale"
11/23/2019	vs	ILLINOIS	19	10	W	-15.5	L	48.5	U	
11/29/2019	@	Nebraska	27	24	W	-3.5	L	46.0	O	"Heroes Trophy"
12/27/2019	vs	Usc	49	24	W	1.5	W	54.5	O	Holiday Bowl
Coach: Kirk Ferentz		Season Record >>	335	182	10-3	ATS>>	6-6-1	O/U>>	4-8-1	
2018-Iowa		Opponent	Iowa	Opp	S/U	Line	ATS	Total	O/U	
9/1/2018	vs	NORTHERN ILLINOIS	33	7	W	-9.5	W	46.5	U	
9/8/2018	vs	IOWA STATE	13	3	W	-3.5	W	47.0	U	"Cy-Hawk Trophy"
9/15/2018	vs	NORTHERN IOWA	38	14	W	-18.0	W	NT	---	
9/22/2018	vs	WISCONSIN	17	28	L	3.0	L	43.5	O	"Heartland Trophy"
10/6/2018	@	Minnesota	48	31	W	-7.0	W	41.5	O	"Floyd of Rosedale"
10/13/2018	@	Indiana	42	16	W	-3.5	W	52.5	O	
10/20/2018	vs	MARYLAND	23	0	W	-9.5	W	44.0	U	
10/27/2018	@	Penn State	24	30	L	5.5	L	52.0	O	
11/3/2018	@	Purdue	36	38	L	2.0	T	50.5	O	
11/10/2018	vs	NORTHWESTERN	10	14	L	-11.5	L	44.0	U	
11/17/2018	@	Illinois	63	0	W	-15.0	W	59.5	O	
11/23/2018	vs	NEBRASKA	31	28	W	-7.5	L	52.0	O	"Heroes Trophy"
1/1/2019	vs	Mississippi State	27	22	W	7.0	W	40.0	O	Outback Bowl
Coach: Kirk Ferentz		Season Record >>	405	231	9-4	ATS>>	8-4-1	O/U>>	8-4	
2017-Iowa		Opponent	Iowa	Opp	S/U	Line	ATS	Total	O/U	
9/2/2017	vs	WYOMING	24	3	W	-12.5	W	51.5	U	
9/9/2017	@	Iowa State	44	41	W	-3.0	T	49.0	O	"Cy-Hawk Trophy"
9/16/2017	vs	NORTH TEXAS	31	14	W	-19.5	L	52.0	U	
9/23/2017	vs	PENN STATE	19	21	L	12.5	L	53.0	U	
9/30/2017	@	Michigan State	10	17	L	3.5	L	44.0	U	
10/7/2017	vs	ILLINOIS	45	16	W	-16.0	W	41.5	O	
10/21/2017	@	Northwestern	10	17	L	2.0	L	45.5	U	
10/28/2017	vs	MINNESOTA	17	10	W	-6.5	W	43.0	U	"Floyd of Rosedale"
11/4/2017	vs	OHIO STATE	55	24	W	20.5	W	55.0	O	
11/11/2017	@	Wisconsin	14	38	L	12.0	L	45.5	U	"Heartland Trophy"
11/18/2017	vs	PURDUE	15	24	L	-6.0	L	42.5	U	
11/24/2017	@	Nebraska	56	14	W	-5.0	W	50.0	O	"Heroes Trophy"
12/27/2017	vs	Boston College	27	20	W	-2.0	W	46.0	O	Pinstripe Bowl
Coach: Kirk Ferentz		Season Record >>	367	259	8-5	ATS>>	7-5-1	O/U>>	6-7	

    Copyright © 2021 by Steve's Football Bible, LLC

IOWA HAWKEYES

BIG TEN West

STADIUM: Nile Kinnick Stadium {69,250}		Location: Iowa City, IA							COACH: Kirk Ferentz
DATE		**Opponent**	**Iowa**	**Opp**	**S/U**	**Line**	**ATS**	**Total**	**O/U**	**Trends & Angles**

DATE		Opponent	Iowa	Opp	S/U	Line	ATS	Total	O/U	Trends & Angles
9/4/2021	vs	INDIANA								9-1 O/U vs Indiana as favorite since 2005
9/11/2021	@	*Iowa State*								4-0 S/U @ Iowa State since 2013
9/18/2021	vs	*KENT STATE*								vs Kent State - Iowa leads series 2-0
9/25/2021	vs	*COLORADO STATE*								1st meeting
10/2/2021	@	Maryland								vs Maryland - Iowa leads series 2-1
10/9/2021	vs	PENN STATE								1-6 S/U vs Penn State since 2011
10/23/2021	vs	PURDUE								13-3 S/U @ home vs Purdue since 1981
10/30/2021	@	Wisconsin								6-1 ATS @ Wisconsin since 2003
11/6/2021	@	Northwestern								Game 1-6 O/U @ Northwestern since 2005
11/13/2021	vs	MINNESOTA								9-0 S/U @ home vs Minnesota since 2001
11/20/2021	vs	ILLINOIS								12-1 S/U vs Illinois since 2003
11/27/2021	@	Nebraska								4-0 S/U @ Nebraska since 2013 {3-1 ATS}
12/4/2021	vs									Big Ten Championship
	vs									BOWL GAME

Pointspread Analysis
Non-Conference

0-11 S/U vs Non-Conf. as 7.5 point or more Dog since 1990
7-1 S/U vs Non-Conf. as 3 point or less favorite since 1993
0-5 O/U vs Non-Conf. as 7.5-10 point favorite since 2003
15-3 S/U vs Non-Conf. as 15.5-20 point favorite since 1986
30-2 S/U vs Non-Conf. as 20.5 point or more favorite since 1984
vs Iowa State - Iowa leads series 45-22
Game 3-13 O/U vs Iowa State since 2004
16-2 S/U vs Iowa State as 13.5 point or more favorite since 1984
0-7 O/U vs Iowa State as 13.5 point or more favorite since 1998

Dog

0-6 S/U as 25.5 point or more Dog since 1998
0-6 S/U on road as 20.5-25 point Dog since 1990
1-8 S/U as 15.5-20 point Dog since 1993
0-8 S/U on road as 10.5-15 point Dog since 1998
1-12 S/U as 10.5-15 point Dog since 1996
2-10 O/U as 7.5-10 point Dog since 2005
1-6 O/U on road as 7.5-10 point Dog since 2005
3-9 O/U on road as 3.5-7 point Dog since 2005
2-9 S/U on road as 3.5-7 point Dog since 2007
3-9 S/U @ home as 3 point or less Dog since 1989

Favorite

16-4-2 ATS as a road favorite since 2013
15-3 S/U on road as 3 point or less favorite since 1987
14-1 S/U as 3.5-7 point favorite since 2013
9-2 ATS on road as 3.5-7 point favorite since 2008
19-3 S/U @ home as 7.5-10 point favorite since 1989
17-2 S/U on road as 10.5-15 point favorite since 1984
30-3 S/U @ home as 15.5-20 point favorite since 1983
17-0 S/U @ home as 20.5-25 point favorite since 1983
27-1 S/U as 25.5 point or more favorite since 1986
12-4 ATS as 25.5-30 point favorite since 1990

Bowl Games

2-7 S/U & ATS vs PAC-12 in Bowl Games since 1981
0-4 S/U & ATS in Rose Bowl since 1982
3-0 O/U in Rose Bowl since 1986
0-4 O/U in Alamo Bowl since 1993
9-0 ATS prior to playing Wisconsin since 2010

Pointspread Analysis
Conference

vs Indiana - Iowa leads series 45-28-4
6-0 S/U vs Indiana as 3.5-6.5 point favorite since 1987
9-1 S/U vs Indiana as 13.5 point or more favorite since 1986
1-4 S/U & ATS vs Northwestern since 2016
vs Northwestern - Iowa leads series 51-28-3
0-5 O/U vs Northwestern as Dog since 2000
vs Penn State - Penn State leads series 17-13
0-6 S/U vs Penn State as 4.0-6.5 point Dog since 1993
0-5 ATS @ home vs Purdue since 2008
vs Purdue - Purdue leads series 49-39-3
1-5 S/U vs Purdue as Dog since 1998
18-1 S/U vs Purdue as 6.5 point or more favorite since 1983
6-0 S/U vs Nebraska since 2015
vs Nebraska - Nebraska leads series 28-19-3
5-0 S/U vs Nebraska as favorite since 2015
6-0 S/U vs Minnesota since 2015
vs Minnesota - Minnesota leads series 62-50-2
12-0 S/U vs Minnesota as 2.0-8.5 point favorite since 1986
vs Illinois - Illinois leads series 39-34-2
14-0 S/U vs Illinois as favorite since 1996 {10-4 ATS}
14-1 S/U vs Illinois as 7 point or more favorite since 1985
2-7 S/U vs Wisconsin since 2010
13-2-1 S/U vs Wisconsin as favorite since 1983
vs Wisconsin - Wisconsin leads series 48-44-2
0-8 S/U vs Wisconsin as 7 point or more Dog since 1998
8-0 S/U vs Wisconsin as 8.5 point or more favorite since 1985

INDIANA	17-3 S/U in 1st home game of season since 2001
INDIANA	1-9-1 O/U prior to playing Iowa State since 2006
INDIANA	18-0 S/U prior to playing Iowa State since 2001
Iowa State	8-1 S/U in 1st road game of season since 2012
Iowa State	3-8 S/U after playing Indiana since 2005
Iowa State	2-9 ATS after playing Indiana since 2005
KENT STATE	8-1 S/U after playing Iowa State since 2011
KENT STATE	13-0 S/U in 2nd home game of season since 2008
Maryland	3-13 O/U in 2nd road game of season since 2005
PURDUE	11-3 S/U after playing Penn State since 2002
PURDUE	9-0 S/U prior to playing Wisconsin since 2008
Wisconsin	1-8-2 ATS prior to playing Northwestern since 2010
Northwestern	9-1 O/U prior to playing Minnesota since 2011
MINNESOTA	2-10 O/U prior to playing Illinois since 2004
ILLINOIS	9-1 S/U after playing Minnesota since 2011
Nebraska	8-0 S/U in final road game of season since 2013 {7-1 ATS}

Copyright © 2021 by Steve's Football Bible, LLC

IOWA STATE CYCLONES   BIG TWELVE

2020-Iowa State		Opponent	ISU	Opp	S/U	Line	ATS	Total	O/U	
9/12/2020	vs	LOUISIANA	14	31	L	-11.5	L	56.0	U	
9/26/2020	@	Tcu	37	34	W	-3.0	T	44.0	O	
10/3/2020	vs	OKLAHOMA	37	30	W	7.5	W	62.0	O	
10/10/2020	vs	TEXAS TECH	31	15	W	-10.0	W	63.0	U	
10/24/2020	@	Oklahoma State	21	24	L	2.5	L	54.0	U	
10/31/2020	@	Kansas	52	22	W	-27.5	W	49.5	O	
11/7/2020	vs	BAYLOR	38	31	W	-14.0	L	46.5	O	
11/21/2020	vs	KANSAS STATE	45	0	W	-13.5	W	47.5	U	
11/27/2020	@	Texas	23	20	W	-2.0	W	58.0	U	
12/5/2020	vs	WEST VIRGINIA	42	6	W	-5.5	W	47.5	O	
12/19/2020	vs	Oklahoma	21	27	L	5.5	L	59.5	U	Big 12 Championship
1/2/2021	vs	Oregon	34	17	W	-4.0	W	57.5	U	Fiesta Bowl
Coach: Matt Campbell		Season Record >>	395	257	9-3	ATS>>	7-4-1	O/U>>	5-7	
2019-Iowa State		Opponent	ISU	Opp	S/U	Line	ATS	Total	O/U	
8/31/2019	vs	NORTHERN IOWA	29	26	W	-23.5	L	NT	---	{3 OT}
9/14/2019	vs	IOWA	17	18	L	1.0	T	42.0	U	"Cy-Hawk Trophy"
9/21/2019	vs	LOUISIANA-MONROE	72	20	W	-17.5	W	52.0	O	
9/28/2019	@	Baylor	21	23	L	-2.5	L	55.5	U	
10/5/2019	vs	TCU	49	24	W	-3.5	W	46.5	O	
10/12/2019	@	West Virginia	38	14	W	-10.0	W	55.0	U	
10/19/2019	vs	TEXAS TECH	34	24	W	-7.5	W	57.0	O	
10/26/2019	@	Oklahoma State	27	34	L	-10.5	L	64.0	U	
11/9/2019	@	Oklahoma	41	42	L	14.5	W	70.0	O	
11/16/2019	vs	TEXAS	23	21	W	-7.0	L	64.5	U	
11/23/2019	vs	KANSAS	41	31	W	-26.0	L	58.5	O	
11/30/2019	@	Kansas State	17	27	L	-4.5	L	45.5	U	
12/28/2019	vs	Notre Dame	9	33	L	3.5	L	54.0	U	Camping World Bowl
Coach: Matt Campbell		Season Record >>	418	337	7-6	ATS>>	5-7-1	O/U>>	5-7	
2018-Iowa State		Opponent	ISU	Opp	S/U	Line	ATS	Total	O/U	
9/8/2018	@	Iowa	3	13	L	3.5	L	47.0	U	"Cy-Hawk Trophy"
9/15/2018	vs	OKLAHOMA	27	37	L	18.5	W	54.0	O	
9/22/2018	vs	AKRON	26	13	W	-18.5	L	47.0	U	
9/29/2018	@	Tcu	14	17	L	11.0	W	45.0	U	
10/6/2018	@	Oklahoma State	48	42	W	10.0	W	55.5	O	
10/13/2018	vs	WEST VIRGINIA	30	14	W	4.0	W	55.0	U	
10/27/2018	vs	TEXAS TECH	40	31	W	-4.5	W	59.0	O	
11/3/2018	@	Kansas	27	3	W	-19.0	W	46.5	U	
11/10/2018	vs	BAYLOR	28	14	W	-17.0	L	51.0	U	
11/17/2018	@	Texas	10	24	L	1.5	L	51.0	U	
11/24/2018	vs	KANSAS STATE	42	38	W	-10.5	L	41.0	O	
12/1/2018	vs	DRAKE	27	24	W	-40.5	L	NT	---	
12/28/2018	vs	Washington State	26	28	L	1.5	L	56.0	U	Alamo Bowl
Coach: Matt Campbell		Season Record >>	348	298	8-5	ATS>>	6-7	O/U>>	4-8	
2017-Iowa State		Opponent	ISU	Opp	S/U	Line	ATS	Total	O/U	
9/2/2017	vs	NORTHERN IOWA	42	24	W	-10.0	W	51.5	O	
9/9/2017	vs	IOWA	41	44	L	3.0	T	49.0	O	"Cy-Hawk Trophy"
9/16/2017	@	Akron	41	14	W	-10.0	W	63.0	U	
9/30/2017	vs	TEXAS	7	17	L	5.0	L	61.0	U	
10/7/2017	@	Oklahoma	38	31	W	31.0	W	61.5	O	
10/14/2017	vs	KANSAS	45	0	W	-23.0	W	62.0	U	
10/21/2017	@	Texas Tech	31	13	W	6.5	W	66.0	U	
10/28/2017	vs	TCU	14	7	W	6.5	W	48.0	U	
11/4/2017	@	West Virginia	16	20	L	3.5	L	58.5	U	
11/11/2017	vs	OKLAHOMA STATE	42	49	L	7.0	T	60.5	O	
11/18/2017	@	Baylor	23	13	W	-8.0	W	49.0	U	
11/25/2017	@	Kansas State	19	20	L	2.5	W	50.0	U	
12/30/2017	vs	Memphis	21	20	W	3.5	W	67.5	U	Liberty Bowl
Coach: Matt Campbell		Season Record >>	380	272	8-5	ATS>>	9-2-2	O/U>>	4-9	

Copyright © 2021 by Steve's Football Bible, LLC

IOWA STATE CYCLONES   BIG TWELVE

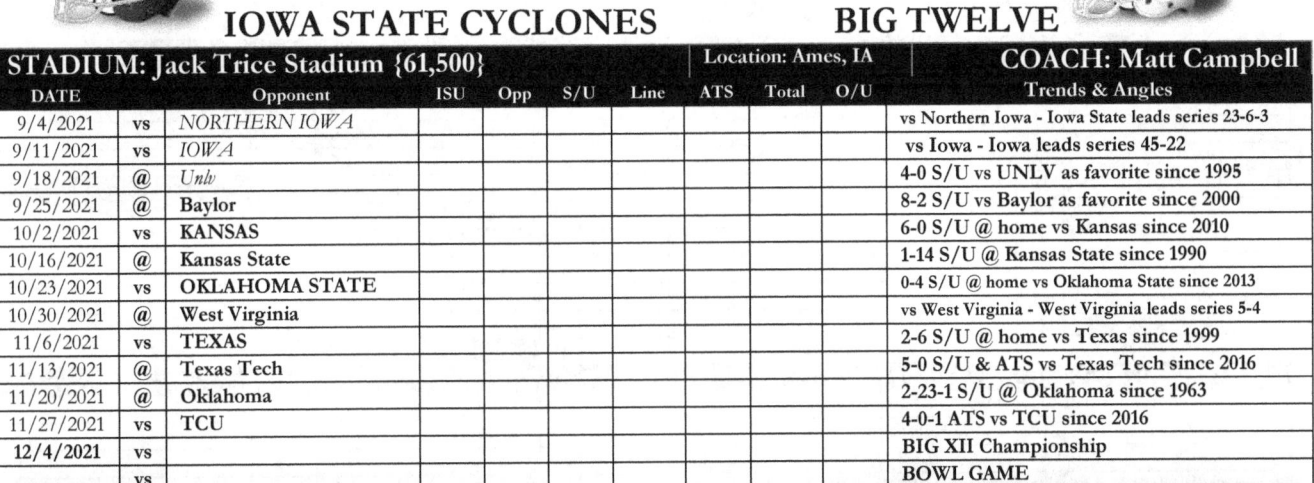

DATE		Opponent	ISU	Opp	S/U	Line	ATS	Total	O/U	Trends & Angles
		STADIUM: Jack Trice Stadium {61,500}				Location: Ames, IA				COACH: Matt Campbell
9/4/2021	vs	NORTHERN IOWA								vs Northern Iowa - Iowa State leads series 23-6-3
9/11/2021	vs	IOWA								vs Iowa - Iowa leads series 45-22
9/18/2021	@	Unlv								4-0 S/U vs UNLV as favorite since 1995
9/25/2021	@	Baylor								8-2 S/U vs Baylor as favorite since 2000
10/2/2021	vs	KANSAS								6-0 S/U @ home vs Kansas since 2010
10/16/2021	@	Kansas State								1-14 S/U @ Kansas State since 1990
10/23/2021	vs	OKLAHOMA STATE								0-4 S/U @ home vs Oklahoma State since 2013
10/30/2021	@	West Virginia								vs West Virginia - West Virginia leads series 5-4
11/6/2021	vs	TEXAS								2-6 S/U @ home vs Texas since 1999
11/13/2021	@	Texas Tech								5-0 S/U & ATS vs Texas Tech since 2016
11/20/2021	@	Oklahoma								2-23-1 S/U @ Oklahoma since 1963
11/27/2021	vs	TCU								4-0-1 ATS vs TCU since 2016
12/4/2021	vs									BIG XII Championship
	vs									BOWL GAME

Pointspread Analysis Non-Conference		Pointspread Analysis Conference
1-15 S/U vs Iowa as 13.5-25 point Dog since 1984		1-8 S/U vs Baylor as Dog since 1988
1-11 S/U vs Non-Conf. as 10.5-15 point Dog since 1983		vs Baylor - Baylor leads series 10-9
28-4 S/U vs Non-Conf. as 7.5 point or more favorite since 1985		16-2-1 S/U vs Kansas as favorite since 1987
13-2 S/U vs Non-Conf. as 7.5-10 point favorite since 1985 {10-5 ATS}		vs Kansas - Kansas leads series 50-44-6
1-12 S/U vs ranked Iowa all time {0-6 S/U @ Iowa}		10-1 S/U vs Kansas since 2010
0-5 O/U vs ranked Iowa since 2005		Game 1-5 O/U @ home vs Kansas since 2010
0-5 S/U @ home vs Iowa as 3 point or less Dog since 1993		1-9 S/U vs Kansas as 7 point or more Dog since 1985
Bowl Games		2-11 S/U vs Kansas State since 2008
1-9 O/U in Bowl Games since 2001		vs Kansas State - Iowa State leads series 50-49-4
Dog		4-22 S/U vs Kansas State as Dog since 1983
1-18 S/U as 30.5 point or more Dog since 1985		8-3 S/U vs Kansas State as favorite since 1985
0-13 S/U on road as 25.5-30 point Dog since 1985		0-9 S/U vs Kansas State as 15 point or more Dog since 1994
0-11 S/U @ home as 20.5-25 point Dog since 1984		1-8 S/U vs Oklahoma State since 2012
2-12 S/U on road as 20.5-25 point Dog since 1984		Game 4-0 O/U @ home vs Oklahoma State since 2011
1-19 S/U on road as 15.5-20 point Dog since 1986		vs Oklahoma State - Oklahoma State leads series 33-19-3
4-15-1 ATS on road as 15.5-20 point Dog since 1986		0-8 S/U vs Oklahoma State as 11-17.5 point Dog since 1983
2-14 S/U on road as 10.5-15 point Dog since 2006		3-1 S/U & ATS vs OK State as favorite since 2000
0-7 S/U @ home as 10.5-15 point Dog since 2008		vs Texas - Texas leads series 14-4
2-9 S/U on road as 7.5-10 point Dog since 1997		Game 0-6 O/U vs Texas since 2015
1-4 S/U @ home as 7.5-10 point Dog since 2008		vs Texas Tech - Texas Tech leads series 11-8
1-9 O/U as 3.5-7 point Dog since 2017		3-48-1 S/U vs Oklahoma since 1962
1-8 S/U @ home as 3 point or less Dog since 2006		vs Oklahoma - Oklahoma leads series 77-7-2
Favorite		Game 8-2 O/U vs Oklahoma since 2012
3-7 O/U @ home as 3.5-7 point favorite since 2004		4-52-1 S/U vs ranked Oklahoma all time
7-0 S/U on road as 7.5-10 point favorite since 1989		1-16 S/U vs Oklahoma as 23 point or less Dog since 1983
15-3 S/U @ home as 7.5-10 point favorite since 1992		vs TCU - TCU leads series 8-4
11-0 S/U on road as 7.5 point or more favorite since 1988		**Favorite**
38-3 S/U as 10.5 point or more favorite since 1986		2-7 O/U @ home as 3.5-7 point favorite since 2004
		7-0 S/U on road as 7.5-10 point favorite since 1989
2-9 O/U in 1st road game of season since 2010	Unlv	14-3 S/U @ home as 7.5-10 point favorite since 1992
7-0 ATS after playing Iowa since 2013	Unlv	11-0 S/U on road as 7.5 point or more favorite since 1988
4-25 S/U in 2nd road game of season since 1992	Baylor	35-2 S/U as 10.5 point or more favorite since 1986
2-7 S/U prior to playing Oklahoma State since 2012	K State	
0-7 O/U after playing Kansas State since 2010	OK STATE	
8-1 ATS prior to playing West Virginia since 2012	OK STATE	0-11 S/U vs #1 ranked teams all time
11-2 ATS after playing Oklahoma State since 2005	West Virginia	1-8 S/U vs #2 ranked teams all time {0-6 on road}
7-1 ATS prior to playing Texas since 2013	West Virginia	1-17-1 S/U vs #3 ranked teams all time
7-1 ATS prior to playing Texas since 2013	Texas Tech	1-12 S/U vs #4 ranked teams all time
10-0 O/U after playing Texas since 2011	Texas Tech	10-2 S/U @ home when ranked since 1981
3-14 S/U & ATS after playing Texas Tech since 1998	Oklahoma	2-13-2 S/U when ranked vs ranked teams all time

Copyright © 2021 by Steve's Football Bible, LLC

KANSAS JAYHAWKS   BIG TWELVE

2020-Kansas		Opponent	KU	Opp	S/U	Line	ATS	Total	O/U	
9/12/2020	@	*Coastal Carolina*	23	35	L	**-40.0**	L	56.0	O	
9/26/2020	@	Baylor	14	47	L	17.5	L	62.0	U	
10/3/2020	vs	OKLAHOMA STATE	7	47	L	21.5	L	53.0	O	
10/17/2020	@	West Virginia	17	38	L	22.5	W	51.5	O	
10/24/2020	@	Kansas State	14	55	L	18.5	L	46.0	O	*"Governor's Cup"*
10/31/2020	vs	IOWA STATE	22	52	L	27.5	L	49.5	O	
11/7/2020	@	Oklahoma	9	62	L	38.5	L	62.0	O	
11/28/2020	vs	TCU	23	59	L	23.0	L	51.0	O	
12/5/2020	@	Texas Tech	13	16	L	27.0	W	63.0	U	
12/12/2021	vs	TEXAS	31	69	L	7.0	L	53.5	O	
Coach: Les Miles		Season Record >>	173	480	0-10	ATS>>	2-8	O/U>>	8-2	
2019-Kansas		Opponent	KU	Opp	S/U	Line	ATS	Total	O/U	
8/31/2019	vs	*INDIANA STATE*	24	17	W	**-12.0**	L	NT	---	
9/7/2019	vs	*COASTAL CAROLINA*	7	12	L	**-7.0**	L	54.0	U	
9/13/2019	@	*Boston College*	48	24	W	19.5	W	51.0	O	
9/21/2019	vs	WEST VIRGINIA	24	29	L	4.5	L	49.5	O	
9/28/2019	@	Tcu	14	51	L	14.5	L	48.0	O	
10/5/2019	vs	OKLAHOMA	20	45	L	31.5	W	67.0	U	
10/19/2019	@	Texas	48	50	L	21.0	W	63.0	O	
10/26/2019	vs	TEXAS TECH	37	34	W	6.0	W	65.5	O	
11/2/2019	vs	KANSAS STATE	10	38	L	4.5	L	54.5	U	*"Governor's Cup"*
11/16/2019	@	Oklahoma State	13	31	L	17.0	L	69.0	O	
11/23/2019	@	Iowa State	31	41	L	26.0	W	58.5	O	
11/30/2019	vs	BAYLOR	6	61	L	14.0	L	58.5	O	
Coach: Les Miles		Season Record >>	282	433	3-9	ATS>>	5-7	O/U>>	7-4	
2018-Kansas		Opponent	KU	Opp	S/U	Line	ATS	Total	O/U	
9/1/2018	vs	*NICHOLLS STATE*	23	26	L	**-7.5**	L	NT	---	{OT}
9/8/2018	@	*Central Michigan*	31	7	W	3.0	W	48.0	U	
9/15/2018	vs	*RUTGERS*	55	14	W	**PK**	W	44.0	O	
9/22/2018	@	Baylor	7	26	L	7.5	L	55.0	U	
9/29/2018	vs	OKLAHOMA STATE	28	48	L	17.0	L	53.5	O	
10/6/2018	@	West Virginia	22	38	L	27.5	W	62.0	U	
10/20/2018	@	Texas Tech	16	48	L	17.5	L	59.0	O	
10/27/2018	vs	TCU	27	26	W	13.5	W	47.0	O	
11/3/2018	vs	IOWA STATE	3	27	L	19.0	L	46.5	U	
11/10/2018	@	Kansas State	17	21	L	8.5	W	46.0	U	*"Governor's Cup"*
11/17/2018	@	Oklahoma	40	55	L	34.5	W	69.5	O	
11/23/2018	vs	TEXAS	17	24	L	15.0	W	50.0	U	
Coach: David Beaty		Season Record >>	286	360	3-9	ATS>>	7-5	O/U>>	5-6	
2017-Kansas		Opponent	KU	Opp	S/U	Line	ATS	Total	O/U	
9/2/2017	vs	*SE MISSOURI*	38	16	W	**-28.5**	L	50.5	O	
9/9/2017	vs	*CENTRAL MICHIGAN*	27	45	L	**-3.0**	L	56.5	O	
9/16/2017	@	*Ohio*	30	42	L	7.0	L	59.5	O	
9/23/2017	vs	WEST VIRGINIA	34	56	L	24.5	W	71.0	O	
10/7/2017	vs	TEXAS TECH	19	65	L	14.5	L	76.0	O	
10/14/2017	@	Iowa State	0	45	L	23.0	L	62.0	U	
10/21/2017	@	Tcu	0	43	L	36.0	L	60.0	U	
10/28/2017	vs	KANSAS STATE	20	30	L	24.0	W	55.5	U	*"Governor's Cup"*
11/4/2017	vs	BAYLOR	9	38	L	7.0	L	59.0	U	
11/11/2017	@	Texas	27	42	L	31.5	W	54.5	O	
11/18/2017	vs	OKLAHOMA	3	41	L	38.5	W	68.0	U	
11/25/2017	@	Oklahoma State	17	58	L	40.5	L	67.5	O	
Coach: David Beaty		Season Record >>	224	521	1-11	ATS>>	4-8	O/U>>	7-5	

Copyright © 2021 by Steve's Football Bible, LLC

 **KANSAS JAYHAWKS**  **BIG TWELVE**

STADIUM: Kansas Memorial Stadium {50,071}					Location: Lawrence, KS				COACH: Lance Leipold	
DATE		Opponent	KU	Opp	S/U	Line	ATS	Total	O/U	Trends & Angles
9/4/2021	vs	*SOUTH DAKOTA*								vs South Dakota - Kansas leads series 2-0
9/11/2021	@	*Coastal Carolina*								vs Coastal Carolina - CCU leads series 2-0
9/18/2021	vs	**BAYLOR**								0-16 S/U vs Baylor as Dog since 1988
9/25/2021	@	*Duke*								vs Duke - Series tied 1-1
10/2/2021	@	Iowa State								vs Iowa State - Kansas leads series 50-44-6
10/16/2021	vs	**TEXAS TECH**								1-10 S/U @ home vs Texas Tech since 1966
10/23/2021	vs	**OKLAHOMA**								0-8 S/U @ home vs Oklahoma since 2001
10/30/2021	@	Oklahoma State								0-5 S/U & ATS @ Oklahoma State since 2011
11/6/2021	vs	**KANSAS STATE**								0-12 S/U vs Kansas State since 2009 {3-9 ATS}
11/13/2021	@	Texas								0-9 S/U @ Texas since 1997
11/20/2021	@	Tcu								1-10-2 S/U @ TCU since 1953
11/27/2021	vs	**WEST VIRGINIA**								0-7 S/U vs West Virginia since 2014
12/4/2021	vs									BIG XII Championship
	vs									BOWL GAME

Pointspread Analysis Non-Conference		Pointspread Analysis Conference
0-6 S/U vs Non-Conf. as 20.5 point or more Dog since 1987		3-0 S/U vs Baylor as favorite since 1999
1-7 S/U vs Non-Conf. as 15.5-25 point Dog since 1984		0-9 ATS vs Baylor as Dog since 2012
2-10 S/U vs Non-Conf. as 10.5-15 point Dog since 1984		0-11-1 S/U @ Iowa State as Dog since 1983
9-1 S/U vs Non-Conf. as 3.5-7 point favorite since 1995		0-16-1 S/U vs Iowa State as 4.5 point or more Dog since 1983
8-2 ATS vs Non-Conf. as 3.5-7 point favorite since 1995		vs Kansas State - Kansas leads series 66-46-5
37-5 S/U vs Non-Conf. as 7.5 point or more favorite since 1986		0-18 S/U vs Kansas State as 6 point or more Dog since 1996
Dog		0-16 S/U vs Oklahoma since 2000
0-74 S/U as 25.5 point or more Dog since 1984		vs Oklahoma - Oklahoma leads series 77-27-6
4-45 S/U as 20.5-25 point Dog since 1983		0-18 S/U vs Oklahoma as 21.5 point or more Dog since 1986
5-11 O/U as 15.5-20 point Dog since 2010		0-11 S/U vs Oklahoma State since 2010
3-34 S/U as 15.5-20 point Dog since 1984		vs Oklahoma State - Oklahoma State leads series 38-29-3
0-15 S/U @ home as 15.5-20 point Dog since 1984		1-22 S/U vs Oklahoma State as Dog since 1983
11-3 O/U @ home as 10.5-15 point Dog since 2001		1-8 S/U vs TCU since 2012
5-32 S/U as 10.5-15 point Dog since 1984		7-3 ATS vs TCU as Dog since 1983
0-7 S/U on road as 7.5-10 point Dog since 1991		vs Tcu - TCU leads series 23-9-4
0-7 S/U on road as 3.5-7 point Dog since 2008		vs Texas - Texas leads series 16-3
1-4 S/U on road as 3 point or less Dog since 1993		1-16 S/U vs Texas as Dog since 1996
Favorite		1-17 S/U vs Texas since 1996
0-5 S/U & ATS as 3 point or less favorite since 2007		vs Texas Tech - Texas Tech leads series 20-1
9-1 S/U @ home as 3.5-7 point favorite since 1993		1-12 S/U vs Texas Tech as Dog since 2004
8-2 ATS @ home as 3.5-7 point favorite since 1993		0-3 S/U & ATS vs Texas Tech as favorite since 1996
9-2 S/U on road as 3.5-7 point favorite since 1985		vs West Virginia - West Virginia leads series 8-1
7-1 S/U @ home as 7.5-10 point favorite since 1993		4-1 ATS vs West Virginia since 2016
15-1 S/U @ home as 10.5-15 point favorite since 1986		**Bowl Games**
30-2 S/U as 15.5 point or more favorite since 1985		5-1 S/U & ATS in Bowl Games since 1992
17-5 S/U in 1st home game of season since 1999	S. DAKOTA	
2-10 ATS in 1st home game of season since 2008	S. DAKOTA	5-0 O/U in 1st home game of season since 2013
1-9 S/U prior to playing Baylor since 2011	Coastal Carolina	8-3-1 ATS prior to playing Baylor since 2007
1-10 S/U in 1st road game of season since 2010	Coastal Carolina	
1-9 S/U after playing Baylor since 2010	Duke	
0-12 S/U in 2nd road game of season since 2009	Duke	2-11 ATS in 2nd road game of season since 2008
2-9 S/U prior to playing Iowa State since 2010	Duke	11-3 O/U prior to playing Iowa State since 2007
3-11 O/U prior to playing Texas Tech since 2001	Iowa State	0-13 S/U in final road game of season since 2008
0-11 S/U prior to playing Oklahoma State since 2010	OKLAHOMA	0-8 O/U prior to playing Oklahoma State since 2013
1-10 S/U after playing Texas Tech since 2009	OKLAHOMA	
0-19 S/U after playing Oklahoma since 1995	OK State	4-15-1 ATS after playing Oklahoma since 1994
2-11 S/U prior to playing Kansas State since 2008	OK State	2-8 O/U prior to playing Kansas State since 2011
7-1 O/U after playing Oklahoma since 2013	OK State	
1-16 S/U prior to playing Texas since 1996	K STATE	5-12 ATS prior to playing Texas since 1996
3-10 ATS after playing Kansas State since 2008	Texas	
1-8 S/U prior to playing West Virginia since 2012	Tcu	2-11 S/U in final home game of season since 2008
1-8 S/U after playing Texas since 2009	Tcu	9-2 ATS after playing Texas since 2004
0-9 S/U after playing TCU since 2012	W.VIRGINIA	

Copyright © 2021 by Steve's Football Bible, LLC

KANSAS STATE WILDCATS   BIG TWELVE

2020-Kansas State		Opponent	KSU	Opp	S/U	Line	ATS	Total	O/U	
9/12/2020	vs	ARKANSAS STATE	31	35	L	-10.5	L	54.0	O	
9/26/2020	@	Oklahoma	38	35	W	27.5	W	61.5	O	
10/3/2020	vs	TEXAS TECH	31	21	W	PK	W	62.0	U	
10/10/2020	@	Tcu	21	14	W	11.0	W	50.0	U	
10/24/2020	vs	KANSAS	55	14	W	-18.5	W	46.0	O	"Governor's Cup"
10/31/2020	@	West Virginia	10	37	L	5.0	L	46.0	O	
11/7/2020	vs	OKLAHOMA STATE	18	20	L	14.0	W	48.5	U	
11/21/2020	@	Iowa State	0	45	L	13.5	L	47.5	U	
11/28/2020	@	Baylor	31	32	L	5.5	W	44.5	O	
12/5/2020	vs	TEXAS	31	69	L	7.0	L	53.5	O	
Coach: Chris Klieman		Season Record >>	266	322	4-6	ATS>>	6-4	O/U>>	6-4	
2019-Kansas State		Opponent	KSU	Opp	S/U	Line	ATS	Total	O/U	
8/31/2019	vs	NICHOLLS STATE	49	14	W	-21.0	W	NT	---	
9/7/2019	vs	BOWLING GREEN	52	0	W	-24.5	W	57.5	U	
9/14/2019	@	Mississippi State	31	24	W	7.0	W	50.5	O	
9/28/2019	@	Oklahoma State	13	26	L	4.0	L	60.0	U	
10/5/2019	vs	BAYLOR	12	31	L	PK	L	48.0	U	
10/19/2019	vs	TCU	24	17	W	4.5	W	44.0	U	
10/26/2019	vs	OKLAHOMA	48	41	W	23.5	W	60.0	O	
11/2/2019	@	Kansas	38	10	W	-4.5	W	54.5	U	"Governor's Cup"
11/9/2019	@	Texas	24	27	L	7.0	W	57.5	U	
11/16/2019	vs	WEST VIRGINIA	20	24	L	-14.0	L	46.5	U	
11/23/2019	@	Texas Tech	30	27	W	PK	W	57.5	U	
11/30/2019	vs	IOWA STATE	27	17	W	4.5	W	45.5	U	
12/31/2019	vs	Navy	17	20	L	1.5	L	52.5	U	Liberty Bowl
Coach: Chris Klieman		Season Record >>	385	278	8-5	ATS>>	9-4	O/U>>	2-10	
2018-Kansas State		Opponent	KSU	Opp	S/U	Line	ATS	Total	O/U	
9/1/2018	vs	SOUTH DAKOTA	27	24	W	-23.5	L	NT	---	
9/8/2018	vs	MISSISSIPPI STATE	10	31	L	7.0	L	52.5	U	
9/15/2018	vs	TEXAS-SAN ANTONIO	41	17	W	-21.0	W	46.5	O	
9/22/2018	@	West Virginia	6	35	L	15.5	L	60.5	U	
9/29/2018	vs	TEXAS	14	19	L	8.5	W	49.0	U	
10/6/2018	@	Baylor	34	37	L	3.5	W	52.5	O	
10/13/2018	vs	OKLAHOMA STATE	31	12	W	9.0	W	61.5	O	
10/27/2018	@	Oklahoma	14	51	L	24.0	L	65.0	T	
11/3/2018	@	Tcu	13	14	L	10.0	W	44.0	U	
11/10/2018	vs	KANSAS	21	17	W	-8.5	L	46.0	U	"Governor's Cup"
11/17/2018	vs	TEXAS TECH	21	6	W	6.5	W	55.0	U	
11/24/2018	@	Iowa State	38	42	L	10.5	W	41.0	O	
Coach: Bill Snyder		Season Record >>	270	305	5-7	ATS>>	7-5	O/U>>	3-7-1	
2017-Kansas State		Opponent	KSU	Opp	S/U	Line	ATS	Total	O/U	
9/2/2017	vs	CENTRAL ARKANSAS	55	19	W	-27.0	W	53.0	O	
9/9/2017	vs	NC-CHARLOTTE	55	7	W	-34.0	W	56.0	O	
9/16/2017	@	Vanderbilt	7	14	L	-4.5	L	48.5	U	
9/30/2017	vs	BAYLOR	33	20	W	-14.5	L	56.0	U	
10/7/2017	@	Texas	34	40	L	5.5	L	47.5	O	{2 OT}
10/14/2017	vs	TCU	6	26	L	7.5	L	49.0	U	
10/21/2017	vs	OKLAHOMA	35	42	L	14.5	W	55.5	O	
10/28/2017	@	Kansas	30	20	W	-24.0	L	55.5	U	"Governor's Cup"
11/4/2017	@	Texas Tech	42	35	W	4.0	W	63.5	O	{OT}
11/11/2017	vs	WEST VIRGINIA	23	38	L	3.0	L	60.0	O	
11/18/2017	@	Oklahoma State	45	40	W	20.0	W	62.5	O	
11/25/2017	vs	IOWA STATE	20	19	W	-2.5	L	50.0	U	
12/26/2017	vs	Ucla	35	17	W	-6.0	W	59.0	U	Cactus Bowl
Coach: Bill Snyder		Season Record >>	420	337	8-5	ATS>>	6-7	O/U>>	7-6	

Copyright © 2021 by Steve's Football Bible, LLC

KANSAS STATE WILDCATS　　BIG TWELVE

STADIUM: Bill Snyder Family Football Stadium {50,000}	Location: Manhattan, KS	COACH: Chris Klieman

DATE		Opponent	KSU	Opp	S/U	Line	ATS	Total	O/U	Trends & Angles
1/6/2021	@	Kansas								vs Kansas - Kansas leads series 67-46-5
9/4/2021	vs	*STANFORD*								vs Stanford - Stanford leads series 1-0
9/11/2021	vs	*SOUTHERN ILLINOIS*								1st meeting
9/18/2021	vs	*NEVADA*								1st meeting
9/25/2021	@	Oklahoma State								1-6 S/U @ Oklahoma State since 2003
10/2/2021	vs	OKLAHOMA								1-7 S/U @ home vs Oklahoma since 2000
10/16/2021	vs	IOWA STATE								vs Iowa State - Iowa State leads series 50-49-4
10/23/2021	@	Texas Tech								9-1 S/U vs Texas Tech since 2011 {8-2 ATS}
10/30/2021	vs	TCU								3-0 S/U vs TCU as favorite since 1983
11/13/2021	vs	WEST VIRGINIA								0-5 S/U vs West Virginia since 2016
11/20/2021	vs	BAYLOR								4-0 S/U @ home vs Baylor as favorite since 1999
11/27/2021	@	Texas								0-4 S/U @ Texas since 2013 {1-3 ATS}
12/4/2021	vs									BIG XII Championship
	vs									BOWL GAME

Pointspread Analysis Non-Conference		Pointspread Analysis Conference
4-21 S/U vs Non-Conf. as 3 point or more Dog since 1982		13-1 S/U @ home vs Iowa State as favorite since 1992
0-5 O/U vs Non-Conf. as 3.5-7 point favorite since 2009		8-0 S/U vs Iowa State as 6 point or less favorite since 1991
8-0 S/U vs Non-Conf. as 7.5-10 point favorite since 1991		9-0 S/U vs Iowa State as 15 point or more favorite since 1994
49-1 S/U vs Non-Conf. as 15.5 point or more favorite since 1992		vs Baylor - Series tied 9-9
Dog		0-4 S/U vs Baylor as 6.5 point or more Dog since 2010
2-46 S/U as 20.5 point or more Dog since 1984		7-1 ATS vs Baylor as Dog since 2010
1-11 S/U @ home as 20.5 point or more Dog since 1984		1-6 S/U @ Kansas as Dog since 1983
5-1 ATS as 15.5-20 point Dog since 2009		18-0 S/U vs Kansas as 6 point or more favorite since 1996
0-11-1 S/U @ home as 10.5-15 point Dog since 1984		1-5 S/U @ home vs Oklahoma as Dog since 2004
5-20 S/U as 10.5-15 point Dog since 1984		Game 1-5 O/U @ home vs Oklahoma since 2008
1-6 S/U @ home as 7.5-10 point Dog since 2005		vs Oklahoma - Oklahoma leads series 76-21-4
3-13 S/U on road as 3.5-7 point Dog since 2013		Game 10-2-1 O/U vs Oklahoma since 2005
12-4-1 ATS as 3 point or less Dog since 1993		12-1 ATS vs Oklahoma as Dog since 1988
4-0 S/U & ATS on road as 3 point or less Dog since 2012		2-14 S/U vs Oklahoma as 16 point or more Dog since 1983
Favorite		13-4 ATS vs Oklahoma State since 1998
11-3 O/U as 3 point or less favorite since 2003		vs Oklahoma State - Oklahoma State leads series 41-26
14-3 S/U @ home as 3.5-7 point favorite since 1990		10-0 S/U vs OK State as 3.5 point or more favorite since 1991
7-0 S/U @ home as 7.5-10 point favorite since 2006		0-6 S/U vs Oklahoma State as 21 point or more Dog since 1984
7-3 S/U @ home as 10.5-15 point favorite since 2011		11-2 ATS vs Oklahoma State as Dog since 1988
7-0 S/U on road as 15.5-20 point favorite since 1994		vs Texas - Texas leads series 11-10
11-0 S/U @ home as 15.5-20 point favorite since 1994		vs Texas - HOME team 7-2 ATS since 2012
5-0 ATS on road as 15.5-20 point favorite since 1995		vs TCU - Series tied 7-7
11-0 S/U on road as 20.5 point or more favorite since 1992		3-7 S/U vs TCU as Dog since 1984
72-1 S/U as 20.5 point or more favorite since 1992		Game 0-5 O/U vs TCU since 2016
		Game 6-1 O/U @ Texas Tech since 2005
29-2 S/U in 1st home game of season since 1990	STANFORD	vs Texas Tech - Kansas State leads series 12-9
14-2 S/U in 2nd home game of season since 2005	S. ILLINOIS	7-1 O/U vs Texas Tech as Dog since 2005
11-3 S/U prior to playing Texas Tech since 2004	IOWA State	Game 2-7 O/U vs West Virginia since 2012
2-9 O/U prior to playing Texas Tech since 2009	IOWA State	vs West Virginia - West Virginia leads series 6-5
6-2-1 O/U prior to playing TCU since 2012	Texas Tech	**Bowl Games**
7-1 S/U prior to playing West Virginia since 2012	TCU	3-0 S/U in Holiday Bowl
12-3 O/U after playing Texas Tech since 2001	TCU	0-3 O/U in Cactus Bowl since 2001
9-2 S/U in final home game of season since 2010	BAYLOR	1-4 S/U & ATS vs Big Ten teams in Bowl Games
		0-3 S/U & ATS in Bowl Games as 7.5-10 point Dog since 2006
1-11 S/U @ home vs ranked teams since 2013		0-7 S/U vs ranked teams in Bowl games since 2001 {0-7 ATS}
0-19 S/U vs #2 ranked teams all time		
0-8 S/U vs #3 ranked teams all time		
18-2 S/U @ home when ranked since 2011		
11-0 S/U when ranked vs Iowa State since 1994		
5-0 S/U @ home when ranked vs Oklahoma State all time		

Copyright © 2021 by Steve's Football Bible, LLC

KENTUCKY WILDCATS

2020-Kentucky		Opponent	UK	Opp	S/U	Line	ATS	Total	O/U	
9/26/2020	@	Auburn	13	29	L	6.5	L	48.0	U	
10/3/2020	vs	MISSISSIPPI	41	42	L	-6.5	L	63.0	O	{OT}
10/10/2020	vs	MISSISSIPPI STATE	24	2	W	-3.0	W	57.5	U	
10/17/2020	@	Tennessee	34	7	W	6.0	W	45.5	U	
10/24/2020	@	Missouri	10	20	L	-3.0	L	47.0	U	
10/31/2020	vs	GEORGIA	3	14	L	16.5	W	41.5	U	
11/14/2020	vs	VANDERBILT	38	35	W	-17.5	L	41.5	O	
11/21/2020	@	Alabama	3	63	L	31.0	L	57.5	O	
11/28/2020	@	Florida	10	34	L	23.5	L	60.5	U	
12/5/2020	vs	SOUTH CAROLINA	41	18	W	-11.5	W	47.5	O	
1/2/2021	vs	**NC State**	**23**	**21**	**W**	-3.5	L	50.0	U	**Gator Bowl**
Coach: Mark Stoops		Season Record >>	240	285	5-6	ATS>>	4-7	O/U>>	4-7	

2019-Kentucky		Opponent	UK	Opp	S/U	Line	ATS	Total	O/U	
8/31/2019	vs	*TOLEDO*	38	24	W	-9.0	W	60.5	O	
9/7/2019	vs	*EASTERN MICHIGAN*	38	17	W	-15.5	W	52.0	O	
9/14/2019	vs	FLORIDA	21	29	L	9.5	W	46.5	O	
9/21/2019	@	Mississippi State	13	28	L	5.5	L	48.0	U	
9/28/2019	@	South Carolina	7	24	L	3.5	L	54.0	U	
10/12/2019	vs	ARKANSAS	24	20	W	-3.0	W	52.0	U	
10/19/2019	@	Georgia	0	21	L	24.0	W	45.5	U	
10/26/2019	vs	MISSOURI	29	7	W	9.5	W	43.5	U	
11/9/2019	vs	TENNESSEE	13	17	L	PK	L	42.0	U	
11/16/2019	@	Vanderbilt	38	14	W	-9.0	W	43.0	O	
11/23/2019	vs	*TENNESSEE-MARTIN*	50	7	W	-30.5	W	NT	---	
11/30/2019	vs	*LOUISVILLE*	45	13	W	-2.5	W	51.5	O	*"Governor's Cup"*
12/31/2019	vs	**Virginia Tech**	**37**	**30**	**W**	2.0	W	46.0	O	**Belk Bowl**
Coach: Mark Stoops		Season Record >>	353	251	8-5	ATS>>	10-3	O/U>>	6-6	

2018-Kentucky		Opponent	UK	Opp	S/U	Line	ATS	Total	O/U	
9/1/2018	vs	*CENTRAL MICHIGAN*	35	20	W	-17.5	L	49.0	O	
9/8/2018	@	Florida	27	16	W	13.5	W	52.5	U	
9/15/2018	vs	*MURRAY STATE*	48	10	W	-39.5	L	NT	---	
9/22/2018	vs	MISSISSIPPI STATE	28	7	W	9.5	W	56.0	U	
9/29/2018	vs	SOUTH CAROLINA	24	10	W	-1.0	W	52.0	U	
10/6/2018	@	Texas A&M	14	20	L	4.5	L	48.5	U	{OT}
10/20/2018	vs	VANDERBILT	14	7	W	-10.0	L	45.0	U	
10/27/2018	@	Missouri	15	14	W	7.5	W	54.5	U	
11/3/2018	vs	GEORGIA	17	34	L	9.0	L	46.0	O	
11/10/2018	@	Tennessee	7	24	L	-6.0	L	42.5	U	
11/17/2018	vs	*MIDDLE TENNESSEE*	34	23	W	-16.5	L	48.0	O	
11/24/2018	@	*Louisville*	56	10	W	-16.5	W	53.0	O	*"Governor's Cup"*
1/1/2019	vs	**Penn State**	**27**	**24**	**W**	4.5	W	47.5	O	**Citrus Bowl**
Coach: Mark Stoops		Season Record >>	346	219	10-3	ATS>>	6-7	O/U>>	5-7	

2017-Kentucky		Opponent	UK	Opp	S/U	Line	ATS	Total	O/U	
9/2/2017	@	*Southern Miss*	24	17	W	-9.5	L	57.0	U	
9/9/2017	vs	*EASTERN KENTUCKY*	27	16	W	-32.5	L	NT	---	
9/16/2017	@	South Carolina	23	13	W	5.5	W	47.0	U	
9/23/2017	vs	FLORIDA	27	28	L	3.0	W	44.5	O	
9/30/2017	vs	*EASTERN MICHIGAN*	24	20	W	-14.0	L	50.0	U	
10/7/2017	vs	MISSOURI	40	34	W	-8.5	L	54.5	O	
10/21/2017	@	Mississippi State	7	45	L	14.0	L	54.5	U	
10/28/2017	vs	TENNESSEE	29	26	W	-4.0	L	46.0	O	
11/4/2017	vs	MISSISSIPPI	34	37	L	-3.5	L	63.5	O	
11/11/2017	@	Vanderbilt	44	21	W	2.0	W	53.0	O	
11/18/2017	@	Georgia	13	42	L	22.5	L	48.5	O	
11/25/2017	vs	*LOUISVILLE*	17	44	L	9.5	L	67.5	U	*"Governor's Cup"*
12/29/2017	vs	**Northwestern**	**23**	**24**	**L**	8.0	W	51.5	U	**Music City Bowl**
Coach: Mark Stoops		Season Record >>	332	367	7-6	ATS>>	4-9	O/U>>	6-6	

Copyright © 2021 by Steve's Football Bible, LLC

KENTUCKY WILDCATS

SEC East

STADIUM: Kroger Stadium {61,000}		Location: Lexington, KY							COACH: Mark Stoops
DATE		Opponent	UK	Opp	S/U	Line	ATS	Total	O/U	Trends & Angles

DATE		Opponent	UK	Opp	S/U	Line	ATS	Total	O/U	Trends & Angles
9/4/2021	vs	LOUISIANA-MONROE								4-0 S/U vs Louisiana-Monroe as favorite since 1997
9/11/2021	vs	MISSOURI								5-1 S/U vs Missouri since 2015 {4-2 ATS}
9/18/2021	vs	CHATTANOOGA								1st meeting
9/25/2021	@	South Carolina								7-1 ATS vs South Carolina since 2013
10/2/2021	vs	FLORIDA								1-33 S/U vs Florida since 1987
10/9/2021	vs	LSU								4-0 ATS @ home vs LSU since 1999
10/16/2021	@	Georgia								1-18 S/U @ Georgia as Dog since 1983
10/30/2021	@	Mississippi State								0-5 S/U @ Mississippi State since 2010
11/6/2021	vs	TENNESSEE								2-17 S/U @ home vs Tennessee since 1982
11/13/2021	@	Vanderbilt								5-0 S/U vs Vanderbilt since 2016
11/20/2021	vs	NEW MEXICO STATE								vs NMSU - Kentucky leads series 1-0
11/27/2021	@	Louisville								Game 4-0 O/U @ Louisville since 2012
12/4/2021	vs									SEC Championship
	vs									BOWL GAME

Pointspread Analysis Non-Conference		Pointspread Analysis Conference
8-1-1 O/U vs Non-Conf. as 3.5-7 point favorite since 2000		vs Florida - Florida leads series 53-18
8-0 S/U vs Non-Conf. as 7.5-10 point favorite since 1989		0-25 S/U vs Florida as 14 point or more Dog since 1983
50-2 S/U vs Non-Conf. as 10.5 point or more favorite since 1984		2-22 S/U vs Georgia since 1997
vs Louisville - Kentucky leads series 17-15		vs Georgia - Georgia leads series 60-12-2
5-1 ATS @ Louisville since 2008		0-13 S/U vs Georgia as 16 point or more Dog since 1983
Bowl Games		0-7 S/U vs Georgia as 10-13 point Dog since 1985
1-4 O/U in Music City Bowl		0-5 S/U & ATS vs Georgia as 6 point or less Dog since 1984
0-3 O/U vs Clemson in Bowl Games		Game 3-0 O/U @ home vs LSU since 2001
Dog		3-9 S/U vs Mississippi State since 2009
6-15 ATS as home Dog since 2012		1-10 S/U @ Mississippi State as Dog since 1995
0-12 S/U @ home as 20.5 point or more Dog since 1990		Game 0-6 O/U @ Mississippi State since 2008
1-45 S/U as 20.5 point or more Dog since 1990		3-0 S/U & ATS @ Mississipi State as favorite since 1984
2-25 S/U as 15.5-20 point Dog since 1983		vs Mississippi State - Mississippi State leads series 25-23
4-11 ATS on road as 10.5-15 point Dog since 2010		0-7 S/U vs Mississippi State as 10 point or more Dog since 1991
1-19 S/U as 10.5-15 point Dog since 2010		vs Missouri - Kentucky leads series 7-4
0-15 S/U @ home as 10.5-15 point Dog since 1983		vs South Carolina - South Carolina leads series 18-13-1
3-10 S/U @ home as 7.5-10 point Dog since 2000		Game 1-5 O/U vs South Carolina since 2015
2-8 S/U @ home as 3 point or less Dog since 1998		3-1 S/U & ATS vs South Carolina as Dog since 2014
Favorite		6-1 S/U vs South Carolina as favorite since 1992
16-2 S/U & ATS @ home as 3 point or less favorite since 1983		6-1 S/U vs South Carolina since 2014
13-2 ATS as 3 point or less favorite since 2004		0-6 S/U vs South Carolina as 12.5 point or more Dog since 2001
0-8 ATS @ home as 3.5-7 point favorite since 2008		1-8 ATS @ home vs Tennessee since 2003
10-2-1 O/U as 3.5-7 point favorite since 2007		3-33 S/U vs Tennessee since 1985
16-0 S/U as 7.5-10 point favorite since 1989		3-11 ATS vs Tennessee since 2007
61-3 S/U as 10.5 point or more favorite since 1984		vs Tennessee - Tennessee leads series 81-26-9
13-2 S/U in 1st home game of season since 2006	UL-MONROE	0-20 S/U vs Tennessee as 9 point or more Dog since 1990
1-8 ATS after playing Missouri since 2012	CHATTANOOGA	1-9 S/U vs Tennessee as 6.5 point or less Dog since 1983
1-8 ATS prior to playing South Carolina since 2012	CHATTANOOGA	vs Vanderbilt - Kentucky leads series 47-42-4
3-14 S/U in 2nd road game of season since 2004	South Carolina	6-0 S/U vs Vanderbilt as 3.5 point or less favorite since 1996
0-9 O/U in 2nd road game of season since 2012	South Carolina	8-0 S/U vs Vanderbilt as 10 point or more favorite since 1986
11-2 O/U prior to playing Mississippi State since 2007	Georgia	
3-11 S/U after playing Georgia since 2007	Mississippi State	5-63 S/U on road vs ranked teams since 1978
3-11 ATS after playing Georgia since 2007	Mississippi State	2-14 S/U vs #1 ranked teams since 1951
2-6 S/U & ATS prior to playing Tennessee since 2013	Mississippi State	0-22 S/U vs #5 #6 ranked teams all time
0-9 O/U prior to playing Vanderbilt since 2012	TENNESSEE	0-15 S/U vs #7 ranked teams since 1972
4-17 S/U in final road game of season since 2000	Louisville	1-32 S/U vs ranked Georgia since 1967

Copyright © 2021 by Steve's Football Bible, LLC

KENT STATE GOLDEN FLASHES   MAC East

2020-Kent State		Opponent	Kent	Opp	S/U	Line	ATS	Total	O/U	
11/4/2020	vs	EASTERN MICHIGAN	27	23	W	-4.5	L	65.5	U	
11/10/2020	@	Bowling Green	62	24	W	-20.5	W	55.0	O	"Anniversary Award"
11/17/2020	vs	AKRON	69	35	W	-26.0	W	60.5	O	"Wagon Wheel"
11/28/2020	@	Buffalo	41	70	L	7.5	L	70.0	O	
Coach: Sean Lewis		Season Record >>	199	152	3-1	ATS>>	2-2	O/U>>	3-1	
2019-Kent State		Opponent	Kent	Opp	S/U	Line	ATS	Total	O/U	
8/29/2019	@	Arizona State	7	30	L	24.5	W	61.0	U	
9/7/2019	vs	KENNESAW STATE	26	23	W	-4.5	L	NT	---	{OT}
9/14/2019	@	Auburn	16	55	L	36.0	L	53.5	O	
9/21/2019	vs	BOWLING GREEN	62	20	W	-11.5	W	62.0	O	"Anniversary Award"
10/5/2019	@	Wisconsin	0	48	L	35.0	L	58.5	U	
10/12/2019	@	Akron	26	3	W	-14.5	W	57.5	U	"Wagon Wheel"
10/19/2019	@	Ohio	38	45	L	9.0	W	64.5	O	
10/26/2019	vs	MIAMI-OHIO	16	23	L	-2.5	L	54.5	U	
11/5/2019	@	Toledo	33	35	L	3.0	W	64.0	O	
11/14/2019	vs	BUFFALO	30	27	W	6.0	W	54.5	O	
11/23/2019	vs	BALL STATE	41	38	W	3.5	W	67.5	O	
11/29/2019	@	Eastern Michigan	34	26	W	3.0	W	68.5	U	
12/20/2019	vs	**Utah State**	**51**	**41**	**W**	**7.0**	**W**	**71.5**	**O**	Frisco Bowl
Coach: Sean Lewis		Season Record >>	380	414	7-6	ATS>>	9-4	O/U>>	7-5	
2018-Kent State		Opponent	Kent	Opp	S/U	Line	ATS	Total	O/U	
9/1/2018	@	Illinois	24	31	L	18.0	W	57.0	U	
9/8/2018	vs	HOWARD	54	14	W	-9.0	W	NT	---	
9/15/2018	@	Penn State	10	63	L	35.0	L	63.0	O	
9/22/2018	@	Mississippi	17	38	L	28.0	W	75.0	U	
9/29/2018	@	Ball State	24	52	L	7.0	L	61.5	O	
10/6/2018	vs	OHIO	26	27	L	11.5	W	68.5	U	
10/13/2018	@	Miami-Ohio	6	31	L	11.5	L	59.0	U	
10/20/2018	vs	AKRON	23	24	L	4.5	W	49.5	U	"Wagon Wheel"
10/30/2018	@	Bowling Green	35	28	W	PK	W	68.0	U	"Anniversary Award"
11/6/2018	@	Buffalo	14	48	L	17.0	L	48.0	O	
11/15/2018	vs	TOLEDO	34	56	L	11.5	L	57.0	O	
11/23/2018	vs	EASTERN MICHIGAN	20	28	L	12.5	W	52.0	U	
Coach: Sean Lewis		Season Record >>	287	440	2-10	ATS>>	7-5	O/U>>	4-7	
2017-Kent State		Opponent	Kent	Opp	S/U	Line	ATS	Total	O/U	
9/2/2017	@	Clemson	3	56	L	38.0	L	52.0	O	
9/9/2017	vs	HOWARD	38	31	W	-25.0	L	NT	---	
9/16/2017	@	Marshall	0	21	L	13.5	L	50.5	U	
9/23/2017	@	Louisville	3	42	L	42.0	W	56.0	U	
9/30/2017	vs	BUFFALO	13	27	L	7.5	L	40.5	U	
10/7/2017	@	Northern Illinois	3	24	L	23.0	L	43.5	U	
10/14/2017	vs	MIAMI-OHIO	17	14	W	8.0	W	42.5	U	
10/21/2017	@	Ohio	3	48	L	17.0	L	47.0	O	
10/31/2017	vs	BOWLING GREEN	16	44	L	1.5	L	48.0	O	"Anniversary Award"
11/8/2017	@	Western Michigan	20	48	L	20.0	L	45.0	O	
11/14/2017	vs	CENTRAL MICHIGAN	23	42	L	17.0	L	44.5	O	
11/21/2017	@	Akron	14	24	L	14.5	W	46.0	U	"Wagon Wheel"
Coach: Paul Haynes		Season Record >>	153	421	2-10	ATS>>	4-8	O/U>>	5-6	

Copyright © 2021 by Steve's Football Bible, LLC

KENT STATE GOLDEN FLASHES   MAC East

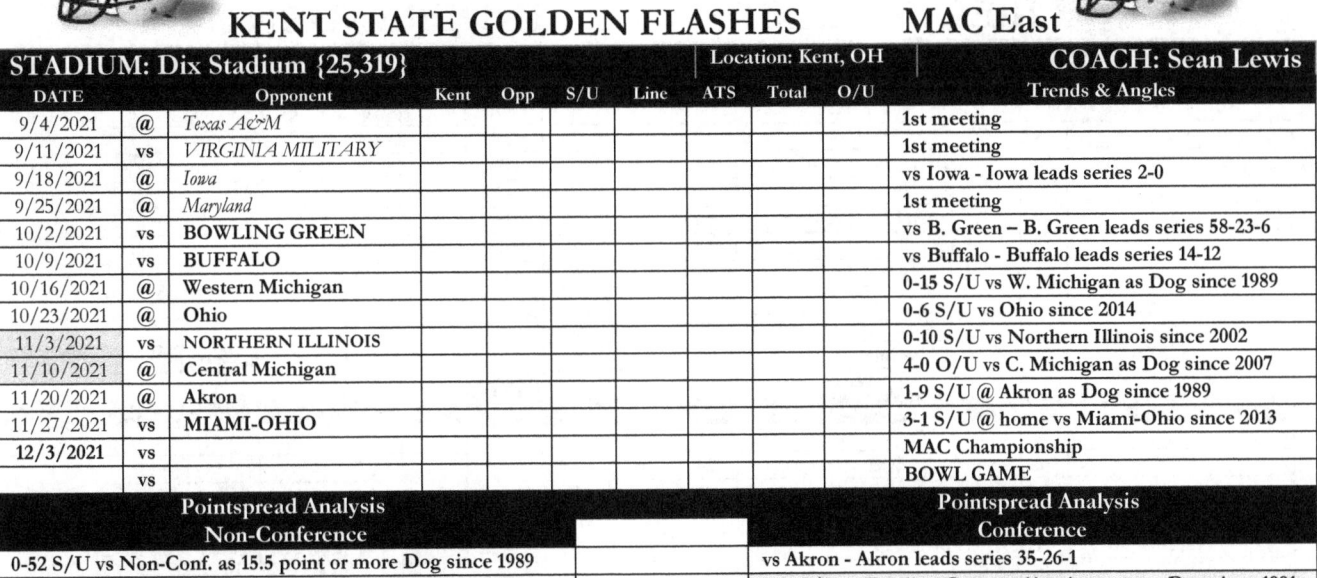

STADIUM: Dix Stadium {25,319}					Location: Kent, OH				COACH: Sean Lewis	
DATE		Opponent	Kent	Opp	S/U	Line	ATS	Total	O/U	Trends & Angles
9/4/2021	@	Texas A&M								1st meeting
9/11/2021	vs	VIRGINIA MILITARY								1st meeting
9/18/2021	@	Iowa								vs Iowa - Iowa leads series 2-0
9/25/2021	@	Maryland								1st meeting
10/2/2021	vs	BOWLING GREEN								vs B. Green – B. Green leads series 58-23-6
10/9/2021	vs	BUFFALO								vs Buffalo - Buffalo leads series 14-12
10/16/2021	@	Western Michigan								0-15 S/U vs W. Michigan as Dog since 1989
10/23/2021	@	Ohio								0-6 S/U vs Ohio since 2014
11/3/2021	vs	NORTHERN ILLINOIS								0-10 S/U vs Northern Illinois since 2002
11/10/2021	@	Central Michigan								4-0 O/U vs C. Michigan as Dog since 2007
11/20/2021	@	Akron								1-9 S/U @ Akron as Dog since 1989
11/27/2021	vs	MIAMI-OHIO								3-1 S/U @ home vs Miami-Ohio since 2013
12/3/2021	vs									MAC Championship
	vs									BOWL GAME

Pointspread Analysis Non-Conference		Pointspread Analysis Conference
0-52 S/U vs Non-Conf. as 15.5 point or more Dog since 1989		vs Akron - Akron leads series 35-26-1
5-21 S/U vs Non-Conf. as a 15 point or less Dog since 1989		1-13 S/U vs Bowling Green as 11 point or more Dog since 1991
4-0 S/U vs Non-Conf. as 15.5 point or more favorite since 2010		0-3 S/U & ATS @ home vs Buffalo as favorite since 2005
Bowl Games		0-10 S/U vs C. Michigan as 7.5 point or more Dog since 1989
1-3 S/U in Bowl Games		vs Miami-Ohio - Miami-Ohio leads series 50-17
Dog		Game 0-7 O/U vs Miami-Ohio since 2013
0-35 S/U on road as 25.5 point or more Dog since 1989		Game 0-8 O/U @ home vs Miami-Ohio since 2005
1-30 S/U as 20.5-25 point Dog since 1993		0-10 S/U vs Miami-Ohio as 14 point or more Dog since 1991
0-9 S/U @ home as 20.5 point or more Dog since 1994		vs Northern Illinois - NIU leads series 21-7
0-27 S/U on road as 15.5-20 point Dog since 1990		0-9 S/U vs Northern Illinois as Dog since 2002
8-152 S/U as 10.5 point or more Dog since 1989		vs Ohio - Ohio leads series 44-26-2
0-12 S/U @ home as 10.5-15 point Dog since 2001		Game 3-9 O/U vs Ohio since 2008
2-13 S/U @ home as 7.5-10 point Dog since 1992		0-5 S/U vs Ohio as 14 point or more Dog since 1997
8-1 O/U @ home as 3.5-7 point Dog since 2011		3-0 S/U & ATS vs Western Michigan as favorite since 2009
1-10 S/U @ home as 3 point or less Dog since 2008		
Favorite	Texas A&M	8-2 O/U in 1st road game of season since 2011
7-0 S/U @ home as 3.5-7 point favorite since 2011 {5-2 ATS}	Texas A&M	1-12 S/U in 1st road game of season since 2008
5-1 ATS @ home as 3.5-7 point favorite since 2011	Iowa	2-26 S/U in 2nd road game of season since 1993
17-2 S/U @ home as 10.5 point or more favorite since 1999	Iowa	0-11 ATS in 2nd road game of season since 2010
	B. GREEN	2-13 S/U prior to playing Buffalo since 2002
	BUFFALO	11-3 O/U after playing Bowling Green since 2006
	W. Michigan	3-9 S/U after playing Buffalo since 2005
	C. Michigan	1-7 S/U prior to playing Akron since 2013
	MIAMI-OHIO	9-2 O/U after playing Akron since 2009
	Akron	1-6 S/U in final road game of season since 2014
	Akron	2-5 O/U in final road game of season since 2014
	MIAMI-OHIO	6-1 O/U in final home game of season since 2014

Copyright © 2021 by Steve's Football Bible, LLC

LIBERTY FLAMES   INDEPENDENT

2020-Liberty		Opponent	Lib	Opp	S/U	Line	ATS	Total	O/U	
9/19/2020	@	Western Kentucky	30	24	W	14.0	W	51.5	O	
9/26/2020	vs	FLORIDA INTERNATIONAL	36	34	W	-7.5	L	60.5	O	
10/3/2020	vs	NORTH ALABAMA	28	7	W	-32.5	L	63.5	U	
10/10/2020	vs	LOUISIANA-MONROE	40	7	W	-17.0	W	63.0	U	
10/17/2020	@	Syracuse	38	21	W	-3.0	W	52.5	O	
10/24/2020	vs	SOUTHERN MISSISSIPPI	56	35	W	-15.0	W	59.5	O	
11/7/2020	@	Virginia Tech	38	35	W	16.5	W	67.5	O	
11/14/2020	vs	WESTERN CAROLINA	58	14	W	-39.0	W	63.0	O	
11/21/2020	@	NC State	14	15	L	4.0	W	66.5	U	
11/27/2020	vs	MASSACHUSETTS	45	0	W	-35.0	W	57.5	U	
12/26/2020	vs	**Coastal Carolina**	37	34	W	6.5	W	60.0	O	**FBC Mortgage Cure Bowl**
Coach: Hugh Freeze		Season Record >>	420	226	10-1	ATS>>	9-2	ATS>>	7-4	
2019-Liberty		Opponent	Lib	Opp	S/U	Line	ATS	Total	O/U	
8/31/2019	vs	SYRACUSE	0	24	L	19.5	L	68.0	U	
9/7/2019	@	Louisiana-Lafayette	14	35	L	14.0	L	65.5	U	
9/14/2019	vs	BUFFALO	35	17	W	6.0	W	55.0	U	
9/21/2019	vs	HAMPTON	62	27	W	NL	---	NT	---	
9/28/2019	vs	NEW MEXICO	17	10	W	-7.0	T	72.0	U	
10/5/2019	@	New Mexico State	20	13	W	-4.0	W	63.5	U	
10/19/2019	vs	MAINE	59	44	W	-14.5	W	NT	---	
10/26/2019	@	Rutgers	34	44	L	-7.5	L	43.5	O	
11/2/2019	@	Massachusetts	63	21	W	-23.5	W	71.0	O	
11/9/2019	@	Byu	24	31	L	17.0	W	62.0	U	
11/23/2019	@	Virginia	27	55	L	16.0	L	58.0	O	
11/30/2019	vs	NEW MEXICO STATE	49	28	W	-14.5	W	68.0	O	
12/21/2019	vs	**Georgia Southern**	23	16	W	5.0	W	58.5	U	**AutoNation Cure Bowl**
Coach: Hugh Freeze		Season Record >>	427	365	8-5	ATS>>	7-4-1	ATS>>	4-7	
2018-Liberty		Opponent	Lib	Opp	S/U	Line	ATS	Total	O/U	
9/1/2018	vs	OLD DOMINION	52	10	W	5.0	W	58.0	O	
9/8/2018	@	Army	14	38	L	7.5	L	59.5	U	
9/22/2018	vs	NORTH TEXAS	7	47	L	11.0	L	67.0	U	
9/29/2018	@	New Mexico	52	43	W	7.0	W	66.0	O	
10/6/2018	@	New Mexico State	41	49	L	-3.5	L	64.0	O	
10/13/2018	vs	TROY	22	16	W	10.0	W	63.0	U	
10/20/2018	vs	IDAHO STATE	48	41	W	NL	---	NT	---	
11/3/2018	@	Massachusetts	59	62	L	1.0	L	67.5	O	{3 OT}
11/10/2018	@	Virginia	24	45	L	23.5	W	59.0	O	
11/17/2018	@	Auburn	0	53	L	28.5	L	64.5	U	
11/24/2018	vs	NEW MEXICO STATE	28	21	W	-5.5	W	72.5	U	
12/1/2018	vs	NORFOLK STATE	52	17	W	-29.5	W	NT	---	
Coach: Turner Gill		Season Record >>	399	442	6-6	ATS>>	6-5	ATS>>	5-5	
2017-Liberty		Opponent	Lib	Opp	S/U	Line	ATS	Total	O/U	
9/2/2017	@	*Baylor*	48	45	W					
9/9/2017	vs	*MOREHEAD STATE*	58	17	W					
9/16/2017	vs	*INDIANA STATE*	42	41	W					
9/23/2017	@	*Jacksonville State*	10	31	L					
9/30/2017	vs	*ST. FRANCIS-PA*	7	13	L					
10/14/2017	vs	KENNESAW STATE	28	42	L					
10/21/2017	@	Monmouth	39	56	L					
10/28/2017	@	Gardner-Webb	33	17	W					
11/4/2017	vs	*DUQUESNE*	27	24	W					
11/11/2017	vs	PRESBYTERIAN	47	28	W					
11/18/2017	@	Charleston Southern	19	20	L					
Coach: Turner Gill		Season Record >>	358	334	6-5					

Copyright © 2021 by Steve's Football Bible, LLC

LIBERTY FLAMES   INDEPENDENT

STADIUM: Williams Stadium {25,000}		Location: Lynchburg, VA					COACH: Hugh Freeze		
DATE		Opponent	Lib	Opp	S/U	Line	ATS	Total	O/U	Trends & Angles

DATE		Opponent	Lib	Opp	S/U	Line	ATS	Total	O/U	Trends & Angles
9/4/2021	vs	CAMPBELL								1st meeting
9/11/2021	@	Troy								vs Troy - Liberty leads series 2-1
9/18/2021	vs	OLD DOMINION								vs Old Dominion- Series tied 1-1
9/25/2021	@	Syracuse								vs Syracuse - Series tied 1-1
10/2/2021	@	Alabama-Birmingham								1st meeting
10/9/2021	vs	MIDDLE TENNESSEE								vs Middle Tennessee - MTSU leads series 1-0
10/16/2021	@	Louisiana-Monroe								vs UL-Monroe - Liberty leads series 1-0
10/23/2021	@	North Texas								vs North Texas - North Texas leads series 1-0
10/30/2021	vs	MASSACHUSETTS								vs Massachusetts - Liberty leads series 2-1
11/6/2021	@	Mississippi								1st meeting
11/20/2021	vs	LOUISIANA								vs Louisiana - Louisiana leads series 1-0
11/27/2021	vs	ARMY								vs Army - Army leads series 1-0
	vs									BOWL GAME

Pointspread Analysis		Pointspread Analysis	
Dog			
2-7 S/U as 11 point or more Dog since 2018	CAMPBELL	16-2 S/U in 1st home game of season since 2003	
5-1 S/U & ATS as 5-10 point Dog since 2018	Ole Miss	0-6 S/U in final road game of season since 2015	
Favorite	ARMY	13-2 S/U in final home game of season since 2006	
9-0 S/U as 14.5 point or more favorite since 2018			
8-1 ATS as 14.5 point or more favorite since 2018			

Steve's Football Bible also offers the Pro Football Bible, the Pro football handicapper's best friend for the 2021 football season.

To order Go to: www.stevesfootballbible.com

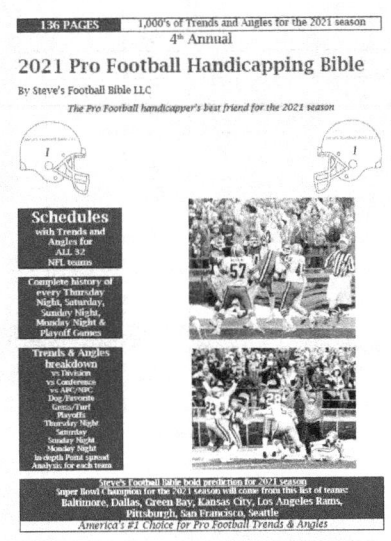

2021 Pro Football Bible $24.95

Copyright © 2021 by Steve's Football Bible, LLC

LOUISIANA RAGIN' CAJUNS SUN BELT West

2020-Louisiana		Opponent	ULL	Opp	S/U	Line	ATS	Total	O/U	
9/12/2020	@	*Iowa State*	31	14	W	11.5	W	56.0	U	
9/19/2020	@	Georgia State	34	31	W	-16.5	L	57.0	O	{OT}
9/26/2020	vs	GEORGIA SOUTHERN	20	18	W	-11.5	L	50.0	U	
10/14/2020	vs	COASTAL CAROLINA	27	30	L	-9.0	L	57.0	T	
10/23/2020	@	*Alabama-Birmingham*	24	20	W	-2.5	W	50.5	U	
10/31/2020	@	Texas State	44	34	W	-16.5	L	56.5	O	
11/7/2020	vs	ARKANSAS STATE	27	20	W	-14.5	L	68.5	U	
11/14/2020	vs	SOUTH ALABAMA	38	10	W	-14.5	W	53.5	U	
11/28/2020	@	Louisiana-Monroe	70	20	W	-29.0	W	58.0	O	*"Battle of the Bayou"*
12/4/2020	@	Appalachian State	24	21	W	3.0	W	51.0	U	
12/26/2020	vs	**Texas-San Antonio**	**31**	**24**	W	-13.5	L	55.0	T	**First Responder Bowl**
Coach: Billy Napier		Season Record >>	370	242	10-1	ATS>>	5-6	O/U>>	3-6-2	
2019-Louisiana		Opponent	ULL	Opp	S/U	Line	ATS	Total	O/U	
8/31/2019	vs	*Mississippi State*	28	38	L	18.5	W	60.5	O	
9/7/2019	vs	*LIBERTY*	35	14	W	-14.0	W	65.5	U	
9/14/2019	vs	*TEXAS SOUTHERN*	77	6	W	-46.5	W	NT	---	
9/21/2019	@	*Ohio*	45	25	W	3.0	W	68.0	O	
9/28/2019	@	Georgia Southern	37	24	W	-3.0	W	55.0	O	
10/9/2019	vs	APPALACHIAN STATE	7	17	L	-3.0	L	69.0	U	
10/17/2019	@	Arkansas State	37	20	W	6.0	W	68.5	U	
11/2/2019	vs	TEXAS STATE	31	3	W	-23.0	W	55.0	U	
11/7/2019	@	Coastal Carolina	48	7	W	-14.0	W	58.0	U	
11/16/2019	@	South Alabama	37	27	W	-27.5	L	52.5	O	
11/23/2019	vs	TROY	53	3	W	-12.5	W	74.0	U	
11/30/2019	vs	LOUISIANA-MONROE	31	30	W	-20.0	L	71.0	U	*"Battle of the Bayou"*
12/7/2019	vs	**Appalachian State**	**38**	**45**	L	5.0	L	57.0	O	**SUN BELT CHAMPIONSHIP**
1/6/2020	vs	**Miami-Ohio**	**27**	**17**	W	-16.0	L	55.0	U	**Lending Tree Bowl**
Coach: Billy Napier		Season Record >>	531	276	11-3	ATS>>	9-5	O/U>>	5-8	
2018-Louisiana		Opponent	ULL	Opp	S/U	Line	ATS	Total	O/U	
9/1/2018	vs	*GRAMBLING STATE*	49	17	W	-13.5	W	NT	---	
9/15/2018	@	*Mississippi State*	10	56	L	33.5	L	63.0	O	
9/22/2018	vs	COASTAL CAROLINA	28	30	L	-3.0	L	63.0	U	
9/29/2018	@	*Alabama*	14	56	L	49.0	W	69.0	O	
10/6/2018	@	Texas State	42	27	W	-3.5	W	58.5	O	
10/13/2018	vs	*NEW MEXICO STATE*	66	38	W	-7.0	W	67.5	O	
10/20/2018	@	Appalachian State	17	27	L	25.5	W	67.0	U	
10/27/2018	vs	ARKANSAS STATE	47	43	W	3.0	W	70.0	O	
11/3/2018	@	Troy	16	26	L	7.5	L	64.5	U	
11/10/2018	vs	GEORGIA STATE	36	22	W	-13.0	W	70.0	U	
11/17/2018	vs	SOUTH ALABAMA	48	38	W	-19.5	L	65.5	O	
11/24/2018	@	Louisiana-Monroe	31	28	W	1.5	W	72.0	U	*"Battle of the Bayou"*
12/1/2018	@	**Appalachian State**	**19**	**30**	L	17.0	W	55.0	U	**SUN BELT CHAMPIONSHIP**
12/15/2018	vs	**Tulane**	**24**	**41**	L	3.0	L	60.5	O	**AutoNation Cure Bowl**
Coach: Billy Napier		Season Record >>	447	479	7-7	ATS>>	9-5	O/U>>	7-6	
2017-Louisiana		Opponent	ULL	Opp	S/U	Line	ATS	Total	O/U	
9/2/2017	vs	*SE LOUISIANA*	51	48	W	-14.0	L	52.0	O	*"Cypress Mug"*
9/9/2017	@	*Tulsa*	42	66	L	14.0	L	60.5	O	
9/16/2017	@	*Texas A&M*	21	45	L	24.5	W	62.0	O	
9/23/2017	vs	LOUISIANA-MONROE	50	56	L	-4.5	L	58.5	O	*"Battle of the Bayou"*
10/7/2017	@	*Idaho*	21	16	W	5.5	W	61.5	U	
10/12/2017	vs	TEXAS STATE	24	7	W	-14.0	W	55.0	U	
10/19/2017	@	Arkansas State	3	47	L	12.0	L	65.5	U	
11/4/2017	@	South Alabama	19	14	W	6.5	W	52.0	U	
11/11/2017	@	*Mississippi*	22	50	L	22.0	L	67.0	O	
11/18/2017	vs	NEW MEXICO STATE	47	34	W	4.0	W	64.0	O	
11/25/2017	vs	GEORGIA SOUTHERN	24	34	L	-4.5	L	56.0	O	
12/2/2017	@	Appalachian State	14	63	L	14.0	L	56.5	O	
Coach: Mark Hudspeth		Season Record >>	338	480	5-7	ATS>>	5-7	O/U>>	8-4	

Copyright © 2021 by Steve's Football Bible, LLC

LOUISIANA RAGIN' CAJUNS   SUN BELT West

STADIUM: Cajun Field {41,264}		Location: Lafayette, LA							COACH: Billy Napier
DATE		Opponent	ULL	Opp	S/U	Line	ATS	Total	O/U	Trends & Angles
9/4/2021	@	*Texas*								vs Texas - Texas leads series 2-0
9/11/2021	vs	*NICHOLLS STATE*								vs Nicholls State - Louisiana leads series 4-0
9/18/2021	vs	*OHIO*								vs Ohio - Ohio leads series 2-1
9/25/2021	@	Georgia Southern								vs Georgia Southern - Louisiana leads series 3-1
10/2/2021	@	South Alabama								5-0 S/U vs South Alabama since 2016
10/12/2021	vs	APPALACHIAN STATE								vs App. State - App. State leads series 7-1
10/21/2021	@	Arkansas State								vs Ark. State - Louisiana leads series 27-21-1
10/30/2021	vs	TEXAS STATE								vs Texas State - Louisiana leads series 8-0
11/4/2021	vs	GEORGIA STATE								5-0 S/U vs Georgia State as favorite since 2013
11/13/2021	@	Troy								vs Troy - Louisiana leads series 12-9
11/20/2021	@	*Liberty*								vs Liberty - Louisiana leads series 1-0
11/27/2021	vs	LOUISIANA-MONROE								0-5 ATS @ home vs UL-Monroe since 2011
12/4/2021	vs									Sun Belt Championship
	vs									BOWL GAME

Pointspread Analysis Non-Conference		Pointspread Analysis Conference
1-58 S/U vs Non-Conf. as 20.5 point or more Dog since 1989		13-2 S/U vs Arkansas State as favorite since 1990
3-21 S/U vs Non-Conf. as 10.5-20 point Dog since 1988		2-7 S/U @ Arkansas State as Dog since 1999
16-1 S/U vs Non-Conf. as 10.5 point or more favorite since 1988		1-6 S/U vs Appalachian State as Dog since 2015
Dog		vs UL-Monroe - Louisiana leads series 31-25
0-41 S/U as 25.5 point or more Dog since 1991		vs Louisiana-Monroe - ROAD team 17-1 ATS since 2003
0-66 S/U on road as 20.5 point or more Dog since 1989		4-0 S/U & ATS vs UL-Monroe as Dog since 2009
3-17 S/U as 15.-20 point Dog since 1988		vs South Alabama - Louisiana leads series 7-2
1-11 S/U as 10.5-15 point Dog since 2009		6-0 S/U vs South Alabama as favorite since 2012
1-7 ATS as 10.5-15 point Dog since 2013		0-3 S/U @ Troy as Dog since 2008
5-0 S/U @ home as 3.5-7 point Dog since 2009		7-0 S/U vs Texas State as favorite since 2013 {6-1 ATS}
6-20-1 O/U as 3.5-7 point Dog since 2001		
9-1 ATS as 3 point or less Dog since 2013		
Favorite	Texas	3-27 S/U in 1st road game of season since 1990
5-0 S/U & ATS on road as 3 point or less favorite since 2012	NICHOLLS	12-1 S/U in 1st home game of season since 2008
5-0 S/U on road as 3.5-7 point favorite since 2013	OHIO	7-3-1 O/U in 2nd home game of season since 2007
15-3 S/U as 7.5-10 point favorite since 1995	G. Southern	4-23 S/U in 2nd road game of season since 1994
7-0 S/U on road as 7.5-10 point favorite since 1995	APP STATE	6-1 ATS prior to playing Arkansas State since 2013
11-0 S/U as 10.5-15 point favorite since 2017	TEXAS STATE	8-1 S/U after playing Arkansas State since 2012
0-8-1 O/U as 10.5-15 point favorite since 2017	UL-MONROE	3-9 ATS in final home game of season since 2009
9-0 S/U on road as 10.5 point or more favorite since 1993		
12-0 S/U @ home as 20.5 point or more favorite since 1996		
Bowl Games		
4-1 S/U & ATS in New Orleans Bowl		
0-3 O/U in New Orleans Bowl since 2013		
0-4 ATS in Bowl Games since 2016		2-30 S/U vs ranked teams since 1985
6-2 S/U in Bowl Games since 2011		8-2 O/U vs ranked teams since 2009

Copyright © 2021 by Steve's Football Bible, LLC

LOUISIANA-MONROE WARHAWKS   SUN BELT West

2020-UL-Monroe		Opponent	ULM	Opp	S/U	Line	ATS	Total	O/U	
9/12/2020	@	Army	7	37	L	22.5	L	53.5	U	
9/19/2020	vs	TEXAS STATE	17	38	L	3.0	L	58.0	U	
9/26/2020	vs	TEXAS-EL PASO	6	31	L	-10.0	L	50.0	U	
10/3/2020	vs	GEORGIA SOUTHERN	30	35	L	18.5	W	49.5	O	
10/10/2020	@	Liberty	7	40	L	17.0	L	63.0	U	
10/24/2020	@	South Alabama	14	38	L	14.5	L	57.0	U	
10/31/2020	vs	APPALACHIAN STATE	13	31	L	29.0	W	56.0	U	
11/7/2020	@	Georgia State	34	52	L	18.5	W	60.0	O	
11/28/2020	vs	LOUISIANA-LAFAYETTE	20	70	L	29.0	L	58.0	O	"Battle of the Bayou"
12/5/2020	@	Arkansas State	15	48	L	20.0	L	71.0	U	"Trail of Tears Classic"
Coach: Matt Viator		Season Record >>	163	420	0-10	ATS>>	3-7	O/U>>	3-7	
2019-UL-Monroe		Opponent	ULM	Opp	S/U	Line	ATS	Total	O/U	
8/31/2019	vs	GRAMBLING STATE	31	9	W	-27.5	L	NT	---	
9/7/2019	@	Florida State	44	45	L	23.0	W	65.5	O	{OT}
9/14/2019	@	Iowa State	20	72	L	17.5	L	52.0	O	
9/28/2019	vs	SOUTH ALABAMA	30	17	W	-14.5	L	58.5	U	
10/5/2019	vs	MEMPHIS	33	52	L	15.0	L	69.0	O	
10/10/2019	@	Texas State	24	14	W	-4.0	W	60.0	U	
10/19/2019	@	Appalachian State	7	52	L	15.5	L	65.5	U	
11/2/2019	vs	ARKANSAS STATE	41	48	L	-1.0	L	69.5	O	"Trail of Tears Classic"
11/9/2019	vs	GEORGIA STATE	45	31	W	2.5	W	76.0	T	
11/16/2019	@	Georgia Southern	29	51	L	6.0	L	58.0	U	
11/23/2019	vs	COASTAL CAROLINA	45	42	W	-6.0	L	63.5	O	
11/30/2019	@	Louisiana-Lafayette	30	31	L	20.0	W	71.0	U	"Battle of the Bayou"
Coach: Matt Viator		Season Record >>	379	464	5-7	ATS>>	4-8	O/U>>	6-4-1	
2018-UL-Monroe		Opponent	ULM	Opp	S/U	Line	ATS	Total	O/U	
9/1/2018	vs	SE LOUISIANA	34	31	W	-20.5	L	NT	---	
9/8/2018	@	Southern Mississippi	21	20	W	5.0	W	67.0	U	
9/15/2018	@	Texas A&M	10	48	L	28.0	L	66.0	U	
9/22/2018	vs	TROY	27	35	L	4.5	L	59.0	O	
9/29/2018	@	Georgia State	14	46	L	-5.5	L	65.5	U	
10/6/2018	@	Mississippi	21	70	L	24.0	L	76.0	O	
10/13/2018	@	Coastal Carolina	45	20	W	6.5	W	67.5	U	
10/20/2018	vs	TEXAS STATE	20	14	W	-10.5	L	59.5	U	
11/3/2018	vs	GEORGIA SOUTHERN	44	25	W	7.0	W	60.5	O	
11/10/2018	@	South Alabama	38	10	W	-7.5	W	62.0	U	
11/17/2018	@	Arkansas State	17	31	L	8.0	L	68.0	U	"Trail of Tears Classic"
11/24/2018	vs	LOUISIANA-LAFAEYTTE	28	31	L	-1.5	L	72.0	U	"Battle of the Bayou"
Coach: Matt Viator		Season Record >>	319	381	6-6	ATS>>	4-8	O/U>>	3-8	
2017-UL-Monroe		Opponent	ULM	Opp	S/U	Line	ATS	Total	O/U	
8/31/2017	@	Memphis	29	37	L	28.0	W	61.0	O	
9/16/2017	vs	SOUTHERN MISS	17	28	L	7.5	L	55.5	U	
9/23/2017	@	Louisiana-Lafayette	56	50	W	4.5	W	58.5	O	"Battle of the Bayou"
9/30/2017	vs	COASTAL CAROLINA	51	43	W	-7.5	W	54.0	O	
10/7/2017	@	Texas State	45	27	W	-5.0	W	54.5	O	
10/14/2017	vs	GEORGIA STATE	37	47	L	-3.5	L	57.0	O	
10/21/2017	@	South Alabama	23	33	L	3.5	L	55.0	O	
10/28/2017	@	Idaho	23	31	L	2.5	L	62.0	U	
11/4/2017	vs	APPALACHIAN STATE	52	45	W	8.0	W	62.0	O	
11/18/2017	@	Auburn	14	42	L	38.0	W	68.0	O	
11/25/2017	vs	ARKANSAS STATE	50	67	L	8.5	L	69.0	O	"Trail of Tears Classic"
12/2/2017	@	Florida State	10	42	L	25.5	L	63.5	U	
Coach: Matt Viator		Season Record >>	407	492	4-8	ATS>>	6-6	O/U>>	8-4	

Copyright © 2021 by Steve's Football Bible, LLC

LOUISIANA-MONROE WARHAWKS   SUN BELT West

STADIUM: Malone Stadium {27,617}							Location: Monroe, LA		COACH: Terry Bowden
DATE		Opponent	ULM	Opp	S/U	Line	ATS	Total	O/U	Trends & Angles
9/4/2021	@	Kentucky								vs Kentucky - Kentucky leads series 4-1
9/18/2021	vs	JACKSON STATE								1st meeting
9/25/2021	vs	TROY								4-1 S/U @ home vs Troy since 2005
10/2/2021	@	Coastal Carolina								vs Coastal Carolina - UL-Monroe leads series 3-0
10/9/2021	@	Lsu								0-3 S/U vs LSU as Dog since 2003
10/9/2021	vs	GEORGIA STATE								vs Georgia State - Series tied 3-3
10/16/2021	vs	LIBERTY								vs Liberty - Liberty leads series 1-0
10/23/2021	vs	SOUTH ALABAMA								3-0 S/U @ home vs South Alabama since 2012
10/30/2021	@	Appalachian State								vs Appalachian State - App. State leads series 5-1
11/6/2021	@	Texas State								5-1 S/U @ Texas State since 1991
11/13/2021	vs	ARKANSAS STATE								vs Arkansas State - Ark State leads series 28-14
11/27/2021	@	Louisiana								vs Louisiana - Louisiana leads series 31-25
12/4/2021	vs									Sun Belt Championship
	vs									BOWL GAME

Pointspread Analysis Non-Conference		Pointspread Analysis Conference
5-91 S/U vs Non-Conf. as 10.5 point or more Dog since 1994		1-5 S/U & ATS vs Arkansas State as favorite since 1998
6-0 S/U vs Non-Conf. as 15.5 point or more favorite since 2011		0-10 S/U vs Arkansas State as 6.5 point or more Dog since 2003
Dog		0-4 S/U & ATS vs Louisiana as favorite since 2009
0-36 S/U as 30.5 point or more Dog since 1994		0-5 O/U vs Louisiana as favorite since 2007
1-20 S/U as 25.5-30 point Dog since 1997		0-4 S/U & ATS @ home vs Louisiana as favorite since 2005
2-19 S/U as 20.5-25 point Dog since 1995		0-4 S/U & ATS @ home vs Louisiana as Dog since 2008
3-13 ATS as 20.5-25 point Dog since 1997		vs South Alabama - UL-Monroe leads series 4-3
2-21 S/U on road as 15.5-20 point Dog since 1994		vs Texas State - Louisiana-Monroe leads series 12-5
12-5 O/U as 15.5-20 point Dog since 2002		4-1 S/U vs Texas State since 2016
3-18 S/U on road as 10.5-15 point Dog since 1994		vs Troy - Troy leads series 11-7-1
11-4-1 O/U as 7.5-10 point Dog since 2001	Kentucky	1-26 S/U in 1st road game of season since 1994
1-10 S/U @ home as 3.5-7 point Dog since 2003	JACKSON STATE	1-12 S/U prior to playing Troy since 2001
Favorite	JACKSON STATE	2-8 O/U in 1st home game of season since 2004
3-0 S/U & ATS on road as 3 point or less favorite since 2004	TROY	1-9 ATS in 2nd home game of season since 2011
1-8 O/U as 10.5-15 point favorite since 2006	Coastal Carolina	2-27 S/U in 2nd road game of season since 1992
10-0 S/U as 15.5 point or more favorite since 2008	Coastal Carolina	0-6 S/U after playing Troy since 2010
	ARK STATE	1-7 S/U prior to playing Louisiana since 2013
	ARK STATE	3-9 S/U in final home game of season since 2009
	ARK STATE	2-10 ATS in final home game of season since 2009
2-33 S/U vs ranked teams all time	Louisiana	7-3 ATS in final road game of season since 2011

Print Version $29.99

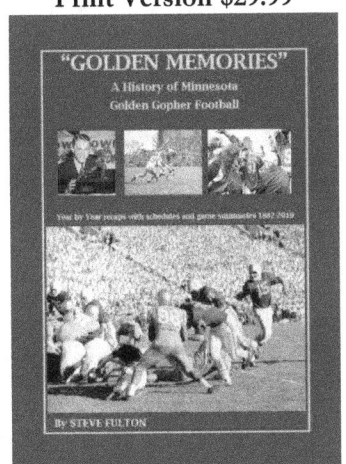

"Golden Gopher Fans" This book is available from Steve's Football Bible LLC

These books available at numerous online retailers

Copyright © 2021 by Steve's Football Bible, LLC

LOUISIANA TECH BULLDOGS   C-USA West

2020-Louisiana Tech		Opponent	Tech	Opp	S/U	Line	ATS	Total	O/U	
9/19/2020	@	Southern Mississippi	31	30	W	7.5	W	58.5	O	"Rivalry in Dixie"
9/26/2020	vs	HOUSTON BAPTIST	66	38	W	-24.0	W	73.5	O	
10/3/2020	@	Byu	14	45	L	24.0	L	61.5	U	
10/10/2020	vs	TEXAS-EL PASO	21	17	W	-14.0	L	56.0	U	
10/17/2020	vs	MARSHALL	17	35	L	11.5	L	48.0	O	
10/24/2020	@	Texas-San Antonio	26	27	L	-2.5	L	54.5	U	
10/31/2020	vs	ALABAMA-BIRMINGHAM	37	34	W	13.0	W	47.0	O	{2 OT}
12/3/2020	@	North Texas	42	31	W	-1.0	W	65.0	O	
12/12/2020	@	Tcu	10	52	L	21.5	L	50.5	O	
12/23/2020	vs	Georgia Southern	3	38	L	7.5	L	47.5	U	New Orleans Bowl
Coach: Skip Holtz		Season Record >>	267	347	5-5	ATS>>	4-6	O/U>>	6-4	
2019-Louisiana Tech		Opponent	Tech	Opp	S/U	Line	ATS	Total	O/U	
8/31/2019	@	Texas	10	45	L	19.0	L	55.5	U	
9/7/2019	vs	GRAMBLING STATE	20	14	W	-30.0	L	NT	---	
9/14/2019	@	Bowling Green	35	17	W	-12.5	W	58.5	U	
9/21/2019	vs	FLORIDA INTERNATIONAL	43	31	W	-6.5	W	51.5	O	
9/28/2019	@	Rice	23	20	W	-8.0	L	49.0	U	{OT}
10/12/2019	vs	MASSACHUSETTS	69	21	W	-31.5	W	64.0	O	
10/19/2019	vs	SOUTHERN MISS	45	30	W	2.5	W	58.0	O	"Rivalry in Dixie"
10/26/2019	@	Texas-El Paso	42	21	W	-18.5	W	50.0	O	
11/9/2019	vs	NORTH TEXAS	52	17	W	-5.0	W	71.5	U	
11/16/2019	@	Marshall	10	31	L	6.0	L	54.5	U	
11/23/2019	@	Alabama-Birmingham	14	20	L	6.5	W	44.0	U	
11/30/2019	vs	TEXAS-SAN ANTONIO	41	27	W	-21.0	L	56.0	O	
12/26/2019	vs	Miami	14	0	W	7.0	W	49.5	U	Independence Bowl
Coach: Skip Holtz		Season Record >>	418	294	10-3	ATS>>	8-5	O/U>>	5-7	
2018-Louisiana Tech		Opponent	Tech	Opp	S/U	Line	ATS	Total	O/U	
9/1/2018	@	South Alabama	30	26	W	-10.5	L	53.0	O	
9/8/2018	vs	SOUTHERN	54	17	W	-34.5	W	NT	---	
9/22/2018	@	Lsu	21	38	L	19.5	W	51.0	O	
9/29/2018	@	North Texas	29	27	W	7.0	W	63.0	U	
10/6/2018	vs	ALABAMA-BIRMINGHAM	7	28	L	-6.5	L	55.5	U	
10/13/2018	@	Texas-San Antonio	31	3	W	-13.0	W	45.5	U	
10/20/2018	vs	TEXAS-EL PASO	31	24	W	-23.0	L	50.5	O	
10/27/2018	@	Florida Atlantic	21	13	W	3.5	W	58.5	U	
11/3/2018	@	Mississippi State	3	45	L	23.0	L	48.5	U	
11/10/2018	vs	RICE	28	13	W	-24.0	L	53.0	U	
11/17/2018	@	Southern Mississippi	20	21	L	2.0	W	47.0	O	"Rivalry in Dixie"
11/24/2018	vs	WESTERN KENTUCKY	15	30	L	-10.5	L	49.0	U	
12/22/2018	vs	Hawaii	31	14	W	1.0	W	61.5	U	HAWAI'I BOWL
Coach: Skip Holtz		Season Record >>	321	299	8-5	ATS>>	7-6	O/U>>	3-9	
2017-Louisiana Tech		Opponent	Tech	Opp	S/U	Line	ATS	Total	O/U	
9/2/2017	vs	NORTHWESTERN STATE	52	29	W	-40.0	L	71.0	O	"State Fair Game"
9/9/2017	vs	MISSISSIPPI STATE	21	57	L	10.5	L	67.0	O	
9/16/2017	@	Western Kentucky	23	22	W	4.5	W	63.0	U	
9/23/2017	@	South Carolina	16	17	L	9.0	W	50.0	U	
9/30/2017	vs	SOUTH ALABAMA	34	16	W	-11.5	W	57.5	U	
10/7/2017	@	Alabama-Birmingham	22	23	L	-9.5	L	64.5	U	
10/21/2017	vs	SOUTHERN MISS {2 OT}	27	34	L	1.0	L	55.5	O	"Rivalry in Dixie"
10/28/2017	@	Rice	42	28	W	-11.5	W	51.5	O	
11/4/2017	vs	NORTH TEXAS	23	24	L	PK	L	67.0	U	
11/11/2017	vs	FLORIDA ATLANTIC	23	48	L	3.5	L	68.0	O	
11/18/2017	@	Texas-El Paso	42	21	W	-17.0	W	48.5	O	
11/25/2017	vs	TEXAS-SAN ANTONIO	20	6	W	1.0	W	52.0	U	
12/20/2017	vs	Smu	51	10	W	4.0	W	71.0	U	Frisco Bowl
Coach: Skip Holtz		Season Record >>	396	335	7-6	ATS>>	7-6	O/U>>	6-7	

Copyright © 2021 by Steve's Football Bible, LLC

LOUISIANA TECH BULLDOGS   C-USA West

STADIUM: Joe Aillet Stadium {28,562}							Location: Ruston, LA		COACH: Skip Holtz

DATE		Opponent	Tech	Opp	S/U	Line	ATS	Total	O/U	Trends & Angles
9/4/2021	@	*Mississippi State*								2-10 S/U @ Mississippi State since 1904
9/11/2021	vs	*SE LOUISIANA*								8-0 S/U vs SE Louisiana since 1971
9/18/2021	vs	*SMU*								vs SMU - Louisiana Tech leads series 4-1
9/25/2021	vs	**NORTH TEXAS**								12-3 S/U vs North Texas since 1983
10/2/2021	@	*NC State*								vs NC State - NC State leads series 1-0
10/16/2021	@	Texas-El Paso								7-0 S/U @ UTEP since 1991
10/23/2021	vs	**TEXAS-SAN ANTONIO**								5-0 S/U @ home vs Texas-San Antonio since 2012
10/30/2021	@	Old Dominion								vs Old Dominion - ODU leads series 1-0
11/6/2021	@	Alabama-Birmingham								vs UAB - La Tech leads series 6-3
11/13/2021	vs	**CHARLOTTE**								1st meeting
11/20/2021	vs	**SOUTHERN MISSISSIPPI**								vs Southern Miss - Southern Miss leads series 36-16
11/27/2021	@	Rice								6-0 S/U vs Rice since 2014
12/4/2021	vs									C-USA Championship
	vs									BOWL GAME

Pointspread Analysis Non-Conference		Pointspread Analysis Conference
0-30 S/U vs Non-Conf. as 20.5 point or more Dog since 1989		vs North Texas - Louisiana Tech leads series 12-7
2-10 S/U vs Non-Conf. as 15.5-20 point Dog since 1990		5-0 S/U & ATS vs North Texas as favorite since 2005
2-17 S/U vs Non-Conf. as 10.5-15 point Dog since 1993		7-0 S/U vs Rice as favorite since 2012
1-12 ATS vs Non-Conf. as 10.5-15 point Dog since 2001		vs Rice - Louisiana Tech leads series 9-4
4-15 S/U vs Non-Conf. as 3.5-10 point Dog since 1992		6-1 S/U vs Texas-San Antonio as favorite since 2012
4-0 S/U & ATS vs Non-Conf. as 3.5-7 point favorite since 1999		vs Texas-San Antonio - Louisiana Tech leads series 7-2
4-0 S/U vs Non-Conf. as 15.5-20 point favorite since 1990		Game 5-1 O/U @ UTEP since 2001
8-0 S/U vs Non-Conf. as 25.5 point or more favorite since 2010		8-0 S/U vs UTEP since 2013
vs Mississippi State - Mississippi State leads series 11-3		vs Texas-El Paso - Louisiana Tech leads series 14-2-1
vs SE Louisiana - La Tech leads series 28-7-2		10-0 S/U vs UTEP as 12.5 point or more favorite since 2001

Dog		
0-21 S/U as 25.5 point or more Dog since 1993		
6-1 O/U as 25.5 point or more Dog since 2006		Bowl Games
1-22 S/U as 20.5-25 point Dog since 1989		6-0 S/U in Bowl Games since 2014
0-7 S/U @ home as 20.5 point or more Dog since 1995		
0-9 S/U as 15.5-20 point Dog since 2000		
1-13 S/U on road as 10.5-15 point Dog since 2005		2-38 S/U on road vs ranked teams all time
2-15 S/U as 10.5-15 point Dog since 2005		0-25 S/U vs Top 10 ranked teams all time
1-15 S/U on road as 7.5-10 point Dog since 1992		
0-6 S/U @ home as 3.5-7 point Dog since 2008		
10-2 ATS on road as 3.5-7 point Dog since 2008		

Favorite		
19-3 S/U as 3.5-7 point favorite since 2003		
8-0 S/U on road as 3.5-7 point favorite since 2003		
7-1 ATS on road as 3.5-7 point favorite since 2003		
17-5 ATS as 3.5-7 point favorite since 2003	M State	4-19 S/U in 1st road game of season since 1997
8-1 S/U on road as 7.5-10 point favorite since 1990	SE LOUISIANA	15-1 S/U in 1st home game of season since 2004
12-1 S/U @ home as 10.5-15 point favorite since 1993	SE LOUISIANA	2-8 ATS in 1st home game of seaosn since 2010
14-0 S/U on road as 15.5 point or more favorite since 1997	NC State	3-13 S/U in 2nd road game of season since 2004
53-1 S/U as 15.5 point or more favorite since 1990	NC State	7-2 ATS in 2nd road game of season since 2011
9-1 O/U as 15.5-20 point favorite since 2009	NC State	7-2 O/U prior to playing Texas-El Paso since 2003

Copyright © 2021 by Steve's Football Bible, LLC

LOUISVILLE CARDINALS   ACC Atlantic

2020-Louisville		Opponent	Ville	Opp	S/U	Line	ATS	Total	O/U	
9/12/2020	vs	WESTERN KENTUCKY	35	21	W	-12.5	W	56.5	U	
9/19/2020	vs	MIAMI	34	47	L	2.5	L	66.0	O	
9/26/2020	@	Pittsburgh	20	23	L	3.0	T	54.0	U	
10/9/2020	@	Georgia Tech	27	46	L	-4.5	L	63.0	O	
10/17/2020	@	Notre Dame	7	12	L	17.0	W	62.0	U	
10/24/2020	vs	FLORIDA STATE	48	16	W	-5.0	W	62.0	O	
10/31/2020	vs	VIRGINIA TECH	35	42	L	2.5	L	67.5	O	
11/7/2020	@	Virginia	17	31	L	5.5	L	63.0	U	
11/20/2020	vs	SYRACUSE	30	0	W	-19.5	W	56.0	U	
11/28/2020	@	Boston College	27	34	L	1.0	L	57.0	O	
12/12/2020	vs	WAKE FOREST	45	21	W	2.0	W	61.0	O	
Coach: Scott Satterfield		Season Record >>	325	293	4-7	ATS>>	5-5-1	O/U>>	6-5	
2019-Louisville		Opponent	Ville	Opp	S/U	Line	ATS	Total	O/U	
9/2/2019	vs	NOTRE DAME	17	35	L	19.0	W	54.5	U	
9/7/2019	vs	EASTERN KENTUCKY	42	0	W	-20.0	W	NT	---	
9/14/2019	vs	Western Kentucky	38	21	W	-10.5	W	49.0	O	Nissan Stadium
9/21/2019	@	Florida State	24	35	L	7.0	L	61.0	U	
10/5/2019	vs	BOSTON COLLEGE	41	39	W	-3.5	L	61.0	O	
10/12/2019	@	Wake Forest	62	59	W	7.0	W	65.5	O	
10/19/2019	vs	CLEMSON	10	45	L	25.0	L	62.0	U	
10/26/2019	vs	VIRGINIA	28	21	W	4.0	W	51.0	U	
11/9/2019	@	Miami	27	52	L	6.5	L	49.0	O	
11/16/2019	@	NC State	34	20	W	-4.0	W	52.0	O	
11/23/2019	vs	SYRACUSE	56	34	W	-7.5	W	65.0	O	
11/30/2019	@	Kentucky	13	45	L	2.5	L	51.5	O	"Governor's Cup"
12/30/2019		Mississippi State	38	28	W	4.5	W	63.5	O	Music City Bowl
Coach: Scott Satterfield		Season Record >>	430	434	8-5	ATS>>	8-5	O/U>>	8-4	
2018-Louisville		Opponent	Ville	Opp	S/U	Line	ATS	Total	O/U	
9/1/2018	vs	Alabama	14	51	L	23.5	L	60.0	O	Camping World Stadium
9/8/2018	vs	INDIANA STATE	31	7	W	-42.0	L	NT	---	
9/15/2018	vs	WESTERN KENTUCKY	20	17	W	-23.5	L	53.5	U	
9/22/2018	@	Virginia	3	27	L	5.0	L	51.5	U	
9/29/2018	vs	FLORIDA STATE	24	28	L	5.0	W	46.0	O	
10/5/2018	vs	GEORGIA TECH	31	66	L	5.5	L	56.0	O	
10/13/2018	@	Boston College	20	38	L	12.0	L	56.5	O	
10/27/2018	vs	WAKE FOREST	35	56	L	-2.5	L	67.5	O	
11/3/2018	@	Clemson	16	77	L	38.0	L	61.0	O	
11/9/2018	@	Syracuse	23	54	L	20.5	L	69.0	O	
11/17/2018	vs	NC STATE	10	52	L	16.0	L	65.5	U	
11/24/2018	vs	KENTUCKY	10	56	L	16.5	L	53.0	O	"Governor's Cup"
Coach: Bobby Petrino		Season Record >>	237	529	2-10	ATS>>	1-11	O/U>>	8-3	
2017-Louisville		Opponent	Ville	Opp	S/U	Line	ATS	Total	O/U	
9/2/2017	@	Purdue	35	28	W	-26.5	L	65.5	U	Lucas Oil Stadium
9/9/2017	@	North Carolina	47	35	W	-12.0	T	66.0	O	
9/16/2017	vs	CLEMSON	21	47	L	3.0	L	61.5	O	
9/23/2017	vs	KENT STATE	42	3	W	-42.0	L	56.0	U	
9/30/2017	vs	MURRAY STATE	55	10	W	-48.0	L	NT	---	
10/5/2017	@	NC State	25	39	L	-3.0	L	66.0	U	
10/14/2017	vs	BOSTON COLLEGE	42	45	L	-19.0	L	60.0	O	
10/21/2017	@	Florida State	31	28	W	7.0	W	58.5	O	
10/28/2017	@	Wake Forest	32	42	L	-2.5	L	66.5	O	
11/11/2017	vs	VIRGINIA	38	21	W	-11.5	W	66.0	U	
11/18/2017	vs	SYRACUSE	56	10	W	-14.5	W	69.5	U	
11/25/2017	@	Kentucky	44	17	W	-9.5	W	67.5	U	"Governor's Cup"
12/30/2017	vs	Mississippi State	27	31	L	-6.5	L	60.5	U	Gator Bowl
Coach: Bobby Petrino		Season Record >>	495	356	8-5	ATS>>	4-8-1	O/U>>	5-7	

Copyright © 2021 by Steve's Football Bible, LLC

LOUISVILLE CARDINALS   ACC Atlantic

STADIUM: Papa John's Cardinal Stadium {61,000}　　Location: Louisville, KY　　**COACH:** Scott Satterfield

DATE		Opponent	UL	Opp	S/U	Line	ATS	Total	O/U	Trends & Angles
9/6/2021	vs	*Mississippi {@ Atlanta}*								1st meeting
9/11/2021	vs	EASTERN KENTUCKY								vs Eastern Kent. - Louisville leads series 11-1
9/18/2021	vs	CENTRAL FLORIDA								vs Central Florida - Series tied 1-1
9/25/2021	@	Florida State								vs Florida State - Florida State leads series 16-5
10/2/2021	@	Wake Forest								Game 4-0 O/U vs Wake Forest since 2017
10/9/2021	vs	VIRGINIA								4-0 S/U @ home vs Virginia since 1988
10/23/2021	vs	BOSTON COLLEGE								vs Boston College - Louisville leads series 7-6
10/30/2021	@	NC State								vs NC State - Louisville leads series 7-3
11/6/2021	vs	CLEMSON								vs Clemson - Clemson leads series 6-0
11/13/2021	vs	SYRACUSE								6-0 S/U @ home vs Syracuse since 2009 {5-1 ATS}
11/18/2021	@	Duke								vs Duke - Louisville leads series 2-0
11/27/2021	vs	*KENTUCKY*								vs Kentucky - Kentucky leads series 17-15
12/4/2021	vs									ACC Championship
	vs									BOWL GAME

Pointspread Analysis Non-Conference		Pointspread Analysis Conference
1-14 S/U vs Non-Conf. as 15.5 point or more Dog since 1984		0-5 S/U vs Clemson as Dog since 2014
1-10 S/U vs Non-Conf. as 10.5-15 point Dog since 1992		4-1 O/U vs Florida State as Dog since 2014
1-7 ATS vs Non-conf. as 3 point or less Dog since 2002		6-1 ATS vs Syracuse since 2014
1-7 S/U vs Non-conf. as 3 point or less Dog since 2002		vs Syracuse - Louisville leads series 12-7
0-5 S/U vs Non-Conf. as 7.5-10 point favorite since 2004		6-0 S/U & ATS vs Syracuse as favorite since 2014
13-4 S/U vs Non-Conf. as 10.5-15 point favorite since 2002		9-2 S/U vs Syracuse since 2009
37-1 S/U vs Non-conf. as 20.5 point or more favorite since 1990		Game 0-5 O/U vs Virginia since 2016
Dog		vs Virginia - Louisville leads series 5-4
5-1 ATS as 30.5 point or more Dog since 1984		3-0 S/U vs Virginia as favorite since 2015
0-9 S/U @ home as 15.5 point or more Dog since 1984		vs Wake Forest - Louisville leads series 6-2
2-33 S/U as 15.5 point or more Dog since 1984		0-5 ATS vs Wake Forest as favorite since 2014
1-8 ATS @ home as 15.5-25 point Dog since 1984		2-5 ATS vs Wake Forest since 2014
2-15 S/U on road as 10.5-15 point Dog since 1989		**Bowl Games**
1-9 S/U as 7.5-10 point Dog since 1995		0-3 S/U & ATS in Bowl Games as 3 point or less Dog since 2002
0-5 S/U & ATS @ home as 7.5-10 point Dog since 1985		3-0 S/U & ATS in Bowl Games as 3 point or less favorite since 2001
2-7 S/U & ATS @ home as 3.5-7 point Dog since 2008		1-5 O/U in Bowl Games since 2013
2-9 S/U & ATS @ home as 3 point or less Dog since 1997		
Favorite		44-8 S/U @ home when ranked all time
9-18 O/U as 3.5-7 point favorite since 2001		0-7 S/U on road when ranked vs ranked teams all time
13-4 S/U as 3.5-7 point favorite since 2008		13-0 S/U when ranked #5 #6 #7 all time
3-10 O/U @ home as 3.5-7 point favorite since 2001		4-40 S/U on road vs ranked teams all time
2-9 O/U as 7.5-10 point favorite since 2001		0-3 S/U vs #1 ranked teams all time
6-1 S/U on road as 7.5-10 point favorite since 1988		0-5 S/U & ATS vs ranked Clemson all time
12-1 S/U on road as 10.5-15 point favorite since 2000		
1-8 O/U on road as 10.5-15 point favorite since 2005		
27-7 S/U @ home as 10.5-15 point favorite since 1989	C. FLORIDA	17-4 S/U in 2nd home game of season since 2000
14-1 S/U @ home as 15.5-20 point favorite since 1990	C. FLORIDA	3-10 ATS in 2nd home game of season since 2007
14-0 S/U @ home as 20.5-25 point favorite since 1990	Wake Forest	1-8-1 ATS after playing Florida State since 1991
1-7 O/U @ home as 20.5-25 point favorite since 2005	VIRGINIA	2-9 ATS prior to playing Boston College since 1990
18-0 S/U on road as 20.5 point or more favorite since 1990	NC State	7-1 S/U after playing Boston College since 1998
1-6 O/U as 25.5-30 point favorite since 2004	CLEMSON	6-2 S/U prior to playing Syracuse since 2012
24-1 S/U as 30.5 point or more favorite since 2000	CLEMSON	1-7 ATS after playing NC State since 1994
3-13-1 ATS as 30.5 point or more favorite since 2006	KENTUCKY	3-10 ATS in final home game of season since 2008

Copyright © 2021 by Steve's Football Bible, LLC

LSU TIGERS

SEC West

2020-LSU		Opponent	LSU	Opp	S/U	Line	ATS	Total	O/U	
9/26/2020	vs	MISSISSIPPI STATE	34	44	L	-14.0	L	57.0	O	
10/3/2020	@	Vanderbilt	41	7	W	-21.0	W	50.0	U	
10/10/2020	@	Missouri	41	45	L	-13.5	L	53.0	O	
10/24/2020	vs	SOUTH CAROLINA	52	24	W	-5.0	W	55.0	O	
10/31/2020	@	Auburn	11	48	L	PK	L	63.5	U	
11/21/2020	@	Arkansas	27	24	W	-1.5	W	65.0	U	"The Golden Boot"
11/28/2020	@	Texas A&M	7	20	L	16.0	W	59.5	U	
12/5/2020	vs	ALABAMA	17	55	L	28.5	L	63.5	O	
12/12/2020	@	Florida	37	34	W	23.0	W	66.0	O	
12/19/2020	vs	MISSISSIPPI	53	48	W	PK	W	74.5	O	"Magnolia Bowl Trophy"
Coach: Ed Orgeron		Season Record >>	320	349	5-5	ATS>>	6-4	O/U>>	6-4	
2019-LSU		Opponent	LSU	Opp	S/U	Line	ATS	Total	O/U	
8/31/2019	vs	GEORGIA SOUTHERN	55	3	W	-27.0	W	52.5	O	
9/7/2019	@	Texas	45	38	W	-7.0	T	57.0	O	
9/14/2019	vs	NORTHWESTERN STATE	65	14	W	-51.5	L	NT	---	
9/21/2019	@	Vanderbilt	66	38	W	-24.0	W	62.5	O	
10/5/2019	vs	UTAH STATE	42	6	W	-27.5	W	72.5	U	
10/12/2019	vs	FLORIDA	42	28	W	-14.0	T	55.0	O	
10/19/2019	@	Mississippi State	36	13	W	-19.0	W	62.5	U	
10/26/2019	vs	AUBURN	23	20	W	-11.5	L	59.5	U	
11/9/2019	@	Alabama	46	41	W	4.5	W	65.0	O	
11/16/2019	@	Mississippi	58	37	W	-21.5	W	67.0	O	"Magnolia Bowl Trophy"
11/23/2019	vs	ARKANSAS	56	20	W	-40.0	L	69.5	O	"The Golden Boot"
11/30/2019	vs	TEXAS A&M	50	7	W	-18.0	W	64.5	U	
12/7/2019	vs	Georgia	37	10	W	-7.0	W	57.0	U	SEC Championship
12/28/2019	vs	Oklahoma	63	28	W	-12.0	W	75.0	O	Peach Bowl (National Semifinal)
1/13/2020	vs	Clemson	42	25	W	-4.0	W	66.5	O	CFB Championship Game
Coach: Ed Orgeron		Season Record >>	726	328	15-0	ATS>>	10-3-2	O/U>>	9-5	SEC Champions/National Champs
2018-LSU		Opponent	LSU	Opp	S/U	Line	ATS	Total	O/U	
9/2/2018	vs	Miami	33	17	W	3.0	W	47.5	O	AT&T Stadium
9/8/2018	vs	SE LOUISIANA	31	0	W	-40.0	L	NT	---	
9/15/2018	@	Auburn	22	21	W	10.0	W	45.0	U	
9/22/2018	vs	LOUISIANA TECH	38	21	W	-19.5	L	51.0	O	
9/29/2018	vs	MISSISSIPPI	45	16	W	-11.5	W	59.0	O	"Magnolia Bowl Trophy"
10/6/2018	@	Florida	19	27	L	-1.5	L	44.5	O	
10/13/2018	vs	GEORGIA	36	16	W	6.5	W	50.5	O	
10/20/2018	vs	MISSISSIPPI STATE	19	3	W	-6.0	W	45.0	U	
11/3/2018	vs	ALABAMA	0	29	L	13.5	L	51.5	U	
11/10/2018	@	Arkansas	24	17	W	-13.0	L	49.5	U	"The Golden Boot"
11/17/2018	vs	RICE	42	10	W	-42.0	L	51.5	U	
11/24/2018	@	Texas A&M	72	74	L	2.5	W	45.5	O	{7 OT}
1/1/2019	vs	Central Florida	40	32	W	-7.0	W	58.5	O	Fiesta Bowl
Coach: Ed Orgeron		Season Record >>	421	283	10-3	ATS>>	7-6	O/U>>	8-4	
2017-LSU		Opponent	LSU	Opp	S/U	Line	ATS	Total	O/U	
9/2/2017	vs	Byu	27	0	W	-14.0	W	47.5	U	Mercedes Benz Superdome
9/9/2017	vs	TENNESSEE-CHATT.	45	10	W	-36.5	L	NT	---	
9/16/2017	@	Mississippi State	7	37	L	-7.5	L	54.0	U	
9/23/2017	vs	SYRACUSE	35	26	W	-21.0	L	56.5	O	
9/30/2017	vs	TROY	21	24	L	-20.5	L	49.0	U	
10/7/2017	@	Florida	17	16	W	-1.5	L	44.5	U	
10/14/2017	vs	AUBURN	27	23	W	6.5	W	45.0	O	
10/21/2017	@	Mississippi	40	24	W	-6.5	W	59.5	O	"Magnolia Bowl Trophy"
11/4/2017	@	Alabama	10	24	L	20.5	W	46.5	U	
11/11/2017	vs	ARKANSAS	33	10	W	-18.0	W	53.5	U	"The Golden Boot"
11/18/2017	@	Tennessee	30	10	W	-17.0	W	42.0	U	
11/25/2017	vs	TEXAS A&M	45	21	W	-11.0	W	50.5	O	
1/1/2018	vs	Notre Dame	17	21	L	-2.0	L	53.0	U	Citrus Bowl
Coach: Ed Orgeron		Season Record >>	354	246	9-4	ATS>>	7-6	O/U>>	4-8	

Copyright © 2021 by Steve's Football Bible, LLC

LSU TIGERS

SEC West

STADIUM: Tiger Stadium (Death Valley) {102,321}			Location: Baton Rouge, LA					COACH: Ed Orgeron		

DATE		Opponent	LSU	Opp	S/U	Line	ATS	Total	O/U	Trends & Angles
9/4/2021	@	*Ucla*								1st meeting
9/11/2021	vs	*MCNEESE STATE*								1st meeting
9/18/2021	vs	*CENTRAL MICHIGAN*								1st meeting
9/25/2021	@	Mississippi State								9-1 S/U @ Mississippi State since 2001
10/2/2021	vs	**AUBURN**								9-0 S/U @ home vs Auburn as favorite since 2001
10/9/2021	vs	*LOUISIANA-MONROE*								vs Louisiana-Monroe - LSU leads series 3-0
10/9/2021	@	Kentucky								vs Kentucky - LSU leads series 40-16-1
10/16/2021	vs	**FLORIDA**								6-1 S/U @ home vs Florida as favorite since 2005
10/23/2021	@	Mississippi								5-0 S/U & ATS vs Ole Miss since 2016
11/6/2021	@	Alabama								1-9 S/U vs Alabama as Dog since 2012
11/13/2021	vs	**ARKANSAS**								vs Arkansas - LSU leads series 42-22-2
11/27/2021	vs	**TEXAS A&M**								5-0 ATS @ home vs Texas A&M since 1994
12/4/2021	vs									SEC Championship
	vs									BOWL GAME

Pointspread Analysis		Pointspread Analysis
Non-Conference		**Conference**
0-7 S/U vs Non-Conf. as 10.5 point or more Dog since 1990		vs Alabama - Alabama leads series 54-26-5
4-0 S/U vs Non-Conf. as 3.5-7 point Dog since 2004		6-0 S/U vs Alabama as favorite since 2000
11-2 S/U vs Non-Conf. as 3.5-7 point favorite since 1995		Game 2-7-2 O/U vs Alabama since 2011
9-1 O/U vs Non-Conf. as 3.5-7 point favorite since 1997		5-0 S/U @ Alabama as favorite since 1987
0-4 ATS vs Non-Conf. as 7.5-10 point favorite since 2010		12-1 S/U vs Arkansas as 9.5 point or more favorite since 1996
12-1 S/U vs Non-Conf. as 10.5-15 point favorite since 1984		vs Auburn - LSU leads series 31-23-1
11-1 S/U vs Non-Conf. as 15.5-20 point favorite since 1985		10-1 S/U vs Auburn as 5.5 point or more favorite since 1998
60-1 S/U vs Non-conf. as 20.5 point or more favorite since 1983		vs Florida - Florida leads series 33-31-3
Dog		vs Mississippi - LSU leads series 64-41-4
8-1 ATS as 20.5 point or more Dog since 1991		10-1 S/U vs Ole Miss as 12 point or more favorite since 1987
2-7 S/U as 20.5 point or more Dog since 1991		18-3 S/U vs Mississippi State since 2000
1-6 S/U as 15.5-20 point Dog since 1990		25-3 S/U vs Mississippi State as favorite since 1985
0-16 S/U as 10.5-15 point Dog since 1990		Game 1-5 O/U vs Mississippi State since 2015
3-13 ATS as 10.5-15 point Dog since 1990		vs Mississippi State - LSU leads series 73-38-3
0-7-1 O/U as 7.5-10 point Dog since 2000		6-0 ATS vs Mississippi State as Dog since 1992
2-6 S/U on road as 7.5-10 point Dog since 1994		10-0 ATS vs Texas A&M since 2011
Favorite		8-2 S/U vs Texas A&M since 2011
2-8 ATS @ home as 3 point or less favorite since 1989		10-1 S/U vs Texas A&M as favorite since 1986
1-7 O/U as 3 point or less favorite since 2014		vs Texas A&M - LSU leads series 34-22-3
1-7 O/U on road as 3 point or less favorite since 2008		0-7 S/U vs Texas A&M as Dog since 1991
2-8 ATS @ home as 3 point or less favorite since 1989		
16-2 S/U on road as 3.5-7 point favorite since 1997	Ucla	2-9 O/U in 1st road game of season since 2010
13-3 S/U @ home as 3.5-7 point favorite since 1998	MCNEESE	24-2 S/U in 1st home game of season since 1995
9-1 S/U @ home as 7.5-10 point favorite since 2003	C. MICHIGAN	22-1 S/U in 2nd home game of season since 1998
24-4 S/U @ home as 10.5-15 point favorite since 1987	C. MICHIGAN	1-9-1 ATS in 2nd home game of season since 2010
14-2 S/U on road as 10.5-15 point favorite since 1984	M State	11-0 S/U prior to playing Auburn since 2010
10-0 S/U on road as 15.5-20 point favorite since 1997	UL-MONROE	18-1 S/U after playing Auburn since 2002
25-0 S/U as 15.5-20 point favorite since 1997	FLORIDA	17-1 S/U prior to playing Mississippi since 2003
78-1 S/U as 20.5 point or more favorite since 1983	Ole Miss	12-1 S/U after playing Florida since 2008
Bowl Games	Ole Miss	17-2 S/U prior to playing Alabama since 2002
6-1 S/U in Chick-Fil-A Peach Bowl	Ole Miss	9-1 ATS prior to playing Alabama since 2011
0-4 S/U vs Nebraska in Bowl Games	Alabama	1-7 S/U after playing Mississippi since 2012
10-2 S/U vs ACC teams in Bowl Games	ARKANSAS	19-2 S/U after playing Alabama since 2000
1-4 O/U in Peach Bowl since 1996	TEXAS A&M	5-12 ATS in final home game of season since 2004
3-0 S/U & ATS in Sugar Bowl since 2002		0-7 S/U when ranked vs #1 Alabama all time
0-3 O/U in Citrus Bowl since 2010		0-8 S/U vs #1 ranked teams since 2008
0-3 S/U in Orange Bowl since 1971		0-4 S/U on road vs #1 ranked teams all time

Copyright © 2021 by Steve's Football Bible, LLC

MARSHALL THUNDERING HERD   C-USA East

2020-Marshall		Opponent	Marsh	Opp	S/U	Line	ATS	Total	O/U	
9/5/2020	@	EASTERN KENTUCKY	59	0	W	-25.5	W	55.0	O	
9/19/2020	vs	APPALACHIAN STATE	17	7	W	6.0	W	59.5	U	
10/10/2020	@	Western Kentucky	38	14	W	-6.5	W	43.0	O	
10/17/2020	@	Louisiana Tech	35	17	W	-11.5	W	48.0	O	
10/24/2020	vs	FLORIDA ATLANTIC	20	9	W	-19.5	L	51.0	U	
11/7/2020	vs	MASSACHUSETTS	51	10	W	-44.0	L	55.5	O	
11/14/2020	vs	MIDDLE TENNESSEE	42	14	W	-23.5	W	55.5	O	
12/5/2020	vs	RICE	0	20	L	-24.5	L	42.5	U	
12/18/2020	vs	**ALABAMA-BIRMINGHAM**	13	22	L	-4.0	L	44.0	U	**C-USA CHAMPIONSHIP GAME**
12/25/2020	vs	**Buffalo**	10	17	L	5.0	L	53.5	U	Camelia Bowl
Coach: Doc Holliday		Season Record >>	285	130	7-3	ATS>>	5-5	O/U>>	5-5	
2019-Marshall		Opponent	Marsh	Opp	S/U	Line	ATS	Total	O/U	
8/31/2019	vs	VIRGINIA MILITARY	56	17	W	-41.0	L	NT	---	
9/6/2019	@	Boise State	7	14	L	14.0	W	57.0	U	
9/14/2019	vs	OHIO	33	31	W	-4.5	L	47.5	O	"Battle for the Bell"
9/28/2019	vs	CINCINNATI	14	52	L	4.0	L	47.5	O	
10/5/2019	@	Middle Tennessee	13	24	L	-4.0	L	53.5	U	
10/12/2019	vs	OLD DOMINION	31	17	W	-16.0	L	46.5	O	
10/19/2019	@	Florida Atlantic	36	31	W	4.0	W	58.0	O	
10/26/2019	vs	WESTERN KENTUCKY	26	23	W	-3.5	L	45.0	O	
11/2/2019	@	Rice	20	7	W	-12.0	W	48.0	U	
11/16/2019	vs	LOUISIANA TECH	31	10	W	-6.0	W	54.5	U	
11/23/2019	@	Charlotte	13	24	L	-7.0	L	55.5	U	
11/30/2019	vs	FLORIDA INTERNATIONAL	30	27	W	-10.0	L	49.5	O	
12/23/2019	vs	**Central Florida**	25	48	L	15.5	L	59.5	O	**Gasparilla Bowl**
Coach: Doc Holliday		Season Record >>	335	325	8-5	ATS>>	4-9	O/U>>	7-5	
2018-Marshall		Opponent	Marsh	Opp	S/U	Line	ATS	Total	O/U	
9/1/2018	@	Miami-Ohio	35	28	W	1.5	W	51.5	O	
9/8/2018	vs	EASTERN KENTUCKY	32	16	W	-31.0	L	NT	---	
9/22/2018	vs	NC STATE	20	37	L	5.5	L	57.0	T	
9/29/2018	@	Western Kentucky	20	17	W	-3.5	L	51.5	U	
10/5/2018	vs	MIDDLE TENNESSEE	24	34	L	-3.0	L	50.5	U	
10/13/2018	@	Old Dominion	42	20	W	-3.5	W	57.0	O	
10/20/2018	vs	FLORIDA ATLANTIC	31	7	W	2.5	W	60.0	U	
11/3/2018	@	Southern Mississippi	24	26	L	-2.5	L	45.5	O	
11/10/2018	vs	CHARLOTTE	30	13	W	-12.0	W	41.5	O	
11/17/2018	vs	TEXAS-SAN ANTONIO	23	0	W	-27.5	L	47.0	U	
11/24/2018	@	Florida International	28	25	W	-3.0	T	52.5	O	
12/1/2018	@	Virginia Tech	20	41	L	4.0	L	51.5	O	
12/20/2018	vs	**South Florida**	38	20	W	-3.0	W	50.0	O	**Gasparilla Bowl**
Coach: Doc Holliday		Season Record >>	367	284	9-4	ATS>>	5-7-1	O/U>>	8-3-1	
2017-Marshall		Opponent	Marsh	Opp	S/U	Line	ATS	Total	O/U	
9/2/2017	vs	MIAMI-OHIO	31	26	W	3.5	W	48.0	O	
9/9/2017	@	NC State	20	37	L	21.0	W	55.0	O	
9/16/2017	vs	KENT STATE	21	0	W	-13.5	W	50.5	U	
9/30/2017	@	Cincinnati	38	21	W	3.0	W	52.5	O	
10/7/2017	@	Charlotte	14	3	W	-14.5	L	51.0	U	
10/14/2017	vs	OLD DOMINION	35	3	W	-12.5	W	48.5	U	
10/20/2017	@	Middle Tennessee	38	10	W	-1.5	W	49.5	U	
10/28/2017	vs	FLORIDA INTERNATIONAL	30	41	L	-14.0	L	47.0	O	
11/3/2017	@	Florida Atlantic	25	30	L	6.0	W	63.0	U	
11/11/2017	vs	WESTERN KENTUCKY	30	23	W	-10.0	L	52.0	O	
11/18/2017	@	Texas-San Antonio	7	9	L	3.0	W	45.0	U	
11/25/2017	vs	SOUTHERN MISS	27	28	L	PK	L	47.0	O	
12/16/2017	vs	**Colorado State**	31	28	W	3.0	W	58.5	O	**New Mexico Bowl**
Coach: Doc Holliday		Season Record >>	347	259	8-5	ATS>>	9-4	O/U>>	7-6	

Copyright © 2021 by Steve's Football Bible, LLC

MARSHALL THUNDERING HERD   C-USA East

STADIUM: Joan C. Edwards Stadium {38,227}				Location: Huntington, WV					COACH: Charles Huff	

DATE		Opponent	Herd	Opp	S/U	Line	ATS	Total	O/U	Trends & Angles
9/4/2021	@	*Navy*								1st meeting
9/11/2021	vs	*N.C. CENTRAL*								1st meeting
9/18/2021	vs	*EAST CAROLINA*								0-4 S/U vs East Carolina as Dog since 2008
9/25/2021	@	*Appalachian State*								vs Appalachian State - App State leads series 14-7
10/2/2021	@	Middle Tennessee								vs Middle Tennessee - Marshall leads series 6-4
10/9/2021	vs	OLD DOMINION								5-0 S/U vs Old Dominion as favorite since 2014
10/16/2021	@	North Texas								vs North Texas - Marshall leads series 2-1
10/30/2021	vs	FLA INTERNATIONAL								vs Florida International - Marshall leads series 6-2
11/6/2021	@	Florida Atlantic								vs Florida Atlantic - Marshall leads series 7-1
11/13/2021	vs	ALABAMA-BIRMINGHAM								4-1 S/U @ home vs UAB as favorite since 2007
11/20/2021	@	Charlotte								vs Charlotte - Marshall leads series 3-2
11/27/2021	vs	WESTERN KENTUCKY								1-6 ATS vs Western Kentucky since 2014
12/4/2021	vs									C-USA Championship
	vs									BOWL GAME

Pointspread Analysis Non-Conference		Pointspread Analysis Conference
1-28 S/U vs Non-Conf. as 7.5 point or more Dog since 1997		3-0 S/U & ATS vs Alabama-Birmingham as Dog since 2005
8-2 S/U & ATS vs Non-conf. as 3 point or less Dog since 1997		5-0 S/U vs Florida Atlantic as favorite since 2013
2-6 O/U vs Non-Conf. as 3 point or less favorite since 1999		vs Old Dominion - Marshall leads series 5-1
11-0 S/U vs Non-Conf. as 20.5 point or more favorite since 2012		4-1 ATS vs Old Dominion as favorite since 2014
Dog		vs Rice - Marshall leads series 5-4
1-23 S/U on road as 15.5 point or more Dog since 1997		Game 0-4 O/U @ home vs Rice since 2007
0-6 S/U @ home as 10.5 point or more Dog since 2007		Game 6-1 O/U vs Western Kentucky since 2014
11-3 O/U as 20.5 point or more Dog since 2005		vs Western Kentucky - Marshall leads series 8-4
2-12 S/U as 10.5-15 point Dog since 2002		**Bowl Games**
1-12 O/U as 10.5-15 point Dog since 2003		12-4 S/U in Bowl Games
1-8 S/U on road as 7.5-10 point Dog since 2000		12-2 ATS in Bowl Games since 1998
2-7 S/U on road as 3.5-7 point Dog since 2006		
Favorite		
6-1 S/U & ATS @ home as 3 point or less favorite since 1998		9-1 S/U @ home when ranked all time
9-3 S/U on road as 3.5-7 point favorite since 1999		1-7 ATS on road vs ranked teams since 2006
10-1 S/U @ home as 3.5-7 point favorite since 2009		0-17 S/U vs ranked teams since 2003
8-1 S/U @ home as 7.5-10 point favorite since 1997		
3-9 O/U as 10.5-15 point favorite since 2011		
12-2 S/U @ home as 10.5-15 point favorite since 1997	Navy	3-18 S/U in 1st road game of season since 2000
14-3 S/U on road as 10.5-15 point favorite since 1997	Navy	5-0 ATS in 1st road game of season since 2016
2-6 ATS on road as 10.5-15 point favorite since 2004	Navy	9-3 O/U in 1st road game of season since 2008
16-2 S/U as 15.5-20 point favorite since 1998	NC CENTRAL	9-0 S/U in 1st home game of season since 2011
0-5 O/U on road as 15.5-20 point favorite since 2002	App. State	2-6 O/U prior to playing Middle Tennessee since 2013
9-3 O/U as 20.5 point or more favorite since 2001	Charlotte	1-5 O/U prior to playing Western Kentucky since 2014
10-0 S/U on road as 20.5 point or more favorite since 1997	Charlotte	4-13 S/U in final road game of season since 2004
47-2 S/U as 20.5 point or more favorite since 1997	W. KENTUCKY	13-3 O/U in final home game of season since 2005

Copyright © 2021 by Steve's Football Bible, LLC

MARYLAND TERRAPINS   BIG TEN East

2020-Maryland		Opponent	MD	Opp	S/U	Line	ATS	Total	O/U	
10/24/2020	@	Northwestern	3	43	L	14.0	L	52.5	U	
10/30/2020	vs	MINNESOTA	45	44	W	17.0	W	60.5	O	{OT}
11/7/2020	@	Penn State	35	19	W	27.0	W	62.5	U	
11/28/2020	@	Indiana	11	27	L	12.0	L	64.5	U	
12/12/2020	vs	RUTGERS	27	27	L	-3.0	L	54.0	U	{OT}
Coach:Mike Locksley		Season Record >>	121	160	2-3	ATS>>	2-3	O/U>>	1-4	
2019-Maryland		Opponent	MD	Opp	S/U	Line	ATS	Total	O/U	
8/31/2019	vs	HOWARD	79	0	W	-32.0	W	NT	---	
9/7/2019	vs	SYRACUSE	63	20	W	-1.0	W	58.5	O	
9/14/2019	@	Temple	17	20	L	-5.5	L	66.0	U	
9/27/2019	vs	PENN STATE	0	59	L	6.5	L	61.0	U	
10/5/2019	@	Rutgers	48	7	W	-14.5	W	55.5	U	
10/12/2019	@	Purdue	14	40	L	-4.5	L	52.0	O	
10/19/2019	vs	INDIANA	28	34	L	6.5	W	59.0	O	
10/26/2019	@	Minnesota	10	52	L	14.5	L	58.5	O	
11/2/2019	vs	MICHIGAN	7	38	L	21.0	L	57.5	U	
11/9/2019	@	Ohio State	14	73	L	42.5	L	64.5	O	
11/23/2019	vs	NEBRASKA	7	54	L	6.5	L	62.5	U	
11/30/2019	@	Michigan State	16	19	L	22.0	W	47.5	U	
Coach: Mike Locksley		Season Record >>	303	416	3-9	ATS>>	5-7	O/U>>	5-6	
2018-Maryland		Opponent	MD	Opp	S/U	Line	ATS	Total	O/U	
9/1/2018	vs	TEXAS	34	29	W	12.0	W	54.5	O	FedEx Field
9/8/2018	@	Bowling Green	45	14	W	-13.5	W	66.0	U	
9/15/2018	vs	TEMPLE	14	35	L	-15.0	L	53.5	U	
9/29/2018	vs	MINNESOTA	42	13	W	PK	W	46.5	O	
10/6/2018	@	Michigan	21	42	L	17.5	L	44.0	O	
10/13/2018	vs	RUTGERS	34	7	W	-24.0	W	50.5	U	
10/20/2018	@	Iowa	0	23	L	9.5	L	44.0	U	
10/27/2018	vs	ILLINOIS	63	33	W	-16.5	W	53.5	O	
11/3/2018	vs	MICHIGAN STATE	3	24	L	3.5	L	42.5	U	
11/10/2018	@	Indiana	32	34	L	1.0	L	55.0	O	
11/17/2018	vs	OHIO STATE	51	52	L	14.0	W	61.5	O	{OT}
11/24/2018	@	Penn State	3	38	L	14.0	L	50.5	U	
Coach: DJ Durkin		Season Record >>	342	344	5-7	ATS>>	6-6	O/U>>	6-6	
2017-Maryland		Opponent	MD	Opp	S/U	Line	ATS	Total	O/U	
9/2/2017	@	Texas	51	41	W	19.0	W	57.0	O	
9/9/2017	vs	TOWSON	63	17	W	-34.0	W	NT	---	
9/23/2017	vs	CENTRAL FLORIDA	10	38	L	-5.0	L	61.5	U	
9/30/2017	@	Minnesota	31	24	W	12.5	W	45.0	O	
10/7/2017	@	Ohio State	14	62	L	29.5	L	60.0	O	
10/14/2017	vs	NORTHWESTERN	21	37	L	2.5	L	49.5	O	
10/21/2017	@	Wisconsin	13	38	L	23.0	L	50.0	O	
10/28/2017	vs	INDIANA	42	39	W	6.5	W	53.0	O	
11/4/2017	vs	Rutgers	24	31	L	-3.5	L	49.0	O	Yankee Stadium
11/11/2017	vs	MICHIGAN	10	35	L	15.0	L	46.5	U	
11/18/2017	@	Michigan State	7	17	L	14.0	W	44.0	U	
11/25/2017	vs	PENN STATE	3	66	L	20.5	L	57.0	O	
Coach: DJ Durkin		Season Record >>	289	445	4-8	ATS>>	5-7	O/U>>	8-3	

Copyright © 2021 by Steve's Football Bible, LLC

MARYLAND TERRAPINS BIG TEN East

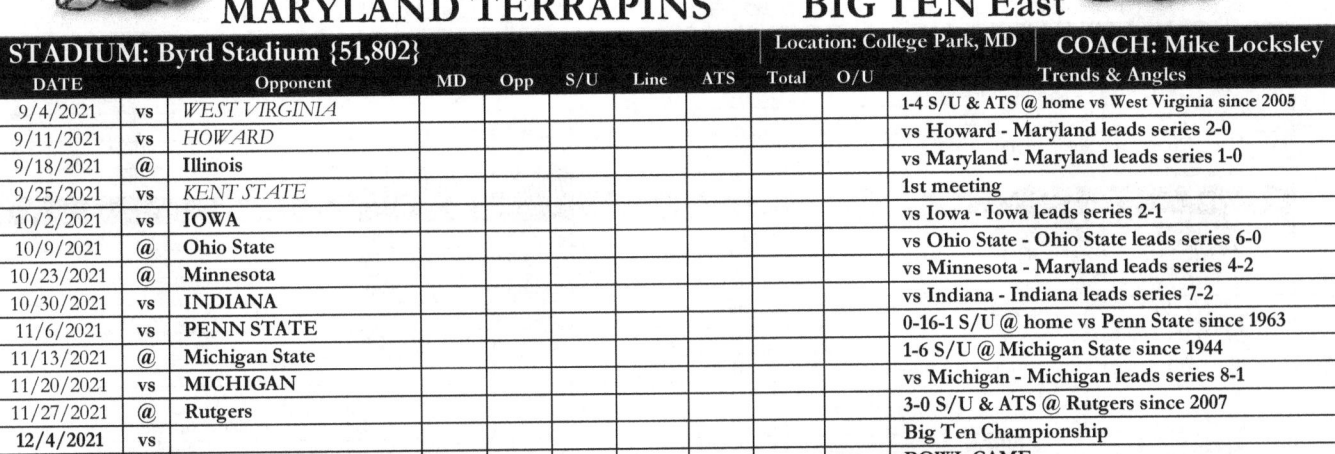

STADIUM: Byrd Stadium {51,802}						Location: College Park, MD		COACH: Mike Locksley	

DATE		Opponent	MD	Opp	S/U	Line	ATS	Total	O/U	Trends & Angles
9/4/2021	vs	WEST VIRGINIA								1-4 S/U & ATS @ home vs West Virginia since 2005
9/11/2021	vs	HOWARD								vs Howard - Maryland leads series 2-0
9/18/2021	@	Illinois								vs Maryland - Maryland leads series 1-0
9/25/2021	vs	KENT STATE								1st meeting
10/2/2021	vs	IOWA								vs Iowa - Iowa leads series 2-1
10/9/2021	@	Ohio State								vs Ohio State - Ohio State leads series 6-0
10/23/2021	@	Minnesota								vs Minnesota - Maryland leads series 4-2
10/30/2021	vs	INDIANA								vs Indiana - Indiana leads series 7-2
11/6/2021	vs	PENN STATE								0-16-1 S/U @ home vs Penn State since 1963
11/13/2021	@	Michigan State								1-6 S/U @ Michigan State since 1944
11/20/2021	vs	MICHIGAN								vs Michigan - Michigan leads series 8-1
11/27/2021	@	Rutgers								3-0 S/U & ATS @ Rutgers since 2007
12/4/2021	vs									Big Ten Championship
	vs									BOWL GAME

Pointspread Analysis
Non-Conference

0-8 S/U vs Non-Conf. as 20.5 point or more Dog since 1987	
1-9 S/U vs Non-Conf. as 7.5-10 point Dog since 1984	
11-3 S/U vs Non-Conf. as 10.5-15 point favorite since 1988	
24-0 S/U vs Non-Conf. as 15.5 point or more favorite since 1983	
1-14 S/U vs West Virginia as 6.5 point or more Dog since 1988	
0-6 S/U vs West Virginia as Dog since 2004	
vs West Virginia - WVU leads series 28-22-2	

Pointspread Analysis
Conference

5-1 O/U vs Indiana as Dog since 2015
Game 0-6 O/U vs Michigan State since 2014
vs Michigan State - Michigan State leads series 9-2
Game 6-0 O/U vs Ohio State since 2014
vs Penn State - Penn State leads series 39-3-1
1-10 S/U vs Penn State as 7.5 point or more Dog since 1984
vs Rutgers - Maryland leads series 9-7

Dog

2-23 S/U on road as 20.5 point or more Dog since 1987
0-11 S/U @ home as 20.5 point or more Dog since 1991
12-5 O/U as 20.5 point or more Dog since 2000
4-19 S/U on road as 15.5-20 point Dog since 1986
0-4 S/U @ home as 15.5-20 point Dog since 2002
3-27 S/U on road as 10.5-15 point Dog since 1987
3-13 ATS as 10.5-15 point Dog since 2011
1-10 S/U @ home as 7.5-10 point Dog since 1987
4-0 O/U @ home as 7.5-10 point Dog since 2000
1-10 S/U @ home as 3.5-7 point Dog since 2009

Bowl Games

0-3 S/U in Orange Bowl
3-0-1 S/U in Gator Bowl

1-13 S/U @ home vs ranked teams since 2011
2-31 S/U vs ranked teams since 2011
1-20 S/U on road vs ranked teams since 2008
0-21-1 S/U vs ranked Penn State all time

Favorite

9-3 O/U as 3 point or less favorite since 2005	
5-14 ATS as 3 point or less favorite since 1998	
14-5 S/U on road as 3.5-7 point favorite since 1983	
15-4 S/U @ home as 10.5-15 point favorite since 1983	
8-0 S/U on road as 15.5 point or more favorite since 1983	
30-1 S/U @ home as 15.5 point or more favorite since 1983	

W. VIRGINIA	22-1 S/U in 1st home game of season since 1998
INDIANA	2-9 S/U prior to playing Penn State since 1990
Michigan State	1-5 S/U prior to playing Michigan since 2014
Michigan State	3-9 S/U after playing Penn State since 1987
MICHIGAN	2-11 S/U in final home game of season since 2008
MICHIGAN	8-3 O/U in final home game of season since 2010
Rutgers	1-6 S/U after playing Michigan since 1990

Print Version $24.99   **Print Version $29.99**   **Print Version $29.99**

These books available at numerous online retailers

Copyright © 2021 by Steve's Football Bible, LLC

MASSACHUSETTS MINUTEMEN   INDEPENDENT

2020 - Massachusetts		Opponent	Umass	Opp	S/U	Line	ATS	Total	O/U	
10/17/2020	@	Georgia Southern	0	41	L	30.0	L	62.0	U	
11/7/2020	@	Marshall	10	51	L	44.0	W	55.5	U	
11/20/2020	@	Florida Atlantic	2	24	L	34.0	W	50.5	U	
11/27/2020	@	Liberty	0	45	L	35.0	L	57.5	U	
Coach: Walt Bell		Season Record >>	12	161	0-4	ATS>>	2-2	O/U>>	0-4	
2019 - Massachusetts		Opponent	Umass	Opp	S/U	Line	ATS	Total	O/U	
8/30/2019	@	Rutgers	21	48	L	16.5	L	54.5	O	
9/7/2019	vs	SOUTHERN ILLINOIS	20	45	L	-5.5	L	NT	---	
9/14/2019	@	Charlotte	17	52	L	21.0	L	66.5	O	
9/21/2019	vs	COASTAL CAROLINA	28	62	L	17.0	L	62.0	O	
9/28/2019	vs	AKRON	37	29	W	9.5	W	60.5	O	
10/5/2019	@	Florida International	0	44	L	28.0	L	70.0	U	
10/12/2019	@	Louisiana Tech	21	69	L	31.5	L	64.0	O	
10/26/2019	vs	CONNECTICUT	35	56	L	9.5	L	62.0	O	Gillette Stadium
11/2/2019	vs	LIBERTY	21	63	L	23.5	L	71.0	O	
11/9/2019	@	Army	7	63	L	34.5	L	61.0	O	
11/16/2019	@	Northwestern	6	45	L	38.0	L	57.5	U	
11/23/2019	vs	BYU	24	56	L	42.0	W	69.0	O	
Coach: Walt Bell		Season Record >>	237	632	1-11	ATS>>	2-10	O/U>>	9-2	
2018 - Massachusetts		Opponent	Umass	Opp	S/U	Line	ATS	Total	O/U	
8/25/2018	vs	DUQUESNE	63	15	W	-21.0	W	68.5	O	
9/1/2018	@	Boston College	21	55	L	20.5	L	62.5	O	"Battle of The Bay State"
9/8/2018	@	Georgia Southern	13	34	L	1.5	L	61.0	U	
9/15/2018	@	Florida International	24	63	L	3.5	L	66.5	O	
9/22/2018	vs	CHARLOTTE	49	31	W	-6.0	W	55.0	O	
9/29/2018	@	Ohio	42	58	L	11.5	L	70.0	O	
10/6/2018	vs	SOUTH FLORIDA	42	58	L	16.0	T	71.0	O	
10/20/2018	vs	COASTAL CAROLINA	13	24	L	-2.0	L	74.0	U	
10/27/2018	@	Connecticut	22	17	W	-3.5	W	62.5	U	
11/3/2018	vs	LIBERTY	62	59	W	-1.0	W	67.5	O	{3 OT}
11/10/2018	vs	BYU	16	35	L	14.0	L	57.5	U	Gillette Stadium
11/17/2018	@	Georgia	27	66	L	41.5	W	67.0	O	
Coach: Mark Whipple		Season Record >>	394	515	4-8	ATS>>	5-6-1	O/U>>	8-4	
2017 - Massachusetts		Opponent	Umass	Opp	S/U	Line	ATS	Total	O/U	
8/26/2017	vs	HAWAII	35	38	L	-3.0	L	59.5	O	
9/2/2017	@	Coastal Carolina	28	38	L	-2.5	L	56.0	O	
9/9/2017	vs	OLD DOMINION	7	17	L	3.5	L	60.5	U	
9/15/2017	@	Temple	21	29	L	14.0	W	52.0	U	
9/23/2017	@	Tennessee	13	17	L	27.5	W	58.0	U	
9/30/2017	vs	OHIO	50	58	L	4.0	L	52.5	O	
10/21/2017	vs	GEORGIA SOUTHERN	55	20	W	-7.0	W	53.0	O	
10/28/2017	vs	APPALACHIAN STATE	30	27	W	4.0	W	57.0	T	{2 OT}
11/4/2017	@	Mississippi State	23	34	L	33.5	W	56.5	O	
11/11/2017	vs	MAINE	44	31	W	-16.0		NT	---	
11/18/2017	@	Byu	16	10	W	3.0	W	51.5	U	
12/2/2017	@	Florida International	45	63	L	-2.5	L	56.5	O	
Coach: Mark Whipple		Season Record >>	367	382	4-8	ATS>>	6-6	O/U>>	6-4-1	

Copyright © 2021 by Steve's Football Bible, LLC

MASSACHUSETTS MINUTEMEN   INDEPENDENT

STADIUM: McGuirk Stadium {17,000}								Location: Amherst, MA		COACH: Walt Bell	
DATE		Opponent	Mass	Opp	S/U	Line	ATS	Total	O/U	Trends & Angles	
9/4/2021	@	Pittsburgh								1st meeting	
9/11/2021	vs	BOSTON COLLEGE								0-4 S/U vs Boston College as Dog since 2011	
9/18/2021	vs	EASTERN MICHIGAN								vs E. Michigan - U Mass leads series 2-0	
9/25/2021	@	Coastal Carolina								vs Coastal Carolina - Coastal leads series 3-0	
10/2/2021	vs	TOLEDO								0-4 S/U vs Toledo since 1983	
10/9/2021	vs	CONNECTICUT								vs Connecticut - U Mass leads series 37-35-2	
10/23/2021	@	Florida State								1st meeting	
10/30/2021	@	Liberty								vs Liberty - Series tied 1-1	
11/6/2021	vs	RHODE ISLAND								5-0 S/U @ home vs Rhode Island since 2003	
11/13/2021	vs	MAINE								vs Maine - U Mass leads series 41-17-1	
11/20/2021	@	Army								vs Army - Army leads series 3-0	
11/27/2021	@	New Mexico State								1st meeting	
	vs									BOWL GAME	

Pointspread Analysis Dog			Pointspread Analysis Conference	
0-46 S/U as 15.5 point or more Dog since 2012			vs Rhode Island - U Mass leads series 47-37-2	
0-18 S/U @ home as 10.5 point or more Dog since 2012			vs Toledo - Toledo leads series 4-1	
1-13 S/U as 10.5-15 point Dog since 2011		Pittsburgh	0-9 S/U in 1st road game of season since 2012	
Favorite		BOSTON C.	1-7 S/U in 1st home game of season since 2012	
3-0 S/U as 15 point or more favorite since 2014		C. Carolina	0-12 S/U in 2nd road game of season since 2008	
		NMSU	2-11 S/U in final road game of season since 2008	

Baseball Fans – We have books on Baseball as well

Print Version $39.99

Print Version $39.99

These books available at numerous online retailers

Copyright © 2021 by Steve's Football Bible, LLC

MEMPHIS TIGERS   AMERICAN West

2020-Memphis		Opponent	Mem	Opp	S/U	Line	ATS	Total	O/U	
9/5/2020	vs	ARKANSAS STATE	37	24	W	-18.5	L	72.5	U	"Paint Bucket Bowl"
10/1/2020	@	Smu	27	30	L	2.0	L	75.0	U	
10/16/2020	vs	CENTRAL FLORIDA	50	49	W	3.0	W	74.0	O	
10/24/2020	vs	TEMPLE	41	29	W	-14.0	L	70.5	U	
10/31/2020	@	Cincinnati	10	49	L	6.5	L	56.5	O	
11/7/2020	vs	SOUTH FLORIDA	34	33	W	-17.5	L	67.0	T	
11/21/2020	vs	STEPHEN F. AUSTIN	56	14	W	-32.5	W	61.5	O	
11/28/2020	@	Navy	10	7	W	-13.0	L	63.5	U	
12/5/2020	@	Tulane	21	35	L	3.5	L	64.0	U	
12/12/2020	vs	HOUSTON	30	27	W	4.5	W	63.0	U	
12/23/2020	vs	Florida Atlantic	25	10	W	-9.5	W	52.5	U	Montgomery Bowl
Coach: Ryan Silverfield		Season Record >>	341	307	8-3	ATS>>	4-7	O/U>>	3-7-1	
2019-Memphis		Opponent	Mem	Opp	S/U	Line	ATS	Total	O/U	
8/31/2019	vs	MISSISSIPPI	15	10	W	-3.5	W	64.5	U	
9/7/2019	vs	SOUTHERN	55	24	W	-41.0	L	NT	---	
9/14/2019	@	South Alabama	42	6	W	-20.5	W	55.0	U	
9/26/2019	vs	NAVY	35	23	W	-10.5	W	53.5	O	
10/5/2019	@	Louisiana-Monroe	52	33	W	-15.0	W	69.0	O	
10/12/2019	@	Temple	28	30	L	-4.0	L	50.0	O	
10/19/2019	vs	TULANE	47	17	W	-2.5	W	60.5	O	
10/26/2019	@	Tulsa	42	41	W	-9.5	L	59.0	O	
11/2/2019	vs	SMU	54	48	W	-5.5	W	72.0	O	
11/16/2019	@	Houston	45	27	W	-9.5	W	71.5	O	
11/23/2019	@	South Florida	49	10	W	-14.5	W	59.5	U	
11/30/2019	vs	CINCINNATI	34	24	W	-13.5	L	59.5	U	
12/7/2019	vs	CINCINNATI	29	24	W	-8.0	L	58.0	U	AAC CHAMPIONSHIP
12/28/2019	vs	Penn State	39	53	L	6.5	L	59.0	O	Cotton Bowl
Coach: Mike Norvell		Season Record >>	566	370	12-2	ATS>>	8-6	O/U>>	8-5	AAC CHAMPIONS
2018-Memphis		Opponent	Mem	Opp	S/U	Line	ATS	Total	O/U	
9/1/2018	vs	MERCER	66	14	W	-30.0	W	NT	---	
9/8/2018	@	Navy	21	22	L	-6.5	L	67.0	U	
9/14/2018	vs	GEORGIA STATE	59	22	W	-28.5	W	59.0	O	
9/22/2018	vs	SOUTH ALABAMA	52	35	W	-32.0	L	66.0	O	
9/28/2018	@	Tulane	24	40	L	-14.5	L	66.0	U	
10/6/2018	vs	CONNECTICUT	55	14	W	-36.0	W	76.0	U	
10/13/2018	vs	CENTRAL FLORIDA	30	31	L	5.5	W	80.5	U	
10/20/2018	@	Missouri	33	65	L	8.5	L	69.5	O	
11/3/2018	@	East Carolina	59	41	W	-10.5	W	66.0	O	
11/10/2018	vs	TULSA	47	21	W	-16.5	W	64.5	O	
11/16/2018	@	Smu	28	18	W	-8.5	W	74.5	U	
11/23/2018	vs	HOUSTON	52	31	W	-9.5	W	74.5	O	
12/1/2018	@	Central Florida	41	56	L	PK	L	65.0	O	AAC Championship
12/22/2018	vs	Wake Forest	34	37	L	-2.0	L	71.5	U	Birmingham Bowl
Coach: Mike Norvell		Season Record >>	601	447	8-6	ATS>>	8-6	O/U>>	7-6	
2017-Memphis		Opponent	Mem	Opp	S/U	Line	ATS	Total	O/U	
8/31/2017	vs	LOUISIANA-MONROE	37	29	W	-28.0	L	61.0	O	
9/16/2017	vs	UCLA	48	45	W	3.0	W	70.5	O	
9/23/2017	vs	SOUTHERN ILLINOIS	44	31	W	NL	---	NT	---	
9/30/2017	@	Central Florida	13	40	L	5.5	L	68.5	U	
10/6/2017	@	Connecticut	70	31	W	-16.0	W	76.0	O	
10/14/2017	vs	NAVY	30	27	W	-3.5	L	73.0	U	
10/19/2017	@	Houston	42	38	W	PK	W	62.0	O	
10/27/2017	vs	TULANE	56	26	W	-10.0	W	61.0	O	
11/3/2017	@	Tulsa	41	14	W	-14.0	W	80.5	U	
11/18/2017	vs	SMU	66	45	W	-11.0	W	70.0	O	
11/25/2017	vs	EAST CAROLINA	70	13	W	-29.5	W	81.5	O	
12/2/2017	@	Central Florida	55	62	L	6.5	L	80.0	O	AAC Championship
12/30/2017	vs	Iowa State	20	21	L	-3.5	L	67.5	U	Liberty Bowl
Coach: Mike Norvell		Season Record >>	592	422	10-3	ATS>>	7-5	O/U>>	8-4	

Copyright © 2021 by Steve's Football Bible, LLC

MEMPHIS TIGERS   AMERICAN West

STADIUM: Liberty Bowl Memorial Stadium {58,318}			Location: Memphis, TN		COACH: Ryan Silverfield						
DATE		Opponent	Mem	Opp	S/U	Line	ATS	Total	O/U	Trends & Angles		
9/4/2021	vs	*NICHOLLS STATE*								vs Nicholls State - Memphis leads series 1-0		
9/11/2021	@	*Arkansas State*								11-1-1 S/U vs Ark. State as favorite since 1990		
9/18/2021	vs	*MISSISSIPPI STATE*								0-8 S/U @ home vs M State since 1990 {2-6 ATS}		
9/25/2021	vs	*TEXAS-SAN ANTONIO*								1st meeting		
10/2/2021	@	Temple								0-6 ATS vs Temple since 2013		
10/9/2021	@	Tulsa								6-2-1 ATS @ Tulsa since 1987		
10/14/2021	vs	NAVY								vs Navy - Series tied 3-3		
10/22/2021	@	Central Florida								1-10 S/U vs UCF as Dog since 2006		
11/6/2021	vs	SMU								6-1 S/U & ATS vs SMU since 2014		
11/13/2021	vs	EAST CAROLINA								5-0 S/U vs ECU as favorite since 2003		
11/19/2021	@	Houston								2-5 S/U vs Houston as Dog since 2006		
11/27/2021	vs	TULANE								13-1 S/U @ home vs Tulane since 1983		
12/4/2021	vs									AAC Championship		
	vs									BOWL GAME		

Pointspread Analysis Non-Conference		Pointspread Analysis Conference
2-15 S/U vs Non-Conf. as 20.5 point or more Dog since 1986		1-12 S/U vs East Carolina as Dog since 1991
2-13 S/U vs Non-Conf. as 15.5-20 point Dog since 1985		vs Smu - Memphis leads series 9-4
2-14 S/U vs Non-Conf. as 10.5-15 point Dog since 1984		vs Temple - Series tied 3-3
4-14 S/U vs Non-Conf. as 3 point or less Dog since 1984		0-3 ATS @ Temple since 2014
7-1 S/U vs Non-Conf. as 3.5-7 point favorite since 1990		vs Tulane - Memphis leads series 23-13-1
33-1 S/U vs Non-Conf. as 10.5 point or more favorite since 1991		12-2 S/U vs Tulane since 2002
0-12 S/U vs Mississippi State since 1994		5-1-1 ATS vs Tulane as Dog since 1988
0-6 ATS vs Mississippi State since 2000		11-1-1 ATS @ home vs Tulane since 1985
vs Mississippi State - M State leads series 34-10		11-0 S/U @ home vs Tulane as favorite since 1985 {9-1-1 ATS}
0-11 S/U vs Mississippi State as Dog since 1994		14-1 S/U vs Tulane as 3 point or more favorite since 1985
0-5 ATS vs Mississippi State as Dog since 2000		vs Tulsa - Memphis leads series 19-11
Dog		0-4 S/U vs Tulsa as Dog since 2005
1-10 S/U as 25.5 point or more Dog since 1986		5-0 S/U @ Tulsa as favorite since 1987
0-13 S/U on road as 20.5-25 point Dog since 1993		Game 6-1 O/U @ Tulsa since 1992
0-15 S/U as 20.5-25 point Dog since 1993		
1-17 S/U on road as 15.5-20 point Dog since 1991		
0-5 S/U @ home as 15.5-20 point Dog since 1998		**Bowl Games**
0-13 S/U @ home as 10.5-15 point Dog since 1989		1-5 S/U & ATS in Bowl Game since 2015
4-18 S/U on road as 10.5-15 point Dog since 1984		
1-7 O/U as 7.5-10 point Dog since 2008	Arkansas State	2-14 S/U in 1st road game of season since 2005
1-12 S/U on road as 7.5-10 point Dog since 1988	M STATE	19-3 S/U in 2nd home game of season since 1999
1-10 S/U on road as 3.5-7 point Dog since 2006	Temple	3-9 ATS in 2nd road game of season since 2009
2-12 S/U on road as 3 point or less Dog since 1994	NAVY	1-9 O/U prior to playing Central Florida since 2007
Favorite	E. CAROLINA	8-0-1 O/U after playing SMU since 2011
9-4 S/U on road as 3.5-7 point favorite since 1995	Houston	4-1 S/U in final road game of season since 2016
2-12 ATS @ home as 7.5-10 point favorite since 2003		
8-1 O/U @ home as 7.5-10 point favorite since 2006		
18-0 S/U @ home as 10.5-15 point favorite since 1993		
13-3 ATS @ home as 10.5-15 point favorite since 1994		
5-13-1 O/U as 10.5-15 point favorite since 2002		0-15 S/U on road vs ranked teams since 1993
33-0 S/U @ home as 15.5 point or more favorite since 1991		0-3 S/U vs ranked Central Florida all time
38-1 S/U as 15.5 point or more favorite since 1991		1-7 S/U vs ranked Houston all time

Copyright © 2021 by Steve's Football Bible, LLC

MIAMI HURRICANES

ACC Coastal

2020-MIAMI		Opponent	Miami	Opp	S/U	Line	ATS	Total	O/U	
9/10/2020	vs	ALABAMA-BIRMINGHAM	31	14	W	-14.5	W	54.5	U	
9/19/2020	@	Lousiville	47	34	W	-2.5	W	66.0	O	
9/26/2020	vs	FLORIDA STATE	52	10	W	-10.5	W	54.0	O	
10/10/2020	@	Clemson	17	42	L	14.0	L	60.5	U	
10/17/2020	vs	PITTSBURGH	31	19	W	-13.5	L	47.5	O	
10/24/2020	vs	VIRGINIA	19	14	W	-13.5	L	54.5	U	
11/6/2020	@	NC State	44	41	W	-11.0	L	58.0	O	
11/14/2020	@	Virginia Tech	25	24	W	2.0	W	67.5	O	
12/5/2020	@	Duke	48	0	W	-14.0	W	62.5	U	
12/12/2020	vs	NORTH CAROLINA	26	62	L	-3.0	L	72.5	O	
12/29/2020	vs	**Oklahoma State**	34	37	L	1.5	L	63.0	O	**Cheez-it Bowl**
Coach: Manny Diaz		Season Record >>	374	297	8-3	ATS>>	5-6	O/U>>	6-5	
2019-MIAMI		Opponent	Miami	Opp	S/U	Line	ATS	Total	O/U	
8/24/2019	vs	Florida	20	24	L	7.0	W	46.0	U	"Seminole War Canoe Trophy"
9/7/2019	@	North Carolina	25	28	L	-5.0	L	46.0	O	
9/14/2019	vs	BETHUNE-COOKMAN	63	0	W	-40.5	W	NT	---	
9/21/2019	vs	CENTRAL MICHIGAN	17	12	W	-30.5	L	48.5	U	
10/5/2019	vs	VIRGINIA TECH	35	42	L	-14.0	L	45.0	O	
10/11/2019	vs	VIRGINIA	17	9	W	-3.0	W	43.5	U	
10/19/2019	vs	GEORGIA TECH	21	28	L	-18.0	L	46.0	O	{OT}
10/26/2019	@	Pittsburgh	16	12	W	4.5	W	41.5	U	
11/2/2019	@	Florida State	27	10	W	3.0	W	50.5	U	
11/9/2019	vs	LOUISVILLE	52	27	W	-6.5	W	49.0	U	
11/23/2019	@	Florida International	24	30	L	-21.0	L	51.5	O	
11/30/2019	vs	DUKE	17	27	L	-9.0	L	44.0	T	
12/26/2019	vs	**Louisiana Tech**	0	14	L	-7.0	L	49.5	U	**Independence Bowl**
Coach: Manny Diaz		Season Record >>	334	263	6-7	ATS>>	6-7	O/U>>	5-6-1	
2018-MIAMI		Opponent	Miami	Opp	S/U	Line	ATS	Total	O/U	
9/2/2018	vs	Lsu	17	33	L	-3.0	L	47.5	O	**AT&T Stadium**
9/8/2018	vs	SAVANNAH STATE	77	0	W	-61.5	W	NT	---	
9/15/2018	@	Toledo	49	24	W	-12.0	W	58.5	O	
9/22/2018	vs	FLORIDA INTERNATIONAL	31	17	W	-25.5	L	56.5	U	
9/29/2018	vs	NORTH CAROLINA	47	10	W	-18.5	W	55.0	O	
10/6/2018	vs	FLORIDA STATE	28	27	W	-14.0	L	48.0	O	
10/13/2018	@	Virginia	13	16	L	-7.0	L	46.5	U	
10/27/2018	@	Boston College	14	27	L	-4.0	L	49.0	U	
11/3/2018	vs	DUKE	12	20	L	-8.5	L	50.5	U	
11/10/2018	@	Georgia Tech	21	27	L	1.0	L	50.5	U	
11/17/2018	@	Virginia Tech	38	14	W	-6.5	W	52.5	U	
11/24/2018	vs	PITTSBURGH	24	3	W	-5.0	W	46.5	U	
12/27/2018	vs	**Wisconsin**	3	35	L	-2.5	L	44.0	U	**Pinstripe Bowl**
Coach: Mark Richt		Season Record >>	374	253	7-6	ATS>>	5-8	O/U>>	4-8	
2017-MIAMI		Opponent	Miami	Opp	S/U	Line	ATS	Total	O/U	
9/2/2017	vs	BETHUNE-COOKMAN	41	13	W	-46.0	L	63.5	U	
9/23/2017	vs	TOLEDO	52	30	W	-13.0	W	59.5	O	
9/29/2017	@	Duke	31	6	W	-5.0	W	55.0	U	
10/7/2017	@	Florida State	24	20	W	-2.5	W	45.0	U	
10/14/2017	vs	GEORGIA TECH	25	24	W	-6.5	L	53.0	U	
10/21/2017	vs	SYRACUSE	27	19	W	-17.0	L	61.0	U	
10/28/2017	@	North Carolina	24	19	W	-21.0	L	55.5	U	
11/4/2017	vs	VIRGINIA TECH	28	10	W	-2.0	W	49.5	U	
11/11/2017	vs	NOTRE DAME	41	8	W	3.5	W	59.0	U	
11/18/2017	vs	VIRGINIA	44	28	W	-19.5	L	49.0	O	
11/24/2017	@	Pittsburgh	14	24	L	-12.0	L	53.0	U	
12/2/2017	vs	**Clemson**	3	38	L	12.5	L	47.5	U	**ACC CHAMPIONSHIP**
12/30/2017	vs	**Wisconsin**	24	34	L	6.5	L	45.5	O	**Orange Bowl**
Coach: Mark Richt		Season Record >>	378	273	10-3	ATS>>	5-8	O/U>>	3-10	

Copyright © 2021 by Steve's Football Bible, LLC

MIAHMI HURRICANES   ACC Coastal

STADIUM: Hard Rock Stadium {64,767}						Location: Coral Gables, FL				COACH: Manny Diaz		

DATE		Opponent	Mia	Opp	S/U	Line	ATS	Total	O/U	Trends & Angles
9/4/2021	vs	*Alabama {@ Atlanta}*								vs Alabama - Alabama leads series 14-3
9/11/2021	vs	*APPALACHIAN STATE*								vs Appalachian State - Miami leads series 1-0
9/18/2021	vs	*MICHIGAN STATE*								vs Michigan State - Miami leads series 4-0
9/25/2021	vs	*CENTRAL CONNECTICUT*								1st meeting
9/30/2021	vs	**VIRGINIA**								4-0 S/U @ home vs Virginia since 2013
10/16/2021	@	North Carolina								0-4 ATS @ North Carolina since 2013
10/23/2021	vs	**NC STATE**								vs NC State - Miami leads series 10-5-1
10/30/2021	@	Pittsburgh								7-1 S/U @ Pittsburgh since 1999
11/6/2021	vs	**GEORGIA TECH**								6-1 S/U vs Georgia Tech as favorite since 2009
11/13/2021	@	Florida State								2-6 ATS vs Florida State as favorite since 2005
11/20/2021	vs	**VIRGINIA TECH**								Game 2-7 O/U @ home vs Va Tech since 2004
11/27/2021	@	Duke								13-3 S/U vs Duke as favorite since 1983
12/4/2021	vs									ACC Championship
	vs									BOWL GAME

Pointspread Analysis Non-Conference		Pointspread Analysis Conference
0-7 S/U vs Non-Conf. as 10.5 point or more Dog since 1993		vs Duke - Miami leads series 15-3
1-4 O/U vs Non-Conf. as 3 point or less Dog since 2004		8-0 S/U vs Duke as 15.5 point or more favorite since 1983
8-2 S/U vs Non-Conf. as 3 point or less favorite since 1985		vs Florida State - Miami leads series 35-29
0-4 O/U vs Non-Conf. as 7.5-10 point favorite since 2004		1-5 S/U vs Florida State as Dog since 2011
63-1 S/U vs Non-Conf. as 15.5 point or more favorite since 1984		0-6 O/U vs Florida State as Dog since 2011
Dog		10-1 ATS vs Florida State as 3.0-7.0 Dog since 1983
0-6 S/U as 15.5 point or more Dog since 1995		0-8 S/U vs Florida State as 9.5 point or more Dog since 1993
1-9 S/U as 10.5-15 point Dog since 1993		vs Georgia Tech - G Tech leads series 13-12
7-0 O/U on road as 7.5-10 point Dog since 1996		vs North Carolina - UNC leads series 13-11
1-6 S/U as 7.5-10 point Dog since 2010		6-0 S/U vs North Carolina as 9.0-21 point favorite since 2005
4-14 O/U as 3 point or less Dog since 2004		21-3 S/U vs Pittsburgh since 1984
Favorite		vs Pittsburgh - Miami leads series 28-11-1
13-4 S/U & ATS as 3 point or less favorite since 2011		7-0 S/U vs Pittsburgh as 9 point or less favorite since 1989
7-0 S/U & ATS on road as 3 point or less favorite since 2010		9-0 S/U vs Pittsburgh as 19.5 point or more favorite since 1986
3-9 O/U as 3 point or less favorite since 2014		vs Virginia - Miami leads series 11-7
10-2 S/U @ home as 3.5-7 point favorite since 2010		3-11 ATS vs Virginia as favorite since 2005
10-2 S/U on road as 7.5-10 point favorite since 1988		vs Virginia Tech - Miami leads series 23-15
1-9 ATS @ home as 7.5-10 point favorite since 1991		Game 4-14 O/U vs Virginia Tech since 2003
5-11 ATS as 10.5-15 point favorite since 2010		2-8 O/U vs Virginia Tech as favorite since 2003
2-9 O/U on road as 10.5-15 point favorite since 2000		4-1 S/U & ATS vs Virginia Tech as favorite since 2014
14-1 S/U @ home as 15.5-20 point favorite since 2005		2-7 S/U vs Virginia Tech as 2 point or more Dog since 1997
18-1 S/U as 15.5-20 point favorite since 2005		6-1 S/U vs Virginia Tech as 14 point or more favorite since 1987
14-0 S/U on road as 15.5-20 point favorite since 1985		**Bowl Games**
0-8 ATS as 20.5-25 point favorite since 2004		0-4 S/U in Fiesta Bowl
33-2 S/U on road as 20.5 point or more favorite since 1984		5-2 S/U in Orange Bowl since 1984
83-0 S/U @ home as 20.5 point or more favorite since 1984		1-10 S/U in Bowl Games since 2008
0-8 O/U as 25.5-30 point favorite since 2002		2-11 ATS in Bowl Games since 2005
0-4 ATS on road as 30.5 point or more favorite since 1994		3-9 O/U in Bowl Games since 2006
		0-3 S/U & ATS vs Wisconsin in Bowl Games
59-12 S/U @ home when ranked since 2000	APP STATE	22-1 S/U in 1st home game of season since 1998
20-0 S/U @ home when #1 ranked all time	APP STATE	0-12 O/U in 1st home game of season since 2004
14-0 S/U on road when #1 ranked since 1991	MICHIGAN ST	9-0 S/U in 2nd home game of season since 2012
28-0 S/U when #1 ranked in regular season since 1991	CENTRAL CONN.	10-3 S/U prior to playing Virginia since 2008
24-0 S/U @ home when #2 ranked all time	NC STATE	2-8 O/U after playing North Carolina since 2009
	NC STATE	2-8 ATS prior to playing Pittsburgh since 2003
3-17 S/U on road vs ranked teams since 2006	Pittsburgh	10-2 S/U prior to playing Georgia Tech since 2008
6-0 S/U @ home vs #1 ranked teams since 1981	GEORGIA TECH	7-0 S/U after playing Pittsburgh since 2000
4-0 ATS @ home vs #1 ranked team since 1986	Florida State	2-10 O/U prior to playing Virginia Tech since 2008
0-6 S/U vs ranked Florida State since 2010	VPI	12-3 S/U after playing Florida State since 2006
1-5 S/U vs ranked Virginia Tech since 2006	Duke	4-11 O/U in final road game of season since 2006
	Duke	9-3 S/U & ATS in final road game of season since 2009

Copyright © 2021 by Steve's Football Bible, LLC

2020-Miami-Ohio		Opponent	M-O	Opp	S/U	Line	ATS	Total	O/U	
11/4/2020	vs	BALL STATE	38	31	W	1.0	W	56.5	O	
11/10/2020	@	Buffalo	10	42	L	7.0	L	56.0	U	
11/28/2020	@	Akron	38	7	W	-14.0	W	55.0	U	
Coach: Chuck Martin		Season Record >>	86	80	2-1	ATS>>	2-1	O/U>>	1-2	
2019-Miami-Ohio		Opponent	M-O	Opp	S/U	Line	ATS	Total	O/U	
8/31/2019	@	Iowa	14	38	L	24.5	W	47.0	O	
9/7/2019	vs	TENNESSEE TECH	48	17	W	-37.0	L	NT	---	
9/14/2019	@	Cincinnati	13	35	L	17.5	L	49.5	U	"Victory Bell"
9/21/2019	@	Ohio State	5	76	L	38.5	L	57.0	O	
9/28/2019	vs	BUFFALO	34	20	W	2.5	W	48.5	O	
10/12/2019	@	Western Michigan	16	38	L	12.0	L	57.5	U	
10/19/2019	vs	NORTHERN ILLINOIS	27	24	W	1.5	W	48.0	O	
10/26/2019	@	Kent State	23	16	W	2.5	W	54.5	U	
11/6/2019	@	Ohio	24	21	W	7.0	W	57.5	U	"Battle of the Bricks"
11/13/2019	vs	BOWLING GREEN	44	3	W	-17.0	W	47.4	U	
11/20/2019	vs	AKRON	20	17	W	-28.5	L	45.0	U	
11/29/2019	@	Ball State	27	41	L	3.0	L	55.5	O	
12/7/2019	vs	**Central Michigan**	26	21	W	5.5	W	56.5	U	MAC Championship Game
1/6/2020	vs	**Louisiana**	17	27	L	16.0	W	55.0	U	Lending Tree Bowl
Coach: Chuck Martin		Season Record >>	338	394	8-6	ATS>>	8-6	O/U>>	5-8	MAC Champions
2018-Miami-Ohio		Opponent	M-O	Opp	S/U	Line	ATS	Total	O/U	
9/1/2018	vs	MARSHALL	28	35	L	-1.5	L	51.5	O	
9/8/2018	@	Cincinnati	0	21	L	-1.5	L	45.5	U	"Victory Bell"
9/15/2018	@	Minnesota	3	26	L	13.5	L	46.5	U	
9/22/2018	@	Bowling Green	38	23	W	-6.5	W	54.5	O	
9/29/2018	vs	WESTERN MICHIGAN	39	40	L	2.5	W	52.0	O	
10/6/2018	@	Akron	41	17	W	5.0	W	47.5	O	
10/13/2018	vs	KENT STATE	31	6	W	-11.5	W	59.0	U	
10/20/2018	@	Army	30	31	L	6.5	W	47.0	O	{2 OT}
10/30/2018	@	Buffalo	42	51	L	7.0	L	53.0	O	
11/7/2018	vs	OHIO	30	28	W	4.5	W	59.0	U	"Battle of the Bricks"
11/14/2018	@	Northern Illinois	13	7	W	6.0	W	48.0	U	
11/20/2018	vs	BALL STATE	42	21	W	-14.5	W	55.0	O	
Coach: Chuck Martin		Season Record >>	337	306	6-6	ATS>>	8-4	O/U>>	7-5	
2017-Miami-Ohio		Opponent	M-O	Opp	S/U	Line	ATS	Total	O/U	
9/2/2017	@	Marshall	26	31	L	-3.5	L	48.0	O	
9/9/2017	vs	AUSTIN PEAY	31	10	W	-36.5	L	NT	---	
9/16/2017	vs	CINCINNATI	17	21	L	-3.0	L	49.0	U	"Victory Bell"
9/23/2017	@	Central Michigan	31	14	W	1.5	W	50.5	U	
9/30/2017	@	Notre Dame	17	52	L	20.5	L	53.0	O	
10/7/2017	vs	BOWLING GREEN	29	37	L	-16.5	L	50.5	O	
10/14/2017	@	Kent State	14	17	L	-8.0	L	42.5	U	
10/21/2017	vs	BUFFALO	24	17	W	-2.5	W	46.5	U	
10/31/2017	@	Ohio	28	45	L	7.0	L	53.5	O	"Battle of the Bricks"
11/7/2017	vs	AKRON	24	14	W	-11.5	L	50.5	U	
11/15/2017	vs	EASTERN MICHIGAN	24	27	L	-1.5	L	51.0	T	
11/21/2017	@	Ball State	28	7	W	-17.5	W	53.5	U	
Coach: Chuck Martin		Season Record >>	293	292	5-7	ATS>>	3-9	O/U>>	4-6-1	

  Copyright © 2021 by Steve's Football Bible, LLC

MIAMI-OHIO REDHAWKS   MAC East

STADIUM: Yager Stadium {24,2863}									Location: Oxford, OH	COACH: Chuck Martin

DATE		Opponent	M-O	Opp	S/U	Line	ATS	Total	O/U	Trends & Angles
9/4/2021	@	*Cincinnati*								0-14 S/U vs Cincinnati since 2006
9/11/2021	@	*Minnesota*								vs Minnesota - Minnesota leads series 4-0
9/18/2021	vs	*LONG ISLAND U*								1st meeting
9/25/2021	@	*Army*								vs Army - Series tied 3-3
10/2/2021	vs	**CENTRAL MICHIGAN**								1-6 S/U in 2nd home game of season since 2013
10/9/2021	@	Eastern Michigan								
10/16/2021	vs	**AKRON**								11-0 S/U @ home vs Akron as favorite since 1994
10/23/2021	@	Ball State								3-9 S/U prior to playing Ohio since 2008
11/2/2021	@	Ohio								1-6 S/U @ Ohio since 2007
11/9/2021	vs	**BUFFALO**								1-8 S/U vs Buffalo as Dog since 2008
11/16/2021	vs	**BOWLING GREEN**								3-11-1 ATS in final home game of season since 2005
11/27/2021	@	Kent State								vs Kent State - Miami-Ohio leads series 50-17
12/3/2021	vs									MAC Championship
	vs									BOWL GAME

Pointspread Analysis Non-Conference		Pointspread Analysis Conference
0-25 S/U vs Non-Conf. as 20.5 point or more Dog since 1989		vs Akron - Miami-Ohio leads series 20-8-1
0-14 S/U vs Non-Conf. as 15.5-20 point Dog since 2005		1-6 S/U vs Akron as Dog since 1993
0-22-1 S/U vs Non-Conf. as 7.5-15 point Dog since 1986		11-0 S/U vs Akron as favorite since 2001
4-0 S/U vs Non-Conf. as 15.5 point or more favorite since 2012		0-4 S/U vs Ball State as 8 point or more Dog since 1989
vs Cincinnati - Miami-Ohio leads series 59-58-7		8-0 S/U vs Ball State as 6-19 point favorite since 1996
0-12 S/U vs Cincinnati as 8 point or more Dog since 1989		vs Bowling Green - Miami-Ohio leads series 45-24-5
1-28 S/U vs Big Ten teams as Dog since 1989		6-1 ATS vs Bowling Green as 6 point or less Dog since 1989
Dog		vs Buffalo - Miami-Ohio leads series 15-8
0-29 S/U as 20.5 point or more Dog since 1989		13-0 S/U vs Buffalo as favorite since 1999
0-10 S/U @ home as 15.5 point or more Dog since 2008		5-0 S/U @ Eastern Michigan as favorite since 1992
0-15 S/U on road as 15.5-20 point Dog since 2005		13-1 S/U vs Kent State as 10.5 point or more favorite since 1990
1-30-1 S/U as 10.5-15 point Dog since 1989		vs Ohio - Miami-Ohio leads series 56-40-1
0-7 O/U as 10.5-15 point Dog since 2015		11-2 S/U vs Ohio as favorite since 1991
1-8 S/U @ home as 7.5-15 point Dog since 1989		8-2 ATS vs Ohio as favorite since 1994
2-8 O/U as 7.5-10 point Dog since 2003		3-11 S/U vs Ohio since 2006
8-1 ATS as 3 point or less Dog since 2016		1-6 S/U @ Ohio as Dog since 2007
Favorite		
6-2 S/U & ATS on road as 3 point or less favorite since 1994	Cincinnati	0-13 S/U in 1st road game of season since 2008
9-1 S/U on road as 7.5-10 point favorite since 1991	Minnesota	2-13 S/U in 2nd road game of season since 2006
2-9 O/U @ home as 10.5-15 point favorite since 2002	C. MICHIGAN	3-10 O/U in 2nd home game of season since 2006
17-4 S/U @ home as 10.5-15 point favorite since 1990	Ball State	2-9 O/U prior to playing Ohio since 2009
5-0 S/U on road as 10.5-15 point favorite since 1991	Ohio	3-12 S/U prior to playing Buffalo since 2006
16-0 S/U on road as 15.5 point or more favorite since 1997	B. GREEN	2-6 S/U prior to playing Kent State since 2012
24-4 S/U @ home as 15.5 point or more favorite since 1991	Kent State	1-7 O/U after playing Bowling Green since 2010

Print Version $34.99   Print Version $39.99   Print Version $39.99

These books available at numerous online retailers

Copyright © 2021 by Steve's Football Bible, LLC

2020-Michigan		Opponent	UM	Opp	S/U	Line	ATS	Total	O/U	
10/24/2020	@	Minnesota	49	24	W	-2.5	W	54.5	O	*"Little Brown Jug"*
10/31/2020	vs	MICHIGAN STATE	24	27	L	-22.0	L	51.5	U	*"Paul Bunyan Trophy"*
11/7/2020	@	Indiana	21	38	L	-4.5	L	54.5	O	
11/14/2020	vs	WISCONSIN	11	49	L	7.0	L	51.5	O	
11/21/2020	@	Rutgers	48	42	W	-11.5	L	52.0	O	{3 OT}
11/28/2020	vs	PENN STATE	17	27	L	PK	L	56.0	U	
Coach: Jim Harbaugh		Season Record >>	170	207	2-4	ATS>>	1-5	O/U>>	4-2	
2019-Michigan		Opponent	UM	Opp	S/U	Line	ATS	Total	O/U	
8/31/2019	vs	*MIDDLE TENNESSEE*	40	21	W	-36.5	L	55.0	O	
9/7/2019	vs	*ARMY*	24	21	W	-22.0	L	47.5	U	{2 OT}
9/21/2019	@	Wisconsin	14	35	L	3.0	L	45.0	O	
9/28/2019	vs	RUTGERS	52	0	W	-27.5	W	49.0	O	
10/5/2019	vs	IOWA	10	3	W	-4.0	W	49.0	U	
10/12/2019	@	Illinois	42	25	W	-24.5	L	48.5	O	
10/19/2019	@	Penn State	21	28	L	7.5	W	46.5	O	
10/26/2019	vs	*NOTRE DAME*	45	14	W	-1.0	W	46.5	O	
11/2/2019	@	Maryland	38	7	W	-21.0	W	57.5	U	
11/16/2019	vs	MICHIGAN STATE	44	10	W	-14.0	W	43.5	O	*"Paul Bunyan Trophy"*
11/23/2019	@	Indiana	39	14	W	-10.0	W	54.0	U	
11/30/2019	vs	OHIO STATE	27	56	L	8.5	L	53.0	O	*"100 Yard War"*
1/1/2020	vs	**Alabama**	16	35	L	8.0	L	60.0	U	**Citrus Bowl**
Coach: Jim Harbaugh		Season Record >>	412	269	9-4	ATS>>	7-6	O/U>>	8-5	
2018-Michigan		Opponent	UM	Opp	S/U	Line	ATS	Total	O/U	
9/1/2018	@	*Notre Dame*	17	24	L	-3.0	L	48.0	U	
9/8/2018	vs	*WESTERN MICHIGAN*	49	3	W	-28.0	W	55.0	U	
9/15/2018	vs	*SMU*	45	20	W	-36.0	L	54.0	O	
9/22/2018	vs	NEBRASKA	56	10	W	-17.0	W	50.5	O	
9/29/2018	@	Northwestern	20	17	W	-14.5	L	46.5	U	
10/6/2018	vs	MARYLAND	42	21	W	-17.5	W	44.0	O	
10/13/2018	vs	WISCONSIN	38	13	W	-9.5	W	48.0	O	
10/20/2018	@	Michigan State	21	7	W	-7.0	W	39.0	U	*"Paul Bunyan Trophy"*
11/3/2018	vs	PENN STATE	42	7	W	-11.0	W	49.5	U	
11/10/2018	@	Rutgers	42	7	W	-37.0	L	44.5	O	
11/17/2018	vs	INDIANA	31	20	W	-28.0	L	53.5	U	
11/24/2018	@	Ohio State	39	62	L	-4.0	L	53.5	O	*"100 Yard War"*
12/29/2018	vs	**Florida**	15	41	L	-4.0	L	51.0	O	**Chick-Fil-A Peach Bowl**
Coach: Jim Harbaugh		Season Record >>	457	252	10-3	ATS>>	6-7	O/U>>	7-6	
2017-Michigan		Opponent	UM	Opp	S/U	Line	ATS	Total	O/U	
9/2/2017	vs	*Florida*	33	17	W	-4.0	W	46.0	O	**AT&T Stadium**
9/9/2017	vs	*CINCINNATI*	36	14	W	-12.0	L	51.0	O	
9/16/2017	vs	*AIR FORCE*	29	13	W	-23.0	L	52.5	U	
9/23/2017	@	Purdue	28	10	W	-13.5	W	51.0	U	
10/7/2017	vs	MICHIGAN STATE	10	14	L	-12.5	L	40.0	U	*"Paul Bunyan Trophy"*
10/14/2017	@	Indiana	27	20	W	-7.0	T	44.0	O	{OT}
10/21/2017	@	Penn State	13	42	L	7.5	L	42.5	O	
10/28/2017	vs	RUTGERS	35	14	W	-22.0	L	42.0	O	
11/4/2017	vs	MINNESOTA	33	10	W	-15.5	W	39.0	O	*"Little Brown Jug"*
11/11/2017	@	Maryland	35	10	W	-15.0	W	46.5	U	
11/18/2017	@	Wisconsin	10	24	L	6.5	L	42.0	U	
11/25/2017	vs	OHIO STATE	20	31	L	12.5	W	49.5	O	*"100 Yard War"*
1/1/2018	vs	**South Carolina**	19	26	L	-9.0	L	41.5	O	**Outback Bowl**
Coach: Jim Harbaugh		Season Record >>	328	245	8-5	ATS>>	6-7	O/U>>	7-6	

Copyright © 2021 by Steve's Football Bible, LLC

MICHIGAN WOLVERINES   BIG TEN East

STADIUM: Michigan Stadium {107,601}							Location: Ann Arbor, MI		COACH: Jim Harbaugh	
DATE		Opponent	Mich	Opp	S/U	Line	ATS	Total	O/U	Trends & Angles
9/4/2021	vs	*WESTERN MICHIGAN*								vs Western Michigan - Michigan leads series 7-0
9/11/2021	vs	*WASHINGTON*								vs Washington - Michigan leads series 7-5
9/18/2021	vs	*NORTHERN ILLINOIS*								vs Northern Illinois - Michigan leads series 1-0
9/25/2021	vs	RUTGERS								6-0 S/U vs Rutgers since 2015
10/2/2021	@	Wisconsin								0-6 ATS @ Wisconsin since 2001
10/9/2021	@	Nebraska								vs Nebraska - Michigan leads series 5-4-1
10/23/2021	vs	NORTHWESTERN								21-2 S/U @ home vs Northwestern since 1960
10/30/2021	@	Michigan State								2-11 ATS vs Michigan State since 2008
11/6/2021	vs	INDIANA								20-0 S/U @ home vs Indiana since 1971
11/13/2021	@	Penn State								1-5 S/U @ Penn State since 2008
11/20/2021	@	Maryland								vs Maryland - Michigan leads series 8-1
11/27/2021	vs	OHIO STATE								1-7 S/U @ home vs Ohio State since
12/4/2021	vs									Big Ten Championship
	vs									BOWL GAME

Pointspread Analysis
Non-Conference

0-5 S/U vs Non-Conf. as 3.5-7 point Dog since 2012

14-2 S/U vs Non-Conf. as 10.5-15 point favorite since 1983

51-1 S/U vs Non-Conf. as 15.5 point or more favorite since 1986

5-0 ATS vs Western Michigan since 2001

Game 0-4 O/U vs Western Michigan since 2002

1-5 ATS vs ranked Washington since 1983

Dog

0-6 S/U as 7.5-10 Point Dog since 2009

1-6 S/U on road as 10.5 point or more Dog since 1996

0-11 S/U as 3.5-7 point Dog since 2012

3-8 O/U as 3.5-7 point Dog since 2012

Favorite

1-6 ATS on road as 3 point or less favorite since 2007

9-2 O/U as 3.5-7 point favorite since 2015

7-0 S/U @ home as 7.5-10 point favorite since 2007

13-1 S/U on road as 10.5-15 point favorite since 1996

27-2 S/U @ home as 10.5-15 point favorite since 1995

2-12 O/U @ home as 10.5-15 point favorite since 2006

19-2 S/U @ home as 15.5-20 point favorite since 1983

30-2 S/U as 15.5-20 point favorite since 1983

8-0 O/U @ home as 15.5-20 point favorite since 2009

11-0 S/U on road as 15.5-20 point favorite since 1992

0-5 O/U on road as 15.5-20 point favorite since 2004

41-4 S/U as 20.5-25 point favorite since 1983

1-8 ATS as 20.5-25 point favorite since 2016

61-0-1 S/U as 25.5 point or more favorite since 1983

Bowl Games

1-6 S/U & ATS vs USC in Bowl Games since 70

4-12 S/U in Rose Bowl since 1969

10-3 O/U in Bowl Games since 2005

3-8 S/U vs ranked teams in Bowl games since 2004

3-1 S/U & ATS vs Florida in Bowl Games since 2003

4-0 O/U vs Florida in Bowl Games since 2003

1-11 S/U in Bowl Games as 3.5-7 point Dog since 1976

5-1 O/U in Citrus Bowl since 1999

4-2 S/U in Citrus Bowl since 1999

5-1 O/U in Outback Bowl since 1988

2-20 S/U on road vs ranked teams since 2006

0-9 S/U vs #1 ranked teams since 1984

0-7 S/U on road vs #1 ranked teams all time

Pointspread Analysis
Conference

25-0 S/U vs Indiana as 9 point or more favorite since 1983

vs Indiana - Michigan leads series 59-10

Game 3-9 O/U vs Michigan State since 2009

vs Michigan State - Michigan leads series 71-37-5

0-5 S/U & ATS vs Michigan State as Dog since 2008

9-1 S/U vs Michigan State as 13.5 point or more favorite since 1983

14-2 S/U vs Northwestern since 1997

Game 5-0 O/U @ home vs Ohio State since 2011

1-15 S/U vs Ohio State since 2004

Game 7-0 O/U vs Ohio State since 2013

0-14 S/U vs Ohio State as Dog since 2002

6-0 O/U vs Ohio State as Dog since 2013

vs Ohio State - Michigan leads series 58-52-6

8-2 S/U @ home vs Ohio State as favorite since 1983

1-8 S/U vs Ohio State as 7.5 point or more Dog since 1996

vs Penn State - Michigan leads series 14-10

Game 6-0 O/U @ Penn State since 2008

0-4 S/U vs Penn State as Dog since 2008

8-0 S/U vs Penn State as 3.5 point or more favorite since 2000

vs Rutgers - Michigan leads series 6-1

Game 7-0 O/U vs Rutgers since 2014

0-5 S/U @ Wisconsin since 2005

2-11-1 ATS vs Wisconsin since 2000

vs Wisconsin - Michigan leads series 51-17-1

0-5 S/U & ATS vs Wisconsin as Dog since 2009

vs Wisconsin - HOME team 10-2 S/U since 2002

16-1 S/U vs Wisconsin as 3.5 point or more favorite since 1983

42-6 S/U @ home when ranked since 2009

7-0 S/U & ATS when ranked vs Maryland all time

9-3 ATS in 1st home game of season since 2009

11-1 S/U in 1st home game of season since 2009

12-1 S/U in 2nd home game of season since 2008

15-3 S/U prior to playing Wisconsin since 1994

10-3 O/U in 2nd road game of season since 2008

12-0 S/U prior to playing Michigan State since 2009

20-1 S/U prior to playing Northwestern since 1988

9-1 ATS prior to playing Northwesern since 2005

9-1 O/U prior to playing Penn State since 2009

4-11 S/U in final road game of season since 2006

2-9 ATS after playing Penn State since 2007

| W. MICHIGAN |
| W. MICHIGAN |
| WASHINGTON |
| RUTGERS |
| Nebraska |
| NORTHWESTERN |
| Nebraska |
| Nebraska |
| INDIANA |
| Maryland |
| Maryland |

Copyright © 2021 by Steve's Football Bible, LLC

MICHIGAN STATE SPARTANS   BIG TEN East

2020-Michigan State		Opponent	MSU	Opp	S/U	Line	ATS	Total	O/U	
10/24/2020	vs	RUTGERS	27	38	L	-9.5	L	45.0	O	
10/31/2020	@	Michigan	27	24	W	22.0	W	51.5	U	"Paul Bunyan Trophy"
11/7/2020	@	Iowa	7	49	L	5.5	L	45.5	U	
11/14/2020	vs	INDIANA	0	24	L	7.5	L	52.5	U	"Old Brass Spittoon"
11/28/2020	vs	NORTHWESTERN	23	20	W	13.5	W	40.0	L	
12/5/2020	vs	OHIO STATE	12	52	L	22.0	L	58.5	O	
12/12/2020	@	Penn State	24	39	L	14.5	L	46.5	O	"Land Grant Trophy"
Coach: Mel Tucker		Season Record >>	120	246	2-5	ATS>>	2-5	O/U>>	4-3	
2019-Michigan State		Opponent	MSU	Opp	S/U	Line	ATS	Total	O/U	
8/30/2019	vs	TULSA	28	7	W	-23.5	L	47.0	U	
9/7/2019	vs	WESTERN MICHIGAN	51	17	W	-15.0	W	46.0	O	
9/14/2019	vs	ARIZONA STATE	7	10	L	-15.5	L	42.0	U	
9/21/2019	@	Northwestern	31	10	W	-7.5	W	35.5	O	
9/28/2019	vs	INDIANA	40	31	W	-14.0	L	43.0	O	"Old Brass Spittoon"
10/5/2019	@	Ohio State	10	34	L	20.0	L	51.0	U	
10/12/2019	@	Wisconsin	0	38	L	8.0	L	40.5	U	
10/26/2019	vs	PENN STATE	7	28	L	4.5	L	42.0	U	"Land Grant Trophy"
11/9/2019	vs	ILLINOIS	34	37	L	-15.5	L	47.5	O	
11/16/2019	@	Michigan	10	44	L	14.0	L	43.5	O	"Paul Bunyan Trophy"
11/23/2019	@	Rutgers	27	0	W	-22.0	W	43.5	U	
11/30/2019	vs	MARYLAND	19	16	W	-22.0	L	47.5	U	
12/27/2019	vs	Wake Forest	27	21	W	-4.0	W	51.5	U	Pinstripe Bowl
Coach: Mark Dantonio		Season Record >>	291	293	7-6	ATS>>	4-9	O/U>>	5-8	
2018-Michigan State		Opponent	MSU	Opp	S/U	Line	ATS	Total	O/U	
8/31/2018	vs	UTAH STATE	38	31	W	-23.5	L	52.0	O	
9/8/2018	@	Arizona State	13	16	L	-4.5	L	54.0	U	
9/22/2018	@	Indiana	35	21	W	-6.5	W	51.0	O	"Old Brass Spittoon"
9/29/2018	vs	CENTRAL MICHIGAN	31	20	W	-28.0	L	45.0	O	
10/6/2018	vs	NORTHWESTERN	19	29	L	-10.0	L	43.5	O	
10/13/2018	@	Penn State	21	17	W	13.5	W	53.5	U	"Land Grant Trophy"
10/20/2018	vs	MICHIGAN	7	21	L	7.0	L	39.0	U	"Paul Bunyan Trophy"
10/27/2018	vs	PURDUE	23	13	W	2.5	W	49.0	U	
11/3/2018	@	Maryland	24	3	W	-3.5	W	42.5	U	
11/10/2018	vs	OHIO STATE	6	26	L	3.5	L	49.5	U	
11/17/2018	@	Nebraska	6	9	L	1.0	L	48.0	U	
11/24/2018	vs	RUTGERS	14	10	W	-24.5	L	37.0	U	
12/31/2018	vs	Oregon	6	7	L	-1.5	L	47.0	U	Redbox Bowl
Coach: Mark Dantonio		Season Record >>	243	223	7-6	ATS>>	4-9	O/U>>	4-9	
2017-Michigan State		Opponent	MSU	Opp	S/U	Line	ATS	Total	O/U	
9/2/2017	vs	BOWLING GREEN	35	10	W	-17.0	W	56.0	U	
9/9/2017	vs	WESTERN MICHIGAN	28	14	W	-7.0	W	51.0	U	
9/23/2017	vs	NOTRE DAME	18	38	L	3.5	L	54.0	O	"Megaphone Trophy"
9/30/2017	vs	IOWA	17	10	W	-3.5	W	44.0	U	
10/7/2017	@	Michigan	14	10	W	12.5	W	40.0	U	"Paul Bunyan Trophy"
10/14/2017	@	Minnesota	30	27	W	-4.5	L	41.0	O	
10/21/2017	vs	INDIANA	17	9	W	-6.5	W	47.0	U	"Old Brass Spittoon"
10/28/2017	@	Northwestern	31	39	L	-1.5	L	40.0	O	{3 OT}
11/4/2017	vs	PENN STATE	27	24	W	9.5	W	46.5	U	"Land Grant Trophy"
11/11/2017	@	Ohio State	3	48	L	17.0	L	55.0	U	
11/18/2017	vs	MARYLAND	17	7	W	-14.0	L	44.0	U	
11/25/2017	@	Rutgers	40	7	W	-14.0	W	42.0	O	
12/28/2017	vs	Washington State	42	17	W	-2.5	W	47.5	O	Holiday Bowl
Coach: Mark Dantonio		Season Record >>	319	260	10-3	ATS>>	8-5	O/U>>	6-7	

Copyright © 2021 by Steve's Football Bible, LLC

MICHIGAN STATE SPARTANS   BIG TEN East

STADIUM: Spartan Stadium {75,005}									Location: East Lansing, MI		COACH: Mel Tucker	
DATE		Opponent	MSU	Opp	S/U	Line	ATS	Total	O/U	Trends & Angles		
9/4/2021	@	Northwestern								6-1 S/U @ Northwestern since 2006		
9/11/2021	vs	*YOUNGSTOWN STATE*								vs Youngstown State - MSU leads series 2-0		
9/18/2021	@	*Miami*								vs Miami - Miami leads series 4-0		
9/25/2021	vs	**NEBRASKA**								1-8 ATS vs Nebraska since 1995		
10/2/2021	vs	*WESTERN KENTUCKY*								1st meeting		
10/9/2021	@	Rutgers								6-1 S/U vs Rutgers since 2014		
10/16/2021	@	Indiana								vs Indiana - Michigan State leads series 49-16-2		
10/30/2021	vs	**MICHIGAN**								Game 1-5 O/U @ Michigan State since 2009		
11/6/2021	@	Purdue								8-0 S/U vs Purdue since 2007		
11/13/2021	vs	**MARYLAND**								vs Maryland - Michigan State leads series 9-2		
11/20/2021	@	Ohio State								Game 0-5 O/U @ Ohio State since 2007		
11/27/2021	vs	**PENN STATE**								4-14 S/U vs Penn State as Dog since 1993		
12/4/2021	vs									Big Ten Championship		
	vs									BOWL GAME		

Pointspread Analysis
Non-Conference

0-8 S/U vs Non-Conf. as 10.5-15 point Dog since 1988	
0-5 S/U vs Non-Conf. as 7.5-10 point Dog since 2009	
9-1 S/U vs Non-Conf. as 15.5-20 point favorite since 1996	
34-1 S/U vs Non-Conf. as 20.5 point or more favorite since 1989	

Dog

0-6 S/U @ home as 15.5 point or more Dog since 1983
3-14 S/U on road as 15.5 point or more Dog since 1983
3-13 S/U on road as 10.5-15 point Dog since 1991
2-5 S/U @ home as 10.5-15 point Dog since 1983
2-11 S/U as 7.5-10 point Dog since 2005
0-7 S/U & ATS @ home as 3.5-7 point Dog since 2003
7-1 S/U & ATS as 3 point or less Dog since 2010
15-6 O/U as 3 point or less Dog since 2010
7-2 O/U @ home as 3 point or less Dog since 1999

Favorite

1-6 S/U & ATS @ home as 3 point or less favorite since 2001
13-5 S/U as 7.5-10 point favorite since 2001
14-4 S/U @ home as 7.5-10 point favorite since 1994
3-10 ATS @ home as 10.5-15 point favorite since 2000
6-0 S/U on road as 10.5-15 point favorite since 2007
11-0 S/U as 10.5-15 point favorite since 2009
15-3 S/U @ home as 15.5-20 point favorite since 1993
9-0 S/U on road as 15.5-20 point favorite since 1987
55-2 S/U @ home as 20.5 point or more favorite since 1985
6-0 S/U on road as 20.5 point or more favorite since 1987

Pointspread Analysis
Conference

15-0 S/U vs Indiana as 8 point or more favorite since 1987
vs Michigan - Michigan leads series 71-37-5
5-0 S/U & ATS vs Michigan as favorite since 2008
0-4 O/U vs Michigan as favorite since 2009
1-9 S/U vs Michigan as 13.5 point or more Dog since 1983
vs Nebraska - Nebraska leads series 9-2
0-5 S/U & ATS vs Nebraska as Dog since 1995
vs Northwestern - Michigan State leads series 40-19
Game 4-1 O/U vs Northwestern since 2016
6-0 S/U vs Northwestern as 19.5 point or more favorite since 1985
vs Ohio State - Ohio State leads series 34-15
2-13 S/U vs Ohio State as 6.5 point or more Dog since 1983
vs Penn State - Michigan State leads series 17-16-1
vs Penn State - Game 16-5-1 O/U since 1996
2-10 S/U vs Penn State as 6.5 point or more Dog since 1994
1-4 ATS vs Purdue since 2010
vs Purdue - Michigan State leads series 37-27-3
8-2 ATS vs Purdue as Dog since 1983
6-0 S/U vs Purdue as favorite since 2008
0-4 ATS vs Purdue as favorite since 2010
12-0 S/U vs Purdue as 8 point or more favorite since 1986
vs Rutgers - Michigan State leads series 8-4
Game 2-6 O/U vs Rutgers since 2004

Bowl Games

4-1 S/U in Rose Bowl
0-4 S/U & ATS in Bowl Games as 7.5-10 point Dog since 2009
3-0 ATS in Bowl Games as 3.5-7 point Dog since 2001

YOUNGSTOWN	21-1 S/U in 1st home game of season since 1999
Miami	8-3 S/U in 2nd road game of season since 2010
Miami	6-1 S/U & ATS prior to playing Nebraska since 1996
WKU	1-7 S/U prior to playing Rutgers since 1991
MICHIGAN	6-1 S/U prior to playing Purdue since 2008
MICHIGAN	3-11 ATS after playing Indiana since 2004
MICHIGAN	3-11 O/U after playing Indiana since 2004
Purdue	11-3 S/U after playing Michigan since 2007
Purdue	6-2 O/U after playing Michigan since 2013
MARYLAND	11-0 S/U prior to playing Ohio State since 2007
MARYLAND	9-2 ATS prior to playing Ohio State since 2007
Ohio State	9-3 S/U in final road game of season since 2009
Ohio State	9-3 ATS in final road game of season since 2009

12-1 S/U @ home when #1 ranked all time
21-4 S/U when ranked vs Indiana all time
4-0 S/U & ATS when ranked vs Penn State since 2010
2-11 S/U on road vs #1 ranked teams all time
0-6 S/U @ home vs #2 ranked teams since 1967
1-9 S/U vs #3 ranked teams since 1960
9-2 ATS vs ranked Michigan since 2009
10-3 O/U vs ranked Penn State since 1996

Copyright © 2021 by Steve's Football Bible, LLC

MIDDLE TENNESSEE BLUE RAIDERS   C-USA East

2020-Middle Tennessee		Opponent	MTSU	Opp	S/U	Line	ATS	Total	O/U	
9/5/2020	@	Army	0	42	L	3.5	L	54.0	U	
9/19/2020	vs	TROY	14	47	L	2.5	L	65.0	U	"The Palladium Trophy"
9/26/2020	@	Texas-San Antonio	35	37	L	-16.5	L	58.5	O	
10/3/2020	vs	WESTERN KENTUCKY	17	20	L	7.0	W	51.0	U	100 Miles of Hate Rivalry
10/10/2020	@	Florida International	38	28	W	6.5	W	56.5	O	
10/17/2020	vs	NORTH TEXAS	35	52	L	-3.5	L	70.5	O	
10/24/2020	@	Rice	40	34	W	4.0	W	48.0	O	{OT}
11/14/2020	@	Marshall	14	42	L	23.5	L	55.5	O	
11/21/2020	@	Troy	20	17	W	10.5	W	60.5	U	"The Palladium Trophy"
Coach: Rick Stockstill		Season Record >>	213	319	3-6	ATS>>	4-5	O/U>>	5-4	
2019-Middle Tennessee		Opponent	MTSU	Opp	S/U	Line	ATS	Total	O/U	
8/31/2019	@	Michigan	21	40	L	36.5	W	55.0	O	
9/7/2019	vs	TENNESSEE STATE	45	26	W	-26.5	L	NT	---	
9/14/2019	vs	DUKE	18	41	L	6.5	L	51.0	O	
9/28/2019	@	Iowa	3	48	L	23.5	L	51.0	T	
10/5/2019	vs	MARSHALL	24	13	W	4.0	W	53.5	U	
10/12/2019	@	Florida Atlantic	13	28	L	12.5	L	63.5	U	
10/19/2019	@	North Texas	30	33	L	7.0	W	59.5	O	
10/26/2019	vs	FLORIDA INTERNATIONAL	50	17	W	1.5	W	57.5	O	
11/2/2019	@	Charlotte	20	34	L	-3.5	L	65.5	U	
11/16/2019	vs	RICE	28	31	L	-13.0	L	47.0	O	
11/23/2019	vs	OLD DOMINION	38	17	W	-13.5	W	47.0	O	
11/30/2019	@	Western Kentucky	26	31	L	10.0	W	46.0	O	100 Miles of Hate Rivalry
Coach: Rick Stockstill		Season Record >>	316	359	4-8	ATS>>	6-6	O/U>>	7-3-1	
2018-Middle Tennessee		Opponent	MTSU	Opp	S/U	Line	ATS	Total	O/U	
9/1/2018	@	Vanderbilt	7	35	L	3.0	L	56.5	U	
9/8/2018	vs	TENNESSEE-MARTIN	61	37	W	-19.5	W	NT	---	
9/15/2018	@	Georgia	7	49	L	33.5	L	59.5	U	
9/29/2018	vs	FLORIDA ATLANTIC	25	24	W	2.5	W	62.0	U	
10/6/2018	@	Marshall	34	24	W	3.0	W	50.5	O	
10/13/2018	@	Florida International	21	24	L	1.5	L	60.5	U	
10/20/2018	vs	CHARLOTTE	21	13	W	-15.0	W	50.0	U	
10/27/2018	@	Old Dominion	51	17	W	-4.5	W	62.0	O	
11/3/2018	vs	WESTERN KENTUCKY	29	10	W	-11.5	W	52.5	U	100 Miles of Hate Rivalry
11/10/2018	@	Texas-El Paso	48	32	W	-13.5	W	48.0	O	
11/17/2018	@	Kentucky	23	34	L	16.5	W	48.0	O	
11/24/2018	vs	ALABAMA-BIRMINGHAM	27	3	W	3.0	W	52.0	U	
12/1/2018	vs	ALABAMA-BIRMINGHAM	25	27	L	-1.0	L	44.0	O	C-USA Championship Game
12/15/2018	vs	Appalachian State	13	45	L	6.5	L	49.0	O	New Orleans Bowl
Coach: Rick Stockstill		Season Record >>	392	374	8-6	ATS>>	8-6	O/U>>	6-7	
2017-Middle Tennessee		Opponent	MTSU	Opp	S/U	Line	ATS	Total	O/U	
9/2/2017	vs	VANDERBILT	6	28	L	2.0	L	57.0	U	
9/9/2017	@	Syracuse	30	23	W	7.5	W	72.0	U	
9/16/2017	@	Minnesota	3	34	L	14.0	L	49.5	U	
9/23/2017	vs	BOWLING GREEN	24	13	W	-7.0	W	53.5	U	
9/30/2017	@	Florida Atlantic	20	38	L	2.5	L	60.0	U	
10/7/2017	vs	FLORIDA INTERNATIONAL	37	17	W	-8.0	W	53.5	O	
10/14/2017	@	Alabama-Birmingham	23	25	L	-4.0	L	55.0	U	
10/20/2017	vs	MARSHALL	10	38	L	1.5	L	49.5	U	
11/4/2017	vs	TEXAS-EL PASO	30	3	W	-20.5	W	50.5	O	
11/11/2017	@	Charlotte	35	21	W	-16.0	L	50.0	O	
11/17/2017	@	Western Kentucky	38	41	L	PK	L	56.0	O	100 Miles of Hate Rivalry
11/25/2017	vs	OLD DOMINION	41	10	W	-14.0	W	48.5	O	
12/16/2017	vs	Arkansas State	35	30	W	3.5	W	60.5	O	Camelia Bowl
Coach: Rick Stockstill		Season Record >>	332	321	7-6	ATS>>	6-7	O/U>>	5-8	

Copyright © 2021 by Steve's Football Bible, LLC

MIDDLE TENNESSEE BLUE RAIDERS   C-USA East

STADIUM: Johnny "Red" Floyd Stadium {30,788}			Location: Murfreesboro, TN					COACH: Rick Stockstill	
DATE		Opponent	Mtsu	Opp	S/U	Line	ATS	Total	O/U	Trends & Angles
9/4/2021	vs	*MONMOUTH*								1st Meeting
9/11/2021	@	*Virginia Tech*								1st Meeting
9/18/2021	@	Texas-San Antonio								vs Texas-San Antonio - UTSA leads series 2-1
9/25/2021	@	Charlotte								vs Charlotte - MTSU leads series 4-1
10/2/2021	vs	MARSHALL								vs Marshall - Marshall leads series 6-4
10/9/2021	@	*Liberty*								vs Liberty - MTSU leads series 1-0
10/23/2021	@	*Connecticut*								vs Connecticut - MTSU leads series 2-0
10/30/2021	vs	SOUTHERN MISS								vs Southern Miss - MTSU leads series 3-0
11/6/2021	@	Western Kentucky								0-3 S/U @ Western Kentucky since 2015
11/13/2021	vs	FLA INTERNATIONAL								vs Florida International - MTSU leads series 11-5
11/20/2021	vs	OLD DOMINION								vs Old Dominion - MTSU leads series 4-0
11/27/2021	@	Florida Atlantic								vs Florida Atlantic - MTSU leads series 12-4
12/4/2021	vs									C-USA Championship
	vs									BOWL GAME

Pointspread Analysis Non-Conference		Pointspread Analysis Conference
1-35 S/U vs Non-Conf. as 15.5 point or more Dog since 1999		10-0 S/U vs Florida Atlantic as favorite since 2005
0-8 S/U vs Non-conf. as 3 point or less Dog since 2010		0-5 O/U vs Florida Atlantic as Dog since 2007
8-0 S/U vs Non-Conf. as 20.5 point or more favorite since 2001		8-1 S/U vs Florida International as favorite since 2006
Dog		5-1 S/U vs Western Kentucky as favorite since 2008
1-38 S/U as 15.5 point or more Dog since 1999		vs Western Kentucky - Series tied 34-34-1
3-15 S/U as 10.5-15 point Dog since 1999		Game 7-2 O/U vs Western Kentucky since 2011
6-0 ATS as 7.5-10 point Dog since 2012		
2-8 S/U on road as 3.5-7 point Dog since 2011		**Bowl Games**
4-11 S/U as 3 point or less Dog since 2014		1-5 S/U & ATS in Bowl Games since 2011
2-9 O/U @ home as 3 point or less Dog since 2010		
Favorite	Charlotte	1-7 ATS prior to playing Marshall since 2013
6-2 S/U @ home as 3 point or less favorite since 2007	MARSHALL	9-2 S/U in 2nd home game of season since 2010
2-6 O/U @ home as 3 point or less favorite since 2007	Liberty	6-2 S/U after playing Marshall since 2013
15-4 S/U on road as 3.5-7 point favorite since 2006	FIU	10-1 S/U after playing Western Kentucky since 2008
5-1 S/U @ home as 3.5-7 point favorite since 2012	FIU	9-2 ATS after playing Western Kentucky since 2008
8-1 S/U @ home as 7.5-10 point favorite since 2001	ODU	1-9 ATS after playing Florida International since 2011
12-2 S/U @ home as 15.5-20 point favorite since 2000	ODU	8-1 S/U in final home game of season since 2012
10-2 O/U @ home as 15.5-20 point favorite since 2001	ODU	9-3-1 ATS in final home game of season since 2008
15-0 S/U as 20.5 point or more favorite since 2000	FAU	3-13 S/U in final road game of season since 2005
		0-18 S/U vs ranked teams all time

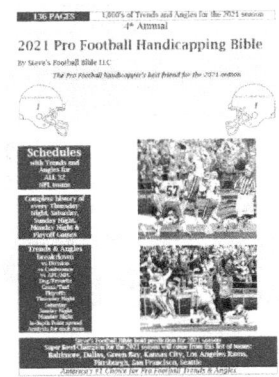

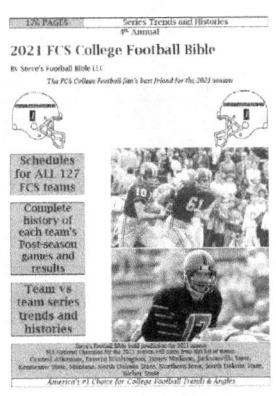

2021 Pro Football Bible $24.95   2021 FCS College Football Bible $19.95

www.stevesfootballbible.com

Copyright © 2021 by Steve's Football Bible, LLC

MINNESOTA GOLDEN GOPHERS BIG TEN West

2020-Minnesota		Opponent	MN	Opp	S/U	Line	ATS	Total	O/U	
10/24/2020	vs	MICHIGAN	24	49	L	2.5	L	54.5	O	*"Little Brown Jug"*
10/30/2020	@	Maryland	44	45	L	-17.0	L	60.5	O	{OT}
11/7/2020	@	Illinois	41	14	W	-7.5	W	64.5	O	
11/13/2020	vs	IOWA	7	35	L	3.0	L	58.0	U	*"Floyd of Rosedale"*
11/20/2020	vs	PURDUE	34	31	W	2.5	W	62.5	O	
12/12/2020	@	Nebraska	24	17	W	8.5	W	61.5	U	
12/19/2020	@	Wisconsin	17	20	L	10.0	W	47.0	U	*"Paul Bunyan Axe"*
Coach: P.J. Fleck		Season Record >>	191	211	3-4	ATS>>	4-3	O/U>>	4-3	

2019-Minnesota		Opponent	MN	Opp	S/U	Line	ATS	Total	O/U	
8/30/2019	vs	*SOUTH DAKOTA STATE*	28	21	W	-14.0	L	NT	---	
9/7/2019	@	*Fresno State*	38	35	W	-3.0	T	46.0	O	{2 OT}
9/14/2019	vs	*GEORGIA SOUTHERN*	35	32	W	-17.0	L	45.5	O	
9/28/2019	@	Purdue	38	31	W	1.5	W	56.0	O	
10/5/2019	vs	ILLINOIS	40	17	W	-14.5	W	57.0	T	
10/12/2019	vs	NEBRASKA	34	7	W	-7.5	W	47.5	U	
10/19/2019	@	Rutgers	42	7	W	-28.5	W	46.5	O	
10/26/2019	vs	MARYLAND	52	10	W	-14.5	W	58.5	O	
11/9/2019	vs	PENN STATE	31	26	W	5.5	W	48.5	O	*"Governor's Victory Bell"*
11/16/2019	@	Iowa	19	23	L	3.0	L	45.0	U	*"Floyd of Rosedale"*
11/23/2019	@	Northwestern	38	22	W	-15.5	W	41.5	O	
11/30/2019	vs	WISCONSIN	17	38	L	3.0	L	45.0	O	*"Paul Bunyan Axe"*
1/1/2020	vs	**Auburn**	**31**	**24**	**W**	7.0	**W**	**53.5**	**O**	Outback Bowl
Coach: P.J. Fleck		Season Record >>	443	293	11-2	ATS>>	8-4-1	O/U>>	9-2-1	

2018-Minnesota		Opponent	MN	Opp	S/U	Line	ATS	Total	O/U	
8/30/2018	vs	*NEW MEXICO STATE*	48	10	W	-21.5	W	47.5	O	
9/8/2018	vs	*FRESNO STATE*	21	14	W	PK	W	50.0	U	
9/15/2018	vs	*MIAMI-OHIO*	26	3	W	-13.5	W	46.5	U	
9/29/2018	@	Maryland	13	42	L	PK	L	46.5	O	
10/6/2018	vs	IOWA	31	48	L	7.0	L	41.5	O	*"Floyd of Rosedale"*
10/13/2018	@	Ohio State	14	30	L	29.5	W	60.0	U	
10/20/2018	@	Nebraska	28	53	L	5.5	L	55.0	O	
10/26/2019	vs	INDIANA	38	31	W	2.5	W	54.0	O	
11/3/2018	@	Illinois	31	55	L	-10.0	L	62.0	O	
11/10/2018	vs	PURDUE	41	10	W	10.5	W	58.0	U	
11/17/2018	vs	NORTHWESTERN	14	24	L	-3.0	L	48.5	U	
11/24/2018	@	Wisconsin	37	15	W	12.5	W	54.0	U	*"Paul Bunyan Axe"*
12/26/2018	vs	**Georgia Tech**	**34**	**10**	**W**	5.0	**W**	**57.0**	**U**	Quick Lane Bowl
Coach: P.J. Fleck		Season Record >>	376	345	7-6	ATS>>	8-5	O/U>>	6-7	

2017-Minnesota		Opponent	MN	Opp	S/U	Line	ATS	Total	O/U	
8/31/2017	vs	*BUFFALO*	17	7	W	-22.0	L	51.5	U	
9/9/2017	@	*Oregon State*	48	14	W	2.5	W	50.5	O	
9/16/2017	vs	*MIDDLE TENNESSEE*	34	3	W	-14.0	W	49.5	U	
9/30/2017	vs	MARYLAND	24	31	L	-12.5	L	45.0	O	
10/7/2017	@	Purdue	17	31	L	3.0	L	45.0	O	
10/14/2017	vs	MICHIGAN STATE	27	30	L	4.5	W	41.0	O	
10/21/2017	vs	ILLINOIS	24	17	W	-13.5	L	48.0	U	
10/28/2017	@	Iowa	10	17	L	6.5	L	43.0	U	*"Floyd of Rosedale"*
11/4/2017	@	Michigan	10	33	L	15.5	L	39.0	O	*"Little Brown Jug"*
11/11/2017	vs	NEBRASKA	54	21	W	-2.0	W	47.5	O	
11/18/2017	@	Northwestern	0	39	L	7.0	L	39.0	T	
11/25/2017	vs	WISCONSIN	0	31	L	19.5	L	43.0	U	*"Paul Bunyan Axe"*
Coach: P.J. Fleck		Season Record >>	265	274	5-7	ATS>>	4-8	O/U>>	6-5-1	

Copyright © 2021 by Steve's Football Bible, LLC

MINNESOTA GOLDEN GOPHERS BIG TEN West

STADIUM: TCF Bank Stadium {50,805}								Location: Mpls, MN		COACH: P.J. Fleck
DATE		Opponent	Minn	Opp	S/U	Line	ATS	Total	O/U	Trends & Angles
9/2/2021	vs	OHIO STATE								0-13 S/U @ home vs Ohio State since 1984
9/11/2021	vs	*MIAMI-OHIO*								vs Miami-Ohio - Minnesota leads series 4-0
9/18/2021	@	*Colorado*								vs Colorado - Colorado leads series 3-0
9/25/2021	vs	*BOWLING GREEN*								vs Bowling Green - Minnesota leads series 2-1
10/2/2021	@	Purdue								3-10 S/U @ Purdue since 1992
10/16/2021	vs	NEBRASKA								Game 3-1 O/U @ home vs Nebraska since 2013
10/23/2021	vs	MARYLAND								vs Maryland - Maryland leads series 4-2
10/30/2021	@	Northwestern								10-2 ATS @ Northwestern since 1993
11/6/2021	vs	ILLINOIS								vs Illinois - Minnesota leads series 40-30-3
11/13/2021	@	Iowa								0-13 S/U @ Iowa as Dog since 1991
11/20/2021	@	Indiana								1-7 S/U @ Indiana as Dog since 1983
11/27/2021	vs	WISCONSIN								0-8 S/U @ home vs Wisconsin since 2005
12/4/2021	vs									Big Ten Championship
	vs									BOWL GAME

Pointspread Analysis Non-Conference		Pointspread Analysis Conference
0-10 S/U vs Non-Conf. as 10.5 point or more Dog since 1985		5-0 S/U vs Illinois as 4.5 point or less favorite since 1996
6-0 S/U vs Non-Conf. as 3 point or less Dog since 1989		3-0 S/U & ATS vs Illinois as Dog since 2008
5-0 S/U vs Non-Conf. as 3 point or less favorite since 1998		vs Indiana - Minnesota leads series 39-26-3
7-1 S/U vs Non-Conf. as 7.5-10 point favorite since 2000		vs Iowa - Minnesota leads series 63-49-2
14-2 S/U vs Non-Conf. as 10.5-15 point favorite since 1994		vs Nebraska - Minnesota leads series 34-25-2
22-3 S/U vs Non-Conf. as 15.5 point or more favorite since 1995		0-6 S/U vs Nebraska as 19 point or more Dog since 1983
Dog		vs Northwestern - Minnesota leads series 54-36-5
0-15 S/U on road as 25.5 point or more Dog since 1983		Game 1-7-1 O/U vs Northwestern since 2011
0-11 S/U @ home as 20.5 point or more Dog since 1983		0-5 S/U vs Northwestern as 5-10.5 point Dog since 1996
2-15 S/U on road as 20.5-25 point Dog since 1989		7-0-1 S/U vs Northwestern as 10.5 point or more favorite since 1985
0-4 O/U @ home as 15.5-20 point Dog since 2011		6-0 S/U @ Northwestern as favorite since 1985
0-18 S/U on road as 15.5-20 point Dog since 1985		2-38 S/U vs Ohio State since 1969
3-10 ATS on road as 15.5-20 point Dog since 1990		vs Ohio State - Ohio State leads series 46-7
1-26 S/U as 15.5-20 point Dog since 1985		1-25 S/U vs Ohio State as Dog since 1983
14-3-1 ATS as 10.5-15 point Dog since 2007		1-9 S/U @ Purdue as Dog since 1992 {2-8 ATS}
3-12 S/U @ home as 10.5-15 point Dog since 1994		10-2 S/U vs Purdue as favorite since 1983
2-21 S/U on road as 3.5-7 point Dog since 1993		Game 8-1 O/U vs Purdue since 2011
5-32 S/U as 3.5-7 point Dog since 1993		vs Purdue - Minnesota leads series 40-33-3
9-19-1 ATS as 3.5-7 point Dog since 2000		vs Wisconsin - Wisconsin leads series 62-60-8
0-11 S/U @ home as 3.5-7 point Dog since 1992		1-16 S/U vs Wisconsin since 2004
7-0 O/U @ home as 3.5-7 point Dog since 2001		2-21 S/U vs Wisconsin as Dog since 1995
Favorite		1-7 ATS vs Wisconsin as favorite since 1987
7-3 S/U @ home as 3 point or less favorite since 1998		
10-4-1 ATS as 3 point or less favorite since 2006		1-17 S/U vs ranked Wisconsin since 1954
7-2-1 ATS on road as 3 point or less favorite since 1986		6-76 S/U on road vs ranked teams since 1970
8-2 S/U on road as 3 point or less favorite since 1986		2-16 S/U when ranked vs ranked teams since 1962
8-2 S/U on road as 3.5-7 point favorite since 1985		1-13 S/U on road when ranked vs ranked teams since 1942
5-0 O/U on road as 7.5-10 point favorite since 2000		
2-6 ATS @ home as 7.5-10 point favorite since 2003	MIAMI-OHIO	5-1 ATS after playing Ohio State since 2008
7-2 S/U on road as 10.5-15 point favorite since 1985	MIAMI-OHIO	9-1 S/U in 2nd home game of season since 2011
19-2 S/U @ home as 10.5-15 point favorite since 1994	Purdue	5-12 S/U in 2nd road game of season since 2004
8-0 S/U @ home as 15.5-20 point favorite since 2002	Purdue	10-2 O/U in 2nd road game of season since 2008
18-3 S/U @ home as 20.5 point or more favorite since 1995	NEBRASKA	2-13 S/U after playing Purdue since 2005
Bowl Games	ILLINOIS	8-3 O/U after playing Northwestern since 2009
0-4 S/U vs Big 12 in Bowl Games	Indiana	11-3-1 ATS in final road game of season since 2006
4-0 S/U & ATS in Bowl Games since 2015	Indiana	2-8 S/U in final road game of season since 2011
1-3 O/U in Bowl Games since 2015	WISCONSIN	5-1 ATS after playing Indiana since 2005
	WISCONSIN	3-8 O/U in final home game of season since 2010

Copyright © 2021 by Steve's Football Bible, LLC

MISSISSIPPI REBELS   SEC West

2020-Mississippi		Opponent	Miss	Opp	S/U	Line	ATS	Total	O/U	
9/26/2020	vs	FLORIDA	35	51	L	14.0	L	58.5	O	
10/3/2020	@	Kentucky	42	41	W	6.5	W	63.0	O	{OT}
10/10/2020	vs	ALABAMA	48	63	L	24.0	W	74.0	O	
10/17/2020	@	Arkansas	20	33	L	-1.5	L	75.0	U	
10/24/2020	vs	AUBURN	28	35	L	3.5	L	73.5	U	
10/31/2020	@	Vanderbilt	54	21	W	-17.0	W	63.5	O	
11/14/2020	vs	SOUTH CAROLINA	59	42	W	-12.0	W	73.0	O	
11/28/2020	vs	MISSISSIPPI STATE	31	24	W	-10.0	L	70.5	U	""Egg Bowl" - "Golden Egg Trophy""
12/19/2020	@	Lsu	48	53	L	PK	L	74.5	O	
1/2/2021	vs	Indiana	26	20	W	7.5	W	67.5	U	Outback Bowl
Coach: Lane Kiffin		Season Record >>	391	383	5-5	ATS>>	5-5	O/U>>	6-4	
2019-Mississippi		Opponent	Miss	Opp	S/U	Line	ATS	Total	O/U	
8/31/2019	@	Memphis	10	15	L	3.5	L	64.5	U	
9/7/2019	vs	ARKANSAS	31	17	W	-5.5	W	51.5	U	
9/14/2019	vs	SE LOUISIANA	40	29	W	-30.5	L	NT	---	
9/21/2019	vs	CALIFORNIA	20	28	L	-3.0	L	41.5	O	
9/28/2019	@	Alabama	31	59	L	37.5	W	62.5	O	
10/5/2019	vs	VANDERBILT	31	6	W	-7.0	W	64.5	U	
10/12/2019	@	Missouri	27	38	L	11.5	W	56.5	O	
10/19/2019	vs	TEXAS A&M	17	24	L	6.0	L	55.5	U	
11/2/2019	@	Auburn	14	20	L	17.5	W	53.5	U	
11/9/2019	vs	NEW MEXICO STATE	41	3	W	-29.0	W	65.0	U	
11/16/2019	vs	LSU	37	58	L	21.5	W	67.0	O	"Magnolia Bowl Trophy"
11/28/2019	@	Mississippi State	20	21	L	-2.0	L	59.0	U	""Egg Bowl" - "Golden Egg Trophy""
Coach: Matt Luke		Season Record >>	319	318	4-8	ATS>>	7-5	O/U>>	4-7	
2018-Mississippi		Opponent	Miss	Opp	S/U	Line	ATS	Total	O/U	
9/1/2018	vs	Texas Tech	47	27	W	-2.0	W	71.5	O	NRG Stadium
9/8/2018	vs	SOUTHERN ILLINOIS	76	41	W	-27.5	W	NT	---	
9/15/2018	vs	ALABAMA	7	62	L	22.5	L	71.0	U	
9/22/2018	vs	KENT STATE	38	17	W	-28.0	L	75.0	U	
9/29/2018	@	Lsu	16	45	L	11.5	L	59.0	O	"Magnolia Bowl Trophy"
10/6/2018	vs	LOUISIANA-MONROE	70	21	W	-24.0	W	76.0	O	
10/13/2018	@	Arkansas	37	33	W	-6.5	L	66.5	O	War Memorial Stadium
10/20/2018	vs	AUBURN	16	31	L	5.0	L	63.5	U	
11/3/2018	vs	SOUTH CAROLINA	44	48	L	-2.5	L	69.5	O	
11/10/2018	@	Texas A&M	24	38	L	13.0	L	67.5	U	
11/17/2018	@	Vanderbilt	29	36	L	3.0	L	73.0	U	{OT}
11/22/2018	vs	MISSISSIPPI STATE	3	35	L	12.5	L	61.0	U	""Egg Bowl" - "Golden Egg Trophy""
Coach: Matt Luke		Season Record >>	407	434	5-7	ATS>>	3-9	O/U>>	5-6	PROBATION
2017-Mississippi		Opponent	Miss	Opp	S/U	Line	ATS	Total	O/U	
9/2/2017	vs	SOUTH ALABAMA	47	27	W	-22.0	L	59.0	O	
9/9/2017	vs	TENNESSEE-MARTIN	45	23	W	-33.5	L	62.0	O	
9/16/2017	@	California	16	27	L	-7.0	L	68.5	U	
9/30/2017	@	Alabama	3	66	L	29.0	L	55.0	O	
10/7/2017	@	Auburn	23	44	L	21.0	T	55.5	O	
10/14/2017	vs	VANDERBILT	57	35	W	-3.0	W	56.0	O	
10/21/2017	vs	LSU	24	40	L	6.5	L	59.5	O	"Magnolia Bowl Trophy"
10/28/2017	vs	ARKANSAS	37	38	L	-2.0	L	63.0	O	
11/4/2017	@	Kentucky	37	34	W	3.5	W	63.5	O	
11/11/2017	vs	LOUISIANA-LAFAYETTE	50	22	W	-22.0	W	67.0	O	
11/18/2017	vs	TEXAS A&M	24	31	L	3.0	L	69.0	U	
11/23/2017	@	Mississippi State	31	28	W	14.0	W	64.5	U	""Egg Bowl" - "Golden Egg Trophy""
Coach: Matt Luke (I)		Season Record >>	394	415	6-6	ATS>>	4-7-1	O/U>>	9-3	PROBATION

Copyright © 2021 by Steve's Football Bible, LLC

MISSISSIPPI REBELS   SEC West

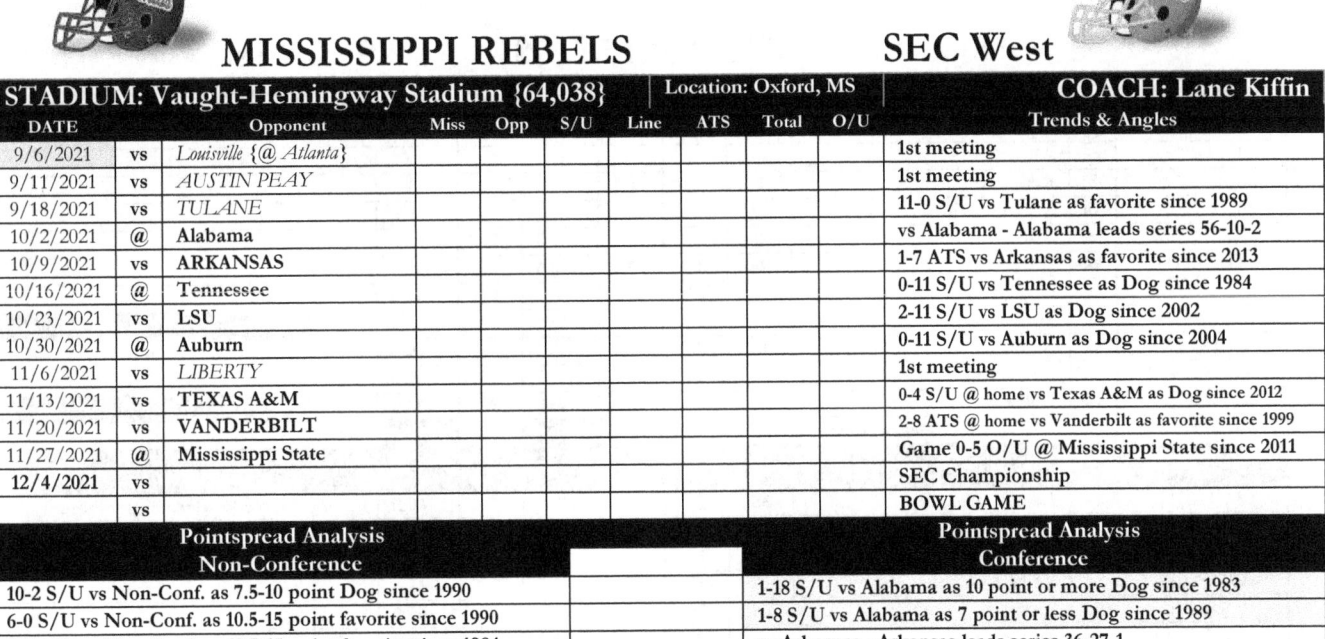

STADIUM: Vaught-Hemingway Stadium {64,038}		Location: Oxford, MS							COACH: Lane Kiffin	
DATE		Opponent	Miss	Opp	S/U	Line	ATS	Total	O/U	Trends & Angles
9/6/2021	vs	*Louisville {@ Atlanta}*								1st meeting
9/11/2021	vs	*AUSTIN PEAY*								1st meeting
9/18/2021	vs	*TULANE*								11-0 S/U vs Tulane as favorite since 1989
10/2/2021	@	Alabama								vs Alabama - Alabama leads series 56-10-2
10/9/2021	vs	ARKANSAS								1-7 ATS vs Arkansas as favorite since 2013
10/16/2021	@	Tennessee								0-11 S/U vs Tennessee as Dog since 1984
10/23/2021	vs	LSU								2-11 S/U vs LSU as Dog since 2002
10/30/2021	@	Auburn								0-11 S/U vs Auburn as Dog since 2004
11/6/2021	vs	*LIBERTY*								1st meeting
11/13/2021	vs	TEXAS A&M								0-4 S/U @ home vs Texas A&M as Dog since 2012
11/20/2021	vs	VANDERBILT								2-8 ATS @ home vs Vanderbilt as favorite since 1999
11/27/2021	@	Mississippi State								Game 0-5 O/U @ Mississippi State since 2011
12/4/2021	vs									SEC Championship
	vs									BOWL GAME

Pointspread Analysis Non-Conference		Pointspread Analysis Conference
10-2 S/U vs Non-Conf. as 7.5-10 point Dog since 1990		1-18 S/U vs Alabama as 10 point or more Dog since 1983
6-0 S/U vs Non-Conf. as 10.5-15 point favorite since 1990		1-8 S/U vs Alabama as 7 point or less Dog since 1989
2-7 ATS vs Non-Conf. as 10.5-15 point favorite since 1984		vs Arkansas - Arkansas leads series 36-27-1
46-1 S/U vs Non-Conf. as 15.5 point or more favorite since 1990		9-3 S/U vs Arkansas as favorite since 1991
6-0 S/U vs Tulane as 7.5 point or less favorite since 1985		1-6 S/U @ home vs Arkansas as Dog since 1985
6-0 S/U vs Tulane as 15.5 point or more favorite since 1992		0-6 S/U vs Arkansas as 4.0-6.0 point Dog since 1985
14-2 S/U @ home vs Tulane since 1959		0-5 ATS vs Arkansas as 4.0-6.0 point Dog since 1987
vs Tulane - Ole Miss leads series 42-29		vs Auburn - Auburn leads series 33-10
Dog		0-14 S/U vs Auburn as 10 point or more Dog since 1984
1-20 S/U as 20.5 point or more Dog since 1994		vs LSU - LSU leads series 64-41-4
0-11 S/U @ home as 15.5 point or more Dog since 1994		1-10 S/U vs LSU as 12 point or more Dog since 1987
0-12 S/U as 15.5-20 point Dog since 2004		7-0-1 O/U vs LSU as 12 point or more Dog since 1987
8-2 ATS as 15.5-20 point Dog since 2006		vs Mississippi State - Mississippi leads series 62-48-6
4-19 S/U on road as 10.5-15 point Dog since 1987		Game 4-15 O/U vs Mississippi State since 2002
4-9 O/U on road as 10.5-15 point Dog since 2002		0-8 S/U @ Tennessee since 1985
1-10 S/U @ home as 10.5-15 point Dog since 1983		vs Texas A&M - Texas A&M leads series 9-3
3-12 S/U on road as 7.5-10 point Dog since 1991		Game 0-6 O/U vs Texas A&M since 2014
2-19 S/U @ home as 3.5-7 point Dog since 1995		vs Vanderbilt - Mississippi leads series 53-40-2
1-7 O/U @ home as 3 point or less Dog since 2006		2-9 ATS vs Vanderbilt as 12 point or more favorite since 1990
9-3 S/U on road as 3 point or less Dog since 1988		
10-3 ATS on road as 3 point or less Dog since 1985		4-0 ATS vs ranked Texas A&M since 2013
Favorite		0-13 S/U vs #1 ranked teams all time
9-0 O/U @ home as 3 point or less favorite since 2008		0-19 S/U vs ranked Auburn all time
0-7 O/U on road as 3 point or less favorite since 2007		14-1 S/U when ranked vs Vanderbilt since 1948 {5-0 @ home}
1-8 ATS on road as 3 point or less favorite since 2001		**Bowl Games**
10-0 S/U @ home as 3.5-7 point favorite since 2008		4-0 S/U in Liberty Bowl
1-10 O/U as 3.5-7 point favorite since 2013		4-0 S/U & ATS in Independence Bowl since 1986
2-7 S/U on road as 3.5-7 point favorite since 2009		7-2 S/U & ATS vs Big 12 in Bowl Games since 1986
1-10 ATS on road as 3.5-7 point favorite since 2004		3-0 S/U & ATS vs Oklahoma State in Bowl Games since 2004
4-13 ATS as 10.5-15 point favorite since 1984		0-3 O/U vs Oklahoma State in Bowl Games since 2004
12-4 ATS as 15.5-20 point favorite since 1990		4-0 S/U vs ACC in Bowl Games since 1968
8-0 S/U on road as 15.5 point or more favorite since 1994		12-2 S/U in Bowl Games since 1992
25-1 S/U @ home as 15.5 point or more favorite since 1990		12-2 ATS in Bowl Games since 1992
55-2 S/U as 15.5 point or more favorite since 1990		6-1 S/U in Sugar Bowl since 1958
	AUSTIN PEAY	8-1 S/U in 1st home game of season since 2012
	TULANE	10-2 S/U prior to playing Alabama since 2009
	LSU	2-9 S/U prior to playing Auburn since 2010
	LSU	3-12-2 O/U prior to playing Auburn since 2004
	VANDERBILT	2-9 S/U prior to playing Mississippi State since 2010
	M State	3-14 S/U in final road game of season since 2004

Copyright © 2021 by Steve's Football Bible, LLC

MISSISSIPPI STATE BULLDOGS   SEC West

2020-Mississippi State		Opponent	MSU	Opp	S/U	Line	ATS	Total	O/U	
9/26/2020	@	Lsu	44	34	W	14.0	W	57.0	O	
10/3/2020	vs	ARKANSAS	14	21	L	-17.0	L	68.5	U	
10/10/2020	@	Kentucky	2	24	L	3.0	L	57.5	U	
10/17/2020	vs	TEXAS A&M	14	28	L	3.5	L	57.0	U	
10/31/2020	@	Alabama	0	41	L	29.0	L	63.5	U	
11/7/2020	vs	VANDERBILT	24	17	W	-18.5	L	45.0	U	
11/21/2020	@	Georgia	24	31	L	26.5	W	44.0	O	
11/28/2020	@	Mississippi	24	31	L	10.0	W	70.5	U	""Egg Bowl" - "Golden Egg Trophy""
12/12/2020	vs	AUBURN	10	24	L	5.5	L	50.5	U	
12/19/2020	vs	MISSOURI	51	32	W	1.5	W	49.0	O	
12/31/2020	vs	Tulsa	28	26	W	-1.0	W	44.5	O	Armed Forces Bowl
Coach: Mike Leach		Season Record >>	235	309	4-7	ATS>>	5-6	O/U>>	4-7	
2019-Mississippi State		Opponent	MSU	Opp	S/U	Line	ATS	Total	O/U	
8/31/2019	vs	Louisiana-Lafayette	38	28	W	-18.5	L	60.5	O	Mercedes Benz Superdome
9/7/2019	vs	SOUTHERN MISSISSIPPI	35	15	W	-15.5	W	51.0	U	
9/14/2019	vs	KANSAS STATE	24	31	L	-7.0	L	50.5	O	
9/21/2019	vs	KENTUCKY	28	13	W	-5.5	W	48.0	U	
9/28/2019	@	Auburn	23	56	L	8.0	L	60.0	O	
10/12/2019	@	Tennessee	10	20	L	-5.0	L	52.0	U	
10/19/2019	vs	LSU	13	36	L	19.0	L	62.5	U	
10/26/2019	@	Texas A&M	30	49	L	10.5	L	50.0	O	
11/2/2019	@	Arkansas	54	24	W	-7.0	W	59.0	O	
11/16/2019	vs	ALABAMA	7	38	L	19.0	L	61.5	U	
11/23/2019	vs	ABILENE CHRISTIAN	45	7	W	-37.0	W	NT	---	
11/28/2019	vs	MISSISSIPPI	21	20	W	2.0	W	59.0	U	""Egg Bowl" - "Golden Egg Trophy""
12/30/2019	vs	Louisville	28	38	L	-4.5	L	63.5	O	Music City Bowl
Coach: Joe Moorhead		Season Record >>	356	375	6-7	ATS>>	5-8	O/U>>	6-6	
2018-Mississippi State		Opponent	MSU	Opp	S/U	Line	ATS	Total	O/U	
9/1/2018	vs	STEPHEN F. AUSTIN	63	6	W	-48.0	W	NT	---	
9/8/2018	@	Kansas State	31	10	W	-7.0	W	52.5	U	
9/15/2018	vs	LOUISIANA-LAFAYETTE	56	10	W	33.5	W	63.0	O	
9/22/2018	@	Kentucky	7	28	L	-9.5	L	56.0	U	
9/29/2018	vs	FLORIDA	6	13	L	-7.0	L	51.0	U	
10/6/2018	vs	AUBURN	23	9	W	3.0	W	45.0	U	
10/20/2018	@	Lsu	3	19	L	6.0	L	45.0	U	
10/27/2018	vs	TEXAS A&M	28	13	W	-1.0	W	42.5	U	
11/3/2018	vs	LOUISIANA TECH	45	3	W	-23.0	W	48.5	U	
11/10/2018	@	Alabama	0	24	L	21.5	L	51.0	U	
11/17/2018	vs	ARKANSAS	52	6	W	-22.5	W	48.0	O	
11/22/2018	@	Mississippi	35	3	W	-12.5	W	61.0	U	""Egg Bowl" - "Golden Egg Trophy""
1/1/2019	vs	Iowa	22	27	L	-7.0	L	40.0	O	Outback Bowl
Coach: Joe Moorhead		Season Record >>	371	171	8-5	ATS>>	8-5	O/U>>	3-9	
2017-Mississippi State		Opponent	MSU	Opp	S/U	Line	ATS	Total	O/U	
9/2/2017	vs	CHARLESTON SOUTHERN	49	0	W	-21.5	W	62.5	U	
9/9/2017	@	Louisiana Tech	57	21	W	-10.5	W	67.0	O	
9/16/2017	vs	LSU	37	7	W	7.5	W	54.0	U	
9/23/2017	@	Georgia	3	31	L	2.5	L	50.0	U	
9/30/2017	@	Auburn	10	49	L	7.0	L	51.0	O	
10/14/2017	vs	BYU	35	10	W	-23.5	W	50.5	U	
10/21/2017	vs	KENTUCKY	45	7	W	-14.0	W	54.5	U	
10/28/2017	@	Texas A&M	35	14	W	-3.5	W	57.0	U	
11/4/2017	vs	MASSACHUSETTS	34	23	W	-33.5	L	56.5	O	
11/11/2017	vs	ALABAMA	24	31	L	14.0	W	49.5	U	
11/18/2017	@	Arkansas	28	21	W	-13.5	L	57.0	U	
11/23/2017	vs	MISSISSIPPI	28	31	L	-14.0	L	64.5	U	""Egg Bowl" - "Golden Egg Trophy""
12/30/2017	vs	Louisville	31	27	W	6.5	W	60.5	U	Gator Bowl
Coach: Dan Mullen		Season Record >>	416	272	9-4	ATS>>	8-5	O/U>>	4-9	

Copyright © 2021 by Steve's Football Bible, LLC

MISSISSIPPI STATE BULLDOGS   SEC West

STADIUM: Davis Wade Stadium @ Scott Field {61,337}		Location: Starkville, MS		COACH: Mike Leach					
DATE		Opponent	MSU	Opp	S/U	Line	ATS	Total	O/U	Trends & Angles
9/4/2021	vs	*LOUISIANA TECH*								4-0 S/U vs Louisiana Tech as favorite since 2011
9/11/2021	vs	*NC STATE*								vs NC State - Series tied 3-3
9/18/2021	@	*Memphis*								12-0 S/U vs Memphis since 1994
9/25/2021	vs	LSU								vs LSU - LSU leads series 73-38-3
10/2/2021	@	Texas A&M								1-4 S/U @ Texas A&M since 1937
10/16/2021	vs	**ALABAMA**								0-13 S/U vs Alabama as Dog since 2008
10/23/2021	@	Vanderbilt								6-0 S/U vs Vanderbilt as favorite since 1989
10/30/2021	vs	**KENTUCKY**								10-1 S/U @ home vs Kentucky as favorite since 1995
11/6/2021	@	Arkansas								3-13-1 S/U Arkansas as Dog since 1993
11/13/2021	@	Auburn								5-26 S/U vs Auburn as Dog since 1983
11/20/2021	vs	*TENNESSEE STATE*								1st meeting
11/27/2021	vs	**MISSISSIPPI**								vs Mississippi - Ole Miss leads series 62-48-6
12/4/2021	vs									SEC Championship
	vs									BOWL GAME

Pointspread Analysis Non-Conference		Pointspread Analysis Conference
0-7 S/U vs Non-Conf. as 10.5 point or more Dog since 1980		vs Alabama - Alabama leads series 85-17-3
5-1 S/U & ATS vs Non-Conf. as 3 point or less Dog since 1992		0-15 S/U vs Alabama as 16 point or more Dog since 1983
18-2 S/U vs Non-Conf. as 10.5-15 point favorite since 1983		0-9 S/U vs Alabama as 6.0-11.0 point Dog since 1985
12-1 S/U vs Non-Conf. as 15.5-20 point favorite since 2010		6-1 S/U vs Arkansas as favorite since 2012
20-1-1 S/U vs Non-Conf. as 25.5 point or more favorite since 1991		vs Arkansas - Arkansas leads series 17-12-1
11-0 S/U vs Memphis as favorite since 1994		0-11 S/U vs Arkansas as 7 point or more Dog since 1995
5-0 ATS vs Memphis as favorite since 2000		7-0 O/U vs Arkansas as Dog since 2007
Dog		vs Auburn - Auburn leads series 62-29-3
0-20 S/U on road as 20.5 point or more Dog since 1987		1-13 S/U vs Auburn as 13.5 point or more Dog since 1983
1-23 S/U as 15.5-20 point Dog since 1983		vs Kentucky - Mississippi State leads series 25-23
0-11 S/U @ home as 10.5-15 point Dog since 2002		2-8 S/U vs Kentucky as Dog since 1984
0-13 S/U as 10.5-15 point Dog since 2007		0-9 O/U @ home vs Kentucky as favorite since 1999
7-1 ATS as 7.5-10 point Dog since 2014		1-5 S/U vs LSU as favorite since 1992
2-12 O/U as 3.5-7 point Dog since 2011		0-6 ATS vs LSU as favorite since 1992
2-10 S/U on road as 3.5-7 point Dog since 1998		0-6 S/U vs LSU as 7 point or less Dog since 1989
2-14 S/U @ home as 3.5-7 point Dog since 1996		0-5 O/U vs LSU as 7 point or less Dog since 1998
2-12 ATS @ home as 3.5-7 point Dog since 2002		1-14 S/U vs LSU as 12.5 point or more Dog since 1987
3-13 O/U as 3 point or less Dog since 2006		8-2 O/U vs LSU as 12.5 point or more Dog since 2004
Favorite		vs Texas A&M - Series tied 7-7
8-2 S/U & ATS as 3 point or less favorite since 2010		3-0 S/U & ATS vs Texas A&M as favorite since 2014
13-3 S/U @ home as 3.5-7 point favorite since 1997		8-2 S/U & ATS vs Vanderbilt since 1988
6-1 S/U @ home as 7.5-10 point favorite since 1983		vs Vanderbilt - M State leads series 14-7-2
14-2 S/U @ home as 10.5-15 point favorite since 1992	NC STATE	0-5 O/U after playing Louisiana Tech since 2008
7-0 S/U on road as 10.5-15 point favorite since 1998	NC STATE	8-2 S/U in 2nd home game of season since 2011
22-2 S/U as 10.5-15 point favorite since 1992	Memphis	6-1 S/U prior to playing LSU since 2013
38-6-1 S/U @ home as 15.5 point or more favorite since 1991	Texas A&M	9-3 ATS prior to playing Alabama since 2009
6-0 S/U on road as 15.5 point or more favorite since 1986	Texas A&M	6-2 O/U prior to playing Alabama since 2013
Bowl Games	Texas A&M	10-2 S/U prior to playing Alabama since 2009
10-3 ATS in Bowl Games since 1999	KENTUCKY	2-11 S/U prior to playing Arkansas since 2008
1-5 S/U vs ranked teams in Bowl games since 1980 {1-5 ATS}		
		12-95-1 S/U on road vs ranked teams since 1958
		1-10 S/U vs #1 ranked teams all time
		0-11 S/U vs #4 ranked teams since 1961
		0-11 S/U vs #5 ranked teams since 1971
		0-12 S/U when ranked vs ranked Alabama since 1974
		1-14 S/U vs ranked LSU since 2000

Copyright © 2021 by Steve's Football Bible, LLC

MISSOURI TIGERS

SEC East

2020-Missouri		Opponent	Mizzu	Opp	S/U	Line	ATS	Total	O/U	
9/26/2020	vs	ALABAMA	19	38	L	29.0	W	55.5	O	
10/3/2020	@	Tennessee	12	35	L	10.0	L	48.5	U	
10/10/2020	vs	LSU	45	41	W	13.5	W	53.0	O	
10/24/2020	vs	KENTUCKY	20	10	W	3.0	W	47.0	U	
10/31/2020	@	Florida	17	41	L	13.5	L	62.5	U	
11/21/2020	@	South Carolina	17	10	W	-4.5	W	57.5	U	
11/28/2020	vs	VANDERBILT	41	0	W	-14.0	W	51.5	U	
12/5/2020	vs	ARKANSAS	50	48	W	-2.0	T	55.5	O	"Battle Line Trophy"
12/12/2020	vs	GEORGIA	14	49	L	14.0	L	54.5	O	
12/19/2020	@	Mississippi State	32	51	L	-1.5	L	49.0	O	
Coach: Eli Drinkwitz		Season Record >>	267	323	5-5	ATS>>	5-4-1	O/U>>	5-5	
2019-Missouri		Opponent	Mizzu	Opp	S/U	Line	ATS	Total	O/U	
8/31/2019	@	Wyoming	31	37	L	-15.5	L	52.5	O	
9/7/2019	vs	WEST VIRGINIA	38	7	W	-13.5	W	62.5	U	
9/14/2019	vs	SE MISSOURI STATE	50	0	W	-34.0	W	NT	---	
9/21/2019	vs	SOUTH CAROLINA	34	14	W	-9.5	W	60.5	U	
10/5/2019	vs	TROY	42	10	W	-25.5	W	65.5	U	
10/12/2019	vs	MISSISSIPPI	38	27	W	-11.5	L	56.5	O	
10/19/2019	@	Vanderbilt	14	21	L	-21.0	L	55.5	U	
10/26/2019	@	Kentucky	7	29	L	-9.5	L	43.5	U	
11/9/2019	@	Georgia	0	27	L	18.5	L	47.5	U	
11/16/2019	vs	FLORIDA	6	23	L	6.5	L	51.0	U	
11/23/2019	vs	TENNESSEE	20	24	L	-2.0	L	47.5	U	
11/30/2019	@	Arkansas	24	14	W	-14.5	L	52.5	U	"Battle Line Trophy"
Coach: Barry Odom		Season Record >>	304	233	6-6	ATS>>	4-8	O/U>>	2-9	
2018-Missouri		Opponent	Mizzu	Opp	S/U	Line	ATS	Total	O/U	
9/1/2018	vs	TENNESSEE-MARTIN	51	14	W	-34.0	W	NT	---	
9/8/2018	vs	WYOMING	40	13	W	-19.5	W	52.5	O	
9/15/2018	@	Purdue	40	37	W	-5.0	L	67.5	O	
9/22/2018	vs	GEORGIA	29	43	L	14.5	W	68.0	O	
10/6/2018	@	South Carolina	35	37	L	PK	L	63.0	O	
10/13/2018	@	Alabama	10	39	L	28.0	L	72.5	U	
10/20/2018	vs	MEMPHIS	65	33	W	-8.5	W	69.5	O	
10/27/2018	vs	KENTUCKY	14	15	L	-7.5	L	54.5	U	
11/3/2018	@	Florida	38	17	W	5.0	W	58.5	U	
11/10/2018	vs	VANDERBILT	33	28	W	-14.0	L	64.5	U	
11/17/2018	@	Tennessee	50	17	W	-6.0	W	57.0	O	
11/24/2018	vs	ARKANSAS	38	0	W	-24.0	W	59.0	U	"Battle Line Trophy"
12/31/2018	vs	**Oklahoma State**	33	38	L	-9.5	L	72.5	U	Liberty Bowl
Coach: Barry Odom		Season Record >>	476	331	8-5	ATS>>	7-6	O/U>>	6-6	
2017-Missouri		Opponent	Mizzu	Opp	S/U	Line	ATS	Total	O/U	
9/2/2017	vs	MISSOURI STATE	72	43	W	-36.0	L	63.0	O	
9/9/2017	vs	SOUTH CAROLINA	13	31	L	-2.5	L	71.5	U	
9/16/2017	vs	PURDUE	3	35	L	-5.5	L	75.0	U	
9/23/2017	vs	AUBURN	14	51	L	18.0	L	60.5	O	
10/7/2017	@	Kentucky	34	40	L	8.5	W	59.5	O	
10/14/2017	@	Georgia	28	53	L	28.5	W	58.5	O	
10/21/2017	vs	IDAHO	68	21	W	-14.5	W	64.0	O	
10/28/2017	@	Connecticut	52	12	W	-13.0	W	75.5	U	
11/4/2017	vs	FLORIDA	45	16	W	-1.0	W	61.5	U	
11/11/2017	vs	TENNESSEE	50	17	W	-12.0	W	63.0	O	
11/18/2017	@	Vanderbilt	45	17	W	-7.5	W	64.5	U	
11/25/2017	@	Arkansas	48	45	W	-10.0	L	65.0	O	"Battle Line Trophy"
12/27/2017	vs	**Texas**	16	33	L	-3.0	L	62.0	U	Texas Bowl
Coach: Barry Odom		Season Record >>	488	414	7-6	ATS>>	7-6	O/U>>	7-6	

Copyright © 2021 by Steve's Football Bible, LLC

 **MISSOURI TIGERS**  **SEC East**

STADIUM: Faurot Field @ Memorial Stadium {60,168}								Location: Columbia, MO		COACH: Eli Drinkwitz	
DATE		Opponent	Mizz	Opp	S/U	Line	ATS	Total	O/U	Trends & Angles	
9/4/2021	vs	*CENTRAL MICHIGAN*								1st meeting	
9/11/2021	@	Kentucky								vs Kentucky - Kentucky leads series 7-4	
9/18/2021	vs	*SE MISSOURI*								vs SE Missouri - Missouri leads series 4-0	
9/25/2021	@	*Boston College*								1st meeting	
10/2/2021	vs	TENNESSEE								vs Tennessee - Missouri leads series 5-4	
10/9/2021	vs	*NORTH TEXAS*								vs North Texas - Missouri leads series 1-0	
10/16/2021	vs	TEXAS A&M								3-0 S/U @ home vs Texas A&M since 2003	
10/30/2021	@	Vanderbilt								Game 0-7 O/U vs Vanderbilt since 2014	
11/6/2021	@	Georgia								vs Georgia - Georgia leads series 9-1	
11/13/2021	vs	FLORIDA								vs Florida - Series tied 5-5	
11/20/2021	vs	SOUTH CAROLINA								Game 1-8 O/U vs South Carolina since 2012	
11/27/2021	@	Arkansas								6-0 S/U vs Arkansas as favorite since 2004	
12/4/2021	vs									SEC Championship	
	vs									BOWL GAME	

Pointspread Analysis Non-Conference		Pointspread Analysis Conference
0-4 S/U vs Non-Conf. as 15.5 point or more Dog since 1988		vs Arkansas - Missouri leads series 9-3
8-1 S/U vs Non-Conf. as 10.5-15 point favorite since 2006		0-7 S/U vs Georgia as Dog since 2014
10-1 O/U vs Non-Conf. as 10.5-15 point favorite since 2002		vs South Carolina - Missouri series 6-5
36-0 S/U vs Non-Conf. as 15.5 point or more favorite since 1986		3-1 S/U & ATS vs Tennessee as favorite since 2013
Dog		6-1 S/U vs Vanderbilt as favorite since 2013
7-2 ATS as 30.5 point or more Dog since 1986		vs Vanderbilt - Missouri leads series 8-4-1
5-14 ATS as 20.5-25 point Dog since 1985		**Bowl Games**
0-63 S/U as 15.5 point or more Dog since 1983		0-4 S/U in Bowl Games as 3.5 point or less Dog since 1983
1-36 S/U @ home as 10.5 point or more Dog since 1983		
4-39 S/U as 10.5-15 point Dog since 1983		
1-7 S/U on road as 7.5-10 point Dog since 2001		
5-0 ATS @ home as 7.5-10 point Dog since 1986		
8-1 S/U & ATS on road as 3.5-7 point Dog since 2010		30-7 S/U @ home when ranked since 1998
2-10 S/U @ home as 3.5-7 point Dog since 1999		0-6 S/U when ranked vs #1 ranked teams all time
Favorite		7-54 S/U on road vs ranked teams since 1982
1-6 O/U @ home as 3 point or less favorite since 2006		0-10 S/U @ home vs ranked teams since 2014
4-1 S/U & ATS on road as 3 point or less favorite since 2009		0-15 S/U vs #1 ranked teams all time
1-8 O/U @ home as 3.5-7 point favorite since 2005		0-8 S/U @ home vs #2 ranked teams since 1979
4-1 S/U on road as 7.5-10 point favorite since 2009		
13-1 S/U @ home as 10.5-15 point favorite since 2009	C. MICHIGAN	18-1 S/U in 1st home game of season since 2002
13-2 S/U on road as 10.5-15 point favorite since 1983	Boston College	2-7 O/U prior to playing Tennessee since 2012
18-1 S/U as 10.5-15 point favorite since 2009	NORTH TEXAS	1-6 O/U after playing Tennessee since 2014
11-4 ATS on road as 10.5-15 point favorite since 1983	Georgia	0-7 O/U prior to playing Florida since 2014
10-4 ATS as 10.5-15 point favorite since 2010	FLORIDA	7-1 O/U after playing Georgia since 2013
54-2-1 S/U @ home as 15.5 point or more favorite since 1983	S. CAROLINA	12-4 S/U in final home game of season since 2005
2-9 O/U as 20.5-25 point favorite since 2006	Arkansas	0-9 O/U after playing South Carolina since 2012

Copyright © 2021 by Steve's Football Bible, LLC

NAVY MIDSHIPMEN   AMERICAN West

2020-Navy		Opponent	Navy	Opp	S/U	Line	ATS	Total	O/U	
9/7/2020	vs	BYU	3	55	L	1.0	L	48.5	O	
9/19/2020	@	Tulane	27	24	W	6.5	W	47.5	O	
9/26/2020	@	Air Force	7	40	L	-6.0	L	47.5	U	
10/3/2020	vs	TEMPLE	31	29	W	4.0	W	51.0	O	
10/17/2020	@	East Carolina	27	23	W	-3.0	W	55.5	U	
10/24/2020	vs	HOUSTON	21	37	L	15.5	L	57.0	O	
10/31/2020	@	Smu	37	51	L	12.5	L	59.0	O	"Ganzs Trophy"
11/28/2020	vs	MEMPHIS	7	10	L	13.0	W	63.5	U	
12/5/2020	vs	TULSA	6	19	L	12.0	L	45.5	U	
12/12/2020	@	Army	0	15	L	7.0	L	35.5	U	"Thompson Cup"
Coach: Ken Niumatalolo		Season Record >>	166	303	3-7	ATS>>	4-6	O/U>>	5-5	
2019-Navy		Opponent	Navy	Opp	S/U	Line	ATS	Total	O/U	
8/31/2019	vs	HOLY CROSS	45	7	W	-24.0	W	NT	---	
9/14/2019	vs	EAST CAROLINA	42	10	W	-7.5	W	54.0	U	
9/26/2019	@	Memphis	23	35	L	10.5	L	53.5	O	
10/5/2019	vs	AIR FORCE	34	25	W	3.0	W	46.5	O	
10/12/2019	@	Tulsa	45	17	W	2.0	W	52.0	O	
10/19/2019	vs	SOUTH FLORIDA	35	3	W	-15.5	W	51.0	U	
10/26/2019	vs	TULANE	41	38	W	-4.5	L	58.5	O	
11/1/2019	@	Connecticut	56	10	W	-26.5	W	54.5	O	
11/16/2019	@	Notre Dame	20	52	L	7.0	L	56.0	O	"Rip Miller Trophy"
11/23/2019	vs	SMU	35	28	W	-3.0	W	69.0	U	"Ganzs Trophy"
11/30/2019	@	Houston	56	41	W	-9.5	W	56.5	O	
12/14/2019	vs	Army	31	7	W	-11.5	W	41.5	U	"Thompson Cup"
12/31/2019	vs	Kansas State	20	17	W	-1.5	W	52.5	U	Liberty Bowl
Coach: Ken Niumatalolo		Season Record >>	483	290	11-2	ATS>>	10-3	O/U>>	7-5	"Commander-in-Chief Trophy"
2018-Navy		Opponent	Navy	Opp	S/U	Line	ATS	Total	O/U	
9/1/2018	@	Hawaii	41	59	L	-13.0	L	61.5	O	
9/8/2018	vs	MEMPHIS	22	21	W	6.5	W	67.0	U	
9/15/2018	vs	LEHIGH	51	21	W	-33.0	L	NT	---	
9/22/2018	@	Smu	30	31	L	-6.0	L	58.0	O	"Ganzs Trophy"
10/6/2018	@	Air Force	7	35	L	-3.0	L	47.0	U	
10/13/2018	vs	TEMPLE	17	24	L	6.5	L	49.0	U	
10/20/2018	vs	HOUSTON	36	49	L	11.0	L	58.5	O	
10/27/2018	vs	Notre Dame	22	44	L	22.5	W	57.0	O	"Rip Miller Trophy"
11/3/2018	@	Cincinnati	0	42	L	13.0	L	48.0	U	
11/10/2018	@	Central Florida	24	35	L	23.5	W	68.0	U	
11/17/2018	vs	TULSA	37	29	W	-5.0	W	51.0	O	
11/24/2018	@	Tulane	28	29	L	6.5	W	53.0	O	
12/8/2018	vs	Army	10	17	L	9.0	W	38.5	U	"Thompson Cup"
Coach: Ken Niumatalolo		Season Record >>	325	436	3-10	ATS>>	6-7	O/U>>	6-6	
2017-Navy		Opponent	Navy	Opp	S/U	Line	ATS	Total	O/U	
9/2/2017	@	Florida Atlantic	42	19	W	-8.5	W	65.0	U	
9/9/2017	vs	TULANE	23	21	W	-8.0	L	50.0	U	
9/23/2017	vs	CINCINNATI	42	32	W	-7.0	W	52.0	O	
9/30/2017	@	Tulsa	31	21	W	-8.5	W	70.5	U	
10/7/2017	vs	AIR FORCE	48	45	W	-9.5	L	52.0	O	
10/14/2017	@	Memphis	27	30	L	3.5	W	73.0	U	
10/21/2017	vs	CENTRAL FLORIDA	21	31	L	10.0	T	65.0	U	
11/3/2017	@	Temple	26	34	L	-5.5	L	51.0	O	
11/11/2017	vs	SMU	43	40	W	-1.5	W	66.0	O	"Ganzs Trophy"
11/18/2017	@	Notre Dame	17	24	L	20.5	W	58.5	U	"Rip Miller Trophy"
11/24/2017	@	Houston	14	24	L	6.5	L	55.0	U	
12/9/2017	vs	Army	13	14	L	-2.5	L	44.0	U	"Thompson Cup"
12/28/2017	vs	Virginia	49	7	W	-2.5	W	50.0	O	Military Bowl
Coach: Ken Niumatalolo		Season Record >>	396	342	7-6	ATS>>	7-5-1	O/U>>	5-8	

Copyright © 2021 by Steve's Football Bible, LLC

 **NAVY MIDSHIPMEN** **AMERICAN West**

STADIUM: Navy-Marine Corps Memorial Stadium {34,000}				Location: Annapolis, MD		COACH: Ken Niumatalolo	

DATE		Opponent	Navy	Opp	S/U	Line	ATS	Total	O/U	Trends & Angles
9/4/2021	vs	*MARSHALL*								1st meeting
9/11/2021	vs	*AIR FORCE*								6-1 S/U @ home vs Air Force as favorite since 2005
9/25/2021	@	Houston								vs Houston - Houston leads series 5-2
10/2/2021	vs	**CENTRAL FLORIDA**								vs Central Florida - UCF leads series 2-0
10/9/2021	vs	**SMU**								5-0 S/U & ATS @ home vs SMU since 2008
10/14/2021	@	Memphis								vs Memphis - Series tied 3-3
10/23/2021	vs	**CINCINNATI**								vs Cincinnati - Navy leads series 3-1
10/29/2021	@	Tulsa								4-0 S/U @ Tulsa since 2004 {4-0 ATS}
11/6/2021	@	*Notre Dame*								2-26 S/U @ Notre Dame since 1965
11/20/2021	vs	**EAST CAROLINA**								vs East Carolina - Navy leads series 7-1
11/27/2021	@	Temple								vs Temple - Temple leads series 9-6
12/4/2021	vs									AAC Championship
12/11/2021	vs	*Army*								1-8 S/U vs Army as Dog since 1992
	vs									BOWL GAME

Pointspread Analysis		Pointspread Analysis
Non-Conference		**Conference**
vs Notre Dame - Notre Dame leads series 79-13-1		9-2 S/U vs SMU since 2002
0-28 S/U vs Notre Dame as 13 point or more Dog since 1983		6-2 ATS vs SMU since 2010
9-1 O/U vs Notre Dame as 13 point or more Dog since 2002		vs Smu - Navy leads series 13-9
Game 8-2 O/U vs Notre Dame since 2010		1-6 ATS vs Temple as favorite since 2007
4-52 S/U vs Notre Dame since 1964		1-4 S/U vs Temple as Dog since 1988
3-8 O/U vs Air Force as Dog since 2001		vs Tulane - Series tied 12-12-1
2-14 S/U vs Air Force as 9.5 point or more Dog since 1984		vs Tulsa - Navy leads series 6-2
vs Air Force - Air Force leads series 30-23		4-0 S/U vs Tulsa as favorite since 2015
11-2 ATS vs Air Force as Dog since 1999		5-1 S/U vs Tulsa since 2015
vs Army - Navy leads series 61-52-7		
1-8 S/U vs Army as 6.5 point or less Dog since 1984		5-32 S/U on road vs ranked teams since 1975
0-13 O/U vs Army as favorite since 2006		2-14 S/U @ home vs ranked teams since 1985
15-0 S/U vs Army as 6.5 point or more favorite since 1997		0-14 S/U vs #1 ranked teams all time
8-2-1 S/U when ranked vs Army since 1963		0-31 S/U on Neutral fields vs ranked teams since 1958
1-40 S/U vs ranked Notre Dame since 1964		30-1-3 S/U @ home when ranked all time
Dog		**Bowl Games**
9-0 ATS as 25.5-30 point Dog since 1991		6-0 ATS in Bowl Games since 2013
0-51 S/U as 20.5 point or more Dog since 1983		5-0 S/U & ATS in Bowl Games as 3 point or less favorite since 1996
2-17 S/U as 15.5-20 point Dog since 1996		4-1 O/U in Bowl Games as 3 point or less favorite since 1996
1-13 S/U @ home as 10.5-15 point Dog since 1989		
13-1-1 ATS as 7.5-10 point Dog since 1999		
1-10 S/U on road as 3.5-7 point Dog since 2011		
5-11 O/U as 3.5-7 point Dog since 2010		
2-10 O/U @ home as 3.5-7 point Dog since 1999		
11-1 S/U & ATS on road as 3 point or less Dog since 2004		
3-9 S/U @ home as 3 point or less Dog since 1993		
Favorite		
9-2 S/U @ home as 3 point or less favorite since 2007		
8-2 S/U @ home as 3.5-7 point favorite since 2011	MARSHALL	11-2 S/U in 1st home game of season since 2008
13-1 S/U @ home as 7.5-10 point favorite since 2003	MARSHALL	2-8 O/U prior to playing Air Force since 2011
7-0 S/U on road as 7.5-10 point favorite since 2011	Houston	8-3 S/U in 1st road game of season since 2010
20-2 S/U as 7.5-10 point favorite since 2003	Houston	8-3-1 ATS in 1st road game of season since 2009
18-3 S/U as 10.5-15 point favorite since 2004	UCF	8-1 O/U prior to playing SMU since 2008
15-2 S/U @ home as 10.5-15 point favorite since 2003	E. CAROLINA	3-8 ATS after playing Notre Dame since 2009
6-0 S/U on road as 15.5 point or more favorite since 1983	E. CAROLINA	1-5 O/U prior to playing Temple since 2008
24-1 S/U @ home as 15.5 point or more favorite since 1986	E. CAROLINA	17-1 S/U in final home game of season since 2003

Copyright © 2021 by Steve's Football Bible, LLC

NEBRASKA CORNHUSKERS   BIG TEN West

2020-Nebraska		Opponent	Neb	Opp	S/U	Line	ATS	Total	O/U	
10/24/2020	@	Ohio State	17	52	L	27.5	L	70.5	U	
11/7/2020	@	Northwestern	13	21	L	4.0	L	53.0	U	
11/14/2020	vs	PENN STATE	30	23	W	2.5	W	57.5	U	
11/21/2020	vs	ILLINOIS	23	41	L	-16.5	L	62.0	O	
11/27/2020	@	Iowa	20	26	L	12.5	W	53.0	U	"Heroes Trophy"
12/5/2020	@	Purdue	37	27	W	2.0	W	64.5	U	
12/12/2020	vs	MINNESOTA	17	24	L	-8.5	L	61.5	U	
12/18/2020	@	Rutgers	28	21	W	-6.5	W	51.5	U	
Coach: Scott Frost		Season Record >>	185	235	3-5	ATS>>	4-4	O/U>>	1-7	
2019-Nebraska		Opponent	Neb	Opp	S/U	Line	ATS	Total	O/U	
8/31/2019	vs	SOUTH ALABAMA	35	21	W	-36.0	L	64.5	U	
9/7/2019	@	Colorado	31	34	L	-4.0	L	64.5	O	{OT}
9/14/2019	vs	NORTHERN ILLINOIS	44	8	W	-14.0	W	54.0	U	
9/21/2019	@	Illinois	42	38	W	-13.0	L	62.0	O	
9/28/2019	vs	OHIO STATE	7	48	L	17.0	L	66.0	U	
10/5/2019	vs	NORTHWESTERN	13	10	W	-7.5	L	48.5	U	
10/12/2019	@	Minnesota	7	34	L	7.5	L	47.5	U	
10/26/2019	vs	INDIANA	31	38	L	-2.5	L	54.5	O	
11/2/2019	@	Purdue	27	31	L	-3.5	L	58.0	T	
11/16/2019	vs	WISCONSIN	21	37	L	14.0	L	50.0	O	"Freedom Trophy"
11/23/2019	@	Maryland	54	7	W	-6.5	W	62.5	U	
11/29/2019	vs	IOWA	24	27	L	3.5	W	46.0	O	"Heroes Trophy"
Coach: Scott Frost		Season Record >>	336	333	5-7	ATS>>	3-9	O/U>>	5-6-1	
2018-Nebraska		Opponent	Neb	Opp	S/U	Line	ATS	Total	O/U	
9/8/2018	vs	COLORADO	28	33	L	-3.0	L	63.5	U	
9/15/2018	vs	TROY	19	24	L	-10.5	L	55.5	U	
9/22/2018	@	Michigan	10	56	L	17.0	L	50.5	O	
9/29/2018	vs	PURDUE	28	42	L	3.0	L	57.5	O	
10/6/2018	@	Wisconsin	24	41	L	18.0	W	60.5	O	"Freedom Trophy"
10/13/2018	@	Northwestern	31	34	L	3.5	W	59.5	O	{OT}
10/20/2018	vs	MINNESOTA	53	28	W	-5.5	W	55.0	O	
10/27/2018	vs	BETHUNE-COOKMAN	45	9	W	-46.5	L	NT	---	
11/3/2018	@	Ohio State	31	36	L	17.0	W	75.5	U	
11/10/2018	vs	ILLINOIS	54	35	W	-17.5	W	71.0	O	
11/17/2018	vs	MICHIGAN STATE	9	6	W	-1.0	W	48.0	U	
11/23/2018	@	Iowa	28	31	L	7.5	W	52.0	O	"Heroes Trophy"
Coach: Scott Frost		Season Record >>	360	375	4-8	ATS>>	7-5	O/U>>	7-4	
2017-Nebraska		Opponent	Neb	Opp	S/U	Line	ATS	Total	O/U	
9/2/2017	vs	ARKANSAS STATE	43	36	W	-14.5	L	51.0	O	
9/9/2017	@	Oregon	35	42	L	10.5	L	67.5	O	
9/16/2017	vs	NORTHERN ILLINOIS	17	21	L	-10.5	L	56.5	U	
9/23/2017	vs	RUTGERS	27	17	W	-12.0	L	47.5	U	
9/30/2017	@	Illinois	28	6	W	-6.0	W	46.5	U	
10/7/2017	vs	WISCONSIN	17	38	L	12.5	L	47.5	O	"Freedom Trophy"
10/14/2017	vs	OHIO STATE	14	56	L	24.0	L	57.5	O	
10/28/2017	@	Purdue	25	24	W	3.5	W	53.5	U	
11/4/2017	vs	NORTHWESTERN	24	31	L	PK	L	55.0	T	{OT}
11/11/2017	@	Minnesota	21	54	L	2.0	L	47.5	O	
11/18/2017	@	Penn State	44	56	L	27.5	W	56.0	O	
11/24/2017	vs	IOWA	14	56	L	5.0	L	50.0	O	"Heroes Trophy"
Coach: Mike Riley		Season Record >>	309	437	4-8	ATS>>	4-8	O/U>>	7-4-1	

Copyright © 2021 by Steve's Football Bible, LLC

NEBRASKA CORNHUSKERS   BIG TEN West

STADIUM: Memorial Stadium {85,458}				Location: Lincoln, NE						COACH: Scott Frost
DATE		Opponent	Neb	Opp	S/U	Line	ATS	Total	O/U	Trends & Angles
8/28/2021	vs	Illinois {@ Dublin, IRE}								vs Illinois - Nebraska leads series 13-4-1
9/11/2021	vs	BUFFALO								1st meeting
9/18/2021	@	Oklahoma								0-3 S/U @ Oklahoma since 2000
9/25/2021	@	Michigan State								vs Michigan State - Nebraska leads series 9-2
10/2/2021	vs	NORTHWESTERN								0-5 ATS @ home vs Northwestern since 2011
10/9/2021	vs	MICHIGAN								vs Michigan - Michigan leads series 5-4-1
10/16/2021	@	Minnesota								vs Minnesota - Minnesota leads series 34-25-2
10/30/2021	@	Purdue								vs Purdue - Nebraska leads series 5-4
11/6/2021	vs	OHIO STATE								0-6 S/U vs Ohio State since 2012
11/13/2021	vs	SE LOUISIANA								1st meeting
11/20/2021	@	Wisconsin								0-7 S/U vs Wisconsin since 2012
11/26/2021	vs	IOWA								0-6 S/U vs Iowa as Dog since 2015
12/4/2021	vs									Big Ten Championship
	vs									BOWL GAME

Pointspread Analysis Non-Conference		Pointspread Analysis Conference
2-9 S/U vs Non-Conf. as 7.5 point or more Dog since 1992		vs Iowa - Nebraska leads series 28-19-3
2-8 S/U vs Non-Conf. as 3.5-7 point Dog since 1986		4-1 S/U vs Iowa as favorite since 1999
9-0 S/U vs Non-Conf. as 7.5-10 point favorite since 1984		5-0 S/U & ATS vs Michigan State as favorite since 1995
9-0 S/U vs Non-Conf. as 15.5-20 point favorite since 1983		8-3 S/U vs Minnesota as favorite since 1983
14-0 S/U vs Non-Conf. as 20.5-25 point favorite since 1998		vs Northwestern - Nebraska leads series 8-6
53-0 S/U vs Non-Conf. as 25.5 point or more favorite since 1983		1-6 ATS vs Ohio State since 2011
vs Oklahoma - Oklahoma leads series 45-38-3		vs Ohio State - Ohio State leads series 8-1
1-8 S/U vs Oklahoma as Dog since 1979		0-6 S/U vs Ohio State as Dog since 2012
Dog		vs Penn State - Nebraska leads series 10-8
2-25 S/U as 10.5 point or more Dog since 1979		0-7 S/U vs Wisconsin since 2012
6-2 O/U as 10.5-15 point Dog since 1998		vs Wisconsin - Wisconsin leads series 10-4
2-12 S/U on road as 3.5-7 point Dog since 2003		0-7 S/U vs Wisconsin as Dog since 2011
Favorite		**Bowl Games**
10-3 S/U on road as 3.5-7 point favorite since 2008		0-4 S/U vs Florida State in Bowl Games
6-1 S/U on road as 7.5-10 point favorite since 2006		0-3 S/U & ATS in Citrus Bowl
17-3 S/U @ home as 7.5-10 point favorite since 1984		3-0 S/U & ATS in Alamo Bowl
18-4 S/U @ home as 10.5-15 point favorite since 1984		4-0 S/U vs LSU in Bowl Games
14-2 S/U on road as 10.5-15 point favorite since 1983		3-0 S/U in Sugar Bowl since 1974
2-8 ATS @ home as 10.5-15 point favorite since 2008		2-8 S/U in Bowl Games as 7.5 point or more Dog since 1979
16-4 S/U @ home as 15.5-20 point favorite since 1987		1-5 S/U in Bowl Games as 3.5-7 point Dog since 1986
10-0 S/U on road as 15.5-20 point favorite since 1989		0-3 O/U in Bowl Games as 3 point or less Dog since 2007
2-8 ATS as 15.5-20 point favorite since 2008		
129-0 S/U @ home as 20.5 point or more favorite since 1983		
39-3 S/U on road as 20.5 point or more favorite since 1983		
	BUFFALO	0-8 O/U after playing Illinois since 2013
	BUFFALO	7-1 ATS after playing Illinois since 2013
	BUFFALO	33-2 S/U in 1st home game of season since 1986
	Oklahoma	6-1 S/U & ATS prior to playing Michigan State since 1995
	NORTHWESTERN	10-3 S/U in 2nd home game of season since 2008
170-15 S/U @ home when ranked since 1982	MICHIGAN	7-2 S/U after playing Northwestern since 2011
17-3 S/U @ home when ranked vs ranked teams since 1991	SE LOUISIANA	6-1 S/U after playing Ohio State since 2011
1-9 S/U when ranked vs #1 ranked teams all time	SE LOUISIANA	1-6 O/U after playing Ohio State since 2011
13-2 S/U when ranked vs Minnesota since 1967	SE LOUISIANA	1-5-1 O/U prior to playing Wisconsin since 2011
0-11 S/U on road vs ranked teams since 2011	IOWA	1-6 S/U after playing Wisconsin since 2012
1-12 S/U vs #1 ranked teams all time	IOWA	2-6 ATS after playing Wisconsin since 2011
0-7 S/U vs ranked ranked Ohio State all time	IOWA	6-2 O/U after playing Wisconsin since 2011

Copyright © 2021 by Steve's Football Bible, LLC

NEVADA WOLFPACK   MOUNTAIN WEST West

2020-Nevada		Opponent	Nev	Opp	S/U	Line	ATS	Total	O/U	
10/24/2020	vs	WYOMING	37	34	W	3.0	W	53.5	O	{OT}
10/31/2020	@	Unlv	37	19	W	-13.5	W	60.0	U	*"Fremont Cannon"*
11/6/2020	vs	UTAH STATE	34	9	W	-17.0	W	58.0	U	
11/14/2020	@	New Mexico	27	20	W	-17.5	L	63.0	U	
11/21/2020	vs	SAN DIEGO STATE	26	21	W	1.5	W	46.0	O	
11/28/2020	@	Hawaii	21	24	L	-7.0	L	63.0	U	
12/5/2020	vs	FRESNO STATE	37	26	W	-5.5	W	60.0	O	
12/12/2020	@	San Jose State	20	30	L	-2.5	L	62.0	U	
12/22/2020	vs	**Tulane**	**38**	**27**	W	-1.0	W	**56.5**	O	**Famous Idaho Potato Bowl**
Coach: Jay Norvell		Season Record >>	277	210	7-2	ATS>>	6-3	O/U>>	4-5	
2019-Nevada		Opponent	Nev	Opp	S/U	Line	ATS	Total	O/U	
8/30/2019	vs	*PURDUE*	34	31	W	11.0	W	58.5	O	
9/7/2019	@	*Oregon*	6	77	L	24.5	L	61.5	O	
9/14/2019	vs	*WEBER STATE*	19	13	W	-7.0	L	NT	---	
9/21/2019	@	*Texas-El Paso*	37	21	W	-14.0	W	52.0	O	
9/28/2019	vs	HAWAII	3	54	L	-1.5	L	63.0	U	
10/12/2019	vs	SAN JOSE STATE	41	38	W	-2.5	W	58.5	O	
10/19/2019	@	Utah State	10	36	L	21.5	L	59.0	U	
10/26/2019	@	Wyoming	3	31	L	14.0	L	43.5	U	
11/2/2019	vs	NEW MEXICO	21	10	W	-3.5	W	57.5	U	
11/9/2019	@	San Diego State	17	13	W	17.0	W	34.5	U	
11/23/2019	@	Fresno State	35	28	W	13.0	W	51.5	O	
11/30/2019	vs	UNLV	30	33	L	-6.5	L	52.0	O	*"Fremont Cannon"*
1/3/2020	vs	**Ohio**	**21**	**30**	L	10.0	W	62.0	U	**Famous Idaho Potato Bowl**
Coach: Jay Norvell		Season Record >>	277	415	7-6	ATS>>	7-6	O/U>>	6-6	
2018-Nevada		Opponent	Nev	Opp	S/U	Line	ATS	Total	O/U	
8/31/2018	vs	*PORTLAND STATE*	72	19	W	-28.0	W	NT	---	
9/8/2018	@	*Vanderbilt*	10	41	L	10.0	L	61.0	U	
9/15/2018	vs	*OREGON STATE*	37	35	W	-3.5	L	67.5	O	
9/22/2018	@	*Toledo*	44	63	L	12.0	L	69.0	O	
9/29/2018	@	Air Force	28	25	W	3.5	W	63.0	U	
10/6/2018	vs	FRESNO STATE	3	21	L	16.0	L	58.5	U	
10/13/2018	vs	BOISE STATE	27	31	L	14.0	W	58.0	T	
10/20/2018	@	Hawaii	40	22	W	2.0	W	67.5	U	
10/27/2018	vs	SAN DIEGO STATE	28	24	W	1.0	W	46.0	O	
11/10/2018	vs	COLORADO STATE	49	10	W	-14.0	W	62.0	U	
11/17/2018	@	San Jose State	21	12	W	-14.5	L	58.5	U	
11/24/2018	@	Unlv	29	34	L	-14.0	L	61.0	O	*"Fremont Cannon"*
12/29/2018	vs	**Arkansas State**	**16**	**13**	W	PK	W	57.0	U	**Arizona Bowl**
Coach: Jay Norvell		Season Record >>	404	350	8-5	ATS>>	7-6	O/U>>	4-7-1	
2017-Nevada		Opponent	Nev	Opp	S/U	Line	ATS	Total	O/U	
9/2/2017	@	*Northwestern*	20	31	L	24.0	W	60.5	U	
9/9/2017	vs	*TOLEDO*	24	37	L	10.5	L	69.5	U	
9/16/2017	vs	*IDAHO STATE*	28	30	L	-33.5	L	NT	---	
9/23/2017	@	*Washington State*	7	45	L	28.5	L	66.0	U	
9/30/2017	@	Fresno State	21	41	L	7.5	L	59.5	O	
10/7/2017	vs	HAWAII	35	21	W	3.5	W	62.5	U	
10/14/2017	@	Colorado State	42	44	L	24.5	W	65.5	O	
10/20/2017	vs	AIR FORCE	42	45	L	6.0	W	64.0	O	
11/4/2017	@	Boise State	14	41	L	20.0	L	61.0	U	
11/11/2017	vs	SAN JOSE STATE	59	14	W	-18.0	W	67.0	O	
11/18/2017	@	San Diego State	23	42	L	17.0	L	55.5	O	
11/25/2017	vs	UNLV	23	16	W	3.0	W	70.5	U	*"Fremont Cannon"*
Coach: Jay Norvell		Season Record >>	338	407	3-9	ATS>>	6-6	O/U>>	5-6	

Copyright © 2021 by Steve's Football Bible, LLC

NEVADA WOLFPACK   MOUNTAIN WEST West

STADIUM: Mackay Stadium {27,000}					Location: Reno, NV				COACH: Jay Norvell
DATE		Opponent	UNR	Opp	S/U	Line	ATS	Total	O/U	Trends & Angles

DATE		Opponent	UNR	Opp	S/U	Line	ATS	Total	O/U	Trends & Angles
9/4/2021	@	California								vs California - California leads series 22-3-1
9/11/2021	vs	IDAHO STATE								11-1 vs Idaho State since 1982
9/18/2021	@	Kansas State								1st meeting
10/2/2021	@	Boise State								1-15 S/U vs Boise State as Dog since 2001
10/9/2021	vs	NEW MEXICO STATE								vs New Mexico State - Nevada leads series 13-2
10/16/2021	vs	HAWAII								5-1 S/U @ home vs Hawaii as favorite since 2005
10/23/2021	@	Fresno State								2-6 S/U @ Fresno State as Dog since 2000
10/30/2021	vs	UNLV								Game 2-8 O/U @ home vs UNLV since 2001
11/6/2021	vs	SAN JOSE STATE								9-0 S/U @ home vs San Jose since 2002 {8-1 ATS}
11/13/2021	@	San Diego State								1-5 S/U @ San Diego State since 1995
11/20/2021	vs	AIR FORCE								vs Air Force - Air Force leads series 3-2
11/27/2021	@	Colorado State								1-10 S/U vs Colorado State as Dog since 1997
12/4/2021	vs									MWC Championship
	vs									BOWL GAME

Pointspread Analysis Non-Conference		Pointspread Analysis Conference
0-13 S/U vs Non-Conf. as 20.5 point or more Dog since 2000		vs Fresno State - Fresno leads series 29-22-1
2-17 S/U vs Non-Conf. as 7.5-20 point Dog since 1996		6-1 S/U vs Fresno State as favorite since 2009
vs Idaho State - Nevada leads series 16-12		vs Hawaii - Nevada leads series 14-11
Game 6-1 O/U vs New Mexico State since 2005		5-2 S/U vs Hawaii as favorite since 2011
Dog		4-0 ATS @ home vs Hawaii as Dog since 2001
0-27 S/U on road as 20.5 point or more Dog since 2000		4-0 ATS vs Hawaii as Dog since 2006
3-10 S/U on road as 15.5-20 point Dog since 1996		vs Unlv - Nevada leads series 27-19
3-14 S/U on road as 10.5-15 point Dog since 2000		12-4 S/U vs UNLV since 2005
9-3 ATS as 10.5-15 point Dog since 2009		4-0 S/U & ATS vs UNLV as Dog since 2005
1-12 S/U as 7.5-10 point Dog since 2005		vs San Jose State - Nevada leads series 22-10-2
2-7 S/U on road as 3.5-7 point Dog since 1995		15-3 S/U vs San Jose State since 2002
6-1 O/U on road as 3.5-7 point Dog since 2001		8-1 S/U vs San Jose State as favorite since 2008
5-0 S/U & ATS as 3 point or less Dog since 2017		7-0 S/U @ home vs San Jose State as favorite since 2002
Favorite		vs San Diego State - San Diego State leads series 7-6
3-11 O/U as 3.5-7 point favorite since 2013		1-4 ATS @ San Diego State since 2004
18-0 S/U as 7.5-10 point favorite since 1995		1-5 S/U @ San Diego State as Dog since 1995
9-0 S/U on road as 7.5-10 point favorite since 1995		
11-5 O/U as 10.5-15 point favorite since 2008		1-17 S/U on road vs ranked teams all time
13-1 S/U @ home as 10.5-15 point favorite since 1995		5-0 S/U @ home when ranked all time
10-1 S/U on road as 10.5-15 point favorite since 1995		
31-3 S/U @ home as 15.5 point or more favorite since 1995		
9-0 S/U on road as 15.5 point or more favorite since 1995		
Bowl Games	California	3-22 S/U in 1st road game of season since 1996
3-8 S/U in Bowl Games since 2006	NMSU	16-3 S/U in 2nd home game of season since 2002
3-0 ATS in Bowl Games as 3.5-7 point Dog since 1992	Fresno State	11-2 S/U after playing Hawaii since 2008
1-3 ATS in Bowl Games as 3 point or less favorite since 2005	AIR FORCE	10-2 ATS in final home game of season since 2009

Copyright © 2021 by Steve's Football Bible, LLC

NEVADA-LAS VEGAS REBELS   MOUNTAIN WEST West

2020-Nevada-Las Vegas		Opponent	Unlv	Opp	S/U	Line	ATS	Total	O/U	
10/24/2020	@	San Diego State	6	34	L	13.5	L	49.5	U	
10/31/2020	vs	NEVADA	19	37	L	13.5	L	60.0	U	"Fremont Cannon"
11/7/2020	vs	FRESNO STATE	27	40	L	11.0	L	57.5	O	
11/14/2020	@	San Jose State	17	34	L	17.0	T	61.5	U	
11/27/2020	vs	WYOMING	14	45	L	17.0	L	52.0	O	
12/12/2020	@	Hawaii	21	38	L	18.5	W	60.0	U	
Coach: Marcus Arroyo		Season Record >>	104	228	0-6	ATS>>	1-4-1	O/U>>	2-4	
2019-Nevada-Las Vegas		Opponent	Unlv	Opp	S/U	Line	ATS	Total	O/U	
8/31/2019	vs	SOUTHERN UTAH	56	23	W	-24.0	W	NT	---	
9/7/2019	vs	ARKANSAS STATE	17	43	L	PK	L	64.0	U	
9/14/2019	@	Northwestern	14	30	L	18.5	W	51.5	U	
9/28/2019	@	Wyoming	17	53	L	8.0	L	44.5	O	
10/5/2019	vs	BOISE STATE	13	38	L	24.5	L	57.5	U	
10/12/2019	@	Vanderbilt	34	10	W	15.5	W	57.5	U	
10/19/2019	@	Fresno State	27	56	L	16.0	L	52.0	O	
10/26/2019	vs	SAN DIEGO STATE	17	20	L	11.5	W	44.5	U	
11/2/2019	@	Colorado State	17	37	L	7.0	L	64.0	U	
11/16/2019	vs	HAWAII	7	21	L	7.0	L	72.5	U	
11/23/2019	vs	SAN JOSE STATE	38	35	W	7.0	W	65.0	O	
11/30/2019	@	Nevada	33	30	W	6.5	W	52.0	O	"Fremont Cannon"
Coach: Tony Sanchez		Season Record >>	290	396	4-8	ATS>>	6-6	O/U>>	4-7	
2018-Nevada-Las Vegas		Opponent	Unlv	Opp	S/U	Line	ATS	Total	O/U	
9/1/2018	@	Usc	21	43	L	24.5	W	59.0	O	
9/8/2018	vs	TEXAS-EL PASO	52	24	W	-22.0	W	53.5	O	
9/15/2018	vs	PRAIRIE VIEW A&M	46	17	W	-31.0	L	NT	---	
9/22/2018	@	Arkansas State	20	27	L	8.0	W	66.5	U	
10/6/2018	vs	NEW MEXICO	14	50	L	-7.5	L	62.5	O	
10/13/2018	@	Utah State	28	59	L	27.0	L	65.5	O	
10/19/2018	vs	AIR FORCE	35	41	L	9.5	W	54.0	O	
10/27/2018	@	San Jose State	37	50	L	2.5	L	57.0	O	
11/3/2018	vs	FRESNO STATE	3	48	L	27.0	L	60.0	U	
11/10/2018	@	San Diego State	27	24	W	24.0	W	51.5	U	
11/17/2018	@	Hawaii	28	35	L	7.0	T	72.5	U	
11/24/2018	vs	NEVADA	34	29	W	14.0	W	61.0	O	"Fremont Cannon"
Coach: Tony Sanchez		Season Record >>	345	447	4-8	ATS>>	6-5-1	O/U>>	7-4	
2017-Nevada-Las Vegas		Opponent	Unlv	Opp	S/U	Line	ATS	Total	O/U	
9/2/2017	vs	HOWARD	40	43	L	-45.5	L	66.5	O	
9/9/2017	@	Idaho	44	16	W	4.0	W	69.5	U	
9/23/2017	@	Ohio State	21	54	L	41.0	W	66.5	O	
9/30/2017	vs	SAN JOSE STATE	41	13	W	-17.0	W	63.0	U	
10/7/2017	vs	SAN DIEGO STATE	10	41	L	9.5	L	56.0	U	
10/14/2017	@	Air Force	30	34	L	9.0	W	64.0	T	
10/21/2017	vs	UTAH STATE	28	52	L	-3.5	L	60.0	O	
10/28/2017	@	Fresno State	26	16	W	22.5	W	58.0	U	
11/4/2017	vs	HAWAII	31	23	W	-7.0	W	58.5	U	
11/10/2017	vs	BYU	21	31	L	PK	W	49.0	O	
11/18/2017	@	New Mexico	38	35	W	3.0	W	55.0	O	
11/25/2017	@	Nevada	16	23	L	-3.0	L	70.5	U	"Fremont Cannon"
Coach: Tony Sanchez		Season Record >>	346	381	5-7	ATS>>	8-4	O/U>>	5-6-1	

Copyright © 2021 by Steve's Football Bible, LLC

NEVADA-LAS VEGAS REBELS   MOUNTAIN WEST West

STADIUM: Allegiant Stadium {65,000}					Location: Las Vegas, NV				COACH: Marcus Arroyo	
DATE		Opponent	Unlv	Opp	S/U	Line	ATS	Total	O/U	Trends & Angles
9/2/2021	vs	EASTERN WASHINGTON								1st meeting
9/11/2021	@	Arizona State								vs Arizona State - UNLV leads series 1-0
9/18/2021	vs	IOWA STATE								vs Iowa State - Iowa State leads series 4-1
9/25/2021	@	Fresno State								vs Fresno State - Fresno leads series 16-7
10/2/2021	@	Texas-San Antonio								1st meeting
10/16/2021	vs	UTAH STATE								0-5 S/U vs Utah State since 2012
10/23/2021	vs	SAN JOSE STATE								2-9 S/U vs San Jose State since 1995
10/30/2021	@	Nevada								vs Nevada - Nevada leads series 27-19
11/6/2021	@	New Mexico								vs New Mexico - Series tied 12-12
11/13/2021	vs	HAWAII								vs Hawaii - Hawaii leads series 18-12
11/20/2021	vs	SAN DIEGO STATE								3-12 S/U vs San Diego State since 2006
11/27/2021	@	Air Force								2-8 S/U @ Air Force as Dog since 1997
12/4/2021	vs									MWC Championship
	vs									BOWL GAME

Pointspread Analysis Non-Conference			Pointspread Analysis Conference	
0-12 S/U vs Non-Conf. as 25.5 point or more Dog since 1996			9-1-1 O/U vs Air Force as Dog since 2006	
4-28 S/U vs Non-Conf. as 3.5-20 point Dog since 1985			2-9 S/U vs Hawaii as Dog since 1995	
Dog			6-0 S/U @ home vs Hawaii as favorite since 1997	
0-23 S/U on road as 25.5 point or more Dog since 1995			0-4 S/U & ATS vs Nevada as favorite since 2005	
1-13 S/U as 25.5-30 point Dog since 1996			vs San Diego State - San Diego State leads series 20-10	
2-15 S/U as 20.5-25 point Dog since 2008			vs San Jose State - San Jose State leads series 17-7-1	
0-6 S/U @ home as 20.5-25 point Dog since 1998			1-7 S/U vs San Jose State as Dog since 1995 {2-5-1 ATS}	
3-35 S/U as 15.5-20 point Dog since 1994			vs Utah State - Utah State leads series 17-7	
0-13 S/U on road as 10.5-15 point Dog since 2002				
4-31 S/U as 10.5-15 point Dog since 1985				
6-0 O/U on road as 3 point or less Dog since 2002				
1-6 S/U @ home as 3 point or less Dog since 1998				
Favorite		Arizona State	2-19 S/U in 1st road game of season since 2000	
0-7-1 ATS as 3 point or less favorite since 2012		IOWA STATE	2-8 S/U prior to playing Fresno State since 1985	
0-5 S/U on road as 3 point or less favorite since 2012		Fresno State	2-15 S/U in 2nd road game of season since 2004	
8-2 O/U as 10.5-15 point favorite since 2002		UTAH STATE	7-3 ATS prior to playing San Jose State since 1996	
3-14 ATS as road favorite since 2003		SAN JOSE STATE	6-1-1 ATS prior to playing Nevada since 2013	
10-1 S/U @ home as 15.5 point or more favorite since 1985		SAN JOSE STATE	9-4 O/U prior to playing Nevada since 2008	
		Nevada	2-15 S/U prior to playing New Mexico since 1999	
		Nevada	6-0 ATS prior to playing New Mexico since 2012	
0-22 S/U vs ranked teams since 2008		Nevada	3-9 S/U after playing San Jose State since 1994	
0-21 S/U @ home vs ranked teams all time		New Mexico	3-11 S/U prior to playing Hawaii since 2006	
1-15 S/U on road vs ranked teams since 2004		HAWAII	1-7 S/U after playing New Mexico since 2009	
		SAN DIEGO STATE	3-9 S/U after playing Hawaii since 2009	
		SAN DIEGO STATE	0-6 S/U prior to playing Air Force since 2011	
		SAN DIEGO STATE	3-8 S/U in final home game of season since 2010	
		Air Force	2-15 S/U in final road game of season since 2004	
		Air Force	10-3 O/U in final road game of season since 2008	
		Air Force	5-11-1 ATS in final road game of season since 2004	

Copyright © 2021 by Steve's Football Bible, LLC

NEW MEXICO LOBOS   MOUNTAIN WEST Mountain

2020-New Mexico		Opponent	UNM	Opp	S/U	Line	ATS	Total	O/U	
10/31/2020	@	San Jose State	21	38	L	13.5	L	56.5	O	
11/7/2020	@	Hawaii	33	39	L	13.0	W	66.5	O	
11/14/2020	vs	NEVADA	20	27	L	17.5	W	63.0	U	
11/21/2020	@	Air Force	0	28	L	8.0	L	55.5	U	
11/26/2020	@	Utah State	27	41	L	-6.5	L	49.0	O	
12/5/2020	vs	WYOMING	17	16	W	15.0	W	51.0	U	
12/12/2020	vs	FRESNO STATE	49	39	W	16.5	W	55.5	O	
Coach: Danny Gonzales		Season Record >>	167	228	2-5	ATS>>	4-3	O/U>>	4-3	
2019-New Mexico		Opponent	UNM	Opp	S/U	Line	ATS	Total	O/U	
8/31/2019	vs	SAM HOUSTON STATE	39	31	W	-6.0	W	NT	---	
9/14/2019	@	Notre Dame	14	66	L	34.5	L	64.0	O	
9/21/2019	vs	NEW MEXICO STATE	55	52	W	-4.0	L	69.0	O	"Rio Grande Rivalry"
9/28/2019	@	Liberty	10	17	L	7.0	T	72.0	U	
10/5/2019	@	San Jose State	21	32	L	7.0	W	69.5	U	
10/12/2019	vs	COLORADO STATE	21	35	L	5.0	L	66.0	U	
10/19/2019	@	Wyoming	10	23	L	17.5	W	49.0	U	
10/26/2019	vs	HAWAII	31	45	L	10.0	L	71.5	O	
11/2/2019	@	Nevada	10	21	L	3.5	L	57.5	U	
11/9/2019	vs	AIR FORCE	9	42	L	26.0	L	57.5	U	
11/16/2019	@	Boise State	22	44	L	24.0	W	56.5	O	
11/30/2019	vs	UTAH STATE	25	38	L	12.0	L	64.0	U	
Coach: Bob Davie		Season Record >>	267	446	2-10	ATS>>	4-7-1	O/U>>	4-7	
2018-New Mexico		Opponent	UNM	Opp	S/U	Line	ATS	Total	O/U	
9/1/2018	vs	INCARNATE WORD	62	30	W	-35.5	L	NT	---	
9/8/2018	@	Wisconsin	14	45	L	35.0	W	58.5	O	
9/15/2018	@	New Mexico State	42	25	W	-3.0	W	59.0	O	"Rio Grande Rivalry"
9/29/2018	vs	LIBERTY	43	52	L	-7.0	L	66.0	O	
10/6/2018	@	Unlv	50	14	W	7.5	W	62.5	O	
10/13/2018	@	Colorado State	18	20	L	-2.5	L	64.0	U	
10/20/2018	vs	FRESNO STATE	7	38	L	14.0	L	52.5	U	
10/27/2018	@	Utah State	19	61	L	19.5	L	64.0	O	
11/3/2018	vs	SAN DIEGO STATE	23	31	L	12.5	W	45.0	O	
11/10/2018	@	Air Force	24	42	L	13.0	L	55.5	O	
11/17/2018	vs	BOISE STATE	14	45	L	22.0	L	61.5	U	
11/27/2018	vs	WYOMING	3	31	L	7.0	L	43.0	U	
Coach: Bob Davie		Season Record >>	319	434	3-9	ATS>>	4-8	O/U>>	7-4	
2017-New Mexico		Opponent	UNM	Opp	S/U	Line	ATS	Total	O/U	
9/2/2017	vs	ABILENE CHRISTIAN	38	14	W	-34.0	L	67.5	U	
9/9/2017	vs	NEW MEXICO STATE	28	30	L	-7.5	L	68.5	U	"Rio Grande Rivalry"
9/14/2017	@	Boise State	14	28	L	16.5	W	56.0	U	
9/23/2017	@	Tulsa	16	13	W	7.5	W	68.0	U	
9/30/2017	vs	AIR FORCE	56	38	W	3.0	W	50.5	O	
10/14/2017	@	Fresno State	0	38	L	-2.0	L	53.0	U	
10/20/2017	vs	COLORADO STATE	24	27	L	10.0	L	60.0	U	
10/28/2017	@	Wyoming	3	42	L	2.5	L	47.5	U	
11/4/2017	vs	UTAH STATE	10	24	L	-3.0	L	51.0	U	
11/11/2017	@	Texas A&M	14	55	L	18.0	L	52.5	O	
11/18/2017	vs	UNLV	38	38	L	-3.0	L	55.0	O	
11/25/2017	@	San Diego State	10	35	L	20.0	L	46.5	U	
Coach: Bob Davie		Season Record >>	251	382	3-9	ATS>>	3-9	O/U>>	3-9	

Copyright © 2021 by Steve's Football Bible, LLC

NEW MEXICO LOBOS   MOUNTAIN WEST Mountain

STADIUM: Dreamstyle Stadium {39,224}		Location: Albuquerque, NM							COACH: Danny Gonzales	
DATE		Opponent	Nmex	Opp	S/U	Line	ATS	Total	O/U	Trends & Angles
9/4/2021	vs	*HOUSTON BAPTIST*								1st meeting
9/11/2021	vs	*NEW MEXICO STATE*								13-3 S/U @ home vs NMSU as favorite since 1986
9/18/2021	@	*Texsas A&M*								0-3 S/U & ATS vs Texas A&M as Dog since 2008
9/25/2021	@	*Texas-El Paso*								1-5 S/U @ Texas-El Paso as Dog since 1987
10/2/2021	vs	**AIR FORCE**								vs Air Force - Air Force leads series 23-13
10/9/2021	@	San Diego State								0-4 S/U @ San Diego State since 2009
10/16/2021	vs	**COLORADO STATE**								vs Colorado State - Colorado State leads series 42-25
10/23/2021	@	Wyoming								1-5 S/U @ Wyoming since 2009
11/6/2021	vs	**UNLV**								vs UNLV - Series tied 12-12
11/13/2021	@	Fresno State								1-6 S/U & ATS vs Fresno State as Dog since 1995
11/20/2021	@	Boise State								1-9 S/U vs Boise State as Dog since 2000
11/27/2021	vs	**UTAH STATE**								0-4 S/U & ATS vs Utah State since 2017
12/4/2021	vs									MWC Championship
	vs									BOWL GAME

Pointspread Analysis Non-Conference		Pointspread Analysis Conference
0-18 S/U vs Non-Conf. as 20.5 point or more Dog since 1985		5-2 O/U vs Air Force as Dog since 2014
1-9 S/U vs Non-Conf. as 10.5-15 point Dog since 1998		vs Boise State - Boise State leads series 10-1
10-1 S/U vs Non-Conf. as 15.5 point or more favorite since 1986		0-9 S/U vs Colorado State as Dog since 2010
vs New Mexico State - New Mexico leads series 71-33-5		1-11 S/U vs Colorado State as 5-10 point Dog since 1986
1-5 ATS vs New Mexico State since 2014		1-6 S/U vs Colorado State as favorite since 1985
10-2 O/U vs New Mexico State as favorite since 2005		0-7 ATS vs Colorado State as favorite since 1985
Game 6-1 O/U vs New Mexico State since 2013		1-10 S/U vs Fresno State as 5.5 point or more Dog since 1990
vs Texas-El Paso - New Mexico leads series 43-31-1		0-7 S/U vs San Diego State since 2009
vs Texas A&M - Texas A&M leads series 4-0		vs San Diego State - San Diego State leads series 27-15
Dog		1-17 S/U vs San Diego State as 5 point or more Dog since 1985
1-38 S/U as 25.5 point or more Dog since 1985		Game 2-5 O/U vs Utah State since 2014
0-8 S/U @ home as 25.5 point or more Dog since 1985		vs Utah State - Utah State leads series 14-13
2-22 S/U as 20.5-25 point Dog since 1984		vs Wyoming - Wyoming leads series 38-35
0-13 S/U on road as 20.5-25 point Dog since 1986		7-2 ATS @ Wyoming since 2003
5-34 S/U as 15.5-20 point Dog since 1985		1-11 S/U vs Wyoming as 10 point or more Dog since 1987
0-15 S/U on road as 10.5-15 point Dog since 2001		7-0 S/U vs Wyoming as favorite since 1985
0-5 O/U on road as 3 point or less Dog since 2010		
Favorite		0-22 S/U vs ranked teams since 2004
0-7 ATS as 7.5-10 point favorite since 2004	NMSU	3-10 S/U in 2nd home game of season since 2008
0-7-1 O/U as 7.5-10 point favorite since 2003	NMSU	10-3 O/U in 2nd home game of season since 2008
3-0 S/U on road as 7.5-10 point favorite since 1997	NMSU	2-11 ATS in 2nd home game of season since 2008
16-2 S/U @ home as 10.5-15 point favorite since 1989	Texas A&M	2-12 S/U in 1st road game of season since 2007
5-0 O/U as 10.5-15 point favorite since 2013	Texas A&M	0-11 S/U after playing New Mexico State since 2009
11-0 S/U @ home as 15.5 point or more favorite since 1986	AIR FORCE	1-7 S/U prior to playing San Diego State since 2008
	San Diego State	3-10 O/U prior to playing Colorado State since 2007
	San Diego State	2-12 S/U after playing Air Force since 2006
	Wyoming	0-12 S/U prior to playing UNLV since 2004
	Wyoming	7-1 O/U prior to playing UNLV since 2009
	Fresno State	1-8 S/U after playing UNLV since 2008
	Boise State	1-4 O/U after playing Fresno State since 2012
	Boise State	1-14 S/U in final road game of season since 2006
	UTAH STATE	6-2 O/U in final home game of seaosn since 2013

Copyright © 2021 by Steve's Football Bible, LLC

NEW MEXICO STATE AGGIES INDEPENDENT

2019-New Mexico State		Opponent	NNSU	Opp	S/U	Line	ATS	Total	O/U	
8/31/2019	@	Washington State	7	58	L	33.5	L	65.5	U	
9/7/2019	@	Alabama	10	62	L	55.0	W	64.0	O	
9/14/2019	vs	SAN DIEGO STATE	10	31	L	17.0	L	51.0	U	
9/21/2019	@	New Mexico	52	55	L	4.0	W	69.0	O	"Rio Grande Rivalry"
9/28/2019	vs	FRESNO STATE	17	30	L	20.5	W	62.5	U	
10/5/2019	vs	LIBERTY	13	20	L	4.0	L	63.5	U	
10/12/2019	@	Central Michigan	28	42	L	10.5	L	56.5	O	
10/26/2019	@	Georgia Southern	7	41	L	14.0	L	54.5	U	
11/9/2019	@	Mississippi	3	41	L	29.0	L	65.0	U	
11/16/2019	vs	INCARNATE WORD	41	28	W	-7.5	W	NT	---	
11/23/2019	vs	TEXAS-EL PASO	44	35	W	-7.0	W	55.5	O	"Brass Spittoon"
11/30/2019	@	Liberty	28	49	L	14.5	L	68.0	O	
Coach: Doug Martin		Season Record >>	260	492	2-10	ATS>>	5-7	O/U>>	5-6	
2018-New Mexico State		Opponent	NNSU	Opp	S/U	Line	ATS	Total	O/U	
8/25/2018	vs	WYOMING	7	29	L	5.0	L	45.5	U	
8/30/2018	@	Minnesota	10	48	L	21.5	L	47.5	O	
9/8/2018	@	Utah State	13	60	L	21.5	L	62.0	O	
9/15/2018	vs	NEW MEXICO	25	42	L	3.0	L	59.0	O	"Rio Grande Rivalry"
9/22/2018	@	Texas-El Paso	27	20	W	-4.5	W	50.0	U	"Brass Spittoon"
10/6/2018	vs	LIBERTY	49	41	W	3.5	W	64.0	O	
10/13/2018	@	Louisiana-Lafayette	38	66	L	7.0	L	67.5	O	
10/20/2018	vs	GEORGIA SOUTHERN	31	48	L	10.0	L	52.5	O	
10/27/2018	@	Texas State	20	27	L	PK	L	56.0	U	
11/3/2018	vs	ALCORN STATE	52	42	W	-12.5	L	NT	---	
11/17/2018	@	Byu	10	45	L	25.5	L	59.0	U	
11/24/2018	@	Liberty	21	28	L	5.5	L	72.5	U	
Coach: Doug Martin		Season Record >>	303	496	3-9	ATS>>	2-10	O/U>>	6-5	
2017-New Mexico State		Opponent	NNSU	Opp	S/U	Line	ATS	Total	O/U	
8/31/2017	@	Arizona State	31	37	L	25.5	W	68.5	U	
9/9/2017	@	New Mexico	30	28	W	7.5	W	68.5	U	"Rio Grande Rivalry"
9/16/2017	vs	TROY	24	27	L	9.5	W	60.0	U	
9/23/2017	vs	TEXAS-EL PASO	41	14	W	-17.5	W	58.5	U	"Brass Spittoon"
9/30/2017	@	Arkansas	24	42	L	18.5	W	61.0	O	
10/7/2017	@	Appalachian State	31	45	L	12.5	L	55.5	O	
10/14/2017	@	Georgia Southern	35	27	W	-5.0	W	58.0	O	
10/28/2017	vs	ARKANSAS STATE	21	37	L	3.5	L	71.5	U	
11/4/2017	@	Texas State	45	35	W	-9.0	W	56.0	O	
11/18/2017	@	Louisiana-Lafayette	34	47	L	-4.0	L	64.0	O	
11/25/2017	vs	IDAHO	17	10	W	-10.0	L	56.5	U	
12/2/2017	vs	SOUTH ALABAMA	22	17	W	-12.0	L	54.5	U	
12/29/2017	vs	**Utah State**	26	20	W	5.5	W	64.0	U	Arizona Bowl
Coach: Doug Martin		Season Record >>	381	386	7-6	ATS>>	8-5	O/U>>	5-8	
2016-New Mexico State		Opponent	NNSU	Opp	S/U	Line	ATS	Total	O/U	
9/3/2016	@	Texas-El Paso	22	38	L	9.0	L	58.0	O	"Brass Spittoon"
9/10/2016	vs	NEW MEXICO	32	31	W	11.5	W	61.5	O	"Rio Grande Rivalry"
9/17/2016	@	Kentucky	42	62	L	22.0	W	66.0	O	
9/24/2016	@	Troy	6	52	L	20.0	L	66.5	U	
10/1/2016	vs	LOUISIANA-LAFAYETTE	37	31	W	-5.5	W	68.0	T	{2 OT}
10/15/2016	@	Idaho	23	55	L	4.0	L	67.5	O	
10/22/2016	vs	GEORGIA SOUTHERN	19	22	L	14.0	W	64.0	U	
10/29/2016	@	Texas A&M	10	52	L	42.5	W	71.0	U	
11/12/2016	@	Arkansas State	22	41	L	18.5	L	63.0	T	
11/19/2016	vs	TEXAS STATE	50	10	W	-10.0	W	67.0	U	
11/26/2016	vs	APPALACHIAN STATE	7	37	L	20.0	L	60.0	U	
12/3/2016	@	South Alabama	28	35	L	11.0	W	58.5	O	
Coach: Doug Martin		Season Record >>	298	466	3-9	ATS>>	7-5	O/U>>	5-5-2	

Copyright © 2021 by Steve's Football Bible, LLC

NEW MEXICO STATE AGGIES INDEPENDENT

STADIUM: Aggie Memorial Stadium {30,343}			Location: Las Cruces, NM						COACH: Doug Martin	
DATE		Opponent	Nmsu	Opp	S/U	Line	ATS	Total	O/U	Trends & Angles
8/28/2021	vs	TEXAS-EL PASO								3-0 S/U & ATS vs Texas-El Paso since 2017
9/4/2021	@	San Diego State								0-8 S/U vs San Diego State since 1969
9/11/2021	@	New Mexico								3-13 S/U @ New Mexico as Dog since 1986
9/25/2021	vs	HAWAII								0-7 S/U vs Hawaii as Dog since 2005
10/2/2021	@	San Jose State								0-4 S/U @ San Jose State since 2005
10/9/2021	@	Nevada								6-1 O/U vs Nevada as Dog since 2005
10/16/2021	vs	DIXIE STATE								1st meeting
10/23/2021	@	Hawaii								1-8 S/U prior to playing Utah State since 2005
11/6/2021	vs	UTAH STATE								vs Utah State - Utah State leads series 31-8
11/13/2021	@	Alabama								vs Alabama - Alabama leads series 1-0
11/20/2021	@	Kentucky								0-13 S/U in final road game of season since 2007
11/27/2021	vs	MASSACHUSETTS								1st meeting
	vs									BOWL GAME

Pointspread Analysis Non-Conference		Pointspread Analysis Bowl Games
vs New Mexico - New Mexico leads series 71-33-5		3-0 S/U in Bowl Games since 1959
10-2 O/U vs New Mexico as Dog since 2005		
0-4 S/U vs San Diego State as Dog since 2009	San Diego State	3-12 S/U after playing Texas-El Paso since 2005
vs San Diego State - San Diego State leads series 10-1-1	San Diego State	5-1 ATS after playing Texas-El Paso since 2014
vs San Jose State - SJSU leads series 17-3	San Diego State	6-1 O/U after playing Texas-El Paso since 2013
1-13 S/U vs San Jose State as 4 point or more Dog since 1985	San Diego State	0-11 S/U prior to playing New Mexico since 2009
vs UTEP - Texas-El Paso leads series 57-38-2	New Mexico	2-18 S/U in 2nd road game of season since 2000
0-7 S/U vs Texas-El Paso as Dog since 2009	New Mexico	12-1 O/U in 2nd road game of season since 2007
0-11 S/U vs UTEP as 9 point or more Dog since 1989	HAWAII	1-7 S/U after playing New Mexico since 2012
0-4 O/U vs Texas-El Paso as favorite since 2007	Alabama	2-13 S/U after playing Utah State since 1998
1-11 S/U vs Utah State as 6 point or more Dog since 1986	Kentucky	1-9 ATS in final road game of season since 2010
1-7 S/U & ATS vs Utah State as favorite since 1992	Kentucky	7-1 O/U in final road game of season since 2012
Game 1-7 O/U vs Utah State since 2007		
Dog		
0-62 S/U as 25.5 point or more Dog since 1985		
2-35 S/U as 20.5-25 point Dog since 1987		
9-1 O/U as 20.5-25 point Dog since 2012		
0-21 S/U @ home as 20.5 point or more Dog since 1986		
4-16 S/U on road as 15.5-20 point Dog since 1985		
0-12 S/U @ home as 15.5-20 point Dog since 1988		
2-25 S/U on road as 10.5-15 point Dog since 1989		
9-2 O/U as 10.5-15 point Dog since 2012		
2-12 S/U @ home as 10.5-15 point Dog since 1990		
2-15 S/U on road as 7.5-10 point Dog since 1985		
4-13 S/U @ home as 3.5-7 point Dog since 2004		
2-11 S/U on road as 3.5-7 point Dog since 2002		
3-10 ATS on road as 3.5-7 point Dog since 2002		
2-8 S/U & ATS as 3 point or less Dog since 2005		
Favorite		
10-1 S/U @ home as 10.5 point or more favorite since 1999		

Copyright © 2021 by Steve's Football Bible, LLC

2020-North Carolina		Opponent	UNC	Opp	S/U	Line	ATS	Total	O/U	
9/12/2020	vs	SYRACUSE	31	6	W	-23.0	W	65.5	U	
10/3/2020	@	Boston College	26	22	W	-14.5	L	52.5	U	
10/10/2020	vs	VIRGINIA TECH	56	45	W	-3.0	W	58.5	O	
10/17/2020	@	Florida State	28	31	L	-13.5	L	65.0	U	
10/24/2020	vs	NC STATE	48	21	W	-16.0	W	61.5	O	
10/31/2020	@	Virginia	41	44	L	-8.0	L	61.5	O	*"South's Oldest Rivalry"*
11/7/2020	@	Duke	56	24	W	-11.0	W	63.0	O	*"Victory Bell"*
11/14/2020	vs	WAKE FOREST	59	53	W	-13.0	L	70.5	O	
11/27/2020	vs	NOTRE DAME	17	31	L	4.5	L	69.5	U	
12/5/2020	vs	*WESTERN CAROLINA*	49	9	W	-48.5	L	69.5	U	
12/12/2020	@	Miami	62	26	W	3.0	W	72.5	O	
1/2/2021	**vs**	**Texas A&M**	**27**	**41**	**L**	**10.0**	**L**	**65.5**	**O**	**Orange Bowl**
Coach: Mack Brown		Season Record >>	500	353	8-4	ATS>>	5-7	O/U>>	7-5	
2019-North Carolina		Opponent	UNC	Opp	S/U	Line	ATS	Total	O/U	
8/31/2019	vs	*South Carolina*	24	20	W	12.0	W	62.5	U	**Bank Of America Stadium**
9/7/2019	vs	MIAMI	28	25	W	5.0	W	46.0	O	
9/12/2019	@	Wake Forest	18	24	L	3.0	L	65.0	U	
9/21/2019	vs	*APPALACHIAN STATE*	31	34	L	-2.0	L	58.0	O	
9/28/2019	vs	CLEMSON	20	21	L	27.5	W	60.0	U	
10/5/2019	@	Georgia Tech	38	22	W	-10.0	W	47.0	O	
10/19/2019	@	Virginia Tech	41	43	L	-4.0	L	57.0	O	{6 OT}
10/26/2019	vs	DUKE	20	17	W	-3.0	T	53.5	U	*"Victory Bell"*
11/2/2019	vs	VIRGINIA	31	38	L	1.0	L	47.5	O	*"South's Oldest Rivalry"*
11/14/2019	@	Pittsburgh	27	34	L	4.5	L	48.5	O	{OT}
11/23/2019	vs	*MERCER*	56	7	W	-38.5	W	NT	---	
11/30/2019	@	NC State	41	10	W	-11.5	W	58.0	U	
12/27/2019	**vs**	**Temple**	**55**	**13**	**W**	**-6.5**	**W**	**56.5**	**O**	**Military Bowl**
Coach: Mack Brown		Season Record >>	430	308	7-6	ATS>>	7-5-1	O/U>>	7-5	
2018-North Carolina		Opponent	UNC	Opp	S/U	Line	ATS	Total	O/U	
9/1/2018	@	*California*	17	24	L	7.0	T	58.0	U	
9/8/2018	@	*East Carolina*	19	41	L	-15.5	L	59.0	O	
9/22/2018	vs	PITTSBURGH	38	35	W	2.5	W	48.0	O	
9/27/2018	@	Miami	10	47	L	18.5	L	55.0	O	
10/13/2018	vs	VIRGINIA TECH	19	22	L	6.5	W	57.5	U	
10/20/2018	@	Syracuse	37	40	L	10.0	W	67.0	O	{2 OT}
10/27/2018	@	Virginia	21	31	L	9.0	L	50.5	O	*"South's Oldest Rivalry"*
11/3/2018	vs	GEORGIA TECH	28	38	L	3.5	L	65.0	O	
11/10/2018	@	Duke	35	42	L	7.5	W	58.5	O	*"Victory Bell"*
11/17/2018	vs	*WESTERN CAROLINA*	49	26	W	-30.5	L	NT	---	
11/24/2018	vs	NC STATE	28	34	L	7.0	W	59.0	O	{OT}
Coach: Larry Fedora		Season Record >>	731	688	2-9	ATS>>	5-5-1	O/U>>	8-2	
2017-North Carolina		Opponent	UNC	Opp	S/U	Line	ATS	Total	O/U	
9/2/2017	vs	*CALIFORNIA*	30	35	L	-13.0	L	57.0	O	
9/9/2017	vs	LOUISVILLE	35	47	L	12.0	T	66.0	O	
9/16/2017	@	*Old Dominion*	53	23	W	-11.0	W	56.5	O	
9/23/2017	vs	DUKE	17	27	L	-1.5	L	61.5	U	*"Victory Bell"*
9/30/2017	@	Georgia Tech	7	33	L	10.0	L	58.0	U	
10/7/2017	vs	*NOTRE DAME*	10	33	L	13.5	L	63.5	U	
10/14/2017	vs	VIRGINIA	14	20	L	3.0	L	53.0	U	*"South's Oldest Rivalry"*
10/21/2017	@	Virginia Tech	7	59	L	20.5	L	53.5	O	
10/28/2017	vs	MIAMI	19	24	L	21.0	W	55.5	U	
11/9/2017	@	Pittsburgh	34	31	W	10.0	W	50.0	O	
11/18/2017	vs	*WESTERN CAROLINA*	65	10	W	-21.0	W	NT	---	
11/25/2017	@	NC State	21	33	L	14.5	W	56.0	U	
Coach: Larry Fedora		Season Record >>	312	375	3-9	ATS>>	5-6-1	O/U>>	5-6	

Copyright © 2021 by Steve's Football Bible, LLC

NORTH CAROLINA TAR HEELS   ACC Coastal

STADIUM: Kenan Memorial Stadium {50,500}		Location: Chapel Hill, NC								COACH: Mack Brown
DATE		**Opponent**	**Unc**	**Opp**	**S/U**	**Line**	**ATS**	**Total**	**O/U**	**Trends & Angles**
9/2/2021	@	Virginia Tech								1-11 S/U vs Virginia Tech as Dog since 2004
9/11/2021	vs	*GEORGIA STATE*								1st meeting
9/18/2021	vs	**VIRGINIA**								Game 2-7 O/U @ home vs Virginia since 2003
9/25/2021	vs	**WAKE FOREST**								vs Wake Forest - HOME team 6-0 S/U since 2007
9/25/2021	@	Georgia Tech								vs Georgia Tech - Georgia Tech leads series 30-22-3
10/2/2021	vs	**DUKE**								vs Duke - UNC leads series 61-40-4
10/9/2021	vs	**FLORIDA STATE**								vs Florida State - FSU leads series 16-3-1
10/16/2021	vs	**MIAMI**								vs Miami - UNC leads series 13-11
10/30/2021	@	*Notre Dame*								0-12 S/U @ Notre Dame since 1950
11/11/2021	@	Pittsburgh								4-1 S/U & ATS @ Pittsburgh since 2000
11/20/2021	vs	*WOFFORD*								1st meeting
11/26/2021	@	NC State								4-0 ATS @ NC State since 2013
12/4/2021	vs									ACC Championship
	vs									BOWL GAME

Pointspread Analysis Non-Conference		Pointspread Analysis Conference
1-16 S/U vs Non-Conf. as 10.5 point or more Dog since 1987		5-0 ATS vs Duke as Dog since 1990
1-8 S/U vs Non-Conf. as 3.5-7 point Dog since 2003		9-0 S/U vs Duke as 6.5-10 point favorite since 1991
0-7 S/U vs Non-Conf. as 3 point or less Dog since 2003		11-0 S/U vs Duke as 12.5 point or more favorite since 1983
7-2 S/U vs Non-Conf. as 3 point or less favorite sicne 1990		1-8 S/U vs Georgia Tech as Dog since 2005
2-8-1 O/U vs Non-Conf. as 3.5-7 point favorite since 1998		7-0 S/U vs Georgia Tech as 8 point or more favorite since 1983
5-0 S/U vs Non-Conf. as 7.5-10 point favorite since 2003		0-8-1 S/U vs Georgia Tech as 10 point or more Dog since 1989
6-1 S/U vs Non-Conf. as 15.5-20 point favorite since 2000		0-6 S/U vs Miami as 9 point or more Dog since 2005
24-0 S/U vs Non-Conf. as 20.5 point or more favorite since 1987		6-1 S/U & ATS vs Miami as 7.5 point or less Dog since 2007
0-4 S/U vs Notre Dame as Dog since 2006		vs NC State - North Carolina leads series 68-36-6
vs Notre Dame - Notre Dame leads series 19-2		11-2 ATS vs NC State as Dog since 1990
Dog		1-5 S/U & ATS vs NC State as 8-11.5 point favorite since 1986
0-16 S/U on road as 20.5 point or more Dog since 1987		vs Pittsburgh - North Carolina leads series 10-4
1-13 S/U on road as 15.5-20 point Dog since 1989		Game 6-1 O/U vs Pittsburgh since 2013
1-7 S/U @ home as 15.5-20 point Dog since 1989		6-1 S/U vs Pittsburgh since 2013
3-16 S/U on road as 10.5-15 point Dog since 1984		8-2 ATS vs Pittsburgh since 1998
2-7-1 S/U @ home as 10.5-15 point Dog since 1989		5-1 ATS vs Pittsburgh as Dog since 2000
2-10 S/U as 7.5-10 point Dog since 2004		4-0 S/U vs Pittsburgh as favorite since 1998
1-7 S/U on road as 7.5-10 point Dog since 2011		vs Virginia - North Carolina leads series 63-57-4
2-10 S/U @ home as 7.5-10 point Dog since 1985		0-4 S/U & ATS vs Virginia since 2017
2-8 S/U as 3.5-7 point Dog since 2015		7-0 S/U vs Virginia as favorite since 2010
4-13 S/U as 3 point or less Dog since 2003		0-7 S/U vs Virginia as 8 point or more Dog since 1989
Favorite		vs Virginia Tech - Virginia Tech leads series 24-13-6
1-5 O/U on road as 3 point or less favorite since 1996		2-6 ATS vs Virginia Tech since 2013
17-4 S/U on road as 3.5-7 point favorite since 1992		Game 4-10 O/U vs Virginia Tech since 2007
13-3 S/U as 7.5-10 point favorite since 2001		4-13 S/U vs Virginia Tech since 2004
5-1 S/U on road as 7.5-10 point favorite since 2003		vs Wake Forest - North Carolina leads series 70-36-2
10-1 S/U as 15.5-20 point favorite since 1998		8-0 S/U vs Wake Forest as 17 point or more favorite since 1983
41-0 S/U as 20.5 point or more favorite since 1983		5-0 S/U & ATS vs Wake Forest as 4.5-9 point favorite since 1985

Bowl Games		
5-2 S/U in Gator Bowl	GEORGIA ST.	12-2 S/U in 1st home game of season since 2007
0-3 S/U vs Pacific-12 in Bowl Games	GEORGIA ST.	6-1-1 ATS after playing Virginia Tech since 2013
0-4 S/U in Bowl Games as 3 point or less Dog since 1994	WAKE FOREST	9-3 ATS prior to playing Georgia Tech since 2008
1-4 O/U in Bowl Games as 3.5-7 point favorite since 1993	DUKE	3-14 O/U after playing Georgia Tech since 2003
	WOFFORD	8-1 S/U after playing Pittsburgh since 1998
	NC State	9-1 ATS in final road game of season since 2011

18-3 S/U @ home when ranked since 1996
9-1 S/U when ranked vs Duke since 1972 {5-0 @ home}
19-79-2 S/U on road vs ranked teams all time
0-11 S/U vs #1 ranked teams all time
0-9 S/U vs #2 ranked teams all time

Copyright © 2021 by Steve's Football Bible, LLC

NORTH CAROLINA STATE WOLFPACK   ACC Atlantic

2020-North Carolina State		Opponent	NCS	Opp	S/U	Line	ATS	Total	O/U	
9/19/2020	vs	WAKE FOREST	45	42	W	2.5	W	53.0	O	
9/26/2020	@	Virginia Tech	24	45	L	6.5	L	57.5	O	
10/3/2020	@	Pittsburgh	30	29	W	14.0	W	46.0	O	
10/10/2020	@	Virginia	38	21	W	7.0	W	58.5	O	
10/17/2020	vs	DUKE	31	20	W	-4.5	W	60.0	U	
10/24/2020	@	North Carolina	21	48	L	16.0	L	61.5	O	
11/6/2020	vs	MIAMI	41	44	L	11.0	W	58.0	O	
11/14/2020	vs	FLORIDA STATE	38	22	W	-12.0	W	60.5	U	
11/21/2020	vs	LIBERTY	15	14	W	-4.0	L	66.5	U	
11/28/2020	@	Syracuse	36	29	W	-17.5	L	49.5	O	
12/5/2020	vs	GEORGIA TECH	23	13	W	-7.0	W	61.0	U	
1/2/2021	vs	Kentucky	21	23	L	3.5	W	50.0	U	Gator Bowl
Coach: Dave Doeren		Season Record >>	363	350	8-4	ATS>>	8-4	O/U>>	7-5	
2019-North Carolina State		Opponent	NCS	Opp	S/U	Line	ATS	Total	O/U	
8/31/2019	vs	EAST CAROLINA	34	6	W	-17.5	W	51.5	U	"Victory Barrel"
9/7/2019	vs	WESTERN CAROLINA	41	0	W	-40.5	W	NT	---	
9/14/2019	@	West Virginia	27	44	L	-7.0	L	45.5	O	
9/21/2019	vs	BALL STATE	34	23	W	-19.5	L	58.5	U	
9/28/2019	@	Florida State	13	31	L	7.0	L	62.0	U	
10/10/2019	vs	SYRACUSE	16	10	W	-4.0	W	55.5	U	
10/19/2019	@	Boston College	24	45	L	-4.0	L	54.5	O	
11/2/2019	@	Wake Forest	10	44	L	7.5	L	60.5	U	
11/9/2019	vs	CLEMSON	10	55	L	35.0	L	54.0	O	"Textile Bowl"
11/16/2019	vs	LOUISVILLE	20	34	L	4.0	L	52.0	O	
11/21/2019	@	Georgia Tech	26	28	L	-2.5	L	46.5	O	
11/30/2019	vs	NORTH CAROLINA	10	41	L	11.5	L	58.0	U	
Coach: Dave Doeren		Season Record >>	265	361	4-8	ATS>>	3-9	O/U>>	5-6	
2018-North Carolina State		Opponent	NCS	Opp	S/U	Line	ATS	Total	O/U	
9/1/2018	vs	JAMES MADISON	24	13	W	-14.0	L	NT	---	
9/8/2018	vs	GEORIGA STATE	41	7	W	-24.5	W	56.0	U	
9/22/2018	@	Marshall	37	20	W	-5.5	W	57.0	T	
9/29/2018	vs	VIRGINIA	35	21	W	-6.0	W	52.5	O	
10/6/2018	vs	BOSTON COLLEGE	28	23	W	-6.5	L	60.5	U	
10/20/2018	@	Clemson	7	41	L	18.5	L	58.0	U	"Textile Bowl"
10/27/2018	@	Syracuse	41	51	L	-2.0	L	64.5	O	
11/3/2018	vs	FLORIDA STATE	47	28	W	-9.0	W	52.0	O	
11/8/2018	vs	WAKE FOREST	23	27	L	-19.0	L	66.5	U	
11/17/2018	@	Louisville	52	10	W	-16.0	W	65.5	U	
11/24/2018	@	North Carolina	34	28	W	-7.0	L	59.0	O	{OT}
12/1/2018	vs	EAST CAROLINA	58	3	W	-26.0	W	60.5	O	
12/31/2018	vs	Texas A&M	13	52	L	7.5	L	58.0	O	Gator Bowl
Coach: Dave Doeren		Season Record >>	440	324	9-4	ATS>>	6-7	O/U>>	6-5-1	
2017-North Carolina State		Opponent	NCS	Opp	S/U	Line	ATS	Total	O/U	
9/2/2017	vs	South Carolina	28	35	L	-7.5	L	50.0	O	Bank of America Stadium
9/9/2017	vs	MARSHALL	37	20	W	-21.0	L	55.0	O	
9/16/2017	vs	FURMAN	49	16	W	-36.5	L	NT	---	
9/23/2017	@	Florida State	27	21	W	11.5	W	50.5	U	
9/30/2017	vs	SYRACUSE	33	25	W	-14.0	L	61.0	U	
10/5/2017	vs	LOUISVILLE	39	25	W	3.0	W	66.0	U	
10/14/2017	@	Pittsburgh	35	17	W	-11.5	W	54.5	U	
10/28/2017	@	Notre Dame	14	35	L	7.0	L	59.5	U	
11/4/2017	vs	CLEMSON	31	38	L	10.0	W	51.5	O	"Textile Bowl"
11/11/2017	@	Boston College	17	14	W	-3.0	T	52.5	U	
11/18/2017	@	Wake Forest	24	30	L	2.5	L	62.5	U	
11/25/2017	vs	NORTH CAROLINA	33	21	W	-14.5	L	56.0	U	
12/29/2017	vs	Arizona State	52	31	W	-4.5	W	62.0	O	Sun Bowl
Coach: Dave Doeren		Season Record >>	419	328	9-4	ATS>>	5-7-1	O/U>>	4-8	

Copyright © 2021 by Steve's Football Bible, LLC

NORTH CAROLINA STATE WOLFPACK ACC Atlantic

STADIUM: Carter-Finley Stadium {57,583}		Location: Raleigh, NC				COACH: Dave Doeren			
DATE		Opponent	NCS	Opp	S/U	Line	ATS	Total	O/U	Trends & Angles
9/2/2021	vs	*SOUTH FLORIDA*								vs South Florida - NC State leads series 2-1
9/11/2021	@	*Mississippi State*								vs Mississippi State - Series tied 3-3
9/18/2021	vs	*FURMAN*								vs Furman - Furman leads series 8-5-4
9/25/2021	vs	**CLEMSON**								1-15 S/U vs Clemson as Dog since 2000
10/2/2021	vs	*LOUISIANA TECH*								vs Louisiana Tech - NC State leads series 1-0
10/16/2021	@	Boston College								vs Boston College - Boston College leads series 10-7
10/23/2021	@	Miami								vs Miami - Miami leads series 10-5-1
10/30/2021	vs	**LOUISVILLE**								vs Louisville - Louisville leads series 7-3
11/6/2021	@	Florida State								14-4 ATS vs Florida State as Dog since 2001
11/13/2021	@	Wake Forest								1-8 S/U @ Wake Forest since 2003
11/20/2021	vs	**SYRACUSE**								6-1 S/U @ home vs Syracuse since 1972
11/26/2021	vs	**NORTH CAROLINA**								vs North Carolina - UNC leads series 67-37-6
12/4/2021										ACC Championship
	vs									BOWL GAME

Pointspread Analysis Non-Conference		Pointspread Analysis Conference
1-7 S/U vs Non-Conf. as 7.5-10 point Dog since 1984		0-5 S/U vs Boston College as Dog since 2005 {1-4 ATS}
0-6 S/U vs Non-Conf. as 3.5-7 point Dog since 2008		4-0 O/U vs Boston College as Dog since 2007
5-0 S/U vs Non-Conf. as 3 point or less favorite since 2010		1-7 O/U vs Boston College as favorite since 2011
0-4 S/U & ATS vs Non-Conf. as 7.5-10 point favorite since 2006		vs Clemson - Clemson leads series 59-28-1
42-0 S/U vs Non-Conf. as 10.5 point or more favorite since 1989		1-15 S/U vs Clemson as 10 point or more Dog since 1983
Dog		vs Florida State - Florida State leads series 27-14
1-8 S/U on road as 20.5 point or more Dog since 1993		2-11 S/U vs Florida State as 18 point or more Dog since 1993
1-13 S/U on road as 15.5-20 point Dog since 1987		2-11 ATS vs North Carolina as favorite since 1990
1-8 S/U @ home as 10.5-15 point Dog since 1990		5-0 S/U & ATS vs UNC as 8.5-11 point Dog since 1986
1-8 S/U @ home as 7.5-10 point Dog since 1996		vs Syracuse - NC State leads series 12-2
2-13 S/U as 3.5-7 point Dog since 2012		3-0 S/U & ATS vs Syracuse as Dog since 1997
4-11 ATS as 3.5-7 point Dog since 2012		3-0 S/U & ATS vs Syracuse as Dog since 1997
Favorite		1-3 ATS @ home vs Syracuse since 2013
2-10 O/U @ home as 3 point or less favorite since 2000		vs Wake Forest - NC State leads series 67-41-6
6-0 S/U @ home as 3.5-7 point favorite since 2018		1-11 ATS @ Wake Forest since 1997
1-7 O/U @ home as 3.5-7 point favorite since 2013		14-1 S/U vs Wake Forest as 9 point or more favorite since 1990
1-8 O/U as 10.5-15 point favorite since 2012		2-5 S/U & ATS vs Wake Forest as Dog since 1987
45-1 S/U as 15.5 point or more favorite since 1989		vs Wake Forest - HOME team 12-2 S/U since 2007
Bowl Games	S. FLORIDA	11-0 S/U in 1st home game of season since 2010
6-1 O/U in Bowl Games since 2011	FURMAN	14-0 S/U in 2nd home game of season since 2007
10-2 ATS in Bowl Games since 2003	LA TECH	3-11 S/U prior to playing Boston College since 2006
5-2 O/U in Bowl Games as 3.5-7 point Dog since 1995	LA TECH	11-3 O/U prior to playing Boston College since 2006
3-0 S/U & ATS in Bowl Games as 3.5-7 point favorite since 2005	Boston College	4-13 S/U in 2nd road game of season since 2003
	Miami	1-11 S/U after playing Boston College since 2007
	Miami	1-8 O/U after playing Boston College since 2010
0-8-1 S/U when ranked vs Top #10 teams all time	Florida State	2-5 O/U after playing Louisville since 2007
0-4 S/U when ranked vs Florida State since 1992	Wake Forest	1-10 O/U after playing Florida State since 2010
1-14 S/U on road vs ranked teams since 2005	Wake Forest	2-7 S/U prior to playing Syracuse since 1998
10-2 ATS vs ranked Florida State since 2001	Wake Forest	0-8 O/U prior to playing Syracuse since 2013
0-6 ATS vs ranked North Carolina since 1993	Wake Forest	5-14 S/U in final road game of season since 2002

Copyright © 2021 by Steve's Football Bible, LLC

NORTHERN ILLINOIS HUSKIES MAC West

2020-Northern Illinois		Opponent	NIU	Opp	S/U	Line	ATS	Total	O/U	
11/4/2020	vs	BUFFALO	30	49	L	14.5	L	53.0	O	
11/11/2020	vs	CENTRAL MICHIGAN	10	40	L	6.0	L	57.0	O	
11/18/2020	@	Ball State	25	31	L	14.5	W	58.5	U	"Bronze Stalk Trophy"
11/28/2020	@	Western Michigan	27	30	L	18.5	W	64.5	U	
12/5/2020	vs	TOLEDO	24	41	L	9.0	L	53.5	O	
12/12/2020	@	Eastern Michigan	33	41	L	6.0	L	55.5	O	
Coach: Thomas Hammock		Season Record >>	149	232	0-6	ATS>>	2-4	O/U>>	3-3	
2019-Northern Illinois		Opponent	NIU	Opp	S/U	Line	ATS	Total	O/U	
8/31/2019	vs	ILLINOIS STATE	24	10	W	-6.5	W	NT	---	
9/7/2019	@	Utah	17	35	L	23.0	W	45.0	O	
9/14/2019	@	Nebraska	8	44	L	14.0	L	54.0	U	
9/28/2019	@	Vanderbilt	18	24	L	7.0	W	51.5	U	
10/5/2019	vs	BALL STATE	20	27	L	-4.0	L	54.5	U	"Bronze Stalk Trophy"
10/12/2019	@	Ohio	39	36	W	4.5	W	50.5	O	
10/19/2019	@	Miami-Ohio	24	27	L	-1.5	L	48.0	O	
10/26/2019	vs	AKRON	49	0	W	-22.5	W	41.5	O	
11/2/2019	@	Central Michigan	10	48	L	-1.5	L	49.5	O	
11/13/2019	@	Toledo	31	28	W	1.5	W	55.5	O	
11/19/2019	vs	EASTERN MICHIGAN	17	45	L	-3.5	L	57.5	O	
11/26/2019	vs	WESTERN MICHIGAN	17	14	W	9.5	W	51.5	U	
Coach: Thomas Hammock		Season Record >>	274	338	5-7	ATS>>	7-5	O/U>>	7-4	
2018-Northern Illinois		Opponent	NIU	Opp	S/U	Line	ATS	Total	O/U	
9/1/2018	@	Iowa	7	33	L	9.5	L	46.5	U	
9/8/2018	vs	UTAH	6	17	L	10.0	L	47.0	U	
9/15/2018	vs	CENTRAL MICHIGAN	24	16	W	-14.0	L	48.0	U	
9/22/2018	@	Florida State	19	37	L	10.0	L	44.5	O	
9/29/2018	@	Eastern Michigan	26	23	W	3.5	W	50.5	U	{3 OT}
10/6/2018	@	Ball State	24	16	W	-3.0	W	53.0	U	"Bronze Stalk Trophy"
10/13/2018	vs	OHIO	24	21	W	-6.0	L	51.5	U	
10/27/2018	@	Byu	7	6	W	6.5	W	43.0	U	
11/1/2018	@	Akron	36	26	W	-6.0	W	37.0	O	
11/7/2018	vs	TOLEDO	38	15	W	-3.5	W	54.0	U	
11/14/2018	vs	MIAMI-OHIO	7	13	L	-6.0	L	48.0	U	
11/20/2018	@	Western Michigan	21	28	L	-6.5	L	48.5	O	
11/30/2018	vs	Buffalo	30	29	W	3.0	W	51.5	O	MAC CHAMPIONSHIP
12/18/2018	vs	Alabama-Birmingham	13	37	L	1.0	L	41.0	O	Boca Raton Bowl
Coach: Rod Carey		Season Record >>	282	317	8-6	ATS>>	6-8	O/U>>	5-9	
2017-Northern Illinois		Opponent	NIU	Opp	S/U	Line	ATS	Total	O/U	
9/1/2017	vs	BOSTON COLLEGE	20	23	L	3.5	W	46.0	U	
9/9/2017	vs	EASTERN ILLINOIS	38	10	W	-14.0	W	NT	---	
9/16/2017	@	Nebraska	21	17	W	10.5	W	56.5	U	
9/30/2017	@	San Diego State	28	34	L	9.0	W	47.0	O	
10/7/2017	vs	KENT STATE	24	3	W	-23.0	L	43.5	U	
10/14/2017	@	Buffalo	14	13	W	-7.0	L	49.5	U	
10/21/2017	@	Bowling Green	48	17	W	-14.0	W	56.5	O	
10/26/2017	vs	EASTERN MICHIGAN	30	27	W	-7.5	L	47.0	O	{OT}
11/2/2017	@	Toledo	17	27	L	7.5	L	57.0	U	
11/9/2017	vs	BALL STATE	63	17	W	-29.0	W	51.0	O	"Bronze Stalk Trophy"
11/15/2017	vs	WESTERN MICHIGAN	35	31	W	-8.5	L	50.0	O	
11/24/2017	@	Central Michigan	24	31	L	-2.5	L	51.5	O	
12/26/2017	vs	Duke	14	36	L	5.5	L	47.0	O	Quick Lane Bowl
Coach: Rod Carey		Season Record >>	376	286	8-5	ATS>>	6-7	O/U>>	7-5	

Copyright © 2021 by Steve's Football Bible, LLC

NORTHERN ILLINOIS HUSKIES   MAC West

STADIUM: Huskie Stadium {24,000}			Location: DeKalb, IL				COACH: Thomas Hammock	

DATE		Opponent	NIU	Opp	S/U	Line	ATS	Total	O/U	Trends & Angles
9/4/2021	@	*Georgia Tech*								1st meeting
9/11/2021	vs	*WYOMING*								vs Wyoming - Wyoming leads series 1-0
9/18/2021	@	*Michigan*								vs Michigan - Michigan leads series 1-0
9/25/2021	vs	*MAINE*								1st meeting
10/2/2021	vs	EASTERN MICHIGAN								vs E. Michigan - NIU leads series 33-16-2
10/9/2021	@	Toledo								4-1 S/U & ATS @ Toledo since 2011
10/16/2021	vs	BOWLING GREEN								6-1 S/U vs B. Green as favorite since 2004
10/23/2021		Central Michigan								vs C. Michigan - CMU leads series 30-25-1
11/3/2021	@	Kent State								9-0 S/U vs Kent State as favorite since 2002
11/10/2021	vs	BALL STATE								16-2 S/U vs Ball State as favorite since 1997
11/17/2021	@	Buffalo								
11/23/2021	vs	WESTERN MICHIGAN								6-0 S/U @ home vs W. Michigan since 2009
12/3/2021	vs									MAC Championship
	vs									BOWL GAME

Pointspread Analysis Non-Conference		Pointspread Analysis Conference
0-39 S/U vs Non-Conf. as 15.5 point or more Dog since 1989		vs Ball State - NIU leads series 25-21-2
1-13 S/U vs Non-Conf. as 7.5-10 point Dog since 1991		1-5 S/U vs Ball State as Dog since 1997 {5-1 ATS}
12-3 S/U vs Non-conf. as 3.5-7 point favorite since 1989		1-4 S/U & ATS vs Bowling Green as Dog since 1997
15-1 S/U vs Non-Conf. as 10.5 point or more favorite since 1993		10-0 S/U vs Buffalo as favorite since 1999
Dog		1-5 S/U vs Central Michigan as favorite since 2014 {0-6 ATS}
14-5-1 ATS as road Dog since 2010		10-1 S/U vs Eastern Michigan as favorite since 2008
0-49 S/U as 15.5 point or more Dog since 1989		8-0 S/U @ Eastern Michigan as favorite since 2002
1-9 O/U as 15.5-20 point Dog since 2004		Game 2-7 O/U vs Toledo since 2012
0-13 S/U @ home as 10.5 point or more Dog since 1995		vs Toledo - Toledo leads series 32-16
3-10 ATS as 10.5-15 point Dog since 2006		1-8 O/U vs Toledo as favorite since 2004
0-7 O/U @ home as 3.5-7 point Dog since 2001		5-0 S/U @ home vs Toledo as favorite since 2008
8-1 ATS on road as 3.5-7 point Dog since 2010		10-1-1 ATS vs Western Michigan as Dog since 1997
Favorite		6-0 S/U @ home vs Western Michigan as favorite since 2003
13-2 S/U @ home as 7.5-10 point favorite since 1989		9-3 S/U vs Western Michigan since 2009
7-1 S/U on road as 7.5-10 point favorite since 1989		vs Western Michigan - WMU leads series 26-20
7-0 S/U on road as 10.5-15 point favorite since 2005		0-5 S/U vs W. Michigan as 8.5 point or more Dog since 1997
12-1 S/U @ home as 10.5-15 point favorite since 2008		5-0 ATS vs W. Michigan as 8.5 point or more Dog since 1997
17-1 S/U as 10.5-15 point favorite since 2008		
7-0 S/U as 15.5-20 point favorite since 2011	MAINE	2-11 O/U in 2nd home game of season since 2006
8-0 S/U on road as 15.5-20 point favorite since 2003	MAINE	9-2 S/U prior to playing Eastern Michigan since 2009
18-0 S/U @ home as 20.5 point or more favorite since 2006	E. MICHIGAN	11-2 S/U prior to playing Toledo since 2008
8-0 S/U on road as 20.5 point or more favorite since 2002	B. GREEN	15-1 S/U after playing Toledo since 2003
Bowl Games	B. GREEN	7-2 ATS after playing Toledo since 2010
0-6 S/U & ATS in Bowl Games since 2013	Kent State	9-2 S/U after playing Central Michigan since 2008
0-3 S/U & ATS in Bowl Games as 10.5-15 point Dog since 2006	Buffalo	8-2 S/U & ATS prior to playing Western Michigan since 2010
0-3 S/U & ATS in Bowl Games as 3.5-7 point Dog since 2010	Buffalo	8-2 S/U after playing Ball State since 2010
4-0 O/U in Bowl Games since 2014	Buffalo	8-2 S/U in final road game of season since 2010
	Buffalo	14-2 ATS in final road game of season since 2004
	W. MICHIGAN	3-14 O/U in final home game of season since 2004
	W. MICHIGAN	1-8-1 ATS in final home game of season since 2011

Copyright © 2021 by Steve's Football Bible, LLC

NORTH TEXAS MEAN GREEN   C-USA West

2020-North Texas		Opponent	UNT	Opp	S/U	Line	ATS	Total	O/U	
9/5/2020	vs	HOUSTON BAPTIST	57	31	W	-23.5	W	73.0	O	
9/19/2020	vs	SMU	35	65	L	14.5	L	71.0	O	"Safeway Bowl"
10/3/2020	vs	SOUTHERN MISSISSIPPI	31	41	L	-1.5	L	75.0	U	
10/10/2020	vs	CHARLOTTE	21	49	L	3.0	L	66.5	O	
10/17/2020	@	Middle Tennessee	52	35	W	3.5	W	70.5	O	
11/21/2020	vs	RICE	27	17	W	-1.0	W	65.0	U	
11/28/2020	@	Texas-San Antonio	17	49	L	1.5	L	67.0	U	
12/3/2020	vs	LOUISIANA TECH	31	42	L	1.0	L	65.0	O	
12/11/2020	vs	TEXAS-EL PASO	45	43	W	-9.5	L	66.0	O	
12/21/2020	**vs**	**Appalachian State**	**28**	**56**	**L**	22.5	**L**	**68.0**	**O**	**Myrtle Beach Bowl**
Coach: Seth Littrell		Season Record >>	344	428	4-6	ATS>>	3-7	O/U>>	7-3	

2019-North Texas		Opponent	UNT	Opp	S/U	Line	ATS	Total	O/U	
8/31/2019	vs	ABILENE CHRISTIAN	51	31	W	-22.5	L	NT	---	
9/7/2019	@	Smu	27	49	L	3.5	L	73.0	O	"Safeway Bowl"
9/14/2019	@	California	17	23	L	14.5	W	50.5	U	
9/21/2019	vs	TEXAS-SAN ANTONIO	45	3	W	-17.0	W	55.5	U	
9/28/2019	vs	HOUSTON	25	46	L	-8.0	L	59.0	O	
10/12/2019	@	Southern Miss	27	45	L	3.0	L	59.0	O	
10/19/2019	vs	MIDDLE TENNESSEE	33	30	W	-7.0	L	59.5	O	
10/26/2019	@	Charlotte	38	39	L	-4.0	L	64.0	O	
11/2/2019	vs	TEXAS-EL PASO	52	26	W	-23.0	W	59.0	O	
11/9/2019	@	Louisiana Tech	17	52	L	5.0	L	71.5	U	
11/23/2019	@	Rice	14	20	L	-6.5	L	55.5	U	
11/30/2019	vs	ALABAMA-BIRMINGHAM	21	26	L	3.0	L	49.5	U	
Coach: Seth Littrell		Season Record >>	367	390	4-8	ATS>>	3-9	O/U>>	6-5	

2018-North Texas		Opponent	UNT	Opp	S/U	Line	ATS	Total	O/U	
9/1/2018	vs	SMU	46	23	W	-3.5	W	71.5	U	"Safeway Bowl"
9/8/2018	vs	INCARNATE WORD	58	16	W	-43.0	L	NT	----	
9/15/2018	@	Arkansas	44	17	W	5.5	W	63.0	U	
9/22/2018	@	Liberty	47	7	W	-11.0	W	67.0	U	
9/29/2018	vs	LOUISIANA TECH	27	29	L	-7.0	L	63.0	U	
10/6/2018	@	Texas-El Paso	27	24	W	-25.5	L	53.0	U	
10/13/2018	vs	SOUTHERN MISSISSIPPI	30	7	W	-7.0	W	53.0	U	
10/20/2018	@	Alabama-Birmingham	21	29	L	1.5	L	53.5	U	
10/27/2018	vs	RICE	41	17	W	-29.0	L	58.5	U	
11/10/2018	@	Old Dominion	31	34	L	-14.5	L	66.0	U	
11/17/2018	vs	FLORIDA ATLANTIC	41	38	W	-4.0	L	63.5	O	
11/24/2018	@	Texas-San Antonio	24	21	W	-24.5	L	51.5	U	
12/15/2018	**vs**	**Utah State**	**13**	**52**	**L**	7.0	**L**	**67.5**	**U**	**New Mexico Bowl**
Coach: Seth Littrell		Season Record >>	450	314	9-4	ATS>>	4-9	O/U>>	1-11	

2017-North Texas		Opponent	UNT	Opp	S/U	Line	ATS	Total	O/U	
9/2/2017	vs	LAMAR	59	14	W	-17.5	W	54.0	O	
9/9/2017	@	Smu	32	54	L	12.0	L	64.0	O	"Safeway Bowl"
9/16/2017	@	Iowa	14	31	L	19.5	W	52.0	U	
9/23/2017	vs	ALABAMA-BIRMINGHAM	46	43	W	-9.5	L	59.5	O	
9/30/2017	@	Southern Miss	43	28	W	7.5	W	56.5	O	
10/14/2017	vs	TEXAS-SAN ANTONIO	29	26	W	2.5	W	58.0	U	
10/21/2017	@	Florida Atlantic	31	69	L	3.5	L	67.0	O	
10/28/2017	vs	OLD DOMINION	45	38	W	-12.0	L	60.0	O	
11/4/2017	@	Louisiana Tech	24	23	W	PK	W	67.0	U	
11/11/2017	vs	TEXAS-EL PASO	45	10	W	-24.0	W	53.0	O	
11/18/2017	vs	ARMY	52	49	W	-2.0	W	59.5	O	
11/25/2017	@	Rice	30	14	W	-12.0	W	61.5	U	
12/2/2017	**@**	**Florida Atlantic**	**17**	**41**	**L**	10.5	**L**	**71.0**	**U**	**Conference USA Championship**
12/16/2017	**vs**	**Troy**	**30**	**50**	**L**	5.0	**L**	**61.5**	**O**	**New Orleans Bowl**
Coach: Seth Littrell		Season Record >>	497	490	9-5	ATS>>	8-6	O/U>>	9-5	

Copyright © 2021 by Steve's Football Bible, LLC

NORTH TEXAS MEAN GREEN   C-USA West

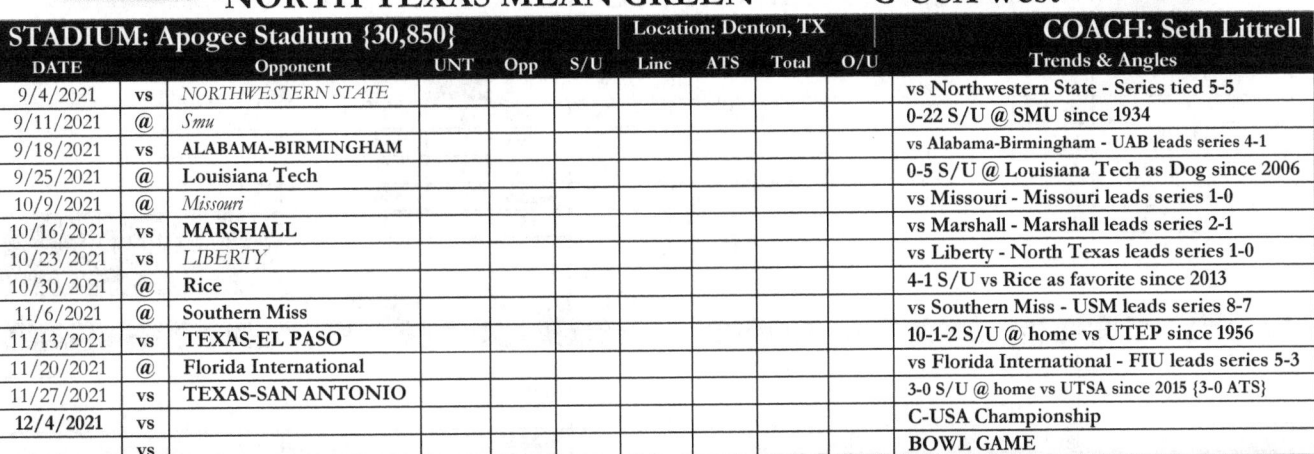

STADIUM: Apogee Stadium {30,850}					Location: Denton, TX				COACH: Seth Littrell	
DATE		Opponent	UNT	Opp	S/U	Line	ATS	Total	O/U	Trends & Angles
9/4/2021	vs	NORTHWESTERN STATE								vs Northwestern State - Series tied 5-5
9/11/2021	@	Smu								0-22 S/U @ SMU since 1934
9/18/2021	vs	ALABAMA-BIRMINGHAM								vs Alabama-Birmingham - UAB leads series 4-1
9/25/2021	@	Louisiana Tech								0-5 S/U @ Louisiana Tech as Dog since 2006
10/9/2021	@	Missouri								vs Missouri - Missouri leads series 1-0
10/16/2021	vs	MARSHALL								vs Marshall - Marshall leads series 2-1
10/23/2021	vs	LIBERTY								vs Liberty - North Texas leads series 1-0
10/30/2021	@	Rice								4-1 S/U vs Rice as favorite since 2013
11/6/2021	@	Southern Miss								vs Southern Miss - USM leads series 8-7
11/13/2021	vs	TEXAS-EL PASO								10-1-2 S/U @ home vs UTEP since 1956
11/20/2021	@	Florida International								vs Florida International - FIU leads series 5-3
11/27/2021	vs	TEXAS-SAN ANTONIO								3-0 S/U @ home vs UTSA since 2015 {3-0 ATS}
12/4/2021	vs									C-USA Championship
	vs									BOWL GAME

Pointspread Analysis Non-Conference		Pointspread Analysis Conference
1-40 S/U vs Non-Conf. as 20.5 or more Dog since 1995		0-4 S/U & ATS vs Fla International as Dog since 2008
2-20 S/U vs Non-Conf. as 10.5-20 point Dog since 1995		vs Louisiana Tech - La Tech leads series 12-7
3-13 S/U vs Non-Conf. as 3.5-7 point Dog since 1997		0-5 S/U vs Louisiana Tech as Dog since 2005
7-1 S/U vs Non-Conf. as 10.5 point or more favorite since 2003		4-1 S/U vs Rice since 2016
vs Smu - SMU leads series 33-6-1		vs Rice - North Texas leads series 6-5
0-6 S/U vs SMU as Dog since 2007 {1-5 ATS}		4-1 O/U vs Rice as Dog since 2008
Dog		vs Texas-El Paso - North Texas leads series 18-8-3
1-25 S/U as 30.5 point or more Dog since 1995		Game 0-6 O/U vs Texas-San Antonio since 2015
6-0 ATS as 30.5 point or more Dog since 2011		vs Texas-San Antonio - Series tied 4-4
1-32 S/U as 20.5-30 point Dog since 1995		**Bowl Games**
3-19 S/U as 15.5-20 point Dog since 1995		1-4 S/U in New Orleans Bowl since 2001
0-15 S/U @ home as 15.5 point or more Dog since 1995		2-8 S/U in Bowl Games since 1948
0-8 S/U on road as 10.5-15 point Dog since 2011		0-3 S/U in Bowl Games as 10.5-15 point Dog since 2001
4-14 S/U on road as 3.5-7 point Dog since 2005		0-4 S/U & ATS in Bowl Games as 3.5-7 point Dog since 2003
3-11 ATS as 3.5-7 point Dog since 2012		
3-12 O/U @ home as 3.5-7 point Dog since 2005	NW STATE	8-3 O/U in 1st home game of season since 2008
0-5 S/U on road as 3 point or less Dog since 2009 {0-5 ATS}	NW STATE	2-5 S/U & ATS prior to playing SMU since 2006
Favorite	Smu	2-9 S/U in 1st road game of season since 2010
0-5 ATS @ home as 7.5-10 point Favorite since 2013	UAB	4-12 ATS in 2nd home game of season since 2005
6-1 S/U on road as 7.5-15 point favorite since 2002	UAB	7-2 ATS prior to playing Louisiana Tech since 2005
8-0 S/U @ home as 10.5-15 point favorite since 2001	UAB	2-7 O/U prior to playing Louisiana Tech since 2005
16-0 S/U @ home as 15.5 point or more favorite since 2002	Louisiana Tech	2-19 S/U in 2nd road game of season since 2000
	Southern Miss	1-8 O/U after playing Rice since 2008

Print Version $34.99   Print Version $39.99   Print Version $39.99

These books available at numerous online retailers

Copyright © 2021 by Steve's Football Bible, LLC

NORTHWESTERN WILDCATS   BIG TEN West

2020-Northwestern		Opponent	NW	Opp	S/U	Line	ATS	Total	O/U	
10/24/2020	vs	MARYLAND	43	3	W	-14.0	W	52.5	U	
10/31/2020	@	Iowa	21	20	W	-1.0	T	43.0	U	
11/7/2020	vs	NEBRASKA	21	13	W	-4.0	W	53.0	U	
11/14/2020	@	Purdue	27	20	W	-3.5	W	48.5	U	
11/21/2020	vs	WISCONSIN	17	7	W	7.0	W	43.0	U	
11/28/2020	@	Michigan State	20	23	L	-13.5	L	40.0	O	
12/12/2020	vs	ILLINOIS	28	10	W	-13.0	W	41.0	U	"Land of Lincoln Trophy"
12/19/2020	vs	Ohio State	10	22	L	16.5	W	57.5	U	Big Ten Championship
1/1/2021	vs	Auburn	35	19	W	-3.5	W	45.0	O	Citrus Bowl
Coach: Pat Fitzgerald		Season Record >>	222	137	7-2	ATS>>	7-1-1	O/U>>	2-7	
2019-Northwestern		Opponent	NW	Opp	S/U	Line	ATS	Total	O/U	
8/31/2019	@	Stanford	7	17	L	6.5	L	47.0	U	
9/14/2019	vs	UNLV	30	14	W	-18.5	L	51.5	U	
9/21/2019	vs	MICHIGAN STATE	10	31	L	7.5	L	35.5	O	
9/28/2019	@	Wisconsin	15	24	L	23.5	W	46.0	U	
10/5/2019	@	Nebraska	10	13	L	7.5	W	48.5	U	
10/19/2019	vs	OHIO STATE	3	52	L	27.0	L	50.0	O	
10/26/2019	vs	IOWA	0	20	L	8.5	L	36.5	U	
11/2/2019	@	Indiana	3	34	L	8.5	L	44.0	U	
11/9/2019	vs	PURDUE	22	24	L	PK	L	39.0	O	
11/16/2019	vs	MASSACHUSETTS	45	6	W	-38.0	W	57.5	U	
11/23/2019	vs	MINNESOTA	22	38	L	15.5	L	41.5	O	
11/30/2019	@	Illinois	29	10	W	6.0	W	39.0	T	"Land of Lincoln Trophy"
Coach: Pat Fitzgerald		Season Record >>	196	283	3-9	ATS>>	4-8	O/U>>	4-7-1	
2018-Northwestern		Opponent	NW	Opp	S/U	Line	ATS	Total	O/U	
8/30/2018	@	Purdue	31	27	W	PK	W	51.0	O	
9/8/2018	@	Duke	7	21	L	-2.5	L	47.5	U	
9/15/2018	vs	AKRON	34	39	L	-21.0	L	46.5	O	
9/29/2018	vs	MICHIGAN	17	20	L	14.5	W	46.5	U	
10/6/2018	@	Michigan State	29	19	W	10.0	W	43.5	O	
10/13/2018	vs	NEBRASKA	34	31	W	-3.5	L	59.5	O	{OT}
10/20/2018	@	Rutgers	18	15	W	-20.0	L	49.0	U	
10/27/2018	vs	WISCONSIN	31	17	W	5.0	W	50.5	U	
11/3/2018	vs	NOTRE DAME	21	31	L	10.0	T	49.5	O	
11/10/2018	@	Iowa	14	10	W	11.5	W	44.0	U	
11/17/2018	@	Minnesota	24	14	W	3.0	W	48.5	U	
11/24/2018	vs	ILLINOIS	24	16	W	-14.5	L	57.5	U	"Land of Lincoln Trophy"
12/1/2018	vs	Ohio State	24	45	L	16.5	L	63.0	O	BIG TEN Championship
12/31/2018	vs	Utah	31	20	W	6.5	W	44.5	O	Holiday Bowl
Coach: Pat Fitzgerald		Season Record >>	339	325	9-5	ATS>>	7-6-1	O/U>>	7-7	
2017-Northwestern		Opponent	NW	Opp	S/U	Line	ATS	Total	O/U	
9/2/2017	vs	NEVADA	31	20	W	-24.0	L	60.5	U	
9/9/2017	@	Duke	17	41	L	-2.0	L	54.5	O	
9/16/2017	vs	BOWLING GREEN	49	7	W	-21.0	W	56.0	T	
9/30/2017	@	Wisconsin	24	33	L	16.5	W	50.0	O	
10/7/2017	vs	PENN STATE	7	31	L	14.5	L	51.5	U	
10/14/2017	@	Maryland	37	21	W	-2.5	W	49.5	O	
10/21/2017	vs	IOWA	17	10	W	-2.0	W	45.5	U	{OT}
10/28/2017	vs	MICHIGAN STATE	39	31	W	1.5	W	40.0	O	{3 OT}
11/4/2017	@	Nebraska	31	24	W	PK	W	55.0	T	{OT}
11/11/2017	vs	PURDUE	23	13	W	-6.5	W	48.5	U	
11/18/2017	vs	MINNESOTA	39	0	W	-7.0	W	39.0	T	
11/25/2017	@	Illinois	42	7	W	-15.5	W	46.0	O	"Land of Lincoln Trophy"
12/29/2017	vs	Kentucky	24	23	W	-8.0	L	51.5	U	Music City Bowl
Coach: Pat Fitzgerald		Season Record >>	380	261	10-3	ATS>>	9-4	O/U>>	5-5-3	

Copyright © 2021 by Steve's Football Bible, LLC

NORTHWESTERN WILDCATS   BIG TEN West

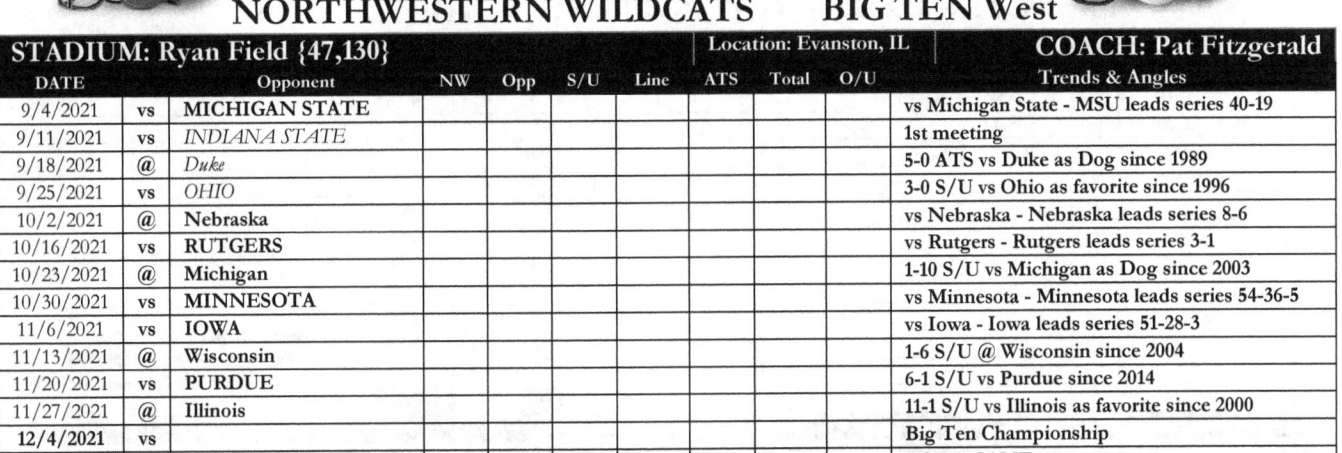

STADIUM: Ryan Field {47,130}					Location: Evanston, IL					COACH: Pat Fitzgerald	
DATE		Opponent	NW	Opp	S/U	Line	ATS	Total	O/U	Trends & Angles	
9/4/2021	vs	MICHIGAN STATE								vs Michigan State - MSU leads series 40-19	
9/11/2021	vs	INDIANA STATE								1st meeting	
9/18/2021	@	Duke								5-0 ATS vs Duke as Dog since 1989	
9/25/2021	vs	OHIO								3-0 S/U vs Ohio as favorite since 1996	
10/2/2021	@	Nebraska								vs Nebraska - Nebraska leads series 8-6	
10/16/2021	vs	RUTGERS								vs Rutgers - Rutgers leads series 3-1	
10/23/2021	@	Michigan								1-10 S/U vs Michigan as Dog since 2003	
10/30/2021	vs	MINNESOTA								vs Minnesota - Minnesota leads series 54-36-5	
11/6/2021	vs	IOWA								vs Iowa - Iowa leads series 51-28-3	
11/13/2021	@	Wisconsin								1-6 S/U @ Wisconsin since 2004	
11/20/2021	vs	PURDUE								6-1 S/U vs Purdue since 2014	
11/27/2021	@	Illinois								11-1 S/U vs Illinois as favorite since 2000	
12/4/2021	vs									Big Ten Championship	
	vs									BOWL GAME	

Pointspread Analysis Non-Conference		Pointspread Analysis Conference
0-7-1 S/U vs Non-Conf as 10.5-15 point favorite since 1988		vs Illinois - Series tied 54-54-5
16-0 S/U vs Non-Conf. as 15.5 point or more favorite since 2009		5-0 S/U @ Illinois as favorite since 1997
3-0 S/U vs Duke as Dog since 1999		4-0 S/U & ATS vs Illinois as 5 point or less Dog since 1995
Dog		0-6 S/U vs Iowa as 21 point or more Dog since 1985
12-3 ATS as road Dog last 10 times		1-6 S/U & ATS vs Iowa as 6 point or less Dog since 1993
9-3 ATS as 25.5 point or more Dog since 1992		0-10 S/U vs Michigan as 17.5 point or more Dog since 1983
2-20 S/U on road as 25.5 point or more Dog since 1983		0-6 S/U vs Michigan as 8.5-16.5 point Dog since 1998
0-7 S/U @ home as 25.5 or more Dog since 1988		0-6 S/U @ home vs Minnesota as Dog since 1985
0-18 S/U on road as 20.5-25 point Dog since 1984		6-1 S/U vs Minnesota as 5 point or more favorite since 1996
1-8 S/U @ home as 20.5-25 point Dog since 1984		1-6 ATS vs Minnesota as 5 point or more favorite since 1996
6-0 ATS on road as 15.5-20 point Dog since 2006		vs Purdue - Purdue leads series 51-33-1
0-10 S/U @ home as 15.5-20 point Dog since 1987		1-7 O/U vs Purdue as Dog since 2002
3-21-1 S/U @ home as 10.5-15 point Dog since 1983		7-1 S/U vs Purdue as favorite since 1995
2-8 S/U @ home as 3.5-7 point Dog since 2010 {3-7 ATS}		1-7 S/U vs Purdue as 13 point or more Dog since 1983
10-3 ATS as 3 point or less Dog since 2006		Game 2-6 O/U @ home vs Purdue since 2002
Favorite		0-7 S/U vs Wisconsin as 16.5 point or more Dog since 1984
1-6 O/U @ home as 3 point or less favorite since 2004		6-0 S/U & ATS vs Wisconsin as 7-10 point Dog since 1987
13-2 S/U @ home as 3.5-7 point favorite since 2002		vs Wisconsin - Wisconsin leads series 60-37-5
1-8-1 O/U @ home as 3.5-7 point favorite since 2012		Game 1-7 O/U vs Wisconsin since 2013
14-2 S/U on road as 3.5-7 point favorite since 1996		
7-1 S/U @ home vs Big Ten as 10.5-15 point Favorite since 2004		
25-0 S/U @ home as 15.5 point or more favorite since 1996	MICHIGAN ST.	3-9 O/U in 1st home game of season since 2007
5-0 S/U vs Big Ten as 15.5 point or more favorite since 2011	MICHIGAN ST.	11-3 S/U in 1st home game of season since 2007
Bowl Games	INDIANA ST.	10-1 S/U after playing Michigan State since 2007
0-5 S/U in Bowl Games as 7.5-10 point Dog since 1997	Duke	9-2 S/U in 1st road game of season since 2010
	Duke	7-2-1 ATS in 1st road game of season since 2011
	Nebraska	2-8 S/U in 2nd road game of season since 2011
1-21-1 S/U @ ranked Michigan since 1940	MINNESOTA	3-10-1 ATS prior to playing Iowa since 2007
2-12-1 S/U vs ranked Minnesota since 1940	MINNESOTA	2-10 S/U prior to playing Iowa since 2009
7-0 S/U when ranked vs Minnesota since 1959	Wisconsin	8-1 ATS after playing Iowa since 2012
	PURDUE	3-9 O/U after playing Wisconsin since 2003
	PURDUE	3-10-1 O/U prior to playing Illinois since 2007
	Illinois	10-3 S/U in final road game of season since 2008

Copyright © 2021 by Steve's Football Bible, LLC

NOTRE DAME FIGHTING IRISH   INDEPENDENT

2020-Notre Dame		Opponent	ND	Opp	S/U	Line	ATS	Total	O/U	
9/12/2020	vs	DUKE	27	13	W	-21.5	L	51.5	U	
9/19/2020	vs	SOUTH FLORIDA	52	0	W	-23.0	W	49.5	O	
10/10/2020	vs	FLORIDA STATE	42	26	W	-21.0	L	54.0	O	
10/17/2020	vs	LOUISVILLE	12	7	W	-17.0	L	62.0	U	
10/24/2020	@	Pittsburgh	45	3	W	-10.0	W	43.5	O	
10/31/2020	@	Georgia Tech	31	13	W	-20.5	L	58.0	U	
11/7/2020	vs	CLEMSON	47	40	W	4.5	W	50.5	O	{2 OT}
11/14/2020	@	Boston College	45	31	W	-13.0	W	52.0	O	"Holy War"
11/27/2020	@	North Carolina	31	17	W	-4.5	W	69.5	U	
12/5/2020	vs	SYRACUSE	45	21	W	-35.0	L	51.0	O	
12/19/2020	vs	**Clemson**	13	34	L	11.0	L	58.0	U	**ACC CHAMPIONSHIP GAME**
1/1/2021	vs	**Alabama**	14	31	L	18.0	W	65.5	U	**Rose Bowl {CFP Semifinal}**
Coach: Brian Kelly		Season Record >>	404	236	10-2	ATS>>	6-6	O/U>>	6-6	
2019-Notre Dame		Opponent	ND	Opp	S/U	Line	ATS	Total	O/U	
9/2/2019	@	Louisville	35	17	W	-19.0	L	54.5	U	
9/14/2019	vs	NEW MEXICO	66	14	W	-34.5	W	64.0	O	
9/21/2019	@	Georgia	17	23	L	15.5	W	58.5	U	
9/28/2019	vs	VIRGINIA	35	20	W	-11.0	W	46.5	O	
10/5/2019	vs	BOWLING GREEN	52	0	W	-46.0	W	64.5	U	
10/12/2019	vs	USC	30	27	W	-10.5	L	59.0	U	"Jeweled Shillelagh"
10/26/2019	@	Michigan	14	45	L	1.0	L	46.5	O	
11/2/2019	vs	VIRGINIA TECH	21	20	W	-17.5	L	58.0	U	
11/9/2019	@	Duke	37	7	W	-7.0	W	49.5	U	
11/16/2019	vs	NAVY	52	20	W	-7.0	W	56.0	O	"Rip Miller Trophy"
11/23/2019	vs	BOSTON COLLEGE	40	7	W	-21.0	W	65.5	U	"Holy War"
11/30/2019	@	Stanford	45	24	W	-17.5	W	45.5	O	"Legends Trophy"
12/28/2019	vs	**Iowa State**	33	9	W	-3.5	W	54.0	U	**Camping World Bowl**
Coach: Brian Kelly		Season Record >>	477	233	11-2	ATS>>	9-4	O/U>>	5-8	
2018-Notre Dame		Opponent	ND	Opp	S/U	Line	ATS	Total	O/U	
9/1/2018	vs	MICHIGAN	24	17	W	3.0	W	48.0	U	
9/8/2018	vs	BALL STATE	24	16	W	-34.0	L	60.5	U	
9/15/2018	vs	VANDERBILT	22	17	W	-13.5	L	51.5	U	
9/22/2018	@	Wake Forest	56	27	W	-6.0	W	59.5	O	
9/29/2018	vs	STANFORD	38	17	W	-5.0	W	54.0	O	"Legends Trophy"
10/6/2018	@	Virginia Tech	45	23	W	-6.5	W	55.0	O	
10/13/2018	vs	PITTSBURGH	19	14	W	-21.0	L	55.5	U	
10/27/2018	vs	Navy	44	22	W	-22.5	L	57.0	O	"Rip Miller Trophy"
11/3/2018	@	Northwestern	31	21	W	-10.0	T	49.5	O	
11/10/2018	vs	Syracuse	42	13	W	-17.0	W	51.0	O	Yankee Stadium
11/17/2018	vs	FLORIDA STATE	36	3	W	-10.0	W	64.5	U	
11/24/2018	@	Usc	24	17	W	-14.0	L	54.0	U	"Jeweled Shillelagh"
12/29/2018	vs	**Clemson**	3	30	L	10.0	L	58.0	U	**Cotton Bowl (National Semi-Final)**
Coach: Brian Kelly		Season Record >>	408	237	12-1	ATS>>	6-6-1	O/U>>	6-7	
2017-Notre Dame										
9/2/2017	vs	TEMPLE	49	16	W	-19.5	W	56.0	O	
9/9/2017	vs	GEORGIA	19	20	L	-5.0	L	57.0	U	
9/16/2017	@	Boston College	49	20	W	-14.0	W	53.0	O	"Holy War"
9/23/2017	@	Michigan State	38	18	W	-3.5	W	59.0	U	"Megaphone Trophy"
9/30/2017	vs	MIAMI-OHIO	52	17	W	-20.5	W	53.0	O	
10/7/2017	@	North Carolina	33	10	W	-13.5	W	63.5	U	
10/21/2017	vs	USC	49	14	W	-3.5	W	61.0	O	"Jeweled Shillelagh"
10/28/2017	vs	NC STATE	35	14	W	-7.0	W	59.5	U	
11/4/2017	vs	WAKE FOREST	48	37	W	-15.5	L	55.0	O	
11/11/2017	@	Miami	8	41	L	-3.5	L	59.0	U	
11/18/2017	vs	NAVY	24	17	W	-20.5	L	58.5	U	"Rip Miller Trophy"
11/25/2017	@	Stanford	20	38	L	-3.0	L	57.5	O	"Legends Trophy"
1/1/2018	vs	**LSU**	21	17	W	2.0	W	53.0	U	**Citrus Bowl**
Coach: Brian Kelly		Season Record >>	445	279	10-3	ATS>>	8-5	O/U>>	6-7	

Copyright © 2021 by Steve's Football Bible, LLC

NOTRE DAME FIGHTING IRISH   INDEPENDENT

STADIUM: Notre Dame Stadium {77,622}					Location: South Bend, IN				COACH: Brian Kelly	
DATE		Opponent	ND	Opp	S/U	Line	ATS	Total	O/U	Trends & Angles
9/5/2021	@	Florida State								vs Florida State - FSU leads series 6-3
9/11/2021	vs	TOLEDO								1st meeting
9/18/2021	vs	PURDUE								13-1 S/U @ home vs Purdue since 1986
9/25/2021	vs	Wisconsin {@ Chicago}								vs Wisconsin - Notre Dame leads series 8-6-2
10/2/2021	vs	CINCINNATI								vs Cincinnati - Notre Dame leads series 1-0
10/9/2021	@	Virginia Tech								vs Virginia Tech - Notre Dame leads series 2-1
10/23/2021	vs	USC								4-0 S/U @ home vs USC since 2013 {3-1 ATS}
10/30/2021	vs	NORTH CAROLINA								vs North Carolina - Notre Dame leads series 19-2
11/6/2021	vs	NAVY								vs Navy - Notre Dame leads series 79-13-1
11/13/2021	@	Virginia								vs Virginia - Notre Dame leads series 3-0
11/20/2021	vs	GEORGIA TECH								vs Georgia Tech - Notre Dame leads series 29-6-1
11/27/2021	@	Stanford								1-5 S/U @ Stanford since 2009
	vs									BOWL GAME

Pointspread Analysis Dog		Pointspread Analysis Non-Conference
2-10 S/U on road as 10.5-20 point Dog since 1985		0-3 S/U vs Florida State as Dog since 2003
1-6 S/U @ home as 10.5-20 point Dog since 2000		28-0 S/U vs Navy as 13 point or more favorite since 1983
3-19 S/U as 10.5-20 point Dog since 1985		21-1 S/U vs Purdue as favorite since 1986
2-11 S/U on road as 7.5-10 point Dog since 1998		vs Purdue - Notre Dame leads series 58-26-2
6-1 O/U as 7.5-10 point Dog since 2008		vs Stanford - Notre Dame leads series 21-13
7-0 O/U as 3.5-7 point Dog since 2013		16-2 S/U vs Stanford as 5 point or more favorite since 1988
Favorite		0-3 S/U & ATS vs Stanford as 3 point or less favorite since 1997
10-1 S/U as 3.5-7 point favorite since 2017 {10-1 ATS}		0-4 S/U @ Stanford as Dog since 2009
3-9 O/U as 7.5-10 point favorite since 2009		vs USC - Notre Dame leads series 49-37-5
9-2 S/U @ home as 7.5-10 point favorite since 2003		3-0 S/U vs USC since 2017
17-0 S/U on road as 10.5-15 point favorite since 1997		1-11 S/U vs USC as Dog since 1998
22-0 S/U as 10.5-15 point favorite since 2011		6-0-1 S/U vs USC as 4.5 point or less Dog since 1984 {7-0 ATS}
15-2 S/U @ home as 15.5-20 point favorite since 1995		9-1 S/U vs USC as 7.5 point or less favorite since 1986
11-1 S/U on road as 15.5-20 point favorite since 1991		0-11 S/U vs USC as 6.5 point or more Dog since 1998
6-2 O/U @ home as 15.5-20 point favorite since 2012		
39-2 S/U as 20.5-25 point favorite since 1984	Florida State	9-3 O/U in 1st road game of season since 2009
13-0 S/U on road as 20.5-25 point favorite since 1986	TOLEDO	11-1 S/U in 1st home game of season since 2008
37-1 S/U as 25.5 point or more favorite since 1983	TOLEDO	0-6 ATS after playing Florida State since 1994
3-9 O/U as 25.5 point or more favorite since 2005	PURDUE	3-8 O/U in 2nd home game of season since 2010
Bowl Games	Virginia Tech	9-3 S/U in 2nd road game of season since 2009
0-4 S/U & ATS in Fiesta Bowl since 1995	N. CAROLINA	2-11 O/U prior to playing Navy since 2006
5-2 S/U in Cotton Bowl since 1971	N. CAROLINA	5-1 S/U after playing USC since 2009
0-6 S/U & ATS in Bowl Games as 3.5-7 point Dog since 1995	G TECH	1-8 O/U prior to playing Stanford since 2011
3-0 S/U & ATS in Bowl Games as 3 point or less favorite since 1989	G TECH	4-12 O/U in final home game of season since 2005
		45-4 S/U @ home when ranked since 2011
		37-1 S/U when ranked vs Navy since 1964
		12-0 S/U @ home when ranked vs Purdue since 1980
		5-0 S/U when ranked vs USC since 2012
		0-6 S/U @ ranked Stanford all time
		1-9 S/U vs ranked USC since 2002

Copyright © 2021 by Steve's Football Bible, LLC

 **OHIO BOBCATS**   **MAC East**

2020-Ohio		Opponent	Ohio	Opp	S/U	Line	ATS	Total	O/U	
11/4/2020	@	Central Michigan	27	30	L	-3.0	L	54.5	O	
11/10/2020	vs	AKRON	24	10	W	-27.0	L	58.0	U	
11/28/2020	vs	BOWLING GREEN	52	10	W	-22.5	W	55.0	O	
Coach: Frank Solich		Season Record >>	103	50	2-1	ATS>>	1-2	O/U>>	2-1	
2019-Ohio		Opponent	Ohio	Opp	S/U	Line	ATS	Total	O/U	
8/31/2019	vs	RHODE ISLAND	41	20	W	-25.0	L	NT	---	
9/7/2019	@	Pittsburgh	10	20	L	4.0	L	54.5	U	
9/14/2019	@	Marshall	31	33	L	4.5	W	47.5	O	"Battle for the Bell"
9/21/2019	vs	LOUISIANA-LAFAYETTE	25	45	L	-3.0	L	68.0	O	
10/5/2019	@	Buffalo	21	20	W	-3.0	L	51.5	U	{OT}
10/12/2019	vs	NORTHERN ILLINOIS	36	39	L	-4.5	L	50.5	O	
10/19/2019	vs	KENT STATE	45	38	W	-9.0	L	64.5	O	
10/26/2019	@	Ball State	34	21	W	2.0	W	59.5	U	
1/6/2019	vs	MIAMI-OHIO	21	24	L	-7.0	L	57.5	U	"Battle of the Bricks"
11/12/2019	vs	WESTERN MICHIGAN	34	37	L	-1.5	L	63.5	O	{OT}
11/19/2019	@	Bowling Green	66	24	W	-21.0	W	55.5	O	
11/26/2019	@	Akron	52	3	W	-27.5	W	52.5	O	
1/3/2020	vs	Nevada	30	21	W	-10.0	L	62.0	U	Famous Idaho Potato Bowl
Coach: Frank Solich		Season Record >>	446	345	7-6	ATS>>	4-9	O/U>>	7-5	
2018-Ohio		Opponent	Ohio	Opp	S/U	Line	ATS	Total	O/U	
9/1/2018	vs	HOWARD	38	32	W	-31.0	L	NT	---	
9/15/2018	@	Virginia	31	45	L	5.5	L	53.5	O	
9/22/2018	@	Cincinnati	30	34	L	7.0	W	54.5	O	
9/29/2018	vs	MASSACHUSETTS	58	42	W	-11.5	W	70.0	O	
10/6/2018	@	Kent State	27	26	W	-11.5	L	68.5	U	
10/13/2018	@	Northern Illinois	21	24	L	6.0	L	51.5	U	
10/20/2018	vs	BOWLING GREEN	49	14	W	-16.5	W	66.5	U	
10/25/2018	vs	BALL STATE	52	14	W	-10.0	W	65.5	O	
11/1/2018	@	Western Michigan	59	14	W	-3.0	W	65.0	O	
11/17/2018	@	Miami-Ohio	28	30	L	-4.5	L	59.0	U	"Battle of the Bricks"
11/14/2018	vs	BUFFALO	52	17	W	-2.5	W	65.0	O	
11/23/2018	vs	AKRON	49	28	W	-23.5	L	56.5	O	
12/19/2018	vs	San Diego State	27	0	W	-2.0	W	47.5	U	Frisco Bowl
Coach: Frank Solich		Season Record >>	521	320	9-4	ATS>>	8-5	O/U>>	7-5	
2017-Ohio		Opponent	Ohio	Opp	S/U	Line	ATS	Total	O/U	
9/2/2017	vs	HAMPTON	59	0	W	-35.5	W	47.5	O	
9/8/2017	@	Purdue	21	44	L	3.0	L	54.5	O	
9/16/2017	vs	KANSAS	42	30	W	-7.0	W	59.5	O	
9/23/2017	@	Eastern Michigan	27	20	W	1.5	W	53.5	U	{2 OT}
9/30/2017	@	Massachusetts	58	50	W	-4.0	W	52.5	O	
10/7/2017	vs	CENTRAL MICHIGAN	23	26	L	-10.5	L	54.0	U	
10/14/2017	@	Bowling Green	48	30	W	-9.5	W	62.0	O	
10/21/2017	vs	KENT STATE	48	3	W	-17.0	W	47.0	O	
10/31/2017	vs	MIAMI-OHIO	45	28	W	-7.0	W	53.5	O	"Battle of the Bricks"
11/8/2017	vs	TOLEDO	38	10	W	3.0	W	64.5	U	
11/14/2017	@	Akron	34	37	L	-14.5	L	51.0	O	
11/24/2017	@	Buffalo	24	31	L	-7.0	L	55.0	T	
12/22/2017	vs	Alabama-Birmingham	41	6	W	-6.5	W	54.5	U	Bahamas Bowl
Coach: Frank Solich		Season Record >>	508	315	9-4	ATS>>	9-4	O/U>>	8-4-1	

Copyright © 2021 by Steve's Football Bible, LLC

 **OHIO BOBCATS**  **MAC East**

STADIUM: Peden Stadium {27,000}					Location: Athens, OH					COACH: Frank Solich
DATE		Opponent	Ohio	Opp	S/U	Line	ATS	Total	O/U	Trends & Angles
9/4/2021	vs	SYRACUSE								vs Syracuse - Syracuse leads series 3-1
9/11/2021	vs	DUQUESNE								vs Duquesne - Ohio leads series 1-0
9/18/2021	@	Louisiana								vs Louisiana - Ohio leads series 2-1
9/25/2021	@	Northwestern								0-3 S/U vs Northwestern as Dog since 1996
10/2/2021	@	Akron								vs Akron - Ohio leads series 23-12-1
10/9/2021	vs	CENTRAL MICHIGAN								
10/16/2021	@	Buffalo								vs Buffalo - HOME team 9-1 S/U since 2010
10/23/2021	vs	KENT STATE								vs Kent State - Ohio leads series 44-26-2
11/2/2021	vs	MIAMI-OHIO								vs Miami-Ohio - Miami leads series 56-40-1
11/9/2021	@	Eastern Michigan								
11/16/2021	vs	TOLEDO								1-6 S/U @ home vs Toledo since 1990
11/26/2021	@	Bowling Green								vs B. Green – B. Green leads series 40-30-2
12/3/2021	vs									Big Ten Championship
	vs									BOWL GAME

Pointspread Analysis		Pointspread Analysis
Non-Conference		**Conference**
4-45 S/U vs Non-Conf. as 10.5 point or more Dog since 1989		8-1 S/U vs Akron as 11 point or more favorite since 1997
11-0 S/U vs Non-Conf. as 3.5-15 point favorite since 2010		3-13 S/U vs Bowling Green as Dog since 1991
10-1 S/U vs Non-Conf. as 15.5 point or more favorite since 2010		8-0 S/U vs B. Green as 9 point or more favorite since 1997
Dog		vs Buffalo - Ohio leads series 16-10
3-21-1 S/U @ home as 7.5 point or more Dog since 1989		1-4 S/U @ Buffalo as favorite since 2007
1-33 S/U on road as 20.5 point or more Dog since 1989		0-5 ATS @ Buffalo as favorite since 2007
2-23-1 S/U as 15.5-20 point Dog since 1989		0-11-1 S/U vs Central Michigan as Dog since 1989
6-29 S/U as 10.5-15 point Dog since 1989		2-7 S/U vs Eastern Michigan as Dog since 1989 {6-1-2 ATS}
0-8-1 O/U as 10.5-15 point Dog since 2005		9-1 S/U vs Eastern Michigan as favorite since 1993
3-17 S/U as 7.5-10 point Dog since 1989		2-11-1 S/U vs Miami-Ohio as Dog since 1989
1-12 S/U on road as 3.5-7 point Dog since 2008		6-1 S/U @ home vs Miami-Ohio as favorite since 2007
1-11 O/U as 3 point or less Dog since 2011		6-0 S/U vs Miami-Ohio as 3 point or less favorite since 2006
Favorite		1-10 S/U vs Miami-Ohio as 6 point or more Dog since 1991
13-3 S/U on road as 3 point or less favorite since 2004		1-8 S/U vs Toledo as 6.5 point or more Dog since 1989
9-1 O/U @ home as 3 point or less favorite since 2003		6-1 ATS vs Toledo as 6.5 point or more Dog since 1991
8-3 S/U & ATS @ home as 3.5-7 point favorite since 2006		
13-3 S/U @ home as 10.5-15 point favorite since 1997	SYRACUSE	10-1 S/U in 1st home game of season since 2010
15-3 S/U as 15.5-20 point favorite since 1997	DUQUESNE	9-3 ATS in 2nd home game of season since 2007
21-0 S/U as 20.5 point or more favorite since 1997	DUQUESNE	9-1 S/U in 2nd home game of season since 2011
Bowl Games	Northwestern	3-16 S/U in 2nd road game of season since 2001
4-8 S/U in Bowl Games	C. MICHIGAN	6-1-1 O/U prior to playing Buffalo since 2012
	C. MICHIGAN	1-11-1 ATS prior to playing Buffalo since 2007
	KENT STATE	2-6 O/U after playing Buffalo since 2011
	KENT STATE	0-8 ATS after playing Buffalo since 2011
	TOLEDO	1-7 ATS prior to playing Bowling Green since 2013
	TOLEDO	12-3 S/U in final home game of season since 2006
	B. Green	2-7-1 ATS in final road game of season since 2010
	B. Green	1-8-1 O/U in final road game of season since 2010

Copyright © 2021 by Steve's Football Bible, LLC

OHIO STATE BUCKEYES   BIG TEN East

2020-Ohio State		Opponent	OSU	Opp	S/U	Line	ATS	Total	O/U	
10/24/2020	vs	NEBRASKA	52	17	W	-27.5	W	70.5	U	
10/31/2020	@	Penn State	38	23	W	-10.0	W	63.0	U	
11/7/2020	vs	RUTGERS	49	27	W	-37.5	L	63.0	O	
11/21/2020	vs	INDIANA	42	35	W	-20.5	L	67.0	O	
12/5/2020	@	Michigan State	52	12	W	-22.0	W	58.5	O	
12/19/2020	vs	Northwestern	22	10	W	-16.5	L	57.5	U	Big Ten Championship
1/1/2021	vs	Clemson	49	28	W	7.5	W	69.0	O	Sugar Bowl {National Semifinal}
1/11/2021	vs	Alabama	24	52	L	9.5	L	75.5	O	CFB Championship Game
Coach: Ryan Day		Season Record >>	328	204	7-1	ATS>>	4-4	O/U>>	5-3	Big Ten Champions
2019-Ohio State		Opponent	OSU	Opp	S/U	Line	ATS	Total	O/U	
8/31/2019	vs	FLORIDA ATLANTIC	45	21	W	-27.5	L	65.5	O	
9/7/2019	vs	CINCINNATI	42	0	W	-14.5	W	52.5	U	
9/14/2019	@	Indiana	51	10	W	-17.5	W	60.5	O	
9/21/2019	vs	MIAMI-OHIO	76	5	W	-38.5	W	57.0	O	
9/28/2019	@	Nebraska	48	7	W	-17.0	W	66.0	U	
10/5/2019	vs	MICHIGAN STATE	34	10	W	-20.0	W	51.0	U	
10/18/2019	@	Northwestern	52	3	W	-27.0	W	52.0	O	
10/26/2019	vs	WISCONSIN	38	7	W	-14.5	W	47.5	U	
11/9/2019	vs	MARYLAND	73	14	W	-42.5	W	64.5	O	
11/16/2019	@	Rutgers	56	21	W	-52.0	L	62.5	O	
11/23/2019	vs	PENN STATE	28	17	W	-19.5	L	58.0	U	
11/30/2019	@	Michigan	56	27	W	-8.5	W	53.0	O	"100 Yard War"
12/7/2019	vs	Wisconsin	34	21	W	-16.5	L	58.0	U	Big Ten Championship
12/28/2019	vs	Clemson	23	29	L	2.5	L	62.0	U	Fiesta Bowl (National Semi-Final)
Coach: Ryan Day		Season Record >>	656	192	13-1	ATS>>	9-5	O/U>>	7-7	Big Ten Champions
2018-Ohio State		Opponent	OSU	Opp	S/U	Line	ATS	Total	O/U	
9/1/2018	vs	OREGON STATE	77	31	W	-40.0	W	63.0	O	
9/8/2018	vs	RUTGERS	52	3	W	-35.0	W	59.0	U	
9/15/2018	vs	Tcu	40	28	W	-12.5	L	58.5	O	AT&T Stadium
9/22/2018	vs	TULANE	49	6	W	-38.0	W	67.5	U	
9/29/2018	@	Penn State	27	26	W	-3.5	L	69.5	U	
10/6/2018	vs	INDIANA	49	26	W	-28.0	L	64.5	O	
10/13/2018	vs	MINNESOTA	30	14	W	-29.5	L	60.0	U	
10/20/2018	@	Purdue	20	49	L	-12.0	L	66.0	O	
11/3/2018	vs	NEBRASKA	36	31	W	-17.0	L	75.5	U	
11/10/2018	@	Michigan State	26	6	W	-3.5	W	49.5	U	
11/17/2018	@	Maryland	52	51	W	-14.0	L	61.5	O	{OT}
11/24/2018	vs	MICHIGAN	62	39	W	4.0	W	53.5	O	"100 Yard War"
12/1/2018	vs	Northwestern	45	24	W	-16.5	W	63.0	O	Big Ten Championship
1/1/2019	vs	Washington	28	23	W	-5.5	L	55.0	U	Rose Bowl
Coach: Urban Meyer		Season Record >>	593	357	13-1	ATS>>	6-8	O/U>>	7-7	Big Ten Champions
2017-Ohio State		Opponent	OSU	Opp	S/U	Line	ATS	Total	O/U	
8/31/2017	@	Indiana	49	21	W	-20.5	W	55.0	O	
9/9/2017	vs	OKLAHOMA	16	31	L	-7.0	L	65.0	U	
9/16/2017	vs	ARMY	38	7	W	-31.5	L	54.5	U	
9/23/2017	vs	UNLV	54	21	W	-41.0	L	66.5	O	
9/30/2017	@	Rutgers	56	0	W	-28.0	W	53.5	O	
10/7/2017	vs	MARYLAND	62	14	W	-29.5	W	60.0	O	
10/14/2017	@	Nebraska	56	14	W	-24.0	W	57.5	O	
10/28/2017	vs	PENN STATE	39	38	W	-7.0	L	57.5	O	
11/4/2017	@	Iowa	24	55	L	-20.5	L	55.0	O	
11/11/2017	vs	MICHIGAN STATE	48	3	W	-17.0	W	55.0	U	
11/18/2017	vs	ILLINOIS	52	14	W	-41.0	L	53.0	O	"Illibuck Trophy"
11/25/2017	@	Michigan	31	20	W	-12.5	L	49.5	O	"100 Yard War"
12/2/2017	vs	Wisconsin	27	21	W	-3.5	W	51.0	U	Big Ten Championship
12/29/2017	vs	USC	24	7	W	-9.5	W	65.0	U	Cotton Bowl
Coach: Urban Meyer		Season Record >>	576	266	12-2	ATS>>	7-7	O/U>>	9-5	Big Ten Champions

Copyright © 2021 by Steve's Football Bible, LLC

OHIO STATE BUCKEYES   BIG TEN East

STADIUM: Ohio Stadium {102,082}		Location: Columbus, OH							COACH: Ryan Day	
DATE		Opponent	OSU	Opp	S/U	Line	ATS	Total	O/U	Trends & Angles
9/2/2021	@	Minnesota								25-1 S/U vs Minnesota as favorite since 1983
9/11/2021	vs	*OREGON*								vs Oregon - Ohio State leads series 9-0
9/18/2021	vs	*TULSA*								vs Tulsa - Ohio State leads series 1-0
9/25/2021	vs	*AKRON*								vs Akron - Ohio State leads series 7-1
10/2/2021	@	Rutgers								vs Rutgers - Ohio State leads series 7-0 {5-2 ATS}
10/9/2021	vs	MARYLAND								vs Maryland - Ohio State leads series 5-0
10/23/2021	@	Indiana								vs Indiana - Ohio State leads series 77-12-4
10/30/2021	vs	PENN STATE								12-2 S/U @ home vs Penn State since 1993
11/6/2021	@	Nebraska								vs Indiana - Ohio State leads series 77-12-4
11/13/2021	vs	PURDUE								6-0 S/U vs Nebraska as favorite since 2012
11/20/2021	vs	MICHIGAN STATE								vs Michigan State - Ohio State leads series 33-15
11/27/2021	@	Michigan								14-1 S/U vs Michigan since 2004
12/4/2021	vs									Big Ten Championship
	vs									BOWL GAME

Pointspread Analysis Non-Conference		Pointspread Analysis Conference
9-1 S/U vs Non-Conf. as 7.5-10 point favorite since 1984		27-0 S/U vs Indiana as favorite since 1989
19-2 S/U vs Non-Conf. as 10.5-15 point favorite since 1981		6-0 O/U vs Maryland as favorite since 2014
69-0 S/U vs Non-Conf. as 15.5 point or more favorite since 1983		vs Michigan - Michigan leads series 58-52-6
Dog		2-9 S/U @ Michigan as Dog since 1983
14-4 ATS as a Dog since 2009		14-0 S/U vs Michigan as favorite since 2002
1-7 S/U on road as 10.5 point or more Dog since 1988		8-0 S/U vs Michigan as 3-8.5 point favorite since 1984
7-1 ATS as 7.5-10 point Dog since 1992		13-2 S/U vs Michigan State as 6.5 point or more favorite since 1983
7-0 S/U as 3.5-7 point Dog since 2009		vs Nebraska - Ohio State leads series 8-1
8-0 ATS as 3.5-7 point Dog since 2009		vs Penn State - Ohio State leads series 22-14
1-8 O/U on road as 3 point or less Dog since 1993		1-4 S/U vs Penn State as Dog since 1994
0-8 O/U as 3 point or less Dog since 2004		12-1 S/U vs Penn State as 7 point or more favorite since 1996
1-6 S/U @ home as 3 point or less Dog since 1986		12-1 S/U @ home vs Penn State as favorite since 1993
Favorite		vs Purdue - Ohio State leads series 40-15-2
7-0 S/U on road as 3 point or less favorite since 2004		9-0 S/U @ home vs Purdue as favorite since 1989
6-0-1 ATS on road as 3 point or less favorite since 2004		10-0 S/U vs Purdue as 16.5 point or more favorite since 1983
13-2 S/U @ home as 3.5-7 point favorite since 2001		
10-1 S/U on road as 3.5-7 point favorite since 2005	Minnesota	9-0 S/U in 1st road game of season since 2012
9-2 ATS on road as 3.5-7 point favorite since 2005	Minnesota	8-1 ATS in 1st road game of season since 2012
9-1 S/U on road as 7.5-10 point favorite since 2000	OREGON	40-2 S/U in 1st home game of season since 1979
6-1 O/U on road as 7.5-10 point favorite since 2003	OREGON	20-1 S/U after playing Minnesota since 1989
14-1 S/U @ home as 7.5-10 point favorite since 1983	OREGON	2-8 O/U after playing Minnesota since 2002
22-3 S/U on road as 10.5-15 point favorite since 1985	TULSA	10-0 S/U in 2nd home game of season since 2010
41-2 S/U @ home as 15.5-20 point favorite since 1985	TULSA	3-12 O/U in 2nd home game of season since 2006
40-1 S/U as 15.5-20 point favorite since 1997	Rutgers	11-1 S/U prior to playing Michigan State since 2006
12-2 S/U on road as 15.5-20 point favorite since 1986	Rutgers	8-2 O/U after playing Purdue since 2003
134-2 S/U as 20.5 point or more favorite since 1983	Rutgers	8-1 S/U after playing Purdue since 2004
32-1 S/U on road as 20.5 point or more favorite since 1983	MARYLAND	2-9 ATS after playing Indiana since 2010
100-1 S/U @ home as 20.5 point or more favorite since 1983	MARYLAND	27-1 S/U prior to playing Penn State since 1993
Bowl Games	MARYLAND	8-3 O/U prior to playing Penn State since 2010
1-4 S/U vs Clemson in Bowl Games	PENN STATE	2-8 O/U prior to playing Michigan since 2010
0-7 O/U in Rose Bowl since 1975	PENN STATE	0-7 ATS prior to playing Michigan since 2013
0-3 S/U & ATS in Citrus Bowl since 1993	PENN STATE	1-7 ATS in final home game of season since 2013
4-10 S/U vs SEC teams in Bowl Games {3-11 ATS}	Nebraska	8-1 S/U in 2nd road game of season since 2012
0-4 S/U & ATS in Outback Bowl	Nebraska	8-2 O/U in 2nd road game of season since 2011
4-0 S/U in Sugar Bowl since 1999	Nebraska	12-1 S/U prior to playing Purdue since 2000
6-2 ATS in Fiesta Bowl since 1984	PURDUE	7-0 S/U after playing Nebraska since 2011
5-1 S/U & ATS in Bowl Games as 3.5-7 point Dog since 2004	MICH. STATE	13-0 S/U prior to playing Indiana since 2005
1-6 S/U & ATS in Bowl Games as 3 point or less Dog since 1978	Michigan	15-1 S/U in final road game of season since 2005
0-5 ATS in Bowl Games as 10.5-15 point favorite since 1976	Michigan	6-0 S/U after playing Michigan State since 2012
	Michigan	24-2 S/U after playing Penn State since 1994

    Copyright © 2021 by Steve's Football Bible, LLC

OKLAHOMA SOONERS   BIG TWELVE

2020-Oklahoma		Opponent	OU	Opp	S/U	Line	ATS	Total	O/U	
9/12/2020	vs	MISSOURI STATE	48	0	W	-49.5	L	73.0	U	
9/26/2020	vs	KANSAS STATE	35	38	L	-27.5	L	61.5	O	
10/3/2020	@	Iowa State	30	37	L	-7.5	L	62.0	O	
10/10/2020	vs	Texas	53	45	W	-3.0	W	74.0	O	*"Red River Rivalry - Golden Hat"*
10/24/2020	@	Tcu	33	14	W	-6.5	W	58.5	U	
10/31/2020	@	Texas Tech	62	28	W	-17.0	W	65.0	O	
11/7/2020	vs	KANSAS	62	9	W	-38.5	W	62.0	O	
11/21/2020	vs	OKLAHOMA STATE	41	13	W	-6.5	W	60.5	U	*"The Bedlam Series" (Bedlam Bell)*
12/5/2020	vs	BAYLOR	27	14	W	-23.5	L	60.5	U	
12/19/2020	vs	**Iowa State**	27	21	W	-5.5	W	59.5	U	**Big 12 Championship**
12/30/2020	vs	**Florida**	55	20	W	-8.5	W	65.0	O	**Cotton Bowl**
Coach: Lincoln Riley		Season Record >>	473	239	9-2	ATS>>	7-4	O/U>>	6-5	Big 12 Champions
2019-Oklahoma		Opponent	OU	Opp	S/U	Line	ATS	Total	O/U	
8/31/2019	vs	HOUSTON	49	31	W	-22.0	L	79.5	U	
9/7/2019	vs	SOUTH DAKOTA	70	14	W	-45.5	W	NT	---	
9/14/2019	@	Ucla	48	14	W	-23.0	W	72.0	U	
9/28/2019	vs	TEXAS TECH	55	16	W	-27.0	W	69.0	O	
10/5/2019	@	Kansas	45	20	W	-31.5	L	67.0	U	
10/12/2019	vs	Texas	34	27	W	-10.5	L	77.5	U	*"Red River Rivalry - Golden Hat"*
10/19/2019	vs	WEST VIRGINIA	52	14	W	-32.0	W	63.5	O	
10/26/2019	@	Kansas State	41	48	L	-23.5	L	60.0	O	
11/9/2019	vs	IOWA STATE	42	41	W	-14.5	L	70.0	O	
11/16/2019	@	Baylor	34	31	W	-10.5	L	68.5	U	
11/23/2019	vs	TCU	28	24	W	-18.5	L	64.5	U	
11/30/2019	@	Oklahoma State	34	16	W	-14.0	W	68.0	U	*"The Bedlam Series" (Bedlam Bell)*
12/7/2019	vs	**Baylor**	30	23	W	-9.0	L	66.0	U	**Big 12 Championship**
12/28/2019	vs	**Lsu**	28	63	L	12.0	L	75.0	O	**Chick-Fil-A Peach Bowl (National Semifinal)**
Coach: Lincoln Riley		Season Record >>	590	382	12-2	ATS>>	5-9	O/U>>	6-7	Big 12 Champions
2018-Oklahoma		Opponent	OU	Opp	S/U	Line	ATS	Total	O/U	Heisman Trophy: Kyler Murray
9/1/2018	vs	FLORIDA ATLANTIC	63	14	W	-19.0	W	68.0	O	
9/8/2018	vs	UCLA	49	21	W	-31.0	L	65.5	O	
9/15/2018	@	Iowa State	37	27	W	-18.5	L	54.0	O	
9/22/2018	vs	ARMY	28	21	W	-28.5	L	60.5	U	{OT}
9/29/2018	vs	BAYLOR	66	33	W	-21.0	W	68.0	O	
10/6/2018	vs	Texas	45	48	L	-7.0	L	60.0	O	*"Red River Rivalry - Golden Hat"*
10/20/2018	@	Tcu	52	27	W	-7.5	W	61.5	O	
10/27/2018	vs	KANSAS STATE	51	14	W	-24.0	W	65.0	T	
11/3/2018	@	Texas Tech	51	46	W	-14.0	L	78.5	O	
11/10/2018	vs	OKLAHOMA STATE	48	47	W	-21.5	L	80.0	O	*"The Bedlam Series" (Bedlam Bell)*
11/17/2018	vs	KANSAS	55	40	W	-34.5	L	69.5	O	
11/24/2018	@	West Virginia	59	56	W	-3.0	T	87.0	O	
12/1/2018	vs	**Texas**	39	27	W	-9.5	W	79.5	U	**Big 12 Championship**
12/29/2018	vs	**Alabama**	34	45	L	15.0	W	80.5	U	**Orange Bowl {National Semifinal}**
Coach: Lincoln Riley		Season Record >>	677	466	12-2	ATS>>	6-7-1	O/U>>	11-3	Big 12 Champions
2017-Oklahoma		Opponent	OU	Opp	S/U	Line	ATS	Total	O/U	Heisman Trophy: Baker Mayfield
9/2/2017	vs	TEXAS-EL PASO	56	7	W	-42.5	W	63.0	T	
9/9/2017	@	Ohio State	31	16	W	7.0	W	65.0	U	
9/16/2017	vs	TULANE	56	14	W	-33.5	W	52.5	O	
9/23/2017	@	Baylor	49	41	W	-28.0	L	60.5	O	
10/7/2017	vs	IOWA STATE	31	38	L	-31.0	L	61.5	O	
10/14/2017	vs	Texas	29	24	W	-9.0	L	61.5	U	*"Red River Rivalry - Golden Hat"*
10/21/2017	@	Kansas State	42	35	W	-14.5	L	55.5	O	
10/28/2017	vs	TEXAS TECH	49	27	W	-19.5	W	77.5	U	
11/4/2017	@	Oklahoma State	62	52	W	1.0	W	76.0	O	*"The Bedlam Series" (Bedlam Bell)*
11/11/2017	vs	TCU	38	20	W	-6.0	W	63.5	U	
11/18/2017	@	Kansas	41	3	W	-38.5	L	68.0	U	
11/25/2017	vs	WEST VIRGINIA	59	31	W	-23.0	W	69.5	O	
12/2/2017	vs	**TCU**	41	17	W	-7.5	W	64.0	U	**Big 12 Championship**
1/1/2018	vs	**Georgia**	48	54	L	2.5	L	62.5	O	**Rose Bowl (National Semifinal)**
Coach: Lincoln Riley		Season Record >>	632	379	12-2	ATS>>	8-6	O/U>>	7-6-1	Big 12 Champions

Copyright © 2021 by Steve's Football Bible, LLC

OKLAHOMA SOONERS   BIG TWELVE

STADIUM: Oklahoma Memorial Stadium {86,112}			Location: Norman, OK				COACH: Lincoln Riley	
DATE		**Opponent**	**OK**	**Opp**	**S/U**	**Line**	**ATS**	**Total**	**O/U**	**Trends & Angles**

DATE		Opponent	OK	Opp	S/U	Line	ATS	Total	O/U	Trends & Angles
9/4/2021	@	*Tulane*								vs Tulane - Oklahoma leads series 1-0
9/11/2021	vs	*WESTERN CAROLINA*								1st meeting
9/18/2021	vs	*NEBRASKA*								8-1 S/U vs Nebraska as favorite since 1979
9/25/2021	vs	WEST VIRGINIA								8-0 S/U vs West Virginia since 2012
10/2/2021	@	Kansas State								vs Kansas State - Oklahoma leads series 76-21-4
10/9/2021	vs	Texas								2-7 ATS vs Texas since 2013
10/16/2021	vs	TCU								5-0 S/U @ home vs TCU since 2008
10/23/2021	@	Kansas								16-0 S/U vs Kansas as favorite since 2000
10/30/2021	vs	TEXAS TECH								11-1 S/U @ home vs Texas Tech since 1998
11/13/2021	@	Baylor								22-2 S/U vs Baylor as favorite since 1984
11/20/2021	vs	IOWA STATE								vs Iowa State - Oklahoma leads series 77-7-2
11/27/2021	@	Oklahoma State								8-1 S/U @ Oklahoma State since 2004
12/4/2021	vs									BIG XII Championship
	vs									BOWL GAME

Pointspread Analysis Non-Conference		Pointspread Analysis Conference
1-7 S/U vs Non-Conf. as 3.5-7 point Dog since 1996		vs Baylor - Oklahoma leads series 27-3
2-7 ATS vs Non-Conf. as 7.5-10 point favorite since 1989		16-1 S/U vs Iowa State as 23 point or less favorite since 1983
12-0 S/U vs Non-Conf. as 15.5-20 point favorite since 1984		18-0 S/U vs Kansas as 16.5 point or more favorite since 1986
55-1 S/U vs Non-Conf. as 20.5 point or more favorite since 1986		vs Kansas - Oklahoma leads series 78-27-6
1-7 O/U vs Nebraska as favorite since 1984		13-2 S/U vs Kansas State as 16 point or more favorite since 1983
Dog		16-2 S/U vs Oklahoma State since 2003
12-4 ATS as a road Dog since 1999		vs Oklahoma State - Oklahoma leads series 91-17-7
0-7 S/U on road as 10.5-20 point Dog since 1989		17-0 S/U vs Oklahoma State as 14 point or less favorite since 1983
5-0 ATS as 7.5-10 point Dog since 1998		7-1 ATS @ Oklahoma State since 2006
6-20-1 S/U as 3.5-7 point Dog since 1983		vs TCU - Oklahoma leads series 16-5
6-0 S/U & ATS on road as 3 point or less Dog since 1994		Game 0-6 O/U @ home vs TCU since 2005
Favorite		10-0 S/U vs TCU as 6-19 point favorite since 1998
9-1 S/U as 3 point or less favorite since 1999		vs Texas - Texas leads series 65-49-5
11-2 S/U @ home as 3.5-7 point favorite since 1998		0-3 S/U vs Texas as Dog since 2005
8-1 S/U & ATS on road as 3.5-7 point favorite since 2011		0-6 ATS vs Texas as 12-17.5 point favorite since 1988
6-0 S/U @ home as 7.5-10 point favorite since 1997		Game 9-1 O/U vs Texas Tech since 2011
13-1 S/U as 7.5-10 point favorite since 2009		9-0 S/U vs Texas Tech since 2012
11-1 S/U on road as 10.5-15 point favorite since 2004		vs Texas Tech - Oklahoma leads series 22-6
11-3 O/U on road as 10.5-15 point favorite since 2002		7-1 ATS @ home vs Texas Tech since 2006
19-1 S/U @ home as 10.5-15 point favorite since 1999		13-1 S/U vs Texas Tech as 13.5 point or more favorite since 1994
26-2 S/U @ home as 15.5-20 point favorite since 1984		Game 8-1 O/U vs West Virginia since 2008
16-1 S/U on road as 15.5-20 point favorite since 1983		vs West Virginia - Oklahoma leads series 10-2
16-0 S/U @ home as 20.5-25 point favorite since 2010		5-0-1 ATS vs West Virginia since 2014
17-1 S/U on road as 20.5-25 point favorite since 1985	Tulane	9-2 S/U in 1st road game of season since 2010
23-0 S/U on road as 25.5 point or more favorite since 1984	W. CAROLINA	23-1 S/U in 1st home game of season since 1997
71-4 S/U @ home as 25.5 point or more favorite since 1983	NEBRASKA	19-3 S/U in 2nd home game of season since 1999
Bowl Games	NEBRASKA	8-0 S/U prior to playing West Virginia since 2012
3-0 S/U in Sun Bowl	K State	7-2 O/U in 2nd road game of season since 2012
12-7 S/U in Orange Bowl since 1954	K State	10-0 S/U in 2nd road game of season since 2011
3-0 O/U in Fiesta Bowl since 2007	Texas	9-1 O/U prior to playing TCU since 2008
7-0 S/U vs Big Ten in Bowl Games	Texas	9-2 S/U prior to playing TCU since 1998
6-2 S/U in Sugar Bowl	Texas	9-1 S/U after playing Kansas State since 2011
0-3 S/U & ATS vs Clemson in Bowl Games	TCU	21-1 S/U after playing Texas since 1999
0-3 O/U vs Clemson in Bowl Games	TEXAS TECH	12-4 ATS prior to playing Baylor since 2005
1-4 S/U & ATS in Bowl Games as 3 point or less Dog since 1994	TEXAS TECH	12-4 O/U after playing Kansas since 2000
0-5 O/U in Bowl Games as 3 point or less favorite since 1988	TEXAS TECH	11-0 S/U prior to playing Baylor since 2010
0-9 O/U in Bowl Games as 3.5-7 point favorite since 1986	Baylor	16-1 S/U after playing Texas Tech since 2004
	Baylor	14-3 ATS after playing Texas Tech since 2004
	IOWA STATE	11-0 S/U prior to playing Oklahoma State since 2010
	IOWA STATE	18-1 S/U in final home game of season since 2002
	IOWA STATE	8-2 S/U after playing Baylor since 2010
	OK State	9-0 S/U in final road game of season since 2012

Copyright © 2021 by Steve's Football Bible, LLC

OKLAHOMA STATE COWBOYS   BIG TWELVE

2020-Oklahoma State		Opponent	OSU	Opp	S/U	Line	ATS	Total	O/U	
9/19/2020	vs	TULSA	16	7	W	-23.0	L	66.0	U	
9/26/2020	vs	WEST VIRGINIA	27	13	W	-6.5	W	49.0	U	
10/3/2020	@	Kansas	47	7	W	-21.5	W	53.0	O	
10/24/2020	vs	IOWA STATE	24	21	W	-2.5	W	54.0	U	
10/31/2020	vs	TEXAS	34	41	L	-3.5	L	58.0	O	{OT}
11/7/2020	@	Kansas State	20	18	W	-14.0	L	48.5	U	
11/21/2020	@	Oklahoma	13	41	L	6.5	L	60.5	U	"The Bedlam Series"
11/28/2020	vs	TEXAS TECH	50	44	W	-12.0	L	57.0	O	
12/5/2020	@	Tcu	22	29	L	-2.5	L	53.0	U	
12/12/2020	@	Baylor	42	3	W	-6.0	W	49.5	U	
12/29/2020	vs	Miami	37	34	W	-1.5	W	63.0	O	Cheez-it Bowl
Coach: Mike Gundy		Season Record >>	332	258	8-3	ATS>>	5-6	O/U>>	4-7	
2019-Oklahoma State		Opponent	OSU	Opp	S/U	Line	ATS	Total	O/U	
8/30/2019	@	Oregon State	52	36	W	-13.0	W	72.5	O	
9/7/2019	vs	MCNEESE STATE	56	14	W	-42.0	T	NT	---	
9/14/2019	@	Tulsa	40	21	W	-13.5	W	64.5	U	
9/21/2019	@	Texas	30	36	L	7.0	W	72.5	U	
9/28/2019	vs	KANSAS STATE	26	13	W	-4.0	W	60.0	U	
10/5/2019	@	Texas Tech	35	45	L	-9.5	L	62.5	O	
10/19/2019	vs	BAYLOR	27	45	L	-5.5	L	68.5	O	
10/26/2019	@	Iowa State	34	27	W	10.5	W	64.0	U	
11/2/2019	vs	TCU	34	27	W	-1.5	W	59.0	O	
11/16/2019	vs	KANSAS	31	13	W	-17.0	W	69.0	U	
11/23/2019	@	West Virginia	20	13	W	-6.5	W	56.5	U	
11/30/2019	vs	OKLAHOMA	16	34	L	14.0	L	68.0	U	"The Bedlam Series"
12/27/2019	vs	Texas A&M	21	24	L	5.0	W	55.5	U	Texas Bowl
Coach: Mike Gundy		Season Record >>	422	348	8-5	ATS>>	9-3-1	O/U>>	4-8	
2018-Oklahoma State		Opponent	OSU	Opp	S/U	Line	ATS	Total	O/U	
9/1/2018	vs	MISSOURI STATE	58	17	W	-44.0	L	NT	---	
9/8/2018	vs	SOUTH ALABAMA	55	13	W	-30.5	W	64.0	O	
9/15/2018	vs	BOISE STATE	44	21	W	2.0	W	66.5	U	
9/22/2018	vs	TEXAS TECH	17	41	L	-14.5	L	74.5	U	
9/29/2018	@	Kansas	48	28	W	-17.0	W	53.5	O	
10/6/2018	vs	IOWA STATE	42	48	L	-10.0	L	55.5	O	
10/13/2018	@	Kansas State	12	31	L	-9.0	L	61.5	U	
10/27/2018	vs	TEXAS	38	35	W	1.0	W	59.5	O	
11/3/2018	@	Baylor	31	35	L	-6.5	L	68.5	U	
11/10/2018	@	Oklahoma	47	48	L	21.5	W	80.0	O	"The Bedlam Series"
11/17/2018	vs	WEST VIRGINIA	45	41	W	6.0	W	73.5	O	
11/24/2018	@	Tcu	24	31	L	-5.5	L	54.0	O	
12/31/2018	vs	Missouri	38	33	W	9.5	W	72.5	U	Liberty Bowl
Coach: Mike Gundy		Season Record >>	499	422	7-6	ATS>>	7-6	O/U>>	7-5	
2017-Oklahoma State		Opponent	OSU	Opp	S/U	Line	ATS	Total	O/U	
8/31/2017	vs	TULSA	59	24	W	-20.0	W	70.5	O	
9/9/2017	@	South Alabama	44	7	W	-28.0	W	67.0	U	
9/16/2017	@	Pittsburgh	59	21	W	-11.0	W	66.0	O	
9/23/2017	vs	TCU	31	44	L	-9.5	L	67.5	O	
9/30/2017	@	Texas Tech	41	34	W	-11.0	L	85.0	U	
10/14/2017	vs	BAYLOR	59	16	W	-26.0	W	67.5	O	
10/21/2017	@	Texas	13	10	W	-7.0	L	65.0	U	{OT}
10/28/2017	@	West Virginia	50	39	W	-7.5	W	79.0	O	
11/4/2017	vs	OKLAHOMA	52	62	L	-1.0	L	76.0	O	"The Bedlam Series"
11/11/2017	@	Iowa State	49	42	W	-7.0	T	60.5	O	
11/18/2017	vs	KANSAS STATE	40	45	L	-20.0	L	62.5	O	
11/25/2017	vs	KANSAS	58	17	W	-40.5	W	67.5	O	
12/28/2017	vs	Virginia Tech	30	21	W	-6.5	W	60.5	U	Camping World Bowl
Coach: Mike Gundy		Season Record >>	585	382	10-3	ATS>>	7-5-1	O/U>>	9-4	

Copyright © 2021 by Steve's Football Bible, LLC

OKLAHOMA STATE COWBOYS   BIG TWELVE

STADIUM: Boone-Pickens Stadium {56,790}				Location: Stillwater, OK					COACH: Mike Gundy	
DATE		Opponent	OSU	Opp	S/U	Line	ATS	Total	O/U	Trends & Angles
9/4/2021	vs	MISSOURI STATE								vs Missouri State - OK State leads series 8-0
9/11/2021	vs	TULSA								22-0 S/U @ home vs Tulsa since 1953
9/18/2021	@	Boise State								vs Boise State - OK State leads series 1-0
9/25/2021	vs	KANSAS STATE								2-11 ATS vs Kansas State as favorite since 1988
10/2/2021	vs	BAYLOR								8-1 S/U @ home vs Baylor as favorite since 1998
10/16/2021	@	Texas								5-1 S/U @ Texas since 2010
10/23/2021	@	Iowa State								vs Iowa State - OK State leads series 33-19-3
10/30/2021	vs	KANSAS								22-1 S/U vs Kansas as favorite since 1983
11/6/2021	@	West Virginia								6-0 S/U & ATS vs West Virginia since 2015
11/13/2021	vs	TCU								5-1 S/U @ home vs TCU since 1993
11/20/2021	@	Texas Tech								5-1 S/U @ Texas Tech since 2010
11/27/2021	vs	OKLAHOMA								vs Oklahoma - Oklahoma leads series 91-17-7
12/4/2021	vs									BIG XII Championship
	vs									BOWL GAME

Pointspread Analysis Non-Conference		Pointspread Analysis Conference
1-9 S/U vs Non-Conf as 7.5 point or more Dog since 1990		vs Baylor - Oklahoma State leads series 21-18
10-1 S/U vs Non-Conf. as 3.5-7 point favorite since 1987		14-0 S/U vs Baylor as 7 point or more favorite since 1997
11-0 S/U vs Non-Conf. as 10.5-15 point favorite since 2000		0-10 S/U vs Baylor as 9.5 point or more Dog since 1989
36-2 S/U vs Non-Conf. as 15.5 point or more favorite since 1985		1-3 S/U & ATS vs Iowa State as Dog since 2000
11-0 S/U vs Tulsa as 9 point or more favorite since 1985		8-0 S/U vs Iowa State as 11-17.5 point favorite since 1983
8-0 S/U vs Tulsa since 1999		vs Kansas - Oklahoma State leads series 39-29-3
Dog		19-3-1 ATS vs Kansas as favorite since 1983
1-20 S/U as 25.5 point or more Dog since 1986		vs Kansas State - Oklahoma State leads series 41-26
8-0 ATS as 25.5 point or more Dog since 1995		2-10 S/U vs Kansas State as Dog since 1991
1-13 S/U as 20.5-25 point Dog since 1983		0-10 S/U vs Kansas State as 3.5 point or more Dog since 1991
2-13 S/U as 15.5-20 point Dog since 1990		6-0 S/U vs Kansas State as 21 point or more favorite since 1984
5-1 O/U as 15.5-20 point Dog since 2001		0-17 S/U vs Oklahoma as 14 point or less Dog since 1983
4-25-1 S/U as 10.5-15 point Dog since 1985		vs TCU - Oklahoma State leads series 16-13-2
4-11 ATS on road as 10.5-15 point Dog since 1999		vs Texas - Texas leads series 25-9
0-10 S/U & ATS on road as 7.5-10 point Dog since 1984		6-1 S/U vs Texas as favorite since 2010
2-9 S/U @ home as 7.5-10 point Dog since 1983		1-15 S/U vs Texas as Dog since 1998
6-1 O/U on road as 3 point or less Dog since 2002		Game 11-1 O/U @ home vs Texas since 1997
Favorite		10-2 S/U vs Texas Tech since 2009
8-1 O/U @ home as 3 point or less favorite since 2006		vs Texas Tech - Texas Tech leads series 24-21-3
9-2 S/U @ home as 3.5-7 point favorite since 2009		1-7 S/U @ Texas Tech as Dog since 1996
15-3 S/U on road as 3.5-7 point favorite since 1995		10-2 S/U vs Texas Tech as favorite since 1999
5-14 O/U as 3.5-7 point favorite since 2010		vs West Virginia - Oklahoma State leads series 8-4
14-0 S/U on road as 10.5-15 point favorite since 1983		
10-4 O/U as 10.5-15 point favorite since 2013	MISSOURI ST.	25-0 S/U in 1st home game of season since 1996
16-2 S/U @ home as 10.5-15 point favorite since 1986	TULSA	10-4 O/U in 2nd home game of season since 2006
22-5 S/U as 15.5-20 point favorite since 1985	BAYLOR	12-3 S/U prior to playing Texas since 2006
9-0 S/U on road as 20.5-25 point favorite since 1984	BAYLOR	10-3 ATS prior to playing Texas since 2008
13-0 S/U @ home as 20.5-25 point favorite since 1984	BAYLOR	8-3 S/U after playing Kansas State since 2010
29-0 S/U @ home as 25.5 point or more favorite since 1984	Texas	2-11 O/U in 2nd road game of season since 2008
Bowl Games	Texas	10-3 S/U in 2nd road game of season since 2008
0-3 S/U & ATS vs Mississippi in Bowl Games	Iowa State	10-2 S/U after playing Texas since 2008
0-3 O/U vs Mississippi in Bowl Games	KANSAS	7-2 S/U after playing West Virginia since 2012
0-3 S/U in Cotton Bowl since 2004	W. Virginia	9-0 S/U prior to playing TCU since 2012
12-2 S/U as a favorite in Bowl Games since 1976	TCU	7-3 O/U prior to playing Texas Tech since 2010
11-3 ATS as a favorite in Bowl Games since 1976	TCU	10-2 S/U prior to playing Texas Tech since 2008
2-8 S/U as a Dog in Bowl Games since 1981		
3-7 ATS as a Dog in Bowl Games since 1981		
5-1 S/U & ATS in Bowl Games as 3 point or less favorite since 1984		
4-0 S/U in Bowl Games as 3.5-7 point favorite since 2007		
3-0 S/U & ATS in Bowl Games as 7.5-20 point favorite since 1976		

Copyright © 2021 by Steve's Football Bible, LLC

OLD DOMINION MONARCHS

C-USA East

2019-Old Dominion		Opponent	ODU	Opp	S/U	Line	ATS	Total	O/U	
8/31/2019	vs	NORFOLK STATE	24	21	W	-24.5	L	NT	---	
9/7/2019	@	Virginia Tech	17	31	L	28.5	W	56.5	U	
9/21/2019	@	Virginia	17	28	L	27.0	W	46.5	U	
9/28/2019	vs	EAST CAROLINA	21	24	L	-3.0	L	46.5	U	
10/5/2019	vs	WESTERN KENTUCKY	3	20	L	3.0	L	42.0	U	
10/12/2019	@	Marshall	17	31	L	16.0	W	56.5	U	
10/19/2019	@	Alabama-Birmingham	14	38	L	17.0	L	41.5	O	
10/26/2019	vs	FLORIDA ATLANTIC	3	41	L	14.0	L	50.5	U	
11/2/2019	@	Florida International	17	24	L	17.0	W	47.0	U	
11/9/2019	vs	TEXAS-SAN ANTONIO	23	24	L	-3.0	L	41.5	O	
11/23/2019	@	Middle Tennessee	17	38	L	13.5	L	47.0	O	
11/30/2019	vs	CHARLOTTE	22	38	L	10.0	L	50.5	O	
Coach: Bobby Wilder		Season Record >>	195	358	1-11	ATS>>	4-8	O/U>>	4-7	
2018-Old Dominion		Opponent	ODU	Opp	S/U	Line	ATS	Total	O/U	
9/1/2018	@	Liberty	10	52	L	-5.0	L	58.0	O	
9/8/2018	vs	FLORIDA INTERNATIONAL	20	28	L	2.5	L	51.5	U	
9/15/2018	@	Charlotte	25	28	L	-1.5	L	48.0	O	
9/22/2018	vs	VIRGINIA TECH	49	35	W	29.0	W	53.0	O	
9/29/2018	@	East Carolina	35	37	L	7.0	W	60.5	O	
10/6/2018	@	Florida Atlantic	33	52	L	13.0	L	63.5	O	
10/13/2018	vs	MARSHALL	20	42	L	3.5	L	57.0	O	
10/20/2018	@	Western Kentucky	37	34	W	4.0	W	55.5	O	
10/27/2018	vs	MIDDLE TENNESSEE	17	51	L	4.5	L	62.0	O	
11/10/2018	vs	NORTH TEXAS	34	31	W	14.5	W	66.0	U	
11/17/2018	vs	VIRGINIA MILITARY	77	14	W	-31.0	W	NT	---	
11/24/2018	@	Rice	13	27	L	-7.0	L	62.0	U	
Coach: Bobby Wilder		Season Record >>	370	431	4-8	ATS>>	5-7	O/U>>	8-3	
2017-Old Dominion		Opponent	ODU	Opp	S/U	Line	ATS	Total	O/U	
9/2/2017	vs	SUNY-ALBANY	31	17	W	-23.5	L	52.5	U	
9/9/2017	@	Massachusetts	17	7	W	-3.5	W	60.5	U	
9/16/2017	vs	NORTH CAROLINA	23	53	L	11.0	L	56.5	O	
9/23/2017	@	Virginia Tech	0	38	L	29.5	L	51.5	U	
10/7/2017	vs	FLORIDA ATLANTIC	28	58	L	5.0	L	57.0	O	
10/14/2017	@	Marshall	3	35	L	12.5	L	48.5	U	
10/20/2017	vs	WESTERN KENTUCKY	31	35	L	6.5	W	50.0	O	
10/28/2017	@	North Texas	38	45	L	12.0	W	60.0	O	
11/4/2017	vs	CHARLOTTE	6	0	W	-9.5	L	50.0	U	
11/11/2017	@	Florida International	37	30	W	10.5	W	48.0	O	
11/18/2017	vs	RICE	24	21	W	-7.0	L	51.5	U	
11/25/2017	@	Middle Tennessee	10	41	L	14.0	L	48.5	O	
Coach: Bobby Wilder		Season Record >>	248	380	5-7	ATS>>	4-8	O/U>>	6-6	
2016-Old Dominion		Opponent	ODU	Opp	S/U	Line	ATS	Total	O/U	
9/4/2016	vs	HAMPTON	54	21	W	-21.0	W	NT	---	
9/10/2016	@	Appalchian State	7	31	L	21.0	L	54.0	U	
9/17/2016	@	NC State	22	49	L	24.5	L	58.0	O	
9/24/2016	vs	TEXAS-SAN ANTONIO	33	19	W	-5.5	W	49.5	O	
10/1/2016	@	NC-Charlotte	52	17	W	-8.5	W	57.5	O	
10/8/2016	vs	MASSACHUSETTS	36	16	W	-12.0	W	54.5	U	
10/22/2016	@	Western Kentucky	24	59	L	15.5	L	65.0	O	
10/29/2016	@	Texas-El Paso	31	21	W	-5.0	W	53.5	U	
11/5/2016	vs	MARSHALL	38	14	W	-8.0	W	58.0	U	
11/12/2016	vs	SOUTHERN MISS	51	35	W	1.0	W	63.5	O	
11/19/2016	@	Florida Atlantic	42	24	W	-8.0	W	61.0	O	
11/26/2016	vs	FLORIDA INTERNATIONAL	42	28	W	-14.0	T	60.0	O	
12/23/2016	vs	Eastern Michigan	24	20	W	-5.0	L	63.0	U	Bahamas Bowl
Coach: Bobby Wilder		Season Record >>	456	354	10-3	ATS>>	8-4-1	O/U>>	7-5	

Copyright © 2021 by Steve's Football Bible, LLC

OLD DOMINION MONARCHS

C-USA East

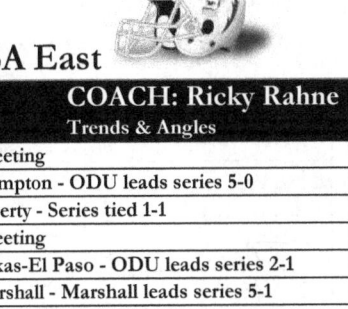

STADIUM: Foreman Field {22,480}			Location: Norfolk, VA						COACH: Ricky Rahne	
DATE		Opponent	ODU	Opp	S/U	Line	ATS	Total	O/U	Trends & Angles
9/3/2021	@	*Wake Forest*								1st Meeting
9/11/2021	vs	*HAMPTON*								vs Hampton - ODU leads series 5-0
9/18/2021	@	*Liberty*								vs Liberty - Series tied 1-1
9/25/2021	vs	*BUFFALO*								1st Meeting
10/2/2021	@	Texas-El Paso								vs Texas-El Paso - ODU leads series 2-1
10/9/2021	@	Marshall								vs Marshall - Marshall leads series 5-1
10/16/2021	vs	WESTERN KENTUCKY								vs Western Kentucky - WKU leads series 5-1
10/30/2021	vs	LOUISIANA TECH								vs Louisiana Tech - ODU lead series 1-0
11/6/2021	@	Florida International								vs Florida International - Series tied 2-2
11/13/2021	vs	FLORIDA ATLANTIC								vs Florida Atlantic - FAU leads series 3-1
11/20/2021	@	Middle Tennessee								vs Middle Tennessee - MTSU leads series 4-0
11/27/2021	vs	CHARLOTTE								vs Charlotte - Old Dominion leads series 3-2
12/4/2021	vs									C-USA Championship
	vs									BOWL GAME

Pointspread Analysis Non-Conference		Pointspread Analysis Conference	
1-11 S/U vs Non-conf. as 3.0 point or more Dog since 2014		Game 5-1 O/U vs Western Kentucky since 2014	
10-3 S/U vs Non-Conf. as 3.0 point or more favorite since 2014			
Dog		HAMPTON	8-1 S/U in 1st home game of season since 2011
1-18 S/U as 15.5 point or more Dog since 2013		CHARLOTTE	9-2 S/U in final home game of season since 2009
1-23 S/U on road as 10.5 or more Dog since 2013			
13-3 O/U as 3.5-7 point Dog since 2014			
Favorite			
0-7 ATS as 3.0-10 point favorite since 2017			
10-0 S/U as 10.5 point favorite since 2013			
16-3 S/U @ home as 3 point or more favorite since 2014			

College Football
"Bowl Games of the 20th Century" {1902-1999}

The most complete and in depth historical accounts of all the Major Bowl Games of the 20th Century

A CELEBRATION OF 150 YEARS OF COLLEGE FOOTBALL

BY STEVE FULTON

1961 Rose Bowl

This book is for football fans of all ages. It is both educational and entertaining as you can read nostalgically about former great College teams and players, as well as some of the great Bowl Games from the past. This book covers all the Bowl Games of the 20th Century (1902-1999), so you can read about your football heroes, past and present.

College Football History "Bowl Games of the 20th Century"

8.5" x 11" {596 pages} Price $34.99 + $5.00 Shipping & Handling

$39.99

These books available at numerous online retailers

Copyright © 2021 by Steve's Football Bible, LLC

OREGON DUCKS PACIFIC-12 North

2020-Oregon		Opponent	ORE	Opp	S/U	Line	ATS	Total	O/U	
11/7/2020	vs	STANFORD	35	14	W	-12.5	W	49.0	T	
11/14/2020	@	Washington State	43	29	W	-10.0	W	58.5	O	
11/20/2020	vs	UCLA	38	35	W	-18.0	L	62.0	O	
11/27/2020	@	Oregon State	38	41	L	-13.0	L	64.5	O	"Civil War" (Platypus Trophy)
12/5/2020	@	California	17	21	L	-8.0	L	59.0	U	
12/18/2020	@	Usc	31	24	W	3.0	W	65.5	U	PAC-12 Championship
1/2/2021	vs	Iowa State	17	34	L	4.0	L	57.5	U	Fiesta Bowl
Coach: Mario Cristobal		Season Record >>	219	198	4-3	ATS>>	3-4	O/U>>	3-3-1	PAC-12 Champions
2019-Oregon		Opponent	ORE	Opp	S/U	Line	ATS	Total	O/U	
8/31/2019	vs	Auburn	21	27	L	3.5	L	55.5	U	AT&T Stadium
9/7/2019	vs	MONTANA	77	6	W	-24.5	W	61.5	O	
9/14/2019	vs	NEVADA	35	3	W	-38.0	L	NT	---	
9/21/2019	@	Stanford	21	6	W	-12.5	W	55.5	U	
10/5/2019	vs	CALIFORNIA	17	7	W	-21.5	L	46.5	U	
10/12/2019	vs	COLORADO	45	3	W	-22.5	W	62.0	U	
10/19/2019	@	Washington	35	31	W	-2.5	W	48.5	O	
10/26/2019	vs	WASHINGTON STATE	37	35	W	-19.5	L	67.5	O	
11/2/2019	@	Usc	56	24	W	-3.5	W	60.0	O	
11/16/2019	vs	ARIZONA	34	6	W	-27.0	W	68.5	U	
11/23/2019	@	Arizona State	28	31	L	-13.5	L	55.0	O	
11/30/2019	vs	OREGON STATE	24	10	W	-20.5	L	65.0	U	"Civil War" (Platypus Trophy)
12/6/2019	vs	Utah	37	15	W	6.5	W	45.0	O	PAC-12 Championship
1/1/2020	vs	Wisconsin	28	27	W	3.0	W	52.5	O	Rose Bowl
Coach: Mario Cristobal		Season Record >>	495	231	12-2	ATS>>	8-6	O/U>>	7-6	PAC-12 Champions
2018-Oregon		Opponent	ORE	Opp	S/U	Line	ATS	Total	O/U	
9/1/2018	vs	BOWLING GREEN	58	24	W	-34.0	T	70.0	O	
9/8/2018	vs	PORTLAND STATE	62	14	W	-49.5	L	NT	---	
9/15/2018	vs	SAN JOSE STATE	35	22	W	-42.5	L	69.5	U	
9/22/2018	vs	STANFORD	31	38	L	3.0	L	59.0	O	{OT}
9/29/2018	@	California	42	24	W	-2.0	W	57.5	O	
10/13/2018	vs	WASHINGTON	30	27	W	3.5	W	58.0	U	{OT}
10/20/2018	@	Washington State	20	34	L	3.0	L	69.5	U	
10/27/2018	@	Arizona	15	44	L	-7.5	L	66.0	U	
11/3/2018	vs	UCLA	42	21	W	-11.0	W	59.0	O	
11/10/2018	@	Utah	25	32	L	6.0	L	51.0	O	
11/17/2018	vs	ARIZONA STATE	31	29	W	-3.5	L	66.0	U	
11/24/2018	@	Oregon State	55	15	W	-17.5	W	70.0	T	"Civil War" (Platypus Trophy)
12/31/2018	vs	Michigan State	7	6	W	1.5	W	47.0	U	Redbox Bowl
Coach: Mario Cristobal		Season Record >>	453	330	9-4	ATS>>	5-7-1	O/U>>	5-6-1	
2017-Oregon		Opponent	ORE	Opp	S/U	Line	ATS	Total	O/U	
9/2/2017	vs	SOUTHERN UTAH	77	21	W	-39.5	W	74.0	O	
9/9/2017	vs	NEBRASKA	42	35	W	-10.5	L	67.5	O	
9/16/2017	@	Wyoming	49	13	W	-14.0	W	66.0	U	
9/23/2017	@	Arizona State	35	37	L	-15.0	L	75.0	U	
9/30/2017	vs	CALIFORNIA	45	24	W	-16.5	W	67.0	O	
10/7/2017	vs	WASHINGTON STATE	10	33	L	2.0	L	59.5	U	
10/14/2017	@	Stanford	7	49	L	9.5	L	56.5	U	
10/21/2017	@	Ucla	14	31	L	6.0	L	68.5	U	
10/28/2017	vs	UTAH	41	20	W	2.0	W	49.5	O	
11/4/2017	@	Washington	3	38	L	17.0	L	53.0	U	
11/18/2017	vs	ARIZONA	48	28	W	-3.0	W	77.5	U	
11/25/2017	vs	OREGON STATE	69	10	W	-25.5	W	62.5	O	"Civil War" (Platypus Trophy)
12/16/2017	vs	Boise State	28	38	L	-7.0	L	62.5	O	Las Vegas Bowl
Coach: Willie Taggert		Season Record >>	468	377	7-6	ATS>>	6-7	O/U>>	6-7	

Copyright © 2021 by Steve's Football Bible, LLC

OREGON DUCKS   PACIFIC-12 North

STADIUM: Autzen Stadium {54,000}					Location: Eugene, OR				COACH: Mario Cristobal	
DATE		Opponent	Ore	Opp	S/U	Line	ATS	Total	O/U	Trends & Angles
9/4/2021	vs	FRESNO STATE								7-0 S/U vs Fresno State as favorite since 1996
9/11/2021	@	Ohio State								vs Ohio State - Ohio State leads series 9-0
9/18/2021	vs	SUNY-STONY BROOK								1st meeting
9/25/2021	vs	ARIZONA								vs Arizona - Oregon leads series 27-17
10/2/2021	@	Stanford								vs Stanford - Stanford leads series 49-34-1
10/15/2021	vs	CALIFORNIA								vs California - California leads series 41-40-2
10/23/2021	@	Ucla								8-1 S/U vs UCLA since 2008
10/30/2021	@	Colorado								6-1 S/U & ATS vs Colorado as favorite since 2011
11/6/2021	@	Washington								6-1 S/U & ATS @ Washington since 2007
11/13/2021	vs	WASHINGTON STATE								1-8 ATS vs Washington State as favorite since 2010
11/20/2021	@	Utah								9-3 S/U vs Utah since 1995
11/27/2021	vs	OREGON STATE								12-1 S/U @ home vs Oregon State since 1995
12/3/2021	vs									PAC-12 Championship
	vs									BOWL GAME

Pointspread Analysis Non-Conference			Pointspread Analysis Conference
0-6 S/U vs Non-Conf. as 15.5 point or more Dog since 1983			0-7 O/U vs Arizona as favorite since 2012
9-3 ATS vs Non-Conf. as 3.5-15 point Dog since 1983			10-1 S/U @ home vs California as favorite since 1989 {8-3 ATS}
1-8 O/U vs Non-Conf. as 3 point or less Dog since 1990			9-0 S/U vs California as 13 point or more favorite since 2000
10-1 S/U vs Non-conf. as 10.5-15 point favorite since 1999			vs Colorado - Oregon leads series 13-9
40-1 S/U vs Non-Conf. as 15.5 point or more favorite since 1985			Game 13-4-2 O/U vs Oregon State since 2002
0-7 S/U vs ranked Ohio State all time			vs Oregon State - Oregon leads series 66-49-9
Dog			11-2 S/U vs Oregon State since 2008
2-8 S/U as 20.5 point or more Dog since 1983			19-2-1 S/U vs Oregon State as 9.5 point or more favorite since 1983
2-11 S/U as 15.5-20 point Dog since 1984			Game 7-1 O/U @ home vs Oregon State since 2005
1-9 S/U as 10.5-15 point Dog since 1987			1-6 S/U vs Stanford as 5.5 point or more Dog since 1986
3-12 S/U on road as 3.5-7 point Dog since 1996			vs Ucla - UCLA leads series 40-30
11-3-1 ATS on road as 3 point or less Dog since 1999			8-0 S/U vs UCLA as favorite since 2008
Favorite			vs Utah - Oregon leads series 23-10
16-2 S/U @ home as 3 point or less favorite since 1985			Game 7-1 O/U vs Utah since 2009
15-3 ATS @ home as 3 point or less favorite since 1985			14-2 S/U & ATS vs Washington since 2004
19-2 S/U on road as 3.5-7 point favorite since 1993			vs Washington - Washington leads series 59-47-6
12-2 O/U on road as 3.5-7 point favorite since 2000			15-1 S/U vs Washington as favorite since 1988
6-0 S/U @ home as 7.5-10 point favorite since 2003			1-8 S/U vs Washington as 10 point or more Dog since 1983
9-2 S/U on road as 7.5-10 point favorite since 2000			vs Washington State - Oregon leads series 51-40-7
13-5 S/U on road as 10.5-15 point favorite since 1992			1-10 ATS vs Washington State since 2010
9-0-1 O/U @ home as 10.5-15 point favorite since 2007			Game 5-1 O/U @ home vs Wazzu since 2009
24-4 S/U @ home as 15.5-20 point favorite since 1985			10-0 S/U vs Wash. State as 16 point or more favorite since 1999
8-1 S/U on road as 15.5-20 point favorite since 2007	FRESNO STATE		10-0-1 O/U in 1st home game of season since 2009
10-0 S/U on road as 20.5 point or more favorite since 1990	FRESNO STATE		10-0-1 O/U in 1st home game of season since 2009
51-1 S/U @ home as 20.5 point or more favorite since 1990	FRESNO STATE		16-0 S/U in 1st home game of season since 2005
Bowl Games	STONY BROOK		25-0 S/U in 2nd home game of season since 1996
1-6 O/U in Bowl Games as 3 point or less Dog since 1999	STONY BROOK		9-2 S/U prior to playing Arizona since 2007
1-4 S/U & ATS in Bowl Games as 3.5-7 point favorite since 1998	STONY BROOK		1-6 ATS prior to playing Arizona since 2010
3-0 S/U in Bowl Games as 10.5-15 point favorite since 1989	ARIZONA		13-4 S/U prior to playing California since 2004
	ARIZONA		11-4 ATS prior to playing California since 2006
0-11 S/U vs #1 ranked teams all time	ARIZONA		12-2 O/U prior to playing California since 2007
38-4 S/U @ home when ranked since 2012	Stanford		17-4 S/U in 2nd road game of season since 2000
12-0 S/U & ATS when ranked vs Washington since 2005	Stanford		16-5 ATS in 2nd road game of season since 2000
	CALIFORNIA		11-2 S/U after playing Stanford since 2008
	CALIFORNIA		1-8 ATS prior to playing UCLA since 2006
	Ucla		15-2 S/U after playing California since 2005
	Colorado		10-1-1 O/U after playing UCLA since 2002
	Colorado		10-2 S/U prior to playing Washington since 2007
	Colorado		9-0-1 ATS prior to playing Washington since 2010
	Washington		11-1 S/U prior to playing Washington State since 2009
2-7 ATS prior to playing Utah since 2001	WAZZU		11-2 S/U after playing Washington since 2007
	OREGON STATE		0-7 O/U after playing Utah since 2008
13-4 O/U in final home game of season since 2004	OREGON STATE		11-2 S/U in final home game of season since 2008

Copyright © 2021 by Steve's Football Bible, LLC

2020-Oregon State		Opponent	State	Opp	S/U	Line	ATS	Total	O/U	
11/7/2020	vs	WASHINGTON STATE	28	38	L	-3.5	L	64.0	O	
11/14/2020	@	Washington	21	27	L	13.5	W	51.0	U	
11/21/2020	vs	CALIFORNIA	31	27	W	1.0	W	46.5	O	
11/27/2020	vs	OREGON	41	38	W	13.0	W	64.5	O	"Civil War" (Platypus Trophy)
12/5/2020	@	Utah	24	30	L	13.5	W	51.0	O	
12/12/2020	vs	STANFORD	24	27	L	2.0	L	55.5	U	
12/19/2020	vs	ARIZONA STATE	33	46	L	7.5	L	54.5	O	
Coach: Jonathan Smith		Season Record >>	202	233	2-5	ATS>>	4-3	O/U>>	5-2	
2019-Oregon State		Opponent	State	Opp	S/U	Line	ATS	Total	O/U	
8/30/2019	vs	OKLAHOMA STATE	36	52	L	13.0	L	72.5	O	
9/7/2019	@	Hawaii	28	31	L	7.0	W	77.0	U	
9/14/2019	vs	CAL POLY-SLO	45	7	W	-16.5	W	NT	---	
9/28/2019	vs	STANFORD	28	31	L	3.0	T	55.5	O	
10/5/2019	@	Ucla	48	31	W	4.5	W	63.5	O	
10/12/2019	vs	UTAH	7	52	L	15.0	L	59.5	U	
10/19/2019	@	California	21	17	W	11.0	W	51.0	U	
11/2/2019	@	Arizona	56	38	W	5.0	W	71.5	O	
11/9/2019	vs	WASHINGTON	7	19	L	10.5	L	64.5	U	
11/16/2019	vs	ARIZONA STATE	35	34	W	1.5	W	56.5	O	
11/23/2019	@	Washington State	53	54	L	10.5	W	77.5	O	
11/30/2019	@	Oregon	10	24	L	20.5	W	65.0	U	"Civil War" (Platypus Trophy)
Coach: Jonathan Smith		Season Record >>	374	390	5-7	ATS>>	8-3-1	O/U>>	6-5	
2018-Oregon State		Opponent	State	Opp	S/U	Line	ATS	Total	O/U	
9/1/2018	@	Ohio State	31	77	L	40.0	L	63.0	O	
9/8/2018	vs	SOUTHERN UTAH	48	25	W	-13.0	W	NT	---	
9/15/2018	@	Nevada	35	37	L	3.5	W	67.5	O	
9/22/2018	vs	ARIZONA	14	35	L	4.0	L	73.5	U	
9/29/2018	@	Arizona State	24	52	L	22.0	L	64.5	O	
10/6/2018	vs	WASHINGTON STATE	37	56	L	18.5	L	64.5	O	
10/20/2018	vs	CALIFORNIA	7	49	L	8.5	L	58.5	U	
10/27/2018	@	Colorado	41	34	W	24.5	W	60.0	O	{OT}
11/3/2018	vs	USC	21	38	L	15.0	L	65.5	U	
11/10/2018	@	Stanford	17	48	L	24.0	L	60.5	O	
11/17/2018	@	Washington	23	42	L	32.5	L	58.5	O	
11/23/2018	vs	OREGON	15	55	L	17.5	L	70.0	T	"Civil War" (Platypus Trophy)
Coach: Jonathan Smith		Season Record >>	313	548	2-10	ATS>>	4-8	O/U>>	7-3-1	
2017-Oregon State		Opponent	State	Opp	S/U	Line	ATS	Total	O/U	
8/26/2017	@	Colorado State	27	58	L	3.5	L	60.0	O	
9/2/2017	vs	PORTLAND STATE	35	32	W	-25.5	L	60.0	O	
9/9/2017	vs	MINNESOTA	14	48	L	-2.5	L	50.5	O	
9/16/2017	@	Washington State	23	52	L	18.0	L	65.5	O	
9/30/2017	vs	WASHINGTON	7	42	L	26.0	L	59.0	U	
10/7/2017	@	Usc	10	38	L	32.0	W	56.5	U	
10/14/2017	vs	COLORADO	33	36	L	10.0	W	56.0	O	
10/26/2017	vs	STANFORD	14	15	L	17.0	W	56.0	U	
11/4/2017	@	California	23	37	L	7.0	L	54.5	O	
11/11/2017	@	Arizona	28	49	L	21.0	T	69.5	O	
11/18/2017	vs	ARIZONA STATE	24	40	L	7.0	L	59.0	O	
11/24/2017	@	Oregon	10	69	L	25.5	L	62.5	O	"Civil War" (Platypus Trophy)
Coach: Gary Anderson		Season Record >>	248	516	1-11	ATS>>	3-8-1	O/U>>	9-3	

Copyright © 2021 by Steve's Football Bible, LLC

OREGON STATE BEAVERS   PACIFIC-12 North

STADIUM: Reser Stadium {43,363}		Location: Corvallis, OR								COACH: Jonathan Smith	
DATE		Opponent	OSU	Opp	S/U	Line	ATS	Total	O/U	Trends & Angles	
9/4/2021	@	*Purdue*								vs Purdue - Oregon State leads series 1-0	
9/11/2021	vs	*HAWAII*								3-0 S/U vs Hawaii as favorite since 2008	
9/18/2021	vs	*IDAHO*								10-0 S/U @ home vs Idaho since 1954	
9/25/2021	@	Usc								0-24 S/U @ USC since 1963	
10/2/2021	vs	WASHINGTON								0-4 S/U & ATS @ home vs Washington since 2013	
10/9/2021	@	Washington State								0-7 S/U vs Washington State since 2014	
10/23/2021	vs	UTAH								1-8 S/U vs Utah as Dog since 1992	
10/30/2021	@	California								1-3 S/U & ATS @ California as Dog since 2011	
11/6/2021	@	Colorado								1-4 S/U vs Colorado as Dog since 1983	
11/13/2021	vs	STANFORD								0-7 S/U @ home vs Stanford as Dog since 2011	
11/20/2021	vs	ARIZONA STATE								5-0 S/U vs Arizona State as favorite since 2003	
11/27/2021	@	Oregon								vs Oregon - Oregon leads series 66-49-9	
12/3/2021	vs									PAC-12 Championship	
	vs									BOWL GAME	

Pointspread Analysis Non-Conference		Pointspread Analysis Conference
1-14 S/U vs Non-conf. as 15.5 point or more Dog since 1984		1-15 S/U vs Arizona State as 9 point or more Dog since 1983
1-10 S/U vs Non-Conf. as 10.5-15 point Dog since 1986		vs California - California leads series 38-35
14-2 S/U vs Non-Conf. as 3.5-7 point favorite since 1994		8-0 S/U vs California as favorite since 1999
16-2 S/U vs Non-Conf. as 15.5 point or more favorite since 1994		2-19 S/U vs Oregon as 9.5 point or more Dog since 1985
vs Hawaii - Oregon State leads series 7-4		vs Stanford - Stanford leads series 59-25-3
27-2 S/U vs Idaho since 1939		0-11 S/U vs Stanford since 2010 {2-8-1 ATS}
vs Idaho - Oregon State leads series 36-7		0-15 S/U vs Stanford as 10 point or more Dog since 1985
Dog		5-0 S/U vs Stanford as 9.5 point or more favorite since 2003
1-11 S/U as 30.5 point or more Dog since 1985		Game 3-7 O/U @ home vs Stanford since 2000
9-3 ATS as 30.5 point or more Dog since 1985		0-4 O/U @ home vs Stanford as favorite since 2000
0-13 S/U as 25.5-30 point Dog since 1983		vs USC - USC leads series 63-11-4
1-23 S/U on road as 20.5-25 point Dog since 1983		Game 0-5 O/U vs USC since 2010
2-11 S/U @ home as 20.5-25 point Dog since 1983		0-14 S/U @ USC as Dog since 1985
1-17 S/U @ home as 15.5-20 point Dog since 1985		1-18 S/U vs USC as 12 point or more Dog since 1983
2-26 S/U on road as 15.5-20 point Dog since 1983		vs Utah - Series tied 11-11-1
2-35 S/U on road as 10.5-15 point Dog since 1984		0-5 S/U vs Utah since 2014
3-14 S/U @ home as 10.5-15 point Dog since 1992		Game 1-4 O/U vs Utah since 2014
8-3 O/U @ home as 10.5-15 point Dog since 2006		vs Washington - Washington leads series 66-34-4
0-6 S/U as 7.5-10 point Dog since 2015		Game 7-2 O/U @ home vs Washington since 2001
4-14 S/U on road as 7.5-10 point Dog since 1995		0-9 S/U vs Washington since 2012
3-11 S/U @ home as 3.5-7 point Dog since 1994		5-1 S/U & ATS vs Washington as favorite since 2004
2-10 S/U as 3.5-7 point Dog since 2012		0-16 S/U vs Washington as 10 point or more Dog since 1986
44-208-4 S/U as 3.5 point or more Dog since 1983		vs Washington State - Washington State leads series 55-47-3
10-2 S/U on road as 3 point or less Dog since 1999		10-0 O/U @ Washington State as Dog since 1993
11-1 ATS on road as 3 point or less Dog since 1999		Game 8-0 O/U vs Washington State since 2013
5-0 O/U on road as 3 point or less Dog since 2010		0-19 S/U vs Washington State as 7.5 point or more Dog since 1983
Favorite		3-0 S/U & ATS @ Wazzu as 3 point or less Dog since 2013

4-12 ATS as 3 point or less favorite since 2006	HAWAII	2-9 ATS in 1st home game of season since 2010
1-6-1 O/U on road as 3 point or less favorite since 2002	HAWAII	15-4 S/U in 1st home game of season since 2002
18-5 S/U @ home as 3.5-7 point favorite since 1994	IDAHO	2-7 O/U prior to playing USC since 2006
0-7 ATS on road as 3.5-7 point favorite since 2000	WASHINGTON	11-2 O/U prior to playing Washington State since 2007
9-2 S/U as 7.5-10 point favorite since 2004	Wazzu	2-6 S/U after playing Washington since 2013
13-1 S/U @ home as 10.5-15 point favorite since 1993	UTAH	1-10 S/U prior to playing California since 2010
12-0 S/U as 15.5-20 point favorite since 1994	California	0-5 O/U prior to playing Colorado since 2014
0-6 ATS @ home as 20.5 point favorite since 2013	Colorado	10-3 ATS prior to playing Stanford since 2007
Bowl Games	ARIZONA STATE	2-12 S/U after playing Stanford since 2007
5-0 S/U in Bowl Games as 3.5-7 point favorite since 2001	Oregon	8-2 O/U in final road game of season since 2011
	Oregon	0-12 S/U in final road game of season since 2009

0-7 S/U on road when ranked vs ranked teams since 1968		6-75 S/U on road vs ranked teams since 1970
0-8 S/U when ranked vs ranked teams since 2009		0-11 S/U vs #3 ranked teams all time
4-0 S/U when ranked vs Washington State since 1962		0-11 S/U vs #4 ranked teams all time
0-4 S/U when ranked vs Washington since 2000		0-11 S/U vs ranked Stanford since 1969

Copyright © 2021 by Steve's Football Bible, LLC

PENN STATE NITTANY LIONS   BIG TEN East

2020-Penn State		Opponent	State	Opp	S/U	Line	ATS	Total	O/U	
10/24/2020	@	Indiana	35	36	L	-6.5	L	61.5	O	{OT}
10/31/2020	vs	OHIO STATE	23	38	L	10.0	L	63.0	U	
11/7/2020	vs	MARYLAND	19	35	L	-27.0	L	62.5	U	
11/14/2020	@	Nebraska	23	30	L	-2.5	L	57.5	U	
11/21/2020	vs	IOWA	21	41	L	1.0	L	45.5	O	
11/28/2020	@	Michigan	27	17	W	PK	W	56.0	U	
12/5/2020	@	Rutgers	23	7	W	-13.0	W	51.5	U	
12/12/2020	vs	MICHIGAN STATE	39	24	W	-14.5	W	46.5	O	"Land Grant Trophy"
12/19/2020	vs	ILLINOIS	56	21	W	-16.0	W	53.5	O	
Coach: James Franklin		Season Record >>	266	249	4-5	ATS>>	4-5	O/U>>	4-5	
2019-Penn State		Opponent	State	Opp	S/U	Line	ATS	Total	O/U	
8/31/2019	vs	IDAHO	79	7	W	-41.5	W	NT	---	
9/7/2019	vs	BUFFALO	45	13	W	-31.5	W	55.0	O	
9/14/2019	vs	PITTSBURGH	17	10	W	-17.0	L	53.0	U	
9/27/2019	@	Maryland	59	0	W	-6.5	W	61.0	U	
10/5/2019	vs	PURDUE	35	7	W	-28.5	L	55.0	U	
10/12/2019	@	Iowa	17	12	W	-3.5	W	43.5	U	
10/19/2019	vs	MICHIGAN	28	21	W	-7.5	L	46.5	O	
10/26/2019	@	Michigan State	28	7	W	-4.5	W	42.0	U	"Land Grant Trophy"
11/9/2019	@	Minnesota	26	31	L	-5.5	L	48.5	O	"Governor's Victory Bell"
11/16/2019	vs	INDIANA	34	27	W	-14.5	L	55.0	O	
11/23/2019	@	Ohio State	17	28	L	19.5	W	58.0	O	
11/30/2019	vs	RUTGERS	27	6	W	-39.0	L	50.5	U	
12/28/2019	vs	**Memphis**	53	39	W	-6.5	W	59.0	O	Cotton Bowl
Coach: James Franklin		Season Record >>	465	208	11-2	ATS>>	7-6	O/U>>	5-7	
2018-Penn State		Opponent	State	Opp	S/U	Line	ATS	Total	O/U	
9/1/2018	vs	APPALACHIAN STATE	45	38	W	-24.0	L	54.0	O	{OT}
9/8/2018	@	Pittsburgh	51	6	W	-7.0	W	50.0	O	
9/15/2018	vs	KENT STATE	63	10	W	-35.0	W	63.0	O	
9/22/2018	@	Illinois	63	24	W	-27.0	W	60.0	O	
9/29/2018	vs	OHIO STATE	26	27	L	3.5	W	69.5	U	
10/13/2018	vs	MICHIGAN STATE	17	21	L	-13.5	L	53.5	U	"Land Grant Trophy"
10/19/2019	@	Indiana	33	28	W	-14.0	L	57.0	O	
10/27/2018	vs	IOWA	30	24	W	-5.5	W	52.0	U	
11/3/2018	@	Michigan	7	42	L	11.0	L	49.5	U	
11/10/2018	vs	WISCONSIN	22	10	W	-7.5	W	54.0	U	
11/17/2018	@	Rutgers	20	7	W	-28.0	L	51.5	U	
11/24/2018	vs	MARYLAND	38	3	W	-12.0	W	50.5	U	
1/1/2019	vs	**Kentucky**	24	27	L	-4.5	L	47.5	O	Citrus Bowl
Coach: James Franklin		Season Record >>	439	267	9-4	ATS>>	7-6	O/U>>	7-6	
2017-Penn State		Opponent	State	Opp	S/U	Line	ATS	Total	O/U	
9/2/2017	vs	AKRON	52	0	W	-30.0	W	62.5	U	
9/9/2017	vs	PITTSBURGH	33	14	W	-19.0	T	64.0	U	
9/16/2017	vs	GEORGIA STATE	56	0	W	-38.0	W	54.5	O	
9/23/2017	@	Iowa	21	19	W	-12.5	L	53.0	U	
9/30/2017	vs	INDIANA	45	14	W	-18.5	W	60.5	U	
10/7/2017	@	Northwestern	31	7	W	-14.5	W	51.5	U	
10/21/2017	vs	MICHIGAN	42	13	W	-7.5	W	42.5	O	
10/28/2017	@	Ohio State	38	39	L	7.0	W	57.5	O	
11/4/2017	@	Michigan State	24	27	L	-9.5	L	46.5	O	"Land Grant Trophy"
11/11/2017	vs	RUTGERS	35	6	W	-31.0	L	56.0	U	
11/18/2017	vs	NEBRASKA	56	44	W	-27.5	L	56.0	O	
11/25/2017	@	Maryland	66	3	W	-23.5	W	57.0	O	
12/30/2017	vs	**Washington**	35	28	W	-3.0	W	54.5	O	Fiesta Bowl
Coach: James Franklin		Season Record >>	534	214	11-2	ATS>>	8-4-1	O/U>>	7-6	

Copyright © 2021 by Steve's Football Bible, LLC

PENN STATE NITTANY LIONS   BIG TEN East

STADIUM: Beaver Stadium {106,572}					Location: University Park, PA				COACH: James Franklin	
DATE		**Opponent**	**PSU**	**Opp**	**S/U**	**Line**	**ATS**	**Total**	**O/U**	**Trends & Angles**
9/4/2021	@	Wisconsin								Game 5-1 O/U vs Wisconsin since 2008
9/11/2021	vs	*BALL STATE*								1st meeting
9/18/2021	vs	*AUBURN*								vs Auburn - Series tied 1-1
9/25/2021	vs	*VILLANOVA*								vs Villanova - Penn State leads series 6-2-1
10/2/2021	vs	**INDIANA**								vs Indiana - Penn State leads series 22-2
10/9/2021	@	Iowa								vs Iowa - Penn State leads series 17-13
10/23/2021	vs	**ILLINOIS**								11-0 S/U vs Illini as 9.5 point or more favorite s/1993
10/30/2021	@	Ohio State								1-12 S/U @ Ohio State as Dog since 1993
11/6/2021	@	Maryland								vs Maryland - Penn State leads series 39-3-1
11/13/2021	vs	**MICHIGAN**								4-0 S/U vs Michigan as favorite since 2008
11/20/2021	vs	**RUTGERS**								15-1 S/U @ home vs Rutgers since 1950
11/27/2021	@	Michigan State								10-1 S/U vs Michigan State as favorite since 1994
12/4/2021	vs				·					Big Ten Championship
	vs									BOWL GAME

Pointspread Analysis Non-Conference		Pointspread Analysis Conference
2-12 S/U vs Non-Conf. as 7.5 point or more Dog since 1975		0-7 ATS @ home vs Illinois as 5 point or more favorite since 1998
4-10 O/U vs Non-Conf. as 3.5-7 point favorite since 1999		22-2 S/U vs Indiana as favorite since 1993
65-1 S/U vs Non-Conf. as 10.5 point or more favorite since 1985		6-0 S/U & ATS vs Iowa as 4-6.5 point favorite since 1993
Dog		12-1-1 S/U vs Maryland as 5.5 point or more favorite since 1984
1-8 S/U on road as 15.5 point or more Dog since 1988		vs Michigan - Michigan leads series 14-10
2-7 ATS on road as 15.5 point or more Dog since 1988		0-8 S/U vs Michigan as 3.5 point or more Dog since 2000
0-4 S/U @ home as 10.5-15 point Dog since 2001		vs Michigan State - Series tied 17-17-1
1-10 S/U on road as 10.5-15 point Dog since 1988		0-3 S/U & ATS vs Michigan State as Dog since 2010
0-11 S/U on road as 7.5-10 point Dog since 1991		4-1 S/U vs Ohio State as favorite since 1994
1-10 S/U on road as 3.5-7 point Dog since 2000		vs Ohio State - Ohio State leads series 22-14
Favorite		1-12 S/U vs Ohio State as 7 point or more Dog since 1996
6-2 ATS on road as 3.5-7 point favorite since 2015		1-6 S/U vs Ohio State as 4.5 point or less Dog since 1993
3-8 O/U @ home as 3.5-7 point favorite since 2011		14-0 S/U vs Rutgers since 1989
5-0 O/U on road as 7.5-10 point favorite since 2007		Game 0-7 O/U vs Rutgers since 2014
10-3 S/U on road as 7.5-10 point favorite since 1983		vs Rutgers - Penn State leads series 29-2
44-0 S/U on road as 10.5 point or more favorite since 1983		19-1 S/U vs Rutgers as favorite since 1983
31-4 S/U @ home as 10.5-15 point favorite since 1985		
33-2 S/U @ home as 15.5-20 point favorite since 1984		22-0-1 S/U when ranked vs Maryland all time
62-1 S/U @ home as 20.5 point or more favorite since 1986		0-12 S/U when ranked vs Top #5 ranked Ohio State all time
Bowl Games		17-1 S/U when ranked vs Rutgers all time {6-0 on road}
7-0 S/U & ATS in Fiesta Bowl		3-24 S/U on road vs ranked teams since 2002
3-0 S/U in Liberty Bowl	BALL STATE	17-2 S/U in 1st home game of season since 2002
3-0 O/U in Rose Bowl since 1995	AUBURN	14-3 S/U in 2nd home game of season since 2004
3-0 S/U & ATS vs Tennessee in Bowl Games	VILLANOVA	8-1 S/U prior to playing Iowa since 2008
0-3 S/U vs Florida in Bowl Games	Iowa	9-3 S/U after playing Indiana since 2008
4-1 S/U in Orange Bowl	Iowa	10-2 ATS after playing Indiana since 2008
3-1 S/U & ATS in Outback Bowl	ILLINOIS	9-3-1 ATS prior to playing Ohio State since 2008
2-7 S/U in Bowl Games as 3.5-7 point Dog since 1976	ILLINOIS	11-3 S/U prior to playing Ohio State since 2007
6-0 S/U in Bowl Games as 3 point or less favorite since 1979	MICHIGAN	0-6 O/U after playing Maryland since 1993
4-0-2 ATS in Bowl Games as 3 point or less favorite since 1979	MICHIGAN	9-2 S/U prior to playing Rutgers since 1992
3-0 S/U in Bowl Games as 7.5-10 point fvorite since 1977	MICHIGAN	11-2 ATS prior to playing Rutgers since 1990

Copyright © 2021 by Steve's Football Bible, LLC

PITTSBURGH PANTHERS   ACC Coastal

2020-Pittsburgh		Opponent	Pitt	Opp	S/U	Line	ATS	Total	O/U	
9/12/2020	vs	AUSTIN PEAY	55	0	W	-29.0	W	48.5	O	
9/19/2020	vs	SYRACUSE	21	10	W	-21.0	L	49.0	U	
9/26/2020	vs	LOUISVILLE	23	20	W	-3.0	T	54.0	U	
10/3/2020	vs	NC STATE	29	30	L	-14.0	L	46.0	O	
10/10/2020	@	Boston College	30	31	L	-6.0	L	42.0	O	{OT}
10/17/2020	@	Miami	19	31	L	13.5	W	47.5	O	
10/24/2020	vs	NOTRE DAME	3	45	L	10.0	L	43.5	O	
11/7/2020	@	Florida State	41	17	W	-1.5	W	52.5	O	
11/21/2020	vs	VIRGINIA TECH	47	14	W	6.0	W	52.0	O	
11/28/2020	@	Clemson	17	52	L	23.5	L	58.5	O	
12/10/2020	@	Georgia Tech	34	20	W	-7.0	W	54.0	U	
Coach: Pat Narduzzi		Season Record >>	319	270	6-5	ATS>>	5-5-1	O/U>>	8-3	
2019-Pittsburgh		Opponent	Pitt	Opp	S/U	Line	ATS	Total	O/U	
8/31/2019	vs	VIRGINIA	14	30	L	2.5	L	45.5	U	
9/7/2019	vs	OHIO	20	10	W	-4.0	W	54.5	U	
9/14/2019	@	Penn State	10	17	L	17.0	W	53.0	U	
9/21/2019	vs	CENTRAL FLORIDA	35	34	W	10.0	W	60.5	O	
9/28/2019	vs	DELAWARE	17	14	W	-27.0	L	NT	---	
10/5/2019	@	Duke	33	30	W	3.5	W	47.0	O	
10/18/2019	@	Syracuse	27	20	W	-3.5	W	53.5	U	
10/26/2019	vs	MIAMI	12	16	L	-4.5	L	41.5	U	
11/2/2019	@	Georgia Tech	20	10	W	-9.0	W	44.0	U	
11/14/2019	vs	NORTH CAROLINA	34	27	W	-4.5	W	48.5	O	{OT}
11/23/2019	@	Virginia Tech	0	28	L	4.0	L	43.5	U	
11/30/2019	vs	BOSTON COLLEGE	19	26	L	-8.5	L	51.5	U	
12/26/2019	vs	**Eastern Michigan**	34	30	W	-12.5	L	51.0	O	Quick Lane Bowl
Coach: Pat Narduzzi		Season Record >>	275	292	8-5	ATS>>	7-6	O/U>>	4-8	
2018-Pittsburgh		Opponent	Pitt	Opp	S/U	Line	ATS	Total	O/U	
9/1/2018	vs	SUNY-ALBANY	33	7	W	-25.5	W	NT	---	
9/8/2018	vs	PENN STATE	6	51	L	7.0	L	50.0	O	
9/15/2018	vs	GEORGIA TECH	24	19	W	3.5	W	54.5	U	
9/22/2018	@	North Carolina	35	38	L	-2.5	L	48.0	O	
9/29/2018	@	Central Florida	15	45	L	13.0	L	65.5	U	
10/6/2018	vs	SYRACUSE	44	37	W	3.0	W	58.5	O	{OT}
10/13/2018	@	Notre Dame	14	19	L	21.0	W	55.5	U	
10/27/2018	vs	DUKE	54	45	W	3.0	W	45.5	O	
11/2/2018	@	Virginia	23	13	W	7.0	W	45.5	U	
11/10/2018	vs	VIRGINIA TECH	52	22	W	-3.0	W	54.0	O	
11/17/2018	@	Wake Forest	34	13	W	-5.0	W	62.5	U	
11/24/2018	@	Miami	3	24	L	5.0	L	46.5	U	
12/1/2018	vs	**Clemson**	10	42	L	27.5	L	53.0	U	**ACC CHAMPIONSHIP**
12/31/2018	vs	**Stanford**	13	14	L	3.0	W	52.5	U	**Sun Bowl**
Coach: Pat Narduzzi		Season Record >>	360	389	7-7	ATS>>	9-5	O/U>>	5-8	
2017-Pittsburgh		Opponent	Pitt	Opp	S/U	Line	ATS	Total	O/U	
9/2/2017	vs	YOUNGSTGOWN STATE	28	21	W	-13.0	L	64.5	U	**OT**
9/9/2017	@	Penn State	14	33	L	19.0	T	64.0	U	
9/16/2017	vs	OKLAHOMA STATE	21	59	L	11.0	L	66.0	O	
9/23/2017	@	Georgia Tech	17	35	L	7.5	L	54.0	U	
9/30/2017	vs	RICE	42	10	W	-20.0	W	52.0	T	
10/7/2017	@	Syracuse	24	27	L	3.0	T	64.0	U	
10/14/2017	vs	NC STATE	17	35	L	11.5	L	54.5	U	
10/21/2017	@	Duke	24	17	W	9.0	W	49.0	U	
10/28/2017	vs	VIRGINIA	31	14	W	PK	W	49.5	U	
11/9/2017	vs	NORTH CAROLINA	31	34	L	-10.0	L	50.0	O	
11/18/2017	@	Virginia Tech	14	20	L	14.0	W	48.5	U	
11/24/2017	vs	MIAMI	24	14	W	12.0	W	53.0	U	
Coach: Pat Narduzzi		Season Record >>	287	319	5-7	ATS>>	5-5-2	O/U>>	2-9-1	

Copyright © 2021 by Steve's Football Bible, LLC

PITTSBURGH PANTHERS ACC Coastal

STADIUM: Heinz Field {68,400}		Location: Pittsburgh, PA							COACH: Pat Narduzzi
DATE		Opponent	Pitt	Opp	S/U	Line	ATS	Total	O/U	Trends & Angles
9/4/2021	vs	MASSACHUSETTS								1st meeting
9/11/2021	@	Tennessee								vs Tennessee - Pitt leads series 2-0
9/18/2021	vs	WESTERN MICHIGAN								1st meeting
9/25/2021	vs	NEW HAMPSHIRE								vs New Hampshire - Pitt leads series 1-0
10/2/2021	@	Georgia Tech								vs Georgia Tech - Pittsburgh leads series 10-5
10/16/2021	@	Virginia Tech								12-2 ATS vs Virginia Tech since 1999
10/23/2021	vs	CLEMSON								vs Clemson - Series tied 2-2
10/30/2021	vs	MIAMI								vs Miami - Miami leads series 28-11-1
11/6/2021	@	Duke								vs Duke - Pittsburgh leads series 15-9
11/11/2021	vs	NORTH CAROLINA								vs North Carolina - UNC leads series 10-4
11/20/2021	vs	VIRGINIA								5-1 S/U @ home vs Virginia since 1955
11/27/2021	@	Syracuse								Game 0-5 O/U @ Syracuse since 2012
12/4/2021	vs									ACC Championship
	vs									BOWL GAME

Pointspread Analysis Non-Conference		Pointspread Analysis Conference
1-15 S/U vs Non-conf. as 15.5 point or more Dog since 1992		0-9 S/U vs Miami as 19.5 point or more Dog since 1986
2-10 S/U vs Non-Conf. as 7.5-15 point Dog since 1993		0-7 S/U & ATS vs Miami as 9 point or less Dog since 1989
0-7 S/U vs Non-Conf. as 3 point or less Dog since 2003		0-4 S/U vs North Carolina as Dog since 1998
29-2 S/U vs Non-Conf. as 15.5 point or more favorite since 1990		1-5 ATS vs North Carolina as favorite since 2000 {2-4 S/U}
Dog		0-5 ATS vs North Carolina as favorite since 2000 {1-4 S/U}
1-12 S/U as 25.5 or more Dog since 1993		vs Syracuse - Pittsburgh leads series 41-32-3
4-1 ATS as 25.5 point or more Dog since 1997		14-2 S/U vs Syracuse since 2005
1-12 S/U as 20.5-25 point Dog since 1990		2-17-1 S/U vs Syracuse as Dog since 1984
0-9 S/U on road as 15.5-20 point Dog since 1990		15-0 S/U vs Syracuse as favorite since 1989
1-12 S/U @ home as 15.5 point or more Dog since 1986		0-14 S/U vs Syracuse as 3.5 point or more Dog since 1984
2-12 S/U as 10.5-15 point Dog since 2005		vs Virginia - Pittsburgh leads series 8-4
1-6 O/U on road as 10.5-15 Dog since 2007		4-0 S/U vs Virginia as favorite since 2006
2-7 S/U on road as 7.5-10 point Dog since 1994		vs Virginia Tech - Virginia Tech leads series 11-9
2-7 O/U on road as 7.5-10 point Dog since 1993		Game 0-4 O/U @ VPI since 2013
4-20 S/U on road as 3.5-7 point Dog since 1988		2-7 S/U @ Virginia Tech since 1994
5-16 S/U @ home as 3.5-7 point Dog since 1985		0-5 S/U @ Virginia Tech as 14 point or more Dog since 1994
Favorite		
4-1 S/U on road as 3 point or less favorite since 2010		
5-1 S/U & ATS on road as 3.5-7 point favorite since 2014		0-6 S/U when ranked vs #1 ranked teams all time
10-2 S/U as 7.5-10 point favorite since 2009		1-12 S/U when ranked vs Top #4 ranked teams all time
15-5 S/U @ home as 10.5-15 point favorite since 1983		0-4 S/U when ranked vs Miami since 1989
9-2 S/U on road as 10.5-15 point favorite since 1992		10-1-1 S/U when ranked vs Syracuse since 1976
7-0 S/U on road as 15.5 point or more favorite since 1983		6-43-1 S/U on road vs ranked teams since 1984
18-1 S/U @ home as 15.5-20 point favorite since 1983		0-12-1 S/U vs #1 ranked teams all time
8-1 S/U as 20.5-25 point favorite since 2001		1-11 S/U on road vs #2 ranked teams all time
17-0 S/U @ home as 25.5 point or more favorite since 1989		2-15 S/U vs ranked Miami since 1984
Bowl Games		
5-1 S/U & ATS vs SEC teams in Bowl Games	U MASS	3-9 ATS in 1st home game of season since 2008
3-10 ATS in Bowl Games since 2003	W. MCIHIGAN	5-12 ATS in 2nd home game of season since 2003
0-4 S/U & ATS vs AAC teams in Bowl Games	Georgia Tech	3-10 S/U in 2nd road game of season since 2009
3-1 S/U & ATS in Bowl Games as 3.5-7 point Dog since 1975	Syracuse	2-12 O/U in final road game of season since 2007
1-5 S/U in Bowl Games as 3 point or less Dog since 1984	Syracuse	8-2-1 ATS in final road game of season since 2010
1-5 S/U & ATS in Bowl Games as 3.5-7 point favorite since 1978	Syracuse	7-1 ATS after playing Virginia since 2006

Copyright © 2021 by Steve's Football Bible, LLC

PURDUE BOILERMAKERS BIG TEN West

2020-Purdue		Opponent	Purd	Opp	S/U	Line	ATS	Total	O/U	
10/24/2020	vs	IOWA	24	20	W	3.0	W	52.5	U	
10/31/2020	@	Illinois	31	24	W	-10.0	L	54.5	O	"Purdue Cannon"
11/14/2020	vs	NORTHWESTERN	20	27	L	3.5	L	48.5	U	
11/20/2020	@	Minnesota	31	34	L	-2.5	L	62.5	O	
11/28/2020	vs	RUTGERS	30	37	L	-12.0	L	61.0	O	
12/5/2020	vs	NEBRASKA	27	37	L	-2.0	L	64.5	U	
Coach: Jeff Brohm		Season Record >>	163	179	2-4	ATS>>	1-5	O/U>>	3-3	
2019-Purdue		Opponent	Purd	Opp	S/U	Line	ATS	Total	O/U	
8/30/2019	@	Nevada	31	34	L	-11.0	L	58.5	O	
9/7/2019	vs	VANDERBILT	42	24	W	-7.0	W	55.5	O	
9/14/2019	vs	TCU	13	34	L	3.5	L	52.5	U	
9/28/2019	vs	MINNESOTA	31	38	L	-1.5	L	56.0	O	
10/5/2019	@	Penn State	7	35	L	28.5	W	55.0	U	
10/12/2019	vs	MARYLAND	40	14	W	4.5	W	52.0	O	
10/19/2019	@	Iowa	20	26	L	17.5	W	48.0	U	
10/26/2019	vs	ILLINOIS	6	24	L	-9.5	L	53.5	U	"Purdue Cannon"
11/2/2019	vs	NEBRASKA	31	27	W	3.5	W	58.0	T	
11/9/2019	@	Northwestern	24	22	W	PK	W	39.0	O	
11/23/2019	@	Wisconsin	24	45	L	24.5	W	48.5	O	
11/30/2019	vs	INDIANA	41	44	L	7.0	W	56.5	O	"Old Oaken Bucket"
Coach: Jeff Brohm		Season Record >>	310	367	4-8	ATS>>	8-4	O/U>>	7-4-1	
2018-Purdue		Opponent	Purd	Opp	S/U	Line	ATS	Total	O/U	
8/30/2018	vs	NORTHWESTERN	27	31	L	PK	L	51.0	O	
9/8/2018	vs	EASTERN MICHIGAN	19	20	L	-15.0	L	50.0	U	
9/15/2018	vs	MISSOURI	37	40	L	5.0	W	67.5	O	
9/22/2018	vs	BOSTON COLLEGE	30	13	W	6.5	W	62.5	U	
9/29/2018	@	Nebraska	42	28	W	-3.0	W	57.5	O	
10/13/2018	@	Illinois	46	7	W	-10.0	W	64.0	U	"Purdue Cannon"
10/20/2018	vs	OHIO STATE	49	20	W	12.0	W	66.0	O	
10/27/2018	@	Michigan State	13	23	L	-2.5	L	49.0	U	
11/3/2018	vs	IOWA	38	36	W	-2.0	T	50.5	O	
11/10/2018	@	Minnesota	10	41	L	-10.5	L	58.0	U	
11/17/2018	vs	WISCONSIN	44	47	L	-3.5	L	56.0	O	{2 OT}
11/24/2018	@	Indiana	28	21	W	-3.5	W	65.0	U	"Old Oaken Bucket"
12/28/2018	vs	Auburn	14	63	L	3.5	L	58.0	O	Music City Bowl
Coach: Jeff Brohm		Season Record >>	397	390	6-7	ATS>>	6-6-1	O/U>>	7-6	
2017-Purdue		Opponent	Purd	Opp	S/U	Line	ATS	Total	O/U	
9/2/2017	vs	Louisville	28	35	L	26.5	W	65.5	U	Lucas Oil Stadium
9/8/2017	vs	OHIO	44	21	W	-3.0	W	54.5	O	
9/16/2017	@	Missouri	35	3	W	5.5	W	75.0	U	
9/23/2017	vs	MICHIGAN	10	28	L	13.5	L	51.0	U	
10/7/2017	vs	MINNESOTA	31	17	W	-3.0	W	45.5	O	
10/14/2017	@	Wisconsin	9	17	L	17.0	U	49.0	U	
10/21/2017	@	Rutgers	12	14	L	-8.5	L	48.0	U	
10/28/2017	vs	NEBRASKA	24	25	L	-3.5	L	53.5	U	
11/4/2017	vs	ILLINOIS	29	10	W	-14.0	W	49.5	U	"Purdue Cannon"
11/11/2017	@	Northwestern	13	23	L	6.5	L	48.5	U	
11/18/2017	@	Iowa	24	15	W	6.0	W	42.5	U	
11/25/2017	vs	INDIANA	31	24	W	-1.0	W	51.0	O	"Old Oaken Bucket"
12/27/2017	vs	Arizona	38	35	W	2.5	W	64.0	O	Foster Farms Bowl
Coach: Jeff Brohm		Season Record >>	328	267	7-6	ATS>>	9-4	O/U>>	4-9	

Copyright © 2021 by Steve's Football Bible, LLC

PURDUE BOILERMAKERS BIG TEN West

STADIUM: Ross-Ade Stadium {57,326}				Location: West Lafayette, IN						COACH: Jeff Brohm
DATE		Opponent	Pur	Opp	S/U	Line	ATS	Total	O/U	Trends & Angles
9/4/2021	vs	OREGON STATE								vs Oregon State - Oregon St. leads series 1-0
9/11/2021	@	Connecticut								1st meeting
9/18/2021	@	Notre Dame								1-21 S/U vs Notre Dame as Dog since 1986
9/25/2021	vs	ILLINOIS								8-1 S/U vs Illinois as favorite since 2003
10/2/2021	vs	MINNESOTA								vs Minnesota - Minnesota leads series 40-33-3
10/16/2021	@	Iowa								vs Iowa - Purdue leads series 49-39-3
10/23/2021	vs	WISCONSIN								0-8 S/U @ home vs Wisconsin since 1999
10/30/2021	@	Nebraska								vs Nebraska - Nebraska leads series 5-4
11/6/2021	vs	MICHIGAN STATE								0-6 S/U vs Michigan State as Dog since 2008
11/13/2021	@	Ohio State								0-9 S/U @ Ohio State as Dog since 1989
11/20/2021	@	Northwestern								1-7 S/U vs Northwestern as Dog since 1995
11/27/2021	vs	INDIANA								0-6 S/U vs Indiana as Dog since 2001
12/4/2021	vs									Big Ten Championship
	vs									BOWL GAME

Pointspread Analysis Non-Conference		Pointspread Analysis Conference
0-13 S/U vs Non-Conf. as 20.5 point or more Dog since 1986		vs Illinois - Series tied 45-45-6
3-17 S/U vs Non-Conf. as 7.5-15 point Dog since 1983		6-6 O/U vs Illinois as favorite since 2005
2-13 S/U vs Non-Conf. as 3.5-7 point Dog since 1986		vs Indiana - Purdue leads series 50-32-1
4-0 O/U vs Non-Conf. as 3 point or less Dog since 2002		11-0 S/U vs Indiana as 7.5 point or more favorite since 1984
0-9 ATS vs Non-Conf. as 7.5-10 point favorite since 1987		5-1 S/U vs Iowa as favorite since 1998
27-0 S/U vs Non-Conf. as 15.5 point or more favorite since 1989		1-17 S/U vs Iowa as 6.5 point or more Dog since 1983
Dog		0-12 S/U vs Michigan State as 8 point or more Dog since 1986
7-23 ATS as a home Dog since 2012		9-1 S/U @ home vs Minnesota as favorite since 1992 {8-2 ATS}
17-4 ATS as a road Dog since 2014		8-0 S/U vs Minnesota as 3.0-6.0 point favorite since 1983
0-45 S/U as 20.5 point or more Dog since 1983		4-0 S/U vs Minnesota as 13 point or more favorite since 1984
10-0 ATS as 20.5-25 point Dog since 2013		7-1 S/U vs Northwestern as 13 point or more favorite since 1983
0-10 S/U on road as 15.5-20 point Dog since 1995		0-10 S/U vs Ohio State as 16.5 point or more Dog since 1983
8-1 ATS on road as 15.5-20 point Dog since 2006		0-5 S/U vs Ohio State as 7 point or less Dog since 1999
1-10 S/U @ home as 15.5-20 point Dog since 1986		vs Wisconsin - Wisconsin leads series 50-29-8
0-14 S/U as 15.5-20 point Dog since 2006		1-18-1 S/U vs Wisconsin as Dog since 1983
1-7 S/U @ home as 10.5-15 point Dog since 2010		0-14 S/U vs Wisconsin since 2004
2-6 ATS @ home as 10.5-15 point Dog since 2010		3-0 S/U @ Wisconsin as favorite since 1988
1-15 S/U as 10.5-15 point Dog since 2010	OREGON STATE	16-1 S/U in 1st home game of season since 2004
0-17-1 S/U on road as 10.5-15 point Dog since 1993	Notre Dame	9-2 ATS in 2nd road game of season since 2010
3-12 S/U @ home as 3.5-7 point Dog since 2012	Notre Dame	3-10 S/U in 2nd road game of season since 2008
1-6 S/U & ATS @ home as 3 point or less Dog since 2006	ILLINOIS	1-8 S/U prior to playing Minnesota since 2011
2-9 S/U on road as 3 point or less Dog since 1985	ILLINOIS	1-10 O/U prior to playing Minnesota since 2010
Favorite	ILLINOIS	0-8 S/U in 2nd home game of season since 2013
8-3 S/U @ home as 3 point or less favorite since 2003	Iowa	0-10 S/U after playing Minnesota since 2010
7-2-1 ATS @ home as 3 point or less favorite since 2003	Iowa	2-8 S/U prior to playing Wisconsin since 2010
10-3-1 O/U @ home as 3 point or less favorite since 2000	WISCONSIN	1-6 S/U prior to playing Nebraska since 2013
5-0 S/U on road as 3.5-7 point favorite since 2002	Ohio State	4-12 S/U prior to playing Northwestern since 2001
2-14 ATS as 7.5-10 point favorite since 2000	Northwestern	7-2 O/U after playing Ohio State since 2003
7-2 S/U on road as 10.5-15 point favorite since 1997	Northwestern	0-8 S/U after playing Ohio State since 2007
13-4 S/U @ home as 10.5-15 point favorite since 2003	Northwestern	10-3 ATS in final road game of season since 2009
40-0 S/U as 15.5 point or more favorite since 1983	Northwestern	2-11 S/U prior to playing Indiana since 2007
Bowl Games	INDIANA	2-10 S/U in final home game of season since 2009
5-0 O/U in Bowl Games since 2007	INDIANA	12-2 O/U in final home game of season since 2007
	INDIANA	2-11 S/U after playing Northwestern since 2005

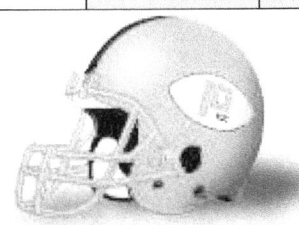

Copyright © 2021 by Steve's Football Bible, LLC

2020-Rice		Opponent	Rice	Opp	S/U	Line	ATS	Total	O/U	
10/24/2020	vs	MIDDLE TENNESSEE	34	40	L	-4.0	L	48.0	O	{2 OT}
10/31/2020	@	Southern Mississippi	30	6	W	-1.5	W	58.5	U	
11/21/2020	@	North Texas	17	27	L	1.0	L	65.0	U	
12/5/2020	@	Marshall	20	0	W	24.5	W	42.5	U	
12/12/2020	vs	ALABAMA-BIRMINGHAM	16	21	L	7.0	W	42.0	U	
Coach: Mike Bloomgren		Season Record >>	117	94	2-3	ATS>>	3-2	O/U>>	1-4	
2019-Rice		Opponent	Rice	Opp	S/U	Line	ATS	Total	O/U	
8/30/2019	@	Army	7	14	L	23.0	W	47.5	U	
9/7/2019	vs	WAKE FOREST	21	41	L	19.5	L	58.5	O	
9/14/2019	vs	Texas	13	48	L	32.0	L	57.0	O	NRG Stadium
9/21/2019	vs	BAYLOR	13	21	L	27.0	W	57.5	U	
9/28/2019	vs	LOUISIANA TECH	20	23	L	8.0	W	49.0	U	{OT}
10/5/2019	@	Alabama-Birmingham	20	35	L	10.0	L	43.5	O	
10/19/2019	@	Texas-San Antonio	27	31	L	-5.5	L	42.0	O	
10/26/2019	vs	SOUTHERN MISS	6	20	L	10.0	L	51.5	U	
11/2/2019	vs	MARSHALL	7	20	L	12.0	L	48.0	U	
11/16/2019	@	Middle Tennessee	31	28	W	13.0	W	47.0	O	
11/23/2019	vs	NORTH TEXAS	20	14	W	6.5	W	55.5	U	
11/30/2019	@	Texas-El Paso	30	16	W	-6.5	W	43.5	O	
Coach: Mike Bloomgren		Season Record >>	215	311	3-9	ATS>>	6-6	O/U>>	6-6	
2018-Rice		Opponent	Rice	Opp	S/U	Line	ATS	Total	O/U	
8/25/2018	vs	PRAIRIE VIEW A&M	31	28	W	-22.0	L	58.5	O	
9/1/2018	vs	HOUSTON	27	45	L	26.0	W	56.0	O	"Bayou Bucket Classic"
9/8/2018	@	Hawaii	29	43	L	17.0	W	68.5	O	
9/22/2018	@	Southern Mississippi	22	40	L	13.5	L	54.5	O	
9/29/2018	@	Wake Forest	24	56	L	27.5	L	66.0	O	
10/6/2018	vs	TEXAS-SAN ANTONIO	3	20	L	-1.0	L	50.0	U	
10/13/2018	vs	ALABAMA-BIRMINGHAM	0	42	L	16.5	L	52.0	U	
10/20/2018	@	Florida International	17	36	L	23.0	W	53.5	U	
10/27/2018	@	North Texas	17	41	L	29.0	W	58.5	U	
11/3/2018	vs	TEXAS-EL PASO	26	34	L	2.5	L	44.5	O	
11/10/2018	@	Louisiana Tech	13	28	L	24.0	W	53.0	U	
11/17/2018	@	Lsu	10	42	L	42.0	W	51.5	O	
11/24/2018	vs	OLD DOMINION	27	13	W	7.0	W	62.0	U	
Coach: Mike Bloomgren		Season Record >>	246	468	2-11	ATS>>	7-6	O/U>>	7-6	
2017-Rice		Opponent	Rice	Opp	S/U	Line	ATS	Total	O/U	
8/26/2017	vs	Stanford	7	62	L	30.0	L	50.5	O	Allianz Stadium
9/9/2017	@	Texas-El Paso	31	14	W	1.0	W	55.5	U	
9/16/2017	@	Houston	3	38	L	22.5	L	54.0	U	"Bayou Bucket Classic"
9/23/2017	vs	FLORIDA INTERNATIONAL	7	13	L	PK	L	52.5	U	
9/30/2017	@	Pittsburgh	10	42	L	20.0	L	52.0	T	
10/7/2017	vs	ARMY	12	49	L	13.0	L	47.0	O	
10/21/2017	@	Texas-San Antonio	7	20	L	20.0	W	52.0	U	
10/28/2017	vs	LOUISIANA TECH	28	42	L	11.5	L	51.5	O	
11/4/2017	@	Alabama-Birmingham	21	52	L	8.5	L	50.5	O	
11/11/2017	vs	SOUTHERN MISS	34	43	L	10.5	L	49.0	O	
11/18/2017	@	Old Dominion	21	24	L	7.0	W	51.5	U	
11/25/2017	vs	NORTH TEXAS	14	30	L	12.0	L	61.5	U	
Coach: David Bailiff		Season Record >>	195	429	1-11	ATS>>	3-9	O/U>>	5-6-1	

Copyright © 2021 by Steve's Football Bible, LLC

RICE OWLS

C-USA West

STADIUM: Rice Stadium {47,000}							COACH: Mike Bloomgren		

DATE		Opponent	Rice	Opp	S/U	Line	ATS	Total	O/U	Trends & Angles
9/4/2021	@	*Arkansas*								1-8 S/U vs Arkansas as Dog since 1983
9/11/2021	vs	*HOUSTON*								0-13 S/U vs Houston as 10.5 point or more Dog s/ 1983
9/18/2021	@	*Texas*								0-23 S/U @ Texas since 1967
9/25/2021	vs	*TEXAS SOUTHERN*								1st meeting
10/2/2021	vs	SOUTHERN MISS								1-5 S/U vs Southern Miss since 2015
10/16/2021	@	Texas-San Antonio								0-5 S/U vs Texas-San Antonio since 2015
10/23/2021	@	Alabama-Birmingham								vs Alabama-Birmingham - UAB leads series 6-3
10/30/2021	vs	NORTH TEXAS								vs North Texas - North Texas leads series 6-5
11/6/2021	@	Charlotte								vs Charlotte - Rice leads series 2-0
11/13/2021	vs	WESTERN KENTUCKY								vs Western Kentucky - WKU leads series 2-0
11/20/2021	@	Texas-El Paso								14-3 ATS vs Texas-El Paso since 2003
11/27/2021	vs	LOUISIANA TECH								0-7 S/U vs Louisiana Tech as Dog since 2012
12/4/2021	vs									C-USA Championship
	vs									BOWL GAME

Pointspread Analysis Non-Conference		Pointspread Analysis Conference
0-39 S/U vs Non-Conf. as 15.5 point or more Dog since 1983		vs Louisiana Tech - Louisiana Tech leads series 9-4
4-22-1 S/U vs Non-Conf. as 3.0-15 point Dog since 1983		4-0 O/U vs North Texas as favorite since 2008
4-0 S/U & ATS vs Non-Conf. as 3 point or less favorite since 2008		vs Southern Mississippi - Southern Miss leads series 6-5
9-1 S/U vs Non-Conf. as 7.5 point or more favorite since 1990		Game 9-2 O/U vs Southern Mississippi since 2007
vs Texas - Texas leads series 73-21-1		0-6 S/U vs Southern Miss as Dog since 2011
1-24 S/U vs Texas as Dog since 1984		vs Texas-El Paso - Rice leads series 15-8
1-42 S/U vs Texas since 1966		0-4 S/U vs UTEP as 9.5 point or more Dog since 2000
Dog		5-1 S/U & ATS vs UTEP as 9 point or less Dog since 2006
0-47 S/U as 25.5 point or more Dog since 1983		Game 2-6 O/U vs Texas-San Antonio since 2012
8-2 O/U as 25.5-30 point Dog since 2009		vs Texas-San Antonio - UTSA leads series 5-3
1-24 S/U on road as 20.5-25 point Dog since 1983		0-3 S/U vs Texas-San Antonio as Dog since 2015
0-8 S/U @ home as 20.5-25 point Dog since 1983		Game 0-4 O/U @ home vs UTSA since 2012
0-27 S/U as 15.5-20 point Dog since 1991		**Bowl Games**
0-19 S/U on road as 15.5-20 point Dog since 1992		3-0 S/U & ATS in Bowl Games as 3 point or less favorite since 2008
0-15 S/U @ home as 15.5-20 point Dog since 1983		
0-15 S/U @ home as 10.5-15 point Dog since 1987		1-71 S/U on road vs ranked teams since 1971
0-7 ATS @ home as 10.5-15 point Dog since 2011		3-31 S/U @ home vs ranked teams since 1975
8-2 ATS on road as 10.5-15 point Dog since 2003		0-18-1 S/U vs ranked Arkansas since 1959
2-12 S/U on road as 7.5-10 point Dog since 1990		0-11 S/U @ ranked Arkansas since 1954
0-7 ATS on road as 7.5-10 point Dog since 2007		0-15 S/U @ ranked Texas since 1969
11-5 O/U as 7.5-10 point Dog since 2007	Texas	1-22 S/U in 2nd road game of season since 1998
0-6 O/U as 3.5-7 point Dog since 2015	Texas	3-14 ATS in 2nd road game of season since 2004
0-6 O/U @ home as 3.5-7 point Dog since 2009	TEXAS SOUTH	2-9 ATS prior to playing Southern Mississippi since 2007
Favorite	TEXAS SOUTH	1-10 S/U prior to playing Southern Mississippi since 2007
6-1 S/U & ATS @ home as 3 point or less favorite since 2008	UTSA	6-2 S/U prior to playing Alabama-Birmingham since 2005
13-1 S/U & ATS as 3 point or less favorite since 2008	UAB	9-0 ATS prior to playing North Texas since 2010
5-0 S/U @ home as 7.5-10 point favorite since 2002	NORTH TEXAS	1-5 ATS after playing Alabama-Birmingham since 2009
1-5 O/U @ home as 7.5-10 point favorite since 2002	Texas-El Paso	12-3 O/U in final road game of season since 2006
13-1 S/U @ home as 10.5-15 point favorite since 1993	Texas-El Paso	8-2-1 ATS prior to playing Louisiana Tech since 2002
0-3 S/U & ATS on road as 10.5-15 point favorite since 1996	LA TECH	13-3 ATS in final home game of season since 2008
13-0 S/U as 20.5 point or more favorite since 1997	LA TECH	2-10 O/U in final home game of season since 2009
8-3 ATS as 20.5 point or more favorite since 1998	LA TECH	11-2 S/U in final home game of season since 2008

Copyright © 2021 by Steve's Football Bible, LLC

RUTGERS SCARLET KNIGHTS   BIG TEN East

2020-Rutgers		Opponent	Rutg	Opp	S/U	Line	ATS	Total	O/U	
10/24/2020	@	Michigan State	38	27	W	9.5	W	45.0	O	
10/31/2020	vs	INDIANA	21	37	L	11.5	L	54.0	O	
11/7/2020	@	Ohio State	27	49	L	37.5	W	63.0	O	
11/14/2020	vs	ILLINOIS	20	23	L	-5.5	L	51.5	U	
11/21/2020	vs	MICHIGAN	42	48	L	11.5	W	52.0	O	{3 OT}
11/28/2020	@	Purdue	37	30	W	12.0	W	61.0	O	
12/5/2020	vs	PENN STATE	7	23	L	13.0	L	51.5	U	
12/12/2020	@	Maryland	27	24	W	3.0	W	54.0	U	{OT}
12/19/2020	vs	NEBRASKA	21	28	L	6.5	L	51.5	U	
Coach: Greg Schiano		Season Record >>	240	289	3-6	ATS>>	5-4	O/U>>	5-4	
2019-Rutgers		Opponent	Rutg	Opp	S/U	Line	ATS	Total	O/U	
8/30/2019	vs	MASSACHUSETTS	48	21	W	-16.5	W	54.5	O	
9/7/2019	@	Iowa	0	30	L	18.0	L	48.0	U	
9/21/2019	vs	BOSTON COLLEGE	16	30	L	7.5	L	57.5	U	
9/28/2019	@	Michigan	0	52	L	27.5	L	49.0	O	
10/5/2019	vs	MARYLAND	7	48	L	14.5	L	55.5	U	
10/12/2019	@	Indiana	0	35	L	27.5	L	49.5	U	
10/19/2019	vs	MINNESOTA	7	42	L	28.5	L	46.5	O	
10/26/2019	vs	LIBERTY	44	34	W	7.5	W	43.5	O	
11/2/2019	@	Illinois	10	38	L	18.5	L	48.5	U	
11/16/2019	vs	OHIO STATE	21	56	L	52.0	W	62.5	O	
11/23/2019	vs	MICHIGAN STATE	0	27	L	22.0	L	43.5	U	
11/30/2019	@	Penn State	6	27	L	39.0	W	50.5	U	
Coach: Chris Ash		Season Record >>	159	440	2-10	ATS>>	4-8	O/U>>	5-7	
2018-Rutgers		Opponent	Rutg	Opp	S/U	Line	ATS	Total	O/U	
9/1/2018	vs	TEXAS STATE	35	7	W	-16.5	W	48.0	U	
9/8/2018	@	Ohio State	3	52	L	35.0	L	59.0	U	
9/15/2018	@	Kansas	14	55	L	PK	L	44.0	O	
9/22/2018	vs	BUFFALO	13	42	L	6.0	L	52.0	O	
9/29/2018	vs	INDIANA	17	24	L	16.5	W	49.0	U	
10/6/2018	vs	ILLINOIS	17	38	L	4.5	L	50.5	O	
10/13/2018	@	Maryland	7	34	L	24.0	L	50.5	U	
10/20/2018	vs	NORTHWESTERN	15	18	L	20.0	W	49.0	U	
11/3/2018	@	Wisconsin	17	31	L	28.5	W	50.5	U	
11/10/2018	vs	MICHIGAN	7	42	L	37.0	W	44.5	O	
11/17/2018	vs	PENN STATE	7	20	L	28.0	W	51.5	U	
11/24/2018	@	Michigan State	10	14	L	24.5	W	37.0	U	
Coach: Chris Ash		Season Record >>	162	377	1-11	ATS>>	7-5	O/U>>	4-8	
2017-Rutgers		Opponent	Rutg	Opp	S/U	Line	ATS	Total	O/U	
9/1/2017	vs	WASHINGTON	14	30	L	28.0	L	54.0	U	
9/9/2017	vs	EASTERN MICHIGAN	13	16	L	-5.0	L	51.0	U	
9/16/2017	vs	MORGAN STATE	65	0	W	-41.5	W	NT	---	
9/23/2017	@	Nebraska	17	27	L	12.0	W	47.5	U	
9/30/2017	vs	OHIO STATE	0	56	L	28.0	L	53.5	O	
10/14/2017	@	Illinois	35	24	W	-1.5	W	47.0	O	
10/21/2017	vs	PURDUE	14	12	W	8.5	W	48.0	U	
10/28/2017	@	Michigan	14	35	L	22.0	W	42.0	O	
11/4/2017	vs	Maryland	31	24	W	3.5	W	49.0	O	Yankee Stadium
11/11/2017	@	Penn State	6	35	L	31.0	W	56.0	U	
11/18/2017	@	Indiana	0	41	L	10.5	L	46.5	U	
11/25/2017	vs	MICHIGAN STATE	7	40	L	14.0	L	42.0	O	
Coach: Chris Ash		Season Record >>	216	340	4-8	ATS>>	8-4	O/U>>	5-6	

Copyright © 2021 by Steve's Football Bible, LLC

RUTGERS SCARLET KNIGHTS BIG TEN East

STADIUM: High Point Solutions Stadium {52,454}		Location: Piscataway, NJ					COACH: Greg Schiano		
DATE		Opponent	Rut	Opp	S/U	Line	ATS	Total	O/U	Trends & Angles

DATE		Opponent	Rut	Opp	S/U	Line	ATS	Total	O/U	Trends & Angles
9/4/2021	vs	TEMPLE								4-0 S/U vs Temple since 2003
9/11/2021	@	Syracuse								vs Syracuse - Syracuse leads series 30-13-1
9/18/2021	vs	DELAWARE								vs Delaware - Rutgers leads series 14-13-1
9/25/2021	@	Michigan								vs Michigan - Michigan leads series 6-1
10/2/2021	vs	OHIO STATE								vs Ohio State - Ohio State leads series 7-0
10/9/2021	vs	MICHIGAN STATE								vs Michigan St. - Michigan St. leads series 8-4
10/16/2021	@	Northwestern								vs Northwestern - Rutgers leads series 3-1
10/30/2021	@	Illinois								vs Illinois - Illinois leads series 5-2
11/6/2021	vs	WISCONSIN								vs Wisconsin - Wisconsin leads series 3-0
11/13/2021	@	Indiana								vs Indiana - Indiana leads series 5-2
11/20/2021	@	Penn State								1-19 S/U vs Penn State as Dog since 1983
11/27/2021	vs	MARYLAND								vs Maryland - Maryland leads series 9-7
12/4/2021	vs									Big Ten Championship
	vs									BOWL GAME

Pointspread Analysis Non-Conference		Pointspread Analysis Conference
2-32-1 S/U vs Non-Conf. as 10.5 point or more Dog since 1983		vs Penn State - Penn State leads series 29-2
8-1 ATS vs Non-Conf. as 7.5-10 point Dog since 1989		
7-3 S/U vs Non-Conf. as 3.5-7 point Dog since 2002		1-37-1 S/U vs Top #10 ranked teams all time
5-0 S/U & ATS vs Non-Conf. as 3 point or less favorite since 2009		1-37-1 S/U on road vs ranked teams since 1989
45-3-1 S/U vs Non-Conf. as 7.5 point or more favorite since 1984		0-13 S/U @ home vs ranked teams since 2009
1-12 S/U vs Syracuse as 7 point or more Dog since 1985		0-4 S/U vs ranked Michigan all time
Game 0-4 O/U @ Syracuse since 2005		0-6 S/U vs ranked Ohio State all time
Game 0-4 O/U vs Syracuse since 2009		1-16 S/U vs ranked Penn State all time
vs Temple - Rutgers leads series 20-16		**Bowl Games**
8-0 S/U vs Temple as favorite since 1991		7-2 ATS in Bowl Games
0-7 S/U vs Temple as 6 point or more Dog since 1985		
Game 1-5 O/U vs Temple since 2001		
Dog		**Favorite**
1-22 S/U as 30.5 point or more Dog since 1993		5-1 S/U & ATS on road as 3 point or less favorite since 2009
0-24 S/U on road as 25.5 point or more Dog since 1993		1-6 ATS @ home as 3 point or less favorite since 2005
1-17 S/U on road as 20.5-25 point Dog since 1983		6-1 O/U @ home as 3 point or less favorite since 2005
0-9 S/U @ home as 20.5-25 point or more Dog since 1996		6-1 O/U on road as 3.5-7 point favorite since 2003
0-37 S/U as 20.5 point or more Dog since 1996		4-0 S/U & ATS as 7.5-10 point favorite since 2011
0-24 S/U on road as 15.5-20 point Dog since 1988		20-1 S/U as 10.5-15 point favorite since 1991
1-12 S/U @ home as 15.5-20 point Dog since 1983		1-9 O/U as 15.5-20 point favorite since 2007
0-20 S/U @ home as 10.5-15 point Dog since 1983		7-0-1 S/U on road as 15.5-20 point favorite since 1986
1-18-1 S/U on road as 10.5-15 point Dog since 1991		16-0 S/U as 20.5 point or more favorite since 1984
16-4 ATS as 7.5-10 point Dog since 1998		
12-1 ATS on road as 7.5-10 point Dog since 1998	TEMPLE	9-2 S/U in 1st home game of season since 2010
0-6 S/U @ home as 3.5-7 point Dog since 2011 {1-5 ATS}	WISCONSIN	1-6 S/U prior to playing Indiana since 2014
5-0 S/U & ATS on road as 3.5-7 point Dog since 2006	Penn State	0-7 S/U after playing Indiana since 2014 {1-6 ATS}
1-11 O/U as 3 point or less Dog since 2008	Penn State	1-8 O/U in final road game of season since 2012

Copyright © 2021 by Steve's Football Bible, LLC

SAN DIEGO STATE AZTECS   MOUNTAIN WEST West

2020-San Diego State		Opponent	SDSU	Opp	S/U	Line	ATS	Total	O/U	
10/24/2020	vs	UNLV	34	6	W	-13.5	W	49.5	U	
10/31/2020	@	Utah State	38	7	W	-8.5	W	40.5	O	
11/6/2020	vs	SAN JOSE STATE	17	28	L	-10.0	L	50.0	U	"El Camino Real Rivalry"
11/14/2020	vs	HAWAII	34	10	W	-9.5	W	51.0	U	
11/21/2020	@	Nevada	21	26	L	-1.5	L	46.0	O	
11/27/2020	@	Colorado	10	20	L	6.0	L	51.5	U	
12/5/2020	vs	COLORADO STATE	29	17	W	-8.0	W	45.5	O	
12/12/2020	@	Byu	14	28	L	16.5	W	47.5	U	
Coach: Brady Hoke		Season Record >>	197	142	4-4	ATS>>	5-3	O/U>>	3-5	
2019-San Diego State		Opponent	SDSU	Opp	S/U	Line	ATS	Total	O/U	
8/31/2019	vs	WEBER STATE	6	0	W	-13.5	L	NT	---	
9/7/2019	@	Ucla	23	14	W	7.5	W	45.0	U	
9/14/2019	@	New Mexico State	31	10	W	-17.0	W	51.0	U	
9/21/2019	vs	UTAH STATE	17	23	L	4.0	L	53.0	U	
10/5/2019	@	Colorado State	24	10	W	-6.5	W	48.0	U	
10/12/2019	vs	WYOMING	26	22	W	-3.5	W	38.0	O	
10/19/2019	@	San Jose State	27	17	W	-7.5	W	45.5	U	"El Camino Real Rivalry"
10/26/2019	@	Unlv	20	17	W	-11.5	L	44.5	U	
11/9/2019	vs	NEVADA	13	17	L	-17.0	L	34.5	U	
11/16/2019	vs	FRESNO STATE	17	7	W	-2.5	W	43.5	U	"Battle for the Oil Can"
11/23/2019	@	Hawaii	11	14	L	-1.5	L	46.5	U	
11/30/2019	vs	BYU	13	3	W	4.0	W	38.5	U	
12/21/2019	vs	Central Michigan	48	11	W	-4.0	W	40.5	O	New Mexico Bowl
Coach: Rocky Long		Season Record >>	276	165	10-3	ATS>>	8-5	O/U>>	2-10	
2018-San Diego State		Opponent	SDSU	Opp	S/U	Line	ATS	Total	O/U	
8/31/2018	@	Stanford	10	31	L	13.5	L	49.5	U	
9/8/2018	vs	SACRAMENTO STATE	28	14	W	-25.0	L	NT	---	
9/15/2018	vs	ARIZONA STATE	28	21	W	5.0	W	47.5	O	
9/22/2018	vs	EASTERN MICHIGAN	23	20	W	-11.0	L	48.0	U	
10/6/2018	@	Boise State	19	13	W	14.0	W	51.0	U	
10/13/2018	vs	AIR FORCE	21	17	W	-11.0	L	42.5	U	
10/20/2018	vs	SAN JOSE STATE	16	13	W	-25.5	L	45.5	U	"El Camino Real Rivalry"
10/27/2018	@	Nevada	24	28	L	-1.0	L	46.0	O	
11/3/2018	@	New Mexico	31	23	W	-12.5	L	45.0	O	
11/10/2018	vs	UNLV	24	27	L	-24.0	L	51.5	U	
11/17/2018	@	Fresno State	14	23	L	10.0	W	42.0	U	"Battle for the Oil Can"
11/24/2018	vs	HAWAII	30	31	L	-18.5	L	54.0	O	{OT}
12/19/2018	vs	Ohio	0	27	L	2.0	L	47.5	U	Frisco Bowl
Coach: Rocky Long		Season Record >>	268	288	7-6	ATS>>	3-10	O/U>>	4-8	
2017-San Diego State		Opponent	SDSU	Opp	S/U	Line	ATS	Total	O/U	
9/2/2017	vs	CAL-DAVIS	38	17	W	-35.0	L	55.0	T	
9/9/2017	@	Arizona State	30	20	W	3.0	W	53.0	U	
9/16/2017	vs	STANFORD	20	17	W	8.5	W	47.5	U	
9/23/2017	@	Air Force	28	24	W	1.0	W	48.5	O	
9/30/2017	vs	NORTHERN ILLINOIS	34	28	W	-9.0	L	47.0	O	
10/7/2017	@	Unlv	41	10	W	-9.5	W	56.0	U	
10/14/2017	vs	BOISE STATE	14	31	L	-4.5	L	47.0	U	
10/21/2017	vs	FRESNO STATE	3	27	L	-6.5	L	50.0	U	"Battle for the Oil Can"
10/28/2017	@	Hawaii	28	7	W	-8.0	W	54.5	U	
11/4/2017	@	San Jose State	52	7	W	-23.5	W	51.0	O	"El Camino Real Rivalry"
11/18/2017	vs	NEVADA	42	23	W	-17.0	W	55.5	O	
11/25/2017	vs	NEW MEXICO	35	10	W	-20.0	W	46.5	U	
12/23/2017	vs	Army	35	42	L	-6.5	L	46.0	O	Armed Forces Bowl
Coach: Rocky Long		Season Record >>	400	263	10-3	ATS>>	8-5	O/U>>	5-7-1	

Copyright © 2021 by Steve's Football Bible, LLC

SAN DIEGO STATE AZTECS   MOUNTAIN WEST West

STADIUM: Dignity Health Sports Park {27,000}	Location: San Diego, CA	COACH: Brady Hoke

DATE		Opponent	Sdsu	Opp	S/U	Line	ATS	Total	O/U	Trends & Angles
9/4/2021	vs	*NEW MEXICO STATE*								vs New Mexico State - SDSU leads series 10-1-1
9/11/2021	@	*Arizona*								0-3 S/U vs Arizona as Dog since 1997
9/18/2021	vs	*UTAH*								0-4 S/U @ home vs Utah since 2004 {0-4 ATS}
9/25/2021	vs	*TOWSON*								1st meeting
10/9/2021	vs	NEW MEXICO								7-0 S/U vs New Mexico as favorite since 2009
10/16/2021	@	San Jose State								Game 1-6 O/U vs San Jose State since 2014
10/23/2021	@	Air Force								5-0 S/U vs Air Force as favorite since 2012
10/30/2021	vs	FRESNO STATE								vs Fresno State - SDSU leads series 30-25-4
11/6/2021	@	Hawaii								14-2 S/U vs Hawaii as favorite since 1986
11/13/2021	vs	NEVADA								vs Nevada - San Diego State leads series 7-6
11/20/2021	@	Unlv								3-0 S/U @ UNLV since 2015
11/27/2021	vs	BOISE STATE								5-0 ATS vs Boise State as Dog since 2011
12/4/2021	vs									MWC Championship
	vs									BOWL GAME

Pointspread Analysis
Non-Conference

2-45 S/U vs Non-Conf. as 7.5 point or more Dog since 1985		
8-0 S/U vs Non-Conf. as 20.5 point or more favorite since 2010		
0-5 S/U vs Utah as 14.5 point or more Dog since 2001		
vs Utah - Utah leads series 17-12-1		
0-5 S/U & ATS vs Utah as Dog since 2006		

Dog

4-0-1 ATS @ home as a Dog since 2013	
0-22 S/U as 20.5 point or more Dog since 1988	
1-7 O/U as 20.5-25 point Dog since 1990	
2-15 S/U on road as 15.5-20 point Dog since 1984	
6-0 ATS as 15.5-20 point Dog since 2009	
0-7 S/U @ home as 15.5-20 point Dog since 1989	
3-27 S/U on road as 10.5-15 point Dog since 1985	
3-10 S/U @ home as 10.5-15 point Dog since 1986	
1-12 S/U @ home as 7.5-10 point Dog since 1988	
8-3-1 ATS as 3.5-7 point Dog since 2011	
4-13 O/U as 3 point or less Dog since 1999	
1-5 O/U @ home as 3 point or less Dog since 1999	

Favorite

1-8 S/U & ATS on road as 3 point or less favorite since 1992	
7-1 S/U on road as 3.5-7 point favorite since 2012	
11-1 S/U @ home as 7.5-10 point favorite since 2001	
22-4 S/U @ home as 10.5-15 point favorite since 1985	
12-0 S/U on road as 10.5-15 point favorite since 1985	
13-4 S/U @ home as 15.5-20 point favorite since 1991	
5-2 ATS @ home as 15.5-20 point favorite since 2015	
30-2 S/U as 20.5 point or more favorite since 1985	
25-1 S/U @ home as 20.5 point or more favorite since 1987	

Bowl Games

0-3 O/U in Bowl Games as 3 point or less favorite since 1991	
1-4 ATS in Bowl Games as 3.5-7 point favorite since 2011	

Pointspread Analysis
Conference

8-0 ATS vs Air Force as 7 point or less Dog since 1991	
0-5 S/U vs Fresno State as Dog since 2002	
7-1 S/U vs Fresno State as favorite since 1995	
vs Hawaii - San Diego State leads series 22-11-2	
11-2-1 ATS vs Hawaii as favorite since 1992	
8-1 ATS vs Hawaii as Dog since 1985	
17-1 S/U vs New Mexico as 5 point or more favorite since 1985	
1-10 ATS vs New Mexico as 5 point or more favorite since 1993	
0-7 S/U vs New Mexico as Dog since 2001 {1-6 ATS}	
vs San Jose State - San Diego State leads series 22-20-2	
7-1 S/U vs San Jose State since 2013	
6-2 ATS vs San Jose State since 2013	
10-1 S/U vs San Jose State as 5 point or more favorite since 1995	
9-2 ATS vs San Jose State as 5 point or more favorite since 1995	
vs UNLV - San Diego State leads series 20-10	
12-3 S/U vs UNLV since 2006	
Game 0-5 O/U vs UNLV since 2016	
Game 0-5 O/U @ home vs UNLV since 2012	
4-0 ATS vs UNLV as Dog since 2003	
12-1 S/U vs UNLV as 7-18 point favorite since 1997	

NMSU	11-1 S/U in 1st home game of season since 2009
NMSU	0-5-1 O/U in 1st home game of season since 2012
Arizona	3-12 O/U in 1st road game of season since 2006
UTAH	10-4 S/U in 2nd home game of season since 2007
NEW MEXICO	9-0 S/U prior to playing San Jose State since 2012
San Jose State	5-0 ATS prior to playing Air Force since 2013
Air Force	7-3 O/U after playing San Jose State since 2006
FRESNO STATE	10-4 S/U prior to playing Hawaii since 1996
FRESNO STATE	9-3 ATS prior to playing Hawaii since 1998
Hawaii	9-0 S/U prior to playing Nevada since 2012
Hawaii	6-2 S/U after playing Fresno State since 2012
Unlv	2-7 O/U after playing Nevada since 2004
Unlv	0-6 O/U prior to playing Boise State since 2011
Unlv	6-0 S/U prior to playing Boise State since 2011
BOISE STATE	0-7 O/U after playing UNLV since 2012
BOISE STATE	9-2 S/U in final home game of season since 2010

Copyright © 2021 by Steve's Football Bible, LLC

SAN JOSE STATE SPARTANS   MOUNTAIN WEST West

2020-San Jose State		Opponent	SJSU	Opp	S/U	Line	ATS	Total	O/U	
10/24/2020	vs	AIR FORCE	17	6	W	7.5	W	64.5	U	
10/31/2020	vs	NEW MEXICO	38	21	W	-13.5	W	56.5	O	
11/6/2020	@	San Diego State	28	17	W	10.0	W	50.0	U	"El Camino Real Rivalry"
11/14/2020	vs	UNLV	34	17	W	-17.0	T	61.5	U	
12/5/2020	vs	HAWAII	35	24	W	-2.5	W	59.5	U	
12/11/2020	vs	NEVADA	30	20	W	2.5	W	62.0	U	
12/19/2020	vs	**Boise State**	**34**	20	W	6.5	W	59.5	U	MWC CHAMPIONSHIP
12/31/2020	vs	**Ball State**	**13**	34	L	-7.5	L	66.0	U	Arizona Bowl
Coach: Brent Brennan		Season Record >>	229	159	7-1	ATS>>	6-1-1	O/U>>	1-7	MWC CHAMPIONS
2019-San Jose State		Opponent	SJSU	Opp	S/U	Line	ATS	Total	O/U	
8/29/2019	vs	NORTHERN COLORADO	35	18	W	-17.0	T	NT	---	
9/7/2019	vs	TULSA	16	34	L	6.5	L	53.5	U	
9/21/2019	@	Arkansas	31	24	W	20.5	W	61.0	U	
9/28/2019	@	Air Force	24	41	L	19.0	W	58.0	O	
10/5/2019	vs	NEW MEXICO	32	21	W	-7.0	L	69.5	U	
10/12/2019	@	Nevada	38	41	L	2.5	L	58.5	O	
10/19/2019	vs	SAN DIEGO STATE	17	27	L	7.5	L	45.5	U	"El Camino Real Rivalry"
10/26/2019	@	Army	34	29	W	9.5	W	54.0	O	
11/2/2019	vs	BOISE STATE	42	52	L	16.5	W	61.0	O	
11/9/2019	@	Hawaii	40	42	L	7.5	W	78.5	O	
11/23/2019	@	Unlv	35	38	L	-7.0	L	65.0	O	
11/30/2019	vs	FRESNO STATE	17	16	W	-2.5	L	59.5	U	"Valley Rivalry"
Coach: Brent Brennan		Season Record >>	361	383	5-7	ATS>>	5-6-1	O/U>>	6-5	
2018-San Jose State		Opponent	SJSU	Opp	S/U	Line	ATS	Total	O/U	
8/30/2018	vs	CALIFORNIA-DAVIS	38	44	L	-3.5	L	NT	---	
9/8/2018	@	Washington State	0	31	L	30.0	L	62.5	U	
9/15/2018	@	Oregon	22	35	L	42.5	W	69.5	U	
9/29/2018	vs	HAWAII	41	44	L	9.5	W	62.0	O	{5 OT}
10/6/2018	vs	COLORADO STATE	30	42	L	3.0	L	59.5	O	
10/13/2018	vs	ARMY	3	52	L	17.0	L	49.5	O	
10/20/2018	@	San Diego State	13	16	L	25.5	W	45.5	U	"El Camino Real Rivalry"
10/27/2018	vs	UNLV	50	37	W	-2.5	W	57.0	O	
11/3/2018	@	Wyoming	9	24	L	17.0	W	39.0	U	
11/10/2018	@	Utah State	24	62	L	31.0	L	63.5	O	
11/17/2018	vs	NEVADA	12	21	L	14.5	W	58.5	U	
11/24/2018	@	Fresno State	13	31	L	32.0	W	52.0	U	"Valley Rivalry"
Coach: Brent Brennan		Season Record >>	255	439	1-11	ATS>>	7-5	O/U>>	5-6	
2017-San Jose State		Opponent	SJSU	Opp	S/U	Line	ATS	Total	O/U	
8/26/2017	vs	SOUTH FLORIDA	22	42	L	21.0	W	68.5	U	
9/2/2017	vs	CAL POLY-SLO	34	13	W	-10.5	W	58.0	U	
9/9/2017	@	Texas	0	56	L	26.5	L	62.5	U	
9/16/2017	@	Utah	16	54	L	28.0	L	59.5	O	
9/23/2017	vs	UTAH STATE	10	61	L	1.5	L	55.5	O	
9/30/2017	@	Unlv	13	41	L	17.0	L	63.0	U	
10/7/2017	vs	FRESNO STATE	10	27	L	17.0	T	60.0	U	"Valley Rivalry"
10/14/2017	@	Hawaii	26	37	L	17.0	W	58.5	O	
10/28/2017	@	Byu	20	41	L	8.5	L	51.0	O	
11/4/2017	vs	SAN DIEGO STATE	7	52	L	23.5	L	51.0	O	"El Camino Real Rivalry"
11/11/2017	@	Nevada	14	59	L	18.0	L	67.0	O	
11/18/2017	@	Colorado State	14	42	L	32.5	W	67.5	U	
11/25/2017	vs	WYOMING	20	17	W	19.0	W	48.5	U	
Coach: Brent Brennan		Season Record >>	206	542	2-11	ATS>>	5-6-1	O/U>>	6-6	

Copyright © 2021 by Steve's Football Bible, LLC

SAN JOSE STATE SPARTANS   MOUNTAIN WEST West

STADIUM: Spartan Stadium {30,456}					Location: San Jose, CA				COACH: Brent Brennan	
DATE		Opponent	Sjsu	Opp	S/U	Line	ATS	Total	O/U	Trends & Angles
8/28/2021	vs	*SOUTHERN UTAH*								vs Southern Utah - SJSU leads series 2-0
9/4/2021	@	*Usc*								0-4 S/U vs USC as Dog since 1995
9/18/2021	@	Hawaii								4-0 S/U & ATS @ Hawaii as favorite since 1998
9/25/2021	@	*Western Michigan*								1st meeting
10/2/2021	vs	*NEW MEXICO STATE*								vs NMSU - San Jose State leads series 17-3
10/9/2021	@	Colorado State								vs Colorado State - CSU leads series 6-4
10/16/2021	vs	SAN DIEGO STATE								vs San Diego State - SDSU leads series 22-20-2
10/23/2021	@	Unlv								vs UNLV - San Jose State leads series 17-7-1
10/30/2021	vs	WYOMING								vs Wyoming - Wyoming leads series 7-4
11/6/2021	@	Nevada								vs Nevada - Nevada leads series 22-10-2
11/13/2021	vs	UTAH STATE								0-5 ATS vs Utah State since 2012
11/27/2021	vs	FRESNO STATE								vs Fresno State - Fresno State leads series 42-38-3
12/4/2021	vs									MWC Championship
	vs									BOWL GAME

Pointspread Analysis Non-Conference		Pointspread Analysis Conference
2-38 S/U vs Non-Conf. as 20.5 point or more Dog since 1985		3-20 S/U vs Fresno State as Dog since 1985
0-12 S/U vs Non-Conf. as 15.5-20 point Dog since 2001		6-1 S/U vs Fresno State as favorite since 1987
1-5 S/U & ATS vs Non-Conf. as 7.5-10 point Dog since 2008		0-16 S/U vs Fresno State as 9.5 point or more Dog since 1985
14-1 S/U vs New Mexico State as 4 point or more favorite since 1985		0-9 S/U vs Hawaii as 9.5 point or more Dog since 2001
Dog		0-3 S/U & ATS @ home vs Hawaii as favorite since 1999
0-42 S/U as 25.5 point or more Dog since 1989		vs Hawaii - Hawaii leads series 22-20-1
0-9 S/U @ home as 20.5 point or more Dog since 1996		0-7 S/U @ Nevada as Dog since 2002
2-57 S/U on road as 20.5 point or more Dog since 1985		0-11 S/U vs Nevada as 6 point or more Dog since 1994
1-25 S/U as 15.5-20 point Dog since 2001		7-1 S/U vs UNLV as favorite since 1995 {5-2-1 ATS}
0-18 S/U on road as 15.5-20 point Dog since 2001		1-10 S/U vs San Diego State as 5 point or more Dog since 1995
0-9 S/U @ home as 10.5-15 point Dog since 2004		Game 6-1 O/U vs Utah State sinice 2010
0-17 S/U on road as 10.5-15 point Dog since 1998		0-8 S/U vs Utah State since 2009
2-9 S/U on road as 7.5-10 point Dog since 1999		1-9 S/U vs Utah State as Dog since 1985
4-14 S/U as 7.5-10 point Dog since 2008		9-1 S/U vs Utah State as favorite since 1986
14-6 O/U as 7.5-10 point Dog since 2003		
1-6 S/U & ATS as 3.5-7 point Dog since 2014	S. UTAH	1-7 O/U in 1st home game of season since 2009
Favorite	S. UTAH	7-1-1 ATS in 1st home game of season since 2012
20-5 ATS as a road favorite since 1998	Usc	2-16 S/U in 1st road game of season since 2003
6-1 S/U & ATS on road as 3 point or less favorite since 2000	Usc	1-11 S/U prior to playing Hawaii since 2008
10-3 S/U on road as 3.5-7 point favorite since 1987	Usc	7-3 O/U prior to playing Hawaii since 2010
5-1 O/U @ home as 3.5-7 point favorite since 2009	Hawaii	2-18 S/U in 2nd road game of season since 2001
6-1 S/U on road as 7.5-10 point favorite since 1986	Western Michigan	1-11 S/U prior to playing Hawaii since 2008
8-1 S/U @ home as 7.5-10 point favorite since 2001	WYOMING	3-8 S/U after playing UNLV since 1994
12-2 S/U @ home as 10.5-15 point favorite since 1986	WYOMING	2-10 S/U prior to playing Nevada since 2007
14-0 S/U on road as 10.5 point or more favorite since 1986	WYOMING	2-9 ATS prior to playing Nevada since 2008
10-1 S/U @ home as 15.5-20 point favorite since 1987	WYOMING	3-10 O/U prior to playing Nevada since 2006
13-0 S/U as 20.5 point or more favorite since 1986	UTAH STATE	4-14 S/U after playing Nevada since 2001
Bowl Games	UTAH STATE	2-10 O/U after playing Nevada since 2008
4-1 S/U & ATS in Bowl Games since 1990	UTAH STATE	1-11 S/U prior to playing Fresno State since 2007
	FRESNO STATE	2-10 O/U after playing Utah State since 2005

Copyright © 2021 by Steve's Football Bible, LLC

2020-South Alabama		Opponent	USA	Opp	S/U	Line	ATS	Total	O/U	
9/3/2020	@	Southern Mississippi	32	21	W	13.5	W	54.5	U	
9/12/2020	vs	TULANE	24	27	L	10.5	W	52.0	U	
9/24/2020	vs	ALABAMA-BIRMINGHAM	10	42	L	7.0	L	47.5	O	
10/17/2020	vs	TEXAS STATE	30	20	W	-3.0	W	58.0	U	
10/24/2020	vs	LOUISIANA-MONROE	38	14	W	-14.5	W	57.0	U	
10/29/2020	@	Georgia Southern	17	24	L	3.5	L	51.5	U	
11/7/2020	@	Coastal Carolina	6	23	L	17.0	T	57.0	U	
11/14/2020	@	Louisiana	10	38	L	14.5	L	53.5	U	
11/21/2020	vs	GEORGIA STATE	14	31	L	3.5	L	58.5	U	"Clash of the Claws"
11/28/2020	@	Arkansas State	38	31	W	7.0	W	63.5	O	
12/5/2020	vs	TROY	0	29	L	4.0	L	54.0	U	"The Championship Belt"
Coach: Steve Campbell		Season Record >>	219	300	4-7	ATS>>	5-5-1	O/U>>	2-9	

2019-South Alabama		Opponent	USA	Opp	S/U	Line	ATS	Total	O/U	
8/31/2019	@	Nebraska	21	35	L	36.0	W	64.5	U	
9/7/2019	vs	JACKSON STATE	37	14	W	-25.5	L	NT	---	
9/14/2019	vs	MEMPHIS	6	42	L	20.5	L	55.0	U	
9/21/2019	@	Alabama-Birmingham	3	35	L	12.0	L	48.0	U	
9/28/2019	@	Louisiana-Monroe	17	30	L	14.5	W	58.5	U	
10/3/2019	vs	GEORGIA SOUTHERN	17	20	L	10.0	W	44.5	U	{2 OT}
10/16/2019	@	Troy	13	37	L	17.0	L	54.5	U	"The Championship Belt"
10/26/2019	vs	APPALACHIAN STATE	3	30	L	26.5	L	51.0	U	
11/9/2019	@	Texas State	28	30	L	7.0	W	41.5	O	
11/16/2019	vs	LOUISIANA-LAFAYETTE	27	37	L	27.5	W	52.5	O	
11/23/2019	@	Georgia State	15	28	L	9.5	L	56.0	U	
11/30/2019	vs	ARKANSAS STATE	34	30	W	10.0	W	53.0	O	
Coach: Steve Campbell		Season Record >>	221	368	2-10	ATS>>	6-6	O/U>>	3-8	

2018-South Alabama		Opponent	USA	Opp	S/U	Line	ATS	Total	O/U	
9/1/2018	vs	LOUISIANA TECH	26	30	L	10.5	W	53.0	O	
9/8/2018	@	Oklahoma State	13	55	L	30.5	L	64.0	O	
9/15/2018	vs	TEXAS STATE	41	31	W	-9.5	W	49.0	O	
9/22/2018	@	Memphis	35	52	L	32.0	W	66.0	O	
9/29/2018	@	Appalachian State	7	52	L	25.0	L	56.5	O	
10/6/2018	@	Georgia Southern	13	48	L	12.0	L	57.5	O	
10/13/2018	vs	ALABAMA STATE	45	7	W	-27.0	W	NT	---	
10/23/2018	vs	TROY	17	38	L	11.5	L	52.0	O	"The Championship Belt"
11/3/2018	@	Arkansas State	14	38	L	14.0	L	61.5	U	
11/10/2018	vs	LOUISIANA-MONROE	10	38	L	7.5	L	62.0	U	
11/17/2018	@	Louisiana-Lafayette	38	48	L	19.5	W	65.5	O	
11/24/2018	vs	COASTAL CAROLINA	31	28	W	1.0	W	58.5	O	
Coach: Steve Campbell		Season Record >>	290	465	3-9	ATS>>	6-6	O/U>>	9-2	

2017-South Alabama		Opponent	USA	Opp	S/U	Line	ATS	Total	O/U	
9/2/2017	@	Mississippi	27	47	L	22.0	W	59.0	O	
9/9/2017	vs	OKLAHOMA STATE	7	44	L	28.0	L	67.0	U	
9/16/2017	vs	ALABAMA A&M	45	0	W	-36.0	W	NT	---	
9/23/2017	vs	IDAHO	23	29	L	-7.0	L	55.5	U	{2 OT}
9/30/2017	@	Louisiana Tech	16	34	L	11.5	L	57.5	U	
10/11/2017	@	Troy	19	8	W	18.5	W	51.5	U	"The Championship Belt"
10/21/2017	vs	LOUISIANA-MONROE	33	23	W	-3.5	W	55.0	O	
10/26/2017	@	Georgia State	13	21	L	1.0	L	51.0	U	"Clash of the Claws"
11/4/2017	vs	LOUISIANA-LAFAYETTE	14	19	L	-6.5	L	52.0	U	
11/11/2017	vs	ARKANSAS STATE	24	19	W	12.5	W	54.5	U	
11/18/2017	@	Georgia Southern	0	52	L	-6.0	L	43.5	O	
12/2/2017	@	New Mexico State	17	22	L	12.0	W	54.5	U	
Coach: Joey Jones		Season Record >>	238	318	4-8	ATS>>	6-6	O/U>>	3-8	

Copyright © 2021 by Steve's Football Bible, LLC

SOUTH ALABAMA JAGUARS   SUN BELT West

STADIUM: Ladd Peebles Stadium {40,000}					Location: Mobile, AL				COACH: Kane Wommack	
DATE		Opponent	USA	Opp	S/U	Line	ATS	Total	O/U	Trends & Angles
9/4/2021	vs	*SOUTHERN MISS*								vs Southern Miss - South Alabama leads series 1-0
9/11/2021	@	*Bowling Green*								vs Bowling Green - BGU leads series 1-0
9/18/2021	vs	*ALCORN STATE*								1st meeting
10/2/2021	vs	**LOUISIANA**								vs Louisiana - Louisiana leads series 7-2
10/9/2021	@	Texas State								vs Texas State - HOME team 6-0 S/U since 2013
10/14/2021	vs	**GEORGIA SOUTHERN**								vs Ga Southern - Ga Southern leads series 7-0
10/23/2021	@	Louisiana-Monroe								vs UL-Monroe - UL-Monroe leads series 4-3
10/30/2021	vs	**ARKANSAS STATE**								vs Arkansas State - Arkansas State leads series 6-3
11/6/2021	@	Troy								vs Troy - Troy leads Series 6-3
11/13/2021	@	Appalachian State								vs Appalachian State - App State leads series 2-1
11/20/2021	@	*Tennessee*								vs Tennessee- Tennessee leads series 1-0
11/27/2021	vs	**COASTAL CAROLINA**								vs Coastal Carolina - Series tied 1-1
12/4/2021	vs									**Sun Belt Championship**
	vs									**BOWL GAME**

Pointspread Analysis Non-Conference		Pointspread Analysis Conference
1-11 S/U vs Non-Conf. as 20.5 point or more Dog since 2011		0-6 S/U vs Georgia Southern as Dog since 2014 {1-5 ATS}
2-10 S/U vs Non-Conf. as 7.5-15 point Dog since 2011		0-6 S/U vs Louisiana as Dog since 2012
Dog		vs Texas State - Series tied 3-3
1-17 S/U as 20.5 point or more Dog since 2011		
6-2-1 ATS as 15.5-20 point Dog since 2013		
2-14 S/U as 10.5-15 point Dog since 2014		
1-8 S/U as 7.5-10 point Dog since 2011	SOUTHERN MISS	2-7 ATS in 1st home game of season since 2012
3-14 S/U as 7 point or less Dog since 2013	ALCORN STATE	2-7 O/U prior to playing Louisiana since 2012
4-11-1 ATS as 7 point or less Dog since 2014	Texas State	1-6 O/U prior to playing Georgia Southern since 2014
Favorite	Troy	1-6 ATS after playing Arkansas State since 2012
11-0 S/U @ home as 7.5 point or more favorite since 2014	Tennessee	2-8 S/U in final road game of season since 2011

This book is for football fans of all ages. It is both educational and entertaining as you can read nostalgically about former great College teams and players, as well as some of the great Bowl Games from the past. This book covers all the Bowl Games of the 21st Century (2000-2020), so you can read about your football heroes, past and present.

College Football History "Bowl Games of the 21st Century"

8.5" x 11" {728 pages}

$39.99

Copyright © 2021 by Steve's Football Bible, LLC

SOUTH CAROLINA GAMECOCKS   SEC East

2020-South Carolina		Opponent	USC	Opp	S/U	Line	ATS	Total	O/U	
9/26/2020	vs	TENNESSEE	27	31	L	4.0	T	44.5	O	
10/3/2020	@	Florida	24	38	L	15.0	W	56.5	O	
10/10/2020	@	Vanderbilt	41	7	W	-14.0	W	41.5	O	
10/17/2020	vs	AUBURN	30	22	W	3.0	W	51.5	O	
10/24/2020	@	Lsu	24	52	L	5.0	L	55.0	O	
11/7/2020	vs	TEXAS A&M	3	48	L	9.0	L	58.0	U	
11/14/2020	@	Mississippi	42	59	L	12.0	L	73.0	O	
11/21/2020	vs	MISSOURI	10	17	L	4.5	L	57.5	U	
11/28/2020	vs	GEORGIA	16	45	L	23.0	L	50.0	O	
12/5/2020	@	Kentucky	18	41	L	11.5	L	47.5	O	
Coach: Will Muschamp		Season Record >>	235	360	2-8	ATS>>	3-6-1	O/U>>	8-2	
2019-South Carolina		Opponent	USC	Opp	S/U	Line	ATS	Total	O/U	
8/31/2019	vs	North Carolina	20	24	L	-12.0	L	62.5	U	Bank Of America Stadium
9/7/2019	vs	CHARLESTON SOUTHERN	72	10	W	-36.0	W	NT	---	
9/14/2019	vs	ALABAMA	23	47	L	26.0	W	59.5	O	
9/21/2019	@	Missouri	14	34	L	9.5	L	60.5	U	
9/28/2019	vs	KENTUCKY	24	7	W	-3.5	W	54.0	U	
10/12/2019	@	Georgia	20	17	W	21.0	W	52.5	U	{2 OT}
10/19/2019	vs	FLORIDA	27	38	L	3.5	L	45.0	O	
10/26/2019	@	Tennessee	21	41	L	-4.0	L	47.0	O	
11/2/2019	vs	VANDERBILT	24	7	W	-15.5	W	51.5	U	
11/9/2019	vs	APPALACHIAN STATE	15	20	L	-6.5	L	51.0	L	
11/16/2019	@	Texas A&M	6	30	L	10.5	L	47.0	L	
11/30/2019	vs	CLEMSON	3	38	L	27.0	L	50.5	U	"Palmetto Bowl"
Coach: Will Muschamp		Season Record >>	269	313	4-8	ATS>>	5-7	O/U>>	3-8	
2018-South Carolina		Opponent	USC	Opp	S/U	Line	ATS	Total	O/U	
9/1/2018	vs	COASTAL CAROLINA	49	15	W	-31.0	W	55.5	O	
9/8/2018	vs	GEORGIA	17	41	L	8.0	L	54.0	O	
9/22/2018	@	Vanderbilt	37	14	W	-1.5	W	54.5	U	
9/29/2018	@	Kentucky	10	24	L	1.0	L	52.0	U	
10/6/2018	vs	MISSOURI	37	35	W	PK	W	63.0	O	
10/13/2018	vs	TEXAS A&M	23	26	L	2.5	L	50.0	U	
10/27/2018	vs	TENNESSEE	27	24	W	-10.5	L	53.0	U	
11/3/2018	@	Mississippi	48	44	W	2.5	W	69.5	O	
11/10/2018	@	Florida	31	35	L	6.5	W	54.0	O	
11/17/2018	vs	TENNESSEE-CHATTANOOGA	49	9	W	-30.5	W	NT	---	
11/24/2018	@	Clemson	35	56	L	25.5	W	58.5	O	"Palmetto Bowl"
12/1/2018	vs	AKRON	28	3	W	-28.5	L	56.5	U	
12/29/2018	vs	Virginia	0	28	L	-3.5	L	54.0	U	Belk Bowl
Coach: Will Muschamp		Season Record >>	391	354	7-6	ATS>>	7-6	O/U>>	6-6	
2017-South Carolina		Opponent	USC	Opp	S/U	Line	ATS	Total	O/U	
9/2/2017	vs	NC State	35	28	W	7.5	W	50.0	O	Bank Of America Stadium
9/9/2017	@	Missouri	31	13	W	2.5	W	71.5	U	
9/16/2017	vs	KENTUCKY	13	23	L	-5.5	L	47.0	U	
9/23/2017	vs	LOUISIANA TECH	17	16	W	-9.0	L	50.0	U	
9/30/2017	@	Texas A&M	17	24	L	8.0	W	49.5	U	
10/7/2017	vs	ARKANSAS	48	22	W	2.5	W	45.0	O	
10/14/2017	@	Tennessee	15	9	W	2.0	W	45.0	U	
10/28/2017	vs	VANDERBILT	34	27	W	-7.0	T	43.5	O	
11/4/2017	@	Georgia	10	24	L	23.5	W	45.0	U	
11/11/2017	vs	FLORIDA	28	20	W	-4.5	W	40.5	O	
11/18/2017	vs	WOFFORD	31	10	W	-23.0	L	NT	---	
11/25/2017	vs	CLEMSON	10	34	L	13.0	L	47.0	U	"Palmetto Bowl"
1/1/2018	vs	Michigan	26	19	W	9.0	W	41.5	O	Outback Bowl
Coach: Will Muschamp		Season Record >>	315	269	9-4	ATS>>	8-4-1	O/U>>	5-7	

Copyright © 2021 by Steve's Football Bible, LLC

SOUTH CAROLINA GAMECOCKS   SEC East

STADIUM: Williams-Brice Stadium {80,250}			Location: Columbia, SC				COACH: Shane Beamer	
DATE		Opponent	SC	Opp	S/U	Line	ATS	Total	O/U	Trends & Angles

DATE		Opponent	SC	Opp	S/U	Line	ATS	Total	O/U	Trends & Angles
9/4/2021	vs	EASTERN ILLINOIS								1st meeting
9/11/2021	@	East Carolina								vs East Carolina - USC leads series 14-5
9/18/2021	@	Georgia								vs Georgia - Georgia leads series 51-19-2
9/25/2021	vs	KENTUCKY								vs Kentucky - South Carolina leads series 18-13-1
10/2/2021	vs	TROY								3-0 S/U vs Troy as favorite since 2004
10/9/2021	@	Tennessee								3-17 S/U @ Tennessee since 1916
10/16/2021	vs	VANDERBILT								12-0 S/U vs Vanderbilt since 2009
10/23/2021	@	Texas A&M								vs Texas A&M - Texas A&M leads series 7-0
11/6/2021	vs	FLORIDA								vs Florida - Florida leads series 29-9-3
11/13/2021	@	Missouri								vs Missouri - Missouri leads series 6-5
11/20/2021	vs	AUBURN								1-7 S/U vs Auburn as Dog since 1996
11/27/2021	vs	CLEMSON								vs Clemson - Clemson leads series 71-41-4
12/4/2021	vs									SEC Championship
	vs									BOWL GAME

Pointspread Analysis Non-Conference		Pointspread Analysis Conference
1-14 S/U vs Non-Conf. as 10.5 point or more Dog since 1983		6-0 O/U vs Auburn as Dog since 2005
0-5 O/U vs Non-Conf. as 3.5-7 point Dog since 2009		3-0 S/U vs Florida as favorite since 2011
7-2 S/U vs Non-Conf. as 3 point or less favorite since 1990		0-20 S/U vs Florida as 7 point or more Dog since 1992
54-2-1 S/U vs Non-Conf. as 10.5 point or more favorite since 1984		5-0 S/U vs Georgia as favorite since 1988
1-12 S/U vs Clemson as 7.5 point or more Dog since 1983		1-7 S/U vs Georgia as 14 point or more Dog since 1983
5-0 S/U vs Clemson as favorite since 1987		1-11 S/U vs Georgia as 5.5-8.5 point Dog since 1985
10-0 S/U vs East Carolina as 9 point or more favorite since 1984		5-0 S/U vs Kentucky as 13 point or more favorite since 2001
Dog		1-3 S/U & ATS vs Kentucky as favorite since 2014
1-39 S/U as 15.5 point or more Dog since 1986		vs Tennessee - Tennessee leads series 27-10-2
1-6 S/U @ home as 10.5-15 point Dog since 1993		0-5 ATS vs Tennessee as favorite since 2012
1-14 S/U on road as 10.5-15 point Dog since 1998		0-8 S/U vs Tennessee as 15.5 point or more Dog since 1993
0-10 S/U on road as 7.5-10 point Dog since 1998		1-8 S/U vs Tennessee as 7.5 point or less Dog since 1994
2-13-1 S/U @ home as 7.5-10 point Dog since 1983		Game 0-5 O/U vs Texas A&M since 2016
1-6 O/U on road as 3 point or less Dog since 2013		22-3 S/U vs Vanderbilt as favorite since 1993
Favorite		vs Vanderbilt - South Carolina leads series 26-4
9-0 S/U as 3 point or less favorite since 2011		7-0 S/U vs Vanderbilt as 6.5 point or less favorite since 1993
1-11 O/U as 3 point or less favorite since 2010		11-1 S/U vs Vanderbilt as 12 point or more favorite since 1995
8-0 S/U on road as 3 point or less favorite since 1997		Game 2-5 O/U @ Vanderbilt since 2008
9-3 S/U on road as 3.5-7 point favorite since 2004	East Carolina	14-4 S/U prior to playing Georgia since 2003
5-0 S/U @ home as 7.5-10 point favorite since 2000	Georgia	10-4 S/U prior to playing Kentucky since 2007
0-8 ATS as 7.5-10 point favorite since 2001	Georgia	1-9 O/U prior to playing Kentucky since 2011
0-4 O/U on road as 7.5-10 point favorite since 2001	KENTUCKY	7-1-1 O/U after playing Georgia since 2012
20-3 S/U @ home as 10.5-15 point favorite since 1997	KENTUCKY	10-3 S/U after playing Georgia since 2008
56-2 S/U as 15.5 point or favorite since 1984	KENTUCKY	11-4 S/U in 2nd home game of season since 2006
12-2 O/U as 20.5 point or more favorite since 2009	TROY	3-9 O/U after playing Kentucky since 2007
Bowl Games	TROY	7-1 O/U prior to playing Tennessee since 2012
5-2 S/U & ATS in Bowl Games since 2013	Missouri	9-1 O/U after playing Florida since 2008
1-5 ATS in Bowl Games as 3.5-7 point favorite since 1987	Missouri	9-3 S/U after playing Florida since 2009
		29-5 S/U @ home when ranked since 2009
		5-1 S/U @ home when ranked vs Clemson all time
		5-0 S/U when ranked vs East Carolina all time
		5-0 S/U @ home when ranked vs Kentucky all time
		0-11 S/U on road vs ranked teams since 2014
		1-6 S/U vs #1 ranked teams all time {0-3 on road}
		0-13 S/U vs #2 ranked teams all time
		2-21 S/U vs ranked Florida all time

Copyright © 2021 by Steve's Football Bible, LLC

SOUTHERN CALIFORNIA TROJANS   PACIFIC-12 South

2020-Southern California		Opponent	USC	Opp	S/U	Line	ATS	Total	O/U	
11/7/2020	vs	ARIZONA STATE	28	27	W	-11.5	L	57.5	U	
11/14/2020	@	Arizona	34	30	W	-14.5	L	67.0	U	
11/21/2020	@	Utah	33	17	W	-2.5	W	58.5	U	
12/6/2020	vs	WASHINGTON STATE	38	13	W	-11.0	W	68.0	U	
12/12/2020	@	Ucla	43	38	W	-3.5	W	65.0	O	"Victory Bell"
12/18/2020	vs	OREGON	24	31	L	-3.0	L	65.5	U	PAC-12 Championship
Coach: Clay Helton		Season Record >>	200	156	5-1	ATS>>	3-3	O/U>>	1-5	
2019-Southern California		Opponent	USC	Opp	S/U	Line	ATS	Total	O/U	
8/31/2019	vs	FRESNO STATE	31	23	W	-14.0	L	50.0	O	
9/7/2019	vs	STANFORD	45	20	W	-3.0	W	43.0	O	
9/14/2019	@	Byu	27	30	L	-4.5	L	57.5	U	{OT}
9/20/2019	vs	UTAH	30	23	W	3.5	W	53.0	T	
9/28/2019	@	Washington	14	28	L	11.0	L	60.5	U	
10/12/2019	@	Notre Dame	27	30	L	10.5	W	59.0	U	"Jeweled Shillelagh"
10/19/2019	vs	ARIZONA	41	14	W	-10.0	W	69.0	U	
10/25/2019	@	Colorado	35	31	W	-10.5	L	64.5	O	
11/2/2019	vs	OREGON	24	56	L	3.5	L	60.0	O	
11/9/2019	@	Arizona State	31	26	W	-4.5	W	54.0	O	
11/16/2019	@	California	41	17	W	-4.0	W	48.5	O	
11/23/2019	vs	UCLA	52	35	W	-13.0	W	66.5	O	"Victory Bell"
12/27/2019	vs	Iowa	24	49	L	-1.5	L	54.5	O	Holiday Bowl
Coach: Clay Helton		Season Record >>	422	382	8-5	ATS>>	7-6	O/U>>	8-4-1	
2018-Southern California		Opponent	USC	Opp	S/U	Line	ATS	Total	O/U	
9/1/2018	vs	UNLV	43	21	W	-24.5	L	59.0	O	
9/8/2018	@	Stanford	3	17	L	4.5	L	54.5	U	
9/15/2018	@	Texas	14	37	L	3.5	L	47.5	O	
9/21/2018	vs	WASHINGTON STATE	39	36	W	-4.5	L	50.5	O	
9/29/2018	@	Arizona	24	20	W	-3.0	W	61.5	U	
10/13/2018	vs	COLORADO	31	20	W	-7.0	W	57.5	U	
10/20/2018	@	Utah	28	41	L	6.5	L	48.0	O	
10/27/2018	vs	ARIZONA STATE	35	38	L	-3.0	L	52.0	O	
11/3/2018	@	Oregon State	38	21	W	-15.0	W	65.5	U	
11/10/2018	vs	CALIFORNIA	14	15	L	-4.0	L	45.5	U	
11/17/2018	@	Ucla	27	34	L	-2.5	L	54.5	O	"Victory Bell"
11/24/2018	vs	NOTRE DAME	17	24	L	14.0	W	54.0	U	"Jeweled Shillelagh"
Coach: Clay Helton		Season Record >>	313	324	5-7	ATS>>	4-8	O/U>>	6-6	
2017-Southern California		Opponent	USC	Opp	S/U	Line	ATS	Total	O/U	
9/2/2017	vs	WESTERN MICHIGAN	49	31	W	-29.0	L	59.5	O	
9/9/2017	vs	STANFORD	42	24	W	-4.0	W	55.0	O	
9/16/2017	vs	TEXAS	27	24	W	-16.5	L	65.5	U	{2 OT}
9/23/2017	@	California	30	20	W	-17.0	L	63.0	U	
9/29/2017	@	Washington State	27	30	L	-4.5	L	58.5	U	
10/7/2017	vs	OREGON STATE	38	10	W	-32.0	L	56.5	U	
10/14/2017	vs	UTAH	28	27	W	-13.0	L	52.0	O	
10/21/2017	@	Notre Dame	14	49	L	3.5	L	61.0	O	"Jeweled Shillelagh"
10/28/2017	@	Arizona State	48	17	W	-5.5	W	58.5	O	
11/4/2017	vs	ARIZONA	49	35	W	-6.5	W	76.5	O	
11/11/2017	@	Colorado	38	24	W	-13.5	W	62.5	U	
11/18/2017	vs	UCLA	28	23	W	-14.5	L	69.5	U	"Victory Bell"
12/2/2017	vs	Stanford	31	28	W	-3.5	L	58.5	O	PAC-12 Championship
12/29/2017	vs	Ohio State	7	24	L	9.5	L	65.0	U	Cotton Bowl
Coach: Clay Helton		Season Record >>	456	366	11-3	ATS>>	4-10	O/U>>	7-7	PAC-12 Champions

Copyright © 2021 by Steve's Football Bible, LLC

SOUTHERN CALIFORNIA TROJANS   PACIFIC-12 South

STADIUM: Los Angeles Memorial Coliseum {78,500}		Location: Los Angeles, CA						COACH: Clay Helton	
DATE		Opponent	USC	Opp	S/U	Line	ATS	Total	O/U	Trends & Angles

DATE		Opponent	USC	Opp	S/U	Line	ATS	Total	O/U	Trends & Angles
9/4/2021	vs	*SAN JOSE STATE*								4-0 S/U vs San Jose State as favorite since 1995
9/11/2021	vs	**STANFORD**								Game 5-1 O/U @ home vs Stanford since 2009
9/18/2021	@	Colorado								vs Colorado - USC leads series 14-0
9/25/2021	vs	**OREGON STATE**								14-0 S/U @ home vs Oregon State as favorite since 1985
10/2/2021	@	Washington State								11-2 S/U vs Washington State since 2003
10/9/2021	vs	**UTAH**								9-0 S/U @ home vs Utah since 1919
10/23/2021	@	*Notre Dame*								vs Notre Dame - Notre Dame leads series 49-37-5
10/30/2021	vs	**ARIZONA**								vs Arizona - USC leads series 36-8
11/6/2021	@	Arizona State								10-0 S/U @ Arizona State as favorite since 1988
11/13/2021	@	California								15-1 S/U vs California as favorite since 2004
11/20/2021	vs	**UCLA**								10-1 S/U @ home vs UCLA since 1999
11/27/2021	vs	*BYU*								vs BYU - USC leads series 2-1
12/4/2021	vs									PAC-12 Championship
	vs									BOWL GAME

Pointspread Analysis — Non-Conference

1-6-1 O/U vs Non-Conf. as 3 point or less Dog since 1990
13-1 S/U vs Non-Conf. as 7.5-10 point favorite since 1993
10-0 S/U vs Non-Conf. as 10.5-15 point favorite since 1990
12-2 S/U vs Non-Conf. as 15.5-20 point favorite since 1993
29-1 S/U vs Non-Conf. as 20.5 point or more favorite since 1983
1-11 S/U Notre Dame as 7.5 point or less Dog since 1986
11-1 S/U vs Notre Dame as favorite since 1998

Dog
3-15 ATS as a Dog since 2015
1-9 S/U & ATS as 3.5-7 point Dog since 2014
1-5 S/U & ATS on road as 3 point or less Dog since 2002
1-6 S/U @ home as 3 point or less Dog since 1983

Favorite
20-5 S/U as 3.5-7 point favorite since 2013
10-2 S/U @ home as 3.5-7 point favorite since 2013
1-8 O/U as 7.5-10 point favorite since 2011
7-1 S/U on road as 7.5-10 point favorite since 1998
18-2 S/U @ home as 10.5-15 point favorite since 2002
11-0 S/U on road as 10.5-15 point favorite since 2008
25-2 S/U as 10.5-15 point favorite since 2008
3-12 O/U on road as 10.5-15 point favorite since 2005
15-2 S/U on road as 15.5-20 point favorite since 1988
16-2 S/U @ home as 15.5-20 point favorite since 1998
5-21-1 O/U as 15.5-20 point favorite since 2004
50-2 S/U @ home as 20.5 point or more favorite since 1983
21-1 S/U on road as 20.5 point or more favorite since 1983
4-12 O/U as 25.5 point or more favorite since 2006

Bowl Games
25-9 S/U in Rosé Bowl
7-0 S/U vs Big Ten in Rose Bowl since 1990 {6-1 ATS}
8-3 S/U vs Big Ten in Bowl Games since 1996
6-1 S/U & ATS vs Michigan in bowl Games since 1970
0-3 S/U & ATS in Sun Bowl
1-4 ATS in Bowl Games as 7.5-10 point favorite since 1980

1-8 ATS in 2nd road game of season since 2012
2-8 O/U after playing Washington State since 2006
2-9 ATS prior to playing Arizona State since 2009
15-2 S/U prior to playing California since 2003

Pointspread Analysis — Conference

11-1 S/U vs Arizona as 6.5 point or less favorite since 1984
9-0 S/U vs Arizona as 14 point or more favorite since 2003
0-6 O/U vs Arizona as 14 point or more favorite since 2006
vs Arizona State - USC leads series 24-13
5-0 O/U vs Arizona State as Dog since 1996
1-5 S/U vs Arizona State as Dog since 1983
13-1 S/U vs Arizona State as 9 point or more favorite since 1988
vs California - USC leads series 71-31-5
3-13 O/U vs California as favorite since 2004
9-0 S/U vs CAL as 16 point or more favorite since 1986
18-1 S/U vs Oregon State as 12 point or more favorite since 1983
10-2 O/U @ home vs Stanford as favorite since 1993
14-1 S/U vs Stanford as 10.5 point or more favorite since 1983
vs Stanford - USC leads series 64-33-3
2-7 ATS vs UCLA as 5 point or less favorite since 1990
10-0 S/U vs UCLA as 13 point or more favorite since 2003
1-6 O/U vs UCLA as 13 point or more favorite since 2007
vs Ucla - USC leads series 51-32-7
vs Utah - USC leads series 13-6
vs Washington State - USC Leads series 61-10-4
9-0 S/U vs Washington State as 7.5-9.5 point favorite since 1983
8-0 S/U vs Wash. State as 16.5 point or more favorite since 1987

SAN JOSE STATE	22-1 S/U in 1st home game of season since 1998
SAN JOSE STATE	16-2 S/U prior to playing Stanford since 2002
STANFORD	18-1 S/U in 2nd home game of season since 2002
STANFORD	9-1 ATS in 2nd home game of season since 2011
STANFORD	8-0 S/U prior to playing Colorado since 2012
STANFORD	2-9 O/U prior to playing Colorado since 2000
STANFORD	8-0 S/U prior to playing Colorado since 2012
Colorado	2-10 ATS in 1st road game of season since 2009
Colorado	0-9 O/U in 1st road game of season since 2012
Colorado	14-4 S/U after playing Stanford since 2002
OREGON STATE	2-9 ATS after playing Colorado since 2000
OREGON STATE	12-3 S/U prior to playing Washington State since 2000
OREGON STATE	1-7 O/U prior to playing Washington State since 2008
OREGON STATE	1-6 ATS prior to playing Washington State since 2009
Wazzu	1-7 S/U in 2nd road game of season since 2013
UTAH	15-1 S/U after playing Washington State since 1999
ARIZONA	9-2 O/U prior to playing Arizona State since 2009
Arizona State	3-11-1 O/U after playing Arizona since 2005
UCLA	2-5 O/U after playing California since 2013
BYU	3-10-1 O/U in final home game of season since 2007
BYU	8-3 S/U after playing UCLA since 1996 {8-3 ATS}

Copyright © 2021 by Steve's Football Bible, LLC

SOUTH FLORIDA BULLS   AMERICAN East

2020-South Florida		Opponent	USF	Opp	S/U	Line	ATS	Total	O/U	
9/12/2020	vs	THE CITADEL	27	6	W	-17.5	W	53.5	U	
9/19/2020	@	Notre Dame	0	52	L	23.0	L	49.5	O	
10/3/2020	@	Cincinnati	7	28	L	22.5	W	45.5	U	
10/10/2020	vs	EAST CAROLINA	24	44	L	-5.0	L	58.0	O	
10/17/2020	@	Temple	37	39	L	10.5	W	54.0	O	
10/23/2020	vs	TULSA	13	42	L	12.5	L	52.0	O	
11/7/2020	@	Memphis	33	34	L	17.5	W	67.0	T	
11/14/2020	@	Houston	21	56	L	15.0	L	58.5	O	
11/27/2020	vs	CENTRAL FLORIDA	46	58	L	25.0	W	70.5	O	"War on I-4 Trophy"
Coach: Jeff Scott		Season Record >>	208	359	1-8	ATS>>	5-4	O/U>>	6-2-1	
2019-South Florida		Opponent	USF	Opp	S/U	Line	ATS	Total	O/U	
8/30/2019	vs	WISCONSIN	0	49	L	10.5	L	58.5	U	
9/7/2019	@	Georgia Tech	10	14	L	4.5	W	58.5	U	
9/14/2019	vs	SOUTH CAROLINA STATE	55	16	W	-26.0	W	NT	---	
9/28/2019	vs	SMU	21	48	L	7.0	L	62.0	O	
10/5/2019	@	Connecticut	48	22	W	-11.0	W	48.0	O	
10/12/2019	vs	BYU	27	23	W	4.5	W	49.5	O	
10/19/2019	@	Navy	3	35	L	15.5	L	51.0	U	
10/26/2019	@	East Carolina	45	20	W	-1.5	W	51.0	O	
11/7/2019	vs	TEMPLE	7	17	L	PK	L	50.5	U	
11/16/2019	vs	CINCINNATI	17	20	L	13.0	W	46.5	U	
11/23/2019	vs	MEMPHIS	10	49	L	14.5	L	59.5	O	
11/29/2019	@	Central Florida	7	34	L	24.0	L	61.5	U	"War on I-4 Trophy"
Coach: Charlie Strong		Season Record >>	250	347	4-8	ATS>>	6-6	O/U>>	5-6	
2018-South Florida		Opponent	USF	Opp	S/U	Line	ATS	Total	O/U	
9/1/2018	vs	ELON	34	14	W	-27.0	L	NT	---	
9/8/2018	vs	GEORGIA TECH	49	38	W	3.0	W	60.0	O	
9/15/2018	@	Illinois	25	19	W	-14.0	L	58.5	U	Soldier Field
9/22/2018	vs	EAST CAROLINA	20	13	W	-19.5	L	68.5	U	
10/6/2018	@	Massachusetts	58	42	W	-16.0	T	71.0	O	
10/12/2018	@	Tulsa	25	24	W	-10.0	L	60.5	U	
10/20/2018	vs	CONNECTICUT	38	30	W	-33.5	L	67.5	O	
10/27/2018	@	Houston	36	57	L	9.5	L	77.5	O	
11/3/2018	vs	TULANE	15	41	L	-5.5	L	61.5	U	
11/10/2018	@	Cincinnati	23	35	L	16.0	W	52.5	O	
11/17/2018	@	Temple	17	27	L	14.0	W	62.5	U	
11/23/2018	vs	CENTRAL FLORIDA	10	38	L	15.5	L	69.5	U	"War on I-4 Trophy"
12/20/2018	vs	**Marshall**	20	38	L	2.0	L	50.0	O	Gasparilla Bowl
Coach: Charlie Strong		Season Record >>	370	416	7-6	ATS>>	3-9-1	O/U>>	6-6	
2017-South Florida		Opponent	USF	Opp	S/U	Line	ATS	Total	O/U	
8/26/2017	@	San Jose State	42	22	W	-21.0	L	68.5	U	
9/2/2017	vs	SUNY-STONY BROOK	31	17	W	-36.0	L	58.5	U	
9/15/2017	vs	ILLINOIS	47	23	W	-16.5	W	55.0	O	
9/21/2017	vs	TEMPLE	43	7	W	-17.5	W	61.5	U	
9/30/2017	@	East Carolina	61	31	W	-22.5	W	73.0	O	
10/14/2017	vs	CINCINNATI	33	3	W	-23.5	W	62.5	U	
10/21/2017	@	Tulane	34	28	W	-10.5	L	54.0	O	
10/28/2017	vs	HOUSTON	24	28	L	-10.0	L	52.5	U	
11/4/2017	@	Connecticut	37	20	W	-23.5	L	63.5	U	
11/16/2017	vs	TULSA	27	20	W	-22.5	L	66.0	U	
11/24/2017	@	Central Florida	42	49	L	10.0	W	65.0	O	"War on I-4 Trophy"
12/23/2017	vs	**Texas Tech**	38	34	W	-2.0	W	65.5	O	Birmingham Bowl
Coach: Charlie Strong		Season Record >>	459	282	10-2	ATS>>	6-6	O/U>>	5-7	

Copyright © 2021 by Steve's Football Bible, LLC

SOUTH FLORIDA BULLS   AMERICAN East

STADIUM: Raymond James Stadium {65,618}		Location: Tampa, FL							COACH: Jeff Scott

DATE		Opponent	USF	Opp	S/U	Line	ATS	Total	O/U	Trends & Angles
9/2/2021	@	NC State								vs NC State - NC State leads series 2-1
9/11/2021	vs	FLORIDA								vs Florida - Florida leads series 1-0
9/18/2021	vs	FLORIDA A&M								vs Florida A&M - USF leads series 3-0
9/24/2021	@	Byu								vs BYU - USF leads series 1-0
10/2/2021	@	Smu								1-4 ATS vs SMU since 2013
10/16/2021	vs	TULSA								vs Tulsa - South Florida leads series 3-1
10/23/2021	vs	TEMPLE								vs Temple - Temple leads series 5-2
10/30/2021	@	East Carolina								vs East Carolina - USF leads series 9-2
11/6/2021	vs	HOUSTON								vs Houston - Houston leads series 5-2
11/12/2021	vs	CINCINNATI								vs Cincinnati - Cincinnati leads series 11-7
11/20/2021	@	Tulane								vs Tulane - Series tied 1-1
11/26/2021	@	Central Florida								0-6 S/U vs Central Florida as Dog since 2013
12/4/2021	vs									AAC Championship
	vs									BOWL GAME

Pointspread Analysis Non-Conference		Pointspread Analysis Conference
1-8 S/U vs non-Conf. as 15.5 point or more Dog since 2001		vs Central Florida - Series tied 6-6
1-7 S/U vs Non-Conf. as 3.5-7 point Dog since 2005		6-0 S/U vs Central Florida as favorite since 2005
7-1 S/U vs Non-Conf. as 7 point or less favoroite since 2002		7-1 S/U vs East Carolina as favorite since 2003
29-2 S/U vs Non-Conf. as 10.5 point or more favorite since 2001		Game 1-4 O/U vs SMU since 2013
Dog		vs SMU - South Florida leads series 3-2
9-3 ATS as 20.5 point or more Dog since 2001		3-0 S/U vs SMU as favorite since 2014
2-9 O/U as 20.5 point or more Dog since 2002		3-0 S/U vs Tulsa as favorite since 2014
6-2 ATS as 15.5-20 point Dog since 2012		
0-5 O/U @ home as 15.5-20 point Dog since 2005		
1-8 S/U as 15.5-20 point Dog since 2006		
0-11 S/U as 10.5-15 point Dog since 2012		
1-7 S/U @ home as 3.5-7 point Dog since 2009		
1-8 S/U on road as 3.5-7 point Dog since 2008		
4-10 O/U as 3.5-7 point Dog since 2012		
3-9-1 ATS as 3.5-7 point Dog since 2012		
10-1 O/U as 3 point or less Dog since 2003		
Favorite		9-1 S/U @ home when ranked since 2011
0-4 S/U @ home as 7.5-10 point favorite since 2012		0-8 S/U on road vs ranked teams since 2012
0-7 ATS @ home as 7.5-10 point favorite since 2008		8-1 ATS on road vs ranked teams since 2011
0-11 ATS as 7.5-10 point favorite since 2008		2-11 S/U @ home vs ranked teams since 2009
19-0 S/U on road as 10.5 point or more favorite since 2002		
36-3 S/U @ home as 10.5 point or more favorite since 2001	NC State	1-7 O/U in 1st road game of season since 2013
Bowl Games	FLORIDA	22-2 S/U in 1st home game of season since 1997
	Byu	6-1 O/U in 2nd road game of season since 2014
5-0 O/U in Bowl Games since 2010	HOUSTON	5-2 S/U after playing East Carolina since 2014
3-0 S/U in Birmingham Bowl since 2006		

Copyright © 2021 by Steve's Football Bible, LLC

SOUTHERN METHODIST MUSTANGS   AMERICAN West

2020-Southern Methodist		Opponent	SMU	Opp	S/U	Line	ATS	Total	O/U	
9/5/2020	@	Texas State	31	24	W	-24.0	L	70.0	U	
9/19/2020	@	North Texas	65	35	W	-14.5	W	71.0	O	"Safeway Bowl"
9/26/2020	vs	STEPHEN F. AUSTIN	50	7	W	-38.0	W	63.5	U	
10/1/2020	vs	MEMPHIS	30	27	W	-2.0	W	75.0	U	
10/16/2020	@	Tulane	37	34	W	-6.5	L	64.5	O	{OT}
10/24/2020	vs	CINCINNATI	13	42	L	1.0	L	57.5	U	
10/31/2020	vs	NAVY	51	37	W	-12.5	W	59.0	O	"Ganzs Trophy"
11/7/2020	@	Temple	47	23	W	-17.0	W	63.5	O	
11/14/2020	@	Tulsa	24	28	L	-2.0	L	63.5	U	
11/28/2020	@	East Carolina	38	52	L	-12.5	L	72.0	O	
Coach: Sonny Dykes		Season Record >>	386	309	7-3	ATS>>	5-5	O/U>>	5-5	

2019-Southern Methodist		Opponent	SMU	Opp	S/U	Line	ATS	Total	O/U	
8/31/2019	@	Arkansas State	37	30	W	2.5	W	56.0	O	
9/7/2019	vs	NORTH TEXAS	49	27	W	-3.5	W	73.0	O	"Safeway Bowl"
9/14/2019	vs	TEXAS STATE	47	17	W	-17.5	W	62.5	O	
9/21/2019	@	Tcu	41	38	W	7.5	W	54.0	O	"Iron Skillet"
9/28/2019	@	South Florida	48	21	W	-7.0	W	62.0	O	
10/5/2019	vs	TULSA	43	37	W	-12.0	L	63.0	O	{3 OT}
10/19/2019	vs	TEMPLE	45	21	W	-9.5	W	60.0	O	
10/24/2019	@	Houston	34	31	W	-12.0	L	65.0	T	
11/2/2019	@	Memphis	48	54	L	5.5	L	72.0	O	
11/9/2019	vs	EAST CAROLINA	59	51	W	-22.5	L	74.0	O	
11/23/2019	@	Navy	28	35	L	3.0	L	69.0	U	"Ganzs Trophy"
11/30/2019	vs	TULANE	37	20	W	-3.0	W	72.0	U	
12/21/2019	@	**Florida Atlantic**	28	52	L	-7.0	L	63.5	O	Boca Raton Bowl
Coach: Sonny Dykes		Season Record >>	544	434	10-3	ATS>>	7-6	O/U>>	10-2-1	

2018-Southern Methodist		Opponent	SMU	Opp	S/U	Line	ATS	Total	O/U	
9/1/2018	vs	NORTH TEXAS	23	46	L	3.5	L	71.5	U	"Safeway Bowl"
9/7/2018	@	Tcu	12	42	L	23.5	L	59.0	U	"Iron Skillet"
9/15/2018	@	Michigan	20	45	L	36.0	W	54.0	O	
9/22/2018	vs	NAVY	31	30	W	6.0	W	58.0	O	"Ganzs Trophy"
9/29/2018	vs	HOUSTON BAPTIST	63	27	W	-43.5	L	NT	---	
10/6/2018	@	Central Florida	20	48	L	25.0	L	74.0	U	
10/20/2018	@	Tulane	27	23	W	7.0	W	55.5	U	
10/27/2018	vs	CINCINNATI	20	26	L	9.5	W	49.5	U	{OT}
11/3/2018	vs	HOUSTON	45	31	W	13.5	W	70.5	O	
11/10/2018	@	Connecticut	62	50	W	-18.0	W	65.5	O	
11/16/2018	vs	MEMPHIS	18	28	L	8.5	L	74.5	U	
11/24/2018	@	Tulsa	24	27	L	-2.5	L	53.5	U	
Coach: Sonny Dykes		Season Record >>	365	423	5-7	ATS>>	6-6	O/U>>	5-7	

2017-Southern Methodist		Opponent	SMU	Opp	S/U	Line	ATS	Total	O/U	
9/2/2017	vs	STEPHEN F. AUSTIN	58	14	W	-30.0	W	70.5	O	
9/9/2017	vs	NORTH TEXAS	54	32	W	-12.0	W	64.0	O	"Safeway Bowl"
9/16/2017	@	Tcu	36	56	L	22.5	W	65.0	O	"Iron Skillet"
9/23/2017	vs	ARKANSAS STATE	44	21	W	-2.5	W	72.0	U	
9/30/2017	vs	CONNECTICUT	49	28	W	-16.0	W	74.5	O	
10/7/2017	@	Houston	22	35	L	10.0	L	60.0	U	
10/21/2017	@	Cincinnati	31	28	W	-5.5	L	65.5	U	{OT}
10/27/2017	vs	TULSA	38	34	W	-12.0	L	78.0	U	
11/4/2017	vs	CENTRAL FLORIDA	24	31	L	14.0	W	75.0	U	
11/11/2017	@	Navy	40	43	L	1.5	L	66.0	O	"Ganzs Trophy"
11/18/2017	@	Memphis	45	66	L	11.0	L	70.0	O	
11/25/2017	vs	TULANE	41	38	W	-7.5	L	65.0	O	
12/20/2017	vs	**Louisiana Tech**	10	51	L	-4.0	L	71.0	U	Frisco Bowl
Coach: Chad Morris		Season Record >>	492	477	7-6	ATS>>	6-7	O/U>>	7-6	

Copyright © 2021 by Steve's Football Bible, LLC

SOUTHERN METHODIST MUSTANGS   AMERICAN West

STADIUM: Gerald R. Ford Stadium {32,000}					Location: Dallas, TX			COACH: Sonny Dykes	
DATE		Opponent	SMU	Opp	S/U	Line	ATS	Total	O/U	Trends & Angles

DATE		Opponent	SMU	Opp	S/U	Line	ATS	Total	O/U	Trends & Angles
9/4/2021	vs	ABILENE CHRISTIAN								vs Abilene Christian - SMU leads series 1-0
9/11/2021	vs	NORTH TEXAS								6-0 S/U vs North Texas as favorite since 2007
9/18/2021	@	Louisiana Tech								vs Louisiana Tech - La Tech leads series 4-1
9/25/2021	@	Tcu								2-11 S/U @ TCU since 1997
10/2/2021	vs	SOUTH FLORIDA								vs South Florida - South Florida leads series 3-2
10/9/2021	@	Navy								vs Navy - Navy leads series 13-9
10/21/2021	vs	TULANE								5-0 S/U @ home vs Tulane since 2009
10/30/2021	@	Houston								1-6 S/U @ Houston as Dog since 2007
11/6/2021	@	Memphis								vs Memphis - Memphis leads series 9-4
11/13/2021	vs	CENTRAL FLORIDA								vs Central Florida - UCF leads series 8-1
11/20/2021	@	Cincinnati								0-4 S/U vs Cincinnati as Dog since 2013
11/27/2021	vs	TULSA								10-2 S/U @ home vs Tulsa since 1996
12/5/2020	vs									AAC Championship
	vs									BOWL GAME

Pointspread Analysis Non-Conference		Pointspread Analysis Conference
0-28 S/U vs Non-Conf. as 15.5 point or more Dog since 1994		0-8 S/U vs Central Florida as Dog since 2007
1-6 O/U vs Non-Conf. as 10.5-15 point Dog since 2002		vs Houston - Houston leads series 21-13-1
1-6 S/U vs Non-Conf. as 7.5-10 point Dog since 1998		1-7 S/U vs Houston as 19.5 point or more Dog since 1989
1-8 S/U vs Non-Conf. as 3.5-7 point Dog since 1998		0-6 S/U & ATS vs Memphis as Dog since 2014
1-5 S/U & ATS vs Non-conf. as 3 point or less Dog since 2003		1-10 S/U vs Navy as Dog since 1996
5-22 S/U vs TCU as Dog since 1984		vs Tulane - SMU leads series 14-13
6-1 S/U vs TCU as favorite since 1983		6-0 S/U vs Tulane since 2015
3-17 S/U vs TCU since 1999		6-1 O/U vs Tulane as favorite since 2011
vs Tcu - TCU leads series 51-40-7		Game 6-2 O/U vs Tulane since 2011
Game 6-1 O/U @ TCU since 2009		2-8 ATS @ home vs Tulane since 1992
vs North Texas - SMU leads series 33-6-1		0-3 S/U & ATS @ home vs Tulane as Dog since 1998
3-0 S/U when ranked vs North Texas all time		vs Tulsa - SMU leads series 15-12
6-0 S/U when ranked vs TCU since 1979		9-2 S/U vs Tulsa as favorite since 1997
Dog		1-6 O/U vs Tulsa as favorite since 2001
0-34 S/U as 25.5 point or more Dog since 1989		0-6 ATS vs Tulsa as favorite since 2002
1-7 ATS as 25.5-30 point Dog since 1991		9-0 ATS vs Tulsa as 5.5 point or more Dog since 2004
1-16 S/U on road as 20.5-25 point Dog since 1994		**Bowl Games**
1-12 S/U @ home as 20.5-25 point Dog since 1995		3-0 S/U in Hawaii Bowl since 1984
1-21 S/U on road as 15.5-20 point Dog since 1990		1-5 O/U in Bowl Games since 2009
1-7 S/U @ home as 15.5-20 point Dog since 1989		0-4 S/U & ATS in Bowl Games as 3.5-7 point favorite since 1983
1-6 S/U as 10.5-15 point Dog since 2015		
1-7 O/U @ home as 10.5-15 point Dog since 2008	ABILENE	2-7 O/U prior to playing North Texas since 1990
1-10 S/U @ home as 10.5-15 point Dog since 2007	La Tech	4-20 S/U in 1st road game of season since 1997
12-3 ATS @ home as 10.5-15 point Dog since 2002	La Tech	2-6 S/U after playing North Texas since 2007
1-20 S/U as 7.5-10 point Dog since 1998	Tcu	2-6 S/U in 2nd road game of season since 2013
3-11 O/U as 7.5-10 point Dog since 2002	TULANE	5-1 O/U prior to playing Houston since 2014
4-15 ATS as 7.5-10 point Dog since 1999	TULANE	2-11 S/U prior to playing Houston since 2007
19-4 O/U as 3.5-7 point Dog since 2005	Houston	6-2-1 O/U prior to playing Memphis since 2012
2-15 S/U & ATS as 3 point or less Dog since 2000	Memphis	8-3 S/U after playing Houston since 2009
4-11 O/U as 3 point or less Dog since 2003	Memphis	8-3 S/U after playing Houston since 2009
Favorite	Cincinnati	2-6 S/U after playing Central Florida since 2007
6-2 S/U & ATS as 3 point or less favorite since 2010		
5-0 S/U on road as 3.5-7 point favorite since 2013		
5-0 S/U @ home as 3.5-7 point favorite since 2009		2-33 S/U on road vs ranked teams since 1989
5-0 S/U on road as 7.5-10 point favorite since 1985		5-21-1 S/U @ home vs ranked teams since 1986
14-1 S/U @ home as 10.5-15 point favorite since 2000		6-55-1 S/U vs ranked teams since 1986
17-0 S/U @ home as 15.5 point or more favorite since 1997		25-5-1 S/U @ home when ranked since 1979

Copyright © 2021 by Steve's Football Bible, LLC

SOUTHERN MISS GOLDEN EAGLES   C-USA West

2020-Southern Mississippi		Opponent	USM	Opp	S/U	Line	ATS	Total	O/U	
9/3/2020	vs	SOUTH ALABAMA	21	32	L	-13.5	L	54.5	U	
9/19/2020	vs	LOUISIANA TECH	30	31	L	-7.5	L	58.5	O	"Rivalry in Dixie"
9/26/2020	vs	TULANE	24	66	L	3.5	L	54.5	O	"Battle for the Bell"
10/3/2020	@	North Texas	41	31	W	1.5	W	75.0	U	
10/24/2020	@	Liberty	35	56	L	15.0	L	59.5	O	
10/31/2020	vs	RICE	6	30	L	1.5	L	58.5	U	
11/7/2020	vs	NORTH ALABAMA	24	13	W	-15.5	L	51.0	U	
11/14/2020	@	Western Kentucky	7	10	L	8.0	W	45.0	U	
11/21/2020	vs	TEXAS-SAN ANTONIO	20	23	L	9.0	W	53.5	U	
12/10/2020	vs	FLORIDA ATLANTIC	45	31	W	9.0	W	43.0	O	
Coach: Jay Hopson		Season Record >>	253	323	3-7	ATS>>	4-6	O/U>>	4-6	
2019-Southern Mississippi		Opponent	USM	Opp	S/U	Line	ATS	Total	O/U	
8/31/2019	vs	ALCORN STATE	38	10	W	-24.5	W	NT	---	
9/7/2019	@	Mississippi State	15	35	L	15.5	L	51.0	U	
9/14/2019	@	Troy	47	42	W	3.0	W	49.0	O	
9/21/2019	@	Alabama	7	49	L	38.0	L	63.0	U	
9/28/2019	vs	TEXAS-EL PASO	31	13	W	-26.0	L	49.5	U	
10/12/2019	vs	NORTH TEXAS	45	27	W	-3.0	W	59.0	O	
10/19/2019	@	Louisiana Tech	30	45	L	-2.5	L	58.0	O	"Rivalry in Dixie"
10/26/2019	@	Rice	20	6	W	-10.0	W	51.5	U	
11/9/2019	vs	ALABAMA-BIRMINGHAM	37	2	W	-7.5	W	50.0	U	
11/16/2019	@	Texas-San Antonio	36	17	W	-17.0	W	55.5	U	
11/23/2019	vs	WESTERN KENTUCKY	10	28	L	-3.5	L	51.0	U	
11/30/2019	@	Florida Atlantic	17	34	L	9.0	L	58.5	U	
1/4/2020	vs	Tulane	13	30	L	7.5	L	57.5	U	Armed Forces Bowl
Coach: Jay Hopson		Season Record >>	346	338	7-6	ATS>>	6-7	O/U>>	3-9	
2018-Southern Mississippi		Opponent	USM	Opp	S/U	Line	ATS	Total	O/U	
9/1/2018	vs	JACKSON STATE	55	7	W	-33.0	W	NT	---	
9/8/2018	vs	LOUISIANA-MONROE	20	21	L	-5.0	L	67.0	U	
9/22/2018	vs	RICE	40	22	W	-13.5	L	54.5	O	
9/29/2018	@	Auburn	13	24	L	27.0	W	50.0	U	
10/13/2018	@	North Texas	7	30	L	7.0	L	53.0	U	
10/20/2018	vs	TEXAS-SAN ANTONIO	27	17	W	-16.0	L	43.5	O	
10/27/2018	@	Charlotte	17	20	L	-6.5	L	45.0	U	
11/3/2018	vs	MARSHALL	26	24	W	2.5	W	45.5	O	
11/10/2018	@	Alabama-Birmingham	23	26	L	13.5	W	45.0	O	{OT}
11/17/2018	vs	LOUISIANA TECH	21	20	W	-2.0	L	47.0	U	"Rivalry in Dixie"
11/24/2018	@	Texas-El Paso	39	7	W	-14.0	W	45.0	O	
Coach: Jay Hopson		Season Record >>	634	556	6-5	ATS>>	6-5	O/U>>	5-5	
2017-Southern Mississippi		Opponent	USM	Opp	S/U	Line	ATS	Total	O/U	
9/2/2017	vs	KENTUCKY	17	24	L	9.5	W	57.0	U	
9/9/2017	vs	SOUTHERN U	45	0	W	-29.5	W	NT	---	
9/16/2017	@	Louisiana-Monroe	28	17	W	-7.5	W	55.5	U	
9/30/2017	vs	NORTH TEXAS	28	43	L	-7.5	L	56.5	O	
10/7/2017	@	Texas-San Antonio	31	29	W	10.5	W	49.5	O	
10/14/2017	vs	TEXAS-EL PASO	24	0	W	-22.5	W	52.0	U	
10/21/2017	@	Louisiana Tech	34	27	W	-1.0	W	55.5	O	{2 OT}
10/28/2017	vs	ALABAMA-BIRMINGHAM	12	30	L	-11.5	L	50.5	U	
11/4/2017	@	Tennessee	10	24	L	7.0	L	48.5	U	
11/11/2017	@	Rice	43	34	W	-10.5	L	49.0	O	
11/18/2017	vs	CHARLOTTE	66	21	W	-17.0	W	47.0	O	
11/25/2017	@	Marshall	28	27	W	PK	W	47.0	O	
12/27/2017	vs	Florida State	13	42	L	11.5	L	48.0	O	Independence Bowl
Coach: Jay Hopson		Season Record >>	379	318	8-5	ATS>>	8-5	O/U>>	7-5	

Copyright © 2021 by Steve's Football Bible, LLC

SOUTHERN MISS GOLDEN EAGLES   C-USA West

STADIUM: M.M Roberts Stadium {36,000}				Location: Hattiesburg, MS						COACH: Will Hall
DATE		Opponent	USM	Opp	S/U	Line	ATS	Total	O/U	Trends & Angles
9/4/2021	@	South Alabama								vs South Alabama - USA lead series 1-0
9/11/2021	vs	GRAMBLING STATE								1st meeting
9/18/2021	vs	TROY								8-1 S/U vs Troy since 1936
9/25/2021	@	Alabama								vs Alabama - Alabama leads series 37-5-2
10/2/2021	@	Rice								0-4 S/U & ATS vs Rice as Dog since 2008
10/9/2021	vs	TEXAS-EL PASO								5-0 S/U vs Texas-El Paso since 2015
10/16/2021	vs	ALABAMA-BRIMINGHAM								vs UAB - Southern Miss leads series 17-7
10/30/2021	@	Middle Tennessee								vs Middle Tennessee - MTSU leads series 3-0
11/6/2021	vs	NORTH TEXAS								vs North Texas - USM leads series 8-7
11/13/2021	@	Texas-San Antonio								vs UTSA - Southern Miss leads series 4-3
11/20/2021	@	Louisiana Tech								vs La Tech - Southern Miss leads series 36-16
11/27/2021	vs	FLA INTERNATIONAL								vs Florida International - FIU leads series 1-0
12/4/2021	vs									C-USA Championship
	vs									BOWL GAME

Pointspread Analysis Non-Conference		Pointspread Analysis Conference
1-34 S/U vs Non-Conf. as 15.5 point or more Dog since 1985		4-0 O/U vs Alabama-Birmingham as Dog since 2005
2-18 S/U vs Non-Conf. as 10.5-15 point Dog since 1992		1-5 S/U & ATS vs UAB as favorite since 2009
1-13 S/U vs Non-Conf. as 7.5-10 point Dog since 1983		3-1 O/U vs Rice as Dog since 2008
9-2 S/U vs Non-Conf. as 3.5-7 point favorite since 1995		6-0 S/U vs Rice as favorite since 2011
15-1 S/U vs Non-Conf. as 10.5 point or more favorite since 1985		6-1 O/U vs Rice as favorite since 2007
vs Troy - Southern Miss leads series 8-2		6-0 S/U vs Texas-El Paso as favorite since 2011
1-15 S/U vs Alabama as 7.5 point or more Dog since 1983		vs Texas-El Paso - Southern Miss leads series 8-4
Dog		Game 1-5 O/U vs Texas-El Paso since 2014
0-6 S/U @ home as 15.5 point or more Dog since 1987		7-1 S/U vs UAB as 9.5 point or less favorite since 2000
1-36 S/U on road as 15.5 point or more Dog since 1985		**Bowl Games**
3-10 ATS as 25.5 point or more Dog since 1988		4-1 S/U in New Orleans Bowl
10-1 O/U on road as 10.5-15 point Dog since 2005		0-5 S/U in Bowl Games as 7.5-15 point Dog since 2002
8-28 S/U as 10.5-15 point Dog since 1983		6-1 S/U in Bowl Games as 3.5-10 point favorite since 1999
1-6 S/U @ home as 7.5-10 point Dog since 2003		1-6 O/U in Bowl Games as 3.5-10 point favorite since 1999
1-10 O/U on road as 7.5-10 point Dog since 1998		0-3 O/U in Liberty Bowl since 1997
3-19 S/U as 3.5-7 point Dog since 2001		0-3 S/U in Citrus Bowl since 1957
11-4 O/U as 3.5-7 point Dog since 2006		
7-3-1 O/U as 3 point or less Dog since 2008		
Favorite	GRAMBLING	0-8 O/U in 1st home game of season since 2010
16-5 S/U as 3 point or less favorite since 2003	Alabama	6-2 ATS in 2nd road game of season since 2013
14-1 S/U @ home as 3 point or less favorite since 1988	UTEP	8-2 O/U prior to playing Alabama-Birmingham since 2008
14-6-1 ATS as 3 point or less favorite since 2003	UAB	7-0 O/U after playing Texas-El Paso since 2011
1-5 O/U @ home as 3 point or less favorite since 2007	Middle Tenn	1-13-1 O/U after playing Alabama-Birmingham since 2002
9-3 S/U on road as 3.5-7 point favorite since 2003	FIU	10-3 ATS in final home game of season since 2008
2-7 ATS @ home as 7.5-10 point favorite since 2010		
11-3 O/U @ home as 7.5-10 point favorite since 2008		
11-2 S/U on road as 7.5-10 point favorite since 1997		4-30 S/U on road vs ranked teams since 1992
12-1 S/U on road as 10.5-15 point favorite since 1996		1-11 S/U @ home vs ranked teams since 1987
10-2 ATS on road as 10.5-15 point favorite since 1997		3-22-1 S/U vs ranked Alabama all time
20-4 S/U @ home as 10.5-15 point favorite since 1994		
18-3 S/U @ home as 15.5-20 point favorite since 1984		
2-9 ATS as 15.5-20 point favorite since 2005		
22-1 S/U @ home as 20.5 point or more favorite since 1991		

Copyright © 2021 by Steve's Football Bible, LLC

STANFORD CARDINAL   PACIFIC-12 North

2020-Stanford		Opponent	Stan	Opp	S/U	Line	ATS	Total	O/U	
11/7/2020	@	Oregon	14	35	L	12.5	L	49.0	T	
11/14/2020	vs	COLORADO	32	35	L	-10.0	L	55.5	O	
11/28/2020	@	California	24	23	W	-2.0	L	51.0	U	"Big Game" (Stanford Axe)
12/5/2020	@	Washington	31	26	W	12.0	W	49.5	O	
12/12/2020	@	Oregon State	27	24	W	-2.0	W	55.5	U	
12/19/2020	@	Ucla	48	47	W	7.0	W	61.0	O	{2 OT}
Coach: David Shaw		Season Record >>	176	190	4-2	ATS>>	3-3	O/U>>	3-2-1	
2019-Stanford		Opponent	Stan	Opp	S/U	Line	ATS	Total	O/U	
8/31/2019	vs	NORTHWESTERN	17	7	W	-6.5	W	47.0	U	
9/7/2019	@	Usc	20	45	L	3.0	L	43.0	O	
9/14/2019	@	Central Florida	27	45	L	9.5	L	59.0	O	
9/21/2019	vs	OREGON	6	21	L	12.5	L	55.5	U	
9/28/2019	@	Oregon State	31	28	W	-3.0	T	55.5	O	
10/12/2019	vs	WASHINGTON	23	13	W	12.5	W	52.0	U	
10/17/2019	vs	UCLA	16	34	L	-4.0	L	48.5	O	
10/26/2019	vs	ARIZONA	41	31	W	-3.0	W	54.0	O	
11/9/2019	@	Colorado	13	16	L	-4.0	L	56.5	U	
11/16/2019	@	Washington State	22	49	L	11.0	L	66.0	O	
11/23/2019	vs	CALIFORNIA	20	24	L	1.0	L	41.5	O	"Big Game" (Stanford Axe)
11/30/2019	vs	NOTRE DAME	24	45	L	17.5	L	45.5	O	"Legends Trophy"
Coach: David Shaw		Season Record >>	260	358	4-8	ATS>>	3-8-1	O/U>>	8-4	
2018-Stanford		Opponent	Stan	Opp	S/U	Line	ATS	Total	O/U	
9/1/2018	vs	SAN DIEGO STATE	31	10	W	-13.5	W	49.5	U	
9/8/2018	vs	USC	17	3	W	-4.5	W	54.5	U	
9/15/2018	vs	CALIFORNIA-DAVIS	30	10	W	-30.5	L	NT	---	
9/22/2018	@	Oregon	38	31	W	-3.0	W	59.0	O	{OT}
9/29/2018	@	Notre Dame	17	38	L	5.0	L	54.0	O	"Legends Trophy"
10/6/2018	vs	UTAH	21	40	L	-4.0	L	45.0	O	
10/18/2018	@	Arizona State	20	13	W	-2.5	W	57.5	U	
10/27/2018	vs	WASHINGTON STATE	38	41	L	-2.5	L	55.0	O	
11/3/2018	@	Washington	23	27	L	9.5	W	44.0	U	
11/10/2018	vs	OREGON STATE	48	17	W	-24.0	W	60.5	O	
11/24/2018	@	Ucla	49	42	W	-7.0	T	60.5	O	
12/1/2018	@	California	23	13	W	-3.0	W	46.0	U	"Big Game" (Stanford Axe)
12/31/2018	vs	Pittsburgh	14	13	W	-3.0	L	52.5	U	Sun Bowl
Coach: David Shaw		Season Record >>	369	298	9-4	ATS>>	7-5-1	O/U>>	7-5	
2017-Stanford		Opponent	Stan	Opp	S/U	Line	ATS	Total	O/U	
8/26/2017	vs	Rice	62	7	W	-30.0	W	50.5	O	Allianz Stadium
9/9/2017	@	Usc	24	42	L	4.0	L	55.0	O	
9/16/2017	@	San Diego State	17	20	L	-8.5	L	47.5	U	
9/23/2017	vs	UCLA	58	34	W	-6.5	W	60.5	O	
9/30/2017	vs	ARIZONA STATE	34	24	W	-16.5	L	60.0	U	
10/7/2017	@	Utah	23	20	W	-3.0	T	51.5	U	
10/14/2017	vs	OREGON	49	7	W	-9.5	W	56.5	U	
10/26/2017	@	Oregon State	15	14	W	-17.0	L	56.0	U	
11/4/2017	@	Washington State	21	24	L	-1.0	L	55.0	U	
11/10/2017	vs	WASHINGTON	30	22	W	6.5	W	50.0	O	
11/18/2017	vs	CALIFORNIA	17	14	W	-14.0	L	56.0	U	"Big Game" (Stanford Axe)
11/25/2017	vs	NOTRE DAME	38	20	W	3.0	W	57.5	O	"Legends Trophy"
12/1/2017	vs	Usc	28	31	L	3.5	W	58.5	O	PAC-12 CHAMPIONSHIP
12/28/2017	vs	TCU	37	39	L	3.0	W	49.5	O	Alamo Bowl
Coach: David Shaw		Season Record >>	453	318	9-5	ATS>>	7-6-1	O/U>>	7-7	

Copyright © 2021 by Steve's Football Bible, LLC

STANFORD CARDINAL   PACIFIC-12 North

STADIUM: Stanford Stadium {50,424}		Location: Palo Alto, CA		COACH: David Shaw						
DATE		Opponent	Stan	Opp	S/U	Line	ATS	Total	O/U	Trends & Angles
9/4/2021	vs	*Kansas State {@ Arlington}*								vs Kansas State - Stanford leads series 1-0
9/11/2021	@	Usc								vs USC - USC leads series 64-33-3
9/18/2021	@	*Vanderbilt*								1st meeting
9/25/2021	vs	UCLA								6-1 S/U @ home vs UCLA since 2009
10/2/2021	vs	OREGON								vs Oregon - Stanford leads series 49-34-1
10/8/2021	@	Arizona State								vs Arizona State - ASU leads series 17-15
10/16/2021	@	Washington State								0-4 S/U vs Washington State since 2016
10/30/2021	vs	WASHINGTON								6-0 S/U @ home vs Washington since 2009 {5-1 ATS}
11/5/2021	vs	UTAH								0-4 S/U & ATS @ home vs Utah since 1989
11/13/2021	@	Oregon State								vs Oregon State - Stanford leads series 59-25-3
11/20/2021	vs	CALIFORNIA								10-0 S/U vs California as favorite since 2010
11/27/2021	vs	*NOTRE DAME*								vs Notre Dame - Notre Dame leads series 21-13
12/4/2021	vs									PAC-12 Championship
	vs									BOWL GAME

Pointspread Analysis Non-Conference		Pointspread Analysis Conference
3-12 S/U vs Non-Conf. as 10.5 point or more Dog since 1983		0-8 S/U vs Arizona State as 11 point or more Dog since 1983
0-6 S/U vs Non-Conf. as 7.5-10 point Dog since 1999		9-2 S/U vs Arizona State as 2 point or more favorite since 1988
0-7 S/U vs Non-Conf. as 3.5-7 point Dog since 2003		vs California - Stanford leads series 60-45-9
10-2 S/U vs Non-Conf. as 3.5-7 point favorite since 1999		2-6 O/U vs California as Dog since 2002
5-0 S/U vs Non-Conf. as 10.5-15 point favorite since 2003		1-7 S/U vs California as Dog since 2002
7-0 S/U & ATS vs Non-Conf. as 15.5-20 point favorite since 2001		2-8 S/U vs Oregon State as Dog since 1998
15-0 S/U vs Non-Conf. as 20.5 point or more favorite since 1992		11-0 S/U vs Oregon State as favorite since 1990
0-9 S/U vs Notre Dame as 5-11.5 point Dog since 1991		10-1 S/U vs UCLA as favorite since 2009
7-2 S/U vs Notre Dame as favorite since 1999 {2-7 ATS}		vs Ucla - UCLA leads series 46-43-3
2-12 S/U vs Notre Dame as 7.5 point or more Dog since 1988		12-1 S/U vs Ucla since 2009
6-1 O/U @ home vs Notre Dame as Dog since 1991		10-2-1 ATS vs Ucla since 2009
Dog		0-5 S/U vs UCLA as 14 point or more Dog since 1987
1-6 O/U as 20.5 point or more Dog since 2006		8-3 ATS vs USC as Dog since 2004
1-14 S/U as 20.5 point or more Dog since 1989		1-13 S/U vs USC as 13.5 point or more Dog since 1983
0-5 S/U @ home as 15.5-20 point Dog since 2002		Game 1-4 O/U vs Utah since 1996
5-0 O/U @ home as 15.5-20 point Dog since 2002		vs Utah - Utah leads series 5-4
3-14 S/U as 15.5-20 point Dog since 1983		vs Washington - Stanford leads series 44-43-4
4-13 S/U on road as 10.5-15 point Dog since 2000		7-1 S/U vs Washington as favorite since 2004
1-9-1 O/U @ home as 10.5-15 point Dog since 2000		10-3 S/U vs Washington since 2008
1-10 S/U on road as 7.5-10 point Dog since 2002		2-14 S/U vs Washington as 7 point or more Dog since 1983
2-13 S/U as 7.5-10 point Dog since 2002		vs Washington State - Stanford leads sereies 40-29-1
13-3 O/U as 3.5-7 point Dog since 2009		0-5 ATS vs Washington State since 2015
7-3 S/U on road as 3 point or less Dog since 1996		7-3 S/U @ Washington State since 2000
9-2 S/U on road as 3 point or less favorite since 2012		Game 2-8 O/U @ Washington State since 2000
Favorite		1-6 O/U vs Washington State as Dog since 2002
11-2 S/U on road as 3 point or less favorite since 2012		10-0 S/U vs Wash. State as 8 point or more favorite since 1986
9-3 ATS @ home as 3.5-7 point favorite since 2011	Kansas State	9-0 S/U & ATS prior to playing USC since 2011
10-2 S/U @ home as 3.5-7 point favorite since 2011	Vanderbilt	11-2 S/U prior to playing UCLA since 2008
2-10 O/U on road as 3.5-7 point favorite since 2010	Vanderbilt	2-12 O/U prior to playing UCLA since 2006
0-5 O/U on road as 7.5-10 point favorite since 2013	UCLA	13-0 S/U in 1st home game of season since 2008
0-5 ATS on road as 7.5-10 point favorite since 2013	UCLA	13-1 S/U prior to playing Oregon since 2004
14-0 S/U as 10.5-15 point favorite since 2003	OREGON	11-2 S/U in 2nd home game of season since 2007 {10-3 ATS}
12-2 ATS as 10.5-15 point favorite since 2003	OREGON	7-1 O/U prior to playing Arizona State since 2007
4-0 S/U on road as 10.5-15 point favorite since 1997	Wazzu	5-1 S/U after playing Arizona State since 2009
10-1 S/U on road as 15.5 point or more favorite since 1986	Wazzu	11-2 S/U prior to playing Washington since 2008
11-0 S/U @ home as 15.5-20 point favorite since 2002	WASHINGTON	0-6 ATS prior to playing Utah since 1989
29-0 S/U as 20.5 point or more favorite since 1990	UTAH	2-7 ATS after playing Washington since 2012
Bowl Games	UTAH	12-3 S/U prior to playing Oregon State since 2006 {15-2 ATS}
8-2 ATS in Bowl Games since 2009	Oregon State	5-0 S/U after playing Utah since 1996
4-1 S/U in Sun Bowl	Oregon State	11-4-1 ATS prior to playing California since 2003
5-0 ATS in Bowl Games as 3.5-15 point Dog since 1996	Oregon State	9-3 S/U & ATS in final road game of season since 2009
3-0 S/U & ATS in Bowl Games as 3.5-7 point favorite since 2011	CALIFORNIA	8-2 S/U prior to playing Notre Dame since 2010
9-2 S/U in final home game of season since 2009	NOTRE DAME	10-1 S/U after playing California since 2009

Copyright © 2021 by Steve's Football Bible, LLC

2020-Syracuse		Opponent	Cuse	Opp	S/U	Line	ATS	Total	O/U	
9/12/2020	@	North Carolina	6	31	L	23.0	L	65.5	U	
9/19/2020	@	Pittsburgh	10	21	L	21.0	W	49.0	U	
9/26/2020	vs	GEORGIA TECH	37	20	W	7.0	W	51.5	O	
10/10/2020	vs	DUKE	24	38	L	2.5	L	51.5	O	
10/17/2020	vs	LIBERTY	21	38	L	3.0	L	52.5	O	
10/24/2020	@	Clemson	21	47	L	46.5	W	64.5	O	
10/31/2020	vs	WAKE FOREST	14	38	L	14.0	L	59.5	U	
11/7/2020	vs	BOSTON COLLEGE	13	16	L	15.0	W	53.5	U	
11/20/2020	@	Louisville	0	30	L	19.5	L	56.0	U	
11/28/2020	vs	NC STATE	29	36	L	17.5	W	49.5	O	
12/5/2020	@	Notre Dame	21	45	L	35.0	W	51.0	O	
Coach: Dino Babers		Season Record >>	196	360	1-10	ATS>>	6-5	O/U>>	6-5	

2019-Syracuse		Opponent	Cuse	Opp	S/U	Line	ATS	Total	O/U	
8/31/2019	@	Liberty	24	0	W	-19.5	W	68.0	U	
9/7/2019	@	Maryland	20	63	L	1.0	L	58.5	O	
9/14/2019	vs	CLEMSON	6	41	L	28.0	L	64.5	U	
9/21/2019	vs	WESTERN MICHIGAN	52	33	W	-3.5	W	66.5	O	
9/28/2019	vs	HOLY CROSS	41	3	W	-41.5	L	NT	---	
10/10/2019	@	NC State	10	16	L	4.0	L	55.5	U	
10/18/2019	vs	PITTSBURGH	20	27	L	3.5	L	53.5	U	
10/26/2019	@	Florida State	17	35	L	12.0	L	59.5	U	
11/2/2019	vs	BOSTON COLLEGE	27	58	L	-3.0	L	59.0	O	
11/16/2019	@	Duke	49	6	W	9.0	W	49.0	O	
11/23/2019	@	Louisville	34	56	L	7.5	L	65.0	O	
11/30/2019	vs	WAKE FOREST	39	30	W	6.5	W	66.5	O	{OT}
Coach: Dino Babers		Season Record >>	339	368	5-7	ATS>>	4-8	O/U>>	6-5	

2018-Syracuse		Opponent	Cuse	Opp	S/U	Line	ATS	Total	O/U	
9/1/2018	@	Western Michigan	55	42	W	-5.0	W	66.0	O	
9/8/2018	vs	WAGNER	62	10	W	-45.0	W	NT	---	
9/15/2018	vs	FLORIDA STATE	30	7	W	3.0	W	69.5	U	
9/22/2018	vs	CONNECTICUT	51	21	W	-30.5	L	75.5	U	
9/29/2018	@	Clemson	23	27	L	24.5	W	64.5	U	
10/6/2018	@	Pittsburgh	37	44	L	-3.0	L	58.5	O	{OT}
10/20/2018	vs	NORTH CAROLINA	40	37	W	-10.0	L	67.0	O	{2 OT}
10/27/2018	vs	NC STATE	51	41	W	2.0	W	64.5	O	
11/3/2018	@	Wake Forest	41	24	W	-6.5	W	77.5	U	
11/9/2018	vs	LOUISVILLE	54	23	W	-20.5	W	69.0	O	
11/17/2018	vs	Notre Dame	3	36	L	10.0	L	64.5	U	Yankee Stadium
11/24/2018	@	Boston College	42	21	W	6.0	W	60.5	O	
12/28/2018	vs	West Virginia	34	18	W	-3.0	W	67.0	U	Camping World Bowl
Coach: Dino Babers		Season Record >>	523	351	10-3	ATS>>	9-4	O/U>>	6-6	

2017-Syracuse		Opponent	Cuse	Opp	S/U	Line	ATS	Total	O/U	
9/1/2017	vs	CENTRAL CONNECTICUT	50	7	W	-46.0	L	70.5	O	
9/9/2017	vs	MIDDLE TENNESSEE	23	30	L	-7.5	L	72.0	U	
9/16/2017	vs	CENTRAL MICHIGAN	41	17	W	-8.5	W	66.5	U	
9/23/2017	@	Lsu	26	35	L	21.0	W	56.5	O	
9/30/2017	@	NC State	25	33	L	14.0	W	61.0	U	
10/7/2017	vs	PITTSBURGH	27	24	W	-3.0	T	64.0	U	
10/13/2017	vs	CLEMSON	27	24	W	23.5	W	58.0	U	
10/21/2017	@	Miami	19	27	L	17.0	W	61.0	U	
11/4/2017	@	Florida State	24	27	L	7.5	W	50.5	O	
11/11/2017	vs	WAKE FOREST	43	64	L	2.5	L	66.0	O	
11/18/2017	@	Louisville	10	56	L	14.5	L	69.5	U	
11/25/2017	vs	BOSTON COLLEGE	14	42	L	4.0	L	56.5	U	
Coach: Dino Babers		Season Record >>	329	386	4-8	ATS>>	6-5-1	O/U>>	3-9	

Copyright © 2021 by Steve's Football Bible, LLC

SYRACUSE ORANGEMEN   ACC Atlantic

STADIUM: Carrier Dome {49,262}			Location: Syracuse, NY						COACH: Dino Babers	
DATE		Opponent	Cuse	Opp	S/U	Line	ATS	Total	O/U	Trends & Angles
9/4/2021	@	*Ohio*								vs Ohio - Syracuse leads series 2-0
9/11/2021	vs	*RUTGERS*								1-4 S/U vs Rutgers as Dog since 2007
9/18/2021	vs	*SUNY-ALBANY*								1st meeting
9/25/2021	vs	*LIBERTY*								vs Liberty - Series tied 1-1
10/2/2021	@	Florida State								vs Florida State - Florida State leads series 11-2
10/9/2021	vs	WAKE FOREST								5-0 S/U & ATS vs Wake as favorite since 2011
10/15/2021	vs	CLEMSON								vs Clemson - Clemson leads series 7-2
10/23/2021	@	Virginia Tech								1-5 S/U @ Virginia Tech since 1993 {1-5 ATS}
10/30/2021	vs	BOSTON COLLEGE								vs Boston College - Syracuse leads series 32-21
11/13/2021	@	Louisville								0-6 S/U & ATS vs Louisville as Dog since 2014
11/20/2021	@	NC State								3-1 ATS @ NC State as Dog since 2013
11/27/2021	vs	PITTSBURGH								0-15 S/U vs Pittsburgh as Dog since 1989
12/4/2021	vs									ACC Championship
	vs									BOWL GAME

Pointspread Analysis Non-Conference		Pointspread Analysis Conference
2-25 S/U vs Non-Conf. as 10.5 point or more Dog since 1983		12-4 S/U vs Boston College as favorite since 1985
6-2 ATS vs Non-Conf. as 7.5-10 point Dog since 1991		0-10 S/U vs Florida State as 5 point or more Dog since 1989
11-4 ATS vs Non-Conf. as 3.5-7 point Dog since 1987		vs Louisville - Louisville leads series 11-8
10-2 ATS vs Non-Conf. as 3.5-7 point favorite since 1995		vs NC State - NC State leads series 12-2
14-3 S/U vs Non-Conf. as 10.5-15 point favorite since 1984		0-4 S/U vs NC State as favorite since 1997 {1-3 ATS}
26-1 S/U vs Non-Conf. as 15.5 point or more favorite since 1987		vs Pittsburgh - Pittsburgh leads series 41-23-2
11-1 S/U vs Rutgers as 10 point or more favorite since 1985		17-2-1 S/U vs Pittsburgh as favorite since 1984
Dog		0-8 S/U vs Pittsburgh as 10 point or more Dog since 1983
1-14 S/U as 25.5 point or more Dog since 2004		14-0 S/U vs Pittsburgh as 3.5 point or more favorite since 1984
9-3 O/U as 25.5 point or more Dog since 2006		5-0 S/U vs Virginia Tech as favorite since 1987
8-2 ATS as 20.5-25 point Dog since 2012		vs Virginia Tech - Syracuse leads series 10-8
0-13 S/U on road as 20.5-25 point Dog since 1983		vs VPI - HOME team 12-2 S/U since 1988
1-11 S/U on road as 15.5-20 point Dog since 2003		vs Wake Forest - Syracuse leads series 6-4
0-8 S/U @ home as 15.5-20 point Dog since 2004		1-4 S/U vs Wake Forest as Dog since 2006
7-2 O/U as 15.5-20 point Dog since 2011		**Bowl Games**
2-6 O/U @ home as 15.5-20 point Dog since 2004		0-3 S/U in Orange Bowl
1-13 S/U on road as 10.5-15 point Dog since 2005		4-0 S/U & ATS in Bowl Games as 3 point or less favorite since 1989
0-10 S/U as 10.5-15 point Dog since 2013		
1-10 S/U as 7.5-10 point Dog since 2011		
2-8 S/U on road as 7.5-10 point Dog since 2002	RUTGERS	9-3 O/U in 1st home game of season since 2007
1-8 S/U @ home as 7.5-10 point Dog since 1994	RUTGERS	7-1 S/U in 1st home game of season since 2013
2-8 S/U @ home as 3.5-7 point Dog since 2006	LIBERTY	1-5 S/U prior to playing Florida State since 2014
4-10 O/U as 3.5-7 point Dog since 2012	LIBERTY	0-6 O/U prior to playing Florida State since 2013
Favorite	LIBERTY	8-0 O/U prior to playing Wake Forest since 2013
1-8-2 ATS as 3 point or less favorite since 2011	WAKE FOREST	2-9 ATS after playing Florida State since 1989
5-12-1 O/U as 3 point or less favorite since 2005	CLEMSON	2-6 O/U after playing Wake Forest since 2006
9-0 S/U & ATS as 3.5-7 point favorite since 2011	Virginia Tech	1-6 S/U after playing Clemson since 2014
2-8 O/U on road as 3.5-7 point favorite since 1996	Virginia Tech	1-9 S/U prior to playing Boston College since 2003
8-2 S/U @ home as 7.5-10 point favorite since 1994	NC State	0-10 S/U prior to playing Pittsburgh since 2011
10-2 S/U on road as 7.5-10 point favorite since 1985	NC State	1-7 S/U in final road game of season since 2013
9-0 S/U @ home as 10.5-15 point favorite since 1992	PITTSBURGH	1-6 O/U after playing NC State since 2014
9-0 S/U as 10.5-15 point favorite since 1998		
13-2 S/U on road as 10.5-15 point favorite since 1984		0-5 S/U @ home vs #1 ranked teams since 1992
20-2 S/U as 15.5-20 point favorite since 1988		1-13 S/U vs #2 ranked teams all time {0-6 on road}
8-0 S/U on road as 15.5 point or more favorite since 1991		7-0 S/U @ home when ranked since 1998
16-1 S/U as 20.5-25 point favorite since 1991		4-0 S/U when ranked vs Boston College since 1995
18-0 S/U @ home as 25.5 point or more favorite since 1987		7-0 S/U when ranked vs Pittsburgh since 1991
23-1 S/U as 25.5 point or more favorite since 1987		5-0 S/U @ home when ranked vs Pittsburgh since 1968

Copyright © 2021 by Steve's Football Bible, LLC

TEXAS CHRISTIAN HORNED FROGS   BIG TWELVE

2020-Texas Christian		Opponent	TCU	Opp	S/U	Line	ATS	Total	O/U	
9/26/2020	vs	IOWA STATE	34	37	L	3.0	T	44.0	O	
10/3/2020	@	Texas	33	31	W	10.5	W	61.5	O	
10/10/2020	vs	KANSAS STATE	14	21	L	-11.0	L	50.0	U	
10/24/2020	vs	OKLAHOMA	14	33	L	6.5	L	58.5	U	
10/31/2020	@	Baylor	33	23	W	-2.5	W	47.5	O	
11/7/2020	vs	TEXAS TECH	34	18	W	-9.5	W	60.0	U	"Saddle Trophy"
11/14/2020	@	West Virginia	6	24	L	3.0	L	44.0	U	
11/28/2020	@	Kansas	59	23	W	-23.0	W	51.0	O	
12/5/2020	vs	OKLAHOMA STATE	29	22	W	2.5	W	53.0	U	
12/12/2020	vs	LOUISIANA TECH	52	10	W	-21.5	W	50.5	O	
Coach: Gary Patterson		Season Record >>	308	242	6-4	ATS>>	6-3-1	O/U>>	4-6	
2019-Texas Christian		Opponent	TCU	Opp	S/U	Line	ATS	Total	O/U	
8/31/2019	vs	*ARKANSAS-PINE BLUFF*	39	7	W	-53.5	L	NT	---	
9/14/2019	@	*Purdue*	34	13	W	-3.5	W	52.5	U	
9/21/2019	vs	*SMU*	38	41	L	-7.5	L	54.0	O	"Iron Skillet"
9/28/2019	vs	KANSAS	51	14	W	-14.5	W	48.0	O	
10/5/2019	@	Iowa State	24	49	L	3.5	L	46.5	O	
10/19/2019	@	Kansas State	17	24	L	-4.5	L	44.0	U	
10/26/2019	vs	TEXAS	37	27	W	-1.0	W	56.5	O	
11/2/2019	@	Oklahoma State	27	34	L	1.5	L	59.0	O	
11/9/2019	vs	BAYLOR	23	29	L	2.0	L	48.5	O	{3 OT}
11/16/2019	@	Texas Tech	33	31	W	-3.5	L	53.5	O	"Saddle Trophy"
11/23/2019	@	Oklahoma	24	28	L	18.5	W	64.5	U	
11/30/2019	vs	WEST VIRGINIA	17	20	L	-14.0	L	44.0	U	
Coach: Gary Patterson		Season Record >>	364	317	5-7	ATS>>	4-8	O/U>>	7-4	
2018-Texas Christian		Opponent	TCU	Opp	S/U	Line	ATS	Total	O/U	
9/1/2018	vs	*SOUTHERN U*	55	7	W	-50.0	L	NT	---	
9/8/2018	@	*Smu*	42	12	W	-23.5	W	59.0	U	"Iron Skillet"
9/15/2018	vs	*Ohio State*	28	40	L	12.5	W	58.5	O	
9/22/2018	@	Texas	16	31	L	-2.5	L	50.0	U	
9/29/2018	vs	IOWA STATE	17	14	W	-11.0	L	45.0	U	
10/11/2018	vs	TEXAS TECH	14	17	L	-7.0	L	57.5	U	"Saddle Trophy"
10/20/2018	vs	OKLAHOMA	27	52	L	7.5	L	61.5	O	
10/27/2018	@	Kansas	26	27	L	-13.5	L	47.0	O	
11/3/2018	vs	KANSAS STATE	14	13	W	-10.0	L	44.0	U	
11/10/2018	@	West Virginia	10	47	L	12.0	L	56.0	O	
11/17/2018	@	Baylor	16	9	W	1.0	W	50.0	U	
11/24/2018	vs	OKLAHOMA STATE	31	24	W	5.5	W	54.0	O	
12/26/2018	vs	**California**	10	7	W	-2.5	W	38.0	U	**Cheez-it Bowl**
Coach: Gary Patterson		Season Record >>	306	300	7-6	ATS>>	5-8	O/U>>	5-7	
2017-Texas Christian		Opponent	TCU	Opp	S/U	Line	ATS	Total	O/U	
9/2/2017	vs	*JACKSON STATE*	63	0	W	-59.0	W	NL	---	
9/9/2017	@	*Arkansas*	28	7	W	-2.5	W	57.0	U	
9/16/2017	vs	*SMU*	56	36	W	-22.5	L	65.0	O	"Iron Skillet"
9/23/2017	@	Oklahoma State	44	31	W	9.5	W	67.5	O	
10/7/2017	vs	WEST VIRGINIA	31	24	W	-12.0	L	68.0	U	
10/14/2017	@	Kansas State	26	6	W	-7.5	W	49.0	U	
10/21/2017	vs	KANSAS	43	0	W	-36.0	W	60.0	U	
10/28/2017	@	Iowa State	7	14	L	-6.5	L	48.0	U	
11/4/2017	vs	TEXAS	24	7	W	-7.5	W	44.0	U	
11/11/2017	@	Oklahoma	20	38	L	6.0	L	63.5	U	
11/18/2017	@	Texas Tech	27	3	W	-6.5	W	52.0	U	"Saddle Trophy"
11/25/2017	vs	BAYLOR	45	22	W	-24.5	L	52.0	O	
12/2/2017	vs	**Oklahoma**	17	41	L	7.5	L	64.0	U	**Big 12 Championship**
12/28/2017	vs	**Stanford**	39	37	W	-3.0	L	49.5	O	**Alamo Bowl**
Coach: Gary Patterson		Season Record >>	470	266	11-3	ATS>>	7-7	O/U>>	4-9	

Copyright © 2021 by Steve's Football Bible, LLC

TEXAS CHRISTIAN HORNED FROGS   BIG TWELVE

STADIUM: Amon Carter Stadium {45,000}		Location: Fort Worth, TX				COACH: Gary Patterson		
DATE		Opponent	TCU	Opp	S/U	Line	ATS	Total	O/U	Trends & Angles

DATE		Opponent	TCU	Opp	S/U	Line	ATS	Total	O/U	Trends & Angles
9/4/2021	vs	DUQUESNE								1st meeting
9/11/2021	vs	CALIFORNIA								vs California - TCU leads series 1-0
9/25/2021	vs	SMU								19-3 S/U vs SMU as favorite since 1994
10/2/2021	vs	TEXAS								3-0 S/U @ home vs Texas since 2015 {3-0 ATS}
10/9/2021	@	Texas Tech								3-0 S/U @ Texas Tech since 2015
10/16/2021	@	Oklahoma								1-10 S/U vs Oklahoma as Dog since 2008
10/23/2021	vs	WEST VIRGINIA								vs West Virginia - WVU leads series 6-4
10/30/2021	@	Kansas State								vs Kansas State - Series tied 7-7
11/6/2021	vs	BAYLOR								vs Baylor - TCU leads series 57-50-7
11/13/2021	@	Oklahoma State								vs OK State – OK State leads series 16-13-2
11/20/2021	vs	KANSAS								vs Kansas - TCU leads series 24-9-4
11/27/2021	@	Iowa State								vs Iowa State - TCU leads series 8-4
12/4/2021	vs									BIG XII Championship
	vs									BOWL GAME

Pointspread Analysis

Non-Conference		Conference
2-12 S/U vs Non-Conf. as 10.5 point or more Dog since 1988		7-1 ATS vs Baylor as Dog since 1995
2-6-2 ATS vs Non-Conf. as 3 point or less favorite since 1983		1-8 S/U vs Baylor as 7.5 point or more Dog since 1983
10-2 S/U vs Non-Conf. as 3.5-7 point favorite since 1990		0-3 O/U @ Iowa State as favorite since 2013
1-7 ATS vs Non-Conf. as 7.5-10 point favorite since 1993		0-3 S/U vs Kansas as Dog since 1995
44-1-1 S/U vs Non-Conf. as 10.5 point or more favorite since 1985		8-1 S/U vs Kansas as favorite since 2012 {2-6 ATS}
vs SMU - TCU leads series 51-40-7		0-3 S/U vs Kansas State as Dog since 1983
1-6 S/U vs SMU as Dog since 1983		7-3 S/U vs Kansas State as favorite since 1984
16-0 S/U vs SMU as 15 point or more favorite since 1989		vs Oklahoma - Oklahoma leads series 16-5
17-3 S/U vs SMU since 1999		vs Texas - Texas leads series 63-27-1
Dog		6-1 S/U & ATS vs Texas since 2014
2-15 S/U as 20.5 point or more Dog since 1985		2-7 S/U vs Texas as 8.5 point or more Dog since 1985
1-12 S/U on road as 15.5-20 point Dog since 1986		vs Texas Tech - Texas Tech leads series 38-29-3
0-5 S/U & ATS @ home as 15.5-20 point Dog since 1985		2-9 ATS @ Texas Tech since 1985
4-15 S/U on road as 10.5-15 point Dog since 1986		1-4 S/U vs Texas Tech as 4 point or less favorite since 1987
3-9 S/U @ home as 3.5-7 point Dog since 1996		0-5 ATS vs Texas Tech as 4 point or less favorite since 1987
5-2 S/U & ATS @ home as 3 point or less Dog since 2004		0-4 S/U & ATS vs Texas Tech as 4 point or less favorite since 1987
Favorite		0-5 ATS vs West Virginia since 2016
23-4 S/U on road as 3.5-7 point favorite since 1995		Game 1-6 O/U vs West Virginia since 2014
3-11 O/U as 7.5-10 point favorite since 2007		3-1 S/U vs West Virginia as favorite since 2014
2-7 ATS on road as 7.5-10 point favorite since 1994	DUQUESNE	18-1 S/U in 1st home game of season since 2002
14-6 S/U as 10.5-15 point favorite since 2006	DUQUESNE	6-0 O/U in 1st home game of season since 2010
8-3 S/U on road as 10.5-15 point favorite since 1985	CALIFORNIA	11-1 S/U prior to playing SMU since 2008
22-0 S/U as 15.5-20 point favorite since 1995	CALIFORNIA	20-3 S/U in 2nd home game of season since 1998
0-6 O/U as 15.5-20 point favorite since 2010	CALIFORNIA	9-4 O/U in 2nd home game of seaosn since 2008
66-0 S/U as 20.5 point or more favorite since 1986	SMU	1-7-1 ATS prior to playing Texas since 2012
8-1 ATS on road as 20.5-25 point favorite since 2000	TEXAS	6-0 O/U after playing SMU since 2014
Bowl Games	Texas Tech	11-2 S/U in 1st road game of seaosn since 2008
1-6 S/U vs SEC in Bowl Games since 1942	Texas Tech	8-2 S/U prior to playing Oklahoma since 2008
0-3 O/U in Bowl Games as 3.5-7 point Dog since 1999	Texas Tech	3-11 S/U after playing Texas since 1992
1-5 ATS in Bowl Games as 3 point or less favorite since 2008	Texas Tech	1-12 ATS after playing Texas since 1993
	W. VIRGINIA	9-2 S/U prior to playing Kansas State since 1985
	OK State	8-2 O/U after playing Baylor since 2007
	Iowa State	2-7 O/U after playing Kansas since 2012
	Iowa State	12-4 S/U in final road game of season since 2005
	Iowa State	12-0 ATS in final road game of season since 2009

Copyright © 2021 by Steve's Football Bible, LLC

TEMPLE OWLS

AMERICAN East

2020-Temple		Opponent	Temp	Opp	S/U	Line	ATS	Total	O/U	
10/10/2020	@	Navy	29	31	L	-4.0	L	51.0	O	
10/17/2020	vs	SOUTH FLORIDA	39	37	W	-10.5	L	54.0	O	
10/24/2020	@	Memphis	29	41	L	14.0	W	70.5	U	
10/31/2020	@	Tulane	3	38	L	7.0	L	56.0	U	
11/7/2020	vs	SMU	23	47	L	17.0	L	63.5	O	
11/14/2020	@	Central Florida	13	38	L	29.0	W	71.5	U	
11/21/2020	vs	EAST CAROLINA	3	28	L	7.0	L	53.0	U	
Coach: Rod Carey		Season Record >>	139	260	1-6	ATS>>	2-5	O/U>>	3-4	
2019-Temple		Opponent	Temp	Opp	S/U	Line	ATS	Total	O/U	
8/31/2019	vs	*BUCKNELL*	56	12	W	-39.0	W	NT	---	"The Old Shoes Trophy"
9/14/2019	vs	*MARYLAND*	20	17	W	5.5	W	66.0	U	
9/21/2019	@	*Buffalo*	22	38	L	-14.0	L	51.0	O	
9/28/2019	vs	*GEORGIA TECH*	24	3	W	-9.5	W	48.0	U	
10/3/2019	@	East Carolina	27	17	W	-12.5	L	46.5	U	
10/12/2019	vs	MEMPHIS	30	28	W	4.0	W	50.0	O	
10/19/2019	@	Smu	21	45	L	9.5	L	60.0	O	
10/26/2019	vs	CENTRAL FLORIDA	21	63	L	10.5	L	61.0	O	
11/7/2019	@	South Florida	17	7	W	PK	W	50.5	U	
11/16/2019	vs	TULANE	29	21	W	6.5	W	52.5	U	
11/23/2019	@	Cincinnati	13	15	L	8.5	W	45.5	U	
11/30/2019	vs	CONNECTICUT	49	17	W	-27.0	W	48.0	O	
12/27/2019	vs	**North Carolina**	13	55	L	6.5	L	56.5	O	**Military Bowl**
Coach: Rod Carey		Season Record >>	342	338	8-5	ATS>>	8-5	O/U>>	6-6	
2018-Temple		Opponent	Temp	Opp	S/U	Line	ATS	Total	O/U	
9/1/2018	vs	*VILLANOVA*	17	19	L	-15.0	L	NT	---	"Mayor's Cup"
9/8/2018	vs	*BUFFALO*	26	36	L	-4.0	L	52.0	O	
9/15/2018	@	*Maryland*	35	14	W	15.0	W	55.5	U	
9/20/2018	vs	*TULSA*	31	17	W	-6.0	W	54.0	U	
9/29/2018	@	*Boston College*	35	45	L	11.5	W	54.0	O	
10/6/2018	vs	EAST CAROLINA	49	6	W	-10.5	W	52.0	O	
10/13/2018	@	Navy	24	17	W	-6.5	W	49.0	U	
10/20/2018	vs	CINCINNATI	24	17	W	-2.5	W	47.0	U	{OT}
11/1/2018	@	Central Florida	40	52	L	10.0	L	60.0	O	
11/10/2018	@	Houston	59	49	W	3.5	W	69.5	O	
11/17/2018	vs	SOUTH FLORIDA	27	17	W	-14.0	L	62.5	U	
11/24/2018	@	Connecticut	57	7	W	-31.0	W	69.0	U	
12/27/2018	vs	**Duke**	27	56	L	-3.5	L	56.5	O	**Independence Bowl**
Coach: Geoff Collins		Season Record >>	451	352	8-5	ATS>>	8-5	O/U>>	6-6	
2017-Temple		Opponent	Temp	Opp	S/U	Line	ATS	Total	O/U	
9/2/2017	@	*Notre Dame*	16	49	L	19.5	L	56.0	O	
9/9/2017	vs	*VILLANOVA*	16	13	W	-17.0	L	NT	---	"Mayor's Cup"
9/15/2017	vs	*MASSACHUSETTS*	29	21	W	-14.0	L	52.0	U	
9/21/2017	@	South Florida	7	43	L	17.5	L	61.5	U	
9/30/2017	vs	HOUSTON	13	20	L	10.5	W	44.0	U	
10/7/2017	@	East Carolina	34	10	W	-3.5	W	58.5	U	
10/14/2017	vs	CONNECTICUT	24	28	L	-10.5	L	57.5	U	
10/21/2017	@	*Army*	28	31	L	7.0	W	47.0	O	
11/3/2017	vs	NAVY	34	26	W	5.5	W	51.0	O	
11/10/2017	@	Cincinnati	35	24	W	-3.0	W	49.5	O	
11/18/2017	vs	CENTRAL FLORIDA	19	45	L	12.0	L	58.5	O	
11/25/2017	@	Tulsa	43	22	W	-4.5	W	57.0	O	
12/21/2017	vs	**Florida International**	28	3	W	-7.0	W	56.5	U	**Gasparilla Bowl**
Coach: Geoff Collins		Season Record >>	326	335	7-6	ATS>>	7-6	O/U>>	6-6	

Copyright © 2021 by Steve's Football Bible, LLC

TEMPLE OWLS AMERICAN East

STADIUM: Lincoln Financial Field {69,176}				Location: Philadelphia, PA					COACH: Rod Carey	
DATE		Opponent	Tem	Opp	S/U	Line	ATS	Total	O/U	Trends & Angles
9/4/2021	@	*Rutgers*								0-8 S/U vs Rutgers as Dog since 1991
9/11/2021	@	*Akron*								vs Akron - Temple leads series 13-6
9/18/2021	vs	*BOSTON COLLEGE*								vs Boston College - BC leads series 29-7-2
9/25/2021	vs	*WAGNER*								1st meeting
10/2/2021	vs	**MEMPHIS**								6-0 ATS vs Memphis as Dog since 2013
10/8/2021	@	Cincinnati								1-6 S/U vs Cincinnati as Dog since 2002
10/23/2021	@	South Florida								vs South Florida - Temple leads series 5-2
10/30/2021	vs	**CENTRAL FLORIDA**								vs Central Florida - UCF leads series 6-2
11/4/2021	@	East Carolina								vs East Carolina - Temple leads series 10-8
11/13/2021	vs	**HOUSTON**								1-6 S/U vs Houston as Dog since 1987
11/20/2021	@	Tulsa								3-0 S/U vs Tulsa since 2014
11/27/2021	vs	**NAVY**								vs Navy - Temple leads series 9-6
12/4/2021	vs									AAC Championship
	vs									BOWL GAME

Pointspread Analysis Non-Conference		Pointspread Analysis Conference
0-46 S/U vs Non-Conf. as 15.5 point or more Dog since 1983		1-6 S/U vs Central Florida as Dog since 2013
2-8 S/U vs Non-Conf. as 7.5-10 point Dog since 1985		vs Cincinnati - Temple leads series 13-8-1
14-4 S/U vs Non-Conf. as 10.5 point or more favorite since 1987		5-0 S/U vs Cincinnati as favorite since 1984
7-0 S/U vs Rutgers as 6 point or more favorite since 1985		5-0 S/U vs East Carolina as favorite since 1990
0-7 S/U vs Boston College as 14.5 point or more Dog since 1984		4-1 ATS vs East Carolina as favorite since 1990
0-6 S/U vs ranked Boston College all time		vs Memphis - Series tied 3-3
Dog		4-1 S/U vs Navy as favorite since 1988
1-32 S/U as 30.5 point or more Dog since 1989		0-4 S/U vs Navy as 12.5 point or more Dog since 1997
11-4 O/U as 30.5 point or more Dog since 2002		vs Tulsa - Tulsa leads series tied 3-2
0-28 S/U as 25.5-30 point Dog since 1989		3-0 S/U vs Tulsa as favorite since 2014
0-6 O/U as 25.5-30 point Dog since 2007		**Bowl Games**
0-22 S/U @ home as 20.5 point or more Dog since 1989		3-6 S/U in Bowl games
0-29 S/U as 20.5-25 point Dog since 1987		
7-1 ATS as 20.5-25 point Dog since 2003	Rutgers	10-4 ATS in 1st road game of season since 2007
2-31 S/U as 15.5-20 point Dog since 1983	Akron	2-12 S/U after playing Boston College since 1989
9-2 O/U as 15.5-20 point Dog since 2002	South Florida	9-3 S/U after playing Cincinnati since 1984
0-8 S/U @ home as 10.5-15 point Dog since 2002	UCF	10-2 ATS prior to playing East Carolina since 1988
3-11 S/U on road as 10.5-15 point Dog since 2000	HOUSTON	9-1 ATS after playing East Carolina since 1988
13-2-1 ATS on road as 10.5-15 point Dog since 1998	Tulsa	6-1 O/U after playing Navy since 2007
3-17 S/U on road as 7.5-10 point Dog since 1985		
2-11 S/U @ home as 7.5-10 point Dog since 1995		
14-3-1 ATS @ home as 3.5-7 point Dog since 2005		
0-6 O/U as 3 point or less Dog since 2010		
1-6-1 ATS @ home as 3 point or less Dog since 1985		
1-8 S/U @ home as 3 point or less Dog since 1985		
Favorite		
14-5 S/U as 3.5-7 point favorite since 2008		
13-5-1 ATS as 3.5-7 point favorite since 2008		
0-5 O/U on road as 7.5-10 point favorite since 2002		4-63-1 S/U on road vs ranked teams all time
5-1 S/U on road as 7.5-10 point favorite since 1993		5-45 S/U @ home vs ranked teams all time
16-3 S/U @ home as 10.5-15 point favorite since 1999		0-40 S/U vs Top #1 - #9 ranked teams all time
22-1 S/U as 15.5 point or more favorite since 1986		0-10 S/U vs #11 #12 ranked teams all time

Copyright © 2021 by Steve's Football Bible, LLC

TENNESSEE VOLUNTEERS   SEC East

2020-Tennessee		Opponent	Tenn	Opp	S/U	Line	ATS	Total	O/U	
9/26/2020	@	South Carolina	31	27	W	-4.0	T	44.5	O	
10/3/2020	vs	MISSOURI	35	12	W	-10.0	W	48.5	U	
10/10/2020	@	Georgia	21	44	L	12.0	L	43.5	O	
10/17/2020	vs	KENTUCKY	7	34	L	-6.0	L	45.5	U	
10/24/2020	vs	ALABAMA	17	48	L	22.0	L	66.5	U	Third Saturday in October Rivalry
11/7/2020	@	Arkansas	13	24	L	-2.5	L	54.5	U	
11/21/2020	@	Auburn	17	30	L	10.0	L	51.0	U	
12/5/2020	vs	FLORIDA	19	31	L	18.5	W	63.0	U	
12/12/2020	@	Vanderbilt	42	17	W	-15.0	W	51.0	O	
12/19/2020	vs	TEXAS A&M	13	34	L	13.5	L	50.0	U	
Coach: Jeremy Pruitt		Season Record >>	215	301	3-7	ATS>>	3-6-1	O/U>>	3-7	
2019-Tennessee		Opponent	Tenn	Opp	S/U	Line	ATS	Total	O/U	
8/31/2019	vs	GEORGIA STATE	30	38	L	-24.5	L	58.0	O	
9/7/2019	vs	BYU	26	29	L	-3.5	L	52.5	O	{2 OT}
9/14/2019	vs	TENNESSEE-CHATT	45	0	W	-30.0	W	NT	---	
9/21/2019	@	Florida	3	34	L	14.0	L	48.5	U	
10/5/2019	vs	GEORGIA	14	43	L	24.0	L	51.0	O	
10/12/2019	vs	MISSISSIPPI STATE	20	10	W	5.0	W	52.0	U	
10/19/2019	@	Alabama	13	35	L	34.5	W	62.5	U	Third Saturday in October Rivalry
10/26/2019	vs	SOUTH CAROLINA	41	21	W	4.0	W	47.0	O	
11/2/2019	vs	ALABAMA-BIRMINGHAM	30	7	W	-13.5	W	49.0	U	
11/9/2019	@	Kentucky	17	13	W	PK	W	42.0	U	
11/23/2019	@	Missouri	24	20	W	2.0	W	47.5	U	
11/30/2019	vs	VANDERBILT	28	10	W	-23.5	L	48.0	U	
1/2/2020	vs	Indiana	23	22	W	-3.5	L	56.0	U	Gator Bowl
Coach: Jeremy Pruitt		Season Record >>	314	282	8-5	ATS>>	7-6	O/U>>	4-8	
2018-Tennessee		Opponent	Tenn	Opp	S/U	Line	ATS	Total	O/U	
9/1/2018	vs	West Virginia	14	40	L	10.0	L	59.5	U	Bank of America Stadium
9/8/2018	vs	EAST TENNESSEE STATE	59	3	W	-37.5	W	NT	---	
9/15/2018	vs	TEXAS-EL PASO	24	0	W	-34.0	L	51.5	U	
9/22/2018	vs	FLORIDA	21	47	L	3.5	L	45.5	O	
9/29/2018	@	Georgia	12	38	L	27.5	W	55.0	U	
10/13/2018	@	Auburn	30	24	W	14.5	W	47.0	O	
10/20/2018	vs	ALABAMA	21	58	L	28.5	L	57.5	O	Third Saturday in October Rivalry
10/27/2018	@	South Carolina	24	27	L	10.5	W	53.0	U	
11/3/2018	vs	CHARLOTTE	14	3	W	-21.5	L	45.0	U	
11/10/2018	vs	KENTUCKY	24	7	W	6.0	W	42.5	U	
11/17/2018	vs	MISSOURI	17	50	L	6.0	L	57.0	O	
11/24/2018	@	Vanderbilt	13	38	L	3.0	L	51.5	U	
Coach: Jeremy Pruitt		Season Record >>	273	335	5-7	ATS>>	5-7	O/U>>	4-7	
2017-Tennessee		Opponent	Tenn	Opp	S/U	Line	ATS	Total	O/U	
9/4/2017	vs	Georgia Tech	42	41	W	-4.0	L	54.0	O	2 OT
9/9/2017	vs	INDIANA STATE	42	7	W	-35.5	L	NT	---	
9/16/2017	@	Florida	20	26	L	6.5	W	51.0	U	
9/23/2017	vs	MASSACHUSETTS	17	13	W	-27.5	L	58.0	U	
9/30/2017	vs	GEORGIA	0	41	L	10.0	L	47.0	U	
10/14/2017	vs	SOUTH CAROLINA	9	15	L	-2.0	L	45.0	U	
10/21/2017	@	Alabama	7	45	L	37.0	L	50.5	O	Third Saturday in October Rivalry
10/28/2017	@	Kentucky	26	29	L	4.0	W	46.0	O	
11/4/2017	vs	SOUTHERN MISS	24	10	W	-7.5	W	48.5	U	
11/11/2017	@	Missouri	17	50	L	12.0	L	63.0	O	
11/18/2017	vs	LSU	10	30	L	17.0	L	42.0	U	
11/25/2017	vs	VANDERBILT	24	42	L	-2.5	L	45.5	O	
Coach: Butch Jones		Season Record >>	238	349	4-8	ATS>>	3-9	O/U>>	5-6	

Copyright © 2021 by Steve's Football Bible, LLC

TENNESSEE VOLUNTEERS   SEC East

STADIUM: Neyland Stadium {102,455}		Location: Knoxville, TN							COACH: Josh Heupel

DATE		Opponent	Tenn	Opp	S/U	Line	ATS	Total	O/U	Trends & Angles
9/4/2021	vs	BOWLING GREEN								vs Bowling Green - Tennessee leads series 1-0
9/11/2021	vs	PITTSBURGH								vs Pittsburgh - Pitt leads series 2-0
9/18/2021	vs	TENNESSEE TECH								vs Tennessee Tech - Tennessee leads series 6-0
9/25/2021	@	Florida								vs Florida - Florida leads series 30-20
10/2/2021	@	Missouri								vs Missouri - Missouri leads series 5-4
10/9/2021	vs	SOUTH CAROLINA								vs South Carolina - Tennessee leads series 27-10-2
10/16/2021	vs	MISSISSIPPI								11-0 S/U vs Mississippi as favorite since 1984
10/23/2021	@	Alabama								0-20-1 S/U vs Alabama as Dog since 1983
11/6/2021	@	Kentucky								31-3 S/U vs Kentucky as favorite since 1983
11/13/2021	vs	GEORGIA								1-10 S/U vs Georgia as Dog since 2008
11/20/2021	vs	SOUTH ALABAMA								vs South Alabama - Tennessee leads series 1-0
11/27/2021	vs	VANDERBILT								19-3 S/U @ home vs Vandy since 1977
12/4/2021	vs									SEC Championship
	vs									BOWL GAME

Pointspread Analysis Non-Conference				Pointspread Analysis Conference
11-2 S/U vs Non-Conf. as 7.5-10 point favorite since 1989				10-2 S/U vs Alabama as favorite since 1995
10-3 ATS vs Non-Conf. as 7.5-10 point favorite since 1989				vs Alabama - Alabama leads series 57-37-8
13-2 S/U vs Non-Conf. as 10.5-15 point favorite since 1983				8-1 S/U vs Arkansas as 9 point or more favorite since 1996
20-0 S/U vs Non-Conf. as 15.5-20 point favorite since 1986				4-20 S/U vs Florida as Dog since 1984
18-1 S/U vs Non-Conf. as 20.5-25 point favorite since 1986				0-6 ATS vs Florida as 3.5 point or less favorite since 1993 {1-5 S/U}
33-2 S/U vs Non-Conf. as 25.5 point or more favorite since 1986				vs Georgia - Georgia leads series 25-23-2
Dog				10-2 S/U vs Georgia as favorite since 1989
0-9 S/U as 20.5 point or more Dog since 2009				vs Kentucky - Tennessee leads series 81-26-9
0-6 S/U @ home as 15.5-20 point Dog since 2010				1-3 S/U & ATS vs Missouri as Dog since 2013
0-5 S/U on road as 15.5-20 point Dog since 2010				10-0 S/U vs South Carolina as favorite since 1993
6-1 ATS on road as 15.5-20 point Dog since 1989				vs Vanderbilt - Tennessee leads series 77-32-5
1-11 S/U on road as 10.5-15 point Dog since 2008				2-7 ATS vs Vanderbilt since 2012
0-6 S/U @ home as 10.5-15 point Dog since 1986				24-0 S/U vs Vanderbilt as 12 point or more favorite since 1985
1-7 S/U @ home as 7.5-10 point Dog since 1984				**Bowl Games**
0-7 S/U on road as 7.5-10 point Dog since 1985				3-0 S/U in Liberty Bowl
1-9 S/U on road as 3.5-7 point Dog since 2005				0-3 S/U & ATS vs Penn State in Bowl Games
3-8 S/U @ home as 3.5-7 point Dog since 1994				0-3 S/U vs ACC teams in Bowl Games since 2002
Favorite				1-4 S/U in Peach Bowl {0-5 ATS}
0-5 S/U & ATS as 3 point or less favorite since 2013				3-0 S/U in Sugar Bowl since 1971
5-0 O/U on road as 3 point or less favorite since 2003				0-3 S/U in Orange Bowl since 1947
10-3 S/U on road as 3 point or less favorite since 1988				5-1 O/U in Bowl Games since 2009
10-2 S/U on road as 3.5-7 point favorite since 1995				3-0 O/U in Bowl Games as 3 point or less Dog since 1990
13-0 S/U @ home as 7.5-10 point favorite since 1989				4-0 S/U in Bowl Games as 7.5-10 point favorite since 1994
0-6 O/U @ home as 7.5-10 point favorite since 2000				4-0 O/U in Bowl Games as 7.5-10 point favorite since 1994
6-1 S/U on road as 7.5-10 point favorite since 2001				
9-1 S/U @ home as 10.5-15 point favorite since 2006	B. GREEN			25-1 S/U in 1st home game of season since 1995
11-1 S/U on road as 10.5-15 point favorite since 1994	B. GREEN			10-2 S/U in 1st game of season since 2009
13-2 S/U as 10.5-15 point favorite since 2006	PITTSBURGH			3-15 ATS in 2nd home game of season since 2003
32-0 S/U @ home as 15.5-20 point favorite since 1986	Florida			2-12 S/U in 1st road game of season since 2007
11-0 S/U on road as 15.5-20 point favorite since 1983	Florida			7-0 S/U prior to playing Missouri since 2014
25-1 S/U @ home as 20.5-25 point favorite since 1993	Missouri			9-3 S/U after playing Florida since 2009
42-1 S/U @ home as 25.5 point or more favorite since 1986	Missouri			1-12 S/U prior to playing South Carolina since 2007
	Missouri			6-2 S/U prior to playing South Carolina since 2012
23-0 S/U when ranked vs Kentucky since 1967	Missouri			1-13 S/U in 2nd road game of season since 2007
8-0 S/U @ home when ranked vs Mississippi since 1968	Ole Miss			10-2 S/U after playing South Carolina since 2009
38-1 S/U when ranked vs Vanderbilt all time {22-0 @ home}	Alabama			1-8 ATS after playing Missouri since 2012
0-12 S/U vs #1 ranked teams since 1990	Kentucky			2-7 ATS prior to playing Georgia since 2012
0-7 S/U on road vs #1 ranked teams all time	GEORGIA			5-2 S/U after playing Kentucky since 2014
0-13 S/U vs ranked Alabama since 2005	SO. ALABAMA			9-3 O/U prior to playing Vanderbilt since 2009
0-7 S/U @ ranked Florida since 2005	SO. ALABAMA			3-9 S/U after playing Georgia since 2009

Copyright © 2021 by Steve's Football Bible, LLC

TEXAS LONGHORNS   BIG TWELVE

2020-Texas		Opponent	Texas	Opp	S/U	Line	ATS	Total	O/U	
9/12/2020	vs	*TEXAS-EL PASO*	59	3	W	-49.5	W	57.5	O	
9/26/2020	@	Texas Tech	63	56	W	-17.5	L	71.0	O	*"Chancellor's Spurs"*
10/3/2020	vs	TCU	31	33	L	-10.5	L	61.5	O	
10/10/2020	vs	Oklahoma	45	53	L	3.0	L	74.0	O	*"Red River Rivalry - Golden Hat"*
10/24/2020	vs	BAYLOR	27	16	W	-10.5	W	61.0	U	
10/31/2020	@	Oklahoma State	41	34	W	3.5	W	58.0	O	{OT}
11/7/2020	vs	WEST VIRGINIA	17	13	W	-6.0	L	55.5	U	
11/28/2020	vs	IOWA STATE	20	23	L	2.0	L	58.0	U	
12/5/2020	@	Kansas State	69	31	W	-7.0	W	53.5	O	
12/12/2020	@	Kansas	69	31	W	-7.0	W	53.5	O	
12/29/2020	vs	**Colorado**	**55**	**23**	**W**	**-9.0**	**W**	**67.0**	**O**	**Alamo Bowl**
Coach: Tom Herman		Season Record >>	496	316	8-3	ATS>>	6-5	O/U>>	8-3	
2019-Texas		Opponent	Texas	Opp	S/U	Line	ATS	Total	O/U	
8/31/2019	vs	*LOUISIANA TECH*	45	10	W	-19.0	W	55.5	U	
9/7/2019	vs	*LSU*	38	45	L	7.0	T	57.0	O	
9/14/2019	@	*Rice*	48	13	W	-32.0	W	57.0	O	
9/21/2019	vs	OKLAHOMA STATE	36	30	W	-7.0	L	72.5	U	
10/5/2019	@	West Virginia	42	31	W	-10.5	W	62.0	O	
10/12/2019	vs	Oklahoma	27	34	L	10.5	W	77.5	U	*"Red River Rivalry - Golden Hat"*
10/19/2019	vs	KANSAS	50	48	W	-21.0	L	63.0	O	
10/26/2019	@	Tcu	27	37	L	1.0	L	56.5	O	
11/9/2019	vs	KANSAS STATE	27	24	W	-7.0	L	57.5	U	
11/16/2019	@	Iowa State	21	23	L	7.0	W	64.5	U	
11/23/2019	@	Baylor	10	24	L	4.0	L	57.5	U	
11/30/2019	vs	TEXAS TECH	49	24	W	-8.0	W	65.0	O	*"Chancellor's Spurs"*
12/31/2019	vs	**Utah**	**38**	**10**	**W**	**7.0**	**W**	**56.0**	**U**	**Alamo Bowl**
Coach: Tom Herman		Season Record >>	458	353	8-5	ATS>>	7-4-1	O/U>>	6-7	
2018-Texas		Opponent	Texas	Opp	S/U	Line	ATS	Total	O/U	
9/1/2018	@	*Maryland*	29	34	L	-12.0	L	54.5	O	FedEx Field
9/8/2018	vs	*TULSA*	28	21	W	-21.5	L	59.5	U	
9/15/2018	vs	USC	37	14	W	-3.5	W	47.5	O	
9/22/2018	vs	TCU	31	16	W	2.5	W	50.0	L	
9/29/2018	@	Kansas State	19	14	W	-8.5	L	49.0	U	
10/6/2018	vs	Oklahoma	48	45	W	7.0	W	60.0	O	*"Red River Rivalry - Golden Hat"*
10/13/2018	vs	BAYLOR	23	17	W	-13.0	L	58.5	U	
10/27/2018	@	Oklahoma State	35	38	L	-1.0	L	59.5	O	
11/3/2018	vs	WEST VIRGINIA	41	42	L	1.0	T	58.0	O	
11/10/2018	@	Texas Tech	41	34	W	-2.0	W	62.0	O	*"Chancellor's Spurs"*
11/17/2018	vs	IOWA STATE	24	10	W	-1.5	W	51.0	U	
11/24/2018	@	Kansas	24	17	W	-15.0	L	50.0	U	
12/1/2018	vs	**Oklahoma**	**27**	**39**	**L**	**9.5**	**L**	**79.5**	**U**	**Big 12 Championship**
1/1/2019	vs	**Georgia**	**28**	**21**	**W**	**13.5**	**W**	**60.5**	**U**	**Sugar Bowl**
Coach: Tom Herman		Season Record >>	435	362	10-4	ATS>>	6-7-1	O/U>>	6-8	
2017-Texas		Opponent	Texas	Opp	S/U	Line	ATS	Total	O/U	
9/2/2017	vs	*MARYLAND*	41	51	L	-19.0	L	57.0	O	
9/9/2017	vs	*SAN JOSE STATE*	56	0	W	-26.5	W	62.5	U	
9/16/2017	@	*Usc*	24	27	L	16.5	W	65.5	U	{2 OT}
9/30/2017	@	Iowa State	17	7	W	-5.0	W	61.0	U	
10/7/2017	vs	KANSAS STATE	40	34	W	-5.5	W	47.5	O	{2 OT}
10/14/2017	vs	Oklahoma	24	29	L	9.0	W	61.5	U	*"Red River Rivalry - Golden Hat"*
10/21/2017	vs	OKLAHOMA STATE	10	13	L	7.0	W	65.0	U	{OT}
10/28/2017	@	Baylor	38	7	W	-10.0	W	53.5	U	
11/4/2017	@	Tcu	7	24	L	7.5	L	44.0	U	
11/11/2017	vs	KANSAS	42	27	W	-31.5	L	54.5	O	
11/18/2017	@	West Virginia	28	14	W	3.0	W	54.5	U	
11/25/2017	vs	TEXAS TECH	23	27	L	-7.5	L	58.0	U	*"Chancellor's Spurs"*
12/27/2017	vs	**Missouri**	**33**	**16**	**W**	**3.0**	**W**	**62.0**	**U**	**Texas Bowl**
Coach: Tom Herman		Season Record >>	383	276	7-6	ATS>>	9-4	O/U>>	3-10	

Copyright © 2021 by Steve's Football Bible, LLC

TEXAS LONGHORNS   BIG TWELVE

STADIUM: Darrell K. Royal Texas Memorial Stadium {100,119}									Location: Austin, TX	COACH: Steve Sarkisian
DATE		Opponent	TEX	Opp	S/U	Line	ATS	Total	O/U	Trends & Angles
9/4/2021	vs	LOUISIANA								vs Louisiana - Texas leads series 2-0
9/11/2021	@	Arkansas								5-1 S/U @ Arkansas since 1983
9/18/2021	vs	RICE								24-1 S/U vs Rice as favorite since 1984
9/25/2021	vs	TEXAS TECH								15-3 S/U vs Texas Tech since 2003
10/2/2021	@	Tcu								vs TCU - Texas leads series 63-27-1
10/9/2021	vs	Oklahoma								vs Oklahoma - Texas leads series 65-49-5
10/16/2021	vs	OKLAHOMA STATE								vs Oklahoma State - Texas leads series 25-9
10/30/2021	@	Baylor								16-1 S/U vs Baylor as favorite since 1998
11/6/2021	@	Iowa State								vs Iowa State - Texas leads series 14-4
11/13/2021	vs	KANSAS								17-1 S/U vs Kansas as favorite since 1996
11/20/2021	@	West Virginia								vs West Virginia - Series tied 5-5
11/27/2021	vs	KANSAS STATE								vs Kansas State - Texas leads series 11-10
12/4/2021	vs									BIG XII Championship
	vs									BOWL GAME

Pointspread Analysis Non-Conference		Pointspread Analysis Conference
1-5 S/U vs Non-Conf. as 10.5-20 point Dog since 1987		vs Baylor - Texas leads series 78-27-5
7-2 O/U vs Non-Conf. as 3.5-7 point Dog since 1996		0-5 O/U vs Baylor as Dog since 2013
7-2 S/U & ATS vs Non-Conf. as 3 point or less Dog since 1982		16-0 S/U vs Baylor as 10 point or more favorite since 1983
2-11 ATS vs Non-Conf. as 7.5-10 point favorite since 1984		13-2 S/U vs Iowa State as favorite since 1998
8-2 S/U vs Non-Conf. as 10.5-15 point favorite since 1987		vs Kansas - Texas leads series 17-3
33-0 S/U vs Non-Conf. as 20.5 point or more favorite since 1988		0-4-1 ATS vs Oklahoma as 3 point or less favorite since 1984
vs Arkansas - Texas leads series 55-21		6-0 S/U vs Oklahoma as 3.5-14 point favorite since 1983
26-1 S/U when ranked vs Rice since 1968 {13-0 @ home}		6-0 ATS vs Oklahoma as 12-17.5 point Dog since 1988
Dog		1-6 S/U vs Oklahoma State as Dog since 2010 {2-5 ATS}
8-1 ATS as 15.5-20 point Dog since 1988		15-1 S/U vs Oklahoma State as favorite since 1998
4-17 S/U as 10.5-15 point Dog since 1987		8-0 S/U @ home vs Oklahoma State as favorite since 1996
1-10 S/U on road as 10.5-15 point Dog since 1987		7-2 S/U vs TCU as 8.5 point or more favorite since 1985
0-7 S/U as 7.5-10 point Dog since 2014		vs Texas Tech - Texas leads series 53-17
1-10 O/U as 7.5-10 point Dog since 1999		14-0 S/U vs Texas Tech as 10 point or more favorite since 1983
1-8 S/U @ home as 3 point or less Dog since 2010		
1-7-1 ATS @ home as 3 point or less Dog since 2010	LOUISIANA	20-1 S/U in 1st home game of season since 2000
Favorite	RICE	3-10 O/U prior to playing Texas Tech since 2008
1-4 S/U & ATS @ home as 3 point or less favorite since 1997	TEXAS TECH	12-2 S/U prior to playing TCU since 1992
14-0 S/U @ home as 3.5-7 point favorite since 2000	Tcu	3-9 ATS prior to playing Oklahoma since 2009
16-1 S/U as 3.5-7 point favorite since 2011 {12-5 ATS}	Tcu	1-7 O/U after playing Texas Tech since 2011
3-9 ATS as 7.5-10 point favorite since 2011	OK STATE	3-9 O/U after playing Oklahoma since 2009
1-6 ATS @ home as 7.5-10 point favorite since 2010	KANSAS	8-1 S/U prior to playing West Virginia since 2012
8-2 S/U on road as 7.5-10 point favorite since 1999	W. VIRGINIA	1-7 O/U prior to playing Kansas since 2013
15-2 S/U as 10.5-15 point favorite since 2008	W. VIRGINIA	1-7 O/U in final road game of season since 2013
14-1 S/U on road as 10.5-15 point favorite since 2000		
17-2 S/U @ home as 15.5-20 point favorite since 1991		
11-1 S/U on road as 15.5-20 point favorite since 1983		
9-1 S/U on road as 20.5-25 point favorite since 1991		
15-1 S/U @ home as 20.5-25 point favorite since 1985		
66-0 S/U as 25.5 point or more favorite since 1983		
1-4 O/U on road as 25.5 point or more favorite since 2007		
Bowl Games		
4-1-1 S/U vs Alabama in Bowl Games		8-0 S/U @ home when #1 ranked since 1965
0-3 S/U & ATS in Bowl Games as 7.5-15 point Dog since 1991		19-1 S/U on road when #2 ranked all time
1-5 ATS in Bowl Games as 7.5-10 point favorite since 1984		20-2 S/U @ home when ranked vs Texas Tech all time

Copyright © 2021 by Steve's Football Bible, LLC

2020-Texas A&M		Opponent	A&M	Opp	S/U	Line	ATS	Total	O/U	
9/26/2020	vs	VANDERBILT	17	12	W	-31.0	L	45.5	U	
10/3/2020	@	Alabama	24	52	L	18.0	L	54.0	O	
10/10/2020	vs	FLORIDA	41	38	W	5.5	W	60.0	O	
10/17/2020	@	Mississippi State	28	14	W	-3.5	W	57.0	U	
10/31/2020	vs	ARKANSAS	42	31	W	-14.5	L	54.5	O	"Southwest Classic"
11/7/2020	@	South Carolina	48	3	W	-9.0	W	58.0	U	
11/28/2020	vs	LSU	20	7	W	-16.0	L	59.5	U	
12/5/2020	@	Auburn	31	20	W	-5.0	W	49.0	O	
12/19/2020	@	Tennessee	34	13	W	-13.5	W	50.0	U	
1/2/2021	vs	North Carolina	41	27	W	-10.0	W	65.5	O	Orange Bowl
Coach: Jimbo Fisher		Season Record >>	326	217	9-1	ATS>>	6-4	O/U>>	5-5	
2019-Texas A&M		Opponent	A&M	Opp	S/U	Line	ATS	Total	O/U	
8/29/2019	vs	TEXAS STATE	41	7	W	-33.5	W	57.0	U	
9/7/2019	@	Clemson	10	24	L	16.0	W	62.5	U	
9/14/2019	vs	LAMAR	62	3	W	-45.0	W	NT	---	
9/21/2019	vs	AUBURN	20	28	L	-4.0	L	48.0	T	
9/28/2019	vs	Arkansas	31	27	W	-23.0	L	60.0	U	"Southwest Classic"
10/12/2019	vs	ALABAMA	28	47	L	17.0	L	61.0	O	
10/19/2019	@	Mississippi	24	17	W	-6.0	W	55.5	U	
10/26/2019	vs	MISSISSIPPI STATE	49	30	W	-10.5	W	50.0	O	
11/2/2019	vs	TEXAS-SAN ANTONIO	45	14	W	-38.0	L	53.0	O	
11/16/2019	vs	SOUTH CAROLINA	30	6	W	-10.5	W	47.0	U	
11/23/2019	@	Georgia	13	19	L	12.5	W	43.5	U	
11/30/2019	@	Lsu	7	50	L	18.0	L	64.5	U	
12/27/2019	vs	Oklahoma State	24	21	W	-5.0	L	55.5	U	Texas Bowl
Coach: Jimbo Fisher		Season Record >>	384	293	8-5	ATS>>	7-6	O/U>>	3-8-1	
2018-Texas A&M		Opponent	A&M	Opp	S/U	Line	ATS	Total	O/U	
9/1/2018	vs	NORTHWESTERN STATE	59	7	W	-46.5	W	NT	---	
9/8/2018	vs	CLEMSON	26	28	L	12.0	W	52.5	O	
9/15/2018	vs	LOUISIANA-MONROE	48	10	W	-28.0	W	66.0	U	
9/22/2018	@	Alabama	23	45	L	23.5	W	58.5	O	
9/29/2018	vs	Arkansas	24	17	W	-20.0	L	54.0	U	"Southwest Classic"
10/6/2018	vs	KENTUCKY	20	14	W	-4.5	W	48.5	U	{OT}
10/13/2018	@	South Carolina	26	23	W	-2.5	W	50.0	U	
10/27/2018	@	Mississippi State	13	28	L	1.0	L	42.5	U	
11/3/2018	@	Auburn	24	28	L	3.5	L	47.5	O	
11/10/2018	vs	MISSISSIPPI	38	24	W	-13.0	W	67.5	U	
11/17/2018	vs	ALABAMA-BIRMINGHAM	41	20	W	-17.0	W	46.5	U	
11/24/2018	vs	LSU	74	72	W	-2.5	L	45.5	O	{7 OT}
12/31/2018	vs	NC State	52	13	W	-7.5	W	58.0	O	Gator Bowl
Coach: Jimbo Fisher		Season Record >>	468	329	9-4	ATS>>	9-4	O/U>>	6-6	
2017-Texas A&M		Opponent	A&M	Opp	S/U	Line	ATS	Total	O/U	
9/2/2017	@	Ucla	44	45	L	6.5	W	61.5	O	
9/9/2017	vs	NICHOLLS STATE	24	14	W	-37.0	L	NT	---	
9/16/2017	vs	LOUISIANA-LAFAYETTE	45	21	W	-24.5	L	62.0	O	
9/23/2017	vs	Arkansas	50	43	W	-2.0	W	56.5	O	"Southwest Classic"
9/30/2017	vs	SOUTH CAROLINA	24	17	W	-8.0	L	49.5	U	
10/7/2017	vs	ALABAMA	19	27	L	25.5	W	56.0	U	
10/14/2017	@	Florida	19	17	W	3.5	W	49.5	U	
10/28/2017	vs	MISSISSIPPI STATE	14	35	L	3.5	L	57.0	U	
11/4/2017	vs	AUBURN	27	42	L	15.0	T	52.0	O	
11/11/2017	vs	NEW MEXICO	55	14	W	-18.0	W	52.5	O	
11/18/2017	@	Mississippi	31	24	W	-3.0	W	69.0	U	
11/25/2017	@	Lsu	21	45	L	11.0	L	50.5	O	
12/29/2017	vs	Wake Forest	52	55	L	3.5	W	62.0	O	Belk Bowl
Coach: Kevin Sumlin		Season Record >>	425	399	7-6	ATS>>	7-5-1	O/U>>	7-5	

Copyright © 2021 by Steve's Football Bible, LLC

TEXAS A&M AGGIES

SEC West

STADIUM: Kyle Field {102,733}					Location: College Station, TX				COACH: Jimbo Fisher	
DATE		Opponent	A&M	Opp	S/U	Line	ATS	Total	O/U	Trends & Angles
9/4/2021	vs	*KENT STATE*								1st meeting
9/11/2021	@	*Colorado*								2-7 ATS vs Colorado since 1995
9/18/2021	vs	*NEW MEXICO*								vs New Mexico - A&M leads series 4-0 {3-0 ATS{
9/25/2021	vs	Arkansas {@ Arlington, TX}								9-0 S/U vs Arkansas as favorite since 2012
10/2/2021	vs	**MISSISSIPPI STATE**								vs Mississippi State - Series tied 7-7
10/9/2021	vs	**ALABAMA**								0-8 S/U vs Alabama as Dog since 2013
10/16/2021	@	Missouri								1-4 S/U & ATS vs Missouri as favorite since 2002
10/23/2021	vs	**SOUTH CAROLINA**								vs South Carolina - Texas A&M leads series 7-0
11/6/2021	vs	**AUBURN**								vs Auburn - Texas A&M leads series 6-5
11/13/2021	@	Mississippi								0-5 O/U vs Mississippi as favorite since 2014
11/20/2021	vs	*PRAIRIE VIEW A&M*								vs Prairie View - Texas A&M leads series 1-0
11/27/2021	@	Lsu								vs LSU - LSU leads series 34-22-3
12/4/2021	vs									SEC Championship
	vs									BOWL GAME

Pointspread Analysis Non-Conference		Pointspread Analysis Conference
0-7 S/U vs Non-Conf. as 7.5-15 point Dog since 1994		vs Alabama - Aalabama leads series 11-2
2-8 S/U vs Non-Conf. as 3.5-7 point Dog since 1992		vs Arkansas - Arkansas leads series 41-33-3
1-7 S/U & ATS vs Non-Conf. as 3 point or less Dog since 2000		0-4 S/U & ATS vs Arkansas as Dog since 1984
3-11 ATS vs Non-Conf. as 3.5-7 point favorite since 1983		11-0 S/U vs Arkansas as 5 point or more favorite since 1987
7-0 S/U vs Non-Conf. as 7.5-10 point favorite since 1992		7-0 S/U vs LSU as favorite since 1991
13-0 S/U vs Non-Conf. as 10.5-15 point favorite since 1987		1-10 S/U & ATS vs LSU as Dog since 1987
12-1 ATS vs Non-Conf. as 10.5-15 point favorite since 1987		vs Mississippi - Texas A&M leads series 9-3
11-2 S/U & ATS vs Non-conf. as 15.5-20 point favorite since 1986		vs Mississippi State - Series tied 7-7
44-1 S/U vs Non-Conf. as 20.5 point or more favorite since 1990		0-3 S/U & ATS vs Mississippi State as Dog since 2014
9-2 ATS vs Non-Conference since 2018		6-0 S/U vs South Carolina as favorite since 2015
1-4 S/U & ATS vs Colorado as Dog since 1995		**Bowl Games**
vs Colorado - Colorado leads series 6-3		1-6 S/U in Cotton Bowl since 1992
Dog		0-4 S/U vs PAC-12 teams in Bowl Games
4-1 ATS @ home as 20.5 point or more Dog since 2005		6-1 S/U vs Big 12 teams in Bowl Games
0-5 S/U @ home as 20.5 point or more Dog since 2005		5-2 ATS vs Big 12 teams in Bowl Games
0-7 S/U on road as 15.5-20 point Dog since 2001		0-3 S/U & ATS in Alamo Bowl since 1999
3-11 S/U on road as 10.5-15 point Dog since 1999		1-4 S/U in Bowl Games as 7.5-20 point Dog since 1994
0-4 S/U @ home as 10.5-15 point Dog since 2001		4-1 ATS in Bowl Games as 7.5-20 point Dog since 1994
8-1 O/U as 7.5-10 point Dog since 1994		2-7 S/U in Bowl Games as 3.5-7 point Dog since 1992
2-10 S/U as 7.5-10 point Dog since 1983		
1-7 S/U @ home as 3.5-7 point Dog since 2008		12-0 S/U @ home when #5 ranked all time
2-9 S/U on road as 3.5-7 point Dog since 2000		0-7 S/U when ranked vs Alabama since 2013
3-16 S/U as 3.5-7 point Dog since 2007		2-16 S/U vs #1 ranked teams all time
2-8 ATS as 3 point or less Dog since 2009		2-10 S/U vs #2 ranked teams all time
3-10 O/U @ home as 3 point or less Dog since 1999		0-5 S/U @ ranked LSU since 1986
1-7 S/U @ home as 3 point or less Dog since 2006		
Favorite	KENT STATE	31-2 S/U in 1st home game of season since 1988
5-0 S/U as 3 point or less favorite since 2015	NEW MEXICO	10-2 O/U in 2nd home game of season since 2006
4-0 S/U & ATS on road as 3 point or less favorite since 2010	NEW MEXICO	16-2 S/U in 2nd home game of season since 2003
2-9-2 O/U @ home as 3.5-7 point favorite since 2007	NEW MEXICO	7-2 S/U prior to playing Arkansas since 2012
6-0 S/U on road as 3.5-7 point favorite since 2012 {5-1 ATS}	Arkansas	9-0 S/U prior to playing Mississippi State since 2012
12-2 S/U as 7.5-10 point favorite since 2003	Arkansas	1-7 O/U prior to playing Mississippi State since 2013
1-7 ATS @ home as 7.5-10 point favorite since 1998	M STATE	3-8 ATS after playing Arkansas since 2010
11-4 O/U as 10.5-15 point favorite since 2009	M STATE	8-2 S/U after playing Arkansas since 2011
21-3 S/U @ home as 10.5-15 point favorite since 1990	ALABAMA	0-7-1 ATS after playing Mississippi State since 2013
19-1 S/U on road as 10.5-15 point favorite since 1987	ALABAMA	2-6 S/U after playing Mississippi State since 2013
11-2 S/U on road as 15.5-20 point favorite since 1983	Missouri	12-0 S/U in 2nd road game of season since 2009
1-8 ATS on road as 15.5-20 point favorite since 1990	Missouri	9-1 S/U after playing Alabama since 1985
32-1 S/U @ home as 15.5-20 point favorite since 1984	Missouri	1-7 O/U after playing Alabama since 2013
7-1 O/U @ home as 15.5-20 point favorite since 2009	S. CAROLINA	2-7 ATS prior to playing Auburn since 2012
18-1-1 S/U @ home as 20.5-25 point favorite since 1986	AUBURN	8-0 O/U prior to playing Mississippi since 2012
8-2 S/U on road as 20.5-25 point favorite since 1985	PRAIRIE VIEW	2-6 ATS after playing Mississippi since 2012
54-0 S/U as 25.5 point or more favorite since 1986	PRAIRIE VIEW	9-2 S/U prior to playing LSU since 1990

Copyright © 2021 by Steve's Football Bible, LLC

2020-Texas-El Paso		Opponent	UTEP	Opp	S/U	Line	ATS	Total	O/U	
9/5/2020	vs	STEPHEN F. AUSTIN	24	14	W	-5.0	W	54.5	U	
9/12/2020	@	Texas	3	59	L	49.5	L	57.5	O	
9/19/2020	vs	ABILENE CHRISTIAN	17	13	W	-8.5	L	47.5	U	
9/26/2020	@	Louisiana-Monroe	31	6	W	10.0	W	50.0	U	
10/10/2020	@	Louisiana Tech	17	21	L	14.0	W	56.0	U	
10/24/2020	@	Charlotte	28	38	L	17.5	W	50.5	O	
11/14/2020	@	Texas-San Antonio	21	52	L	5.5	L	45.0	O	
12/11/2020	@	North Texas	43	45	L	9.5	W	66.0	O	
Coach: Dana Dimel		Season Record >>	184	248	3-5	ATS>>	5-3	O/U>>	4-4	
2019-Texas-El Paso		Opponent	UTEP	Opp	S/U	Line	ATS	Total	O/U	
8/31/2019	vs	HOUSTON BAPTIST	36	34	W	-16.5	L	NT	---	
9/7/2019	@	Texas Tech	3	38	L	34.5	L	64.5	U	
9/21/2019	vs	NEVADA	21	37	L	14.0	L	52.0	O	
9/28/2019	@	Southern Miss	13	31	L	26.0	W	49.5	U	
10/5/2019	vs	TEXAS-SAN ANTONIO	16	26	L	-1.0	L	45.0	U	
10/19/2019	@	Florida International	17	32	L	24.5	W	51.0	U	
10/26/2019	vs	LOUISIANA TECH	21	42	L	18.5	L	50.0	O	
11/2/2019	@	North Texas	26	52	L	23.0	L	59.0	O	
11/9/2019	vs	CHARLOTTE	21	28	L	12.0	W	55.5	U	
11/16/2019	@	Alabama-Birmingham	10	37	L	14.5	L	42.0	O	
11/23/2019	@	New Mexico State	35	44	L	7.0	L	55.5	O	"Brass Spittoon"
11/30/2019	vs	RICE	16	30	L	6.5	L	43.5	O	
Coach: Dana Dimel		Season Record >>	235	431	1-11	ATS>>	3-9	O/U>>	6-5	
2018-Texas-El Paso		Opponent	UTEP	Opp	S/U	Line	ATS	Total	O/U	
9/1/2018	vs	NORTHERN ARIZONA	10	30	L	7.0	L	NT	---	
9/8/2018	@	Unlv	24	52	L	22.0	L	53.5	O	
9/15/2018	@	Tennessee	0	24	L	34.0	W	51.5	U	
9/22/2018	vs	NEW MEXICO STATE	20	27	L	4.5	L	50.0	U	"Brass Spittoon"
9/29/2018	@	Texas-San Antonio	21	30	L	10.0	W	45.5	O	
10/6/2018	vs	NORTH TEXAS	24	27	L	25.5	W	53.0	U	
10/20/2018	@	Louisiana Tech	24	31	L	23.0	W	50.5	O	
10/27/2018	vs	ALABAMA-BIRMINGHAM	0	19	L	15.0	L	49.5	U	
11/3/2018	@	Rice	34	26	W	-2.5	W	44.5	O	
11/10/2018	vs	MIDDLE TENNESSEE	32	48	L	13.5	L	48.0	O	
11/17/2018	@	Western Kentucky	16	40	L	6.5	L	47.5	O	
11/24/2018	vs	SOUTHERN MISSISSIPPI	7	39	L	14.0	L	45.0	O	
Coach: Dana Dimel		Season Record >>	212	393	1-11	ATS>>	5-7	O/U>>	7-4	
2017-Texas-El Paso		Opponent	UTEP	Opp	S/U	Line	ATS	Total	O/U	
9/2/2017	@	Oklahoma	7	56	L	42.5	L	63.0	T	
9/9/2017	vs	RICE	14	31	L	-1.0	L	55.5	U	
9/16/2017	vs	ARIZONA	16	63	L	26.0	L	57.5	O	
9/23/2017	@	New Mexico State	14	41	L	17.5	L	58.5	U	"Brass Spittoon"
9/30/2017	@	Army	21	35	L	22.5	W	47.5	O	
10/7/2017	vs	WESTERN KENTUCKY	14	15	L	16.0	W	53.5	U	
10/14/2017	@	Southern Miss	0	24	L	22.5	L	52.0	U	
10/28/2017	vs	TEXAS-SAN ANTONIO	14	31	L	16.0	L	47.0	U	
11/4/2017	@	Middle Tennessee	3	30	L	20.5	L	50.5	U	
11/11/2017	@	North Texas	10	45	L	24.0	L	53.0	O	
11/18/2017	vs	LOUISIANA TECH	21	42	L	17.0	L	48.5	O	
11/25/2017	@	Alabama-Birmingham	7	28	L	21.0	T	47.0	U	
Coach: Sean Kugler		Season Record >>	141	441	0-12	ATS>>	2-9-1	O/U>>	4-7-1	

Copyright © 2021 by Steve's Football Bible, LLC

TEXAS-EL PASO MINERS C-USA West

STADIUM: Sun Bowl Stadium {51,500}					Location: El Paso, TX				**COACH: Dana Dimel**	
DATE		Opponent	Utep	Opp	S/U	Line	ATS	Total	O/U	Trends & Angles
8/28/2021	@	*New Mexico State*								vs New Mexico State - UTEP leads series 57-38-2
9/4/2021	vs	*BETHUNE-COOKMAN*								1st meeting
9/11/2021	@	*Boise State*								0-5 S/U vs Boise State as Dog since 2000
9/25/2021	vs	*NEW MEXICO*								vs New Mexico - New Mexico leads series 43-31-3
10/2/2021	vs	OLD DOMINION								vs Old Dominion - ODU leads series 2-1
10/9/2021	@	Southern Mississippi								0-6 S/U vs Southern Miss as Dog since 2011
10/16/2021	vs	LOUISIANA TECH								0-8 S/U vs Louisiana Tech as Dog since 2013
10/30/2021	@	Florida Atlantic								vs Florida Atlantic - Series tied 1-1
11/6/2021	vs	TEXAS-SAN ANTONIO								vs UTSA - ROAD team 7-1 ATS 2013
11/13/2021	@	North Texas								vs North Texas - North Texas leads series 18-8-3
11/20/2021	vs	RICE								vs Rice - Rice leads series 15-8
11/27/2021	@	Alabama-Birmingham								vs Alabama-Birmingham - UAB leads series 6-1
12/4/2021	vs									C-USA Championship
	vs									BOWL GAME

Pointspread Analysis Non-Conference		Pointspread Analysis Conference
0-45 S/U vs Non-Conf. as 15.5 point or more Dog since 1986		vs Texas-San Antonio - UTSA leads series 6-2
13-1 S/U vs Non-Conf. as 10.5 point or more favorite since 1989		vs Louisiana Tech - Louisiana Tech leads series 14-2-1
1-4 O/U vs New Mexico State as Dog since 2007		0-3 S/U vs Middle Tennessee as Dog since 2013
13-1 S/U vs NMSU as 7.5 point or more favorite since 1987		vs Southern Miss - Southern Miss leads series 8-4
0-4 S/U vs New Mexico as 13.5 point or more Dog since 1993		**Bowl Games**
5-1 S/U @ home vs New Mexico as favorite since 1987		0-6 S/U & ATS in Bowl Games since 1988
Game 1-7-1 O/U vs New Mexico since 1998		5-1 S/U in Sun Bowl since 1950
Dog		
0-19 S/U as 30.5 point or more Dog since 1985		
0-71 S/U as 20.5 point or more Dog since 1985		
0-13 S/U @ home as 20.5 point or more Dog since 1985		1-37 S/U on road vs ranked teams all time
0-8 S/U @ home as 15.5-20 point Dog since 2002		2-22 S/U @ home vs ranked teams all time
1-22 S/U on road as 15.5-20 point Dog since 1987		
3-16 S/U on road as 10.5-15 point Dog since 1998		
13-5 O/U as 10.5-15 point Dog since 2009		
2-10 O/U as 7.5-10 point Dog since 2009		
1-6-1 S/U @ home as 7.5-10 point Dog since 1987		
1-11 S/U on road as 3.5-7 point Dog since 2001		
5-1 O/U @ home as 3 point or less Dog since 2003	BETHUNE	1-8 S/U after New Mexico State since 2011
0-4 S/U & ATS @ home as 3 point or less Dog since 2007	Boise State	1-8 S/U in 2nd road game of season since 2012
Favorite	Southern Miss	1-7 S/U prior to playing Louisiana Tech since 2013
15-3 S/U @ home as 3.5-7 point favorite since 1988	LA TECH	1-6 S/U after playing Southern Mississippi since 2011
8-0 S/U on road as 10.5 point or more favorite since 1988	LA TECH	0-5 O/U after playing Southern Mississippe since 2014
1-7 O/U @ home as 10.5-15 point favorite since 2005	UAB	2-27 S/U in final road game of season since 1992
14-0 S/U as 15.5 point or more favorite since 1987	UAB	3-14-1 ATS in final road game of season since 2003

Copyright © 2021 by Steve's Football Bible, LLC

TEXAS-SAN ANTONIO ROADRUNNERS C-USA West

2020-Texas-San Antonio		Opponent	UTSA	Opp	S/U	Line	ATS	Total	O/U	
9/12/2020	@	Texas State	51	48	W	6.5	W	56.0	O	{OT}
9/19/2020	vs	STEPHEN F. AUSTIN	24	10	W	-16.0	L	54.5	U	
9/25/2020	vs	MIDDLE TENNESSEE	37	35	W	16.5	W	58.5	O	
10/3/2020	@	Alabama-Birmingham	13	21	L	21.5	W	55.0	U	
10/10/2020	@	Byu	20	27	L	34.0	W	63.0	U	
10/17/2020	vs	ARMY	16	28	L	7.5	L	49.0	U	
10/24/2020	vs	LOUISIANA TECH	27	26	W	2.5	W	54.5	U	
10/31/2020	@	Florida Atlantic	3	24	L	4.5	L	47.0	U	
11/14/2020	vs	TEXAS-EL PASO	52	21	W	-5.5	W	45.0	O	
11/21/2020	@	Southern Mississippi	23	20	W	-9.0	L	53.5	U	
11/28/2020	@	NORTH TEXAS	49	17	W	-1.5	W	67.0	U	
12/19/2020	vs	Louisiana	24	31	L	13.5	W	55.0	T	First Responder Bowl
Coach: Frank Wilson		Season Record >>	339	308	7-5	ATS>>	8-4	O/U>>	3-8-1	
2019-Texas-San Antonio		Opponent	UTSA	Opp	S/U	Line	ATS	Total	O/U	
8/31/2019	vs	INCARNATE WORD	35	7	W	-7.0	W	NT	---	
9/7/2019	@	Baylor	14	63	L	25.0	L	58.0	O	
9/14/2019	vs	ARMY	13	31	L	14.5	L	49.0	U	
9/21/2019	@	North Texas	3	45	L	17.0	L	55.5	U	
10/5/2019	@	Texas-El Paso	26	16	W	1.0	W	45.0	U	
10/12/2019	vs	ALABAMA-BIRMINGHAM	14	33	L	12.5	L	47.0	T	
10/19/2019	vs	RICE	31	27	W	5.5	W	42.0	O	
11/2/2019	@	Texas A&M	14	45	L	38.0	W	53.0	O	
11/9/2019	@	Old Dominion	24	23	W	3.0	W	41.5	O	
11/16/2019	vs	SOUTHERN MISS	17	36	L	17.0	L	55.5	U	
11/23/2019	vs	FLORIDA ATLANTIC	26	40	L	21.5	W	57.0	O	
11/30/2019	@	Louisiana Tech	27	41	L	21.0	W	56.0	O	
Coach: Frank Wilson		Season Record >>	244	407	4-8	ATS>>	7-5	O/U>>	6-4-1	
2018-Texas-San Antonio		Opponent	UTSA	Opp	S/U	Line	ATS	Total	O/U	
9/1/2018	@	Arizona State	7	49	L	17.5	L	52.0	O	
9/8/2018	vs	BAYLOR	20	37	L	17.0	T	55.0	O	
9/15/2018	@	Kansas State	17	41	L	21.0	L	46.5	O	
9/22/2018	vs	TEXAS STATE	25	21	W	-7.0	L	49.0	U	
9/29/2018	vs	TEXAS-EL PASO	30	21	W	-10.0	L	45.5	O	
10/6/2018	@	Rice	20	3	W	1.0	W	50.0	U	
10/13/2018	vs	LOUISIANA TECH	3	31	L	13.0	L	45.5	U	
10/20/2018	@	Southern Mississippi	17	27	L	16.0	W	43.5	O	
11/3/2018	@	Alabama-Birmingham	3	52	L	21.5	L	42.0	O	
11/10/2018	vs	FLORIDA INTERNATIONAL	7	45	L	10.5	L	47.0	O	
11/17/2018	@	Marshall	0	23	L	27.5	W	47.0	U	
11/24/2018	vs	NORTH TEXAS	21	24	L	24.5	W	51.5	U	
Coach: Frank Wilson		Season Record >>	170	374	3-9	ATS>>	4-7-1	O/U>>	7-5	
2017-Texas-San Antonio		Opponent	UTSA	Opp	S/U	Line	ATS	Total	O/U	
9/9/2017	@	Baylor	17	10	W	11.0	W	57.0	U	
9/16/2017	vs	SOUTHERN U	51	17	W	-36.0	L	NT	---	
9/23/2017	@	Texas State	44	14	W	-13.5	W	45.0	O	
10/7/2017	vs	SOUTHERN MISS	29	31	L	-10.5	L	49.5	O	
10/14/2017	@	North Texas	26	29	L	-2.5	L	58.0	U	
10/21/2017	vs	RICE	20	7	W	-20.0	L	52.0	U	
10/28/2017	@	Texas-El Paso	31	14	W	-16.0	W	47.0	U	
11/4/2017	@	Florida International	7	14	L	-6.5	L	53.0	U	
11/11/2017	vs	ALABAMA-BIRMINGHAM	19	24	L	-7.0	L	50.0	U	
11/18/2017	vs	MARSHALL	9	7	W	-3.0	L	45.0	U	
11/25/2017	@	Louisiana Tech	6	20	L	-1.0	L	52.0	U	
Coach: Frank Wilson		Season Record >>	429	561	6-5	ATS>>	3-8	O/U>>	2-8	

Copyright © 2021 by Steve's Football Bible, LLC

TEXAS-SAN ANTONIO ROADRUNNERS C-USA West

STADIUM: AlamoDome {64,000}				Location: San Antonio, TX			COACH: Jeff Traylor	

DATE		Opponent	Utsa	Opp	S/U	Line	ATS	Total	O/U	Trends & Angles
9/4/2021	@	*Illinois*								1st meeting
9/11/2021	vs	*LAMAR*								1st meeting
9/18/2021	vs	**MIDDLE TENNESSEE**								vs MTSU - UTSA leads series 2-1
9/25/2021	@	*Memphis*								1st meeting
10/2/2021	vs	*UNLV*								1st meeting
10/9/2021	@	Western Kentucky								vs Western Kentucky - WKU leads series 1-0
10/16/2021	vs	**RICE**								vs Rice - UTSA leads series 5-3
10/23/2021	@	Louisiana Tech								1-6 S/U vs Louisiana Tech as Dog since 2012
11/6/2021	@	Texas-El Paso								vs Texas-El Paso - UTSA leads series 6-2
11/13/2021	vs	**SOUTHERN MISS**								vs Southern Miss - Southern Miss leads series 4-3
11/20/2021	vs	**ALABAMA-BIRMINGHAM**								vs Alabama-Birmingham - UAB leads series 4-1
11/27/2021	@	North Texas								vs North Texas - Series tied 4-4
12/4/2021	vs									C-USA Championship
	vs									BOWL GAME

Pointspread Analysis Non-Conference		Pointspread Analysis Conference
6-24 S/U vs Non-Conf. as Dog since 2012		vs Louisiana Tech - Louisiana Tech leads series 7-2
Dog		1-4 O/U vs Rice as Dog since 2012
0-19 S/U as 20.5 point or more Dog since 2012		3-0 S/U vs Rice as favorite since 2015
4-20 S/U @ home as Dog since 2012		
5-2 O/U on road as 10.5 point or more Dog since 2014		
0-5 S/U on road as 7.5-10 point Dog since 2014		
1-9 O/U as 7.5-10 point Dog since 2013		
Favorite	MIDDLE TENN	1-7 S/U in 2nd home game of season since 2013
1-4 ATS as 3 point or less favorite since 2016	Memphis	5-2 O/U in 2nd road game of season since 2014
0-5 O/U as 3 point or less favorite since 2016	RICE	6-2 S/U prior to playing Louisiana Tech since 2013
1-6 O/U as 3.5-7 point favorite since 2015	UTEP	1-5 O/U after playing Louisiana Tech since 2013
7-1 S/U as 7.5-10 point favorite since 2012	UAB	1-6 S/U prior to playing North Texas since 2014
0-6 ATS as 7.5-10 point favorite since 2013	UAB	1-7 ATS prior to playing North Texas since 2013
1-8 ATS @ home as 10.5 point or more favorite since 2014	UAB	2-5 ATS after playing Southern Miss since 2014

This book takes a comprehensive look at College Football's most memorable plays and memorable moments throughout the years. You will read about games most people have never heard of, but have played an important role in shaping College Football as we know it today. It is a must read for fans of College Football. Games include all divisions of College Football (FBS, FCS, Division II and Division III). It is truly a walk down memory lane for fans who enjoy the rich traditions and history of college football.

College Football History "Memorable Plays and Memorable Moments" {8.5" x 11"} {156 pages}

Price $24.99 + $5.00 Shipping & Handling

This books is available from Steve's Football Bible LLC
These books available at numerous online retailers

Copyright © 2021 by Steve's Football Bible, LLC

  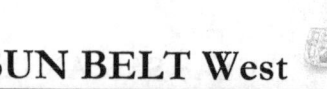 

TEXAS STATE BOBCATS   SUN BELT West

2020-Texas State		Opponent	State	Opp	S/U	Line	ATS	Total	O/U	
9/5/2020	vs	SMU	24	31	L	24.0	W	70.0	U	
9/12/2020	vs	TEXAS-SAN ANTONIO	48	51	L	-6.5	L	56.0	O	{OT}
9/19/2020	@	Louisiana-Monroe	38	17	W	-3.0	W	58.0	U	
9/26/2020	@	Boston College	21	24	L	20.5	W	56.5	U	
10/10/2020	@	Troy	17	37	L	7.0	L	59.5	U	
10/17/2020	@	South Alabama	20	30	L	3.0	L	58.0	U	
10/24/2020	@	Byu	14	52	L	30.0	L	61.5	O	
10/31/2020	vs	LOUISIANA	34	44	L	16.5	W	56.5	O	
11/7/2020	vs	APPALACHIAN STATE	17	38	L	21.5	W	59.0	U	
11/14/2020	@	Georgia Southern	38	40	L	13.0	W	50.0	O	
11/21/2020	vs	ARKANSAS STATE	47	45	W	4.5	W	69.0	O	
11/28/2020	vs	COASTAL CAROLINA	14	49	L	16.5	L	59.0	O	
Coach: Everett Withers		Season Record >>	332	458	2-10	ATS>>	7-5	O/U>>	6-6	

2019-Texas State		Opponent	State	Opp	S/U	Line	ATS	Total	O/U	
8/29/2019	@	Texas A&M	7	41	L	33.5	L	57.0	U	
9/7/2019	vs	WYOMING	14	23	L	7.0	L	47.5	U	
9/14/2019	@	Smu	17	47	L	17.5	L	62.5	O	
9/21/2019	vs	GEORGIA STATE	37	34	W	-3.0	T	62.5	O	{3 OT}
9/28/2019	vs	NICHOLLS STATE	24	3	W	NL	---	NT	---	"Battle for the Paddle"
10/10/2019	vs	LOUISIANA-MONROE	14	24	L	4.0	L	60.0	U	
10/26/2019	@	Arkansas State	14	38	L	11.0	L	60.5	U	
11/2/2019	@	Louisiana-Lafayette	3	31	L	23.0	L	55.0	U	
11/9/2019	vs	SOUTH ALABAMA	30	28	W	-7.0	L	41.5	O	
11/16/2019	vs	TROY	27	63	L	7.0	L	64.5	O	
11/23/2019	@	Appalachian State	13	35	L	28.0	W	50.0	U	
11/30/2019	@	Coastal Carolina	21	24	L	7.0	W	52.0	U	
Coach: Everett Withers		Season Record >>	221	391	3-9	ATS>>	2-8-1	O/U>>	4-7	

2018-Texas State		Opponent	State	Opp	S/U	Line	ATS	Total	O/U	
9/1/2018	@	Rutgers	7	35	L	16.5	L	48.0	U	
9/8/2018	vs	TEXAS SOUTHERN	36	20	W	-31.5	L	NT	---	
9/15/2018	@	South Alabama	31	41	L	9.5	L	49.0	O	
9/22/2018	@	Texas-San Antonio	21	25	L	7.0	W	49.0	U	
10/6/2018	vs	LOUISIANA-LAFAYETTE	27	42	L	3.5	L	58.5	O	
10/13/2018	vs	GEORGIA SOUTHERN	13	15	L	17.0	W	51.0	U	
10/20/2018	@	Louisiana-Monroe	14	20	L	10.5	W	59.5	U	
10/27/2018	vs	NEW MEXICO STATE	27	20	W	PK	W	56.0	U	
11/3/2018	@	Georgia State	40	31	W	7.0	W	52.5	O	
11/10/2018	vs	APPALACHIAN STATE	7	38	L	19.0	L	45.5	U	
11/17/2018	@	Troy	7	12	L	22.0	W	47.5	U	
11/24/2018	vs	ARKANSAS STATE	7	33	L	13.0	L	48.5	U	
Coach: Everett Withers		Season Record >>	237	332	3-9	ATS>>	6-6	O/U>>	3-8	

2017-Texas State		Opponent	State	Opp	S/U	Line	ATS	Total	O/U	
9/2/2017	vs	HOUSTON BAPTIST	20	11	W	-16.0	L	57.0	U	
9/9/2017	@	Colorado	3	37	L	35.5	W	56.5	U	
9/16/2017	vs	APPALACHIAN STATE	13	20	L	21.5	W	49.5	U	
9/23/2017	vs	TEXAS-SAN ANTONIO	14	44	L	13.5	L	45.0	O	
9/30/2017	@	Wyoming	10	45	L	16.0	L	45.0	O	
10/7/2017	vs	LOUISIANA-MONROE	27	45	L	5.0	L	54.5	O	
10/12/2017	@	Louisiana-Lafayette	7	24	L	14.0	L	55.0	U	
10/28/2017	@	Coastal Carolina	27	7	W	9.5	W	54.0	U	
11/4/2017	vs	NEW MEXICO STATE	35	45	L	9.0	L	56.0	O	
11/11/2017	vs	GEORGIA STATE	30	33	L	5.5	W	51.0	O	
11/18/2017	@	Arkansas State	12	30	L	26.5	W	57.5	U	
11/25/2017	@	Troy	9	62	L	23.0	L	53.0	O	
Coach: Everett Withers		Season Record >>	207	403	2-10	ATS>>	5-7	O/U>>	6-6	

Copyright © 2021 by Steve's Football Bible, LLC

TEXAS STATE BOBCATS SUN BELT West

STADIUM: Jim Wacker Field at Bobcat Stadium {30,008}				Location: Mc Allen, TX			COACH: Jake Spavital		
DATE		**Opponent**	**State**	**Opp**	**S/U**	**Line**	**ATS**	**Total**	**O/U**	**Trends & Angles**
9/4/2021	vs	*BAYLOR*								vs Baylor - Baylor leads series 7-0
9/11/2021	@	*Florida International*								1st meeting
9/18/2021	vs	*INCARNATE WORD*								vs Incarnate Word - Texas State leads series 1-0
9/25/2021	@	*Eastern Michigan*								1st meeting
10/9/2021	vs	SOUTH ALABAMA								vs South Alabama - Series tied 3-3
10/16/2021	vs	TROY								0-9 S/U vs Troy since 1998
10/23/2021	@	Georgia State								vs Georgia State - Texas State leads series 4-3
10/30/2021	@	Louisiana								vs Louisiana - Louisiana leads series 8-0
11/6/2021	vs	LOUISIANA-MONROE								vs Louisiana-Monroe - ULM leads series 12-5
11/13/2021	vs	GEORGIA SOUTHERN								0-4 S/U vs Georgia Southern as Dog since 2014
11/20/2021	@	Coastal Carolina								vs Coastal Carolina - Coastal leads series 2-1
11/27/2021	@	Arkansas State								vs Arkansas State - Ark State leads series 6-2
12/4/2021	vs									Sun Belt Championship
	vs									BOWL GAME

Pointspread Analysis Non-Conference		Pointspread Analysis Conference
2-17 S/U vs Non-Conf. as 15.5 point or more Dog since 2012		0-5 O/U vs Appalachian State as Dog since 2016
7-0 S/U vs Non-Conf. as 10.5 point or more favorite since 2013		4-0 O/U vs Georgia Southern as Dog since 2014
Dog		0-7 S/U vs Louisiana as Dog since 2013
0-22 S/U as 20.5 point or more Dog since 2012		vs Troy - Troy leads series 10-1
3-14 O/U as 20.5 point more Dog since 2016		0-6 S/U vs Troy as Dog since 2013
1-12 S/U as 15.5-20 point Dog since 2012		
0-9 S/U as 10.5-15 point Dog since 2013		
0-3 S/U & ATS @ home as 7.5-10 point Dog since 2014		
1-8 S/U on road as 3.5-7 point Dog since 2012		
1-7 S/U @ home as 3.5-7 point Dog since 2016	BAYLOR	21-4 S/U in 1st home game of season since 1996
4-1 S/U & ATS as 3 point or less Dog since 2013	E. Michigan	1-11 S/U in 2nd road game of season since 2009
Favorite	Louisiana	1-7 S/U prior to playing UL-Monroe since 2013
1-4 S/U @ home as 3 point or less favorite since 2012	Louisiana	1-6 ATS prior to playing Louisiana-Monroe since 2013
0-4-1 ATS @ home as 3 point or less favorite since 2012	UL-MONROE	6-1 ATS after playing Louisiana since 2014
11-3 S/U @ home as 6 point or more favorite since 2012	Coastal Carolina	0-7 S/U prior to playing Arkansas State since 2014
3-0 S/U & ATS on road as 6 point or more favorite since 2013	Arkansas State	1-10 S/U in final road game of season since 2010

Steve's Football Bible also offers the Pro Football Bible, the Pro football handicapper's best friend for the 2021 football season. To order Go to: www.stevesfootballbible.com

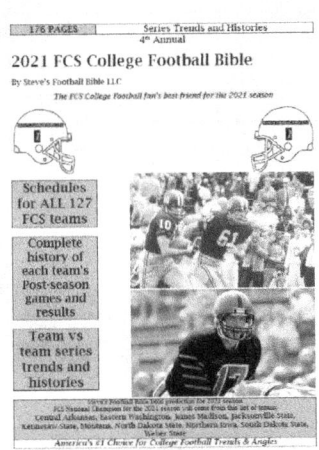

2021 FCS Football Bible $19.95

Copyright © 2021 by Steve's Football Bible, LLC

TEXAS TECH RED RAIDERS   BIG TWELVE

2020-Texas Tech		Opponent	Tech	Opp	S/U	Line	ATS	Total	O/U	
9/12/2020	vs	HOUSTON BAPTIST	35	33	W	-39.5	L	71.5	U	
9/26/2020	vs	TEXAS	56	63	L	17.5	W	71.0	O	"Chancellor's Spurs"
10/3/2020	@	Kansas State	21	31	L	PK	L	62.0	U	
10/10/2020	@	Iowa State	15	31	L	10.0	L	63.0	U	
10/24/2020	vs	WEST VIRGINIA	34	27	W	2.0	W	54.0	O	
10/31/2020	vs	OKLAHOMA	28	62	L	17.0	L	65.0	O	
11/7/2020	@	Tcu	18	34	L	9.5	L	60.0	U	"Saddle Trophy"
11/14/2020	vs	BAYLOR	24	23	W	-1.0	T	54.0	U	
11/28/2020	@	Oklahoma State	44	50	L	12.0	W	57.0	O	
12/5/2020	vs	KANSAS	16	13	W	-27.0	L	63.0	U	
Coach: Matt Wells		Season Record >>	291	367	4-6	ATS>>	3-6-1	O/U>>	4-6	
2019-Texas Tech		Opponent	Tech	Opp	S/U	Line	ATS	Total	O/U	
8/31/2019	vs	MONTANA STATE	45	10	W	-28.5	W	NT	---	
9/7/2019	vs	TEXAS-EL PASO	38	3	W	-34.5	W	64.5	U	
9/14/2019	@	Arizona	14	28	L	-2.0	L	74.0	U	
9/28/2019	@	Oklahoma	16	55	L	27.0	L	69.0	O	
10/5/2019	vs	OKLAHOMA STATE	45	35	W	9.5	W	62.5	O	
10/12/2019	@	Baylor	30	33	L	10.5	W	60.0	O	{2 OT}
10/19/2019	vs	IOWA STATE	24	34	L	7.5	L	57.0	O	
10/26/2019	@	Kansas	34	37	L	-6.0	L	65.5	O	
11/9/2019	@	West Virginia	38	17	W	-2.5	W	56.5	U	
11/16/2019	vs	TCU	31	33	L	3.5	W	53.5	O	"Saddle Trophy"
11/23/2019	vs	KANSAS STATE	27	30	L	PK	L	57.5	U	
11/30/2019	@	Texas	24	49	L	8.0	L	65.0	O	"Chancellor's Spurs"
Coach: Matt Wells		Season Record >>	366	364	4-8	ATS>>	6-6	O/U>>	7-4	
2018-Texas Tech		Opponent	Tech	Opp	S/U	Line	ATS	Total	O/U	
9/1/2018	vs	Mississippi	27	47	L	2.0	L	71.5	O	NRG Stadium
9/8/2018	vs	LAMAR	77	0	W	-48.0	W	NT	---	
9/15/2018	vs	HOUSTON	63	49	W	PK	W	69.0	O	
9/22/2018	@	Oklahoma State	41	17	W	14.5	W	74.5	U	
9/29/2018	vs	WEST VIRGINIA	34	42	L	3.5	L	73.0	O	
10/13/2018	@	Tcu	17	14	W	7.0	W	57.5	U	"Saddle Trophy"
10/20/2018	vs	KANSAS	48	16	W	-17.5	W	59.0	O	
10/27/2018	@	Iowa State	31	40	L	4.5	L	59.0	O	
11/3/2018	vs	OKLAHOMA	46	51	L	14.0	W	78.5	O	
11/10/2018	vs	TEXAS	34	41	L	2.0	L	62.0	O	"Chancellor's Spurs"
11/17/2018	@	Kansas State	6	21	L	-6.5	L	55.0	U	
11/24/2018	vs	Baylor	24	35	L	-6.5	L	63.5	U	AT&T Stadium
Coach: Kliff Kingsbury		Season Record >>	448	373	5-7	ATS>>	6-6	O/U>>	7-4	
2017-Texas Tech		Opponent	Tech	Opp	S/U	Line	ATS	Total	O/U	
9/2/2017	vs	EASTERN WASHINGTON	56	10	W	-12.5	W	87.5	U	
9/16/2017	vs	ARIZONA STATE	52	45	W	-7.0	T	74.0	O	
9/23/2017	@	Houston	27	24	W	7.0	W	68.0	U	
9/30/2017	vs	OKLAHOMA STATE	34	41	L	11.0	W	85.0	U	
10/7/2017	@	Kansas	65	19	W	-14.5	W	76.0	O	
10/14/2017	@	West Virginia	35	46	L	5.5	L	77.5	O	
10/21/2017	vs	IOWA STATE	13	31	L	-6.5	L	66.0	U	
10/28/2017	@	Oklahoma	27	49	L	19.5	L	77.5	U	
11/4/2017	vs	KANSAS STATE	35	42	L	-4.0	L	63.5	O	{OT}
11/11/2017	vs	Baylor	38	24	W	-9.0	W	68.0	U	
11/18/2017	vs	TCU	3	27	L	6.5	L	52.0	U	"Saddle Trophy"
11/25/2017	@	Texas	27	23	W	7.5	W	58.0	U	"Chancellor's Spurs"
12/23/2017	vs	South Florida	34	38	L	2.0	L	65.5	O	Birmingham Bowl
Coach: Kliff Kingsbury		Season Record >>	446	419	6-7	ATS>>	6-6-1	O/U>>	5-8	

Copyright © 2021 by Steve's Football Bible, LLC

TEXAS TECH RED RAIDERS   BIG TWELVE

STADIUM: Jones AT&T Stadium {60,454}							Location: Lubbock, TX		COACH: Matt Wells		
DATE		Opponent	Tech	Opp	S/U	Line	ATS	Total	O/U	Trends & Angles	
9/4/2021	@	*Houston*								8-1 S/U vs Houston since 1991 {7-2 ATS{	
9/11/2021	vs	*STEPHEN F. AUSTIN*								vs Stephen F. Austin – T. Tech leads series 3-0	
9/18/2021	vs	*FLA INTERNATIONAL*								vs FIU - Texas Tech leads series 1-0	
9/25/2021	@	Texas								3-16 S/U vs Texas as Dog since 1999	
10/2/2021	@	West Virginia								vs West Virginia – W VA leads series 6-4	
10/9/2021	vs	TCU								vs TCU - Texas Tech leads series 38-29-3	
10/16/2021	@	Kansas								12-1 S/U vs Kansas as favorite since 2004	
10/23/2021	vs	KANSAS STATE								vs Kansas State - K State leads series 12-9	
10/30/2021	@	Oklahoma								0-9 S/U vs Oklahoma as Dog since 2012	
11/13/2021	vs	IOWA STATE								vs Iowa State - Texas Tech leads series 11-8	
11/20/2021	vs	OKLAHOMA STATE								vs OK State - Texas Tech leads series 23-22-3	
11/27/2021	@	Baylor								vs Baylor - Baylor leads series 39-38-1	
12/4/2021	vs									BIG XII Championship	
	vs									BOWL GAME	

Pointspread Analysis		Pointspread Analysis
Non-Conference		**Conference**
0-5 S/U vs Non-Conf. as 15.5 point or more Dog since 1986		7-0 O/U vs Baylor as Dog since 2011
1-7 S/U vs Non-Conf. as 3.5-7 point Dog since 1986		18-1 S/U vs Baylor as favorite since 1992
0-10 S/U & ATS vs Non-Conf. as 3 point or less favorite since 1992		vs Kansas - Texas Tech leads series 20-2
7-0-1 O/U vs Non-Conf. as 3.5-7 point favorite since 2002		3-0 S/U & ATS vs Kansas as Dog since 1996
61-3 S/U vs Non-Conf. as 7.5 point or more favorite since 1985		7-1 O/U vs Kansas State as favorite since 2005
6-0-1 S/U vs Houston as favorite since 1986		1-4 S/U & ATS vs Kansas State as favorite since 2011
Dog		1-5 S/U @ Kansas State as Dog since 1996
2-19 S/U as 20.5 point or more Dog since 1983		vs Oklahoma - Oklahoma leads series 22-6
8-3 ATS on road as 20.5 point or more Dog since 1994		1-13 S/U vs Oklahoma as 13.5 point or more Dog since 1994
6-1 O/U as 20.5 point or more Dog since 2001		2-10 S/U vs Oklahoma State as Dog since 1999
0-15 S/U on road as 15.5-20 point Dog since 1983		5-0-1 S/U vs TCU as 6 point or more favorite since 1983
1-22 S/U as 15.5-20 point Dog since 1983		5-1 ATS vs TCU as 6 point or more favorite since 1985
6-0 ATS @ home as 10.5-15 point Dog since 1999		vs Texas - Texas leads series 53-17
3-13 S/U on road as 10.5-15 point Dog since 1985		0-14 S/U vs Texas as 10 point or more Dog since 1983
0-7 S/U @ home as 3.5-7 point Dog since 2012		2-5 S/U vs West Virginia since 2014
3-20 S/U on road as 3.5-7 point Dog since 1998		
4-18 ATS on road as 3.5-7 point Dog since 1999	Houston	10-4 ATS in 1st road game of season since 2007
10-2 S/U on road as 3 point or less Dog since 1996	Houston	13-4 S/U in 1st road game of season since 2004
11-2 ATS on road as 3 point or less Dog since 1993	Houston	9-4-1 ATS in 1st game of season since 2005
1-6 S/U & ATS as 3 point or less Dog since 2015	Houston	17-1 S/U in 1st game of season since 2003
Favorite	S.F. AUSTIN	21-0 S/U in 1st home game of season since 2000
1-5 S/U & ATS @ home as 3 point or less favorite since 2002	FLORIDA	15-3 S/U in 2nd home game of season since 2003
13-5-2 O/U as 3.5-7 point favorite since 2007	Texas	7-3 ATS in 2nd road game of season since 2011
10-0 S/U @ home as 7.5-10 point favorite since 1985	W. Virginia	6-2-1 ATS prior to playing TCU since 2012
7-2-1 ATS @ home as 7.5-10 point favorite since 1985	W. Virginia	7-3 S/U prior to playing TCU since 2006
8-1 S/U on road as 7.5-10 point favorite since 1984	TCU	7-1 ATS prior to playing Kansas since 2013
5-0 S/U & ATS on road as 10.5-15 point favorite since 1993	K STATE	2-8 S/U after playing Kansas since 2009
23-4 S/U @ home as 10.5-15 point favorite since 1985	K STATE	8-1 O/U after playing Kansas since 2011
22-0 S/U as 15.5-20 point favorite since 1983	K STATE	2-6 O/U prior to playing Oklahoma since 2013
17-4 ATS as 15.5-20 point favorite since 1987	K STATE	1-7 ATS prior to playing Oklahoma since 2013
30-1 S/U @ home as 20.5 point or more favorite since 2000	Oklahoma	7-1 O/U prior to playing Iowa State since 2013
12-1 S/U on road as 20.5 point or more favorite since 1989	OK STATE	3-13 S/U prior to playing Baylor since 2005
Bowl Games		
0-4 S/U in Cotton Bowl		
1-7 S/U in Sun Bowl		
0-5 S/U vs SEC in Bowl Games since 1986		
7-1-1 O/U in Bowl Games since 2006		
2-8 ATS in Bowl Games since 2006		
0-4 S/U in Bowl Games as 3.5-7 point Dog since 1986		
0-3 S/U & ATS in Bowl Games as 3 point or less favorite since 2000		11-0 O/U on road when ranked since 2008
3-0 S/U in Bowl Games as 7.5-10 point favorite since 2006		0-11 ATS @ home when ranked since 2008

Copyright © 2021 by Steve's Football Bible, LLC

TOLEDO ROCKETS   MAC West

2020-Toledo		Opponent	Tol	Opp	S/U	Line	ATS	Total	O/U	
11/4/2020	vs	BOWLING GREEN	38	3	W	-24.0	W	62.0	U	"Battle of I-75 Trophy"
11/11/2020	@	Western Michigan	38	41	L	1.0	L	58.5	O	
11/18/2020	@	Eastern Michigan	45	28	W	-6.5	W	62.5	O	
11/28/2020	vs	BALL STATE	24	27	L	-9.5	L	67.0	U	
12/5/2020	@	Northern Illinois	41	24	W	-9.0	W	53.5	O	
12/12/2020	vs	CENTRAL MICHIGAN	24	23	W	-10.0	L	55.0	U	
Coach: Jason Candle		Season Record >>	210	146	4-2	ATS>>	3-3	O/U>>	3-3	
2019-Toledo		Opponent	Tol	Opp	S/U	Line	ATS	Total	O/U	
8/31/2019	@	Kentucky	24	38	L	9.0	L	60.5	O	
9/14/2019	vs	MURRAY STATE	45	0	W	-36.0	W	NT	---	
9/21/2019	@	Colorado State	41	35	W	-6.0	T	67.0	O	
9/28/2019	vs	BYU	28	21	W	1.5	W	62.5	U	
10/5/2019	vs	WESTERN MICHIGAN	31	24	W	-1.5	W	73.5	U	
10/12/2019	@	Bowling Green	7	20	L	-27.0	L	65.0	U	"Battle of I-75 Strophy"
10/19/2019	@	Ball State	14	52	L	3.0	L	58.0	O	
10/26/2019	vs	EASTERN MICHIGAN	37	34	W	-2.5	W	53.5	O	{OT}
11/5/2019	vs	KENT STATE	35	33	W	-3.0	L	64.0	O	
11/13/2019	vs	NORTHERN ILLINOIS	28	31	L	-1.5	L	55.5	O	
11/20/2019	@	Buffalo	30	49	L	10.0	L	54.0	O	
11/29/2019	@	Central Michigan	7	49	L	14.5	L	63.5	U	
Coach: Jason Candle		Season Record >>	327	386	6-6	ATS>>	4-7-1	O/U>>	7-4	
2018-Toledo		Opponent	Tol	Opp	S/U	Line	ATS	Total	O/U	
9/1/2018	vs	VIRGINIA MILITARY	66	3	W	-48.5	W	NT	---	
9/15/2018	vs	MIAMI-FL	24	49	L	12.0	L	58.5	O	
9/22/2018	vs	NEVADA	63	44	W	-12.0	W	69.0	O	
9/29/2018	@	Fresno State	27	49	L	10.0	L	62.0	O	
10/6/2018	vs	BOWLING GREEN	52	36	W	-23.0	L	71.0	O	"Battle of I-75 Trophy"
10/13/2018	@	Eastern Michigan	26	28	L	-2.0	L	63.0	U	
10/20/2018	vs	BUFFALO	17	31	L	-3.0	L	62.5	U	
10/25/2018	@	Western Michigan	51	24	W	4.0	W	68.0	O	
10/31/2018	vs	BALL STATE	45	13	W	-20.0	W	63.5	U	
11/7/2018	@	Northern Illinois	15	38	L	3.5	L	54.0	U	
11/15/2018	@	Kent State	56	34	W	-11.5	W	57.0	O	
11/23/2018	vs	CENTRAL MICHIGAN	51	13	W	-18.5	W	57.5	O	
12/21/2018	vs	Florida International	18	49	L	-7.0	L	57.5	O	Bahamas Bowl
Coach: Jason Candle		Season Record >>	511	411	7-6	ATS>>	6-7	O/U>>	8-4	
2017-Toledo		Opponent	Tol	Opp	S/U	Line	ATS	Total	O/U	
8/31/2017	vs	ELON	47	13	W	-45.0	L	55.5	O	
9/9/2017	@	Nevada	37	24	W	-10.5	W	69.5	U	
9/16/2017	vs	TULSA	54	51	W	-7.0	L	74.5	O	
9/23/2017	@	Miami	30	52	L	13.0	L	59.5	O	
10/7/2017	vs	EASTERN MICHIGAN	20	15	W	-13.5	L	61.0	U	
10/14/2017	@	Central Michigan	30	10	W	-9.0	W	54.5	U	
10/21/2017	vs	AKRON	48	21	W	-14.5	W	58.5	O	
10/26/2017	@	Ball State	58	17	W	-26.5	W	54.5	O	
11/2/2017	vs	NORTHERN ILLINOIS	27	17	W	-7.5	W	57.0	U	
11/8/2017	@	Ohio	10	38	L	-3.0	L	64.5	U	
11/15/2017	@	Bowling Green	66	37	W	-17.0	W	65.5	O	"Battle of I-75 Trophy"
11/24/2017	vs	WESTERN MICHIGAN	37	10	W	-12.0	W	62.0	U	
12/2/2017	vs	Akron	41	17	W	-21.0	L	61.0	U	MAC Championship
12/23/2017	vs	Appalachian State	0	34	L	-6.0	L	61.0	U	Dollar General Bowl
Coach: Jason Candle		Season Record >>	505	356	11-3	ATS>>	8-6	O/U>>	6-8	MAC Champions

Copyright © 2021 by Steve's Football Bible, LLC

TOLEDO ROCKETS

MAC West

STADIUM: Glass Bowl {26,038}						Location: Toledo, OH			COACH: Jason Candle	
DATE		Opponent	Tol	Opp	S/U	Line	ATS	Total	O/U	Trends & Angles
9/4/2021	vs	*NORFOLK STATE*								1st meeting
9/11/2021	@	*Notre Dame*								1st meeting
9/18/2021	vs	*COLORADO STATE*								vs Colorado State - Toledo leads series 2-1
9/25/2021	@	**Ball State**								vs Ball State - Toledo leads series 24-21-1
10/2/2021	@	*Massachusetts*								vs UMASS - Toledo leads series 4-1
10/9/2021	vs	NORTHERN ILLINOIS								
10/16/2021	@	Central Michigan								20-3 S/U vs C Michigan as favorite since 1993
10/23/2021	vs	WESTERN MICHIGAN								13-3 S/U @ home vs WMU since 1989
11/2/2021	vs	EASTERN MICHIGAN								vs E Michigan - Toledo leads series 36-12
11/10/2021	@	Bowling Green								10-1 S/U vs B. Green as favorite since 2002
11/16/2021	@	Ohio								
11/27/2021	vs	AKRON								9-1 S/U vs Akron as favorite since 1994
12/3/2021	vs									MAC Championship
	vs									BOWL GAME

Pointspread Analysis Non-Conference		Pointspread Analysis Conference
1-9 S/U vs Non-Conf. as 20.5 point or more Dog since 1989		0-6 S/U vs Ball State as Dog since 1993
1-6 O/U vs Non-Conf. as 20.5 point or more Dog since 2007		10-1 S/U vs Ball State as 14 point or more favorite since 1998
1-7 S/U & ATS vs Non-Conf. as 10.5-15 point Dog since 1993		vs Bowling Green - Toledo leads series 41-40-4
3-7 S/U vs Non-Conf. as 3 point or less Dog since 1996		0-5 O/U vs Bowling Green as Dog since 2007
8-3 S/U vs Non-Conf. as 3.5-7 point favorite since 1990		12-1 S/U vs Bowling Green as 6.5 point or more favorite since 1990
9-1 S/U vs Non-Conf. as 7.15-15 point favorite since 1990		vs Central Michigan - Toledo leads series 27-19
6-0 ATS vs Non-Conf. as 10.5-15 point favorite since 1992		0-6 S/U vs Central Michigan as Dog since 1992 {1-5 ATS}
7-0 S/U vs Non-Conf. as 20.5 point or more favorite since 2001		16-0 S/U vs C. Michigan as 8 point or more favorite since 1995
Dog		18-1 S/U vs Eastern Michigan as favorite since 2000
1-10 S/U as 20.5 point or more Dog since 1989		15-0 S/U vs E. Michigan as 13 point or more favorite since 1992
1-7 O/U as 20.5 point or more Dog since 1999		11-1 S/U vs Kent State as favorite since 1989
0-5 S/U as 15.5-20 point Dog since 2008		0-5 S/U vs Northern Illinois as Dog since 2010
1-5 O/U as 15.5-20 point Dog since 2008		vs Northern Illinois - Toledo leads series 32-16
2-12 S/U as 10.5-15 point Dog since 1993		1-8 O/U vs Northern Illinois as Dog since 2004
8-3 ATS as 3.5-7 point Dog since 2009		8-1 S/U vs Ohio as 6.5 point or more favorite since 1989
Favorite		9-3 ATS vs Western Michigan as Dog since 1989
9-3 O/U @ home as 3 point or less favorite since 2002		vs Western Michigan - Toledo leads series 44-31
0-5 O/U as 3 point or less favorite since 2012		Game 6-2 O/U @ home vs Western Michigan since 2005
13-1 S/U on road as 3.5-7 point favorite since 1990		7-0 S/U vs W. Michigan as 11.5 point or more favorite since 2001
7-1 S/U & ATS as 7.5-10 point favorite since 2015		**Bowl Games**
1-7 O/U as 7.5-10 point favorite since 2015		0-5 S/U in Bowl Games as 3.0-15 point Dog since 1997
9-2 S/U on road as 7.5-10 point favorite since 1993		
15-1 S/U @ home as 10.5-15 point favorite since 2001	NORFOLK	10-0 S/U in 1st home game of season since 2011
20-1 S/U as 10.5-15 point favorite since 2010	NORFOLK	11-2 ATS in 1st home game of season since 2008
9-0 S/U on road as 10.5-15 point favorite since 2010	COLORADO ST.	9-1 ATS prior to playing Ball State since 2010
5-0 S/U on road as 15.5-20 point favorite since 1994	Massachusetts	13-3 S/U prior to playing Northern Illinois since 2005
17-1 S/U @ home as 15.5-20 point favorite since 1990	N. ILLINOIS	9-2 S/U prior to playing Central Michigan since 2010
5-1 S/U on road as 20.5 point or more favorite since 2002	E. MICHIGAN	8-2 ATS after playing Western Michigan since 2006
30-0 S/U @ home as 20.5 point or more favorite since 1995	E. MICHIGAN	10-2 S/U after playing Western Michigan since 2004
9-1 O/U @ home as 20.5 point or more favorite since 2005	B. Green	7-2 S/U after playing Eastern Michigan since 2011
	Ohio	10-3 S/U after playing Bowling Green since 1997

Copyright © 2021 by Steve's Football Bible, LLC

TROY TROJANS

SUN BELT East

2020-Troy		Opponent	Troy	Opp	S/U	Line	ATS	Total	O/U	
9/19/2020	@	Middle Tennessee	47	14	W	-2.5	W	65.0	U	"The Palladium Trophy"
9/26/2020	@	Byu	7	48	L	14.0	L	56.5	U	
10/10/2020	vs	TEXAS STATE	37	17	W	-7.0	W	59.5	U	
10/17/2020	vs	EASTERN KENTUCKY	31	29	W	-28.5	L	60.0	T	
10/24/2020	vs	GEORGIA STATE	34	36	L	-2.5	L	68.5	O	
10/31/2020	@	Arkansas State	38	10	W	3.5	W	70.0	U	
11/7/2020	@	Georgia Southern	13	20	L	-2.5	L	52.0	U	
11/21/2020	vs	MIDDLE TENNESSEE	17	20	L	-10.5	L	60.5	U	
11/28/2020	@	Appalachian State	10	47	L	14.0	L	50.5	O	
12/5/2020	@	South Alabama	29	0	W	-4.0	W	54.0	U	"The Championship Belt"
12/12/2020	vs	COASTAL CAROLINA	38	42	L	11.5	W	53.0	O	
Coach: Chip Lindsey		Season Record >>	301	283	5-6	ATS>>	5-6	O/U>>	3-7-1	
2019-Troy		Opponent	Troy	Opp	S/U	Line	ATS	Total	O/U	
8/31/2019	vs	CAMPBELL	43	14	W	-36.5	L	NT	---	
9/14/2019	vs	SOUTHERN MISS	42	47	L	-3.0	L	49.0	O	
9/21/2019	@	Akron	35	7	W	-18.5	W	57.0	U	
9/28/2019	vs	ARKANSAS STATE	43	50	L	-7.0	L	59.5	O	
10/5/2019	@	Missouri	10	42	L	25.5	L	65.5	U	
10/16/2019	vs	SOUTH ALABAMA	17	13	W	-17.0	W	54.5	U	"The Championship Belt"
10/26/2019	@	Georgia State	33	52	L	1.0	L	67.0	O	
11/2/2019	@	Coastal Carolina	35	36	L	PK	L	60.0	O	
11/9/2019	vs	GEORGIA SOUTHERN	49	28	W	2.5	W	57.0	O	
11/16/2019	@	Texas State	63	27	W	-7.0	W	64.5	O	
11/23/2019	@	Louisiana-Lafayette	3	53	L	12.5	L	74.0	U	
11/30/2019	vs	APPALACHIAN STATE	13	48	L	11.0	L	64.0	U	
Coach: Neal Brown		Season Record >>	386	417	5-7	ATS>>	4-8	O/U>>	6-5	
2018-Troy		Opponent	Troy	Opp	S/U	Line	ATS	Total	O/U	
9/1/2018	vs	BOISE STATE	20	56	L	9.0	L	48.0	O	
9/8/2018	vs	FLORIDA A&M	59	7	W	-35.0	W	NT	---	
9/15/2018	@	Nebraska	24	19	W	10.5	W	55.5	U	
9/22/2018	@	Louisiana-Monroe	35	27	W	-4.5	W	59.0	O	
9/29/2018	vs	COASTAL CAROLINA	45	21	W	-13.5	W	57.0	O	
10/4/2018	vs	GEORGIA STATE	37	20	W	-17.0	T	55.5	O	
10/13/2018	@	Liberty	16	22	L	-10.0	L	63.0	U	
10/23/2018	@	South Alabama	38	17	W	-11.5	W	52.0	O	"The Championship Belt"
11/3/2018	vs	LOUISIANA-LAFAYETTE	26	16	W	-7.5	W	64.5	U	
11/10/2018	@	Georgia Southern	35	21	W	-2.5	W	44.5	O	
11/17/2018	vs	TEXAS STATE	12	7	W	-22.0	L	47.5	U	
11/24/2018	@	Appalachian State	10	21	L	11.5	L	45.5	U	
12/22/2018	vs	Buffalo	42	32	W	2.5	W	51.5	O	Dollar General Bowl
Coach: Neal Brown		Season Record >>	399	286	10-3	ATS>>	9-3-1	O/U>>	7-5	
2017-Troy		Opponent	Troy	Opp	S/U	Line	ATS	Total	O/U	
9/2/2017	@	Boise State	13	24	L	10.5	L	59.0	U	
9/9/2017	vs	ALABAMA STATE	34	7	W	-42.5	L	NT	---	
9/16/2017	@	New Mexico State	27	24	W	-9.5	L	60.0	U	
9/23/2017	vs	AKRON	22	17	W	-17.0	L	55.5	U	
9/30/2017	@	Lsu	24	21	W	20.5	W	49.0	U	
10/11/2017	vs	SOUTH ALABAMA	8	19	L	-18.5	L	51.5	U	"The Championship Belt"
10/21/2017	@	Georgia State	34	10	W	-7.0	W	50.5	U	
10/28/2017	vs	GEORGIA SOUTHERN	38	16	W	-22.5	L	49.0	O	
11/2/2017	vs	IDAHO	24	21	W	-18.0	L	50.0	U	
11/11/2017	@	Coastal Carolina	42	17	W	-17.0	W	53.0	O	
11/25/2017	vs	TEXAS STATE	62	9	W	-23.0	W	53.0	O	
12/2/2017	@	Arkansas State	32	25	W	-1.0	W	60.0	U	
12/16/2017	vs	North Texas	50	30	W	-5.0	W	61.5	O	New Orleans Bowl
Coach: Neal Brown		Season Record >>	410	240	11-2	ATS>>	6-7	O/U>>	4-8	SUN BELT CHAMPIONS

Copyright © 2021 by Steve's Football Bible, LLC

TROY TROJANS

SUN BELT East

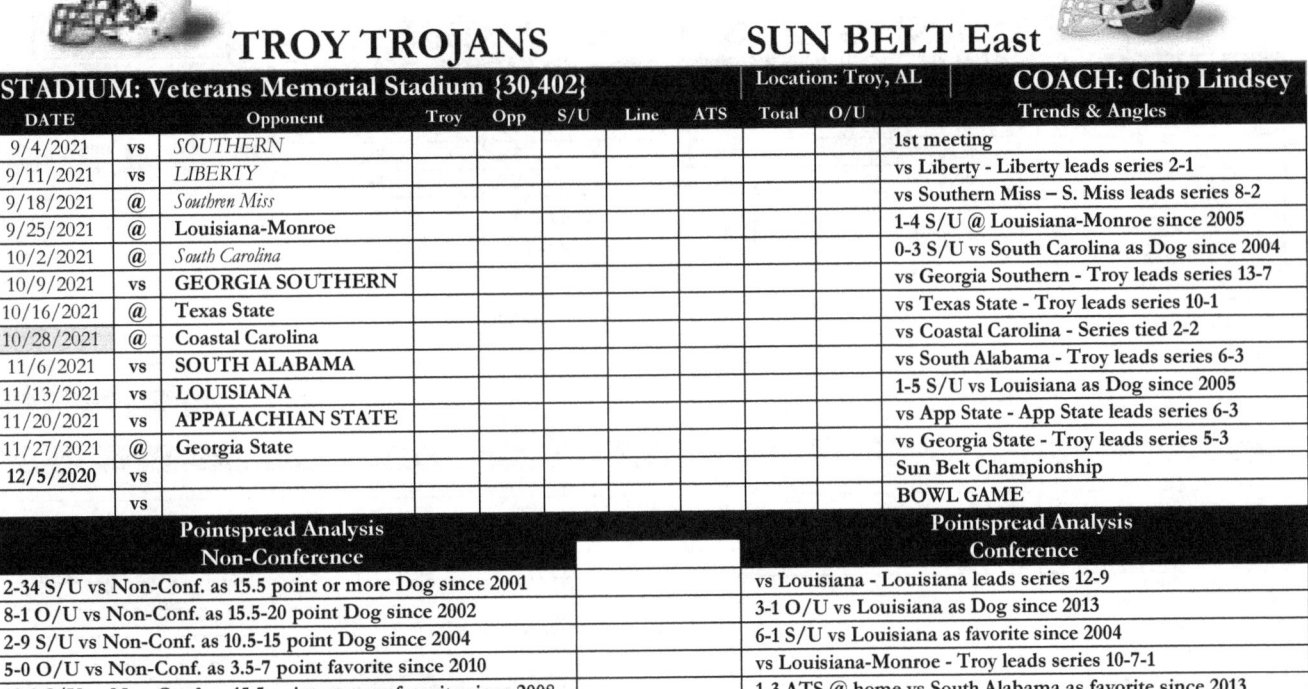

STADIUM: Veterans Memorial Stadium {30,402}											Location: Troy, AL	COACH: Chip Lindsey
DATE		Opponent	Troy	Opp	S/U	Line	ATS	Total	O/U			Trends & Angles
9/4/2021	vs	SOUTHERN										1st meeting
9/11/2021	vs	LIBERTY										vs Liberty - Liberty leads series 2-1
9/18/2021	@	Southren Miss										vs Southern Miss – S. Miss leads series 8-2
9/25/2021	@	Louisiana-Monroe										1-4 S/U @ Louisiana-Monroe since 2005
10/2/2021	@	South Carolina										0-3 S/U vs South Carolina as Dog since 2004
10/9/2021	vs	GEORGIA SOUTHERN										vs Georgia Southern - Troy leads series 13-7
10/16/2021	@	Texas State										vs Texas State - Troy leads series 10-1
10/28/2021	@	Coastal Carolina										vs Coastal Carolina - Series tied 2-2
11/6/2021	vs	SOUTH ALABAMA										vs South Alabama - Troy leads series 6-3
11/13/2021	vs	LOUISIANA										1-5 S/U vs Louisiana as Dog since 2005
11/20/2021	vs	APPALACHIAN STATE										vs App State - App State leads series 6-3
11/27/2021	@	Georgia State										vs Georgia State - Troy leads series 5-3
12/5/2020	vs											Sun Belt Championship
	vs											BOWL GAME

Pointspread Analysis Non-Conference		Pointspread Analysis Conference
2-34 S/U vs Non-Conf. as 15.5 point or more Dog since 2001		vs Louisiana - Louisiana leads series 12-9
8-1 O/U vs Non-Conf. as 15.5-20 point Dog since 2002		3-1 O/U vs Louisiana as Dog since 2013
2-9 S/U vs Non-Conf. as 10.5-15 point Dog since 2004		6-1 S/U vs Louisiana as favorite since 2004
5-0 O/U vs Non-Conf. as 3.5-7 point favorite since 2010		vs Louisiana-Monroe - Troy leads series 10-7-1
12-0 S/U vs Non-Conf. as 15.5 point or more favorite since 2008		1-3 ATS @ home vs South Alabama as favorite since 2013
Dog		6-0 S/U vs Texas State as favorite since 2013
0-17 S/U as 25.5 point or more Dog since 2001		
1-13 S/U as 20.5-25 point Dog since 2001	South Carolina	6-1 ATS prior to playing Georgia Southern since 2014
0-10 S/U as 15.5-20 point Dog since 2002	South Carolina	3-9 O/U after playing Louisiana-Monroe since 2001
9-1 O/U as 15.5-20 point Dog since 2002	APP STATE	1-5-1 O/U prior to playing Georgia State since 2014
2-17 S/U as 10.5-15 point Dog since 2004	APP STATE	1-5 S/U after playing Louisiana since 2010
0-3 S/U & ATS @ home as 3.5-7 point Dog since 2005		
1-7 O/U on road as 3.5-7 point Dog since 2005		
Favorite		
11-4 S/U @ home as 3.5-7 point favorite since 2001		
9-2-1 O/U @ home as 3.5-7 point favorite since 2012		
6-1 S/U on road as 7.5-10 point favorite since 2007		
3-9-1 ATS @ home as 7.5-10 point favorite since 2002		
15-2 S/U @ home as 10.5-15 point favorite since 2003		
13-3 S/U as 15.5-20 point favorite since 2007		
1-7 O/U @ home as 15.5-20 point favorite since 2011		
17-0 S/U as 20.5 point or more favorite since 2004		
Bowl Games		
8-0 O/U in Bowl Games		

Copyright © 2021 by Steve's Football Bible, LLC

TULANE GREEN WAVE   AMERICAN West

2020-Tulane		Opponent	Wave	Opp	S/U	Line	ATS	Total	O/U	
9/12/2020	@	South Alabama	27	24	W	-10.5	L	52.0	U	
9/19/2020	vs	NAVY	24	27	L	-6.5	L	47.5	O	
9/26/2020	@	Southern Mississippi	66	24	W	-3.5	W	54.5	O	"Battle for the Bell"
10/8/2020	@	Houston	31	49	L	7.0	L	58.0	O	
10/16/2020	vs	SMU	34	37	L	6.5	W	64.5	O	{OT}
10/24/2020	@	Central Florida	34	51	L	21.5	W	71.0	O	
10/31/2020	vs	TEMPLE	38	3	W	-7.0	W	56.0	U	
11/7/2020	@	East Carolina	38	21	W	-3.5	W	63.5	U	
11/14/2020	vs	ARMY	38	12	W	-3.0	W	46.5	O	
11/19/2020	@	Tulsa	24	30	L	4.5	L	56.5	U	{2 OT}
12/5/2020	vs	MEMPHIS	35	21	W	-3.5	W	64.0	U	
12/22/2020	vs	Nevada	27	38	L	1.0	L	56.5	O	Famous Idaho Potato Bowl
Coach: Willie Fritz		Season Record >>	416	337	6-6	ATS>>	7-5	O/U>>	7-5	
2019-Tulane		Opponent	Wave	Opp	S/U	Line	ATS	Total	O/U	
8/29/2019	vs	FLORIDA INTERNATIONAL	42	14	W	-3.0	W	58.5	U	
9/7/2019	@	Auburn	6	24	L	16.0	L	51.0	U	
9/14/2019	vs	MISSOURI STATE	58	6	W	-32.0	W	NT	---	
9/19/2019	vs	HOUSTON	38	31	W	-4.5	W	57.5	O	
10/5/2019	@	Army	42	33	W	-2.5	W	42.5	O	
10/12/2019	vs	CONNECTICUT	49	7	W	-33.5	W	57.5	U	
10/19/2019	@	Memphis	17	47	L	2.5	L	60.5	O	
10/26/2019	@	Navy	38	41	L	4.5	L	58.5	O	
11/2/2019	vs	TULSA	38	26	W	-9.5	W	59.0	O	
11/16/2019	@	Temple	21	29	L	-6.5	L	52.5	U	
11/23/2019	vs	CENTRAL FLORIDA	31	34	L	7.0	W	74.0	U	
11/30/2019	@	Smu	20	37	L	3.0	L	72.0	U	
1/4/2020	vs	Southern Mississippi	30	13	W	-7.5	W	57.5	U	Armed Forces Bowl
Coach: Willie Fritz		Season Record >>	430	342	7-6	ATS>>	8-5	O/U>>	5-7	
2018-Tulane		Opponent	Wave	Opp	S/U	Line	ATS	Total	O/U	
8/30/2018	vs	WAKE FOREST	17	23	L	7.0	W	55.5	U	{OT}
9/8/2018	vs	NICHOLLS STATE	42	17	W	-15.5	W	NT	---	
9/15/2018	@	Alabama-Birmingham	24	31	L	-3.5	L	57.0	U	
9/22/2018	@	Ohio State	6	49	L	38.0	L	67.5	U	
9/28/2018	vs	MEMPHIS	40	24	W	14.5	W	66.0	U	
10/6/2018	@	Cincinnati	21	37	L	7.0	L	48.0	O	
10/20/2018	vs	SMU	23	27	L	-7.0	L	55.5	U	
10/27/2018	@	Tulsa	24	17	W	-1.5	W	48.5	U	
11/3/2018	@	South Florida	41	15	W	5.5	W	61.5	U	
11/10/2018	vs	EAST CAROLINA	24	18	W	-10.5	L	54.0	U	
11/15/2018	@	Houston	17	48	L	7.5	L	68.0	U	
11/24/2018	vs	NAVY	29	28	W	-6.5	L	53.0	O	
12/15/2018	vs	Louisiana-Lafayette	41	24	W	-3.0	W	60.5	O	AutoNation Cure Bowl
Coach: Willie Fritz		Season Record >>	349	358	7-6	ATS>>	6-7	O/U>>	3-9	
2017-Tulane		Opponent	Wave	Opp	S/U	Line	ATS	Total	O/U	
9/2/2017	vs	GRAMBLING STATE	44	14	W	-22.5	W	54.0	O	
9/9/2017	@	Navy	21	23	L	8.0	W	50.0	U	
9/16/2017	@	Oklahoma	14	56	L	33.5	L	52.5	O	
9/23/2017	vs	ARMY	21	17	W	-3.0	W	45.5	U	
10/7/2017	vs	TULSA	62	28	W	-6.5	W	53.5	O	
10/14/2017	@	Florida International	10	23	L	-12.0	L	50.5	U	
10/21/2017	vs	SOUTH FLORIDA	28	34	L	10.5	W	54.0	O	
10/27/2017	@	Memphis	26	56	L	10.0	L	61.0	O	
11/4/2017	vs	CINCINNATI	16	17	L	-5.5	L	52.0	U	
11/11/2017	@	East Carolina	31	24	W	-6.5	W	64.0	U	{OT}
11/18/2017	vs	HOUSTON	20	17	W	9.5	W	47.0	U	
11/25/2017	@	Smu	38	41	L	7.5	W	65.0	O	
Coach: Willie Fritz		Season Record >>	331	350	5-7	ATS>>	8-4	O/U>>	6-6	

Copyright © 2021 by Steve's Football Bible, LLC

TULANE GREEN WAVE   AMERICAN West

STADIUM: Yulman Stadium {30,000}							Location: New Orleans, LA			COACH: Willie Fritz	
DATE		Opponent	Wave	Opp	S/U	Line	ATS	Total	O/U	Trends & Angles	
9/4/2021	vs	OKLAHOMA								vs Oklahoma - Oklahoma leads series 1-0	
9/11/2021	vs	MORGAN STATE								1st meeting	
9/18/2021	@	Mississippi								0-11 S/U vs Mississippi as Dog since 1989	
9/25/2021	vs	ALABAMA-BIRMINGHAM								vs UAB - Series tied 5-5	
10/2/2021	@	East Carolina								5-0 S/U vs East Carolina as favorite since 2003	
10/7/2021	vs	HOUSTON								vs Houston - Houston leads series 18-7	
10/21/2021	@	Smu								1-8 S/U vs SMU as Dog since 2009	
10/30/2021	vs	CINCINNATI								vs Cincinnati -Tulane leads series 11-6	
11/6/2021	@	Central Florida								0-5 S/U @ Central Florida as Dog since 2005	
11/13/2021	vs	TULSA								4-12 ATS vs Tulsa since 2005	
11/20/2021	vs	SOUTH FLORIDA								vs South Florida - Series tied 1-1	
11/27/2021	@	Memphis								0-11 S/U @ Memphis as Dog since 1985 {1-9-1 ATS}	
12/4/2021	vs									AAC Championship	
	vs									BOWL GAME	

Pointspread Analysis Non-Conference		Pointspread Analysis Conference
0-34 S/U vs Non-Conf. as 20.5 point or more Dog since 1986		vs Central Florida - UCF leads series 8-2
2-21 S/U vs Non-Conf. as 15.5-20 point Dog since 1984		0-8 S/U vs Central Florida as 5.5 point or more Dog since 2001
4-21 S/U vs Non-Conf. as 10.5-15 point Dog since 1985		1-11 S/U vs East Carolina as Dog since 1991
0-12 S/U vs Non-Conf. as 7.5-10 point Dog since 1990		3-14 S/U vs Houston as Dog since 1999
1-10 S/U vs Non-Conf. as 3.5-7 point Dog since 1990		1-10 S/U vs Houston as 12.5 point or more Dog since 1999
8-2 S/U vs Non-Conf. as 3.5-7 point favorite since 1987		vs Memphis - Memphis leads series 23-13-1
11-2 S/U vs Non-Conf. as 15.5 point or more favorite since 1988		1-5-1 ATS vs Memphis as favorite since 1988
5-1 ATS vs Alabama-Birmingham as Dog since 2001		2-17 S/U vs Memphis as Dog since 1985
5-1 O/U vs Alabama-Birmingham as Dog since 2001		6-2 S/U vs SMU as favorite since 1990
0-9 S/U vs ranked Mississippi since 1957		vs SMU - SMU leads series 14-13
Dog		6-1 O/U vs SMU as Dog since 2011
0-51 S/U as 20.5 point or more Dog since 1986		0-3 S/U vs Temple as Dog since 2014
3-10 ATS as 30.5 point or more Dog since 1991		vs Tulsa - Tulsa leads series 12-5
4-0 ATS as 25.5-30 point Dog since 2011		1-12 S/U vs Tulsa as Dog since 2005
1-6 O/U as 25.5-30 point Dog since 2008		**Bowl Games**
2-5 ATS on road as 20.5-25 point Dog since 2001		6-9 S/U in Bowl Games
2-5 O/U as 20.5-25 point Dog since 2005		
2-19 S/U on road as 15.5-20 point Dog since 1995		
2-9 S/U @ home as 15.5-20 point Dog since 1985		7-0 S/U @ home when ranked since 1974
2-19 S/U @ home as 10.5-15 point Dog since 1984		1-56 S/U vs ranked teams since 1984
2-9-1 O/U @ home as 10.5-15 point Dog since 2001		0-32 S/U on road vs ranked teams since 1984
2-12 S/U on road as 10.5-15 point Dog since 2006		1-24 S/U @ home vs ranked teams since 1985
2-18 S/U on road as 7.5-10 point Dog since 1990		
3-15 S/U @ home as 3.5-7 point Dog since 2003	Mississippi	1-6 S/U prior to playing Alabama-Birmingham since 2003
3-17 S/U on road as 3.5-7 point Dog since 1990	UAB	2-9 O/U prior to playing East Carolina since 2002
4-11 ATS on road as 3 point or less Dog since 1983	East Carolina	7-1 O/U in 2nd road game of season since 2013
5-1 O/U on road as 3 point or less Dog since 2012	East Carolina	4-10 S/U in 2nd road game of season since 2007
Favorite	East Carolina	2-8 S/U after playing Alabama-Birmingham since 1999
9-1 S/U as 3 point or less favorite since 2014	HOUSTON	1-5 O/U after playing East Carolina since 2012
22-5 S/U @ home as 3.5-7 point favorite since 1987	Smu	3-9 S/U after playing Houston since 2007
1-6 O/U on road as 3.5-7 point favorite since 2000	CINCY	1-6 S/U after playing SMU since 2010
7-0 S/U as 7.5-10 point favorite since 1997	CINCY	3-7 ATS after playing SMU since 2007
6-1 S/U @ home as 10.5-15 point favorite since 1997	UCF	4-1 ATS after playing Cincinnati since 2001
8-2 S/U @ home as 15.5-20 point favorite since 1990	UCF	6-1 S/U after playing Cincinnati since 1998
5-0 S/U on road as 15.5-20 point favorite since 1998	USF	2-7 S/U after playing Tulsa since 2012
10-0 S/U as 20.5 point or more favorite since 1988	Memphis	1-15 S/U in final road game of seson since 2005

Copyright © 2021 by Steve's Football Bible, LLC

TULSA GOLDEN HURRICANE   AMERICAN West

2020-Tulsa		Opponent	Tulsa	Opp	S/U	Line	ATS	Total	O/U	
9/19/2020	@	Oklahoma State	7	16	L	23.0	W	66.0	U	
10/3/2020	@	Central Florida	34	26	W	20.0	W	70.0	U	
10/23/2020	@	South Florida	42	13	W	-12.5	W	52.0	O	
10/30/2020	vs	EAST CAROLINA	34	30	W	-17.0	L	59.5	O	
11/14/2020	vs	SMU	28	24	W	2.0	W	63.5	U	
11/21/2020	vs	TULANE	30	24	W	-4.5	W	56.5	U	{2 OT}
12/5/2020	@	Navy	19	6	W	-12.0	W	45.5	U	
12/19/2020	**@**	**Cincinnati**	**24**	**27**	L	14.0	W	**44.5**	O	**AAC CHAMPIONSHIP**
12/31/2020	**vs**	**Mississippi State**	**26**	**28**	L	1.0	L	**44.5**	O	**Armed Forces Bowl**
Coach: Philip Montgomery		Season Record >>	244	194	6-3	ATS>>	7-2	O/U>>	4-5	
2019-Tulsa		Opponent	Tulsa	Opp	S/U	Line	ATS	Total	O/U	
8/30/2019	@	Michigan State	7	28	L	23.5	W	47.0	U	
9/7/2019	@	San Jose State	34	16	W	-6.5	W	53.5	U	
9/14/2019	vs	OKLAHOMA STATE	21	40	L	13.5	L	64.5	U	
9/21/2019	vs	WYOMING	24	21	W	-6.0	L	46.0	U	
10/5/2019	@	Smu	37	43	L	12.0	W	63.0	O	{3 OT}
10/12/2019	vs	NAVY	17	45	L	-2.0	L	52.0	O	
10/19/2019	@	Cincinnati	13	24	L	15.5	W	47.0	U	
10/26/2019	vs	MEMPHIS	41	42	L	9.5	W	59.0	O	
11/2/2019	@	Tulane	26	38	L	9.5	L	59.0	O	
11/8/2019	vs	CENTRAL FLORIDA	34	31	W	16.0	W	68.5	U	
11/23/2019	vs	HOUSTON	14	24	L	-6.5	L	57.0	U	"Battle for the Best City"
11/30/2019	@	East Carolina	49	24	W	-7.0	W	64.0	O	
Coach: Philip Montgomery		Season Record >>	317	376	4-8	ATS>>	7-5	O/U>>	5-7	
2018-Tulsa		Opponent	Tulsa	Opp	S/U	Line	ATS	Total	O/U	
9/1/2018	vs	CENTRAL ARKANSAS	38	27	W	-12.0	L	NT	---	
9/8/2018	@	Texas	21	28	L	21.5	W	59.5	U	
9/15/2018	vs	ARKANSAS STATE	20	29	L	-1.5	L	71.5	U	
9/20/2018	@	Temple	17	31	L	6.0	L	54.0	U	
10/4/2018	@	Houston	26	41	L	17.5	W	70.0	U	"Battle for the Best City"
10/12/2018	vs	SOUTH FLORIDA	24	25	L	10.0	W	60.5	U	
10/20/2018	@	Arkansas	0	23	L	7.5	L	53.0	U	
10/27/2018	vs	TULANE	17	24	L	1.5	L	48.5	U	
11/3/2018	vs	CONNECTICUT	49	14	W	-19.0	W	60.0	O	
11/10/2018	@	Memphis	21	47	L	16.5	L	64.5	O	
11/17/2018	@	Navy	29	37	L	5.0	L	51.0	O	
11/24/2018	vs	SMU	27	24	W	2.5	W	53.5	U	
Coach: Philip Montgomery		Season Record >>	289	350	3-9	ATS>>	5-7	O/U>>	3-8	
2017-Tulsa		Opponent	Tulsa	Opp	S/U	Line	ATS	Total	O/U	
8/31/2017	@	Oklahoma State	24	59	L	20.0	L	70.5	O	
9/9/2017	vs	LOUISIANA-LAFAYETTE	66	42	W	-14.0	W	60.5	O	
9/16/2017	@	Toledo	51	54	L	7.0	W	74.5	O	
9/23/2017	vs	NEW MEXICO	13	16	L	-7.5	L	68.0	U	
9/30/2017	vs	NAVY	21	31	L	8.5	L	70.5	U	
10/7/2017	@	Tulane	28	62	L	6.5	L	53.5	O	
10/14/2017	vs	HOUSTON	45	17	W	14.0	W	63.5	U	"Battle for the Best City"
10/21/2017	@	Connecticut	14	20	L	-4.0	L	76.5	U	
10/27/2017	@	Smu	34	38	L	12.0	W	78.0	U	
11/3/2017	vs	MEMPHIS	14	41	L	14.0	L	80.5	U	
11/17/2017	@	South Florida	20	27	L	22.5	W	66.0	U	
11/25/2017	vs	TEMPLE	22	43	L	4.5	L	57.0	O	
Coach: Philip Montgomery		Season Record >>	352	450	2-10	ATS>>	4-8	O/U>>	5-7	

Copyright © 2021 by Steve's Football Bible, LLC

TULSA GOLDEN HURRICANE   AMERICAN West

STADIUM: Chapman Stadium {30,000}								Location: Tulsa, OK		COACH: Philip Montgomery	
DATE		Opponent	Tuls	Opp	S/U	Line	ATS	Total	O/U	Trends & Angles	
9/2/2021	vs	CALIFORNIA-DAVIS								1st meeting	
9/11/2021	@	Oklahoma State								0-12 S/U @ OK State as Dog since 1985	
9/18/2021	@	Ohio State								vs Ohio State - Ohio State leads series 1-0	
9/25/2021	vs	ARKANSAS STATE								vs Arkansas State - Ark. State leads series 3-2	
10/1/2021	vs	HOUSTON								1-5 S/U vs Houston as Dog since 2011	
10/9/2021	vs	MEMPHIS								4-0 S/U vs Memphis as favorite since 2005	
10/16/2021	@	South Florida								0-3 S/U vs South Florida as Dog since 2014	
10/29/2021	vs	NAVY								0-4 S/U vs Navy as Dog since 2015	
11/6/2021	@	Cincinnati								0-5 S/U vs Cincinnati as Dog since 1995	
11/13/2021	@	Tulane								Game 5-2 O/U vs Tulane since 2014	
11/20/2021	vs	TEMPLE								vs Temple - Temple leads series 3-2	
11/27/2021	@	Smu								vs SMU - SMU leads series 15-12	
12/4/2021	vs									AAC Championship	
	vs									BOWL GAME	

Pointspread Analysis
Non-Conference

2-38 S/U vs Non-Conf as 15.5 point or more Dog since 1985
2-11 S/U vs Non-Conf. as 10.5-15 point Dog since 1985
1-8 S/U & ATS vs Non-Conf. as 3 point or less favorite since 1993
1-8 ATS vs Non-Conf. as 3.5-7 point favorite since 1985
16-0 S/U vs Non-Conf. as 7.5 point or more favorite since 1985
0-11 S/U vs Oklahoma State as 9 point or more Dog since 1985
vs Oklahoma State - OK State leads series 42-27-5
0-7 S/U vs ranked Oklahoma State all time

Dog

0-42 S/U as 20.5 point or more Dog since 1985
1-59 S/U on road as 15.5 point or more Dog since 1984
4-0 O/U @ home as 20.5-25 point Dog since 2002
1-8 S/U @ home as 10.5-15 point Dog since 1999
2-16 S/U on road as 10.5-15 point Dog since 1994
2-10 S/U @ home as 7.5-10 point Dog since 2001
2-12 S/U on road as 7.5-10 point Dog since 1998
2-11 S/U @ home as 3.5-7 point Dog since 1987
2-10-1 ATS @ home as 3.5-7 point Dog since 1987
5-0 O/U @ home as 3.5-7 point Dog since 2002
2-8 O/U on road as 3 point or less Dog since 1993

Favorite

1-6 S/U & ATS as 3 point or less favorite since 2013
8-2 S/U @ home as 3.5-7 point favorite since 2010
8-2 S/U as 7.5-10 point favorite since 2003
6-1 S/U on road as 7.5-10 point favorite since 1987
8-0 S/U @ home as 10.5-15 point favorite since 2007
5-0 O/U @ home as 10.5-15 point favorite since 2008
11-0 S/U on road as 10.5-15 point favorite since 2005
8-0 S/U on road as 15.5 or more favorite since 1991
31-1 S/U @ home as 15.5 point or more favorite since 1986

Bowl Games

0-3 S/U in Independence Bowl
6-2 ATS in Bowl Games since 2008
3-7 O/U in Bowl Games since 2005

Pointspread Analysis
Conference

0-7 O/U vs Central Florida as Dog since 2007
5-0 S/U vs Central Florida as favorite since 2008
vs Cincinnati - Tulsa leads series 17-16-2
0-5 S/U vs East Carolina as Dog since 1994
11-2 ATS vs Houston as Dog since 1985
vs Houston - Houston leads series 24-19
vs Memphis - Memphis leads series 19-11
0-5 S/U @ home vs Memphis as Dog since 1987
vs Navy - Navy leads series 6-2
12-1 S/U & ATS vs Tulane as favorite since 2005
2-9 S/U vs SMU as Dog since 1997
1-6 O/U vs SMU as Dog since 2001
2-9 ATS vs SMU as favorite since 2004
6-1 S/U @ home vs SMU as favorite since 2003
12-1 S/U & ATS vs Tulane as favorite since 2005

	2-43 S/U on road vs ranked teams since 1977
	1-11 S/U @ home vs ranked teams since 2007
	7-0 S/U @ home when ranked since 1945
	0-7 S/U when ranked vs ranked teams all time
CAL-DAVIS	13-2 S/U in 1st home game of season since 2006
Oklahoma State	1-10 S/U in 1st road game of season since 2010
Cincinnati	2-10 S/U prior to playing Tulane since 2008
TEMPLE	11-2 S/U after playing Tulane since 2007
Smu	7-1 ATS in final road game of season since 2013

Copyright © 2021 by Steve's Football Bible, LLC

2020-UCLA		Opponent	UCLA	Opp	S/U	Line	ATS	Total	O/U	
11/7/2020	@	Colorado	42	48	L	-7.0	L	56.0	O	
11/13/2020	vs	CALIFORNIA	34	10	W	3.0	W	58.0	U	
11/20/2020	@	Oregon	35	38	L	18.0	L	62.0	O	
11/28/2020	vs	ARIZONA	27	10	W	-7.5	W	70.5	U	
12/5/2020	@	Arizona State	25	18	W	2.5	W	57.5	U	
12/12/2020	vs	USC	38	43	L	3.0	L	65.0	O	"Victory Bell"
12/19/2020	vs	STANFORD	47	48	L	-7.0	L	61.0	O	{2 OT}
Coach: Chip Kelly		Season Record >>	248	215	3-4	ATS>>	4-3	O/U>>	4-3	
2019-UCLA		Opponent	UCLA	Opp	S/U	Line	ATS	Total	O/U	
8/31/2019	@	Cincinnati	14	24	L	2.5	L	55.5	U	
9/7/2019	vs	SAN DIEGO STATE	14	23	L	-7.5	L	45.0	U	
9/14/2019	vs	OKLAHOMA	14	48	L	23.0	L	72.0	U	
9/21/2019	@	Washington State	67	63	W	18.0	W	59.5	O	
9/28/2019	@	Arizona	17	20	L	3.0	T	68.0	U	
10/5/2019	vs	OREGON STATE	31	48	L	-4.5	L	63.5	O	
10/17/2019	@	Stanford	34	16	W	4.0	W	48.5	O	
10/26/2019	vs	ARIZONA STATE	42	32	W	3.0	W	56.0	O	
11/2/2019	vs	COLORADO	31	14	W	-6.5	W	64.5	U	
11/16/2019	@	Utah	3	49	L	20.5	L	51.5	O	
11/23/2019	@	Usc	35	52	L	13.0	L	66.5	O	"Victory Bell"
11/30/2019	vs	CALIFORNIA	18	28	L	-1.0	L	51.0	U	
Coach: Chip Kelly		Season Record >>	320	417	4-8	ATS>>	4-7-1	O/U>>	6-6	
2018-UCLA		Opponent	UCLA	Opp	S/U	Line	ATS	Total	O/U	
9/1/2018	vs	CINCINNATI	17	26	L	-14.5	L	62.5	U	
9/8/2018	@	Oklahoma	21	49	L	31.0	W	65.5	O	
9/15/2018	vs	FRESNO STATE	14	38	L	2.5	L	51.5	O	
9/28/2018	@	Colorado	16	38	L	10.0	L	56.5	U	
10/6/2018	vs	WASHINGTON	24	31	L	21.5	W	53.5	O	
10/13/2018	@	California	37	7	W	6.5	W	53.5	U	
10/20/2018	vs	ARIZONA	31	30	W	-10.0	L	57.0	O	
10/26/2018	vs	UTAH	10	41	L	11.0	L	54.0	U	
11/3/2018	@	Oregon	21	42	L	11.0	L	59.0	O	
11/10/2018	@	Arizona State	28	31	L	11.5	W	64.5	U	
11/17/2018	vs	USC	34	27	W	2.5	W	54.5	O	"Victory Bell"
11/24/2018	vs	STANFORD	42	49	L	7.0	T	60.5	O	
Coach: Chip Kelly		Season Record >>	295	409	3-9	ATS>>	5-6-1	O/U>>	7-5	
2017-UCLA		Opponent	UCLA	Opp	S/U	Line	ATS	Total	O/U	
9/3/2017	vs	TEXAS A&M	45	44	W	-6.5	L	61.5	O	
9/9/2017	vs	HAWAII	56	23	W	-24.0	W	62.5	O	
9/16/2017	@	Memphis	45	48	L	-3.0	L	70.5	O	
9/23/2017	@	Stanford	34	58	L	6.5	L	60.5	O	
9/30/2017	vs	COLORADO	27	23	W	-7.5	L	66.0	U	
10/14/2017	@	Arizona	30	47	L	-3.0	L	77.0	T	
10/21/2017	vs	OREGON	31	14	W	-6.0	W	68.5	U	
10/28/2017	@	Washington	23	44	L	17.5	L	59.5	O	
11/3/2017	@	Utah	17	48	L	9.5	L	54.0	O	
11/11/2017	vs	ARIZONA STATE	44	37	W	-3.0	W	65.5	O	
11/18/2017	@	Usc	23	28	L	14.5	W	69.5	U	"Victory Bell"
11/24/2017	vs	CALIFORNIA	30	27	W	-7.0	L	66.0	U	
12/26/2017	vs	Kansas State	17	35	L	6.0	L	59.0	U	Cactus Bowl
Coach: Jim Mora		Season Record >>	422	476	6-7	ATS>>	4-9	O/U>>	7-5-1	

Copyright © 2021 by Steve's Football Bible, LLC

UCLA BRUINS

PACIFIC-12 South

STADIUM: Rose Bowl Stadium {92,542}					Location: Westwood, CA					COACH: Chip Kelly	
DATE		Opponent	Ucla	Opp	S/U	Line	ATS	Total	O/U	Trends & Angles	
8/28/2021	vs	*HAWAII*								vs Hawaii - UCLA leads series 3-0	
9/4/2021	vs	*LSU*								1st meeting	
9/18/2021	vs	*FRESNO STATE*								vs Fresno State - UCLA leads series 6-3	
9/25/2021	@	Stanford								1-6 S/U @ Stanford since 2009	
10/2/2021	vs	ARIZONA STATE								6-1 S/U @ home vs AZ State as favorite since 2000	
10/9/2021	@	Arizona								vs Arizona - UCLA leads series 26-17-2	
10/16/2021	@	Washington								0-3 S/U vs Washington as Dog since 2010	
10/23/2021	vs	OREGON								0-7 S/U vs Oregon as Dog since 2008	
10/30/2021	@	Utah								0-4 S/U & ATS vs Utah as Dog since 2011	
11/13/2021	vs	COLORADO								7-1 S/U vs Colorado as favorite since 2011	
11/20/2021	@	Usc								vs USC - USC leads series 51-32-7	
11/27/2021	vs	CALIFORNIA								6-1 S/U @ home vs California as favorite since 2001	
12/3/2021	vs									PAC-12 Championship	
	vs									BOWL GAME	

Pointspread Analysis Non-Conference		Pointspread Analysis Conference
9-3 S/U vs Non-Conf. as 7.5-10 point favorite since 1991		10-0 S/U vs Arizona as 9.5 point or more favorite since 1987
13-2 S/U vs Non-Conf. as 10.5-15 point favorite since 1985		6-0-1 O/U vs Arizona as 4.5 point or less favorite since 1983
7-1 S/U vs Non-Conf. as 15.5-20 point favorite since 1987		10-0 S/U vs Arizona as 9.5 point or more favorite since 1987
9-1 S/U vs Non-Conf. as 20.5-25 point favorite since 1988		1-5 S/U vs Arizona State as 7 point or more Dog since 2004
10-0 S/U vs Non-Conf. as 25.5 point or more favorite since 1987		vs Arizona State - UCLA leads series 23-13-1
4-1 S/U vs Fresno State as favorite since 1987 {1-4 ATS}		vs California - UCLA leads series 56-34-1
Dog		0-6 O/U vs California as favorite since 2013
0-11 S/U as 20.5 point or more Dog since 2003		10-0 S/U vs California as 14 point or more favorite since 1985
2-13 S/U as 15.5-20 point Dog since 1983		2-13-1 ATS vs California as 13 point or less favorite since 1983
3-11 O/U as 10.5-15 point Dog since 2003		vs Colorado - UCLA leads series 11-5
1-12 S/U on road as 10.5-15 point Dog since 1994		0-3 S/U vs Colorado as Dog since 2003
0-14 S/U on road as 7.5-10 point Dog since 1990		0-3 O/U vs Colorado as Dog since 2003
2-5 S/U as 3.5-7 point Dog since 2015		1-5 ATS vs Colorado as favorite since 2013
2-5 S/U & ATS @ home as 3 point or less Dog since 2012		vs Stanford - UCLA leads series 46-43-3
Favorite		1-12 S/U vs Stanford since 2009
5-2 S/U & ATS @ home as 3 point or less favorite since 2005		2-10-1 ATS vs Stanford since 2009
0-6 S/U & ATS on road as 3 point or less favorite since 2006		1-10 S/U vs Stanford as Dog since 2009 {2-8-1 ATS}
21-4 S/U @ home as 3.5-7 point favorite since 1996		2-6 O/U vs Stanford as favorite since 2002
8-2 S/U on road as 3.5-7 point favorite since 2005		5-0 S/U vs Stanford as 14 point or more favorite since 1987
5-12 O/U on road as 3.5-7 point favorite since 1995		0-10 S/U vs USC as 13 point or more Dog since 2003
4-10 O/U @ home as 3.5-7 point favorite since 2009		1-6 O/U vs USC as 13 point or more Dog since 2007
13-3 S/U @ home as 7.5-10 point favorite since 1995		6-2 S/U & ATS vs USC as 1.5-5 point Dog since 1993
1-5 ATS @ home as 7.5-10 point favorite since 2012		0-4 S/U & ATS vs Utah since 2016
1-7 ATS on road as 7.5-10 point favorite since 1997		vs Utah - UCLA leads series 11-7
14-2 S/U on road as 10.5-15 point favorite since 1983		vs Washington - UCLA leads series 40-32-2
10-0 S/U on road as 15.5-20 point favorite since 1986		5-1 O/U vs Washington as Dog since 2000
7-0 S/U @ home as 15.5-20 point favorite since 1989		4-1 S/U @ Washington as favorite since 1988
0-6 O/U @ home as 15.5-20 point favorite since 1991		1-4 O/U @ Washington as favorite since 1988
0-4 ATS on road as 20.5-25 point favorite since 1988		8-0 S/U vs Washington as 6 point or more favorite since 1987

7-1 S/U on road as 20.5 point or more favorite since 1987	HAWAII	1-6 ATS in 1st home game of season since 2014
31-1 S/U @ home as 20.5 point or more favorite since 1985	HAWAII	13-3 S/U in 1st home game of season since 2005
Bowl Games	Stanford	10-3 S/U prior to playing Arizona State since 2008
0-3 S/U vs Wisconsin in Bowl Games	AZ STATE	8-2 S/U prior to playing Arizona since 2010
0-3 S/U & ATS in Foster Farms Bowl	AZ STATE	4-10 S/U prior to playing Arizona since 2007
3-1 S/U in Sun Bowl	AZ STATE	2-6 S/U after playing Stanford since 2009
0-3 O/U in Las Vegas Bowl	Arizona	8-3 S/U in 2nd road game of season since 2010
0-3 S/U & O/U in Bowl Games as 3.5-7 point Dog since 2000	Arizona	4-11 O/U after playing Arizona State since 2006
4-0 O/U in Bowl Games as 3.5-7 point favorite since 1995	Arizona	5-1 ATS prior to playing Washington since 2009
0-4 O/U in Bowl Games as 10.5-15 point favorite since 1986	Washington	0-6 S/U & ATS prior to playing Oregon since 2009
	OREGON	6-2 O/U prior to playing Utah since 2011
	Utah	3-8 ATS prior to playing Colorado since 1984
	CALIFORNIA	4-11 O/U in final home game of season since 2006
	CALIFORNIA	0-8-1 ATS in final home game of season since 2012

Copyright © 2021 by Steve's Football Bible, LLC

UTAH UTES

PACIFIC-12 South

2020-Utah		Opponent	Utah	Opp	S/U	Line	ATS	Total	O/U	
11/21/2020	vs	USC	17	33	L	2.5	L	58.5	U	
11/29/2020	@	Washington	21	24	L	9.5	W	47.0	U	
12/5/2020	vs	OREGON STATE	30	24	W	-13.5	L	51.0	O	
12/12/2020	@	Colorado	38	21	W	-2.5	W	49.0	O	*"Rumble in the Rockies"*
12/19/2020	vs	WASHINGTON STATE	45	28	W	-12.0	W	54.5	O	
Coach: Kyle Whittingham		Season Record >>	151	130	3-2	ATS>>	3-2	O/U>>	3-2	
2019-Utah		Opponent	Utah	Opp	S/U	Line	ATS	Total	O/U	
8/29/2019	@	*Byu*	30	12	W	-5.5	W	49.0	U	*"Holy War" (Beehive Boot)*
9/7/2019	vs	NORTHERN ILLINOIS	35	17	W	-23.0	L	45.0	O	
9/14/2019	vs	*IDAHO STATE*	31	0	W	-37.0	L	NT	---	
9/20/2019	@	*Usc*	23	30	L	-3.5	L	53.0	T	
9/28/2019	vs	WASHINGTON STATE	38	13	W	-5.5	W	56.5	U	
10/12/2019	@	Oregon State	52	7	W	-15.0	W	59.5	U	
10/19/2019	vs	ARIZONA STATE	21	3	W	-14.5	W	46.0	U	
10/26/2019	vs	CALIFORNIA	35	0	W	-21.0	W	36.5	U	
11/2/2019	@	Washington	33	28	W	-3.0	W	48.0	O	
11/16/2019	vs	UCLA	49	3	W	-20.5	W	51.5	O	
11/23/2019	@	Arizona	35	7	W	-23.5	W	56.5	U	
11/30/2019	vs	COLORADO	45	15	W	-28.0	W	50.0	O	*"Rumble in the Rockies"*
12/6/2019	vs	**Oregon**	**15**	**37**	L	-6.5	L	45.0	**O**	PAC-12 Championship
12/31/2019	vs	**Texas**	**10**	**38**	L	-7.0	L	56.0	U	Alamo Bowl
Coach: Kyle Whittingham		Season Record >>	452	210	11-3	ATS>>	9-5	O/U>>	5-7-1	
2018-Utah		Opponent	Utah	Opp	S/U	Line	ATS	Total	O/U	
8/30/2018	vs	*WEBER STATE*	41	10	W	-29.0	W	NT	---	
9/8/2018	@	*Northern Illinois*	17	6	W	-10.0	W	47.0	U	
9/15/2018	vs	WASHINGTON	7	21	L	4.0	L	46.0	U	
9/29/2018	@	Washington State	24	28	L	-1.5	L	50.0	O	
10/6/2018	@	Stanford	40	21	W	4.0	W	45.0	O	
10/13/2018	vs	ARIZONA	42	10	W	-13.5	W	52.5	U	
10/20/2018	vs	USC	41	28	W	-6.5	W	48.0	O	
10/27/2018	@	Ucla	41	10	W	-11.0	W	54.0	U	
11/3/2018	@	Arizona State	20	38	L	-7.5	L	54.0	O	
11/10/2018	vs	OREGON	32	25	W	-6.0	W	51.0	O	
11/17/2018	@	Colorado	30	7	W	-7.0	W	45.5	U	*"Rumble in the Rockies"*
11/24/2018	vs	BYU	35	27	W	-10.5	L	44.5	O	*"Holy War" (Beehive Boot)*
12/1/2018	vs	**Washington**	**3**	**10**	L	4.5	L	46.0	U	PAC-12 Championship
12/31/2018	vs	**Northwestern**	**20**	**31**	L	-6.5	L	44.5	O	Holiday Bowl
Coach: Kyle Whittingham		Season Record >>	393	272	9-5	ATS>>	8-6	O/U>>	7-6	
2017-Utah		Opponent	Utah	Opp	S/U	Line	ATS	Total	O/U	
8/31/2017	vs	*NORTH DAKOTA*	37	16	W	-20.0	W	59.0	U	
9/9/2017	@	*Byu*	19	13	W	-5.0	W	46.0	U	*"Holy War" (Beehive Boot)*
9/16/2017	vs	*SAN JOSE STATE*	54	16	W	-28.0	W	59.5	U	
9/22/2017	@	Arizona	30	24	W	-5.0	W	61.5	U	
10/7/2017	vs	STANFORD	20	23	L	3.0	T	51.5	U	
10/14/2017	@	Usc	27	28	L	13.0	W	52.0	O	
10/21/2017	vs	ARIZONA STATE	10	30	L	-10.5	L	54.0	U	
10/28/2017	@	Oregon	20	41	L	-2.0	L	49.5	O	
11/3/2017	vs	UCLA	48	17	W	-9.5	W	54.0	O	
11/11/2017	vs	WASHINGTON STATE	25	33	L	PK	L	50.5	O	
11/18/2017	@	Washington	30	33	L	17.5	W	47.0	O	
11/25/2017	vs	COLORADO	34	13	W	-9.0	W	57.0	U	*"Rumble in the Rockies"*
12/26/2017	vs	**West Virginia**	**30**	**14**	W	-7.0	W	56.0	U	Heart of Dallas Bowl
Coach: Kyle Whittingham		Season Record >>	384	301	7-6	ATS>>	9-3-1	O/U>>	6-7	

Copyright © 2021 by Steve's Football Bible, LLC

UTAH UTES   PACIFIC-12 South

| STADIUM: Rice-Eccles Stadium {45,807} | | Location: Salt Lake City, UT | | | | COACH: Kyle Whittingham | | | | |

DATE		Opponent	Utah	Opp	S/U	Line	ATS	Total	O/U	Trends & Angles
9/2/2021	vs	WEBER STATE								vs Weber State - Utah leads series 5-0
9/11/2021	@	Byu								9-1 ATS vs BYU as Dog since 1997
9/18/2021	@	San Diego State								5-0 S/U & ATS vs San Diego State since 2005
9/25/2021	vs	WASHINGTON STATE								Game 6-2 O/U vs Washington State snice 2011
10/9/2021	@	Usc								0-4 S/U @ USC as Dog since 2011
10/16/2021	vs	ARIZONA STATE								vs Arizona State - Arizona State leads series 21-9
10/23/2021	@	Oregon State								8-1 S/U vs Oregon State as favorite since 1992
10/30/2021	vs	UCLA								4-0 S/U & ATS vs UCLA as favorite since 2011
11/5/2021	@	Stanford								4-0-1 ATS vs Stanford since 1996
11/13/2021	@	Arizona								vs Arizona - Utah leads series 24-19-2
11/20/2021	vs	OREGON								Game 7-1 O/U vs Oregon since 2009
11/26/2021	vs	COLORADO								8-0 S/U vs Colorado as favorite since 2012
12/3/2021	vs									PAC-12 Championship
	vs									BOWL GAME

Pointspread Analysis
Non-Conference

5-12 S/U vs Non-Conf. as 10.5-15 point Dog since 1985
8-1 ATS vs Non-Conf. as 7.5-10 point Dog since 1993
5-0 S/U & ATS on road vs Non-Conf. as 3.5-7 point Dog since 2011
8-1 S/U & ATS vs Non-Conf. as 3 point or less Dog since 1994
11-0 S/U vs Non-Conf. as 3 point or less favorite since 2003
9-1-1 ATS vs Non-Conf. as 3 point or less favorite since 2003
9-3 S/U vs Non-Conf. as 3.5-7 point favorite since 2007
1-8 O/U vs Non-Conf. as 3.5-7 point favorite since 2010
8-1 S/U on road vs Non-Conf. as 7.5-10 point favorite since 1998
15-0 S/U @ home vs Non-Conf. as 10.5-15 point favorite since 1994
12-2 ATS @ home vs Non-Conf. as 10.5-15 point favorite since 1994
8-0 S/U @ home vs Non-Conf. as 15.5-20 point favorite since 1998
36-0 S/U vs Non-Conf. as 20.5 point or more favorite since 1985
vs BYU - Utah leads series 59-31-4
3-0 S/U & ATS vs BYU as Dog since 2011
10-0 S/U vs BYU as favorite since 2002
5-0 S/U & ATS vs San Diego State as favorite since 2006
5-0 S/U vs San Diego State as 14.5 point or more favorite since 2001

Dog

0-17 S/U as 15.5 point or more Dog since 1985
8-0 ATS as 10.5-15 point Dog since 2002
15-4 ATS as 7.5-10 point Dog since 1992
7-18 O/U on road as 3.5-7 point Dog since 1997
2-14 S/U @ home as 3.5-7 point Dog since 1986
5-1-1 ATS @ home as 3 point or less Dog since 1996
0-5 O/U @ home as 3 point or less Dog since 2003

Favorite

9-3 S/U on road as 3.5-7 point favorite since 2007
10-2 S/U on road as 7.5-10 point favorite since 1998
3-12 ATS on road as 7.5-10 point favorite since 1994
13-2 S/U as 7.5-10 point favorite since 2007
12-1 S/U on road as 10.5-15 point favorite since 1998
11-0 S/U as 15.5-20 point favorite since 2003
0-5 O/U as 15.5-20 point favorite since 2009
4-0 S/U & ATS on road as 15.5-20 point favorite since 2004
8-0 S/U on road as 20.5 point or more favorite since 2004
6-2 O/U on road as 20.5 point or more favorite since 2004
51-3 S/U @ home as 15.5 point or more favorite since 1985

Pointspread Analysis
Conference

0-5 O/U vs Arizona as 5 point or less favorite since 2000
5-0 S/U vs Arizona as 7.5 point or more favorite since 2004
0-8 S/U vs Arizona State as Dog since 1985
0-4 S/U & ATS vs Arizona as 4.5 point or less favorite since 2000
vs Colorado - Colorado leads series 33-32-3
4-0 O/U vs Oregon as Dog since 2009
vs Oregon State - Series tied 11-11-1
4-0 S/U & ATS @ Stanford as Dog since 1989
vs UCLA - UCLA leads series 11-7
4-1 ATS vs UCLA as Dog since 2007
vs USC - USC leads series 13-6
vs Washington State - Series tied 9-9
Game 4-0 O/U @ Washington State since 2011

Bowl Games

14-3 S/U in Bowl Games since 1999
11-5 ATS in Bowl Games since 2001
4-1 S/U in Las Vegas Bowl since 1999
1-4 O/U in Las Vegas Bowl since 1999
8-1 S/U in Bowl Games as 3.5-10 point favorite since 1999

WEBER STATE	12-1 S/U in 1st home game of season since 2008
Byu	7-1 S/U in 1st road game of season since 2013 {8-0 ATS}
WAZZU	12-2 S/U in 2nd home game of season since 2007
AZ STATE	0-9 O/U after playing USC since 2012
Oregon State	2-6 S/U after playing Arizona State since 2010
Oregon State	6-2 O/U after playing Arizona State since 2010
UCLA	1-6 S/U prior to playing Stanford since 1989
Stanford	5-1 ATS after playing UCLA since 2013
Stanford	9-2 S/U & ATS prior to playing Arizona since 2002
Arizona	8-3 O/U in final road game of season since 2010
OREGON	9-2 S/U after playing Arizona since 2002
COLORADO	8-2 S/U & ATS after playing Oregon since 1997
COLORADO	3-8 ATS in final home game of season since 2010
COLORADO	3-9 O/U in final home game of season since 2009

Copyright © 2021 by Steve's Football Bible, LLC

UTAH STATE AGGIES   MOUNTAIN WEST West

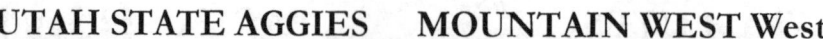

2020-Utah State		Opponent	USU	Opp	S/U	Line	ATS	Total	O/U	
10/24/2020	@	Boise State	13	42	L	17.0	L	51.0	O	
10/31/2020	vs	SAN DIEGO STATE	7	38	L	8.5	L	40.5	O	
11/6/2020	@	Nevada	9	34	L	17.0	L	58.0	U	
11/14/2020	vs	FRESNO STATE	16	35	L	10.5	L	51.5	U	
11/26/2020	vs	NEW MEXICO	41	27	W	6.5	W	49.0	O	
12/3/2020	vs	AIR FORCE	7	35	L	13.5	L	52.5	U	
Coach: Gary Andersen		Season Record >>	93	211	1-5	ATS>>	1-5	O/U>>	3-3	
2019-Utah State		Opponent	USU	Opp	S/U	Line	ATS	Total	O/U	
8/30/2019	@	*Wake Forest*	35	38	L	5.0	W	60.0	O	
9/7/2019	vs	*SUNY-STONY BROOK*	62	7	W	-29.0	W	NT	---	
9/21/2019	@	San Diego State	23	17	W	-4.0	W	53.0	U	
9/28/2019	vs	COLORADO STATE	34	24	W	-24.0	L	69.0	U	
10/5/2019	@	*Lsu*	6	42	L	27.5	L	72.5	U	
10/19/2019	vs	NEVADA	36	10	W	-21.5	W	59.0	U	
10/26/2019	@	Air Force	7	31	L	3.5	L	60.0	U	
11/2/2019	vs	BYU	14	42	L	-3.0	L	52.0	O	*"The Old Wagon Wheel"*
11/9/2019	@	Fresno State	37	35	W	5.5	W	58.0	O	
11/16/2019	vs	WYOMING	26	21	W	-5.0	T	51.5	U	*"Bridger's Battle"*
11/23/2019	vs	BOISE STATE	21	56	L	4.0	L	54.5	O	
11/30/2019	@	New Mexico	38	25	W	-12.0	W	64.0	U	
12/20/2019	vs	**Kent State**	**41**	**51**	L	-7.0	L	71.5	**O**	**Frisco Bowl**
Coach: Gary Andersen		Season Record >>	380	399	7-6	ATS>>	6-6-1	O/U>>	5-6-1	
2018-Utah State		Opponent	USU	Opp	S/U	Line	ATS	Total	O/U	
8/31/2018	@	*Michigan State*	31	38	L	23.5	W	52.0	O	
9/8/2018	vs	*NEW MEXICO STATE*	60	13	W	-31.0	W	62.0	O	
9/13/2018	vs	*TENNESSEE TECH*	73	12	W	-44.5	W	NT	---	
9/22/2018	vs	AIR FORCE	42	32	W	-9.5	W	59.5	O	
10/5/2018	@	*Byu*	45	20	W	-1.0	W	55.0	O	*"The Old Wagon Wheel"*
10/13/2018	vs	UNLV	59	28	W	-27.0	W	65.5	O	
10/20/2018	@	Wyoming	24	16	W	-14.0	L	49.5	U	*"Bridger's Battle"*
10/27/2018	vs	NEW MEXICO	61	19	W	-19.5	W	64.0	O	
11/3/2018	@	Hawaii	56	17	W	-18.0	W	72.0	O	
11/10/2018	vs	SAN JOSE STATE	62	24	W	-31.0	W	63.5	O	
11/17/2018	@	Colorado State	29	24	W	-30.0	L	66.0	U	
11/24/2018	@	Boise State	24	33	L	2.0	L	64.0	U	
12/15/2018	vs	**North Texas**	**52**	**13**	W	-7.0	**W**	67.5	U	**New Mexico Bowl**
Coach: Matt Wells		Season Record >>	618	289	11-2	ATS>>	10-3	O/U>>	8-4	
2017-Utah State		Opponent	USU	Opp	S/U	Line	ATS	Total	O/U	
9/1/2017	@	*Wisconsin*	10	59	L	27.5	L	51.5	O	
9/7/2017	vs	*IDAHO STATE*	51	13	W	-35.0	W	NT	---	
9/16/2017	@	*Wake Forest*	10	46	L	15.5	L	51.5	O	
9/23/2017	@	San Jose State	61	10	W	-1.5	W	55.5	O	
9/29/2017	vs	BYU	40	24	W	-1.0	W	49.5	O	*"The Old Wagon Wheel"*
10/7/2017	vs	COLORADO STATE	14	27	L	9.5	L	65.0	U	
10/14/2017	vs	WYOMING	23	28	L	2.0	L	50.0	O	*"Bridger's Battle"*
10/21/2017	@	Unlv	52	28	W	3.5	W	60.0	O	
10/28/2017	vs	BOISE STATE	14	41	L	13.0	L	51.5	O	
11/4/2017	@	New Mexico	24	10	W	3.0	W	51.0	U	
11/18/2017	vs	HAWAII	38	0	W	-10.0	W	56.0	U	
11/25/2017	@	Air Force	35	38	L	2.0	L	57.0	O	
12/29/2017	vs	**New Mexico State**	**20**	**26**	L	-5.5	L	64.0	U	**Arizona Bowl**
Coach: Matt Wells		Season Record >>	392	350	6-7	ATS>>	6-7	O/U>>	8-4	

Copyright © 2021 by Steve's Football Bible, LLC

UTAH STATE AGGIES   MOUNTAIN WEST West

STADIUM: Romney Stadium {25,100}						Location: Logan, UT			COACH: Blake Andersen	
DATE		Opponent	USU	Opp	S/U	Line	ATS	Total	O/U	Trends & Angles
9/4/2021	@	*Washington State*								vs Washington State - WAZZU leads series 2-1
9/11/2021	vs	*NORTH DAKOTA*								1st meeting
9/18/2021	@	Air Force								vs Air Force - Air Force leads series 6-3
9/25/2021	vs	BOISE STATE								1-16 S/U vs Boise State as Dog since 1998
10/1/2021	vs	*BYU*								3-21 S/U vs BYU as Dog since 1985
10/16/2021	@	Unlv								5-0 S/U vs UNLV as favorite since 1995
10/23/2021	vs	COLORADO STATE								vs Colorado State - CSU leads series 39-35-2
10/30/2021	vs	HAWAII								4-0 S/U & ATS vs Hawaii as favorite since 2013
11/6/2021	@	*New Mexico State*								10-1 S/U vs NMSU as 6 point or more favorite s/1986
11/13/2021	@	San Jose State								1-9 S/U vs San Jose State as Dog since 1986
11/20/2021	vs	WYOMING								vs Wyoming - Utah State leads series 40-26-4
11/27/2021	@	New Mexico								vs New Mexico - Utah State leads series 14-13
12/4/2021	vs									MWC Championship
	vs									BOWL GAME

Pointspread Analysis Non-Conference		Pointspread Analysis Conference
1-11 S/U vs Non-Conf. as 25.5-30 point Dog since 1986		3-10 S/U @ home vs MWC teams as 3.5-7 point Dog since 1991
7-1 ATS vs Non-Conf. as 20.5-25 point Dog since 2005		4-0 O/U vs Air Force as favorite since 2013
0-8 S/U on road vs Non-Conf. as 10.5-15 point Dog since 1996		vs Boise State - Boise State leads series 20-5
8-2 ATS on road vs Non-Conf. as 10.5-15 point Dog since 1986		0-5 S/U vs Colorado State as Dog since 1994
1-18 S/U vs BYU as 13.5 point or more Dog since 1985		1-6 S/U vs Fresno State as Dog since 2007
vs BYU - BYU leads series 49-37-3		vs Nevada - Nevada leads series 19-7
1-13 S/U vs ranked BYU all time		5-1 ATS vs UNLV as Dog since 1985
1-8 O/U vs New Mexico State as favorite since 2003		6-0 S/U vs Wyoming as favorite since 2011 {4-1-1 ATS}
8-1 S/U & ATS vs New Mexico State as Dog since 1992		0-5 S/U vs Wyoming as Dog since 2003 {1-4 ATS}
Dog		Game 5-2 O/U @ home vs Wyoming since 2001
0-22 S/U as 30.5 point or more Dog since 1985		**Bowl Games**
0-33 S/U on road as 25.5 point or more Dog since 1986		1-3 S/U & ATS in Famous Idaho Potato Bowl since 1997
1-28-1 S/U as 20.5-25 point Dog since 1985		1-3 O/U Famous Idaho Potato Bowl since 1997
1-21 S/U on road as 15.5-20 point Dog since 1985		1-6 O/U in Bowl Games since 2011
0-9 S/U @ home as 15.5-20 point Dog since 1987		
1-15 S/U on road as 10.5-15 point Dog since 1993	Washington St.	0-23 S/U in 1st road game of season since 1998
1-6 O/U on road as 10.5-15 point Dog since 2006	NORTH DAKOTA	11-1 S/U in 1st home game of season since 2009
1-8 S/U @ home as 10.5-15 point Dog since 1996	Air Force	5-21 S/U in 2nd road game of season since 1995
1-7 S/U @ home as 7.5-10 point Dog since 1994	BYU	7-1 O/U after playing Boise State since 2008
8-3 ATS @ home as 7.5-10 point Dog since 1987	COLORADO STATE	1-7 O/U after playing UNLV since 2006
1-9 S/U on road as 7.5-10 point Dog since 1985	HAWAII	6-0 ATS prior to playing New Mexico State since 2008
3-12 S/U on road as 3.5-7 point Dog since 2002	San Jose State	6-0 ATS after playing New Mexico State since 2007
0-6 S/U & ATS @ home as 3 point or less Dog since 2003	New Mexico	1-7 ATS in final road game of season since 2013
7-1 O/U @ home as 3 point or less Dog since 2002		
Favorite		
46-1 S/U @ home as 7.5 point or more favorite since 1995		
8-0 S/U @ home as 7.5-10 point favorite since 1995		
5-0 S/U on road as 7.5-10 point favorite since 1987		
13-0 S/U as 10.5-15 point favorite since 2011		2-54 S/U on road vs ranked teams all time
6-1 O/U @ home as 10.5-15 point favorite since 2011		2-13 S/U @ home vs ranked teams all time
11-1 S/U @ home as 10.5-15 point favorite since 1993		0-25 S/U vs Top #10 ranked teams all time
29-0 S/U @ home as 15.5 point or more favorite since 1990		0-16 S/U vs #11 - #17 ranked teams all time

Copyright © 2021 by Steve's Football Bible, LLC

VANDERBILT COMMODORES   SEC East

2020-Vanderbilt		Opponent	Vandy	Opp	S/U	Line	ATS	Total	O/U	
9/26/2020	@	Texas A&M	12	17	L	31.0	W	45.5	U	
10/3/2020	vs	LSU	7	41	L	21.0	L	50.0	U	
10/10/2020	vs	SOUTH CAROLINA	7	41	L	14.0	L	41.5	O	
10/31/2020	vs	MISSISSIPPI	21	54	L	17.0	L	63.5	O	
11/7/2020	@	Mississippi State	17	24	L	18.5	W	45.0	U	
11/14/2020	@	Kentucky	35	38	L	17.5	W	41.5	O	
11/21/2020	vs	FLORIDA	17	38	L	31.0	W	68.0	U	
11/28/2020	@	Missouri	0	41	L	14.0	L	51.5	U	
12/12/2020	vs	TENNESSEE	17	42	L	15.0	L	51.0	O	
Coach: Derek Mason		Season Record >>	133	336	0-9	ATS>>	4-5	O/U>>	4-5	
2019-Vanderbilt		Opponent	Vandy	Opp	S/U	Line	ATS	Total	O/U	
8/31/2019	vs	GEORGIA	6	30	L	22.5	L	57.0	U	
9/7/2019	@	Purdue	24	42	L	7.0	L	55.5	O	
9/21/2019	vs	LSU	38	66	L	24.0	L	62.5	O	
9/28/2019	vs	NORTHERN I.ILLINOIS	24	18	W	-7.0	L	51.5	U	
10/5/2019	@	Mississippi	6	31	L	7.0	L	64.5	U	
10/12/2019	vs	UNLV	10	34	L	-15.5	L	57.5	U	
10/19/2019	vs	MISSOURI	21	14	W	21.0	W	55.5	U	
11/2/2019	@	South Carolina	7	24	L	15.5	L	51.5	U	
11/9/2019	@	Florida	0	56	L	27.0	L	49.5	O	
11/16/2019	vs	KENTUCKY	14	38	L	9.0	L	43.0	O	
11/23/2019	vs	EAST TENNESSEE STATE	38	0	W	-20.5	W	NT	---	
11/30/2019	@	Tennessee	10	28	L	23.5	W	48.0	U	
Coach: Derek Mason		Season Record >>	198	381	3-9	ATS>>	3-9	O/U>>	4-7	
2018-Vanderbilt		Opponent	Vandy	Opp	S/U	Line	ATS	Total	O/U	
9/1/2018	vs	MIDDLE TENNESSEE	35	7	W	-3.0	W	56.5	U	
9/8/2018	vs	NEVADA	41	10	W	-10.0	W	60.0	U	
9/15/2018	@	Notre Dame	17	22	L	13.5	W	51.5	U	
9/22/2018	vs	SOUTH CAROLINA	14	37	L	1.5	L	54.5	U	
9/29/2018	vs	TENNESSEE STATE	31	27	W	-28.5	L	NT	---	
10/6/2018	@	Georgia	13	41	L	26.0	L	55.5	U	
10/13/2018	vs	FLORIDA	27	37	L	10.0	T	52.0	O	
10/20/2018	@	Kentucky	7	14	L	10.0	W	45.0	U	
10/27/2018	@	Arkansas	45	31	W	PK	W	53.0	O	
11/10/2018	@	Missouri	28	33	L	14.0	W	64.5	U	
11/17/2018	vs	MISSISSIPPI	36	29	W	-3.0	W	73.0	U	{OT}
11/24/2018	vs	TENNESSEE	38	13	W	-3.0	W	51.5	U	
12/27/2018	vs	**Baylor**	38	45	L	-4.5	L	56.5	O	**Texas Bowl**
Coach: Derek Mason		Season Record >>	370	346	6-7	ATS>>	8-4-1	O/U>>	3-9	
2017-Vanderbilt		Opponent	Vandy	Opp	S/U	Line	ATS	Total	O/U	
9/2/2017	@	Middle Tennessee	28	6	W	-2.0	W	57.0	U	
9/9/2017	vs	ALABAMA A&M	42	0	W	-49.5	L	NT	---	
9/16/2017	vs	KANSAS STATE	14	7	W	4.5	W	48.5	U	
9/23/2017	vs	ALABAMA	0	59	L	19.5	L	42.0	O	
9/30/2017	@	Florida	24	38	L	9.0	L	39.0	O	
10/7/2017	vs	GEORGIA	14	45	L	17.0	L	41.5	O	
10/14/2017	@	Mississippi	35	57	L	3.0	L	56.0	O	
10/28/2017	@	South Carolina	27	34	L	7.0	T	43.5	O	
11/4/2017	vs	WESTERN KENTUCKY	31	17	W	-12.5	W	53.5	U	
11/11/2017	vs	KENTUCKY	21	44	L	-2.0	L	53.0	O	
11/18/2017	vs	MISSOURI	17	45	L	7.5	L	64.5	U	
11/25/2017	@	Tennessee	42	24	W	2.5	W	45.5	O	
Coach: Derek Mason		Season Record >>	295	376	5-7	ATS>>	4-7-1	O/U>>	7-4	

Copyright © 2021 by Steve's Football Bible, LLC

VANDERBILT COMMODORES   SEC East

STADIUM: Vanderbilt Stadium {40,550}		Location: Nashville, TN							COACH: Clark Lea
DATE		Opponent	Vand	Opp	S/U	Line	ATS	Total	O/U	Trends & Angles

DATE		Opponent	Vand	Opp	S/U	Line	ATS	Total	O/U	Trends & Angles
9/4/2021	vs	*EAST TENNESEE ST.*								vs East Tennessee - Vandy leads series 1-0
9/11/2021	@	*Colorado State*								1st meeting
9/18/2021	vs	*STANFORD*								1st meeting
9/25/2021	vs	**GEORGIA**								1-13 S/U @ home vs Georgia as Dog since 1993
10/2/2021	vs	*CONNECTICUT*								vs U Conn - Vandy leads series 2-1
10/9/2021	@	Florida								9-4 ATS @ Florida as Dog since 1995
10/16/2021	@	South Carolina								0-11 S/U vs South Carolina as Dog since 2009
10/23/2021	vs	MISSISSIPPI STATE								0-6 S/U & ATS vs M State as Dog since 1989
10/30/2021	vs	MISSOURI								1-6 S/U vs Missouri as Dog since 2013
11/13/2021	vs	KENTUCKY								0-8 S/U vs Kentucky as Dog since 2009
11/20/2021	@	Mississippi								8-2 ATS @ Mississippi as Dog since 1999
11/27/2021	@	Tennessee								vs Tennessee - Tennessee leads series 77-32-5
12/4/2021	vs									SEC Championship
	vs									BOWL GAME

Pointspread Analysis Non-Conference		Pointspread Analysis Conference
0-8 S/U vs Non-Conf. as 10.5-15 point Dog since 1986		vs Florida - Florida leads series 42-10-2
1-6 S/U @ home vs Non-Conf. as 3.5-7 point favorite since 1998		1-29 S/U vs Florida as Dog since 1989
0-7 ATS @ home vs Non-Conf. as 3.5-7 point favorite since 1998		vs Georgia - Georgia leads series 58-20-2
Dog		0-10 S/U vs Georgia as 21.5 point or more Dog since 1990
1-63 S/U as 20.5 point or more Dog since 1986		1-11 S/U vs Georgia as 12 point or less Dog since 1983
0-26 S/U as 15.5-20 point Dog since 2000		vs Kentucky - Kentucky leads series 47-42-4
0-26 S/U @ home as 10.5-15 point Dog since 1983		0-8 S/U vs Kentucky as 10 point or more Dog since 1986
16-5 ATS on road as 10.5-15 point Dog since 2005		0-6 S/U vs Kentucky as 3.5 point or less Dog since 1996 {1-5 ATS}
2-18 S/U @ home as 7.5-10 point Dog since 1989		11-1 ATS vs Kentucky as 5-13 point Dog since 1985
2-11 S/U on road as 7.5-10 point Dog since 1983		vs Mississippi - Ole Miss leads series 53-40-2
1-10 S/U @ home as 3 point or less Dog since 1984		8-2 ATS vs Mississippi as 12 point or more Dog since 1990
1-9-1 ATS @ home as 3 point or less Dog since 1984		vs Missouri - Mizzu leads series 8-4-1
Favorite		0-6 O/U vs Missouri as Dog since 2014
8-1 S/U & ATS as 3 point or less favorite since 2012		vs South Carolina - South Carolina leads series 26-4
4-0 S/U on road as 3.5-7 point favorite since 1993		0-4 ATS vs South Carolina as favorite since 1992
1-9 ATS @ home as 3.5-7 point favorite since 1998		1-12 S/U vs South Carolina as 12 point or more Dog since 1995
5-0 S/U on road as 10.5 point or more favorite since 1992		0-7 S/U vs South Carolina as 6.5 point or less Dog since 1993
20-1 S/U as 15.5 point or more favorite since 1989		0-24 S/U vs Tennessee as 12 point or more Dog since 1985
Bowl Games		
5-0 O/U in Bowl Games since 2011	Colorado State	3-12-1 O/U in 1st road game of season since 2005
	STANFORD	1-5 S/U prior to playing Georgia since 2013
	Florida	0-20 S/U in 6th game of season since 2001 {4-16 ATS}
0-24 S/U vs ranked Florida since 1989	South Carolina	2-7 O/U after playing Florida since 2012
1-9 S/U @ home vs ranked Georgia since 1997	MISSOURI	8-1-1 ATS prior to playing Kentucky since 2011
1-15 S/U vs ranked Mississippi since 1948 {0-6 on road}	KENTUCKY	5-2 S/U & ATS after playing Missouri since 2013
1-38 S/U vs ranked Tennessee all time {0-21 on road}	KENTUCKY	1-6 ATS prior to playing Mississippi since 2014

Copyright © 2021 by Steve's Football Bible, LLC

VIRGINIA CAVALIERS

ACC Coastal

2020-Virginia		Opponent	UVA	Opp	S/U	Line	ATS	Total	O/U	
9/26/2020	vs	DUKE	38	20	W	-4.5	W	45.5	O	
10/3/2020	@	Clemson	23	41	L	27.5	W	55.5	O	
10/10/2020	vs	NC STATE	21	38	L	-7.0	L	58.5	O	
10/17/2020	@	Wake Forest	23	40	L	2.5	L	57.5	O	
10/24/2020	@	Miami	14	19	L	13.5	W	54.5	U	
10/31/2020	vs	NORTH CAROLINA	44	41	W	8.0	W	61.5	O	"South's Oldest Rivalry"
11/14/2020	vs	LOUISVILLE	31	17	W	-5.5	W	63.0	U	
11/21/2020	vs	ABILENE CHRISTIAN	55	15	W	-38.5	W	61.0	O	
12/5/2020	vs	BOSTON COLLEGE	43	32	W	-6.5	W	53.0	O	
12/12/2020	@	Virginia Tech	15	33	L	3.0	L	64.0	U	"Commonwealth Cup"
Coach: Bronco Mendenhall		Season Record >>	307	296	5-5	ATS>>	7-3	O/U>>	7-3	
2019-Virginia		Opponent	UVA	Opp	S/U	Line	ATS	Total	O/U	
8/31/2019	@	Pittsburgh	30	14	W	-2.5	W	45.5	U	
9/6/2019	vs	WILLIAM & MARY	52	17	W	-32.5	W	NT	---	
9/14/2019	vs	FLORIDA STATE	31	24	W	-7.0	T	54.5	O	"Jefferson-Eppes Trophy"
9/21/2019	vs	OLD DOMINION	28	17	W	-27.0	L	46.5	U	
9/28/2019	@	Notre Dame	20	35	L	11.0	L	46.5	O	
10/11/2019	@	Miami	9	17	L	3.0	L	43.5	U	
10/19/2019	vs	DUKE	48	14	W	-3.0	W	45.0	O	
10/26/2019	@	Louisville	21	28	L	-4.0	L	51.0	U	
11/2/2019	@	North Carolina	38	31	W	-1.0	W	47.5	O	"South's Oldest Rivalry"
11/9/2019	vs	GEORGIA TECH	33	28	W	-16.0	L	45.5	O	
11/23/2019	vs	LIBERTY	55	27	W	-16.0	W	58.0	O	
11/30/2019	vs	VIRGINIA TECH	39	30	W	2.5	W	48.5	O	"Commonwealth Cup"
12/7/2019	vs	Clemson	17	62	L	30.0	L	57.5	O	ACC CHAMPIONSHIP GAME
12/30/2019	vs	Florida	28	36	L	16.5	W	55.0	O	Orange Bowl
Coach: Bronco Mendenhall		Season Record >>	449	380	9-5	ATS>>	7-6-1	O/U>>	9-4	
2018-Virginia		Opponent	UVA	Opp	S/U	Line	ATS	Total	O/U	
9/1/2018	vs	RICHMOND	42	13	W	-14.5	W	NT	---	
9/8/2018	@	Indiana	16	20	L	5.0	W	50.0	U	
9/15/2018	vs	OHIO	45	31	W	-5.5	W	53.5	O	
9/22/2018	vs	LOUISVILLE	27	3	W	-5.0	W	51.5	U	
9/29/2018	@	NC State	21	35	L	6.0	L	52.5	O	
10/13/2018	vs	MIAMI	16	13	W	7.0	W	46.5	U	
10/20/2018	@	Duke	28	14	W	6.5	W	44.5	U	
10/27/2018	vs	NORTH CAROLINA	31	21	W	-9.0	W	50.5	O	"South's Oldest Rivalry"
11/2/2018	vs	PITTSBURGH	13	23	L	-7.0	L	45.5	U	
11/10/2018	vs	LIBERTY	45	24	W	-23.5	L	59.0	O	
11/17/2018	@	Georgia Tech	27	30	L	6.5	W	52.0	O	{OT}
11/23/2018	@	Virginia Tech	31	34	L	-5.0	L	50.0	O	"Commonwealth Cup"
12/29/2018	vs	South Carolina	28	0	W	3.5	W	54.0	U	Belk Bowl
Coach: Bronco Mendenhall		Season Record >>	370	261	8-5	ATS>>	9-4	O/U>>	6-6	
2017-Virginia		Opponent	UVA	Opp	S/U	Line	ATS	Total	O/U	
9/2/2017	vs	WILLIAM & MARY	28	10	W	-27.0	L	50.0	U	
9/9/2017	vs	INDIANA	17	34	L	4.0	L	55.0	U	
9/16/2017	vs	CONNECTICUT	38	16	W	-11.5	W	51.5	O	
9/22/2017	@	Boise State	42	23	W	13.5	W	50.5	O	
10/7/2017	vs	DUKE	28	21	W	PK	W	52.0	U	
10/14/2017	@	North Carolina	20	14	W	-3.0	W	53.0	U	"South's Oldest Rivalry"
10/21/2017	vs	BOSTON COLLEGE	10	41	L	-6.5	L	47.5	O	
10/28/2017	@	Pittsburgh	14	31	L	PK	L	49.5	U	
11/4/2017	vs	GEORGIA TECH	40	36	W	7.5	W	50.5	O	
11/11/2017	@	Louisville	21	38	L	11.5	L	66.0	U	
11/18/2017	@	Miami	28	44	L	19.5	W	49.0	O	
11/25/2017	vs	VIRGINIA TECH	0	10	L	6.5	L	48.5	U	"Commonwealth Cup"
12/28/2017	vs	Navy	7	49	L	2.5	L	50.0	O	Military Bowl
Coach: Bronco Mendenhall		Season Record >>	293	367	6-7	ATS>>	6-7	O/U>>	6-7	

Copyright © 2021 by Steve's Football Bible, LLC

VIRGINIA CAVALIERS ACC Coastal

STADIUM: Scott Stadium {61,500}					Location: Charlottesville, VA				COACH: Bronco Mendenhall	
DATE		Opponent	UVA	Opp	S/U	Line	ATS	Total	O/U	Trends & Angles
9/4/2021	vs	WILLIAM & MARY								10-1 S/U vs William & Mary since 1988
9/11/2021	vs	ILLINOIS								vs Illinois - Illinois leads series 2-0
9/18/2021	@	North Carolina								1-6 S/U vs UNC as Dog since 2010 {2-5 ATS}
9/24/2021	vs	WAKE FOREST								11-2 S/U @ home vs Wake Forest since 1982
9/30/2021	@	Miami								vs Miami - Miami leads series 11-7
10/9/2021	@	Louisville								vs Louisville - Louisville leads series 5-4
10/16/2021	vs	DUKE								vs Duke - Virginia leads series 39-33
10/23/2021	vs	GEORGIA TECH								vs Georgia Tech - G TECH leads series 21-20-1
10/30/2021	@	Byu								vs BYU - Virginia leads series 3-2
11/13/2021	vs	NOTRE DAME								vs Notre Dame - Notre Dame leads series 3-0
11/20/2021	@	Pittsburgh								vs Pittsburgh - PITT leads series 8-4
11/27/2021	vs	VIRGINIA TECH								1-7 S/U @ home vs Virginia Tech since 2005
12/4/2021	vs									ACC Championship
	vs									BOWL GAME

Pointspread Analysis

Non-Conference		Conference
0-7 S/U vs Non-Conf. as 15.5-20 point Dog since 1987		3-0 S/U & ATS vs Duke as Dog since 2015
1-7 S/U vs Non-Conf. as 10.5-15 point Dog since 1987		16-1 S/U vs Duke as 9.5 point or more favorite since 1985
4-1 ATS vs Non-Conf. as 10.5-15 point Dog since 2009		6-0 S/U @ home vs Georgia Tech as favorite since 1992
7-0 O/U vs Non-Conf. as 10.5-15 point Dog since 2008		0-6 S/U vs Georgia Tech as 9.5-12 point Dog since 1991
10-2 ATS vs Non-Conf. as 3.5-7 point Dog since 2001		0-3 S/U vs Louisville as Dog since 2015
1-5 S/U vs Non-Conf. as 3 point or less Dog since 1988		11-3 ATS vs Miami as Dog since 2005
9-1 O/U vs Non-Conf. as 3.5-7 point favorite since 1995		vs North Carolina - UNC leads series 63-57-4
1-6 ATS vs Non-Conf. as 7.5-10 point favorite since 2000		9-1 S/U & ATS vs North Carolina as favorite since 1998
7-2 S/U vs Non-Conf. as 7.5-10 point favorite since 1991		0-4 S/U vs Pittsburgh as Dog since 2006
30-0 S/U vs Non-Conf. as 15.5 point or more favorite since 1990		vs Virginia Tech - Virginia Tech leads series 59-38-5
vs William & Mary - Virginia leads series 30-6-1		1-16 S/U vs Virginia Tech since 2004

Dog

		1-18 S/U vs Virginia Tech as Dog since 1999
0-16 S/U as 20.5 point or more Dog since 1987		1-10 S/U @ home vs Virginia Tech as Dog since 1983
1-15 S/U on road as 15.5-20 point Dog since 1983		Game 1-4 O/U @ home vs Virginia Tech since 2011
0-4 S/U @ home as 15.5-20 point Dog since 1997		5-0 O/U vs Virginia Tech as favorite since 1995
3-9 S/U @ home as 10.5-15 point Dog since 1984		vs Wake Forest - Virginia leads series 34-16
0-10 S/U on road as 7.5-10 point Dog since 2000		0-4 S/U & ATS vs Wake Forest since 2008
1-10 S/U on road as 3.5-7 point Dog since 2008		1-6-1 ATS @ home vs Wake Forest since 1993
4-13 O/U @ home as 3.5-7 point Dog since 2008		15-0 S/U vs Wake Forest as 4.5 point or more favorite since 1984
2-7 O/U on road as 3 point or less Dog since 2004		

Favorite

	ILLINOIS	3-8 ATS prior to playing North Carolina since 2010
4-0 S/U & ATS as 3 point or less favorite since 2017	ILLINOIS	10-3 O/U prior to playing North Carolina since 2008
20-5 S/U @ home as 7.5-10 point favorite since 1984	UNC	3-12 S/U in 1st road game of season since 2006
6-0 S/U on road as 7.5-10 point favorite since 1997	WAKE F	3-7 S/U after playing North Carolina since 2011
1-6 O/U as 7.5-10 point favorite since 2006	Miami	8-1 ATS prior to playing Louisville since 1988
9-1 S/U @ home as 10.5-15 point favorite since 1995	Louisville	4-11 S/U after playing Miami since 2006
19-0 S/U on road as 10.5 point or more favorite since 1985	DUKE	7-0 O/U after playing Louisville since 2014
31-1 S/U @ home as 20.5 point or more favorite since 1990	G TECH	1-7 S/U after playing Duke since 2012

Bowl Games

	Byu	1-11 S/U after playing Georgia Tech since 2008
11-2-1 O/U in Bowl Games since 1995	Byu	3-9 ATS after playing Georgia Tech since 2008
5-1 O/U vs SEC in Bowl Games since 1995	NOTRE DAME	6-0 O/U prior to playing Pittsburgh since 2007
0-3 S/U & ATS in Bowl Games as 3 point or less Dog since 1990	Pittsburgh	3-18 S/U in final road game of season since 2000
	Pittsburgh	7-1 O/U in final road game of season since 2013
6-0 S/U when ranked vs Duke since 1995	VA TECH	1-7 ATS after playing Pittsburgh since 2006
6-0 S/U when ranked vs Wake Forest all time		
5-0 S/U when ranked vs William & Mary all time		
13-2 ATS vs ranked teams since 2014		
2-23 S/U on road vs ranked teams since 2001		
0-5 S/U vs #1 ranked teams all time		
0-7 S/U @ North Carolina all time		

Copyright © 2021 by Steve's Football Bible, LLC

VIRGINIA TECH HOKIES   ACC Coastal

2020-Virginia Tech		Opponent	VPI	Opp	S/U	Line	ATS	Total	O/U	
9/26/2020	vs	NC STATE	45	24	W	-6.5	W	57.5	O	
10/3/2020	@	Duke	38	31	W	-10.5	L	54.0	O	
10/10/2020	@	North Carolina	45	56	L	3.0	L	58.5	O	
10/17/2020	vs	BOSTON COLLEGE	40	14	W	-13.5	W	61.5	U	
10/24/2020	@	Wake Forest	16	23	L	-10.5	L	69.0	U	
10/31/2020	@	Louisville	42	35	W	-2.5	W	67.5	O	
11/7/2020	vs	LIBERTY	35	38	L	-16.5	L	67.5	O	
11/14/2020	vs	MIAMI	24	25	L	-2.0	L	67.5	U	
11/21/2020	@	Pittsburgh	14	47	L	-6.0	L	52.0	O	
12/5/2020	vs	CLEMSON	10	45	L	23.0	L	66.5	U	
12/12/2020	vs	VIRGINIA	33	15	W	-3.0	W	64.0	U	"Commonwealth Cup"
Coach: Justin Fuente		Season Record >>	342	353	5-6	ATS>>	4-7	O/U>>	6-5	

2019-Virginia Tech		Opponent	VPI	Opp	S/U	Line	ATS	Total	O/U	
8/31/2019	@	Boston College	28	35	L	-4.0	L	58.0	O	
9/7/2019	vs	OLD DOMINION	31	17	W	-28.5	L	56.5	U	
9/14/2019	vs	FURMAN	24	17	W	-23.5	L	NT	---	
9/27/2019	vs	DUKE	10	45	L	-2.5	L	51.5	O	
10/5/2019	@	Miami	42	35	W	14.0	W	45.0	O	
10/12/2019	vs	RHODE ISLAND	34	17	W	-26.5	L	NT	---	
10/19/2019	vs	NORTH CAROLINA	43	41	W	4.0	W	57.0	O	{6 OT}
11/2/2019	@	Notre Dame	20	21	L	17.5	W	58.0	U	
11/9/2019	vs	WAKE FOREST	36	17	W	2.5	W	60.0	U	
11/16/2019	@	Georgia Tech	45	0	W	-6.0	W	51.5	U	"Battle of the Techs"
11/23/2019	vs	PITTSBURGH	28	0	W	-4.0	W	43.5	U	
11/29/2019	@	Virginia	30	39	L	-2.5	L	48.5	O	"Commonwealth Cup"
12/31/2019	vs	Kentucky	30	37	L	-2.0	L	46.0	O	Belk Bowl
Coach: Justin Fuente		Season Record >>	401	321	8-5	ATS>>	6-7	O/U>>	6-5	

2018-Virginia Tech		Opponent	VPI	Opp	S/U	Line	ATS	Total	O/U	
9/3/2018	@	Florida State	24	3	W	7.5	W	54.0	U	
9/8/2018	vs	WILLIAM & MARY	62	17	W	-42.0	W	NT	---	
9/22/2018	@	Old Dominion	35	49	L	-29.0	L	53.0	O	
9/29/2018	@	Duke	31	14	W	6.5	W	52.5	U	
10/6/2018	vs	NOTRE DAME	23	45	L	6.5	L	55.0	O	
10/13/2018	@	North Carolina	22	19	W	-6.5	L	57.5	U	
10/25/2018	vs	GEORGIA TECH	28	49	L	-3.0	L	58.5	O	"Battle of the Techs"
11/3/2018	vs	BOSTON COLLEGE	21	31	L	2.0	L	57.0	U	
11/10/2018	@	Pittsburgh	22	52	L	3.0	L	54.0	O	
11/17/2018	vs	MIAMI	14	38	L	6.5	L	52.5	U	
11/23/2018	vs	VIRGINIA	34	31	W	5.0	W	50.0	O	"Commonwealth Cup"
12/1/2018	vs	MARSHALL	41	20	W	-4.0	W	51.5	O	
12/31/2018	vs	Cincinnati	31	35	L	5.5	W	48.5	O	Military Bowl
Coach: Justin Fuente		Season Record >>	388	403	6-7	ATS>>	6-7	O/U>>	7-5	

2017-Virginia Tech		Opponent	VPI	Opp	S/U	Line	ATS	Total	O/U	
9/2/2017	vs	West Virginia	31	24	W	-5.0	W	55.0	T	"Black Diamond Trophy"
9/9/2017	vs	DELAWARE	27	0	W	-40.0	L	NT	---	
9/16/2017	@	East Carolina	64	17	W	-27.0	W	60.0	O	
9/23/2017	vs	OLD DOMINION	38	0	W	-29.5	W	51.5	U	
9/30/2017	vs	CLEMSON	17	31	L	7.0	L	49.0	U	
10/7/2017	@	Boston College	23	10	W	-15.5	L	46.5	U	
10/21/2017	vs	NORTH CAROLINA	59	7	W	-20.5	W	53.5	O	
10/28/2017	vs	DUKE	24	3	W	-17.0	W	48.5	U	
11/4/2017	@	Miami	10	28	L	2.0	L	49.5	U	
11/11/2017	@	Georgia Tech	22	28	L	-3.0	L	47.5	O	"Battle of the Techs"
11/18/2017	vs	PITTSBURGH	20	14	W	-14.0	L	48.5	U	
11/24/2017	@	Virginia	10	0	W	-6.5	W	48.5	U	"Commonwealth Cup"
12/28/2017	vs	Oklahoma State	21	30	L	6.5	L	60.5	U	Camping World Bowl
Coach: Justin Fuente		Season Record >>	366	192	9-4	ATS>>	6-7	O/U>>	3-8-1	

Copyright © 2021 by Steve's Football Bible, LLC

VIRGINIA TECH HOKIES   ACC Coastal

STADIUM: Lane Stadium {65,632}			Location: Blacksburg, VA						COACH: Justin Fuentes
DATE		Opponent	VPI	Opp	S/U	Line	ATS	Total	O/U	Trends & Angles
9/2/2021	vs	NORTH CAROLINA								vs North Carolina - VPI leads series 24-13-6
9/11/2021	vs	*MIDDLE TENNESSEE*								1st meeting
9/18/2021	@	*West Virginia*								6-0 ATS vs West Virginia as Dog since 1986
9/25/2021	vs	*RICHMOND*								12-1 S/U @ home vs Richmond since 1957
10/9/2021	vs	*NOTRE DAME*								vs Notre Dame - Notre Dame leads series 2-1
10/16/2021	vs	PITTSBURGH								vs Pittsburgh - VPI leads series 11-9
10/23/2021	vs	SYRACUSE								6-1 S/U @ home vs Syracuse as favorite since 1985
10/30/2021	@	Georgia Tech								2-9 ATS vs Georgia Tech as favorite since 2006
11/5/2021	@	Boston College								vs Boston College - VPI leads series 18-10
11/13/2021	vs	DUKE								vs Duke - VPI leads series 18-10
11/20/2021	@	Miami								vs Miami - Miami leads series 23-15
11/27/2021	@	Virginia								18-1 S/U vs Virginia as favorite since 1999
12/4/2021	vs									ACC Championship
	vs									BOWL GAME

Pointspread Analysis Non-Conference		Pointspread Analysis Conference
2-10 S/U vs Non-Conf. as 3.5-7 point Dog since 1987		13-1 S/U vs Boston College as 6.5 point or more favorite since 1997
14-3 S/U vs Non-Conf. as 3.5-7 point favorite since 1994		14-1 S/U vs Duke as 7.5 point or more favorite since 1983
7-2 S/U vs Non-Conf. as 15.5-20 point favorite since 2003		vs Georgia Tech - VPI leads series 10-7
42-1 S/U vs Non-Conf. as 20.5-30 point favorite since 1987		3-0 S/U vs Georgia Tech as Dog since 2007
5-0 S/U vs W. Virginia as 2-5 point favorite since 1995		4-0 ATS vs Georgia Tech as Dog since 1990
4-0 S/U vs W. Virginia as 15 point or more favorite since 1994		0-3 O/U vs Georgia Tech as Dog since 2007
vs West Virginia - WVU leads series 28-23-1		1-4 S/U vs Georgia Tech as favorite since 2014
vs Richmond - VPI leads series 37-10-4		1-4 S/U & ATS vs Miami as Dog since 2014
Dog		2-8 O/U vs Miami as Dog since 2014
0-9 S/U as 20.5 point or more Dog since 1987		1-6 S/U vs Miami as 14 point or more Dog since 1987
5-2 ATS as 20.5 point or more Dog since 1988		11-1 S/U vs North Carolina as favorite since 2004
1-14 S/U as 15.5-20 point Dog since 1985		2-11 ATS vs Pittsburgh as favorite since 1999
0-10 S/U @ home as 10.5 point or more Dog since 1987		6-0 S/U @ home vs PITT as 14 point or more favorite since 1994
7-0 O/U as 10.5-15 point Dog since 2007		0-5 S/U vs Syracuse as Dog since 1987 {1-4 ATS}
2-6 S/U as 7.5-10 point Dog since 1989		vs Virginia - Virginia Tech leads series 59-38-5
2-5 ATS as 7.5-10 point Dog since 1991		10-1 S/U @ Virginia as favorite since 1983
Favorite		8-2 ATS vs Virginia as 4 point or more Dog since 1985
6-2 O/U as 3 point or less favorite since 2017		
2-6 S/U & ATS as 3 point or less favorite since 2017	UNC	23-2 S/U in 1st home game of season since 1996
21-5 S/U on road as 3.5-7 point favorite since 1994	MTSU	22-3 S/U in 2nd home game of season since 1996
18-8 ATS on road as 3.5-7 point favorite since 1994	MTSU	3-9-1 O/U in 2nd home game of season since 2006
4-13 ATS as 7.5-10 point favorite since 2006	MTSU	1-7 O/U after playing North Carolina since 2013
7-2 S/U on road as 7.5-10 point favorite since 1984	MTSU	12-4 S/U after playing North Carolina since 2004
0-4 ATS on road as 7.5-10 point favorite since 2008	West Virginia	11-2 S/U in 1st road game of season since 2008
2-12 ATS as 10.5-15 point favorite since 2010	SYRACUSE	0-8-1 O/U prior to playing Georgia Tech since 2010
9-3 S/U on road as 10.5-15 point favorite since 2005	SYRACUSE	1-9 O/U after playing Pittsburgh since 2003
12-3 S/U @ home as 15.5-20 point favorite since 2003	Georgia Tech	0-8 S/U prior to playing Boston College since 2012
8-1 S/U on road as 15.5-20 point favorite since 1997	Georgia Tech	0-7 ATS prior to playing Boston College since 2013
1-5 ATS on road as 15.5-20 point favorite since 2001	Boston College	8-2 S/U after playing Georgia Tech since 2010
14-2 S/U on road as 20.5 point or more favorite since 1996	DUKE	9-2 S/U after playing Boston College since 2010
43-0 S/U @ home as 20.5-30 point favorite since 1985	DUKE	15-2 S/U in final home game of season since 2004
33-1 S/U as 20.5-25 point favorite since 1987	Miami	2-7 S/U & ATS after playing Duke since 2012
22-1 S/U as 25.5-30 point favorite since 1985	Virginia	8-2 S/U in final road game of season since 2009
Bowl Games	Virginia	1-7 ATS after playing Miami since 2013
0-3 S/U in Sugar Bowl since 2000	Virginia	9-0 O/U after playing Miami since 2011
3-0 S/U in Peach Bowl since 1986		
0-3 S/U in Orange Bowl since 2008		0-5 ATS when ranked @ Boston College since 2000
0-10 S/U in Bowl Games as 3.5-20 point Dog since 1981		14-2 S/U when ranked vs Virginia since 1996 {6-0 @ home}
1-9 ATS in Bowl Games as 3.5-20 point Dog since 1981		1-12 S/U @ home vs ranked teams since 2010
4-1 S/U & ATS in Bowl Games as 3 point or less Dog since 1986		0-9 S/U vs #1 ranked teams all time

Copyright © 2021 by Steve's Football Bible, LLC

WAKE FOREST DEMON DEACONS ACC Atlantic

2020-Wake Forest		Opponent	Wake	Opp	S/U	Line	ATS	Total	O/U	
9/12/2020	vs	CLEMSON	13	37	L	34.0	W	59.0	U	
9/19/2020	@	NC State	42	45	L	-2.5	L	53.0	O	
10/2/2020	vs	CAMPBELL	66	14	W	-34.0	W	69.0	O	
10/17/2020	vs	VIRGINIA	40	23	W	-2.5	W	57.5	O	
10/24/2020	vs	VIRGINIA TECH	23	16	W	10.5	W	69.0	U	
10/31/2020	@	Syracuse	38	14	W	-14.0	W	59.5	U	
11/14/2020	@	North Carolina	53	59	L	13.0	W	70.5	O	
12/12/2020	@	Louisville	21	45	L	-2.0	L	61.0	O	
12/30/2020	vs	Wisconsin	28	42	L	10.5	L	51.5	O	Duke's Mayo Bowl
Coach: Dave Clawson		Season Record >>	324	295	4-5	ATS>>	6-3	O/U>>	6-3	
2019-Wake Forest		Opponent	Wake	Opp	S/U	Line	ATS	Total	O/U	
8/30/2019	vs	UTAH STATE	38	35	W	-5.0	L	60.0	O	
9/7/2019	@	Rice	41	21	W	-19.5	W	58.5	O	
9/12/2019	vs	NORTH CAROLINA	24	18	W	-3.0	W	65.0	U	
9/21/2019	vs	ELON	49	7	W	-30.0	W	NT	---	
9/28/2019	@	Boston College	27	24	W	-5.0	L	69.5	U	
10/12/2019	vs	LOUISVILLE	59	62	L	-7.0	L	65.5	O	
10/19/2019	vs	FLORIDA STATE	22	20	W	3.0	W	69.0	U	
11/2/2019	vs	NC STATE	44	10	W	-7.5	W	60.5	U	
11/9/2019	@	Virginia Tech	17	36	L	-2.5	L	60.0	U	
11/16/2019	@	Clemson	3	52	L	34.5	L	59.0	U	
11/23/2019	vs	DUKE	39	27	W	-6.0	W	50.0	O	
11/30/2019	@	Syracuse	30	39	L	-6.5	L	66.5	O	{OT}
12/27/2019	vs	Michigan State	21	27	L	4.0	L	51.5	U	Pinstripe Bowl
Coach: Dave Clawson		Season Record >>	414	378	8-5	ATS>>	6-7	O/U>>	5-7	
2018-Wake Forest		Opponent	Wake	Opp	S/U	Line	ATS	Total	O/U	
8/30/2018	@	Tulane	23	17	W	-7.0	L	55.5	U	{OT}
9/8/2018	vs	TOWSON	51	20	W	-34.0	L	NT	---	
9/13/2018	vs	BOSTON COLLEGE	34	41	L	6.5	L	57.5	O	
9/22/2018	vs	NOTRE DAME	27	56	L	6.0	L	59.5	O	
9/29/2018	vs	RICE	56	24	W	-27.5	W	66.0	O	
10/6/2018	vs	CLEMSON	3	63	L	20.5	L	61.0	O	
10/20/2018	@	Florida State	17	38	L	10.5	L	57.5	U	
10/27/2018	@	Louisville	56	35	W	2.5	W	67.5	O	
11/3/2018	vs	SYRACUSE	24	41	L	6.5	L	77.5	U	
11/8/2018	@	NC State	27	23	W	19.0	W	66.5	U	
11/17/2018	vs	PITTSBURGH	13	34	L	5.0	L	62.5	U	
11/24/2018	@	Duke	59	7	W	9.5	W	60.5	O	
12/22/2018	vs	Memphis	37	34	W	2.0	W	71.5	U	Birmingham Bowl
Coach: Dave Clawson		Season Record >>	427	433	7-6	ATS>>	5-7	O/U>>	6-6	
2017-Wake Forest		Opponent	Wake	Opp	S/U	Line	ATS	Total	O/U	
8/31/2017	vs	PRESBYTERIAN	51	7	W	-42.5	W	53.5	O	
9/9/2017	@	Boston College	34	10	W	PK	W	45.5	U	
9/16/2017	vs	UTAH STATE	46	10	W	-15.5	W	51.5	O	
9/23/2017	@	Appalachian State	20	19	W	-5.0	L	48.5	U	
9/30/2017	vs	FLORIDA STATE	19	26	L	7.0	T	46.0	U	
10/7/2017	@	Clemson	14	28	L	21.5	W	50.5	U	
10/21/2017	@	Georgia Tech	24	38	L	3.5	L	49.0	O	
10/28/2017	vs	LOUISVILLE	42	32	W	2.5	W	66.5	O	
11/4/2017	@	Notre Dame	37	48	L	15.5	W	55.0	O	
11/11/2017	@	Syracuse	64	43	W	-2.5	W	66.0	O	
11/18/2017	vs	NC STATE	30	24	W	-2.5	W	62.5	U	
11/25/2017	vs	DUKE	23	31	L	-10.0	L	58.5	U	
12/29/2017	vs	Texas A&M	55	52	W	-3.5	L	62.0	O	Belk Bowl
Coach: Dave Clawson		Season Record >>	459	368	8-5	ATS>>	8-4-1	O/U>>	7-6	

Copyright © 2021 by Steve's Football Bible, LLC

WAKE FOREST DEMON DEACONS ACC Atlantic

STADIUM: BB&T Field {31,500}					Location: Winston-Salem, NC				COACH: Dave Clawson	
DATE		Opponent	Wake	Opp	S/U	Line	ATS	Total	O/U	Trends & Angles
9/3/2021	vs	OLD DOMINION								1st Meeting
9/11/2021	vs	NORFOLK STATE								1st Meeting
9/18/2021	vs	FLORIDA STATE								1-7 S/U vs Florida State as Dog since 2012
9/24/2021	@	Virginia								vs Virginia - Virginia leads series 34-16
9/25/2021	@	North Carolina								1-7 S/U @ North Carolina as Dog since 1991
10/2/2021	vs	LOUISVILLE								vs Louisville - Louisville leads series 6-2
10/9/2021	@	Syracuse								4-1 S/U vs Syracuse as favorite since 2006
10/23/2021	@	Army								7-1 S/U vs Army as favorite since 1992
10/30/2021	vs	DUKE								vs Duke - Duke leads series 58-40-2
11/13/2021	vs	NC STATE								vs NC State - NC State leads series 67-41-6
11/20/2021	@	Clemson								0-10 S/U @ Clemson as Dog since 2000
11/27/2021	@	Boston College								vs Boston College - BC leads series 14-11-2
12/4/2021	vs									ACC Championship
	vs									BOWL GAME

Pointspread Analysis Non-Conference		Pointspread Analysis Conference
5-1 ATS vs Non-Conf. as 15.5-20 point Dog since 1985		0-3 S/U @ home vs Boston College as Dog since 2010
6-1 ATS vs Non-Conf. as 7.5-10 point Dog since 1995		vs Clemson - Clemson leads series 68-17-1
11-0 S/U vs Non-Conf. as 3.5-7 point favorite since 1991		0-19 S/U vs Clemson as 16 point or more Dog since 1983
Dog		11-4 ATS vs Clemson as 16 point or more Dog since 1990
0-26 S/U as 25.5 point or more Dog since 1983		0-3 S/U & ATS vs Duke as 13 point or more Dog since 1989
1-24 S/U as 20.5-25 point Dog since 1989		11-1 S/U vs Duke as 6 point or more favorite since 1984
0-14 S/U @ home as 20.5 point or more Dog since 1990		vs Florida State - FSU leads series 30-7-1
1-36 S/U on road as 20.5 point or more Dog since 1983		0-6 O/U vs Florida State as Dog since 2014
7-1 ATS as 20.5-25 point Dog since 2013		0-21 S/U vs Florida State as 10.5 point or more Dog since 1992
2-7 O/U as 20.5-25 point Dog since 2012		5-0 ATS vs Louisville as Dog since 2014
2-17 S/U on road as 15.5-20 point Dog since 1983		vs North Carolina - UNC leads series 69-36-2
3-8 ATS on road as 15.5-20 point Dog since 2003		0-8 S/U vs North Carolina as 17 point or more Dog since 1983
1-10 S/U @ home as 15.5-20 point Dog since 1983		0-5 S/U & ATS vs North Carolina as 4.5-9 point Dog since 1986
0-9 S/U on road as 10.5-15 point Dog since 2004		1-14 S/U vs NC State as 9 point or more Dog since 1990
4-18 S/U @ home as 10.5-15 point Dog since 1993		9-2 ATS vs NC State as 7 point or less Dog since 1984
1-9 O/U @ home as 10.5-15 point Dog since 2002		5-0 S/U & ATS @ home vs NC State as favorite since 1987
8-2 ATS on road as 10.5-15 point Dog since 2003		vs Syracuse - Syracuse leads series 6-4
8-2 O/U on road as 10.5-15 point Dog since 2003		0-5 S/U & ATS vs Syracuse as Dog since 2011
3-7 O/U @ home as 3.5-7 point Dog since 2013		0-15 S/U vs Virginia as 4.5 point or more Dog since 1984
0-8 S/U @ home as 3.5-7 point Dog since 2013		Game 3-0 O/U vs Virginia as favorite since 2002
0-7-1 ATS @ home as 3.5-7 point Dog since 2013		
2-6 O/U on road as 3 point or less Dog since 2007	OLD DOMINION	10-1 S/U in 1st home game of season since 2010
Favorite	NORFOLK ST.	13-4 S/U in 2nd home game of season since 2004
11-1 S/U @ home as 3.5-7 point favorite since 2007	Virginia	1-6 O/U after playing Florida State since 2013
8-3-1 ATS @ home as 3.5-7 point favorite since 2007	UNC	2-11 O/U in 2nd road game of season since 2008
11-1 S/U on road as 7.5 point or more favorite since 1984	Clemson	1-8 O/U after playing NC State since 2012
27-1 S/U @ home as 7.5 point or more favorite since 1989	Clemson	0-5 O/U prior to playing Boston College since 2012
Bowl Games	Army	1-5 O/U after playing Syracuse since 2014
8-4 S/U & ATS in Bowl Games since 1992	Syracuse	1-5 S/U after playing Louisville since 2014
	NC STATE	7-1-1 ATS prior to playing Clemson since 2011
2-47 S/U on road vs ranked teams since 1980	NC STATE	1-9 O/U prior to playing Clemson since 2010
0-9 S/U vs #1 ranked teams all time	NC STATE	1-5 S/U prior to playing Clemson since 2014
0-6 S/U vs #2 ranked teams all time	NC STATE	6-1 O/U after playing Duke since 2007
0-9 S/U vs #3 ranked teams all time	NC STATE	3-9 S/U & ATS in final home game of season since 2009
0-28 S/U vs ranked Clemson since 1948	Boston College	1-6 S/U & ATS after playing Clemson since 2014

Copyright © 2021 by Steve's Football Bible, LLC

WASHINGTON HUSKIES   PACIFIC-12 North

2020-Washington		Opponent	UW	Opp	S/U	Line	ATS	Total	O/U	
11/14/2020	vs	OREGON STATE	27	21	W	-13.5	L	51.0	U	
11/21/2020	vs	ARIZONA	44	27	W	-12.5	W	53.5	O	
11/28/2020	vs	UTAH	24	21	W	-9.5	L	47.0	U	
12/5/2020	vs	STANFORD	26	31	L	-12.0	L	49.5	O	
Coach: Jimmy Lake		Season Record >>	121	100	3-1	ATS>>	1-3	O/U>>	2-2	
2019-Washington		Opponent	UW	Opp	S/U	Line	ATS	Total	O/U	
8/31/2019	vs	EASTERN WASHINGTON	47	14	W	-24.5	W	NT	---	
9/7/2019	vs	CALIFORNIA	19	20	L	-13.5	L	43.0	U	
9/14/2019	vs	HAWAII	52	20	W	-21.5	W	59.0	O	
9/21/2019	@	Byu	45	19	W	-6.5	W	51.0	O	
9/28/2019	vs	USC	28	14	W	-11.0	W	60.5	U	
10/5/2019	@	Stanford	13	23	L	-12.5	L	52.0	U	
10/12/2019	@	Arizona	51	27	W	-6.0	W	62.0	O	
10/19/2019	vs	OREGON	31	35	L	2.5	L	48.5	O	
11/2/2019	vs	UTAH	28	33	L	3.0	L	48.0	O	
11/8/2019	@	Oregon State	19	7	W	-10.5	W	64.5	U	
11/23/2019	@	Colorado	14	20	L	-14.0	L	53.0	U	
11/29/2019	vs	WASHINGTON STATE	31	13	W	-7.0	W	65.0	U	"Apple Cup"
12/21/2019	vs	**Boise State**	38	7	W	-4.0	W	48.0	U	Las Vegas Bowl
Coach: Chris Peterson		Season Record >>	416	252	8-5	ATS>>	8-5	O/U>>	5-7	
2018-Washington		Opponent	UW	Opp	S/U	Line	ATS	Total	O/U	
9/1/2018	vs	Auburn	16	21	L	1.5	L	50.5	U	Mercedes Benz Stadium
9/8/2018	vs	NORTH DAKOTA	45	3	W	-46.0	L	NT	---	
9/15/2018	@	Utah	21	7	W	-4.0	W	46.0	U	
9/22/2018	vs	ARIZONA STATE	27	20	W	-18.5	L	53.0	U	
9/29/2018	vs	BYU	35	7	W	-19.0	W	47.5	U	
10/6/2018	@	Ucla	31	24	W	-21.5	L	53.5	O	
10/13/2018	@	Oregon	27	30	L	-3.5	L	58.0	U	
10/20/2018	vs	COLORADO	27	13	W	-17.0	L	50.5	U	
10/27/2018	@	California	10	12	L	-11.5	L	45.5	U	
11/3/2018	vs	STANFORD	27	23	W	-9.5	L	44.0	O	
11/17/2018	vs	OREGON STATE	42	23	W	-32.5	L	58.5	O	
11/23/2018	@	Washington State	28	15	W	3.0	W	49.5	U	"Apple Cup"
11/30/2018	vs	**Utah**	10	3	W	-4.5	W	46.0	U	PACIFIC 12 Championship
1/1/2019	vs	**Ohio State**	23	28	L	5.5	W	55.0	U	Rose Bowl
Coach: Chris Peterson		Season Record >>	369	229	10-4	ATS>>	5-9	O/U>>	3-10	PACIFIC 12 Champions
2017-Washington		Opponent	UW	Opp	S/U	Line	ATS	Total	O/U	
9/1/2017	@	Rutgers	30	14	W	-28.0	L	54.0	U	
9/9/2017	vs	MONTANA	63	7	W	-39.0	W	NT	---	
9/16/2017	vs	FRESNO STATE	48	16	W	-35.0	L	56.5	O	
9/23/2017	@	Colorado	37	10	W	-11.0	W	54.5	U	
9/30/2017	@	Oregon State	42	7	W	-26.0	W	59.0	U	
10/7/2017	vs	CALIFORNIA	38	7	W	-28.5	W	55.0	U	
10/14/2017	@	Arizona State	7	13	L	-17.5	L	59.0	U	
10/28/2017	vs	UCLA	44	23	W	-17.5	W	59.5	O	
11/4/2017	vs	OREGON	38	3	W	-17.0	W	53.0	U	
11/10/2017	@	Stanford	22	30	L	-6.5	L	50.0	O	
11/18/2017	vs	UTAH	33	30	W	-17.5	L	47.0	O	
11/25/2017	vs	WASHINGTON STATE	41	14	W	-9.5	W	49.0	O	"Apple Cup"
12/30/2017	vs	**Penn State**	28	35	L	3.0	L	54.5	O	Fiesta Bowl
Coach: Chris Peterson		Season Record >>	471	209	10-3	ATS>>	7-6	O/U>>	6-6	

Copyright © 2021 by Steve's Football Bible, LLC

WASHINGTON HUSKIES   PACIFIC-12 North

STADIUM: Husky Stadium {70,083}					Location: Seattle, WA				COACH: Jimmy Lake
DATE		Opponent	Wash	Opp	S/U	Line	ATS	Total	O/U	Trends & Angles
9/4/2021	vs	MONTANA								17-0-1 S/U vs Montana since 1921
9/11/2021	@	Michigan								1-3 S/U @ Michigan since 1953
9/18/2021	vs	ARKANSAS STATE								1st meeting
9/25/2021	vs	CALIFORNIA								18-3 S/U vs California as favorite since 1984
10/2/2021	@	Oregon State								vs Oregon State - Washington leads series 67-34-4
10/16/2021	vs	UCLA								vs UCLA - UCLA leads series 40-32-2
10/22/2021	@	Arizona								0-4 S/U @ Arizona as Dog since 2008
10/30/2021	@	Stanford								vs Stanford - Stanford leads series 44-43-4
11/6/2021	vs	OREGON								1-15 S/U vs Oregon as Dog since 1988 {2-14 ATS}
11/13/2021	vs	ARIZONA STATE								vs Arizona State - ASU leads series 20-16
11/20/2021	@	Colorado								vs Colorado - Washington leads series 12-7-1
11/27/2021	vs	WASHINGTON STATE								6-0 S/U @ home vs Washington State since 2009
12/3/2021	vs									PAC-12 Championship
	vs									BOWL GAME

Pointspread Analysis Non-Conference		Pointspread Analysis Conference
0-6 S/U vs Non-Conf. as 15.5 point or more Dog since 2001		vs Arizona - Washington leads series 23-11-1
1-10 S/U vs Non-Conf. as 10.5-15 point Dog since 1996		6-0 S/U vs Arizona as favorite since 2011
0-6 S/U vs Non-Conf. as 7.5-10 point Dog since 1981		8-1 S/U vs Arizona as 9 point or more favorite since 1990
6-2 O/U vs Non-Conf. as 3.5-7 point Dog since 1998		0-9 S/U & ATS vs Arizona State as Dog since 2002
14-3 S/U vs Non-Conf. as 3.5-7 point favorite since 1983		6-1 S/U vs Arizona State as 15 point or more favorite since 1991
13-0 S/U vs Non-Conf. as 7.5-15 point favorite since 1984		vs California - Washington leads series 52-41-4
8-1 S/U vs Non-Conf. as 15.5-20 point favorite since 1983		0-5 O/U vs California as Dog since 2009
1-7 ATS vs Non-Conf. as 15.5-20 point favorite since 1983		3-0 S/U & ATS vs Colorado as Dog since 1999
36-0 S/U vs Non-Conf. as 20.5 point or more favorite since 1984		7-1 S/U vs Colorado as favorite since 1985
Dog		8-1 S/U vs Oregon as 10 point or more favorite since 1983
0-15 S/U as 20.5 point or more Dog since 2001		vs Oregon - Washington leads series 59-47-6
0-5 ATS as 20.5-25 point Dog since 2008		16-0 S/U vs Oregon State as 10 point or more favorite since 1986
1-7 S/U on road as 15.5-20 point Dog since 2004		1-5 S/U & ATS vs Oregon State as Dog since 2004
1-12 S/U on road as 10.5-15 point Dog since 2004		1-7 S/U vs Stanford as Dog since 2004
0-7 S/U @ home as 10.5-15 point Dog since 1988		13-3 S/U vs Stanford as 7 point or more favorite since 1983
0-6 O/U as 10.5-15 point Dog since 2010		0-8 S/U vs UCLA as 6 point or more Dog since 1987
4-11 ATS as 10.5-15 point Dog since 2006		vs Washington State - Washington leads series 74-32-6
0-6 S/U @ home as 7.5-10 point Dog since 2004		7-0 S/U vs Washington State since 2013
4-17 S/U as 7.5-10 point Dog since 1981		6-0 ATS vs Washington State since 2014
1-5 S/U & ATS on road as 3 point or less Dog since 1997		7-1 ATS vs Washington State as Dog since 1988
2-8 O/U @ home as 3 point or less Dog since 2001		5-0 S/U vs Wash. State as 16 point or more favorite since 1986
Favorite		7-0 S/U vs Wash. State as 7.5-13 point favorite since 1993
4-12 ATS as 3 point or less favorite since 2002		
12-4 S/U on road as 3.5-7 point favorite since 1995	MONTANA	11-0 S/U in 1st home game of season since 2010
8-0 S/U & ATS @ home as 3.5-7 point favorite since 2011	Michigan	3-9 O/U in 1st road game of season since 2008
12-2 S/U & ATS vs PAC-12 as 3.5-7 point favorite since 2010	ARKANSAS STATE	9-1 S/U in 2nd home game of season since 2011
13-3 S/U @ home as 7.5-10 point favorite since 1984	ARKANSAS STATE	10-3 O/U in 2nd home game of season since 2008
21-3 S/U @ home as 10.5-15 point favorite since 1992	CALIFORNIA	3-9 S/U prior to playing Oregon State since 2008
9-2 S/U on road as 15.5-20 point favorite since 1983	Oregon State	8-3 ATS in 2nd road game of season since 2009
23-3 S/U @ home as 15.5-20 point favorite since 1983	Oregon State	6-2 O/U prior to playing UCLA since 2007
3-13 ATS @ home as 15.5-20 point favorite since 1997	UCLA	8-1 S/U after playing Oregon State since 2011
10-0 S/U on road as 20.5 point or more favorite since 1984	Arizona	8-2 S/U prior to playing Stanford since 2011
50-1 S/U @ home as 20.5 point or more favorite since 1986	Stanford	8-1 S/U prior to playing Oregon since 2011
Bowl Games	Stanford	8-1 ATS prior to playing Oregon since 2011
3-0 ATS in Holiday Bowl since 1999	AZ STATE	2-7 S/U after playing Oregon since 2011
0-3 S/U in Sun Bowl since 1986	AZ STATE	0-7 ATS after playing Oregon since 2013
0-3 S/U vs Alabama in Bowl Games	AZ STATE	6-2 S/U prior to playing Colorado since 2000
3-0 ATS in Bowl Games as 10.5-15 point Dog since 1978	Colorado	7-1 S/U prior to playing Washington State since 2012
0-3 S/U in Bowl Games as 7.5-10 point Dog since 1981	Colorado	5-2-1 O/U after playing Arizona State since 2009
0-4 S/U in Bowl Games as 3.5-7 point Dog since 1996	Colorado	7-0 S/U after playing Arizona State since 2010
3-1 O/U in Bowl Games as 3.5-7 point Dog since 1996	Colorado	12-4-1 O/U in final road game of season since 2003
0-3 S/U & ATS in Bowl Games as 3 point or less Dog since 1983	WAZZU	2-6 S/U after playing Colorado since 2000
3-0 O/U in Bowl Games as 3 point or less favorite since 1989	WAZZU	11-1 S/U in final home game of season since 2009

Copyright © 2021 by Steve's Football Bible, LLC

WASHINGTON STATE COUGARS   PACIFIC-12 North

2020-Washington State		Opponent	Wazzu	Opp	S/U	Line	ATS	Total	O/U	
11/7/2020	@	Oregon State	38	28	W	3.5	W	64.0	O	
11/14/2020	vs	OREGON	29	43	L	10.0	L	58.5	O	
12/6/2020	@	Usc	13	38	L	11.0	L	68.0	U	
12/19/2020	@	Utah	28	45	L	12.0	L	54.5	O	
Coach: Nick Rolovich		Season Record >>	108	154	1-3	ATS>>	1-3	O/U>>	3-1	
2019-Washington State		Opponent	Wazzu	Opp	S/U	Line	ATS	Total	O/U	
8/31/2019	vs	NEW MEXICO STATE	58	7	W	-33.5	W	65.5	U	
9/7/2019	vs	NORTHERN COLORADO	59	17	W	-43.0	L	NT	---	
9/13/2019	@	Houston	31	24	W	-8.5	L	74.0	U	NRG Stadium
9/21/2019	vs	UCLA	63	67	L	-18.0	L	59.5	O	
9/28/2019	@	Utah	13	38	L	5.5	L	56.5	U	
10/12/2019	@	Arizona State	34	38	L	-1.5	L	60.5	O	
10/19/2019	vs	COLORADO	41	10	W	-13.0	W	68.5	U	
10/26/2019	@	Oregon	35	37	L	19.5	W	67.5	O	
11/9/2019	@	California	20	33	L	-8.5	L	52.0	O	
11/16/2019	vs	STANFORD	49	22	W	-11.0	W	66.0	O	
11/23/2019	vs	OREGON STATE	54	53	W	-10.5	L	77.5	O	
11/29/2019	@	Washington	13	31	L	7.0	L	65.0	U	"Apple Cup"
12/27/2019	vs	Air Force	21	31	L	2.5	L	71.5	U	Cheez-it Bowl
Coach: Mike Leach		Season Record >>	491	408	6-7	ATS>>	4-9	O/U>>	6-6	
2018-Washington State		Opponent	Wazzu	Opp	S/U	Line	ATS	Total	O/U	
9/1/2018	@	Wyoming	41	19	W	-3.0	W	44.0	O	
9/8/2018	vs	SAN JOSE STATE	31	0	W	-30.0	W	62.5	U	
9/15/2018	vs	EASTERN WASHINGTON	59	24	W	-20.0	W	NT	---	
9/21/2018	@	Usc	36	39	L	4.5	W	50.5	O	
9/29/2018	vs	UTAH	28	24	W	1.5	W	50.0	O	
10/6/2018	@	Oregon State	56	37	W	-18.5	W	64.5	O	
10/20/2018	vs	OREGON	34	20	W	-3.0	W	69.5	U	
10/27/2018	@	Stanford	41	38	W	2.5	W	55.0	O	
11/3/2018	vs	CALIFORNIA	19	13	W	-7.0	L	51.0	U	
11/10/2018	@	Colorado	31	7	W	-5.5	W	59.5	U	
11/17/2018	vs	ARIZONA	69	28	W	-10.5	W	63.5	O	
11/23/2018	vs	WASHINGTON	15	28	L	-3.0	L	49.5	U	"Apple Cup"
12/28/2018	vs	Iowa State	28	26	W	-1.5	W	56.0	U	Alamo Bowl
Coach: Mike Leach		Season Record >>	488	303	11-2	ATS>>	11-2	O/U>>	6-6	
2017-Washington State		Opponent	Wazzu	Opp	S/U	Line	ATS	Total	O/U	
9/2/2017	vs	MONTANA STATE	31	0	W	-41.0	L	62.0	U	
9/9/2017	vs	BOISE STATE	47	44	W	-7.5	L	57.5	O	{3 OT}
9/16/2017	vs	OREGON STATE	52	23	W	-18.0	W	65.5	O	
9/23/2017	vs	NEVADA	45	7	W	-28.5	W	66.0	U	
9/29/2017	vs	USC	30	27	W	4.5	W	58.5	U	
10/7/2017	@	Oregon	33	10	W	-2.0	W	59.5	U	
10/13/2017	@	California	3	37	L	-16.5	L	55.0	U	
10/21/2017	vs	COLORADO	28	0	W	-9.0	W	52.0	U	
10/28/2017	@	Arizona	37	58	L	PK	L	63.0	O	
11/4/2017	vs	STANFORD	24	21	W	1.0	W	55.0	U	
11/11/2017	@	Utah	33	25	W	PK	W	50.5	O	
11/25/2017	@	Washington	14	41	L	9.5	L	49.0	O	"Apple Cup"
12/28/2017	vs	Michigan State	17	42	L	2.5	L	47.5	O	Holiday Bowl
Coach: Mike Leach		Season Record >>	394	335	9-4	ATS>>	7-6	O/U>>	6-7	

Copyright © 2021 by Steve's Football Bible, LLC

WASHINGTON STATE COUGARS   PACIFIC-12 North

STADIUM: Martin Stadium {32,952}					Location: Pullman, WA			COACH: Nick Rolovich	

DATE		Opponent	WSU	Opp	S/U	Line	ATS	Total	O/U	Trends & Angles
9/4/2021	vs	*UTAH STATE*								vs Utah State - WAZZU leads series 2-1
9/11/2021	vs	*PORTLAND STATE*								vs Portland State - WAZZU leads series 2-1
9/18/2021	vs	USC								vs USC - USC leads series 61-10-4
9/25/2021	@	Utah								vs Utah - Washington State leads series 9-8
10/2/2021	@	California								0-9 S/U vs California as Dog since 2005
10/9/2021	vs	OREGON STATE								vs Oregon State - WAZZU leads series 54-47-3
10/16/2021	vs	STANFORD								vs Stanford - Stanford leads series 40-29-1
10/23/2021	vs	*BYU*								vs BYU - BYU leads series 3-1
10/30/2021	@	Arizona State								vs Arizona State - ASU leads series 27-14-2
11/13/2021	@	Oregon								8-1 ATS vs Oregon as Dog since 2010
11/19/2021	vs	ARIZONA								7-1 S/U vs Arizona as favorite since 1997
11/27/2021	@	Washington								vs Washington - Washington leads series 73-32-6
12/3/2021	vs									PAC-12 Championship
	vs									BOWL GAME

Pointspread Analysis Non-Conference		Pointspread Analysis Conference
0-16 S/U vs Non-Conf. as 10.5 point or more Dog since 1983		1-13 S/U vs Arizona State as Dog since 1997
9-2 ATS vs Non-Conf. as 3.5-7 point Dog since 1988		0-5 S/U @ home vs Arizona as Dog since 1989
10-2 S/U vs Non-Conf. as 7.5-10 point favorite since 1996		5-1 ATS @ home vs Arizona as Dog since 1987
0-5-1 ATS vs Non-Conf. as 7.5-10 point favorite since 2010		0-7 S/U vs Arizona as 13 point or more Dog since 1993
8-1 S/U vs Non-Conf. as 10.5-15 point favorite since 1995		vs California - California leads series 48-28-5
Dog		vs Oregon - Oregon 51-40-7
0-21 S/U as 25.5 point or more Dog since 1991		12-3 O/U vs Oregon as Dog since 2003
5-0 ATS as 30.5 point or more Dog since 2010		0-10 S/U vs Oregon as 16 point or more favorite since 1999
0-13 S/U @ home as 20.5 point or more Dog since 1990		18-0 S/U vs Oregon State as 7.5 point or more favorite since 1984
1-26 S/U on road as 20.5 point or more Dog since 1987		1-5 O/U vs Stanford as favorite since 2002
0-7 O/U as 20.5-25 point Dog since 2010		1-7 S/U @ home vs Stanford as Dog since 1991
0-5 S/U @ home as 15.5-20 point Dog since 1986		0-10 S/U vs Stanford as 8 point or more Dog since 1986
2-11 S/U on road as 15.5-20 point Dog since 1990		0-8 S/U vs USC as 16.5 point or more Dog since 1987
7-1 ATS as 15.5-20 point Dog since 2012		0-9 S/U vs USC as 7.5-9.5 point Dog since 1983
3-8 O/U on road as 10.5-15 point Dog since 2007		0-6 S/U vs Washington as Dog since 2013
0-13 S/U @ home as 7.5-10 point Dog since 1989		1-7 ATS vs Washington as favorite since 1988
3-17 S/U on road as 7.5-10 point Dog since 1984		0-5 S/U vs Washington as 16 point or more Dog since 1986
3-15 ATS on road as 7.5-10 point Dog since 1984		0-6 S/U vs Washington as 9.5-13 point Dog since 1993
1-5 S/U @ home as 3.5-7 point Dog since 2010		
11-3 O/U on road as 3.5-7 point Dog since 2001		
11-4 O/U as 3 point or less Dog since 2002		
Favorite	PORTLAND ST.	7-0 S/U in 2nd home game of season since 2013
10-3 S/U & ATS on road as 3 point or less favorite since 2001	USC	5-2 ATS prior to playing Utah since 2011
3-9 S/U & ATS @ home as 3 point or less favorite since 1999	Utah	7-1 O/U after playing USC since 2007
1-6 ATS as 3.5-7 point favorite since 2003	Utah	5-0 ATS after playing USC since 2010
12-4 S/U @ home as 7.5-10 point favorite since 1985	California	7-3-1 ATS in 2nd road game of season since 2010
10-1 S/U on road as 7.5-10 point favorite since 1996	California	1-8 S/U after playing Utah since 1985
7-0 S/U on road as 10.5-15 point favorite since 1990	OREGON STATE	8-3 ATS prior to playing Stanford since 2009
16-1 S/U @ home as 10.5-15 point favorite since 2001	BYU	2-9 ATS after playing Stanford since 2009
32-5 S/U @ home as 15.5 point or more favorite since 1992	Arizona State	7-0 ATS prior to playing Oregon since 2014
Bowl Games	Washington	2-9 S/U after playing Arizona since 2004
0-3 S/U in Rose Bowl since 1931	Washington	1-9 S/U in final road game of season since 2011
0-3 O/U in Bowl Games as 3.5-7 point Dog since 1988	Washington	2-8 ATS in final road game of season since 2011

Copyright © 2021 by Steve's Football Bible, LLC

WESTERN KENTUCKY HILLTOPPERS   C-USA East

2020-Western Kentucky		Opponent	WKU	Opp	S/U	Line	ATS	Total	O/U	
9/12/2020	@	Louisville	21	35	L	12.5	L	56.5	U	
9/19/2020	vs	LIBERTY	24	30	L	-14.0	L	51.5	O	
10/3/2020	@	Middle Tennessee	20	17	W	-7.0	L	51.0	U	*100 Miles of Hate Rivalry*
10/10/2020	vs	MARSHALL	14	38	L	6.5	L	43.0	O	
10/17/2020	@	Alabama-Birmingham	14	37	L	13.5	L	44.5	O	
10/24/2020	vs	CHATTANNOGA	13	10	W	-13.5	L	54.0	U	
10/31/2020	@	Byu	10	41	L	30.5	L	52.0	U	
11/7/2020	@	Florida Atlantic	6	10	L	6.5	W	37.5	U	
11/14/2020	vs	SOUTHERN MISSISSIPPI	10	7	W	-8.0	L	45.0	U	
11/21/2020	vs	FLORIDA INTERNATIONAL	38	21	W	-7.0	W	41.5	O	
12/1/2020	@	Charlotte	37	19	W	3.0	W	47.0	O	
12/26/2020	vs	**Georgia State**	21	39	L	3.0	L	49.0	O	**Lending Tree Bowl**
Coach: Tyson Helton		Season Record >>	228	304	5-7	ATS>>	3-9	O/U>>	6-6	
2019-Western Kentucky		Opponent	WKU	Opp	S/U	Line	ATS	Total	O/U	
8/29/2019	vs	CENTRAL ARKANSAS	28	35	L	-10.0	L	NT	---	
9/7/2019	@	Florida International	20	14	W	9.0	W	57.0	U	
9/14/2019	vs	Louisville	21	38	L	10.5	L	49.0	O	**Nissan Stadium**
9/28/2019	vs	ALABAMA-BIRMINGHAM	20	13	W	3.5	W	47.0	U	
10/5/2019	@	Old Dominion	20	3	W	-3.0	W	42.0	U	
10/12/2019	vs	ARMY	17	8	W	5.0	W	43.5	U	
10/19/2019	vs	CHARLOTTE	30	14	W	-9.5	W	48.5	U	
10/26/2019	@	Marshall	23	26	L	3.5	W	45.0	O	
11/2/2019	vs	FLORIDA ATLANTIC	24	35	L	PK	L	51.0	O	
11/9/2019	@	Arkansas	45	19	W	PK	W	51.5	O	**Razorback Stadium**
11/23/2019	@	Southern Miss	28	10	W	3.5	W	51.0	U	
11/30/2019	vs	MIDDLE TENNESSEE	31	26	W	-10.0	L	46.0	O	*100 Miles of Hate Rivalry*
12/30/2019	vs	**Western Michigan**	23	20	W	-3.0	T	55.5	U	**First Responder Bowl**
Coach: Tyson Helton		Season Record >>	330	261	9-4	ATS>>	8-4-1	O/U>>	5-7	
2018-Western Kentucky		Opponent	WKU	Opp	S/U	Line	ATS	Total	O/U	
8/31/2018	@	Wisconsin	3	34	L	36.0	W	52.0	U	
9/8/2018	vs	MAINE	28	31	L	-9.0	L	NT	---	
9/15/2018	@	Louisville	17	20	L	23.5	W	53.5	U	
9/22/2018	@	Ball State	28	20	W	3.0	W	54.0	U	
9/29/2018	vs	MARSHALL	17	20	L	3.5	W	51.5	U	
10/13/2018	@	Charlotte	14	40	L	-9.5	L	44.0	O	
10/20/2018	vs	OLD DOMINION	34	37	L	-4.0	L	55.5	O	
10/27/2018	vs	FLORIDA INTERNATIONAL	17	38	L	3.0	L	54.0	O	
11/3/2018	@	Middle Tennessee	10	29	L	11.5	L	52.5	U	*100 Miles of Hate Rivalry*
11/10/2018	@	Florida Atlantic	15	34	L	18.0	L	59.5	U	
11/17/2018	vs	TEXAS-EL PASO	40	16	W	-6.5	W	47.5	O	
11/24/2018	@	Louisiana Tech	30	15	W	10.5	W	49.0	U	
Coach: Mike Sanford		Season Record >>	253	334	3-9	ATS>>	6-6	O/U>>	4-7	
2017-Western Kentucky		Opponent	WKU	Opp	S/U	Line	ATS	Total	O/U	
9/2/2017	vs	EASTERN KENTUCKY	31	17	W	-38.5	L	67.0	U	**"Battle of the Bluegrass"**
9/9/2017	@	Illinois	7	20	L	-5.0	L	51.0	U	
9/16/2017	vs	LOUISIANA TECH	22	23	L	-4.5	L	63.0	U	
9/23/2017	vs	BALL STATE	33	21	W	-11.0	W	50.0	O	
10/7/2017	@	Texas-El Paso	15	14	W	-16.0	L	53.5	U	
10/14/2017	vs	CHARLOTTE	45	14	W	-19.0	W	47.5	O	
10/20/2017	@	Old Dominion	35	31	W	-6.5	L	50.0	O	
10/28/2017	vs	FLORIDA ATLANTIC	28	42	L	6.5	L	67.0	O	
11/4/2017	@	Vanderbilt	17	31	L	12.5	L	53.5	U	
11/11/2017	@	Marshall	23	30	L	10.0	W	52.0	O	
11/18/2017	vs	MIDDLE TENNESSEE	41	38	W	PK	W	56.0	O	*100 Miles of Hate Rivalry*
11/25/2017	@	Florida International	17	41	L	-3.0	L	57.0	O	
12/16/2017	vs	**Georgia State**	17	27	L	-5.0	L	54.5	U	**AutoNation Cure Bowl**
Coach: Mike Sanford		Season Record >>	331	349	6-7	ATS>>	4-9	O/U>>	7-6	

Copyright © 2021 by Steve's Football Bible, LLC

WESTERN KENTUCKY HILLTOPPERS   C-USA East

STADIUM: L.T. Smith Stadium {22,113}			Location: Bowling Green, KY					COACH: Tyson Helton	
DATE		Opponent	WKU	Opp	S/U	Line	ATS	Total	O/U	Trends & Angles

DATE		Opponent	WKU	Opp	S/U	Line	ATS	Total	O/U	Trends & Angles
9/4/2021	vs	TENNESSEE-MARTIN								vs UT-Martin - WKU leads series 4-0
9/11/2021	@	Army								vs Army - Western Kentucky leads series 3-0
9/25/2021	vs	INDIANA								0-3 S/U vs Indiana as Dog since 2010
10/2/2021	@	Michigan State								1st meeting
10/9/2021	vs	TEXAS-SAN ANTONIO								vs UTSA - WKU leads series 1-0
10/16/2021	@	Old Dominion								vs Old Dominion - WKU leads series 5-1
10/23/2021	@	Florida International								vs Florida International - WKU leads series 7-6
10/30/2021	vs	CHARLOTTE								vs Charlotte - WKU leads series 3-1
11/6/2021	vs	MIDDLE TENNESSEE								vs Middle Tennessee - Series tied 34-34-1
11/13/2021	@	Rice								vs Rice - WKU leads series 2-0
11/20/2021	vs	FLORIDA ATLANTIC								vs Florida Atlantic - FAU leads series 9-3
11/27/2021	@	Marshall								vs Marshall - Marshall leads series 8-4
12/4/2021	vs									C-USA Championship
	vs									BOWL GAME

Pointspread Analysis Non-Conference		Pointspread Analysis Conference
0-25 S/U vs Non-Conf. as 10.5 point or more Dog since 2005		1-6 S/U vs Florida Atlantic as Dog since 2008
7-0 S/U vs Non-Conf. as 15.5 point or more favorite since 2012		1-5 S/U vs Middle Tennessee as Dog since 2008
Dog		5-1 S/U vs Old Dominion as favorite since 2014
1-24 S/U as 15.5 point or more Dog since 2008		5-1 O/U vs Old Dominion as favorite since 2014
0-8 S/U @ home as 7.5 point or more Dog since 2008		
6-1 ATS as 3.5-7 point Dog since 2018		**Bowl Games**
4-1 ATS @ home as 3 point or less Dog since 2010		6-2 S/U in Bowl Games
Favorite		
8-3 O/U as 3 point or less favorite since 2010	Army	3-17 S/U in 1st road game of season since 2001
6-1 S/U @ home as 10.5-15 point favorite since 2012	Michigan State	2-6 ATS in 2nd road game of season since 2013
5-1 O/U @ home as 10.5-15 point favorite since 2014	Rice	7-2 O/U prior to playing Florida Atlantic since 2011
8-0 S/U as 15.5-20 point favorite since 2013	FAU	10-0 S/U in final home game of season since 2011
11-0 S/U as 20.5 point or momre favorite since 2012	FAU	9-3 ATS in final home game of season since 2009
	Marshall	9-1 ATS in final road game of season since 2011
	Marshall	7-2-1 O/U after playing Florida Atlantic since 2010

"Golden Memories" is a comprehensive historical look at 138 years of the University of Minnesota Football teams. From the glory years of the 1930's and 1940's through the 2020 season, it is truly a walk down memory lane for fans who enjoy the rich traditions and history of college football. A must read for all Golden Gopher football fans as well as all College Football fans.

"Golden Memories" – History of Minnesota Gophers Football

8.5" x 11" {288 pages} {Paperback} **$29.99**

Order at: www.stevesfootballbible.com

These books available at numerous online retailers

Copyright © 2021 by Steve's Football Bible, LLC

2020-Western Michigan		Opponent	WMU	Opp	S/U	Line	ATS	Total	O/U	
11/4/2020	@	Akron	58	13	W	-20.0	W	52.0	O	
11/11/2020	vs	TOLEDO	41	38	W	-1.0	W	58.5	O	
11/18/2020	@	Central Michigan	52	44	W	-1.0	W	59.5	O	*"Victory Cannon"*
11/28/2020	vs	NORTHERN ILLINOIS	30	27	W	-18.5	L	64.5	U	
12/5/2020	vs	EASTERN MICHIGAN	42	53	L	-13.0	L	67.5	U	
12/12/2020	@	Ball State	27	30	L	-2.0	L	66.0	U	
Coach: Tim Lester		Season Record >>	250	205	4-2	ATS>>	3-3	O/U>>	4-2	
2019-Western Michigan		Opponent	WMU	Opp	S/U	Line	ATS	Total	O/U	
8/31/2019	vs	*MONMOUTH*	48	13	W	-24.5	W	NT	---	
9/7/2019	@	*Michigan State*	17	51	L	15.0	L	46.0	O	
9/14/2019	vs	*GEORGIA STATE*	57	10	W	-9.0	W	69.5	U	
9/21/2019	@	*Syracuse*	33	52	L	3.5	L	66.5	O	
9/28/2019	vs	CENTRAL MICHIGAN	31	15	W	-15.0	W	60.0	U	*"Victory Cannon"*
10/5/2019	@	Toledo	24	31	L	1.5	L	73.5	U	
10/12/2019	vs	MIAMI-OHIO	38	16	W	-12.0	W	57.5	U	
10/19/2019	@	Eastern Michigan	27	34	L	-9.5	L	61.0	T	
10/26/2019	vs	BOWLING GREEN	49	10	W	-26.5	W	65.5	U	
11/5/2019	vs	BALL STATE	35	31	W	-6.0	L	65.0	O	
11/12/2019	@	Ohio	37	34	W	1.5	W	63.5	O	{OT}
11/26/2019	@	Northern Illinois	14	17	L	-9.5	L	51.5	U	
12/30/2019	vs	**Western Kentucky**	20	23	L	3.0	T	55.5	U	**First Responder Bowl**
Coach: Tim Lester		Season Record >>	430	337	7-6	ATS>>	6-6-1	O/U>>	4-7-1	
2018-Western Michigan		Opponent	WMU	Opp	S/U	Line	ATS	Total	O/U	
8/31/2018	vs	*SYRACUSE*	42	55	L	5.0	L	66.0	O	
9/8/2018	@	*Michigan*	3	49	L	28.0	L	55.0	U	
9/15/2018	vs	*DELAWARE STATE*	68	0	W	-46.0	W	NT	---	
9/22/2018	@	*Georgia State*	34	15	W	-9.0	W	61.0	U	
9/29/2018	@	Miami-Ohio	40	39	W	-2.5	L	52.0	O	
10/6/2018	vs	EASTERN MICHIGAN	27	24	W	-4.5	L	58.5	U	*"MICHIGAN MAC TROPHY"*
10/13/2018	@	Bowling Green	42	35	W	-14.5	L	69.5	O	
10/20/2018	@	Central Michigan	35	10	W	-6.5	W	54.0	U	*"Victory Cannon"*
10/25/2018	vs	TOLEDO	24	51	L	-4.0	L	68.0	O	
11/1/2018	vs	OHIO	14	59	L	3.0	L	65.0	O	
11/13/2018	@	Ball State	41	42	L	-9.5	L	57.5	O	{OT}
11/20/2018	vs	NORTHERN ILLINOIS	28	21	W	6.5	W	48.5	O	
12/21/2018	vs	**Byu**	18	49	L	10.0	L	52.0	O	**Famous Idaho Potato Bowl**
Coach: Tim Lester		Season Record >>	416	449	7-6	ATS>>	4-9	O/U>>	8-4	
2017-Western Michigan		Opponent	WMU	Opp	S/U	Line	ATS	Total	O/U	
9/2/2017	@	*Usc*	31	49	L	29.0	W	59.5	O	
9/9/2017	@	*Michigan State*	14	28	L	7.0	L	51.0	U	
9/16/2017	vs	*IDAHO*	37	28	W	-17.0	L	55.0	O	
9/23/2017	vs	*WAGNER*	49	14	W	-38.0	L	NT	---	
9/30/2017	vs	BALL STATE	55	3	W	-12.5	W	54.0	O	
10/7/2017	@	Buffalo	71	68	W	-7.5	L	50.5	O	{7 OT}
10/14/2017	vs	AKRON	13	14	L	-12.5	L	54.5	U	
10/21/2017	@	Eastern Michigan	20	17	W	-2.0	W	51.5	U	{OT}
11/1/2017	vs	CENTRAL MICHIGAN	28	35	L	-4.0	L	48.0	O	*"Victory Cannon"*
11/8/2017	vs	KENT STATE	48	20	W	-20.0	W	45.0	O	
11/15/2017	@	Northern Illinois	31	35	L	8.5	W	50.0	O	
11/24/2017	@	Toledo	10	37	L	12.0	L	62.0	U	
Coach: Tim Lester		Season Record >>	407	348	6-6	ATS>>	5-7	O/U>>	7-4	

Copyright © 2021 by Steve's Football Bible, LLC

WESTERN MICHIGAN BRONCOS   MAC West

STADIUM: Waldo Stadium {30,200}					Location: Kalamazoo, MI						COACH: Tim Lester
DATE		Opponent	WMU	Opp	S/U	Line	ATS	Total	O/U		Trends & Angles
9/4/2021	@	*Michigan*									0-5 S/U & ATS vs Michigan as Dog since 2001
9/11/2021	vs	*ILLINOIS STATE*									vs Illinois State - WMU leads series 7-1
9/18/2021	@	*Pittsburgh*									1st meeting
9/25/2021	vs	*SAN JOSE STATE*									1st meeting
10/2/2021	@	**Buffalo**									
10/9/2021	vs	**BALL STATE**									vs Ball State - WMU leads series 26-21
10/16/2021	vs	**KENT STATE**									15-0 S/U vs Kent State as favorite since 1989
10/23/2021	@	**Toledo**									vs Toledo - Toledo leads series 44-31
11/3/2021	vs	**CENTRAL MICHIGAN**									vs C. Michigan - WMU leads series 52-39-2
11/9/2021	vs	**AKRON**									
11/16/2021	@	**Eastern Michigan**									vs E. Michigan - WMU leads series 34-19-2
11/23/2021	@	**Northern Illinois**									0-6 S/U @ N. Illinois as Dog since 2003
12/3/2021	vs										MAC Championship
	vs										BOWL GAME

Pointspread Analysis Non-Conference		Pointspread Analysis Conference
0-27 S/U vs Non-Conf. as 15.5 point or more Dog since 1991		3-0 S/U & ATS vs Akron as Dog since 1990
1-12 S/U vs Non-Conf. as 10.5-15 point Dog since 1988		4-0 S/U & ATS vs Akron as 7.5 point or less favorite since 1991
16-0 S/U vs Non-Conf. as 7.5 point or more favorite since 2006		6-0 S/U vs Akron as 13 point or more favorite since 1994
14-2 ATS vs Non-Conf. as 7.5 point or more favorite since 2006		0-3 S/U & ATS @ home vs Ball State as Dog since 1996
Dog		7-0 S/U vs Ball State as 12 point or more favorite since 1999
0-18 S/U as 25.5 point or more Dog since 1991		9-1 S/U @ home vs Central Michigan as favorite since 1995
14-3 ATS as 25.5 point or more Dog since 1995		8-0 S/U vs C. Michigan as 6.5-17.5 point favorite since 1995
1-10 S/U as 20.5-25 point Dog since 2002		1-7 S/U vs Central Michigan as Dog since 1996
2-8-1 ATS as 20.5-25 point Dog since 2002		5-2 S/U vs Eastern Michigan as favorite since 2014
7-1-1 O/U as 20.5-25 point Dog since 2004		10-0 S/U vs E. Michigan as 15 point or more favorite since 1992
0-12 S/U as 15.5-20 point Dog since 1992		0-3 S/U & ATS vs Kent State as Dog since 2009
8-1 O/U as 15.5-20 point Dog since 1999		8-1 ATS vs Kent State as favorite since 1995
1-18 S/U on road as 10.5-15 point Dog since 1989		1-10-1 ATS vs Northern Illinois as favorite since 1997
0-7 S/U as 7.5-10 point Dog since 2010		3-9 ATS vs Toledo as favorite since 1989
10-3 ATS on road as 7.5-10 point Dog since 1993		0-7 S/U vs Toledo as 11.5 point or more Dog since 2001
1-10 S/U @ home as 3.5-7 point Dog since 1996		0-5 S/U vs Toledo as 2.5-6.5 point Dog since 1992 {1-4 ATS}
6-2 S/U & ATS on road as 3 point or less Dog since 2014		1-7 S/U & ATS vs Toledo as 4 point or less favorite since 1989
0-5 S/U @ home as 3 point or less Dog since 2007		
Favorite		**Bowl Games**
10-1 S/U & ATS @ home as 3 point or less favorite since 1992		1-9 S/U in Bowl Games
10-5 ATS on road as 3 point or less favorite since 1995		3-1 ATS in Bowl Games as 3.5-15 point Dog since 1988
11-1 O/U @ home as 3.5-7 point favorite since 2004		0-7 S/U in Bowl Games as 3.0-15 point Dog since 1988
13-4 S/U as 3.5-7 point favorite since 2008		
11-4-1 O/U as 7.5-10 point favorite since 2001		
17-7 S/U as 7.5-10 point favorite since 1990		
10-1 S/U on road as 10.5-15 point favorite since 1990		
1-5 O/U on road as 10.5-15 point favorite since 2002	Michigan	2-24 S/U in 1st road game of season since 1995
21-6 S/U @ home as 10.5-15 point favorite since 1989	ILL. STATE	10-2 ATS in 1st home game of season since 2009
34-0 S/U @ home as 15.5 point or more favorite since 1994	KENT STATE	12-1 ATS prior to playing Toledo since 1995
8-2 O/U as 15.5-20 point favorite since 2009	Toledo	6-2 ATS prior to playing Central Michigan since 2013
7-1 S/U on road as 15.5 point or more favorite since 1998	Northern Illinois	3-9 O/U in final road game of season since 2009

Copyright © 2021 by Steve's Football Bible, LLC

WEST VIRGINIA MOUNTAINEERS   BIG TWELVE

2020-West Virginia		Opponent	Wva	Opp	S/U	Line	ATS	Total	O/U	
9/12/2020	vs	EASTERN KENTUCKY	56	10	W	-44.5	W	57.5	O	
9/26/2020	@	Oklahoma State	13	27	L	6.5	L	49.0	U	
10/3/2020	vs	BAYLOR	27	21	W	1.0	W	54.0	U	{2 OT}
10/17/2020	vs	KANSAS	38	17	W	-22.5	L	51.5	O	
10/24/2020	@	Texas Tech	27	34	L	-2.0	L	54.0	O	
10/31/2020	vs	KANSAS STATE	37	10	W	-5.0	W	46.0	O	
11/7/2020	@	Texas	13	17	L	6.0	L	55.5	U	
11/14/2020	vs	TCU	24	6	W	-3.0	W	44.0	U	
12/5/2020	@	Iowa State	6	42	L	5.5	L	47.5	O	
12/31/2020	vs	Army	24	21	W	-9.0	L	41.0	O	Liberty Bowl
Coach: Neal Brown		Season Record >>	265	205	6-4	ATS>>	5-5	O/U>>	6-4	
2019-West Virginia		Opponent	Wva	Opp	S/U	Line	ATS	Total	O/U	
8/31/2019	vs	JAMES MADISON	20	13	W	-7.0	T	NT	---	
9/7/2019	@	Missouri	7	38	L	13.5	L	62.5	O	
9/14/2019	vs	NC STATE	44	27	W	7.0	W	45.5	O	
9/21/2019	@	Kansas	29	24	W	-4.5	W	49.5	O	
10/5/2019	vs	TEXAS	31	42	L	10.5	L	62.0	O	
10/12/2019	vs	IOWA STATE	14	38	L	10.0	L	55.0	U	
10/19/2019	@	Oklahoma	14	52	L	32.0	L	63.5	O	
10/31/2019	@	Baylor	14	17	L	17.5	W	56.5	U	
11/9/2019	vs	TEXAS TECH	17	38	L	2.5	L	56.5	U	
11/16/2019	@	Kansas State	24	20	W	14.0	W	46.5	U	
11/23/2019	vs	OKLAHOMA STATE	13	20	L	6.5	L	56.5	U	
11/29/2019	@	Tcu	20	17	W	14.0	W	44.0	U	
Coach: Neal Brown		Season Record >>	247	346	5-7	ATS>>	5-6-1	O/U>>	4-7	
2018-West Virginia		Opponent	Wva	Opp	S/U	Line	ATS	Total	O/U	
9/1/2018	vs	Tennessee	40	14	W	-10.0	W	59.5	U	Bank of America Stadium
9/8/2018	vs	YOUNGSTOWN STATE	52	17	W	-30.5	W	NT	---	
9/22/2018	vs	KANSAS STATE	35	6	W	-15.5	W	60.5	U	
9/29/2018	@	Texas Tech	42	34	W	-3.5	W	73.0	O	
10/6/2018	vs	KANSAS	38	22	W	-27.5	L	62.0	U	
10/13/2018	@	Iowa State	14	30	L	-4.0	L	55.0	U	
10/25/2018	vs	BAYLOR	58	14	W	-15.0	W	67.0	O	
11/3/2018	@	Texas	42	41	W	-1.0	T	58.0	O	
11/10/2018	vs	TCU	47	10	W	-12.0	W	56.0	O	
11/17/2018	@	Oklahoma State	41	45	L	-6.0	L	73.5	O	
11/23/2018	vs	OKLAHOMA	56	59	L	3.0	T	87.0	O	
12/28/2018	vs	Syracuse	18	34	L	3.0	L	67.0	U	Camping World Bowl
Coach: Dana Holgerson		Season Record >>	730	672	8-4	ATS>>	6-4-1	O/U>>	6-5	
2017-West Virginia		Opponent	Wva	Opp	S/U	Line	ATS	Total	O/U	
9/2/2017	vs	Virginia Tech	24	31	L	5.0	L	55.0	T	"Black Diamond Trophy"
9/9/2017	vs	EAST CAROLINA	56	20	W	-25.5	W	67.5	O	
9/16/2017	vs	DELAWARE STATE	59	16	W	NL	---	NT	---	
9/23/2017	@	Kansas	56	34	W	-24.5	L	71.0	O	
10/7/2017	@	Tcu	24	31	L	12.0	W	68.0	U	
10/14/2017	vs	TEXAS TECH	46	35	W	-5.5	W	77.5	O	
10/21/2017	@	Baylor	38	36	W	-10.5	L	67.0	O	
10/28/2017	vs	OKLAHOMA STATE	39	50	L	7.5	L	79.0	O	
11/4/2017	vs	IOWA STATE	20	16	W	-3.5	W	58.5	U	
11/11/2017	@	Kansas State	28	23	W	-3.0	W	60.0	U	
11/18/2017	vs	TEXAS	14	28	L	-3.0	L	54.5	U	
11/25/2017	@	Oklahoma	31	59	L	23.0	L	69.5	O	
12/26/2017	vs	Utah	14	30	L	7.0	L	56.0	U	Heart of Dallas Bowl
Coach: Dana Holgerson		Season Record >>	449	409	7-6	ATS>>	4-8	O/U>>	6-5-1	

Copyright © 2021 by Steve's Football Bible, LLC

WEST VIRGINIA MOUNTAINEERS   BIG TWELVE

STADIUM: Milan Pusker Stadium {60,000}		Location: Morgantown, WV								COACH: Neal Brown
DATE		Opponent	WVU	Opp	S/U	Line	ATS	Total	O/U	Trends & Angles
9/4/2021	@	*Maryland*								6-0 S/U vs Maryland as favorite since 2004
9/11/2021	vs	*LONG ISLAND U*								1st meeting
9/18/2021	vs	*VIRGINIA TECH*								0-7-1 ATS vs Va Tech as favorite since 1986
9/25/2021	@	Oklahoma								0-8 S/U vs Oklahoma as Dog since 2012
10/2/2021	vs	TEXAS TECH								vs Texas Tech - West Virginia leads series 6-4
10/9/2021	@	Baylor								vs Baylor - West Virginia leads series 6-3
10/23/2021	@	Tcu								vs TCU - West Virginia leads series 6-4
10/30/2021	vs	IOWA STATE								vs Iowa State - West Virginia leads series 5-4
11/6/2021	vs	OKLAHOMA STATE								vs Oklahoma State - OK State leads series 8-4
11/13/2021	@	Kansas State								1-6 O/U vs Kansas State as favorite since 2012
11/20/2021	vs	TEXAS								vs Texas - Series tied 5-5
11/27/2021	@	Kansas								vs Kansas - West Virginia leads series 9-1
12/4/2021	vs									BIG XII Championship
	vs									BOWL GAME

Pointspread Analysis Non-Conference		Pointspread Analysis Conference
0-15 S/U vs Non-Conf. as 15.5 point or more Dog since 1986		4-0 S/U vs Baylor as favorite since 2012
1-11 S/U vs Non-Conf. as 10.5-15 point Dog since 1987		vs Kansas State - WVU leads series 6-5
7-0 S/U vs Non-Conf. as 7.5-10 point favorite since 2009		vs Oklahoma - Oklahoma leads series 10-2
0-6 S/U vs Maryland as 4 point or more Dog since 1985 {1-5 ATS}		6-0 O/U vs Oklahoma as Dog since 2014
5-1 S/U & ATS vs Maryland as 3.5 point or less Dog since 1983		0-3 S/U & ATS vs Oklahoma State as favorite since 2015
14-2 S/U vs Maryland as 6.5 point or more favorite since 1984		1-3 S/U vs TCU as Dog since 2014
0-4 S/U & ATS vs Maryland as 6 point or less favorite since 1990		5-1 S/U vs Texas Tech as favorite since 2014
4-0 S/U when ranked @ Maryland all time		**Bowl Games**
2-8 S/U vs Virginia Tech as 2 point or more Dog since 1994		1-6 S/U in Gator Bowl
4-1 S/U @ home when ranked vs Virginia Tech all time		0-7 ATS in Gator Bowl
Dog		1-10 ATS in Bowl Games since 2008
0-12 S/U as 20.5 point or more Dog since 1986		0-3 S/U vs Florida State in Bowl Games
0-12 S/U on road as 15.5 point or more Dog since 1987		2-7 S/U in Bowl Games as 3.5-7 point Dog since 1989
3-14 S/U on road as 10.5-15 point Dog since 1987		1-5 S/U & ATS in Bowl Games as 3 point or less Dog since 1982
2-8 S/U @ home as 7.5-10 point Dog since 1987		0-5 ATS in Bowl Games as 3 point or less favorite since 1995
5-12 ATS as 3.5-7 point Dog since 2009		0-3 S/U & ATS in Bowl Games as 3.5-7 point favorite since 2002
1-6 S/U @ home as 3.5-7 point Dog since 2011		
5-1 S/U & ATS on road as 3 point or less Dog since 2005	LONG ISLAND U	17-0 S/U in 1st home game of season since 2004
Favorite	VIRGINIA TECH	16-1 S/U in 2nd home game of season since 2004
4-12 O/U as 3 point or less favorite since 2010	Oklahoma	2-9 S/U in 2nd road game of season since 2010
1-4 S/U & ATS @ home as 3 point or less favorite since 2000	Oklahoma	1-6 O/U prior to playing Texas Tech since 2014
6-1 S/U on road as 3 point or less favorite since 2012	Baylor	7-0 S/U after playing Texas Tech since 2014
5-1-1 ATS on road as 3 point or less favorite since 2012	IOWA STATE	1-7 ATS after playing TCU since 2012
2-6 O/U on road as 3 point or less favorite since 2012	K State	8-1 S/U prior to playing Texas since 2012
6-0 S/U @ home as 3.5-7 point favorite since 2016 {4-1-1 ATS}	TEXAS	3-11 O/U in final home game of season since 2007
7-1 S/U on road as 7.5-10 point favorite since 1989		
6-1 ATS on road as 7.5-10 point favorite since 1989		
14-2 S/U as 7.5-10 point favorite since 2000		
7-1 S/U @ home as 7.5-10 point favorite since 2000		
12-1 S/U on road as 10.5-15 point favorite since 1986		
12-2 S/U @ home as 10.5-15 point favorite since 1998		
30-2 S/U @ home as 15.5-20 point favorite since 1983		
19-1 S/U on road as 15.5 point or more favorite since 1988		0-9 S/U vs #1 ranked teams all time
22-1 S/U @ home as 20.5-25 point favorite since 1983		0-9 S/U vs #2 ranked teams all time
2-6 O/U @ home as 20.5-25 point favorite since 2007		0-9 S/U vs #5 ranked teams all time
29-1 S/U @ home as 25.5 point or more favorite since 1984		0-7 S/U vs ranked Oklahoma since 2013

Copyright © 2021 by Steve's Football Bible, LLC

WISCONSIN BADGERS   BIG TEN West

2020-Wisconsin		Opponent	UW	Opp	S/U	Line	ATS	Total	O/U	
10/23/2020	vs	ILLINOIS	45	7	W	-20.5	W	51.5	O	
11/14/2020	@	Michigan	49	11	W	-7.0	W	51.5	O	
11/21/2020	@	Northwestern	7	17	L	-7.0	L	43.0	U	
12/5/2020	vs	INDIANA	6	14	L	-13.0	L	44.5	U	
12/12/2020	@	Iowa	7	28	L	-1.0	L	39.5	U	"Heartland Trophy"
12/19/2020	vs	MINNESOTA	20	17	W	-10.0	L	47.0	U	"Paul Bunyan Axe"
12/30/2020	vs	**Wake Forest**	42	28	W	-10.5	W	51.5	O	Duke's Mayo Bowl
Coach: Paul Chryst		Season Record >>	176	122	4-3	ATS>>	3-4	O/U>>	3-4	
2019-Wisconsin		Opponent	UW	Opp	S/U	Line	ATS	Total	O/U	
8/31/2019	@	*South Florida*	49	0	W	-10.5	W	58.5	U	
9/7/2019	vs	*CENTRAL MICHIGAN*	61	0	W	-35.0	W	54.0	O	
9/21/2019	vs	MICHIGAN	35	14	W	-3.0	W	45.0	U	
9/28/2019	vs	NORTHWESTERN	24	15	W	-23.5	L	46.0	U	
10/5/2019	vs	*KENT STATE*	48	0	W	-35.0	W	58.5	U	
10/12/2019	vs	MICHIGAN STATE	38	0	W	-8.0	W	40.5	U	
10/19/2019	@	Illinois	23	24	L	-31.0	L	52.0	U	
10/26/2019	@	Ohio State	7	38	L	14.5	L	47.5	U	
11/9/2019	vs	IOWA	24	22	W	-7.5	L	37.5	O	"Heartland Trophy"
11/16/2019	@	Nebraska	37	21	W	-14.0	W	50.0	O	"Freedom Trophy"
11/23/2019	vs	PURDUE	45	24	W	-24.5	L	48.5	O	
11/30/2019	@	Minnesota	38	17	W	-3.0	W	45.0	O	"Paul Bunyan Axe"
12/7/2019	vs	**Ohio State**	21	34	L	16.5	W	58.0	U	Big Ten Championship
1/1/2020	vs	**Oregon**	27	28	L	-3.0	L	52.5	O	Rose Bowl
Coach: Paul Chryst		Season Record >>	477	237	10-4	ATS>>	8-6	O/U>>	7-7	
2018-Wisconsin		Opponent	UW	Opp	S/U	Line	ATS	Total	O/U	
8/31/2018	vs	*WESTERN KENTUCKY*	34	3	W	-36.0	L	52.0	U	
9/8/2018	vs	*NEW MEXICO*	45	14	W	-35.0	L	58.5	U	
9/15/2018	vs	*BYU*	21	24	L	-23.5	L	51.5	U	
9/22/2018	@	Iowa	28	17	W	-3.0	W	43.5	O	"Heartland Trophy"
10/6/2018	vs	NEBRASKA	41	24	W	-18.0	L	60.5	O	"Freedom Trophy"
10/13/2018	@	Michigan	13	38	L	9.5	L	48.0	O	
10/20/2018	vs	ILLINOIS	49	20	W	-24.0	W	53.0	O	
10/27/2018	@	Northwestern	17	31	L	-5.0	L	50.5	U	
11/3/2018	vs	RUTGERS	31	17	W	-28.5	L	50.5	U	
11/10/2018	@	Penn State	10	22	L	7.5	L	54.0	U	
11/17/2018	@	Purdue	47	44	W	3.5	W	56.0	O	{2 OT}
11/24/2018	vs	MINNESOTA	15	37	L	-12.5	L	54.0	U	"Paul Bunyan Axe"
12/27/2018	vs	**Miami**	35	3	W	2.5	W	44.0	U	Pinstripe Bowl
Coach: Paul Chryst		Season Record >>	386	294	8-5	ATS>>	4-9	O/U>>	5-8	
2017-Wisconsin		Opponent	UW	Opp	S/U	Line	ATS	Total	O/U	
9/1/2017	vs	*UTAH STATE*	59	10	W	-27.5	W	51.5	O	
9/9/2017	vs	*FLORIDA ATLANTIC*	31	14	W	-34.5	L	59.5	U	
9/16/2017	@	*Byu*	40	6	W	-14.0	W	41.5	O	
9/30/2017	vs	NORTHWESTERN	33	24	W	-16.5	L	50.0	O	
10/7/2017	@	Nebraska	38	17	W	-12.5	W	47.5	O	"Freedom Trophy"
10/14/2017	vs	PURDUE	17	9	W	-17.0	L	49.0	U	
10/21/2017	vs	MARYLAND	38	13	W	-23.0	W	50.0	O	
10/28/2017	@	Illinois	24	10	W	-27.0	L	51.5	U	
11/4/2017	@	Indiana	45	17	W	-10.5	W	49.0	O	
11/11/2017	vs	IOWA	38	14	W	-12.0	W	45.5	O	"Heartland Trophy"
11/18/2017	vs	MICHIGAN	24	10	W	-6.5	W	42.0	U	
11/25/2017	@	Minnesota	31	0	W	-19.5	W	43.0	U	"Paul Bunyan Axe"
12/2/2017	vs	**Ohio State**	21	27	L	3.5	L	51.0	U	Big Ten Championship
12/30/2017	vs	**Miami**	34	24	W	-6.5	W	45.5	O	Orange Bowl
Coach: Paul Chryst		Season Record >>	473	195	13-1	ATS>>	9-5	O/U>>	8-6	

Copyright © 2021 by Steve's Football Bible, LLC

WISCONSIN BADGERS   BIG TEN West

DATE		Opponent	UW	Opp	S/U	Line	ATS	Total	O/U	Trends & Angles
		STADIUM: Camp Randall Stadium {80,321}				Location: Madison, WI				**COACH:** Paul Chryst
9/4/2021	vs	PENN STATE								Game 3-0 O/U @ home vs Penn State since 2008
9/11/2021	vs	*EASTERN MICHIGAN*								3-0 S/U vs Eastern Michigan as favorite since 1991
9/25/2021	vs	*Notre Dame {@ Chicago}*								vs Notre Dame - Notre Dame leads series 8-6-2
10/2/2021	vs	MICHIGAN								vs Michigan - Michigan leads series 51-17-1
10/9/2021	@	Illinois								13-1 S/U vs Illinois as favorite since 2003
10/16/2021	vs	*ARMY*								1st meeting
10/23/2021	@	Purdue								14-0 S/U vs Purdue as favorite since 1996
10/30/2021	vs	IOWA								2-12 S/U vs Iowa as Dog since 1985
11/6/2021	@	Rutgers								3-0 S/U vs Rutgers as favorite since 2014
11/13/2021	vs	NORTHWESTERN								vs Northwestern - Wisconsin leads series 60-37-5
11/20/2021	vs	NEBRASKA								7-0 S/U vs Nebraska as favorite since 2011
11/27/2021	@	Minnesota								21-2 S/U vs Minnesota as favorite since 1995
12/4/2021	vs									Big Ten Championship
	vs									BOWL GAME

Pointspread Analysis
Non-Conference

10-2 S/U vs Non-Conf. as 3.5-7 point favorite since 1989	
1-6 O/U vs Non-Conf. as 3.5-7 point favorite since 2002	
12-0 S/U vs Non-conf. as 7.5-10 point favorite since 1990	
17-1 S/U vs Non-Conf. as 10.5-15 point favorite since 1985	
7-0 S/U vs Non-Conf. as 15.5-20 point favorite since 1991	
11-2 S/U vs Non-Conf. as 20.5-25 point favorite since 1994	
32-1 S/U vs Non-Conf. as 25.5 or more favorite since 1994	

Dog

0-20 S/U as 20.5 point or more Dog since 1986
0-18 S/U on road as 15.5 point or more Dog since 1986
1-7 O/U on road as 10.5-15 point Dog since 2001
0-7 S/U on road as 10.5-15 point Dog since 2002
14-6-1 ATS as 10.5-15 point Dog since 1986
0-8 S/U on road as 7.5-10 point Dog since 1985
2-11-1 S/U @ home as 3.5-7 point Dog since 1983

Favorite

9-2 S/U on road as 3 point or less favorite since 2003
9-3 O/U on road as 3 point or less favorite since 2001
1-5 O/U @ home as 3.5-7 point favorite since 2006
16-6 S/U on road as 3.5-7 point favorite since 1996
13-6 ATS on road as 3.5-7 point favorite since 1998
25-0 S/U @ home as 7.5-10 point favorite since 1983
2-8 O/U as 7.5-10 point favorite since 2013
1-7 ATS as 7.5-10 point favorite since 2014
15-3 S/U @ home as 10.5-15 point favorite since 2002
13-0 S/U on road as 10.5-15 point favorite since 2004
12-3-1 ATS as 10.5-15 point favorite since 2012
10-0 S/U on road as 15.5-25 point favorite since 1983
11-0 S/U @ home as 15.5-20 point favorite since 2004
25-4 S/U @ home as 20.5-25 point favorite since 1984
16-6 O/U as 20.5-25 point favorite since 2005
7-2 S/U on road as 25.5 point or more favorite since 1996
34-0 S/U @ home as 25.5 point or more favorite since 1994

Bowl Games

3-0 S/U vs UCLA in Bowl Games
3-0 S/U & ATS vs Miami in Bowl Games
1-3 S/U in Outback Bowl
5-1 S/U in Bowl Games since 2015
0-4 S/U in Rose Bowl since 2011
0-5 ATS in Rose Bowl since 2000
7-3 S/U vs PAC-12 in Bowl Games since 1994
0-5 O/U in Bowl Games as 3 point or less Dog since 2003
3-0 S/U in Bowl Games as 7.5-10 point favorite since 1995

Pointspread Analysis
Conference

	vs Illinois - Wisconsin leads series 42-37-7
	1-10 S/U vs Illinois as Dog since 1983
	9-1 S/U @ Illinois as favorite since 1993
	vs Iowa - Wisconsin leads series 48-44-2
	1-16 S/U vs Michigan as 3.5 point or more Dog since 1983
	vs Minnesota - Wisconsin leads series 62-60-8
	6-0 ATS @ Minnesota as Dog since 1987
	vs Nebraska - Wisconsin leads series 10-4
	7-0 S/U vs Northwestern as 16.5 point or more favorite since 1984
	vs Purdue - Wisconsin leads series 50-29-8
	11-0-1 S/U @ home vs Purdue as favorite since 1994
	0-3 S/U @ home vs Purdue as Dog since 1988
	0-5 S/U & ATS vs Penn State as Dog since 2005
	0-4 S/U & ATS vs Penn State since 2012
	64-8 S/U @ home when ranked since 2006
	13-1 S/U when ranked vs Illinois since 1962 {6-0 @ home}
	9-1-1 S/U @ home when ranked vs Purdue all time
	4-0 S/U @ home vs ranked Michigan since 2005
	5-0 ATS @ home vs ranked Michigan since 2001
	7-1 S/U vs ranked Minnesota since 1961

PENN STATE	25-0 S/U in 1st home game of season since 1996
E. MICHIGAN	16-1 S/U in 2nd home game of season since 2004
Notre Dame	8-0 S/U prior to playing Michigan since 2008
Notre Dame	10-2 ATS prior to playing Michigan since 2005
ARMY	8-2 S/U after playing Illinois since 2011
ARMY	9-2 ATS after playing Illinois since 2008
ARMY	8-3 O/U after playing Illinois since 2008
IOWA	12-2 S/U after playing Purdue since 2004
Rutgers	12-1 S/U prior to playing Northwestern since 2004
NEBRASKA	12-3 S/U prior to playing Minnesota since 2006
NEBRASKA	11-1 S/U after playing Northwestern since 2004
NEBRASKA	10-3 O/U after playing Northwestern since 2003
NEBRASKA	12-3 ATS after playing Northwestern since 1999
Minnesota	14-2 S/U in final road game of season since 2005
Minnesota	7-1 S/U after playing Nebraska since 2011

Copyright © 2021 by Steve's Football Bible, LLC

WYOMING COWBOYS MOUNTAIN WEST Mountain

2020-Wyoming		Opponent	WYO	Opp	S/U	Line	ATS	Total	O/U	
10/24/2020	@	Nevada	34	37	L	-3.0	L	53.5	O	{OT}
10/30/2020	vs	HAWAII	38	7	W	3.0	W	59.5	U	
11/6/2020	@	Colorado State	24	34	L	-3.5	L	63.0	U	*"Bronze Boot"*
11/27/2020	@	Unlv	45	14	W	-17.0	W	52.0	O	
12/5/2020	@	New Mexico	16	17	L	-15.0	L	51.0	U	
12/12/2020	vs	BOISE STATE	9	17	L	9.5	W	47.0	U	
Coach: Craig Bohl		Season Record >>	166	126	2-4	ATS>>	3-3	O/U>>	2-4	
2019-Wyoming		Opponent	WYO	Opp	S/U	Line	ATS	Total	O/U	
8/31/2019	vs	*MISSOURI*	37	31	W	15.5	W	52.5	O	
9/7/2019	@	*Texas State*	23	14	W	-7.0	W	47.5	U	
9/14/2019	vs	*IDAHO*	21	16	W	-27.0	L	NT	---	
9/21/2019	@	*Tulsa*	21	24	L	6.0	W	46.0	U	
9/28/2019	vs	UNLV	53	17	W	-8.0	W	44.5	O	
10/12/2019	@	San Diego State	22	26	L	3.5	L	38.0	O	
10/19/2019	vs	NEW MEXICO	23	10	W	-17.5	L	49.0	U	
10/26/2019	vs	NEVADA	31	3	W	-14.0	W	43.5	U	
11/9/2019	@	Boise State	17	20	L	16.5	W	48.0	U	
11/16/2019	@	Utah State	21	26	L	5.0	T	51.5	U	*"Bridger's Battle"*
11/23/2019	vs	COLORADO STATE	17	7	W	-4.0	W	51.0	U	*"Bronze Boot"*
11/30/2019	@	Air Force	6	20	L	13.0	L	41.5	U	
12/31/2019	vs	**Georgia State**	38	17	W	-7.0	W	49.0	O	**Arizona Bowl**
Coach: Craig Bohl		Season Record >>	330	231	8-5	ATS>>	8-4-1	O/U>>	4-8	
2018-Wyoming		Opponent	WYO	Opp	S/U	Line	ATS	Total	O/U	
8/25/2018	@	*New Mexico State*	29	7	W	-5.0	W	45.5	U	
9/1/2018	vs	*WASHINGTON STATE*	19	41	L	3.0	L	44.0	O	
9/8/2018	@	*Missouri*	13	40	L	19.5	L	52.5	O	
9/15/2018	vs	*WOFFORD*	17	14	W	-14.0	L	NT	---	
9/29/2018	vs	BOISE STATE	14	34	L	16.0	L	46.0	O	
10/6/2018	@	Hawaii	13	17	L	-3.0	L	52.0	U	*"Paniola Trophy"*
10/13/2018	@	Fresno State	3	27	L	18.0	L	44.0	U	
10/20/2018	vs	UTAH STATE	16	24	L	14.0	W	49.5	U	*"Bridger's Battle"*
10/27/2018	@	Colorado State	34	21	W	-3.0	W	47.5	O	*"Bronze Boot"*
11/3/2018	vs	SAN JOSE STATE	24	9	W	-17.0	L	39.0	U	
11/17/2018	vs	AIR FORCE	35	27	W	-2.5	W	43.0	O	
11/24/2018	@	New Mexico	31	3	W	-7.0	W	43.0	U	
Coach: Craig Bohl		Season Record >>	248	264	6-6	ATS>>	5-7	O/U>>	5-6	
2017-Wyoming		Opponent	WYO	Opp	S/U	Line	ATS	Total	O/U	
9/2/2017	@	*Iowa*	3	24	L	12.5	L	51.5	U	
9/9/2017	vs	*GARDNER-WEBB*	27	0	W	-37.5	L	NT	---	
9/16/2017	vs	*OREGON*	13	49	L	14.0	L	66.0	U	
9/23/2017	vs	HAWAII	28	21	W	-4.5	W	55.0	U	*"Paniola Trophy"*
9/30/2017	vs	*TEXAS STATE*	45	10	W	-16.0	W	45.0	O	
10/14/2017	@	Utah State	28	23	W	-2.0	W	50.0	O	*"Bridger's Battle"*
10/21/2017	@	Boise State	14	24	L	14.5	W	44.5	U	
10/28/2017	vs	NEW MEXICO	42	3	W	-2.5	W	47.5	U	
11/4/2017	vs	COLORADO STATE	16	13	W	4.0	W	47.5	U	*"Bronze Boot"*
11/11/2017	@	Air Force	28	14	W	2.5	W	50.5	U	
11/18/2017	vs	FRESNO STATE	7	13	L	PK	L	38.5	U	
11/25/2017	@	San Jose State	17	20	L	-19.0	L	48.5	U	
12/22/2017	vs	**Central Michigan**	37	14	W	-2.5	W	47.0	O	**Famous Idaho Potato Bowl**
Coach: Craig Bohl		Season Record >>	305	228	8-5	ATS>>	8-5	O/U>>	3-9	

Copyright © 2021 by Steve's Football Bible, LLC

WYOMING COWBOYS MOUNTAIN WEST Mountain

STADIUM: War Memorial Stadium {29,181}					Location: Laramie, WY				COACH: Craig Bohl	
DATE		Opponent	WYO	Opp	S/U	Line	ATS	Total	O/U	Trends & Angles
9/4/2021	vs	*MONTANA STATE*								8-0 S/U vs Montana State since 1934
9/11/2021	@	*Northern Illinois*								vs Northern Illinois - WYO leads series 1-0
9/18/2021	vs	*BALL STATE*								1st meeting
9/25/2021	@	*Connecticut*								1st meeting
10/9/2021	@	Air Force								vs Air Force - Air Force leads series 28-26-3
10/16/2021	vs	FRESNO STATE								vs Fresno State - Fresno leads series 7-5
10/23/2021	vs	NEW MEXICO								vs New Mexico - Wyoming leads series 38-35
10/30/2021	@	San Jose State								vs San Jose State - WYO leads series 7-4
11/6/2021	vs	COLORADO STATE								vs Colorado State - CSU leads series 59-48-5
11/13/2021	@	Boise State								vs Boise State - Boise State leads series 14-1
11/20/2021	@	Utah State								5-0 S/U vs Utah State as favorite since 2003 {4-1 ATS}
11/27/2021	vs	HAWAII								8-2 S/U vs Hawaii since 1993 {7-3 ATS}
12/4/2021	vs									MWC Championship
	vs									BOWL GAME

Pointspread Analysis		Pointspread Analysis
Non-Conference		**Conference**
1-11 S/U vs Non-Conf. as 15.5-20 point Dog since 1976		1-9 O/U vs Air Force as Dog since 2007
1-20 S/U vs Non-Conf. as 10.5-15 point Dog since 1985		12-2 ATS vs Air Force as Dog since 2001
18-1 S/U vs Non-Conf. as 15.5 point or more favorite since 1988		1-7 S/U vs Air Force as 3-11 point Dog since 1985
		8-1 ATS vs Air Force as 11 point or more Dog since 2001
Dog		1-14 S/U vs Boise State as Dog since 2002
5-0 ATS as 30.5 point or more Dog since 2011		5-0 ATS vs Colorado State as 11 point or more Dog since 1994
0-13 S/U as 30.5 point or more Dog since 1994		5-0 O/U vs Colorado State as 11 point or more Dog since 1994
3-9 O/U as 30.5 point or more Dog since 1997		3-0 S/U & ATS @ home vs Fresno State as favorite since 1993
1-9 S/U as 25.5-30 point Dog since 1982		5-0 S/U @ home vs Hawaii as favorite since 1993
0-16 S/U as 20.5-25 point Dog since 1991		1-8 S/U vs New Mexico as Dog since 1985
0-6 O/U as 20.5-25 point Dog since 2010		11-1 S/U vs New Mexico as 10 point or more favorite since 1987
0-6 O/U on road as 20.5-25 point Dog since 2003		vs Utah State - Utah State leads series 40-26-4
1-7 ATS as 20.5-25 point Dog since 2008		0-6 S/U vs Utah State as Dog since 2011 {1-4-1 ATS}
0-8 S/U @ home as 20.5 point or more Dog since 2001		
2-13 S/U on road as 15.5-20 point Dog since 1998		3-39 S/U on road vs ranked teams all time
2-23 S/U on road as 10.5-15 point Dog since 1985		2-22 S/U vs ranked teams since 2004
1-7 S/U @ home as 7.5-10 point Dog since 2001		0-29 S/U vs Top #10 ranked teams all time
1-9 S/U on road as 7.5-10 point Dog since 2001		0-7-1 ATS on road when ranked since 1988
7-2 S/U & ATS as 3 point or less Dog since 2009		14-2 S/U @ home when ranked all time

Favorite		
8-1 S/U @ home as 3.5-7 point favorite since 2008	MONTANA ST.	15-3 S/U in 1st home game of season since 2003
7-1 S/U as 3.5-7 point favorite since 2016	Northern Ill.	3-16 S/U in 1st road game of season since 2002
6-0 O/U as 7.5-10 point favorite since 2006	Northern Ill.	5-12 O/U in 1st road game of season since 2004
8-1 S/U @ home as 7.5-10 point favorite since 1995	Connecticut	7-2 ATS prior to playing Air Force since 2011
23-3-1 S/U @ home as 10.5-15 point favorite since 1986	Connecticut	2-7 S/U prior to playing Air Force since 2011
2-9 ATS as 10.5-15 point favorite since 2006	Air Force	0-5 S/U prior to playing Fresno State since 1997
14-1 S/U @ home as 15.5-20 point favorite since 1987	FRESNO STATE	2-9 O/U after playing Air Force since 2008
16-1 S/U as 20.5 point or more favorite since 1988	San Jose State	3-7 S/U after playing New Mexico since 2007
Bowl Games	San Jose State	3-11 S/U prior to playing Colorado State since 2007
3-0 S/U in Sun Bowl	Boise State	5-1 ATS prior to playing Utah State since 2014
5-1 ATS in Bowl Games since 2004	Utah State	2-12 ATS prior to playing Hawaii since 1988
0-4 S/U in Bowl Games as 3.5-7 point Dog since 1987	Utah State	1-7 S/U & ATS in final road game of season since 2013

Copyright © 2021 by Steve's Football Bible, LLC

Books available from Steve's Football Bible LLC

Print Version $34.99   **Print Version $34.99**

Print Version $34.99   **Print Version $29.99**

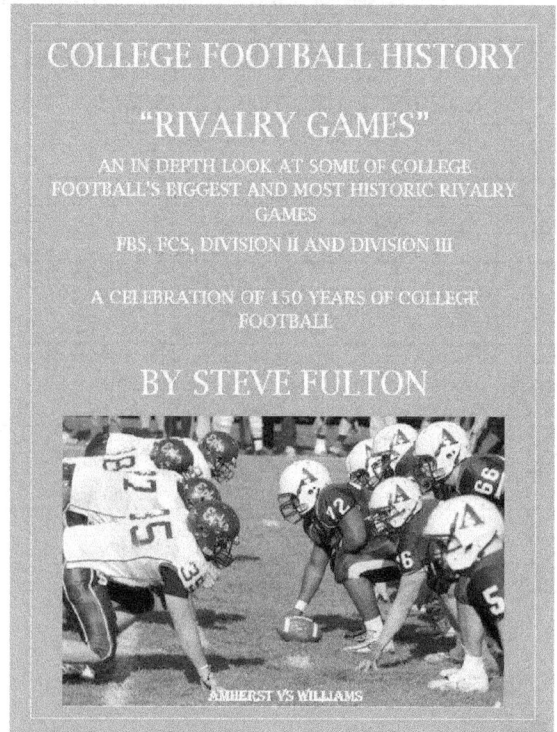

These books available at numerous online retailers

Copyright © 2021 by Steve's Football Bible, LLC

Books available from Steve's Football Bible LLC
Print Version $39.99   Print Version $39.99

Print Version $29.99   Print Version $19.95

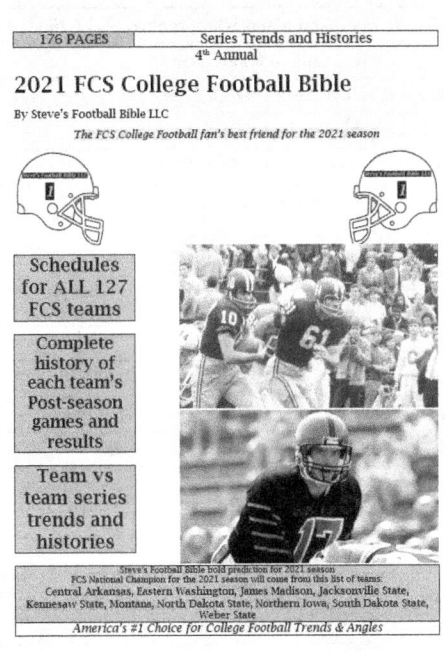

These books available at numerous online retailers

Copyright © 2021 by Steve's Football Bible, LLC

Team Trends when ranked in the Polls / vs Ranked teams in the Polls

Air Force {When Ranked}
5-1 S/U when ranked #10 all time
4-0 S/U vs when ranked #13 all time
5-0 S/U when ranked #20 since 1969
4-0 S/U when ranked #7 all time
7-1 S/U vs Colorado State {4-0 on road}

Air Force {vs Ranked}
0-12 S/U on road vs ranked teams since 2004
13-5 ATS on road vs ranked teams since 1996
0-12 S/U vs #3 - #5 ranked teams all time
1-10 S/U vs #11 - #14 ranked teams all time

Akron {When Ranked}
NEVER RANKED

Akron {vs Ranked}
1-19 S/U vs ranked teams since 1999 {0-17 on road}
2-7 O/U vs ranked teams since 2009

Alabama {When Ranked}
44-6 S/U on road when ranked since 2008
54-1 S/U @ home when ranked since 2013
80-8 S/U when ranked #1 since 2009
38-9 S/U when ranked #1 vs ranked teams since 1978
12-0 S/U on road when ranked #2 since 1992
11-0 S/U at Neutral sites when ranked #2 since 1979
7-1 S/U on road when ranked #2 vs ranked teams all time
35-0 S/U when ranked #2 vs unranked teams since 1986
21-0 S/U @ home when ranked #3 since 1964
5-0 S/U @ home vs ranked teams when ranked #3 all time
21-1 S/U on road when ranked #4 all time
27-1 S/U @ home when ranked #4 all time
12-1 S/U @ home when ranked #5 since 1961
8-0 S/U on road when ranked #6 since 1981
18-2 S/U when ranked #6 since 1971
16-0-1 S/U @ home when ranked #7 since 1945
10-1 S/U @ home when ranked #8 all time
17-3-1 S/U when ranked #9 all time
9-2 S/U when ranked #10 since 1977
3-17 O/U when ranked #11 since 1983
8-1 S/U when ranked #12 since 1981
15-2 S/U when ranked #13 since 1985 {5-0 on road}
12-1 S/U when ranked #14 all time
12-2 S/U @ home when ranked #15 all time
8-1 S/U @ home when ranked #16 since 1983
1-5 ATS when ranked #18 since 1983
5-0 S/U @ home when ranked #20 since 1985
10-1-1 S/U when ranked #20 since 1976
0-4 S/U when ranked #22 since 1998
3-0 S/U when ranked #24 all time
9-2 S/U vs #1 ranked teams when ranked since 1977
0-4 S/U on road vs #2 ranked teams when ranked all time
2-10 S/U vs #2 ranked teams when ranked all time
7-0 S/U vs #3 ranked teams when ranked since 2008

(Air Force / Alabama continued)
4-0 S/U on road vs #5 ranked teams when ranked since 1971
1-5 S/U on road vs #6 ranked teams when ranked all time
8-1-1 S/U vs #10 ranked teams when ranked since 1977
5-0 S/U vs #12 ranked teams when ranked all time
10-1 S/U vs #14 ranked teams when ranked all time
5-0 ATS vs #14 ranked teams when ranked since 1989
5-1 S/U vs #16 ranked teams when ranked since 1975
0-5 O/U vs #17 ranked teams when ranked since 2001
5-0 S/U vs #18 ranked teams when ranked since 2006
6-1 S/U vs #20 ranked teams when ranked all time
13-0 S/U vs Arkansas when ranked since 2008
5-2 S/U vs Clemson when ranked all time
7-0 S/U vs Florida when ranked since 2009
7-1 S/U @ Florida when ranked all time
2-7-2 O/U vs LSU when ranked since 2011
20-2 S/U vs Mississippi when ranked since 1989
23-3 S/U vs Southern Miss when ranked since 1966
15-0 S/U vs Tennessee when ranked since 2002
5-0 S/U @ Texas A&M when ranked all time
8-0 S/U vs Texas A&M when ranked since 2013

Alabama {vs Ranked}
119-84-5 S/U @ home vs ranked teams all time
54-47-3 S/U on road vs ranked teams all time
9-3 S/U vs #1 ranked teams since 1977
7-0 S/U vs #3 ranked teams since 2008
2-14 S/U vs #2 ranked teams all time {0-5 on road}
1-6 O/U vs #5 ranked teams since 1987
1-5 S/U on road vs #6 ranked teams all time
1-5 S/U on road vs #7 ranked teams all time
6-1 ATS vs #8 ranked teams since 1987
4-0 S/U & ATS vs #9 ranked teams since 2008
1-7 S/U vs #11 ranked teams since 2001 {1-7 ATS}
5-1 ATS vs #12 ranked teams since 1984
5-0 ATS vs #13 ranked teams since 1992
5-0 S/U & ATS vs #14 ranked teams since 1999
4-0 S/U on road vs #14 ranked teams since 1974
6-1 S/U vs #16 ranked teams since 1975
5-0 S/U @ home vs #16 ranked teams all time
0-7 O/U vs #17 ranked teams since 2001
5-0 S/U vs #18 ranked teams since 2006
5-1 S/U vs #19 ranked teams since 1946
6-0 S/U & ATS vs #20 ranked teams since 1990
3-0 S/U on road vs #20 ranked teams since 1958
4-0 ATS vs #21 ranked teams since 1995
1-4 ATS vs #22 ranked teams since 2003
0-3 ATS vs #25 ranked teams since 2000
0-3 O/U vs #25 ranked teams since 2000
7-1 S/U vs ranked Arkansas all time
2-9 S/U @ ranked Auburn all time
1-9 O/U @ home vs ranked Auburn since 1988
6-0 S/U vs ranked Florida since 2009

Copyright © 2021 by Steve's Football Bible, LLC

8-1 S/U vs ranked LSU since 2012
1-7-2 O/U vs ranked LSU since 2011
16-2 S/U vs ranked Mississippi State since 1944
7-0 S/U vs ranked Texas A&M since 2013

Alabama-Birmingham {When Ranked}

NEVER RANKED

Alabama-Birmingham {vs Ranked}

1-16 S/U on road vs ranked teams since 1997

Appalachian State {When Ranked}

7-3 S/U when ranked all time

Appalachian State {vs Ranked}

1-11 S/U vs ranked teams all time

Arizona {When Ranked}

1-8 S/U on road when ranked vs ranked teams since 1999
10-1 S/U on road when ranked vs ranked teams since 1998
26-5 S/U @ home when ranked vs unranked teams since 1993
0-3 S/U when ranked vs #3 ranked teams all time
4-1 S/U when ranked #7 all time
0-4 ATS when ranked #7 since 1993
0-3 S/U on road when #13 ranked all time
5-0 S/U @ home when #14 ranked since 1986
11-2 S/U when #15 ranked all time
11-2 S/U when #17 ranked all time {7-0 @ home}
0-5 S/U when ranked vs #17 #18 ranked teams all time
0-4 ATS when #18 ranked all time
5-0 ATS when ranked #21 since 1992
1-5 ATS when ranked #22 since 1992
4-0 O/U when ranked #23 all time
4-0 S/U vs Arizona State when ranked since 1993
1-9 ATS vs California when ranked all time {0-4 @ home}
0-4 S/U when ranked vs Oregon since 2000
0-5 S/U @ Oregon when ranked since 1989
3-0 S/U vs San Diego State when ranked all time
0-8 ATS vs UCLA when ranked since 1993
0-5 S/U & ATS when ranked vs ranked UCLA since 1993
1-8 S/U vs USC when ranked all time
0-6 S/U when ranked vs ranked USC all time
4-0 S/U vs Washington when ranked since 1992
11-0 S/U vs Washington State when ranked all time

Arizona {vs Ranked}

0-6 ATS on road vs ranked teams since 2015
5-1 O/U on road vs ranked teams since 2015
0-5 S/U on road vs #1 ranked teams since 1984
5-30 S/U on road vs ranked teams since 1999
2-19-1 S/U on road vs #3 - #9 ranked teams since 1970
0-4 S/U on road vs #10 ranked teams all time
4-0 ATS vs #11 ranked teams since 1989
0-3 S/U on road vs #13 ranked teams since 1987
1-4 S/U vs #14 ranked teams all time
0-7 S/U vs #16 ranked teams all time
0-4 S/U on road vs #17 ranked teams all time

0-4 S/U on road vs #18 ranked teams since 1981
1-4 S/U vs #19 ranked teams all time
4-0 S/U & ATS on road vs #20 ranked teams since 1994
4-1 ATS vs #22 ranked teams all time
0-3 S/U vs #24 ranked teams all time
5-1 O/U vs #25 ranked teams since 2003
1-9 S/U @ ranked Arizona State all time
0-3 S/U vs ranked Colorado all time
0-6 O/U vs ranked Oregon since 2012
0-4 S/U & ATS vs ranked UCLA since 2012
0-7-1 S/U @ ranked UCLA all time
7-1 ATS vs ranked USC since 2005
1-4 S/U @ ranked USC since 2004
0-5 S/U vs ranked Washington since 2000
1-4 S/U @ ranked Washington State since 1997

Arizona State {When Ranked}

10-2 S/U @ home when ranked since 2011
6-0 S/U when #4 ranked since 1996
3-0 S/U when #5 ranked all time
7-1 S/U when #9 ranked all time {4-0 @ home}
8-0 S/U when #10 ranked all time
10-0-1 S/U when ranked #11 since 1973
0-6 S/U when ranked #12 since 1977
10-2 S/U @ home when ranked #13 all time
0-6 ATS when ranked #15 since 2004
6-2 S/U when ranked #17 all time
6-0 S/U @ home when #18 ranked since 1981
8-0 S/U when #19 ranked all time
8-0 S/U @ home when #20 ranked since 1981
5-0 S/U @ home when #21 ranked since 2003
3-0 S/U @ home when ranked #23 all time
0-3 S/U vs #7 ranked teams when ranked all time
8-1 S/U @ home vs Arizona when ranked all time
4-1 S/U @ home vs BYU when ranked all time
5-0 S/U @ home vs Stanford when ranked all time
7-1 S/U vs Utah when ranked since 1974
5-0 S/U vs Washington State when ranked since 2004

Arizona State {vs Ranked}

7-30 S/U on road vs ranked teams since 1998
0-6 S/U vs ranked teams in Bowl Games since 1997
5-0 S/U vs ranked Non-Conference teams since 2011
0-7 S/U vs #2 ranked teams all time
1-5 S/U vs #5 ranked teams all time
3-18 S/U vs #7 - #9 ranked teams all time {1-10 on road}
0-6 S/U vs #11 ranked teams since 1990
0-6 S/U vs #13 ranked teams since 1992 {1-5 ATS}
1-5 S/U vs #14 ranked teams all time
5-1 ATS vs #16 ranked teams since 1992
4-0 O/U vs #16 ranked teams since 2004
0-7 S/U vs #17 ranked teams all time
4-0 S/U @ home vs #20 ranked teams all time

Copyright © 2021 by Steve's Football Bible, LLC

Team Trends when ranked in the Polls / vs Ranked teams in the Polls

1-6 S/U vs #21 ranked teams all time
0-6 ATS vs #21 ranked teams since 1994
4-0 ATS vs #23 ranked teams all time
6-0 O/U vs UCLA since 1995
1-9 S/U @ home vs USC since 1988
0-6 S/U @ Washington since 1991

Arkansas {When Ranked}

9-1 O/U on road when ranked since 2007
20-4 S/U @ home when ranked since 2007
6-1 S/U @ home when #2 ranked since 1965
3-0 S/U on road when ranked #2 all time
4-0 S/U @ home when ranked #3 all time
1-4 S/U @ home when #4 ranked since 1970
6-0 S/U @ home when #6 ranked all time
4-0 S/U on road when #7 ranked since 1962
7-1 S/U on road when #8 ranked all time
8-2 S/U @ home when #8 ranked since 1977
10-0 S/U @ home when #9 ranked since 1970
6-0 S/U on road when #11 ranked all time
6-0 S/U on road when #13 ranked all time
8-2 S/U @ home when #13 ranked since 1959
9-0 S/U @ home when #14 ranked since 1976
9-1 S/U @ home when #15 ranked all time
10-0 S/U @ home when #17 ranked all time
8-2 S/U @ home when ranked #18 all time
5-0 S/U when ranked #19 since 1959
7-1 S/U @ home when ranked #20 all time
0-4 O/U when #22 ranked all time
0-6 S/U when ranked vs #1 ranked teams since 1969
0-7 S/U when ranked vs #3 ranked teams all time
5-0 S/U when ranked vs #14 ranked teams all time
1-7 S/U when ranked vs Alabama all time
0-5 S/U when ranked @ LSU all time
4-0 S/U when ranked vs Mississippi State since 1999
4-0 S/U when ranked vs Mississippi since 2006
4-0 S/U @ home when ranked vs Mississippi since 1998
19-0-1 S/U when ranked vs Rice since 1959

Arkansas {vs Ranked}

4-23 S/U vs #1 ranked teams all time {12 straight L}
1-12 S/U vs #3 ranked teams all time
0-6 S/U vs #4 ranked teams since 1994
0-3 S/U on road vs #5 ranked teams all time
1-5 S/U on road vs #6 ranked teams all time
1-4 S/U @ home vs #6 ranked teams all time
0-6 S/U vs #7 ranked teams since 2004
0-4 S/U on road vs #7 ranked teams all time
1-11 S/U vs #8 ranked teams since 1949
5-1 ATS vs #11 ranked teams since 1985
0-5 S/U on road vs #12 ranked teams all time
5-0 S/U @ home vs #15 ranked teams all time
1-8 S/U vs #16 ranked teams all time

0-5 S/U on road vs #17 ranked teams all time
3-0 S/U @ home vs #18 ranked teams all time
1-4 S/U @ home vs #19 ranked teams all time
0-3 S/U on road vs #20 ranked teams since 1940
0-5-1 S/U vs #21 ranked teams all time
0-5 ATS vs #21 ranked teams since 1993
4-0 O/U vs #21 ranked teams since 2005
0-14 S/U vs ranked Alabama since 2005
0-7 S/U vs ranked Auburn since 2013 {1-6 ATS}
0-7 S/U vs ranked Georgia since 2000
3-0 ATS @ ranked LSU since 2013
9-2 ATS vs ranked LSU since 2007
0-6 S/U vs ranked Texas A&M since 2013

Arkansas State {When Ranked}

NEVER RANKED

Arkansas State {vs Ranked}

1-23 S/U vs ranked teams since 1994

ARMY {When Ranked}

13-1 S/U @ home when ranked since 1956
21-0-2 S/U when #1 ranked all time
13-1-1 S/U when #2 ranked all time
8-1-1 S/U when #3 ranked all time {4-0 on road}
6-1 S/U when #5 ranked all time
1-4 S/U when #19 ranked all time
7-0 S/U when ranked vs #15 - #19 ranked teams all time

ARMY {vs Ranked}

0-48 S/U vs ranked teams since 1973
0-34 S/U on road vs ranked teams since 1963
0-7 O/U vs ranked teams since 2014
0-4 S/U vs #5 ranked teams since 1980
0-4 S/U vs #6 ranked teams since 1954
0-6 S/U vs #7 ranked teams since 1960
0-6 S/U vs #8 ranked teams since 1957
0-5 S/U vs #14 ranked teams all time
0-4 S/U vs #15 ranked teams since 1969
0-3 ATS vs #19 ranked teams all time
0-4 S/U vs #20 ranked teams since 1970

AUBURN {When Ranked}

5-16 S/U on road when ranked vs ranked teams since 2007
43-4 S/U @ home when ranked since 2009
17-4 S/U @ home when ranked vs ranked teams since 2004
0-5 S/U in Bowl Games vs ranked teams since 2014 {-14 ATS}
7-1 S/U @ home when #2 ranked all time
5-1-1 S/U on road when #2 ranked since 1957
10-1-2 S/U @ home when #3 ranked all time
16-1-3 S/U When #3 ranked since 1983 {4-0-1 on road}
11-0-2 S/U when #3 ranked vs ranked team all time
12-0 S/U @ home when #4 ranked all time
11-1 S/U @ home when #5 ranked since 1983
10-2 S/U @ home when #6 ranked since 1988
5-2 S/U on road when #7 ranked since 1983

Copyright © 2021 by Steve's Football Bible, LLC

Team Trends when ranked in the Polls / vs Ranked teams in the Polls

14-1 S/U @ home when #8 ranked all time	**BAYLOR {When Ranked}**
12-2 S/U @ home when #9 ranked all time	28-4 S/U @ home when ranked since 2011
13-0 S/U @ home when #10 ranked all time	3-0 S/U when #2 ranked all time
9-1 S/U @ home when #11 ranked since 1969	4-0 S/U @ home when #5 ranked all time
16-0 S/U when #12 ranked since 1970 {6-0 on road}	5-0 S/U on road when #10 ranked all time
5-0 S/U when #12 ranked vs ranked teams since 1972	6-0 S/U when #11 ranked since 1980
6-0 S/U @ home when #14 ranked since 1955	3-0 S/U on road when #12 ranked all time
1-7 O/U when #16 ranked since 2005	1-4 ATS when #13 ranked since 1986
3-7 S/U when #16 ranked vs ranked teams all time	3-0 S/U & ATS when #14 ranked all time
1-9 ATS when #17 ranked since 2000	4-0 S/U on road when #16 ranked since 1956
4-0 S/U @ home when #18 ranked since 1984	6-0 S/U when #17 ranked since 1985 {4-0 @ home}
0-4 S/U on road when #19 ranked all time	8-0 S/U when #19 ranked since 1948
7-0 S/U @ home when #19 ranked since 1980	3-0 S/U when #21 ranked all time
8-2 S/U @ home when #20 ranked all time	4-0 S/U when #23 ranked all time
0-3 S/U when #20 ranked vs ranked team all time	0-4 S/U when ranked vs #7 ranked teams all time
6-1 O/U when #21 ranked since 1995	0-4 S/U on road when ranked vs #5 ranked teams since 1976
6-0 S/U when #22 ranked all time	0-4 S/U when ranked vs #19 ranked teams all time
3-0 S/U on road when #24 ranked all time	5-0 S/U when ranked vs Iowa State all time
1-7 ATS when #25 ranked all time	5-0 S/U when ranked vs Kansas all time
0-6 O/U when #25 ranked since 1998	5-0 S/U when ranked vs Texas Tech since 2011
12-5 S/U when ranked vs ranked Alabama since 1983	5-0 O/U when ranked vs Texas Tech since 2011
6-0 S/U @ home when ranked vs Arkansas since 2010	0-5 O/U when ranked vs Texas since 2013
0-6 S/U when ranked @ Georgia since 2007	**BAYLOR {vs Ranked}**
19-1 S/U @ home when ranked vs Mississippi State all time	2-46-1 S/U on road vs ranked teams since 1992 {11 L}
2-5 O/U when ranked vs Mississippi State since 2006	0-16 S/U vs ranked teams since 2016
19-0 S/U when ranked vs Mississippi all time	1-10 S/U vs #1 ranked teams since 1955
7-0 S/U when ranked vs South Carolina all time	0-7 S/U vs #2 ranked teams since 1957
AUBURN {vs Ranked}	0-5 S/U @ home vs #3 ranked teams all time
13-5-1 ATS @ home vs ranked teams since 2013	0-5 S/U @ home vs #4 ranked teams all time
0-6 S/U vs ranked teams in Bowl Games since 2014	0-5 S/U on road vs #6 ranked teams all time
0-7 S/U on road vs #1 ranked teams since 1996	0-8 S/U on road vs #7 ranked teams all time
1-5 S/U @ home vs #2 ranked teams since 2009	0-9 S/U vs #8 ranked teams all time
0-12 S/U vs #3 ranked teams all time	0-8 S/U on road vs #10 ranked teams since 1967
1-7 ATS vs #3 ranked teams since 1972	0-7 S/U vs #11 ranked teams since 1957
1-7 S/U on road vs #5 ranked teams all time	1-5 S/U vs #12 ranked teams since 1992
0-4 S/U @ home vs #8 ranked teams since 1982	0-11 S/U vs #13 ranked teams since 1952
1-9 O/U vs #10 ranked teams since 2000	1-5 ATS vs #13 ranked teams since 1983
1-4 S/U on road vs #12 ranked teams all time	0-5 S/U on road vs #14 ranked teams since 1981
3-0 S/U @ home vs #15 ranked teams since 1953	0-6 S/U vs #15 ranked teams since 1959
5-1-1 O/U vs #17 ranked teams since 1995	0-3 S/U & ATS @ home vs #16 ranked teams since 2005
3-0 S/U @ home vs #18 ranked teams since 1977	0-4 S/U on road vs #18 ranked teams since 1946
1-5 O/U vs #19 ranked teams since 1983	0-10 S/U vs #19 ranked teams since 1945
1-7 S/U vs #20 ranked teams since 1973	0-3 S/U vs #21 ranked teams all time
4-0 S/U vs #24 ranked teams all time	1-5 S/U vs #22 ranked teams all time {0-3 on road}
3-0 S/U & ATS vs #25 ranked teams all time	1-6 S/U @ Oklahoma State all time
1-12 S/U @ ranked LSU all time {9 straight L}	0-4 S/U @ ranked TCU since 2007
3-0 S/U & ATS vs South Carolina all time	0-3 S/U @ ranked Texas Tech all time
Ball State {When Ranked}	1-14 S/U vs ranked Texas since 1990
5-2 S/U when ranked all time	0-4 S/U vs ranked West Virginia all time
Ball State {vs Ranked}	**Boise State {When Ranked}**
3-12 S/U vs ranked teams since 2005	54-4 S/U @ home when ranked all time

Copyright © 2021 by Steve's Football Bible, LLC

7-1 S/U when #3 ranked all time	0-6 S/U vs #3 ranked teams all time
0-5 O/U when #3 ranked since 2010	0-4 S/U @ home vs #4 ranked teams since 1968
4-0 S/U when #4 ranked all time	4-1 ATS vs #4 ranked teams since 2000
6-1 S/U when #5 ranked all time	0-15 S/U vs #5 & #6 ranked teams all time
9-0 S/U when #6 ranked all time	0-3 S/U on road vs #7 ranked teams all time
4-0 S/U when #8 ranked all time	1-5 S/U @ home vs #8 ranked teams all time
3-0 S/U when #11 ranked all time	3-0 ATS on road vs #9 ranked teams since 1984
6-0 S/U when #15 ranked all time	0-3 S/U @ home vs #10 ranked teams since 1974
5-0 S/U when #16 ranked all time	0-4 S/U vs #11 ranked teams since 1995
0-5 O/U when #16 ranked all time	0-4 S/U @ home vs #15 ranked teams all time {0-3 ATS}
4-1 S/U when #18 ranked all time	0-8-1 S/U vs #16 ranked teams all time
8-1 S/U when #21 ranked all time	1-6 S/U @ home vs #17 ranked teams since 1985
6-0 S/U @ home when #22 ranked all time	1-8 S/U vs #17 ranked teams since 1990
6-0 S/U when #23 ranked all time	0-4 S/U on road vs #22 ranked teams all time
6-1 S/U when #24 ranked all time	0-7 S/U vs #23 ranked teams all time
5-0 S/U when #25 ranked all time	0-10 S/U vs ranked Clemson since 2011
5-0 O/U when #25 ranked all time	1-8 S/U vs ranked Florida State all time {0-3 @ home}
0-6 S/U on road when ranked vs ranked teams all time	0-5 S/U vs ranked Syracuse since 1995
5-0 S/U when ranked vs Colorado State all time	5-0 ATS @ home vs ranked Virginia Tech since 2000
0-4 O/U when ranked vs Fresno State since 2012	**Bowling Green {When Ranked}**
8-1 S/U when ranked vs Nevada all time {3-0 @ home}	5-0 S/U @ home when ranked all time
0-4 ATS when ranked vs Nevada since 2009	**Bowling Green {vs Ranked}**
4-0 S/U when ranked vs New Mexico all time	0-10 S/U vs teams ranked in Top Ten all time
4-0 S/U when ranked vs New Mexico State all time	0-3 S/U vs ranked teams in Bowl games all time
8-1 S/U when ranked vs Utah State all time {5-0 @ home}	0-3 S/U vs #24 ranked teams all time
Boise State {vs Ranked}	0-3 S/U vs #25 ranked teams snice 2009
3-13 S/U on road vs ranked teams since 1996	0-3 S/U vs ranked Miami-Ohio all time
2-8 O/U vs ranked teams since 2014	0-5 S/U vs ranked Ohio State all time
Boston College {When Ranked}	**BYU {When Ranked}**
13-2 S/U @ home when ranked since 2005	1-8 S/U on road when ranked vs ranked teams since 1991
4-1 S/U when #4 ranked all time	26-3 S/U @ home when ranked since 2001
4-0 S/U when ranked #5 #6 #7 all time	4-0 S/U @ home when #4 ranked all time
4-0 S/U when #10 ranked all time	4-0 S/U when ranked #5 all time
1-4 S/U when #13 ranked all time	0-4 ATS when ranked #7 since 1984
6-0 S/U when #14 #15 ranked all time	1-6 ATS when #9 ranked since 1985
0-5-1 S/U @ home when #17 ranked all time	7-0 S/U When #10 ranked all time
5-1 S/U when #18 ranked since 1976	10-1 S/U when ranked #11 all time {7-0 @ home}
7-1 S/U when ranked #19 since 1983	5-0 S/U when #12 ranked all time
5-0 S/U @ home when #25 ranked all time	6-0 S/U @ home when #13 ranked all time
7-0 O/U when #25 ranked since 1999	10-1 S/U when ranked #15 all time {5-0 @ home}
0-4 S/U & ATS when ranked vs #5 ranked teams all time	4-0 S/U on road when #16 ranked all time
3-0 S/U when ranked vs #9 ranked teams all time	9-1 S/U when #17 ranked since 1977 {3-0 on road}
1-4 S/U when ranked vs Florida State all time	10-2 S/U when #18 ranked all time
6-0 S/U when ranked vs Temple all time	0-6 S/U when #19 ranked vs ranked teams all time
Boston College {vs Ranked}	5-1 S/U @ home when #20 ranked all time
6-16 O/U on road vs ranked teams since 2005	10-1 S/U when #21 ranked all time {6-0 @ home}
1-31 S/U vs ranked teams last 32 {0-15 on road}	0-5 O/U when #22 ranked all time
2-6 S/U vs ranked teams in Bowl games all time	5-0-1 S/U when #23 ranked all time
0-4 S/U vs #1 ranked teams since 2001	5-0 S/U when #24 ranked since 1996
0-3 O/U vs #3 ranked teams since 2001	4-0 S/U @ home when #25 ranked since 1994
0-9 S/U vs #2 ranked teams all time	0-3 S/U & ATS when ranked vs #7 ranked teams all time

Copyright © 2021 by Steve's Football Bible, LLC

13-1 S/U when ranked vs Utah State all time {5-0 on road}
9-1 S/U @ home when ranked vs Utah all time
1-6 ATS when ranked vs Utah since 1999

BYU {vs Ranked}

10-3 ATS on road vs ranked teams since 2010
2-11 O/U on road vs ranked teams since 2010
4-21 S/U on road vs ranked teams since 1998
2-9-1 S/U vs ranked teams in Bowl games since 1985
0-13 S/U vs #10 - #13 ranked teams all time
1-9 O/U vs #14 ranked teams since 1979
4-0 S/U vs #19 ranked teams since 1980
1-4 ATS vs #20 ranked teams all time
0-8 S/U vs #21 - #22 ranked teams all time
0-4 O/U vs #21 ranked teams since 2002
0-6 O/U vs #23 #24 ranked teams all time
4-0 O/U vs #25 ranked teams all time
6-0 ATS vs ranked Boise State all time

Buffalo {When Ranked}

1-1 S/U when ranked all time

Buffalo {vs Ranked}

1-13 S/U vs ranked teams all time

California {When Ranked}

2-10 S/U on road when ranked since 2007
22-6 S/U @ home when ranked since 2004
13-3 S/U when ranked vs Non-Conference since 2005
5-1 S/U when #2 ranked all time {3-0 on road}
6-0-1 S/U @ home when #4 ranked since 1948
9-1 S/U when #5 ranked all time {5-0 @ home - 4-0 on road}
3-0 S/U @ home when #6 ranked all time
0-5 O/U when #7 ranked since 1991
5-0 S/U @ home when #8 ranked all time
0-3 S/U on road when #9 ranked since 1951
5-0 S/U @ home when #9 ranked all time
9-1 S/U when #10 ranked all time {5-0 @ home}
5-0 S/U when #12 ranked since 2004
4-1 S/U @ home when ranked #17 all time
4-1 S/U @ home when ranked #19 all time
3-0 S/U @ home when #21 ranked all time
1-4 S/U when ranked #23 all time
1-4 O/U when ranked #23 all time
0-6 ATS when #24 ranked all time
0-3 S/U when ranked vs #1 ranked team all time
0-5 S/U when ranked vs #7 ranked team all time
8-1 S/U @ home when ranked vs Oregon all time
5-1 S/U when ranked @ Stanford all time
1-5 S/U when ranked @ UCLA since 1951
0-5 S/U when ranked @ USC since 1952
4-0 S/U when ranked vs unranked USC all time
6-0 S/U @ home when ranked vs Washington State all time
10-2-2 S/U when ranked vs unranked Washington all time
0-3 S/U when ranked vs ranked Washington since 1991

California {vs Ranked}

0-9 O/U on road vs ranked teams since 2015
1-17 S/U on road vs ranked teams since 2010
4-0 O/U vs ranked teams in Bowl games since 1992
0-11 S/U vs #1 ranked teams all time
0-9 S/U vs #2 ranked teams all time
1-11-1 S/U vs #3 ranked teams since 1954
1-16 S/U vs #4 ranked teams since 1946 {0-8 on road}
0-6 ATS vs #4 ranked teams since 1996
0-22-1 S/U vs #5 & #6 ranked teams all time
1-9 S/U vs #7 ranked teams all time
1-6 S/U vs #8 ranked teams all time {0-4 on road}
0-8 S/U vs #9 ranked teams all time
0-9 S/U vs #10 ranked teams since 1978
4-0 ATS @ home vs #13 ranked teams since 1993
0-3 S/U & ATS on road vs #15 ranked teams since 2005
1-5-1 S/U on road vs #16 ranked teams all time
1-4 S/U vs #17 ranked teams all time
4-0 ATS vs #18 ranked teams since 1992
0-3 S/U @ home vs #19 ranked teams since 1970
0-4 S/U on road vs #20 ranked teams since 1984
4-1 O/U vs #21 ranked teams all time
1-4 S/U vs #22 ranked teams all time
9-1 ATS vs ranked Arizona all time
1-7 S/U vs ranked Oregon since 2010
0-7 S/U vs ranked Stanford since 2010
1-13 S/U @ ranked UCLA since 1953
1-8 S/U @ home vs ranked USC since 1979
0-8 S/U vs ranked USC since 2004
0-8 O/U vs ranked USC since 2004
2-9 S/U @ ranked Washington since 1960

Central Florida {When Ranked}

37-5 S/U when ranked all time
5-1 S/U when ranked vs ranked teams all time
13-2 S/U on road when ranked all time
3-0 S/U when ranked #10 all time
0-3 O/U when ranked #10 all time
4-0 S/U when ranked #17 all time

Central Florida {vs Ranked}

1-19 S/U on road vs ranked teams all time
0-3 S/U vs ranked Virginia Tech all time

Central Michigan {when Ranked}

1-0 S/U when ranked all time

Central Michigan {vs Ranked}

1-13 S/U vs ranked teams all time
0-3 S/U vs ranked Michigan all time
0-4 S/U vs ranked Michigan State all time

Charlotte {When Ranked}

NEVER RANKED

Charlotte {vs Ranked}

0-3 S/U & ATS vs ranked teams all time {3-0 O/U}

Copyright © 2021 by Steve's Football Bible, LLC

Team Trends when ranked in the Polls / vs Ranked teams in the Polls

Cincinnati {When Ranked}

20-2 S/U @ home when ranked since 2008
6-0 S/U when #5 ranked all time

Cincinnati {vs Ranked}

4-16 S/U vs ranked teams since 2010
2-31 S/U vs Top 10 ranked teams all time
0-18 S/U on road vs Top 10 ranked teams all time
0-12 S/U vs #10 - #13 ranked teams all time
3-0 ATS vs #12 ranked teams all time
3-17 S/U vs #16 - #18 ranked teams all time
4-0 S/U vs #21 ranked teams since 2004
6-0 ATS vs #21 ranked teams since 1995
0-3 S/U & ATS vs #25 ranked teams all time

Clemson {When Ranked}

27-2 S/U on road when ranked since 2015
43-1 S/U @ home when ranked since 2014
19-3 S/U when ranked #1 all time
22-3 S/U when ranked #2 all time {10-0 @ home}
23-4 S/U when ranked #3 all time {8-0 on road}
6-0 ATS on road when #3 ranked since 2013
16-0 S/U when #4 ranked all time
10-1 ATS when #4 ranked since 2016
10-1 S/U when #5 ranked all time {4-0 on road}
4-0 S/U @ home when #7 ranked since 1989
9-0 S/U @ home when #8 ranked all time
6-0 ATS when #8 ranked 1991
5-0 S/U @ home when #9 ranked all time
5-0 S/U @ home when #10 ranked all time
11-1 S/U when #12 ranked since 1959
1-5 ATS when #13 ranked since 1991
6-1 S/U & ATS when #14 ranked since 1989
13-2-1 S/U when #15 ranked since 1977
10-3 ATS when #15 ranked since 1988
0-4 S/U & ATS when #16 ranked since 2007
7-0 S/U @ home when ranked #17 all time
0-4 S/U & ATS on road when #18 ranked since 1992
5-0-1 S/U @ home when ranked #18 all time
3-11 ATS when #19 ranked since 1986
6-0 S/U when #21 ranked all time
2-6 ATS when #22 ranked since 1990
4-0 S/U @ home when #23 ranked all time
4-0 S/U on road when #24 ranked all time
5-0 S/U when ranked vs #16 ranked teams all time
3-0 S/U when ranked vs #17 ranked teams all time
1-4 S/U on road when ranked vs #20 ranked teams all time
0-4 S/U when ranked vs #24 ranked teams all time
3-0 S/U when ranked vs #25 ranked teams all time
10-0 S/U when ranked vs Boston College since 2011
6-0 S/U @ home when ranked vs Georgia Tech since 2006
4-0 S/U when ranked vs Louisville all time
12-1 S/U when ranked vs NC State since 1997 {5-0 @ home}

(Clemson When Ranked continued)

3-1 S/U when ranked vs Ohio State all time
3-0 S/U when ranked vs Oklahoma all time
2-7 O/U when ranked vs Syracuse all time
28-0 S/U when ranked vs Wake Forest since 1948 {12-0 on road}

Clemson {vs Ranked}

23-5 S/U vs ranked teams since 2015
2-6 S/U vs #1 ranked teams all time
5-1 ATS vs #1 ranked teams since 1995
2-5 S/U vs #2 ranked teams all time
5-1 S/U & ATS vs #3 ranked teams since 2003
0-6 S/U on road vs #4 ranked teams all time
1-5 S/U @ home vs #5 ranked teams all time
4-1 ATS vs #5 ranked teams since 1992
0-3 S/U on road vs #6 ranked teams all time
0-3 S/U on road vs #7 ranked teams all time
4-0 O/U vs #8 ranked teams since 2001
0-4 S/U @ home vs #9 ranked teams all time
3-0 S/U & ATS vs #11 ranked teams since 2004
0-3 S/U on road vs #13 ranked teams all time
0-3 S/U @ home vs #14 ranked teams since 1980
1-5 S/U & ATS vs #14 ranked teams since 1990
1-5 S/U on road vs #15 ranked teams all time
5-1 ATS vs #17 ranked teams since 1989
1-5 O/U vs #17 ranked teams since 1989
4-1 S/U @ home vs #18 ranked teams all time
1-6 S/U on road vs #20 ranked teams all time
6-0 ATS vs #22 ranked teams all time
0-4 S/U & ATS on road vs #24 ranked teams all time
0-4 S/U & ATS vs #24 ranked teams since 2008
5-0 S/U vs #25 ranked teams all time
11-3 O/U vs Florida State since 2000
1-4 S/U @ NC State all time
0-4 S/U & ATS vs South Carolina since 2010
0-7 O/U vs South Carolina since 2000

Coastal Carolina {When Ranked}

7-1 S/U when ranked all time

Coastal Carolina {vs Ranked}

2-1 S/U vs Ranked teams all time

Colorado {When Ranked}

0-6 S/U on road when ranked vs ranked teams since 1996
23-5 S/U @ home when ranked since 1996
5-0 S/U @ home when #2 ranked all time
5-1 S/U when #4 ranked all time {2-0 on road}
1-6 ATS when #5 ranked since 1990
5-0 S/U @ home when #6 ranked all time
10-2 S/U when #7 ranked since 1993
6-0 S/U @ home when #8 ranked since 1967
0-3 S/U on road when #8 ranked since 1970
7-0 S/U @ home when #9 ranked since 1972
5-0 S/U on road when #9 ranked since 1990
7-0 S/U @ home when #10 ranked all time

Copyright © 2021 by Steve's Football Bible, LLC

Team Trends when ranked in the Polls / vs Ranked teams in the Polls

9-1 S/U @ home when #12 ranked all time	1-5 S/U vs #17 ranked teams since 1982
4-0 S/U on road when #12 ranked all time	4-0 S/U @ home vs #22 ranked teams all time
4-0 S/U @ home when #14 ranked all time	6-1 O/U vs #25 ranked teams all time
4-0 S/U on road when #15 ranked all time	0-6 S/U & ATS vs ranked Oregon since 2011
7-1 S/U @ home when #16 ranked all time	4-0 ATS vs ranked UCLA since 2002
0-3 S/U on road when #17 ranked since 1973	4-0 O/U vs ranked UCLA since 2002
5-0 S/U @ home when #19 ranked all time	0-8 S/U vs ranked USC all time
8-1 S/U when #20 ranked all time {4-0 on road}	0-4 S/U & O/U vs ranked Washington since 2000
4-1 S/U @ home when #21 ranked all time	**Colorado State {When Ranked}**
1-4 O/U when #21 ranked since 2002	0-3 O/U when ranked vs Air Force all time
4-0 S/U when #25 ranked all time	4-0 S/U when ranked vs New Mexico all time
0-4 S/U on road when ranked vs #2 ranked teams all time	**Colorado State {vs Ranked}**
0-4 ATS when ranked vs #2 ranked teams since 1995	5-0 ATS on road vs ranked teams since 2012
0-3 S/U when ranked vs #6 ranked teams since 1972	0-22 S/U vs ranked teams since 2004
0-3 S/U when ranked vs #8 ranked teams since 1991	0-25 S/U on road vs ranked teams all time
0-4 ATS when ranked vs #8 ranked teams all time	0-3 S/U vs #1 ranked teams all time
0-4 O/U when ranked vs #9 ranked teams since 1991	0-8 S/U vs #8 - #9 ranked teams all time
5-0 S/U when ranked vs #10 ranked teams all time	0-5 S/U vs #13 ranked teams all time
3-0 S/U when ranked vs #12 ranked teams all time	0-3 ATS vs #13 ranked teams since 1990
4-0 S/U when ranked vs #22 ranked teams all time	0-9 S/U vs #15 - #18 ranked teams all time
3-0 S/U when ranked vs Arizona all time	4-0 ATS vs #19 ranked teams since 1990
3-0 S/U when ranked vs Minnesota all time	0-8 S/U vs #20 ranked teams all time
0-3 S/U when ranked vs USC all time	1-3 ATS vs #20 ranked teams since 1994
0-3 O/U when ranked vs USC all time	0-6 S/U vs #24 - #25 ranked teams all time
Colorado {vs Ranked}	0-4 S/U @ home vs ranked Air Force all time
4-34 S/U vs ranked teams since 2009	0-5 S/U vs ranked ranked Boise State all time
1-31 S/U on road vs ranked teams since 2002	**Connecticut {When Ranked}**
1-10 S/U vs #1 ranked all time	0-3 S/U & ATS on road when ranked all time
1-17 S/U vs #2 ranked teams all time	**Connecticut {vs Ranked}**
1-7 ATS vs #2 ranked teams since 2002	1-8 O/U @ home vs ranked teams since 2005
1-8 S/U on road vs #3 ranked teams all time	1-22 S/U on road vs ranked teams all time
3-0 ATS @ home vs #3 ranked teams since 1995	0-4 S/U vs ranked Central Florida all time
1-7 S/U vs #4 ranked teams since 1970	0-5 S/U vs West Virginia all time
0-6 S/U @ home vs #5 ranked teams since 1978	**DUKE {When Ranked}**
0-7 S/U vs #6 ranked teams since 1972	6-0 S/U & ATS on road when ranked since 2010
1-5 S/U on road vs #7 ranked teams all time	1-8 S/U @ home when ranked since 1994
1-5 S/U @ home vs #7 ranked teams all time	1-7 ATS @ home when ranked since 2007
0-4 O/U vs #7 ranked teams since 1995	5-0-1 S/U @ home when #4 ranked all time
0-5-1 S/U vs #8 ranked teams all time	3-0 S/U @ home when ranked #7 all time
0-5 ATS vs #8 ranked teams since 1990	6-0-1 S/U when #10 ranked all time
1-10-1 S/U @ home vs #9 ranked teams all time	8-2 S/U when #11 ranked all time
0-6 S/U vs #9 ranked teams since 2000	9-2-1 S/U when #13 ranked all time
1-5 O/U @ home vs #9 ranked teams since 1991	0-3 S/U when #14 ranked all time
0-4 ATS @ home vs #9 ranked teams since 2000	6-1 S/U when #15 ranked all time {3-0 @ home}
5-1 O/U vs #10 ranked teams since 1989	0-4 S/U & ATS when #16 ranked since 1958
0-7 S/U vs #11 ranked teams since 1977	4-0 S/U on road when #20 ranked all time
0-5 O/U vs #11 ranked teams since 1996	3-0 S/U on road when #25 ranked all time
0-4 S/U vs #14 ranked teams all time	0-4 S/U when ranked vs #1 ranked teams all time
0-5 S/U vs #15 ranked teams since 2007	5-1 S/U when ranked @ North Carolina since 1943
0-5 S/U on road vs #15 ranked teams all time	6-0 S/U when ranked vs Virginia all time
1-6 S/U vs #16 ranked teams since 1976	13-1 S/U when ranked vs Wake Forest all time {6-0 on road}

Copyright © 2021 by Steve's Football Bible, LLC

Team Trends when ranked in the Polls / vs Ranked teams in the Polls

DUKE {vs Ranked}
0-6 O/U @ home vs ranked teams since 2015
3-28 S/U @ home vs ranked teams since 1996
2-60 S/U on road vs ranked teams since 1972
0-12 S/U vs #1 ranked teams all time
0-6 S/U vs #2 ranked teams all time
0-4 S/U on road vs #4 ranked teams all time
0-5 S/U vs #5 ranked teams since 1958
0-8 S/U @ home vs #6 ranked teams since 1948
0-3 S/U on road vs #7 ranked teams since 1972
0-3 O/U vs #7 ranked teams since 2005
0-4 S/U vs #8 ranked teams all time
0-4 ATS vs #9 ranked teams since 1994
0-6 S/U vs #11 ranked teams since 1981
0-5 ATS vs #11 ranked teams since 1988
0-10-1 S/U vs #12 ranked teams since 1953
1-8 S/U vs #13 ranked teams since 1947 {0-4 on road}
6-1 ATS vs #13 ranked teams since 1991
0-6 S/U vs #14 ranked teams since 1959
0-3 S/U @ home vs #16 ranked teams all time
0-4 S/U vs #17 ranked teams since 1980
0-3 ATS vs #17 ranked teams since 1986
0-6 S/U vs #18 ranked teams all time
0-7 S/U vs #19 ranked teams all time
4-0 ATS vs #19 ranked teams since 1990
0-4 S/U vs #21 ranked teams all time
0-6 S/U vs #23 ranked teams all time
1-10 S/U @ home vs ranked Georgia Tech since 1946
1-6 S/U @ ranked North Carolina all time
1-8 S/U vs ranked Virginia Tech all time {0-5 @ home}
0-5 O/U vs ranked Virginia Tech since 2010
0-6 S/U vs ranked Virginia since 1995
0-4 S/U @ ranked Virginia since 1993

East Carolina {When Ranked}
0-5 ATS on road when ranked since 2008
0-4 ATS @ home when ranked since 2007
3-0 S/U when #16 ranked all time

East Carolina {vs Ranked}
4-40 S/U on road vs ranked teams all time
2-26 S/U vs Top 10 ranked teams all time
8-1 O/U vs ranked teams since 2017
0-5 S/U vs #10 ranked teams all time
0-4 S/U vs #13 ranked teams all time
0-6 S/U vs #19 ranked teams all time
0-3 ATS vs #19 ranked teams since 1994
0-5 S/U vs ranked South Carolina all time

Eastern Michigan {When Ranked}
NEVER RANKED

Eastern Michigan {vs Ranked}
5-0 O/U on road vs ranked teams since 2013

Florida {When Ranked}
13-0 S/U @ home when #1 ranked since 1996
12-1 S/U when #1 ranked since 2009
6-1 S/U @ home when #2 ranked all time
7-1 S/U on road when #3 ranked all time
14-2 S/U @ home when #3 ranked since 1995
5-1 S/U on road when #4 ranked since 2001
13-2 S/U @ home when #4 ranked since 1992
17-0 S/U @ home when ranked #5 all time
8-0 ATS when #5 ranked since 2006
14-2 S/U @ home when #6 ranked all time
8-1 S/U @ home when #7 ranked all time
15-1 S/U when #8 ranked since 1993 {8-0 @ home}
8-0 S/U @ home when #9 ranked since 1983
4-10 O/U when #10 ranked since 2000
14-1 S/U @ home when #10 ranked all time
8-1 S/U @ home when #11 ranked all time
9-1-1 ATS when #11 ranked since 2004
1-5 ATS when #12 ranked since 2002
1-9 ATS when #13 ranked since 1986
10-2 S/U @ home when #14 ranked since 1970
5-0 S/U @ home when #15 ranked all time
5-0 S/U when #16 ranked since 2004
1-6 ATS when #17 ranked since 2003
5-0 S/U @ home when #18 ranked since 1987
9-0 ATS when #18 ranked since 1983
0-5 S/U on road when #19 ranked since 1980
10-0 S/U @ home when #19 ranked since 1959
1-6 ATS when #19 ranked since 2004
5-0 S/U @ home when #20 ranked since 1988
5-0 ATS when #20 ranked since 1992
4-0 S/U @ home when #22 ranked since 2011
7-0 S/U when #23 ranked all time
0-5 ATS when #23 ranked since 2002
0-4 O/U when #25 ranked since 2003
0-3 S/U on road when ranked vs #1 ranked team all time
0-5 S/U on road when ranked vs #3 ranked team all time
10-0 S/U when ranked vs #4 ranked team since 1990
9-0-1 ATS when ranked vs #4 ranked team since 1990
0-4 S/U on road when ranked vs #5 ranked team all time
5-2 S/U & ATS when ranked vs #8 ranked teams since 1995
7-1 O/U when ranked vs #8 ranked teams since 1990
1-5 O/U when ranked vs #10 ranked teams since 1987
3-0 S/U @ home when ranked vs #11 ranked team since 1976
0-4 S/U & ATS when ranked vs #12 ranked teams since 2003
1-7 S/U & ATS when ranked vs #14 ranked teams since 1992
0-4 O/U when ranked vs #15 ranked teams since 1994
5-1 S/U & ATS when ranked vs #21 ranked teams all time
6-1 S/U when ranked vs #23 ranked teams all time
3-0 S/U when ranked vs #25 ranked teams all time
0-6 S/U when ranked vs Alabama since 2009

Copyright © 2021 by Steve's Football Bible, LLC

3-0 S/U when ranked vs Florida Atlantic all time	28-3 S/U when #5 ranked all time {11-1 on road}
31-1 S/U when ranked vs Kentucky since 1980 {16-0 on road}	24-3 S/U when #6 rnaked since 1985 {13-1 @ home}
22-2 S/U when ranked vs South Carolina all time	8-0-1 S/U @ home when #7 ranked all time
7-0 S/U @ home when ranked vs Tennessee since 2005	17-0 S/U when #8 ranked all time
25-0 S/U when ranked vs Vanderbilt since 1989	1-6 ATS when #9 ranked since 2004
16-0 S/U @ home when ranked vs Vanderbilt since 1969	6-0 O/U when #10 ranked since 2006

Florida {vs Ranked}

0-4 S/U on road vs #1 ranked team all time	8-1 S/U @ home when #11 ranked all time
1-6 S/U @ home vs #2 ranked team all time	5-1 S/U on road when #12 ranked all time
0-7 S/U on road vs #3 ranked team since 1964	9-0 S/U when #13 ranked since 1978
10-0 S/U vs #4 ranked teams since 1990	8-2 S/U when #14 ranked all time
9-0-1 ATS vs #4 ranked teams since 1990	0-4 O/U when #14 ranked since 2002
0-6 S/U on road vs #5 ranked team since 1963	4-0-1 S/U @ home when #15 ranked all time
1-4 O/U on road vs #6 ranked teams since 1987	2-7 ATS when #16 ranked since 1989
9-3 ATS vs #8 ranked teams since 1974	4-0 S/U @ home when #17 ranked all time
8-1 O/U vs #8 ranked teams since 1990	0-3 S/U on road when #20 ranked since 1986
5-1 ATS vs #10 ranked team since 1987	3-0 S/U & ATS when #22 ranked all time
1-7 O/U vs #10 ranked teams since 1987	0-5 S/U when ranked vs #1 ranked teams since 1999
5-1 O/U vs #11 ranked teams since 1998	0-5 O/U when ranked vs #1 ranked teams since 1999
0-4 S/U & ATS vs #12 ranked teams since 2003	1-7 S/U when ranked vs #3 ranked teams since 1995
1-7 S/U & ATS vs #14 ranked teams since 1992	1-5 S/U when ranked vs #5 ranked teams all time
0-4 ATS vs #15 ranked teams since 2001	0-5 O/U when ranked vs #7 ranked teams all time
0-5 O/U vs #15 ranked teams since 1994	5-0 S/U @ home when ranked vs #10 ranked teams since 1991
0-3 S/U on road vs #17 ranked teams since 1969	6-0 S/U when ranked vs #11 ranked teams since 1989
5-1 S/U & ATS vs #21 ranked teams all time	0-3 S/U when ranked vs #12 ranked teams all time
0-4 S/U & ATS vs #22 ranked teams since 2010	4-0 O/U when ranked vs #12 ranked teams since 1985
5-0 S/U vs #23 ranked teams since 2005	6-0 S/U when ranked vs #15 ranked teams all time
4-0 S/U vs #25 ranked teams all time	3-0 S/U when ranked vs #16 ranked teams all time
7-3 S/U vs ranked teams in Bowl games since 2006	6-1 S/U when ranked vs #19 ranked teams all time {3-0 @ home}
8-2 O/U vs ranked teams in Bowl games since 2006	4-0 S/U & ATS when ranked vs #25 ranked all time
0-7 S/U vs ranked Alabama since 2009	8-1 S/U when ranked vs Boston College all time
1-6 S/U @ home vs ranked Alabama all time	1-5 S/U when ranked @ Clemson since 2003
5-0 O/U vs ranked Alabama since 2011	3-10 O/U when ranked vs Florida since 2000
0-4 S/U vs ranked Florida State since 2013	6-0 S/U @ home when ranked vs Louisville all time

Florida Atlantic {When Ranked}

NEVER RANKED

	6-0 S/U when ranked vs Miami since 2010
	2-11 O/U when ranked vs Miami since 2002

Florida Atlantic {vs Ranked}

	2-11 ATS when ranked vs NC State since 2001
0-23 S/U vs ranked teams all time	6-1 S/U when ranked @ North Carolina all time

Florida Int'l {When Ranked}

	9-0 S/U when ranked vs Syracuse all time
NEVER RANKED	

Florida State {vs Ranked}

	0-8 S/U on road vs ranked teams since 2017

Florida International {vs Ranked}

0-10 S/U vs ranked teams all time	0-6 S/U vs #1 ranked teams since 1999
	0-6 O/U vs #1 ranked teams since 1999

Florida State {When Ranked}

19-3 S/U on road when ranked since 2012	1-5-1 S/U on road vs #2 ranked teams all time
25-0 S/U @ home when #1 ranked since 1993	0-4 S/U vs #3 ranked teams since 2015
1-8 ATS when #1 ranked since 2014	5-1 O/U vs #3 ranked teams since 2006
13-0 S/U @ home when #2 ranked all time	0-4 S/U vs #4 ranked teams since 2003
8-2 O/U when #2 ranked since 2013	1-7 S/U on road vs #5 ranked teams all time
18-0 S/U @ home when #3 ranked all time	1-4 O/U on road vs #5 ranked teams since 1990
8-0 S/U @ home when #4 ranked since 1987	5-1 S/U vs #7 ranked teams all time
0-6 ATS on road when #4 ranked since 1994	0-5 O/U vs #7 ranked teams since 1989
	3-0 S/U & ATS vs #9 ranked teams since 1992

Copyright © 2021 by Steve's Football Bible, LLC

Team Trends when ranked in the Polls / vs Ranked teams in the Polls

5-0 S/U @ home vs #10 ranked teams since 1991	7-0 S/U @ home when #12 ranked since 1999
6-0 O/U @ home vs #10 ranked teams since 1989	11-1 S/U @ home when #13 ranked all time
6-1 S/U vs #11 ranked teams since 1989	10-0 S/U when #13 ranked since 2011
0-7 S/U on road vs #12 ranked teams all time	10-0 S/U on road when #14 ranked all time
6-0 O/U vs #12 ranked teams since 1983	0-5 O/U on road when #15 ranked since 1983
0-3 S/U on road vs #14 ranked teams all time	8-0 S/U @ home when #15 ranked all time
6-0 S/U vs #15 ranked teams since 1988	6-0 S/U @ home when #18 ranked since 1985
4-0 S/U vs #16 ranked teams since 1992	6-0 S/U @ home when ranked #20 all time
3-0 S/U on road vs #16 ranked teams since 1982	5-0 S/U when #21 ranked since 1997
5-0 ATS vs #17 ranked teams since 1989	6-0 S/U when #24 ranked all time
4-1 S/U & ATS vs #25 ranked teams all time	4-1 ATS when ranked vs #2 ranked teams since 1984
3-0 S/U @ ranked Boston College all time	0-3 S/U & ATS when ranked vs #5 ranked teams since 1999
0-5 S/U vs ranked Clemson since 2015	2-6 S/U when ranked vs #8 ranked teams since 1982
15-3 O/U vs ranked Clemson since 1988	6-1 O/U when ranked vs #8 ranked teams since 1987
6-2 ATS vs ranked Miami since 2005	0-4 O/U when ranked vs #17 ranked teams since 1987
3-8 O/U vs ranked Miami since 2002	4-0 ATS when ranked vs #20 ranked teams since 1999
4-0 S/U vs ranked North Carolina all time	4-0 S/U when ranked vs #22 ranked teams since 2002
4-0 S/U & ATS vs ranked NC State since 1992	0-5 O/U when ranked vs #22 ranked teams since 2002
1-5 ATS vs ranked Notre Dame all time	1-6 O/U when ranked vs #24 ranked teams all time
Fresno State {When Ranked}	10-0 S/U when ranked vs Arkansas since 1987
5-0 S/U @ home when ranked since 2013	7-0 S/U when ranked @ Georgia Tech since 2001
Fresno State {vs Ranked}	10-0 ATS when ranked @ Georgia Tech since 1991
2-23 S/U vs ranked teams since 2005	20-0 S/U when ranked vs Kentucky since 1991 {10-0 on road}
3-37 S/U on road vs ranked teams all time	15-0 S/U @ home when ranked vs Kentucky all time
0-5 S/U vs #1 ranked teams all time	5-0 S/U when ranked @ Missouri all time
3-0 ATS vs #1 ranked teams since 2003	9-1 S/U when ranked @ Vanderbilt since 1997
1-5 S/U vs #10 ranked teams all time	**Georgia {vs Ranked}**
3-0 ATS vs #13 ranked teams all time	0-5 S/U vs #1 ranked teams since 1996
0-12 S/U vs #14 - #17 ranked teams all time	5-0 O/U vs #2 ranked teams since 1990
0-3 S/U vs #21 ranked teams all time	0-6 S/U @ home vs #3 ranked teams since 1952
3-0 ATS vs #23 ranked teams since 2001	1-8 S/U vs #4 ranked teams all time
2-9 S/U vs Boise State all time	1-5 S/U vs #5 ranked teams since 1970
0-4 S/U vs Oregon all time	3-0 O/U vs #5 ranked teams since 2006
0-3 S/U vs UCLA all time	9-4 O/U vs #6 ranked teams since 1991
3-0 ATS vs UCLA all time	7-2 O/U vs #8 ranked teams since 1987
0-6 S/U vs San Diego State all time	0-4-1 S/U on road vs #9 ranked teams all time
Georgia {When Ranked}	5-1 ATS vs #9 ranked teams since 1993
22-1 S/U @ home when ranked since 2017	0-6 S/U on road vs #10 ranked teams all time
4-0 S/U @ home when #1 ranked all time	0-3 S/U & ATS @ home vs #12 ranked teams all time
5-0 S/U @ home when #2 ranked all time	4-0 O/U vs #12 ranked teams since 2004
6-1 S/U on road when #3 ranked since 1982	0-3 S/U on road vs #14 ranked teams all time
10-1 S/U @ home when #4 ranked all time	0-4 O/U vs #17 ranked teams since 1987
1-9-1 O/U when #4 ranked since 1983	5-0 ATS vs #20 ranked teams since 1995
13-0 S/U @ home when #5 ranked all time	4-0 S/U vs #22 ranked teams since 2002
11-0 S/U @ home when #6 ranked all time	0-5 O/U vs #22 ranked teams since 2002
20-2 S/U when ranked #6 since 1971	1-6 O/U vs #24 ranked teams since 2001
11-1 S/U when #7 ranked since 2005 {4-0 on road}	4-0 O/U @ Auburn since 2006
2-7 ATS when #8 ranked since 2004	4-20 S/U vs ranked Florida since 1990
14-2 S/U when #9 ranked since 1966 {5-0 on road}	4-0 S/U & ATS @ ranked Georgia Tech since 2001
12-1 S/U when #10 ranked since 2002 {5-0 on road}	0-4 O/U @ ranked Georgia Tech since 2001
9-1 S/U @ home when #11 ranked since 1971	1-5 S/U @ ranked South Carolina all time

Copyright © 2021 by Steve's Football Bible, LLC

Team Trends when ranked in the Polls / vs Ranked teams in the Polls

3-0 S/U @ ranked Tennessee since 2001	1-4 S/U on road vs #11 ranked teams all time
4-0 O/U @ ranked Tennessee since 1999	1-4 S/U on road vs #12 ranked teams since 1948
Georgia South {When Ranked}	0-4 O/U vs #13 ranked teams since 2007
NEVER RANKED	0-3 S/U on road vs #13 ranked teams all time
Georgia Southern {vs Ranked}	0-7 S/U @ home vs #14 ranked teams all time
2-4 S/U vs ranked teams all time	0-6 S/U vs #14 ranked teams since 1993
Georgia State {When Ranked}	1-10 S/U vs #15 ranked teams since 1960
NEVER RANKED	8-1 S/U @ home vs #17 ranked teams since 1955
Georgia State {vs Ranked}	8-1 ATS vs #17 ranked teams since 1986
0-7 S/U vs ranked teams all time	0-5 O/U vs #19 ranked teams since 2000
Georgia Tech {When Ranked}	0-4 S/U on road vs #20 ranked teams since 1988
10-2 S/U when #2 ranked all time	1-4 S/U vs #25 ranked teams all time
12-1-2 S/U when #3 ranked all time {9-0-1 @ home}	0-6 S/U @ ranked Clemson since 2006
9-2 S/U when ranked #4 all time	0-6 S/U @ home vs ranked Georgia since 2001
14-2 S/U when #6 ranked all time	0-8 ATS @ home vs ranked Georgia since 1999
6-1 S/U @ home when #8 ranked all time	0-4 S/U vs ranked Miami since 2009
4-0-1 S/U on road when #8 ranked all time	3-0 ATS @ home vs ranked North Carolina since 1997
10-3 S/U when ranked #9 all time	**Hawaii {When Ranked}**
4-0-1 S/U on road when #11 ranked all time	5-0 S/U on road when ranked since 2007
7-1-1 S/U when #11 ranked since 1951	8-0 S/U @ home when ranked since 2007
0-4 ATS when #14 ranked since 2008	4-0 S/U when ranked #16 ranked all time
0-4 S/U on road when #15 ranked all time	0-4 ATS when ranked #16 ranked all time
1-6 ATS when #15 ranked since 2000	**Hawaii {vs Ranked}**
11-2 S/U when #16 ranked all time	1-20 S/U on road vs ranked teams all time
4-0 S/U on road when #17 ranked since 1991	0-4 S/U vs #1 ranked teams all time
6-0 S/U when #18 ranked since 1984	0-3 S/U & ATS vs #5 ranked teams all time
3-0 S/U @ home when #19 ranked all time	0-4 S/U vs #13 ranked teams all time
0-3 S/U on road when #19 ranked since 1960	0-10 S/U vs #14 - #17 ranked teams all time
0-4 S/U & ATS when #20 ranked since 2008	1-9 S/U vs #24 - #25 ranked teams all time
3-0 S/U @ home when #23 ranked all time	**Houston {When Ranked}**
0-3 S/U when ranked vs #3 ranked teams all time	29-1 S/U @ home when ranked since 1988
5-1 S/U when ranked vs #9 ranked teams all time {3-0 @ home}	10-1 S/U when #6 ranked all time {6-0 @ home}
0-5 O/U when ranked vs #19 ranked teams since 2000	5-1 S/U when #11 ranked since 1978
9-1 S/U when ranked @ Duke since 1946	0-3 S/U on road when #12 ranked all time
0-4 S/U @ home when ranked vs Georgia since 2001	5-0 S/U @ home when #12 ranked all time
1-7 O/U when ranked vs Georgia since 2000	4-0 S/U @ home when #13 ranked all time
4-0 S/U @ home when ranked vs North Carolina all time	4-0 S/U on road when #14 ranked since 1973
1-5 S/U when ranked @ Virginia since 1992	10-1 S/U @ home when #14 ranked since 1989
Georgia Tech {vs Ranked}	5-0 S/U when ranked #16 all time
2-14 S/U on road vs ranked teams since 2009	8-1 S/U when #17 ranked all time {4-0 @ home}
1-8 S/U on road vs #1 ranked teams all time	7-1 S/U @ home when #18 ranked all time
1-8-1 S/U vs #2 ranked teams all time	11-1 S/U when ranked #19 all time {6-0 on road}
1-10 S/U vs #3 ranked teams all time {0-5 at home}	3-0 O/U when #21 ranked since 2011
1-11 S/U vs #4 ranked teams all time	3-0 S/U when #24 ranked all time
0-7 S/U @ home vs #5 ranked teams since 1971	3-0 S/U when ranked vs #20 ranked teams all time
1-4 S/U @ home vs #6 ranked teams since 1959	7-1 S/U when ranked vs Memphis all time {4-0 @ home}
0-6 S/U on road vs #7 ranked teams all time	10-0 S/U when ranked vs Rice all time
1-5 S/U @ home vs #7 ranked teams since 1971	4-0 S/U when ranked vs SMU since 1979
0-5 S/U on road vs #8 ranked teams since 1970	5-0 S/U when ranked vs Texas Tech since 1979
1-7 S/U vs #10 ranked teams since 1968	4-0 S/U when ranked vs Tulane all time
1-5 S/U @ home vs #10 ranked teams all time	3-0 S/U @ home when ranked vs Tulsa all time

Copyright © 2021 by Steve's Football Bible, LLC

Team Trends when ranked in the Polls / vs Ranked teams in the Polls

Houston {vs Ranked}
7-2 ATS on road vs ranked teams since 2008
1-6 O/U on road vs ranked teams since 2012
3-33 S/U on road vs ranked teams since 1985
0-3 S/U vs #1 ranked teams all time
0-4 S/U vs #2 ranked teams all time
4-0 ATS vs #3 ranked teams since 1984
0-6 S/U vs #4 ranked teams since 1992
0-5 S/U vs #8 ranked teams all time
0-3 S/U vs #9 ranked teams since 1958
0-10-1 S/U vs #13 ranked teams all time
1-8 S/U vs #14 ranked teams all time {0-4 on road}
0-4 S/U vs #15 ranked teams since 1987
0-3 S/U on road vs #15 ranked teams since 1974
0-3 S/U on road vs #16 ranked teams all time
0-3 S/U vs #19 ranked teams since 1982
0-4 S/U on road vs #20 ranked teams since 1980
0-3 S/U & ATS vs #22 ranked teams all time
1-5 S/U vs ranked SMU all time

Illinois {When Ranked}
2-17 ATS @ home when ranked since 1990
3-0 S/U on road when #4 ranked all time
7-2 S/U when #5 ranked all time
9-1 S/U when #8 ranked all time {4-0 on road}
3-0 S/U when #9 ranked all time
4-1 S/U on road when #11 ranked all time
0-4 S/U when #17 ranked all time
5-0 S/U when #19 ranked since 1983
4-0 S/U @ home when #20 ranked all time
4-0 S/U when #21 ranked all time
0-3 S/U on road when #22 ranked since 2000
4-0 O/U when #22 ranked since 2000
3-0 S/U when #24 ranked all time
0-3 S/U when #25 ranked all time
3-0 S/U when ranked vs #20 ranked teams all time
0-4 S/U on road when ranked vs #8 ranked teams all time
9-1 S/U when ranked vs Northwestern since 1951 {4-0 @ home}
4-0 S/U when ranked vs Wisconsin since 1963

Illinois {vs Ranked}
1-25 S/U vs ranked teams since 2011
2-26 S/U on road vs ranked teams since 2003
4-28 S/U @ home vs ranked teams since 2002
1-9 S/U vs #1 ranked teams since 1966
0-11 S/U vs #2 ranked teams since 1940
0-7-1 S/U vs #3 ranked teams since 1971
1-10-1 S/U vs #4 ranked teams since 1964
5-0 ATS vs #5 ranked teams since 1985
1-7 S/U vs #6 ranked teams since 1985
2-6 ATS vs #6 ranked since 1985
1-8 S/U vs #7 ranked teams all time
1-9-1 S/U vs #8 ranked teams since 1959

(Illinois vs Ranked continued)
0-9-1 S/U on road vs #8 ranked teams since 1952
1-4 S/U on road vs #9 ranked all time
0-10 S/U vs #10 ranked since 1954
2-10-1 S/U vs #11 ranked teams all time
0-6 S/U on road vs #11 ranked teams all time
0-7 S/U vs #12 ranked teams all time
1-8 S/U on road vs #13 ranked teams all time
0-6 S/U vs #13 ranked teams since 1995
0-5 S/U @ home vs #13 ranked teams since 1969
0-7-1 S/U vs #14 ranked teams all time
0-10 S/U vs #15 ranked teams since 1971
5-0 ATS vs #15 ranked since 1993
0-4 S/U vs #17 ranked since 2001
0-5 ATS vs #17 ranked since 1995
0-6 S/U vs #18 ranked teams all time
0-7 S/U vs #19 ranked since 1990
4-0 S/U @ home vs #20 ranked teams all time
6-1 ATS vs #20 ranked since 1988
1-4 S/U vs #22 ranked teams all time
0-5 S/U vs #23 ranked teams all time {1-4 ATS}
4-1 O/U vs #23 ranked teams all time
0-9 S/U vs ranked Iowa since 1990
0-5 S/U @ ranked Iowa since 1985
0-4 S/U vs ranked Nebraska all time
1-13 S/U vs ranked Penn State all time {0-5 on road}
4-16 S/U vs ranked Wisconsin since 1952

Indiana {When Ranked}
3-10 S/U on road when ranked since 1987
8-0-1 S/U @ home when ranked since 1987
5-1 S/U when ranked #6 #7 #8 all time
0-4 S/U when #19 ranked since 1950
2-10 S/U on road when ranked vs ranked teams all time
4-0 S/U when ranked vs Purdue since 1942

Indiana {vs Ranked}
2-25 S/U on road vs ranked teams since 2005
14-122-1 S/U on road vs ranked teams all time
1-81 S/U vs Top #1 - #7 ranked teams all time
0-57 S/U on road vs Top #1 - #7 ranked teams all time
3-20 S/U @ home vs ranked teams since 2006
9-1 O/U @ home vs ranked teams last 10
0-16 S/U vs #1 ranked teams all time
0-15 S/U vs #2 ranked teams all time
1-9 S/U vs #3 ranked teams all time
0-30 S/U vs #4 #5 #6 ranked teams all time
0-11 S/U vs #7 ranked since 1953
1-8 S/U vs #8 ranked since 1976
0-10 S/U vs #10 ranked teams all time
0-4 ATS vs #10 ranked since 1991
0-10 S/U vs #12 ranked since 1950
1-11 S/U vs #13 ranked teams all time
1-9 S/U vs #15 ranked since 1948

Copyright © 2021 by Steve's Football Bible, LLC

Team Trends when ranked in the Polls / vs Ranked teams in the Polls

0-7 S/U vs #16 ranked teams since 1957	10-0 S/U when ranked vs Illinois since 1990
1-5 ATS vs #16 ranked teams since 1984	13-1 S/U when ranked vs Indiana since 1957 {8-0 @ home}
1-11 S/U vs #17 ranked teams since 1969	12-1 S/U when ranked vs Iowa State all time {6-0 @ home}
2-10 S/U vs #18 ranked teams since 1957	0-5 O/U when ranked vs Iowa State since 2005
0-7 S/U vs #19 ranked teams since 1978	8-0 S/U @ home when ranked vs Minnesota since 1983
5-1 O/U vs #22 ranked teams since 1993	10-0 S/U @ home when ranked vs Purdue all time
6-0 ATS vs #23 ranked teams since 1995	**Iowa {vs Ranked}**
0-7 S/U vs #24 & #25 teams all time	9-3 O/U on road vs ranked teams since 2009
1-6 ATS vs #24 & #25 teams all time	0-10-1 S/U vs #1 ranked teams all time
0-8 S/U @ ranked Iowa all time	3-14 S/U vs #2 ranked teams all time {0-6 on road}
1-13 S/U vs ranked Iowa since 1957	0-6 S/U on road vs #3 ranked teams all time
4-21 S/U vs ranked Michigan State all time	1-10 S/U vs #4 ranked teams all time
1-4 ATS @ ranked Michigan State since 2003	0-4 O/U vs #5 ranked teams since 2003
3-42 S/U vs ranked Michigan all time	1-7 S/U @ home vs #5 ranked teams all time
6-0-1 ATS vs ranked Michigan since 2009	0-8 S/U on road vs #6 ranked teams since 1957
3-0 S/U @ home vs ranked Minnesota since 1977	1-11 S/U vs #7 ranked teams since 1955 {0-4 on road}
1-43 S/U vs ranked Ohio State since 1952	1-11 S/U vs #8 ranked teams since 1978 {0-6 @ home}
7-2 ATS vs ranked Ohio State since 2012	0-5 O/U on road vs #8 ranked teams since 1985
1-12 S/U vs ranked Penn State all time	3-0 S/U & ATS vs #9 ranked teams since 2003
0-3 O/U @ ranked Penn State since 2008	0-3 S/U on road vs #9 ranked teams since 1963
0-8 S/U vs ranked Purdue since 1968	0-4 S/U @ home vs #10 ranked teams since 1976
0-3 O/U vs ranked Purdue since 1999	3-0 S/U & ATS vs #12 ranked teams since 2000
Iowa {When Ranked}	4-1 S/U @ home vs #13 ranked teams all time
5-14 S/U when ranked vs ranked teams since 1994	3-14 S/U vs #14 ranked teams all time
5-0 S/U @ home when #1 ranked all time	0-5 S/U on road vs #16 ranked teams all time
6-1 S/U when #2 ranked all time {3-0 on road}	1-6 S/U on road vs #17 ranked teams all time
4-0-1 S/U on road when #3 ranked all time	4-0 O/U vs #17 ranked teams since 1998
3-0 S/U @ home when #3 ranked all time	1-6 S/U vs #18 ranked teams since 1999
4-0 S/U when #6 ranked since 2002	0-5 O/U vs #19 ranked teams since 2005
0-4 S/U on road when #8 ranked since 1986	1-3 O/U vs #22 ranked teams all time
0-4 ATS when #8 ranked since 1997	3-0 S/U vs ranked Illinois since 1990
5-0 S/U @ home when #9 ranked since 1991	0-6 S/U @ ranked Nebraska all time
1-5 S/U on road when #9 ranked since 1954	7-3 ATS vs ranked Penn State since 1996
6-0 S/U @ home when #10 ranked all time	**Iowa State {When Ranked}**
8-1 S/U when #11 ranked all time {4-0 on road}	3-11-1 S/U on road when ranked since 1978
5-0 S/U @ home when #12 ranked all time	2-6 ATS on road when ranked since 2002
7-0 S/U @ home when #15 ranked all time	14-3 S/U @ home when ranked since 1981
6-0 S/U @ home when #16 ranked since 1997	4-15-2 S/U when ranked vs ranked teams all time
5-1 S/U @ home when #17 ranked since 1997	0-5 S/U when ranked vs Oklahoma State all time
5-0 S/U on road when #17 ranked all time	0-4-1 S/U when ranked vs Oklahoma all time
8-1 S/U when #17 ranked since 1991	**Iowa State {vs Ranked}**
7-2-2 ATS when #19 ranked since 1997	0-11 S/U vs #1 ranked teams all time
10-1 S/U @ home when #19 ranked since 1960	1-8 S/U vs #2 ranked teams all time {0-6 on road}
5-1 ATS when #20 ranked since 1996	1-17-1 S/U vs #3 ranked teams all time
0-4 O/U when #21 ranked since 1996	2-7 ATS vs #3 ranked teams since 1984
4-0 S/U @ home when #22 ranked all time	1-12 S/U vs #4 ranked teams all time
3-0 S/U on road when #23 ranked all time	0-5 ATS on road vs #4 ranked teams since 1993
0-4 S/U when ranked vs #6 ranked teams since 1957	0-9-1 S/U vs #5 ranked teams all time
1-5 S/U when ranked vs #8 ranked teams since 1985	0-6 S/U on road vs #6 ranked teams all time
0-4 O/U when ranked vs #8 ranked teams since 2002	0-6 S/U on road vs #7 ranked teams since 1979
4-0 S/U when ranked vs #9 ranked teams all time	4-0 ATS on road vs #7 ranked teams since 1994

Copyright © 2021 by Steve's Football Bible, LLC

Team Trends when ranked in the Polls / vs Ranked teams in the Polls

1-5 S/U @ home vs #9 ranked teams all time	0-5 ATS vs #4 ranked teams since 1986
4-0 ATS vs #9 ranked teams since 1995	1-6 S/U @ home vs #5 ranked teams all time
0-10 S/U vs #10 ranked teams all time	0-3 S/U on road vs #5 ranked teams all time
0-4 ATS vs #10 ranked teams since 1995	0-17 S/U vs #6 ranked teams since 1952
0-16 S/U vs #11 #12 ranked teams all time	4-1 O/U vs #6 ranked teams since 2008
1-8 S/U vs #13 ranked teams all time	0-7 S/U vs #7 ranked teams all time
1-18 S/U vs #14 #15 ranked teams all time	0-4 ATS vs #7 ranked teams since 1992
1-10 S/U vs #16 ranked teams all time	4-0 O/U vs #7 ranked teams since 1992
0-8 S/U vs #17 ranked teams all time	2-9 S/U vs #8 ranked teams all time
0-4 ATS vs #17 ranked teams since 2002	0-10 S/U vs #9 ranked teams since 1973
1-8 S/U vs #19 ranked teams all time	1-6 S/U vs #10 ranked teams all time
0-6 S/U vs #21 ranked teams all time	0-5 S/U on road vs #11 ranked teams all time
3-0 ATS on road vs #22 ranked teams since 2007	0-3 ATS on road vs #11 ranked teams since 1997
0-3 S/U & ATS vs #23 ranked teams all time	0-7 S/U vs #12 ranked teams all time
0-5 S/U vs ranked Baylor all time	0-3 ATS vs #12 ranked teams since 1984
3-0 ATS vs ranked Baylor since 2014	0-8 S/U vs #13 ranked teams since 1971
4-1 O/U vs ranked Baylor all time	3-0 ATS vs #13 ranked teams since 1999
1-12 S/U vs ranked Iowa all time {0-6 S/U @ Iowa}	0-10 S/U vs #14 ranked teams all time
0-5 O/U vs ranked Iowa since 2005	4-0 O/U vs #14 ranked teams since 2002
0-9 S/U vs ranked Kansas all time	0-11 S/U vs #16 ranked teams since 1972
0-11 S/U vs ranked Kansas State since 1994	1-4 S/U vs #17 ranked teams since 1974
0-6 S/U @ ranked Kansas State all time	0-5 S/U on road vs #18 ranked teams all time
4-52-1 S/U vs ranked Oklahoma all time	4-0 O/U vs #18 ranked teams since 1999
8-2 O/U vs ranked Oklahoma since 2012	0-3 S/U & ATS vs #19 ranked teams since 1994
1-7 S/U @ ranked Oklahoma State all time	0-7 S/U vs #20 #21 ranked teams all time
4-0 O/U @ home vs ranked Oklahoma State since 2011	0-4 S/U vs #25 ranked teams since 1998
3-9 S/U vs ranked Texas all time {1-4 @ home}	0-4 S/U & ATS vs ranked Baylor since 2013

Kansas {When Ranked}	1-12 S/U & ATS vs ranked Kansas State all time
12-2 S/U @ home when ranked since 1996	2-29 S/U vs ranked Oklahoma since 1978
4-0 S/U when #7 ranked since 1960	0-19 S/U @ home vs ranked Oklahoma since 1952
4-0-1 S/U when #9 ranked all time	0-12 S/U vs ranked ranked Oklahoma State all time
0-3 S/U on road when #18 ranked all time	1-9-1 ATS vs ranked ranked Oklahoma State all time
4-0 S/U @ home when #19 ranked since 1952	0-3 S/U @ ranked TCU all time
3-0 S/U on road when #24 ranked all time	0-4 S/U vs ranked TCU since 2012
3-0 S/U when #25 ranked all time	0-8 S/U vs ranked Texas all time {2-6 ATS}

	Kansas State {When Ranked}
0-4 S/U when ranked vs #3 ranked teams all time	19-2 S/U @ home when ranked since 2011
0-4 S/U when ranked vs #6 ranked teams all time	5-0 O/U when #2 ranked all time
0-7 S/U @ home when ranked vs ranked teams since 1974	4-0 S/U @ home when #4 ranked all time
9-0 S/U when ranked vs Iowa State all time	4-0 S/U & ATS on road when #4 ranked all time
5-1 S/U when ranked vs Kansas State all time	3-0 S/U @ home when #5 ranked all time
6-1 S/U when ranked vs Oklahoma State all time {3-0 @ home}	5-1 S/U when #6 ranked all time

Kansas {vs Ranked}	0-4 O/U when #6 ranked since 1999
0-39 S/U vs ranked teams since 2010	7-0 S/U @ home when #7 ranked since 2000
1-40 S/U on road vs ranked teams since 1995	5-0 S/U & ATS @ home when #9 ranked all time
0-18 S/U @ home vs ranked teams since 2010	4-0 S/U @ home when #11 ranked all time
0-12 S/U vs #1 ranked teams since 1960	3-0 S/U on road when #12 ranked since 2001
0-9 S/U @ home vs #1 ranked teams all time	3-0 S/U on road when #14 ranked all time
0-7 S/U & ATS vs #2 ranked teams since 1985	4-0 S/U when #15 ranked since 1994
4-0 O/U vs #2 ranked teams since 2001	5-0 S/U when #19 ranked since 1995
0-13-1 S/U vs #3 ranked teams all time	10-2 S/U when #20 ranked since 1993 {3-1 on road}
1-9 S/U vs #4 ranked teams all time	

Copyright © 2021 by Steve's Football Bible, LLC

Team Trends when ranked in the Polls / vs Ranked teams in the Polls

6-0 S/U when #21 ranked all time	4-0 O/U vs ranked Texas Tech all time

3-0 S/U @ home when #25 ranked all time	**Kent State {When Ranked}**
0-4 S/U when ranked vs #2 ranked teams all time	0-2 S/U when ranked vs ranked teams all time
0-3 S/U when ranked vs #3 ranked teams all time	**Kent State {vs Ranked}**
0-3 S/U when ranked vs #5 ranked teams all time	2-30 S/U vs ranked teams all time
0-3 O/U when ranked vs #5 ranked teams all time	0-3 S/U vs ranked Toledo all time
0-8 S/U when ranked vs #7 #8 #9 ranked teams all time	**Kentucky {When Ranked}**
0-7 ATS when ranked vs #7 #8 #9 ranked teams all time	24-8 S/U @ home when ranked since 1950
3-0 S/U when ranked vs #25 ranked teams all time	3-0 S/U when #4 ranked all time
11-0 S/U when ranked vs Iowa State since 1994	3-0 S/U @ home when #6 ranked all time
13-1 S/U when ranked vs Kansas all time {7-0 on road}	6-0 S/U when #7 ranked since 1951
11-0 S/U when ranked vs Missouri since 1993	3-0 S/U when #10 ranked all time
0-4 S/U when ranked @ Oklahoma State since 2003	5-0 S/U @ home when #13 ranked since 1949
5-1 O/U when ranked vs Oklahoma State since 2003	7-1 S/U when #14 ranked all time {3-0 on road}
6-1 S/U when ranked vs Texas Tech all time {4-0 @ home}	0-3 O/U when #14 ranked since 2007
7-1 ATS when ranked vs Texas all time {4-0 on road}	4-0-1 S/U when #17 ranked since 1977
Kansas State {vs Ranked}	1-4 S/U when ranked vs #11 ranked teams all time
1-12 S/U @ home vs ranked teams since 2013	0-7 S/U when ranked vs #6 #8 #9 ranked teams all time
0-7 S/U vs ranked teams in Bowl games since 2001 {0-7 ATS}	6-1 S/U when ranked vs Vanderbilt all time
1-9 S/U vs #1 ranked teams all time	**Kentucky {vs Ranked}**
0-19 S/U vs #2 ranked teams all time	5-63 S/U on road vs ranked teams since 1978
4-0 ATS vs #2 ranked teams since 2001	2-14 S/U vs #1 ranked teams since 1951
1-8 S/U vs #3 ranked teams all time	0-6 S/U vs #2 ranked teams all time
0-5 S/U on road vs #4 ranked teams all time {0-3 ATS}	0-9 S/U vs #3 ranked teams all time
1-7 S/U vs #5 ranked teams all time	0-4 ATS vs #3 ranked teams since 1999
2-16 S/U vs #6 ranked teams all time	1-10 S/U vs #4 ranked teams all time
1-13 S/U vs #7 ranked teams all time	0-21 S/U vs #5 #6 ranked teams all time
1-7 ATS vs #7 ranked teams since 1984	1-6 ATS vs #6 ranked teams since 1987
5-1 O/U vs #7 ranked teams since 1999	4-0 O/U @ home vs #6 ranked teams since 1990
1-11 S/U vs #8 ranked teams all time	0-15 S/U vs #7 ranked teams since 1972
0-6 ATS vs #8 ranked teams since 1990	0-4 ATS @ home vs #7 ranked teams since 1993
0-13 S/U vs #9 ranked teams all time	0-8 S/U vs #8 ranked teams since 1970
1-7 S/U vs #10 ranked teams all time	0-7 S/U on road vs #9 ranked teams all time
0-4 S/U vs #12 ranked teams all time	0-3 ATS on road vs #9 ranked teams since 1994
1-8 S/U vs #13 ranked teams all time	1-4 ATS vs #11 ranked teams since 1989
4-0 ATS vs #15 ranked teams since 1999	0-9 S/U vs #12 ranked teams since 1970
0-4-1 S/U vs #16 ranked teams all time	4-0 ATS vs #12 ranked teams since 1987
1-6 S/U vs #18 ranked teams all time	1-9 S/U vs #13 ranked teams since 1976
1-6 S/U vs #19 ranked teams all time	0-8 S/U on road vs #14 ranked teams since 1959
0-7 S/U vs #20 ranked teams all time	0-4 ATS on road vs #14 ranked teams since 1999
0-3 S/U vs #22 ranked teams all time	0-8 S/U vs #16 ranked teams since 1978
3-0 O/U vs #22 ranked teams all time	3-0 ATS on road vs #17 ranked teams since 1996
6-0 ATS vs #25 ranked teams since 1994	1-6 S/U vs #18 ranked teams all time
0-3 S/U vs ranked Baylor since 2013	4-1 ATS vs #19 ranked teams since 1976
1-5 S/U vs ranked Kansas all time	0-4 S/U vs #24 ranked teams all time
4-24 S/U @ home vs ranked Oklahoma all time	5-1 ATS vs #25 ranked teams all time
6-0 O/U @ home vs ranked Oklahoma since 2008	0-16 S/U @ home vs ranked Florida since 1980
1-12 S/U vs ranked Oklahoma State all time	1-32 S/U vs ranked Georgia since 1967
4-1 O/U vs ranked Oklahoma State since 2013	0-16 S/U @ ranked Georgia all time
0-3 S/U vs ranked TCU all time	4-1 ATS vs ranked LSU since 1998
5-0 ATS vs ranked Texas since 2003	2-11 S/U @ home vs ranked LSU all time

Copyright © 2021 by Steve's Football Bible, LLC

Team Trends when ranked in the Polls / vs Ranked teams in the Polls

1-6 S/U vs ranked Mississippi State since 1992	5-1 S/U on road when #18 ranked all time
1-5 O/U vs ranked Mississippi State since 1999	14-1 S/U when #19 ranked since 1946 {10-0 @ home}
6-0 O/U vs ranked South Carolina since 2007	6-1 S/U @ home when #20 ranked all time
0-4 S/U @ ranked South Carolina all time	5-0 S/U when #21 ranked since 2001
1-23 S/U vs ranked Tennessee since 1967	0-7 S/U when ranked vs #1 ranked teams since 2008

Liberty {When Ranked}

3-1 S/U when ranked all time	0-5-1 O/U when ranked vs #1 ranked teams since 2009

Liberty {vs Ranked}

1-2 S/U vs ranked teams all time	0-6 S/U when ranked vs #1 Alabama all time

Louisiana {When Ranked}

6-1 S/U when ranked all time	0-5 S/U when ranked on road vs #3 ranked teams all time

Louisiana {vs Ranked}

2-30 S/U vs ranked teams since 1985	6-0 S/U @ home when ranked vs #7 ranked teams all time
8-2 O/U vs ranked teams since 2009	4-0 S/U when ranked vs #8 ranked teams all time

Louisiana-Monroe {When Ranked}

NEVER RANKED	6-1 S/U @ home when ranked vs #9 ranked teams all time

Louisiana-Monroe {vs Ranked}

2-34 S/U vs ranked teams all time	1-5 S/U @ home when ranked vs #12 ranked teams all time

Louisiana Tech {When Ranked}

5-1 O/U when ranked all time	0-5 ATS @ home when ranked vs #12 ranked teams since 1983
1-5 ATS when ranked all time	7-2 S/U when ranked vs #14 ranked teams all time

Louisiana Tech {vs Ranked}

2-38 S/U on road vs ranked teams all time	3-0 S/U on road when ranked vs #15 ranked teams all time
0-25 S/U vs Top 10 ranked teams all time	6-1 S/U when ranked vs #16 ranked teams since 1970

LSU {When Ranked}

55-10 S/U @ home when ranked since 2010	3-0 S/U @ home when ranked vs #17 ranked teams all time
15-1 S/U @ home when #1 ranked all time	5-0 S/U when ranked vs #18 ranked teams all time
10-2 S/U on road when #1 ranked all time	5-0 O/U when ranked vs #18 ranked teams all time
7-0 S/U @ home when #2 ranked all time	4-0 S/U @ home when ranked vs #19 ranked teams all time
13-1 S/U when #2 ranked since 2004	3-0 ATS when ranked vs #20 ranked teams since 1985
9-0 S/U @ home when #3 ranked all time	3-0 S/U @ home when ranked vs #22 ranked teams all time
1-3 S/U @ home when #4 ranked since 2005	3-0 S/U & ATS when ranked vs #25 ranked teams all time
12-2-1 S/U @ home when #5 ranked all time	0-3 O/U when ranked vs #25 ranked teams all time
13-3 S/U @ home when #6 ranked all time	1-8 S/U when ranked vs Alabama since 2012
6-1 S/U on road when #7 ranked all time	1-7-2 O/U when ranked vs Alabama since 2011
10-0 S/U when #7 ranked since 1998	8-2 S/U @ home when ranked vs Arkansas all time
6-1 O/U when #8 ranked since 2006	12-1 S/U @ home when ranked vs Auburn all time
24-2 S/U @ home when #9 ranked all time	24-4 S/U when ranked vs Kentucky since 1957
15-1 S/U @ home when #10 ranked all time	3-0 S/U when ranked vs Louisiana-Monroe all time
6-0 S/U when #11 ranked team since 2009	22-3 S/U when ranked vs Mississippi State since 1985
1-7 ATS @ home when #11 ranked since 1988	5-0 S/U @ home when ranked vs Texas A&M since 1986
12-2 S/U @ home when #12 ranked since 1978	10-1 ATS when ranked vs Texas A&M since 1986

LSU {vs Ranked}

14-1 S/U @ home when #13 ranked all time	0-8 S/U vs #1 ranked teams since 2008
15-1 S/U when #13 ranked since 1988	0-4 S/U on road vs #1 ranked teams all time
8-2 O/U when #13 ranked since 2003	1-5-1 O/U vs #1 ranked teams since 2009
10-1 S/U @ home when #14 ranked since 1971	5-0 S/U vs #3 ranked teams since 2011
0-5 O/U when #14 ranked since 2006	0-9 S/U on road vs #3 ranked teams all time
1-7-1 ATS when #15 ranked since 2008	0-4 ATS on road vs #3 ranked teams since 1995
2-9 O/U when #15 ranked since 1985	5-0-1 ATS vs #7 ranked teams since 2001
5-0 S/U on road when #16 ranked since 1978	7-2 O/U vs #9 ranked teams since 2003
12-2 S/U when #17 ranked since 1979 {9-1 @ home}	1-7 S/U @ home vs #12 ranked teams all time
	0-5 ATS @ home vs #12 ranked teams since 1983
	0-4 O/U on road vs #12 ranked teams since 1999
	4-0 ATS on road vs #14 ranked teams since 1996
	1-6 O/U vs #15 ranked teams since 1987
	4-0 ATS @ home vs #17 ranked teams since 1999
	6-0 S/U vs #18 ranked teams since 1988
	4-0 O/U vs #18 ranked teams since 2007
	3-0 S/U & ATS vs #25 ranked teams since 2001

Copyright © 2021 by Steve's Football Bible, LLC

Team Trends when ranked in the Polls / vs Ranked teams in the Polls

0-3 O/U vs #25 ranked teams since 2001
2-7-2 O/U vs ranked Alabama since 2005
5-0 S/U @ home vs ranked Arkansas all time
13-1 S/U @ home vs ranked Auburn all time
4-1 O/U @ home vs ranked Auburn since 2007
5-0 S/U vs ranked Mississippi State since 2000
8-0 ATS vs ranked Mississippi State since 1992
4-1 S/U vs ranked Texas A&M since 2011 {5-0 ATS}

Louisville {When Ranked}

21-8 S/U on road when ranked since 2005
44-9 S/U @ home when ranked all time
0-8 S/U on road when ranked vs ranked teams all time
1-6 ATS on road when ranked vs ranked teams all time
13-0 S/U when ranked #5 #6 #7 all time
6-1 S/U when #8 ranked all time
0-6 ATS when #8 ranked since 2004
3-0 S/U when #10 ranked all time
5-0 S/U when #12 ranked all time
4-0 S/U when #16 ranked all time
5-1 S/U when #18 ranked all time
4-0 S/U when #19 ranked since 2013
0-3 ATS when #21 ranked all time
0-3 O/U when #21 ranked all time
3-0 S/U @ home when #22 ranked all time
5-0 S/U when #23 ranked all time
5-1 S/U when #24 ranked all time
5-1 S/U when #25 ranked all time
1-4 ATS When ranked vs Syracuse all time

Louisville {vs Ranked}

4-40 S/U on road vs ranked teams all time
0-3 S/U vs #1 ranked teams all time
0-3 S/U on road vs #2 ranked teams all time
3-0 O/U vs #2 ranked teams since 2014
3-1 O/U vs #3 ranked teams since 2004
4-0 ATS vs #4 ranked teams all time
0-5 S/U vs #6 ranked teams all time
1-6 S/U vs #9 ranked teams all time
0-4 S/U & ATS vs #11 ranked teams all time
3-0 ATS vs #15 ranked teams all time
0-4 S/U @ home vs #17 ranked teams all time
1-4 S/U on road vs #19 ranked teams all time
1-6 S/U vs #24 ranked teams all time
1-4 ATS vs #24 ranked teams since 2002
0-5 S/U & ATS vs ranked Clemson all time
2-9 S/U vs ranked Florida State all time

Marshall {When Ranked}

12-2 S/U @ home when ranked all time

Marshall {vs Ranked}

1-7 ATS on road vs ranked teams since 2006
5-1 O/U on road vs ranked teams since 2009
0-17 S/U vs ranked teams since 2003

Maryland {When Ranked}

24-8 S/U @ home when ranked since 1976
0-6 O/U @ home when ranked since 2001
0-4 S/U on road when ranked since 2006
4-0 S/U @ home when #1 ranked all time
12-0 S/U @ home when #2 ranked all time
7-2 S/U when #3 ranked all time
3-0 S/U @ home when #4 ranked all time
6-1 S/U when #5 ranked all time {4-0 @ home}
3-0 S/U @ home when #6 ranked since 1976
3-0 S/U when #9 ranked all time
5-1 S/U on road when #10 ranked all time
4-0 S/U when #12 ranked all time
6-0 S/U @ home when #15 ranked all time
3-0 S/U on road when #16 ranked all time
4-0 S/U when #19 ranked since 1982
5-0 S/U when #20 ranked since 1975
0-3 S/U when #21 ranked all time
0-3 O/U when #22 ranked all time
0-3 S/U when ranked vs #14 ranked teams all time
0-8 S/U when ranked vs #4 - #9 ranked teams all time
0-4 S/U when ranked vs Penn State all time

Maryland {vs Ranked}

1-13 S/U @ home vs ranked teams since 2011
2-30 S/U vs ranked teams since 2011
1-20 S/U on road vs ranked teams since 2008
0-4 S/U vs #1 ranked teams since 1956
0-7 S/U vs #2 ranked teams since 1957
1-7 S/U vs #3 ranked teams all time
0-5 ATS vs #3 ranked teams since 1983
0-7 S/U vs #4 ranked teams all time
0-7 S/U on road vs #5 ranked teams all time
1-4 ATS vs #5 ranked teams since 2002
1-10 S/U vs #6 ranked teams all time
0-5 ATS vs #6 ranked teams since 1990
0-13 S/U vs #9 ranked teams all time
4-0 ATS vs #9 ranked teams since 1998
1-8 S/U vs #10 ranked teams all time
0-9 S/U vs #12 ranked teams all time
1-6 ATS vs #12 ranked teams since 1985
0-5 S/U on road vs #13 ranked teams all time
0-4 S/U on road vs #14 ranked teams all time
1-6 S/U on road vs #15 ranked teams since 1959
1-5 ATS on road vs #15 ranked teams since 1991
0-5 S/U vs #16 ranked teams all time
1-6 S/U on road vs #17 ranked teams all time
1-4 S/U on road vs #19 ranked teams since 1998
0-4 S/U & ATS @ home vs #20 ranked teams since 2000
0-6 S/U vs #22 ranked teams all time
4-0 O/U vs #23 ranked teams since 2005
5-1 ATS vs #23 ranked teams since 2003

Copyright © 2021 by Steve's Football Bible, LLC

Team Trends when ranked in the Polls / vs Ranked teams in the Polls

0-8 S/U vs ranked Michigan all time	1-5 O/U when #10 ranked since 2003
0-6 ATS vs ranked Michigan since 1990	6-0 S/U on road when #11 ranked all time
0-6 S/U vs ranked Ohio State all time	4-0 S/U on road when #13 ranked since 1981
6-0 O/U vs ranked Ohio State all time	8-0 S/U when #14 ranked since 1984 {4-0 S/U & ATS on road}
0-21-1 S/U vs ranked Penn State all time	7-0 S/U @ home when #14 ranked all time
0-6 ATS vs ranked Penn State since 1991	5-0 S/U @ home when #17 ranked all time
0-6 S/U vs ranked West Virginia since 2004	3-0 S/U on road when #18 ranked all time

Massachusetts {When Ranked}
NEVER RANKED

Massachusetts {vs Ranked}

0-13 S/U vs ranked teams all time	

Memphis {When Ranked}

9-3 S/U on road when ranked all time	3-0 S/U @ home when #19 ranked all time
6-2 O/U @ home when ranked all time	4-0 S/U when #20 ranked all time
4-1 S/U when #25 ranked all time	5-1 S/U when #23 ranked all time
3-0 S/U when ranked vs Cincinnati since 2016	0-4 ATS when #24 ranked since 2009
0-3 O/U when ranked vs Cincinnati since 2016	7-0 S/U when #25 ranked all time {6-1 ATS}
3-1 S/U when ranked vs SMU since 2017	4-0 S/U & ATS @ home when ranked vs #1 ranked team all time

Memphis {vs Ranked}

0-15 S/U on road vs ranked teams since 1993	0-3 S/U on road when ranked vs #2 ranked teams all time
0-3 S/U vs #5 ranked teams all time	6-0 O/U when ranked vs #2 ranked teams since 1990
0-3 S/U on road vs #6 ranked teams all time	3-0 S/U @ home when ranked vs #8 ranked teams all time
4-0 ATS vs #6 ranked teams since 1984	0-6 O/U when ranked vs #8 ranked teams all time
0-5 S/U vs #7 ranked teams since 1987	4-0 S/U when ranked vs #9 ranked teams since 1991
0-6 S/U vs #8 #9 ranked teams all time	5-0 S/U when ranked vs #13 ranked teams all time
0-6 S/U vs #10 ranked teams since 1967	4-0 ATS when ranked vs #13 ranked teams since 1993
0-3 S/U vs #11 ranked teams all time	1-4 S/U @ home when ranked vs #14 ranked teams all time
1-4 S/U vs #14 ranked teams all time	0-5 O/U when ranked vs #14 ranked teams since 1989
1-5 S/U vs #16 ranked teams all time	6-0 S/U when ranked vs #20 ranked teams all time
0-3 S/U vs #19 ranked teams all time	3-9 O/U when ranked vs Florida State since 2002
0-3 S/U vs ranked Central Florida all time	2-6 ATS when ranked vs Florida State since 2005
1-7 S/U vs ranked Houston all time	4-0 S/U when ranked vs Georgia Tech since 2009

Miami {When Ranked}

59-12 S/U @ home when ranked since 2000	3-0 S/U when ranked vs Michigan State all time
20-0 S/U @ home when #1 ranked all time	3-0 S/U when ranked vs NC State all time
14-0 S/U on road when #1 ranked since 1991	0-4 ATS when ranked @ North Carolina all time
28-0 S/U when #1 ranked in regular season since 1991	2-8 O/U when ranked vs Pittsburgh since 1997
24-0 S/U @ home when #2 ranked all time	4-10 ATS when ranked vs Virginia Tech since 1995
16-1 S/U @ home when #3 ranked all time	1-7 O/U when ranked vs Virginia Tech since 2003
11-1 S/U on road when #3 ranked all time	4-0 S/U when ranked @ home vs Virginia all time
5-0 S/U @ home when #4 ranked since 1985	

Miami {vs Ranked}

12-0 S/U when #5 ranked all time	3-17 S/U on road vs ranked teams since 2006
7-0 S/U @ home when #7 ranked all time	3-13 O/U @ home vs ranked teams since 2009
0-7 O/U when #7 ranked since 2000	6-0 S/U @ home vs #1 ranked teams since 1981
4-0 S/U on road when #8 ranked since 1983	4-0 ATS @ home vs #1 ranked team since 1986
5-1 S/U @ home when #8 ranked all time	1-6 S/U on road vs #1 ranked teams all time
0-4 ATS when #8 ranked since 1999	0-6 S/U on road vs #2 ranked teams all time
9-3 S/U @ home when #9 ranked since 1956	6-1 O/U vs #2 ranked teams since 1990
7-0 S/U on road when #10 ranked all time	1-6 S/U on road vs #4 ranked teams all time
7-1 S/U @ home when #10 ranked all time	1-6 S/U vs #5 ranked teams since 1973 {0-3 @ home}
0-4 ATS when #10 ranked since 2005	1-5 S/U on road vs #6 ranked teams all time
	4-0 O/U vs #6 ranked teams since 2002
	0-3 S/U @ home vs #7 ranked teams all time
	2-5-1 ATS vs #8 ranked teams since 1986
	0-8 O/U vs #8 ranked teams since 1986
	3-0 S/U @ home vs #9 ranked teams since 1980
	0-6 S/U vs #10 ranked teams since 2004 {1-5 ATS}
	4-1 ATS vs #12 ranked teams since 1983

Copyright © 2021 by Steve's Football Bible, LLC

Team Trends when ranked in the Polls / vs Ranked teams in the Polls

6-0 S/U & ATS vs #13 ranked teams since 1983	11-0 S/U @ home when #14 ranked since 1982
1-6 S/U @ home vs #14 ranked teams all time	11-0 S/U when #15 ranked since 1998
0-6 O/U vs #14 ranked teams since 1989	7-1 S/U when #16 ranked since 1981
3-0 O/U vs #15 ranked teams since 1988	7-1 S/U when #17 ranked since 2011
0-3 S/U on road vs #17 ranked teams all time	6-1 O/U when #17 ranked since 2011
4-0 S/U on road vs #18 ranked teams since 1980	13-0 S/U @ home when #19 ranked since 1960
4-1 S/U @ home vs #20 ranked teams since 1986	6-1 O/U when #19 ranked since 2013
0-5 S/U & ATS vs #21 ranked teams since 1996	7-1 S/U on road when #19 ranked since 1982
1-4 S/U vs #24 ranked teams all time	11-1 S/U @ home when #20 ranked all time
1-4 O/U vs #24 ranked teams all time	5-1 S/U when #22 ranked all time
0-6 S/U vs ranked Florida State since 2010	0-6 O/U when #22 ranked all time
2-11 O/U vs ranked Florida State since 2002	3-0 S/U @ home when #23 ranked all time
4-0 S/U vs ranked Pittsburgh since 1989	5-0 S/U when #25 ranked all time
0-4 O/U vs ranked Pittsburgh since 1989	0-6 S/U on road when ranked vs #1 ranked teams all time
0-4 O/U @ home vs ranked Virginia Tech since 2004	0-8 S/U when ranked vs #1 ranked teams since 1985
Miami-Ohio {When Ranked}	6-1 O/U when ranked vs #1 ranked teams since 1988
10-0 S/U @ home when ranked all time	1-6 S/U @ home when ranked vs #2 ranked teams all time
4-0 S/U when #15 ranked all time	1-6 S/U when ranked vs #2 ranked teams since 1998
7-0 S/U when #16 ranked all time	5-0 O/U when ranked vs #2 ranked teams since 2006
3-0 S/U when #17 ranked all time	1-8-2 S/U when ranked vs #3 ranked teams since 1951
3-0 S/U when ranked vs Bowling Green all time	0-4 S/U in Bowl games when ranked vs #3 ranked teams all time
3-0 S/U when ranked vs Cincinnati all time	3-0 S/U @ home when ranked vs #4 ranked teams all time
3-0 S/U when ranked vs Kent State all time	0-3-1 S/U on road when ranked vs #4 ranked teams since 1945
3-0 S/U when ranked vs Ohio all time	0-4 ATS when ranked vs #8 ranked teams since 2002
3-0 S/U when ranked vs Toledo all time	5-0-1 S/U @ home when ranked vs #10 ranked teams all time
3-0 S/U when ranked vs Western Michigan all time	7-1 O/U when ranked vs #11 ranked teams since 1993
Miami-Ohio {vs Ranked}	4-0 S/U @ home when ranked vs #14 ranked teams since 1977
2-13 S/U vs Top 10 ranked teams all time	6-0 S/U @ home when ranked vs #15 ranked teams all time
0-3 S/U vs #17 ranked teams all time	2-7 O/U when ranked vs #15 ranked teams since 1985
Michigan {When Ranked}	0-4 ATS when ranked vs #16 ranked teams since 1984
42-6 S/U @ home when ranked since 2009	6-1 S/U @ home when ranked vs #17 ranked teams all time
298-61-9 S/U @ home when ranked all time	4-0 O/U when ranked vs #19 ranked teams since 1995
175-79-6 S/U on road when ranked all time	21-0 S/U when ranked vs Indiana since 1988
14-1 S/U @ home when #1 ranked all time	1-5-1 ATS when ranked vs Indiana since 2009
11-2-1 S/U @ home when #2 ranked since 1947	7-0 S/U & ATS when ranked vs Maryland all time
0-4 S/U on road when #3 ranked since 1999	2-9 ATS when ranked vs Michigan State since 2009
1-6 ATS when #3 ranked since 2000	24-1-2 S/U @ home when ranked vs Northwestern all time
22-1 S/U @ home when #4 ranked since 1976	7-0 S/U when ranked vs Northwestern since 2003
19-2 S/U on road when #4 ranked since 1971	9-1 O/U when ranked vs Ohio State since 2003
10-2 S/U @ home when #5 ranked since 1986	3-0 S/U & ATS when ranked vs Western Michigan all time
10-1 S/U on road when #5 ranked since 1970	0-3 S/U when ranked @ Wisconsin since 2005
11-0 S/U @ home when #6 ranked since 1983	**Michigan {vs Ranked}**
0-3 S/U on road when #7 ranked since 1995	5-13 ATS on road vs ranked teams since 2009
11-1 S/U @ home when #8 ranked since 1970	2-20 S/U on road vs ranked teams since 2006
5-0 S/U when #10 ranked since 1995	13-4 O/U @ home vs ranked teams since 2010
9-1 S/U @ home when #11 ranked since 1972	3-8 S/U vs ranked teams in Bowl games since 2004
5-12 O/U when #11 ranked since 1989	0-9 S/U vs #1 ranked teams since 1984
0-4 ATS @ home when ranked #11 since 1995	0-7 S/U on road vs #1 ranked teams all time
5-1 O/U when #12 ranked since 2004	6-1 O/U vs #1 ranked teams since 1988
7-1 ATS when #13 ranked since 2002	1-8 S/U @ home vs #2 ranked teams all time
3-10 O/U when #14 ranked since 1997	4-0 O/U vs #2 ranked teams since 2006

Copyright © 2021 by Steve's Football Bible, LLC

Team Trends when ranked in the Polls / vs Ranked teams in the Polls

1-9-1 S/U vs #3 ranked teams since 1957
4-0 O/U vs #3 ranked teams since 1994
4-0 S/U @ home vs #4 ranked teams all time
3-0 S/U @ home vs #5 ranked teams since 1975
3-0 O/U vs #6 ranked teams since 1999
0-6 S/U vs #7 ranked teams since 1994
2-5 S/U & ATS vs #8 ranked teams since 2007
6-2 ATS vs #9 ranked teams since 1993
0-3 S/U on road vs #10 ranked teams all time
4-0 S/U @ home vs #10 ranked teams since 1962
8-1 O/U vs #11 ranked teams since 1993
5-0 S/U @ home vs #14 ranked teams since 1977
6-1 S/U @ home vs #15 ranked teams all time
0-4 O/U on road vs #15 ranked teams since 1985
1-5 S/U vs #16 ranked teams since 1983
0-5 ATS vs #16 ranked teams since 1984
7-1 S/U @ home vs #17 ranked teams all time
9-1-1 S/U vs #17 ranked teams since 1985
0-3 S/U @ home vs #19 ranked teams all time
4-0 O/U vs #19 ranked teams since 1995
4-1 S/U @ home vs #20 ranked teams all time
1-5 ATS vs #20 ranked teams since 1986
0-3 S/U on road vs #22 ranked teams all time
0-3 ATS on road vs #23 ranked teams all time
3-0 S/U & ATS vs #25 ranked teams all time
2-9 S/U @ home vs ranked Michigan State all time
1-5 S/U & ATS vs ranked Michigan State since 2010
1-5 O/U vs ranked Michigan State since 2010
0-14 S/U vs ranked Ohio State since 2005
7-0 O/U vs ranked Ohio State since 2013
6-0 O/U @ ranked Penn State since 1995
1-6 S/U & ATS vs ranked USC since 1970
1-4 ATS vs ranked Washington since 1984

Michigan State {When Ranked}

12-1 S/U @ home when #1 ranked all time
10-2 S/U on road when #1 ranked all time
24-2-1 S/U when #2 ranked all time
13-1-1 S/U when #4 ranked all time
0-4-1 ATS when #5 ranked since 1999
4-0 S/U @ home when #6 ranked all time
0-3 S/U on road when #6 ranked since 1961
6-0 O/U when #7 ranked since 2011
9-1 S/U when #8 ranked since 1957 {3-0 on road}
4-0 S/U on road when #10 ranked all time
4-0 S/U @ home when #11 ranked since 2010
11-1 S/U when #12 ranked all time {7-0 @ home}
10-1 S/U when #13 ranked since 1960 {6-0 @ home}
0-4 O/U when #13 ranked since 2012
5-1 S/U & ATS when #18 ranked since 2002
6-0 S/U @ home when #19 ranked all time
0-4 S/U & ATS @ home when #20 ranked since 1997

4-0 S/U when #21 ranked since 2012
5-1 O/U when #21 ranked all time
0-6 ATS when #22 ranked since 1993
4-0 S/U @ home when #23 ranked all time
5-1 ATS when #23 ranked all time
4-0 S/U @ home when #25 ranked since 1997
3-1 ATS @ home when #25 ranked since 1997
6-1 S/U when ranked vs #4 ranked teams all time
6-1 S/U when ranked vs #6 ranked teams all time {3-0 on road}
0-5 S/U when ranked vs #8 ranked teams since 1960
0-3 S/U when ranked vs #15 ranked teams since 2005
3-0 O/U when ranked vs #15 ranked teams since 2005
21-4 S/U when ranked vs Indiana all time
6-2 ATS when ranked vs Indiana since 2003
0-3 O/U when ranked vs Maryland since 2014
9-1 S/U when ranked @ Michigan all time
1-5 O/U when ranked vs Michigan since 2010
4-0 S/U & ATS when ranked vs Penn State since 2010
6-1 S/U @ home when ranked vs Penn State all time
3-0 S/U when ranked vs Rutgers all time

Michigan State {vs Ranked}

2-11 S/U on road vs #1 ranked teams all time
0-6 S/U @ home vs #2 ranked teams since 1967
1-9 S/U vs #3 ranked teams since 1960
4-1 S/U vs #4 ranked teams since 1997
1-6 S/U on road vs #4 ranked teams since 1971
1-5 S/U @ home vs #5 ranked teams since 1973
1-6 S/U @ home vs #6 ranked teams since 1967
3-0 S/U @ home vs #7 ranked teams since 1995
1-4 S/U on road vs #7 ranked teams since 1994
1-7 S/U @ home vs #8 ranked teams all time
0-4 S/U on road vs #9 ranked teams since 1987
4-1 O/U vs #10 ranked teams since 1993
4-1 S/U @ home vs #10 ranked all time
0-3 S/U on road vs #11 ranked teams all time
1-5 S/U @ home vs #12 ranked teams since 1982
0-10 S/U vs #14 ranked teams since 1983
0-4 S/U on road vs #14 ranked teams all time
0-5 S/U vs #15 ranked teams since 2002
5-0 O/U vs #15 ranked teams since 2002
0-4 S/U vs #16 ranked teams since 2000
0-5 S/U on road vs #16 ranked teams since 1982
0-4 O/U vs #16 ranked teams since 2000
1-5-1 S/U vs #17 ranked teams since 1956
4-1 S/U & ATS vs #18 ranked teams since 1984
4-0 S/U @ home vs #19 ranked teams since 1975
3-0 ATS vs #22 ranked teams since 2007
3-0 ATS vs #23 ranked teams since 2001
0-3 O/U vs #23 ranked teams since 2001
0-3 O/U vs #24 ranked teams all time
9-2 ATS vs ranked Michigan since 2009

Copyright © 2021 by Steve's Football Bible, LLC

1-5 S/U vs ranked Nebraska all time	0-7 S/U vs #16 ranked teams since 1978 {0-4 on road}
0-6 ATS vs ranked Nebraska all time	0-6 S/U vs #17 ranked teams since 1954
1-3 S/U vs ranked Northwestern since 1970	0-6 S/U vs #18 ranked teams since 1987
1-5 O/U vs ranked Ohio State since 2015	0-4 S/U on road vs #18 ranked teams since 1978
10-3 O/U vs ranked Penn State since 1996	0-7 S/U vs #19 ranked teams since 1991
1-6 S/U vs ranked Purdue since 1967	1-6 S/U vs #20 ranked teams since 1957

Middle Tennessee {When Ranked}

NEVER RANKED	4-0-1 ATS vs #21 ranked teams since 2005

Middle Tennessee {vs Ranked}

0-19 S/U vs ranked teams all time	1-5 S/U vs #22 ranked teams all time

Minnesota {When Ranked}

5-1 S/U @ home when #1 ranked all time	0-3 S/U vs ranked Colorado all time
4-0 S/U @ home when #2 ranked all time	0-8 S/U @ ranked Iowa since 1983
4-0 S/U when #6 ranked since 1957	1-6 S/U @ home vs ranked Nebraska since 1968
4-0 S/U @ home when #10 ranked all time	1-6 S/U @ ranked Northwestern since 1943
6-1 S/U when #14 ranked all time {3-0 on road}	0-4 S/U vs ranked Northwestern since 1959
3-0 S/U @ home when #18 ranked all time	2-34 S/U vs ranked Ohio State since 1950
0-4 S/U on road when #19 ranked all time	4-0 O/U vs ranked Purdue since 1999
2-5 S/U when #20 ranked all time	1-17 S/U vs ranked Wisconsin since 1954

	Mississippi {When Ranked}
2-16 S/U when ranked vs ranked teams since 1962	4-16-1 O/U on road when ranked since 2002
1-13 S/U on road when ranked vs ranked teams since 1942	15-3 S/U @ home when ranked since 2014
0-4 S/U when ranked vs #20 ranked teams since 1957	5-1 S/U when #1 ranked all time
0-4 S/U when ranked vs #6 ranked teams all time	10-1-2 S/U when #2 ranked all time
0-3 S/U when ranked @ Indiana all time	7-0 S/U @ home when #3 ranked all time
0-3 S/U @ home when ranked vs Ohio State all time	0-5 O/U when #3 ranked since 2014
7-2 S/U when ranked vs Purdue all time	7-0 S/U @ home when #5 ranked all time
1-7 S/U when ranked vs Wisconsin since 1961 {0-2 on road}	5-0 S/U on road when #5 ranked since 1959

Minnesota {vs Ranked}	7-1 S/U when #6 ranked since 1958 {2-0 @ home}
6-76 S/U on road vs ranked teams since 1970	13-2-1 S/U when #7 ranked since 1954
10-48 S/U @ home vs ranked teams since 1983	6-0 S/U @ home when #9 ranked all time
7-3 ATS @ home vs ranked teams since 2013	3-0 S/U @ home when #11 ranked all time
0-12 S/U on road vs #1 ranked teams all time	5-0 S/U @ home when #13 ranked all time
0-8 S/U @ home vs #2 ranked teams all time	8-0 S/U when #14 ranked since 1952
4-1 ATS vs #2 ranked teams since 1985	5-0 S/U on road when #15 ranked since 1955
0-8 S/U on road vs #3 ranked teams since 1948	6-0 S/U when #17 ranked since 1976
0-11 S/U vs #3 ranked teams since 1962	4-0 ATS when #17 ranked since 1990
0-8 S/U vs #4 ranked teams since 1944	9-1 S/U when #18 ranked since 1952 {3-0 on road}
0-8 S/U on road vs #5 ranked teams since 1957	3-0 S/U on road when #19 ranked since 1957
0-8 S/U vs #5 ranked teams since 1967	0-3 O/U when #21 ranked since 2002
0-4 S/U @ home vs #6 ranked teams since 1970	0-5 S/U when ranked vs #1 ranked teams all time
0-5-1 S/U vs #7 ranked teams since 1963	0-3 S/U & ATS when ranked vs Arkansas since 2014
0-13-1 S/U vs #8 ranked teams since 1951	0-4 S/U @ home when ranked vs Auburn since 1972
4-1 ATS vs #8 ranked teams since 1998	7-1 ATS when ranked vs Mississippi State since 1990
1-7 S/U vs #9 ranked teams since 1959	9-0 S/U when ranked vs Tulane since 1957
2-8-1 S/U vs #10 ranked teams all time	14-1 S/U when ranked vs Vanderbilt since 1948 {5-0 @ home}

	Mississippi {vs Ranked}
0-3 S/U on road vs #11 ranked teams since 1979	0-13 S/U vs #1 ranked teams all time
2-7 S/U vs #12 ranked teams since 1945	1-9 S/U vs #2 ranked teams all time
0-5 S/U vs #13 ranked teams since 1997	1-7 S/U vs #3 ranked teams since 1995
0-5 S/U vs #14 ranked teams since 1988	0-5 S/U vs #5 ranked teams since 1982
0-6 S/U vs #15 ranked teams since 1996	0-5 S/U on road vs #6 ranked teams all time
0-5 S/U on road vs #15 ranked teams since 1943	0-4 O/U vs #6 ranked teams since 2002
	1-6 S/U vs #7 ranked teams since 1971

Copyright © 2021 by Steve's Football Bible, LLC

1-7 S/U on road vs #8 ranked teams all time	6-1 S/U when ranked vs Kentucky since 1992
0-8 S/U on road vs #9 ranked teams all time	1-5 O/U when ranked vs Kentucky since 1999
0-6 S/U vs #9 ranked teams since 1975	0-4 S/U when ranked vs ranked LSU since 2011
4-0 ATS on road vs #10 ranked teams since 1991	1-7 ATS when ranked vs LSU since 1992
0-6 S/U vs #11 ranked teams since 1981	3-9 O/U when ranked vs Mississippi since 1992
0-3 S/U @ home vs #13 ranked teams since 1987	3-0 S/U when ranked vs Vanderbilt all time
0-4 S/U @ home vs #14 ranked teams all time	**Mississippi State {vs Ranked}**
0-7 S/U on road vs #15 ranked teams all time	12-95-1 S/U on road vs ranked teams since 1958
1-4 S/U on road vs #16 ranked teams all time	0-5 S/U on road vs #1 ranked teams all time
4-0 ATS vs #16 ranked teams since 1992	1-10 S/U vs #1 ranked teams all time
0-4 S/U vs #17 ranked teams since 1972	1-12 S/U vs #2 ranked teams all time
1-8 S/U vs #18 ranked teams since 1984	1-9-1 S/U vs #3 ranked teams all time
1-4 S/U vs #19 ranked teams all time	0-6 S/U on road vs #3 ranked teams all time
1-6 O/U vs #21 ranked teams since 1999	0-11 S/U vs #4 ranked teams since 1961
0-3 O/U vs #22 ranked teams since 1997	0-10 S/U on road vs #5 ranked teams all time
4-1 S/U vs ranked teams in Bowl games since 2004	0-11 S/U vs #5 ranked teams since 1971
3-25 S/U vs ranked Alabama since 1977	1-5 S/U on road vs #6 ranked teams all time
0-19 S/U vs ranked Auburn all time	5-1 O/U vs #6 ranked teams since 1991
4-1 O/U vs ranked Auburn since 2010	0-6 S/U on road vs #7 ranked teams all time
0-4 S/U vs ranked Arkansas since 2006	0-7 S/U on road vs #9 ranked teams all time
3-15 S/U @ ranked LSU since 1970	0-7 S/U @ home vs #10 ranked teams all time
0-4 O/U vs ranked Mississippi State since 2014	1-4 ATS vs #10 ranked teams since 1988
4-0 ATS @ ranked Mississippi State since 1997	1-10 S/U vs #11 ranked teams since 1969
0-9 S/U vs ranked Tennessee since 1985	1-7 S/U vs #12 ranked teams since 1960
0-9 S/U @ ranked Tennessee since 1968	0-6 S/U on road vs #13 ranked teams all time
6-1 ATS vs ranked Tennessee since 1989	1-8 S/U vs #14 ranked teams since 1955
3-0 S/U vs ranked Texas A&M since 2014	0-5 O/U vs #14 ranked teams since 1991
4-0 ATS vs ranked Texas A&M since 2013	0-8 S/U on road vs #16 ranked teams all time
Mississippi State {When Ranked}	0-5 S/U @ home vs #18 ranked teams all time
0-3 ATS when #8 ranked all time	0-5 ATS vs #18 ranked teams since 1996
5-1 S/U when #11 ranked all time	1-9 S/U vs #19 ranked teams all time
0-4 S/U when #13 ranked since 1986	0-4 ATS vs #19 ranked teams since 1988
0-5 ATS when #13 ranked since 1986	1-5 S/U vs #20 ranked teams since 1971
3-0 S/U & ATS when #15 ranked since 1999	1-4 S/U & ATS vs #25 ranked teams since 2005
0-3 O/U when #15 ranked since 1999	1-5 S/U vs ranked teams in Bowl games since 1980 {1-5 ATS}
0-3 S/U on road when #15 ranked since 1945	0-23 S/U @ ranked Alabama since 1961
0-5 ATS when #17 ranked since 2001	3-19 S/U @ home vs ranked Alabama since 1962
0-5 O/U when #17 ranked since 2001	2-15-1 O/U vs ranked Alabama since 1995
4-0 S/U when #19 ranked since 1992	0-5-1 S/U vs ranked Arkansas since 1995
1-5 O/U @ home when #23 ranked since 1999	1-20 S/U @ ranked Auburn all time
3-0 S/U @ home when #24 ranked all time	2-14 S/U vs ranked LSU since 2000
0-4 S/U when ranked vs #1 ranked teams all time	1-11 S/U @ home vs ranked LSU since 1986
0-3 S/U when ranked vs #3 ranked teams all time	0-5 O/U vs ranked LSU since 2015
0-3 S/U when ranked vs #5 ranked teams all time	1-7 ATS vs ranked Mississippi since 1990
0-3 S/U when ranked vs #8 ranked teams all time	**Missouri {When Ranked}**
0-3 S/U & ATS when ranked vs #11 ranked teams since 1999	6-2 S/U on road when ranked since 2013
0-4 S/U when ranked vs #14 ranked teams all time	30-7 S/U @ home when ranked since 1998
0-3 O/U when ranked vs #14 ranked teams since 1991	1-9 O/U @ home when ranked since 2013
0-3 S/U when ranked vs #18 ranked teams since 1976	4-0 S/U when ranked #6 since 2007
0-12 S/U when ranked vs ranked Alabama since 1974	5-1 S/U when #8 ranked all time
4-1 S/U when ranked vs Arkansas since 2014	6-0 S/U on road when #9 ranked since 1965

Copyright © 2021 by Steve's Football Bible, LLC

Team Trends when ranked in the Polls / vs Ranked teams in the Polls

	NAVY {When Ranked}
0-3-1 S/U on road when #10 ranked since 1961	30-1-3 S/U @ home when ranked all time
9-2 S/U when #12 ranked all time {3-0 on road}	4-0 S/U when #5 ranked since 1955
3-0 S/U @ home when #13 ranked since 1981	4-0 S/U when #8 ranked all time
1-4 S/U on road when #14 ranked since 1972	3-0-1 S/U when #9 ranked since 1955
11-2 S/U when #16 ranked all time	5-0 S/U when #10 ranked since 1954
5-0 S/U @ home when #17 ranked since 1978	6-0-1 S/U when #12 ranked all time
1-8 S/U when #19 ranked since 1981	3-0 S/U when #19 ranked all time
8-1 S/U when #20 ranked all time	4-0 S/U when #21 ranked all time
4-1 S/U when #24 ranked since 2010	3-0 S/U when #24 ranked all time
8-1 S/U when #25 ranked all time	0-3 S/U when ranked #25 all time
0-6 S/U when ranked vs #1 ranked teams all time	0-5 S/U when ranked vs #1 ranked teams all time
0-5 S/U when ranked vs #6 ranked teams all time	8-2-1 S/U when ranked vs Army since 1963
3-0 S/U @ home when ranked vs #14 ranked teams all time	**NAVY {vs Ranked}**
3-0 S/U when ranked vs #22 ranked teams all time	5-32 S/U on road vs ranked teams since 1975
3-0 S/U when ranked vs #25 ranked teams all time	11-5 ATS on road vs ranked teams since 1995
3-0 S/U when ranked vs Texas A&M since 2007	2-14 S/U @ home vs ranked teams since 1985
Missouri {vs Ranked}	0-31 S/U on Neutral fields vs ranked teams since 1958
7-54 S/U on road vs ranked teams since 1982	0-14 S/U vs #1 ranked teams all time
0-10 S/U @ home vs ranked teams since 2014	2-10 S/U vs #2 ranked teams since 1946
0-15 S/U vs #1 ranked teams all time	0-3 S/U on road vs #2 ranked teams all time
4-1 O/U vs #1 ranked teams since 2008	0-4 S/U vs #3 ranked teams since 1969
0-8 S/U @ home vs #2 ranked teams since 1979	0-7 S/U vs #5 ranked teams since 1958
5-1 ATS & O/U vs #2 ranked teams since 1998	1-5 S/U vs #6 ranked teams all time
2-12 S/U vs #3 ranked teams all time	0-8 S/U vs #7 ranked teams since 1948
1-4 ATS vs #3 ranked teams since 1989	1-7 S/U vs #8 ranked teams since 1944
0-4 S/U on road vs #4 ranked teams all time	0-6 S/U vs #9 ranked teams since 1962
0-4 S/U @ home vs #4 ranked teams since 1977	4-0 ATS vs #9 ranked teams since 1986
1-4 ATS vs #4 ranked team since 1986	0-7 S/U vs #10 ranked teams since 1967
0-5 S/U @ home vs #5 ranked teams since 1955	0-6 S/U vs #11 ranked teams all time
0-12 S/U vs #6 ranked teams all time	0-8 S/U vs #12 ranked teams all time
1-12 S/U vs #7 ranked teams since 1977	0-5 S/U vs #13 ranked teams since 1951
0-9 S/U @ home vs #7 ranked teams since 1977	0-3 S/U vs #19 ranked teams since 1983
0-4 S/U @ home vs #8 ranked teams all time	0-4 S/U vs #20 ranked teams since 1989
0-4 S/U on road vs #9 ranked teams since 1991	0-9 S/U vs #23 #24 #25 ranked teams all time
0-7 S/U vs #9 ranked teams since 1983	0-3 S/U & ATS vs ranked Air Force since 1985
1-9 S/U vs #11 ranked teams all time	2-9-1 S/U vs ranked Army since 1944
0-5 S/U vs #12 ranked teams since 1975	1-40 S/U vs ranked Notre Dame since 1964
5-1 S/U on road vs #13 ranked teams all time	9-2 O/U vs ranked Notre Dame since 2002
0-5 S/U on road vs #14 ranked teams all time	**Nebraska {When Ranked}**
3-0 S/U @ home vs #14 ranked teams since 1975	5-19 S/U on road when ranked vs ranked teams since 1998
1-4 S/U on road vs #15 ranked teams all time	17-3 S/U @ home when ranked vs ranked teams since 1991
1-6 S/U vs #17 ranked teams all time	170-15 S/U @ home when ranked since 1982
0-3 S/U & ATS vs #18 ranked teams since 1997	19-4-1 S/U on road when #1 ranked all time
0-3 O/U vs #19 ranked teams since 2003	23-2 S/U @ home when #1 ranked all time
1-5 S/U vs #20 ranked teams since 1991	9-0 S/U on road when #2 ranked vs unranked teams since 1979
0-3 O/U vs #21 ranked teams since 2004	23-0 S/U @ home when #2 ranked since 1979
3-0 S/U vs #22 ranked teams since 2007	7-0 S/U @ home when #2 ranked vs ranked teams all time
3-0 S/U vs #25 ranked teams since 2007	12-1 S/U @ home when #3 ranked since 1982
1-8 S/U vs ranked Georgia all time	26-2 S/U when #4 ranked since 1982
6-2 O/U vs ranked Georgia since 2012	10-1 S/U on road when #4 ranked since 1975
0-3 O/U vs ranked South Carolina since 2012	

Copyright © 2021 by Steve's Football Bible, LLC

Team Trends when ranked in the Polls / vs Ranked teams in the Polls

	Nebraska {vvs Ranked}
15-0 S/U @ home when #4 ranked since 1984	0-11 S/U on road vs ranked teams since 2011
14-0 S/U on road when #5 ranked all time	1-12 S/U vs #1 ranked teams all time
14-2 S/U @ home when #5 ranked since 1976	0-4 S/U on road vs #1 ranked teams all time
10-0 S/U on road when #6 ranked all time	1-4 ATS vs #1 ranked teams since 1982
17-0 S/U @ home when #6 ranked since 1975	2-6 S/U on road vs #2 ranked teams all time
13-3 S/U on road when #7 ranked all time	6-0 ATS vs #2 ranked teams since 1994
11-1 S/U @ home when #7 ranked all time	0-4-1 S/U on road vs #3 ranked teams all time
18-0 S/U @ home when #8 ranked all time	1-4 S/U @ home vs #3 ranked teams all time
1-5 ATS on road when #8 ranked since 1992	1-5 S/U @ home vs #4 ranked teams all time
7-2 ATS @ home when #8 ranked since 1984	1-5 S/U on road vs #4 ranked teams all time
11-2 S/U @ home when #9 ranked since 1986	0-4 ATS vs #4 ranked teams since 1991
0-5 O/U @ home when #9 ranked since 1999	4-0 O/U vs #6 ranked teams since 2000
10-2 S/U @ home when #10 ranked all time	1-7 S/U on road vs #8 ranked teams all time
11-0 S/U @ home when #11 ranked all time	0-5 S/U vs #10 ranked teams since 2007
0-4 O/U when #12 ranked since 1992	0-5 O/U vs #10 ranked teams since 2006
4-0 S/U @ home when #12 ranked since 1977	3-0 S/U @ home vs #10 ranked teams since 1973
8-2 S/U when #13 ranked all time {2-0 on road}	0-3 S/U vs #13 ranked teams since 2002
4-0 S/U & ATS on road when #14 ranked all time	4-1 ATS vs #13 ranked teams since 1992
8-1 S/U @ home when #14 ranked all time	7-1 S/U vs #12 ranked teams since 1973
6-1 S/U @ home when #16 ranked all time	0-3 S/U on road vs #14 ranked teams all time
4-0-1 O/U when #16 ranked since 2010	0-6 S/U vs #16 ranked teams since 2000
6-1 S/U when #17 ranked all time {3-0 @ home}	0-3 S/U on road vs #18 ranked teams all time
8-1 S/U @ home when #18 ranked all time	5-0 S/U @ home or neutral field vs #18 ranked teams all time
0-4-1 ATS when #18 ranked since 2003	5-1 S/U @ home vs #19 ranked teams all time
3-0 S/U @ home when #19 ranked all time	1-4 S/U on road vs #19 ranked teams all time
2-7 O/U when #19 ranked since 2003	7-1 S/U vs #20 ranked teams since 1970
9-0 S/U @ home when #22 ranked all time	4-0 S/U vs #23 ranked teams all time
0-4 ATS when #23 ranked all time	5-0 ATS vs #24 ranked teams since all time
7-0 O/U when #25 ranked all time	1-8 S/U @ ranked Oklahoma since 1973
1-9 S/U when ranked vs #1 ranked teams all time	1-10 O/U vs ranked Oklahoma since 1987
5-0 ATS when ranked vs #2 ranked teams since 1994	0-6 S/U vs ranked Wisconsin all time
0-3 S/U on road when ranked vs #3 ranked teams since 1973	5-1 O/U vs ranked Wisconsin all time
1-5 S/U when ranked vs #4 ranked teams all time	**Nevada {When Ranked}**
1-4 S/U on road when ranked vs #7 ranked teams all time	5-0 S/U @ home when ranked all time
0-5 S/U when ranked vs #10 ranked teams since 2006	7-2 S/U on road when ranked all time
0-5 O/U when ranked vs #10 ranked teams since 2006	**Nevada {vs Ranked}**
7-1 S/U when ranked vs #12 ranked teams all time	1-17 S/U on road vs ranked teams all time
5-1 S/U when ranked vs #13 ranked teams all time {3-0 @ home}	2-12 S/U @ home vs ranked teams all time
3-0-1 S/U when ranked vs #15 ranked teams all time	0-3 O/U vs #12 ranked teams all time
0-3 S/U on road when ranked vs #18 ranked teams all time	0-3 S/U vs #12 ranked teams all time
5-0 S/U @ home when ranked vs #19 ranked teams all time	0-3 S/U & ATS vs #18 ranked teams all time
0-4 ATS when ranked vs #19 ranked teams since 1988	0-3 O/U vs #18 ranked teams all time
4-0 ATS when ranked vs #24 ranked teams all time	0-3 S/U vs #22 ranked teams all time
4-0 S/U when ranked vs Illinois all time	0-3 S/U vs #25 ranked teams all time
6-0 S/U @ home when ranked vs Iowa all time	1-8 S/U vs ranked Boise State all time
6-0 ATS when ranked vs Michigan State all time	**UNLV {When Ranked}**
5-1 S/U when ranked vs Michigan State all time	**NEVER RANKED**
13-2 S/U when ranked vs Minnesota since 1967	**UNLV {vs Ranked}**
1-6 S/U when ranked @ ranked Oklahoma since 1973	0-22 S/U vs ranked teams since 2008
3-0 S/U @ home when ranked vs Wisconsin all time	0-21 S/U @ home vs ranked teams all time

Copyright © 2021 by Steve's Football Bible, LLC

Team Trends when ranked in the Polls / vs Ranked teams in the Polls

1-15 S/U on road vs ranked teams since 2004	**North Carolina {vs Ranked}**
0-8 S/U vs #10 #11 #12 #13 ranked teams all time	19-79-2 S/U on road vs ranked teams all time
0-3 O/U vs #24 ranked teams all time	2-11 S/U @ home vs ranked teams since 2010
0-30 S/U vs #18 - #25 ranked teams all time	0-11 S/U vs #1 ranked teams all time
New Mexico {When Ranked}	1-4 ATS vs #1 ranked teams since 1987
0-1 S/U when ranked all time	0-9 S/U vs #2 ranked teams all time
New Mexico {vs Ranked}	1-6 S/U vs #3 ranked teams all time
0-22 S/U vs ranked teams since 2004	3-0 ATS vs #3 ranked teams since 1994
2-33 S/U on road vs ranked teams all time	0-6 S/U vs #4 ranked teams since 1961
4-28 S/U @ home vs ranked teams all time	0-3 ATS vs #4 ranked teams since 1988
0-11 S/U vs #4 #5 #6 #7 #8 ranked teams all time	0-8 S/U vs #5 ranked teams all time
4-0 ATS vs #9 ranked teams since 1985	0-7 S/U on road vs #6 ranked teams all time
0-6 S/U vs #10 #11 #12 ranked teams all time	5-1 ATS vs #6 ranked teams since 1995
0-13 S/U vs #14 #15 #16 #17 ranked teams all time	0-4 S/U vs #8 ranked teams since 1992
0-8 ATS vs #14 #15 #16 #17 ranked teams since 1988	2-10-1 S/U vs #11 ranked teams all time
0-17 S/U vs #19 #20 #21 #22 ranked teams all time	1-6 S/U vs #12 ranked teams since 1952
0-5 S/U vs ranked Boise State all time	2-9 S/U vs #16 ranked teams all time
0-4 S/U vs ranked Colorado State all time	1-8 S/U vs #17 ranked teams all time {0-4 @ home}
New Mexico State {When Ranked	5-0 ATS @ home vs #19 ranked teams since 1984
5-0 S/U when ranked all time	0-4 S/U on road vs #20 ranked teams all time
New Mexico State {vs Ranked}	0-4 S/U vs #21 ranked teams all time
0-7 S/U @ home vs ranked all time	3-0 S/U & ATS vs #23 ranked teams since 2005
1-29 S/U on road vs ranked teams all time	1-6 S/U vs #24 ranked teams since 1996
2-7 ATS on road vs ranked teams since 2010	1-5 ATS on road vs #24 ranked teams all time
0-9-1 ATS vs #14 - #18 ranked teams all time	1-5 O/U vs #25 ranked teams since 1997
3-0 ATS vs #22 ranked teams all time	2-8 S/U @ home vs Duke all time
North Carolina {When Ranked}	1-6 S/U @ home vs Florida State all time
4-12 ATS on road when ranked since 2001	0-4 S/U @ Georgia Tech all time
4-10 O/U on road when ranked since 1997	4-0 ATS @ home vs Georgia Tech all time
21-4 S/U @ home when ranked since 1996	4-0 ATS @ home vs Miami all time
4-0 S/U when #4 ranked all time	0-14 S/U vs ranked Notre Dame all time
5-1 S/U @ home when #5 ranked all time	2-8 S/U vs ranked Virginia Tech all time {1-4 @ home}
7-0 S/U @ home when #8 ranked since 1983	2-5 O/U vs ranked Virginia Tech since 2007
4-0 S/U when #9 ranked since 1981	3-0 S/U @ home vs Virginia since 1992
6-1 S/U when #11 ranked since 1981 {3-0 @ home}	5-0 ATS @ home vs Virginia since 1984
4-1 S/U on road when #13 ranked all time	**NC State {When Ranked}**
3-0 S/U @ home when #13 ranked since 1993	2-10 S/U on road when ranked since 2002
7-0 S/U when #14 ranked since 1980	5-0 S/U when ranked #4 - #9 all time
6-0-1 S/U @ home when #15 ranked since 1946	0-4 S/U when #10 ranked since 1957
7-0 S/U when #16 ranked since 1972	6-0-1 S/U when #13 ranked all time
5-1 S/U on road when #19 ranked since 1947	5-1 S/U @ home when #16 ranked all time
3-0 S/U when #21 ranked all time	4-0 S/U @ home when #17 ranked all time
0-4 S/U when ranked vs #1 ranked teams all time	4-0 S/U on road when #19 ranked since 1979
0-4 S/U when ranked vs #2 ranked teams all time	4-1 S/U @ home when #19 ranked all time
0-3 S/U when ranked vs #13 ranked teams all time	0-3 S/U & ATS on road when #20 ranked since 1998
10-1 S/U when ranked vs Duke since 1972 {5-0 @ home}	1-5 ATS when #21 ranked all time
0-5 S/U when ranked vs Florida State all time	0-4 S/U on road when #22 ranked all time
0-3 S/U when ranked @ Georgia Tech since 2001	0-7 ATS when #22 ranked all time
7-1 S/U when ranked @ NC State all time	4-0 S/U @ home when #24 ranked all time
7-0 S/U @ home when ranked vs Virginia all time	4-1 S/U when #25 ranked all time
4-0 S/U @ home when ranked vs Wake Forest since 1981	0-8-1 S/U when ranked vs Top #10 teams all time

Copyright © 2021 by Steve's Football Bible, LLC

Team Trends when ranked in the Polls / vs Ranked teams in the Polls

1-6 ATS when ranked vs Top #10 teams since 1992	4-12 O/U vs ranked teams since 2002
0-4 S/U when ranked vs Florida State since 1992	0-13 S/U vs Top 10 ranked teams all time
9-3 S/U when ranked vs Wake Forest all time	3-0 ATS vs #20 ranked teams since 2000

NC State {vs Ranked}	Northwestern {When Ranked}
1-14 S/U on road vs ranked teams since 2005	11-2 S/U when ranked @ home since 2013
2-9 S/U @ home vs ranked teams aince 2013	5-1 S/U when #2 ranked all time
0-4 S/U vs #1 ranked teams all time	4-0 S/U when #7 ranked since 1940
1-5 S/U on road vs #2 ranked teams all time	7-0 S/U @ home when #10 ranked all time
0-7 S/U on road vs #3 ranked teams all time	0-3 S/U on road when #13 ranked since 1949
1-15 S/U vs #3 ranked teams all time	3-0 S/U on road when #18 ranked all time
0-5-1 S/U vs #4 ranked teams all time	1-4 S/U on road when #20 ranked all time
0-9 S/U vs #5 #6 ranked teams all time	5-0 ATS when #22 ranked all time
0-3 S/U & ATS vs #7 ranked teams since 2004	5-0 S/U & ATS when #23 ranked all time
0-3 S/U on road vs #9 ranked teams all time	0-3 S/U when ranked vs #1 ranked teams since 1938
0-3 S/U on road vs #11 ranked teams all time	0-4 S/U when ranked vs #4 ranked teams all time
1-4 S/U vs #12 ranked teams all time	0-3 S/U when ranked vs #9 ranked teams all time
1-6 S/U vs #14 ranked teams all time	7-0 S/U @ home when ranked vs Illinois since 1940
0-4 S/U vs #16 ranked teams since 1953	7-1 S/U when ranked vs Indiana all time {2-0 on road}
5-1 ATS @ home vs #16 ranked teams since 1986	7-0 S/U when ranked vs Minnesota since 1959
1-4 S/U @ home vs #18 ranked teams since 1951	5-1 ATS when ranked vs Minnesota since 1995
0-6 S/U vs #19 ranked teams since 1979	1-5 S/U when ranked vs ranked Notre Dame all time
0-3 ATS on road vs #19 ranked teams since 1987	0-6 S/U when ranked vs Ohio State since 1970
0-7 S/U vs #20 ranked teams all time	1-4 ATS when ranked vs Ohio State since 2001
3-0 ATS vs #22 ranked teams all time	Northwestern {vs Ranked}
3-1 ATS vs #23 ranked teams all time	8-2 ATS on road vs ranked teams since 2011
0-4 O/U vs #23 ranked teams all time	7-21 S/U @ home vs ranked teams since 2005
2-7 ATS vs #24 ranked teams all time	0-18 S/U vs #1 ranked teams since 1938
0-3 S/U & ATS vs #25 ranked teams since 1997	0-7 S/U vs #2 ranked teams since 1966
1-8 S/U @ home vs ranked Clemson since 1997	0-7 S/U on road vs #2 ranked teams all time
0-4 S/U vs ranked Florida State since 2013	0-8 S/U vs #3 ranked teams all time
10-2 ATS vs ranked Florida State since 2001	0-15 S/U vs #4 ranked teams since 1948
0-4 S/U vs ranked Miami all time	1-6-1 S/U on road vs #5 ranked teams all time
1-7 S/U @ home vs ranked North Carolina all time	1-5 S/U vs #6 ranked teams since 1997
0-6 ATS vs ranked North Carolina since 1993	1-5 S/U on road vs #6 ranked teams since 1977
3-1-1 S/U vs ranked Wake Forest all time	1-4 S/U @ home vs #8 ranked teams since 1958

North Texas {When Ranked}	2-8 S/U on road vs #8 ranked teams all time
1-1 S/U when ranked all time	1-14 S/U vs #9 ranked teams since 1939

North Texas {vs Ranked}	0-8 S/U @ home vs #9 ranked teams since 1954
0-24 S/U vs Top 10 ranked teams all time	1-5 ATS vs #9 ranked teams since 1997
0-43 S/U on road vs ranked teams all time	1-7 S/U vs #10 ranked teams since 1974
5-0 ATS vs ranked teams since 2011	0-6 S/U on road vs #10 ranked teams all time
0-3 S/U vs ranked SMU all time	0-7 S/U on road vs #11 ranked teams since 1944

Northern Illinois {When Ranked}	1-5 S/U vs #13 ranked teams all time
4-0 S/U & ATS on road when ranked since 2012	0-3 S/U on road vs #14 ranked teams all time
8-0 S/U @ home when ranked all time	0-5 S/U vs #15 ranked teams all time
3-0 S/U & ATS when #20 ranked all time	1-7 S/U on road vs #16 ranked teams all time
4-0 S/U when #23 ranked all time	0-3-1 S/U on road vs #17 ranked teams all time
0-3 O/U when #24 ranked all time	1-4 ATS vs #17 ranked teams since 1996

Northern Illinois {vs Ranked}	2-8 S/U vs #18 ranked teams since 1954
2-21 S/U on road vs ranked teams all time	4-0 O/U vs #18 ranked teams since 2000
9-2 ATS on road vs ranked teams since 2000	0-5 S/U on road vs #19 ranked teams all time

Copyright © 2021 by Steve's Football Bible, LLC

Team Trends when ranked in the Polls / vs Ranked teams in the Polls

0-6 S/U vs #19 ranked teams since 1983	6-0 S/U when #21 ranked all time
0-5-1 ATS vs #19 ranked teams since 1983	1-5 ATS when #22 ranked since 2010
2-6 O/U vs #20 ranked teams since 2002	0-4 O/U when #23 ranked since 2001
6-1 ATS vs #22 ranked teams all time	1-5 S/U when #24 ranked since 1999 {0-6 ATS}
0-4 S/U vs #25 ranked teams all time	0-4-1 S/U on road when ranked vs #1 ranked teams all time
0-4 S/U @ ranked Illinois since 1990	3-0 S/U @ home when ranked vs #2 ranked teams all time
4-1 ATS vs ranked Illinois since 1990	5-1 ATS when ranked vs #3 ranked teams since 1989
1-21-1 S/U @ ranked Michigan since 1940	1-8 S/U when ranked vs #4 ranked teams since 1991
1-21-1 S/U @ ranked Michigan since 1940	1-9 ATS when ranked vs #4 ranked teams since 1990
2-12-1 S/U vs ranked Minnesota since 1940	0-6 O/U when ranked vs #4 ranked teams since 2001
1-11 S/U vs ranked Purdue since 1958	1-5 S/U on road when ranked vs #6 ranked teams since 1958
2-10 S/U @ ranked Wisconsin all time	4-0 O/U when ranked vs #6 ranked teams since 1994
12-2 ATS vs ranked Wisconsin since 1999	5-0 S/U @ home when ranked vs #7 ranked teams all time

Notre Dame {When Ranked}

45-4 S/U @ home when ranked since 2011	0-3 S/U on road when ranked vs #7 ranked teams since 1989
9-1 S/U on road when #1 ranked since 1988	4-1 S/U on road when ranked vs #8 ranked teams since 1941
16-5-1 S/U on road when #1 ranked vs ranked teams all time	7-0 S/U when ranked vs #9 ranked teams since 1979
13-3-1 S/U @ home when #1 ranked vs ranked teams all time	4-0 S/U @ home when ranked vs #10 ranked teams all time
14-2-2 S/U on road when #2 ranked all time	4-0 O/U when ranked vs #11 ranked teams since 2002
19-3-1 S/U @ home when #2 ranked all time	4-0 S/U & ATS when ranked vs #14 ranked teams since 2014
11-2 S/U on road when #3 ranked since 1965	0-4 O/U when ranked vs #14 ranked teams since 2014
8-0-1 S/U @ home when #3 ranked all time	3-0 S/U on road when ranked vs #15 ranked teams all time
14-4 S/U on road when #4 ranked all time	6-0 S/U @ home when ranked vs #17 ranked teams all time
8-2 S/U on road when #5 ranked since 1977	1-4 O/U when ranked vs #18 ranked teams since 1990
17-3 S/U @ home when #5 ranked since 1968	3-0 S/U on road when ranked vs #18 ranked teams all time
5-1 O/U on road when #6 ranked since 2002	3-1 S/U on road when ranked vs #19 ranked teams all time
10-0 S/U @ home when #6 ranked since 1974	5-1 ATS when ranked vs Florida State all time
17-1 S/U @ home when #7 ranked since 1941	8-0 S/U @ home when ranked vs Georgia Tech all time
11-3-1 S/U on road when #8 ranked all time	37-1 S/U when ranked vs Navy since 1964
11-1 S/U @ home when #8 ranked since 1988	0-4 ATS when ranked vs Purdue since 2006
15-2 S/U on road when #9 ranked since 1969	12-0 S/U @ home when ranked vs Purdue since 1980
13-2 S/U @ home when #9 ranked since 1987	0-4 O/U @ home when ranked vs Purdue since 2000
8-2 ATS @ home when #9 ranked since 2002	1-4 S/U when ranked @ Stanford since 2011
2-8 ATS on road when #9 ranked since 1994	5-0 S/U when ranked vs USC since 2012
5-2 O/U on road when #9 ranked since 2002	6-1 ATS @ home when ranked vs USC since 1993

Notre Dame {vs Ranked}

16-1 S/U @ home when #10 ranked all time	3-11 S/U on road vs ranked teams since 2013
9-0 S/U @ home when #11 ranked since 1977	1-7-1 S/U on road vs #1 ranked teams all time
7-0 S/U on road when #11 ranked since 1977	12-5 ATS vs #1 ranked teams since 1970
9-1 S/U on road when #12 ranked all time	1-4 S/U @ home vs #2 ranked teams since 1956
7-0 S/U @ home when #12 ranked since 1968	4-0 ATS on road vs #2 ranked teams since 1988
2-7 S/U on road when #13 ranked since 1976	4-1 S/U vs #3 ranked teams since 1989
1-5 ATS on road when #13 ranked since 1983	0-4-1 S/U @ home vs #3 ranked teams since 1958
5-1 S/U @ home when #13 ranked since 1972	6-0-1 ATS vs #3 ranked teams since 1986
1-4 S/U on road when #14 ranked all time	1-7 S/U on road vs #4 ranked teams since 1957
7-1 S/U @ home when #14 ranked since 1976	2-10 ATS vs #4 ranked teams since 1985
7-0 S/U @ home when #15 ranked all time	0-7 O/U vs #4 ranked teams since 2001
3-8 O/U when #16 ranked since 1987	0-5 S/U & ATS vs #5 ranked teams since 2001
0-3 S/U on road when #18 ranked since 1982	0-5 S/U vs #6 ranked teams since 1994
8-1 S/U when #19 ranked all time {4-0 on road}	7-1 S/U @ home vs #7 ranked teams all time
6-0 S/U when #20 ranked all time	4-0 O/U @ home vs #7 ranked teams since 1989
4-0 ATS when #20 ranked since 2000	4-0 ATS vs #8 ranked teams since 2004

Copyright © 2021 by Steve's Football Bible, LLC

Team Trends when ranked in the Polls / vs Ranked teams in the Polls

9-2 S/U vs #9 ranked teams since 1979	7-1 O/U @ home when #6 ranked since 2005
6-0 S/U @ home vs #10 ranked teams all time	7-2 ATS on road when #7 ranked since 1985
10-2 S/U vs #10 ranked teams since 1944	8-0 S/U @ home when #7 ranked since 1993
4-0 O/U vs #11 ranked teams since 2002	15-0 S/U on road when #8 ranked since 1960
0-4 S/U on road vs #13 ranked teams all time	13-2 S/U @ home when #8 ranked since 1979
4-0 S/U & ATS @ home vs #14 ranked teams since 2014	14-0 S/U when #9 ranked since 2004
0-4 O/U @ home vs #14 ranked teams since 2014	19-0-1 S/U on road when #9 ranked all time
4-1 S/U on road vs #15 ranked teams all time	20-2 S/U @ home when #9 ranked all time {10 straight W}
1-7 O/U vs #15 ranked teams since 1995	5-0 O/U on road when #10 ranked since 1983
0-4 ATS vs #17 ranked teams since 1997	16-2 S/U @ home when #10 ranked all time
0-4 O/U @ home vs #17 ranked teams since 1985	5-0 O/U @ home when #10 ranked since 2008
1-4 O/U vs #18 ranked teams since 1990	7-0 S/U when #11 ranked since 1993
0-4 S/U vs #20 ranked teams since 1981	12-0 S/U @ home when #11 ranked since 1955
3-0 S/U vs #21 ranked teams all time	8-0 S/U when #12 ranked since 2005
0-3 O/U vs #21 ranked teams all time	6-0 S/U @ home when #13 ranked since 1999
4-1 S/U vs #23 ranked teams all time	5-1 S/U on road when #13 ranked since 1971
5-0 O/U vs #23 ranked teams all time	13-0 S/U when #14 ranked since 1979
0-5 O/U vs #25 ranked teams since 2000	5-0 ATS on road when #14 ranked since 1983
0-3 S/U vs ranked Florida State since 2003	3-0 S/U on road when #15 ranked all time
0-6 S/U @ ranked Stanford all time	9-0 S/U when #16 ranked since 1979 {all home}
1-9 S/U vs ranked USC since 2002	0-7 O/U when #17 ranked since 1990
Ohio U {When Ranked}	1-5 S/U on road when #18 ranked all time
4-2 S/U when ranked all time	7-1 S/U @ home when #18 ranked since 1949
Ohio U {vs Ranked}	5-1 ATS @ home when #18 ranked since 1991
0-26 S/U vs ranked teams all time	4-0 S/U on road when #19 ranked all time
1-7 O/U vs ranked teams since 2005	6-1 S/U @ home when #20 ranked all time
0-3 S/U vs Miami-Ohio all time	7-0 S/U @ home when #22 ranked all time
Ohio State {When Ranked}	0-4 S/U & ATS when #25 ranked all time
37-3 S/U on road when ranked since 2012	4-0 O/U when #25 ranked all time
67-3 S/U @ home when ranked since 2010	0-3 S/U on road when ranked vs #1 ranked teams all time
10-0 S/U on road when ranked vs ranked teams since 2010	4-1 S/U @ home when ranked vs #2 ranked teams all time
16-1 S/U on road when #1 ranked since 1975	3-7 ATS when ranked vs #2 ranked teams since 1999
10-4 ATS on road when #1 ranked since 1998	2-7 S/U when ranked vs #3 ranked teams since 1977
48-2 S/U @ home when #1 ranked all time	1-4 S/U @ home when ranked vs #5 ranked teams all time
2-8 ATS @ home when #1 ranked since 2006	1-5 O/U when ranked vs #5 ranked teams since 1986
2-11 ATS when #2 ranked since 2016	0-6-1 S/U when ranked vs #6 ranked teams since 1964
3-8 ATS on road when #2 ranked since 1993	3-0 S/U @ home when ranked vs #9 ranked teams since 1961
21-4 S/U on road when #2 ranked all time	4-0 S/U on road when ranked vs #11 ranked teams since 1975
27-4 S/U @ home when #2 ranked since 1968	5-1 S/U @ home when ranked vs #12 ranked teams all time
3-7-1 ATS on road when #3 ranked since 1983	3-0 S/U on road when ranked vs #13 ranked teams all time
12-2-1 S/U on road when #3 ranked since 1961	3-0 S/U @ home when ranked vs #14 ranked teams all time
19-2 S/U @ home when #3 ranked since 1961	5-1 S/U when ranked vs #17 ranked teams all time
20-0 S/U when #4 ranked since 2006	11-2 S/U when ranked vs #20 ranked teams all time
16-4 ATS when #4 ranked since 2006	5-0 S/U when ranked vs #21 ranked teams since 1997
17-3 S/U on road when #4 ranked since 1964	6-0 S/U when ranked vs #24 ranked teams all time
26-2 S/U @ home when #4 ranked since 1954	5-0 S/U @ home when ranked vs #25 ranked teams all time
1-6 O/U on road when #5 ranked since 1993	5-0 S/U when ranked vs #25 ranked teams since 1995
20-1 S/U @ home when #5 ranked since 1960	3-0 S/U when ranked vs Akron all time
12-1 S/U when #6 ranked since 2009	1-3 S/U when ranked vs Clemson all time
1-7 ATS on road when #6 ranked since 1983	22-0 S/U when ranked vs Indiana since 1991 {12-0 @ home}
11-0 S/U @ home when #6 ranked since 2002	17-0 S/U when ranked @ Indiana all time

Copyright © 2021 by Steve's Football Bible, LLC

Team Trends when ranked in the Polls / vs Ranked teams in the Polls

6-0 S/U when ranked vs Maryland all time	38-0 S/U @ home when #1 ranked all time
6-0 O/U when ranked vs Maryland all time	5-0 S/U on road when #2 ranked since 2002
13-3 S/U @ home when ranked vs Michigan State since 1973	0-6 ATS on road when #2 ranked since 2001
14-0 S/U when ranked vs Michigan since 2005 {7-0 on road}	16-0 S/U @ home when #2 ranked since 1984
35-2 S/U when ranked vs Minnesota since 1950	0-5 ATS on road when #3 ranked since 2010
19-1 S/U when ranked @ Minneosta all time	33-4 S/U @ home when #3 ranked all time
8-0 S/U when ranked vs Nebraska all time	17-1 S/U on road when #4 ranked since 1952
7-0 S/U when ranked vs Oregon all time	22-2 S/U @ home when #4 ranked all time
11-1 S/U @ home when ranked vs Penn State since 1993	16-2 S/U when #5 ranked since 1985
2-7 O/U when ranked vs Purdue since 2002	16-1 S/U @ home when #5 ranked all time
13-0 S/U @ home when ranked vs Purdue since 1968	22-2 S/U @ home when #6 ranked all time
6-0 S/U & ATS when ranked vs Rutgers all time	13-2 S/U on road when #6 ranked all time
1-7 S/U when ranked vs USC since 1975	11-0 S/U on road when #7 ranked all time

Ohio State {vs Ranked}

9-0 S/U on road vs ranked teams since 2012	14-1 S/U @ home when #7 ranked all time
17-4-1 ATS on road vs ranked teams since 2005	1-6-1 O/U @ home when #7 ranked since 2005
13-2 S/U @ home vs ranked teams since 2009	13-1-2 S/U on road when #8 ranked all time
0-5 S/U on road vs #1 ranked teams all time	10-1 S/U @ home when #8 ranked all time
5-1-1 S/U @ home vs #4 ranked teams all time	6-0 S/U on road when #9 ranked all time
1-5 S/U @ home vs #5 ranked teams all time	6-0 S/U when #9 ranked since 2007
4-0 S/U @ home vs #7 ranked teams since 1975	11-1 S/U when #10 ranked since 2000
5-0 S/U & ATS vs #7 ranked teams since 1988	17-2 S/U @ home when #10 ranked all time
0-3-1 S/U @ home vs #8 ranked teams all time	5-1 S/U @ home when #11 ranked all time
8-1 S/U vs #9 ranked teams since 1961	1-9 O/U when #12 ranked since 2009
3-0 S/U @ home vs #10 ranked teams since 2002	5-1 S/U on road when #12 ranked all time
5-0 S/U on road vs #11 ranked teams since 1975 {4-0 ATS}	5-1 S/U @ home when #12 ranked all time
7-1 S/U & ATS vs #11 ranked teams since 1997	10-0 O/U when #14 ranked since 2010
4-0 ATS vs #12 ranked teams since 2002	5-0 S/U on road when #14 ranked since 1995
8-1-1 S/U vs #13 ranked teams since 1942	13-1 S/U @ home when #14 ranked since 1976
3-0 S/U on road vs #13 ranked teams all time	5-1 S/U @ home when #15 ranked all time
4-0 S/U @ home vs #14 ranked teams all time	5-1 S/U on road when #16 ranked since 1948
3-0 O/U vs #16 ranked teams since 1992	8-2 S/U @ home when #16 ranked all time
3-0 S/U & ATS vs #17 ranked teams since 2002	16-0 S/U when #17 ranked all time
4-0 S/U on road vs #20 ranked teams since 1996	5-0 ATS when #17 ranked since 2006
5-0 S/U vs #21 ranked teams since 1997	5-0 O/U when #17 ranked since 2006
3-0 S/U on road vs #21 ranked teams all time	10-2 S/U when #18 ranked all time {4-1 on road}
6-1 S/U & ATS vs #24 ranked teams all time	13-0 S/U when #19 ranked since 1992 {5-0 on road}
5-0 S/U & ATS vs #25 ranked teams since 1995	8-0 S/U @ home when #19 ranked all time
1-4 S/U & ATS vs Ranked Clemson since 1978	7-1 ATS when #19 ranked since 2010
9-2 O/U vs ranked Michigan since 2003	7-0 S/U @ home when #20 ranked all time
3-0 S/U vs ranked Minnesota since 1985	3-0 S/U @ home when #21 ranked all time
0-3 O/U vs ranked Minnesota since 1985	5-0 O/U when #22 ranked all time
3-0 ATS vs ranked Nebraska since 2011	0-5 S/U when ranked vs #1 ranked teams since 2005
3-0 O/U vs ranked Nebraska since 2011	1-8 O/U when ranked vs #1 ranked teams since 1984
2-10 O/U vs ranked Penn State since 1998	4-0 S/U @ home when ranked vs #2 ranked teams all time
7-1 S/U @ home vs ranked Penn State since 1993	0-4 S/U on road when ranked vs #3 ranked teams all time
4-0 S/U @ home vs ranked Purdue since 1968	4-0 O/U when ranked vs #4 ranked teams since 1986

Oklahoma {When Ranked}

34-3 S/U @ home when ranked since 2015	1-4 S/U when ranked vs #7 ranked teams all time
35-5 S/U on road when ranked since 2012	6-0 S/U when ranked vs #8 ranked teams all time
30-3 S/U on road when #1 ranked all time	5-1 S/U on road when ranked vs #10 ranked teams since 1973
	6-0 S/U @ home when ranked vs #11 ranked teams all time
	11-1 S/U when ranked vs #11 ranked teams since 2000

Copyright © 2021 by Steve's Football Bible, LLC

Team Trends when ranked in the Polls / vs Ranked teams in the Polls

8-1 S/U when ranked vs #12 ranked teams since 1949
3-0 S/U @ home when ranked vs #13 ranked teams all time
6-1 S/U when ranked vs #14 ranked teams all time
4-0 S/U @ home when ranked vs #16 ranked teams all time
8-1 S/U when ranked vs #17 ranked teams all time
3-0 O/U when ranked vs #22 ranked teams since 2004
4-0 S/U when ranked vs #23 ranked teams all time
4-0 S/U when ranked vs #24 ranked teams all time
0-3 S/U on road when ranked vs #25 ranked teams all time
52-3-1 S/U when ranked vs Iowa State all time {27-1 on road}
6-0 O/U when ranked @ Kansas State since 2008
7-1 S/U when ranked @ Kansas State since 2000
15-0 S/U when ranked vs Kansas since 2000
21-1 S/U when ranked @ Kansas since 1948
1-13 O/U when ranked vs Nebraska since 1984
18-2 S/U @ home when ranked vs Nebraska all time
28-2 S/U when ranked @ Oklahoma State all time
5-0 S/U @ home when ranked vs TCU since 2008
19-2 S/U when ranked vs Texas Tech all time
8-1 O/U when ranked vs Texas Tech since 2011
1-7 ATS when ranked vs Texas since 2013
8-0 S/U when ranked vs West Virginia since 2012
6-0 O/U when ranked vs West Virginia since 2014

Oklahoma {vs Ranked}

10-1 S/U on road vs ranked teams since 2015
8-2-1 ATS on road vs ranked teams since 2015
1-5 S/U @ home vs #1 ranked teams all time
1-8 S/U vs #1 ranked teams since 1994
1-8 O/U vs #1 ranked teams since 1984
4-0 S/U @ home vs #2 ranked teams since 1975
0-4 S/U on road vs #3 ranked teams since 1970
4-0 O/U vs #4 ranked teams since 1986
1-5 O/U vs #5 ranked teams since 2001
1-5-1 S/U vs #7 ranked teams all time
7-0 S/U vs #8 ranked teams all time
3-0 S/U @ home vs #9 ranked teams all time
1-4 S/U on road vs #9 ranked teams since 1965
5-1 S/U on road vs #10 ranked teams since 1973
12-1 S/U vs #11 ranked teams since 2000
7-0 S/U @ home vs #11 ranked teams all time
4-0 S/U on road vs #12 ranked teams since 1954
7-1 S/U vs #13 ranked teams all time
1-4 S/U vs #15 ranked teams since 1994
0-3 S/U on road vs #16 ranked teams all time
9-1 S/U vs #17 ranked teams all time
0-5-1 S/U vs #18 ranked teams since 1982
1-4 ATS vs #18 ranked teams since 1995
7-1 S/U vs #19 ranked teams since 1990
4-0 S/U vs #21 ranked teams all time
2-5 ATS vs #22 ranked teams all time
3-0 S/U on road vs #23 ranked teams all time

4-0 S/U vs #24 ranked teams all time
0-3 S/U & ATS on road vs #25 ranked teams all time
0-3 S/U & ATS vs ranked Clemson all time
0-3 O/U vs ranked Clemson all time
4-0-1 S/U vs ranked Iowa State all time
4-1-1 S/U @ ranked Kansas all time
0-4 O/U vs ranked Nebraska since 2000
10-1 S/U @ ranked Oklahoma State all time
6-0 ATS vs ranked Oklahoma State since 2013
4-0 S/U @ home vs ranked TCU all time
3-0 S/U vs ranked Texas Tech all time
3-0 S/U vs ranked West Virginia since 2015
4-0 O/U vs ranked West Virginia since 2008

Oklahoma State {When Ranked}

15-4 S/U on road when ranked since 2015
4-0 S/U when #3 ranked since 2011
0-3 ATS when #5 ranked since 1985
3-0 O/U when #5 ranked since 1985
3-0 S/U on road when #6 ranked all time
3-0 ATS when #7 ranked since 2008
3-0 S/U @ home when #8 ranked all time
6-1 S/U when #9 ranked since 1984
1-7 ATS when #10 ranked since 1984
1-5 O/U on road when #11 ranked all time
8-0 S/U when #12 ranked since 2009
6-0-1 ATS when #12 ranked since 2010
6-0 S/U on road when #12 ranked since 1988
4-0 S/U on road when #13 ranked since 1988
3-0 S/U @ home when #14 ranked all time
0-5 O/U when #15 ranked since 2013
8-0 S/U when #16 ranked all time
7-0 S/U on road when #17 ranked all time
5-1 S/U & ATS when #18 ranked since 1988
5-1 O/U when #19 ranked since 1997
3-0 S/U @ home when #19 ranked since 1987
3-0 S/U on road when #20 ranked since 1977
8-1 S/U when #21 ranked since 2013
6-1 S/U @ home when #21 ranked since 2008
5-0 S/U on road when #22 ranked all time
5-0 S/U when #24 ranked since 2003
7-1 ATS when #25 ranked all time
0-3 S/U when ranked vs #1 ranked teams all time
0-5 S/U when ranked vs #2 ranked teams all time
0-4 S/U when ranked vs #9 ranked teams all time
0-3 S/U when ranked vs #14 ranked teams since 2010
0-3 S/U when ranked vs #16 ranked teams all time
3-0 S/U when ranked vs #22 ranked teams all time
3-0 S/U when ranked vs #24 ranked teams all time
8-1 S/U when ranked vs Baylor since 2003
7-1 ATS when ranked vs Baylor since 2004
5-1 S/U When ranked @ Iowa State since 1988

Copyright © 2021 by Steve's Football Bible, LLC

Team Trends when ranked in the Polls / vs Ranked teams in the Polls

12-1 S/U when ranked vs Kansas State all time {7-0 on road}	**Old Dominion {vs Ranked}**
12-0 S/U when ranked vs Kansas all time	1-2 S/U vs ranked teams all time
2-18 S/U when ranked vs Oklahoma since 1972	**Oregon {When Ranked}**
1-6 ATS @ home when ranked vs Oklahoma since 2008	38-4 S/U @ home when ranked since 2012
10-2 S/U when ranked vs Texas Tech since 2009	6-1 S/U when #1 ranked all time {3-0 on road}
5-1 S/U when ranked vs Texas since 2010	0-8 O/U when #2 ranked since 2013
1-5 O/U when ranked vs Texas since 2010	9-1 S/U on road when #2 ranked since 2012
8-0 S/U when ranked vs Tulsa all time	7-1 S/U @ home when #2 ranked since 2012
Oklahoma State {vs Ranked}	0-4 O/U on road when #2 ranked since 2013
19-100-1 S/U on road all time	6-0 S/U when #3 ranked since 2012
0-11 S/U vs #1 ranked teams all time	7-1 S/U when #4 ranked all time
0-16 S/U vs #2 ranked teams all time	4-0 S/U @ home when #5 ranked since 2007
2-7 S/U on road vs #3 ranked teams all time	5-1 S/U on road when #6 ranked since 2001
2-15 S/U vs #4 ranked teams all time	6-1 S/U when #6 ranked since 2011
2-7 S/U vs #5 ranked teams all time	6-0 S/U @ home when #7 ranked since 2001
4-0 O/U vs #5 ranked teams since 2007	0-6 ATS @ home when #7 ranked since 2001
1-12 S/U vs #6 ranked teams all time {0-10 on road}	6-1 ATS on road when #7 ranked since 2001
0-4 S/U on road vs #7 ranked teams since 1973	4-0 S/U when #8 ranked all time
1-5 S/U @ home vs #7 ranked teams all time	7-0 S/U @ home when #9 ranked all time
0-4 S/U @ home vs #8 ranked teams since 1988	9-2 S/U when #9 ranked since 2000
0-6 S/U vs #9 ranked teams all time	4-0 S/U& ATS when #4 ranked since 2005
1-6 S/U on road vs #10 ranked teams all time	8-2 O/U when #11 ranked since 1998
0-4 S/U @ home vs #11 ranked teams since 1981	6-0 S/U @ home when #12 ranked since 1995
0-3 S/U on road vs #11 ranked teams since 1970	0-4-1 ATS @ home when #12 ranked since 1998
2-9 S/U vs #12 ranked teams all time	5-0 S/U on road when #13 ranked all time
0-4 O/U vs #13 ranked teams since 2005	8-1 S/U when #13 ranked since 2001
0-6 S/U vs #14 ranked teams since 1991	6-1 ATS when #13 ranked since 2002
4-0 O/U vs #14 ranked teams since 2007	7-2 S/U when #18 ranked all time
0-7 S/U vs #16 ranked teams since 1978	6-1 S/U & ATS when #20 ranked since 1995
0-6 ATS vs #16 ranked teams since 1989	4-0 S/U @ home when #22 ranked all time
0-5 S/U on road vs #16 ranked teams all time	5-0 S/U @ home when #24 ranked since 2006
0-4 S/U on road vs #17 ranked teams all time	3-0 S/U & ATS when ranked vs #3 ranked teams since 2002
4-0 S/U @ home vs #17 ranked teams since 1972	1-4 O/U when ranked vs #5 ranked teams all time
2-6 S/U vs #18 ranked teams all time	0-4 O/U when ranked vs #6 ranked teams all time
0-4 S/U on road vs #19 ranked teams all time	3-1 S/U & ATS when ranked vs #12 ranked teams all time
0-4 S/U on road vs #20 ranked teams all time	4-0 S/U & ATS when ranked vs #17 ranked teams since 2001
3-0 ATS vs #20 ranked teams since 1993	4-0-1 O/U when ranked vs #18 ranked teams all time
5-0-1 ATS vs #24 ranked teams all time	3-0 S/U & ATS when ranked vs #22 ranked teams all time
0-4 S/U vs ranked Baylor since 2014	0-6 O/U when ranked vs Arizona since 2012
5-0 S/U vs ranked Iowa State all time	7-0 S/U when ranked vs California since 2010
1-6 S/U vs ranked Kansas all time	7-1 S/U @ home when ranked vs California all time
4-0 S/U @ home vs ranked Kansas State since 2003	0-6 O/U @ home when ranked vs California since 2000
5-1 O/U vs ranked Kansas State since 2003	6-0 S/U & ATS when ranked vs Colorado since 2002
1-7 ATS vs ranked Kansas State since 1998	4-0 S/U when ranked vs Fresno State all time
5-55 S/U vs ranked Oklahoma all time	9-0 S/U when ranked vs Oregon State since 2008
4-0 ATS vs ranked Texas since 2013	6-1 ATS when ranked @ UCLA since 1995
0-4 O/U @ ranked Texas since 2006	6-0 S/U when ranked vs UCLA since 2009
3-0 S/U & ATS vs ranked West Virginia since 2016	9-1 S/U when ranked vs Washington State since 2007
Old Dominion {When Ranked}	1-7 ATS when ranked vs Washington State since 2010
NEVER RANKED	12-0 S/U & ATS when ranked vs Washington since 2005

Copyright © 2021 by Steve's Football Bible, LLC

Team Trends when ranked in the Polls / vs Ranked teams in the Polls

Oregon {vs Ranked}
0-11 S/U vs #1 ranked teams all time
0-5 S/U on road vs #2 ranked teams all time
1-5 S/U on road vs #3 ranked teams all time
4-0 ATS vs #3 ranked teams since 1991
0-3 S/U on road vs #4 ranked teams all time
0-6 S/U on road vs #5 ranked teams all time
2-8 S/U vs #5 ranked teams all time
1-5 S/U on road vs #6 ranked teams all time
0-6 O/U vs #6 ranked teams since 2000
1-6 S/U on road vs #9 ranked teams all time
1-4 S/U on road vs #13 ranked teams all time
0-3 S/U on road vs #14 ranked teams all time
0-4 ATS vs #14 ranked teams since 1983
0-4-1 S/U @ home vs #15 ranked teams all time
0-3 ATS @ home vs #15 ranked teams since 1986
4-1 S/U vs #16 ranked teams since 1987
4-1 ATS vs #16 ranked teams since 1987
4-0 S/U vs #17 ranked teams since 2001
4-0 ATS vs #17 ranked teams since 2001
5-0-1 O/U vs #18 ranked teams since 2009
5-1 S/U vs #19 ranked teams since 1955
0-4 S/U vs #20 ranked teams since 1992
0-4 ATS vs #20 ranked teams since 1992
4-0 S/U @ home vs #23 ranked teams since 1998
4-0 ATS @ home vs #23 ranked teams since 1998
4-0 ATS vs #24 ranked teams all time
5-0 S/U @ home vs ranked Arizona since 1989
3-0 S/U vs ranked Arizona State since 2005
3-0 S/U vs ranked Oregon State since 2008
4-0 S/U vs ranked UCLA since 2000
8-0 ATS vs ranked UCLA since 1988
0-4 S/U & ATS vs ranked Washington State since 2002
0-4 S/U @ home vs ranked Washington State all time
0-4 ATS @ home vs ranked Washington State all time

Oregon State {When Ranked}
7-1 O/U on road when ranked since 2009
3-0 S/U @ home when #13 ranked all time
3-0 S/U when #14 ranked all time
4-1 S/U @ home when #15 ranked all time
4-0 S/U when #18 ranked since 1962
0-4 S/U when #24 ranked since 2009
0-7 S/U on road when ranked vs ranked teams since 1968
0-8 S/U when ranked vs ranked teams since 2009
0-4 S/U when ranked @ USC all time
4-0 S/U when ranked vs Washington State since 1962
0-4 S/U when ranked vs Washington since 2000

Oregon State {vs Ranked}
6-75 S/U on road vs ranked teams since 1970
1-10 S/U @ home vs ranked teams since 2012
4-11 O/U @ home vs ranked teams since 2010

1-7 S/U vs #1 ranked teams since 1968
0-11 S/U vs #3 ranked teams all time
4-0 ATS on road vs #3 ranked teams since 1986
0-11 S/U vs #4 ranked teams all time
0-4 S/U on road vs #5 ranked teams all time
1-12 S/U vs #6 ranked teams all time
5-0 ATS on road vs #6 ranked teams since 1984
0-7 S/U on road vs #7 ranked teams all time
0-3 S/U on road vs #8 ranked teams all time
1-4 S/U on road vs #9 ranked teams all time
0-3 S/U on road vs #11 ranked teams all time
0-6 S/U vs #12 ranked teams since 1973
0-4 S/U on road vs #13 ranked teams since 1953
1-10 S/U vs #14 ranked teams all time {0-3 @ home}
1-6 S/U vs #15 ranked teams since 1969
0-11 S/U vs #16 ranked teams all time
0-6 S/U vs #17 ranked teams since 1948
0-4 O/U vs #18 ranked teams since 2002
1-7 S/U vs #19 ranked teams since 1970
0-5 S/U vs #21 ranked teams since 1997
6-1 ATS vs ranked Arizona State since 1996
3-0 S/U & ATS @ ranked California since 2005
2-10 S/U vs ranked Oregon since 2001 {1-4 @ home}
5-0 O/U @ ranked Oregon since 2005
0-9 S/U @ home vs ranked Stanford all time
0-11 S/U vs ranked Stanford since 1969
1-5 ATS vs ranked Stanford since 2010
0-18 S/U @ ranked USC since 1968
1-18 S/U vs ranked Washington since 1959
0-4 S/U @ ranked Washington State since 1988

Penn State {When Ranked}
41-7 S/U @ home when ranked since 2008
7-0 S/U @ home when #1 ranked all time
33-3 S/U when #2 ranked all time {12-1 on road} {4-0 in Bowls}
22-3 S/U when #3 ranked all time {7-0 @ home}
7-1 S/U @ home when #4 ranked all time
6-1 S/U @ home when #5 ranked since 1986
6-1 S/U on road when #5 ranked since 1973
11-0 S/U on road when #6 ranked since 1972
13-4 ATS when #6 ranked since 1986
0-4 S/U on road when #7 ranked since 1974
7-0 S/U @ home when #7 ranked since 1995
9-1 S/U @ home when #8 ranked since 1982
13-3 S/U on road when #9 ranked all time
12-2 S/U @ home when #9 ranked since 1971
32-4 S/U when #10 ranked all time {22-1 @ home}
5-0 S/U on road when #12 ranked since 2005
15-2-1 S/U when #13 ranked all time {6-0 @ home}
14-3 S/U when #14 ranked all time {5-1 @ home}
9-0 ATS when #15 ranked snice 1996
7-0 S/U @ home when #15 ranked since 1993

Copyright © 2021 by Steve's Football Bible, LLC

Team Trends when ranked in the Polls / vs Ranked teams in the Polls

7-0 S/U @ home when #16 ranked all time	3-0 S/U on road vs #10 ranked teams all time
10-1 S/U when #16 ranked since 1987	0-3 S/U @ home vs #10 ranked teams since 2004
6-0 S/U when #17 ranked since 1993	5-1 ATS vs #12 ranked teams since 1975
6-0 S/U @ home when #18 ranked all time	0-4 S/U on road vs #13 ranked teams since 1987
9-0 S/U @ home when #19 ranked since 1984	1-4 O/U vs #13 ranked teams since 1989
10-1 S/U when #19 ranked since 1985	5-1 O/U vs #14 ranked teams since 1988
5-0 S/U @ home when #20 ranked since 1987	0-3 S/U on road vs #15 ranked teams since 1999
3-0 S/U @ home when #21 ranked since 1990	7-0 O/U vs #16 ranked teams since 1996
0-6 O/U when #22 ranked all time	3-0 S/U @ home vs #17 ranked teams all time
1-6 ATS when #24 ranked since 2002	4-0 S/U & ATS @ home vs #18 ranked teams since 1999
0-4 S/U & ATS when ranked vs #1 ranked teams since 1998	0-4 S/U on road vs #18 ranked teams since 2003
2-7 S/U when ranked vs #2 ranked teams all time	7-1-1 ATS vs #19 ranked teams since 1989
0-6 S/U when ranked vs #3 ranked teams all time	0-3 S/U on road vs #20 ranked teams all time
0-4 ATS when ranked vs #3 ranked teams since 1986	0-4 O/U vs #20 ranked teams since 1997
1-9 S/U when ranked vs #4 ranked teams since 1959	4-0 S/U vs #22 rankled teams since 2000
0-3 S/U & ATS when ranked vs #5 ranked teams since 1995	3-0 S/U vs ranked Maryland all time
0-3 S/U on road when ranked vs #6 ranked teams since 1979	0-4 S/U & ATS vs ranked Michigan State since 2010
4-0 ATS when ranked vs #8 ranked teams all time	3-10 S/U vs ranked Michigan since 1997
5-0 S/U when ranked vs #10 ranked teams all time	1-11 S/U @ ranked Ohio State since 1993
6-1 S/U when ranked vs #12 ranked teams since 1972	1-10 S/U vs ranked Ohio State since 2009
0-4 S/U on road when ranked vs #13 ranked teams since 1987	3-0 S/U @ home vs ranked Wisconsin all time
1-4 O/U when ranked vs #13 ranked teams since 1989	**Pittsburgh {When Ranked}**
6-0 O/U when ranked vs #16 ranked teams since 1996	3-0 S/U on road when #1 ranked all time
5-0 S/U when ranked vs #17 ranked teams since 1969	12-0-1 S/U when #2 ranked all time
3-0 S/U when ranked vs #19 ranked teams all time	12-2 S/U when #3 ranked all time
0-3 ATS when ranked vs #22 ranked teams all time	5-1 S/U when #5 ranked all time
13-1 S/U when ranked vs Illinois all time {6-0 @ home}	5-0 S/U @ home when #6 ranked all time
13-1 S/U when ranked vs Indiana all time	0-3 S/U on road when #7 ranked since 1956
5-0 S/U when ranked vs Iowa since 2011	4-1 S/U on road when #8 ranked all time
22-0-1 S/U when ranked vs Maryland all time	5-0 S/U @ home when #9 ranked all time
9-3 O/U when ranked vs Michigan State since 1996	5-1 S/U @ home when #10 ranked all time
0-12 S/U when ranked vs Top #5 ranked Ohio State all time	6-0 S/U when #11 ranked since 1978
17-1 S/U when ranked vs Rutgers all time {6-0 on road}	5-0 S/U when #12 ranked since 1977
0-3 S/U when ranked vs USC since 2000	3-0 S/U @ home when #13 ranked all time
21-1 S/U when ranked vs West Virginia since 1956 {10-0 @ home}	0-5 S/U when #15 ranked since 1978
Penn State {vs Ranked}	0-4 S/U & ATS when #16 ranked since 1983
3-24 S/U on road vs ranked teams since 2002	4-0 S/U on road when #19 ranked all time
5-14-1 ATS on road vs ranked teams since 2006	0-6 S/U on road when #20 ranked all time
10-4 O/U on road vs ranked teams since 2010	0-3 ATS when #22 ranked all time
2-9 S/U on road vs #1 ranked teams all time	0-3 S/U @ home when #23 ranked since 1991
0-5 S/U & ATS vs #1 ranked teams since 1998	3-0 S/U on road when #23 ranked all time
0-5 O/U on road vs #1 ranked teams since 1998	1-6 O/U when #25 ranked all time
0-4 S/U on road vs #3 ranked teams all time	0-6 S/U when ranked vs #1 ranked teams all time
0-5 S/U & ATS vs #3 ranked teams since 1986	1-12 S/U when ranked vs Top #4 ranked teams all time
0-9 S/U on road vs #4 ranked teams all time	0-4 S/U when ranked vs Miami since 1989
0-6 S/U vs #4 ranked teams since 2002 {1-5 ATS}	0-4 O/U when ranked vs Miami since 1989
0-5 S/U on road vs #6 ranked teams since 1979	11-1-1 S/U when ranked vs Syracuse since 1976
3-0 S/U @ home vs #7 ranked teams since 1987	**Pittsburgh {vs Ranked}**
6-0 ATS vs #8 ranked teams since 1982	6-43-1 S/U on road vs ranked teams since 1984
3-0 O/U vs #8 ranked teams since 1999	0-12-1 S/U vs #1 ranked teams all time
3-0 O/U vs #9 ranked teams since 1984	1-11 S/U on road vs #2 ranked teams all time

Copyright © 2021 by Steve's Football Bible, LLC

Team Trends when ranked in the Polls / vs Ranked teams in the Polls

0-6 S/U @ home vs #3 ranked teams since 1945	12-1 S/U when ranked vs Northwestern since 1958 {7-0 @ home}
5-1 ATS vs #3 ranked teams since 1990	0-4 S/U on road when ranked vs Ohio State since 1968
1-11 S/U vs #4 ranked teams all time	3-0 S/U when ranked @ Wisconsin since 1980
0-4 S/U vs #5 ranked teams since 2005	**Purdue {vs Ranked}**
0-7 S/U vs #6 ranked teams since 1965	4-71-1 S/U on road vs ranked teams since 1974
0-5 S/U vs #7 ranked teams since 1972	11-0 ATS on road vs ranked teams since 2012
0-5 S/U on road vs #7 ranked teams since 1957	1-7 O/U on road vs ranked teams since 2012
0-9-1 S/U @ home vs #8 ranked teams all time	5-20 S/U @ home vs ranked teams since 2004
0-11 S/U vs #8 ranked teams since 1954	0-3 S/U vs #1 ranked Ohio State all time
1-5 ATS vs #8 ranked teams since 1987	0-7 S/U @ home vs #3 ranked teams since 1970
0-4-1 S/U vs #9 ranked teams since 1977	1-8 S/U on road vs #3 ranked teams all time
0-3-1 S/U on road vs #9 ranked teams since 1958	4-0-1 ATS vs #3 ranked teams since 1986
2-8 S/U vs #10 ranked teams all time	0-5 S/U @ home vs #4 ranked teams all time
1-9 S/U @ home vs #11 ranked teams since 1940	0-8 S/U on road vs #4 ranked teams since 1953
0-5 S/U vs #11 ranked teams since 1988	0-4 O/U vs #4 ranked teams since 2001
1-4 S/U on road vs #12 ranked teams since 1946	1-5 S/U on road vs #5 ranked teams all time
1-6 S/U vs #13 ranked teams all time	0-7 S/U on road vs #6 ranked teams all time
3-0 S/U @ home vs #14 ranked teams since 1958	1-9 S/U vs #6 ranked teams since 1970
0-3 S/U on road vs #17 ranked teams all time	0-4 ATS @ home vs #6 ranked teams since 1997
0-4 S/U vs #18 ranked teams since 1988	1-6 S/U @ home vs #7 ranked teams all time
1-5 S/U @ home vs #19 ranked teams all time	0-3 S/U on road vs #7 ranked teams since 1978
1-6 S/U vs #19 ranked teams since 1994	0-7 S/U vs #8 ranked teams since 1987
0-6-1 S/U on road vs #20 ranked teams all time	0-6 S/U on road vs #8 ranked teams all time
1-8-1 S/U vs #20 ranked teams since 1946	0-5 S/U on road vs #9 ranked teams all time
0-5 S/U vs #22 ranked teams all time {1-4 ATS}	0-6-1 S/U on road vs #10 ranked teams all time
3-7 S/U vs #24 ranked teams all time	0-14 S/U vs #11 ranked teams since 1977
2-15 S/U vs Miami since 1984	0-8 S/U @ home vs #11 ranked teams all time
2-8 O/U vs Miami since 1997	0-3 S/U on road vs #12 ranked teams since 1987
0-7 S/U vs Syracuse since 1991	0-8 S/U vs #13 ranked teams since 1983
7-2 ATS vs Virginia Tech since 1999	1-6 S/U vs #14 ranked teams all time
Purdue {When Ranked}	4-0 ATS vs #14 ranked teams since 2003
0-6 S/U on road when #10 ranked all time	0-3 O/U vs #16 ranked teams since 1997
0-3 S/U when #11 ranked since 1999	1-5 S/U vs #16 ranked teams since 1980
3-0 S/U @ home when #13 ranked all time	0-3 S/U vs #18 ranked teams since 2008
5-1 S/U @ home when #14 ranked all time	0-4 S/U on road vs #19 ranked teams all time
5-1 S/U on road when #15 ranked all time	0-3 S/U @ home vs #20 ranked teams all time
1-6 O/U when #17 ranked since 1997	1-8 S/U vs #20 ranked teams since 1950
3-0 S/U @ home when #18 ranked since 1978	1-7 S/U vs #21 ranked teams all time
3-0 S/U on road when #19 ranked all time	0-3 S/U on road vs #24 ranked teams all time
6-1 S/U when #20 ranked all time {3-0 on road}	1-6 S/U vs #25 ranked teams all time
3-0 S/U when #21 ranked all time	3-0 ATS on road vs #25 ranked teams all time
4-0 S/U when #24 ranked all time	0-4 S/U vs ranked Indiana since 1942
3-0 S/U when #25 ranked all time	0-9 S/U @ ranked Iowa all time
0-6 S/U when ranked vs #4 ranked teams since 1945	4-1 O/U vs ranked Iowa since 2004
0-3 S/U when ranked vs #11 ranked teams since 1980	1-9 S/U vs ranked Michigan State since 1963
0-3 S/U & ATS when ranked vs #13 ranked teams since 2003	5-1 ATS vs ranked Michigan State since 1993
0-4 S/U & ATS when ranked vs #21 ranked teams all time	2-7 S/U vs ranked Minnesota since 1936
10-2-1 S/U when ranked vs Illinois all time	0-3 S/U & O/U vs ranked Nebraska since 2013
8-0 S/U when ranked vs Indiana since 1968	3-1 ATS vs ranked Northwestern since 1996
6-1 S/U when ranked vs Michigan State since 1967	0-12 S/U @ ranked Notre Dame since 1980
4-0 O/U when ranked vs Minnesota since 1999	2-18 S/U vs ranked Notre Dame since 1987

Copyright © 2021 by Steve's Football Bible, LLC

Team Trends when ranked in the Polls / vs Ranked teams in the Polls

4-0 ATS vs ranked Notre Dame since 2006	1-27 S/U vs ranked ranked Texas since 1968
0-15-1 S/U @ ranked Ohio State since 1957	**Rutgers {When Ranked}**
0-9 S/U vs ranked Wisconsin since 2004 {2-7 ATS}	5-0 S/U when #15 ranked all time
1-9-1 S/U @ ranked Wisconsin all time	0-3 O/U when #22 ranked all time
Rices {When Ranked}	**Rutgers {vs Ranked}**
RICE was last ranked in 1961	1-38-1 S/U vs Top #10 ranked teams all time
3-0 S/U when #14 ranked all time	1-38-1 S/U on road vs ranked teams since 1989
0-5 S/U when #15 ranked since 1950	0-14 S/U @ home vs ranked teams since 2009
7-0 S/U when #16 ranked all time	0-4 S/U vs #1 ranked teams all time
0-3 S/U when #17 ranked all time	0-27-1 S/U vs #3 - #9 ranked teams all time
3-0 S/U when #19 ranked all time	5-0 ATS vs #3 ranked teams since 1985
3-0 S/U when #20 ranked all time	0-4 ATS vs #9 ranked teams all time
1-6 S/U when ranked vs Top #5 ranked teams all time	0-21 S/U vs #10 #11 #12 #13 #14 ranked teams all time
7-0 S/U when ranked vs #10 - #17 ranked teams all time	0-4 ATS vs #10 ranked teams since 1996
5-0 S/U @ home when ranked vs Baylor all time	0-3 ATS vs #13 ranked teams since 1994
1-5 S/U when ranked vs SMU since 1947	4-1 ATS vs #15 ranked teams since 1988
6-1 S/U when ranked vs TCU since 1946	0-6 S/U vs #16 ranked teams all time
6-1 S/U when ranked vs Texas A&M since 1946	3-1 S/U vs #17 ranked teams all time
3-0 S/U when ranked vs Texas Tech all time	0-12-1 S/U vs #20 #21 #22 #23 ranked teams all time
Rice {vs Ranked}	0-4 S/U vs ranked Michigan all time
1-71 S/U on road vs ranked teams since 1971	4-0 O/U vs ranked Michigan all time
3-31 S/U @ home vs ranked teams since 1975	0-7 S/U vs ranked Ohio State all time
0-4-1 S/U vs #1 ranked teams all time	2-5 ATS vs ranked Ohio State all time
0-11 S/U vs #2 ranked teams all time	1-16 S/U vs ranked Penn State all time
0-6 S/U on road vs #3 ranked teams all time	0-3 S/U & ATS vs ranked Syracuse all time
0-10 S/U vs #3 ranked teams since 1947	**San Diego State {When Ranked}**
0-5 S/U on road vs #4 ranked teams all time	4-0 S/U when #20 ranked all time
0-6 S/U vs #4 ranked teams since 1962	**San Diego State {vs Ranked}**
0-6 S/U vs #5 ranked teams since 1980	3-37 S/U on road vs ranked teams all time
0-5 S/U vs #6 ranked teams all time	1-23 S/U vs Top #10 ranked teams all time
0-7 S/U on road vs #7 ranked teams all time	1-15 O/U on road vs ranked teams since 1997
0-11 S/U vs # 7 ranked teams since 1950	12-3-1 O/U @ home vs ranked teams since 2000
1-8 S/U vs #8 ranked teams all time	1-23 S/U vs Top #10 ranked teams all time
0-5 S/U vs #9 ranked teams since 1955	0-3 ATS vs #7 ranked teams since 1985
0-12 S/U vs #10 ranked teams since 1951	0-4 S/U vs #10 #11 ranked teams all time
0-5 S/U vs #11 ranked teams since 1978	0-3 S/U on road vs #12 ranked teams all time
1-6 S/U vs #12 ranked teams since 1959	0-4 S/U vs #17 ranked teams since 1999
0-5 S/U vs #13 ranked team since 1974	4-0 ATS vs #17 ranked teams since 1999
0-9 S/U vs #14 ranked teams all time	0-3 O/U vs #17 ranked teams since 2002
0-6-1 S/U vs #15 ranked teams since 1956	0-7 S/U vs #21 ranked teams all time {1-6 ATS}
0-7-1 S/U vs #16 ranked teams since 1971	0-4 S/U vs #25 ranked teams since 1995
0-6-1 S/U vs #17 ranked teams since 1971	1-4 S/U vs ranked Air Force since 1985
0-9 S/U vs #18 ranked teams since 1972	2-13 S/U vs ranked BYU all time
0-6 S/U vs #19 ranked teams all time	0-4 S/U vs ranked Utah since 2004
0-5 S/U on road vs #20 ranked teams all time	0-4 ATS vs ranked Utah since 2004
0-3 O/U vs #21 ranked teams since 1997	**San Jose State {When Ranked}**
0-18-1 S/U vs ranked Arkansas since 1959	1-2 S/U when ranked all time
0-11 S/U @ ranked Arkansas since 1954	**San Jose State {vs Ranked}**
0-10 S/U vs ranked Houston all time	0-35 S/U on road vs ranked teams since 1981
0-15 S/U @ ranked Texas since 1969	1-10 S/U @ home vs ranked teams since 2001
0-4 ATS @ ranked Texas since 2005	1-15 S/U vs Top #10 ranked teams all time

 Copyright © 2021 by Steve's Football Bible, LLC

5-34 S/U vs #10 - #19 ranked teams all time	2-5 O/U vs #9 ranked teams since 1997
1-3 O/U vs #21 ranked teams all time	3-0 ATS on road vs #9 ranked teams since 2001
0-16 S/U vs #20 - #25 ranked teams all time	2-7 S/U @ home vs #12 ranked teams since 1976
4-1 ATS vs Fresno State since 1986	2-7 S/U vs #12 ranked teams since 1989
0-3 S/U vs Wyoming all time	0-4 S/U & ATS vs #13 ranked teams since 1983

South Alabama {When Ranked}

NEVER RANKED

South Alabama {vs Ranked}

1-6 S/U vs Ranked teams all time	

South Carolina {When Ranked}

29-5 S/U @ home when ranked since 2009	1-5 S/U on road vs #14 ranked teams all time
8-0 S/U when #12 ranked since 2011	1-9-1 S/U vs #14 ranked teams since 1948
7-0 S/U @ home when #12 ranked all time	4-0-1 ATS vs #15 ranked teams since 1992
7-0 S/U when #14 ranked since 2002	0-4 S/U vs #17 ranked teams since 2007
4-0 S/U on road when #14 ranked since 1987	0-4 ATS vs #17 ranked teams since 2007
5-0 S/U @ home when #16 ranked all time	5-0 S/U vs #18 ranked teams since 1970 {3-0 ATS}
9-1 S/U when #17 ranked since 1980	0-3 O/U vs #18 ranked teams since 2001
3-0 S/U on road when #18 ranked since 2000	1-10 S/U vs #20 ranked teams all time {0-6 @ home}
1-4 ATS when #21 ranked all time	1-4 ATS vs #21 ranked teams all time
4-1 S/U @ home when #24 ranked all time	1-6 S/U vs ranked Auburn all time
1-4 S/U & ATS when #25 ranked all time	5-0 O/U vs ranked Auburn since 2006
0-4 S/U when ranked vs #2 ranked teams all time	0-6 S/U vs ranked Clemson since 2014
0-4 S/U when ranked vs #3 ranked teams all time	5-1 ATS @ home vs ranked Clemson since 2007
0-4 S/U when ranked vs #4 ranked teams all time	2-21 S/U vs ranked Florida all time
3-0 S/U when ranked vs #6 ranked teams all time	1-4 S/U @ ranked Georgia since 2009
0-4 S/U when ranked vs #9 ranked teams all time	3-15 S/U vs ranked Tennessee all time
0-3 S/U when ranked vs Auburn all time	5-0 ATS @ ranked Tennessee since 1997
4-0 S/U & ATS when ranked vs Clemson since 2010	0-4 S/U vs ranked Texas A&M all time

USC {When Ranked}

0-7 O/U when ranked vs Clemson since 2000	11-1 S/U @ home when ranked since 2016
5-1 S/U @ home when ranked vs Clemson all time	69-6-2 S/U when #1 ranked all time
5-1 S/U when ranked vs ranked Clemson all time	32-2 S/U on road when #1 ranked all time
5-0 S/U when ranked vs East Carolina all time	16-0 S/U @ home when #1 ranked since 2004
5-0 S/U @ home when ranked vs Kentucky all time	0-4 ATS when #2 ranked since 2006
6-0 O/U when ranked vs Kentucky since 2007	1-6 ATS on road when #3 ranked since 2003
0-3 O/U when ranked vs Missouri since 2012	15-1-1 S/U @ home when #3 ranked since 1962
6-0 S/U when ranked vs Vanderbilt since 2009	22-0 S/U when #4 ranked since 1976 {9-0 on road}

South Carolina {vs Ranked}

0-12 S/U on road vs ranked teams since 2014	18-0 S/U @ home when #4 ranked since 1967
1-6 S/U vs #1 ranked teams all time {0-3 on road}	0-4 ATS on road when #5 ranked since 1995
4-0 ATS vs #1 ranked teams since 1996	15-2 S/U @ home when #5 ranked all time
0-13 S/U vs #2 ranked teams all time	8-1 O/U when #6 ranked since 2002
10-1 ATS vs #2 ranked teams since 1987	9-0 S/U on road when #6 ranked since 1974
2-12 S/U vs #3 ranked teams all time {0-7 @ home}	11-1-1 S/U @ home when #6 ranked since 1966
2-5 ATS vs #3 ranked teams since 1995	16-0-1 S/U @ home when #7 ranked all time
1-11 S/U vs #4 ranked teams all time {0-7 on road}	6-0 S/U when #7 ranked since 2002
0-3 S/U on road vs #6 ranked teams all time	10-1 S/U on road when #8 ranked all time
4-0 ATS vs #6 ranked teams since 1996	12-1-2 S/U @ home when #8 ranked all time
0-9 S/U vs #7 ranked teams all time	13-2-1 S/U @ home when #9 ranked since 1955
0-7 S/U on road vs #8 ranked teams since 1958	4-0 O/U on road when #10 ranked since 1989
4-0 O/U vs #8 ranked teams since 2003	0-4 O/U @ home when #11 ranked since 1995
0-12 S/U vs #9 ranked teams all time	6-1 S/U @ home when #11 ranked since 1959
	9-0 S/U when #12 ranked since 1984
	6-0 S/U @ home when #12 ranked since 1982
	2-9 O/U when #13 ranked since 1992
	12-1 S/U @ home when #13 ranked all time
	4-0 S/U @ home when #14 ranked since 1945

Copyright © 2021 by Steve's Football Bible, LLC

11-3 S/U @ home when #16 ranked all time	4-0 O/U vs #2 ranked teams since 1993
2-7 ATS when #20 ranked since 2010	8-1 ATS vs #3 ranked teams since 1973
6-1 S/U @ home when #20 ranked since 1984	11-3 S/U vs #3 ranked teams all time
6-2 S/U & ATS when #21 ranked since 1995	7-2 S/U vs #4 ranked teams since 1963
0-3 S/U @ home when #23 ranked since 1997	2-8 O/U vs #5 ranked teams since 1987
0-6 ATS when #24 ranked since 2010	10-0 S/U vs #6 ranked teams since 1955
0-3 ATS when #25 ranked all time	7-0 ATS vs #6 ranked teams since 1985
0-3 O/U when #25 ranked all time	3-17 S/U vs #7 ranked teams since 1950
0-5 S/U when ranked vs #1 ranked teams since 1988	4-0-1 S/U @ home vs #8 ranked teams since 1962
7-0 S/U & ATS when ranked vs #3 ranked teams since 1973	5-2 S/U vs #9 ranked teams since 1979
7-0 S/U when ranked in Bowl games vs #3 ranked teams all time	1-6 S/U on road vs #10 ranked teams all time
3-0 S/U on road when ranked vs #4 ranked teams since 1972	0-6 ATS on road vs #10 ranked teams since 1987
10-0 S/U when ranked vs #6 ranked teams all time	1-6 S/U on road vs #11 ranked teams since 1977
7-0 ATS when ranked vs #6 ranked teams since 1985	1-4 S/U on road vs #12 ranked teams since 1957
1-4 S/U on road when ranked vs #7 ranked teams since 1952	5-0 S/U @ home vs #13 ranked teams since 1968
1-4 S/U @ home when ranked vs #7 ranked teams all time	5-1 ATS vs #13 ranked teams since 1992
0-4 S/U on road when ranked vs #10 ranked teams all time	10-2 S/U vs #14 ranked teams all time
1-5 S/U on road when ranked vs #11 ranked teams since 1977	0-6-1 S/U on road vs #17 ranked teams all time
3-0 S/U @ home when ranked vs #11 ranked teams since 1953	0-6 ATS on road vs #17 ranked teams since 1987
5-0 S/U when ranked vs #13 ranked teams all time	3-0 S/U @ home vs #17 ranked teams all time
10-0 S/U when ranked vs #14 ranked teams all time	3-0 S/U & ATS vs #18 ranked teams since 1988
4-0 S/U when ranked vs #15 ranked teams since 1972	1-5 O/U vs #19 ranked teams since 1986
0-5-1 S/U on road when ranked vs #17 ranked teams all time	6-2 S/U vs #19 ranked teams since 1971
1-6 ATS when ranked vs #17 ranked teams since 1987	5-1 S/U vs #20 ranked teams since 1979
3-0-1 S/U @ home when ranked vs #18 ranked teams all time	0-7 O/U vs #21 ranked teams all time
1-3 O/U when ranked vs #19 ranked since 1989	0-3 S/U & ATS on road vs #21 ranked teams all time
0-5 O/U when ranked vs #21 ranked teams all time	5-1 S/U on road vs #25 ranked teams all time
3-0 S/U & ATS when ranked vs #24 ranked teams all time	5-0-1 O/U vs #25 ranked teams since 1999
0-3 O/U when ranked vs #24 ranked teams all time	8-1 S/U vs ranked Arizona all time {3-0 S/U & ATS @ home}
4-0 O/U when ranked vs #25 ranked teams since 2002	3-0 S/U vs ranked Arizona State since 2004
9-1 S/U when ranked @ Arizona State since 1988	5-0 S/U vs ranked California since 2004
1-7 ATS when ranked vs Arizona since 2005	0-5 O/U vs ranked California since 2004
8-0 S/U when ranked vs California since 2004	3-0 S/U vs ranked Colorado since 2002
0-8 O/U when ranked vs California since 2004	0-3 O/U vs ranked Colorado since 2002
8-0 S/U when ranked vs Colorado all time	0-5 S/U vs ranked Notre Dame since 2012
9-1 S/U when ranked vs Notre Dame since 2002	5-2 O/U @ ranked Notre Dame since 1993
7-1 S/U when ranked vs Ohio State since 1975	7-1 S/U vs ranked Ohio State since 1975
17-0 S/U @ home when ranked vs Oregon State since 1968	3-0 S/U @ home vs ranked Oregon State all time
3-0 S/U when ranked vs San Jose State all time	1-5 S/U & ATS vs ranked Oregon since 2009
1-4 S/U @ home when ranked vs Stanford since 2007	**South Florida {When Ranked}**
2-7 ATS @ home when ranked vs Stanford since 1989	9-1 S/U @ home when ranked since 2011
4-0 O/U @ home when ranked vs Stanford since 2009	4-12 ATS on road when ranked since 2007
2-9 O/U when ranked vs UCLA since 2006	4-0 S/U when #18 ranked all time
4-10 ATS when ranked @ UCLA since 1984	4-0 S/U when #19 ranked all time
6-1 S/U @ home when ranked vs UCLA since 2003	5-0 S/U when #23 ranked all time
5-1 S/U when ranked vs Wisconsin all time	**South Florida {vs Ranked}**
USC {vs Ranked}	0-8 S/U on road vs ranked teams since 2012
1-11 S/U on road vs ranked teams since 2014	8-1 ATS on road vs ranked teams since 2011
2-11 ATS on road vs ranked teams since 2014	2-11 S/U @ home vs ranked teams since 2009
7-2 S/U @ home vs ranked teams since 2015	0-7 S/U vs #12 #13 #14 #15 ranked teams all time
0-6 S/U vs #1 ranked teams since 1988	0-6 S/U vs #19 ranked teams all time

Copyright © 2021 by Steve's Football Bible, LLC

Team Trends when ranked in the Polls / vs Ranked teams in the Polls

0-3 S/U vs Central Florida all time

SMU {When Ranked}

25-5-1 S/U @ home when ranked since 1979
3-0-1 S/U when #2 ranked all time
5-1-2 S/U when #3 ranked all time
5-0 S/U on road when #6 ranked since 1981
5-1-1 S/U when #8 ranked all time
5-0 S/U when #10 ranked since 1981
4-0 S/U on road when #10 ranked all time
4-0 S/U when #13 ranked since 1981
0-3 S/U when ranked vs #2 ranked teams all time
5-1 S/U when ranked vs Houston since 1981
3-0 S/U when ranked vs North Texas all time
6-0 S/U when ranked vs TCU since 1979

SMU {vs Ranked}

2-33 S/U on road vs ranked teams since 1989
5-21-1 S/U @ home vs ranked teams since 1986
10-3 ATS @ home vs ranked teams since 2003
6-55-1 S/U vs ranked teams since 1986
0-9 S/U vs #1 ranked teams all time
0-6-1 S/U @ home vs #2 ranked teams all time
0-6-1 S/U on road vs #3 ranked teams all time
0-6 S/U vs #4 ranked teams since 1966
3-0 O/U vs #4 ranked teams since 1985
0-4 S/U on road vs #5 ranked teams since 1962
0-3 S/U @ home vs #6 ranked teams all time
0-3 S/U on road vs #6 ranked teams all time
0-7 S/U on road vs #7 ranked teams all time
0-4 S/U vs #8 ranked teams all time
0-4 S/U on road vs #9 ranked teams all time
0-5 S/U on road vs #10 ranked teams all time
0-3 S/U @ home vs #10 ranked teams all time
0-8 S/U on road vs #11 ranked teams since 1951
1-12 S/U vs #11 ranked teams since 1955
0-8 S/U vs #12 ranked teams all time
1-5 S/U on road vs #13 ranked teams all time
1-7 S/U vs #13 ranked teams since 1969
0-7-1 S/U vs #14 ranked teams all time
0-4 S/U vs #15 ranked teams since 1973
3-0 ATS vs #15 ranked teams since 2012
0-3 O/U vs #15 ranked teams since 2012
0-4 S/U on road vs #17 ranked teams all time
0-8-1 S/U vs #18 ranked teams all time
0-3 ATS on road vs #18 ranked teams since 1985
1-5 S/U @ home vs #19 ranked teams since 1952
3-0 ATS vs #19 ranked teams since 1985
0-5 S/U @ home vs #20 ranked teams since 1954
1-8 S/U vs #20 ranked teams since 1954
3-0 ATS vs #20 ranked teams since 1989
4-1 ATS vs #22 ranked teams since 1991
4-13 S/U vs #21 #22 #23 #24 #25 ranked teams all time

0-3 S/U vs ranked Central Florida all time
0-4 S/U @ ranked Houston since 1979
2-8 S/U @ ranked TCU all time
9-1 ATS vs ranked TCU since 2003

Southern Miss {When Ranked}

0-3 S/U on road when #20 ranked all time
5-0 S/U when #25 ranked since 1999
6-0 S/U when #14 - #17 ranked all time
1-9 ATS when ranked since 2000

Southern Miss {vs Ranked}

4-30 S/U on road vs ranked teams since 1992
1-11 S/U @ home vs ranked teams since 1987
0-8 S/U vs #1 #2 #3 ranked teams all time
0-7 S/U vs #4 ranked teams since 1971
0-6 S/U vs #5 ranked teams all time
0-4 ATS vs #5 ranked teams since 1989
0-6 S/U vs #8 #9 ranked teams all time
0-4 S/U vs #14 ranked teams all time
0-4 S/U vs #15 ranked teams since 2003
0-3 S/U @ home vs #17 ranked teams all time
0-3 S/U vs #19 ranked teams all time
0-3 S/U vs #20 ranked teams since 1985
3-0 ATS vs #20 ranked teams since 1985
0-4 S/U vs #21 #22 ranked teams all time
0-4 S/U vs #24 #25 ranked teams all time
3-22-1 S/U vs ranked Alabama all time

Stanford {When Ranked}

42-6 S/U @ home when ranked since 2010
4-0 S/U @ home when #4 ranked all time
4-0 ATS when #4 ranked since 2011
3-0 S/U @ home when #5 ranked all time
6-0 S/U @ home when #6 ranked all time
5-0 ATS when #6 ranked since 2011
7-1 S/U @ home when #7 ranked all time
5-1 ATS @ home when #7 ranked since 2010
6-0 S/U when #8 ranked since 2012
0-5 O/U when #8 ranked since 2013
4-0 S/U & ATS when #10 ranked since 2010
5-0 S/U when #12 ranked since 1970
8-1 S/U when #13 ranked since 1980
1-7 O/U when #13 ranked since 1993
11-1 S/U @ home when #13 ranked all time
4-0 O/U when #14 ranked since 2017
5-1 S/U @ home when #15 ranked since 1980
5-1 ATS when #15 ranked since 2012
6-0 S/U when #16 ranked since 2001
5-1-1 S/U @ home when #16 ranked all time
1-5 S/U on road when #17 ranked all time
5-1 S/U @ home when #19 ranked since 1972
6-0 S/U when #20 ranked since 1993
5-0 S/U @ home when #21 ranked all time

Copyright © 2021 by Steve's Football Bible, LLC

Team Trends when ranked in the Polls / vs Ranked teams in the Polls

5-0 S/U & ATS when #25 ranked since 2009	0-8 S/U @ ranked Notre Dame since 1994
0-3 S/U when ranked vs #3 ranked teams all time	4-1 S/U @ home vs ranked Notre Dame since 2011
3-0 S/U @ home when ranked vs #4 ranked teams all time	5-0 S/U vs ranked UCLA since 2012
4-0 ATS when ranked vs #7 ranked teams all time	13-4 ATS vs ranked UCLA since 1984 {7-0 @ UCLA}
0-3 S/U when ranked vs #14 ranked teams all time	9-2 ATS vs ranked USC since 2007
3-0 S/U when ranked vs #15 ranked teams all time	7-1 O/U @ ranked USC since 1995
4-0 S/U When ranked vs #20 ranked teams all time	0-5 S/U vs ranked Washington State since 1997
6-0 S/U when ranked vs California since 2010	5-0 S/U @ home vs ranked Washington since 2009
6-0 S/U @ home when ranked vs Notre Dame all time	8-2 O/U @ home vs ranked Washington since 1990
11-0 S/U when ranked vs Oregon State since 1969	**Syracuse {When Ranked}**
9-0 S/U when ranked @ Oregon State all time	5-18 ATS on road when ranked since 1993
6-1 ATS when ranked vs Oregon State since 2010	7-0 S/U @ home when ranked since 1998
8-0 S/U when ranked vs UCLA since 2001	5-0 S/U when #1 ranked all time
7-1 ATS when ranked vs UCLA since 2001	6-0-1 S/U when #6 ranked all time
3-0 S/U @ home when ranked vs Washington since 2011	0-3 S/U on road when #9 ranked all time
Stanford {vs Ranked}	7-1 S/U when #12 ranked all time
19-6 S/U @ home vs ranked teams since 2009	10-2 S/U when #17 ranked since 1956
0-3 S/U @ home vs #1 ranked teams all time	5-0 S/U @ home when #18 ranked all time
5-0 ATS vs #1 ranked teams since 1989	0-6 O/U when #18 ranked since 1988
4-0 ATS vs #2 ranked teams since 1998	5-0 S/U when #19 ranked all time
3-0 S/U vs #2 ranked teams since 2007	3-1 S/U when #21 ranked all time
0-3 O/U vs #2 ranked teams since 2007	5-0 S/U when #22 ranked since 1997
0-6 S/U vs #3 rankeed teams all time	7-0 S/U when #24 ranked all time
3-11 S/U vs #4 ranked teams since 1974	0-3 S/U when ranked vs #1 ranked teams all time
1-9 S/U on road vs #5 ranked teeams all time	4-0 S/U when ranked vs Boston College since 1995
3-0 O/U on road vs #5 ranked teams since 1988	7-0 S/U when ranked vs Pittsburgh since 1991
0-4 S/U @ home vs #6 ranked teams since 2003	5-0 S/U @ home when ranked vs Pittsburgh since 1968
8-2 ATS vs #6 ranked teams since 1988	3-0 S/U & ATS when ranked vs Rutgers all time
5-0 O/U vs #6 ranked teams since 2005	**Syracuse {vs Ranked}**
0-3 S/U on road vs #7 ranked teams since 1981	3-29 S/U on road vs ranked teams since 2001
5-0 ATS vs #7 ranked teams since 1992	6-19 S/U @ home vs ranked teams since 2002
0-8 S/U on road vs #8 ranked teams all time	0-5 S/U @ home vs #1 ranked teams since 1992
0-12 S/U vs #8 ranked teams since 1966	0-7 S/U on road vs #1 ranked teams all time
0-7 S/U vs #10 ranked teams all time	1-13 S/U vs #2 ranked teams all time {0-6 on road}
5-1 ATS vs #11 ranked teams since 1992	0-4 S/U vs #3 ranked teams all time
0-5-1 O/U vs #12 ranked teams since 1995	0-4 S/U & ATS vs #4 ranked teams since 1988
5-0 O/U vs #13 ranked teams since 1990	3-0 ATS vs #5 ranked teams since 2001
0-7 S/U vs #14 ranked teams all time	0-7-1 S/U vs #6 ranked teams since 1985
0-5 S/U vs #16 ranked teams since 1977	1-8 S/U vs #7 ranked teams all time
4-1 S/U @ home vs #17 ranked teams all time	1-7 S/U vs #8 ranked teams all time {0-3 on road}
0-4 S/U on road vs #17 ranked teams since 1989	1-5 S/U vs #9 ranked teams all time
0-4 S/U on road vs #18 ranked teams since 1981	0-3 S/U on road vs #10 ranked teams all time
4-0 S/U vs #19 ranked teams since 1974 {3-0 ATS since 1983}	2-7 S/U @ home vs #10 ranked teams all time
3-0 S/U vs #20 ranked teams since 2011	4-0 ATS @ home vs #10 ranked teams since 1987
3-0-1 ATS vs #20 ranked teams since 2006	0-4 S/U on road vs #12 ranked teams all time
4-0 S/U vs #22 ranked teams since 1989	1-5 S/U @ home vs #13 ranked teams all time
5-0 ATS vs #22 ranked teams all time	0-3 S/U on road vs #14 ranked teams all time
1-4 S/U vs #23 ranked teams all time	0-3 S/U on road vs #15 ranked teams all time
1-4 S/U & ATS vs #25 ranked teams all time	0-3 S/U on road vs #16 ranked teams all time
0-4 O/U vs #25 ranked teams since 2000	3-1 S/U on road vs #18 ranked teams all time
1-5 S/U @ home vs ranked California all time	4-1 S/U vs #18 ranked teams since 1978

Copyright © 2021 by Steve's Football Bible, LLC

Team Trends when ranked in the Polls / vs Ranked teams in the Polls

1-4 S/U on road vs #19 ranked teams all time	0-13 S/U vs #10 ranked teams all time
0-6 S/U on road vs #25 ranked teams all time	0-9 S/U vs #11 ranked teams all time
3-0 ATS @ home vs #25 ranked teams since 2005	0-7 S/U vs #12 ranked teams since 1973
0-9 S/U vs ranked Florida State all time	0-5 ATS vs #12 ranked teams since 1991
0-4 ATS @ ranked Florida State all time	1-8 S/U vs #13 ranked teams since 1957
4-1 ATS vs ranked Louisville all time	1-4 ATS vs #13 ranked teams since 1985
3-0 O/U vs ranked Louisville since 2007	1-8 S/U vs #14 ranked teams all time
1-10-1 S/U vs ranked Pittsburgh since 1976	3-0 S/U vs #15 ranked teams since 2014

TCU {When Ranked}

41-4 S/U @ home when ranked since 2007	2-6 S/U vs #17 ranked teams all time
5-0 S/U when #2 ranked all time	2-13 S/U vs #18 ranked teams all time
7-0 S/U when #3 ranked since 2010	1-7 S/U @ home vs #20 ranked teams since 1947
14-1 S/U when ranked #4 since 2009 {8-0 @ home}	4-0 S/U vs #23 ranked teams since 1998
4-1 S/U when #5 ranked all time	4-1 ATS vs ranked Baylor since 2013
5-1 S/U when #6 ranked since 2009	0-6 S/U vs ranked SMU since 1979
5-1 S/U when #7 ranked since 1955	3-23 S/U vs ranked Texas since 1962
7-0 S/U when #8 ranked all time	0-4 ATS vs ranked West Virginia since 2014

Temple {When Ranked}

0-5 S/U on road when #9 ranked all time	2-5 S/U on road when ranked all time

Temple {vs Ranked}

4-1 S/U on road when #10 ranked all time	4-63-1 S/U on road vs ranked teams all time
0-3 S/U on road when #11 ranked all time	5-45 S/U @ home vs ranked teams all time
4-0 S/U @ home when #11 ranked all time	0-40 S/U vs Top #1 - #9 ranked teams all time
6-1 S/U when #12 ranked all time {3-0 on road}	0-10 S/U vs #11 #12 ranked teams all time
6-0 S/U when #13 ranked since 1959	1-7 S/U vs #14 ranked teams all time
7-1 S/U when #14 ranked all time {3-0 @ home}	0-4 S/U vs #15 ranked teams all time
11-1 S/U when ranked #16 all time {6-0 on road}	0-4 S/U vs #16 ranked teams since 1994
0-4 S/U on road when #17 ranked since 1956	0-17-1 S/U vs #17 #18 #19 ranked teams all time
6-0 S/U when #18 ranked since 1958	1-3 ATS vs #17 ranked teams since 1999
4-0 S/U @ home when #18 ranked all time	0-3 O/U vs #20 ranked teams since 2010
7-1 S/U @ home when #20 ranked all time	2-5 S/U vs #21 ranked teams all time
3-0 S/U on road when #20 ranked since 1958	0-4 O/U vs #21 ranked teams since 2003
6-1 S/U when #25 ranked all time	1-11 S/U vs #22 #23 #24 #25 ranked teams all time
3-0 S/U on road when ranked vs #6 ranked teams all time	0-6 S/U vs ranked Boston College all time
4-0 S/U @ home when ranked vs Baylor since 2007	0-3 S/U vs ranked Central Florida all time

Tennessee {When Ranked}

3-0 S/U when ranked vs Kansas State all time	11-2 O/U on road when ranked since 2007
4-0 S/U when ranked vs Kansas since 2012	16-1 S/U when #1 ranked all time {10-0 @ home}
3-0 S/U @ home vs Kansas all time	9-1 S/U @ home when #2 ranked all time
0-4 S/U when ranked @ Oklahoma all time	0-4 S/U when #2 ranked @ neutral sites since 1940
13-3 S/U when ranked vs SMU since 1937	7-1 S/U @ home when #3 ranked all time
1-9 ATS when ranked vs SMU since 2003	3-8 ATS when #3 ranked since 1990
5-1 S/U when ranked vs Texas Tech since 1984 {3-0 @ home}	8-2 S/U @ home when #4 ranked since 1950
3-0 S/U when ranked vs West Virginia all time	11-0 S/U @ home when #5 ranked all time
0-3 O/U when ranked vs West Virginia all time	11-1 S/U @ home when #6 ranked all time

TCU {vs Ranked}

1-6 S/U vs #1 ranked teams all time	0-5 ATS when #6 ranked since 2000
0-7 S/U vs #2 ranked teams since 1968	5-1 O/U when #6 ranked since 1999
0-8-2 S/U vs #3 ranked teams all time	20-1 S/U when #7 ranked since 1965 {10-1 on road}
0-7 S/U on road vs #4 ranked teams all time	13-0-1 S/U @ home when #7 ranked all time
0-5 S/U @ home vs #5 ranked teams all time	12-3 S/U when #8 ranked since 1992
1-6 S/U on road vs #7 ranked teams all time	4-0 O/U when #8 ranked since 2002
0-3 S/U on road vs #8 ranked teams since 1974	16-4 S/U when #9 ranked since 1971
0-5 S/U @ home vs #9 ranked teams all time	

Copyright © 2021 by Steve's Football Bible, LLC

Team Trends when ranked in the Polls / vs Ranked teams in the Polls

9-1 S/U @ home when #10 ranked since 1985	5-1 O/U vs #1 ranked teams since 2012
14-2 S/U when #11 ranked since 1989	0-7 S/U on road vs #1 ranked teams all time
16-2-1 S/U @ home when #11 ranked all time	0-5 S/U vs #2 ranked teams since 2008
7-1 S/U on road when #11 ranked since 1971	1-14-2 S/U vs #3 ranked teams since 1959
12-0 S/U when #12 ranked since 1960	0-5-1 S/U @ home vs #3 ranked teams since 1962
9-0 S/U @ home when #12 ranked all time	1-7 S/U on road vs #4 ranked teams all time
2-8 ATS when #13 ranked since 1987	2-8 S/U @ home vs #4 ranked teams all time
8-2 S/U when #14 ranked since 1987	0-5 S/U vs #5 ranked teams since 2005
7-0 S/U @ home when #14 ranked since 1970	5-2 ATS vs #5 ranked teams since 1990
6-1 ATS when #14 ranked since 1991	0-4 S/U @ home vs #6 ranked teams since 2000
0-4-1 ATS on road when #15 ranked since 1987	0-12 S/U vs #8 ranked teams since 1957
8-2 ATS when #17 ranked since 1987	5-2 O/U vs #9 ranked teams since 1990
6-1 S/U @ home when #18 ranked since 1949	0-6 S/U on road vs #10 ranked teams all time
10-0 S/U @ home when #19 ranked all time	1-5 S/U & ATS vs #10 ranked teams since 1989
8-0 S/U when #19 ranked since 1985	1-4 ATS vs #11 ranked teams since 1997
5-0 S/U @ home when #20 ranked all time	4-0 S/U @ home vs #12 ranked teams since 2001
6-0 S/U when #25 ranked all time	0-3 S/U on road vs #12 ranked teams since 2007
0-5 S/U when ranked vs #1 ranked teams since 1979	4-0 ATS vs #12 ranked teams since 2010
0-4 ATS when ranked vs #1 ranked teams since 1990	0-3 S/U vs #13 ranked teams since 1994
3-0 S/U & ATS when ranked vs #2 ranked teams since 1998	4-0 S/U @ home vs #15 ranked teams all time
1-7-2 S/U when ranked vs #3 ranked teams since 1952	0-5 O/U vs #15 ranked teams since 1985
1-4 S/U on road when ranked vs #4 ranked teams all time	3-0 S/U & ATS vs #16 ranked teams since 1983
4-1 ATS when ranked vs #5 ranked teams since 1990	0-4 S/U vs #17 ranked teams since 2010
1-5 S/U when ranked vs #6 ranked teams since 1975	0-4 S/U on road vs #19 ranked teams all time
0-6 S/U when ranked vs #8 ranked teams since 1957	1-4 S/U vs #20 ranked teams since 1976
3-0 S/U @ home when ranked vs #9 ranked teams all time	6-0 S/U vs #22 #23 ranked teams all time
0-3 S/U on road when ranked vs #10 ranked teams all time	0-3 O/U vs #22 ranked teams all time
4-0 O/U when ranked vs #10 ranked teams since 1989	3-0 S/U vs #25 ranked teams all time
3-0 S/U when ranked vs #15 ranked teams all time	0-14 S/U vs ranked Alabama since 2005
0-3 O/U when ranked vs #15 ranked teams all time	1-12 S/U vs ranked Florida since 2005
3-0 S/U when ranked vs #16 ranked teams all time	0-7 S/U @ ranked Florida since 2005
4-0 S/U when ranked vs #17 ranked teams all time	0-3 O/U vs ranked Mississippi since 1986
3-0 S/U when ranked vs #22 ranked teams all time	3-0 ATS @ ranked South Carolina since 2000
0-3 O/U when ranked vs #22 ranked teams all time	**Texas {When Ranked}**
3-0 S/U when ranked vs #23 ranked teams all time	5-11 ATS on road when ranked since 2012
3-0 S/U when ranked vs #25 ranked teams all time	15-4 O/U on road when ranked since 2011
7-1 ATS when ranked @ Alabama since 1993	8-0 S/U @ home when #1 ranked since 1965
2-9 S/U when ranked @ Florida since 1985	19-1 S/U on road when #2 ranked all time
1-7 ATS when ranked vs Georgia since 2000	5-1-1 O/U on road when #2 ranked since 2005
5-0 O/U when ranked vs Georgia since 2003	24-2 S/U @ home when #2 ranked since 1962
23-1 S/U when ranked vs Kentucky since 1967	1-5 ATS @ home when #2 ranked since 2006
9-0 S/U when ranked vs Mississippi since 1985	8-0 S/U when #3 ranked since 2006
8-0 S/U @ home when ranked vs Mississippi since 1968	11-1 S/U on road when #3 ranked since 1959
0-4 ATS @ home when ranked vs Mississippi since 1989	18-1 S/U @ home when #3 ranked all time
8-1 S/U @ home when ranked vs South Carolina all time	17-2-1 S/U when #4 ranked since 1963
0-5 ATS @ home when ranked vs South Carolina since 1997	13-0-1 S/U @ home when #4 ranked since 1962
38-1 S/U when ranked vs Vanderbilt all time {22-0 @ home}	0-4 O/U @ home when #4 ranked since 2002
Tennessee {vs Ranked}	7-0 S/U when #5 ranked since 2006
2-31 S/U on road vs ranked teams since 2006	2-9 O/U when #5 ranked since 2003
0-12 S/U vs #1 ranked teams since 1990	7-0 S/U on road when #5 ranked since 2001
1-6 ATS vs #1 ranked teams since 2011	2-6 ATS on road when #5 ranked since 2000

Copyright © 2021 by Steve's Football Bible, LLC

Team Trends when ranked in the Polls / vs Ranked teams in the Polls

9-0 S/U @ home when #5 ranked since 1990	26-1 S/U when ranked vs Rice since 1968 {13-0 @ home}
9-1 S/U when #6 ranked since 2003	21-4 S/U when ranked vs TCU since 1962
15-3 S/U @ home when #6 ranked all time	12-2 S/U when ranked @ TCU since 1950
32-4 S/U when #7 ranked all time {10-2 on road}	20-2 S/U @ home when ranked vs Texas Tech all time
16-1 S/U when #8 ranked since 1975	9-1 S/U when ranked vs Texas Tech since 2003
9-0 S/U on road when #8 ranked since 1968	**Texas {vs Ranked}**
9-0 S/U @ home when #9 ranked since 1972	1-9 O/U on road vs ranked teams since 2013
11-0 S/U when #10 ranked since 1972	4-1 O/U vs #1 ranked teams since 2003
9-0 S/U @ home when #10 ranked since 1952	1-7 S/U vs #2 ranked teams since 1972
9-2 S/U on road when #11 ranked all time	0-3 S/U & ATS vs #3 ranked teams since 1999
7-0 S/U @ home when #12 ranked all time	4-0 S/U @ home vs #3 ranked teams all time
1-4 S/U & ATS on road when #13 ranked since 1991	0-3 S/U @ home vs #4 ranked teams since 1982
4-0 O/U on road when #13 ranked since 1995	4-1 ATS on road vs #4 ranked teams sice 1984
12-1 S/U @ home when #13 ranked since 1957	1-3 S/U on road vs #6 ranked teams all time
5-1 ATS @ home when #13 ranked since 1990	1-6 S/U vs #8 ranked teams since 1988
5-0 S/U on road when #14 ranked all time	0-4 S/U vs #9 ranked teams since 1992
9-0 S/U @ home when #14 ranked all time	1-4 S/U on road vs #9 ranked teams all time
10-1 S/U @ home when #15 ranked all time	0-3 S/U on road vs #10 ranked teams since 1979
4-0 S/U on road when #17 ranked all time	1-4 O/U vs #10 ranked teams since 2013
0-4 O/U when #18 ranked since 1999	0-4 S/U vs #11 ranked teams since 2014
6-1 ATS when #19 ranked since 2000	0-4 S/U on road vs #11 ranked teams since 1980
4-0 S/U on road when #19 ranked since 2000	5-0-1 ATS vs #12 ranked teams since 2013
6-1 S/U @ home when #19 ranked all time	1-6 O/U vs #12 ranked teams since 2010
6-1 S/U when #20 ranked since 1994	4-0 S/U on road vs #12 ranked teams all time
1-6 S/U when #22 ranked since 2010	3-0 S/U & ATS vs #14 ranked teams since 1995
0-6 ATS @ home when #22 ranked all time	6-1 S/U @ home vs #14 ranked teams all time
1-4 S/U & ATS when #23 ranked since 2012	0-6 O/U vs #14 ranked teams since 1984
8-1 O/U when #23 ranked since 1998	0-3 S/U on road vs #15 ranked teams since 1987
3-0 S/U & ATS on road when #25 ranked all time	5-1 S/U vs #16 ranked teams since 1992
1-7 S/U when ranked vs #2 ranked teams since 1972	0-4 O/U vs #16 ranked teams since 1995
4-0 S/U @ home when #3 ranked all time	0-4 O/U vs #17 ranked teams since 2002
3-0 S/U on road when ranked vs #5 ranked teams all time	5-1 S/U @ home vs #17 ranked teams all time
0-6 S/U when ranked vs #6 ranked teams since 1988	6-0 O/U vs #19 ranked teams since 1987
0-3 S/U on road when ranked vs #6 ranked teams all time	3-0 S/U vs #21 ranked teams since 2001
3-0 S/U @ home when ranked vs #7 ranked teams all time	4-1 O/U vs #21 ranked teams since 1992
0-4 S/U & ATS when ranked vs #8 ranked since 1988	3-0 S/U & ATS vs #22 ranked teams all time
3-0 S/U on road when ranked vs #12 ranked teams all time	1-5 O/U vs #24 ranked teams since 2000
4-0 S/U @ home when ranked vs #13 ranked teams all time	10-3 S/U @ ranked Arkansas all time
7-0 S/U when ranked vs #14 ranked teams all time	3-0 ATS @ ranked Arkansas since 1985
0-4 S/U & ATS when ranked vs #15 ranked teams since 1985	1-4 S/U @ ranked Baylor since 1980
4-0 S/U when ranked vs #16 ranked teams since 1994	0-5 O/U vs ranked Baylor since 2013
4-0 S/U when ranked vs #17 ranked teams all time	1-3 S/U vs ranked Kansas State since 2011
4-0 O/U when ranked vs #19 ranked teams since 1996	0-5 ATS vs ranked Kansas State since 2003
19-0 S/U @ home when ranked vs Baylor since 1953	1-5 O/U vs ranked Kansas State since 2002
9-3 S/U when ranked vs Iowa State all time {4-1 on road}	7-1 ATS vs ranked Oklahoma since 2013
1-6 ATS when ranked vs Kansas State all time	1-5 S/U vs ranked Oklahoma State since 2010
9-0 S/U when ranked vs Kansas all time	1-5 O/U vs ranked Oklahoma State since 2010
1-6 S/U when ranked vs Notre Dame all time	1-4 S/U @ ranked TCU all time
1-5-2 S/U when ranked vs #3 ranked Oklahoma all time	3-0 S/U @ home vs ranked Texas Tech all time
1-3 S/U when ranked vs Oklahoma State since 2013	**Texas A&M {When Ranked}**
0-4 ATS when ranked vs Oklahoma State since 2013	6-17 ATS @ home when ranked since 2014

Copyright © 2021 by Steve's Football Bible, LLC

Team Trends when ranked in the Polls / vs Ranked teams in the Polls

4-1 S/U when #1 ranked all time	
5-1 S/U @ home when #2 ranked all time	
4-0 S/U @ home when #3 ranked all time	
7-0 S/U on road when #4 ranked all time	
12-0 S/U @ home when #5 ranked all time	
2-7 ATS when #6 ranked since 1994	
9-1 S/U @ home when #7 ranked all time	
10-1 S/U @ home when #8 ranked since 1974	
2-8 ATS when #9 ranked since 1994	
8-2-1 S/U on road when #9 ranked all time	
9-1 S/U @ home when #9 ranked all time	
17-2 S/U when #10 ranked all time {6-0 on road}	
7-1 S/U @ home when #11 ranked all time	
3-1 S/U on road when #12 ranked all time	
7-0 S/U @ home when #13 ranked since 1986	
5-1 S/U on road when #14 ranked since 1941	
2-7-1 ATS when #15 ranked since 1987	
8-2 S/U when #17 ranked since 1997	
4-1 S/U @ home when #17 ranked since 1977	
0-6 O/U on road when #17 ranked since 1997	
4-0 S/U on road when #18 ranked since 1995	
4-0 S/U @ home when #18 ranked all time	
1-5 ATS when #20 ranked since 1997	
5-1 O/U when #22 ranked since 2012	
6-0 S/U when #23 ranked since 2004	
5-0 S/U on road when #23 ranked all time	
5-2 O/U when #23 ranked since 2002	
8-3 S/U when #24 ranked all time	
0-4 S/U & ATS on road when #25 ranked all time	
1-7 S/U when ranked vs #1 ranked teams all time	
4-0 ATS when ranked vs #2 ranked teams since 1998	
0-5 O/U when ranked vs #5 ranked teams since 1992	
0-4 S/U when ranked vs #6 ranked teams since 1953 {0-3 ATS}	
0-3 O/U when ranked vs #6 ranked teams since 1987	
0-3 S/U & ATS when ranked vs #7 ranked teams since 2002	
0-3 O/U when ranked vs #7 ranked teams since 2002	
0-3 S/U & ATS when ranked vs #12 ranked teams all time	
1-4 S/U when ranked vs #15 ranked all time	
5-1 S/U when ranked vs #16 ranked all time	
1-4 S/U on road when ranked vs #17 ranked all time	
1-4 S/U when ranked vs #18 ranked teams all time	
3-0 S/U @ home when ranked vs #20 ranked teams all time	
0-4 S/U on road when ranked vs #20 ranked teams all time	
0-7 S/U when ranked vs Alabama since 2013	
6-0 S/U when ranked vs Arkansas since 2013	
1-4 S/U when ranked vs LSU since 2011 {0-5 ATS}	
0-3 S/U when ranked vs Mississippi since 2014	
0-4 ATS when ranked vs Mississippi since 2013	
0-3 S/U when ranked vs Notre Dame since 1993	
4-0 S/U when ranked vs South Carolina all time	

Texas A&M {vs Ranked}
2-16 S/U vs #1 ranked teams all time
2-10 S/U vs #2 ranked teams all time
6-1 ATS vs #2 ranked teams since 1998
1-6 S/U vs #3 ranked teams all time
0-5 S/U on road vs #4 ranked teams all time
1-8 S/U vs #4 ranked teams since 1959
0-6 S/U on road vs #5 ranked teams all time
0-7 O/U vs #5 ranked teams since 1992
0-4 S/U & ATS @ home vs #6 ranked teams since 1987
0-5 ATS vs #6 ranked teams since 1987
0-6 S/U vs #7 ranked teams since 2002
0-4 S/U on road vs #10 ranked teams all time
0-4 S/U on road vs #12 ranked teams since 1980
0-6 S/U @ home vs #12 ranked teams all time
0-3 ATS on road vs #12 ranked teams since 1990
5-1 S/U vs #13 ranked teams since 1984
0-3 S/U on road vs #14 ranked teams since 1978
1-6 S/U on road vs #17 ranked teams since 1959
0-5 S/U on road vs #18 ranked teams all time
0-6 S/U vs #18 ranked teams since 1988
1-5 ATS vs #18 ranked teams since 1988
0-4 S/U on road vs #19 ranked teams since 1951
3-0 S/U @ home vs #19 ranked teams since 1985
0-9 S/U on road vs #20 ranked teams all time
0-4 ATS on road vs #20 ranked teams since 1985
5-0 O/U vs #20 ranked teams since 1997
0-4 S/U & ATS vs #24 ranked teams all time
0-5 S/U @ home vs ranked Alabama since 1988
0-8 S/U vs ranked Alabama since 2013
1-4 S/U & ATS vs ranked Arkansas since 1988
4-0-1 O/U vs ranked Auburn since 1986
0-5 S/U @ ranked LSU since 1986
0-7 ATS vs ranked LSU since 2011
0-3 S/U vs ranked Missouri since 2007

Texas-El Paso {When Ranked}
2-2 S/U when ranked all time

Texas-El Paso {vs Ranked}
1-37 S/U on road vs ranked teams all time
10-2-1 O/U on road vs ranked teams since 2000
2-22 S/U @ home vs ranked teams all time
0-8 S/U vs #2 - #6 ranked teams all time
0-5 S/U vs #10 - #11 ranked teams all time {0-3 ATS}
0-7 S/U vs #13 ranked teams all time
0-16 S/U vs #15 - #19 ranked teams all time
0-12 S/U vs #20 - #25 ranked teams all time
7-2 ATS vs #21 - #25 ranked teams all time

Texas-San Antonio {When Ranked}
NEVER RANKED

Texas-San Antonio {vs Ranked}
0-2 S/U vs ranked teams all time

Copyright © 2021 by Steve's Football Bible, LLC

Team Trends when ranked in the Polls / vs Ranked teams in the Polls

Texas State {When Ranked}
NEVER RANKED

Texas State {vs Ranked}
0-9 S/U vs ranked teams all time

Texas Tech {When Ranked}
11-0 O/U on road when ranked since 2008
0-11 ATS @ home when ranked since 2008
4-0 O/U @ home when ranked since 2013
4-0 S/U when ranked #7 since 2008
4-0 S/U when ranked #11 since 1973
6-0 S/U when #12 ranked since 1973
0-3 S/U & ATS when #15 ranked since 2006
3-0 S/U when ranked #16 since 2005
4-0-1 S/U @ home when #17 ranked all time
5-1 S/U when #18 ranked since 1940
3-0 S/U on road when #19 ranked all time
0-3 S/U when #22 ranked since 1998
3-0 O/U when #23 ranked since 1995
0-4 ATS when #24 ranked since 1995
0-4 ATS when #25 ranked since 2012
3-0 O/U when ranked vs #4 ranked teams all time
0-5 S/U when ranked vs #13 ranked teams since 1970
3-0 S/U @ home when ranked vs Baylor all time
4-0 O/U when ranked vs Kansas State all time
4-0 S/U when ranked vs Kansas all time
0-3 S/U when ranked @ Oklahoma all time
0-4 ATS when ranked vs Oklahoma all time
5-1 S/U when ranked vs TCU since 1973
0-3 S/U when ranked @ Texas since 1977

Texas Tech {vs Ranked}
1-19 S/U vs ranked teams since 2014
7-66 S/U on road vs ranked teams since 1977
0-12 S/U @ home vs ranked teams since 2013
1-7 S/U vs #1 ranked teams all time
0-13 S/U vs #2 ranked teams all time
0-4 O/U vs #2 ranked teams since 2004
0-6 S/U on road vs #4 ranked teams all time
6-1 O/U vs #4 ranked teams since 2002
0-5 S/U on road vs #5 ranked teams all time {0-3 ATS}
0-7 S/U vs #6 ranked teams since 1975
0-9 S/U vs #7 ranked teams all time
3-0 ATS & O/U vs #7 ranked teams since 2003
0-5 S/U on road vs #9 ranked teams all time
0-6 S/U vs #9 ranked teams since 1976
0-6 S/U vs #10 ranked teams all time
1-5 S/U vs #11 ranked teams all time
1-5 S/U vs #12 ranked teams all time
0-12 S/U vs #13 ranked teams all time
1-4 S/U vs #14 ranked teams all time
1-5 S/U vs #15 ranked teams since 1992
1-4 S/U on road vs #15 ranked teams all time
1-6 S/U vs #16 ranked teams all time
0-6 S/U vs #17 ranked teams since 2009 {1-5 ATS}
0-5 S/U @ home vs #17 ranked teams since 1986
2-8 S/U on road vs #17 ranked teams all time
5-0 O/U vs #17 ranked teams since 2011
1-5 S/U vs #18 ranked teams since 1990
5-1 ATS vs #19 ranked teams since 1989
0-4 S/U & ATS vs #20 ranked teams since 2000
1-7 S/U vs #21 ranked teams all time {0-4 on road}
1-5-1 ATS vs #21 ranked teams since 1995
0-3 S/U & ATS vs #23 ranked teams since 2006
5-2 ATS vs #24 ranked teams since 2001
1-3 S/U & ATS vs #25 ranked teams all time
0-5 S/U vs ranked Baylor since 2011
5-0 O/U vs ranked Baylor since 2011
0-5 S/U vs ranked Houston since 1979 {0-3 on road}
0-4 S/U @ ranked Kansas State all time
1-5 S/U @ home vs ranked Oklahoma State since 2010
2-9 S/U vs ranked Oklahoma State since 2009
1-11 S/U @ ranked Oklahoma all time
8-1 O/U vs ranked Oklahoma since 2011
0-3 S/U vs ranked TCU since 2014
1-9 S/U vs ranked Texas since 2003
0-15 S/U @ ranked Texas since 1969

Toledo {When Ranked}
11-2 S/U on road when ranked all time
4-0 S/U when #14 ranked all time
4-0 S/U when #15 ranked all time
3-0 S/U when #19 ranked all time
0-3 S/U & ATS when ranked vs Ball State all time
3-0 S/U when ranked vs Kent State all time

Toledo {vs Ranked}
1-14 S/U on road vs ranked teams all time
1-6 S/U vs Top #10 ranked teams all time
0-7 S/U vs #11 - #16 ranked teams all time
0-3 S/U vs Miami-Ohio all time

Troy {When Ranked}
0-1 S/U when ranked all time

Troy {vs Ranked}
1-22 S/U on road vs ranked teams all time
0-8 S/U vs Top #10 ranked teams all time

Tulane {When Ranked}
7-0 S/U @ home when ranked since 1974
0-5 S/U when ranked vs Top #3 ranked teams all time
4-1 S/U when #14 ranked all time
4-0 S/U when #19 ranked since 1948
3-0 S/U when #20 ranked all time

Tulane {vs Ranked}
1-56 S/U vs ranked teams since 1984
0-32 S/U on road vs ranked teams since 1984
3-14 ATS on road vs ranked teams since 1999

Copyright © 2021 by Steve's Football Bible, LLC

Team Trends when ranked in the Polls / vs Ranked teams in the Polls

1-24 S/U @ home vs ranked teams since 1985	15-1 S/U @ home when #4 ranked all time
0-6 S/U vs #1 ranked teams all time	5-0 O/U when #4 ranked since 1986
0-13 S/U vs #2 ranked teams all time	10-0 S/U @ home when #5 ranked all time
0-18-1 S/U vs #3 - #5 ranked teams all time	1-6 ATS when #6 ranked since 1988
0-5 S/U vs #6 ranked teams since 1964	9-1 S/U on road when #7 ranked all time
1-7 S/U vs #7 ranked teams all time	5-1 S/U @ home when #7 ranked all time
1-7 S/U vs #8 ranked teams all time	1-5 S/U on road when #8 ranked since 1972
0-8 S/U vs #10 ranked teams since 1950	1-5 ATS when #8 ranked since 1984
0-6 S/U vs #11 ranked teams all time	5-1 S/U @ home when #9 ranked since 1969
0-4 S/U vs #12 ranked teams since 1951	5-1 S/U @ home when #10 ranked all time
0-5 S/U on road vs #13 ranked teams all time	6-0 S/U @ home when #11 ranked since 1982
0-5 S/U vs #14 ranked teams since 1973	10-1 S/U on road when #12 ranked since 1978
0-3 S/U & ATS vs #15 ranked teams since 1984	9-0 S/U @ home when #13 ranked since 1985
0-5 S/U on road vs #16 ranked teams all time	8-2 S/U on road when #14 ranked all time
0-6 S/U vs #16 ranked teams since 1984	4-0 O/U when #14 ranked since 2005
0-4 S/U vs #18 ranked teams since 1976	5-1 S/U on road when #15 ranked since 1960
0-3 S/U & ATS vs #19 ranked teams since 1985	6-1 S/U when #15 ranked since 1983
0-4 S/U vs #20 ranked teams since 1960	8-0 S/U @ home when #16 ranked since 1973
0-10 S/U vs #22 - #25 ranked teams all time	6-1 S/U @ home when #17 ranked since 1985
0-4 S/U vs ranked Houston all time	1-6 ATS when #18 ranked since 1994
0-3 ATS vs ranked Houston since 2009	4-0-1 S/U on road when #19 ranked since 1956
0-9 S/U vs ranked Mississippi since 1957	0-3 S/U & ATS @ home when #19 ranked since 1990
Tulsa {When Ranked}	3-0 S/U & ATS @ home when #23 ranked all time
7-0 S/U @ home when ranked since 1945	4-0 O/U when #24 ranked since 1995
0-7 S/U when ranked vs ranked teams all time	6-1 O/U when #25 ranked since 1993
Tulsa {vs Ranked}	0-3 S/U & ATS when ranked vs #1 ranked teams since 1984
2-43 S/U on road vs ranked teams since 1977	0-3 S/U @ home when ranked vs #1 ranked teams all time
1-11 S/U @ home vs ranked teams since 2007	2-8 S/U when ranked vs #2 ranked teams all time
0-5 S/U vs #1 ranked teams all time	0-3 S/U on road when ranked vs #4 ranked teams all time
0-3 ATS vs #1 ranked teams since 1987	0-5 S/U when ranked vs #5 ranked teams all time
0-3 S/U vs #2 ranked teams all time	0-3 S/U & ATS when ranked vs #7 ranked teams since 2001
0-5 S/U vs #3 ranked teams all time	4-0 ATS when ranked vs #8 ranked teams since 1978
0-11 S/U vs #4 #5 #6 ranked teams all time	4-0 S/U @ home when ranked vs #9 ranked teams all time
0-4 S/U vs #7 ranked teams since 1992	4-0 S/U when ranked vs #10 ranked teams since 1986
0-4 S/U vs #8 #9 ranked teams all time	5-0 S/U @ home when ranked vs #10 ranked teams all time
0-3 S/U vs #10 ranked teams since 1984	5-0 ATS when ranked vs #10 ranked teams since 1986
1-4 S/U vs #11 ranked teams since 1968	0-3 S/U on road when ranked vs #13 ranked teams all time
1-4 S/U on road vs #11 ranked teams all time	3-0 S/U @ home when ranked vs #13 ranked teams all time
0-3 S/U vs #12 ranked teams since 1986	1-4 S/U when ranked vs #14 ranked teams since 1947
0-6 S/U vs #13 ranked teams since 1979	3-0 S/U & ATS when ranked vs #21 ranked teams all time
0-3 S/U vs #14 ranked teams all time	3-0 S/U & ATS when ranked vs #23 ranked teams since 1998
0-3 S/U vs #16 ranked teams since 1971	6-0 O/U when ranked vs Arizona State since 1995
3-0 S/U vs #17 ranked teams all time	7-1 S/U & ATS when ranked vs Arizona since 1993
0-7 S/U vs #18 ranked teams all time	6-1-1 O/U when ranked vs Arizona since 1993
0-7 S/U vs ranked Oklahoma State all time	13-1 S/U @ home when ranked vs California since 1953
1-3 ATS vs ranked Oklahoma State since 1988	26-3 S/U when ranked vs California since 1952
UCLA {When Ranked}	6-1 S/U when ranked vs Colorado all time {3-0 on road}
7-0 S/U when #2 ranked since 1988	3-0 S/U when ranked vs Fresno State all time
0-6 ATS when #2 ranked since 1988	0-3 ATS when ranked vs Fresno State all time
5-0 S/U @ home when #3 ranked since 1954	0-5 S/U when ranked vs Oregon since 2000
15-3 S/U when #3 ranked since 1954	0-9 ATS when ranked vs Oregon since 1988

Copyright © 2021 by Steve's Football Bible, LLC

Team Trends when ranked in the Polls / vs Ranked teams in the Polls

0-5 S/U when ranked vs Stanford since 2012	**Utah {When Ranked}**
9-0 S/U when ranked vs Washington since 1987	4-0 S/U when #7 ranked all time
8-2 ATS when ranked vs Washington since 1986	3-1 O/U when #7 ranked all time
UCLA {vs Ranked}	4-0 S/U when #8 ranked all time
2-12 S/U vs ranked teams since 2016	4-0 S/U when #9 ranked since 2008
0-5 S/U & ATS on road vs #1 ranked teams all time	5-0-1 O/U when #10 ranked all time
0-7 S/U vs #1 ranked teams since 1983	8-0 S/U when #13 ranked all time {6-2 ATS}
4-1 O/U vs #1 ranked teams since 1986	6-2 O/U when ranked #13 all time
0-4 S/U on road vs #2 ranked teams since 1994	6-0 S/U when #14 ranked all time {5-1 ATS}
3-0 ATS vs #3 ranked teams since 1997	7-0 S/U when #19 ranked all time
0-4 S/U @ home vs #4 ranked teams all time	4-0 S/U on road when #20 ranked all time
0-5 S/U on road vs #4 ranked teams since 1964	8-0 S/U when #23 ranked since 2008
1-10 S/U vs #5 ranked teams since 1947 {0-5 on road}	0-5 O/U when #23 ranked since 2010
0-5 S/U @ home vs #7 ranked teams since 2001	4-0 S/U when #24 ranked since 2009
1-4 S/U on road vs #7 ranked teams all time	3-0 S/U when ranked vs #20 ranked teams all time
9-2 O/U vs #7 ranked teams since 1984	4-0 O/U when ranked vs #4 ranked teams all time
0-6 S/U vs #8 ranked teams since 1993	7-1 S/U when ranked vs BYU all time
0-4 S/U @ home vs #8 ranked teams all time	5-0 S/U when ranked vs Oregon State all time
0-5 S/U on road vs #8 ranked teams since 2004	4-0 S/U & ATS when ranked vs San Diego State since 2004
8-1 ATS vs #8 ranked teams since 1978	4-0 S/U when ranked @ San Diego State all time
6-1 S/U @ home vs #9 ranked teams all time	**Utah {vs Ranked}**
8-1 S/U @ home vs #10 ranked teams all time	8-40 S/U on road vs ranked teams all time
9-1 ATS vs #10 ranked teams since 1986	9-0 ATS on road vs ranked teams since 2013
0-3 S/U on road vs #10 ranked teams since 2006	0-4 S/U vs #4 ranked teams all time (Reg season)
5-1 S/U on road vs #11 ranked teams since 1951	4-0 O/U vs #4 ranked teams since 2009
5-0 O/U vs #11 ranked teams since 1995	0-3 O/U vs #8 ranked teams since 1996
0-4 S/U vs #12 ranked teams since 2003	0-4 S/U vs #9 ranked teams all time
0-5 S/U on road vs #12 ranked teams all time	0-5 S/U vs #10 ranked teams all time {0-3 ATS}
0-4 S/U & ATS vs #13 ranked teams since 1999	0-3 O/U vs #10 ranked teams since 2010
0-4 S/U on road vs #13 ranked teams all time	0-5 S/U on road vs #11 ranked teams all time
2-8-1 S/U vs #14 ranked teams all time	4-0 O/U vs #13 ranked teams since 2012
1-4-1 S/U on road vs #15 ranked teams all time	1-5 S/U on road vs #14 ranked teams since 1958
5-0 O/U vs #15 ranked teams since 1992	3-0 ATS vs #14 ranked teams since 2002
4-0 S/U @ home vs #21 ranked teams all time	0-3 S/U on road vs #15 ranked teams all time
7-0 ATS vs #21 ranked teams all time	1-5 S/U @ home vs #15 ranked teams all time
1-4 S/U vs #22 ranked teams all time	1-8 S/U vs #16 #17 #18 ranked teams all time
6-1 S/U vs #23 ranked teams siknce 1995	3-1 S/U @ home vs #20 ranked teams all time
5-1 ATS vs #24 ranked teams all time	0-3 S/U on road vs #20 ranked teams all time
3-0 S/U @ ranked Arizona since 1998	0-3 O/U vs #23 ranked teams since 2007
6-0 ATS vs ranked Arizona since 1998	1-4 S/U vs ranked Arizona all time
3-0 O/U @ home vs ranked Arizona State since 2011	1-7 S/U vs ranked Arizona State since 1975
3-0 S/U @ home vs ranked California since 2005	1-8 S/U @ ranked BYU all time
4-0 ATS vs ranked California since 2005	0-4 O/U @ ranked BYU since 1999
0-5 S/U vs ranked Oregon since 2009	6-1 ATS vs ranked BYU since 1999
2-9 ATS vs ranked Oregon since 1995	4-0 O/U vs ranked Oregon since 2013
0-8 S/U vs ranked Stanford since 2001 {1-7 ATS}	3-1 ATS vs ranked USC all time
0-5 S/U @ ranked Stanford since 2001	**Utah State {When Ranked}**
1-6 S/U @ ranked USC since 2003	3-0 S/U @ home when ranked all time
1-10 O/U vs ranked USC since 2006	**Utah State {vs Ranked}**
0-4 S/U @ ranked Washington since 1994	2-54 S/U on road vs ranked teams all time
5-0 O/U vs ranked Washington since 2000	2-13 S/U @ home vs ranked teams all time

Copyright © 2021 by Steve's Football Bible, LLC

Team Trends when ranked in the Polls / vs Ranked teams in the Polls

0-25 S/U vs Top #10 ranked teams all time	
0-16 S/U vs #11 - #17 ranked teams all time	
3-0 O/U vs #18 ranked teams since 2008	
0-5 S/U vs #20 ranked teams all time	
0-3 S/U vs #22 ranked teams all time	
3-0 ATS vs #24 ranked teams since 2013	
0-4 O/U vs #24 ranked teams since 2013	
1-13 S/U vs ranked BYU all time	

Vanderbilt {When Ranked}

2-8-1 S/U on road when ranked all time

0-3 S/U when #13 ranked all time

Vanderbilt {vs Ranked}

3-117-1 S/U on road vs ranked teams all time

7-50 S/U @ home vs ranked teams since 1992

4-1 ATS vs #3 ranked teams since 1994

0-5 ATS vs #5 ranked teams since 2002

5-0 O/U vs #5 ranked teams since 2002

5-1 ATS vs #8 ranked teams since 1983

5-114 S/U vs Top #10 ranked teams all time

0-11 S/U vs #11 ranked teams all time

4-0 ATS on road vs #11 ranked teams since 1994

0-3 O/U on road vs #11 ranked teams since 2009

0-6 S/U vs #12 ranked teams since 1972

0-3 O/U vs #12 ranked teams since 2002

0-12 S/U on road vs #13 ranked teams all time

7-0 ATS vs #13 ranked teams since 1997

3-0 O/U on road vs #13 ranked teams since 2005

1-13 S/U vs #14 ranked teams all time {0-7 on road}

1-6-1 S/U vs #15 ranked teams all time

0-5 S/U on road vs #17 ranked teams all time

4-0 ATS vs #17 ranked teams since 1987

0-8-1 S/U on road vs #18 ranked teams all time

1-4 S/U @ home vs #18 ranked teams since 1977

1-10 S/U vs #19 ranked teams all time {0-6 on road}

0-3 ATS @ home vs #19 ranked teams since 2001

1-5 O/U vs #19 ranked teams since 2001

1-6 S/U vs #20 ranked teams since 1947

0-11 S/U vs #21 #22 #23 ranked teams all time

0-3 ATS vs #21 ranked teams since 1997

0-4 O/U vs #23 ranked teams since 2002

4-0 ATS @ home vs #24 ranked teams since 1991

1-4 O/U vs #24 ranked teams since 1995

0-25 S/U vs ranked Florida since 1989

1-9 S/U @ home vs ranked Georgia since 1997

1-6 S/U vs ranked Kentucky all time

0-3 S/U vs ranked Mississippi State all time

1-15 S/U vs ranked Mississippi since 1948 {0-6 on road}

0-3 O/U vs ranked Mississippi since 2009

0-6 S/U vs ranked South Carolina since 2009

3-0 ATS vs ranked South Carolina since 2012

1-38 S/U vs ranked Tennessee all time {0-21 on road}

Virginia {When Ranked}

4-13 ATS on road when ranked since 1999

3-8-1 O/U @ home when ranked since 2004

0-4 S/U when ranked in Bowl games since 1998

6-1 S/U when #11 ranked all time {3-0 on road}

3-0 S/U @ home when #12 ranked all time

0-4 ATS when #12 ranked since 1996

1-4 S/U & ATS when #13 ranked since 1994

8-1 S/U when #16 ranked since 1994

0-3 S/U on road when #17 ranked all time

0-4 S/U & ATS when #18 ranked since 2004

4-0 O/U when #18 ranked since 2004

4-0 S/U when #19 ranked since 1995

4-0 S/U @ home when #20 ranked since 1991

7-0 S/U when #21 ranked all time

0-3 O/U when #23 ranked since 1999

1-4 S/U & ATS when #24 ranked since 1999

1-5 O/U when #24 ranked since 1996

0-3 S/U & ATS when ranked vs #17 ranked teams all time

3-0 O/U when ranked vs #20 ranked teams all time

1-5 S/U when ranked vs #6 ranked teams all time

4-0 S/U @ home when ranked vs Duke since 1993

6-0 S/U when ranked vs Duke since 1995

0-5 S/U & ATS @ home when ranked vs Virginia Tech since 1993

6-0 S/U when ranked vs Wake Forest all time

5-0 S/U when ranked vs William & Mary all time

Virginia {vs Ranked}

10-2 ATS vs ranked teams since 2014

2-23 S/U on road vs ranked teams since 2001

6-17-1 O/U on road vs ranked teams since 2002

0-5 S/U vs #1 ranked teams all time

0-4 S/U vs #2 ranked teams since 2008

0-9 S/U vs #3 #4 ranked teams all time

0-5 S/U on road vs #5 ranked teams all time

3-0 ATS vs #5 ranked teams since 2002

0-3 O/U vs #5 ranked teams since 2002

1-10 S/U vs #6 ranked teams all time {0-4 on road}

0-5 S/U vs #8 ranked teams all time

1-5 S/U vs #9 ranked teams all time

0-12 S/U vs #10 #11 ranked teams all time

4-0 S/U & ATS vs #12 ranked teams since 1984

1-5 S/U vs #13 ranked teams all time

0-5 S/U vs #14 ranked teams since 1995

1-4 O/U vs #14 ranked teams since 1995

0-3 S/U on road vs #15 ranked teams all time

1-6 S/U vs #16 ranked teams all time {1-4 ATS}

1-8 S/U vs #17 ranked teams all time

1-6 ATS vs #17 ranked teams since 1992

7-0 ATS vs #18 ranked teams since 1989

1-6 S/U on road vs #19 ranked teams all time

2-11 S/U vs #19 ranked teams all time

Copyright © 2021 by Steve's Football Bible, LLC

4-1 O/U vs #19 ranked teams since 1996
4-0 O/U vs #20 ranked teams since 1991
0-4 O/U vs #22 ranked teams since 2002
0-3 S/U on road vs #24 ranked teams all time
1-4 S/U & ATS vs #25 ranked teams all time
0-6 S/U vs ranked Duke all time
1-6 S/U vs ranked Miami all time
0-7 S/U @ ranked North Carolina all time
1-12 S/U vs ranked Virginia Tech since 1999
1-9 S/U @ home vs ranked Virginia Tech since 1993
1-8-1 ATS vs ranked Virginia Tech since 2002

Virginia Tech {When Ranked}

7-23 O/U @ home when ranked since 2008
0-5 ATS when #2 ranked since 1999
3-0 S/U @ home when #2 ranked all time
0-4 O/U when #3 ranked since 2005
4-1 S/U on road when #3 ranked all time
7-1 S/U when #4 ranked all time
7-0 S/U when #6 ranked all time
9-1 S/U & ATS when #8 ranked all time
6-1 S/U @ home when #9 ranked all time
0-4 ATS when #9 ranked since 2007
5-0 S/U & ATS when #10 ranked since 2000
10-2 S/U when #11 ranked all time
5-0 S/U when #13 ranked since 2010
3-0 S/U & ATS on road when #14 ranked since 2007
5-0 S/U @ home when #15 ranked all time
4-0 S/U when #15 ranked since 2009
13-1 S/U when #16 ranked all time {5-0 on road}
0-5 S/U & ATS when #17 ranked since 2008
6-1 S/U @ home when #17 ranked all time
2-8 ATS when #18 ranked since 1996
0-4 O/U when #18 ranked since 2000
7-0 S/U when #20 ranked since 1995
2-5 ATS @ home when #20 ranked all time
8-1 S/U when #21 ranked all time {3-0 @ home}
8-2 S/U when #23 ranked all time {3-0 @ home}
7-2 ATS when #23 ranked since 1997
4-1 S/U when #24 ranked all time
1-4 O/U when #24 ranked all time
0-3 S/U when ranked vs #1 ranked teams all time
0-3 S/U & ATS when ranked vs #2 ranked teams since 2007
0-4 S/U when ranked vs #3 ranked teams all time
0-3 S/U & ATS when ranked vs #6 ranked teams all time
0-3 O/U when ranked vs #9 ranked teams since 2004
0-3 O/U when ranked vs #13 ranked teams since 1995
6-0 S/U & ATS when ranked vs #16 ranked teams since 1999
0-4 O/U when ranked vs #19 ranked teams since 2002
3-0 S/U when ranked vs #22 ranked teams all time
0-5 ATS when ranked @ Boston College since 2000
3-7 ATS @ home when ranked vs Boston College since 1995

8-1 S/U when ranked vs Duke all time {5-0 on road}
0-5 O/U when ranked vs Duke since 2010
5-1 S/U when ranked vs Miami since 2006
0-4 O/U When ranked @ Miami since 2004
8-2 S/U when ranked vs North Carolina all time {4-1 on road}
3-7 O/U when ranked vs North Carolina all time
2-7 ATS when ranked vs Pittsburgh since 1999
14-2 S/U when ranked vs Virginia since 1996 {6-0 @ home}
7-1-1 ATS when ranked vs Virginia since 2004

Virginia Tech {vs Ranked}

10-4 S/U on road vs ranked teams since 2010
11-3 ATS on road vs ranked teams since 2010
1-12 S/U @ home vs ranked teams since 2010
0-4 S/U & ATS vs ranked teams in Bowl games since 2011
0-9 S/U vs #1 ranked teams all time
1-7 S/U vs #2 ranked teams all time {0-5 on road}
0-8 S/U vs #3 ranked teams all time
1-5 S/U vs #5 ranked teams all time
0-4 S/U vs #6 ranked teams all time
1-10 S/U vs #7 ranked teams all time {0-6 on road}
0-3 O/U vs #9 ranked teams since 2004
3-0 ATS vs #12 ranked teams since 2007
0-3 O/U vs #12 ranked teams since 2007
0-3 S/U @ home vs #13 ranked teams all time
0-3 O/U vs #13 ranked teams since 1995
0-3 O/U vs #14 ranked teams since 2002
6-1 S/U vs #16 ranked teams since 1999
7-0 ATS vs #16 ranked teams since 1999
5-1-1 O/U vs #16 ranked teams since 1998
4-0 ATS vs #18 ranked teams since 1986
3-0 S/U & ATS on road vs #19 ranked teams all time
0-5 O/U vs #19 ranked teams since 2002
3-0 S/U @ home vs #20 ranked teams all time
5-1 ATS vs #20 ranked teams since 1995
4-1 O/U vs #20 ranked teams since 1996
5-0 S/U vs #22 ranked teams all time
0-3 O/U vs #24 ranked teams since 2008
10-4 ATS vs ranked Miami since 1995
1-7 O/U vs ranked Miami since 2003
4-0 S/U & ATS vs ranked Virginia since 1999
5-0 S/U & ATS @ ranked Virginia since 1993
3-0 S/U vs ranked West Virginia since 1998
8-1 ATS vs ranked West Virginia since 1983

Wake Forest {When Ranked}

4-14 O/U when ranked all time
5-2-1 ATS on road when ranked since 2006
0-3 S/U when #15 ranked all time
4-1 S/U when #18 ranked all time
3-0 S/U when #20 ranked all time

Wake Forest {vs Ranked}

2-46 S/U on road vs ranked teams since 1980

Copyright © 2021 by Steve's Football Bible, LLC

Team Trends when ranked in the Polls / vs Ranked teams in the Polls

7-1 ATS on road vs ranked teams since 2015	6-1 S/U when #14 ranked all time
1-9 O/U on road vs ranked teams since 2013	3-1 ATS when #14 ranked since 1983
2-11 S/U @ home vs ranked teams since 2011	6-0 S/U @ home when #15 ranked since 1996
0-9 S/U vs #1 ranked teams all time	0-4 S/U on road when #15 ranked since 1978
0-6 S/U vs #2 ranked teams all time	9-2 S/U @ home when #16 ranked all time
0-9 S/U vs #3 ranked teams all time	13-1-1 S/U @ home when #17 ranked all time
0-4 ATS vs #3 ranked teams since 2005	6-0 S/U @ home when #18 ranked since 1981
0-6 S/U vs #4 ranked teams since 1983	4-0 S/U @ home when #19 ranked since 1977
6-0 ATS vs #5 ranked teams since 1997	5-1 S/U on road when #20 ranked all time
0-25 S/U vs #5 - #9 ranked teams all time	0-3 S/U & ATS when #20 ranked since 1995
0-12 S/U vs #10 #11 ranked teams all time	3-0 O/U when #20 ranked since 1995
0-3 S/U vs #12 ranked teams since 1982	5-0 ATS when #21 ranked since 1990
1-5-1 S/U vs #13 ranked teams all time {0-3 on road}	3-0 O/U when #21 ranked since 1997
0-4 S/U on road vs #14 ranked teams since 1980	1-3 S/U on road when #22 ranked since 1999
5-0 ATS vs #14 ranked teams since 1992	7-0 S/U @ home when #22 ranked all time
2-9 S/U vs #15 ranked teams all time	0-5-1 ATS @ home when #22 ranked since 1994
0-7 S/U on road vs #16 ranked teams since 1958	5-2 S/U when #25 ranked since 1994
4-1 ATS vs #16 ranked teams since 1983	0-3 S/U when ranked vs #1 ranked teams since 1972
0-8 S/U vs #17 #18 ranked teams all time	0-3 S/U & ATS when ranked vs #2 ranked teams since 2003
0-11 S/U vs #19 ranked teams since 1958 {0-6 @ home}	3-0 O/U when ranked vs #10 ranked teams since 1986
1-5 S/U vs #20 ranked teams all time {0-2 @ home}	4-1 S/U when ranked vs #15 ranked teams all time
0-3 ATS vs #20 ranked teams since 1994	4-0 S/U when ranked vs #18 ranked teams all time
0-28 S/U vs ranked Clemson since 1948	3-0 O/U @ home when ranked vs #20 ranked teams all time
1-12 S/U vs ranked Duke all time {0-7 @ home}	0-3 S/U on road when ranked vs #20 ranked teams all time
0-5 S/U vs ranked Florida State since 2012	0-3 O/U when ranked vs #20 ranked teams since 1992
3-0 S/U & ATS @ home vs ranked NC State since 1999	6-0 S/U @ home when ranked vs Arizona State since 1991
0-7 S/U vs ranked North Carolina since 1980	7-1 O/U when ranked vs Arizona since 1996
0-6 S/U vs ranked Virginia all time	5-0 S/U when ranked vs Arizona since 2000
Washington {When Ranked}	17-3 S/U when ranked vs California since 1959
3-9 O/U on road when ranked since 2017	5-0 S/U when ranked vs Colorado since 2000
42-5 S/U @ home when ranked since 2000	0-5 O/U when ranked vs Colorado since 2000
10-0 S/U @ home when #1 ranked all time	4-1 ATS when ranked vs Michigan since 1984
7-1 S/U when #2 ranked since 1991	19-1 S/U when ranked vs Oregon State since 1950 {9-0 @ home}
8-0 S/U when #8 ranked since 1984 {3-0 on road}	0-6 S/U & ATS when ranked vs ranked Oregon since 1995
6-0 S/U on road when #4 ranked all time	0-5 S/U when ranked @ Stanford since 2009
5-0 O/U on road when #4 ranked since 1991	7-2 O/U when ranked @ Stanford since 1990
6-1 S/U @ home when #6 ranked all time	4-0 S/U @ home when ranked vs UCLA since 1994
14-2 S/U when #7 ranked all time	5-0 O/U when ranked vs UCLA since 2000
7-2-1 ATS when #7 ranked since 1986	3-11-1 S/U when ranked vs ranked USC since 1959
8-0-1 S/U @ home when #8 ranked all time	10-2 S/U @ home when ranked vs Washington State all time
9-0 S/U @ home when ranked #9 all time	**Washington {vs Ranked}**
1-5 ATS when #9 ranked since 2000	5-26 S/U on road vs ranked teams since 2004
6-0-2 S/U @ home when #10 ranked all time	0-10 S/U vs #1 ranked teams since 1967
9-1 S/U when #10 ranked since 1990	0-6 S/U on road vs #1 ranked teams since 1939
5-0 S/U @ home when #11 ranked since 2001	0-4 S/U vs #2 ranked teams since 2003
7-1 S/U @ home when #12 ranked since 1986	1-5 O/U vs #2 ranked teams since 1988
1-5 S/U on road when #12 ranked since 1990	1-4 O/U vs #3 ranked teams since 1998
0-5 ATS on road when #12 ranked since 1993	1-5 S/U on road vs #5 ranked teams all time
5-0 S/U @ home when #13 ranked since 1987	4-1 O/U vs #5 ranked teams since 1994
9-1 S/U on road when #13 ranked all time	0-5 S/U on road vs #6 ranked teams all time
8-1 O/U when #13 ranked since 1990	0-5 S/U vs #6 ranked teams since 1966

Copyright © 2021 by Steve's Football Bible, LLC

Team Trends when ranked in the Polls / vs Ranked teams in the Polls

3-0 S/U & ATS vs #7 ranked teams since 2012
1-5 S/U on road vs #9 ranked teams all time
3-0 O/U on road vs #9 ranked teams since 1991
0-5 S/U on road vs #10 ranked teams all time
3-0 O/U @ home vs #10 ranked teams since 1986
0-4 S/U on road vs #11 ranked teams since 1970
3-0 O/U on road vs #11 ranked teams since 1996
0-4 S/U on road vs #12 ranked teams all time
0-4 S/U vs #13 ranked teams since 2002
1-4 O/U @ home vs #13 ranked teams since 1985
4-0-1 O/U vs #15 ranked teams since 1992
4-0 ATS @ home vs #15 ranked teams since 1989
0-5 S/U @ home vs #16 ranked teams since 1977
1-5 O/U vs #17 ranked teams since 1994
0-7 S/U on road vs #20 ranked teams all time
4-0 S/U @ home vs #20 ranked teams since 1992
4-0 ATS vs #20 ranked teams since 2007
3-0 O/U vs #22 ranked teams all time
0-3-1 O/U vs #23 ranked teams since 2002
4-0 S/U vs #25 ranked teams since 1997
0-4 S/U vs ranked Arizona since 1992
0-4 S/U @ ranked Arizona all time
0-3 S/U & ATS vs ranked Arizona State since 2002
6-1 O/U vs ranked California since 1992
4-1 ATS vs ranked Michigan since 1984
5-0 S/U vs ranked Oregon State since 1960
0-12 S/U vs ranked Oregon since 2005 {0-7 on road}
0-12 ATS vs ranked Oregon since 2005 {0-7 on road}
0-3 S/U @ ranked Stanford since 2011
0-9 S/U vs ranked UCLA since 1987
2-8 ATS vs ranked UCLA since 1986
7-0 S/U & ATS vs ranked Washington State since 2001

Washington State {When Ranked}

32-6 S/U @ home when ranked since 1997
3-0 S/U & ATS @ home when #8 ranked all time
3-0 O/U @ home when #8 ranked all time
0-3 O/U when #10 ranked since 2002
1-4 ATS when #10 ranked since 1997
4-0 S/U & ATS when #11 ranked all time
3-0 S/U & ATS when #13 ranked since 1997
3-0 S/U @ home when #15 ranked since 1997
1-4 S/U on road when #15 ranked since 1942
5-0 S/U when #16 ranked since 1997
4-0 S/U @ home when #17 ranked since 1951
5-0-1 S/U when #18 ranked all time
3-0 S/U on road when #19 ranked all time
1-4 S/U on road when #20 ranked all time
0-6 ATS when #20 ranked since 1988
5-0 O/U when #21 ranked all time
5-0 S/U when #22 ranked all time
3-0 S/U when #24 ranked since 1994

0-4 O/U when #24 ranked all time
5-1 S/U @ home when #25 ranked all time
0-3 S/U when ranked vs #11 ranked teams all time
3-0 S/U @ home when ranked vs Arizona State all time
4-0 O/U when ranked vs Arizona since 2006
4-0 S/U @ home when ranked vs Oregon State since 1988
4-0 S/U & ATS when ranked vs Oregon since 2002
4-0 S/U & ATS when ranked @ Oregon since 1989
5-0 S/U when ranked vs Stanford since 1997
0-7 S/U & ATS when ranked vs Washington since 2001

Washington State {vs Ranked}

4-25 S/U on road vs ranked teams since 2003
5-21 S/U @ home vs ranked teams since 2004
1-7 S/U vs #1 ranked teams all time
0-8 S/U vs #2 ranked teams all time
4-0 ATS vs #2 ranked teams since 1995
0-14 S/U vs #3 & #4 ranked teams all time
3-0 ATS vs #3 ranked teams since 2003
0-6 S/U on road vs #5 ranked teams all time
1-5 S/U vs #6 ranked teams since 1969
0-16 S/U vs #7 & #8 ranked teams all time
0-3 O/U vs #8 ranked teams since 2003
0-3 S/U vs #10 ranked teams since 1990
0-11-1 S/U vs #11 ranked teams all time
1-13 S/U vs #12 ranked teams all time {0-8 on road}
1-6 S/U vs #13 ranked teams all time
0-5 S/U on road vs #14 ranked teams since 1959
4-0 O/U vs #15 ranked teams since 2003
0-6 S/U on road vs #16 ranked teams all time
0-3 S/U @ home vs #17 ranked teams since 1986
1-5 S/U on road vs #17 ranked teams all time
3-0 ATS vs #17 ranked teams since 2003
6-2 ATS vs #18 ranked teams since 1994
0-8 S/U on road vs #19 ranked teams all time
0-3 S/U & ATS vs #20 ranked teams since 2004
3-0 O/U on road vs #20 ranked teams since 1997
0-5 S/U vs #22 ranked teams all time
4-1 O/U vs #23 ranked teams all time
0-5 S/U vs ranked Arizona State since 2004
6-1 O/U vs ranked Arizona State since 1997
0-11 S/U vs ranked Arizona all time
0-6 S/U @ ranked California all time
0-3 O/U vs ranked Oregon State since 2000
0-5 S/U @ ranked Oregon since 2007
7-1 ATS vs ranked Oregon since 2010
2-8-1 S/U @ home vs ranked Stanford all time
3-0 S/U vs ranked Stanford since 2016
4-0 ATS vs ranked Stanford since 2015
3-11 S/U @ home vs ranked USC all time
0-3 S/U & ATS vs ranked Washington since 2016
2-10 S/U @ ranked Washington all time

Copyright © 2021 by Steve's Football Bible, LLC

Team Trends when ranked in the Polls / vs Ranked teams in the Polls

Western Kentucky {When Ranked}
1-0 S/U when ranked all time

Western Kentucky {vs Ranked}
0-3 S/U vs #1 ranked teams all time

Western Michigan {When Ranked}
7-1 S/U when ranked all time

Western Michigan {vs Ranked}
1-28 S/U on road vs ranked teams all time
0-7 S/U @ home vs ranked teams all time
8-2 ATS vs ranked teams since 2011
0-3 S/U vs ranked Miami-Ohio all time
0-3 S/U vs ranked Michigan all time

West Virginia {When Ranked}
4-0 O/U when #3 ranked since 2006
7-0 S/U when #4 ranked since 1988
4-0 S/U @ home when #5 ranked all time
0-3 ATS on road when #5 ranked since 2007
0-4 O/U when #5 ranked since 2007
3-0 S/U @ home when #6 ranked all time
4-1 S/U @ home when #7 ranked since 1983
4-0 S/U @ home when #8 ranked since 1955
6-0 S/U when #9 ranked since 1993
8-2 S/U when #11 ranked since 1975
7-2 ATS when #11 ranked since 1988
6-1 O/U when #11 ranked since 1998
7-1 S/U when #12 ranked since 2004 {3-0 on road}
4-0 S/U when #13 ranked since 2004
5-0 O/U when #13 ranked since 2002
6-0 S/U @ home when #14 ranked all time
6-1 S/U when #15 ranked all time
12-1 S/U when #16 ranked all time {5-0 on road}
4-0 O/U when #16 ranked since 2004
0-6 O/U when #17 ranked since 1989
5-1 S/U @ home when #17 ranked all time
7-0 S/U when #19 ranked since 1989
0-4 S/U when #24 ranked since 2008
0-6 ATS when #24 ranked since 1994
4-0 S/U @ home when #25 ranked since 1993
0-3 S/U when ranked vs #2 ranked teams all time
0-4 O/U when ranked vs #4 ranked teams all time
0-3 S/U when ranked vs #5 ranked teams all time
0-3 S/U when ranked vs #9 ranked teams since 1975
5-0 S/U when ranked vs #19 ranked teams all time
0-3 ATS when ranked vs #21 ranked teams all time
4-0 S/U when ranked vs #25 ranked teams since 2007
4-0 S/U when ranked vs Baylor all time
4-0 S/U when ranked @ Maryland all time
0-3 S/U when ranked vs Oklahoma since 2015
4-0 O/U when ranked vs Oklahoma since 2008
0-3 S/U & ATS when ranked vs Oklahoma State since 2016
4-1 S/U @ home when ranked vs Virginia Tech all time

West Virginia {vs Ranked}
0-9 S/U vs #1 ranked teams all time
4-1 O/U vs #1 ranked teams since 1989
0-9 S/U vs #2 ranked teams all time
3-0 O/U vs #2 ranked teams since 2011
0-5 S/U on road vs #3 ranked teams all time
1-5 S/U @ home vs #3 ranked teams all time
0-3 S/U on road vs #4 ranked teams all time
1-5 O/U vs #4 ranked teams since 1984
0-9 S/U vs #5 ranked teams all time
0-6 S/U vs #6 ranked teams all time
0-3 S/U vs #7 ranked teams all time
1-4 S/U & ATS vs #8 ranked teams all time
0-8-1 S/U vs #10 ranked teams all time
3-0 S/U & ATS vs #11 ranked teams since 1993
0-6 S/U @ home vs #12 ranked teams all time
1-5 S/U vs #15 ranked teams since 2005
3-1 O/U vs #15 ranked teams since 2013
0-4 S/U on road vs #16 ranked teams since 1989
6-0 S/U vs #19 ranked teams since 1982
5-0 S/U @ home vs #19 ranked teams since 1982
1-4 S/U vs #20 ranked teams since 1978
1-4 S/U vs #21 ranked teams since 2002 {0-5 ATS}
4-0 S/U vs #25 ranked teams since 2007
4-1 O/U vs #25 ranked teams since 2001
0-4 ATS vs ranked Maryland since 1985
0-7 S/U vs ranked Oklahoma since 2013
6-0 O/U vs ranked Oklahoma since 2014
0-5-1 ATS vs ranked Oklahoma since 2014
1-5 S/U & ATS vs ranked Oklahoma State all time
0-3 S/U vs ranked TCU all time
0-3 O/U vs ranked TCU all time
3-0 O/U vs ranked Texas Tech all time

Wisconsin {When Ranked}
16-7 S/U on road when ranked since 2014 {15-8 ATS}
64-8 S/U @ home when ranked since 2006
1-4 S/U when #2 ranked all time
5-0 S/U @ home when #4 ranked since 2000
9-0 S/U @ home when #5 ranked all time
7-0 S/U when #5 ranked since 2010
6-1 S/U @ home when #6 ranked all time
7-2 O/U when #6 ranked since 2010
7-0 S/U when #7 ranked since 2007
4-0 S/U on road when #7 ranked all time
9-1 S/U @ home when #8 ranked all time
1-4 S/U on road when #8 ranked since 1963
10-0 S/U @ home when #9 ranked since 1951
2-7 ATS when #9 ranked since 2004
8-2 S/U when #10 ranked since 1999
5-0 S/U @ home when #10 ranked since 1954
10-3 ATS when #10 ranked since 1993

Copyright © 2021 by Steve's Football Bible, LLC

Team Trends when ranked in the Polls / vs Ranked teams in the Polls

8-2 S/U when #11 ranked since 1999 {6-0 @ home}
5-0 S/U @ home when #12 ranked since 1959
0-4 ATS when #12 ranked since 2006
2-8 ATS when #14 ranked since 2003
5-1 S/U when #15 ranked since 2004
5-1 O/U when #15 ranked since 2004
11-1 S/U when #16 ranked since 1953 {6-0 @ home}
8-1 O/U when #16 ranked since 1993
7-1 S/U @ home when #17 ranked all time
0-3 ATS on road when #17 ranked all time
5-2 S/U @ home when #18 ranked all time
4-1 S/U on road when #18 ranked all time
4-0 S/U @ home when #20 ranked since 2004
0-4 O/U on road when #20 ranked since 1999
7-1 S/U when #21 ranked since 2003
1-8 O/U when #21 ranked since 1993
6-0 S/U when #22 ranked since 2002
7-1 ATS when #23 ranked since 2003
6-1 S/U when #24 ranked since 2005
2-9 ATS when #24 ranked since 1995
5-2 S/U when #25 ranked all time
0-3 S/U on road when ranked vs #1 ranked team all time
0-4 S/U & ATS when ranked vs #3 ranked teams since 2011
0-3 S/U when ranked vs #4 ranked teams since 1995
0-3 O/U when ranked vs #4 ranked teams since 1995
2-9 S/U when ranked vs #8 ranked teams all time
1-3 S/U when ranked vs #9 ranked teams since 1995
5-0 S/U when ranked vs #11 ranked teams since 1999
3-0 S/U on road when ranked vs #13 ranked teams all time
4-0 O/U when ranked vs #13 ranked teams since 1995
3-0 S/U when ranked vs #14 ranked teams all time
3-0 S/U when ranked vs #22 ranked teams all time
3-0 S/U when ranked vs #25 ranked teams all time
13-1 S/U when ranked vs Illinois since 1962 {6-0 @ home}
9-2 S/U when ranked vs Iowa since 2006 {6-1 on road}
13-0 S/U when ranked vs Minnesota since 1998
5-0 S/U when ranked vs Nebraska since 2014
9-0 S/U when ranked vs Purdue since 2004 {7-2 ATS}
6-0 S/U when ranked @ Purdue since 1999

Wisconsin {vs Ranked}

12-4 S/U @ home vs ranked teams since 2010
23-90-3 S/U on road vs ranked teams all time
0-10 S/U on road vs #1 ranked teams all time
3-0 ATS @ home vs #1 ranked teams since 1985
0-10 S/U vs #2 ranked teams since 1960
1-7-1 S/U vs #3 ranked teams since 1989
0-8 S/U on road vs #4 ranked teams all time
2-8 S/U @ home vs #4 ranked teams all time
0-4 O/U vs #4 ranked teams since 1995
1-5 S/U on road vs #5 ranked teams all time
0-4 S/U vs #6 ranked teams since 2006

1-6 S/U on road vs #6 ranked teams all time
1-5 S/U @ home vs #6 ranked teams all time
0-4 S/U on road vs #7 ranked teams since 1959
2-14 S/U vs #8 ranked teams all time
1-8 S/U on road vs #9 ranked teams all time
1-10 S/U vs #9 ranked teams since 1960
2-10 S/U vs #10 ranked teams since 1946
4-0 S/U vs #11 ranked teams since 2011
4-0 O/U vs #11 ranked teams since 2011
2-6 O/U vs #12 ranked teams since 1992
5-0 O/U vs #13 ranked teams since 1995
3-0 S/U on road vs #13 ranked teams all time
5-0 S/U & ATS vs #14 ranked teams since 1998
0-3 S/U & ATS vs #15 ranked teams since 1983
0-4 S/U on road vs #16 ranked teams all time
0-5 S/U @ home vs #17 ranked teams since 1983
1-7 S/U vs #20 ranked teams since 1969
4-1 S/U & ATS vs #21 ranked teams all time
3-0 O/U vs #22 ranked teams since 2005
4-0 S/U vs #25 ranked teams since 1993
0-4 S/U vs ranked Illinois since 1963
4-0 S/U @ home vs ranked Michigan since 2005
5-0 ATS @ home vs ranked Michigan since 2001
3-8 O/U vs ranked Michigan since 1999
7-1 S/U vs ranked Minnesota since 1961
4-0 S/U @ home vs Nebraska since 1974
4-1 ATS vs ranked Nebraska since 2011
4-1 O/U vs ranked Nebraska since 2011
0-5 S/U vs ranked USC all time

Wyoming {When Ranked}

0-7-1 ATS on road when ranked since 1988
14-2 S/U @ home when ranked all time
3-0 S/U when #12 ranked all time
4-1 S/U when #16 ranked all time
4-0 S/U when #18 ranked all time
0-4 S/U when ranked vs ranked teams since 1988
3-0 S/U when ranked vs San Jose State all time

Wyoming {vs Ranked}

4-26 S/U @ home vs ranked teams since 1974
3-39 S/U on road vs ranked teams all time
2-22 S/U vs ranked teams since 2004
0-29 S/U vs Top #10 ranked teams all time
0-5 S/U vs #12 ranked teams all time
0-5 S/U on road vs #14 ranked teams all time
0-10 S/U vs #16 #17 #18 ranked teams since 1960
0-4 S/U vs #19 ranked teams all time
1-4 S/U vs Boise State all time

Copyright © 2021 by Steve's Football Bible, LLC

CPSIA information can be obtained
at www.ICGtesting.com
Printed in the USA
BVHW010133060821
613589BV00006B/106